African Development Indicators 2004

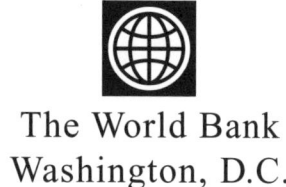

The World Bank
Washington, D.C.

Cover photo collage adapted from collage created by Jeeyeon Seo; photos by © Isaac, John 2002/from *A Day in The Life of Africa* (produce market image); © Jose Luis Pelaez, Inc./Corbis (student image); © James Noble/Corbis (hand/light bulb image); additional images courtesy of World Bank Photo Library; Cover design by Naylor Design.

ISBN 0-8213-5720-4

Contents

6.   External Debt and Related Flows   151

7.   Government Finance   184

Table des matières

Foreword

Making headway against African poverty and meeting the Millennium Development Goals (MDGs) by 2015 are raising difficult challenges in most African countries. Despite pockets of success, nearly half the region's population still lives in extreme poverty, and Africa still houses about three-fourths of the world's poorest countries. Africa urgently needs rich nations to deliver on their promises of more generous aid and wider trade opportunities to reverse the cruel effects of the HIV/AIDS pandemic, civil wars, and persistent low growth rates.

The World Bank's latest annual report on social and economic conditions across the continent, *African Development Indicators (ADI) 2004,* sounds a clear warning that the rapid spread of HIV/AIDS, anemic aid and investment flows, and weak commodity prices threaten to undo some of the hard-fought gains of recent years.

As in previous years, *ADI 2004* assembles economic, social, and environmental data from a variety of sources to present a broad picture of development across Africa. There have been some key improvements in this volume—for example, macroeconomic and other data lags have been reduced, enabling external debt reporting up to 2002, and there have been updates on the HIPC Initiative. In addition, the chapter on Aid Flows includes ODA not allocated by country, and the chapter on Household Welfare contains a new set of standardized household indicators for selected countries.

ADI 2004 depicts a diverse continent. Gross national income (GNI) per head for all Africa averaged $650 in 2002, $1644 and $451 in North and Sub-Saharan Africa (SSA) respectively. But it stood at only $307 per head in SSA, excluding South Africa, ranging from under $100 per head in the Democratic Republic of Congo to over $7,000 in Seychelles. At 2.8 percent in 2002, GDP growth in SSA barely exceeded the growth of its rapidly urbanizing population (cities grew at close to 5 percent), continuing the overall trend of the 1990s. On average, output per head has stagnated.

Yet country performance has diverged widely in SSA—thirteen have averaged more than 5 percent growth for the period 1995–2002, while a few achieved higher growth than the previous decade. Several have seen their economies contract, invariably as a result of severe civil conflict. On average, investment and trade trends have been steady, with a slight increase in the overall current account deficit. Net FDI flows to SSA rose to $8.9 billion in 2002 but were heavily concentrated in oil exporting countries and South Africa.

Access to ICT is still limited but increasing. In 2002, there were about 12 personal computers per thousand population in SSA, over a 30 percent rise from

2000 and 16 percent from 2001. In North Africa, computer ownership was somewhat higher, at about 17 per thousand. Internet use is rising sharply, but of the 6.2 million recorded Internet users in SSA, about half were in South Africa. However, these data may not fully account for multiple user access.

Air transport has declined a bit from 2000 to 2001. All Africa recorded about 30.9 million passengers in 2001, but of this total, 21.7 million are accounted for by North and South Africa.

Net aid to Africa rose about 35 percent in 2002 because of higher DAC and multilateral flows, but on a per capita basis it is still far below ($27 in 2002) what it was in 1992 ($40). Aid flow was $28 per head for SSA. As of July 2003, 16 countries had reached HIPC decision points and 7 had reached completion points. Total debt service relief represented about $43 billion, and pro-poor expenditures had begun to increase in most of the countries. However, nine countries, mostly conflict-affected, had not yet reached the HIPC decision point.

In SSA, death rates have continued to rise because of the HIV/AIDS pandemic, causing life expectancy at birth to fall from 50 in 1990 to 46 in 2002. AIDS-related deaths were 2.2 million in 2001 (for a cumulative total close to 20 million). Almost 30 million were infected and 11 million were orphaned, including a million each in Nigeria and Ethiopia. Under-5 mortality stood at 169 per thousand for SSA; in nine countries it exceeded 200 per thousand. Only half of the children in SSA were immunized. Health expenditures averaged only $13 per head in SSA, excluding South Africa, and were below $10 per head in 16 countries.

But these averages in social indicators conceal wide variation between countries. Maternal mortality, for example, ranges from as low as 45 per 100,000 births to 2,300. Education trends were somewhat more favorable, with a steady fall in illiteracy, from 42 percent in 1997 to 37 percent in 2002. Although there is a lot of catching-up to do, at 87 percent, gross primary enrollment has recovered and exceeded its level in 1980 (80 percent). Social indicators were more favorable in North Africa, with life expectancy at 70 in 2002 and immunization rates near 90 percent.

ADI 2004 draws attention to Africa's rich environmental resources, but also to the stress that environment is coming under. Many countries have large numbers of endangered species, and each year 0.7 percent of forest cover is being lost.

The detailed World Bank Africa Database 2004, consisting of almost 1,200 indicators, including the World Bank's "Country at a Glance" Tables and an electronic copy of *ADI 2004*, is also being made available on CD-ROM, together with a user-friendly interface to facilitate downloading and analysis. Directions for obtaining both the publication and the CD-ROM can be found on the World Bank's external web site (www.worldbank.org). With increased demand for information to monitor the Poverty Reduction Strategy Papers (PRSPs), national development programs, and the Millennium Development Goals, and access to electronic media widening in Africa, *ADI* is expected to evolve further, with the goal of offering the most relevant information to monitor development progress in a combination of information in hardcopy and electronic forms. We welcome user feedback and suggestions for improving *ADI* in future years.

Alan Harold Gelb
Chief Economist, Africa Region

Acknowledgments

This volume was produced by the Operational Quality and Knowledge Services of the Africa Region, in collaboration with the Development Data Group of the Development Economics Vice Presidency.

The volume was prepared by a team led by Tariqul I. Khan and comprising José Delcour, Rose Mungai, Kadra Nour, Joan Pandit, Christophe Rockmore, and Vildan Verbeek-Demiraydin. Valuable guidance was provided by the Africa Chief Economist's office. The chapters on national accounts, balance of payments, trade, and government finance draw heavily on the work of World Bank Africa country desks. The chapters on power, communications and transportation, labor force, and social indicators tap the World Bank's World Development Indicators database. The chapter on external debt is heavily drawn from the Debt Reporting System (DRS) of the World Bank, while the chapter on environment was prepared with data from the World Resources Institute. The update for the chapter on privatization of public enterprises was provided by Nikolay Madinga, and the update for the chapter on the HIPC Initiative was provided by Francis Rowe. The HIV/AIDS table was prepared with data from the Joint United Nations Programme on HIV/AIDS (UNAIDS). In addition, many World Bank staff provided information on their countries or their economic or sectoral specialties.

Lawrence Mastri provided assistance in editing and producing the volume, while the World Bank Office of the Publisher—in particular Richard A. Crabbe, Mary Fisk, and Monika Lynde—prepared and coordinated final production of the book. Other staff aided and advised on the design and content of this volume.

ADI 2004 was produced primarily using the data reporting tool of the Africa Live Database (LDB) system. This tool was programmed to generate automatically all the tables in this volume and can be used for other publications. Using data warehousing technology, the LDB instantly recalculates all indicators and aggregates them once new information is available. This guarantees that the most recent data are reflected in this and future volumes.

Preface

African Development Indicators 2004 continues the data publication series started by the World Bank in 1989 with *African Economic and Financial Data* (published jointly with the United Nations Development Programme), followed by *African Development Indicators 1992, 1994/95, 1996, 1997, 1998/99, 2000, 2001, 2002,* and *2003.* These data volumes are intended to provide Africans and those interested in Africa with a consistent and convenient set of data to monitor development programs and aid flows in the region. Each successive volume provides access to more focused information and represents an improvement in the quality and availability of the data.

The data in this volume derive from a variety of sources. In most cases, the original source is national statistical services in Africa. In addition, many international agencies collect or compile data on Africa and organize national data in a standardized framework. This volume draws heavily from such sources. The data have been supplemented by World Bank staff estimates to help address problems of missing or in-consistent data from standard sources. Some of the estimation methods used here differ from methods used in other sources. This volume addresses these differences in methodologies in the chapter introductions and in the technical notes.

In the tradition of the first nine volumes, this data collection is intended to serve as a prime source of information on Africa. Its wide dissemination to African and non-African analysts and policymakers will contribute to a better understanding of Africa and to development on that continent.

Gerard A. Byam
Director, Operational Quality
and Knowledge Services
Africa Region

Acronyms and Abbreviations

ADB	African Development Bank	DRS	Debtor Reporting System (World Bank)
ADI	*African Development Indicators*	ECA	Economic Commission for Africa
AEFD	African Economic and Financial Data (UNDP/World Bank 1989)	ESAF	Enhanced Structural Adjustment Facility
		FAO	UN Food and Agriculture Organization
AFESD	Arab Fund for Economic and Social Development	FDI	Foreign direct investment
		f.o.b.	Free on board
BADEA	Arab Bank for Economic Development in Africa	GDF	*Global Development Finance* (formerly *World Debt Tables* [*WDT*])
BIS	Bank for International Settlements	GDI	Gross domestic investment
CDIAC	Carbon Dioxide Information Analysis Center	GDP	Gross domestic product
		GDS	Gross domestic savings
CFA	Communauté Financière Africane (franc zone)	*GFS*	*Government Finance Statistics* (IMF)
		GNFS	Goods and nonfactor services
CIDA	Canadian International Development Agency	GNI	Gross national income
		GNP	Gross national product
c.i.f.	Cost, insurance, freight	GNS	Gross national savings
CITES	Convention on International Trade in Endangered Species of Wild Flora and Fauna	HIPC	Heavily indebted poor countries
		IBRD	International Bank for Reconstruction and Development
CMEA	Council for Mutual Economic Assistance	ICP	International Comparison Program
COMTRADE	Commodity Trade database (United Nations)	IDA	International Development Association
		IEA	International Energy Agency
		IFAD	International Fund for Agricultural Development
CPI	Consumer price index		
DAC	Development Assistance Committee of the OECD	*IFS*	*International Financial Statistics* (IMF)
		ILO	International Labour Organization
DDG	Development Data Group, World Bank	IMF	International Monetary Fund

ISIC	UN International Standard Industrial Classification	SNA	System of National Accounts
ITU	International Telecommunication Union	UNAIDS	Joint United Nations Programme on HIV/AIDS
IUCN	International Union for Conservation of Nature and Natural Resources	UNCTAD	United Nations Conference on Trade and Development
LIBOR	London interbank offered rate	UNDP	United Nations Development Programme
LIMIC	Low-income and middle-income countries	UNECE	United Nations Economic Commission for Europe
MBO	Management employee buyout	UNEP	United Nations Environment Programme
METMIN	Metals and Minerals Database (World Bank)	UNESCO	United Nations Education, Scientific, and Cultural Organization
MPA	Marine protected area		
NPV	Net present value	UNHCR	United Nations High Commissioner for Refugees
ODA	Official development assistance		
OECD	Organisation for Economic Co-operation and Development	UNICEF	United Nations Children's Fund
		UNIDO	United Nations Industrial Development Organization
OPEC	Organization of Petroleum Exporting Countries	UNSO	United Nations Statistical Office
ORT	Oral rehydration therapy	UNSTAT	United Nations Statistical Department
PE	Public enterprise	UNTA	United Nations Technical Assistance
PPP	Purchasing power parity	WFP	World Food Programme
SDA	Social dimensions of adjustment	WHO	World Health Organization
SDR	Special drawing right	WRI	World Resources Institute
SIMA	Statistical Information Management and Analysis Database (World Bank)	ZIMCO	Zambia Industrial and Mining Corporation
SITC	UN Standard International Trade Classification		

Introduction

The task of monitoring Africa's development progress and aid flows requires basic empirical data that can be readily used by analysts. This publication—which is the ninth in a series that began with *African Economic and Financial Data (AEFD)* and was followed by *African Development Indicators (ADI)* 1992, 1994/95, 1996, 1997, 1998/99, 2000, 2001, 2002, and *2003*—is meant to provide a starting point to fulfill that task.

This volume has been able to extend the work of the previous volumes in this series. Chiefly,

• Most macroeconomic data (in particular, national accounts, balance of payments, government finance statistics, and trade) reflect data maintained by World Bank country desks, often referred to as operational data. These data are often more up to date and offer better country coverage than the data stored in the Bank's central files, the Statistical Information Management and Analysis Database (SIMA), which were used in publications before 1998. SIMA is a large database that contains some, but not all, data produced by Bank staff—operational and other—and some, but not all, data produced by UN agencies.

• The coverage of many of the data series has been improved, reflecting enhancements in the underlying data series, as well as estimates made by Bank staff.

However, substantial data gaps remain, notably in areas such as public enterprises, gender, and labor. Strengthening the statistical capacity in African countries is an ongoing process, and greater efforts and institutional support will be required if substantial improvements are to be made.

This volume presents the available relevant data for 1980–2002, grouped into 16 chapters: background data; national accounts; prices and exchange rates; money and banking; external sector; external debt and related flows; government finance; agriculture; power, communications, and transportation; public enterprises; labor force and employment; aid flows; social indicators; and environmental indicators. Chapter 14 (environmental indicators) was once again taken from the World Resources Institute's *World Resources 2002–2004: Decisions for Earth: Balance, Voice and Power.*

Each chapter begins with a brief introduction on the nature of the data, followed by a set of charts, statistical tables, and technical notes. These notes define the indicators and identify specific sources.

1

A companion CD-ROM, known as World Bank Africa Database 2004, provides year-by-year time series of most chapters back to 1980. These series will provide analysts with data needed to help place the most recent years in a historical context.

The data in this volume incorporate numerous revisions to those published previously in the series. There are several reasons for this:

• Many of the data that were based on estimates in the earlier volumes have been replaced with updated actual data or improved estimates. In most cases, these changes reflect revisions made by the original reporting authorities or sources, but this volume also includes corrections of errors in previous volumes.

• Data series expressed in constant U.S. dollars and exchange rates use a base year of 1995; previous *ADI*s were based on 1987 exchange rates and prices, and *AEFD* used 1980 exchange rate and prices.

• Some series expressed in constant prices have been revised as a result of updated or revised deflators.

• As in the 2003 volume, macroeconomic data reflect country desk information. The difference is most noticeable in the chapter on government finance, as figures reflect consolidated government data instead of only central government data.

Considerable effort has been made to standardize and to harmonize related data sets drawn from diverse sources. Because statistical methods, coverage, practices, and definitions differ widely among sources, full comparability cannot be ensured, and the indicators must be interpreted with care. In addition, the statistical systems in many developing economies are still weak, which affects the availability and reliability of the data they report. Moreover, intercountry and intertemporal comparisons always involve complex technical problems, which have no full and unequivocal solution.

The data are drawn from sources thought to be the most authoritative, but many data sources are subject to considerable margins of error. To provide reasonably timely data required for meaningful monitoring, the World Bank, the International Monetary Fund (IMF), and other agencies sometimes make estimates on the basis of available secondary information to fill critical gaps in national reporting, especially for the most recent

years, when data cannot be readily produced by national statistical sources. Nonetheless, data gaps exist for many indicators, and some countries are covered only sporadically.

Readers are urged to take these limitations into account in using the data and interpreting the indicators, particularly when making comparisons across economies. Weaknesses in the data point to the need for strengthened statistical systems throughout the region.

As a visual aid to data interpretation and cross-country comparisons, figures for selected indicators are included. As with time series, the figures should also be interpreted with caution—in particular in cross-country analysis because countries with missing data are excluded from the charts.

Throughout this volume (except when otherwise stated), the symbol ".." indicates that data are not available or not applicable. A zero (0) indicates either zero value or an insignificant value, that is, less than one-half of the smallest unit shown. The abbreviation "MR" indicates "most recent year available." In Chapter 13, columns headed by a period (for example, 1993–97) show data for the latest available year in the period.

To facilitate cross-country comparisons, this book has converted values of many national series from the national currencies to U.S. dollars, using the *World Bank Atlas* methodology.

Indicators in this volume generally follow standard definitions as far as possible and cover years through 2002, depending on the chapter. Data for 2002 are preliminary and therefore may not be internally consistent within and across accounts; and data may not be available for all countries. Because data are continually updated, the statistics here may be different from those in other publications.

Shares and ratios are always calculated using current price series; when gross domestic product (GDP) is used as the denominator for these calculations, it is always expressed at market prices (except in Figure 2-3).

In all but the final chapter, the data are arranged by indicator to facilitate cross-country comparisons. For country-specific work, data can be arranged to show all indicators together for each country.

In this volume, the statistical tables are usually arranged as time series, by country and by country groups. The largest country group is All Africa, consisting of two subgroups: North Africa and Sub-Saharan Africa (including South Africa). In turn, the Sub-Saharan Africa group is shown, excluding South Africa and Nigeria. These two are subgroups withing the SSA group, and correspond to the Sub-Saharan Africa and Sub-Saharan Africa, excluding Nigeria groups shown in the *AEFD* and *ADI 1992*, where South Africa was listed separately.

Annual data shown for country groups are totals, averages, or medians for the countries included in the group, as indicated on the table. These group aggregates can be either simple arithmetic—where missing data are not imputed or gap-filled—or weights are used to adjust group totals for missing countries. In the latter case, when values are missing for a country or a year, estimates are made to maintain the same country composition of the groups through time. However, the implicit estimated values for the countries with missing data are not shown separately in the tables. These gap-fill estimates are made and the aggregate statistics are shown only if the countries for which data are available for a given year account for at least two-thirds of the full group, as defined by benchmarks in 1995. This procedure is standard for many World Bank statistical publications.

Most group averages are weighted according to the relative importance of the countries in the group total for that indicator, based on simple addition across countries when the indicator is expressed in reasonably comparable units. Group averages for analytical ratios (for example, imports to GDP) can be either weighted or simple (arithmetic). Usually they are calculated from the group totals for both the numerator and the denominator, which is analytically equivalent to calculating weighted averages, where the weight for each country is its share in the group total for the denominator. Sometimes, however, when it is appropriate to treat the experiences of different countries equally in

determining a representative value for the group, these group averages are arithmetic—that is, each country has equal weight.

Period averages—shown for 1975–1984, 1985–1994, and 1995 to most recent year—are calculated from time series (levels, ratios, growth rates, or medians) for both countries and country groups. They are either simple averages or average annual percentage growth rates. These growth rates always use the least-squares method and are usually computed from real-term series. In this publication, the least-squares growth rates are computed using the level for the year before the first year shown in the label. The least-squares growth rate, r, is estimated by fitting a least-squares linear regression trend line to the logarithmic annual values of the variable in the relevant period. More specifically, the regression equation takes the form: $\log X = a + bt + e$, where this is equivalent to the logarithmic transformation of the compound growth rate equation, $X = X (1 + r)^t$. In these equations X is the variable, t is time, and $a = \log X$ and $b = \log (1 + r)$ are the parameters to be estimated; e is the error term. If b^* is the least-squares estimate of b, then the annual average growth rate, r, is obtained as [anti log (b^*)] – 1 and multiplied by 100 to express it in percentage terms. The least-squares growth rate dampens the influence of exceptional values, particularly at the end points. Least-square growth rates are calculated only if more than two-thirds of consecutive data—carrying the same sign—are present in the time series.

Throughout this volume, data for Ethiopia include Eritrea up to 1992, except when otherwise indicated. Mauritius data are reported for fiscal years ending June 30. The data are published under the second year of the reporting period—for example, July 2000 to June 2001 is published under 2001. Therefore, in some cases (e.g., government finance) data for Mauritius may appear a year off compared to last year's publication, where data were published under the first year of the reporting period.

1

Selected Background Data

The first two tables of the volume provide selected indicators, including a series on population, as background to the data in the rest of the volume. Table 1-1 provides a comparative view, across indicators, of some of the more important indicators for all countries in the most recent year for which relatively complete information is available.

1-1. Basic Indicators

	Population mid-2002 (millions)	Land area (thousands of square km.)	GNI per capita		Life expectancy at birth (years)	Gross school enrollment				Total net ODA per capita
			Atlas dollars	Av. annual percentage growth		Primary		Secondary		
			2002	1990-02	2002	1980	1995-00	1980	1995-00	2002
SUB-SAHARAN AFRICA	689.3	23,626	451	0.02	46	80	87	15	26	28
excluding South Africa	643.9	22,405	307	0.5	46	80	72	15	21	29
excl. S.Africa & Nigeria	511.1	21,494	309	0.5	46	72	85	14	22	36
Angola	13.1	1,247	670	-5.4	47	175	74	21	15	32
Benin	6.6	111	380	2.1	53	67	95	16	22	34
Botswana	1.7	567	3,010	1.8	38	91	108	19	82	22
Burkina Faso	11.8	274	250	1.5	43	17	44	3	10	40
Burundi	7.1	26	100	-3.7	42	26	65	3	7	24
Cameroon	15.8	465	550	-1.0	48	98	108	18	20	40
Cape Verde	0.5	4	1,250	3.0	69	114	139	8	69	201
Central African Republic	3.8	623	250	-0.5	42	71	75	14	10	16
Chad	8.3	1,259	220	-0.8	48	..	73	..	11	28
Comoros	0.6	2	390	-1.3	61	86	86	22	21	55
Congo, Dem. Rep. of	51.6	2,267	90	-7.3	45	92	47	24	18	16
Congo, Rep. of	3.7	342	720	-3.4	52	141	97	74	52	115
Côte d'Ivoire	16.5	318	610	5.7	48	75	81	19	22	65
Djibouti	0.7	23	900	0.0	44	37	40	12	15	112
Equatorial Guinea	0.5	28	..	..	52	..	120	..	31	42
Eritrea	4.3	101	180	0.3	51	..	57	..	28	54
Ethiopia	67.2	1,000	100	1.8	42	37	64	9	5	19
Gabon	1.3	258	3,120	-0.6	53	..	144	..	54	55
Gambia, The	1.4	10	270	0.2	53	53	82	11	27	44
Ghana	20.3	228	270	1.7	55	79	80	41	37	32
Guinea	7.7	246	410	2.0	46	36	67	17	14	32
Guinea-Bissau	1.4	28	150	-2.2	45	68	83	6	20	41
Kenya	31.3	569	360	-0.1	46	115	94	20	30	13
Lesotho	1.8	30	470	-0.5	43	103	115	18	28	43
Liberia	3.3	96	140	0.0	47	48	118	22	23	16
Madagascar	16.4	582	230	-0.7	55	130	103	..	14	23
Malawi	10.7	94	160	0.9	38	60	137	5	45	35
Mali	11.4	1,220	240	1.3	41	26	61	8	15	42
Mauritania	2.8	1,025	280	2.0	51	37	83	11	18	128
Mauritius	1.2	2	3,900	4.1	73	93	109	50	107	20
Mozambique	18.4	784	210	4.2	41	99	92	5	14	112
Namibia	2.0	823	1,960	2.0	42	..	112	..	60	68
Niger	11.4	1,267	170	-1.0	46	25	35	5	7	26
Nigeria	132.8	911	300	0.3	45	109	82	18	30	2
Rwanda	8.2	25	210	-0.3	40	63	119	3	12	44
São Tomé and Principe	0.2	1	290	-0.3	66	..	..	..	..	169
Senegal	9.8	193	460	1.3	52	46	75	11	20	46
Seychelles	0.1	0.5	7,050	1.9	73	..	..	..	..	93
Sierra Leone	5.2	72	140	-5.2	37	52	93	14	24	68
Somalia	9.3	627	..	0.0	47	21	10	9	6	21
South Africa	45.3	1,221	2,600	-0.1	46	90	111	..	90	14
Sudan	32.8	2,376	380	0.3	53	50	55	16	29	11
Swaziland	1.1	17	1,240	0.3	44	103	125	38	60	23
Tanzania	35.2	884	290	1.0	43	93	77	3	5	35
Togo	4.8	54	270	-0.9	50	118	124	33	36	11
Uganda	24.6	197	240	3.7	43	50	136	5	13	26
Zambia	10.2	743	..	-0.8	37	90	78	16	25	63
Zimbabwe	13.0	387	..	-0.8	39	85	95	8	45	15
NORTH AFRICA	142.6	5,738	1,644	1.6	70	84	103	41	69	20
Algeria	31.3	2,382	1,720	0.1	71	94	112	33	67	12
Egypt, Arab Rep.	66.4	995	1,470	2.7	69	73	100	50	84	19
Libya	5.4	1,760	..	0.0	72	125	116	76	79	2
Morocco	29.6	446	1,170	1.0	68	83	94	26	39	21
Tunisia	9.8	155	1,990	3.3	73	102	117	27	75	49
ALL AFRICA	831.8	29,364	650	0.5	50	81	91	20	33	27

Note: 2002 data are preliminary (see page 2). GNI per capita previously called GNP per capita.

Selected Background Data

1-2. Population

	Millions of people											Average annual percentage growth		
	1980	1993	1994	1995	1996	1997	1998	1999	2000	2001	2002	75-84	85-94	95-MR
SUB-SAHARAN AFRICA	383.55	552.51	565.22	580.90	596.71	613.51	628.81	643.86	658.68	674.17	689.26	3.0	2.8	2.5
excluding South Africa	355.97	515.03	526.93	541.78	556.71	572.58	586.91	600.94	614.68	629.36	643.92	3.0	2.8	2.5
excl. S.Africa & Nigeria	284.82	410.14	418.92	430.51	442.22	454.90	466.09	477.04	487.77	499.49	511.13	3.0	2.8	2.5
Angola	7.05	10.29	10.57	10.87	11.16	11.45	11.74	12.05	12.39	12.75	13.12	2.9	2.7	2.7
Benin	3.46	5.18	5.34	5.47	5.61	5.75	5.90	6.06	6.22	6.39	6.55	2.7	3.2	2.6
Botswana	0.91	1.40	1.45	1.50	1.54	1.58	1.61	1.65	1.68	1.70	1.71	3.6	3.3	2.1
Burkina Faso	6.96	9.53	9.76	9.99	10.23	10.47	10.73	11.00	11.27	11.55	11.83	2.4	2.4	2.5
Burundi	4.13	5.89	6.03	6.16	6.29	6.42	6.55	6.68	6.81	6.94	7.07	2.5	2.7	2.0
Cameroon	8.75	12.72	13.07	13.41	13.76	14.11	14.45	14.78	15.12	15.45	15.77	2.9	3.0	2.4
Cape Verde	0.29	0.36	0.37	0.38	0.39	0.40	0.41	0.42	0.44	0.45	0.46	1.0	2.0	2.6
Central African Republic	2.31	3.15	3.25	3.35	3.45	3.54	3.61	3.67	3.72	3.77	3.82	2.5	2.2	2.0
Chad	4.48	6.33	6.52	6.73	6.95	7.17	7.39	7.62	7.86	8.10	8.34	2.3	2.7	3.1
Comoros	0.34	0.47	0.48	0.49	0.51	0.52	0.53	0.54	0.56	0.57	0.59	..	2.7	2.5
Congo, Dem. Rep. of	27.91	41.33	42.81	44.38	45.74	46.85	47.70	48.28	48.57	50.05	51.58	3.1	3.2	2.1
Congo, Rep. of	1.80	2.75	2.84	2.94	3.03	3.13	3.23	3.34	3.45	3.55	3.66	3.2	3.3	3.2
Côte d'Ivoire	8.19	13.04	13.46	13.88	14.29	14.70	15.09	15.47	15.83	16.18	16.51	3.9	3.5	2.6
Djibouti	0.30	0.54	0.56	0.58	0.60	0.62	0.63	0.65	0.67	0.68	0.69	5.9	5.6	2.7
Equatorial Guinea	0.22	0.38	0.39	0.40	0.41	0.42	0.44	0.45	0.46	0.47	0.48	2.2	2.6	2.7
Eritrea	2.38	3.39	3.48	3.57	3.67	3.77	3.88	3.99	4.10	4.20	4.30	2.6	2.9	2.7
Ethiopia	37.72	53.30	54.89	56.53	58.23	59.75	61.27	62.78	64.30	65.78	67.22	2.8	2.9	2.6
Gabon	0.70	1.05	1.08	1.11	1.14	1.17	1.20	1.23	1.26	1.29	1.32	3.2	3.2	2.5
Gambia, The	0.64	1.05	1.08	1.12	1.15	1.19	1.23	1.27	1.31	1.35	1.39	3.1	4.2	3.2
Ghana	11.04	16.51	16.99	17.51	18.00	18.46	18.88	19.26	19.59	19.93	20.27	2.7	2.8	2.2
Guinea	4.46	6.26	6.43	6.59	6.76	6.92	7.09	7.25	7.42	7.58	7.74	1.7	2.9	2.4
Guinea-Bissau	0.79	1.12	1.16	1.19	1.23	1.26	1.29	1.33	1.37	1.41	1.45	3.2	2.9	2.8
Kenya	16.63	25.35	26.02	26.69	27.36	28.04	28.73	29.42	30.09	30.74	31.35	3.8	3.1	2.4
Lesotho	1.28	1.63	1.64	1.66	1.68	1.69	1.71	1.73	1.74	1.76	1.78	2.4	1.5	1.0
Liberia	1.88	2.60	2.66	2.73	2.81	2.88	2.96	3.04	3.13	3.21	3.30	3.2	2.2	2.7
Madagascar	8.87	12.54	12.91	13.30	13.72	14.15	14.59	15.05	15.52	15.98	16.44	2.6	2.7	3.1
Malawi	6.18	8.92	9.07	9.21	9.44	9.67	9.88	10.10	10.31	10.53	10.74	3.3	2.7	2.2
Mali	6.59	9.16	9.39	9.62	9.85	10.09	10.33	10.58	10.84	11.10	11.37	2.2	2.7	2.4
Mauritania	1.61	2.18	2.24	2.30	2.36	2.43	2.50	2.57	2.65	2.72	2.79	2.5	2.4	2.8
Mauritius	0.97	1.10	1.11	1.12	1.13	1.15	1.16	1.17	1.19	1.20	1.21	1.4	0.9	1.1
Mozambique	12.10	15.01	15.42	15.82	16.23	16.63	16.97	17.30	17.69	18.07	18.44	2.7	1.3	2.2
Namibia	1.02	1.57	1.61	1.65	1.69	1.73	1.78	1.84	1.89	1.94	1.99	2.0	4.0	2.8
Niger	5.59	8.43	8.73	9.04	9.36	9.70	10.05	10.40	10.74	11.09	11.43	3.1	3.2	3.5
Nigeria	71.15	104.89	108.01	111.27	114.50	117.68	120.82	123.90	126.91	129.88	132.79	3.1	2.9	2.6
Rwanda	5.16	7.61	5.27	5.70	5.70	7.08	7.28	7.49	7.71	7.93	8.16	3.3	1.0	5.8
São Tomé and Principe	0.09	0.13	0.13	0.13	0.14	0.14	0.14	0.15	0.15	0.15	0.15	1.5	2.9	2.3
Senegal	5.54	7.93	8.13	8.34	8.54	8.75	8.97	9.18	9.39	9.61	9.83	2.9	2.8	2.4
Seychelles	0.06	0.07	0.07	0.08	0.08	0.08	0.08	0.08	0.08	0.08	0.08	1.3	1.0	1.6
Sierra Leone	3.24	4.29	4.40	4.51	4.62	4.73	4.83	4.93	5.03	5.13	5.24	2.0	2.3	2.2
Somalia	6.49	7.76	7.64	7.36	7.61	7.87	8.15	8.43	8.72	9.02	9.32	6.3	2.0	3.0
South Africa	27.58	37.47	38.28	39.12	40.00	40.93	41.90	42.92	44.00	44.81	45.35	2.3	2.3	2.2
Sudan	19.37	26.63	27.32	28.08	28.81	29.52	30.19	30.83	31.44	32.09	32.79	3.0	2.1	2.3
Swaziland	0.57	0.85	0.87	0.90	0.93	0.96	0.99	1.02	1.05	1.07	1.09	3.2	3.2	2.9
Tanzania	18.58	27.94	28.79	29.65	30.49	31.32	32.13	32.92	33.70	34.45	35.18	3.2	3.2	2.5
Togo	2.52	3.70	3.78	3.87	3.97	4.09	4.23	4.38	4.56	4.66	4.76	2.5	2.8	3.1
Uganda	12.81	19.24	19.78	20.27	20.80	21.35	21.95	22.58	23.25	23.93	24.60	2.6	3.5	2.8
Zambia	5.74	8.46	8.68	8.88	9.08	9.29	9.49	9.69	9.89	10.07	10.24	3.4	3.0	2.1
Zimbabwe	7.13	11.03	11.26	11.48	11.70	11.93	12.16	12.40	12.65	12.85	13.00	3.4	3.1	1.9
NORTH AFRICA	88.35	121.52	123.96	126.34	128.62	130.93	133.23	135.55	137.87	140.20	142.56	2.7	2.3	1.8
Algeria	18.67	26.89	27.50	28.06	28.57	29.05	29.51	29.95	30.39	30.84	31.32	3.1	2.6	1.6
Egypt, Arab Rep.	40.88	55.93	57.06	58.18	59.27	60.42	61.58	62.77	63.98	65.18	66.37	2.5	2.3	1.9
Libya	3.04	4.57	4.66	4.75	4.85	4.94	5.04	5.14	5.24	5.34	5.45	4.5	2.4	2.0
Morocco	19.38	25.47	25.93	26.39	26.85	27.31	27.78	28.24	28.71	29.17	29.64	2.3	2.1	1.7
Tunisia	6.38	8.66	8.82	8.96	9.09	9.22	9.33	9.46	9.56	9.67	9.78	2.6	2.2	1.3
ALL AFRICA	471.90	674.03	689.18	707.24	725.33	744.43	762.04	779.41	796.54	814.37	831.82	2.9	2.7	2.4

Note: 2002 data are preliminary (see page 2).

Figure 1-1. Development diamonds for all African countries, 2002*

* Or most recent year available.   (Figure continued on the following page.)

Figure 1-1. *(continued)*

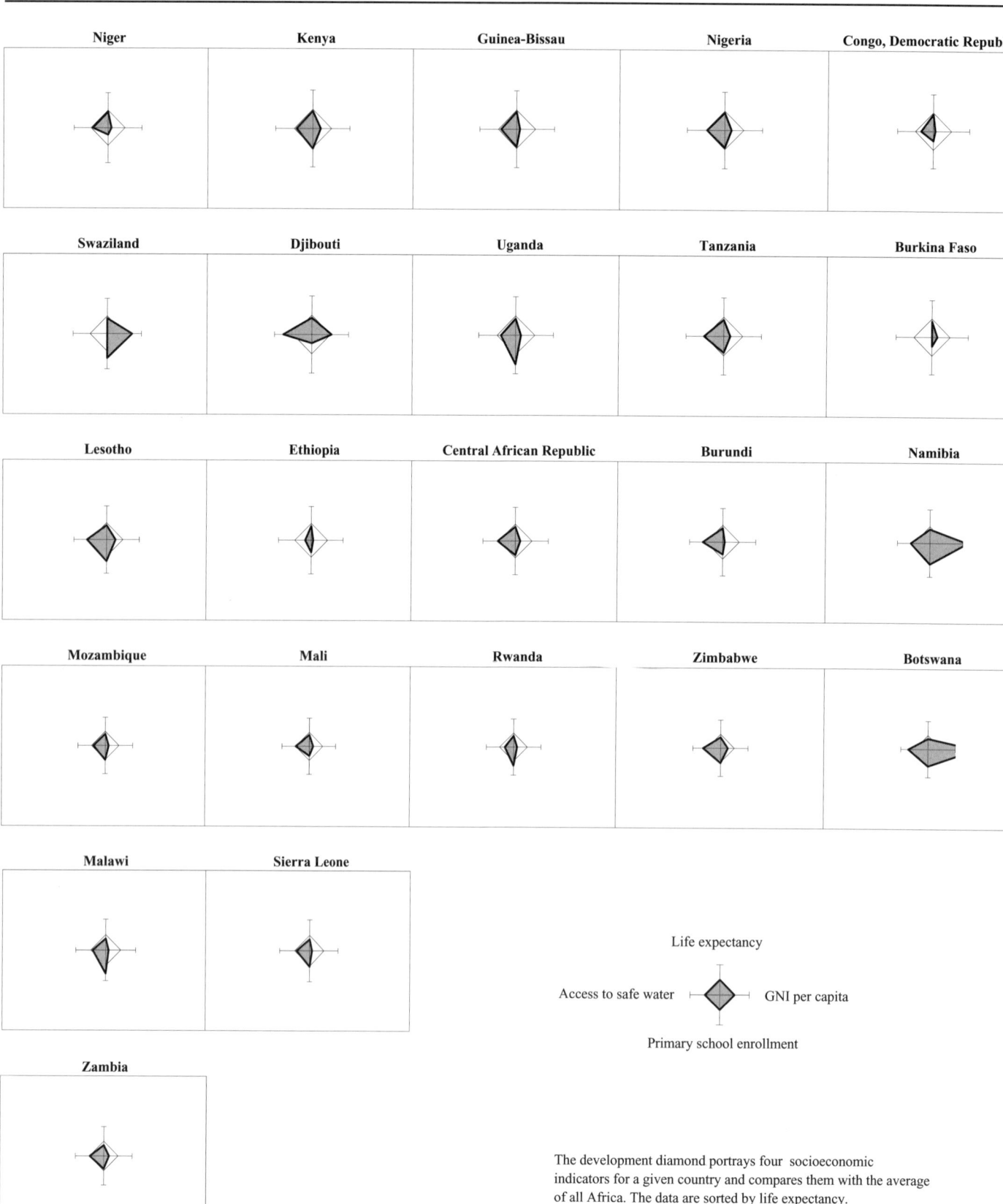

The development diamond portrays four socioeconomic indicators for a given country and compares them with the average of all Africa. The data are sorted by life expectancy.

Figure 1-2. Selected basic indicators, 2002*

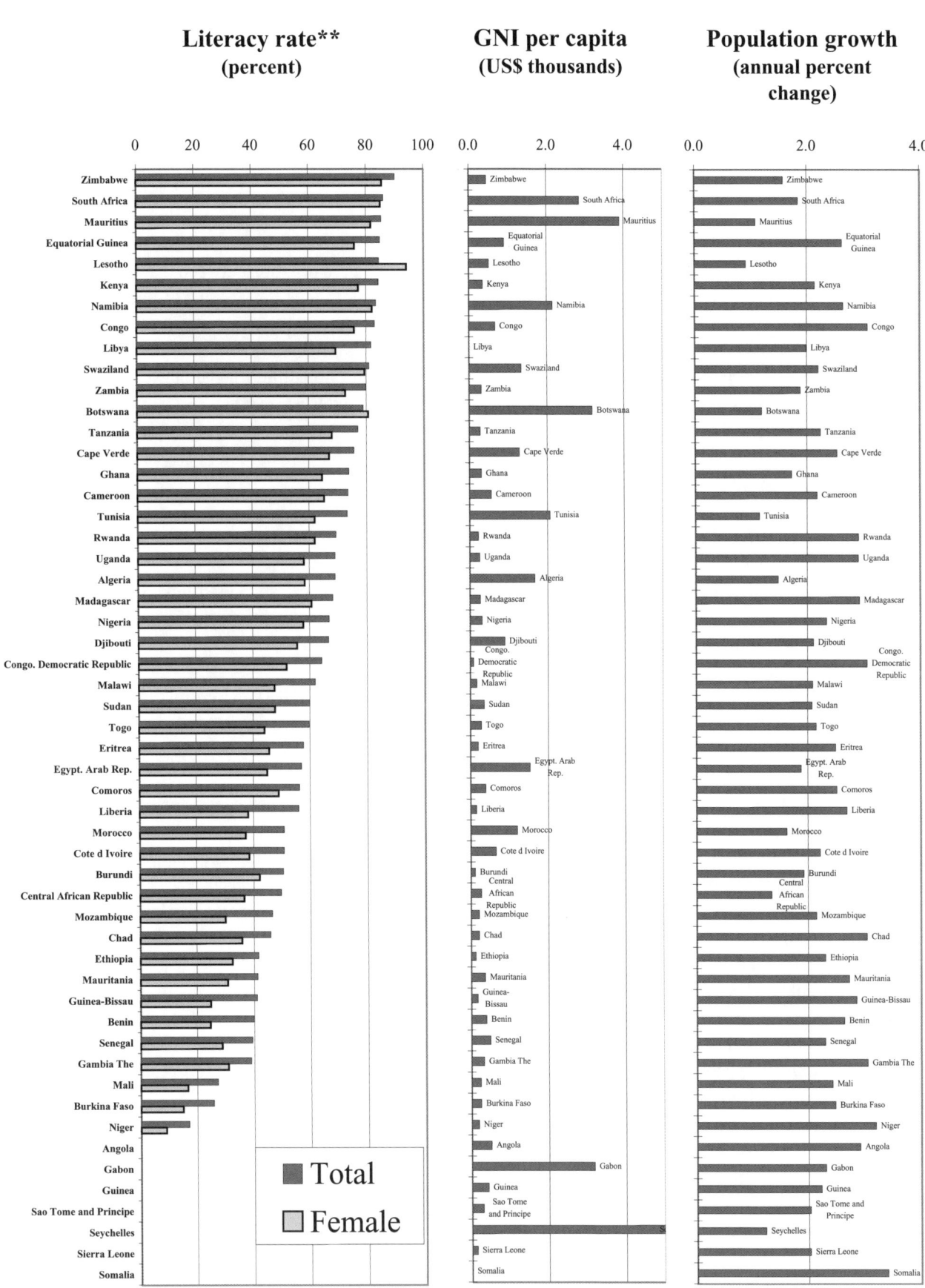

* Or most recent year available.
** Sorted by total literacy rate.

Technical notes

Tables

Table 1-1. Basic indicators. The data for this table are from the World Bank's Statistical Information Management and Analysis Database (SIMA), except for aid flows, which are from the Organisation for Economic Co-operation and Development (OECD), Geographic Distribution of Aid Flows to Developing Countries database (see technical notes to Chapter 12). Regional aggregates for GNP per capita, life expectancy, and education are weighted by population.

Population estimates for mid-2002 are World Bank estimates. These are usually projections from the most recent population censuses or surveys (mostly from 1980–2002). Refugees not permanently settled in the country of asylum are generally considered to be part of the population of their country of origin (see technical notes to Tables 13-1, 13-4, and 13-5).

Land area refers to the land surface area of a country, excluding inland waters.

Gross national income (GNI) per capita figures in U.S. dollars are calculated according to the *World Bank Atlas* method described below. GNI measures the total domestic and foreign value added claimed by residents. It comprises GDP (defined in the note for Table 2-5) plus net factor income from abroad, which is the income residents receive from abroad for factor services (labor and capital) less similar payments made to nonresidents who contributed to the domestic economy. The data are from the Food and Agriculture Organization (FAO).

The *World Bank Atlas* method uses a three-year average of conversion factors to convert GNI data, expressed in different national currencies, to a common denomination, conventionally U.S. dollars. The *Atlas* conversion factor for any year is the average of the official exchange rate (Table 3-4) or alternative conversion factor (Table 3-6) for that year and for the two preceding years, after adjusting them for differences in relative inflation between that country and the United States. This three-year average smoothes fluctuations in prices and exchange rates for each country. The resulting GNI in U.S. dollars is divided by the midyear population for the latest of the three years to derive GNI per capita.

The following formulas describe the procedures for computing the conversion factor for year t:

$$e^*_{t-2,t} = \tfrac{1}{3}\left[e_{t-2}\left(\frac{P_t}{P_{t-2}} \Big/ \frac{P^\$_t}{P^\$_{t-2}} \right) + e_{t-1}\left(\frac{P_t}{P_{t-1}} \Big/ \frac{P^\$_t}{P^\$_{t-1}} \right) + e_t \right]$$

and for calculating per capita GNI in U.S. dollars for year t:

$$Y^\$_t = (Y_t/N_t) + e^*_{t-2,t}$$

where Y_t = current GNI (local currency) for year t, P_t = GNI deflator for year t, N_t midyear population for year t, and $P^\$_t$ = US GNI deflator for year t.

Growth rates of GNI per capita for this table are shown in real terms. They have been calculated by the least-squares method using constant GNI per capita series in 1995 prices in national currency (World Bank, SIMA). (See also technical notes for Table 2-19.)

Life expectancy at birth indicates the number of years a newborn infant would live if prevailing patterns of mortality at the time of its birth were to remain the same throughout its life. Figures are World Bank estimates based on data from the UN Population Division, the UN Statistical Office, and national statistical offices.

Primary school enrollment is the ratio of children of all ages enrolled in primary school to the population of children of primary school age. While many countries consider the primary school age to be 6 to 11 years, others use different age groups. These different country practices arc also reflected in the ratios. Gross enrollment may be reported in excess of 100 percent if some pupils are younger or older than the country's standard range of primary school age. In practice, enrollment does not necessarily equal attendance, nor does it remain constant throughout the year. Data are from the United Nations Education, Scientific, and Cultural Organization (UNESCO).

Secondary school enrollment is the ratio of children of all ages enrolled in secondary schools to the population of children of secondary school age. The definition of secondary school age differs among countries. It is most commonly considered to be 12 to 17 years. Data are from UNESCO.

Total net ODA per capita consists of net disbursements of loans and grants from all official sources on concessional financial terms, divided by the midyear population for the corresponding year (see the technical notes to Chapter 12).

Table 1-2. Population. Average annual percentage growth shown in this table was calculated using the least-squares method.

Figures

The following indicators have been used to derive the figures in this chapter.

Figure 1-1. Life expectancy (Table 1-1); access to safe water (Table 13-11); GNI per capita (Table 2-19); primary school enrollment (Table 1-1).

Figure 1-2. Literacy rate (Table 13-14); GNI per capita (Table 2-19); population growth (Table 1-2).

Methodology used for regional aggregations and period averages in Chapter 1

Table	Aggregations [a]						Period averages [b]	
	(1)	(2)	(3)	(4)	(5)	(6)	(2)	(3)
Table 1-1								
Column 1	x							
Column 2	x							
Column 3				x				
Column 4				x				x
Column 5					x			
Column 6					x			
Column 7					x			
Column 8					x			
Column 9					x			
Column 10		x						
Table 1-2	x						x	

Note: Regional aggregations are shown in the rows for Sub-Saharan Africa, North Africa, and All Africa. Period averages are shown in column 4 for Table 1-1 and in the last three columns for Table 1-2. This table shows only the methodologies used in this chapter.

a. Regional aggregations: (1) simple total; (2) simple total of the first indicator divided by the simple total of the second indicator (same country coverage); (3) simple total of the gap-filled indicator; (4) simple total of the gap-filled main indicator divided by the simple total of the gap-filled secondary indicator; (5) simple total of the first gap-filled main indicator less the simple total of the second gap-filled main indicator, all divided by the simple total of the secondary indicator; (6) weighted total (by population); (7) median; (8) no aggregation; (9) simple arithmetic mean.

b. Period averages: (1) arithmetic mean (using the same series as shown in the table; i.e., ratio if the rest of the table is shown as ratio, level if the rest of the table is shown as level, growth rate if the rest is shown as growth rate); (2) least-squares growth rate (using main indicator); (3) least-squares growth rate (using main indicator in constant terms, with the rest of the table in current terms).

2

National Accounts

ational accounts data provide the broadest picture of a nation's economic performance. National accounts give information on the structure of production in the form of gross domestic product (GDP) and its components by industrial origin, GDP and its components by expenditure, and information on a nation's economic relations with the outside world. These key statistics are used for assessing a nation's economic condition at a given time or the trends in a nation's economic performance over time. National accounts data also provide a quantitative basis for forecasting and policymaking and as such are used widely by analysts and policymakers.

GDP and its components by industrial origin are compiled following the widely used System of National Accounts (SNA). The SNA methodology accounts for virtually all activities pertinent to the production of goods and the provision of services in an economy by residents and nonresidents, regardless of the allocation to domestic and foreign claims. GDP does not account for the depreciation of fixed capital.

There are three methods of compiling GDP figures: income, expenditure, and production methods. Because of technical and resource constraints, the income method is not used in most developing countries. In this volume, GDP and its components by industrial origin are compiled using the production method. The three components of GDP by industrial origin are value added in agriculture, value added in industry, and value added in services. (See the technical notes at the end of this chapter.) The national accounts are constructed in national currencies and in current prices. Figures reported in this chapter are, however, in U.S. dollars, usually converted from national currency series at the official exchange rate. If the official exchange rate is significantly different from the prevailing market rate or shows extreme volatility, the local currency is converted into U.S. dollars by using an alternative conversion factor. The conversion factors used for this purpose are presented in Table 3-6. Reporting currencies in a common denominator facilitates cross-country comparisons and aggregations in country groups.

In addition, estimates of GDP and its components by industrial origin are converted into constant prices. Reporting figures in constant prices is essential for monitoring real changes in the structure of production and for analyzing relationships among prices, production, employment, and so forth.

Constant price series in U.S. dollars use a 1995 base year and are converted from the national currency series using 1995 exchange rates. As this volume establishes a common base year for all countries, national accounts in national currencies at constant prices based on years other than 1995 have been partly rebased to 1995 by rescaling constant price series of components of GDP.

Using a single base year raises problems when there are profound structural changes or significant changes in relative prices. For example, values expressed in constant U.S. dollars necessarily reflect the exchange rates prevailing during the base year. Where subsequent exchange rate changes have been substantial, as they have for many African countries since 1980, comparisons among countries and aggregate trends will be affected. For this reason alone, the data should be used with considerable caution.

Monitoring resource allocations across sectors in any given point in time requires the use of current prices. Accordingly, in addition to GDP in constant prices, GDP in current prices is provided. Following GDP in current prices are components of GDP by expenditure. Data on consumption, investment, and savings are constructed using the SNA's convention. Conceptually, all income is either consumed or saved; as such the sum of total consumption and gross domestic saving equals GDP.

When viewed from a production point of view, by definition savings equals investment. Investment measures additions to fixed assets of an economy—whether it represents additions to the stock of capital or merely replenishes depreciated capital stock—plus net changes in the level of inventories. It is financed either through domestic savings or by drawing on the savings of foreigners. Data on gross domestic investment and gross domestic savings thus shed light not only on the nature of the domestic inter-temporal resource allocation but also on the size of the resource gap. Gross national savings, however, indicates the amount of savings generated by a nation's residents.

Although this volume includes a chapter on international trade, the fact that balance of payments is an integral part of the national accounts warrants the inclusion of the resource balance and its components in this chapter. Moreover, a closer examination of the fifth edition of the IMF's *Balance of Payments Manual* (1993) reflects differences in concepts, definitions, and classifications from the UN's SNA guidelines. For instance, in the SNA, factor services rendered by residents of another country are excluded from goods and services, but this practice is not universally followed. The tables on resource balance, and on values of exports (free on board [f.o.b.]) and imports (cost, insurance, freight [c.i.f.]) of goods and nonfactor services in current U.S. dollars provide a comprehensive and systematic framework for macroeconomic analysis in general. Those interested in a more specialized and rigorous study of international trade transactions should use the data provided in Chapter 5.

The rate of growth of real domestic product is an important indicator of economic progress and as such is widely monitored. Because these growth rates are calculated from national series, they are suitable for both cross-country comparisons and trend analysis for individual countries. Aggregate values and trends, however, reflect the choice of the base year, as explained above.

Gross national income (GNI) per capita, which is GDP per capita adjusted for changes in international terms of trade and which include net factor income from abroad, and total consumption per capita are also widely monitored indicators of economic progress. When expressed in current U.S. dollars to facilitate comparison and aggregation, however, the values for these indicators necessarily reflect exchange rate fluctuations as well as underlying economic and demographic changes. These indicators may be used with caution for cross-country comparison during any single year. They require special attention when used for trend analysis.

Data for Chapter 2 are from the World Bank's country desks. Estimates are based on data obtained from national sources, usually collected by World Bank staff who review the quality of national accounts data and, in some instances, help adjust the national series.

2-1. Gross domestic product, real

	Millions of U.S. dollars, constant 1995 prices											Average annual percentage growth		
	1980	1993	1994	1995	1996	1997	1998	1999	2000	2001	2002	75-84	85-94	95-MR
SUB-SAHARAN AFRICA	248,355	302,568	309,061	320,712	337,185	348,998	356,862	365,671	377,006	389,124	400,117	2.3	1.7	3.2
excluding South Africa	120,662	160,557	162,433	169,531	179,513	187,174	193,855	199,360	204,871	212,133	217,854	2.1	2.6	3.7
excl. S.Africa & Nigeria	97,602	133,126	134,980	141,401	150,181	157,059	163,184	168,362	172,562	178,892	184,939	2.8	2.2	3.9
Angola	5,076	4,410	4,565	5,040	5,604	6,047	6,458	6,674	6,877	7,095	8,181	..	-1.2	6.7
Benin	1,253	1,840	1,921	2,009	2,121	2,251	2,353	2,464	2,606	2,737	2,901	3.8	2.3	5.3
Botswana	1,394	4,412	4,572	4,773	5,040	5,386	5,710	6,018	6,472	6,813	7,023	11.6	8.9	5.8
Burkina Faso	1,475	2,332	2,355	2,463	2,638	2,775	2,803	2,991	3,039	3,178	3,325	3.6	3.2	4.3
Burundi	728	1,122	1,079	1,000	917	920	964	955	946	977	1,012	3.8	2.7	-0.4
Cameroon	6,319	7,909	7,711	7,965	8,364	8,790	9,233	9,639	10,044	10,576	11,020	8.5	-2.7	4.7
Cape Verde	171	427	456	491	510	538	578	627	669	703	733	10.0	6.4	6.3
Central African Republic	964	998	1,047	1,122	1,077	1,134	1,187	1,230	1,258	1,277	1,267	0.4	-0.5	2.6
Chad	788	1,296	1,427	1,438	1,473	1,536	1,627	1,617	1,608	1,760	1,934	-1.3	3.2	3.5
Comoros	167	236	224	232	229	238	241	246	243	248	254	..	1.2	1.4
Congo, Dem. Rep. of	7,531	5,831	5,604	5,643	5,586	5,272	5,186	4,958	4,611	4,519	4,654	-0.3	-4.0	-3.0
Congo, Rep. of	1,281	2,133	2,015	2,116	2,207	2,194	2,275	2,207	2,388	2,474	2,560	9.2	0.3	2.7
Côte d'Ivoire	5,297	10,185	10,267	10,999	11,850	12,527	13,121	13,330	13,000	13,045	12,812	1.9	4.7	2.8
Djibouti	..	524	509	498	481	478	481	491	495	..	..	..	-1.2	-0.4
Equatorial Guinea	..	137	144	164	212	363	442	625	731	740	742	..	3.0	26.5
Eritrea	..	471	571	587	642	692	705	704	612	674	687	..	..	1.8
Ethiopia	..	5,263	5,447	5,780	6,410	6,755	6,630	7,041	7,445	8,106	8,326	..	1.3	5.2
Gabon	3,565	4,481	4,635	4,958	5,213	5,514	5,628	5,279	5,385	5,520	5,685	-0.2	1.9	2.0
Gambia, The	241	378	379	382	390	410	430	457	483	511	495	4.3	3.4	4.2
Ghana	4,231	6,004	6,202	6,457	6,755	7,038	7,369	7,694	7,978	8,313	8,687	-1.1	4.7	4.3
Guinea	..	3,325	3,536	3,692	3,862	4,055	4,250	4,445	4,530	4,702	4,899	..	3.8	4.2
Guinea-Bissau	134	236	243	254	283	302	217	234	251	252	234	2.1	3.8	-1.1
Kenya	5,612	8,443	8,665	9,047	9,422	9,618	9,773	9,900	9,883	9,995	10,098	4.7	3.6	1.7
Lesotho	498	864	894	933	1,026	1,109	1,058	1,060	1,074	1,109	1,151	6.7	5.4	2.7
Liberia	..	..	..	..	..	..	..	..	..	..	..	..	..	..
Madagascar	3,048	3,109	3,107	3,160	3,228	3,347	3,479	3,641	3,814	4,043	3,529	-0.2	1.2	2.8
Malawi	992	1,363	1,224	1,429	1,533	1,591	1,644	1,710	1,729	1,657	1,687	3.2	2.2	3.5
Mali	2,013	2,301	2,322	2,466	2,546	2,718	2,882	3,076	3,219	3,331	3,653	2.3	2.5	5.7
Mauritania	753	976	1,021	1,068	1,127	1,163	1,206	1,255	1,319	1,371	1,417	1.6	2.6	4.2
Mauritius	1,686	3,512	3,671	3,820	4,018	4,254	4,509	4,748	4,938	5,268	5,500	..	6.5	5.3
Mozambique	1,938	2,061	2,216	2,311	2,475	2,750	3,097	3,330	3,381	3,821	4,115	..	4.1	8.3
Namibia	2,442	3,136	3,365	3,503	3,615	3,768	3,892	4,022	4,156	4,257	4,373	..	3.4	3.3
Niger	1,833	1,762	1,833	1,881	1,945	1,999	2,207	2,194	2,163	2,317	2,386	2.0	1.5	3.4
Nigeria	22,357	27,396	27,423	28,109	29,318	30,109	30,675	31,012	32,315	33,252	32,953	-0.7	5.0	2.5
Rwanda	1,658	1,923	957	1,293	1,458	1,660	1,807	1,944	2,061	2,199	2,405	6.8	-2.7	10.8
São Tomé and Principe	..	44	45	45	46	47	48	49	50	52	55	..	1.7	2.5
Senegal	3,061	4,137	4,256	4,476	4,706	4,943	5,227	5,488	5,795	6,118	6,185	2.1	2.1	5.0
Seychelles	326	517	512	508	533	597	647	659	691	676	678	3.4	5.7	4.4
Sierra Leone	1,123	1,031	1,011	930	987	813	806	741	769	811	862	2.5	-1.7	-2.7
Somalia	..	..	..	..	..	..	..	..	..	..	..	..	..	..
South Africa	127,411	141,957	146,547	151,113	157,621	161,793	163,014	166,329	172,143	177,012	182,281	2.4	0.8	2.6
Sudan	4,929	8,890	8,980	9,519	10,631	11,355	12,074	12,705	13,358	14,174	14,956	8.6	4.1	6.5
Swaziland	640	1,272	1,315	1,364	1,417	1,472	1,519	1,571	1,604	1,632	1,690	3.3	7.3	3.1
Tanzania	..	4,996	5,074	5,255	5,495	5,688	5,899	6,114	6,461	6,854	7,287	..	2.6	4.5
Togo	1,175	1,056	1,214	1,309	1,425	1,486	1,454	1,489	1,461	1,457	1,525	2.1	0.5	2.2
Uganda	..	4,851	5,161	5,756	6,278	6,598	6,922	7,468	7,879	8,277	8,833	..	5.1	6.6
Zambia	3,366	3,916	3,579	3,478	3,719	3,842	3,770	3,854	3,992	4,188	4,326	0.2	0.9	2.5
Zimbabwe	4,354	6,500	7,100	7,111	7,848	8,058	8,291	8,233	7,831	7,172	6,771	3.0	3.3	-0.2
NORTH AFRICA	106,378	165,142	171,630	174,245	185,670	190,423	201,480	209,482	216,741	226,068	234,629	6.0	2.8	4.1
Algeria	31,384	40,601	40,235	41,764	43,476	43,955	46,196	47,675	48,819	50,583	52,328	5.5	0.5	3.3
Egypt, Arab Rep.	29,896	55,295	57,478	60,159	63,173	66,643	70,361	74,599	78,422	81,009	83,440	8.3	3.9	5.0
Libya	..	..	..	..	..	..	..	..	..	..	..	..	..	..
Morocco	21,590	31,995	35,309	32,986	37,016	36,191	38,969	38,984	39,324	41,880	43,722	4.1	3.6	3.0
Tunisia	10,475	17,018	17,579	17,987	19,256	20,304	21,269	22,559	23,623	24,898	26,392	5.3	3.8	5.3
ALL AFRICA	357,329	468,704	481,483	496,071	523,839	540,572	559,009	575,607	594,157	615,439	634,837	3.3	2.0	3.5

Note: 2002 data are preliminary (see page 2).

2-2. Value added in agriculture

				Millions of U.S. dollars, constant 1995 prices								*Average annual percentage growth*		
	1980	*1993*	*1994*	*1995*	*1996*	*1997*	*1998*	*1999*	*2000*	*2001*	*2002*	*75-84*	*85-94*	*95-MR*
SUB-SAHARAN AFRICA	41,986	52,741	53,779	54,737	59,506	61,608	63,078	65,831	68,084	70,040	72,548	1.1	2.6	3.9
excluding South Africa	36,504	46,540	47,083	49,405	52,874	54,924	56,860	59,298	61,049	63,128	65,362	1.2	2.6	4.1
excl. S.Africa & Nigeria	29,791	38,275	38,615	40,631	43,752	45,416	46,965	48,887	50,336	52,007	53,645	2.5	2.2	4.1
Angola	..	275	302	369	423	466	490	496	543	640	704	..	-9.1	9.8
Benin	361	617	673	684	755	798	850	884	941	970	1,041	3.0	4.9	5.7
Botswana	165	195	189	193	192	190	188	173	171	175	176	-3.7	5.5	-1.5
Burkina Faso	448	789	789	783	850	837	896	929	964	928	1,005	1.0	4.6	3.1
Burundi	358	499	448	421	427	429	452	438	455	472	490	2.0	1.9	1.4
Cameroon	2,131	2,782	2,868	3,119	3,350	3,603	3,847	4,109	4,294	4,530	4,815	4.5	0.3	6.6
Cape Verde	31	65	63	67	92	88	90	101	104	106	107	12.7	4.6	6.7
Central African Republic	391	462	468	491	515	547	568	591	628	653	679	0.6	1.1	4.8
Chad	319	406	515	505	519	546	604	585	565	591	618	-1.0	4.6	2.4
Comoros	63	91	87	95	95	102	102	107	123	135	141	..	1.8	6.1
Congo, Dem. Rep. of	2,076	2,883	2,859	3,191	3,258	3,169	3,123	2,964	2,882	2,726	2,808	1.7	2.5	-1.4
Congo, Rep. of	159	200	207	221	232	234	234	221	230	243	253	3.4	1.7	1.7
Côte d'Ivoire	1,816	2,422	2,607	2,720	2,827	2,867	3,031	2,967	3,352	3,368	3,356	2.7	6.0	3.4
Djibouti	..	15	14	15	15	15	16	16	17	..	..	..	-2.4	2.6
Equatorial Guinea	..	64	73	83	95	115	102	112	122	130	136	..	-0.6	7.5
Eritrea	..	92	125	110	104	105	165	152	86	111	72	..	..	-3.7
Ethiopia	..	3,030	2,919	3,018	3,461	3,580	3,180	3,301	3,374	3,761	3,643	..	2.7	2.4
Gabon	431	455	448	398	397	417	395	413	428	446	468	..	-0.3	1.1
Gambia, The	95	91	97	99	96	103	112	140	157	171	123	3.0	-1.2	6.6
Ghana	2,143	2,370	2,415	2,504	2,634	2,748	2,888	3,000	3,070	3,183	3,313	0.2	1.9	4.0
Guinea	..	700	735	761	795	835	879	948	945	1,005	1,056	..	3.6	4.7
Guinea-Bissau	59	117	123	132	152	165	132	142	147	149	143	-2.6	3.5	1.3
Kenya	1,660	2,207	2,275	2,384	2,490	2,520	2,560	2,593	2,541	2,575	2,594	4.1	2.0	1.4
Lesotho	130	152	151	145	166	172	177	184	188	189	184	-0.5	1.7	3.2
Liberia	..	..	..	..	..	..	..	..	..	..	..	..	..	..
Madagascar	593	773	769	784	803	818	836	864	871	906	892	0.2	2.3	2.1
Malawi	261	387	275	384	482	482	495	550	584	547	562	2.2	1.0	7.7
Mali	823	991	1,057	1,082	1,117	1,168	1,202	1,312	1,395	1,215	1,412	3.2	5.2	3.5
Mauritania	160	235	246	251	251	264	281	306	315	314	303	2.9	3.3	3.6
Mauritius	275	366	339	320	340	360	365	368	282	371	395	..	0.7	1.2
Mozambique	..	734	686	805	892	969	1,039	1,099	999	1,125	1,204	..	2.3	6.2
Namibia	248	334	386	376	410	384	407	432	468	419	403	..	4.7	1.5
Niger	577	678	747	756	757	777	941	894	819	940	953	1.1	3.0	3.3
Nigeria	6,432	8,298	8,498	8,809	9,169	9,556	9,942	10,457	10,760	11,169	11,761	-3.0	4.5	4.1
Rwanda	663	640	440	569	682	711	785	853	930	1,008	1,154	5.6	-2.1	11.2
São Tomé and Principe	..	12	12	12	13	13	14	14	15	15	16	..	4.8	3.5
Senegal	669	808	884	903	958	934	909	961	1,063	1,144	917	-1.2	1.7	1.8
Seychelles	28	20	22	21	22	23	23	26	27	26	26	-3.1	-1.7	2.9
Sierra Leone	582	384	403	363	384	366	376	356	363	377	404	7.9	-7.2	0.0
Somalia	..	..	..	..	..	..	..	..	..	..	..	..	..	..
South Africa	5,448	6,166	6,651	5,326	6,603	6,659	6,209	6,523	7,017	6,901	7,174	0.2	2.1	2.0
Sudan	1,904	3,014	2,907	3,082	3,679	4,278	4,788	5,385	5,670	5,986	6,407	6.8	2.9	11.0
Swaziland	180	167	172	168	205	226	236	246	232	211	215	-1.4	-0.4	3.2
Tanzania	..	2,123	2,167	2,294	2,383	2,441	2,488	2,591	2,679	2,825	2,965	..	3.5	3.7
Togo	285	469	468	494	575	601	584	615	587	574	618	2.8	3.2	2.7
Uganda	..	2,420	2,462	2,607	2,718	2,748	2,796	2,959	3,124	3,267	3,428	..	3.6	4.0
Zambia	346	521	423	564	560	531	538	592	601	586	576	0.5	0.8	2.7
Zimbabwe	684	966	1,036	958	1,147	1,184	1,244	1,298	1,337	1,176	1,094	-0.1	1.8	2.1
NORTH AFRICA	16,087	21,536	24,702	21,322	27,210	24,563	27,295	26,752	25,710	..	..	2.0	3.3	2.1
Algeria	2,484	3,811	3,468	3,986	4,939	4,275	4,762	4,891	4,646	4,971	5,170	3.7	4.1	3.9
Egypt, Arab Rep.	6,302	8,846	9,185	9,451	9,742	10,076	10,452	10,839	11,209	..	..	2.8	2.7	3.4
Libya	..	..	..	..	..	..	..	..	..	..	..	..	..	..
Morocco	5,032	5,328	8,599	4,820	8,580	6,309	8,071	6,726	5,639	6,936	7,421	0.4	3.1	-0.5
Tunisia	1,504	2,527	2,275	2,049	2,655	2,734	2,710	3,023	2,993	3,038	3,235	1.2	4.4	5.0
ALL AFRICA	58,053	74,254	78,409	76,053	86,638	86,155	90,318	92,557	93,802	98,009	101,927	1.4	2.8	3.5

Note: 2002 data are preliminary (see page 2).

2-3. Value added in industry

	Millions of U.S. dollars, constant 1995 prices											Average annual percentage growth		
	1980	1993	1994	1995	1996	1997	1998	1999	2000	2001	2002	75-84	85-94	95-MR
SUB-SAHARAN AFRICA	82,276	89,613	90,943	94,006	97,663	101,459	102,376	103,407	106,957	110,234	113,851	2.3	0.8	2.7
excluding South Africa	38,451	44,403	44,578	45,913	48,673	51,169	52,580	53,844	55,939	57,902	60,112	1.8	1.9	3.8
excl. S.Africa & Nigeria	23,817	31,224	31,788	32,974	34,956	37,284	38,969	40,626	41,893	43,671	46,650	..	1.3	4.8
Angola	..	2,718	3,046	3,339	3,707	4,004	4,415	4,700	4,867	5,066	5,917	..	0.2	8.0
Benin	134	272	285	293	316	328	329	336	365	399	423	5.4	3.1	4.8
Botswana	652	2,147	2,188	2,253	2,366	2,531	2,641	2,778	3,119	3,339	3,412	24.0	4.8	6.2
Burkina Faso	286	414	381	414	429	472	426	452	479	519	522	1.6	1.8	3.6
Burundi	142	217	203	168	146	145	147	158	164	191	239	8.9	2.2	2.3
Cameroon	1,478	2,221	1,901	1,855	1,939	2,088	2,248	2,389	2,509	2,672	2,854	18.3	-4.3	5.8
Cape Verde	28	85	88	96	99	96	105	112	125	131	137	6.3	8.8	5.7
Central African Republic	190	191	216	224	199	195	198	206	225	234	244	1.4	0.1	1.5
Chad	88	181	172	206	201	223	263	256	257	323	405	-2.0	1.0	9.4
Comoros	22	27	27	28	27	25	27	27	40	44	46	..	-0.5	7.7
Congo, Dem. Rep. of	2,464	1,084	1,062	952	952	759	776	838	824	855	881	-2.0	-10.7	-2.1
Congo, Rep. of	483	929	901	949	965	1,046	1,104	1,122	1,171	1,135	1,177	11.5	1.9	3.5
Côte d'Ivoire	982	1,988	2,030	2,285	2,500	2,971	3,050	3,099	2,808	2,689	2,588	6.5	7.3	2.9
Djibouti	..	95	87	67	64	63	61	62	62	..	..	..	-1.4	-4.2
Equatorial Guinea	..	35	35	44	84	236	337	543	652	644	1,167	..	15.9	57.0
Eritrea	..	64	73	89	121	145	136	140	131	139	152	..	..	7.6
Ethiopia	..	427	457	494	521	535	548	595	605	636	673	..	-3.5	4.6
Gabon	1,859	2,264	2,469	2,597	2,655	2,679	2,714	2,752	2,797	2,853	2,930	..	2.4	1.8
Gambia, The	31	48	46	44	46	46	51	54	57	60	66	3.1	5.6	5.1
Ghana	1,356	1,456	1,508	1,568	1,642	1,747	1,803	1,892	1,980	2,076	2,206	-7.5	5.0	4.8
Guinea	..	1,081	1,102	1,169	1,271	1,328	1,376	1,449	1,519	1,600	1,676	..	2.6	5.2
Guinea-Bissau	18	28	28	29	31	31	19	19	20	21	24	3.2	3.1	-4.9
Kenya	769	1,162	1,184	1,226	1,268	1,294	1,312	1,325	1,308	1,318	1,333	4.7	3.7	1.3
Lesotho	137	284	296	319	353	384	366	362	378	397	421	14.6	10.0	3.6
Liberia	..	..	..	..	..	..	..	..	..	..	..	..	..	..
Madagascar	306	269	266	271	276	289	304	317	335	360	285	-2.9	1.2	2.7
Malawi	173	231	237	247	268	268	271	278	276	246	228	2.7	3.7	-0.1
Mali	217	398	382	408	435	532	564	578	621	814	908	1.6	3.3	11.1
Mauritania	169	281	288	298	302	287	286	284	303	307	320	0.6	2.8	0.9
Mauritius	372	986	1,032	1,079	1,137	1,200	1,268	1,331	1,413	1,512	1,556	..	9.2	5.5
Mozambique	..	340	361	410	494	625	802	941	1,048	1,259	1,416	..	-3.0	19.6
Namibia	740	777	847	865	821	875	920	926	938	996	1,050	..	2.8	2.7
Niger	368	315	317	325	346	358	368	376	384	393	403	10.4	-1.6	3.0
Nigeria	13,605	13,210	12,845	13,009	13,791	13,992	13,757	13,406	14,224	14,433	13,745	0.0	3.6	1.0
Rwanda	424	402	139	207	242	285	314	331	342	368	398	7.4	-7.2	12.0
São Tomé and Principe	..	9	9	9	9	9	9	10	10	10	11	..	0.9	2.4
Senegal	498	796	793	885	932	987	1,070	1,142	1,211	1,284	1,406	3.7	3.0	7.0
Seychelles	49	91	94	115	136	165	190	176	199	197	203	2.0	6.3	9.6
Sierra Leone	216	231	231	193	203	188	177	151	158	167	178	-3.1	2.5	-3.6
Somalia	..	..	..	..	..	..	..	..	..	..	..	..	..	..
South Africa	43,794	45,169	46,306	48,025	48,956	50,278	49,820	49,614	51,081	52,405	53,827	2.6	-0.1	1.6
Sudan	..	..	..	..	..	..	..	..	..	..	..	..	..	..
Swaziland	139	438	461	484	494	509	525	539	549	566	591	4.4	14.9	2.9
Tanzania	..	708	719	705	753	803	886	932	1,002	1,071	1,171	..	1.0	6.8
Togo	277	190	241	290	306	313	316	315	331	331	348	1.5	0.8	3.5
Uganda	..	555	627	754	879	979	1,065	1,192	1,259	1,315	1,410	..	7.8	10.2
Zambia	1,233	1,413	1,273	1,095	1,101	1,180	1,053	987	1,016	1,109	1,216	-0.4	1.6	-0.8
Zimbabwe	1,353	1,673	1,956	1,828	2,016	2,030	2,008	1,939	1,749	1,578	1,448	-1.0	2.9	-3.2
NORTH AFRICA	42,050	61,314	61,744	64,256	66,620	70,050	73,531	76,421	81,765	..	..	6.2	2.4	4.7
Algeria	15,236	19,041	18,601	19,139	19,723	20,454	21,361	22,332	23,298	23,476	24,271	5.0	0.3	3.6
Egypt, Arab Rep.	9,620	17,145	17,384	18,195	18,886	20,053	21,479	22,263	25,090	..	..	11.0	4.3	6.0
Libya	..	..	..	..	..	..	..	..	..	..	..	..	..	..
Morocco	7,171	10,016	10,416	10,882	11,406	12,038	12,312	12,653	12,973	13,363	13,830	3.4	3.0	3.5
Tunisia	2,945	4,791	4,949	5,224	5,390	5,713	6,001	6,310	6,640	6,985	7,362	7.1	4.0	5.1
ALL AFRICA	125,037	150,498	152,299	157,818	163,835	170,961	175,073	178,773	187,362	192,591	199,167	3.5	1.4	3.4

Note: 2002 data are preliminary (see page 2).

2-4. Value added in services

				Millions of U.S. dollars, constant 1995 prices								*Average annual percentage growth*		
	1980	*1993*	*1994*	*1995*	*1996*	*1997*	*1998*	*1999*	*2000*	*2001*	*2002*	*75-84*	*85-94*	*95-MR*
SUB-SAHARAN AFRICA	104,249	141,327	144,688	151,235	157,707	163,006	167,740	173,108	178,415	184,611	189,324	3.3	1.9	3.4
excluding South Africa	42,519	62,543	63,628	66,549	69,364	72,264	74,915	77,070	78,866	81,673	83,180	3.3	2.7	3.4
excl. S.Africa & Nigeria	38,949	56,670	57,729	60,514	63,149	65,744	68,281	70,393	71,921	74,508	76,336	3.5	2.3	3.5
Angola	..	1,375	1,221	1,332	1,473	1,576	1,581	1,536	1,532	1,465	1,663	..	-3.1	2.7
Benin	783	953	958	1,033	1,040	1,118	1,165	1,237	1,288	1,358	1,423	3.8	0.4	5.0
Botswana	420	1,667	1,835	1,982	2,123	2,281	2,458	2,617	2,758	2,946	3,117	6.3	13.4	6.8
Burkina Faso	736	1,126	1,187	1,266	1,361	1,466	1,486	1,615	1,600	1,733	1,801	6.4	2.9	5.2
Burundi	166	308	298	285	252	253	259	267	276	286	296	6.2	3.5	0.4
Cameroon	2,365	2,332	2,637	2,793	2,714	2,689	2,669	2,663	2,756	2,880	2,926	8.6	-4.3	0.9
Cape Verde	114	279	306	328	326	358	386	419	443	469	491	10.5	6.1	6.4
Central African Republic	358	287	309	347	299	320	345	354	325	308	262	0.3	-3.0	-1.2
Chad	391	662	712	696	707	718	752	765	772	831	894	-0.7	2.9	2.9
Comoros	83	118	111	109	107	111	113	112	79	68	65	..	1.2	-6.7
Congo, Dem. Rep. of	3,286	1,897	1,715	1,501	1,374	1,313	1,263	1,151	904	949	978	-0.5	-6.4	-7.4
Congo, Rep. of	629	1,004	907	945	1,008	918	944	876	997	1,099	1,134	9.3	-1.2	2.2
Côte d'Ivoire	2,479	5,774	5,625	5,995	6,527	6,708	7,057	7,284	6,838	6,982	6,859	0.5	2.4	2.4
Djibouti	..	354	344	355	332	337	349	355	360	..	..	..	-1.0	0.7
Equatorial Guinea	..	32	32	34	38	43	52	59	65	72	81	..	6.5	13.0
Eritrea	..	253	315	328	351	371	344	355	353	369	388	..	..	1.9
Ethiopia	..	1,565	1,689	1,846	1,975	2,111	2,329	2,508	2,745	2,875	3,007	..	1.9	7.7
Gabon	1,326	1,778	1,755	1,963	2,137	2,362	2,447	2,108	2,153	2,213	2,280	..	1.7	2.2
Gambia, The	119	190	186	188	197	212	227	226	229	242	266	4.7	3.5	4.3
Ghana	1,015	2,184	2,282	2,385	2,482	2,569	2,691	2,818	2,950	3,082	3,217	0.1	7.9	4.4
Guinea	..	1,436	1,561	1,604	1,656	1,713	1,800	1,836	1,886	1,924	1,961	..	3.6	3.0
Guinea-Bissau	47	76	77	78	87	91	62	67	75	74	86	10.0	4.2	-0.5
Kenya	2,112	3,714	3,842	4,046	4,256	4,387	4,475	4,548	4,593	4,656	4,716	5.9	4.5	2.4
Lesotho	187	314	332	348	371	391	399	400	400	406	419	5.0	4.6	2.7
Liberia	..	..	..	..	..	..	..	..	..	..	..	..	..	..
Madagascar	1,924	1,844	1,853	1,882	1,922	2,014	2,111	2,226	2,381	2,526	2,136	0.1	1.1	3.4
Malawi	441	616	579	631	626	678	709	727	722	717	748	3.1	2.7	3.0
Mali	552	699	695	695	754	770	802	852	879	936	938	1.6	0.9	4.3
Mauritania	353	384	398	402	437	487	512	538	569	618	673	2.1	2.9	6.9
Mauritius	843	1,700	1,827	1,960	2,079	2,207	2,337	2,480	2,604	2,777	2,932	..	6.4	6.0
Mozambique	..	774	990	907	902	931	1,001	982	992	1,071	1,086	..	8.1	1.9
Namibia	927	1,685	1,773	1,861	1,952	2,032	2,074	2,149	2,229	2,298	2,367	..	4.3	3.6
Niger	888	769	769	800	842	864	898	924	961	984	1,030	-0.1	1.9	3.6
Nigeria	3,488	5,884	5,910	6,049	6,230	6,535	6,651	6,697	6,964	7,185	6,873	1.5	7.4	2.3
Rwanda	571	881	378	518	534	665	708	761	788	823	854	7.6	-0.8	9.7
São Tomé and Principe	..	23	24	25	24	24	25	25	26	27	28	..	0.3	1.9
Senegal	1,891	2,532	2,578	2,687	2,815	3,022	3,249	3,387	3,522	3,690	3,867	3.1	1.9	5.4
Seychelles	260	295	309	308	311	346	361	385	402	390	380	-3.9	4.4	3.7
Sierra Leone	323	353	339	311	327	284	281	257	267	279	297	2.8	0.7	-2.2
Somalia	..	..	..	..	..	..	..	..	..	..	..	..	..	..
South Africa	61,526	78,705	80,975	84,598	88,250	90,653	92,740	95,948	99,448	102,835	106,029	3.2	1.4	3.3
Sudan	2,283	4,698	5,057	5,313	5,212	5,416	5,491	5,940	6,353	6,605	6,850	11.0	5.3	4.0
Swaziland	223	413	419	439	446	460	474	495	519	535	556	5.8	4.8	3.6
Tanzania	..	1,810	1,816	1,866	1,934	1,994	2,077	2,184	2,315	2,442	2,593	..	4.1	4.6
Togo	619	396	506	524	543	571	553	557	541	551	556	2.0	-1.9	0.8
Uganda	..	1,571	1,693	1,917	2,082	2,200	2,387	2,551	2,721	2,901	3,103	..	5.7	7.5
Zambia	1,619	1,621	1,449	1,404	1,628	1,693	1,766	1,876	1,957	2,052	2,132	0.1	0.1	5.4
Zimbabwe	2,076	3,200	3,301	3,500	3,776	3,828	3,937	4,016	3,872	3,667	3,514	5.4	3.8	0.8
NORTH AFRICA	43,389	74,875	78,126	80,857	84,239	87,573	92,228	97,209	99,772	..	..	7.5	3.1	4.4
Algeria	10,209	14,027	14,443	14,848	15,060	15,394	16,049	16,316	16,586	17,083	18,025	6.2	0.9	2.6
Egypt, Arab Rep.	12,243	25,798	27,251	28,682	30,473	32,094	33,819	36,609	37,012	..	..	11.0	3.8	5.5
Libya	..	..	..	..	..	..	..	..	..	..	..	..	..	..
Morocco	9,925	16,753	17,075	17,285	17,801	18,147	19,173	19,864	20,681	21,742	22,671	5.9	4.0	3.8
Tunisia	6,006	9,659	10,344	10,714	11,186	11,834	12,547	13,206	13,981	14,879	15,801	5.7	3.6	5.5
ALL AFRICA	148,711	216,838	223,359	232,720	242,606	251,225	260,481	270,700	278,610	289,110	298,226	4.4	2.3	3.7

Note: 2002 data are preliminary (see page 2).

2-5. Gross domestic product, nominal

	Millions of U.S. dollars, current prices											Annual average		
	1980	*1993*	*1994*	*1995*	*1996*	*1997*	*1998*	*1999*	*2000*	*2001*	*2002*	*75-84*	*85-94*	*95-MR*
SUB-SAHARAN AFRICA	260,862	288,471	279,966	320,712	333,683	345,814	323,648	323,231	326,303	318,646	319,842	199,387	267,105	326,485
excluding South Africa	181,119	158,093	144,066	169,531	190,098	197,155	190,221	192,448	198,685	205,017	216,344	139,094	164,867	194,937
excl. S.Africa & Nigeria	115,762	136,814	120,389	141,401	154,702	160,833	158,041	155,824	156,406	162,152	172,637	96,882	139,662	157,750
Angola	..	5,286	4,060	5,040	7,526	7,675	6,445	6,090	8,858	9,471	11,248	..	7,538	7,794
Benin	1,405	2,106	1,497	2,009	2,208	2,157	2,335	2,387	2,255	2,372	2,695	1,035	1,602	2,302
Botswana	1,061	4,160	4,340	4,773	4,805	5,191	4,932	5,069	5,362	5,252	5,273	818	3,058	5,082
Burkina Faso	1,929	2,345	1,972	2,463	2,773	2,602	2,794	2,811	2,601	2,782	3,127	1,479	2,435	2,744
Burundi	920	939	925	1,000	900	957	878	714	679	689	719	778	1,093	817
Cameroon	6,741	11,891	7,854	7,965	9,109	9,115	8,703	9,186	8,854	8,501	9,374	5,630	10,944	8,851
Cape Verde	107	363	411	491	502	506	540	583	531	572	644	86	303	546
Central African Republic	797	1,299	853	1,122	1,070	1,003	1,047	1,051	953	967	1,046	619	1,223	1,033
Chad	1,033	1,463	1,179	1,438	1,605	1,508	1,741	1,534	1,390	1,670	2,002	928	1,432	1,611
Comoros	124	278	186	232	230	212	216	223	204	219	247	113	215	223
Congo, Dem. Rep. of	14,391	10,708	5,817	5,643	5,771	6,107	6,150	4,727	4,854	5,187	5,707	12,212	8,399	5,518
Congo, Rep. of	1,706	1,919	1,769	2,116	2,541	2,323	1,949	2,354	3,220	2,788	3,017	1,452	2,306	2,538
Côte d'Ivoire	10,175	11,045	8,313	10,999	12,140	11,722	12,782	12,556	10,578	10,742	11,686	7,126	10,458	11,651
Djibouti	..	471	487	498	494	503	514	536	553	..	..	..	425	516
Equatorial Guinea	..	152	126	164	259	498	456	872	1,341	1,846	2,173	104	123	951
Eritrea	..	468	532	587	694	686	745	728	641	708	642	..	492	679
Ethiopia	..	6,250	5,539	5,780	6,010	6,381	6,516	6,498	6,528	6,510	6,059	5,603	7,690	6,285
Gabon	4,279	4,381	4,191	4,958	5,741	5,428	4,619	4,352	4,932	4,334	4,971	3,211	4,357	4,917
Gambia, The	241	366	363	382	392	410	417	432	421	391	357	181	289	400
Ghana	4,445	5,966	5,441	6,457	6,926	6,884	7,474	7,710	4,978	5,309	6,160	3,762	5,606	6,487
Guinea	..	3,279	3,434	3,692	3,869	3,784	3,588	3,461	3,113	3,042	3,213	..	2,750	3,470
Guinea-Bissau	111	237	236	254	271	269	206	224	215	200	203	131	203	230
Kenya	7,265	4,977	7,149	9,047	9,257	10,745	11,229	10,559	10,440	11,234	12,330	5,535	7,493	10,605
Lesotho	432	815	835	933	943	1,024	890	911	859	768	714	310	584	880
Liberia	1,117	..	..	..	..	..	..	..	..	..	..	987	1,143	..
Madagascar	4,042	3,371	2,977	3,160	3,995	3,546	3,739	3,717	3,878	4,530	4,400	3,057	2,873	3,870
Malawi	1,238	2,071	1,182	1,429	2,432	2,534	1,736	1,810	1,707	1,688	1,901	1,018	1,560	1,905
Mali	1,787	2,678	1,763	2,466	2,619	2,475	2,597	2,570	2,443	2,630	3,091	1,285	2,101	2,611
Mauritania	709	944	1,027	1,068	1,116	1,096	1,002	958	936	1,008	984	645	965	1,021
Mauritius	1,153	3,307	3,373	3,820	4,163	4,385	4,146	4,175	4,424	4,526	4,533	1,060	2,309	4,271
Mozambique	3,526	1,981	2,178	2,311	2,841	3,397	3,874	3,985	3,685	3,436	3,599	3,457	2,739	3,391
Namibia	2,169	2,847	3,253	3,503	3,491	3,636	3,399	3,385	3,458	3,163	2,904	1,895	2,289	3,367
Niger	2,509	1,607	1,563	1,881	1,988	1,846	2,077	2,018	1,798	1,945	2,171	1,725	2,036	1,965
Nigeria	64,202	21,353	23,663	28,109	35,299	36,229	32,144	36,511	42,078	42,674	43,540	42,093	25,226	37,073
Rwanda	1,163	1,971	754	1,293	1,382	1,852	1,989	1,931	1,811	1,703	1,732	1,091	1,988	1,712
São Tomé and Principe	47	48	50	45	45	44	41	47	46	47	50	41	52	46
Senegal	2,987	5,431	3,642	4,476	4,636	4,374	4,655	4,751	4,374	4,611	5,037	2,364	4,685	4,614
Seychelles	147	474	487	508	503	563	608	623	618	618	699	112	336	593
Sierra Leone	1,101	769	994	930	942	849	672	669	636	749	783	963	787	779
Somalia	604	..	..	..	..	..	..	..	..	..	..	677	977	..
South Africa	80,544	130,406	135,778	151,113	143,732	148,814	133,663	131,058	127,965	114,174	104,242	61,201	102,551	131,845
Sudan	6,760	5,953	6,496	9,519	8,425	10,277	10,692	10,640	11,249	12,099	13,516	7,025	10,109	10,802
Swaziland	546	1,063	1,146	1,364	1,332	1,436	1,358	1,377	1,394	1,276	1,186	433	782	1,340
Tanzania	..	4,258	4,511	5,255	6,496	7,684	8,383	8,638	9,079	9,341	9,382	5,569	4,539	8,032
Togo	1,136	1,234	983	1,309	1,465	1,499	1,416	1,421	1,221	1,259	1,384	813	1,294	1,372
Uganda	1,245	3,220	3,990	5,756	6,045	6,269	6,534	5,966	5,891	5,641	5,803	2,289	4,318	5,988
Zambia	3,884	3,274	3,347	3,478	3,270	3,910	3,237	3,131	3,238	3,637	3,697	3,159	3,037	3,450
Zimbabwe	6,679	6,564	6,891	7,111	8,553	8,428	5,732	5,494	7,204	9,057	8,304	5,993	7,233	7,485
NORTH AFRICA	125,005	157,899	160,024	174,245	194,559	200,333	211,661	220,001	233,503	237,595	237,340	97,452	149,937	213,655
Algeria	42,345	49,946	42,543	41,764	46,845	47,869	47,357	47,592	53,306	56,689	57,990	34,827	55,135	49,926
Egypt, Arab Rep.	22,912	47,197	51,898	60,159	67,651	75,605	82,704	89,207	98,782	97,545	90,650	20,312	40,682	82,788
Libya	35,545	..	..	..	..	..	..	..	..	..	..	24,534	22,892	..
Morocco	18,821	26,801	30,351	32,986	36,639	33,415	35,817	35,277	33,344	34,219	37,555	13,499	23,292	34,907
Tunisia	8,743	14,609	15,626	17,987	19,587	18,900	19,850	20,970	19,462	20,032	22,067	6,901	11,842	19,857
ALL AFRICA	386,160	447,284	440,364	496,071	528,399	546,409	533,728	541,003	556,694	552,489	553,502	296,948	418,329	538,537

Note: 2002 data are preliminary (see page 2).

2-6. Total consumption

	Percentage of GDP											Annual average		
	1980	1993	1994	1995	1996	1997	1998	1999	2000	2001	2002	75-84	85-94	95-MR
SUB-SAHARAN AFRICA	74.5	85.1	83.0	83.3	80.6	83.7	84.9	84.4	80.6	81.6	81.5	78.7	82.1	82.6
excluding South Africa	80.1	88.5	85.1	85.3	80.2	84.9	86.8	86.5	79.9	82.1	82.5	82.6	85.5	83.5
excl. S.Africa & Nigeria	87.6	89.9	86.2	86.1	83.7	87.1	88.1	87.6	83.6	83.8	82.2	85.2	86.7	85.3
Angola	..	90.1	73.9	73.7	51.2	74.1	80.7	86.9	37.0	65.0	60.8	..	79.7	66.2
Benin	106.3	98.9	94.0	93.3	96.6	94.4	93.4	95.2	94.0	93.5	94.0	101.7	100.0	94.3
Botswana	73.3	63.2	63.0	62.5	58.7	57.0	60.2	61.9	59.7	60.3	61.5	76.7	58.6	60.2
Burkina Faso	107.2	94.8	93.0	91.8	91.7	90.1	88.4	91.9	93.5	94.9	95.2	103.4	96.9	92.2
Burundi	100.6	104.7	107.6	104.8	97.5	96.1	102.9	100.5	105.7	104.8	104.5	95.9	101.0	102.1
Cameroon	78.3	82.4	82.1	80.4	82.7	80.9	80.8	81.6	79.7	79.6	83.2	76.9	79.1	81.1
Cape Verde	124.0	96.3	97.2	97.0	116.7	107.4	116.7	117.6	113.3	110.0	110.1	119.8	102.4	111.1
Central African Republic	108.9	98.2	94.0	93.8	99.4	95.6	94.7	89.0	92.2	88.9	89.7	101.6	98.6	92.9
Chad	..	106.2	101.5	101.7	96.7	97.7	92.8	104.7	97.9	94.9	93.6	97.6	107.4	97.5
Comoros	110.1	98.5	106.5	105.3	103.6	109.0	104.7	105.7	101.4	100.0	99.4	106.5	102.9	103.7
Congo, Dem. Rep. of	89.9	96.0	89.4	85.9	72.5	93.8	101.3	91.0	95.7	93.8	96.0	89.5	90.2	91.2
Congo, Rep. of	64.3	76.4	84.5	62.3	64.3	62.2	69.7	59.0	42.3	46.9	50.0	73.9	77.8	57.1
Côte d'Ivoire	79.6	86.7	75.1	77.1	79.2	77.2	80.3	78.7	82.4	80.4	74.8	76.2	84.6	78.8
Djibouti	..	..	..	108.3	106.9	105.7	100.8	105.5	105.3	..	..	..	..	105.4
Equatorial Guinea	..	113.7	74.9	72.7	69.3	56.9	80.1	35.2	26.0	9.6	7.3	92.4	114.6	44.6
Eritrea	..	124.0	129.7	138.0	130.6	124.9	138.5	139.1	144.2	131.6	130.1	..	126.5	134.6
Ethiopia	..	97.9	94.6	92.0	93.0	92.1	92.3	97.9	99.1	97.4	97.8	93.6	94.3	95.2
Gabon	39.4	63.3	54.7	52.7	49.0	49.0	61.0	65.2	71.7	49.7	51.6	41.9	64.5	56.2
Gambia, The	94.2	96.0	97.2	103.9	94.4	95.5	97.2	96.8	97.4	102.4	96.3	95.7	92.5	98.0
Ghana	95.1	94.0	87.5	88.4	86.8	95.8	89.7	96.1	94.6	93.0	89.7	93.7	94.0	91.8
Guinea	..	88.9	87.9	87.2	82.3	78.6	82.7	82.7	83.2	80.0	88.7	..	84.9	83.2
Guinea-Bissau	101.0	93.0	96.1	101.2	98.2	97.0	110.1	101.1	110.4	113.2	117.4	103.0	98.0	106.1
Kenya	86.6	76.2	80.4	88.7	86.8	92.1	90.7	89.8	94.3	94.5	89.6	82.6	82.5	90.8
Lesotho	152.0	133.8	130.3	131.6	127.4	129.4	123.9	119.8	117.9	109.7	115.1	168.2	152.2	121.9
Liberia	72.7	..	..	..	..	..	..	..	..	..	..	76.7	83.6	..
Madagascar	101.4	97.9	96.7	96.6	93.9	95.3	93.0	92.8	92.3	84.7	92.3	98.1	96.0	92.6
Malawi	89.2	100.9	103.0	100.3	96.9	100.7	92.5	100.2	102.8	110.3	105.7	84.4	91.7	101.2
Mali	98.9	93.6	92.5	92.2	92.8	90.0	89.6	90.5	91.9	95.9	89.8	99.8	96.9	91.6
Mauritania	103.5	95.3	83.1	91.1	93.7	92.1	95.0	92.8	83.8	86.0	91.0	105.6	90.7	90.7
Mauritius	85.5	74.8	76.4	76.6	76.2	75.7	75.1	76.2	75.8	74.0	74.3	83.1	75.4	75.5
Mozambique	110.6	122.4	113.9	101.9	101.8	98.9	93.2	91.0	89.4	72.2	70.0	110.4	112.8	89.8
Namibia	61.6	88.3	81.4	84.5	84.9	89.8	86.3	87.5	86.2	86.2	76.5	90.3	88.1	85.2
Niger	85.4	96.1	100.0	99.8	96.9	96.8	97.3	96.3	96.7	95.9	95.8	91.6	94.7	96.9
Nigeria	68.6	79.8	79.4	81.6	65.1	75.4	80.4	81.8	66.6	75.5	82.6	78.5	78.8	76.1
Rwanda	95.8	98.6	148.5	107.3	105.8	104.1	102.8	99.8	98.6	97.4	98.6	93.2	100.8	101.8
São Tomé and Principe	111.6	131.6	117.5	111.4	113.7	116.5	107.0	110.3	106.0	127.1	124.3	106.6	125.1	114.5
Senegal	105.0	92.3	88.2	88.9	87.8	88.8	86.9	86.5	91.4	91.4	90.1	98.9	93.5	89.0
Seychelles	72.9	81.8	75.9	76.8	70.3	79.1	81.3	74.4	75.7	76.9	72.2	68.1	75.1	75.8
Sierra Leone	99.1	92.6	88.7	102.1	105.7	96.9	101.6	101.6	108.1	112.1	113.6	90.8	88.6	105.2
Somalia	112.9	..	..	..	..	..	..	..	..	..	..	111.4	97.4	..
South Africa	62.2	81.0	80.9	81.1	81.2	82.2	82.3	81.5	81.7	81.3	80.8	69.5	76.4	81.5
Sudan	100.2	88.2	88.3	88.7	84.4	97.5	89.7	85.1	80.0	..	..	94.8	91.5	87.6
Swaziland	90.4	102.1	96.5	98.7	94.1	96.7	96.7	99.7	96.8	94.3	91.0	85.9	89.6	96.0
Tanzania	..	104.6	98.4	98.1	96.4	95.1	100.8	96.6	90.7	91.6	90.3	89.0	94.6	94.9
Togo	76.8	100.2	84.7	88.8	92.1	99.5	94.5	92.4	95.9	96.4	95.3	78.6	92.1	94.4
Uganda	..	98.9	95.7	92.6	95.4	90.6	94.6	92.6	92.1	92.3	93.7	97.0	97.8	93.0
Zambia	80.7	91.8	92.6	87.8	94.7	90.6	96.1	101.1	91.7	90.2	95.9	81.1	88.4	93.5
Zimbabwe	86.2	79.0	78.2	83.0	81.3	88.9	84.7	84.3	85.2	91.0	89.4	84.8	81.8	86.0
NORTH AFRICA	59.5	80.0	82.0	82.1	80.9	78.7	80.2	78.2	74.9	75.1	75.6	64.7	78.6	78.2
Algeria	56.9	72.3	73.4	71.9	68.6	67.8	72.9	68.6	55.8	59.1	62.0	61.4	73.0	65.8
Egypt, Arab Rep.	84.8	86.8	88.6	87.8	89.2	84.5	84.5	83.1	82.7	82.3	82.2	84.6	85.2	84.5
Libya	43.1	..	..	..	..	..	..	..	..	..	..	53.5	..	..
Morocco	86.3	83.5	84.7	85.9	83.8	82.6	81.9	80.4	81.8	80.7	80.9	87.1	82.5	82.2
Tunisia	76.0	78.3	78.5	79.3	76.5	76.0	76.4	75.4	76.1	75.5	75.1	75.8	76.9	76.3
ALL AFRICA	70.1	83.4	82.7	82.9	80.7	82.0	83.2	82.1	78.4	79.0	79.2	74.6	80.9	80.9

Note:2002 is preliminary.Angola's drop is for weakness in nat. acct. stats. Since 1994, Nigeria's ratios are distorted because the off. ex. rt. used by the Govt. for oil exp. and oil val. added is significantly over-valued.

2-7. General government consumption

	Percentage of GDP											Annual average		
	1980	1993	1994	1995	1996	1997	1998	1999	2000	2001	2002	75-84	85-94	95-MR
SUB-SAHARAN AFRICA	14.8	17.9	17.2	15.9	15.7	16.1	15.5	16.1	17.5	18.1	17.9	15.6	17.0	16.6
excluding South Africa	15.2	16.2	14.5	13.8	13.1	13.7	13.0	14.4	16.7	17.8	17.3	15.8	15.6	15.0
excl. S.Africa & Nigeria	16.5	15.9	14.6	14.3	14.3	14.8	13.6	14.8	15.0	14.4	14.7	16.2	15.9	14.5
Angola	..	41.5	40.1	52.6	39.4	54.4	30.0	60.4	43.8	33.0	35.5	..	36.1	43.6
Benin	8.6	10.3	10.1	11.2	10.7	10.2	9.4	10.0	11.6	11.6	13.0	9.9	12.3	11.0
Botswana	21.3	28.0	28.3	28.5	27.3	26.8	28.9	30.1	29.7	31.4	33.0	22.7	25.1	29.5
Burkina Faso	9.2	13.3	16.1	15.0	13.5	13.0	13.2	12.5	12.6	12.3	13.5	11.4	13.1	13.2
Burundi	9.2	13.3	12.7	13.4	12.6	14.5	13.3	16.1	14.7	13.5	12.8	10.3	10.6	13.9
Cameroon	9.7	12.8	10.0	8.6	8.4	8.2	9.2	10.0	10.2	11.2	12.1	9.7	11.6	9.7
Cape Verde	8.2	17.6	18.3	19.8	17.4	16.2	15.0	19.4	21.1	10.8	11.2	10.0	14.3	16.4
Central African Republic	15.1	15.0	17.5	15.2	9.6	10.9	11.6	11.5	11.3	11.4	11.8	15.0	16.0	11.7
Chad	..	10.0	12.7	11.8	8.7	7.9	5.5	6.9	7.9	7.7	7.7	13.0	12.0	8.0
Comoros	30.9	18.9	23.5	22.3	19.0	17.6	15.7	14.6	13.3	16.3	19.3	29.7	24.6	17.3
Congo, Dem. Rep. of	8.4	15.4	4.4	4.9	6.2	7.8	8.2	6.0	6.7	4.7	3.7	9.1	11.5	6.0
Congo, Rep. of	17.6	21.2	16.2	13.0	14.5	20.0	24.2	15.1	11.6	14.1	18.4	17.3	19.6	16.4
Côte d'Ivoire	16.9	15.5	12.0	10.6	10.5	10.0	9.0	9.5	8.8	9.3	7.7	16.6	18.4	9.4
Djibouti	..	..	..	32.4	27.7	27.8	23.5	26.4	25.2	..	..	..	..	27.2
Equatorial Guinea	..	39.3	15.3	16.4	19.8	11.0	21.0	10.3	6.7	4.2	4.6	28.3	29.7	11.7
Eritrea	..	31.2	30.2	43.9	38.7	29.9	52.0	56.5	49.9	39.4	38.0	..	27.7	43.5
Ethiopia	..	10.2	12.5	11.8	11.7	11.4	14.3	18.8	22.7	16.8	19.3	15.3	14.7	15.9
Gabon	13.2	15.3	12.0	14.1	13.6	13.7	16.9	16.6	10.0	..	..	14.5	17.5	14.1
Gambia, The	31.2	14.1	14.5	13.7	14.9	13.9	12.7	13.0	13.7	15.4	13.3	36.6	15.8	13.8
Ghana	11.2	14.4	13.7	12.1	12.0	12.4	10.3	8.0	7.8	7.9	11.4	9.9	11.0	10.2
Guinea	..	7.1	6.6	6.2	6.4	6.2	6.1	5.9	3.8	5.9	7.0	..	8.3	5.9
Guinea-Bissau	27.6	7.1	7.1	6.4	6.6	7.0	9.3	10.8	13.9	12.6	12.8	23.6	10.7	9.9
Kenya	19.8	16.7	15.2	14.8	16.0	16.2	16.4	16.9	17.5	17.0	19.0	18.5	17.4	16.7
Lesotho	22.0	27.9	29.9	30.3	27.1	27.9	34.7	36.9	35.5	31.9	33.3	19.7	27.3	32.2
Liberia	16.3	..	..	..	..	..	..	..	..	..	..	15.8	19.0	..
Madagascar	12.1	7.9	6.9	6.7	9.8	7.8	7.8	7.2	6.8	8.3	8.2	11.1	8.4	7.8
Malawi	19.3	13.0	31.6	18.6	12.5	12.6	13.3	12.4	16.7	18.3	18.2	16.4	17.4	15.3
Mali	11.6	12.8	11.3	9.7	10.2	12.0	14.7	15.9	14.9	13.0	11.6	11.0	13.2	12.7
Mauritania	45.3	20.7	16.5	14.1	14.3	13.8	14.5	15.2	17.3	15.6	18.4	45.2	22.4	15.4
Mauritius	14.4	12.7	13.1	13.4	13.4	13.2	12.9	12.9	13.2	12.9	8.5	14.7	12.7	12.6
Mozambique	12.2	11.7	12.9	7.8	8.0	9.2	10.4	9.5	10.4	10.8	11.0	14.2	11.6	9.6
Namibia	17.4	31.6	28.3	30.2	30.3	30.2	29.6	30.3	28.4	27.8	28.2	26.0	30.9	29.4
Niger	10.4	15.8	16.0	14.1	11.3	13.8	13.1	14.9	13.0	12.4	12.2	11.5	14.4	13.1
Nigeria	12.1	17.5	14.3	11.1	8.0	9.4	9.7	12.8	22.8	30.0	27.2	14.4	14.0	16.4
Rwanda	12.5	14.3	11.2	10.3	11.5	9.6	10.0	11.0	10.5	11.7	11.8	14.7	12.5	10.8
São Tomé and Principe	34.5	34.5	31.9	27.6	27.2	31.9	25.6	29.8	28.0	29.5	24.4	22.1	35.9	28.0
Senegal	20.3	14.8	12.8	12.4	12.1	11.9	11.8	12.7	12.2	14.5	14.3	17.2	15.0	12.7
Seychelles	28.7	29.5	29.3	27.5	29.4	29.5	31.2	26.9	25.2	30.8	25.9	28.5	31.8	28.3
Sierra Leone	8.4	11.2	10.2	13.1	10.9	9.0	8.9	11.5	14.3	17.2	20.8	8.4	8.7	13.2
Somalia	15.6	..	..	..	..	..	..	..	..	..	..	19.8	..	..
South Africa	14.3	20.1	20.0	18.3	19.1	19.2	19.0	18.6	18.7	18.9	19.2	15.7	19.4	18.9
Sudan	12.6	5.9	5.5	4.6	7.3	5.6	4.9	4.7	5.9	..	..	11.8	7.2	5.5
Swaziland	26.9	22.5	21.5	19.2	20.9	24.8	24.2	22.2	20.0	18.4	16.6	22.2	19.3	20.8
Tanzania	..	19.4	17.1	11.5	11.6	8.8	7.8	7.0	6.5	11.7	12.9	13.5	16.6	9.7
Togo	22.4	16.1	13.2	12.1	11.7	10.3	12.2	11.1	10.8	10.2	9.7	20.0	14.9	11.0
Uganda	..	9.8	10.3	9.8	10.3	10.8	13.0	12.9	13.8	13.9	15.7	10.8	9.3	12.5
Zambia	25.5	18.4	13.1	15.4	18.3	17.5	15.8	12.9	9.5	12.9	11.6	25.7	19.7	14.2
Zimbabwe	18.5	14.9	16.7	18.0	16.9	16.3	17.5	15.2	24.2	19.3	16.9	16.9	20.2	18.1
NORTH AFRICA	12.5	14.9	14.8	14.5	14.0	14.0	14.3	14.0	13.0	12.9	12.6	14.3	15.7	13.7
Algeria	15.2	17.3	17.9	16.8	16.4	16.7	18.1	17.1	14.1	14.2	14.8	15.2	17.5	16.0
Egypt, Arab Rep.	15.7	10.2	10.3	10.5	10.4	10.2	10.1	10.1	9.7	10.3	9.5	19.5	12.8	10.1
Libya	21.8	..	..	..	..	..	..	..	..	..	..	27.8	..	..
Morocco	18.3	18.1	17.1	17.4	16.9	17.8	18.0	19.2	19.1	17.9	15.8	18.9	16.1	17.8
Tunisia	14.5	16.3	16.5	16.9	15.6	15.8	15.7	15.5	15.7	13.6	13.7	15.7	16.7	15.3
ALL AFRICA	13.7	17.0	16.4	15.5	15.1	15.4	15.0	15.3	15.7	16.1	15.8	15.0	16.6	15.5

Note: 2002 data are preliminary (see page 2). Since 1994, Nigeria's ratios are distorted because the official exchange rate used by the Government for oil exports and oil value added is significantly over-valued.

National Accounts

2-8. Gross domestic investment

				Percentage of GDP								*Annual average*		
	1980	*1993*	*1994*	*1995*	*1996*	*1997*	*1998*	*1999*	*2000*	*2001*	*2002*	*75-84*	*85-94*	*95-MR*
SUB-SAHARAN AFRICA	23.5	16.4	17.9	18.2	18.3	17.5	19.2	18.3	17.5	18.1	18.9	23.1	16.8	18.2
excluding South Africa	20.5	17.3	18.9	18.3	18.9	18.2	21.0	19.9	18.8	19.9	20.4	21.2	16.4	19.4
excl. S.Africa & Nigeria	19.3	16.4	18.8	18.7	20.0	18.4	20.3	19.3	19.1	19.8	19.6	19.7	16.1	19.4
Angola	..	11.2	16.6	28.1	34.7	25.5	35.5	19.8	35.4	34.6	32.2	..	13.0	30.7
Benin	15.2	15.4	15.8	19.6	17.1	18.4	17.0	17.5	18.9	19.2	17.8	17.7	13.6	18.2
Botswana	40.1	28.8	26.5	24.6	25.0	28.1	33.5	27.5	19.0	21.7	24.8	36.3	27.6	25.5
Burkina Faso	15.1	18.1	19.3	22.8	24.5	25.0	27.2	23.8	22.7	19.1	18.3	17.9	18.9	22.9
Burundi	13.9	16.3	10.6	9.6	12.1	8.1	8.8	9.1	9.1	6.9	7.9	14.3	15.0	8.9
Cameroon	21.0	16.5	15.3	14.5	15.4	16.2	17.5	18.7	16.4	17.7	18.3	25.1	19.4	16.8
Cape Verde	51.6	39.7	43.4	42.4	24.1	22.0	19.8	20.9	19.7	18.3	20.9	49.1	32.8	23.5
Central African Republic	7.0	10.2	11.7	13.5	4.3	9.8	13.5	14.4	10.8	14.0	14.8	10.5	12.1	11.9
Chad	..	9.8	16.6	10.3	14.9	14.8	20.2	10.1	22.4	41.3	58.9	11.9	9.6	24.1
Comoros	33.2	18.3	20.7	19.5	19.4	15.8	17.9	14.9	13.1	13.2	12.9	33.4	21.1	15.8
Congo, Dem. Rep. of	10.0	1.8	7.9	9.4	27.9	2.5	1.8	3.1	3.1	5.1	7.1	12.7	10.0	7.5
Congo, Rep. of	35.8	29.5	31.2	36.6	27.0	22.4	26.7	27.8	21.0	26.4	23.3	36.2	23.1	26.4
Côte d'Ivoire	26.5	9.8	13.7	15.6	12.1	14.4	13.3	13.1	10.6	11.0	10.4	23.1	9.8	12.6
Djibouti	..	..	..	8.4	9.1	9.4	15.3	8.9	12.9	..	..	..	..	10.7
Equatorial Guinea	..	22.0	74.1	76.3	113.6	65.7	91.6	54.7	40.8	52.6	28.3	13.9	18.8	65.4
Eritrea	..	17.0	25.1	22.5	27.6	31.3	26.7	33.9	18.4	28.1	26.5	..	16.6	26.9
Ethiopia	..	14.2	15.2	16.4	16.9	17.0	17.2	16.9	15.9	17.8	20.5	13.7	13.4	17.3
Gabon	27.5	22.4	21.9	23.7	23.3	29.6	37.3	28.0	26.1	30.5	28.4	42.9	29.3	28.4
Gambia, The	26.7	21.0	18.1	20.2	21.6	17.2	18.4	17.8	17.0	17.7	21.5	19.7	19.1	18.9
Ghana	5.6	22.2	24.0	20.0	21.2	24.8	23.1	21.5	24.0	26.6	22.3	6.9	14.3	22.9
Guinea	..	17.8	15.4	16.6	23.1	23.6	21.0	22.1	22.0	21.9	16.8	..	16.7	20.9
Guinea-Bissau	28.2	30.9	21.8	22.3	23.0	21.8	11.4	16.8	16.0	19.7	14.7	23.8	34.0	18.2
Kenya	24.5	17.7	16.4	17.5	16.8	15.4	17.3	16.2	15.4	14.7	13.6	21.6	18.9	15.8
Lesotho	37.0	55.9	57.1	60.1	57.8	52.3	49.5	46.7	43.2	44.9	40.0	32.4	49.5	49.3
Liberia	27.3	..	..	..	..	..	..	..	..	..	..	23.8	9.2	..
Madagascar	15.0	11.4	10.9	10.9	11.6	12.8	14.8	14.9	15.0	18.5	14.3	10.2	11.3	14.1
Malawi	24.7	15.2	29.1	17.0	11.6	12.2	13.5	14.8	9.6	1.0	12.4	25.3	20.2	11.5
Mali	15.5	21.8	27.3	22.9	22.9	20.6	20.9	21.2	20.6	21.0	18.9	14.8	21.7	21.1
Mauritania	26.3	20.6	20.7	19.3	18.6	17.6	19.0	17.8	30.3	26.7	24.7	26.7	23.1	21.7
Mauritius	25.4	30.0	30.9	28.8	25.3	27.2	27.6	26.0	26.1	23.3	21.9	24.7	27.8	25.8
Mozambique	5.9	12.7	19.8	22.8	21.8	20.6	24.2	36.7	36.6	41.5	44.7	5.8	13.1	31.1
Namibia	30.6	16.5	21.4	21.7	23.1	20.2	25.8	23.3	19.3	23.7	24.1	23.1	18.0	22.6
Niger	28.1	6.4	10.4	7.3	9.7	10.9	11.3	10.2	10.8	11.5	12.8	18.2	10.8	10.5
Nigeria	21.3	23.3	19.6	16.3	14.2	17.4	24.1	22.3	17.7	20.1	23.3	22.3	17.9	19.4
Rwanda	16.1	16.7	10.0	13.4	14.4	13.8	14.8	17.2	17.5	18.4	18.8	14.8	14.8	16.0
São Tomé and Principe	16.8	35.3	41.6	68.1	56.2	49.1	35.8	39.0	43.5	29.9	26.6	14.6	24.2	43.5
Senegal	11.7	13.7	18.5	16.7	18.5	17.8	19.8	20.6	18.5	18.1	19.7	13.1	13.2	18.7
Seychelles	38.3	28.4	27.1	30.3	39.1	31.9	34.6	43.3	27.2	41.3	30.5	30.1	24.1	34.8
Sierra Leone	16.2	7.7	7.8	5.2	9.0	5.0	5.6	4.4	8.0	6.1	8.8	15.1	8.9	6.5
Somalia	42.4	..	..	..	..	..	..	..	..	..	..	27.1	26.3	..
South Africa	29.9	15.3	16.8	18.0	17.4	16.6	16.6	15.9	15.6	15.1	15.8	27.4	18.0	16.4
Sudan	9.5	19.8	22.7	16.0	23.4	15.0	26.7	21.0	17.7	18.7	19.5	15.2	14.1	19.7
Swaziland	37.3	23.1	21.5	20.0	31.9	20.6	22.4	18.7	18.5	17.1	17.9	31.8	21.7	20.9
Tanzania	..	25.1	24.6	19.8	16.6	14.9	13.8	15.5	17.6	17.0	16.7	..	23.3	16.5
Togo	28.4	7.5	15.0	16.1	18.8	16.3	20.8	18.9	20.9	20.7	21.7	29.8	16.8	19.3
Uganda	6.2	15.2	14.7	16.4	16.1	16.8	16.2	19.4	19.8	20.1	21.7	7.2	12.3	18.3
Zambia	23.3	15.0	8.2	15.9	12.8	14.6	16.4	17.6	18.7	20.0	17.4	22.3	13.7	16.7
Zimbabwe	16.9	22.8	23.7	19.7	18.5	18.1	17.1	16.1	12.6	7.8	8.3	16.7	18.8	14.8
NORTH AFRICA	28.2	23.4	22.9	22.8	20.6	22.6	25.9	25.8	24.3	24.4	25.4	31.1	26.8	24.0
Algeria	39.1	29.1	31.2	31.8	25.1	23.8	28.7	27.8	23.8	25.8	28.4	41.7	30.5	26.9
Egypt, Arab Rep.	27.5	16.2	16.6	17.2	16.6	21.7	25.6	25.5	23.9	22.7	23.0	29.9	24.4	22.0
Libya	22.1	..	..	..	..	..	..	..	..	..	..	26.3	..	..
Morocco	24.2	22.5	21.3	20.7	19.6	20.7	22.2	23.4	24.4	24.6	25.0	26.5	23.1	22.6
Tunisia	29.4	29.2	24.5	24.8	25.1	26.4	27.0	26.8	27.4	28.1	28.6	31.2	27.7	26.8
ALL AFRICA	24.3	18.7	19.6	19.7	19.1	19.2	21.6	21.1	20.1	20.6	21.5	25.1	20.2	20.4

Note: 2002 data are preliminary (see page 2). Since 1994, Nigeria's ratios are distorted because the official exchange rate used by the Government for oil exports and oil value added is significantly over-valued.

2-9. Gross public investment

				Percentage of GDP									*Annual average*		
	1980	1993	1994	1995	1996	1997	1998	1999	2000	2001	2002	75-84	85-94	95-MR
SUB-SAHARAN AFRICA	..	..	..	..	..	..	..	..	..	..	..	..	..	..
excluding South Africa	..	6.6	6.1	6.2	5.8	6.3	7.2	7.3	6.3	7.6	7.1	..	6.9	6.7
excl. S.Africa & Nigeria	..	5.9	6.6	6.4	6.0	6.1	6.2	6.6	5.4	5.7	5.8	..	6.2	6.0
Angola	..	..	..	..	..	4.7	5.9	12.9	6.3	6.0	6.9	..	..	7.1
Benin	..	7.1	9.3	10.4	7.5	6.8	5.8	6.3	7.6	7.8	6.4	..	8.1	7.3
Botswana	..	12.8	13.0	11.0	11.4	12.4	13.2	13.1	12.3	10.7	11.7	..	13.0	12.0
Burkina Faso	..	7.7	7.4	9.8	11.0	12.7	12.4	14.9	12.1	8.3	7.4	..	6.8	11.1
Burundi	12.8	12.9	9.0	8.3	10.4	5.0	5.6	6.2	5.6	3.6	4.0	14.1	12.6	6.1
Cameroon	4.4	1.8	1.3	1.2	0.5	1.0	2.0	2.3	1.4	2.1	1.6	4.7	6.0	1.5
Cape Verde	..	28.2	32.0	27.1	20.5	18.0	15.9	14.5	12.0	10.0	11.2	..	20.7	16.2
Central African Republic	3.7	6.2	7.2	9.8	1.8	3.9	7.1	6.8	7.1	7.4	7.6	4.7	6.4	6.4
Chad	..	5.8	7.3	6.3	3.5	5.6	7.6	9.6	10.5	9.1	10.0	2.2	5.6	7.8
Comoros	23.2	6.8	10.4	6.4	5.8	6.0	7.7	5.4	3.8	4.5	4.8	23.3	10.8	5.5
Congo, Dem. Rep. of	5.1	0.9	0.6	4.4	0.5	0.5	0.1	1.1	0.2	0.1	0.1	3.9	3.5	0.9
Congo, Rep. of	35.8	7.1	12.8	9.3	5.2	3.6	4.7	6.1	7.0	10.1	8.6	35.5	9.0	6.8
Côte d'Ivoire	11.4	4.9	5.1	5.1	4.9	5.4	6.0	4.2	2.8	1.8	3.2	9.9	4.2	4.2
Djibouti	..	..	..	3.6	3.9	4.3	6.6	..	..	..	..	..	..	4.6
Equatorial Guinea	..	8.9	4.1	1.9	1.2	4.4	7.5	1.3	0.8	0.4	0.4	..	4.7	2.2
Eritrea	..	14.5	10.8	12.3	15.4	18.1	20.4	29.5	11.7	20.3	17.3	..	9.5	18.1
Ethiopia	..	5.0	7.1	7.5	7.5	8.3	7.4	8.1	5.2	8.5	11.5	..	5.8	8.0
Gabon	5.3	5.1	5.6	5.1	5.9	9.2	13.4	7.3	4.8	5.6	5.4	15.8	5.5	7.1
Gambia, The	..	7.5	7.0	10.0	12.9	7.9	5.2	4.7	3.8	5.8	7.8	13.8	7.5	7.3
Ghana	..	11.1	13.3	14.0	13.3	12.4	11.3	9.8	10.4	10.4	9.6	2.5	8.6	11.4
Guinea	..	6.2	5.9	6.3	7.4	8.2	5.6	7.2	7.1	7.1	7.8	..	7.2	7.1
Guinea-Bissau	..	24.6	20.4	15.2	14.8	15.6	6.2	10.8	10.0	13.7	8.7	..	25.9	11.9
Kenya	10.1	8.0	8.5	7.4	7.0	6.4	3.3	3.0	3.1	2.7	2.7	8.9	8.1	4.5
Lesotho	..	14.9	14.5	15.6	19.6	18.4	12.0	8.7	8.5	11.3	10.2	20.0	19.0	13.0
Liberia	..	..	..	..	..	..	..	..	..	..	..	..	..	..
Madagascar	..	7.8	6.2	5.8	6.7	6.5	7.9	6.9	6.7	7.3	4.8	6.4	7.0	6.6
Malawi	17.5	8.4	15.1	9.4	6.1	7.1	8.7	10.6	10.0	8.4	7.9	13.6	9.0	8.5
Mali	..	9.3	13.7	9.4	9.2	8.2	9.5	9.4	9.1	7.8	8.2	..	10.6	8.9
Mauritania	..	4.3	4.3	3.8	6.1	5.6	5.6	6.0	7.5	8.3	10.7	..	6.0	6.7
Mauritius	9.1	4.1	3.8	3.5	3.3	3.1	3.1	3.4	3.7	6.7	3.9	7.8	4.5	3.9
Mozambique	7.6	12.3	14.0	12.0	10.3	12.1	9.8	11.6	10.6	16.6	14.3	10.4	10.5	12.2
Namibia	15.7	6.1	7.0	7.1	7.3	8.5	7.7	11.0	6.0	9.3	9.5	13.9	7.7	8.3
Niger	20.4	4.9	6.6	5.2	4.6	5.8	6.4	6.4	5.9	6.5	7.4	13.8	7.1	6.0
Nigeria	..	10.7	3.6	5.3	5.2	7.1	11.3	9.9	9.3	14.1	11.7	..	10.0	9.2
Rwanda	12.2	7.7	2.7	8.1	9.3	8.3	6.8	6.3	6.0	6.6	6.8	13.7	8.4	7.3
São Tomé and Principe	..	20.3	26.6	33.1	29.2	22.1	19.8	26.0	26.0	19.3	12.4	..	24.4	23.5
Senegal	5.5	3.8	5.0	4.4	6.4	6.4	7.2	8.3	6.2	6.4	9.1	4.1	4.2	6.8
Seychelles	..	11.1	7.5	18.7	19.4	7.5	2.9	1.4	13.7	5.8	9.4	16.3	9.2	9.9
Sierra Leone	5.3	5.3	4.0	2.4	3.3	1.5	4.9	2.4	5.2	4.8	5.3	5.1	3.7	3.7
Somalia	..	..	..	..	..	..	..	..	..	..	..	..	..	..
South Africa	..	..	..	..	..	..	1.9	1.6	1.4	2.0	2.2	..	..	1.8
Sudan	..	..	..	..	..	..	..	2.6	2.6	2.5	3.3	..	..	2.7
Swaziland	8.6	9.5	8.6	5.9	5.2	4.9	6.5	7.3	6.2	6.7	5.9	10.9	9.3	6.1
Tanzania	..	7.5	6.0	3.4	3.5	2.9	3.3	3.1	3.4	3.5	3.3	..	7.0	3.3
Togo	20.2	2.3	2.3	3.5	5.0	2.0	4.3	3.4	3.3	2.5	2.6	12.2	7.1	3.3
Uganda	..	6.7	5.4	5.4	5.3	5.4	4.7	5.5	6.4	6.4	5.8	..	5.5	5.6
Zambia	4.0	4.5	4.0	5.1	6.1	5.4	11.3	10.6	10.0	11.9	11.8	4.1	5.3	9.0
Zimbabwe	1.8	3.7	3.1	2.9	2.3	2.8	1.8	4.1	0.0	1.0	1.7	2.9	3.0	2.1
NORTH AFRICA	..	9.4	8.3	7.5	6.8	9.2	9.5	..	..	..	..	..	9.6	8.2
Algeria	11.0	8.7	7.9	7.3	6.8	7.3	7.6	5.9	8.0	0.0	0.0	12.9	10.2	5.4
Egypt, Arab Rep.	..	7.1	6.1	5.5	5.5	10.6	11.3	9.8	7.5	6.4	6.1	..	9.9	7.9
Libya	19.4	..	..	..	..	..	..	..	..	..	..	21.1	..	..
Morocco	9.8	11.8	10.1	8.9	6.8	7.1	6.5	..	..	..	..	13.5	9.4	7.3
Tunisia	15.0	15.3	13.7	12.3	11.0	11.9	11.6	12.4	12.5	0.0	0.0	17.2	11.9	9.0
ALL AFRICA	..	..	..	..	..	..	..	..	..	..	..	..	..	..

Note: 2002 data are preliminary (see page 2). Since 1994, Nigeria's ratios are distorted because the official exchange rate used by the Government for oil exports and oil value added is significantly over-valued.

2-10. Gross private investment

					Percentage of GDP								Annual average		
	1980	1993	1994	1995	1996	1997	1998	1999	2000	2001	2002	75-84	85-94	95-MR
SUB-SAHARAN AFRICA	13.9	12.9	14.1	14.0	14.1	14.0	14.1	13.8	12.9	12.4	13.0	14.4	12.6	13.5
excluding South Africa	..	11.3	12.9	12.1	12.3	12.0	13.3	13.6	12.6	12.2	12.9	8.2	9.4	12.6
excl. S.Africa & Nigeria	..	11.1	12.2	12.3	13.1	12.4	13.4	13.9	13.7	13.9	13.3	8.9	9.6	13.3
Angola	..	19.8	28.4	21.1	21.7	20.8	29.6	33.9	29.1	28.6	25.4	..	10.7	26.3
Benin	..	7.9	6.2	6.9	9.1	11.6	11.2	11.2	11.3	11.4	11.4	..	5.8	10.5
Botswana	34.5	14.1	12.5	14.6	13.4	12.5	14.2	14.7	12.6	13.2	6.0	29.3	21.5	12.7
Burkina Faso	..	9.4	13.2	12.4	12.4	12.7	14.8	8.9	10.6	10.9	10.9	..	11.8	11.7
Burundi	1.1	3.0	1.6	1.4	1.8	2.2	2.3	1.8	2.4	2.3	2.3	1.5	2.6	2.1
Cameroon	15.6	14.7	14.0	13.3	14.9	15.2	15.5	16.4	15.1	15.6	16.8	24.2	12.6	15.3
Cape Verde	20.8	11.5	11.3	15.3	3.6	4.0	3.9	6.4	7.7	8.3	9.7	10.1	9.6	7.4
Central African Republic	3.2	3.3	4.5	3.4	2.5	5.9	6.5	7.7	3.7	6.6	7.2	4.1	5.0	5.5
Chad	..	1.1	4.4	5.3	5.9	7.0	9.5	4.2	11.9	32.2	48.8	0.3	1.2	15.6
Comoros	5.3	8.1	9.2	9.1	7.9	7.4	7.0	6.5	6.5	6.2	6.2	5.4	6.6	7.1
Congo, Dem. Rep. of	3.7	1.4	7.0	5.3	26.6	14.5	19.9	19.2	4.0	5.0	7.0	5.8	6.6	12.7
Congo, Rep. of	0.0	21.8	16.9	25.0	20.7	18.2	19.6	20.4	12.3	16.3	13.8	0.0	13.8	18.3
Côte d'Ivoire	15.1	4.9	8.6	10.5	7.2	9.0	7.3	8.9	7.8	9.1	7.3	12.8	5.6	8.4
Djibouti	..	..	..	4.8	5.2	5.1	8.6	..	..	..	..	..	..	5.9
Equatorial Guinea	..	13.1	70.0	74.4	112.4	61.3	84.1	29.2	16.7	13.9	12.4	..	14.2	50.5
Eritrea	..	2.5	14.3	10.3	12.2	13.2	6.3	4.4	6.6	7.8	9.2	..	7.1	8.8
Ethiopia	..	9.2	8.0	9.0	9.4	8.7	9.8	8.9	10.7	9.3	9.0	..	7.8	9.3
Gabon	21.4	17.8	15.4	17.6	17.3	20.4	23.9	20.8	21.3	24.9	23.0	24.0	23.8	21.2
Gambia, The	..	13.5	11.1	10.2	8.6	9.3	13.2	13.1	13.2	11.9	13.7	7.4	11.6	11.7
Ghana	..	12.7	9.3	7.1	7.0	11.4	11.1	10.7	12.7	16.7	9.2	4.4	5.7	10.7
Guinea	..	10.6	11.1	10.3	14.0	14.0	14.0	14.0	14.0	14.0	8.8	..	9.4	12.9
Guinea-Bissau	..	6.3	1.4	7.1	8.3	6.2	5.2	6.0	6.0	6.0	6.0	..	9.2	6.4
Kenya	8.2	8.9	7.5	9.7	9.2	8.1	13.2	12.2	11.5	11.4	10.4	8.8	7.6	10.7
Lesotho	35.6	41.6	43.8	45.1	38.4	34.9	38.6	38.2	36.5	36.0	31.4	25.2	36.3	37.4
Liberia	..	..	..	..	..	..	..	..	..	..	..	..	..	..
Madagascar	..	3.7	4.7	5.2	5.0	6.3	6.9	8.0	8.3	11.2	9.4	2.2	4.3	7.5
Malawi	4.7	4.6	11.6	7.6	5.4	2.7	2.4	2.3	2.6	2.9	1.7	7.0	8.3	3.4
Mali	..	12.5	13.7	13.5	13.7	12.4	11.4	11.8	11.5	13.2	10.7	..	11.1	12.3
Mauritania	..	16.4	16.4	15.5	12.5	12.0	13.3	11.8	22.8	18.4	14.0	..	17.2	15.0
Mauritius	15.1	23.7	25.1	23.7	21.7	22.9	21.7	22.0	21.8	16.4	18.0	15.1	20.7	21.0
Mozambique	0.0	0.4	5.8	10.8	11.6	8.5	14.5	25.1	25.9	24.9	30.4	0.0	2.6	19.0
Namibia	11.4	15.0	12.2	15.1	16.2	11.1	15.3	12.0	12.5	12.8	13.0	8.3	9.6	13.5
Niger	5.1	1.9	2.3	1.8	4.7	4.8	4.6	3.6	4.6	4.8	5.2	3.6	2.6	4.3
Nigeria	..	12.5	16.0	11.1	8.9	10.3	12.8	12.4	8.4	5.9	11.6	5.2	8.3	10.2
Rwanda	..	9.1	7.3	5.3	5.1	5.6	8.0	10.9	11.6	11.8	12.0	..	7.6	8.8
São Tomé and Principe	..	15.0	15.0	35.0	27.0	27.0	16.0	14.0	17.5	10.6	14.2	..	13.8	20.2
Senegal	7.7	9.7	11.1	10.2	9.9	9.4	10.5	11.3	11.1	11.3	10.3	7.9	9.0	10.5
Seychelles	..	15.5	18.9	11.6	20.4	20.6	31.1	40.1	13.0	35.5	21.0	5.4	14.1	24.2
Sierra Leone	9.5	2.4	3.8	2.8	5.6	3.5	0.7	2.0	2.8	1.3	3.5	9.0	4.8	2.8
Somalia	..	..	..	..	..	..	..	..	..	..	..	..	..	..
South Africa	25.9	14.7	15.2	15.9	16.3	16.5	15.1	13.8	13.4	12.7	12.9	26.9	18.2	14.6
Sudan	..	..	..	..	..	12.0	11.1	16.1	16.1	16.2	16.2	..	..	14.6
Swaziland	19.6	12.7	12.1	13.3	25.8	15.7	15.9	11.4	12.4	10.4	11.9	18.5	11.4	14.6
Tanzania	..	17.4	18.5	16.2	13.0	11.8	10.3	12.3	14.1	13.3	13.2	8.6	14.5	13.0
Togo	8.0	8.6	9.7	10.1	12.2	11.0	12.9	12.6	14.5	17.2	17.6	8.0	10.0	13.5
Uganda	..	8.5	9.2	10.2	11.3	11.7	11.0	13.7	13.1	13.4	15.4	..	6.7	12.5
Zambia	17.2	7.0	7.3	7.3	5.2	7.7	3.5	5.4	7.2	6.8	4.2	12.6	5.0	5.9
Zimbabwe	12.3	19.9	18.3	21.7	15.7	15.3	15.7	10.8	12.4	6.7	7.4	13.3	15.1	13.2
NORTH AFRICA	..	14.7	15.3	15.4	14.1	14.6	15.4	16.2	15.0	19.2	18.8	13.0	15.9	16.1
Algeria	22.8	18.3	20.7	21.9	18.1	17.4	19.0	20.1	13.5	24.6	19.2	25.3	17.9	19.2
Egypt, Arab Rep.	..	9.2	10.5	10.7	10.5	12.1	12.3	13.0	14.1	14.4	16.1	7.1	12.6	12.9
Libya	1.8	..	..	..	..	..	..	..	..	..	..	3.6	..	..
Morocco	16.7	18.6	17.2	17.7	16.3	17.3	19.3	20.7	20.7	21.2	21.7	18.1	18.2	19.4
Tunisia	13.3	12.8	13.3	11.9	12.2	12.7	13.2	12.9	13.8	23.7	24.2	13.2	14.7	15.6
ALL AFRICA	14.1	13.5	14.5	14.4	14.1	14.2	14.6	14.7	13.7	15.1	15.3	14.9	13.7	14.5

Note: 2002 data are preliminary (see page 2). Since 1994, Nigeria's ratios are distorted because the official exchange rate used by the Government for oil exports and oil value added is significantly over-valued.

2-11. Gross domestic savings

	Percentage of GDP											Annual average		
	1980	*1993*	*1994*	*1995*	*1996*	*1997*	*1998*	*1999*	*2000*	*2001*	*2002*	*75-84*	*85-94*	*95-MR*
SUB-SAHARAN AFRICA	25.5	14.9	17.0	16.7	19.4	16.3	15.1	15.6	19.4	18.4	18.5	21.3	17.9	17.4
excluding South Africa	19.9	11.5	14.9	14.7	19.8	15.1	13.2	13.5	20.1	17.9	17.5	17.4	14.5	16.5
excl. S.Africa & Nigeria	12.4	10.1	13.8	13.9	16.3	12.9	11.9	12.4	16.4	16.2	17.8	14.8	13.3	14.7
Angola	..	9.9	26.1	26.9	48.8	25.9	19.3	13.1	63.0	35.0	39.2	..	20.3	33.9
Benin	-6.3	1.1	6.0	6.7	3.4	5.6	6.6	4.8	6.0	6.5	6.0	-1.7	0.0	5.7
Botswana	26.7	36.8	37.0	37.5	41.3	43.0	39.8	38.1	40.3	39.7	38.5	23.3	41.4	39.8
Burkina Faso	-7.2	5.2	7.0	8.2	8.3	9.9	11.6	8.1	6.5	5.1	4.8	-3.4	3.1	7.8
Burundi	-0.6	-4.7	-7.6	-4.8	2.5	3.9	-2.9	-0.5	-5.7	-4.8	-4.5	4.1	-1.0	-2.1
Cameroon	21.7	17.6	17.9	19.6	17.3	19.1	19.2	18.4	20.3	20.4	16.8	23.1	20.9	18.9
Cape Verde	-24.0	3.7	2.8	3.0	-16.7	-7.4	-16.7	-17.6	-13.3	-10.0	-10.1	-19.8	-2.4	-11.1
Central African Republic	-8.9	1.8	6.0	6.2	0.6	4.4	5.3	11.0	7.8	11.1	10.3	-1.6	1.4	7.1
Chad	..	-6.2	-1.5	-1.7	3.3	2.3	4.3	-0.9	2.1	5.1	6.4	2.4	-7.4	2.6
Comoros	-10.1	1.5	-6.5	-5.3	-3.6	-9.0	-4.7	-5.7	-1.4	0.0	0.6	-6.5	-2.9	-3.7
Congo, Dem. Rep. of	10.1	4.0	10.6	14.1	27.5	6.2	-1.3	9.0	4.3	6.2	4.0	10.5	9.8	8.8
Congo, Rep. of	35.7	23.6	15.5	37.7	35.7	37.8	30.3	41.0	57.7	53.1	50.0	26.1	22.2	42.9
Côte d'Ivoire	20.4	13.3	24.9	22.9	20.8	22.8	19.7	21.3	17.6	19.6	25.2	23.8	15.4	21.2
Djibouti	..	..	..	-8.3	-6.9	-5.7	-0.8	-5.5	-5.3	..	..	..	..	-5.4
Equatorial Guinea	..	-13.7	25.1	27.3	30.7	43.1	19.9	64.8	74.0	82.6	90.2	7.6	-14.6	54.1
Eritrea	..	-24.0	-29.7	-38.0	-30.6	-24.9	-38.5	-39.1	-44.2	-31.6	-30.1	..	-26.5	-34.6
Ethiopia	..	2.1	5.4	8.0	7.0	7.9	7.7	2.1	0.9	2.6	2.2	6.4	5.7	4.8
Gabon	60.6	36.7	45.3	47.3	51.0	51.0	39.0	34.8	28.3	50.3	48.4	58.1	35.5	43.8
Gambia, The	5.8	4.0	2.8	-3.9	5.6	4.5	2.8	3.2	2.6	-2.4	3.7	4.3	7.5	2.0
Ghana	4.9	6.0	12.5	11.6	13.2	4.2	10.3	3.9	5.4	7.0	10.3	6.3	6.0	8.2
Guinea	..	11.1	12.1	12.8	17.7	21.4	17.3	17.3	16.8	20.0	11.3	..	15.1	16.8
Guinea-Bissau	-1.0	7.0	3.9	-1.2	1.8	3.0	-10.1	-1.1	-10.4	-13.2	-17.4	-4.3	2.0	-6.1
Kenya	13.4	23.8	19.6	11.3	13.2	7.9	9.7	10.4	5.9	3.4	9.5	17.4	17.5	8.9
Lesotho	-52.0	-33.8	-30.3	-31.6	-27.4	-29.4	-23.9	-19.8	-17.9	-9.7	-15.1	-68.2	-52.2	-21.9
Liberia	27.3	..	..	..	..	..	..	..	..	..	..	23.3	16.4	..
Madagascar	-1.4	2.1	3.3	3.4	6.1	4.7	7.0	7.2	7.7	15.3	7.7	1.9	4.0	7.4
Malawi	10.8	-0.9	-3.0	-0.3	3.1	-0.7	7.5	-0.2	-2.8	-10.3	-5.7	15.6	8.3	-1.2
Mali	1.1	6.4	7.5	7.8	7.2	10.0	10.4	9.5	8.1	4.1	10.2	0.2	3.1	8.4
Mauritania	-3.5	4.7	16.9	8.9	6.3	7.9	5.0	7.2	16.2	14.0	9.0	-5.6	9.3	9.3
Mauritius	14.5	25.2	23.6	23.4	23.8	24.3	24.9	23.8	24.2	26.0	25.7	16.9	24.6	24.5
Mozambique	-10.6	-22.4	-13.9	-1.9	-1.8	1.1	6.8	9.0	10.6	27.8	30.0	-10.4	-12.8	10.2
Namibia	38.4	11.7	18.6	15.5	15.1	10.2	13.7	12.5	13.8	13.8	23.5	9.7	11.9	14.8
Niger	14.6	3.9	0.0	0.2	3.1	3.2	2.7	3.7	3.3	4.1	4.2	8.4	5.3	3.1
Nigeria	31.4	20.2	20.6	18.4	34.9	24.6	19.6	18.2	33.4	24.5	17.4	21.5	21.2	23.9
Rwanda	4.2	1.4	-48.5	-7.3	-5.8	-4.1	-2.8	0.2	1.4	2.6	1.4	6.8	-0.8	-1.8
São Tomé and Principe	-11.6	-31.6	-17.5	-11.4	-13.7	-16.5	-7.0	-10.3	-6.0	-27.1	-24.3	-6.6	-25.1	-14.5
Senegal	-5.0	7.7	11.8	11.1	12.2	11.2	13.1	13.5	8.6	8.6	9.9	1.1	6.5	11.0
Seychelles	27.1	18.2	24.1	23.2	29.7	20.9	18.7	25.6	24.3	23.1	27.8	21.9	24.9	24.2
Sierra Leone	..	7.4	11.3	-2.1	-5.7	3.1	-1.6	-1.6	-8.1	-12.1	-13.6	10.9	11.4	-5.2
Somalia	-12.9	..	..	..	..	..	..	..	..	..	..	-11.4	2.6	..
South Africa	37.8	19.0	19.1	18.9	18.8	17.8	17.7	18.5	18.3	18.7	19.2	30.5	23.6	18.5
Sudan	-0.2	11.8	11.7	11.3	15.6	2.5	10.3	14.9	20.0	19.6	12.2	5.2	8.8	13.3
Swaziland	9.6	-2.1	3.5	1.3	5.9	3.3	3.3	0.3	3.2	5.7	9.0	14.1	10.4	4.0
Tanzania	..	-4.6	1.6	1.9	3.6	4.9	-0.8	3.4	9.3	8.4	9.7	11.0	3.7	5.1
Togo	23.2	-0.2	11.3	11.2	7.9	0.5	5.5	7.6	4.1	3.6	4.7	21.4	7.9	5.6
Uganda	-0.4	1.1	4.3	7.4	4.6	9.4	5.4	7.4	7.9	7.7	6.3	4.1	2.2	7.0
Zambia	19.3	8.2	7.4	12.2	5.3	9.4	3.9	-1.1	8.3	9.8	4.1	18.9	11.6	6.5
Zimbabwe	13.8	21.0	21.8	17.0	18.7	11.1	15.3	15.7	14.8	9.8	11.4	15.2	18.2	14.2
NORTH AFRICA	40.5	20.0	18.0	17.9	19.1	21.3	19.8	21.8	25.1	24.9	24.4	35.3	21.4	21.8
Algeria	43.1	27.7	26.6	28.1	31.4	32.2	27.1	31.4	44.2	40.9	38.0	38.6	27.0	34.2
Egypt, Arab Rep.	15.2	13.2	11.4	12.2	10.8	15.5	15.5	16.9	17.3	17.7	17.8	15.4	14.8	15.5
Libya	56.9	..	..	..	..	..	..	..	..	..	..	46.5	..	..
Morocco	13.7	16.5	15.3	14.1	16.2	17.4	18.1	19.6	18.2	19.3	19.1	12.9	17.5	17.8
Tunisia	24.0	21.3	22.2	20.4	..	..	..	..	25.3	24.5	24.9	22.1	20.2	23.8
ALL AFRICA	29.9	16.6	17.3	17.1	19.3	18.0	16.8	17.9	21.6	21.0	20.8	25.4	19.1	19.1

Note: 2002 data are preliminary (see page 2). Since 1994, Nigeria's ratios are distorted because the official exchange rate used by the Government for oil exports and oil value added is significantly over-valued.

2-12. Gross national savings

	Percentage of GDP											Annual average		
	1980	*1993*	*1994*	*1995*	*1996*	*1997*	*1998*	*1999*	*2000*	*2001*	*2002*	*75-84*	*85-94*	*95-MR*
SUB-SAHARAN AFRICA	25.3	12.3	14.5	14.6	17.6	14.1	13.7	13.6	16.6	16.1	17.0	22.1	15.0	15.4
excluding South Africa	20.8	8.8	12.1	12.7	18.7	13.3	12.8	12.3	17.5	16.4	17.1	20.5	11.9	15.1
excl. S.Africa & Nigeria	15.2	8.1	12.0	12.7	15.8	11.0	12.2	11.9	15.0	14.8	18.1	19.9	11.5	13.9
Angola	..	12.5	26.9	20.3	32.4	11.0	5.1	-3.5	44.6	19.9	26.6	..	17.4	19.6
Benin	1.1	6.7	7.4	8.2	4.5	11.0	11.3	9.9	10.9	12.5	9.8	3.2	3.5	9.8
Botswana	28.7	43.8	33.2	36.0	39.8	44.1	47.1	37.9	37.8	41.0	36.3	27.3	40.4	40.0
Burkina Faso	..	17.1	20.3	15.3	11.9	14.5	15.1	6.6	5.9	7.8	8.0	..	16.4	10.6
Burundi	..	..	..	..	..	..	..	3.7	3.2	6.4	0.1	..	..	3.4
Cameroon	5.1	11.3	11.2	13.7	11.2	13.4	15.0	14.6	14.7	13.6	11.7	12.9	17.5	13.5
Cape Verde	16.4	26.4	36.2	26.1	12.5	14.7	6.7	6.0	10.0	12.1	13.9	4.7	21.7	12.8
Central African Republic	-2.9	1.8	11.4	6.3	-1.6	4.2	5.9	12.0	8.6	13.1	7.6	6.0	3.8	7.0
Chad	..	-5.2	6.4	1.9	5.1	4.5	6.3	0.5	3.8	5.7	6.0	6.9	-1.4	4.2
Comoros	-0.4	15.2	7.6	-1.2	1.8	5.6	8.3	2.5	11.3	13.1	10.6	11.3	14.2	6.5
Congo, Dem. Rep. of	7.9	-4.2	-1.2	1.1	22.9	-0.4	-7.1	1.1	-0.9	2.6	5.1	8.4	2.4	3.0
Congo, Rep. of	26.2	9.4	5.6	-4.2	-7.1	9.1	7.4	11.0	28.5	23.3	23.0	19.8	11.8	11.4
Côte d'Ivoire	..	-0.5	12.8	9.5	10.2	12.7	10.0	11.3	7.3	9.8	16.6	7.2	1.8	10.9
Djibouti	..	..	..	..	..	..	..	..	..	..	..	..	..	..
Equatorial Guinea	..	-16.2	22.5	23.6	10.1	27.7	9.7	18.4	11.2	-23.2	64.4	..	-7.3	17.7
Eritrea	..	50.9	64.0	26.8	30.5	59.7	19.0	22.5	17.9	22.9	30.6	..	50.4	28.7
Ethiopia	..	12.5	13.5	19.7	26.2	23.8	24.0	18.0	10.7	13.7	14.5	7.9	10.5	18.8
Gabon	..	22.0	30.7	29.0	32.3	34.5	23.9	18.9	11.5	33.7	32.9	..	24.5	27.1
Gambia, The	..	..	..	..	..	13.4	15.4	13.5	12.3	10.9	13.6	4.7	..	13.2
Ghana	4.5	12.8	19.1	17.6	18.1	10.4	17.8	19.1	25.3	23.8	29.0	5.9	8.0	20.1
Guinea	..	6.6	8.2	8.8	14.3	17.4	14.3	14.8	14.7	19.5	10.3	..	8.9	14.3
Guinea-Bissau	..	9.8	9.4	4.7	6.6	12.3	-1.8	4.8	2.9	-0.8	0.5	-8.5	8.0	3.7
Kenya	10.7	18.3	16.2	11.8	15.5	10.4	12.4	13.9	12.7	11.1	14.1	14.3	14.0	12.7
Lesotho	49.6	41.3	41.8	37.2	32.3	27.3	23.9	25.0	25.2	32.5	25.3	-1.4	37.1	28.6
Liberia	..	..	..	..	..	..	..	..	..	..	..	..	..	..
Madagascar	-2.4	3.6	1.4	0.4	6.2	7.3	7.3	9.5	9.4	17.2	8.3	1.7	4.6	8.2
Malawi	6.6	0.2	-5.0	-3.9	0.5	0.2	12.6	6.7	-4.6	-11.7	-7.2	13.9	8.1	-0.9
Mali	1.9	14.9	19.1	13.7	12.8	13.0	12.9	11.9	12.1	3.0	6.1	1.0	11.7	10.7
Mauritania	..	13.3	21.2	9.8	14.2	17.6	16.2	23.2	30.1	23.3	28.0	..	21.0	20.3
Mauritius	14.0	28.5	26.0	25.6	25.7	26.0	26.7	25.4	25.5	27.7	27.1	14.0	26.4	26.2
Mozambique	-9.9	-30.9	-22.8	-9.6	-3.2	1.0	5.9	10.0	14.4	25.1	30.2	-10.9	-19.3	9.2
Namibia	26.9	39.1	42.2	49.5	45.3	34.9	36.5	39.8	42.0	39.7	46.9	20.5	24.6	41.8
Niger	17.1	4.2	-4.5	-3.7	0.4	0.4	1.3	2.5	2.6	4.1	4.3	11.7	5.5	1.5
Nigeria	26.1	13.2	12.8	12.9	29.6	12.0	15.4	13.2	27.2	22.9	14.8	19.0	15.0	18.5
Rwanda	..	-0.5	-48.8	-7.1	-7.0	-6.3	-4.0	-1.1	-0.3	0.2	..	..	-16.0	-3.7
São Tomé and Principe	-5.5	-39.9	-21.6	-22.2	-23.0	-25.7	-18.1	-19.0	-12.4	-15.6	-13.3	-4.1	-32.1	-18.7
Senegal	-7.4	7.7	13.5	11.5	14.2	13.6	15.6	14.9	12.3	13.2	11.2	-2.8	3.7	13.3
Seychelles	..	19.4	25.0	20.6	28.7	20.2	16.9	23.2	18.6	18.9	18.8	0.0	21.2	20.7
Sierra Leone	..	-0.6	2.5	-4.6	-2.0	4.0	-0.9	1.1	0.0	-3.3	-1.2	9.7	5.9	-0.9
Somalia	..	..	..	..	..	..	..	..	..	..	..	..	..	..
South Africa	34.0	16.4	16.9	16.5	16.1	15.1	14.9	15.4	15.2	14.8	16.1	26.6	20.4	15.5
Sudan	-0.9	16.4	13.7	..	16.1	3.8	..	..	..	..	..	4.1	8.5	10.0
Swaziland	25.1	5.1	6.0	10.0	15.8	15.5	7.1	5.9	13.8	12.8	13.9	25.8	22.8	11.9
Tanzania	..	4.9	6.6	-1.2	4.2	4.0	-2.1	2.0	7.7	7.3	9.1	13.8	13.3	3.9
Togo	26.4	1.5	9.6	14.2	11.4	3.8	8.8	7.3	6.8	4.8	5.9	23.7	8.8	7.9
Uganda	..	3.0	10.4	12.1	10.8	7.6	5.8	7.5	8.3	7.8	8.2	5.9	3.6	8.5
Zambia	7.3	-0.2	-0.2	4.6	-1.5	3.7	-3.6	-6.6	2.9	4.6	0.1	10.1	-0.8	0.5
Zimbabwe	12.4	20.6	21.7	16.8	18.0	9.1	12.6	14.0	11.2	7.4	8.5	13.1	16.8	12.2
NORTH AFRICA	37.1	16.8	15.2	15.2	16.5	19.4	18.3	20.1	23.3	26.7	26.2	31.7	18.1	20.7
Algeria	..	..	..	..	..	..	..	..	40.6	38.1	35.9	..	..	38.2
Egypt, Arab Rep.	..	..	..	..	..	..	..	..	23.0	22.7	22.5	..	..	22.7
Libya	53.5	..	..	..	..	..	..	..	..	..	..	39.8	..	..
Morocco	..	..	..	..	..	..	21.3	22.5	22.8	23.8	23.2	..	..	22.7
Tunisia	25.0	19.3	20.4	19.3	..	..	..	..	24.7	23.8	24.2	22.5	19.9	23.0
ALL AFRICA	28.7	15.7	16.3	16.2	18.5	17.2	16.8	17.4	20.6	20.3	20.7	24.5	17.6	18.5

Note: 2002 data are preliminary (see page 2). Since 1994, Nigeria's ratios are distorted because the official exchange rate used by the Government for oil exports and oil value added is significantly over-valued.

2-13. Resource balance

	Percentage of GDP											Annual average		
	1980	*1993*	*1994*	*1995*	*1996*	*1997*	*1998*	*1999*	*2000*	*2001*	*2002*	*75-84*	*85-94*	*95-MR*
SUB-SAHARAN AFRICA	2.8	-1.5	-1.0	-1.5	1.1	-1.3	-4.1	-2.7	1.9	-0.1	-1.6	-1.9	0.1	-1.0
excluding South Africa	0.5	-5.8	-4.1	-3.6	0.9	-3.1	-7.7	-6.4	1.3	-2.2	-4.1	-3.9	-3.2	-3.1
excl. S.Africa & Nigeria	-5.8	-6.3	-5.0	-4.8	-3.6	-5.4	-8.4	-6.9	-2.6	-3.9	-3.5	-5.3	-4.4	-4.9
Angola	..	-1.3	9.5	-1.2	14.1	0.4	-16.3	-6.7	27.6	0.4	6.9	..	7.3	3.2
Benin	-21.5	-14.2	-9.8	-12.9	-13.7	-12.8	-10.4	-12.7	-12.9	-12.7	-11.8	-19.4	-13.7	-12.5
Botswana	-13.4	8.0	10.5	12.9	16.3	14.8	6.3	10.6	21.3	18.0	13.7	-13.0	13.8	14.2
Burkina Faso	-22.3	-12.9	-12.3	-14.6	-16.2	-15.1	-15.6	-15.7	-16.2	-14.0	-13.5	-21.3	-15.8	-15.1
Burundi	-14.5	-21.0	-18.2	-14.4	-9.6	-4.2	-11.6	-9.7	-14.7	-11.8	-12.4	-10.2	-16.1	-11.0
Cameroon	0.8	1.1	2.6	5.0	2.0	2.9	1.7	-0.3	3.9	2.7	-1.5	-2.0	1.6	2.0
Cape Verde	-75.6	-36.9	-38.5	-40.0	-32.2	-30.4	-35.1	-38.4	-33.9	-32.9	-35.9	-65.2	-35.1	-34.8
Central African Republic	-15.9	-8.3	-5.7	-7.3	-3.7	-5.4	-8.2	-3.4	-3.1	-2.9	-4.5	-12.0	-10.8	-4.8
Chad	-11.9	-16.0	-18.2	-12.0	-11.6	-12.5	-13.0	-14.7	-20.3	-36.2	-52.4	-10.3	-17.0	-21.6
Comoros	-43.2	-16.8	-27.2	-24.8	-23.1	-24.9	-22.6	-20.7	-14.5	-13.2	-12.3	-39.8	-23.9	-19.5
Congo, Dem. Rep. of	0.1	2.2	2.7	4.8	-0.3	3.8	-3.1	6.0	1.2	1.1	-3.1	-2.2	-0.1	1.3
Congo, Rep. of	-0.1	-5.9	-15.7	1.1	8.8	15.5	3.7	13.2	36.7	26.6	26.7	-10.2	-0.9	16.5
Côte d'Ivoire	-6.2	3.5	11.2	7.3	8.7	8.3	6.4	8.2	7.0	8.6	14.8	0.7	5.7	8.7
Djibouti	..	..	..	-16.7	-16.0	-15.1	-16.1	-14.4	-18.2	..	..	..	..	-16.1
Equatorial Guinea	..	-35.7	-49.0	-49.0	-82.8	-22.5	-71.7	10.3	36.5	25.6	31.0	-6.3	-32.9	-15.3
Eritrea	..	-40.9	-54.8	-60.5	-58.1	-56.2	-65.2	-73.1	-62.6	-59.7	-56.6	..	-43.1	-61.5
Ethiopia	..	-12.1	-9.8	-8.5	-9.9	-9.1	-9.4	-14.8	-15.0	-15.2	-18.3	-7.4	-7.7	-12.5
Gabon	33.1	14.2	23.4	23.6	27.6	21.4	1.7	6.8	2.2	19.8	20.0	15.2	6.2	15.4
Gambia, The	-20.9	-17.0	-15.3	-24.1	-15.9	-12.7	-15.6	-14.6	-14.4	-20.1	-17.8	-15.4	-11.6	-16.9
Ghana	-0.7	-16.2	-11.5	-8.4	-8.0	-20.6	-12.9	-17.6	-18.5	-19.6	-12.1	-0.6	-8.3	-14.7
Guinea	..	-6.7	-3.3	-3.8	-5.4	-2.2	-3.7	-4.8	-5.1	-1.9	-5.5	..	-1.7	-4.0
Guinea-Bissau	-29.2	-23.8	-17.9	-23.5	-21.3	-18.8	-21.5	-18.0	-26.5	-32.9	-32.1	-28.1	-32.0	-24.3
Kenya	-11.1	6.0	3.2	-6.2	-3.6	-7.5	-8.0	-5.9	-9.7	-9.2	-3.2	-4.1	-1.5	-6.7
Lesotho	-89.1	-89.6	-87.4	-91.7	-85.2	-81.7	-73.4	-66.5	-61.1	-54.6	-55.1	-100.6	-101.7	-71.2
Liberia	0.0	..	..	..	..	..	..	..	..	..	..	-0.5	7.2	..
Madagascar	-16.4	-9.3	-7.6	-7.6	-5.5	-8.1	-7.8	-7.7	-7.3	-3.2	-6.6	-8.2	-7.3	-6.7
Malawi	-14.0	-16.1	-32.1	-17.3	-8.5	-12.9	-6.0	-15.0	-12.4	-11.3	-18.1	-9.7	-11.8	-12.7
Mali	-14.4	-15.4	-19.9	-15.1	-15.7	-10.6	-10.5	-11.7	-12.5	-16.9	-8.7	-14.6	-18.6	-12.7
Mauritania	-29.8	-15.9	-3.8	-10.4	-12.3	-9.7	-14.0	-10.6	-14.1	-12.7	-15.7	-32.3	-13.9	-12.4
Mauritius	-10.9	-4.7	-7.4	-5.5	-1.5	-2.9	-2.7	-2.2	-2.0	2.7	3.8	-7.9	-3.2	-1.3
Mozambique	-16.5	-35.1	-33.7	-24.7	-23.7	-19.5	-17.4	-27.6	-26.0	-13.7	-14.7	-16.2	-25.9	-20.9
Namibia	7.8	-4.8	-2.8	-6.2	-8.0	-10.0	-12.0	-10.8	-5.5	-10.0	-0.6	-13.4	-6.1	-7.9
Niger	-13.5	-2.5	-10.3	-7.2	-6.5	-7.6	-8.6	-6.5	-7.5	-7.4	-8.5	-9.8	-5.5	-7.5
Nigeria	10.2	-3.1	1.0	2.1	20.7	7.2	-4.5	-4.0	15.7	4.5	-5.9	-0.8	3.3	4.5
Rwanda	-11.9	-15.3	-58.5	-20.7	-20.2	-17.9	-17.6	-17.1	-16.1	-15.8	-17.5	-8.0	-15.6	-17.9
São Tomé and Principe	-28.4	-66.9	-59.1	-79.5	-69.9	-65.6	-42.8	-49.3	-49.5	-57.0	-50.9	-21.2	-49.3	-58.1
Senegal	-16.7	-6.0	-6.7	-5.6	-6.3	-6.7	-6.7	-7.2	-9.9	-9.6	-9.8	-12.0	-6.7	-7.7
Seychelles	-11.2	-10.2	-2.9	-7.2	-9.4	-11.0	-15.9	-17.6	-2.9	-18.2	-2.7	-8.3	0.8	-10.6
Sierra Leone	-15.4	-0.3	3.5	-7.4	-14.7	-1.9	-7.2	-6.0	-16.1	-18.2	-22.4	-9.0	2.5	-11.7
Somalia	-55.3	..	..	..	..	..	..	..	..	..	..	-38.5	-23.7	..
South Africa	8.0	3.7	2.3	0.9	1.4	1.1	1.2	2.6	2.8	3.6	3.4	3.0	5.6	2.1
Sudan	-9.8	-8.0	-10.9	-4.9	-7.8	-12.5	-16.3	-6.0	2.2	0.9	-7.3	-10.0	-5.3	-6.5
Swaziland	-27.6	-25.2	-18.0	-18.6	-26.0	-17.3	-19.1	-18.4	-15.4	-11.3	-8.9	-17.7	-11.3	-16.9
Tanzania	..	-29.7	-23.0	-17.9	-13.0	-10.0	-14.7	-12.2	-8.3	-8.6	-7.0	-8.5	-20.5	-11.5
Togo	-5.3	-7.7	-3.7	-5.0	-10.9	-15.8	-15.3	-11.2	-16.8	-17.1	-17.0	-8.4	-8.8	-13.6
Uganda	-6.6	-14.1	-14.0	-9.0	-11.5	-7.4	-10.8	-12.1	-11.9	-12.4	-15.4	-3.1	-10.0	-11.3
Zambia	-4.0	-6.8	-0.8	-3.7	-7.5	-5.2	-12.5	-18.7	-10.4	-10.2	-13.3	-3.4	-2.1	-10.2
Zimbabwe	-3.2	-1.7	-1.9	-2.7	0.2	-7.0	-1.8	-0.4	2.2	1.2	..	-1.5	-0.6	-1.2
NORTH AFRICA	8.2	2.1	0.5	0.9	4.1	4.3	-1.2	1.0	6.6	6.3	4.8	0.6	-1.1	3.4
Algeria	4.0	-1.4	-4.6	-3.7	6.3	8.4	-1.6	3.5	20.4	15.0	9.6	-2.7	0.1	7.3
Egypt, Arab Rep.	-12.4	-3.0	-5.2	-5.0	-5.8	-6.3	-10.1	-8.6	-6.6	-5.0	-5.2	-14.5	-9.6	-6.6
Libya	34.8	..	..	..	..	..	..	..	..	..	..	20.1	..	..
Morocco	-10.5	-6.0	-6.0	-6.7	-3.4	-3.3	-4.1	-3.8	-6.1	-5.3	-5.9	-13.6	-5.6	-4.8
Tunisia	-5.4	-7.5	-3.0	-4.1	-1.6	-2.5	-3.4	-2.2	-3.5	-3.6	-3.7	-7.0	-4.7	-3.1
ALL AFRICA	3.9	-0.9	-0.9	-1.2	1.7	0.2	-3.5	-1.8	3.0	1.7	0.2	-1.6	-0.7	0.0

Note: 2002 data are preliminary (see page 2). Since 1994, Nigeria's ratios are distorted because the official exchange rate used by the Government for oil exports and oil value added is significantly over-valued.

2-14. Exports of goods and nonfactor services, nominal

	Millions of U.S. dollars, current prices											Annual average		
	1980	1993	1994	1995	1996	1997	1998	1999	2000	2001	2002	75-84	85-94	95-MR
SUB-SAHARAN AFRICA	80,966	71,926	77,293	91,305	101,978	102,500	91,285	93,777	111,426	106,284	108,286	51,580	67,163	100,855
excluding South Africa	52,831	43,908	47,210	56,622	66,720	65,991	56,903	60,111	74,901	71,356	72,962	33,995	41,929	65,696
excl. S.Africa & Nigeria	32,536	33,859	37,358	44,198	49,729	49,716	46,171	47,310	52,455	52,411	56,611	24,797	33,549	49,825
Angola	..	2,849	3,465	3,843	6,202	5,235	3,666	5,296	8,182	6,737	8,607	..	3,104	5,971
Benin	222	291	302	405	349	347	399	385	342	360	385	168	252	372
Botswana	563	1,959	2,139	2,432	2,601	2,914	2,537	2,743	3,220	2,845	2,667	447	1,713	2,745
Burkina Faso	173	237	244	306	276	267	362	287	237	260	272	126	244	283
Burundi	81	88	95	129	51	96	71	62	62	45	47	86	111	70
Cameroon	1,898	2,032	1,734	2,045	2,048	2,306	2,306	2,241	2,721	2,707	2,572	1,615	2,198	2,368
Cape Verde	19	45	69	94	112	129	109	113	146	167	194	22	43	133
Central African Republic	201	182	205	229	185	196	178	117	126	121	126	145	192	160
Chad	175	195	189	321	281	286	318	242	237	254	245	143	192	273
Comoros	11	53	37	46	42	38	26	29	31	35	39	15	37	36
Congo, Dem. Rep. of	2,371	1,213	1,316	1,607	1,732	1,145	1,848	1,109	964	924	1,048	1,691	1,903	1,297
Congo, Rep. of	1,024	849	1,035	1,369	1,746	1,756	1,487	1,702	2,586	2,232	2,434	782	1,085	1,914
Côte d'Ivoire	3,561	3,252	3,369	4,594	4,991	4,855	5,038	5,067	4,211	4,357	5,381	2,701	3,326	4,812
Djibouti	..	..	..	203	204	209	244	250	247	..	..	..	..	226
Equatorial Guinea	..	3	70	91	201	502	464	818	1,272	974	1,074	34	38	674
Eritrea	..	143	149	131	203	203	110	66	97	147	185	..	115	143
Ethiopia	..	507	554	786	787	1,010	1,034	916	984	958	962	560	595	930
Gabon	2,770	2,136	2,585	2,851	3,489	3,199	2,119	1,964	1,825	2,619	2,957	1,877	2,061	2,628
Gambia, The	103	213	159	187	185	185	213	199	202	212	192	77	157	197
Ghana	376	1,208	1,374	1,582	2,224	2,231	2,532	2,488	2,440	2,399	2,616	336	1,005	2,314
Guinea	..	640	763	766	734	771	770	759	735	822	779	..	694	767
Guinea-Bissau	14	21	39	30	28	56	30	56	68	82	92	11	20	55
Kenya	2,030	2,244	2,647	2,948	3,035	3,013	2,843	2,687	2,743	2,968	3,281	1,533	2,037	2,940
Lesotho	91	169	184	194	245	252	235	231	265	332	367	52	104	265
Liberia	614	..	..	..	..	..	..	..	..	..	..	508	466	..
Madagascar	539	516	656	763	819	775	805	909	1,190	1,317	704	415	469	910
Malawi	307	334	350	424	521	569	563	498	446	481	477	258	353	497
Mali	263	424	406	521	525	646	644	680	649	878	1,095	175	358	705
Mauritania	261	413	431	525	506	430	399	370	378	383	362	255	453	419
Mauritius	539	1,942	1,912	2,219	2,584	2,740	2,653	2,716	2,801	2,978	2,749	490	1,400	2,680
Mozambique	383	262	304	351	346	385	406	403	474	747	846	275	207	495
Namibia	1,712	1,477	1,577	1,734	1,766	1,728	1,562	1,563	1,558	1,403	1,403	1,205	1,244	1,590
Niger	617	251	258	323	337	303	369	321	321	323	353	397	352	331
Nigeria	18,859	10,062	9,881	12,449	16,995	16,286	10,776	12,832	22,416	18,953	16,406	8,898	8,410	15,889
Rwanda	168	102	47	67	83	144	111	113	150	157	132	144	144	120
São Tomé and Principe	10	11	12	9	11	12	12	16	15	17	22	9	11	14
Senegal	803	1,205	1,272	1,544	1,367	1,276	1,413	1,463	1,307	1,401	1,571	775	1,186	1,418
Seychelles	100	257	255	278	334	369	370	422	464	500	546	77	199	410
Sierra Leone	252	165	269	162	164	112	95	92	110	122	142	178	183	125
Somalia	200	..	..	..	..	..	..	..	..	..	..	142	69	..
South Africa	28,267	28,025	30,090	34,703	35,307	36,549	34,403	33,701	36,594	34,993	35,392	17,752	25,253	35,205
Sudan	672	266	311	437	462	516	513	791	1,799	1,685	1,963	695	460	1,021
Swaziland	413	778	837	1,020	958	1,087	1,080	1,006	1,124	1,176	1,078	292	581	1,066
Tanzania	..	766	930	1,089	1,142	1,274	1,144	1,190	1,307	1,431	1,563	581	529	1,267
Togo	580	301	300	425	488	434	471	455	398	411	458	401	463	442
Uganda	242	227	349	679	723	838	635	735	663	677	698	279	380	706
Zambia	1,608	1,099	1,205	1,253	1,024	1,178	865	701	682	985	1,058	1,138	1,054	968
Zimbabwe	1,561	2,016	2,384	2,719	3,090	3,169	2,632	2,538	2,118	1,977	1,999	1,211	1,847	2,530
NORTH AFRICA	47,051	50,307	49,746	57,218	62,364	64,478	58,396	63,127	78,499	79,245	78,840	31,418	41,454	67,771
Algeria	14,541	10,880	9,966	11,325	14,148	14,665	10,829	13,259	22,579	21,701	20,578	10,590	11,177	16,136
Egypt, Arab Rep.	6,992	13,071	11,904	13,506	13,650	14,779	13,442	13,500	15,940	17,072	16,332	5,294	8,686	14,778
Libya	23,523	..	..	..	..	..	..	..	..	..	..	13,757	..	..
Morocco	3,273	6,986	7,555	9,045	9,629	9,510	9,970	10,624	10,409	10,405	11,152	2,580	5,779	10,093
Tunisia	3,518	5,909	7,010	8,031	8,249	8,271	8,529	8,852	8,566	8,863	9,682	2,441	4,720	8,630
ALL AFRICA	123,719	119,057	124,466	145,785	161,585	163,856	146,709	153,237	184,884	179,870	181,729	80,351	106,727	164,707

Note: 2002 data are preliminary (see page 2).

2-15. Imports of goods and nonfactor services, nominal

				Millions of U.S. dollars, current prices								*Annual average*		
	1980	1993	1994	1995	1996	1997	1998	1999	2000	2001	2002	75-84	85-94	95-MR
SUB-SAHARAN AFRICA	73,690	76,302	79,976	96,130	98,306	106,878	104,418	102,521	105,330	106,639	113,468	55,026	67,085	104,211
excluding South Africa	51,877	53,144	53,053	62,782	65,012	72,061	71,635	72,345	72,336	75,854	81,756	39,288	47,161	71,723
excl. S.Africa & Nigeria	39,267	42,418	43,418	50,930	55,359	58,390	59,419	58,040	56,525	58,790	62,739	30,013	39,710	57,524
Angola	..	2,915	3,079	3,903	5,141	5,203	4,714	5,705	5,735	6,697	7,827	..	2,500	5,616
Benin	524	591	448	664	652	623	642	688	634	662	703	373	471	659
Botswana	705	1,627	1,682	1,817	1,816	2,143	2,229	2,204	2,076	1,902	1,947	537	1,355	2,017
Burkina Faso	603	540	488	666	725	660	798	729	658	650	693	442	620	697
Burundi	214	285	263	273	137	136	174	131	162	126	136	175	284	159
Cameroon	1,847	1,904	1,532	1,646	1,867	2,041	2,159	2,268	2,376	2,479	2,713	1,696	2,032	2,194
Cape Verde	100	179	227	290	273	283	298	337	326	355	425	77	146	323
Central African Republic	327	290	253	311	225	250	264	153	155	149	174	220	325	210
Chad	298	429	403	493	467	475	544	467	519	858	1,295	240	426	640
Comoros	64	99	88	103	95	91	75	75	60	64	70	60	86	79
Congo, Dem. Rep. of	2,353	975	1,157	1,339	1,750	916	2,041	827	906	867	1,224	1,916	1,920	1,234
Congo, Rep. of	1,026	962	1,313	1,346	1,523	1,397	1,416	1,391	1,404	1,490	1,629	872	1,083	1,450
Côte d'Ivoire	4,190	2,861	2,437	3,789	3,935	3,879	4,224	4,041	3,471	3,430	3,655	2,714	2,790	3,803
Djibouti	..	..	..	286	282	285	327	327	347	..	..	..	..	309
Equatorial Guinea	..	57	132	171	416	614	791	729	782	502	401	49	80	551
Eritrea	..	335	441	487	606	589	596	597	499	570	549	..	330	562
Ethiopia	..	1,263	1,096	1,276	1,382	1,588	1,648	1,877	1,961	1,945	2,073	973	1,170	1,719
Gabon	1,354	1,513	1,603	1,679	1,904	2,037	2,041	1,669	1,718	1,761	1,962	1,338	1,723	1,846
Gambia, The	153	275	214	279	248	237	278	262	262	291	256	108	191	264
Ghana	407	2,172	2,000	2,126	2,777	3,648	3,492	3,841	3,362	3,437	3,359	360	1,485	3,255
Guinea	..	860	875	906	942	855	903	924	894	880	956	..	752	908
Guinea-Bissau	46	77	81	89	86	107	74	96	125	148	157	48	83	110
Kenya	2,837	1,943	2,420	3,512	3,366	3,817	3,737	3,312	3,757	4,002	3,670	1,791	2,180	3,647
Lesotho	475	900	913	1,050	1,049	1,088	888	836	790	751	761	364	687	902
Liberia	614	..	..	..	..	..	..	..	..	..	..	514	387	..
Madagascar	1,202	830	881	1,002	1,039	1,062	1,095	1,197	1,474	1,463	993	692	682	1,166
Malawi	480	667	730	672	727	894	667	769	657	672	822	352	540	735
Mali	520	836	756	894	936	910	915	982	954	1,322	1,363	364	735	1,035
Mauritania	473	563	470	636	643	536	539	471	510	511	517	463	582	545
Mauritius	665	2,099	2,160	2,428	2,647	2,867	2,767	2,808	2,888	2,854	2,577	573	1,493	2,730
Mozambique	965	958	1,038	922	1,018	1,047	1,081	1,505	1,433	1,218	1,376	836	825	1,200
Namibia	1,542	1,614	1,669	1,950	2,046	2,092	1,972	1,927	1,746	1,717	1,421	1,447	1,407	1,859
Niger	957	291	420	457	466	444	547	452	455	467	538	569	458	478
Nigeria	12,324	10,719	9,646	11,858	9,688	13,677	12,236	14,304	15,794	17,038	18,977	8,996	7,486	14,196
Rwanda	307	404	488	334	362	475	462	443	441	427	435	237	396	422
São Tomé and Principe	24	42	41	46	42	41	30	40	38	44	48	19	36	41
Senegal	1,302	1,529	1,515	1,796	1,660	1,568	1,723	1,803	1,741	1,842	2,066	1,070	1,477	1,775
Seychelles	117	306	269	315	381	431	467	531	482	612	565	89	202	473
Sierra Leone	421	168	234	231	303	128	143	132	212	258	317	268	158	215
Somalia	534	..	..	..	..	..	..	..	..	..	..	400	304	..
South Africa	21,838	23,232	26,965	33,385	33,340	34,878	32,855	30,264	33,066	30,894	31,843	15,866	19,994	32,566
Sudan	1,333	744	1,021	904	1,119	1,799	2,258	1,434	1,546	1,573	2,953	1,387	948	1,698
Swaziland	564	1,046	1,044	1,274	1,304	1,335	1,339	1,260	1,338	1,321	1,183	384	677	1,294
Tanzania	..	2,031	1,968	2,029	1,986	2,040	2,375	2,242	2,064	2,232	2,218	1,058	1,438	2,148
Togo	640	396	337	490	647	672	687	615	603	626	693	471	579	629
Uganda	324	682	762	1,199	1,416	1,304	1,344	1,455	1,366	1,378	1,589	337	807	1,381
Zambia	1,764	1,322	1,232	1,383	1,271	1,381	1,268	1,287	1,018	1,358	1,552	1,249	1,125	1,315
Zimbabwe	1,771	2,130	2,516	2,910	3,074	3,760	2,737	2,561	1,956	1,872	1,807	1,342	1,886	2,585
NORTH AFRICA	36,840	46,963	48,941	55,715	54,331	55,849	60,920	60,884	63,014	64,211	67,506	30,264	42,960	60,304
Algeria	12,847	11,557	11,940	12,855	11,204	10,636	11,592	11,571	11,709	13,177	14,998	11,053	13,298	12,218
Egypt, Arab Rep.	9,822	14,488	14,604	16,544	17,562	19,528	21,812	21,144	22,457	21,963	21,010	8,159	12,443	20,253
Libya	11,167	..	..	..	..	..	..	..	..	..	..	8,634	..	..
Morocco	5,247	8,594	9,377	11,243	10,862	10,627	11,425	11,959	12,458	12,220	13,362	4,374	7,066	11,770
Tunisia	3,987	7,007	7,480	8,766	8,553	8,735	9,194	9,317	9,257	9,583	10,494	2,950	5,290	9,237
ALL AFRICA	108,840	122,939	128,594	151,676	152,658	162,982	165,127	163,119	168,017	170,490	180,648	84,291	109,648	164,340

Note: 2002 data are preliminary (see page 2).

National Accounts

2-16. Exports of goods and nonfactor services, real

| | Millions of U.S. dollars, constant 1995 prices | | | | | | | | | | Average annual percentage growth | | |
	1980	1993	1994	1995	1996	1997	1998	1999	2000	2001	2002	75-84	85-94	95-MR
SUB-SAHARAN AFRICA	65,556	79,892	84,583	91,123	99,527	104,509	108,849	110,994	116,741	120,428	120,212	1.0	3.0	4.5
excluding South Africa	41,427	49,769	53,160	56,439	61,659	64,528	67,873	69,443	71,691	74,257	74,686	1.3	3.0	4.4
excl. S.Africa & Nigeria	28,094	39,864	42,540	44,016	47,771	50,478	53,059	56,497	58,378	61,196	63,980	2.6	2.8	5.4
Angola	2,322	3,117	4,574	3,843	4,370	4,811	5,337	5,345	5,166	4,975	6,103	..	5.6	4.0
Benin	502	446	425	405	398	406	452	443	440	462	461	4.0	0.1	1.7
Botswana	752	2,124	2,269	2,432	2,698	2,943	2,731	2,918	3,506	3,341	3,181	14.2	4.4	4.8
Burkina Faso	335	398	293	306	290	306	439	388	351	361	403	4.7	2.0	4.1
Burundi	51	131	101	129	82	159	153	208	274	328	349	4.7	4.5	18.9
Cameroon	1,402	2,078	1,976	2,045	2,270	2,590	2,878	3,249	3,087	3,145	3,114	14.1	-1.9	6.8
Cape Verde	31	53	76	94	113	137	117	121	184	205	221	11.5	-1.8	13.2
Central African Republic	144	126	239	229	211	293	312	242	310	289	275	-0.4	2.5	3.1
Chad	190	253	258	321	255	289	299	251	268	238	232	-0.3	1.1	-2.3
Comoros	11	60	57	46	44	45	32	35	42	38	41	..	9.7	-3.6
Congo, Dem. Rep. of	1,788	1,443	1,335	1,607	1,855	1,445	1,794	2,681	2,583	2,635	2,846	4.2	-9.1	10.1
Congo, Rep. of	714	1,139	1,104	1,369	1,450	1,606	1,936	1,630	1,651	1,683	1,863	10.1	1.0	5.1
Côte d'Ivoire	3,009	4,125	4,021	4,594	4,742	5,120	5,161	5,260	5,117	5,344	5,082	8.5	2.5	2.7
Djibouti	..	..	..	..	..	..	..	..	..	..	..	..	..	..
Equatorial Guinea	..	2	80	91	164	365	449	520	641	723	762	..	-13.0	35.7
Eritrea	..	163	157	131	208	217	130	79	116	178	223	..	..	0.2
Ethiopia	..	779	788	786	992	1,197	1,102	1,191	1,541	1,624	1,839	..	-1.3	11.3
Gabon	1,593	2,787	2,913	2,851	2,969	3,060	2,889	2,698	2,602	2,647	2,729	0.7	6.4	-1.4
Gambia, The	127	219	165	187	184	185	219	210	231	278	267	7.3	1.7	6.3
Ghana	957	1,482	1,562	1,582	2,186	2,191	2,400	2,703	2,726	2,727	2,681	-9.4	9.3	7.7
Guinea	..	652	673	766	791	818	923	953	1,017	1,212	1,133	..	2.7	7.1
Guinea-Bissau	24	19	38	30	28	60	38	62	77	80	77	-1.8	8.7	14.0
Kenya	1,562	3,230	3,193	2,948	3,083	2,637	2,501	2,829	2,935	3,082	3,235	-0.2	7.9	0.3
Lesotho	86	179	195	194	265	272	277	272	329	474	592	9.1	9.6	13.4
Liberia	..	..	..	..	..	..	..	..	..	..	..	..	..	..
Madagascar	800	671	738	763	796	767	732	845	975	1,033	582	-4.1	4.0	0.8
Malawi	353	386	426	424	496	518	632	537	501	557	535	2.7	1.5	3.0
Mali	243	458	490	521	536	777	776	911	890	1,111	1,436	8.9	5.5	13.8
Mauritania	366	323	456	525	522	427	447	469	525	567	647	5.8	-3.9	2.9
Mauritius	733	2,020	2,117	2,219	2,411	2,580	2,732	2,865	2,808	3,108	3,402	..	9.8	5.7
Mozambique	314	284	324	351	430	467	517	509	673	1,067	1,218	..	10.4	17.4
Namibia	1,254	1,636	1,583	1,734	1,781	1,733	1,721	1,798	1,782	1,703	1,824	..	3.4	0.9
Niger	388	326	291	323	382	376	439	394	..	..	..	-1.3	-0.9	7.1
Nigeria	12,962	9,940	10,656	12,449	13,913	14,082	14,846	13,004	13,374	13,137	10,826	-2.9	3.9	0.1
Rwanda	185	158	61	67	95	123	126	149	163	229	219	6.5	-7.9	18.3
São Tomé and Principe	..	11	11	9	8	10	12	16	17	18	19	..	5.3	11.1
Senegal	878	1,241	1,496	1,544	1,457	1,863	2,059	2,206	2,285	2,439	2,481	0.5	2.2	7.7
Seychelles	..	293	278	278	332	390	395	414	509	575	591	..	10.2	10.7
Sierra Leone	375	333	254	162	132	102	15	11	12	14	14	-11.1	-0.6	-35.1
Somalia	..	..	..	..	..	..	..	..	..	..	..	..	..	..
South Africa	24,198	30,141	31,448	34,703	37,889	40,001	41,003	41,580	45,062	46,187	45,551	0.7	2.9	4.6
Sudan	502	397	431	437	563	520	510	932	1,935	1,776	1,822	2.4	-4.5	24.3
Swaziland	485	932	960	1,020	1,020	1,114	1,208	1,148	1,293	1,504	1,535	2.7	9.7	6.1
Tanzania	..	736	821	1,089	1,094	822	903	1,070	1,267	1,315	1,375	..	11.9	5.5
Togo	532	359	352	425	504	465	460	454	450	444	475	4.6	-2.2	1.8
Uganda	..	401	528	679	863	1,118	952	1,314	1,383	1,579	1,759	..	3.5	15.1
Zambia	1,787	1,379	1,500	1,253	1,336	1,593	1,671	1,754	1,501	1,937	2,157	-2.9	-1.0	5.3
Zimbabwe	965	2,067	2,455	2,719	2,829	2,996	3,593	3,781	3,156	3,043	3,019	5.4	7.3	2.7
NORTH AFRICA	28,716	53,738	54,440	57,218	58,900	62,473	63,425	67,488	72,483	74,830	77,483	3.8	5.8	4.6
Algeria	7,239	11,029	10,654	11,325	12,175	12,942	13,162	13,951	14,984	14,814	15,107	1.9	2.3	4.6
Egypt, Arab Rep.	6,537	13,113	12,477	13,506	13,718	14,051	13,547	14,472	15,961	16,993	17,914	5.5	7.6	4.2
Libya	..	..	..	..	..	..	..	..	..	..	..	..	..	..
Morocco	3,401	8,232	8,846	9,045	9,271	9,983	10,576	11,404	11,909	12,074	12,114	4.1	7.3	4.7
Tunisia	3,855	6,985	7,895	8,031	7,975	8,780	9,169	9,602	10,233	10,926	11,615	5.6	7.5	5.2
ALL AFRICA	94,613	130,516	136,207	145,587	156,123	164,440	169,948	175,559	185,859	191,776	193,679	1.8	3.8	4.5

Note: 2002 data are preliminary (see page 2).

2-17. Imports of goods and nonfactor services, real

	Millions of U.S. dollars, constant 1995 prices											Average annual percentage growth		
	1980	1993	1994	1995	1996	1997	1998	1999	2000	2001	2002	75-84	85-94	95-MR
SUB-SAHARAN AFRICA	95,814	81,386	86,166	96,124	102,534	110,497	114,899	116,358	120,148	126,725	137,958	1.8	0.7	5.3
excluding South Africa	73,718	56,887	57,680	62,797	66,294	72,318	76,158	80,546	81,751	88,273	98,355	2.2	-0.4	6.3
excl. S.Africa & Nigeria	44,598	45,424	47,052	50,948	53,874	58,285	62,607	64,952	64,607	69,186	77,644	1.4	0.6	5.8
Angola	2,359	2,427	3,438	3,903	3,886	4,042	3,821	4,243	4,498	5,359	8,662	..	1.8	8.7
Benin	965	700	479	664	656	681	678	744	767	800	808	2.8	-0.6	5.2
Botswana	888	1,700	1,787	1,817	1,974	2,366	2,682	2,646	2,532	2,533	2,631	7.2	6.7	5.4
Burkina Faso	584	763	544	666	710	701	921	849	742	811	860	3.2	0.6	4.6
Burundi	190	313	294	273	162	152	275	311	436	411	504	8.4	1.3	10.7
Cameroon	1,207	1,593	1,628	1,646	1,891	2,203	2,493	2,566	2,979	3,327	3,633	10.5	-4.3	11.2
Cape Verde	160	210	252	290	277	301	319	362	411	436	484	11.9	1.9	8.3
Central African Republic	319	286	305	311	222	291	298	175	199	192	207	3.0	1.4	-6.0
Chad	379	559	460	493	424	480	558	500	635	1,384	2,212	-4.0	-0.7	18.6
Comoros	82	92	79	103	97	109	96	101	96	106	119	..	-1.3	2.7
Congo, Dem. Rep. of	1,872	1,312	980	1,339	1,265	976	1,628	2,595	3,042	3,347	4,585	4.3	-10.1	21.4
Congo, Rep. of	1,330	1,548	1,446	1,346	1,564	1,570	1,401	1,658	1,733	1,842	2,288	8.0	-3.8	5.2
Côte d'Ivoire	5,896	2,307	2,946	3,789	3,645	3,948	4,163	4,097	3,475	3,431	3,353	3.2	-5.2	0.3
Djibouti	..	..	..	..	..	..	..	..	..	..	..	..	..	..
Equatorial Guinea	..	37	151	171	340	447	767	987	1,063	373	285	..	2.9	14.2
Eritrea	..	374	475	487	604	626	656	680	582	676	640	..	..	3.7
Ethiopia	..	1,366	1,166	1,276	1,322	1,578	1,740	2,033	2,032	2,031	2,226	..	-0.1	8.9
Gabon	1,900	2,048	1,723	1,679	1,918	2,295	2,297	1,920	1,964	2,008	2,064	4.0	-4.3	1.9
Gambia, The	342	283	223	279	247	237	286	277	301	381	355	5.3	3.7	5.7
Ghana	1,991	2,228	2,024	2,126	2,770	3,817	3,873	4,304	3,529	3,802	3,636	-9.8	7.7	8.1
Guinea	..	837	858	906	881	883	959	993	1,375	1,442	1,546	..	2.0	8.2
Guinea-Bissau	98	98	96	89	84	109	80	102	139	157	134	0.1	-3.0	6.8
Kenya	2,115	2,558	2,989	3,512	3,576	3,670	3,472	3,292	3,873	4,100	3,417	-3.9	7.6	1.8
Lesotho	592	952	971	1,050	1,139	1,174	1,050	984	983	1,077	1,229	7.2	4.0	0.9
Liberia	..	..	..	..	..	..	..	..	..	..	..	..	..	..
Madagascar	1,889	974	973	1,002	1,041	1,122	1,178	1,250	1,524	1,703	1,176	-3.0	0.1	5.5
Malawi	853	834	757	672	737	906	732	836	699	737	867	-2.1	3.9	1.1
Mali	506	895	835	894	963	1,062	1,121	1,211	1,188	1,485	1,611	7.0	2.6	8.2
Mauritania	471	517	473	636	609	538	612	605	694	728	800	2.9	-3.2	4.9
Mauritius	935	2,240	2,389	2,428	2,531	2,796	3,033	3,215	3,256	3,331	3,504	..	12.1	5.3
Mozambique	1,253	926	1,194	922	968	972	1,054	1,479	1,346	1,168	1,330	..	2.1	3.8
Namibia	1,531	1,722	1,787	1,950	2,256	2,334	2,512	2,548	2,415	2,510	2,896	..	2.2	5.0
Niger	1,151	453	465	457	461	452	529	428	..	..	..	4.9	-6.2	0.0
Nigeria	27,928	11,458	10,640	11,858	12,430	14,036	13,575	15,597	17,117	19,044	20,677	5.8	-3.2	8.4
Rwanda	175	455	514	334	346	480	524	492	436	453	451	10.4	7.0	1.5
São Tomé and Principe	..	47	43	46	41	43	35	44	43	54	58	..	1.5	3.0
Senegal	1,434	1,682	1,513	1,796	1,871	1,839	2,095	1,992	1,947	1,973	2,012	2.3	0.0	2.7
Seychelles	..	317	272	315	381	428	529	522	514	689	598	..	12.8	11.1
Sierra Leone	454	239	229	231	354	132	60	38	71	114	154	-7.8	0.8	-12.7
Somalia	..	..	..	..	..	..	..	..	..	..	..	..	..	..
South Africa	22,394	24,600	28,557	33,385	36,294	38,248	38,825	35,945	38,507	38,607	39,814	-1.4	3.4	3.1
Sudan	910	1,112	1,412	904	1,366	1,813	2,244	1,691	1,663	1,658	3,267	9.9	0.0	9.6
Swaziland	662	1,252	1,197	1,274	1,388	1,368	1,498	1,438	1,540	1,689	1,685	10.1	9.4	4.2
Tanzania	..	1,999	1,911	2,029	1,866	1,339	1,887	2,051	2,053	2,569	2,628	..	2.9	4.4
Togo	702	430	378	490	624	717	770	704	685	723	748	6.0	-4.6	7.0
Uganda	..	692	772	1,199	1,355	1,382	1,425	1,584	1,447	1,468	1,765	..	2.3	7.2
Zambia	2,287	1,080	1,217	1,383	1,322	1,385	1,441	1,473	1,177	1,497	1,550	-10.7	-3.3	1.7
Zimbabwe	959	2,198	2,610	2,910	2,823	3,534	3,743	3,830	3,004	2,983	2,840	3.7	9.8	1.0
NORTH AFRICA	52,209	51,292	52,529	55,715	53,159	55,918	61,853	63,302	67,201	70,141	74,729	4.9	-1.0	4.6
Algeria	18,603	11,878	12,603	12,855	11,145	11,413	12,246	12,454	13,326	15,617	17,038	5.1	-6.4	3.8
Egypt, Arab Rep.	16,885	15,385	15,675	16,544	16,801	17,123	18,494	18,804	19,270	18,532	19,368	4.5	-1.4	2.6
Libya	..	..	..	..	..	..	..	..	..	..	..	..	..	..
Morocco	5,495	10,004	9,802	11,243	10,687	11,800	14,334	14,804	15,955	16,319	17,419	2.7	7.3	7.7
Tunisia	5,316	8,217	8,504	8,766	8,507	9,252	9,777	10,074	11,043	11,733	12,445	8.5	4.9	5.1
ALL AFRICA	147,873	132,248	138,365	151,675	155,961	166,801	176,891	179,754	187,320	196,886	212,820	2.9	0.0	5.0

Note: 2002 data are preliminary (see page 2).

2-18. GDP growth

	Percent annual change											Average annual percentage growth		
	1980	*1993*	*1994*	*1995*	*1996*	*1997*	*1998*	*1999*	*2000*	*2001*	*2002*	*75-84*	*85-94*	*95-MR*
SUB-SAHARAN AFRICA	5.7	1.9	2.1	3.8	5.1	3.5	2.3	2.5	3.1	3.2	2.8	2.3	1.7	3.2
excluding South Africa	1.2	2.6	1.2	4.4	5.9	4.3	3.6	2.8	2.8	3.5	2.7	2.1	2.6	3.7
excl. S.Africa & Nigeria	0.3	2.6	1.4	4.8	6.2	4.6	3.9	3.2	2.5	3.7	3.4	2.8	2.2	3.9
Angola	..	-24.7	3.5	10.4	11.2	7.9	6.8	3.3	3.0	3.2	15.3	..	-1.2	6.7
Benin	6.8	3.5	4.4	4.6	5.5	6.1	4.5	4.7	5.8	5.0	6.0	3.8	2.3	5.3
Botswana	12.0	1.9	3.6	4.4	5.6	6.9	6.0	5.4	7.5	5.3	3.1	11.6	8.9	5.8
Burkina Faso	0.8	4.6	1.0	4.6	7.1	5.2	1.0	6.7	1.6	4.6	4.6	3.6	3.2	4.3
Burundi	1.0	-5.7	-3.9	-7.3	-8.4	0.4	4.8	-1.0	-0.9	3.2	3.6	3.8	2.7	-0.4
Cameroon	-2.0	-3.2	-2.5	3.3	5.0	5.1	5.0	4.4	4.2	5.3	4.2	8.5	-2.7	4.7
Cape Verde	37.7	7.1	6.9	7.5	4.0	5.4	7.4	8.6	6.6	5.1	4.3	10.0	6.4	6.3
Central African Republic	-4.5	0.3	4.9	7.2	-4.0	5.3	4.7	3.6	2.3	1.5	-0.8	0.4	-0.5	2.6
Chad	-6.0	-15.7	10.1	0.8	2.4	4.3	5.9	-0.6	-0.6	9.5	9.9	-1.3	3.2	3.5
Comoros	..	3.0	-5.3	3.6	-1.3	4.2	1.2	1.9	-1.1	1.9	2.5	..	1.2	1.4
Congo, Dem. Rep. of	2.2	-13.5	-3.9	0.7	-1.0	-5.6	-1.6	-4.4	-7.0	-2.0	3.0	-0.3	-4.0	-3.0
Congo, Rep. of	17.6	-1.0	-5.5	5.0	4.3	-0.6	3.7	-3.0	8.2	3.6	3.5	9.2	0.3	2.7
Côte d'Ivoire	-18.4	52.0	0.8	7.1	7.7	5.7	4.7	1.6	-2.5	0.3	-1.8	1.9	4.7	2.8
Djibouti	..	-3.9	-2.9	-2.3	-3.3	-0.6	0.5	2.2	0.7	..	..	..	-1.2	-0.4
Equatorial Guinea	..	6.3	5.1	14.3	29.1	71.2	21.9	41.4	16.9	1.3	0.2	..	3.0	26.5
Eritrea	..	13.4	21.2	2.9	9.2	7.9	1.8	0.0	-13.2	10.2	1.8	..	..	1.8
Ethiopia	..	13.4	3.5	6.1	10.9	5.4	-1.9	6.2	5.7	8.9	2.7	..	1.3	5.2
Gabon	2.6	2.4	3.4	7.0	5.2	5.8	2.1	-6.2	2.0	2.5	3.0	-0.2	1.9	2.0
Gambia, The	6.3	3.0	0.2	0.9	2.2	4.9	4.9	6.4	5.6	5.8	-3.1	4.3	3.4	4.2
Ghana	0.5	4.9	3.3	4.1	4.6	4.2	4.7	4.4	3.7	4.2	4.5	-1.1	4.7	4.3
Guinea	..	4.2	6.3	4.4	4.6	5.0	4.8	4.6	1.9	3.8	4.2	..	3.8	4.2
Guinea-Bissau	-16.0	2.1	3.2	4.4	11.6	6.5	-28.1	7.8	7.5	0.2	-7.2	2.1	3.8	-1.1
Kenya	5.6	0.4	2.6	4.4	4.1	2.1	1.6	1.3	-0.2	1.1	1.0	4.7	3.6	1.7
Lesotho	7.4	3.5	3.4	4.4	10.0	8.1	-4.6	0.2	1.3	3.2	3.8	6.7	5.4	2.7
Liberia	..	..	..	..	..	..	..	..	..	..	..	..	..	..
Madagascar	0.8	2.1	-0.1	1.7	2.1	3.7	3.9	4.7	4.8	6.0	-12.7	-0.2	1.2	2.8
Malawi	0.4	9.7	-10.2	16.7	7.3	3.8	3.3	4.0	1.1	-4.2	1.8	3.2	2.2	3.5
Mali	-4.3	-2.1	0.9	6.2	3.2	6.8	6.0	6.7	4.7	3.5	9.7	2.3	2.5	5.7
Mauritania	3.4	5.5	4.6	4.6	5.5	3.2	3.7	4.1	5.1	4.0	3.3	1.6	2.6	4.2
Mauritius	..	5.9	4.5	4.1	5.2	5.9	6.0	5.3	4.0	6.7	4.4	..	6.5	5.3
Mozambique	..	8.7	7.5	4.3	7.1	11.1	12.6	7.5	1.5	13.0	7.7	..	4.1	8.3
Namibia	..	-2.0	7.3	4.1	3.2	4.2	3.3	3.3	3.3	2.4	2.7	..	3.4	3.3
Niger	-2.2	1.4	4.0	2.6	3.4	2.8	10.4	-0.6	-1.4	7.1	3.0	2.0	1.5	3.4
Nigeria	4.2	2.2	0.1	2.5	4.3	2.7	1.9	1.1	4.2	2.9	-0.9	-0.7	5.0	2.5
Rwanda	9.0	-8.1	-50.2	35.2	12.7	13.8	8.9	7.6	6.0	6.7	9.4	6.8	-2.7	10.8
São Tomé and Principe	..	1.1	2.2	2.0	1.5	1.0	2.5	2.5	3.0	4.0	4.1	..	1.7	2.5
Senegal	-3.3	-2.2	2.9	5.2	5.1	5.0	5.7	5.0	5.6	5.6	1.1	2.1	2.1	5.0
Seychelles	-4.2	6.2	-0.8	-0.8	4.9	12.0	8.4	1.9	4.8	-2.2	0.3	3.4	5.7	4.4
Sierra Leone	4.8	1.4	-1.9	-8.0	6.1	-17.6	-0.9	-8.1	3.8	5.4	6.3	2.5	-1.7	-2.7
Somalia	..	..	..	..	..	..	..	..	..	..	..	..	..	..
South Africa	9.2	1.2	3.2	3.1	4.3	2.6	0.8	2.0	3.5	2.8	3.0	2.4	0.8	2.6
Sudan	-6.0	4.6	1.0	6.0	11.7	6.8	6.3	5.2	5.1	6.1	5.5	8.6	4.1	6.5
Swaziland	12.4	3.6	3.4	3.8	3.9	3.8	3.2	3.4	2.1	1.7	3.6	3.3	7.3	3.1
Tanzania	..	1.2	1.6	3.6	4.6	3.5	3.7	3.6	5.7	6.1	6.3	..	2.6	4.5
Togo	14.6	-15.1	15.0	7.8	8.8	4.3	-2.1	2.4	-1.9	-0.2	4.6	2.1	0.5	2.2
Uganda	..	8.3	6.4	11.5	9.1	5.1	4.9	7.9	5.5	5.1	6.7	..	5.1	6.6
Zambia	3.0	6.8	-8.6	-2.8	6.9	3.3	-1.9	2.2	3.6	4.9	3.3	0.2	0.9	2.5
Zimbabwe	14.4	1.1	9.2	0.2	10.4	2.7	2.9	-0.7	-4.9	-8.4	-5.6	3.0	3.3	-0.2
NORTH AFRICA	5.0	0.5	3.9	1.5	6.6	2.6	5.8	4.0	3.5	4.3	3.8	6.0	2.8	4.1
Algeria	0.8	-2.1	-0.9	3.8	4.1	1.1	5.1	3.2	2.4	3.6	3.4	5.5	0.5	3.3
Egypt, Arab Rep.	10.0	2.9	3.9	4.7	5.0	5.5	5.6	6.0	5.1	3.3	3.0	8.3	3.9	5.0
Libya	..	..	..	..	..	..	..	..	..	..	..	..	..	..
Morocco	3.6	-1.0	10.4	-6.6	12.2	-2.2	7.7	0.0	0.9	6.5	4.4	4.1	3.6	3.0
Tunisia	7.4	2.2	3.3	2.3	7.1	5.4	4.8	6.1	4.7	5.4	6.0	5.3	3.8	5.3
ALL AFRICA	5.5	1.5	2.7	3.0	5.6	3.2	3.4	3.0	3.2	3.6	3.2	3.3	2.0	3.5

Note: 2002 data are preliminary (see page 2).

2-19. Gross national income (GNI) per capita

	U.S. dollars, Atlas method											*Annual average*		
	1980	*1993*	*1994*	*1995*	*1996*	*1997*	*1998*	*1999*	*2000*	*2001*	*2002*	*75-84*	*85-94*	*95-MR*
SUB-SAHARAN AFRICA	661	536	515	523	541	546	516	497	481	468	451	540	525	503
excluding South Africa	525	324	290	290	310	322	318	309	302	306	307	423	357	308
excl. S.Africa & Nigeria	444	346	309	310	326	335	333	323	312	308	309	367	378	319
Angola	..	330	210	340	410	500	490	410	440	500	670	..	644	470
Benin	410	380	330	350	350	390	380	380	390	380	380	314	346	375
Botswana	1,110	3,320	2,950	3,190	3,100	3,260	3,290	3,020	3,040	3,170	3,010	931	2,309	3,135
Burkina Faso	290	280	230	240	260	270	250	260	250	240	250	223	290	253
Burundi	220	180	160	150	140	140	140	120	110	100	100	186	222	125
Cameroon	620	900	730	660	610	620	610	600	580	560	550	600	949	599
Cape Verde	..	1,110	1,150	1,210	1,270	1,300	1,300	1,340	1,320	1,280	1,250	..	1,031	1,284
Central African Republic	340	440	360	350	290	310	290	280	280	260	250	271	416	289
Chad	240	260	250	230	220	230	230	210	200	200	220	221	264	218
Comoros	..	640	500	480	440	450	410	400	380	380	390	327	499	416
Congo, Dem. Rep. of	630	190	160	140	120	60	110	90	90	80	90	483	222	98
Congo, Rep. of	880	900	720	460	500	620	610	520	600	670	720	833	996	588
Côte d'Ivoire	1,140	780	710	730	740	790	780	750	680	640	610	855	780	715
Djibouti	..	..	..	880	870	850	830	850	880	890	900	..	..	869
Equatorial Guinea	..	420	370	390	430	860	1,060	790	680	900	..	..	363	730
Eritrea	..	..	230	200	220	240	220	210	180	190	180	..	230	205
Ethiopia	..	170	140	120	120	120	110	120	110	110	100	145	171	114
Gabon	4,820	4,570	4,140	3,930	4,130	4,400	3,980	3,300	3,190	3,160	3,120	4,344	4,438	3,651
Gambia, The	380	350	340	340	340	340	340	340	340	320	270	295	307	329
Ghana	430	410	370	360	370	390	390	390	330	300	270	355	399	350
Guinea	..	540	560	560	570	560	520	500	450	420	410	..	490	499
Guinea-Bissau	150	230	220	230	240	240	160	170	180	160	150	184	211	191
Kenya	440	250	240	260	320	350	350	360	350	350	360	340	335	338
Lesotho	470	700	700	710	710	720	600	580	550	510	470	414	565	606
Liberia	530	..	..	..	..	100	110	110	130	140	140	441	370	122
Madagascar	450	240	240	240	250	250	260	250	250	260	230	352	253	249
Malawi	190	240	170	170	190	220	220	190	170	160	160	164	190	185
Mali	270	300	250	250	240	260	250	250	230	230	240	201	250	244
Mauritania	460	510	490	460	470	450	420	390	350	350	280	404	507	396
Mauritius	..	3,100	3,170	3,390	3,610	3,840	3,800	3,760	3,730	3,890	3,900	1,137	2,175	3,740
Mozambique	..	..	..	..	..	..	180	..	..	200	210	240	217	197
Namibia	..	2,160	2,310	2,640	2,610	2,470	2,280	2,280	2,280	2,150	1,960	1,557	1,677	2,334
Niger	430	240	210	190	200	200	200	190	180	180	170	316	280	189
Nigeria	780	240	220	210	250	270	260	260	270	300	300	601	275	265
Rwanda	250	260	140	200	200	210	230	240	240	220	210	207	305	219
São Tomé and Principe	..	370	350	340	320	290	270	270	290	290	290	..	426	295
Senegal	530	740	590	550	530	530	510	500	490	480	460	436	633	506
Seychelles	2,110	6,390	6,530	6,460	6,740	7,330	7,320	7,290	7,310	7,220	7,050	1,666	4,618	7,090
Sierra Leone	380	150	170	180	210	170	150	130	130	130	140	305	188	155
Somalia	100	..	..	..	..	..	..	..	..	..	..	124	147	..
South Africa	2,550	3,460	3,610	3,740	3,770	3,700	3,320	3,180	3,060	2,840	2,600	2,139	2,823	3,276
Sudan	470	290	260	260	300	310	340	360	350	350	380	415	527	331
Swaziland	960	1,290	1,300	1,510	1,590	1,640	1,400	1,420	1,390	1,330	1,240	811	1,073	1,440
Tanzania	..	170	160	160	190	210	230	250	270	270	290	..	174	234
Togo	450	360	330	330	340	360	330	320	290	270	270	334	373	314
Uganda	..	190	200	250	290	320	310	300	280	250	240	180	284	280
Zambia	630	380	350	340	360	360	310	..	..	..	..	562	360	343
Zimbabwe	960	650	640	610	670	660	540	450	..	..	..	858	787	586
NORTH AFRICA	1,304	1,255	1,300	1,337	1,439	1,487	1,525	1,566	1,630	1,673	1,644	1,068	1,349	1,538
Algeria	2,080	1,780	1,660	1,590	1,550	1,540	1,560	1,540	1,580	1,660	1,720	1,772	2,341	1,593
Egypt, Arab Rep	530	800	880	990	1,100	1,200	1,270	1,370	1,490	1,530	1,470	483	792	1,303
Libya	10,460	..	..	..	..	..	..	..	..	..	..	7,921	6,190	..
Morocco	970	1,060	1,170	1,120	1,300	1,250	1,260	1,210	1,180	1,190	1,170	733	943	1,210
Tunisia	1,360	1,690	1,740	1,820	2,000	2,080	2,050	2,080	2,080	2,060	1,990	1,093	1,427	2,020
ALL AFRICA	772	669	657	669	701	712	691	680	676	671	650	631	676	681

Note: 2002 data are preliminary (see page 2). Gross National Income (GNI) previously called Gross National Product (GNP).

National Accounts

2-20. Total consumption per capita

	Current U.S. dollars											Annual average		
	1980	1993	1994	1995	1996	1997	1998	1999	2000	2001	2002	75-84	85-94	95-MR
SUB-SAHARAN AFRICA	507	444	411	460	451	472	437	424	399	386	378	411	434	426
excluding South Africa	408	272	233	267	274	292	281	277	258	267	277	326	301	274
excl. S.Africa & Nigeria	356	300	248	283	293	308	299	286	268	272	278	293	325	286
Angola	..	463	284	342	345	497	443	439	264	483	521	..	640	417
Benin	432	402	264	343	380	354	369	375	341	347	387	305	343	362
Botswana	858	1,874	1,888	1,995	1,833	1,876	1,840	1,905	1,910	1,869	1,895	670	1,392	1,890
Burkina Faso	297	233	188	226	249	224	230	235	216	229	252	221	268	233
Burundi	224	167	165	170	140	143	138	108	105	104	106	179	206	127
Cameroon	603	771	493	477	547	523	487	507	467	438	494	486	755	492
Cape Verde	458	961	1,070	1,246	1,496	1,353	1,528	1,622	1,384	1,411	1,547	349	900	1,448
Central African Republic	375	405	247	314	308	271	275	255	237	228	246	273	413	267
Chad	..	246	184	217	223	206	219	211	173	196	225	200	265	209
Comoros	406	586	412	497	473	446	425	433	371	384	419	343	512	431
Congo, Dem. Rep. of	464	249	121	109	91	122	131	89	96	97	106	399	206	105
Congo, Rep. of	608	533	526	449	539	461	420	416	395	368	413	543	729	433
Côte d'Ivoire	989	734	464	611	673	616	680	639	551	534	529	671	770	604
Djibouti	..	..	..	929	883	862	818	869	874	..	..	..	..	873
Equatorial Guinea	..	455	241	297	436	669	840	688	762	378	328	440	413	550
Eritrea	..	171	198	227	247	227	266	254	226	222	195	..	183	233
Ethiopia	..	115	96	94	96	98	98	101	101	96	88	130	146	97
Gabon	2,424	2,652	2,127	2,355	2,470	2,272	2,349	2,307	2,810	1,672	1,949	1,938	2,966	2,273
Gambia, The	354	336	326	356	321	329	330	330	312	296	247	272	291	315
Ghana	383	340	280	326	334	357	355	385	240	248	273	318	350	315
Guinea	..	466	470	489	471	430	419	395	349	321	368	..	403	405
Guinea-Bissau	141	196	196	216	217	207	175	171	174	161	165	179	193	186
Kenya	378	150	221	301	294	353	354	322	327	345	352	278	273	331
Lesotho	514	670	662	740	717	783	646	632	581	479	463	401	553	630
Liberia	433	..	..	..	..	..	..	..	..	..	..	408	411	..
Madagascar	462	263	223	230	273	239	238	229	231	240	247	341	242	241
Malawi	179	234	134	156	250	264	163	180	170	177	187	140	172	193
Mali	268	273	174	236	247	221	225	220	207	227	244	196	241	228
Mauritania	456	412	381	423	442	416	381	346	297	319	322	425	433	368
Mauritius	1,020	2,255	2,316	2,609	2,798	2,892	2,685	2,710	2,826	2,789	2,780	910	1,630	2,761
Mozambique	322	162	161	149	178	202	213	210	186	137	137	300	215	176
Namibia	1,313	1,605	1,645	1,798	1,757	1,887	1,647	1,614	1,573	1,403	1,119	1,595	1,444	1,600
Niger	384	183	179	208	206	184	201	187	162	168	182	281	256	187
Nigeria	619	162	174	206	201	232	214	241	221	248	271	464	210	229
Rwanda	216	255	212	244	257	272	281	257	232	209	209	196	290	245
São Tomé and Principe	588	501	451	384	378	368	308	357	333	395	405	490	579	366
Senegal	566	632	395	477	476	444	451	448	426	439	462	428	600	453
Seychelles	1,678	5,309	4,993	5,206	4,655	5,780	6,258	5,791	5,777	5,791	6,011	1,284	3,618	5,659
Sierra Leone	337	166	200	211	216	174	141	138	137	164	170	271	175	169
Somalia	105	..	..	..	..	..	..	..	..	..	..	128	144	..
South Africa	1,816	2,820	2,869	3,135	2,918	2,991	2,624	2,488	2,375	2,072	1,857	1,527	2,243	2,557
Sudan	350	197	210	301	247	340	317	294	286	..	..	346	379	297
Swaziland	873	1,283	1,269	1,496	1,349	1,446	1,325	1,346	1,292	1,126	992	674	906	1,297
Tanzania	..	159	154	174	205	233	263	254	244	248	241	246	172	233
Togo	347	334	230	301	340	365	317	299	257	260	277	253	349	302
Uganda	..	165	193	263	277	266	282	245	233	218	221	186	253	251
Zambia	546	355	357	344	341	382	328	327	300	326	346	455	350	337
Zimbabwe	807	470	479	515	594	628	399	373	485	642	571	711	592	526
NORTH AFRICA	842	1,040	1,059	1,132	1,224	1,204	1,274	1,269	1,269	1,272	1,258	707	1,048	1,238
Algeria	1,291	1,342	1,136	1,070	1,125	1,117	1,170	1,091	979	1,087	1,148	1,125	1,663	1,098
Egypt, Arab Rep.	476	732	806	908	1,018	1,058	1,135	1,180	1,277	1,232	1,122	417	668	1,116
Libya	5,040	..	..	..	..	..	..	..	..	..	..	4,322	..	..
Morocco	838	879	991	1,074	1,143	1,011	1,056	1,004	950	947	1,025	610	801	1,026
Tunisia	1,041	1,321	1,392	1,593	1,648	1,559	1,625	1,672	1,550	1,563	1,694	820	1,116	1,613
ALL AFRICA	574	554	528	582	588	602	583	570	548	536	527	470	548	567

Note: 2002 data are preliminary (see page 2).

Figure 2-1. Gross domestic product, 2002*

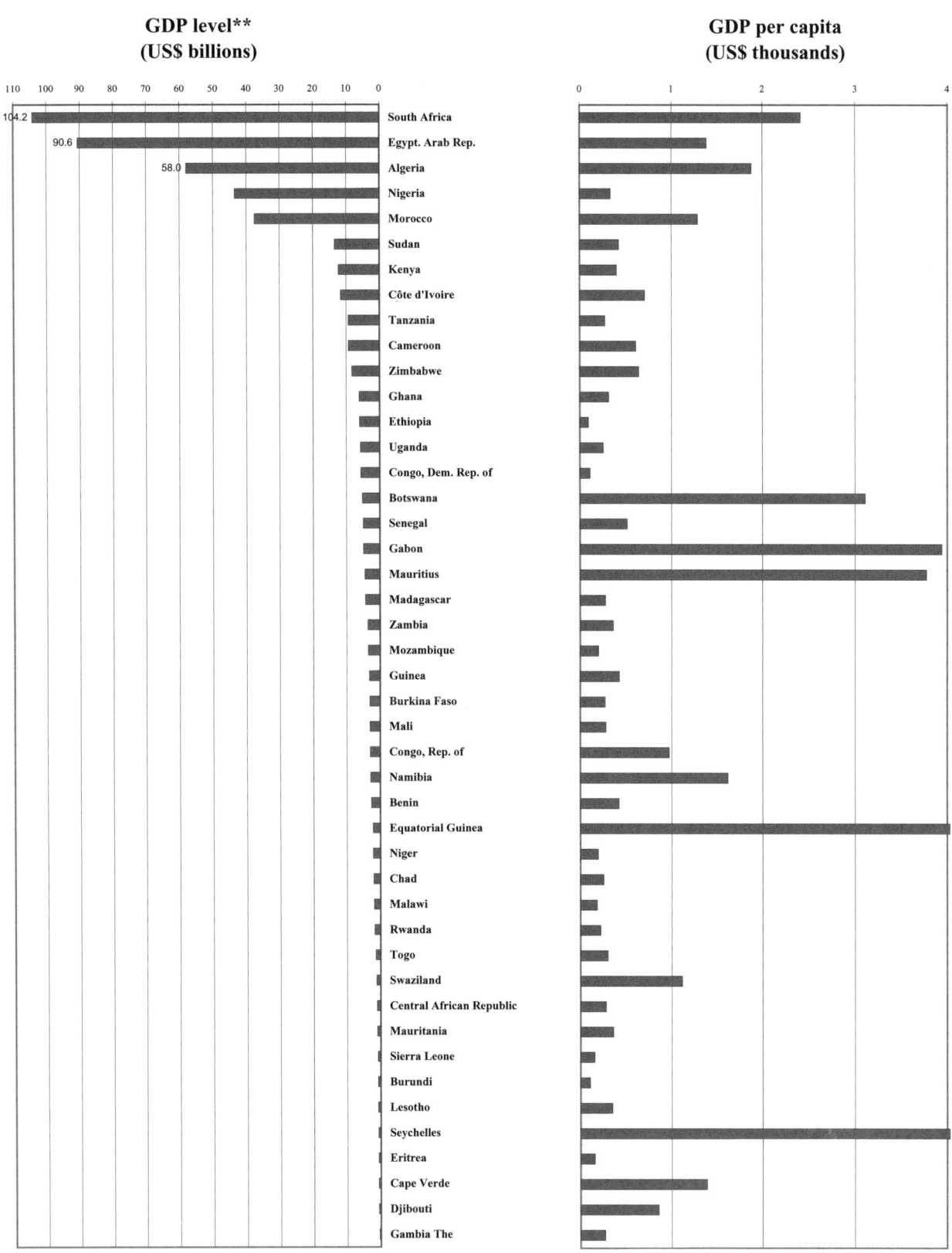

GDP level**
(US$ billions)

GDP per capita
(US$ thousands)

* Or most recent year available.
** Sorted by GDP level.

Figure 2-2. GDP and export growth rates, average 2001-2002*

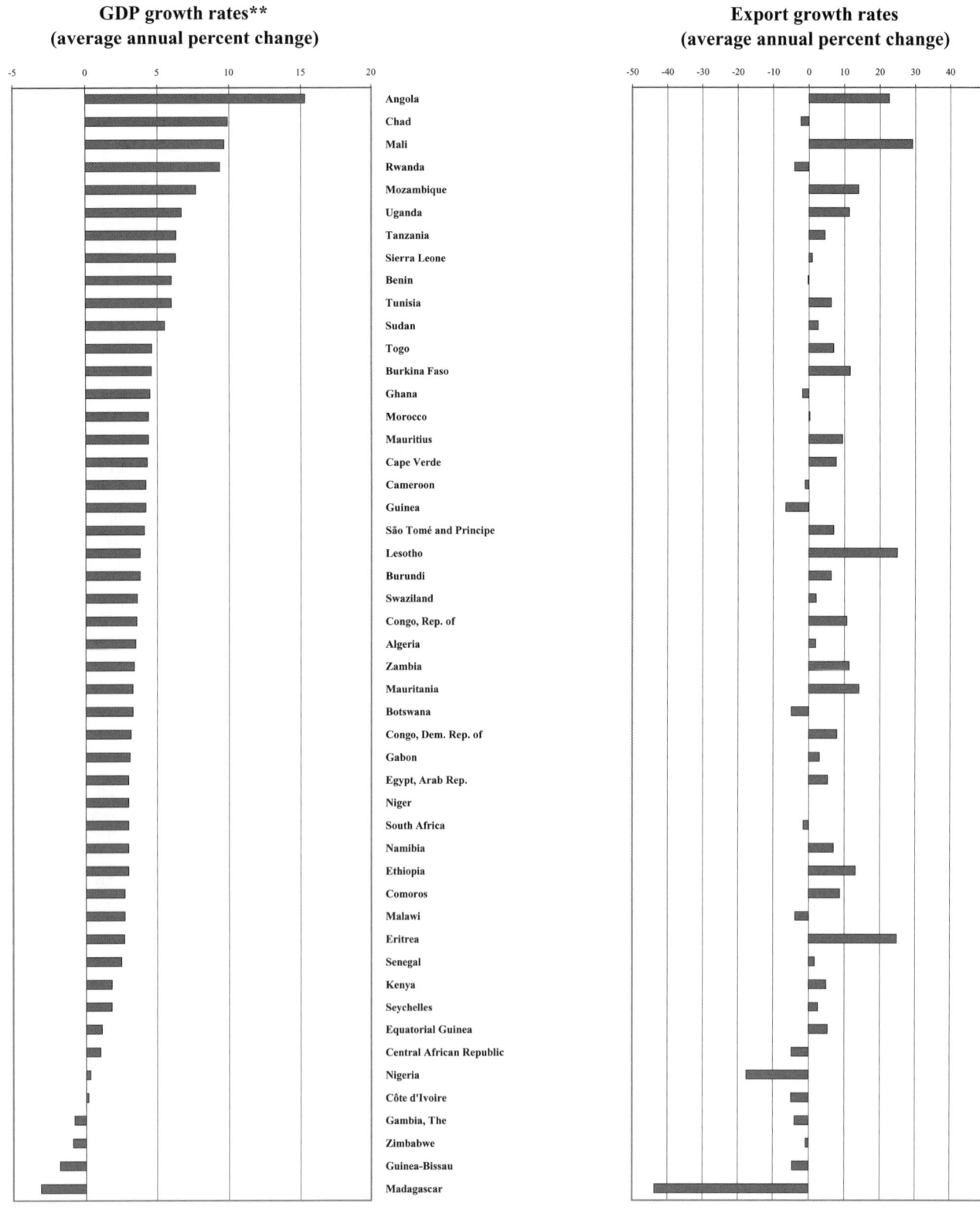

GDP growth rates**
(average annual percent change)

Export growth rates
(average annual percent change)

* Or most recent year available.
** Sorted by GDP.

Figure 2-3. Composition of GDP, 2002*

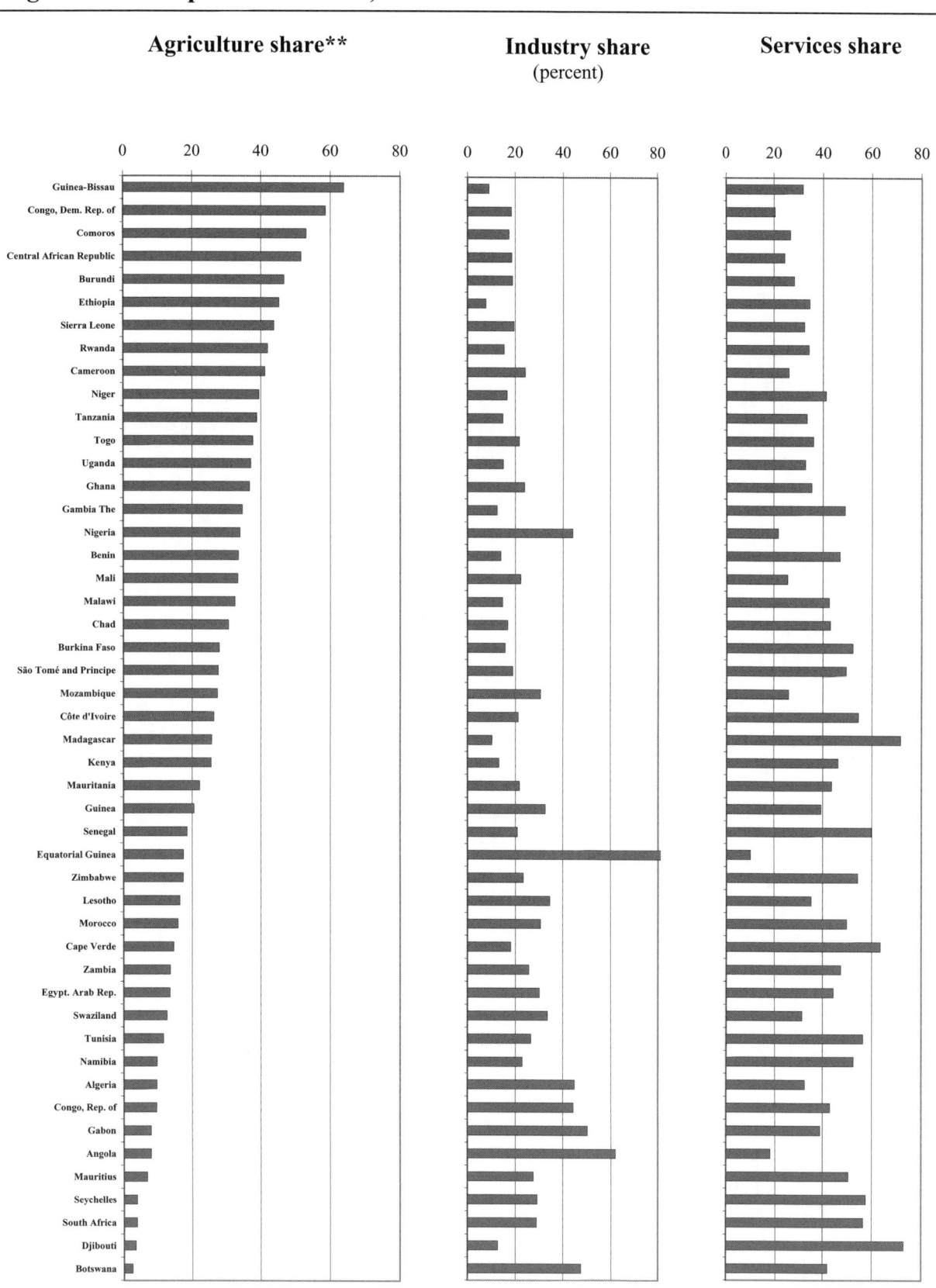

* Or most recent year available.
** Sorted by agriculture share.

Technical notes

Tables

Table 2-1. Gross domestic product, real. Gross domestic product (GDP) measures the total output of goods and services for final use produced by residents and nonresidents, regardless of the allocation to domestic and foreign claims (World Bank country desks). It is calculated without making deductions for depreciation of "manmade" assets or depletion and degradation of natural resources. In this table, GDP figures are shown at market prices (also known as purchaser values) and have been converted to U.S. dollars using constant (1995) exchange rates. For a few countries where the official exchange rate does not effectively reflect the rate applied to actual foreign exchange transactions, an alternative currency conversion factor has been used (Table 3-6). The sum of the components of GDP by industrial origin (presented in this volume in the form of value added) will not normally equal total GDP for several reasons. First, components of GDP by expenditure are individually rescaled and summed to provide a partially rebased series for total GDP. Second, total GDP is shown at purchaser value, while value added components are conventionally reported at producer prices. As explained above, the former excludes net indirect taxes, while the latter includes indirect taxes. Third, certain items, such as imputed bank charges, are added in total GDP.

Table 2-2. Value added in agriculture. Value added in agriculture is shown at factor cost (World Bank country desks). It comprises the gross output of forestry, hunting, and fishing less the value of their intermediate inputs. However, for Botswana, Cameroon, Chad, Congo, Gabon, Guinea, Madagascar, Mali, Morocco, Niger, Rwanda, Senegal, Togo, Zaire, and Zambia, it is shown at market prices, that is, including intermediate inputs.

Table 2-3. Value added in industry. Value added in industry is shown at factor cost (World Bank country desks). It comprises the gross output of mining, manufacturing, construction, electricity, water, and gas, less the value of their intermediate inputs. However, for Botswana, Cameroon, Chad, Congo, Gabon, Guinea, Madagascar, Mali, Morocco, Niger, Rwanda, Senegal, Togo, Zaire, and Zambia, it is shown at market prices, that is, including intermediate inputs.

Table 2-4. Value added in services. Also shown at factor cost, this table consists of the gross output of all other branches of economic activity, including government, less the value of their intermediate inputs (World Bank country desks). However, for Botswana, Cameroon, Chad, Congo, Gabon, Guinea, Madagascar, Mali, Morocco, Niger, Rwanda, Senegal, Togo, Zaire, and Zambia, it is shown at market prices, that is, including intermediate inputs. Other items, such as imputed bank service charges (which are difficult to assess in the same fashion for all countries) and any corrections for statistical discrepancies, are not included.

Table 2-5. Gross domestic product, nominal. This table, presented at market prices, is obtained by converting national currency GDP series in current prices (World Bank country desks) to U.S. dollars at official annual exchange rates (Table 3-4; see also the note for Table 2-1). GDP growth rates are presented in real terms.

Table 2-6. Total consumption. Total consumption is the sum of private consumption (World Bank country desks) and general government consumption (Table 2-7). Private consumption, not separately shown here, is the value of all goods and services purchased or received as income in kind by households and nonprofit institutions. It excludes purchases of dwellings, but includes imputed rent for owner-occupied dwellings. In practice, it includes any statistical discrepancy in the use of resources.

Table 2-7. General government consumption. This indicator includes all current expenditure for purchases of goods and services by all levels of government, including capital expenditure on national defense and security (World Bank country desks). Other capital expenditure by government is included in investment.

Tables 2-8, 2-9, and 2-10. Gross domestic, public, and private investment. Gross domestic investment (GDI) consists of gross domestic fixed capital formation plus net changes in the level of inventories (World Bank country desks). GDI comprises outlays by the public sector (Table 2-9) and the private sector (Table 2-10). Examples include improvements in land, dwellings, machinery, and other equipment. For some countries the sum of gross private investment and gross public investment does not add up to gross domestic investment due to statistical discrepancies.

Table 2-11. Gross domestic savings. Gross domestic savings (GDS) is calculated by deducting total consumption (Table 2-6) from gross domestic product in current prices (Table 2-5).

Table 2-12. Gross national savings. Gross national savings (GNS) is the sum of gross domestic savings (Table 2-11), net factor income from abroad (World Bank country desks), and net private transfers from abroad (Table 5-5). The estimate here also includes net public transfers from abroad (Table 5-6).

Table 2-13. Resource balance. The table indicates the difference between exports f.o.b. (Table 2-14) and imports c.i.f. (Table 2-15) of goods and nonfactor services (or the difference between GDS and GDI). The resource balance is shown as a share of GDP in U.S. dollars at current prices (Table 2-5).

Tables 2-14 and 2-15. Exports and imports of goods and nonfactor services, nominal. Data for exports and imports of goods and nonfactor services are from the World Bank country desks and refer to all goods and nonfactor services (GNFS) provided to, or by, the rest of the world, including merchandise, freight, insurance, travel, and other nonfactor services. The value of factor services, such as investment income, interest, and labor income, is not included. These series are generally estimated on the basis of foreign trade statistics from customs declarations. They are not fully comparable with the series from the balance of payments, which are based on changes in ownership between residents of a country and the rest of the world. Exports, as well as imports of GNFS, are shown in current U.S. dollars.

Tables 2-16 and 2-17. Exports and imports of goods and nonfactor services, real. These are defined as in Tables 2-14 and 2-15, but expressed in constant 1995 U.S. dollars.

Table 2-18. GDP growth. This table (World Bank country desks) provides average annual growth rates calculated from GDP at constant 1995 prices (Table 2-1).

Table 2-19. GNI per capita. Figures presented here (World Bank country desks) are calculated using the *World Bank Atlas* method, as described in the technical notes for Table 1-1; they are similar in concept to GNI per capita in current prices, except that the use of three-year averages of exchange rates smoothes out sharp fluctuations from year to year.

Table 2-20. Total consumption per capita. This table is obtained by dividing total consumption at current U.S. dollars (Table 2-6) by the corresponding midyear population (Table 1-2).

Figures

The following indicators have been used to derive the figures in this chapter.

Figure 2-1. Gross domestic product (Table 2-5); GDP per capita (Tables 1-2 and 2-5).

Figure 2-2. GDP growth (Table 2-1); export growth (Table 2-16).

Figure 2-3. Value added in agriculture (Table 2-2); value added in industry (Table 2-3); value added in services (Table 2-4); gross domestic product (Table 2-1).

Methodology used for regional aggregations and period averages in Chapter 2

Table	Aggregations[a]			Period averages[b]	
	(3)	(4)	(5)	(1)	(2)
2-1	x				x
2-2	x				x
2-3	x				x
2-4	x				x
2-5	x			x	
2-6		x		x	
2-7		x		x	
2-8		x		x	
2-9		x		x	
2-10		x		x	
2-11		x		x	
2-12		x		x	
2-13			x	x	
2-14	x			x	
2-15	x			x	
2-16	x				x
2-17	x				x
2-18	x				x
2-19		x		x	
2-20		x		x	

Note: Regional aggregations are shown in the rows for Sub-Saharan Africa, North Africa, and All Africa. Period averages are shown in the last three columns. This table shows only the methodologies used in this chapter.

a. Regional aggregations: (1) simple total; (2) simple total of the first indicator divided by the simple total of the second indicator (same country coverage); (3) simple total of the gap-filled indicator; (4) simple total of the gap-filled main indicator divided by the simple total of the gap-filled secondary indicator; (5) simple total of the first gap-filled main indicator less the simple total of the second gap-filled main indicator, all divided by the simple total of the secondary indicator; (6) weighted total (by population); (7) median; (8) no aggregation; (9) simple arithmetic mean.

b. Period averages: (1) arithmetic mean (using the same series as shown in the table; i.e., ratio if the rest of the table is shown as ratio, level if the rest of the table is shown as level, growth rate if the rest is shown as growth rate); (2) least-squares growth rate (using main indicator); (3) least-squares growth rate (using main indicator in constant terms, with the rest of the table in current terms).

3

Prices and Exchange Rates

nformation on prices and exchange rates are important in monitoring national economic performance. This chapter provides three sets of price deflators and six exchange rate indicators. The GDP deflator for national currency series shows changes in domestic prices only. The U.S. dollar series GDP deflator includes the effects of both domestic price changes, as reflected in the national currency series GDP implicit deflator, and changes in the exchange rate between national currencies and U.S. dollars. The consumer price index measures the price changes of a selected bundle of consumer goods, which differs among countries.

The U.S. dollar exchange rate (units of national currency per US dollar) is reported because of extensive use of U.S. dollars to denominate international transactions; U.S. dollars are also widely used for statistical comparisons across countries. The special drawing right (SDR) exchange rate index (based on SDRs per unit of national currency) is a broader measure of the changes in the international value of domestic currencies because it is based on five major currencies. For Sub-Saharan Africa, it may be more representative of movements in non-dual exchange rates than that expressed in U.S. dollars alone because a large share of the region's foreign trade and debt is not denominated in U.S. dollars. A decrease in the index shows that the currency has depreciated, which indicates that foreign goods have become relatively more expensive than domestic goods. We have included information on the parallel market exchange rate and the ratio of the parallel to the official exchange rates to provide a measure of the premium on the official rate. It is tempting to view the difference between the official and parallel rates as a measure of the disequilibrium in the official exchange rate. However, this is not necessarily true. Conversion factors are sometimes used in place of official exchange rates when the latter are considered to be especially unrepresentative of rates effectively applied to international transactions.

3-1. GDP deflator (local currency series)

	1980	*1993*	*1994*	*1995*	*1996*	*1997*	*1998*	*1999*	*2000*	*2001*	*2002*	*75-84*	*85-94*	*95-MR*
					Index 1995 = 100								*Annual average*	
SUB-SAHARAN AFRICA	23.1	71.4	90.4	100.0	109.9	117.6	124.4	132.2	147.4	162.4	166.2	24.0	58.5	132.5
excluding South Africa	24.8	71.4	90.1	100.0	110.6	118.0	123.7	131.6	152.5	163.4	168.0	25.8	59.7	133.5
excl. S.Africa & Nigeria	26.4	71.4	90.4	100.0	109.9	117.6	122.8	129.0	141.7	162.4	164.6	28.0	60.9	131.0
Angola	..	0.2	5.0	100.0	5,500	10,687	14,461	93,904	477,055	1,086,173	2,207,860	..	0.5	486,967
Benin	47.5	64.9	86.7	100.0	106.7	112.0	117.3	119.5	123.4	127.3	129.7	45.9	63.8	117.0
Botswana	21.3	82.4	91.9	100.0	114.3	126.9	131.7	140.5	152.5	162.4	171.4	19.2	61.2	137.5
Burkina Faso	55.3	78.3	93.2	100.0	107.7	109.7	117.8	115.9	122.1	128.6	131.3	54.3	80.6	116.6
Burundi	45.5	81.3	86.7	100.0	119.0	146.8	163.2	168.8	206.9	234.6	264.8	38.2	67.7	175.5
Cameroon	43.0	77.0	85.4	100.0	105.4	108.2	109.5	108.2	111.9	115.3	120.2	42.9	75.8	109.8
Cape Verde	32.6	89.1	95.9	100.0	105.8	114.1	119.3	125.3	123.8	130.5	133.8	34.3	78.7	119.1
Central African Republic	35.0	73.9	90.7	100.0	101.8	103.2	104.2	105.4	108.0	111.2	115.3	35.1	75.0	106.1
Chad	55.5	64.1	91.9	100.0	111.7	114.8	126.5	116.8	123.5	139.1	144.3	54.4	70.6	122.1
Comoros	41.6	88.9	92.3	100.0	103.2	104.0	105.7	111.8	119.9	130.1	135.9	52.2	81.2	113.8
Congo, Dem. Rep. of	0.0	0.1	17.7	100.0	738.2	2,160.3	2,718.0	14,930	103,402	490,227	604,418	0.0	1.8	152,337
Congo, Rep. of	56.4	71.4	97.7	100.0	118.0	123.8	101.3	131.6	192.4	165.5	164.6	57.2	76.2	137.1
Côte d'Ivoire	81.3	61.5	90.1	100.0	105.0	109.4	115.1	116.2	116.1	120.9	127.4	68.9	95.0	113.8
Djibouti	..	89.9	95.7	100.0	102.6	105.1	106.9	109.1	111.7	..	..	..	80.4	105.9
Equatorial Guinea	..	63.2	97.5	100.0	125.4	160.5	121.9	172.1	261.8	366.1	409.1	..	67.2	214.6
Eritrea	..	82.5	91.1	100.0	109.1	113.3	123.7	133.7	159.5	181.6	207.9	..	85.7	141.1
Ethiopia	..	86.4	88.7	100.0	100.9	104.7	115.4	118.2	121.9	114.1	106.0	42.4	63.8	110.2
Gabon	50.8	68.5	100.6	100.0	112.8	115.1	97.0	101.7	130.6	115.3	122.1	46.6	70.1	111.8
Gambia, The	18.0	92.7	96.2	100.0	102.9	106.9	108.1	112.8	116.8	125.7	150.4	17.6	69.6	115.4
Ghana	0.8	53.7	69.9	100.0	139.8	167.0	195.5	222.8	283.5	381.5	468.5	1.6	30.3	244.8
Guinea	..	95.0	95.7	100.0	101.5	103.1	105.3	109.0	121.1	127.1	130.7	..	63.4	112.2
Guinea-Bissau	0.2	56.1	69.1	100.0	139.3	186.8	201.0	212.4	219.4	208.2	218.2	0.3	22.0	185.7
Kenya	18.7	66.5	89.9	100.0	109.1	126.0	138.1	146.0	156.6	171.7	186.6	19.0	49.2	141.8
Lesotho	18.6	85.0	91.5	100.0	109.0	117.3	128.2	144.7	153.0	164.3	180.4	17.8	58.1	137.1
Liberia	..	..	..	..	..	..	..	..	..	..	..	..	..	..
Madagascar	6.6	48.6	68.9	100.0	117.8	126.4	137.1	150.4	161.3	173.1	199.7	7.7	34.6	145.7
Malawi	6.6	43.7	55.2	100.0	158.9	171.3	214.8	305.3	384.5	481.4	565.6	6.9	27.5	297.7
Mali	37.6	66.0	84.4	100.0	105.4	106.5	106.5	103.1	108.3	116.0	118.1	37.1	64.6	108.0
Mauritania	33.3	90.0	95.7	100.0	104.7	110.3	120.7	123.2	130.7	144.8	145.4	33.3	72.4	122.5
Mauritius	28.0	87.9	96.1	100.0	105.3	112.8	119.1	125.1	131.0	135.8	142.7	33.9	67.5	121.5
Mozambique	0.6	41.3	65.8	100.0	143.6	157.4	164.6	169.4	182.9	202.3	225.0	0.8	19.0	168.1
Namibia	19.1	81.8	94.6	100.0	114.5	122.6	133.1	141.8	159.2	176.4	193.0	22.5	59.3	142.6
Niger	57.9	71.5	94.9	100.0	104.7	108.0	111.2	113.4	118.6	123.3	127.0	55.9	77.2	113.3
Nigeria	3.2	50.2	64.1	100.0	136.9	138.8	131.1	154.5	188.2	202.9	226.4	3.2	22.2	159.8
Rwanda	24.8	56.4	66.1	100.0	110.9	128.2	131.1	126.5	130.6	130.8	130.8	25.0	42.8	123.6
São Tomé and Principe	..	33.0	57.3	100.0	150.8	302.0	413.9	480.1	517.4	556.7	588.3	..	19.3	388.6
Senegal	41.3	74.5	95.2	100.0	101.0	103.5	105.3	106.8	107.7	110.7	113.7	40.7	75.0	106.1
Seychelles	60.6	99.8	100.8	100.0	98.5	99.5	103.9	106.0	107.3	112.4	118.6	53.4	89.5	105.8
Sierra Leone	0.1	56.0	76.3	100.0	116.3	135.8	172.6	215.8	229.1	243.0	252.5	0.2	22.5	183.1
Somalia	..	..	..	..	..	..	..	..	..	..	..	..	..	..
South Africa	13.6	82.8	90.7	100.0	108.1	116.9	125.0	132.7	142.2	153.1	166.2	13.1	54.7	130.5
Sudan	0.1	18.4	36.1	100.0	170.7	245.5	306.1	364.1	372.7	380.2	409.7	0.2	7.4	293.6
Swaziland	18.3	75.2	85.3	100.0	110.6	123.9	135.0	147.6	165.5	183.1	202.9	18.7	53.1	146.1
Tanzania	..	60.1	78.8	100.0	119.3	143.9	164.3	183.1	195.7	207.8	216.5	..	43.0	166.3
Togo	41.0	66.3	90.0	100.0	105.4	118.0	115.1	117.7	119.2	126.8	126.7	42.2	68.4	116.1
Uganda	..	85.6	91.4	100.0	104.6	107.8	116.4	116.7	121.2	128.8	123.6	0.2	36.7	114.9
Zambia	0.1	43.8	72.4	100.0	122.9	154.8	185.0	224.5	292.0	362.9	435.0	0.1	14.9	234.6
Zimbabwe	11.4	75.4	91.3	100.0	125.8	146.2	188.9	294.9	471.6	802.3	1,664.9	11.8	43.8	474.3
NORTH AFRICA	26.0	87.5	91.2	100.0	105.9	111.1	114.9	118.1	123.0	126.4	131.9	25.4	64.6	116.4
Algeria	10.9	60.3	77.8	100.0	123.8	131.9	126.3	139.4	172.4	181.6	185.3	9.9	35.2	145.1
Egypt, Arab Rep.	16.3	83.9	89.8	100.0	107.1	113.4	117.4	119.6	126.5	130.5	138.2	14.4	54.1	119.1
Libya	..	..	..	..	..	..	..	..	..	..	..	..	..	..
Morocco	40.2	91.2	92.6	100.0	101.0	103.0	103.4	103.9	105.5	108.1	110.8	38.8	77.6	104.5
Tunisia	35.7	91.1	95.1	100.0	104.7	108.8	112.4	116.6	119.4	122.4	125.7	36.5	75.4	113.7
ALL AFRICA	23.1	72.7	90.4	100.0	109.1	117.1	122.8	129.0	136.6	153.1	164.6	24.0	58.9	129.0

Note: 2002 data are preliminary (see page 2). Group data are medians of individual country values for each year.

3-2. GDP deflator (U.S. dollar series)

| | *Index 1995 = 100* | | | | | | | | | | | *Annual average* | | |
	1980	1993	1994	1995	1996	1997	1998	1999	2000	2001	2002	75-84	85-94	95-MR
SUB-SAHARAN AFRICA	105.0	95.3	90.6	100.0	99.0	99.1	90.7	88.4	86.6	81.9	79.9	82.0	91.8	90.7
excluding South Africa	150.1	98.5	88.7	100.0	105.9	105.3	98.1	96.5	97.0	96.6	99.3	117.7	110.7	99.9
excl. S.Africa & Nigeria	118.6	102.8	89.2	100.0	103.0	102.4	96.8	92.6	90.6	90.6	93.3	98.9	111.2	96.2
Angola	..	119.8	88.9	100.0	134.3	126.9	99.8	91.2	128.8	133.5	137.5	..	129.5	119.0
Benin	112.1	114.5	77.9	100.0	104.1	95.8	99.2	96.9	86.5	86.7	92.9	83.7	95.1	95.3
Botswana	76.1	94.3	94.9	100.0	95.3	96.4	86.4	84.2	82.9	77.1	75.1	58.4	82.1	87.2
Burkina Faso	130.7	100.6	83.7	100.0	105.1	93.8	99.7	94.0	85.6	87.5	94.0	98.9	116.2	95.0
Burundi	126.4	83.6	85.7	100.0	98.2	104.0	91.0	74.8	71.7	70.6	71.1	102.9	102.1	85.2
Cameroon	106.7	150.4	101.9	100.0	108.9	103.7	94.3	95.3	88.2	80.4	85.1	83.4	122.0	94.5
Cape Verde	62.3	85.1	90.0	100.0	98.4	94.2	93.4	93.0	79.5	81.4	87.8	58.7	80.0	91.0
Central African Republic	82.6	130.2	81.5	100.0	99.4	88.5	88.2	85.5	75.7	75.7	82.5	62.5	116.0	86.9
Chad	131.0	112.9	82.6	100.0	109.0	98.1	107.0	94.9	86.5	94.9	103.5	99.7	108.2	99.2
Comoros	73.8	117.6	83.0	100.0	100.7	89.0	89.4	90.7	84.1	88.6	97.3	61.6	97.6	92.5
Congo, Dem. Rep. of	191.1	183.6	103.8	100.0	103.3	115.8	118.6	95.3	105.3	114.8	122.6	159.3	111.3	109.5
Congo, Rep. of	133.2	90.0	87.8	100.0	115.1	105.9	85.7	106.7	134.9	112.7	117.9	102.2	112.7	109.8
Côte d'Ivoire	192.1	108.4	81.0	100.0	102.5	93.6	97.4	94.2	81.4	82.3	91.2	125.2	147.4	92.8
Djibouti	..	89.9	95.7	100.0	102.6	105.1	106.9	109.1	111.7	..	..	..	80.4	105.9
Equatorial Guinea	..	111.4	87.6	100.0	122.3	137.3	103.1	139.5	183.6	249.3	293.0	..	102.5	166.0
Eritrea	..	99.4	93.1	100.0	108.1	99.2	105.7	103.3	104.7	104.9	93.6	..	102.4	102.4
Ethiopia	..	118.8	101.7	100.0	93.8	94.5	98.3	92.3	87.7	80.3	72.8	120.0	153.0	89.9
Gabon	120.0	97.8	90.4	100.0	110.1	98.5	82.1	82.4	91.6	78.5	87.4	82.9	104.8	91.3
Gambia, The	99.9	96.9	95.9	100.0	100.4	100.0	97.0	94.5	87.2	76.5	72.1	75.8	85.6	90.9
Ghana	105.1	99.4	87.7	100.0	102.5	97.8	101.4	100.2	62.4	63.9	70.9	94.0	109.4	87.4
Guinea	..	98.6	97.1	100.0	100.2	93.3	84.4	77.9	68.7	64.7	65.6	..	90.1	81.8
Guinea-Bissau	82.8	100.5	96.9	100.0	95.4	89.0	94.7	95.9	85.7	79.5	87.0	85.3	95.6	90.9
Kenya	129.5	59.0	82.5	100.0	98.3	111.7	114.9	106.7	105.6	112.4	122.1	103.8	96.2	109.0
Lesotho	86.6	94.3	93.4	100.0	91.9	92.3	84.1	85.9	80.0	69.2	62.1	67.3	77.6	83.2
Liberia	..	..	..	..	..	..	..	..	..	..	..	..	..	..
Madagascar	132.6	108.4	95.8	100.0	123.8	105.9	107.5	102.1	101.7	112.0	124.7	108.3	95.4	109.7
Malawi	124.7	151.9	96.6	100.0	158.6	159.2	105.6	105.8	98.7	101.9	112.7	107.7	128.2	117.8
Mali	88.8	116.4	75.9	100.0	102.9	91.1	90.1	83.6	75.9	79.0	84.6	66.9	99.2	88.4
Mauritania	94.2	96.7	100.5	100.0	99.0	94.2	83.1	76.3	71.0	73.5	69.4	87.4	107.6	83.3
Mauritius	68.4	94.2	91.9	100.0	103.6	103.1	92.0	87.9	89.6	85.9	82.4	61.5	77.5	93.1
Mozambique	182.0	96.1	98.3	100.0	114.8	123.5	125.1	119.6	100.0	89.9	87.5	195.0	156.0	108.7
Namibia	88.8	90.8	96.7	100.0	96.6	96.5	87.3	84.2	83.2	74.3	66.4	77.8	79.6	86.1
Niger	136.9	91.2	85.3	100.0	102.2	92.3	94.1	92.0	83.1	84.0	91.0	100.8	115.1	92.3
Nigeria	287.2	77.9	86.3	100.0	120.4	120.3	104.8	117.7	130.2	128.3	132.1	210.6	108.7	119.2
Rwanda	70.2	102.5	78.8	100.0	94.8	111.5	110.1	99.3	87.9	77.4	72.0	69.7	103.1	94.1
São Tomé and Principe	..	109.1	111.1	100.0	97.2	94.2	85.4	95.8	92.1	89.4	91.9	..	125.8	93.3
Senegal	97.6	131.3	85.6	100.0	98.5	88.5	89.1	86.6	75.5	75.4	81.4	74.4	116.1	86.9
Seychelles	45.2	91.7	95.0	100.0	94.3	94.3	94.0	94.5	89.4	91.4	103.1	38.0	77.5	95.1
Sierra Leone	98.0	74.6	98.3	100.0	95.4	104.5	83.4	90.3	82.7	92.4	90.8	86.7	69.0	92.4
Somalia	..	..	..	..	..	..	..	..	..	..	..	..	..	..
South Africa	63.2	91.9	92.7	100.0	91.2	92.0	82.0	78.8	74.3	64.5	57.2	48.8	72.5	80.0
Sudan	137.1	67.0	72.3	100.0	79.3	90.5	88.5	83.7	84.2	85.4	90.4	140.1	138.4	87.8
Swaziland	85.2	83.6	87.2	100.0	93.9	97.6	89.4	87.6	86.9	78.2	70.2	70.6	71.6	88.0
Tanzania	..	85.2	88.9	100.0	118.2	135.1	142.1	141.3	140.5	136.3	128.7	..	96.2	130.3
Togo	96.7	116.8	80.9	100.0	102.8	100.9	97.4	95.4	83.6	86.4	90.7	77.4	105.8	94.7
Uganda	..	66.4	77.3	100.0	96.3	95.0	94.4	79.9	74.8	68.1	65.7	81.6	112.5	84.3
Zambia	115.4	83.6	93.5	100.0	87.9	101.8	85.9	81.2	81.1	86.9	85.5	92.8	82.4	88.8
Zimbabwe	153.4	100.1	97.1	100.0	109.0	104.6	69.1	66.7	92.0	126.3	122.6	134.9	116.1	98.8
NORTH AFRICA	117.5	95.6	93.2	100.0	104.8	105.2	105.1	105.0	107.7	105.1	101.2	92.8	98.0	104.3
Algeria	134.9	123.0	105.7	100.0	107.7	108.9	102.5	99.8	109.2	112.1	110.8	109.3	136.8	106.4
Egypt, Arab Rep.	76.6	85.4	90.3	100.0	107.1	113.4	117.5	119.6	126.0	120.4	108.6	69.1	83.0	114.1
Libya	..	..	..	..	..	..	..	..	..	..	..	..	..	..
Morocco	87.2	83.8	86.0	100.0	99.0	92.3	91.9	90.5	84.8	81.7	85.9	64.8	75.5	90.8
Tunisia	83.5	85.8	88.9	100.0	101.7	93.1	93.3	93.0	82.4	80.5	83.6	68.3	79.1	90.9
ALL AFRICA	108.1	95.4	91.5	100.0	100.9	101.1	95.5	94.0	93.7	89.8	87.2	84.7	93.9	95.3

Note: 2002 data are preliminary (see page 2). Group data are obtained by dividing GDP in current US$ by GDP in constant US$ series for each group.

3-3. Consumer price index

	Index 1995 = 100											Average annual percentage growth		
	1980	1993	1994	1995	1996	1997	1998	1999	2000	2001	2002	75-84	85-94	95-MR
SUB-SAHARAN AFRICA	16.3	67.9	90.1	100.0	107.4	114.9	124.1	130.4	130.1	142.7	138.2	12.5	11.2	5.6
excluding South Africa	17.0	67.6	89.8	100.0	107.4	114.6	123.7	130.0	129.9	138.3	137.7	11.0	10.7	5.5
excl. S.Africa & Nigeria	18.6	67.9	90.1	100.0	107.3	114.5	123.3	127.7	129.7	133.9	137.2	11.0	9.7	5.2
Angola	..	..	..	100.0	4,257.3	13,587.8	28,159.8	98,053.7	416,724.4	1,052,476.0	2,198,561.0	..	..	266.3
Benin	..	63.1	87.4	100.0	104.9	108.6	114.8	115.2	120.0	124.7	127.9	..	..	4.3
Botswana	20.2	81.9	90.5	100.0	110.1	119.7	127.7	137.5	149.4	159.2	172.1	12.1	11.3	8.2
Burkina Faso	51.7	74.4	93.1	100.0	106.2	108.6	114.1	112.9	112.5	118.2	120.8	11.0	1.3	2.9
Burundi	28.9	73.0	83.8	100.0	126.4	165.8	186.5	192.8	239.7	261.8	258.3	13.4	7.0	15.8
Cameroon	32.2	67.9	91.7	100.0	103.9	108.9	112.4	114.1	111.7	116.8	120.0	11.5	3.6	2.9
Cape Verde	..	89.3	92.2	100.0	106.0	115.1	120.1	125.4	122.3	126.9	129.4	..	6.3	4.2
Central African Republic	53.3	67.4	83.9	100.0	103.7	105.4	103.4	101.9	105.2	108.8	112.4	..	-0.3	2.4
Chad	..	65.3	91.7	100.0	112.4	118.7	133.1	124.1	128.8	144.8	152.3	..	0.8	5.9
Comoros	..	76.1	93.5	100.0	102.0	105.1	108.7	112.5	117.9	121.4	125.4	..	4.6	3.6
Congo, Dem. Rep. of	0.0	0.1	15.6	100.0	641.9	1,768.5	2,284.0	8,791.2	53,969.6	248,226.1	326,473.4	57.3	421.9	241.7
Congo, Rep. of	..	64.1	91.4	100.0	110.0	..	124.1	130.8	129.7	129.8	135.4	..	2.2	4.9
Côte d'Ivoire	38.8	69.4	87.5	100.0	102.5	106.6	111.6	112.5	115.2	120.2	123.9	12.9	4.4	3.8
Djibouti	..	89.5	95.3	100.0	104.2	106.3	..	..	..	..	..	..	6.0	..
Equatorial Guinea	..	64.6	89.8	100.0	106.0	109.2	112.5	119.2	126.4	132.9	136.9	..	0.5	5.1
Eritrea	..	78.9	89.3	100.0	110.3	114.4	125.2	135.7	162.8	186.6	218.1	..	..	11.2
Ethiopia	35.3	84.5	90.9	100.0	94.9	97.2	99.7	107.6	108.3	99.5	101.0	10.6	8.2	1.3
Gabon	47.4	67.0	91.2	100.0	100.7	104.7	106.2	104.2	104.7	..	..	12.5	0.2	2.0
Gambia, The	8.3	91.7	95.4	100.0	102.1	105.0	106.1	110.1	111.1	65.6	74.1	10.5	24.0	-3.4
Ghana	0.1	50.2	62.7	100.0	146.6	187.5	223.7	251.4	314.8	418.7	480.6	67.9	64.6	26.8
Guinea	..	90.9	94.7	100.0	103.0	105.0	110.3	115.4	123.2	129.9	133.8	..	19.2	4.5
Guinea-Bissau	..	59.7	68.8	100.0	150.7	224.7	239.4	237.7	258.2	266.9	276.9	..	52.8	17.4
Kenya	10.9	76.4	98.5	100.0	108.9	121.2	129.4	136.8	150.5	159.1	162.2	13.6	17.8	7.2
Lesotho	15.5	84.6	91.5	100.0	109.3	..	..	137.9	146.3	132.3	177.0	14.3	14.0	7.3
Liberia	..	..	..	..	..	..	..	..	..	..	..	..	..	..
Madagascar	7.0	48.3	67.1	100.0	119.8	125.1	132.9	146.1	163.7	175.0	202.9	15.3	14.6	12.2
Malawi	5.3	40.5	54.5	100.0	137.6	150.2	194.9	282.2	365.6	465.2	..	..	19.3	32.9
Mali	..	71.6	88.2	100.0	106.8	106.4	110.7	109.4	108.6	114.3	120.0	..	1.3	2.9
Mauritania	..	90.1	93.9	100.0	104.7	109.5	118.3	123.1	127.1	133.1	138.2	..	7.4	5.0
Mauritius	32.3	87.9	94.3	100.0	106.6	113.8	121.6	130.0	135.4	142.7	152.3	14.9	7.7	6.2
Mozambique	..	39.7	64.8	100.0	148.5	159.4	161.8	166.4	187.6	204.6	238.9	..	49.8	14.0
Namibia	17.0	82.1	90.9	100.0	108.0	117.5	124.8	135.5	147.7	161.8	180.2	..	13.0	8.6
Niger	62.0	66.5	90.4	100.0	105.3	108.4	113.3	110.7	113.9	118.5	121.6	12.6	-2.0	3.2
Nigeria	2.0	36.9	57.9	100.0	129.3	139.9	154.3	161.7	185.2	209.2	236.1	17.7	28.9	15.6
Rwanda	22.3	50.3	..	100.0	107.4	120.3	127.8	124.7	130.1	133.9	137.2	11.1	5.6	4.3
São Tomé and Principe	..	57.5	72.9	100.0	137.5	230.6	348.0	404.8	449.3	492.0	537.3	..	33.6	29.9
Senegal	40.7	70.1	92.7	100.0	102.8	104.4	105.6	106.5	107.2	110.5	113.0	9.7	1.5	2.0
Seychelles	68.5	98.5	100.2	100.0	98.9	99.5	102.1	108.6	115.4	122.2	122.5	10.6	2.1	3.0
Sierra Leone	0.1	63.9	79.4	100.0	123.1	141.5	191.8	257.2	255.1	260.4	251.8	22.7	75.3	17.2
Somalia	..	..	..	..	..	..	..	..	..	..	..	..	..	..
South Africa	14.9	84.5	92.0	100.0	107.4	117.0	124.9	131.2	138.1	144.8	160.1	12.9	14.3	6.8
Sudan	0.1	27.6	59.4	100.0	232.8	341.4	399.8	463.8	..	525.5	..	22.9	71.0	36.8
Swaziland	15.5	78.3	89.1	100.0	106.4	114.0	123.3	130.8	146.7	155.4	..	14.4	12.6	8.1
Tanzania	2.1	58.5	77.9	100.0	121.0	140.4	158.4	170.9	181.0	190.3	199.0	19.6	29.4	11.8
Togo	42.7	61.7	85.9	100.0	104.7	113.3	114.4	114.3	116.5	121.1	124.8	11.1	1.9	3.9
Uganda	0.1	83.9	92.1	100.0	107.2	114.6	114.6	121.9	125.4	127.9	127.5	..	76.9	4.1
Zambia	..	48.5	74.5	100.0	143.0	177.9	221.5	280.8	353.8	430.6	526.2	..	99.2	27.3
Zimbabwe	8.1	66.7	81.6	100.0	121.4	144.2	190.1	301.3	469.6	829.8	..	11.9	18.4	37.9
NORTH AFRICA	21.5	88.7	93.3	100.0	104.0	107.7	111.7	114.7	120.4	123.0	126.3	13.3	6.9	3.7
Algeria	11.9	59.7	77.1	100.0	118.7	125.5	131.7	135.2	135.6	141.4	143.4	10.9	16.0	6.7
Egypt, Arab Rep.	11.0	79.9	86.4	100.0	107.2	112.1	116.8	120.4	123.7	126.5	129.9	13.2	17.4	4.6
Libya	31.1	88.7	93.3	100.0	104.0	107.7	111.7	114.7	..	..	..	9.4	6.9	4.1
Morocco	37.0	89.6	94.2	100.0	103.0	104.1	106.9	107.7	109.7	110.4	113.5	9.9	5.3	2.0
Tunisia	..	89.9	94.1	100.0	103.7	107.5	110.9	113.9	117.2	119.4	122.7	..	6.8	3.2
ALL AFRICA	16.3	69.7	90.4	100.0	107.2	114.4	122.4	125.4	129.7	133.9	137.2	12.9	10.9	5.2

Note: 2002 data are preliminary (see page 2). Group data are medians of individual country values for each year.

3-4. Official exchange rate

	National currency per U.S. dollar											Annual average		
	1980	1993	1994	1995	1996	1997	1998	1999	2000	2001	2002	75-84	85-94	95-MR
SUB-SAHARAN AFRICA	..	..	..	..	..	..	..	..	..	..	..	..	..	..
excluding South Africa	..	..	..	..	..	..	..	..	..	..	..	..	..	..
excl. S.Africa & Nigeria	..	..	..	..	..	..	..	..	..	..	..	..	..	..
Angola	0.0	0.0	0.0	0.0	0.1	0.2	0.4	2.8	10.0	22.1	43.5	0.0	0.0	9.9
Benin	211.3	283.2	555.2	499.1	511.6	583.7	590.0	615.7	712.0	733.0	697.0	276.7	337.0	617.8
Botswana	0.8	2.4	2.7	2.8	3.3	3.7	4.2	4.6	5.1	5.8	6.3	0.9	2.0	4.5
Burkina Faso	211.3	283.2	555.2	499.1	511.6	583.7	590.0	615.7	712.0	733.0	697.0	276.7	337.0	617.8
Burundi	90.0	242.8	252.7	249.8	302.7	352.4	447.8	563.6	720.7	830.4	930.7	91.8	171.4	549.7
Cameroon	211.3	283.2	555.2	499.1	511.6	583.7	590.0	615.7	712.0	733.0	697.0	276.7	337.0	617.8
Cape Verde	40.2	80.4	81.9	76.9	82.6	93.2	98.2	103.5	119.7	123.2	117.2	46.6	76.6	101.8
Central African Republic	211.3	283.2	555.2	499.1	511.6	583.7	590.0	615.7	712.0	733.0	697.0	276.7	337.0	617.8
Chad	211.3	283.2	555.2	499.1	511.6	583.7	590.0	615.7	712.0	733.0	697.0	276.7	337.0	617.8
Comoros	211.3	283.2	416.4	374.4	383.7	437.7	442.5	461.8	534.0	549.8	522.7	276.7	323.2	463.3
Congo, Dem. Rep. of	0.0	0.0	0.0	0.1	0.5	1.3	1.6	4.0	21.8	206.6	346.5	0.0	0.0	72.8
Congo, Rep. of	211.3	283.2	555.2	499.1	511.6	583.7	590.0	615.7	712.0	733.0	697.0	276.7	337.0	617.8
Côte d'Ivoire	211.3	283.2	555.2	499.1	511.6	583.7	590.0	615.7	712.0	733.0	697.0	276.7	337.0	617.8
Djibouti	177.7	177.7	177.7	177.7	177.7	177.7	177.7	177.7	177.7	177.7	177.7	177.7	177.7	177.7
Equatorial Guinea	211.3	283.2	555.2	499.1	511.6	583.7	590.0	615.7	712.0	733.0	697.0	276.7	337.0	617.8
Eritrea	2.1	5.0	5.5	6.2	6.4	6.8	7.4	8.2	9.6	11.3	14.0	2.1	2.8	8.7
Ethiopia	2.1	5.0	5.5	6.2	6.4	6.7	7.1	7.9	8.2	8.5	8.6	2.1	2.8	7.4
Gabon	211.3	283.2	555.2	499.1	511.6	583.7	590.0	615.7	712.0	733.0	697.0	276.7	337.0	617.8
Gambia, The	1.7	9.1	9.6	9.5	9.8	10.2	10.6	11.4	12.8	15.7	19.9	2.3	7.6	12.5
Ghana	2.8	649.1	956.7	1,200.4	1,637.2	2,050.2	2,314.1	2,669.3	5,455.1	7,170.8	7,932.7	6.1	350.7	3,803.7
Guinea	19.0	955.5	976.6	991.4	1,004.0	1,095.3	1,236.8	1,387.4	1,746.9	1,950.6	1,975.8	21.1	610.0	1,423.5
Guinea-Bissau	0.5	155.1	198.3	278.0	405.7	583.7	590.0	615.7	712.0	733.0	697.0	0.6	60.9	576.9
Kenya	7.4	58.0	56.1	51.4	57.1	58.7	60.4	70.3	76.2	78.6	78.7	9.4	28.4	66.4
Lesotho	0.8	3.3	3.6	3.6	4.3	4.6	5.5	6.1	6.9	8.6	10.5	1.0	2.6	6.3
Liberia	1.0	1.0	1.0	1.0	1.0	1.0	41.5	41.9	41.0	48.6	61.8	1.0	1.0	29.7
Madagascar	211.3	1,913.8	3,067.3	4,265.6	4,061.3	5,090.9	5,441.4	6,283.8	6,767.5	6,588.5	6,832.0	297.7	1,559.3	5,666.4
Malawi	0.8	4.4	8.7	15.3	15.3	16.4	31.1	44.1	59.5	72.2	76.7	1.0	3.3	41.3
Mali	211.3	283.2	555.2	499.1	511.6	583.7	590.0	615.7	712.0	733.0	697.0	276.7	337.0	617.8
Mauritania	45.9	120.8	123.6	129.8	137.2	151.9	188.5	209.5	238.9	255.6	271.7	49.0	87.8	197.9
Mauritius	7.7	17.6	18.0	17.4	17.9	21.1	24.0	25.2	26.2	29.1	30.0	8.5	15.2	23.9
Mozambique	33.0	3,951.1	6,158.4	9,203.4	11,517.8	11,772.6	12,110.2	13,028.6	15,447.1	20,703.6	23,678.0	34.7	1,676.3	14,682.7
Namibia	0.8	3.3	3.6	3.6	4.3	4.6	5.5	6.1	6.9	8.6	10.5	1.0	2.6	6.3
Niger	211.3	283.2	555.2	499.1	511.6	583.7	590.0	615.7	712.0	733.0	697.0	276.7	337.0	617.8
Nigeria	0.5	22.1	22.0	21.9	21.9	21.9	21.9	92.3	101.7	111.2	120.6	0.6	9.8	64.2
Rwanda	86.1	144.2	140.7	262.2	306.1	301.3	313.7	337.8	393.4	442.8	476.3	92.4	105.3	354.2
São Tomé and Principe	34.8	429.9	732.6	1,420.3	2,203.2	4,552.5	6,883.2	7,119.0	7,978.2	8,842.1	9,088.3	36.5	217.7	6,010.9
Senegal	211.3	283.2	555.2	499.1	511.6	583.7	590.0	615.7	712.0	733.0	697.0	276.7	337.0	617.8
Seychelles	6.4	5.2	5.1	4.8	5.0	5.0	5.3	5.3	5.7	5.9	5.5	6.7	5.6	5.3
Sierra Leone	1.0	567.5	586.7	755.2	920.7	981.5	1,563.6	1,804.2	2,092.1	1,986.2	2,099.0	1.3	224.8	1,525.3
Somalia	6.3	..	..	..	..	..	..	..	..	..	..	9.1	175.6	..
South Africa	0.8	3.3	3.6	3.6	4.3	4.6	5.5	6.1	6.9	8.6	10.5	1.0	2.6	6.3
Sudan	0.0	15.9	29.0	58.1	125.1	157.6	200.8	252.6	257.1	258.7	263.3	0.1	5.7	196.7
Swaziland	0.8	3.3	3.6	3.6	4.3	4.6	5.5	6.1	6.9	8.6	10.5	1.0	2.6	6.3
Tanzania	8.2	405.3	509.6	574.8	580.0	612.1	664.7	744.8	800.4	876.4	966.6	9.2	198.4	727.5
Togo	211.3	283.2	555.2	499.1	511.6	583.7	590.0	615.7	712.0	733.0	697.0	276.7	337.0	617.8
Uganda	0.1	1,195.0	979.4	968.9	1,046.1	1,083.0	1,240.3	1,454.8	1,644.5	1,755.7	1,797.6	0.7	486.4	1,373.9
Zambia	0.8	452.8	669.4	864.1	1,207.9	1,314.5	1,862.1	2,388.0	3,110.8	3,610.9	4,398.6	0.9	143.2	2,344.6
Zimbabwe	0.6	6.5	8.2	8.7	10.0	12.1	23.7	38.3	44.4	55.1	55.0	0.8	3.5	30.9
NORTH AFRICA	..	..	..	..	..	..	..	..	..	..	..	..	..	..
Algeria	3.8	23.3	35.1	47.7	54.7	57.7	58.7	66.6	75.3	77.2	79.7	4.3	13.6	64.7
Egypt, Arab Rep.	0.7	3.4	3.4	3.4	3.4	3.4	3.4	3.4	3.5	4.0	4.5	0.6	1.8	3.6
Libya	0.3	0.3	0.3	0.4	0.4	0.5	0.5	0.5	0.5	0.6	1.3	0.3	0.3	0.6
Morocco	3.9	9.3	9.2	8.5	8.7	9.5	9.6	9.8	10.6	11.3	11.0	5.2	8.8	9.9
Tunisia	0.4	1.0	1.0	0.9	1.0	1.1	1.1	1.2	1.4	1.4	1.4	0.5	0.9	1.2
ALL AFRICA	..	..	..	..	..	..	..	..	..	..	..	..	..	..

Note: 2002 data are preliminary. Uganda changed its currency in 1987 and Congo Dem. Rep. in 1993. Angola and Congo Dem. Rep. again changed their currency in 1998. Guinea-Bissau joined W.A.M.U. in 1997.

3-5. SDR exchange rate index

| | SDRs per unit of national currency, index 1995 = 100 | | | | | | | | | | | Annual average | | |
	1980	1993	1994	1995	1996	1997	1998	1999	2000	2001	2002	75-84	85-94	95-MR
SUB-SAHARAN AFRICA	..	..	..	..	..	..	..	..	..	..	..	..	..	..
excluding South Africa	..	..	..	..	..	..	..	..	..	..	..	..	..	..
excl. S.Africa & Nigeria	..	..	..	..	..	..	..	..	..	..	..	..	..	..
Angola	4,972,386	77,622	6,952	100	4	1	0	0	0	0	0	5,637,727	3,513,572	13
Benin	275	192	95	100	102	94	95	90	81	81	84	245	182	91
Botswana	416	124	109	100	88	84	74	66	63	57	51	402	163	73
Burkina Faso	275	192	95	100	102	94	95	90	81	81	84	245	182	91
Burundi	323	112	105	100	86	78	63	49	40	36	32	354	188	61
Cameroon	275	192	95	100	102	94	95	90	81	81	84	245	182	91
Cape Verde	223	104	99	100	97	91	88	83	76	74	77	240	118	86
Central African Republic	275	192	95	100	102	94	95	90	81	81	84	245	182	91
Chad	275	192	95	100	102	94	95	90	81	81	84	245	182	91
Comoros	207	144	95	100	102	94	95	90	81	81	84	184	139	91
Congo, Dem. Rep. of	6.67E+11	423,415	3,019	100	14	5	4	2	0	0	0	1.44E+12	1.17E+10	16
Congo, Rep. of	275	192	95	100	102	94	95	90	81	81	84	245	182	91
Côte d'Ivoire	275	192	95	100	102	94	95	90	81	81	84	245	182	91
Djibouti	117	109	106	100	104	110	112	111	115	119	117	130	117	111
Equatorial Guinea	275	192	95	100	102	94	95	90	81	81	84	245	182	91
Eritrea	347	134	120	100	101	101	94	84	74	66	52	386	305	84
Ethiopia	347	134	120	100	101	101	97	86	86	87	84	386	306	93
Gabon	275	192	95	100	102	94	95	90	81	81	84	245	182	91
Gambia, The	647	114	106	100	102	103	100	93	86	73	57	568	161	89
Ghana	50,406	201	132	100	76	64	57	50	26	20	18	76,474	854	52
Guinea	6,145	109	106	100	104	110	112	111	106	61	59	6,101	783	95
Guinea-Bissau	61,655	193	148	100	73	52	52	50	45	45	46	62,731	3,799	58
Kenya	796	100	98	100	93	96	94	80	77	77	75	727	267	86
Lesotho	543	121	108	100	89	87	74	66	60	51	41	510	168	71
Liberia	117	109	106	100	104	110	3	3	3	2	2	130	117	41
Madagascar	2,349	241	160	100	110	92	87	75	72	77	73	2,029	416	86
Malawi	2,199	377	211	100	104	103	59	38	31	25	23	2,087	684	61
Mali	275	192	95	100	102	94	95	90	81	81	84	245	182	91
Mauritania	329	117	111	100	99	94	77	69	63	60	56	345	181	77
Mauritius	264	107	103	100	101	91	81	77	76	71	68	284	136	83
Mozambique	31,524	259	154	100	81	84	83	76	66	51	43	33,660	6,950	73
Namibia	543	121	108	100	89	87	74	66	60	51	41	510	168	71
Niger	275	192	95	100	102	94	95	90	81	81	84	245	182	91
Nigeria	4,669	108	106	100	105	110	112	27	25	23	21	4,415	822	65
Rwanda	326	181	181	100	82	88	86	79	71	65	59	338	287	79
São Tomé and Principe	4,681	355	210	100	67	36	23	22	20	19	18	5,055	1,897	38
Senegal	275	192	95	100	102	94	95	90	81	81	84	245	182	91
Seychelles	87	100	100	100	100	104	101	99	96	97	102	92	100	100
Sierra Leone	81,552	141	133	100	84	85	53	46	41	44	41	78,935	4,278	62
Somalia	..	..	..	..	..	..	..	..	..	..	..	..	..	..
South Africa	543	121	108	100	89	87	74	66	60	51	41	510	168	71
Sudan	129,561	382	212	100	47	40	31	132	249	256	247	141,389	14,281	138
Swaziland	543	121	108	100	89	87	74	66	60	51	41	510	168	71
Tanzania	8,149	156	119	100	103	103	96	86	82	78	69	8,361	1,098	90
Togo	275	192	95	100	102	94	95	90	81	81	84	245	182	91
Uganda	1,520,277	88	105	100	97	99	88	74	68	66	63	1,025,920	3,825	82
Zambia	126,813	210	121	100	75	72	52	40	32	28	23	127,103	9,896	53
Zimbabwe	1,570	145	113	100	91	80	45	25	23	19	18	1,556	423	50
NORTH AFRICA	..	..	..	..	..	..	..	..	..	..	..	..	..	..
Algeria	1,441	221	150	100	91	91	90	79	73	73	70	1,447	701	83
Egypt, Arab Rep.	565	110	106	100	105	110	112	111	112	102	88	823	368	105
Libya	165	149	129	100	100	100	100	100	94	83	39	183	168	89
Morocco	253	100	98	100	102	99	99	97	92	90	91	225	114	96
Tunisia	272	102	99	100	101	94	93	89	80	78	78	254	125	89
ALL AFRICA	..	..	..	..	..	..	..	..	..	..	..	..	..	..

Note: 2002 data are preliminary.Uganda changed its currency in 1987 and Congo Dem. Rep. in 1993. Angola and Congo Dem. Rep. again changed their currency in 1998. Guinea-Bissau joined W.A.M.U. in 1997.

3-6. Currency conversion factor

	Units of national currency per U.S. dollar											*Annual average*		
	1980	*1993*	*1994*	*1995*	*1996*	*1997*	*1998*	*1999*	*2000*	*2001*	*2002*	*75-84*	*85-94*	*95-MR*
SUB-SAHARAN AFRICA	..	..	..	..	..	..	..	..	..	..	..	..	..	..
excluding South Africa	..	..	..	..	..	..	..	..	..	..	..	..	..	..
excl. S.Africa & Nigeria	..	..	..	..	..	..	..	..	..	..	..	..	..	..
Angola	..	0.0	0.0	0.0	0.1	0.2	0.4	2.8	10.0	22.1	43.5	..	0.0	9.9
Benin	211.3	283.2	555.2	499.1	511.6	583.7	590.0	615.7	712.0	733.0	697.0	276.7	345.6	617.8
Botswana	0.8	2.4	2.7	2.8	3.3	3.7	4.2	4.6	5.1	5.8	6.3	0.9	2.0	4.5
Burkina Faso	211.3	283.2	555.2	499.1	511.5	583.7	590.0	615.7	712.0	733.0	697.0	276.7	350.2	617.8
Burundi	90.0	242.8	252.7	249.8	302.8	352.4	447.8	563.6	720.7	830.3	930.7	91.8	171.4	549.7
Cameroon	209.2	265.4	435.0	518.5	501.8	541.1	602.1	588.5	658.2	743.5	732.7	265.6	333.3	610.8
Cape Verde	40.2	80.4	81.9	76.9	82.6	93.1	98.2	103.5	119.7	123.2	117.2	46.6	76.6	101.8
Central African Republic	211.3	283.2	555.2	499.1	511.6	582.4	590.0	615.7	712.0	733.0	697.0	276.7	337.0	617.6
Chad	211.3	283.2	555.2	499.1	511.6	583.7	590.0	614.8	713.0	732.0	696.0	276.7	337.0	617.5
Comoros	211.3	283.2	416.4	374.4	383.7	437.8	442.5	461.8	534.0	549.8	522.7	276.7	323.2	463.3
Congo, Dem. Rep. of	0.0	0.0	0.0	0.1	0.5	1.3	1.6	11.0	69.0	300.0	346.3	0.0	0.0	91.2
Congo, Rep. of	211.3	283.2	555.2	499.1	511.6	583.7	590.0	615.7	712.0	733.0	697.0	276.7	337.0	617.8
Côte d'Ivoire	211.3	283.2	555.2	499.1	511.5	583.7	590.0	615.7	712.0	733.0	697.0	276.7	337.0	617.8
Djibouti	177.7	177.7	177.7	177.7	177.7	177.7	177.7	177.7	177.7	177.7	177.7	177.7	177.7	177.7
Equatorial Guinea	110.6	283.2	555.2	499.1	511.6	583.7	590.0	615.7	712.0	733.0	697.0	146.9	337.0	617.8
Eritrea	..	5.2	6.2	6.3	6.4	7.2	7.4	8.2	9.6	10.9	14.0	..	5.3	8.7
Ethiopia	2.1	4.3	5.1	5.9	6.3	6.5	6.9	7.5	8.1	8.3	8.5	2.1	2.6	7.3
Gabon	211.3	283.2	555.2	499.1	511.5	583.7	590.0	615.7	712.0	733.0	697.0	276.7	337.0	617.8
Gambia, The	1.7	9.1	9.6	9.5	9.8	10.2	10.6	11.4	12.8	15.7	19.9	2.3	7.6	12.5
Ghana	9.6	649.1	956.7	1,200.4	1,637.2	2,050.2	2,314.1	2,669.3	5,455.1	7,170.8	7,932.7	17.5	352.2	3,803.7
Guinea	19.0	955.5	976.6	991.4	1,004.0	1,095.3	1,236.8	1,387.4	1,746.9	1,947.8	1,976.2	21.1	611.3	1,423.2
Guinea-Bissau	0.8	155.1	198.3	278.0	405.7	583.7	590.0	615.7	712.0	728.0	697.8	0.8	61.2	576.4
Kenya	7.4	58.0	56.1	51.4	57.1	58.0	61.8	70.4	76.3	78.6	78.6	9.4	28.4	66.5
Lesotho	0.8	3.3	3.6	3.6	4.3	4.6	5.5	6.1	6.9	8.6	10.5	1.0	2.6	6.3
Liberia	1.0	1.0	1.0	1.0	1.0	1.0	41.5	41.9	41.0	48.6	61.8	1.0	1.0	29.7
Madagascar	211.3	1,913.8	3,067.3	4,265.6	4,061.3	5,090.9	5,441.4	6,283.8	6,767.5	6,588.5	6,832.0	297.7	1,559.3	5,666.4
Malawi	0.8	4.4	8.7	15.3	15.3	16.4	31.1	44.1	59.5	72.2	76.7	1.0	3.3	41.3
Mali	211.3	283.2	555.2	499.1	511.5	583.7	590.0	615.7	712.0	733.0	697.0	276.7	337.1	617.8
Mauritania	45.9	120.8	123.6	129.8	137.2	151.9	188.5	209.5	238.9	255.6	271.7	49.0	87.8	197.9
Mauritius	7.1	16.3	18.2	17.4	17.7	19.1	22.6	24.8	25.5	27.6	30.2	9.8	15.1	23.1
Mozambique	32.4	3,951.1	6,158.4	9,203.4	11,517.8	11,722.6	12,110.2	13,028.6	15,447.1	20,703.6	23,678.0	34.3	1,673.0	14,676.4
Namibia	0.8	3.3	3.6	3.6	4.3	4.6	5.5	6.1	6.9	8.6	10.5	1.0	2.6	6.3
Niger	211.3	283.2	555.2	499.1	511.5	583.7	590.0	615.7	712.0	733.0	697.0	276.7	337.0	617.8
Nigeria	0.8	45.3	52.3	70.4	80.0	81.1	88.0	92.3	101.7	111.2	120.6	1.1	16.4	93.2
Rwanda	92.8	144.3	220.0	262.2	306.8	301.5	312.3	333.9	389.7	443.0	476.3	93.7	113.0	353.2
São Tomé and Principe	34.8	429.9	732.6	1,420.3	2,203.2	4,552.5	6,883.2	7,119.0	7,978.2	8,842.1	9,088.3	36.5	217.6	6,010.8
Senegal	211.3	283.2	555.2	499.1	511.5	583.7	590.0	615.7	712.0	733.0	697.0	276.7	337.0	617.8
Seychelles	6.4	5.2	5.1	4.8	5.0	5.0	5.3	5.3	5.7	5.9	5.5	6.7	5.6	5.3
Sierra Leone	1.0	567.5	586.7	755.2	920.7	981.9	1,563.6	1,804.2	2,092.1	1,986.2	2,099.0	1.3	224.8	1,525.4
Somalia	28.8	..	..	..	..	..	..	..	..	..	..	28.1	512.9	..
South Africa	0.8	3.3	3.6	3.6	4.3	4.6	5.5	6.1	6.9	8.6	10.5	1.0	2.6	6.3
Sudan	0.1	15.9	29.0	58.1	125.1	157.6	200.8	252.6	257.1	258.7	263.3	0.1	6.0	196.7
Swaziland	0.8	3.3	3.5	3.6	4.3	4.6	5.5	6.1	6.9	8.5	10.5	0.9	2.6	6.2
Tanzania	8.2	405.3	509.6	574.8	580.0	612.1	664.7	744.8	800.4	876.4	966.6	9.2	198.4	727.5
Togo	211.3	283.2	555.2	499.1	511.6	583.7	590.0	615.7	712.0	733.0	697.0	276.7	337.0	617.8
Uganda	1.0	1,201.8	1,102.7	932.5	1,012.8	1,058.1	1,149.7	1,362.0	1,511.4	1,762.9	1,755.0	1.1	440.2	1,318.1
Zambia	0.8	452.8	669.4	864.1	1,207.9	1,314.5	1,862.1	2,388.0	3,110.8	3,610.9	4,398.6	0.9	144.3	2,344.6
Zimbabwe	0.6	6.5	8.1	8.7	10.0	12.1	23.7	38.3	44.4	55.1	117.6	0.8	3.4	38.7
NORTH AFRICA	..	..	..	..	..	..	..	..	..	..	..	..	..	..
Algeria	3.8	23.3	35.1	47.7	54.7	57.7	58.7	66.6	75.3	77.2	79.7	4.3	13.6	64.7
Egypt, Arab Rep.	0.7	3.3	3.4	3.4	3.4	3.4	3.4	3.4	3.4	3.7	4.3	0.7	2.2	3.5
Libya	0.3	0.3	0.3	0.4	0.4	0.5	0.5	0.5	0.5	0.6	1.3	0.3	0.3	0.6
Morocco	3.9	9.3	9.2	8.5	8.7	9.5	9.6	9.8	10.6	11.3	11.0	5.2	8.8	9.9
Tunisia	0.4	1.0	1.0	0.9	1.0	1.1	1.1	1.2	1.4	1.4	1.4	0.5	0.9	1.2
ALL AFRICA	..	..	..	..	..	..	..	..	..	..	..	..	..	..

Note: Official exchange rate adjusted for some countries to better reflect the rate at which international transactions are carried out. Guinea- Bissau joined W.A.M.U. in 1997.

3-7. Parallel market exchange rate

	National currency per U.S. dollar											Annual average		
	1980	1989	1990	1991	1992	1993	1994	1995	1996	1997	1998	75-84	85-94	95-MR
SUB-SAHARAN AFRICA	..	..	..	..	..	..	..	..	..	..	..	..	..	..
excluding South Africa	..	..	..	..	..	..	..	..	..	..	..	..	..	..
excl. S.Africa & Nigeria	..	..	..	..	..	..	..	..	..	..	..	..	..	..
Angola	..	..	..	1,266.7	1,087.5	31,740.0	203,137.5	569,573.8	163,370.0	283,138.8	564,250.0	900.0	30,572.7	395,083.2
Benin	209.5	324.8	281.8	289.0	270.1	288.0	586.4	499.3	516.4	593.3	..	304.2	343.5	536.3
Botswana	0.8	2.3	1.9	2.4	2.5	2.8	2.9	2.8	3.4	3.7	4.4	1.2	2.4	3.6
Burkina Faso	209.5	324.8	281.8	289.0	270.1	..	..	..	..	..	..	304.2	320.0	..
Burundi	106.0	214.0	186.1	269.3	310.9	370.7	409.4	340.8	369.6	459.2	568.1	122.3	235.5	434.4
Cameroon	209.5	324.8	281.8	289.0	270.1	288.0	586.4	499.3	516.4	593.3	..	304.2	343.5	536.3
Cape Verde	..	..	..	88.0	79.5	87.0	92.0	89.3	89.5	99.5	98.2	..	86.6	94.1
Central African Republic	209.5	324.8	281.8	289.0	270.1	288.0	586.4	499.3	516.4	593.3	603.2	304.2	343.5	553.0
Chad	209.5	324.8	281.8	289.0	270.1	288.0	586.4	499.3	516.4	593.3	..	304.2	343.5	536.3
Comoros	209.5	324.8	281.8	289.0	270.1	288.0	446.0	390.6	415.6	467.6	468.3	304.2	329.4	435.5
Congo, Dem. Rep. of	6.4	469.4	738.1	19,318.8	756,558.3	3,112,920.5	1,209.8	7,452.1	52,429.4	160,358.3	69,064.0	14.3	389,165.8	72,325.9
Congo, Rep. of	209.5	324.8	281.8	289.0	270.1	288.0	586.4	499.3	516.4	593.3	..	304.2	343.5	536.3
Côte d'Ivoire	209.5	324.8	281.8	289.0	270.1	288.0	586.4	499.3	516.4	593.3	..	304.2	343.5	536.3
Djibouti	..	217.9	191.8	213.8	205.8	212.0	208.6	198.5	192.1	183.9	184.0	..	207.1	189.6
Equatorial Guinea	209.5	324.8	281.8	289.0	270.1	288.0	586.4	586.4	516.4	593.3	..	304.2	343.5	565.4
Eritrea	..	..	..	..	..	..	..	..	..	..	..	..	..	..
Ethiopia	2.8	5.9	6.0	6.7	9.5	13.3	12.0	10.7	10.2	7.5	7.2	3.5	7.3	8.9
Gabon	209.5	324.8	281.8	289.0	270.1	288.0	586.4	499.3	516.4	593.3	..	334.6	343.5	536.3
Gambia, The	1.7	7.4	8.3	8.8	11.5	9.1	9.0	10.4	10.8	10.8	11.2	2.5	8.2	10.8
Ghana	15.9	328.8	360.8	382.2	451.6	665.7	976.4	1,224.3	1,663.4	2,080.7	2,334.8	41.7	394.7	1,825.8
Guinea	41.7	580.1	693.3	793.0	1,608.1	1,156.9	1,074.1	1,017.9	1,025.9	1,125.3	1,265.8	102.9	759.4	1,108.7
Guinea-Bissau	..	..	..	4,172.5	6,075.0	9,883.3	14,012.5	19,166.7	26,855.0	..	..	..	7,188.7	23,010.8
Kenya	8.2	22.4	23.3	30.0	44.4	91.7	66.8	53.4	59.5	62.1	63.6	11.9	35.1	59.6
Lesotho	..	2.7	2.7	2.9	3.0	3.5	3.8	3.7	4.5	4.7	5.6	1.4	2.8	4.6
Liberia	..	..	..	..	..	40.0	45.0	42.3	45.8	48.5	48.5	..	28.8	46.3
Madagascar	265.0	1,639.1	1,589.2	2,071.3	2,239.2	2,217.9	3,122.9	4,397.5	4,551.7	5,582.1	5,630.6	521.1	1,690.8	5,040.5
Malawi	1.6	3.6	3.3	3.9	4.6	5.9	9.2	16.7	16.5	17.6	33.3	1.7	4.1	21.0
Mali	209.5	324.8	281.8	289.0	270.1	288.0	586.4	499.3	516.4	593.3	..	304.2	343.5	536.3
Mauritania	65.0	..	..	213.3	221.7	247.5	145.0	139.3	144.0	158.9	194.3	93.2	192.4	159.1
Mauritius	..	16.0	15.7	17.1	16.8	18.3	18.4	18.2	19.4	21.4	24.4	..	15.9	20.8
Mozambique	80.0	1,250.0	..	2,100.0	2,800.0	3,950.0	6,875.0	9,865.7	12,172.5	12,533.7	12,851.3	322.2	2,862.5	11,855.8
Namibia	..	..	..	..	..	..	..	..	..	4.9	5.8	..	..	5.3
Niger	209.5	324.8	281.8	289.0	270.1	288.0	586.4	499.3	516.4	593.3	..	304.2	343.5	536.3
Nigeria	0.9	10.7	9.3	6.7	21.9	56.8	71.7	78.3	81.8	84.7	91.5	1.4	19.8	84.1
Rwanda	115.0	109.8	104.2	209.1	238.9	297.4	286.5	268.1	331.8	360.5	642.1	135.4	169.3	400.6
São Tomé and Principe	..	..	..	222.5	360.0	432.5	810.0	1,503.3	2,407.5	7,300.0	..	..	456.3	3,736.9
Senegal	209.5	324.8	281.8	289.0	270.1	288.0	586.4	499.3	516.4	593.3	..	304.2	343.5	536.3
Seychelles	..	..	5.9	5.7	5.5	5.4	5.5	5.5	5.4	5.5	5.7	..	5.6	5.6
Sierra Leone	1.4	180.9	470.6	535.7	845.1	647.5	618.7	741.3	942.1	1,137.9	2,024.4	2.1	355.0	1,211.4
Somalia	9.9	398.8	1,982.1	4,675.0	6,095.0	7,456.3	6,961.3	6,549.2	7,789.8	5,919.3	7,850.0	14.7	2,829.0	7,027.1
South Africa	0.9	2.7	2.7	2.9	3.0	3.5	3.8	3.7	4.5	4.7	5.7	1.2	2.8	4.6
Sudan	1.0	15.9	43.6	105.3	62.4	31.6	45.3	77.5	147.2	171.2	221.6	1.3	33.0	154.4
Swaziland	..	3.0	2.7	3.1	3.3	3.8	3.9	3.9	4.7	4.9	5.8	..	3.0	4.8
Tanzania	21.0	263.5	292.4	348.5	405.9	443.5	523.2	587.3	604.7	656.9	709.8	30.5	289.1	639.7
Togo	209.5	324.8	281.8	289.0	270.1	288.0	586.4	499.3	516.4	593.3	..	304.2	343.5	536.3
Uganda	75.7	597.5	685.8	859.2	1,365.4	1,515.8	1,289.2	1,076.2	1,135.2	1,178.1	1,333.8	203.8	2,412.3	1,180.8
Zambia	1.3	107.8	121.2	133.3	104.2	531.0	805.4	935.6	1,281.8	1,583.0	2,411.7	1.7	186.3	1,553.0
Zimbabwe	1.1	3.5	3.3	5.3	6.7	7.7	9.4	8.9	10.8	13.9	195.0	1.7	4.6	57.1
NORTH AFRICA	..	..	..	..	..	..	..	..	..	..	..	..	..	..
Algeria	10.9	37.1	29.8	33.8	87.4	106.8	128.7	131.9	127.6	129.8	131.4	13.6	52.3	130.2
Egypt, Arab Rep.	0.8	2.6	2.6	3.4	3.4	3.4	3.4	3.4	3.6	3.4	3.4	0.9	2.6	3.5
Libya	0.5	0.9	1.0	1.2	1.6	1.7	1.6	1.3	2.0	2.2	2.5	0.5	1.2	2.0
Morocco	4.1	9.2	9.3	9.2	8.9	9.4	9.4	8.6	8.8	9.7	9.8	6.0	9.2	9.2
Tunisia	0.4	1.0	0.9	1.0	1.0	1.0	1.1	0.9	1.0	1.1	1.2	0.6	0.9	1.0
ALL AFRICA	..	..	..	..	..	..	..	..	..	..	..	..	..	..

Note: Rates are annual average of month-end estimates, based on a sample of transactions. Guinea-Bissau joined the W.A.M.U. in 1997. The new Ugandan shilling was introduced in 1987.

3-8. Ratio of parallel market to official exchange rates

	Ratio of parallel market to official exchange rates											Annual average		
	1980	1989	1990	1991	1992	1993	1994	1995	1996	1997	1998	75-84	85-94	95-MR
SUB-SAHARAN AFRICA	..	..	..	..	..	..	..	..	..	..	..	..	..	..
excluding South Africa	..	..	..	..	..	..	..	..	..	..	..	..	..	..
excl. S.Africa & Nigeria	..	..	..	..	..	..	..	..	..	..	..	..	..	..
Angola	..	..	..	2.30E+10	4.33E+09	1.19E+10	3.41E+09	2.07E+08	1.28E+06	1.24E+06	1.44E+06	3.01E+10	3.60E+10	5.28E+07
Benin	0.99	1.02	1.04	1.02	1.02	1.02	1.06	1.00	1.01	1.02	..	1.03	1.02	1.01
Botswana	1.03	1.14	1.02	1.19	1.18	1.16	1.08	1.01	1.02	1.01	1.03	1.23	1.20	1.02
Burkina Faso	0.99	1.02	1.04	1.02	1.02	..	..	..	..	..	..	1.03	1.01	..
Burundi	1.18	1.35	1.09	1.48	1.49	1.53	1.62	1.36	1.22	1.30	1.27	1.28	1.33	1.29
Cameroon	0.99	1.02	1.04	1.02	1.02	1.02	1.06	1.00	1.01	1.02	..	1.03	1.02	1.01
Cape Verde	..	..	..	1.23	1.17	1.08	1.12	1.16	1.08	1.07	1.00	..	1.15	1.08
Central African Republic	0.99	1.02	1.04	1.02	1.02	1.02	1.06	1.00	1.01	1.02	1.02	1.03	1.02	1.01
Chad	0.99	1.02	1.04	1.02	1.02	1.02	1.06	1.00	1.01	1.02	..	1.03	1.02	1.01
Comoros	0.99	1.02	1.04	1.02	1.02	1.02	1.07	1.04	1.08	1.07	1.06	1.03	1.02	1.06
Congo, Dem. Rep. of	6.86E+11	3.69E+11	3.08E+11	3.72E+11	3.52E+11	1.24E+11	1.01E+05	1.06E+05	1.04E+05	1.22E+05	4.30E+04	6.49E+11	2.78E+11	9.39E+04
Congo, Rep. of	0.99	1.02	1.04	1.02	1.02	1.02	1.06	1.00	1.01	1.02	..	1.03	1.02	1.01
Côte d'Ivoire	0.99	1.02	1.04	1.02	1.02	1.02	1.06	1.00	1.01	1.02	..	1.03	1.02	1.01
Djibouti	..	1.23	1.08	1.20	1.16	1.19	1.17	1.12	1.08	1.03	1.04	..	1.17	1.07
Equatorial Guinea	0.99	1.02	1.04	1.02	1.02	1.02	1.06	1.17	1.01	1.02	..	1.03	1.02	1.07
Eritrea	..	..	..	..	..	..	..	..	..	..	..	..	..	..
Ethiopia	1.35	2.85	2.90	3.24	3.39	2.66	2.20	1.74	1.61	1.12	1.01	1.70	2.68	1.37
Gabon	0.99	1.02	1.04	1.02	1.02	1.02	1.06	1.00	1.01	1.02	..	1.02	1.02	1.01
Gambia, The	0.99	0.98	1.05	1.00	1.29	1.00	0.94	1.09	1.10	1.06	1.05	1.06	1.08	1.08
Ghana	5.78	1.22	1.11	1.04	1.03	1.03	1.02	1.02	1.02	1.01	1.01	7.98	1.36	1.01
Guinea	2.20	0.98	1.05	1.05	1.78	1.21	1.10	1.03	1.02	1.03	1.02	4.62	2.33	1.02
Guinea-Bissau	..	..	..	74.13	56.95	63.72	70.65	68.94	66.19	..	..	..	74.18	67.56
Kenya	1.11	1.09	1.02	1.09	1.38	1.58	1.19	1.04	1.04	1.06	1.05	1.18	1.17	1.05
Lesotho	..	1.03	1.04	1.05	1.05	1.05	1.07	1.07	1.02	1.05	1.02	1.09	1.07	1.03
Liberia	..	..	..	..	..	40.00	45.00	42.30	45.80	48.50	1.17	..	28.83	34.44
Madagascar	1.25	1.02	1.06	1.13	1.20	1.16	1.02	1.03	1.12	1.10	1.03	1.53	1.08	1.07
Malawi	1.97	1.30	1.21	1.39	1.28	1.34	1.05	1.09	1.08	1.07	1.07	1.77	1.25	1.08
Mali	0.99	1.02	1.04	1.02	1.02	1.02	1.06	1.00	1.01	1.02	..	1.03	1.02	1.01
Mauritania	1.42	..	..	2.60	2.55	2.05	1.17	1.07	1.05	1.05	1.03	1.79	2.23	1.05
Mauritius	..	1.05	1.06	1.09	1.08	1.04	1.02	1.05	1.08	1.02	1.01	..	1.04	1.04
Mozambique	2.42	1.65	..	1.44	1.09	1.00	1.12	1.07	1.06	1.06	1.06	8.06	12.60	1.06
Namibia	..	..	..	..	..	..	..	..	..	1.06	1.04	..	..	1.05
Niger	0.99	1.02	1.04	1.02	1.02	1.02	1.06	1.00	1.01	1.02	..	1.03	1.02	1.01
Nigeria	1.65	1.45	1.16	0.68	1.27	2.57	3.26	3.58	3.74	3.87	4.18	2.09	2.01	3.84
Rwanda	1.34	1.37	1.24	1.67	1.78	2.06	2.04	1.02	1.08	1.20	2.05	1.48	1.53	1.34
São Tomé and Principe	..	..	..	1.10	1.12	1.01	1.11	1.06	1.09	1.60	..	..	1.08	1.25
Senegal	0.99	1.02	1.04	1.02	1.02	1.02	1.06	1.00	1.01	1.02	..	1.03	1.02	1.01
Seychelles	..	..	1.11	1.08	1.07	1.04	1.09	1.15	1.09	1.09	1.09	..	1.08	1.11
Sierra Leone	1.33	3.02	3.11	1.81	1.69	1.14	1.05	0.98	1.02	1.16	1.29	1.42	2.11	1.11
Somalia	1.57	0.81	..	..	..	..	..	..	..	..	..	1.45	1.76	..
South Africa	1.16	1.03	1.04	1.05	1.05	1.07	1.07	1.02	1.05	1.02	1.03	1.12	1.07	1.03
Sudan	20.00	35.33	96.89	151.39	6.40	1.98	1.56	1.33	1.18	1.09	1.10	16.25	37.57	1.18
Swaziland	..	1.14	1.04	1.12	1.16	1.16	1.10	1.08	1.09	1.06	1.05	..	1.11	1.07
Tanzania	2.56	1.84	1.50	1.59	1.36	1.09	1.03	1.02	1.04	1.07	1.07	3.02	2.20	1.05
Togo	0.99	1.02	1.04	1.02	1.02	1.02	1.06	1.00	1.01	1.02	..	1.03	1.02	1.01
Uganda	1,020.63	2.68	1.60	1.17	1.20	1.27	1.32	1.11	1.09	1.09	1.08	535.92	76.51	1.09
Zambia	1.65	7.80	4.00	2.06	0.61	1.17	1.20	1.08	1.06	1.20	1.30	1.69	2.49	1.16
Zimbabwe	1.71	1.65	1.35	1.46	1.31	1.19	1.15	1.03	1.08	1.15	8.23	2.09	1.42	2.87
NORTH AFRICA	..	..	..	..	..	..	..	..	..	..	..	..	..	..
Algeria	2.84	4.88	3.33	1.83	4.00	4.57	3.67	2.77	2.33	2.25	2.24	3.08	4.15	2.40
Egypt, Arab Rep.	1.14	3.00	1.68	1.08	1.02	1.01	1.00	1.00	1.06	1.00	1.01	1.42	1.95	1.02
Libya	1.69	3.00	3.53	4.27	5.68	5.59	4.59	3.11	4.58	4.77	5.30	1.64	4.07	4.44
Morocco	1.04	1.08	1.13	1.06	1.04	1.01	1.02	1.01	1.01	1.02	1.02	1.07	1.04	1.01
Tunisia	0.99	1.05	1.02	1.08	1.13	1.00	1.09	0.95	1.03	0.99	1.02	1.02	1.05	1.00
ALL AFRICA	..	..	..	..	..	..	..	..	..	..	..	..	..	..

Note: 2002 data are preliminary (see page 2).Guinea-Bissau joined the WAMU in May 1997.New Ugandan shilling = 100 old Ugandan shillings, introduced in 1987.Values for Angola and Congo, Dem. Rep. are in scientific notation.

3-9. Real effective exchange rate index

	Index 1990 = 100											Annual average		
	1980	1993	1994	1995	1996	1997	1998	1999	2000	2001	2002	75-84	85-94	95-MR
SUB-SAHARAN AFRICA	117.6	91.0	79.9	79.2	83.1	82.4	84.0	81.9	78.5	76.4	75.9	72.8	100.4	80.2
excluding South Africa	115.2	90.9	79.9	79.0	83.0	80.0	83.6	80.7	76.7	77.5	76.1	71.5	100.8	79.6
excl. S.Africa & Nigeria	112.8	91.0	75.8	79.0	82.2	79.9	83.2	80.5	76.1	76.4	75.9	70.6	100.0	79.2
Angola	..	..	..	..	..	..	..	..	..	..	..	..	..	..
Benin	..	102.3	69.0	79.5	81.5	80.0	86.0	83.0	82.9	85.5	89.6	..	93.8	83.5
Botswana	165.4	86.9	79.9	85.9	88.5	72.8	73.8	73.8	74.9	75.9	75.9	160.2	106.2	77.7
Burkina Faso	..	..	..	..	..	..	..	..	..	..	..	..	..	..
Burundi	128.1	90.8	93.8	103.3	109.4	130.1	117.3	97.3	101.1	96.2	81.7	155.7	115.1	104.5
Cameroon	88.0	89.9	57.9	66.8	67.8	64.7	68.1	71.2	63.8	65.8	68.2	82.2	93.4	67.1
Cape Verde	88.7	87.6	88.0	89.6	89.0	92.1	94.2	89.1	85.8	86.0	88.0	97.2	95.5	89.2
Central African Republic	104.9	85.8	53.8	63.4	64.8	62.8	61.2	58.0	56.6	58.5	60.5	100.1	91.2	60.7
Chad	102.3	111.6	58.7	64.4	66.8	66.9	66.9	61.8	65.4	73.6	76.3	114.4	102.2	67.8
Comoros	..	97.3	..	..	..	..	..	..	..	..	..	..	101.3	..
Congo, Dem. Rep. of	387.5	125.5	95.3	83.8	83.3	102.2	106.1	285.1	232.9	208.7	91.5	342.3	114.8	149.2
Congo, Rep. of	102.2	89.2	69.3	79.0	75.2	77.6	79.9	80.3	75.5	78.8	..	102.2	94.9	78.0
Côte d'Ivoire	105.6	99.3	61.2	70.7	71.0	69.9	74.5	73.0	68.1	70.5	73.3	86.3	93.0	71.4
Djibouti	..	..	..	..	..	..	..	..	..	..	..	..	..	..
Equatorial Guinea	..	93.2	66.6	78.6	79.2	77.5	83.2	80.7	80.4	85.1	91.6	..	102.0	82.1
Eritrea	..	..	..	..	..	..	..	..	..	..	..	..	..	..
Ethiopia	92.5	44.5	37.9	38.5	35.4	35.8	35.5	36.2	35.9	31.6	30.6	92.5	93.7	35.0
Gabon	112.8	74.0	49.9	55.1	54.5	53.7	55.5	53.1	49.5	50.1	50.4	101.4	87.8	52.8
Gambia, The	133.3	105.7	98.1	95.1	94.1	98.2	96.6	94.5	89.9	78.9	65.0	127.2	103.5	89.0
Ghana	478.5	79.3	63.8	73.4	80.0	84.7	91.7	92.1	59.4	59.8	59.4	816.4	114.6	75.1
Guinea	..	100.6	98.5	92.8	95.1	94.4	90.9	85.5	76.7	76.4	76.2	..	106.1	86.0
Guinea-Bissau	..	80.8	71.8	66.4	69.6	78.2	81.3	77.2	80.9	78.5	..	..	86.6	76.0
Kenya	138.9	88.2	111.0	110.8	108.5	124.6	130.5	119.9	128.0	134.6	131.8	136.3	108.3	123.6
Lesotho	112.5	114.8	109.3	109.3	99.6	102.5	93.1	91.2	87.5	75.9	66.5	110.9	107.0	90.7
Liberia	..	..	..	..	..	..	..	..	..	..	..	..	..	..
Madagascar	193.1	102.7	90.2	81.9	104.1	93.6	94.5	91.9	101.2	111.6	120.6	200.0	112.4	99.9
Malawi	110.4	97.3	69.1	60.3	83.0	92.1	67.0	67.2	67.9	70.2	69.3	107.7	95.3	72.1
Mali	..	..	..	..	..	..	..	..	..	..	..	..	..	..
Mauritania	120.7	93.8	86.3	78.9	79.6	79.9	..	..	..	..	..	139.8	106.0	79.5
Mauritius	..	..	..	..	..	..	..	..	..	..	..	..	..	..
Mozambique	117.6	63.5	61.4	58.7	67.4	73.7	66.6	67.9	65.4	59.3	55.1	150.1	140.2	64.3
Namibia	..	..	..	..	..	..	..	..	..	..	..	..	..	..
Niger	..	79.3	55.2	62.1	65.5	65.7	67.2	63.2	61.8	..	..	..	91.1	64.3
Nigeria	349.6	77.3	143.5	121.6	150.4	172.7	189.4	96.0	98.4	109.2	109.8	448.7	188.6	130.9
Rwanda	83.3	85.1	128.7	78.0	85.2	102.2	103.2	104.8	106.4	106.4	106.4	60.9	102.8	99.1
São Tomé and Principe	..	..	..	..	..	..	..	..	..	..	..	..	..	..
Senegal	108.2	91.0	58.8	63.7	64.2	59.9	61.2	59.8	56.2	57.3	58.9	98.2	97.1	60.1
Seychelles	90.6	106.0	104.5	102.1	97.3	101.1	101.1	109.7	107.3	116.7	122.6	103.8	105.6	107.2
Sierra Leone	..	102.8	117.5	106.1	107.1	122.8	105.4	123.2	111.0	122.9	99.8	..	116.9	112.3
Somalia	..	..	..	..	..	..	..	..	..	..	..	..	..	..
South Africa	134.2	106.0	101.5	98.7	91.0	97.4	88.2	83.5	81.8	72.2	61.7	134.4	100.6	84.3
Sudan	45.0	27.9	33.0	25.4	25.3	26.2	19.9	18.3	20.0	21.6	22.0	43.4	60.2	22.4
Swaziland	..	..	..	..	..	..	..	..	..	..	..	..	..	..
Tanzania	..	94.0	93.6	97.7	118.3	125.6	135.5	135.5	120.6	121.8	121.8	..	111.0	122.1
Togo	126.3	93.2	62.1	72.0	73.7	75.4	78.5	75.5	70.9	73.2	75.9	118.1	96.6	74.4
Uganda	913.9	73.0	90.8	88.8	88.6	94.9	84.0	78.0	74.6	72.5	68.1	413.8	129.5	81.2
Zambia	134.7	101.6	97.8	93.6	98.0	117.3	107.2	104.8	106.0	115.1	108.3	138.4	94.0	106.3
Zimbabwe	165.4	86.9	79.9	85.9	88.5	72.8	73.8	..	..	..	..	167.1	106.2	80.2
NORTH AFRICA	150.7	103.3	105.4	108.3	109.1	109.5	110.9	112.0	112.7	109.0	108.2	148.0	110.8	110.0
Algeria	143.0	73.8	64.6	53.7	55.8	61.2	64.2	59.0	57.6	59.2	54.6	165.3	117.2	58.1
Egypt, Arab Rep.	..	108.7	112.6	118.9	126.9	131.2	156.3	162.2	174.1	171.7	166.7	..	104.1	151.0
Libya	..	..	..	..	..	..	..	..	..	..	..	..	..	..
Morocco	156.5	105.9	109.3	112.8	113.7	114.7	117.5	118.7	122.0	117.0	116.7	138.7	106.6	116.7
Tunisia	150.7	100.7	101.5	103.7	104.4	104.3	104.2	105.3	103.5	100.9	99.7	148.0	108.9	103.3
ALL AFRICA	123.5	93.2	83.1	80.7	84.2	88.4	86.0	83.2	80.7	78.5	76.2	76.2	101.3	82.3

Note: 2002 data are preliminary (see page 2).

Figure 3-1. Real effective exchange rate, 2002*

(index 1990 = 100)

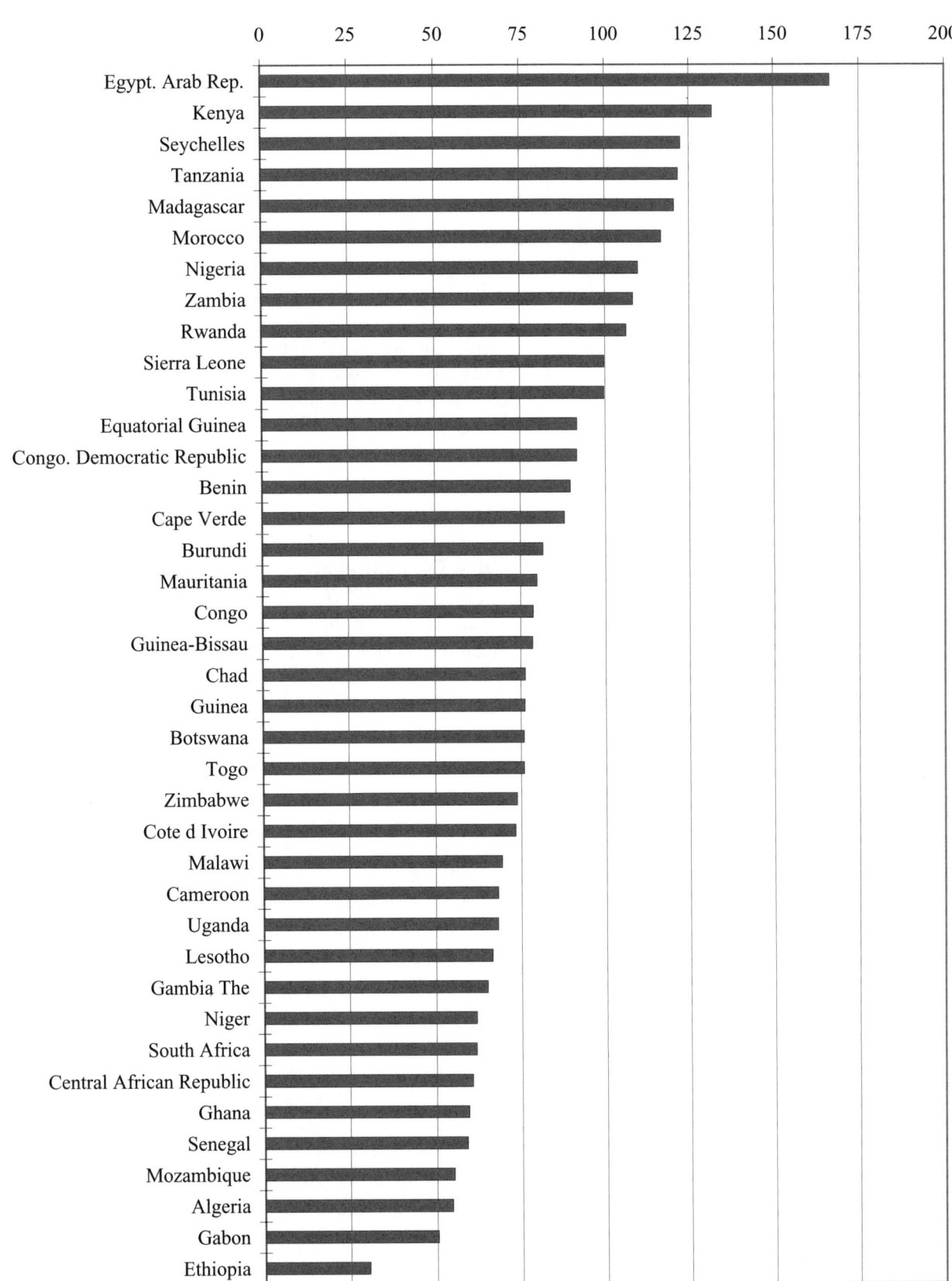

*Or most recent available data.

Technical notes

Tables

Table 3-1. GDP deflator (local currency series). The implicit GDP deflator for the national currency series is obtained by dividing, for each year of the time series, the value of GDP at current prices (World Bank country desks) by the value of GDP at constant 1995 prices (World Bank country desks), both in national currency.

Table 3-2. GDP deflator (U.S. dollar series). The GDP deflator for U.S. dollar series (with base year 1995 = 100) (World Bank country desks) is obtained by dividing, for each year of the time series, the value of GDP at current U.S. dollars (Table 2-5) by the value of GDP at constant 1995 dollars (Table 2-1). GDP at current U.S. dollars was obtained by converting current national series at single-year exchange rates, while GDP at constant 1995 dollars was obtained by converting the constant national series at 1995 prices at a fixed (1995) exchange rate. As a result, the GDP deflator for U.S. dollar series includes both the effects of domestic price changes and the effects of exchange rate variations.

Table 3-3. Consumer price index. Consumer price indexes (IMF, *International Financial Statistics [IFS]*, line 64) are generally compiled using the Laspeyres formula: goods in the consumption basket selected according to consumption patterns in the base year, derived from household expenditure surveys, are weighted by their relative prices in the base year. The data often relate only to selected representative in-

come groups in capital cities or major urban areas. Thus, the consumer price indexes shown for some countries may not accurately represent price movements because the underlying consumption basket may not be representative of overall national consumption patterns, and the weights assigned to prices may be outdated.

Table 3-4. Official exchange rate. The official exchange rate (IMF, *IFS*, line rf) is expressed as the annual average of the official market exchange rate in national currency per U.S. dollar.

Table 3-5. SDR exchange rate index. This index is based on the average annual exchange rate for SDRs per unit of national currency (IMF, *IFS*, line rd-zf).

Table 3-6. Currency conversion factor. These are the annual exchange rates used by the World Bank (World Bank country desks) to convert the national currency series into U.S. dollars. For most countries, in most years, the conversion factor is identical to the average annual official exchange rate. However, where the official exchange rate is judged to diverge by an exceptionally large margin from the rate effectively applied to international transactions, a more appropriate conversion factor is estimated. An alternative conversion factor is used when there are egregious differences between the official and effective transaction rates, when officially recognized multiple exchange rates have analytically significant spreads, or when exchange rates need to be adjusted to a fiscal year base. The objective in estimating alternative conversion factors is to approximate as closely as possible exchange rates actually used. For example, where multiple exchange rates are maintained, a transaction-weighted rate is calculated.

Note that national statistical compilers sometimes use an official exchange rate to assign a national currency value to international transactions originally denominated in foreign currencies. In these cases, the official rate must be used to convert the same items back to dollars, regardless of whether it was the rate actually applied to the international transactions, even if an alternative conversion factor is used for other components of GDP.

Table 3-7. Parallel market exchange rate. Data reported here are from *Pick's Currency Yearbooks* and *Currency Alerts* (now discontinued) and the *Global Currency Report*. They are averages of month-end rates for the period covered, based on a sample of transactions, usually in a capital city or a financial center of the country. They include the rates at the *Bureaux de Change* that have been established in some countries with auction markets as semi-official foreign exchange windows for small transactions. The current table corrects some errors contained in *ADI 1994/95*.

Table 3-8. Ratio of parallel market to official exchange rates. This ratio is obtained by dividing parallel market exchange rates (Table 3-7) by official exchange rates (Table 3-4), to measure the premium on the official exchange rate. The premium is usually high in the presence of an overvalued exchange rate. This table reflects the corrected series for Table 3-7.

Table 3-9. Real effective exchange rate index. This index (World Bank country desks) gives a measure of price competitiveness of the country's exports relative to its trading partners. A decline (increase) in the index indicates real depreciation (appreciation) of the exchange rate. The data have been rebased to 1990. The year 1987 coincided with the early period of massive devaluations in the process of adjustment by several Sub-Saharan African countries. As a result, the substantial devaluations that continued to take place after 1987 may not be very pronounced in the data. Relative movements in the inflation rates between a country and the trading partner (or partners) may diminish the real impact of a devaluation, particularly if inflationary tendencies are stronger domestically than abroad.

Figure

The following indicator has been used to derive the figure in this chapter.

Figure 3-1. Real effective exchange rate (Table 3-9).

Methodology used for regional aggregations and period averages in Chapter 3

Table	Aggregations [a]			Period averages [b]	
	(4)	(7)	(8)	(1)	(2)
3-1		x		x	
3-2	x			x	
3-3		x			x
3-4			x	x	
3-5			x	x	
3-6			x	x	
3-7			x	x	
3-8			x	x	
3-9		x		x	

Note: Regional aggregations are shown in the rows for Sub-Saharan Africa, North Africa, and All Africa. Period averages are shown in the last three columns. This table shows only the methodologies used in this chapter.

a. Regional aggregations: (1) simple total; (2) simple total of the first indicator divided by the simple total of the second indicator (same country coverage); (3) simple total of the gap-filled indicator; (4) simple total of the gap-filled main indicator divided by the simple total of the gap-filled secondary indicator; (5) simple total of the first gap-filled main indicator less the simple total of the second gap-filled main indicator, all divided by the simple total of the secondary indicator; (6) weighted total (by population); (7) median; (8) no aggregation; (9) simple arithmetic mean.

b. Period averages: (1) arithmetic mean (using the same series as shown in the table; i.e., ratio if the rest of the table is shown as ratio, level if the rest of the table is shown as level, growth rate if the rest is shown as growth rate); (2) least-squares growth rate (using main indicator); (3) least-squares growth rate (using main indicator in constant terms, with the rest of the table in current terms).

4

Money and Banking

Monetary variables directly affect prices and exchange rates and indirectly affect real economic performance. Money plays a vital role in any modern economy. Data in this chapter are concerned with the creation of the types of assets that transactors in the economy wish to hold from the types of liabilities that debtors are willing to incur. However, emphasis here is on the creation of the means of payment, that is, on the high end of the liquidity spectrum for assets.

Money and the institutions that deal in money provide cover against credit risks, limit transactions costs, help mobilize savings, allocate credit, and facilitate investment and hence growth of the economy. Data on money and banking help to assess the prevailing financial conditions of a country and to arrive at a proper evaluation of the financial policy options open to a country for achieving its macroeconomic objectives. The government usually intervenes in finance to control the supply of money and credit. The primary objective of such intervention is to maintain price stability. However, the government may also intervene to finance a budget deficit that in turn may threaten price stability. The government also ensures that financial institutions are properly supervised to ensure continued confidence in the financial system and to avoid destabilizing runs on the banking system. Time series are provided for nine indicators in this section.

4-1. Domestic credit

	Level	Percentage annual change											Average annual percentage growth		
	1995	1980	1993	1994	1995	1996	1997	1998	1999	2000	2001	2002	75-84	85-94	95-MR
SUB-SAHARAN AFRICA	..	20	6	20	11	11	13	11	10	13	11	12	21	12	12
excluding South Africa	..	19	6	20	11	11	12	11	10	12	11	12	21	12	11
excl. S.Africa & Nigeria	..	18	6	20	11	11	13	11	10	13	10	12	16	13	11
Angola	8	..	..	..	..	404	340	156	176	-1,191	-91	-2,294	..	..	210
Benin	117,710	49	-26	74	21	4	-24	2	6	36	-42	37	24	-8	-1
Botswana	-4,709	-28	11	20	-3	16	147	19	-1	20	16	-56	7	..	..
Burkina Faso	66,293	3	-5	4	-14	30	116	9	5	23	5	-1	23	1	22
Burundi	39,933	20	6	16	-17	54	19	24	34	12	28	27	32	7	23
Cameroon	791,344	28	-3	-1	-1	-4	6	9	9	-1	9	4	24	0	4
Cape Verde	21,027	39	19	23	19	11	21	6	5	32	7	13	49	18	14
Central African Republic	63,333	39	0	31	-4	-4	-2	11	14	4	11	11	12	1	5
Chad	71,325	-1	-15	30	-10	28	0	2	8	20	21	3	10	0	10
Comoros	12,450	..	-20	9	0	-18	3	-2	20	4	-6	12	..	9	1
Congo, Dem. Rep. of	7	22	1,648	5,299	182	..	..	..	..	..	..	-86	43	441	..
Congo, Rep. of	183,036	17	-32	3	10	8	14	11	9	-28	37	-12	21	-1	5
Côte d'Ivoire	1,540,052	23	-3	6	12	3	8	5	-1	-4	-2	1	21	0	2
Djibouti	45,598	..	-2	10	17	7	-3	-4	-31	12	-10	0	..	3	-5
Equatorial Guinea	20,829	..	-26	47	1	11	16	-15	36	13	-75	-61	..	6	-14
Eritrea	1,853	..	..	..	..	84	6	69	35	23	8	22	..	..	32
Ethiopia	14,087	18	6	9	11	19	8	9	27	16	-3	1	22	12	12
Gabon	453,735	11	1	25	15	-4	14	26	-4	-25	46	-2	15	1	6
Gambia, The	281	23	-17	-13	41	9	35	17	31	16	107	22	28	-8	31
Ghana	1,464,053	29	43	16	53	42	73	18	58	59	19	23	44	32	43
Guinea	282,366	..	9	18	29	17	-7	-7	..	..	13	51	..	..	14
Guinea-Bissau	2,171	..	52	14	-50	58	234	15	44	47	-29	15	..	39	35
Kenya	198,876	13	-2	50	37	19	21	9	10	1	3	9	20	16	12
Lesotho	-270	..	-37	-71	-616	83	52	25	-98	-1,234	59	121	..	-3	..
Liberia	1,692	2	11	6	14	11	5	1,783	-9	12	14	41	21	13	75
Madagascar	2,506,189	50	16	29	-3	-2	2	29	10	13	21	14	28	12	11
Malawi	2,646	6	16	35	-3	16	12	-3	75	17	74	76	22	15	28
Mali	136,883	5	12	20	15	0	29	29	18	-9	34	17	8	-3	16
Mauritania	32,877	13	7	-1	-37	-36	-38	-66	-87	-1,182	-120	-1,927	19	13	-48
Mauritius	46,369	14	25	23	13	6	26	22	9	5	15	7	26	16	13
Mozambique	887,600	..	-39	131	28	-40	107	4	192	97	49	15	..	17	50
Namibia	5,595	..	29	28	31	22	-1	9	9	15	14	14	..	..	12
Niger	81,241	45	-17	25	-17	10	23	3	3	1	-3	13	32	-4	5
Nigeria	474,361	23	64	56	8	-22	-1	40	23	-25	76	60	40	29	13
Rwanda	44,016	12	23	-7	-7	-2	61	13	13	-1	7	-3	10	14	12
São Tomé and Principe	22,359	..	..	..	..	22	-110	-783	-7	-45	350	15	..	..	6
Senegal	538,122	16	-2	7	2	7	2	6	8	16	7	-5	20	-1	6
Seychelles	1,615	12	25	20	15	16	23	31	15	12	11	16	20	16	18
Sierra Leone	426,184	35	1	1,076	-12	6	11	7	13	20	7	3	33	63	9
Somalia	..	31	..	..	..	..	..	..	..	..	..	..	28	63	..
South Africa	333,490	21	12	21	12	18	16	17	9	14	20	8	16	17	15
Sudan	46,238	22	65	48	47	114	18	24	23	43	23	34	27	55	36
Swaziland	328	0	109	163	-36	-45	-15	-269	7	37	71	-206	30	2	8
Tanzania	693,880	24	40	11	11	-15	-1	17	23	5	-8	13	25	35	5
Togo	169,769	13	2	21	44	10	7	11	-7	0	-8	-13	17	3	3
Uganda	234,994	64	-4	-13	-42	34	38	31	15	74	-11	54	50	72	24
Zambia	1,921,138	17	..	123	63	21	0	71	13	60	-5	12	22	85	27
Zimbabwe	20,496	28	59	20	19	27	83	41	7	66	84	129	19	25	49
NORTH AFRICA	..	18	7	10	15	6	15	9	12	11	9	7	30	16	8
Algeria	968,930	17	17	4	25	10	10	9	25	-20	-4	..	23	14	7
Egypt, Arab Rep.	157,300	42	7	13	17	14	16	19	12	11	11	13	30	16	14
Libya	11,529	-11	4	10	8	-4	-16	2	3	2	10	9	21	11	0
Morocco	166,721	18	9	11	15	6	49	9	2	11	-1	4	19	9	12
Tunisia	9,746	19	5	6	7	0	15	8	14	27	9	5	20	10	12
ALL AFRICA	..	18	6	20	11	10	14	11	10	12	10	12	23	11	10

Note: 2002 data are preliminary (see page 2). Levels for 1995 are expressed in millions of units of national currency. Group data are medians of individual country values in each year or period.

4-2. Credit to the private sector

	Level	Percentage annual change											Average annual percentage growth		
	1995	1980	1993	1994	1995	1996	1997	1998	1999	2000	2001	2002	75-84	85-94	95-MR
SUB-SAHARAN AFRICA	..	15	11	14	17	14	18	15	11	13	12	15	18	18	14
excluding South Africa	..	15	11	14	17	13	20	14	11	13	11	15	18	20	14
excl. S.Africa & Nigeria	..	15	10	13	17	13	18	14	11	13	11	15	15	21	14
Angola	1	..	..	..	..	3,595	241	-1	391	318	298	216	..	..	277
Benin	80,447	34	-2	11	7	27	-30	40	61	20	-1	15	22	-7	16
Botswana	1,560	10	12	12	-3	4	9	39	43	23	13	25	17	28	21
Burkina Faso	80,590	4	-9	-17	9	13	80	10	3	16	14	19	16	0	20
Burundi	30,648	14	35	8	-15	31	7	26	29	46	9	30	21	26	22
Cameroon	371,390	29	-8	0	1	4	-10	23	12	13	11	12	27	-9	9
Cape Verde	10,391	-14	59	1	37	17	20	12	12	5	15	12	21	16	15
Central African Republic	23,159	50	-5	17	24	0	4	16	-1	11	12	20	11	-7	9
Chad	27,790	-2	-33	14	17	8	-3	17	0	1	26	30	9	-10	9
Comoros	9,525	..	-12	-3	10	-29	25	-17	23	10	-3	11	..	9	2
Congo, Dem. Rep. of	4	32	1,889	22,432	474	..	..	..	..	..	..	24	33	372	..
Congo, Rep. of	85,683	23	-46	15	13	14	9	5	41	-31	-8	-40	24	-10	0
Côte d'Ivoire	1,016,035	12	-5	-5	19	2	13	1	-7	4	6	0	17	-2	3
Djibouti	37,901	..	-6	2	13	3	-1	9	-35	14	-14	-5	..	0	-5
Equatorial Guinea	3,397	..	-74	13	51	82	94	18	51	27	35	45	..	-10	47
Eritrea	632	..	..	..	..	142	14	47	-27	6	25	17	..	..	17
Ethiopia	3,706	-30	116	47	86	74	24	9	29	6	3	-1	-5	14	23
Gabon	196,080	16	-3	0	25	-2	41	6	0	10	20	11	15	-7	12
Gambia, The	363	19	59	7	-10	0	23	14	20	10	33	37	21	8	16
Ghana	393,289	18	35	46	44	73	70	40	60	47	19	30	32	44	49
Guinea	181,518	..	22	11	26	4	-1	-13	..	..	7	8	..	..	5
Guinea-Bissau	6,129	..	78	53	-8	20	51	13	-22	23	-63	-5	..	59	-3
Kenya	118,189	20	5	28	50	24	25	1	11	4	-4	3	17	16	11
Lesotho	674	-10	59	39	-4	0	46	-15	2	3	7	14	24	25	5
Liberia	191	-39	-12	64	-20	-60	36	1,040	-21	-23	25	24	-1	11	34
Madagascar	1,563,020	26	15	26	16	2	14	1	7	24	15	1	18	14	10
Malawi	1,253	8	-14	54	6	12	14	99	6	50	5	14	19	20	27
Mali	131,787	8	3	-9	52	31	16	27	14	-2	20	20	8	1	19
Mauritania	31,417	13	3	3	-27	13	8	7	18	24	17	20	14	13	11
Mauritius	32,879	9	28	20	15	5	26	31	10	13	10	8	17	23	16
Mozambique	2,374,200	..	14	58	54	46	50	27	32	27	-83	-7	..	35	5
Namibia	4,743	..	30	31	34	19	16	9	4	17	16	20	..	..	15
Niger	42,004	20	-10	10	-41	3	-18	39	-3	29	7	15	21	-5	4
Nigeria	201,785	38	18	61	42	25	23	18	22	30	41	14	27	29	26
Rwanda	28,538	46	17	-9	74	1	56	20	11	17	9	10	21	3	21
São Tomé and Principe	6,694	..	..	..	..	32	36	88	11	6	10	54	..	..	30
Senegal	357,834	16	2	-17	2	16	4	2	11	28	5	5	17	0	9
Seychelles	245	3	10	21	17	10	44	19	9	12	14	17	10	7	18
Sierra Leone	17,600	28	44	12	5	23	25	6	-13	12	25	62	14	72	13
Somalia	..	-5	..	..	..	..	..	..	..	..	..	..	18	95	..
South Africa	327,114	26	11	18	16	17	14	16	10	15	22	5	18	17	15
Sudan	13,068	29	69	96	48	144	23	13	-2	64	41	76	29	48	39
Swaziland	928	15	9	22	2	6	12	6	6	7	6	27	19	22	8
Tanzania	201,015	11	40	20	-10	-42	43	44	26	10	21	41	13	78	15
Togo	131,241	13	-8	-1	28	7	10	4	-10	1	-7	-7	15	4	2
Uganda	246,361	85	56	12	28	31	-1	33	22	12	1	15	36	101	17
Zambia	253,971	10	..	98	81	47	10	3	31	56	10	7	11	72	26
Zimbabwe	15,276	18	44	29	28	21	49	37	13	51	61	186	11	37	43
NORTH AFRICA	..	13	10	11	9	10	12	12	20	11	11	4	29	26	15
Algeria	103,499	14	1	25	7	33	-21	19	35	41	18	..	21	-6	17
Egypt, Arab Rep.	66,777	-9	19	32	37	26	26	27	20	10	12	5	29	18	20
Libya	3,475	8	10	7	8	-17	8	0	28	0	1	-1	17	5	4
Morocco	90,906	13	11	11	15	10	54	12	9	11	0	4	15	13	15
Tunisia	9,274	22	7	8	9	1	12	10	10	24	11	5	19	11	11
ALL AFRICA	..	14	10	14	16	13	16	14	11	13	11	14	23	19	14

Note: 2002 data are preliminary (see page 2). Levels for 1995 are expressed in millions of units of national currency. Group data are medians of individual country values in each year or period.

4-3. Credit to the government

	Level	Percentage annual change											Average annual percentage growth		
	1995	1980	1993	1994	1995	1996	1997	1998	1999	2000	2001	2002	75-84	85-94	95-MR
SUB-SAHARAN AFRICA	..	19	5	35	2	11	2	16	11	1	4	8	51	15	1
excluding South Africa	..	19	4	34	3	9	0	16	13	0	4	6	53	16	1
excl. S.Africa & Nigeria	..	20	2	34	4	11	2	15	11	1	5	6	53	16	1
Angola	7	..	..	..	..	86	538	322	122	-2,024	-44	-140	..	..	153
Benin	36,262	-9	-308	-274	73	-45	8	-125	1,037	-6	95	0	..	4	.
Botswana	-6,388	15	11	19	-2	13	113	23	4	21	15	-41	..	..	.
Burkina Faso	-14,605	46	-25	-115	-704	-63	-500	-7	27	76	-36	-167	..	..	45
Burundi	7,694	9	-58	93	-20	136	64	20	43	-37	78	16	40	-10	29
Cameroon	410,935	40	1	-2	-3	-11	21	-2	8	-15	4	-7	..	46	6
Cape Verde	10,732	188	-3	46	6	4	20	0	-1	69	0	14	57	20	13
Central African Republic	40,174	26	2	38	-15	-6	-6	8	23	1	10	5	14	7	4
Chad	43,535	0	-1	38	-21	40	-1	-9	15	31	20	-6	8	33	9
Comoros	2,924	..	-41	49	-23	17	-41	62	11	-9	-16	15	..	7	-1
Congo, Dem. Rep. of	2	18	1,628	3,914	-3	..	..	..	..	..	..	-185	47	455	.
Congo, Rep. of	96,501	7	-18	-5	8	3	20	17	-16	-24	92	5	9	24	7
Côte d'Ivoire	510,099	-52	2	35	1	6	0	13	11	-19	-18	6	..	7	-1
Djibouti	7,697	..	123	112	37	30	-13	-60	17	-5	21	25	..	..	-6
Equatorial Guinea	17,432	..	5	53	-5	-3	-13	-42	11	-18	-458	79	..	17	-15
Eritrea	1,221	..	..	..	..	54	0	89	79	28	3	..	..	..	43
Ethiopia	9,916	18	19	4	-4	-3	-3	10	24	27	-7	2	39	14	7
Gabon	246,554	-3	7	50	8	-4	-6	52	-9	-63	135	-21	-27	23	-2
Gambia, The	-82	-43	-476	35	-60	-29	-42	-13	-150	268	922	1	28	..	.
Ghana	1,031,892	30	45	7	51	35	75	7	55	61	21	14	47	30	39
Guinea	100,355	..	-13	35	36	42	-15	4	..	..	19	80	..	..	24
Guinea-Bissau	-3,959	..	-979	324	72	-1	-108	85	1,383	73	-2	21	..	-22	138
Kenya	69,644	11	-10	89	17	7	16	10	-8	-6	22	18	26	15	7
Lesotho	-944	329	773	97	44	24	49	2	-51	-25	-12	-53	62	19	.
Liberia	1,498	49	15	-1	20	19	4	1,824	-8	13	14	36	50	13	77
Madagascar	943,169	81	16	33	-24	-7	-21	102	14	-1	31	32	54	9	13
Malawi	1,380	11	41	24	-9	20	11	-93	1,741	-33	297	..	27	11	12
Mali	5,096	2	-239	639	-84	-799	-37	16	-15	82	-65	98	8	-20	.
Mauritania	1,411	13	24	-17	-85	-1,118	77	44	30	38	4	54	25	12	.
Mauritius	13,358	18	20	32	11	9	26	-1	-2	-23	44	6	35	7	5
Mozambique	-1,486,000	..	95	26	75	97	36	36	-4	-10	-269	19	..	..	.
Namibia	796	..	27	4	20	49	-79	16	115	-15	-12	-115	..	..	-7
Niger	39,237	-59	-39	102	50	17	62	-14	8	-19	-14	10	..	0	6
Nigeria	272,350	6	98	55	-8	-56	-57	181	27	-159	-127	1,286	46	30	-7
Rwanda	14,249	109	27	-8	-51	-6	76	-3	22	-40	-4	..	0	37	-2
São Tomé and Principe	15,665	..	..	..	..	18	-178	-68	83	107	-168	-81	..	..	.
Senegal	179,488	53	-23	174	3	-10	-5	18	4	-15	12	-42	57	-4	-3
Seychelles	1,369	118	28	20	15	17	19	33	16	12	10	16	56	18	18
Sierra Leone	408,584	37	-14	1,689	-12	5	10	7	14	18	6	-1	41	61	8
Somalia	..	38	..	..	..	..	..	..	..	..	..	..	68	18	.
South Africa	6,376	0	51	112	-60	81	79	50	-7	3	-27	111	3	9	18
Sudan	33,177	19	65	34	47	101	16	30	34	35	16	13	26	58	34
Swaziland	-600	27	-6	-28	50	34	19	50	6	12	20	-47	..	..	.
Tanzania	446,034	37	46	5	30	3	-12	9	21	2	-25	-16	34	33	0
Togo	38,278	14	-57	-278	177	20	-3	32	0	-2	-12	-30	14	..	9
Uganda	-11,367	58	-21	-28	-105	-26	-1,469	26	-4	302	-24	108	54	75	22
Zambia	1,667,167	20	..	126	60	17	-2	86	11	60	-8	13	35	88	27
Zimbabwe	5,051	41	105	6	-4	43	167	53	-5	90	105	76	26	13	59
NORTH AFRICA	..	21	2	5	8	3	12	3	5	13	-8	10	30	11	-2
Algeria	864,285	24	20	1	28	7	15	8	24	-27	-9	..	29	27	6
Egypt, Arab Rep.	86,799	60	2	5	5	5	7	10	5	13	9	25	30	16	9
Libya	8,055	-20	2	11	8	1	-24	3	-12	-3	26	15	24	14	-2
Morocco	74,178	21	7	10	14	3	12	-1	-11	13	-8	5	21	6	2
Tunisia	473	2	-14	-12	-16	-22	81	-17	97	65	-8	0	20	2	22
ALL AFRICA	..	19	4	32	5	7	7	10	11	2	4	8	39	15	15

Note: 2002 data are preliminary (see page 2). Levels for 1995 are expressed in millions of units of national currency. Group data are medians of individual country values in each year or period.

4-4. Net foreign assets

	Billions of units of national currency											Annual average		
	1980	*1993*	*1994*	*1995*	*1996*	*1997*	*1998*	*1999*	*2000*	*2001*	*2002*	*75-84*	*85-94*	*95-MR*
SUB-SAHARAN AFRICA	..	..	..	..	..	..	..	..	..	..	..	..	..	..
excluding South Africa	..	..	..	..	..	..	..	..	..	..	..	..	..	..
excl. S.Africa & Nigeria	..	..	..	..	..	..	..	..	..	..	..	..	..	..
Angola	..	..	..	0	0	0	0	6	31	48	94	..	..	22
Benin	-23	70	160	146	173	215	206	298	354	481	446	-17	12	290
Botswana	0	11	11	12	19	22	28	30	35	43	31	0	6	28
Burkina Faso	0	106	164	236	220	204	183	170	147	148	171	6	79	185
Burundi	5	35	45	54	47	46	32	33	32	12	18	3	16	34
Cameroon	-14	-236	-318	-343	-302	-204	-195	-191	10	93	264	13	-140	-109
Cape Verde	2	6	6	5	7	6	6	10	7	10	11	2	5	8
Central African Republic	3	21	85	92	101	90	66	66	68	53	46	1	22	73
Chad	-4	-1	14	48	55	47	35	24	21	34	68	0	13	41
Comoros	..	11	16	16	19	19	15	20	23	36	39	4	8	23
Congo, Dem. Rep. of	0	0	0	0	0	0	..	..	..	-72	-222	0	0	-59
Congo, Rep. of	8	-4	4	15	25	18	-44	-11	199	11	23	-3	-16	29
Côte d'Ivoire	-223	-515	-72	58	62	100	114	25	73	396	931	-211	-411	220
Djibouti	..	37	36	34	28	26	24	34	30	38	47	21	35	33
Equatorial Guinea	..	-7	-14	-10	-7	-7	-1	5	16	61	105	..	-6	20
Eritrea	..	..	..	3	3	2	1	1	0	1	1	..	..	1
Ethiopia	0	3	5	6	5	6	6	5	5	6	11	0	1	6
Gabon	16	-33	52	9	86	69	-64	-74	146	-39	8	35	-9	18
Gambia, The	0	1	1	1	1	1	1	1	1	1	2	0	0	1
Ghana	0	-43	217	499	736	981	1,069	333	-9	1,460	3,457	-3	-76	1,066
Guinea	..	159	112	97	80	151	176	0	151	200	119	..	113	122
Guinea-Bissau	..	-5	-6	-4	-3	16	15	14	29	36	55	..	-2	20
Kenya	2	30	16	24	47	56	54	55	87	94	107	1	2	65
Lesotho	0	1	1	2	2	3	4	3	4	5	4	0	0	3
Liberia	0	-1	-1	-1	-1	-1	-28	-25	-27	-31	-44	0	0	-20
Madagascar	-110	-11	1	316	861	1,489	921	1,496	1,919	2,405	2,194	-150	-1,244	1,450
Malawi	0	0	-1	0	2	2	9	9	14	12	4	0	0	6
Mali	-8	74	107	120	184	205	172	126	197	223	324	-29	18	194
Mauritania	-2	-30	-33	-25	-11	-2	0	7	24	26	56	-3	-19	10
Mauritius	0	17	16	19	20	22	20	26	34	36	44	0	9	27
Mozambique	..	-5,671	-3,162	-3,534	-1,627	-861	-243	735	4,348	7,810	12,150	-26	-1,623	2,347
Namibia	..	0	0	0	0	1	1	2	3	3	2	..	0	1
Niger	5	24	23	22	12	0	-9	-17	3	32	29	5	21	9
Nigeria	6	63	56	108	237	228	235	663	1,275	1,433	1,387	3	29	696
Rwanda	14	5	3	28	38	46	40	45	67	81	103	8	8	56
São Tomé and Principe	..	..	..	9	19	101	139	156	169	201	241	..	..	129
Senegal	-97	-207	-130	-70	-46	36	78	119	122	197	345	-102	-204	98
Seychelles	0	0	0	0	0	0	0	0	0	0	0	0	0	0
Sierra Leone	0	-204	-339	-396	-159	-169	-220	-322	-180	-202	-140	0	-99	-224
Somalia	0	..	..	..	..	..	..	..	..	..	..	0	-63	..
South Africa	6	-16	-21	-18	-31	-23	-32	2	11	32	75	2	-4	2
Sudan	0	-59	-122	-202	-444	-494	-687	-724	-677	-697	-626	0	-22	-569
Swaziland	0	1	1	1	2	2	2	3	3	4	3	0	1	2
Tanzania	0	-384	-278	-207	-68	245	275	374	583	898	1,169	0	-164	409
Togo	0	23	43	33	13	14	8	23	67	66	90	21	57	39
Uganda	0	-104	64	177	252	392	655	790	1,197	1,519	1,553	0	-29	817
Zambia	-1	-496	-788	-1,022	-1,287	-1,228	-2,397	-2,572	-3,661	-2,794	-2,599	-1	-150	-2,195
Zimbabwe	0	-3	-2	-3	-3	-13	-30	-12	-8	-11	-12	0	-1	-12
NORTH AFRICA	..	..	..	..	..	..	..	..	..	..	..	..	..	..
Algeria	17	20	60	26	134	350	281	170	776	1,311	..	12	18	435
Egypt, Arab Rep.	-1	46	51	49	54	49	36	25	23	21	19	-1	15	34
Libya	4	2	2	3	3	2	2	3	6	7	15	2	2	5
Morocco	0	35	40	34	36	40	43	59	54	102	110	-1	13	60
Tunisia	0	1	1	1	1	2	1	2	1	2	2	0	0	1
ALL AFRICA	..	..	..	..	..	..	..	..	..	..	..	..	..	..

Note: 2002 data are preliminary (see page 2).

4-5. Growth of money supply

	Level	Percentage annual change											Average annual percentage growth		
	1995	1980	1993	1994	1995	1996	1997	1998	1999	2000	2001	2002	75-84	85-94	95-MI
SUB-SAHARAN AFRICA	..	19	12	32	15	14	16	9	16	13	15	17	16	15	1
excluding South Africa	..	16	12	33	15	14	15	9	16	15	15	18	15	13	1
excl. S.Africa & Nigeria	..	14	12	32	15	14	14	8	16	13	15	18	13	13	1
Angola	3	..	..	..	..	3,393	108	40	343	342	168	134	..	..	23
Benin	161,730	32	-13	67	-13	17	2	-5	47	35	10	-9	18	7	1
Botswana	829	10	15	11	7	15	9	46	17	7	24	7	17	18	1
Burkina Faso	213,703	20	12	39	25	7	18	-3	-2	5	-3	-7	14	8	
Burundi	38,802	3	12	28	-3	12	10	1	42	-1	17	26	15	9	1
Cameroon	319,242	13	-14	35	-12	-2	35	14	11	17	13	14	20	-3	1
Cape Verde	11,868	26	7	8	3	11	22	-2	17	11	3	9	19	10	1
Central African Republic	111,237	32	16	74	8	5	-8	-18	13	3	-3	-4	17	4	-
Chad	85,330	-16	-28	32	43	33	-5	-8	-3	18	22	27	13	-2	1
Comoros	12,040	..	5	10	-5	8	-19	-6	16	21	63	10	..	7	
Congo, Dem. Rep. of	19	73	2,461	5,635	407	..	..	..	..	..	..	47	59	448	
Congo, Rep. of	134,845	37	-20	40	0	14	9	-14	28	68	-23	14	18	1	1
Côte d'Ivoire	944,519	1	1	62	18	2	12	13	-2	-4	15	32	12	0	
Djibouti	36,998	..	4	3	-2	-3	-10	-10	3	-8	3	24	..	7	-
Equatorial Guinea	9,509	..	-29	135	58	50	-4	10	90	35	26	52	..	-11	3
Eritrea	1,135	..	..	..	..	30	36	18	46	13	28	..	..	..	2
Ethiopia	9,280	0	4	21	3	-2	8	-7	12	11	4	15	11	14	
Gabon	219,087	10	-3	42	12	26	8	-5	-5	19	4	4	11	0	
Gambia, The	471	6	6	-12	16	-4	39	0	14	37	14	56	12	15	1
Ghana	925,334	30	28	50	33	32	46	21	16	38	46	61	42	37	3
Guinea	274,125	..	19	-3	9	0	21	9	..	..	12	22	..	..	1
Guinea-Bissau	7,211	..	27	58	47	51	236	-12	22	64	8	22	..	54	4
Kenya	69,333	-8	27	13	4	14	15	3	16	9	6	19	13	18	1
Lesotho	538	..	23	12	11	19	23	25	-3	8	25	12	..	16	1
Liberia	653	-4	60	8	42	7	-1	129	15	-12	7	39	6	16	2
Madagascar	1,848,007	22	12	57	15	17	23	11	20	13	30	7	14	20	1
Malawi	2,211	7	35	51	44	25	17	57	33	37	9	..	7	24	3
Mali	198,195	5	9	48	14	21	6	5	-1	9	30	29	13	2	1
Mauritania	18,202	12	4	-5	-8	-11	8	5	6	23	15	4	14	8	
Mauritius	9,573	21	3	19	8	3	8	9	4	11	16	18	9	17	
Mozambique	3,264,000	..	52	51	35	20	25	15	25	22	18	16	..	43	2
Namibia	1,822	..	46	15	8	54	4	27	22	28	9	6	..	..	2
Niger	100,238	13	11	15	9	-10	-19	-18	15	12	35	-8	17	0	
Nigeria	207,509	50	57	43	16	14	17	19	22	62	26	16	21	32	2
Rwanda	40,658	7	11	16	41	12	23	-1	7	7	1	..	12	6	1
São Tomé and Principe	14,225	..	..	..	..	66	108	-3	5	23	54	14	..	..	3
Senegal	316,756	14	-9	54	4	8	0	16	11	6	15	6	11	2	
Seychelles	335	38	14	-3	3	34	44	20	37	6	13	22	13	10	2
Sierra Leone	49,902	20	12	10	29	7	57	7	49	4	35	31	24	58	2
Somalia	..	19	..	..	..	..	..	..	..	..	..	..	24	87	
South Africa	111,844	36	7	25	18	32	17	23	22	2	17	12	20	17	1
Sudan	40,464	31	76	55	67	86	32	29	28	42	16	30	30	57	3
Swaziland	363	22	14	7	17	16	16	2	32	0	14	9	14	16	1
Tanzania	428,284	28	33	33	30	5	10	10	16	10	10	25	21	32	1
Togo	131,199	5	-18	105	38	-8	2	7	10	22	-9	-8	16	-3	
Uganda	408,701	32	26	36	15	10	14	19	13	17	13	21	40	80	1
Zambia	227,058	0	..	45	61	19	31	17	24	51	34	29	12	67	3
Zimbabwe	11,270	37	95	18	52	23	54	24	35	53	143	170	13	24	5
NORTH AFRICA	..	21	5	11	7	7	13	8	9	8	10	7	25	12	
Algeria	520,286	17	19	8	7	13	15	21	9	17	19	..	21	10	1
Egypt, Arab Rep.	41,540	56	12	11	9	7	9	20	1	5	8	13	25	12	
Libya	6,251	29	4	13	6	1	5	0	5	4	1	4	16	7	
Morocco	135,964	8	5	11	6	6	16	8	12	8	15	9	13	14	1
Tunisia	3,637	21	4	11	10	13	13	8	16	10	10	-2	17	6	1
ALL AFRICA	..	19	12	25	12	13	15	9	16	12	15	15	16	13	1

Note: 2002 data are preliminary (see page 2). Levels for 1995 are expressed in millions of units of national currency. Group data are medians of individual country values in each year or period.

4-6. Discount rate

	Percentage											Annual average		
	1980	*1993*	*1994*	*1995*	*1996*	*1997*	*1998*	*1999*	*2000*	*2001*	*2002*	*75-84*	*85-94*	*95-MR*
SUB-SAHARAN AFRICA	8.5	11.5	12.0	13.0	12.4	12.3	10.0	11.3	10.7	9.3	12.8	8.4	10.7	11.5
excluding South Africa	8.5	11.5	12.0	12.5	11.8	12.0	9.5	11.2	10.4	9.1	11.4	8.4	10.6	11.0
excl. S.Africa & Nigeria	8.5	11.5	11.5	12.0	10.9	11.4	9.1	10.8	10.0	8.9	10.0	8.4	10.6	10.4
Angola	..	..	..	160.0	2.0	48.0	58.0	120.0	150.0	150.0	150.0	..	..	104.8
Benin	10.5	6.0	6.0	6.0	6.0	6.0	6.0	6.0	6.0	6.0	6.0	9.5	9.5	6.0
Botswana	5.8	14.3	13.5	13.0	13.0	12.5	12.5	13.3	14.3	14.3	15.3	8.3	10.2	13.5
Burkina Faso	10.5	6.0	6.0	6.0	6.0	6.0	6.0	6.0	6.0	6.0	6.0	9.5	9.5	6.0
Burundi	7.0	10.0	10.0	10.0	10.0	12.0	12.0	12.0	14.0	14.0	15.5	6.4	8.3	12.4
Cameroon	8.5	11.5	7.8	8.6	7.8	7.5	7.0	7.3	7.0	6.5	6.3	7.6	9.8	7.2
Cape Verde	..	..	..	..	..	..	..	..	..	..	..	..	..	..
Central African Republic	8.5	11.5	7.8	8.6	7.8	7.5	7.0	7.6	7.0	6.5	6.3	7.6	9.8	7.3
Chad	8.5	11.5	7.8	8.6	7.8	7.5	7.0	7.6	7.0	6.5	6.3	7.7	9.8	7.3
Comoros	..	..	..	..	..	..	..	..	..	..	..	10.0	9.3	..
Congo, Dem. Rep. of	12.0	95.0	145.0	125.0	238.0	13.0	22.0	120.0	120.0	140.0	24.0	14.7	56.3	100.3
Congo, Rep. of	8.5	11.5	7.8	8.6	7.8	7.5	7.0	7.6	7.0	6.5	6.3	7.6	9.8	7.3
Côte d'Ivoire	10.5	6.0	6.0	6.0	6.0	6.0	6.0	6.0	6.0	6.0	6.0	9.5	9.5	6.0
Djibouti	..	..	..	..	..	..	..	..	..	..	..	..	..	..
Equatorial Guinea	..	11.5	7.8	8.6	7.8	7.5	7.0	7.6	7.0	6.5	6.3	..	9.8	7.3
Eritrea	..	..	..	..	..	..	..	..	..	..	..	..	..	..
Ethiopia	..	12.0	12.0	12.0	..	..	..	..	..	..	..	..	5.6	12.0
Gabon	8.5	11.5	7.8	8.6	7.8	7.5	7.0	7.6	7.0	6.5	6.3	7.6	9.8	7.3
Gambia, The	8.0	13.5	13.5	14.0	14.0	14.0	12.0	10.5	10.0	13.0	18.0	7.6	16.7	13.2
Ghana	13.5	35.0	33.0	45.0	45.0	45.0	37.0	27.0	27.0	27.0	24.5	12.7	26.6	34.7
Guinea	..	17.0	17.0	18.0	18.0	15.0	..	..	11.5	16.3	16.3	..	14.3	15.8
Guinea-Bissau	..	6.0	6.0	6.0	6.0	6.0	6.0	6.0	6.0	6.0	6.0	..	28.3	6.0
Kenya	8.0	45.5	21.5	24.5	26.9	32.3	17.1	26.5	..	..	..	9.9	19.7	25.4
Lesotho	8.0	13.5	13.5	15.5	17.0	15.6	19.5	19.0	15.0	13.0	16.2	11.8	13.9	16.3
Liberia	..	..	..	..	..	..	..	..	..	..	..	..	..	..
Madagascar	5.5	..	..	..	..	..	..	15.0	..	..	..	8.0	11.5	15.0
Malawi	10.0	25.0	40.0	50.0	27.0	23.0	43.0	47.0	50.2	46.8	40.0	8.5	17.0	40.9
Mali	10.5	6.0	6.0	6.0	6.0	6.0	6.0	6.0	6.0	6.0	6.0	9.5	9.5	6.0
Mauritania	6.0	..	..	..	..	..	..	..	..	..	..	5.5	6.8	..
Mauritius	10.5	8.3	13.8	11.4	11.8	10.5	17.2	..	..	..	..	9.5	10.8	12.7
Mozambique	..	..	69.7	57.8	32.0	13.0	10.0	10.0	10.0	10.0	10.0	..	69.7	19.1
Namibia	..	14.5	15.5	17.5	17.8	16.0	18.8	11.5	11.3	9.3	12.8	..	16.8	14.3
Niger	10.5	6.0	6.0	6.0	6.0	6.0	6.0	6.0	6.0	6.0	6.0	9.5	9.4	6.0
Nigeria	6.0	26.0	13.5	13.5	13.5	13.5	13.5	18.0	14.0	20.5	16.5	5.9	15.5	15.4
Rwanda	9.0	11.0	11.0	16.0	16.0	10.8	11.4	11.2	11.7	13.0	13.0	7.4	10.6	12.9
São Tomé and Príncipe	..	30.0	32.0	50.0	35.0	55.0	29.5	17.0	17.0	15.5	15.5	..	33.7	29.3
Senegal	10.5	6.0	6.0	6.0	6.0	6.0	6.0	6.0	6.0	6.0	6.0	9.5	9.5	6.0
Seychelles	..	1.0	1.0	1.0	1.0	1.0	1.0	1.0	1.0	1.0	1.0	6.0	3.5	1.0
Sierra Leone	12.0	..	..	..	..	..	..	..	..	..	..	10.2	26.9	..
Somalia	..	..	..	..	..	..	..	..	..	..	..	..	..	..
South Africa	6.5	12.0	13.0	15.0	17.0	16.0	19.3	12.0	12.0	9.5	13.5	11.1	13.9	14.3
Sudan	..	..	..	..	..	..	..	..	..	..	..	..	..	..
Swaziland	7.0	11.0	12.0	15.0	16.8	15.8	18.0	12.0	11.0	9.5	13.5	11.1	11.4	13.9
Tanzania	4.8	14.5	67.5	47.9	19.0	16.2	17.6	20.2	10.7	8.7	9.2	4.5	15.2	18.7
Togo	10.5	6.0	6.0	6.0	6.0	6.0	6.0	6.0	6.0	6.0	6.0	9.5	9.5	6.0
Uganda	8.0	24.0	15.0	13.3	15.9	14.1	9.1	15.8	18.9	8.9	13.1	13.7	36.7	13.6
Zambia	6.5	72.5	20.5	40.2	47.0	17.7	..	32.9	25.7	40.1	27.9	7.5	22.5	33.1
Zimbabwe	4.5	28.5	29.5	29.5	27.0	31.5	39.5	74.4	57.8	57.2	29.7	6.3	16.3	43.3
NORTH AFRICA	5.0	8.9	8.9	8.9	7.9	5.5	7.8	7.0	5.5	5.5	5.3	5.7	9.2	6.7
Algeria	2.8	11.5	21.0	14.0	13.0	11.0	9.5	8.5	6.0	6.0	5.5	2.8	9.1	9.2
Egypt, Arab Rep	11.0	16.5	14.0	13.5	13.0	12.3	12.0	12.0	12.0	11.0	10.0	9.7	14.9	12.0
Libya	5.0	5.0	0.0	0.0	0.0	0.0	3.0	5.0	5.0	5.0	5.0	5.0	4.5	2.9
Morocco	4.9	0.0	7.2	0.0	0.0	0.0	6.0	5.4	5.0	4.7	3.8	5.4	4.1	3.1
Tunisia	5.8	8.9	8.9	8.9	7.9	..	..	..	..	..	..	6.1	10.1	8.4
ALL AFRICA	8.5	11.5	12.0	12.5	11.8	11.5	9.5	10.8	10.0	8.9	10.0	8.1	10.6	10.6

Note: 2002 data are preliminary (see page 2). Group data are medians of individual country values in each year or period.

Money and Banking

4-7. Real discount rate

	Percentage											Annual average		
	1980	*1993*	*1994*	*1995*	*1996*	*1997*	*1998*	*1999*	*2000*	*2001*	*2002*	*75-84*	*85-94*	*95-MR*
SUB-SAHARAN AFRICA	-3.6	3.8	-5.7	-0.4	1.5	3.4	4.5	6.5	3.9	2.6	3.2	-3.6	0.9	3.1
excluding South Africa	-3.5	4.6	-6.8	-0.6	1.3	3.4	4.3	6.5	3.7	2.3	3.3	-3.8	1.1	3.0
excl. S.Africa & Nigeria	-3.4	5.4	-5.7	-0.4	1.5	3.4	4.5	6.3	3.9	2.0	3.3	-3.6	1.2	3.1
Angola	..	..	..	..	-97.6	-53.6	-23.8	-36.8	-41.2	-1.0	19.7	..	..	-33.5
Benin	..	5.5	-23.5	-7.4	1.0	2.4	0.2	5.7	1.8	1.9	3.4	..	-9.0	1.1
Botswana	-6.9	-0.1	2.7	2.3	2.6	3.5	5.5	5.1	5.2	7.2	6.6	-3.1	-0.9	4.7
Burkina Faso	-1.5	5.4	-15.3	-1.3	-0.2	3.6	0.9	7.1	6.3	0.9	3.7	-0.5	6.8	2.7
Burundi	4.4	0.3	-4.2	-7.8	-13.0	-14.6	-0.4	8.3	-8.3	4.4	17.1	-5.4	1.2	-1.8
Cameroon	-1.0	15.2	-20.2	-0.4	3.7	2.6	3.7	5.7	9.2	1.9	3.4	-3.8	4.3	3.7
Cape Verde	..	..	..	..	..	..	..	..	..	..	..	..	..	..
Central African Republic	..	14.8	-13.5	-8.9	3.9	5.8	9.1	9.1	3.7	3.0	2.8	1.2	8.3	3.6
Chad	..	20.0	-23.3	-0.4	-4.1	1.8	-4.6	15.5	3.1	-5.3	1.1	-9.4	8.2	0.9
Comoros	..	..	..	..	..	..	..	..	..	..	..	..	5.0	..
Congo, Dem. Rep. of	-23.6	-90.7	-99.0	-64.9	-47.3	-59.0	-5.5	-42.8	-64.2	-47.8	-5.7	-25.6	-48.4	-42.2
Congo, Rep. of	..	6.5	-24.4	-0.7	-2.1	..	..	2.1	8.0	6.4	1.8	..	5.6	2.6
Côte d'Ivoire	-3.7	3.8	-15.9	-7.3	3.4	1.9	1.3	5.2	3.5	1.6	2.8	-2.1	3.8	1.6
Djibouti	..	..	..	..	..	..	..	..	..	..	..	..	..	..
Equatorial Guinea	..	9.7	-22.4	-2.5	1.7	4.4	3.9	1.5	0.9	1.2	3.2	..	9.8	1.8
Eritrea	..	..	..	..	..	..	..	..	..	..	..	..	..	..
Ethiopia	..	8.2	4.1	1.8	..	..	..	..	..	..	..	..	-1.5	1.8
Gabon	-3.4	10.9	-20.8	-1.0	7.0	3.4	5.5	9.7	6.5	..	..	-4.9	7.8	5.2
Gambia, The	1.1	9.1	9.1	8.8	11.7	10.9	10.8	6.5	9.0	91.5	4.5	-4.2	-2.4	19.2
Ghana	-24.4	8.0	6.5	-9.1	-1.1	13.4	14.8	13.0	1.4	-4.5	8.4	-30.2	-6.3	4.5
Guinea	..	22.2	12.3	11.7	14.6	12.9	..	..	4.4	10.3	12.9	..	-2.1	11.1
Guinea-Bissau	..	-28.4	-8.0	-27.1	-29.7	-28.9	-0.5	6.7	-2.4	2.6	2.2	..	-10.7	-9.6
Kenya	-5.1	-0.3	-5.7	22.6	16.5	18.8	9.7	19.6	..	..	..	-3.4	0.9	17.4
Lesotho	-7.1	0.3	4.9	5.7	7.0	..	..	..	8.4	25.0	-13.2	-1.7	0.2	6.6
Liberia	..	..	..	..	..	..	..	..	..	..	..	..	..	..
Madagascar	-10.8	-9.1	-28.0	-32.9	-16.5	-4.3	-5.8	4.6	..	..	..	-5.3	-9.3	-11.0
Malawi	..	1.8	4.0	-18.2	-7.7	12.7	10.2	1.5	15.9	15.4	..	-3.2	-2.5	4.3
Mali	..	6.3	-13.9	-6.6	-0.8	6.4	1.9	7.3	6.7	0.8	0.9	..	7.1	2.1
Mauritania	..	..	..	..	..	..	..	..	..	..	..	..	-0.5	..
Mauritius	-22.2	-2.0	6.0	5.1	4.9	3.4	9.7	..	..	..	..	-3.4	3.3	5.8
Mozambique	..	..	4.0	2.1	-11.1	5.2	8.3	6.9	-2.5	0.8	-5.8	..	4.0	0.5
Namibia	..	5.5	4.3	6.8	9.0	6.6	11.8	2.6	2.1	-0.3	1.3	..	4.1	5.0
Niger	0.2	7.3	-22.1	-4.1	0.7	3.0	1.4	8.5	3.0	1.9	3.3	-2.1	9.9	2.2
Nigeria	-3.6	-19.8	-27.7	-34.3	-12.2	4.9	2.9	12.6	-0.5	6.7	3.2	-11.7	-9.4	-2.1
Rwanda	1.6	-1.2	..	..	8.0	-1.1	4.9	13.9	7.1	9.7	10.3	-3.6	4.5	7.5
São Tomé and Principe	..	3.6	4.2	9.3	-1.8	-7.6	-14.2	0.6	5.4	5.5	5.8	..	-1.0	0.4
Senegal	1.6	6.6	-19.9	-1.7	3.2	4.4	4.8	5.1	5.2	2.8	3.7	-1.2	5.8	3.4
Seychelles	..	-0.4	-0.7	1.2	2.1	0.4	-1.5	-5.0	-5.0	-4.7	0.8	1.2	1.6	-1.5
Sierra Leone	-0.8	..	..	..	..	..	..	..	..	..	..	-11.9	-31.6	..
Somalia	..	..	..	..	..	..	..	..	..	..	..	..	..	..
South Africa	-6.3	2.1	3.7	5.8	9.0	6.4	11.8	6.6	6.4	4.5	2.6	-1.5	-0.1	6.6
Sudan	..	..	..	..	..	..	..	..	..	..	..	..	..	..
Swaziland	-9.8	-0.9	-1.6	2.4	9.7	8.1	9.1	5.6	-1.1	3.4	..	-2.4	-1.4	5.3
Tanzania	-19.5	-8.6	25.9	15.2	-1.6	0.1	4.3	11.4	4.5	3.4	4.4	-13.2	-11.1	5.2
Togo	-1.6	7.1	-23.8	-9.0	1.3	-2.1	5.0	6.1	4.0	2.0	2.8	-0.8	6.1	1.3
Uganda	..	16.9	4.8	4.3	8.0	6.7	9.1	8.8	15.6	6.7	13.4	-23.2	-17.0	9.1
Zambia	..	-40.1	-21.6	4.5	0.5	-5.7	..	..	..	..	..	..	-36.0	-0.2
Zimbabwe	-0.9	0.7	5.9	5.6	4.6	10.7	5.8	10.0	1.3	-11.0	..	-5.5	-2.0	3.9
NORTH AFRICA	-6.4	-4.9	1.9	-5.8	-2.9	2.0	3.8	5.2	5.6	4.1	4.0	-4.8	-1.9	2.0
Algeria	-6.2	-7.5	-6.2	-12.2	-4.8	5.0	4.3	5.7	5.6	1.7	4.0	-6.8	-6.5	1.2
Egypt, Arab Rep.	-8.0	3.9	5.4	-1.9	5.4	7.3	7.5	8.7	9.1	8.5	7.1	-3.1	-1.2	6.5
Libya	-6.6	-5.5	-4.9	-6.7	-3.9	-3.4	-0.7	2.3	..	..	..	-3.8	-2.3	-2.5
Morocco	-4.1	-4.9	1.9	-5.8	-2.9	-1.0	3.2	4.7	3.0	4.1	1.0	-4.0	-1.4	0.8
Tunisia	..	4.7	4.0	2.5	4.0	..	..	..	..	..	..	-1.7	3.3	3.2
ALL AFRICA	-4.1	3.7	-4.5	-0.9	1.3	3.4	4.3	6.3	4.0	2.7	3.3	-4.1	0.7	3.1

Note: 2002 data are preliminary (see page 2). Real discount rate in each year is the nominal discount rate deflated by the annual change in the CPI.

4-8. Commercial bank lending rate

	Percentage										Annual average		
	1980	*1993*	*1994*	*1995*	*1996*	*1997*	*1998*	*1999*	*2000*	*2001*	*2002*	*75-84*	*85-94*	*95-MR*
SUB-SAHARAN AFRICA	12.0	17.5	17.5	18.5	22.0	22.0	22.0	21.9	22.0	20.7	18.2	12.3	15.9	20.9
excluding South Africa	12.3	17.5	17.5	19.3	22.0	22.0	22.0	21.9	22.0	20.7	18.5	12.2	15.7	21.1
excl. S.Africa & Nigeria	12.5	17.5	17.5	18.5	22.0	22.0	22.0	22.0	22.0	20.7	18.2	12.4	15.5	20.9
Angola	..	..	..	206.3	217.9	37.8	45.0	80.3	103.2	96.0	97.3			110.5
Benin	14.5	..										13.8	14.9	..
Botswana	8.5	14.9	13.9	14.3	14.5	14.1	13.5	14.6	15.3	15.8	16.0	13.5	11.1	14.8
Burkina Faso	14.5	..										13.8	14.9	..
Burundi	12.0	13.8	14.2	15.3	..	..	..	15.2	15.8	16.8	19.5	12.0	12.7	16.5
Cameroon	13.0	17.5	17.5	16.0	22.0	22.0	22.0	22.0	22.0	20.7	18.0	13.0	15.9	20.6
Cape Verde	6.5	10.0	10.7	12.0	12.0	12.1	12.5	12.0	11.9	12.8	13.2	6.5	10.1	12.3
Central African Republic	10.5	17.5	17.5	16.0	22.0	22.0	22.0	22.0	22.0	20.7	18.0	11.1	15.1	20.6
Chad	11.0	17.5	17.5	16.0	22.0	22.0	22.0	22.0	22.0	20.7	18.0	10.7	14.5	20.6
Comoros	..	..	..	..	..	..	..	..	..	..	..	15.0	14.0	..
Congo, Dem. Rep. of	..	..	398.3	293.9	247.0	134.6	29.0	124.6	165.0	167.9	66.8	..	398.3	153.6
Congo, Rep. of	11.0	17.5	17.5	16.0	22.0	22.0	22.0	22.0	22.0	20.7	18.0	11.3	14.8	20.6
Côte d'Ivoire	14.5	..	..	..	..	..	..	..	..	..	..	13.8	14.9	..
Djibouti	..	..	..	..	..	..	..	..	..	11.5	11.3	8.5	9.5	11.4
Equatorial Guinea	..	17.5	17.5	16.0	22.0	22.0	22.0	22.0	22.0	20.7	18.0	..	16.3	20.6
Eritrea	..	..	..	..	..	..	..	..	..	..	..		..	..
Ethiopia	..	14.0	14.3	15.1	13.9	10.5	10.5	10.6	10.9	10.9	8.7	..	8.2	11.4
Gabon	12.5	17.5	17.5	16.0	22.0	22.0	22.0	22.0	22.0	20.7	18.0	11.8	14.9	20.6
Gambia, The	15.0	26.1	25.0	25.0	25.5	25.5	25.4	24.0	24.0	24.0	24.0	16.7	25.8	24.7
Ghana	19.0	..										19.3	23.1	
Guinea	..	24.5	22.0	21.5	..	..	19.6	19.9	19.4	..	..		20.8	20.1
Guinea-Bissau	..	63.6	36.3	32.9	51.8	..	..	..	..	..	..		38.6	42.3
Kenya	10.6	30.0	36.2	28.8	33.8	30.2	29.5	22.4	22.3	19.7	18.5	11.8	19.9	25.6
Lesotho	11.0	15.8	14.3	16.4	17.7	18.0	20.1	19.1	17.1	16.6	17.1	15.2	16.5	17.8
Liberia	18.4	..	14.5	15.6	..	16.8	21.7	16.7	20.5	22.1	20.2	19.9	14.9	19.1
Madagascar	..	26.0	30.5	37.5	32.8	30.0	27.0	28.0	26.5	25.3	25.3	..	25.7	29.0
Malawi	16.7	29.5	31.0	47.3	45.3	28.3	37.7	53.6	53.1	56.2	50.5	17.7	22.6	46.5
Mali	14.5	..	..	..	..	..	..	..	..	..	..	13.8	14.9	..
Mauritania	12.0	..	..	..	..	..	..	..	..	..	..	12.0	11.0	..
Mauritius	..	16.6	18.9	20.8	20.8	18.9	19.9	21.6	20.8	21.1	21.0	13.5	16.2	20.6
Mozambique	..	..	..	..	..	..	24.4	19.6	19.0	22.7	26.7	..	..	22.5
Namibia	..	18.0	17.1	18.5	19.2	20.2	20.7	18.5	15.3	14.5	13.8	..	19.7	17.6
Niger	14.5	..	..	..	..	..	..	..	..	..	..	13.8	14.9	..
Nigeria	8.4	31.6	20.5	20.2	19.8	17.8	18.2	20.3	21.3	23.4	24.8	8.0	19.3	20.7
Rwanda	13.5	15.0	..	..	..	..	..	..	..	..	..	13.3	14.3	..
São Tomé and Principe	..	37.0	30.0	52.0	38.0	51.5	55.6	40.3	39.7	37.0	37.1	..	30.2	43.9
Senegal	14.5	..	..	..	..	..	..	..	..	..	..	13.8	14.9	..
Seychelles	..	15.7	15.7	15.8	16.2	14.9	14.4	12.0	11.4	11.1	11.1	..	15.6	13.4
Sierra Leone	11.0	50.5	27.3	28.8	32.1	23.9	23.8	26.8	26.3	24.3	22.2	12.7	37.0	26.0
Somalia	..	..	..	..	..	..	..	..	..	..	..	..	..	..
South Africa	9.5	16.2	15.6	17.9	19.5	20.0	21.8	18.0	14.5	13.8	15.8	14.1	17.5	17.7
Sudan	..	..	..	..	..	..	..	..	..	..	..	..	..	..
Swaziland	9.5	14.3	14.3	17.1	18.7	19.5	19.5	17.4	14.0	13.3	15.3	12.7	14.9	16.8
Tanzania	11.5	31.0	39.0	42.8	34.0	26.3	22.9	21.9	21.6	20.3	16.4	11.4	27.0	25.8
Togo	14.5	..	..	..	..	..	..	..	..	..	..	13.8	15.2	..
Uganda	10.8	..	..	20.2	20.3	21.4	20.9	21.5	22.9	22.7	19.1	15.2	34.3	21.1
Zambia	9.5	113.3	70.6	45.5	53.8	46.7	31.8	40.5	38.8	46.2	45.2	9.7	41.9	43.6
Zimbabwe	17.5	36.3	34.9	34.7	34.2	32.5	42.1	55.4	68.2	38.0	36.5	20.3	18.7	42.7
NORTH AFRICA	7.1	7.0	13.0	8.2	7.8	6.3	12.0	11.5	11.6	11.4	10.8	7.5	8.8	9.9
Algeria	..	..	16.0	19.0	19.0	12.5	11.0	10.0	10.0	9.5	8.5	..	16.0	12.4
Egypt, Arab Rep.	13.3	18.3	16.5	16.5	15.6	13.8	13.0	13.0	13.2	13.3	13.8	12.5	17.3	14.0
Libya	7.0	7.0	..	..	..	..	..	7.0	7.0	7.0	7.0	7.0	7.0	7.0
Morocco	7.0	..	10.0	..	..	..	13.5	13.5	13.3	13.3	13.1	7.0	8.9	13.3
Tunisia	7.3	..	..	..	..	..	..	..	..	..	..	7.9	8.9	..
ALL AFRICA	12.0	17.5	17.5	17.9	21.4	21.4	21.8	21.5	21.3	20.7	18.0	11.9	15.6	20.5

Note: 2002 data are preliminary (see page 2). Group data are medians of individual country values in each year or period.

Money and Banking

4-9. Commercial bank deposit rate

	Percentage											Annual average		
	1980	1993	1994	1995	1996	1997	1998	1999	2000	2001	2002	75-84	85-94	95-MR
SUB-SAHARAN AFRICA	6.2	7.8	8.7	10.0	10.8	9.1	7.6	7.6	7.0	6.2	5.5	6.6	7.8	8.0
excluding South Africa	6.2	7.8	8.4	9.7	10.8	8.5	7.5	7.5	6.7	6.0	5.3	6.6	7.6	7.7
excl. S.Africa & Nigeria	6.2	7.8	8.3	9.4	10.7	9.1	7.3	6.9	6.6	5.9	5.2	6.6	7.6	7.6
Angola	..	..	..	125.9	147.1	29.3	36.9	36.6	39.6	47.9	48.7	..	..	64.0
Benin	6.2	..	..	..	..	..	3.5	3.5	3.5	3.5	3.5	6.5	6.5	3.5
Botswana	5.0	13.5	10.4	10.0	10.4	9.3	8.7	9.5	10.1	10.2	10.3	9.3	9.0	9.8
Burkina Faso	6.2	..	..	..	..	..	3.5	3.5	3.5	3.5	3.5	6.5	6.5	3.5
Burundi	2.5	..	..	..	..	..	..	..	..	..	..	3.4	4.9	..
Cameroon	7.5	7.8	8.1	5.5	5.4	5.0	5.0	5.0	5.0	5.0	5.0	7.3	7.5	5.1
Cape Verde	..	4.0	4.0	5.0	5.0	5.0	5.3	4.8	4.3	4.7	4.9	..	4.0	4.9
Central African Republic	5.5	7.8	8.1	5.5	5.5	5.0	5.0	5.0	5.0	5.0	5.0	6.4	7.5	5.1
Chad	5.5	7.8	8.1	5.5	5.5	5.0	5.0	5.0	5.0	5.0	5.0	5.3	6.3	5.1
Comoros	..	..	..	..	..	..	..	..	..	..	..	7.5	7.0	..
Congo, Dem. Rep. of	..	..	60.0	60.0	60.0	..	..	..	..	..	..	..	60.0	60.0
Congo, Rep. of	6.5	7.8	8.1	5.5	5.5	5.0	5.0	5.0	5.0	5.0	5.0	6.5	7.8	5.1
Côte d'Ivoire	6.2	..	..	..	..	..	3.5	3.5	3.5	3.5	3.5	6.5	6.5	3.5
Djibouti	..	..	..	..	..	..	..	..	..	2.8	1.2	..	..	2.0
Equatorial Guinea	..	7.8	8.1	5.5	5.5	5.0	5.0	5.0	5.0	5.0	5.0	..	7.5	5.1
Eritrea	..	..	..	..	..	..	..	..	..	..	..	..	..	..
Ethiopia	..	11.5	11.5	11.5	9.4	7.0	6.0	6.3	6.7	7.0	4.1	..	6.7	7.2
Gabon	7.5	7.8	8.1	5.5	5.5	5.0	5.0	5.0	5.0	5.0	5.0	7.4	7.9	5.1
Gambia, The	5.0	13.0	12.6	12.5	12.5	12.5	12.5	12.5	12.5	12.5	12.7	7.1	13.3	12.5
Ghana	11.5	23.6	23.1	28.7	34.5	35.8	32.0	23.6	28.6	30.9	16.2	12.0	18.9	28.8
Guinea	..	19.8	18.0	17.5	..	..	6.4	5.7	7.5	8.0	7.4	..	19.4	8.7
Guinea-Bissau	..	53.9	28.7	26.5	47.3	4.6	3.5	3.5	3.5	3.5	3.5	..	34.5	12.0
Kenya	5.8	..	..	13.6	17.6	16.7	18.4	9.6	8.1	6.6	5.5	7.7	11.5	12.0
Lesotho	..	8.1	8.4	13.3	12.7	11.8	10.7	7.5	4.9	4.8	5.2	10.2	10.3	8.9
Liberia	10.3	..	6.3	6.4	..	6.4	6.2	6.3	6.2	5.9	6.2	10.4	6.8	6.2
Madagascar	..	19.5	19.5	18.5	19.0	14.4	8.0	15.3	15.0	12.0	12.0	..	19.7	14.3
Malawi	7.9	21.8	25.0	37.3	26.3	10.2	19.1	33.2	33.3	35.0	28.1	9.8	15.4	27.8
Mali	6.2	..	..	..	..	..	3.5	3.5	3.5	3.5	3.5	6.5	6.5	3.5
Mauritania	..	..	..	..	..	..	..	..	..	..	..	5.5	5.7	..
Mauritius	..	8.4	11.0	12.2	10.8	9.1	9.3	10.9	9.6	9.8	9.9	10.7	10.4	10.2
Mozambique	..	..	33.4	38.8	18.1	25.4	8.2	7.9	9.7	15.0	18.0	..	33.4	17.6
Namibia	..	9.6	9.2	10.8	12.6	12.7	12.9	10.8	7.4	6.8	7.8	..	10.7	10.2
Niger	6.2	..	..	..	..	..	3.5	3.5	3.5	3.5	3.5	6.5	6.5	3.5
Nigeria	5.3	23.2	13.1	13.5	13.1	7.2	10.1	12.8	11.7	15.3	16.7	5.1	14.8	12.5
Rwanda	6.3	5.0	..	..	10.9	9.5	8.5	7.9	8.9	9.2	8.0	5.1	6.6	9.0
São Tomé and Principe	..	35.0	35.0	35.0	31.0	36.8	38.3	27.0	21.0	15.0	15.0	..	28.7	27.4
Senegal	6.2	..	..	..	..	..	3.5	3.5	3.5	3.5	3.5	6.5	6.5	3.5
Seychelles	..	9.5	8.9	9.2	9.9	9.2	7.5	5.1	4.8	4.9	4.9	9.1	9.6	6.9
Sierra Leone	9.2	27.0	11.6	7.0	14.0	9.9	7.1	9.5	9.2	7.7	8.2	9.2	25.6	9.1
Somalia	..	..	..	..	..	..	..	..	..	..	..	..	..	..
South Africa	5.5	11.5	11.1	13.5	14.9	15.4	16.5	12.2	9.2	9.4	10.8	10.0	14.1	12.7
Sudan	6.0	..	..	..	..	..	..	..	..	..	..	9.2	..	..
Swaziland	4.5	7.9	7.5	9.4	11.1	12.0	11.9	9.9	6.5	6.2	8.0	8.6	8.8	9.4
Tanzania	4.0	..	..	24.6	13.6	7.8	7.8	7.8	7.4	4.8	3.3	4.0	12.6	9.6
Togo	6.2	..	..	..	..	..	3.5	3.5	3.5	3.5	3.5	6.5	6.5	3.5
Uganda	6.8	16.3	10.0	7.6	10.6	11.8	11.4	8.7	9.8	8.5	5.6	9.9	24.2	9.3
Zambia	7.0	..	46.1	30.2	42.1	34.5	13.1	20.3	20.2	23.4	23.3	6.2	23.7	25.9
Zimbabwe	3.5	29.4	26.8	25.9	21.6	18.6	29.1	38.5	50.2	13.9	18.4	6.6	15.6	27.0
NORTH AFRICA	4.9	6.8	5.9	5.5	5.3	4.9	7.9	6.9	6.3	5.6	4.9	4.7	7.1	5.9
Algeria	3.0	8.0	12.0	16.0	14.5	9.8	8.5	7.5	7.5	6.3	5.3	3.0	6.7	9.4
Egypt, Arab Rep.	8.3	12.0	11.8	10.9	10.5	9.8	9.4	9.2	9.5	9.5	9.3	8.0	11.6	9.8
Libya	5.1	5.5	..	..	..	..	..	3.2	3.0	3.0	3.0	4.7	5.5	3.1
Morocco	4.9	..	..	..	..	..	7.3	6.4	5.2	5.0	4.5	5.6	8.4	5.7
Tunisia	2.5	..	..	..	..	..	..	..	..	..	..	3.4	6.7	..
ALL AFRICA	6.2	7.8	8.7	10.0	10.7	9.1	7.6	7.5	7.0	6.2	5.3	6.5	7.8	7.9

Note: 2002 data are preliminary (see page 2). Group data are medians of individual country values in each year or period.

Figure 4-1. Credit to private and public sectors as a share of GDP, 2002*

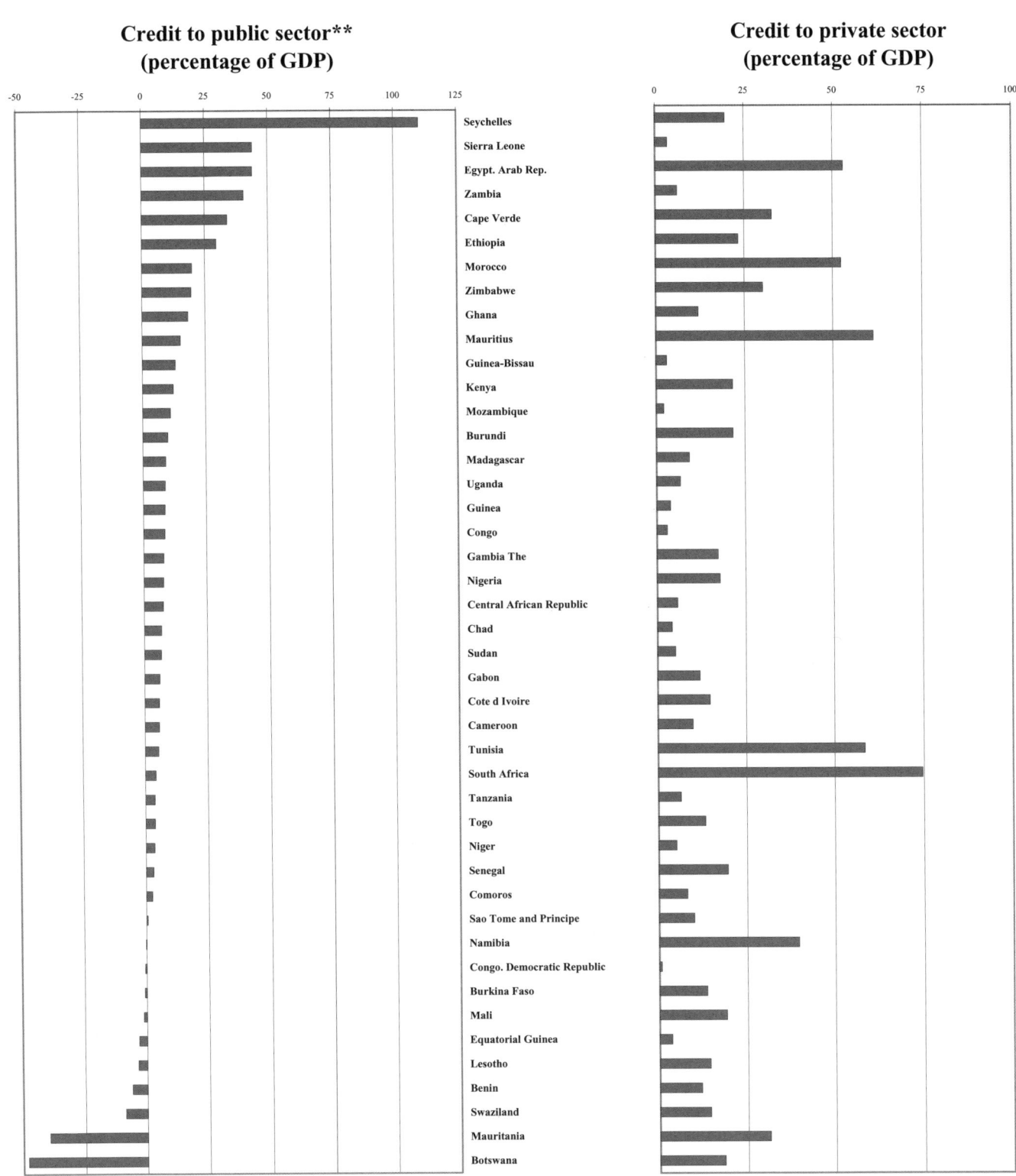

Credit to public sector**
(percentage of GDP)

Credit to private sector
(percentage of GDP)

* Or most recent year available.
** Sorted by credit to public sector.

Figure 4-2. Real discount rate, average 1993-2002*

(percentage)

* Or most recent year available.

Technical notes

Tables

Table 4-1. Domestic credit. Domestic credit (IMF, *IFS*, line 32) includes all domestic assets of the banking system. It is the sum of the claims on the central government (net), on official entities, and on the private sector. Domestic credit comprises credit to the private sector (Table 4-2) and credit to the government (Table 4-3).

Table 4-2. Credit to the private sector. Credit to the private sector is taken from IMF, *IFS* (line 32d).

Table 4-3. Credit to the government. Credit to the government sector is taken from IMF, *IFS* (line 32an). Negative numbers for net claims on the central government indicate that government is a net depositor to the banking system. The government's financial position with the monetary system is always presented on a net basis because its recourse to the monetary system cannot always be analyzed meaningfully in terms of liquidity preferences or by considering debtor and creditor positions separately. Movements in net claims on the central government (that is, claims or credits less government deposits) indicate the impact of government operations on the liquidity of the rest of the economy.

Table 4-4. Net foreign assets. Data for net foreign assets are from the IMF, *IFS* (line 31n). As for credit to the government, the financial position of the foreign sector with the monetary system is presented on a net basis for the same reason as noted above. Movements in net foreign assets (that is, foreign assets less foreign liabilities) indicate the direct monetary impact of a country's transactions with the rest of the world.

Table 4-5. Growth of money supply. This table shows the annual percentage change in money (M1), defined as the sum of currency outside of banks and demand deposits other than those of the central government (IMF, *IFS*, line 34). The presentation of the money supply in the form of growth rates rather than levels reflects the importance from the point of view of macroeconomic stability of the rate of growth rather than the stock of money.

Table 4-6. Discount rate. The discount rate reported here is the nominal interest rate at which the monetary authorities lend to (or discount eligible paper from) deposit money banks (IMF, *IFS*, line 60).

Table 4-7. Real discount rate. The real discount rate in each year is the nominal discount rate (Table 4-6) deflated by the annual change in inflation as reflected by the consumer price index (CPI) (Table 3-3). It has been calculated using the formula:

$$\{[l + (i/100)] / [(\pi_t / \pi_{t-1})] - 1\} \times 100$$

where i is nominal interest rate and ∂ is inflation rate based on the CPI.

Table 4-8. Commercial bank lending rate. The commercial bank lending rate (IMF, *IFS*, line 60p) is the rate charged to borrowers by commercial banks for short- and medium-term use of funds.

Table 4-9. Commercial bank deposit rate. The deposit rate (IMF, *IFS*, line 60l) is the rate paid to depositors on time savings and demand deposits by deposit money banks and similar financial institutions.

Figures

The following indicators have been used to derive the figures in this chapter.

Figure 4-1. Credit to the private sector (Table 4-2); credit to the public sector (Table 4-3); gross domestic product (Table 2-5).

Figure 4-2. Real discount rate (Table 4-7).

Methodology used for regional aggregations and period averages in Chapter 4

Table	Aggregations[a]		Period averages[b]	
	(4)	*(8)*	*(1)*	*(2)*
4-1	x			x
4-2	x			x
4-3	x			x
4-4		x	x	
4-5	x			x
4-6	x		x	
4-7	x		x	
4-8	x		x	
4-9	x		x	

Note: Regional aggregations are shown in the rows for Sub-Saharan Africa, North Africa, and All Africa. Period averages are shown in the last three columns. This table shows only the methodologies used in this chapter. The definitions of the methodologies used throughout the book are given below.

a. Regional aggregations: (1) simple total; (2) simple total of the first indicator divided by the simple total of the second indicator (same country coverage); (3) simple total of the gap-filled indicator; (4) simple total of the gap-filled main indicator divided by the simple total of the gap-filled secondary indicator; (5) simple total of the first gap-filled main indicator less the simple total of the second gap-filled main indicator, all divided by the simple total of the secondary indicator; (6) weighted total (by population); (7) median; (8) no aggregation; (9) simple arithmetic mean.

b. Period averages: (1) arithmetic mean (using the same series as shown in the table; i.e., ratio if the rest of the table is shown as ratio, level if the rest of the table is shown as level, growth rate if the rest is shown as growth rate); (2) least-squares growth rate (using main indicator); (3) least-squares growth rate (using main indicator in constant terms, with the rest of the table in current terms).

5

External Sector

The external sector provides data on economic and financial relations between African countries and the rest of the world, with detailed accounting of commodity trade, one of the principal components of the current account within the balance of payments framework. Commodity trade and price data can also provide a partial basis for analyzing Africa's constraints and performance in the international marketplace, including its terms of trade. Commodity exports are a major source of foreign exchange. Other sources of foreign exchange include receipts from factor and nonfactor services, borrowing from abroad, incoming foreign investment, and foreign transfers and grants.

The balance of payments is a system of accounts covering a given period that is intended to record systematically (a) flows of real resources, including the services of the original factors of production, between the domestic economy of a country and the rest of the world; (b) changes in the country's foreign assets and liabilities that arise from economic transactions; and (c) transfer payments, which are the counterpart of real resources or financial claims provided to, or received from, the rest of the world that carry no provision for repayment.

The tables provide gross entries for goods and services and net entries for unrequited transfers (official and private) and other financial flows; a table for current account balance as traditionally defined (with transfers above the line) is also shown. The information is presented for broad aggregates; fuller detail can be found in the IMF's *Balance of Payments Manual (*1993) and *Balance of Payments Yearbook.*

Unit values for exports (f.o.b.) and imports (c.i.f.) measure changes in the aggregate price level of a country's exports and imports of goods and nonfactor services over time. Unit values reflect average price changes for broad groups of commodities, rather than for any single commodity. The terms of trade indicate relative movements in export and import unit values (here, they are based on goods and nonfactor services from the national accounts). If the prices of exports rise while the prices of imports rise more slowly, stay constant, or decline, the same quantity of exports "buys" a bigger quantity of imports. The effect of such price changes is equivalent to an increase in the real value of output (or increased productivity in value terms) of the export sector. Were import prices to rise more quickly than export prices, the reverse would be true. Export figures for specific commodities show physical quantities rather than value in either current or constant prices. Most of the key nonagricultural primary commodities are exported from a few countries with substantial mineral resources. Variations in export prices and earnings for the five major oil-exporting countries in Sub-Saharan Africa (which in the 1980s accounted for about half of Sub-Saharan export earnings) have dominated trends in this region as a whole.

5-1. Merchandise exports, f.o.b.

	Millions of U.S. dollars (current prices)											Average annual percentage growth		
	1980	*1993*	*1994*	*1995*	*1996*	*1997*	*1998*	*1999*	*2000*	*2001*	*2002*	*75-84*	*85-94*	*95-MR*
SUB-SAHARAN AFRICA	78,719	62,582	65,647	77,877	86,311	87,534	75,895	79,544	97,254	92,691	94,844	6.9	3.1	3.6
excluding South Africa	53,107	37,837	39,307	47,805	56,043	56,351	46,781	50,963	65,586	62,014	62,852	5.4	2.2	4.9
excl. S.Africa & Nigeria	26,479	27,912	29,901	36,079	39,910	40,803	36,690	39,051	44,145	44,050	47,966	6.0	2.8	4.5
Angola	..	2,908	3,016	3,730	5,095	5,006	3,543	5,157	7,921	6,534	8,343	..	6.4	11.7
Benin	222	341	308	235	263	191	239	223	189	210	214	7.1	3.3	-3.8
Botswana	544	1,722	1,874	2,161	2,218	2,822	2,073	2,658	2,683	2,326	2,279	20.0	10.7	2.2
Burkina Faso	161	260	191	237	233	229	323	254	206	224	236	8.1	6.1	0.9
Burundi	66	74	81	113	40	87	64	56	49	39	48	..	-4.5	-8.5
Cameroon	1,506	1,652	1,433	1,655	1,605	1,816	1,800	1,682	2,125	2,129	1,911	18.2	-2.7	4.1
Cape Verde	9	4	20	24	30	38	23	8	40	37	42	15.2	0.5	5.6
Central African Republic	147	132	162	179	142	155	138	96	111	107	110	8.6	1.4	-6.5
Chad	71	152	135	243	238	243	257	188	183	189	172	0.8	6.1	-1.0
Comoros	11	22	11	11	6	6	6	9	14	17	19	..	4.5	9.4
Congo, Dem. Rep. of	2,269	1,144	1,256	1,612	1,652	1,196	1,180	974	892	880	1,088	5.9	-4.9	-6.2
Congo, Rep. of	911	1,119	959	1,282	1,654	1,657	1,369	1,556	2,449	2,055	2,249	22.9	1.0	9.7
Côte d'Ivoire	3,013	2,519	2,869	3,820	4,256	4,275	4,458	4,486	3,739	3,761	4,775	6.4	-0.1	3.0
Djibouti	..	..	..	38	40	43	59	69	72	..	..	..	..	16.1
Equatorial Guinea	..	52	65	86	101	291	460	814	1,363	2,182	2,035	..	9.2	64.0
Eritrea	0	36	65	81	95	54	28	20	37	20	54	..	..	-12.2
Ethiopia	459	222	245	453	413	599	602	484	486	441	431	6.3	-7.8	3.9
Gabon	2,531	2,326	2,365	2,643	3,190	3,043	2,209	2,526	2,750	2,897	3,080	8.9	5.2	1.4
Gambia, The	51	141	124	121	114	108	130	120	126	140	147	3.2	10.5	2.4
Ghana	1,104	1,064	1,227	1,431	1,810	1,810	2,091	2,006	1,936	1,867	2,057	-3.8	6.7	5.3
Guinea	500	672	610	649	610	660	659	646	667	723	700	4.7	3.4	1.7
Guinea-Bissau	..	16	33	24	22	48	26	51	62	46	51	..	6.6	10.3
Kenya	1,363	1,103	1,484	1,924	2,083	2,060	2,012	1,755	1,773	1,881	2,169	5.8	2.0	1.6
Lesotho	58	132	147	154	182	196	193	189	214	276	373	10.4	19.4	10.1
Liberia	600	..	..	..	..	..	..	..	..	..	..	1.4	..	..
Madagascar	437	332	447	566	512	507	522	584	829	965	499	2.0	2.0	5.4
Malawi	281	317	327	404	483	530	528	447	402	426	421	8.8	3.7	1.1
Mali	205	349	337	442	433	561	561	596	547	725	1,002	10.9	7.8	11.2
Mauritania	196	380	393	479	484	408	360	333	345	339	330	6.8	1.4	-4.3
Mauritius	406	1,343	1,334	1,473	1,629	1,727	1,599	1,680	1,523	1,633	1,569	..	14.7	1.3
Mozambique	281	132	164	174	226	230	245	284	364	703	682	..	7.3	20.2
Namibia	1,534	1,293	1,320	1,418	1,463	1,365	1,209	1,196	1,313	1,142	1,205	..	6.1	-2.2
Niger	576	301	225	287	302	272	334	287	283	266	288	14.6	-1.6	1.2
Nigeria	25,956	9,924	9,415	11,734	16,117	15,539	10,114	11,927	21,395	17,949	14,912	3.8	1.1	5.9
Rwanda	134	68	32	50	62	93	64	62	90	93	67	5.6	-10.8	8.9
São Tomé and Principe	17	5	6	5	5	5	5	4	4	4	5	-3.0	-6.5	-4.1
Senegal	480	719	791	968	988	905	988	1,047	920	1,003	1,087	2.1	4.0	2.3
Seychelles	6	49	52	53	78	115	123	146	195	217	236	-1.8	34.7	22.8
Sierra Leone	214	118	194	102	105	88	65	61	75	77	104	-1.0	3.2	-7.0
Somalia	133	..	..	..	..	..	..	..	..	..	..	3.6	-4.1	..
South Africa	25,698	24,750	26,342	30,085	30,306	31,218	29,127	28,610	31,729	30,731	32,042	10.3	4.7	1.4
Sudan	689	306	524	556	620	594	596	780	1,807	1,699	1,948	1.0	-2.4	20.2
Swaziland	368	675	746	868	856	962	976	937	910	1,054	957	6.3	14.2	2.8
Tanzania	508	411	486	593	696	794	588	543	663	776	903	0.1	3.0	4.8
Togo	476	215	226	357	372	352	396	392	327	349	371	7.1	-2.5	3.0
Uganda	319	157	254	595	590	684	458	549	460	458	474	1.3	-8.6	1.7
Zambia	1,457	994	1,067	1,186	993	1,119	816	756	746	884	916	-0.9	3.2	-4.0
Zimbabwe	281	1,610	1,947	2,216	2,496	2,424	1,925	1,924	1,791	1,715	1,730	0.0	4.5	-3.5
NORTH AFRICA	41,259	31,134	30,602	37,625	41,279	43,368	38,416	41,314	56,574	56,637	55,783	9.7	3.0	7.3
Algeria	13,652	10,410	8,892	10,260	13,220	13,820	10,140	12,320	21,700	21,125	19,660	14.3	-0.4	10.9
Egypt, Arab Rep.	3,854	3,725	3,337	4,957	4,609	5,345	5,128	4,445	6,388	7,078	7,005	9.4	0.4	7.8
Libya	21,919	..	..	..	..	..	..	..	..	..	..	6.7	-2.5	..
Morocco	2,414	4,922	5,541	6,871	6,886	7,039	7,144	7,621	7,508	7,256	7,663	5.1	10.5	2.9
Tunisia	2,395	3,746	4,643	5,470	5,519	5,559	5,724	5,873	5,840	6,024	6,528	12.0	11.3	3.1
ALL AFRICA	119,829	93,423	96,343	115,356	127,511	130,527	113,826	120,144	151,767	146,833	148,498	8.0	3.0	4.6

Note: 2002 data are preliminary (see page 2).

5-2. Merchandise imports, f.o.b.

	Millions of U.S. dollars (current prices)											Average annual percentage growth		
	1980	1993	1994	1995	1996	1997	1998	1999	2000	2001	2002	75-84	85-94	95-MR
SUB-SAHARAN AFRICA	60,606	57,007	59,342	71,966	73,931	79,528	77,149	75,626	78,699	80,137	85,547	8.2	4.0	3.1
excluding South Africa	42,350	38,538	37,482	44,560	46,325	50,667	49,931	51,129	51,356	54,328	58,056	8.1	3.3	4.4
excl. S.Africa & Nigeria	27,645	30,229	31,025	36,383	38,119	41,041	40,661	40,593	40,277	42,003	44,703	6.2	4.3	3.4
Angola	..	1,463	1,454	1,852	2,040	2,597	2,079	3,109	3,040	3,179	3,709	..	1.7	11.2
Benin	499	539	374	439	444	426	451	474	447	467	491	8.3	4.3	2.3
Botswana	602	1,455	1,364	1,606	1,468	1,926	1,995	1,874	1,778	1,663	1,596	17.4	12.8	1.8
Burkina Faso	368	534	355	485	563	510	634	581	519	510	549	8.1	3.4	3.2
Burundi	165	173	173	176	100	96	124	97	108	108	115	..	1.0	-4.8
Cameroon	1,452	1,021	1,017	1,074	1,200	1,347	1,452	1,483	1,538	1,617	1,922	12.5	-3.2	7.5
Cape Verde	80	152	191	219	206	211	208	223	233	232	277	10.1	8.9	3.3
Central African Republic	185	158	151	179	125	145	150	86	83	82	97	8.7	0.1	-8.7
Chad	55	205	212	277	243	246	271	239	276	515	812	-1.8	3.8	13.2
Comoros	22	50	45	54	49	48	42	43	37	40	45	..	6.0	-2.5
Congo, Dem. Rep. of	1,519	614	667	997	1,011	694	775	458	680	807	1,061	0.0	-6.3	0.0
Congo, Rep. of	545	500	613	653	586	649	558	523	596	681	706	15.2	-1.0	0.9
Côte d'Ivoire	2,614	1,784	1,608	2,456	2,510	2,537	2,776	2,643	2,300	2,295	2,352	6.1	1.4	2.0
Djibouti	..	..	..	207	201	204	240	252	271	..	..	..	..	6.5
Equatorial Guinea	..	52	67	97	127	206	434	440	464	696	750	..	6.7	37.1
Eritrea	0	275	396	404	514	495	527	495	470	537	520	..	..	3.0
Ethiopia	692	1,052	915	1,063	1,144	1,309	1,357	1,558	1,611	1,556	1,696	16.4	-1.1	7.7
Gabon	829	845	777	898	969	1,018	987	841	887	934	988	4.6	0.3	1.2
Gambia, The	116	205	179	209	189	176	207	194	193	219	232	11.0	11.1	2.2
Ghana	908	1,728	1,580	1,684	2,295	3,042	2,918	3,252	2,759	2,831	2,714	-1.6	10.7	7.2
Guinea	339	602	583	583	584	573	577	582	583	562	650	5.0	4.9	0.6
Guinea-Bissau	..	54	54	59	57	73	51	66	86	92	82	..	1.3	6.4
Kenya	2,585	1,606	2,042	2,666	2,598	2,944	3,028	2,679	3,033	3,176	3,058	8.1	1.8	4.0
Lesotho	424	859	869	983	996	1,012	841	793	737	675	796	14.2	11.1	-3.8
Liberia	478	..	..	..	..	..	..	..	..	..	..	1.8	..	..
Madagascar	764	510	546	628	629	682	672	742	933	950	620	5.4	5.3	4.5
Malawi	308	627	536	474	624	783	579	674	563	584	727	2.7	10.9	2.5
Mali	308	502	466	556	552	556	558	632	595	735	764	9.7	7.1	5.3
Mauritania	321	375	304	395	403	355	358	305	336	372	418	7.0	0.9	1.0
Mauritius	494	1,541	1,556	1,875	1,945	2,013	1,972	2,046	2,006	1,913	1,799	..	16.5	1.2
Mozambique	720	830	881	727	783	760	817	1,200	1,162	1,063	1,263	..	7.6	6.6
Namibia	1,094	1,335	1,406	1,548	1,555	1,644	1,489	1,396	1,432	1,325	1,368	..	9.5	-1.5
Niger	677	259	263	297	306	300	396	317	324	320	374	11.0	0.3	3.0
Nigeria	14,735	8,293	6,470	8,183	8,216	9,630	9,276	10,531	11,068	12,303	13,326	12.7	0.1	8.3
Rwanda	196	268	367	194	213	277	256	249	240	238	234	12.3	3.6	-1.8
São Tomé and Principe	15	26	24	23	20	19	17	22	21	22	22	12.5	2.3	-0.5
Senegal	973	1,102	1,022	1,216	1,264	1,176	1,281	1,373	1,336	1,428	1,603	4.3	3.7	4.3
Seychelles	84	216	188	214	263	304	352	375	304	415	376	12.4	11.3	9.2
Sierra Leone	334	130	131	120	185	81	85	68	137	163	227	1.4	-1.5	4.0
Somalia	402	..	..	..	..	..	..	..	..	..	..	15.0	-8.6	..
South Africa	18,268	18,518	21,875	27,412	27,618	28,880	27,244	24,542	27,373	25,869	27,556	8.7	5.7	1.0
Sudan	1,127	533	1,045	1,066	1,340	1,422	1,732	1,256	1,366	1,395	2,153	0.2	3.5	6.2
Swaziland	538	772	816	1,064	1,062	1,067	1,083	1,068	1,046	1,132	1,037	16.6	11.8	1.9
Tanzania	1,089	1,472	1,591	1,510	1,370	1,388	1,376	1,368	1,368	1,563	1,514	3.6	8.5	-0.2
Togo	524	251	229	350	447	508	553	490	486	506	515	9.4	-1.4	7.8
Uganda	318	523	672	1,085	1,218	899	966	1,039	954	953	1,066	4.5	4.4	1.9
Zambia	1,114	1,019	1,003	1,194	1,056	1,218	971	871	978	1,253	1,204	0.3	6.7	0.6
Zimbabwe	308	1,512	1,778	2,128	2,247	2,654	2,020	1,675	1,520	1,455	1,413	1.4	7.3	-5.4
NORTH AFRICA	31,015	37,896	37,651	45,426	44,783	46,533	46,560	49,505	51,708	52,004	56,342	8.0	3.6	4.0
Algeria	9,596	7,990	9,154	10,100	9,090	8,130	8,630	8,960	9,300	10,795	12,260	5.6	-0.7	2.6
Egypt, Arab Rep.	6,814	12,879	10,377	13,372	14,263	16,718	15,321	16,969	17,861	16,431	17,411	10.2	2.6	5.4
Libya	10,368	..	..	..	..	..	..	..	..	..	..	12.0	0.4	..
Morocco	3,770	6,981	7,648	9,353	9,080	8,903	9,463	9,957	10,601	10,494	11,129	7.3	9.6	3.9
Tunisia	3,453	5,757	6,210	7,458	7,280	7,514	7,875	8,015	8,093	8,397	9,165	13.2	9.3	3.7
ALL AFRICA	90,663	94,454	96,653	116,996	118,444	125,890	123,440	124,587	129,827	131,597	141,250	7.7	3.8	3.5

Note: 2002 data are preliminary (see page 2).

5-3. Exports of total services (nonfactor and factor)

	Millions of U.S. dollars (current prices)											Average annual percentage growth		
	1980	1993	1994	1995	1996	1997	1998	1999	2000	2001	2002	75-84	85-94	95-MR
SUB-SAHARAN AFRICA	12,335	13,236	13,354	16,262	17,375	18,238	18,644	19,004	19,738	19,626	20,589	6.6	5.2	4.4
excluding South Africa	8,812	9,273	8,637	10,512	11,272	11,603	12,097	12,374	12,592	12,852	14,106	8.0	5.0	4.9
excl. S.Africa & Nigeria	6,352	9,126	8,473	10,300	10,872	11,226	10,990	11,177	11,364	11,599	12,834	9.1	5.8	3.6
Angola	..	117	163	129	311	251	158	179	313	252	282	..	3.5	6.7
Benin	84	137	108	162	168	162	191	187	189	160	181	11.3	7.7	4.1
Botswana	203	747	417	744	669	833	929	804	705	718	690	14.8	15.4	3.4
Burkina Faso	65	80	67	80	71	55	53	46	45	52	49	9.2	13.5	-5.9
Burundi	26	25	23	27	17	13	11	8	6	16	18	..	8.5	-8.0
Cameroon	395	394	310	405	456	507	521	574	612	597	674	21.7	-2.9	8.7
Cape Verde	14	46	53	68	85	99	89	108	117	136	159	43.2	6.4	12.7
Central African Republic	58	54	45	53	47	43	40	22	16	22	19	7.0	0.4	-13.9
Chad	0	47	28	79	55	54	65	59	61	67	79	-13.0	-2.3	6.7
Comoros	3	35	29	38	38	35	22	23	19	21	22	..	23.8	-7.4
Congo, Dem. Rep. of	135	151	66	159	73	64	119	48	88	101	123	3.1	-4.7	2.0
Congo, Rep. of	119	68	159	96	101	106	-108	172	149	182	191	7.6	1.0	6.8
Côte d'Ivoire	588	773	536	813	774	741	790	750	626	712	787	8.4	3.7	1.2
Djibouti	..	..	..	192	188	188	206	196	195	..	..	..	..	0.9
Equatorial Guinea	..	5	4	4	4	4	7	7	7	7	614	..	-18.2	47.3
Eritrea	0	57	80	99	113	160	94	54	70	137	141	..	..	2.0
Ethiopia	131	291	283	354	413	441	458	460	514	535	542	5.0	4.6	7.5
Gabon	350	344	231	286	298	263	249	261	280	290	326	12.2	8.5	2.2
Gambia, The	21	77	62	70	75	80	86	82	79	68	85	10.0	13.6	2.3
Ghana	110	156	171	178	451	471	494	498	520	548	571	-5.8	16.2	15.3
Guinea	54	187	153	118	124	111	111	113	68	99	79	..	18.8	-7.0
Guinea-Bissau	..	5	6	6	7	8	4	5	6	7	7	..	-1.9	1.9
Kenya	835	1,146	1,184	1,050	974	955	872	963	1,014	1,130	1,147	7.1	7.4	0.3
Lesotho	305	479	482	519	505	495	415	372	333	267	270	14.8	6.1	-8.7
Liberia	13	..	..	..	..	..	..	..	..	..	..	18.0	..	..
Madagascar	82	187	208	254	292	287	306	347	379	376	257	2.6	13.8	4.7
Malawi	34	18	31	28	44	51	43	59	57	63	58	-5.4	-2.7	9.8
Mali	58	99	78	88	103	102	111	99	110	154	168	10.7	9.1	8.4
Mauritania	73	34	40	48	33	23	41	39	43	48	50	9.6	1.3	3.3
Mauritius	154	660	630	757	890	944	908	1,007	1,113	1,207	1,240	..	19.6	8.0
Mozambique	171	240	246	292	314	342	333	356	405	311	545	..	9.2	6.7
Namibia	205	181	203	348	282	310	289	270	229	175	191	..	-3.6	-4.7
Niger	68	49	37	41	39	39	54	45	53	63	70	7.4	-2.6	7.9
Nigeria	2,164	171	187	239	427	405	1,129	1,219	1,250	1,284	1,318	2.7	-9.6	30.8
Rwanda	49	37	22	38	27	60	57	59	74	77	74	27.2	-3.9	16.0
São Tomé and Principe	6	5	6	6	6	7	7	13	13	14	14	20.0	9.2	14.8
Senegal	416	577	504	604	460	440	502	500	472	465	503	9.0	5.8	-1.0
Seychelles	97	211	201	224	247	265	284	285	280	291	314	15.4	7.3	4.9
Sierra Leone	21	70	76	61	61	24	30	31	35	38	39	42.5	4.3	-8.0
Somalia	71	..	..	..	..	..	..	..	..	..	..	13.9	-8.6	..
South Africa	3,560	3,975	4,720	5,757	6,110	6,641	6,555	6,638	7,153	6,783	6,499	8.5	5.7	3.5
Sudan	341	70	78	127	57	48	30	101	32	32	66	18.6	-13.4	-8.3
Swaziland	83	100	98	152	304	275	262	234	369	285	259	15.4	-2.7	10.5
Tanzania	179	206	369	511	472	520	601	695	694	710	734	-1.1	9.8	8.3
Togo	95	115	81	103	162	117	120	104	105	96	100	17.7	0.5	-0.6
Uganda	11	85	90	87	157	192	218	227	245	264	253	9.2	14.7	15.3
Zambia	168	107	123	152	143	228	144	130	147	192	192	3.7	4.9	3.3
Zimbabwe	34	401	443	542	646	646	660	472	358	293	300	5.2	9.1	-8.0
NORTH AFRICA	11,109	18,463	19,221	21,076	23,231	24,448	23,803	24,938	25,753	27,038	29,306	12.2	8.8	4.5
Algeria	978	760	798	800	750	1,330	1,110	940	1,300	1,551	1,807	7.4	1.2	10.5
Egypt, Arab Rep.	2,662	8,332	8,677	9,556	10,636	11,241	10,455	11,015	11,420	11,696	12,757	19.9	11.8	3.9
Libya	1,446	..	..	..	..	..	..	..	..	..	..	12.8	2.5	..
Morocco	896	2,288	2,238	2,425	2,932	2,643	3,020	3,302	3,281	3,535	3,571	8.1	10.2	5.9
Tunisia	1,214	2,143	2,364	2,657	2,697	2,692	2,848	3,009	2,860	3,022	3,329	11.3	9.3	3.4
ALL AFRICA	21,318	29,313	30,050	34,718	37,667	39,589	39,514	40,820	42,277	43,193	46,069	11.7	7.2	4.5

Note: 2002 data are preliminary (see page 2).

5-4. Imports of total services (nonfactor and factor)

	Millions of U.S. dollars (current prices)											Average annual percentage growth		
	1980	1993	1994	1995	1996	1997	1998	1999	2000	2001	2002	75-84	85-94	95-MR
SUB-SAHARAN AFRICA	32,085	34,368	33,845	39,037	41,047	41,244	41,774	43,806	47,761	48,484	48,459	7.5	4.2	4.2
excluding South Africa	24,449	26,341	25,403	29,098	31,158	30,775	31,806	33,443	36,719	37,349	38,437	8.5	4.6	4.8
excl. S.Africa & Nigeria	15,773	21,541	20,148	23,681	25,916	25,468	25,244	25,882	27,727	29,847	30,052	9.5	5.3	4.2
Angola	..	2,509	2,469	2,726	3,872	3,890	3,885	4,070	4,426	5,128	5,665	..	16.6	9.7
Benin	112	192	171	226	242	234	236	255	238	228	249	11.2	3.4	2.7
Botswana	351	588	778	960	1,106	1,208	1,043	1,222	1,280	1,030	1,140	18.6	7.9	3.5
Burkina Faso	228	230	165	204	198	180	190	179	174	181	177	9.1	4.7	-0.5
Burundi	58	133	110	120	57	61	62	45	53	49	50	..	3.9	-10.0
Cameroon	877	1,626	1,071	1,115	1,270	1,320	1,208	1,267	1,451	1,577	1,364	17.7	1.2	3.8
Cape Verde	8	36	40	62	77	88	98	127	121	132	158	29.4	9.0	16.3
Central African Republic	144	155	126	156	124	123	134	80	84	77	87	7.0	2.1	-7.7
Chad	28	240	188	235	246	250	291	246	269	369	519	-7.6	5.5	9.7
Comoros	12	52	45	52	48	45	34	34	25	25	27	..	2.6	-9.4
Congo, Dem. Rep. of	1,160	1,092	1,186	1,266	845	753	971	692	645	692	673	8.5	1.9	-7.5
Congo, Rep. of	650	1,219	1,253	1,588	2,031	1,416	1,331	1,604	1,766	1,647	1,748	16.3	10.0	2.2
Côte d'Ivoire	2,110	2,484	1,638	2,359	2,383	2,222	2,419	2,381	2,035	1,916	2,019	11.6	5.0	-0.1
Djibouti	..	..	..	88	90	91	98	80	81	..	..	..	..	-2.0
Equatorial Guinea	..	51	82	95	224	345	411	672	1,204	1,894	1,595	..	21.5	51.3
Eritrea	0	1	7	44	70	108	77	105	39	47	45	..	..	11.5
Ethiopia	105	314	273	293	318	406	386	397	425	457	441	-1.9	8.8	6.6
Gabon	1,414	1,688	1,336	1,679	1,985	1,833	1,511	1,663	1,850	1,916	1,939	10.8	3.4	2.8
Gambia, The	44	80	70	79	68	73	81	78	80	73	83	14.3	33.6	1.4
Ghana	355	568	555	602	662	791	780	768	766	730	785	0.4	7.8	3.8
Guinea	238	403	365	407	453	406	455	426	388	385	366	..	3.4	-0.7
Guinea-Bissau	..	39	41	48	48	48	37	45	52	52	45	..	6.0	1.1
Kenya	872	719	787	1,222	1,102	1,036	880	838	899	1,016	769	4.9	2.6	-2.1
Lesotho	58	160	165	201	180	182	165	132	112	102	110	12.9	18.2	-7.9
Liberia	97	..	..	..	..	..	..	..	..	..	..	28.2	..	..
Madagascar	368	443	477	538	536	490	520	518	629	595	506	9.9	4.5	1.5
Malawi	330	82	111	125	149	165	137	146	142	130	217	11.5	-4.9	4.4
Mali	221	356	322	395	446	424	432	417	416	588	693	7.9	4.7	7.1
Mauritania	172	258	221	295	298	233	222	253	223	243	271	13.2	-1.2	-0.4
Mauritius	201	602	583	666	723	792	740	799	794	863	833	..	15.1	4.1
Mozambique	155	366	393	416	404	423	509	592	648	917	804	..	4.8	11.5
Namibia	787	380	358	429	456	397	314	322	310	268	246	..	-4.2	-6.3
Niger	339	143	193	215	193	180	193	166	164	168	182	10.7	-0.7	-2.2
Nigeria	8,498	4,806	5,250	5,420	5,251	5,315	6,559	7,550	8,972	7,510	8,382	5.3	2.2	7.4
Rwanda	139	154	132	156	169	222	223	213	231	225	230	13.4	-0.2	6.7
São Tomé and Principe	7	22	22	28	27	27	18	23	20	25	24	14.7	7.9	-1.3
Senegal	475	787	657	763	550	532	575	606	581	569	622	12.0	3.7	-1.4
Seychelles	43	104	95	115	133	145	165	183	218	241	291	14.6	14.3	14.1
Sierra Leone	95	174	217	135	141	65	75	84	95	102	123	3.4	10.7	-5.9
Somalia	139	..	..	..	..	..	..	..	..	..	..	9.9	6.1	..
South Africa	7,720	8,077	8,485	9,986	9,944	10,519	10,024	10,423	11,109	11,202	10,102	10.5	2.9	2.1
Sudan	449	131	240	177	202	178	215	398	1,227	1,621	1,370	12.4	-6.9	35.1
Swaziland	121	125	96	194	311	290	382	268	405	296	236	9.8	-1.4	9.3
Tanzania	160	723	805	659	759	793	1,168	1,005	852	810	832	5.7	9.6	2.1
Togo	227	201	186	208	272	228	202	205	181	178	208	14.0	1.0	-1.6
Uganda	132	223	241	371	450	460	511	521	596	612	671	6.2	7.4	11.0
Zambia	872	530	566	588	490	622	536	480	519	561	563	3.1	1.0	-0.5
Zimbabwe	330	836	1,016	1,120	1,224	1,415	1,048	993	710	694	661	8.8	7.7	-7.4
NORTH AFRICA	7,995	12,616	16,132	16,894	16,860	15,468	19,536	17,507	18,664	19,324	20,262	12.8	2.6	2.8
Algeria	5,035	3,510	3,770	4,320	4,710	4,630	4,590	5,070	5,500	5,604	5,702	16.1	-1.5	4.8
Egypt, Arab Rep.	2,931	2,620	5,273	4,952	4,688	3,894	7,342	5,069	5,796	6,118	6,452	20.4	-1.5	3.6
Libya	..	..	..	..	..	..	..	..	..	..	..	..	..	..
Morocco	2,076	3,045	3,124	3,459	3,280	3,072	3,190	3,175	3,001	3,079	3,341	9.0	8.1	-0.4
Tunisia	918	2,012	2,138	2,250	2,274	2,121	2,203	2,212	2,254	2,335	2,474	11.5	10.9	1.2
ALL AFRICA	41,760	47,449	50,173	56,278	58,338	57,252	61,576	61,808	66,995	68,361	69,207	8.2	3.8	3.8

Note: 2002 data are preliminary (see page 2).

5-5. Net private transfers

	Millions of U.S. dollars (current prices)											Annual average		
	1980	1993	1994	1995	1996	1997	1998	1999	2000	2001	2002	75-84	85-94	95-MR
SUB-SAHARAN AFRICA	-303	2,437	2,815	2,570	3,037	3,947	3,610	3,891	4,263	4,595	4,571	359	1,470	3,811
excluding South Africa	-397	2,444	2,827	3,215	3,783	4,670	4,349	4,818	5,189	5,334	5,143	240	1,431	4,563
excl. S.Africa & Nigeria	-397	1,652	2,278	2,416	2,839	2,803	2,808	3,193	3,486	3,536	3,310	240	1,217	3,049
Angola	..	-5	-4	-34	11	38	79	110	0	0	0	26	-21	25
Benin	107	94	50	68	67	77	71	74	84	81	71	60	79	74
Botswana	-11	-1	-62	391	173	273	264	252	327	370	435	-5	-21	311
Burkina Faso	112	153	98	106	84	74	74	65	55	35	50	75	144	68
Burundi	3	17	21	16	11	9	6	6	5	8	16	6	12	9
Cameroon	19	-95	-41	-23	7	86	80	100	97	85	93	11	-68	66
Cape Verde	40	71	81	93	96	71	79	107	114	109	127	30	50	100
Central African Republic	0	-31	-10	-11	-10	-10	-9	-6	-8	-8	-20	0	-20	-10
Chad	-4	-23	-8	2	4	4	26	26	38	26	17	-6	-8	18
Comoros	2	11	7	9	12	0	27	28	24	26	28	2	6	19
Congo, Dem. Rep. of	-79	-123	-98	-124	0	0	0	0	0	0	0	-47	-84	-16
Congo, Rep. of	-1	-9	60	-2	-4	-4	-11	-6	7	-3	-2	-44	-32	-3
Côte d'Ivoire	-706	-305	-259	-439	-474	-452	-478	-458	-353	-341	-501	-403	-388	-437
Djibouti	..	..	..	-11	-10	-9	-5	-7	-9	..	..	..	..	-9
Equatorial Guinea	..	-3	0	-3	-3	-1	0	0	0	0	0	0	-2	-1
Eritrea	0	165	276	215	244	352	190	244	196	175	206	0	57	228
Ethiopia	20	248	247	311	313	33	88	289	410	379	364	37	199	273
Gabon	-124	-209	-163	-192	-216	-218	-160	-170	-181	-186	-192	-81	-156	-189
Gambia, The	2	13	15	16	17	17	24	20	16	27	29	2	7	21
Ghana	-3	261	271	263	276	400	454	472	496	600	680	7	189	455
Guinea	-8	-79	-82	-92	-49	-36	-39	-31	-15	-13	-16	-8	-51	-36
Guinea-Bissau	..	1	1	3	2	2	16	5	8	16	21	-10	0	9
Kenya	27	147	147	409	433	497	476	566	769	694	577	56	105	553
Lesotho	2	183	195	217	195	198	155	152	135	123	135	29	94	164
Liberia	-29	..	..	..	..	..	..	..	..	..	..	-32	-25	..
Madagascar	-21	114	46	63	78	102	68	94	102	99	19	-14	68	78
Malawi	..	64	20	-4	-24	-19	-25	9	8	10	10	15	36	-4
Mali	40	93	85	96	90	73	68	68	62	70	76	24	69	75
Mauritania	-28	28	14	30	39	54	56	61	35	48	30	-25	47	44
Mauritius	16	92	93	88	101	109	92	86	90	55	64	21	67	86
Mozambique	0	0	0	0	0	0	0	0	0	0	0	0	0	0
Namibia	0	351	327	409	433	452	435	390	427	342	280	0	186	396
Niger	-57	-34	-41	-23	-25	-22	-6	-5	4	14	16	-40	-34	-6
Nigeria	..	792	549	799	945	1,867	1,541	1,625	1,703	1,798	1,834	-137	306	1,514
Rwanda	0	22	45	16	27	25	18	18	11	22	25	1	15	20
São Tomé and Principe	1	2	3	1	1	1	1	1	0	0	0	1	1	0
Senegal	0	40	39	40	40	35	36	82	162	236	134	7	20	96
Seychelles	0	-6	-7	-5	-6	-6	-8	-7	-6	-6	-10	1	1	-7
Sierra Leone	0	0	0	0	0	6	5	7	7	6	8	1	1	5
Somalia	57	..	..	..	..	..	..	..	..	..	..	43	..	..
South Africa	239	-641	-608	-645	-753	-724	-744	-926	-926	-738	-572	133	-134	-754
Sudan	257	81	68	60	321	429	490	446	315	412	357	267	219	354
Swaziland	0	0	0	0	2	1	3	1	-13	-74	-18	1	1	-12
Tanzania	22	197	465	18	20	26	18	-38	-38	-19	-2	22	305	-2
Togo	1	10	9	11	10	9	11	21	29	30	30	-1	9	19
Uganda	2	108	304	330	421	19	37	21	167	147	228	12	118	171
Zambia	-176	-19	-19	-20	-17	-16	-27	-16	-18	-20	-20	-86	-33	-19
Zimbabwe	120	26	86	120	149	126	128	115	-70	-39	-35	87	27	62
NORTH AFRICA	..	..	..	..	..	..	..	..	..	7,092	7,121	..	..	7,106
Algeria	..	..	..	..	..	..	..	..	0	815	840	..	..	552
Egypt, Arab Rep.	2,791	3,835	3,232	3,279	2,798	3,256	3,718	3,772	3,747	2,973	2,899	2,091	3,285	3,305
Libya	-1,089	..	..	..	..	..	..	..	..	..	..	-1,075	-550	..
Morocco	1,070	2,141	2,096	2,261	2,526	2,158	2,293	2,165	2,332	2,522	2,571	822	1,797	2,354
Tunisia	348	597	688	753	835	766	813	886	807	781	811	255	520	807
ALL AFRICA	2,817	9,010	8,832	8,862	9,197	10,127	10,434	10,715	11,149	11,687	11,692	3,054	6,742	10,483

Note: 2002 data are preliminary (see page 2). Nigeria's series shows a data break between 1991 and 1992.

5-6. Net official current transfers

	Millions of U.S. dollars (current prices)											Annual average		
	1980	*1993*	*1994*	*1995*	*1996*	*1997*	*1998*	*1999*	*2000*	*2001*	*2002*	*75-84*	*85-94*	*95-MR*
SUB-SAHARAN AFRICA	1,495	1,532	1,612	2,055	2,439	1,855	2,270	1,953	2,022	2,644	3,015	1,547	2,098	2,282
excluding South Africa	..	2,166	2,208	2,055	2,439	1,855	2,270	1,953	2,022	2,644	3,015	1,422	2,271	2,282
excl. S.Africa & Nigeria	..	2,112	2,257	2,121	2,507	1,881	2,295	1,933	2,158	2,670	3,037	1,450	2,260	2,325
Angola	..	171	249	190	214	68	91	102	28	91	89	..	92	109
Benin	0	64	5	6	4	70	52	64	40	84	56	0	22	47
Botswana	65	0	0	0	0	0	0	0	0	0	0	31	120	0
Burkina Faso	0	108	129	59	68	61	81	41	40	52	39	0	60	55
Burundi	42	111	144	136	50	51	50	46	71	94	36	45	90	67
Cameroon	83	76	61	80	28	0	25	17	0	34	32	47	76	27
Cape Verde	0	34	40	45	45	36	42	41	22	13	39	0	33	35
Central African Republic	0	50	32	33	8	23	34	30	27	30	26	27	47	26
Chad	0	49	129	78	57	59	24	9	6	8	6	0	97	31
Comoros	11	0	0	27	21	19	4	3	2	4	5	20	19	11
Congo, Dem. Rep. of	267	7	99	153	103	-1	32	18	146	268	363	137	76	135
Congo, Rep. of	0	0	19	44	35	6	8	1	12	6	6	0	5	15
Côte d'Ivoire	..	141	23	43	132	72	81	71	23	45	36	29	104	63
Djibouti	..	..	..	60	57	61	74	68	52	..	..	..	..	62
Equatorial Guinea	..	1	7	7	4	6	4	1	1	2	3	0	5	4
Eritrea	0	17	44	22	27	51	59	77	102	117	43	0	10	62
Ethiopia	60	108	87	148	392	226	261	213	291	395	435	40	61	295
Gabon	..	14	15	0	0	0	17	17	17	17	17	..	15	11
Gambia, The	..	0	30	27	25	28	36	31	31	31	24	1	5	29
Ghana	0	256	201	260	206	160	288	148	154	263	221	0	46	212
Guinea	0	0	0	0	0	0	0	0	0	0	0	0	0	0
Guinea-Bissau	..	21	26	30	30	39	15	23	33	25	24	6	27	27
Kenya	0	94	-1	-4	13	19	0	-2	91	88	0	0	91	26
Lesotho	-90	0	0	0	0	0	0	0	0	0	0	-174	7	0
Liberia	36	..	..	..	..	..	..	..	..	..	..	57	78	..
Madagascar	0	70	44	17	81	80	17	35	34	47	80	37	97	49
Malawi	0	0	0	0	0	0	0	0	0	0	0	0	0	0
Mali	-6	132	143	97	106	56	47	39	65	66	44	2	128	65
Mauritania	118	86	41	32	104	105	87	105	110	74	226	119	88	105
Mauritius	0	5	7	15	12	3	10	5	6	7	-3	3	9	7
Mozambique	0	0	0	0	0	0	0	0	0	0	0	0	0	0
Namibia	0	0	0	0	0	0	0	0	0	0	0	0	148	0
Niger	154	61	0	0	0	0	0	0	0	0	0	127	66	0
Nigeria	-167	54	-49	-66	-68	-26	-25	20	-135	-25	-22	-44	11	-43
Rwanda	104	78	347	231	196	147	149	176	206	170	170	92	118	181
São Tomé and Principe	0	2	3	5	1	10	9	6	6	4	2	0	6	5
Senegal	28	-26	165	132	126	143	135	77	90	68	73	-10	13	106
Seychelles	15	22	15	13	16	15	17	10	9	9	13	13	21	13
Sierra Leone	26	21	25	19	57	19	17	31	64	77	121	11	20	51
Somalia	143	..	..	..	..	..	..	..	..	..	..	111	286	..
South Africa	0	0	0	0	0	0	0	0	0	0	0	0	0	0
Sudan	229	85	82	60	37	129	365	309	198	278	631	146	259	251
Swaziland	79	0	0	0	0	0	0	0	0	0	0	46	30	0
Tanzania	0	266	0	0	0	0	0	0	0	0	0	42	103	0
Togo	86	28	16	26	24	21	22	..	..	..	..	55	52	23
Uganda	0	0	0	0	0	0	0	0	0	0	0	0	0	0
Zambia	0	0	0	0	0	0	0	0	0	0	27	10	0	3
Zimbabwe	0	0	0	0	0	0	0	0	50	70	70	0	0	24
NORTH AFRICA	..	..	..	..	..	..	..	..	..	766	750	..	1,233	758
Algeria	0	0	0	0	0	0	0	0	0	0	0	0	0	0
Egypt, Arab Rep.	..	1,902	814	919	724	890	883	1,097	932	769	754	..	1,471	871
Libya	-46	..	..	..	..	..	..	..	..	..	..	-85	-39	..
Morocco	47	154	173	70	50	48	52	-11	94	-3	-4	15	130	37
Tunisia	42	0	0	0	25	25	18	16	18	0	0	36	4	13
ALL AFRICA	..	3,588	2,598	3,043	3,237	2,817	3,222	3,054	3,067	3,410	3,764	1,432	3,382	3,202

Note: 2002 data are preliminary (see page 2).

External Sector

5-7. Current account balance, excluding net capital grants

	Millions of U.S. dollars (current prices)										*Annual average*		
	1980	*1993*	*1994*	*1995*	*1996*	*1997*	*1998*	*1999*	*2000*	*2001*	*2002*	*75-84*	*85-94*	*95-MR*
SUB-SAHARAN AFRICA	-116	-10,902	-9,144	-11,698	-5,551	-8,862	-18,028	-14,760	-2,658	-8,498	-10,389	-8,245	-7,783	-10,056
excluding South Africa	-3,624	-12,391	-9,238	-9,496	-3,660	-6,599	-15,702	-14,118	-2,131	-8,203	-10,699	-8,044	-9,718	-8,826
excl. S.Africa & Nigeria	-7,934	-10,233	-7,620	-8,598	-7,613	-9,439	-12,627	-10,827	-6,304	-9,396	-7,032	-6,277	-8,345	-8,980
Angola	..	-781	-499	-563	-281	-1,124	-2,094	-1,631	796	-1,430	-660	..	-308	-873
Benin	-197	-95	-73	-194	-185	-159	-133	-181	-183	-162	-218	-174	-85	-177
Botswana	-152	426	87	730	486	793	228	618	656	721	669	-101	264	612
Burkina Faso	-259	-163	-35	-207	-305	-271	-292	-355	-347	-329	-353	-203	-181	-307
Burundi	-86	-79	-15	-4	-39	2	-55	-28	-30	-1	-47	-98	-88	-25
Cameroon	-346	-620	-324	-71	-375	-258	-235	-377	-153	-349	-575	-291	-214	-299
Cape Verde	-25	-33	-38	-51	-27	-55	-74	-87	-62	-68	-69	-38	-19	-61
Central African Republic	-43	-108	-48	-81	-63	-57	-80	-25	-21	-9	-76	-24	-111	-51
Chad	-16	-219	-115	-110	-134	-137	-190	-204	-257	-594	-1,057	-80	-157	-335
Comoros	-9	-34	-43	-21	-20	-33	-18	-14	-3	4	3	-14	-27	-13
Congo, Dem. Rep. of	-87	-528	-530	-465	-28	-188	-415	-113	-199	-250	-160	-366	-627	-227
Congo, Rep. of	-167	-541	-670	-822	-831	-301	-632	-404	256	-88	-10	-258	-345	-354
Côte d'Ivoire	..	-1,140	-78	-579	-204	-123	-344	-174	-300	-34	725	-663	-855	-129
Djibouti	..	..	..	-17	-16	-12	-3	-4	-43	..	..	..	..	-16
Equatorial Guinea	..	-48	-73	-97	-244	-250	-375	-289	-297	-399	244	6	-7	-213
Eritrea	0	55	73	-11	-89	14	-177	-205	-105	-132	-85	0	15	-99
Ethiopia	-126	-497	-291	-90	68	-416	-333	-509	-335	-262	-365	-176	-377	-280
Gabon	514	-58	336	159	317	237	-183	131	128	168	305	157	-216	158
Gambia, The	-86	-54	-18	-54	-26	-15	-13	-19	-20	-26	-29	-47	-38	-25
Ghana	-54	-559	-265	-154	-214	-991	-370	-896	-419	-283	30	-154	-357	-412
Guinea	-32	-225	-267	-316	-352	-244	-239	-253	-226	-73	-208	-64	-238	-239
Guinea-Bissau	..	-50	-29	-45	-45	-24	-27	-27	-28	-50	-23	..	-51	-34
Kenya	-1,233	165	-15	-509	-196	-450	-549	-234	-284	-398	66	-478	-332	-319
Lesotho	-207	-225	-211	-294	-294	-306	-242	-212	-167	-110	-128	-222	-148	-219
Liberia	46	..	..	..	..	..	..	..	..	..	..	15	-15	..
Madagascar	-635	-250	-277	-267	-201	-196	-278	-201	-218	-59	-271	-262	-177	-211
Malawi	-310	-311	-269	-171	-270	-386	-171	-305	-239	-214	-455	-163	-158	-276
Mali	-232	-185	-145	-228	-265	-187	-203	-247	-227	-308	-166	-168	-197	-229
Mauritania	-133	-105	-37	-102	-40	1	-36	-20	-27	-105	-52	-133	-57	-48
Mauritius	-117	-44	-75	-208	-35	-22	-103	-65	-69	126	238	-88	-29	-17
Mozambique	-423	-825	-864	-677	-647	-611	-749	-1,152	-1,042	-967	-841	-489	-711	-835
Namibia	-40	110	86	199	168	85	130	138	227	66	62	33	105	134
Niger	-429	378	187	249	283	252	340	296	308	309	335	-247	92	296
Nigeria	4,310	-2,158	-1,618	-897	3,953	2,840	-3,075	-3,290	4,173	1,193	-3,667	-1,767	-1,373	154
Rwanda	-48	-218	-53	-15	-70	-175	-190	-148	-90	-101	-127	-23	-133	-114
São Tomé and Principe	1	-33	-28	-35	-34	-23	-12	-21	-19	-26	-24	-6	-24	-24
Senegal	-524	-578	-181	-235	-200	-185	-195	-274	-274	-225	-428	-402	-464	-252
Seychelles	-23	-42	-21	-44	-61	-60	-100	-124	-45	-145	-114	-17	-6	-87
Sierra Leone	-168	-95	-53	-73	-103	-9	-44	-22	-51	-67	-79	-128	-57	-56
Somalia	-136	..	..	..	..	..	..	..	..	..	..	-117	-114	..
South Africa	3,508	1,489	94	-2,203	-1,892	-2,263	-2,326	-642	-527	-295	310	-223	1,934	-1,230
Sudan	-289	-129	-560	-500	-827	-828	-957	-465	-411	-912	-843	-124	-158	-718
Swaziland	-129	-122	-68	-238	-52	-3	-94	-35	-66	-55	-46	-61	-27	-74
Tanzania	-540	-1,115	-1,076	-1,047	-942	-842	-1,336	-1,172	-900	-906	-712	-424	-777	-982
Togo	-95	-84	-64	-63	-112	-88	-89	-120	-115	-91	..	-101	-93	-97
Uganda	-117	-396	-265	-444	-500	-464	-764	-763	-678	-696	-782	-58	-276	-636
Zambia	-538	-467	-398	-464	-427	-509	-574	-481	-622	-758	-652	-377	-405	-561
Zimbabwe	-444	-311	-318	-370	-180	-823	-355	-157	-101	-110	-56	-283	-251	-269
NORTH AFRICA	6,271	1,301	-2,805	-3,870	421	2,889	-4,207	-2,186	6,621	5,922	2,259	-3,616	-943	981
Algeria	242	810	-1,839	-2,240	1,050	3,450	-910	20	9,000	7,091	4,346	-1,008	-28	2,726
Egypt, Arab Rep.	-438	2,295	410	386	-185	119	-2,479	-1,709	-1,171	-34	-449	-1,765	6	-690
Libya	8,259	..	..	..	..	..	..	..	..	..	..	1,034	32	..
Morocco	-1,420	-521	-723	-1,186	35	-87	-144	-55	-387	-263	-667	-1,369	-355	-344
Tunisia	-373	-1,283	-654	-830	-479	-593	-675	-443	-821	-873	-971	-507	-585	-710
ALL AFRICA	6,155	-9,601	-11,950	-15,568	-5,130	-5,973	-22,235	-16,946	3,963	-2,577	-8,130	-11,861	-8,726	-9,074

Note: 2002 data are preliminary (see page 2).

5-8. Current account balance, excluding net capital grants/GDP

	Percentage of GDP											Annual average		
	1980	1993	1994	1995	1996	1997	1998	1999	2000	2001	2002	75-84	85-94	95-MR
SUB-SAHARAN AFRICA	0.2	-3.8	-3.3	-3.7	-1.7	-2.6	-5.6	-4.6	-0.8	-2.7	-3.3	-4.3	-2.9	-3.1
excluding South Africa	-1.9	-8.0	-6.5	-5.7	-2.0	-3.4	-8.4	-7.5	-1.1	-4.1	-5.1	-6.0	-6.0	-4.6
excl. S.Africa & Nigeria	-7.9	-7.7	-6.5	-6.2	-5.0	-6.0	-8.1	-7.1	-4.1	-5.9	-4.2	-7.1	-6.1	-5.8
Angola	..	-14.8	-12.3	-11.2	-3.7	-14.6	-32.5	-26.8	9.0	-15.1	-5.9	..	-5.0	-12.6
Benin	-14.0	-4.5	-4.9	-9.7	-8.4	-7.4	-5.7	-7.6	-8.1	-6.8	-8.1	-16.6	-5.4	-7.7
Botswana	-14.3	10.2	2.0	15.3	10.1	15.3	4.6	12.2	12.2	13.7	12.7	-12.0	9.8	12.0
Burkina Faso	-13.4	-6.9	-1.8	-8.4	-11.0	-10.4	-10.4	-12.6	-13.4	-11.8	-11.3	-13.8	-7.7	-11.2
Burundi	-9.3	-8.4	-1.6	-0.4	-4.4	0.3	-6.2	-3.9	-4.5	-0.1	-6.6	-9.8	-8.0	-3.2
Cameroon	-5.1	-5.2	-4.1	-0.9	-4.1	-2.8	-2.7	-4.1	-1.7	-4.1	-6.1	-6.0	-2.0	-3.3
Cape Verde	-23.5	-9.0	-9.1	-10.3	-5.4	-10.8	-13.7	-14.9	-11.6	-11.9	-10.7	-42.3	-8.1	-11.2
Central African Republic	-5.4	-8.3	-5.6	-7.2	-5.9	-5.6	-7.6	-2.4	-2.2	-0.9	-7.3	-4.0	-8.8	-4.9
Chad	-1.5	-15.0	-9.8	-7.7	-8.3	-9.1	-10.9	-13.3	-18.5	-35.6	-52.8	-8.6	-11.3	-19.5
Comoros	-7.2	-12.4	-23.1	-8.9	-8.7	-15.7	-8.4	-6.4	-1.7	1.8	1.1	-13.0	-12.1	-5.9
Congo, Dem. Rep. of	-0.6	-4.9	-9.1	-8.2	-0.5	-3.1	-6.7	-2.4	-4.1	-4.8	-2.8	-3.4	-7.5	-4.1
Congo, Rep. of	-9.8	-28.2	-37.8	-38.8	-32.7	-12.9	-32.4	-17.1	7.9	-3.2	-0.3	-21.5	-16.0	-16.2
Côte d'Ivoire	..	-10.3	-0.9	-5.3	-1.7	-1.1	-2.7	-1.4	-2.8	-0.3	6.2	-9.5	-7.6	-1.1
Djibouti	..	..	..	-3.4	-3.3	-2.3	-0.6	-0.8	-7.7	..	..	..	..	-3.0
Equatorial Guinea	..	-31.6	-58.2	-58.9	-94.3	-50.3	-82.2	-33.2	-22.2	-21.6	11.2	..	-3.0	-43.9
Eritrea	..	11.8	13.7	-1.9	-12.8	2.1	-23.8	-28.1	-16.3	-18.6	-13.2	..	9.9	-14.1
Ethiopia	..	-8.0	-5.2	-1.6	1.1	-6.5	-5.1	-7.8	-5.1	-4.0	-6.0	-5.8	-5.0	-4.4
Gabon	12.0	-1.3	8.0	3.2	5.5	4.4	-4.0	3.0	2.6	3.9	6.1	4.2	-6.3	3.1
Gambia, The	-35.7	-14.6	-5.0	-14.2	-6.7	-3.8	-3.0	-4.3	-4.7	-6.6	-8.2	-22.5	-13.7	-6.4
Ghana	-1.2	-9.4	-4.9	-2.4	-3.1	-14.4	-5.0	-11.6	-8.4	-5.3	0.5	-3.9	-6.3	-6.2
Guinea	..	-6.9	-7.8	-8.6	-9.1	-6.4	-6.7	-7.3	-7.3	-2.4	-6.5	..	-8.8	-6.8
Guinea-Bissau	..	-21.0	-12.4	-17.6	-16.5	-8.8	-13.2	-12.1	-13.2	-24.9	-11.4	..	-23.7	-14.7
Kenya	-17.0	3.3	-0.2	-5.6	-2.1	-4.2	-4.9	-2.2	-2.7	-3.5	0.5	-8.0	-4.1	-3.1
Lesotho	-47.9	-27.6	-25.2	-31.5	-31.2	-29.9	-27.2	-23.3	-19.4	-14.4	-17.9	-71.8	-23.5	-24.3
Liberia	4.1	..	..	..	..	..	..	..	..	..	..	1.9	-1.2	..
Madagascar	-15.7	-7.4	-9.3	-8.4	-5.0	-5.5	-7.4	-5.4	-5.6	-1.3	-6.2	-7.5	-6.1	-5.6
Malawi	-25.0	-15.0	-22.7	-12.0	-11.1	-15.2	-9.8	-16.8	-14.0	-12.7	-23.9	-15.6	-10.3	-14.4
Mali	-13.0	-6.9	-8.3	-9.2	-10.1	-7.6	-7.8	-9.6	-9.3	-11.7	-5.4	-12.9	-10.0	-8.8
Mauritania	-18.8	-11.1	-3.6	-9.5	-3.6	0.1	-3.6	-2.1	-2.8	-10.5	-5.3	-19.9	-5.9	-4.7
Mauritius	-10.2	-1.3	-2.2	-5.5	-0.9	-0.5	-2.5	-1.6	-1.6	2.8	5.2	-7.6	-1.0	-0.5
Mozambique	-12.0	-41.6	-39.7	-29.3	-22.8	-18.0	-19.3	-28.9	-28.3	-28.1	-23.4	-14.2	-29.8	-24.8
Namibia	-1.8	3.9	2.6	5.7	4.8	2.4	3.8	4.1	6.6	2.1	2.1	2.0	5.5	3.9
Niger	-17.1	23.5	11.9	13.3	14.2	13.6	16.4	14.7	17.1	15.9	15.4	-13.6	4.3	15.1
Nigeria	6.7	-10.1	-6.8	-3.2	11.2	7.8	-9.6	-9.0	9.9	2.8	-8.4	-4.5	-6.2	0.2
Rwanda	-4.1	-11.0	-7.0	-1.1	-5.1	-9.4	-9.6	-7.6	-5.0	-5.9	-7.3	-1.6	-6.6	-6.4
São Tomé and Principe	2.1	-70.1	-57.4	-76.7	-76.0	-53.1	-30.5	-45.4	-41.3	-55.2	-47.4	-10.5	-47.8	-53.2
Senegal	-17.5	-10.6	-5.0	-5.3	-4.3	-4.2	-4.2	-5.8	-6.3	-4.9	-8.5	-16.7	-10.3	-5.4
Seychelles	-15.9	-8.9	-4.4	-8.7	-12.0	-10.7	-16.5	-19.8	-7.2	-23.5	-16.3	-15.8	-0.6	-14.4
Sierra Leone	-15.3	-12.4	-5.3	-7.9	-10.9	-1.0	-6.5	-3.2	-8.0	-8.9	-10.1	-11.4	-7.3	-7.1
Somalia	-22.6	..	..	..	..	..	..	..	..	..	..	-17.3	-11.7	..
South Africa	4.4	1.1	0.1	-1.5	-1.3	-1.5	-1.7	-0.5	-0.4	-0.3	0.3	-0.2	2.2	-0.9
Sudan	-4.3	-2.2	-8.6	-5.3	-9.8	-8.1	-8.9	-4.4	-3.7	-7.5	-6.2	-2.4	-2.9	-6.7
Swaziland	-23.7	-11.5	-5.9	-17.4	-3.9	-0.2	-6.9	-2.6	-4.7	-4.3	-3.9	-11.0	-2.1	-5.5
Tanzania	..	-26.2	-23.8	-19.9	-14.5	-11.0	-15.9	-13.6	-9.9	-9.7	-7.6	-10.0	-17.5	-12.8
Togo	-8.4	-6.8	-6.5	-4.8	-7.6	-5.9	-6.3	-8.5	-9.4	-7.3	..	-12.2	-7.3	-7.1
Uganda	-9.4	-12.3	-6.6	-7.7	-8.3	-7.4	-11.7	-12.8	-11.5	-12.3	-13.5	-3.3	-7.0	-10.6
Zambia	-13.8	-14.3	-11.9	-13.3	-13.1	-13.0	-17.7	-15.3	-19.2	-20.8	-17.6	-11.9	-14.2	-16.3
Zimbabwe	-6.6	-4.7	-4.6	-5.2	-2.1	-9.8	-6.2	-2.9	-1.4	-1.2	-0.7	-4.0	-3.5	-3.7
NORTH AFRICA	4.9	0.9	-2.0	-2.5	0.2	1.6	-2.3	-1.1	3.2	2.8	1.1	-4.0	-0.7	0.4
Algeria	0.6	1.6	-4.3	-5.4	2.2	7.2	-1.9	0.0	16.9	12.5	7.5	-4.5	0.0	4.9
Egypt, Arab Rep.	-1.9	4.9	0.8	0.6	-0.3	0.2	-3.0	-1.9	-1.2	0.0	-0.5	-9.6	-0.3	-0.8
Libya	23.2	..	..	..	..	..	..	..	..	..	..	4.8	-2.2	..
Morocco	-7.5	-1.9	-2.4	-3.6	0.1	-0.3	-0.4	-0.2	-1.2	-0.8	-1.8	-10.3	-1.7	-1.0
Tunisia	-4.3	-8.8	-4.2	-4.6	-2.4	-3.1	-3.4	-2.1	-4.2	-4.4	-4.4	-7.4	-4.7	-3.6
ALL AFRICA	1.9	-2.3	-2.9	-3.3	-1.0	-1.2	-4.4	-3.3	0.8	-0.5	-1.6	-4.2	-2.2	-1.8

Note: 2002 data are preliminary (see page 2). Since 1994, Nigeria's ratios are distorted because the official exchange rate used by the Government for oil exports and oil value added is significantly over-valued.

5-9. Net capital grants

	Millions of U.S. dollars (current prices)										*Annual average*		
	1980	*1993*	*1994*	*1995*	*1996*	*1997*	*1998*	*1999*	*2000*	*2001*	*2002*	*75-84*	*85-94*	*95-MR*
SUB-SAHARAN AFRICA	963	4,304	3,789	3,954	3,208	3,303	3,554	2,935	3,021	3,073	2,893	974	3,309	3,243
excluding South Africa	963	4,362	3,723	3,954	3,208	3,303	3,554	2,935	3,021	3,073	2,893	989	3,313	3,243
excl. S.Africa & Nigeria	963	4,362	3,723	3,954	3,208	3,303	3,554	2,935	3,021	3,073	2,893	989	3,313	3,243
Angola	0	0	0	0	0	0	0	0	0	0	0	0	0	0
Benin	63	63	54	70	56	84	62	67	46	44	34	63	59	58
Botswana	8	85	19	14	6	17	32	21	38	18	18	6	14	20
Burkina Faso	211	98	65	74	53	29	33	38	32	37	43	151	143	43
Burundi	34	53	0	0	0	0	0	0	0	0	0	38	42	0
Cameroon	0	0	0	0	0	0	0	0	0	0	0	0	0	0
Cape Verde	29	19	20	20	13	51	70	29	27	4	7	20	11	28
Central African Republic	0	69	63	56	39	..	..	..	..	..	..	0	56	47
Chad	28	95	70	53	46	53	70	49	67	66	101	76	94	63
Comoros	0	26	19	8	4	8	12	11	7	5	4	0	13	7
Congo, Dem. Rep. of	0	19	41	204	0	0	0	0	0	0	0	0	86	26
Congo, Rep. of	0	0	0	21	8	2	6	10	10	5	5	0	0	9
Côte d'Ivoire	..	95	53	70	79	76	86	65	47	55	41	0	29	65
Djibouti	..	..	..	0	0	0	0	0	0	..	..	..	..	0
Equatorial Guinea	..	29	5	3	2	3	3	1	1	2	2	7	23	2
Eritrea	0	52	29	8	4	51	62	78	102	128	84	0	21	65
Ethiopia	0	293	199	280	259	225	229	0	0	0	0	26	216	124
Gabon	0	0	0	0	0	0	0	0	0	0	0	0	0	0
Gambia, The	..	40	35	28	0	0	0	0	0	0	0	17	40	4
Ghana	83	256	201	260	206	61	120	72	62	218	60	69	181	132
Guinea	17	101	104	120	117	114	75	80	72	82	55	13	81	89
Guinea-Bissau	..	37	44	56	41	32	0	21	16	24	12	0	27	25
Kenya	..	65	82	111	112	63	79	64	56	71	89	119	115	81
Lesotho	..	42	39	45	47	169	176	117	53	31	35	6	32	84
Liberia	..	..	..	..	..	..	..	..	..	..	..	..	..	..
Madagascar	0	87	72	85	51	114	119	107	115	113	59	16	23	95
Malawi	50	128	111	152	97	83	157	157	148	98	235	33	80	141
Mali	78	30	57	99	94	92	76	78	123	124	..	95	54	98
Mauritania	0	20	26	30	10	16	25	12	13	15	8	0	32	16
Mauritius	0	-1	-2	-1	-1	-1	-1	-1	0	-1	-1	0	-1	-1
Mozambique	56	503	565	339	225	313	313	434	564	469	420	90	398	385
Namibia	0	0	0	0	0	0	0	0	0	0	0	0	0	0
Niger	0	94	134	120	117	113	129	96	85	93	99	0	90	106
Nigeria	0	0	0	0	0	0	0	0	0	0	0	0	0	0
Rwanda	0	87	7	69	68	116	95	71	73	63	66	10	17	78
São Tomé and Principe	0	8	8	18	20	22	4	9	12	14	12	0	5	14
Senegal	92	266	184	210	164	92	107	95	74	114	86	131	243	118
Seychelles	15	22	15	1	6	7	22	16	9	9	5	10	21	9
Sierra Leone	11	0	0	0	3	0	1	4	4	7	5	5	3	3
Somalia	0	0	0	0	0	0	..	..	..	..	..	0	0	0
South Africa	0	-58	66	0	0	0	0	0	0	0	0	-16	-4	0
Sudan	..	29	15	11	8	4	17	11	24	8	35	7	6	15
Swaziland	-2	0	0	0	0	0	0	0	0	0	0	-1	0	0
Tanzania	108	759	634	525	581	690	682	533	534	486	485	115	517	565
Togo	..	4	7	8	7	13	15	..	..	..	..	24	27	11
Uganda	0	277	228	303	277	307	380	277	369	391	414	15	148	340
Zambia	23	340	338	318	304	198	221	214	185	253	305	13	260	250
Zimbabwe	58	173	181	167	85	85	77	101	53	26	67	39	114	83
NORTH AFRICA	43	104	103	70	46	95	82	73	3	270	200	195	330	105
Algeria	0	0	0	0	0	0	0	0	0	120	100	0	0	28
Egypt, Arab Rep.	2	0	0	0	0	0	0	0	0	0	0	182	231	0
Libya	0	0	0	0	0	0	..	..	..	..	..	0	0	0
Morocco	0	0	0	0	0	0	0	0	0	50	0	0	0	6
Tunisia	42	104	103	70	46	95	82	73	3	100	100	27	100	71
ALL AFRICA	1,006	4,408	3,891	4,024	3,253	3,398	3,636	3,008	3,024	3,343	3,093	1,170	3,640	3,347

Note: 2002 data are preliminary (see page 2).

5-10. Net foreign direct investment

	Millions of U.S. dollars (current prices)											Annual average		
	1980	1993	1994	1995	1996	1997	1998	1999	2000	2001	2002	75-84	85-94	95-MR
SUB-SAHARAN AFRICA	-741	925	712	880	2,500	5,585	4,231	7,585	6,472	18,285	8,904	691	1,250	6,805
excluding South Africa	24	1,213	1,568	2,136	2,726	4,118	5,448	7,663	5,854	7,500	7,810	854	1,621	5,407
excl. S.Africa & Nigeria	763	632	980	1,459	1,966	2,579	4,228	6,190	4,352	5,704	5,860	686	886	4,042
Angola	..	302	327	303	181	412	1,114	2,471	878	2,146	1,312	346	221	1,102
Benin	4	-7	8	4	-6	19	18	77	75	36	41	2	4	33
Botswana	109	-296	-24	30	72	96	92	35	55	55	54	46	6	61
Burkina Faso	0	9	25	14	14	8	1	9	24	12	11	1	6	12
Burundi	1	0	0	1	0	0	0	0	6	6	6	1	1	2
Cameroon	105	134	-228	-154	92	100	-50	7	280	373	703	58	198	169
Cape Verde	..	3	2	26	28	12	9	67	34	34	32	..	1	30
Central African Republic	5	-15	-13	4	12	-5	7	2	3	9	6	6	-1	5
Chad	0	21	35	37	43	37	22	28	101	462	902	11	20	204
Comoros	0	0	0	1	1	0	0	0	0	0	0	0	2	0
Congo, Dem. Rep. of	0	0	0	0	40	0	22	-208	-50	-7	12	91	6	-24
Congo, Rep. of	40	254	285	123	73	76	41	519	478	218	225	24	55	219
Côte d'Ivoire	83	24	-25	234	269	415	383	324	235	271	216	45	3	294
Djibouti	..	..	..	3	3	2	3	4	9	..	..	..	..	4
Equatorial Guinea	..	-10	65	93	264	185	366	30	113	230	106	0	11	173
Eritrea	0	..	..	..	37	39	30	83	28	12	20	0	0	36
Ethiopia	0	0	0	0	0	60	7	136	51	52	0	3	0	38
Gabon	24	-114	-100	-109	-146	-63	-62	129	-15	-33	-39	59	72	-42
Gambia, The	..	9	6	7	9	9	12	7	2	5	7	..	7	7
Ghana	16	106	128	83	70	36	45	63	65	88	50	13	33	62
Guinea	..	6	11	25	17	45	49	34	-47	-58	31	..	25	12
Guinea-Bissau	..	..	..	..	..	..	..	..	..	..	..	..	..	..
Kenya	78	2	4	33	13	40	42	42	127	50	50	25	19	50
Lesotho	4	20	38	30	40	40	172	170	128	110	96	2	31	98
Liberia	..	..	..	..	..	..	..	..	..	..	..	47	2	..
Madagascar	0	15	6	10	10	14	16	58	70	93	9	-1	9	35
Malawi	10	0	0	0	30	24	34	39	27	28	38	4	0	27
Mali	24	-7	38	30	60	-14	-50	24	18	21	..	16	0	13
Mauritania	27	12	3	7	0	-3	0	0	1	4	7	1	4	2
Mauritius	0	-36	-1	22	31	5	20	19	13	197	28	1	11	42
Mozambique	0	32	35	45	73	64	213	382	139	255	156	0	14	166
Namibia	..	47	104	157	152	83	76	110	156	312	247	..	83	162
Niger	44	0	0	0	0	0	0	2	18	30	4	17	-4	7
Nigeria	-739	581	588	677	760	1,539	1,220	1,473	1,502	1,796	1,950	206	736	1,365
Rwanda	16	6	0	2	2	3	7	2	8	4	3	11	12	4
São Tomé and Principe	..	4	2	2	2	0	4	3	3	4	3	..	2	3
Senegal	61	-48	50	35	5	115	75	142	62	39	59	43	-19	67
Seychelles	6	6	17	30	25	38	40	46	14	22	38	5	9	32
Sierra Leone	10	18	17	-5	0	0	4	2	2	2	4	4	5	1
Somalia	..	..	..	..	..	..	..	..	..	..	..	-1	..	..
South Africa	-765	-288	-856	-1,256	-226	1,466	-1,218	-78	617	10,785	1,094	-178	-371	1,398
Sudan	0	0	0	0	0	98	371	371	392	0	633	0	0	233
Swaziland	18	31	23	31	28	-3	130	87	73	69	54	15	36	59
Tanzania	..	62	63	104	134	150	172	517	463	327	240	..	30	264
Togo	42	2	6	5	24	19	1	..	..	..	..	23	11	12
Uganda	0	4	5	2	110	110	158	145	177	144	146	1	13	124
Zambia	62	3	40	97	117	207	198	163	122	72	197	20	4	147
Zimbabwe	-26	32	30	98	35	107	436	50	15	10	153	-18	4	113
NORTH AFRICA	-78	..	..	1,350	1,470	2,409	2,477	2,284	2,886	5,519	4,365	72	221	2,845
Algeria	281	0	0	0	270	260	500	460	400	1,100	900	-2	-43	486
Egypt, Arab Rep.	541	1,021	1,285	735	612	723	967	655	1,613	1,613	1,855	456	542	1,097
Libya	-1,136	..	..	..	..	..	..	..	..	..	..	-564	-19	
Morocco	..	..	..	320	327	1,071	313	831	143	2,298	910	..	..	777
Tunisia	236	545	442	295	261	355	697	337	731	509	700	182	247	486
ALL AFRICA	-819	2,490	2,438	2,230	3,970	7,993	6,707	9,869	9,358	23,805	13,269	763	1,985	9,650

Note: 2002 data are preliminary (see page 2).

5-11. Net long-term borrowing

	Millions of U.S. dollars (current prices)											Annual average		
	1980	*1993*	*1994*	*1995*	*1996*	*1997*	*1998*	*1999*	*2000*	*2001*	*2002*	*75-84*	*85-94*	*95-MR*
SUB-SAHARAN AFRICA	7,739	5,035	4,405	4,045	746	1,540	-539	-234	270	186	1,251	6,024	4,771	908
excluding South Africa	7,739	5,035	2,881	2,566	1,224	1,590	-143	-122	-733	-244	815	6,024	4,619	619
excl. S.Africa & Nigeria	6,229	5,070	3,029	3,052	2,334	2,116	355	308	205	1,404	1,882	5,009	4,703	1,457
Angola	..	622	263	218	125	374	-494	-327	-486	-275	79	..	437	-98
Benin	56	63	84	77	83	23	32	37	-10	91	39	77	68	46
Botswana	21	55	-2	3	-46	-53	-31	-30	-24	-32	-43	27	27	-32
Burkina Faso	55	119	80	83	73	40	58	70	62	121	106	48	87	77
Burundi	35	58	31	27	23	7	18	6	30	2	26	37	73	17
Cameroon	500	267	251	-48	-39	-5	-87	-22	22	-47	-106	313	288	-42
Cape Verde	..	6	23	16	19	11	39	47	18	42	20	18	9	26
Central African Republic	24	48	36	30	25	2	-9	-2	9	-9	1	17	66	6
Chad	3	52	61	55	89	68	31	70	18	33	83	21	64	56
Comoros	13	6	10	9	9	5	3	-1	2	11	9	11	11	6
Congo, Dem. Rep. of	271	53	1	0	3	0	0	8	0	0	167	281	183	22
Congo, Rep. of	488	383	48	-67	-136	-30	-7	0	-5	-17	-7	222	96	-34
Côte d'Ivoire	1,017	278	524	204	64	-580	-225	-577	-294	-291	-213	636	277	-239
Djibouti	8	19	17	9	15	7	2	-3	-1	5	24	8	22	7
Equatorial Guinea	18	9	4	2	0	1	0	3	0	-1	1	8	13	1
Eritrea	..	..	27	7	7	33	67	108	50	103	81	..	27	57
Ethiopia	93	314	168	141	1	127	78	142	114	424	544	426	356	196
Gabon	-109	58	38	57	-43	-23	-66	-197	-157	-245	-156	52	137	-104
Gambia, The	51	7	3	8	43	11	2	11	8	13	40	18	17	17
Ghana	143	327	305	409	696	419	354	128	122	423	137	68	285	336
Guinea	47	245	122	49	85	143	54	30	-20	36	-40	44	142	42
Guinea-Bissau	72	22	25	13	23	25	8	-1	4	-8	-3	22	36	8
Kenya	424	111	-289	111	-142	-197	-92	-202	48	-169	-109	251	253	-94
Lesotho	10	52	47	48	58	45	40	26	36	-21	-15	15	41	27
Liberia	61	20	-14	0	0	0	0	0	0	0	0	61	10	0
Madagascar	333	89	51	66	93	217	44	65	76	106	149	171	128	102
Malawi	120	151	74	149	121	129	121	114	88	95	59	75	88	110
Mali	89	58	69	138	110	86	53	57	50	67	97	78	115	82
Mauritania	108	91	82	42	83	26	-6	-11	68	33	78	100	72	39
Mauritius	79	22	83	255	32	57	-93	38	-269	-62	-14	37	57	-7
Mozambique	..	152	176	196	222	216	185	90	68	63	204	822	216	155
Namibia	0	50	-45	23	19	20	7	59	..	..	..	0	-1	26
Niger	223	44	35	-3	10	51	49	48	62	58	102	107	72	47
Nigeria	1,510	-35	-148	-486	-1,110	-525	-497	-430	-938	-1,648	-1,068	1,015	-84	-838
Rwanda	25	50	20	43	53	62	79	70	27	54	73	27	62	58
São Tomé and Principe	9	14	14	12	10	3	5	14	6	7	1	7	15	7
Senegal	171	100	7	4	66	126	52	-56	6	124	117	166	152	55
Seychelles	12	6	8	-7	2	2	10	-5	8	4	1	11	7	2
Sierra Leone	50	95	45	38	28	33	33	9	67	74	53	25	28	42
Somalia	106	0	0	0	0	0	0	0	0	0	0	136	47	0
South Africa	..	..	1,524	1,478	-478	-51	-396	-111	1,002	431	437	..	1,524	289
Sudan	658	91	9	36	17	5	-1	-6	-4	-2	0	495	130	6
Swaziland	19	-9	-5	2	8	39	17	17	1	22	2	21	-6	13
Tanzania	318	142	164	135	64	161	118	153	87	72	117	290	181	113
Togo	78	14	34	19	81	29	52	15	15	21	12	84	35	31
Uganda	51	299	181	161	170	231	107	113	192	326	139	61	202	180
Zambia	388	99	109	110	80	107	-49	192	163	174	32	205	132	101
Zimbabwe	93	322	57	171	33	63	-198	11	-51	-24	-5	164	144	0
NORTH AFRICA	5,253	688	1,147	1,817	1,007	-260	-1,992	-2,353	-1,780	-347	-2,125	5,240	2,377	-754
Algeria	869	-453	1,432	1,435	920	-377	-1,554	-1,899	-1,508	-1,792	-1,115	1,435	519	-736
Egypt, Arab Rep.	2,337	227	276	-252	-344	-47	-215	-622	-513	802	-743	2,164	840	-242
Libya	110	375	-507	77	-14	1	33	-64	..	..	..	101	157	7
Morocco	1,584	261	-184	93	-28	-492	-85	-298	10	-388	-1,133	1,167	631	-290
Tunisia	352	277	131	465	473	655	-170	529	232	1,030	866	373	231	510
ALL AFRICA	12,992	5,723	5,552	5,862	1,753	1,280	-2,530	-2,587	-1,510	-160	-874	11,264	7,148	154

Note: 2002 data are preliminary (see page 2).

5-12. Other capital flows

	Millions of U.S. dollars (current prices)											Annual average		
	1980	1993	1994	1995	1996	1997	1998	1999	2000	2001	2002	75-84	85-94	95-MR
SUB-SAHARAN AFRICA	2,058	-5,607	37	-7,192	-80	-7,371	295	-11,111	-25,621	-4,719	-9,971	2,009	-1,795	-8,221
excluding South Africa	3,596	-3,922	-2,339	-1,573	-42	-1,405	370	-2,204	-25,090	-4,465	-4,627	1,245	-883	-4,879
excl. S.Africa & Nigeria	3,813	-1,401	-2,477	-2,165	1,482	-628	-264	-1,962	-2,842	-3,037	-2,665	2,417	-597	-1,510
Angola	0	-550	-443	431	2,528	-163	1,164	-879	-613	-940	-479	0	116	131
Benin	116	-109	-65	-1	-25	39	27	187	-36	-1	-78	95	46	14
Botswana	124	477	316	-7	-217	-206	-34	-325	-475	-824	-211	107	142	-287
Burkina Faso	..	-24	-29	-10	-39	-17	-104	-48	-20	-30	12	83	-22	-32
Burundi	-22	-22	34	-1	-55	-29	-16	-7	-9	-19	20	-41	-15	-14
Cameroon	705	-100	-201	-329	76	147	0	10	0	-2	-2	614	-283	-13
Cape Verde	..	-24	-40	-43	-22	-53	-116	-24	-48	28	43	4	-9	-29
Central African Republic	24	-10	-47	-75	-31	4	-19	-54	-30	-90	22	5	-51	-34
Chad	-24	-48	-90	-66	-116	-96	59	19	48	7	13	-27	-31	-16
Comoros	-11	32	16	-17	24	14	-9	-5	-2	-6	-10	-3	12	-1
Congo, Dem. Rep. of	652	-159	-221	-512	665	771	100	30	-242	-144	-149	175	-17	65
Congo, Rep. of	219	463	96	534	468	-117	201	-205	-635	-244	-230	317	449	-28
Côte d'Ivoire	626	355	-40	-51	-46	57	171	-350	-165	-34	-379	224	76	-100
Djibouti	..	..	..	2	-2	-33	..	-2	25	..	..	..	..	-2
Equatorial Guinea	..	7	-8	6	-32	64	9	279	366	373	0	15	-43	133
Eritrea	0	-43	-84	-133	-125	30	-91	-1	5	-60	-6	0	-27	-48
Ethiopia	-7	-41	96	-88	-192	-52	-27	182	-52	-34	220	-4	-119	-5
Gabon	-337	26	-245	-153	-217	-126	-128	-83	-51	-59	-108	-259	-119	-116
Gambia, The	..	1	-36	1	7	2	5	10	14	12	-2	-2	-22	6
Ghana	-168	-7	-129	-338	-733	366	-6	424	129	-301	-40	-20	-38	-62
Guinea	-8	-138	-44	-15	-40	-143	4	-59	167	61	18	6	-12	-1
Guinea-Bissau	..	-29	-52	-12	-17	12	11	30	45	37	31	-8	-11	17
Kenya	683	80	142	195	493	569	485	955	446	472	26	115	165	455
Lesotho	..	204	219	279	247	106	-149	-141	-67	-51	-4	115	67	28
Liberia	..	..	..	..	..	..	..	..	..	..	..	..	..	..
Madagascar	399	-160	-24	-76	-7	-103	-141	-65	-211	-258	-14	66	109	-110
Malawi	62	-12	-8	14	103	144	-97	50	-17	-10	19	31	-19	26
Mali	34	-106	-109	-169	-101	-102	-188	-111	-85	97	19	38	-60	-80
Mauritania	-5	27	-107	98	40	-16	8	15	-149	8	-43	15	-98	-5
Mauritius	84	25	32	60	82	60	7	7	226	-15	11	46	72	55
Mozambique	-85	-551	-554	-316	-113	-322	-360	-544	-621	-439	-707	-90	-424	-428
Namibia	..	-153	-225	-427	-383	-167	-180	-229	-352	-237	-146	..	-222	-265
Niger	0	-527	-456	-451	-502	-560	-572	-462	-467	-471	-497	0	-270	-498
Nigeria	-217	-2,521	137	591	-1,524	-777	634	-242	-22,248	-1,428	-1,962	-783	-286	-3,369
Rwanda	1	13	27	-46	-41	27	-46	-8	-15	-32	15	-14	26	-18
São Tomé and Principe	-22	-1	-9	-15	-23	-22	-8	-11	0	7	18	0	-6	-7
Senegal	-44	0	15	-14	0	4	1	0	-1	0	0	-14	4	-1
Seychelles	0	7	0	26	17	16	-23	3	-40	101	78	-5	-26	22
Sierra Leone	-57	-14	-60	-419	-43	-11	38	40	25	46	13	-25	-28	-39
Somalia	..	..	..	..	..	..	..	..	..	..	..	..	..	..
South Africa	-1,538	-1,685	2,376	-5,618	-38	-5,965	-75	-8,908	-531	-254	-5,344	300	-911	-3,342
Sudan	504	394	501	474	842	605	815	270	467	334	304	287	420	514
Swaziland	129	70	88	288	37	-16	4	9	47	43	19	27	46	54
Tanzania	..	-14	-289	-279	-490	-711	-547	-618	-475	-171	-241	..	-73	-442
Togo	..	..	..	..	..	..	..	..	..	..	..	..	..	..
Uganda	..	-84	29	-127	-71	-131	108	122	-44	36	101	..	-52	-1
Zambia	-123	-552	-295	-380	-331	-229	-439	-404	47	-149	-321	-30	-337	-276
Zimbabwe	365	-101	-176	-6	-132	-235	-182	30	21	-75	-3	66	-92	-73
NORTH AFRICA	-573	561	2,523	-646	179	86	1,797	163	-3,397	-2,018	-1,643	152	80	-685
Algeria	201	-780	574	-180	-10	-40	0	-950	200	-707	0	-19	-180	-211
Egypt, Arab Rep.	0	333	318	-525	237	-138	1,673	-411	-3,152	-1,400	-1,400	0	-280	-639
Libya	-481	..	..	..	..	..	..	..	..	..	..	161	1,100	..
Morocco	-101	610	1,377	43	-144	268	240	1,293	-67	89	-70	97	-171	207
Tunisia	-192	398	255	16	96	-4	-117	231	-378	0	-173	-22	51	-41
ALL AFRICA	1,485	-5,046	2,560	-7,838	99	-7,285	2,092	-10,949	-29,018	-6,737	-11,614	2,417	-1,715	-8,906

Note: 2002 data are preliminary (see page 2). Includes all capital account flows, except changes in reserves, that are not included in the tables on foreign investment or long-term borrowing.

5-13. Use of reserves

	Millions of U.S. dollars (current prices)											Annual average		
	1980	*1993*	*1994*	*1995*	*1996*	*1997*	*1998*	*1999*	*2000*	*2001*	*2002*	*75-84*	*85-94*	*95-MR*
SUB-SAHARAN AFRICA	-4,839	-2,672	-2,056	1,146	-6,527	-1,463	-211	5,169	-4,407	-730	-7,017	1,142	-1,284	-1,755
excluding South Africa	-4,024	57	-3,001	-1,221	-5,339	-3,821	516	938	-5,145	-1,693	-10,422	954	-1,146	-3,273
excl. S.Africa & Nigeria	521	-668	-3,002	-822	-2,986	-760	401	-728	-1,186	-670	-13,413	518	-1,111	-2,520
Angola	0	900	46	33	-245	150	114	-462	-631	508	207	33	49	-41
Benin	19	-30	-75	18	-58	-14	-9	-181	15	-19	-27	10	-44	-34
Botswana	-91	-759	-530	-295	-332	-647	-266	-289	-89	421	-129	-55	-446	-203
Burkina Faso	-11	-72	-119	-145	1	35	35	15	53	-3	-18	-13	-37	-3
Burundi	8	0	-48	-11	62	19	39	14	17	-7	-10	10	-27	15
Cameroon	-162	-291	333	-13	-81	-142	39	-4	-242	-168	-198	-38	-71	-101
Cape Verde	0	4	3	9	-22	3	8	-29	21	-15	-23	-1	-1	-6
Central African Republic	-10	-27	-72	-11	-20	18	41	-6	-11	4	10	-4	-8	3
Chad	5	32	-19	-63	-5	14	20	25	-5	-4	-67	-3	0	-11
Comoros	4	-14	-10	4	-9	4	3	-4	-9	-21	-9	0	-3	-5
Congo, Dem. Rep. of	-35	14	17	39	-15	21	..	694	830	709	-10,168	76	-23	-1,127
Congo, Rep. of	-59	5	-56	-6	-17	20	69	-60	-169	142	36	1	3	2
Côte d'Ivoire	..	-88	-794	-222	-227	-39	3	117	-50	-461	-587	138	-47	-183
Djibouti	..	..	..	7	-1	12	..	-3	-5	..	..	..	..	2
Equatorial Guinea	13	2	-1	-8	-4	-7	2	-29	-176	-199	-230	2	2	-81
Eritrea	0	-109	-78	58	76	-112	129	22	19	-14	-7	0	-28	21
Ethiopia	40	-108	-227	-120	-286	317	147	-23	63	5	-321	27	-42	-27
Gabon	-93	79	-137	42	-83	-39	107	59	-39	-31	-31	-9	-85	-2
Gambia, The	..	-6	5	-11	-8	-7	-10	-3	-1	12	4	5	-1	-3
Ghana	96	-41	-164	-211	14	-25	-100	204	96	-291	-157	25	-59	-59
Guinea	-25	-49	34	-13	27	-47	-71	43	35	-54	44	-5	-15	-4
Guinea-Bissau	0	9	6	1	-12	-25	-1	6	-26	-5	-20	6	-3	-10
Kenya	37	-323	-132	129	-426	0	-58	-68	-148	-191	-21	-63	-163	-98
Lesotho	-41	-92	-119	-109	-112	-89	19	75	78	14	-8	-8	-11	-16
Liberia	41	-1	-3	..	..	..	..	..	..	..	..	27	-2	..
Madagascar	-83	-20	8	-61	-134	-54	104	-46	37	-98	53	6	-13	-25
Malawi	17	0	29	-87	-109	53	-77	-31	17	12	109	16	2	-14
Mali	-9	-28	-87	-68	-128	3	61	56	19	-28	-284	-6	-66	-46
Mauritania	2	-26	11	-131	-67	-61	-19	-23	52	13	2	9	15	-29
Mauritius	-3	56	53	58	-217	-84	-9	-28	-84	-185	-243	2	-89	-99
Mozambique	32	46	-52	-60	-159	-115	-62	-68	-194	6	-94	46	-15	-93
Namibia	..	-91	-75	-24	-23	-22	-53	-57	-14	-29	-45	..	-37	-33
Niger	53	-6	-21	9	11	29	1	22	-29	-24	-5	6	-2	2
Nigeria	-4,545	725	1	-399	-2,353	-3,061	115	1,666	-3,959	-1,023	2,991	436	-35	-753
Rwanda	33	31	-4	-35	-8	-29	4	10	-10	-25	-30	19	51	-15
São Tomé and Principe	12	0	0	-5	0	-8	3	-1	1	-3	-2	0	0	-2
Senegal	135	296	-464	-245	-217	-162	-155	-173	-79	-208	77	87	163	-145
Seychelles	-8	-3	6	3	5	-5	33	-1	12	7	-26	-1	-2	4
Sierra Leone	32	-16	0	23	19	-5	11	20	-23	-18	-28	19	-4	0
Somalia	18	..	..	..	..	..	..	..	..	..	..	5	-18	..
South Africa	-815	-2,729	945	2,367	-1,188	2,357	-727	4,231	737	963	3,404	188	-138	1,518
Sudan	177	2	1	-23	-13	-23	-25	-36	-90	-91	-110	85	64	-51
Swaziland	-34	63	13	-30	-15	-26	-51	-21	6	57	29	-8	-12	-6
Tanzania	66	123	-107	-46	-81	-208	72	-125	-148	-184	-371	9	-21	-136
Togo	2	125	11	-12	12	-35	19	..	..	..	..	-18	10	-4
Uganda	55	-29	-90	-146	-73	-132	-134	-33	15	-41	-167	25	-13	-89
Zambia	162	-17	-77	1,210	-52	-33	211	-19	-138	-84	-229	152	-74	108
Zimbabwe	125	-207	-17	-255	43	739	205	-286	-163	-80	-319	46	-17	-14
NORTH AFRICA	-7,615	-4,370	-3,944	865	-3,638	-6,982	1,164	2,139	-3,918	-7,760	-2,860	434	-1,800	-2,624
Algeria	-1,341	300	-1,122	740	-2,380	-4,180	1,090	2,350	-7,600	-5,741	-3,655	-39	60	-2,422
Egypt, Arab Rep.	168	-4,312	-2,106	-754	-570	-1,912	135	2,117	3,025	685	948	421	-1,173	459
Libya	-6,407	-35	..	..	..	..	..	..	..	..	..	73	-218	..
Morocco	30	-284	-361	982	-292	-553	-247	-1,639	415	-1,985	223	0	-433	-387
Tunisia	-65	-39	-355	-103	-397	-336	187	-690	243	-718	-377	-20	-58	-274
ALL AFRICA	-12,454	-7,042	-6,000	2,012	-10,165	-8,445	953	7,308	-8,325	-8,489	-9,878	1,576	-3,084	-4,379

Note: 2002 data are preliminary (see page 2). Excludes IMF credit transactions, which appear in the table on long-term borrowing.

5-14. Import coverage ratio of reserves

	Reserves in months of imports of goods and services											Annual average		
	1980	1993	1994	1995	1996	1997	1998	1999	2000	2001	2002	75-84	85-94	95-MR
SUB-SAHARAN AFRICA	4	8	8	7	8	7	8	8	8	8	7	3	6	7
excluding South Africa	5	10	10	9	8	9	9	9	9	9	8	3	7	9
excl. S.Africa & Nigeria	3	11	11	9	10	10	11	11	11	11	9	3	8	10
Angola	..	..	..	1	1	1	0	1	2	1	0	..	..	1
Benin	0	4	6	4	5	5	5	7	8	10	10	1	2	6
Botswana	4	24	25	22	23	22	23	24	25	26	24	4	18	24
Burkina Faso	2	6	6	6	5	6	5	5	4	5	5	2	5	5
Burundi	6	7	9	9	11	9	5	4	3	1	4	3	5	6
Cameroon	1	0	0	0	0	0	0	0	1	1	2	1	0	1
Cape Verde	6	4	2	2	1	1	0	1	1	2	2	6	6	1
Central African Republic	2	4	9	9	11	8	6	10	10	9	8	2	4	9
Chad	2	1	2	3	4	3	3	2	3	2	2	1	2	3
Comoros	2	5	6	5	6	5	6	6	8	12	13	2	4	8
Congo, Dem. Rep. of	2	0	1	1	1	..	..	..	..	..	..	1	1	1
Congo, Rep. of	1	0	0	0	0	0	0	0	1	0	0	0	0	0
Côte d'Ivoire	0	0	1	1	1	2	2	2	2	3	5	0	0	2
Djibouti	..	..	..	3	3	3	2	3	2	..	..	..	..	3
Equatorial Guinea	..	0	0	0	0	0	0	0	0	0	0	0	1	0
Eritrea	..	..	..	1	2	5	1	1	1	1	1	..	..	2
Ethiopia	4	4	6	7	7	4	4	3	2	3	5	5	2	5
Gabon	1	0	1	1	1	1	0	0	1	0	1	1	1	1
Gambia, The	0	4	5	4	5	5	4	5	5	4	4	2	3	5
Ghana	3	3	4	4	4	2	1	2	1	1	2	3	4	2
Guinea	..	2	1	1	1	1	3	2	2	3	2	..	1	2
Guinea-Bissau	..	2	2	2	1	3	5	4	6	6	10	..	2	5
Kenya	2	2	2	1	3	2	2	3	3	3	3	2	2	3
Lesotho	1	3	4	5	5	6	7	6	6	6	5	1	2	6
Liberia	0	..	..	..	..	..	..	..	..	..	..	0	0	..
Madagascar	0	1	1	1	2	3	2	2	2	3	4	1	2	2
Malawi	1	1	1	2	4	2	5	4	4	4	2	2	2	3
Mali	1	5	3	4	5	5	5	4	5	3	5	1	2	4
Mauritania	4	1	1	2	2	4	4	5	6	6	7	3	1	5
Mauritius	2	4	4	4	4	3	3	3	4	4	6	1	4	4
Mozambique	..	2	2	2	3	5	6	4	5	4	5	1	2	4
Namibia	..	1	1	1	1	1	2	2	2	2	2	..	1	2
Niger	2	6	3	2	2	1	1	1	2	3	3	2	6	2
Nigeria	5	2	2	2	4	6	6	4	6	6	4	3	2	5
Rwanda	7	1	1	3	3	4	4	5	5	5	6	5	3	4
São Tomé and Principe	..	..	..	1	1	3	3	3	3	4	5	..	..	3
Senegal	0	0	1	2	2	3	3	2	2	3	3	0	0	3
Seychelles	2	1	1	1	1	1	1	1	1	1	1	1	1	1
Sierra Leone	1	1	1	2	1	3	3	3	3	2	3	1	1	2
Somalia	1	..	..	..	..	..	..	..	..	..	..	2	0	..
South Africa	4	1	1	1	1	2	2	3	2	2	2	2	1	2
Sudan	0	1	1	2	1	1	1	1	1	0	2	0	0	1
Swaziland	3	4	4	3	2	3	3	3	3	2	3	3	3	3
Tanzania	0	1	2	1	2	3	3	4	5	6	8	1	1	4
Togo	1	4	3	3	1	2	2	2	3	2	3	3	5	2
Uganda	0	2	4	4	4	6	6	6	6	8	6	1	1	6
Zambia	1	1	2	1	2	2	1	0	2	1	4	3	1	2
Zimbabwe	8	3	3	3	3	1	1	2	2	1	1	3	2	2
NORTH AFRICA	..	8	8	8	9	9	8	7	8	10	12	..	8	9
Algeria	6	4	4	3	5	9	8	5	11	14	17	4	4	9
Egypt, Arab Rep.	3	11	11	11	12	11	10	8	7	7	7	2	5	9
Libya	..	..	..	..	..	..	..	..	..	..	..	..	..	..
Morocco	2	5	5	4	4	4	4	5	4	8	9	1	3	5
Tunisia	2	1	2	2	2	3	2	3	2	2	2	2	2	2
ALL AFRICA	4	8	8	8	8	8	8	7	8	9	10	3	5	8

Note: 2002 data are preliminary (see page 2). Data are based on total reserves, excluding gold, at year-end and on imports of all goods and services at current prices and exchange rates.

5-15. Export unit values

	Index 1995 = 100											Average annual percentage growth		
	1980	1993	1994	1995	1996	1997	1998	1999	2000	2001	2002	75-84	85-94	95-MR
SUB-SAHARAN AFRICA	123.5	90.0	91.4	100.0	102.5	98.1	83.9	84.5	95.4	88.3	90.1	5.9	1.9	-1.2
excluding South Africa	127.5	88.2	88.8	100.0	108.2	102.3	83.8	86.6	104.5	96.1	97.7	4.0	1.8	0.0
excl. S.Africa & Nigeria	115.8	84.9	87.8	100.0	104.1	98.5	87.0	83.7	89.9	85.6	88.5	2.6	0.3	-1.5
Angola	..	91.4	75.8	100.0	141.9	108.8	68.7	99.1	158.4	135.4	141.0	..	-1.5	6.0
Benin	44.2	65.3	71.0	100.0	87.6	85.3	88.4	87.1	77.8	77.9	83.5	5.9	3.0	-0.5
Botswana	74.8	92.2	94.2	100.0	96.4	99.0	92.9	94.0	91.9	85.2	83.8	4.5	6.9	-1.8
Burkina Faso	51.6	59.6	83.4	100.0	95.3	87.1	82.5	73.9	67.6	72.0	67.4	5.1	2.9	-4.4
Burundi	159.5	67.1	93.8	100.0	61.4	60.0	46.8	29.8	22.7	13.6	13.5	6.3	-7.6	-24.0
Cameroon	135.4	97.8	87.8	100.0	90.2	89.0	80.1	69.0	88.1	86.1	82.6	4.8	-0.5	-1.6
Cape Verde	62.3	85.1	90.0	100.0	98.4	94.2	93.4	93.0	79.5	81.4	87.8	9.5	7.2	-1.9
Central African Republic	139.5	144.1	85.7	100.0	87.8	66.9	57.1	48.5	40.5	41.9	45.8	8.4	-1.4	-11.0
Chad	92.3	77.1	73.3	100.0	110.2	98.8	106.3	96.2	88.6	107.0	105.5	-0.7	2.7	2.0
Comoros	101.4	87.3	65.4	100.0	96.7	85.1	81.2	84.2	73.0	92.6	95.3	..	3.0	1.2
Congo, Dem. Rep. of	132.6	84.0	98.6	100.0	93.4	79.3	103.1	41.4	37.3	35.1	36.8	0.9	4.9	-14.7
Congo, Rep. of	143.5	74.5	93.8	100.0	120.4	109.3	76.8	104.4	156.6	132.7	130.7	9.7	-1.2	4.5
Côte d'Ivoire	118.4	78.8	83.8	100.0	105.3	94.8	97.6	96.3	82.3	81.5	105.9	-1.1	-2.2	-0.3
Djibouti	..	..	..	..	..	..	..	..	..	..	..	..	..	..
Equatorial Guinea	..	133.3	87.6	100.0	122.4	137.5	103.2	157.3	198.4	134.6	140.9	..	1.6	6.7
Eritrea	..	87.5	94.7	100.0	97.3	93.7	85.0	83.1	84.3	82.7	83.3	..	..	-2.5
Ethiopia	..	65.1	70.2	100.0	79.3	84.4	93.8	76.9	63.9	59.0	52.3	..	-0.6	-5.3
Gabon	173.9	76.6	88.7	100.0	117.5	104.5	73.3	72.8	70.2	99.0	108.3	8.8	-1.4	-1.0
Gambia, The	81.3	96.9	95.9	100.0	100.4	100.0	97.0	94.5	87.2	76.5	72.1	3.4	7.9	-3.7
Ghana	39.3	81.5	88.0	100.0	101.7	101.8	105.5	92.1	89.5	88.0	97.6	0.9	1.3	-0.5
Guinea	..	98.1	113.3	100.0	92.8	94.2	83.4	79.7	72.2	67.8	68.8	..	-1.2	-6.2
Guinea-Bissau	57.5	109.8	102.2	100.0	102.1	93.9	79.1	90.5	88.5	101.6	120.4	14.1	-1.5	0.6
Kenya	130.0	69.5	82.9	100.0	98.5	114.2	113.6	95.0	93.4	96.3	101.4	5.5	-3.0	0.7
Lesotho	105.8	94.9	94.1	100.0	92.4	92.6	84.9	85.0	80.6	70.0	62.0	5.5	6.9	-5.0
Liberia	..	..	..	..	..	..	..	..	..	..	..	..	..	..
Madagascar	67.4	77.0	88.9	100.0	102.8	101.1	109.8	107.6	122.0	127.5	121.0	6.5	0.9	4.0
Malawi	87.1	86.5	82.3	100.0	104.9	109.9	89.1	92.7	89.1	86.5	89.1	3.8	1.8	-1.0
Mali	108.3	92.6	82.7	100.0	97.8	83.2	82.9	74.6	72.9	79.1	76.3	3.5	1.8	-2.8
Mauritania	71.4	127.8	94.6	100.0	96.9	100.8	82.9	78.8	71.9	67.5	56.0	1.7	5.5	-6.6
Mauritius	73.6	96.2	90.3	100.0	107.1	106.2	97.1	94.8	99.8	95.8	80.8	..	5.1	-1.4
Mozambique	122.0	92.3	93.9	100.0	80.3	82.3	78.7	79.3	70.4	70.0	69.5	..	-0.8	-4.2
Namibia	136.5	90.3	99.6	100.0	99.1	99.7	90.8	86.9	87.4	82.4	76.9	..	2.8	-3.3
Niger	158.9	77.0	88.7	100.0	88.2	80.6	84.0	81.5	..	..	..	12.0	-1.6	-2.9
Nigeria	145.5	101.2	92.7	100.0	122.2	115.6	72.6	98.7	167.6	144.3	151.5	3.1	8.6	6.1
Rwanda	90.9	64.7	77.4	100.0	88.1	117.0	88.3	75.8	91.6	68.7	60.4	8.0	-2.8	-4.0
São Tomé and Principe	..	94.4	110.0	100.0	127.0	130.5	103.6	102.6	88.6	94.6	114.0	..	-6.7	-1.6
Senegal	91.5	97.1	85.1	100.0	93.8	68.5	68.6	66.3	57.2	57.4	63.3	2.5	3.1	-6.2
Seychelles	..	87.7	91.6	100.0	100.4	94.7	93.9	101.7	91.3	86.9	92.5	..	-0.7	-0.8
Sierra Leone	67.2	49.6	106.1	100.0	124.7	110.0	647.1	808.3	898.4	882.0	1,013.8	12.2	7.3	43.1
Somalia	..	..	..	..	..	..	..	..	..	..	..	..	..	..
South Africa	116.8	93.0	95.7	100.0	93.2	91.4	83.9	81.1	81.2	75.8	77.7	9.1	2.1	-3.4
Sudan	133.9	67.0	72.3	100.0	81.9	99.3	100.6	84.8	93.0	94.9	107.7	4.2	-11.7	2.6
Swaziland	85.2	83.6	87.2	100.0	93.9	97.6	89.4	87.6	86.9	78.2	70.2	4.0	3.8	-3.1
Tanzania	..	104.0	113.2	100.0	104.4	155.0	126.7	111.2	103.1	108.8	113.6	..	2.4	-0.1
Togo	109.2	83.9	85.2	100.0	96.8	93.4	102.5	100.3	88.5	92.5	96.4	-1.9	0.5	0.2
Uganda	..	56.7	66.1	100.0	83.7	74.9	66.7	56.0	48.0	42.8	39.7	..	-10.5	-9.5
Zambia	89.9	79.7	80.3	100.0	76.7	73.9	51.7	40.0	45.4	50.9	49.1	2.4	5.0	-9.0
Zimbabwe	161.8	97.5	97.1	100.0	109.2	105.8	73.3	67.1	67.1	65.0	66.2	0.3	-1.5	-6.8
NORTH AFRICA	163.8	93.6	91.4	100.0	105.9	103.2	92.1	93.5	108.3	105.9	101.8	6.5	-0.2	0.9
Algeria	200.9	98.7	93.5	100.0	116.2	113.3	82.3	95.0	150.7	146.5	136.2	11.4	-2.4	5.1
Egypt, Arab Rep.	106.9	99.7	95.4	100.0	99.5	105.2	99.2	93.3	99.9	100.5	91.2	9.8	1.2	-0.5
Libya	..	..	..	..	..	..	..	..	..	..	..	..	..	..
Morocco	96.2	84.9	85.4	100.0	103.9	95.3	94.3	93.2	87.4	86.2	92.1	1.8	2.6	-0.9
Tunisia	91.3	84.6	88.8	100.0	103.4	94.2	93.0	92.2	83.7	81.1	83.4	5.3	3.2	-2.2
ALL AFRICA	130.8	91.2	91.4	100.0	103.5	99.6	86.3	87.3	99.5	93.8	93.8	6.6	1.3	-0.5

Note: 2002 data are preliminary (see page 2).

5-16. Import unit values

	Index 1995 = 100											Average annual percentage growth		
	1980	*1993*	*1994*	*1995*	*1996*	*1997*	*1998*	*1999*	*2000*	*2001*	*2002*	*75-84*	*85-94*	*95-MR*
SUB-SAHARAN AFRICA	76.9	93.8	92.8	100.0	95.9	96.7	90.9	88.1	87.7	84.1	82.2	5.1	4.9	-2.1
excluding South Africa	70.4	93.4	92.0	100.0	98.1	99.6	94.1	89.8	88.5	85.9	83.1	2.2	5.8	-1.9
excl. S.Africa & Nigeria	88.0	93.4	92.3	100.0	102.8	100.2	94.9	89.4	87.5	85.0	80.8	3.9	3.4	-2.4
Angola	..	120.1	89.6	100.0	132.3	128.7	123.4	134.5	127.5	125.0	90.4	..	4.8	1.1
Benin	54.3	84.4	93.6	100.0	99.3	91.5	94.7	92.5	82.6	82.8	87.0	6.3	3.9	-2.0
Botswana	79.3	95.7	94.1	100.0	92.0	90.6	83.1	83.3	82.0	75.1	74.0	7.5	5.4	-3.5
Burkina Faso	103.2	70.8	89.6	100.0	102.1	94.1	86.6	85.8	88.6	80.2	80.5	5.8	-0.4	-2.4
Burundi	112.9	91.2	89.7	100.0	84.5	89.5	63.1	42.1	37.2	30.5	27.0	8.9	0.7	-16.4
Cameroon	153.0	119.5	94.1	100.0	98.8	92.7	86.6	88.4	79.8	74.5	74.7	6.9	0.5	-3.7
Cape Verde	62.3	85.1	90.0	100.0	98.4	94.2	93.4	93.0	79.5	81.4	87.8	-0.5	7.2	-1.9
Central African Republic	102.6	101.4	83.0	100.0	101.7	86.0	88.6	87.5	78.0	77.7	83.8	4.4	-0.8	-2.0
Chad	78.6	76.8	87.7	100.0	110.2	98.9	97.5	93.3	81.7	62.0	58.5	2.2	5.4	-6.0
Comoros	78.5	108.5	111.1	100.0	98.2	83.9	77.6	74.9	63.0	60.4	58.5	..	7.0	-8.1
Congo, Dem. Rep. of	125.7	74.4	118.0	100.0	138.3	93.9	125.4	31.9	29.8	25.9	26.7	-2.6	5.2	-21.0
Congo, Rep. of	77.1	62.2	90.8	100.0	97.4	89.0	101.1	83.9	81.0	80.9	71.2	5.8	5.9	-3.3
Côte d'Ivoire	71.1	124.0	82.7	100.0	108.0	98.2	101.5	98.6	99.9	100.0	109.0	4.4	7.3	1.6
Djibouti	..	..	..	..	..	..	..	..	..	..	..	..	..	..
Equatorial Guinea	..	156.1	87.7	100.0	122.4	137.3	103.1	73.9	73.6	134.4	140.6	..	3.7	1.9
Eritrea	..	89.5	92.7	100.0	100.3	94.1	90.9	87.8	85.6	84.3	85.7	..	..	-2.0
Ethiopia	..	92.5	94.0	100.0	104.5	100.7	94.7	92.3	96.5	95.8	93.1	..	0.1	-0.7
Gabon	71.2	73.9	93.0	100.0	99.3	88.8	88.8	86.9	87.5	87.7	95.0	1.3	4.7	-1.0
Gambia, The	44.8	96.9	95.9	100.0	100.4	100.0	97.0	94.5	87.2	76.5	72.1	7.6	6.3	-3.7
Ghana	20.4	97.5	98.8	100.0	100.2	95.6	90.2	89.3	95.3	90.4	92.4	2.0	5.8	-1.2
Guinea	..	102.8	101.9	100.0	106.9	96.9	94.2	93.0	65.0	61.0	61.9	..	3.2	-7.2
Guinea-Bissau	47.0	79.3	84.3	100.0	102.6	98.4	92.0	94.1	90.6	94.0	117.7	8.1	7.1	1.4
Kenya	134.1	75.9	81.0	100.0	94.1	104.0	107.6	100.6	97.0	97.6	107.4	9.6	-4.3	1.8
Lesotho	80.3	94.6	94.1	100.0	92.0	92.7	84.6	85.0	80.4	69.8	61.9	8.1	6.1	-5.1
Liberia	..	..	..	..	..	..	..	..	..	..	..	..	..	..
Madagascar	63.6	85.2	90.6	100.0	99.8	94.7	92.9	95.8	96.7	85.9	84.4	9.1	5.5	-1.3
Malawi	56.3	80.0	96.4	100.0	98.6	98.7	91.2	91.9	94.1	91.3	94.8	6.4	6.7	-0.8
Mali	102.9	93.4	90.5	100.0	97.2	85.7	81.6	81.1	80.3	89.1	84.6	1.7	3.1	-1.7
Mauritania	100.4	109.0	99.4	100.0	105.7	99.6	88.2	77.9	73.4	70.2	64.6	5.6	2.7	-6.1
Mauritius	71.1	93.7	90.4	100.0	104.6	102.5	91.2	87.3	88.7	85.7	73.5	..	4.2	-2.9
Mozambique	77.0	103.5	86.9	100.0	105.1	107.7	102.5	101.7	106.5	104.3	103.4	..	4.0	1.3
Namibia	100.7	93.7	93.4	100.0	90.7	89.6	78.5	75.6	72.3	68.4	49.0	..	5.1	-7.0
Niger	83.1	64.1	90.4	100.0	101.1	98.1	103.3	105.6	..	..	..	1.8	4.8	2.4
Nigeria	44.1	93.6	90.7	100.0	77.9	97.4	90.1	91.7	92.3	89.5	91.8	-3.4	17.3	0.0
Rwanda	175.7	88.7	94.9	100.0	104.8	98.9	88.0	90.0	101.1	94.1	96.5	5.9	-4.6	-0.5
São Tomé and Principe	..	90.3	94.4	100.0	101.9	95.5	84.6	90.0	88.3	81.3	82.5	..	4.3	-2.5
Senegal	90.8	90.9	100.1	100.0	88.7	85.2	82.2	90.5	89.5	93.3	102.7	3.8	3.8	0.0
Seychelles	..	96.4	99.0	100.0	100.1	100.6	88.2	101.9	93.8	88.8	94.6	..	0.1	-1.1
Sierra Leone	92.7	70.3	102.1	100.0	85.5	97.2	238.6	345.1	298.9	225.6	206.0	11.4	4.8	16.2
Somalia	..	..	..	..	..	..	..	..	..	..	..	..	..	..
South Africa	97.5	94.4	94.4	100.0	91.9	91.2	84.6	84.2	85.9	80.0	80.0	10.3	2.4	-2.5
Sudan	146.6	67.0	72.3	100.0	81.9	99.3	100.6	84.8	93.0	94.9	90.4	-1.0	-11.7	1.4
Swaziland	85.2	83.6	87.2	100.0	93.9	97.6	89.4	87.6	86.9	78.2	70.2	4.2	3.8	-3.1
Tanzania	..	101.6	103.0	100.0	106.4	152.3	125.9	109.3	100.5	86.9	84.4	..	8.2	-2.7
Togo	91.2	92.0	89.1	100.0	103.6	93.7	89.3	87.4	88.0	86.7	92.6	0.2	4.0	-1.1
Uganda	..	98.6	98.8	100.0	104.5	94.3	94.3	91.8	94.4	93.9	90.0	..	-0.3	-1.3
Zambia	77.1	122.5	101.3	100.0	96.2	99.7	87.5	87.4	86.5	90.7	100.1	11.9	9.8	-1.1
Zimbabwe	184.8	96.9	96.4	100.0	108.9	106.4	73.1	66.9	65.1	62.8	63.6	5.7	-1.7	-7.3
NORTH AFRICA	70.6	91.6	93.2	100.0	102.2	99.9	98.5	96.2	93.8	91.5	90.3	5.5	4.2	-1.0
Algeria	69.1	97.3	94.7	100.0	100.5	93.2	94.7	92.9	87.9	84.4	88.0	5.6	3.9	-1.8
Egypt, Arab Rep.	58.2	94.2	93.2	100.0	104.5	114.0	117.9	112.4	116.5	118.5	108.5	8.6	5.6	2.2
Libya	..	..	..	..	..	..	..	..	..	..	..	..	..	..
Morocco	95.5	85.9	95.7	100.0	101.6	90.1	79.7	80.8	78.1	74.9	76.7	3.7	1.8	-3.9
Tunisia	75.0	85.3	88.0	100.0	100.5	94.4	94.0	92.5	83.8	81.7	84.3	5.1	4.8	-1.9
ALL AFRICA	73.6	93.0	92.9	100.0	97.9	97.7	93.3	90.7	89.7	86.6	84.9	5.4	4.6	-1.7

Note: 2002 data are preliminary (see page 2).

5-17. Terms of trade

	Index 1995 = 100											Average annual percentage growth		
	1980	*1993*	*1994*	*1995*	*1996*	*1997*	*1998*	*1999*	*2000*	*2001*	*2002*	*75-84*	*85-94*	*95-MR*
SUB-SAHARAN AFRICA	160.6	96.0	98.5	100.0	106.9	101.4	92.3	95.9	108.9	104.9	109.5	0.8	-2.8	0.9
excluding South Africa	181.2	94.4	96.6	100.0	110.3	102.6	89.1	96.4	118.1	111.8	117.5	1.5	-3.8	2.0
excl. S.Africa & Nigeria	131.5	91.0	95.2	100.0	101.3	98.3	91.7	93.7	102.7	100.8	109.5	-1.3	-3.0	0.9
Angola	..	76.1	84.6	100.0	107.3	84.5	55.7	73.7	124.2	108.4	156.1	..	-6.0	4.9
Benin	81.4	77.3	75.9	100.0	88.2	93.3	93.3	94.1	94.1	94.2	96.0	-0.3	-0.9	1.5
Botswana	94.3	96.4	100.1	100.0	104.8	109.3	111.8	112.8	112.0	113.4	113.3	-2.8	1.4	1.7
Burkina Faso	50.0	84.1	93.1	100.0	93.3	92.6	95.3	86.2	76.3	89.7	83.7	-0.7	3.3	-2.0
Burundi	141.3	73.6	104.6	100.0	72.7	67.1	74.1	70.8	61.1	44.5	50.1	-2.4	-8.2	-9.0
Cameroon	88.5	81.8	93.2	100.0	91.4	96.1	92.5	78.0	110.5	115.5	110.6	-2.0	-1.0	2.2
Cape Verde	100.0	100.0	100.0	100.0	100.0	100.0	100.0	100.0	100.0	100.0	100.0	10.1	0.0	0.0
Central African Republic	136.0	142.1	103.3	100.0	86.4	77.9	64.4	55.4	51.9	53.9	54.7	3.9	-0.6	-9.1
Chad	117.5	100.4	83.6	100.0	100.0	99.9	109.0	103.1	108.4	172.7	180.2	-2.8	-2.5	8.5
Comoros	129.2	80.4	58.8	100.0	98.5	101.4	104.7	112.4	115.9	153.3	162.7	..	-3.8	10.1
Congo, Dem. Rep. of	105.5	113.0	83.5	100.0	67.5	84.4	82.2	129.8	125.3	135.3	137.9	3.6	-0.3	7.9
Congo, Rep. of	186.0	119.8	103.2	100.0	123.6	122.9	76.0	124.5	193.3	164.1	183.5	3.7	-6.7	8.1
Côte d'Ivoire	166.6	63.6	101.3	100.0	97.5	96.5	96.2	97.6	82.4	81.6	97.1	-5.2	-8.8	-1.8
Djibouti	..	..	..	..	..	..	..	..	..	..	..	..	..	..
Equatorial Guinea	..	85.4	100.0	100.0	100.0	100.2	100.2	213.0	269.6	100.2	100.2	..	-2.0	4.7
Eritrea	..	97.7	102.1	100.0	97.0	99.6	93.5	94.6	98.4	98.1	97.2	..	..	-0.5
Ethiopia	..	70.4	74.7	100.0	75.9	83.9	99.1	83.3	66.2	61.6	56.1	..	-0.7	-4.7
Gabon	244.0	103.7	95.4	100.0	118.4	117.7	82.5	83.7	80.2	112.9	114.0	7.5	-5.8	-0.1
Gambia, The	181.6	100.0	100.0	100.0	100.0	100.0	100.0	100.0	100.0	100.0	100.0	-3.9	1.5	0.0
Ghana	192.3	83.6	89.0	100.0	101.5	106.5	117.0	103.1	94.0	97.3	105.6	-1.1	-4.2	0.7
Guinea	..	95.4	111.2	100.0	86.8	97.2	88.5	85.7	111.1	111.1	111.1	..	-4.3	1.1
Guinea-Bissau	122.2	138.4	121.3	100.0	99.6	95.4	86.0	96.2	97.7	108.1	102.4	5.5	-8.0	-0.8
Kenya	96.9	91.5	102.4	100.0	104.6	109.8	105.6	94.4	96.3	98.7	94.4	-3.8	1.4	-1.1
Lesotho	131.8	100.3	100.0	100.0	100.4	99.9	100.4	100.0	100.3	100.3	100.1	-2.4	0.7	0.0
Liberia	..	..	..	..	..	..	..	..	..	..	..	..	..	..
Madagascar	105.9	90.4	98.1	100.0	103.0	106.9	118.2	112.3	126.1	148.4	143.4	-2.4	-4.3	5.4
Malawi	154.7	108.2	85.3	100.0	106.4	111.3	97.7	100.9	94.7	94.8	93.9	-2.4	-4.6	-0.2
Mali	105.3	99.1	91.4	100.0	100.7	97.1	101.6	92.0	90.7	88.8	90.2	1.8	-1.3	-1.1
Mauritania	71.1	117.2	95.1	100.0	91.7	101.2	101.1	101.1	98.0	96.2	86.6	-3.6	2.7	-0.6
Mauritius	103.4	102.6	99.9	100.0	102.5	103.6	106.5	108.5	112.5	111.8	109.9	..	0.9	1.6
Mozambique	158.4	89.2	108.0	100.0	76.4	76.4	76.7	77.9	66.2	67.1	67.2	..	-4.6	-5.5
Namibia	135.5	96.4	106.7	100.0	109.3	111.2	115.7	114.9	120.9	120.4	156.9	..	-2.2	4.0
Niger	191.1	120.1	98.1	100.0	87.2	82.1	81.3	77.1	..	..	..	10.1	-6.1	-5.2
Nigeria	329.7	108.2	102.3	100.0	156.7	118.7	80.5	107.6	181.6	161.3	165.1	6.7	-7.4	6.1
Rwanda	51.7	72.9	81.5	100.0	84.1	118.2	100.3	84.2	90.5	73.0	62.6	2.0	1.9	-3.6
São Tomé and Principe	..	104.6	116.5	100.0	124.6	136.6	122.4	113.9	100.3	116.3	138.2	..	-10.6	0.9
Senegal	100.8	106.9	85.0	100.0	105.8	80.4	83.5	73.3	63.9	61.6	61.7	-1.2	-0.7	-6.2
Seychelles	..	91.0	92.6	100.0	100.3	94.1	106.4	99.8	97.3	97.8	97.8	..	-0.8	0.3
Sierra Leone	72.4	70.6	103.9	100.0	145.9	113.2	271.2	234.2	300.6	390.9	492.1	0.7	2.4	23.1
Somalia	..	..	..	..	..	..	..	..	..	..	..	..	..	..
South Africa	119.8	98.4	101.3	100.0	101.4	100.2	99.1	96.3	94.6	94.7	97.1	-1.2	-0.3	-0.9
Sudan	91.3	100.0	100.0	100.0	100.0	100.0	100.0	100.0	100.0	100.0	119.2	5.2	0.0	1.2
Swaziland	100.0	100.0	100.0	100.0	100.0	100.0	100.0	100.0	100.0	100.0	100.0	-0.2	0.0	0.0
Tanzania	..	102.4	110.0	100.0	98.1	101.7	100.6	101.7	102.6	125.3	134.6	..	-5.4	2.7
Togo	119.7	91.1	95.6	100.0	93.4	99.7	114.8	114.8	100.6	106.8	104.0	-2.1	-3.4	1.4
Uganda	..	57.5	66.9	100.0	80.2	79.4	70.7	60.9	50.8	45.6	44.1	..	-10.2	-8.3
Zambia	116.6	65.1	79.3	100.0	79.7	74.2	59.1	45.7	52.5	56.1	49.0	-8.5	-4.4	-8.0
Zimbabwe	87.6	100.7	100.7	100.0	100.3	99.4	100.2	100.3	103.1	103.6	104.1	-5.1	0.2	0.5
NORTH AFRICA	232.2	102.2	98.1	100.0	103.6	103.3	93.5	97.3	115.5	115.7	112.6	1.0	-4.2	1.9
Algeria	290.9	101.4	98.7	100.0	115.6	121.6	86.9	102.3	171.5	173.6	154.8	5.5	-6.1	7.0
Egypt, Arab Rep.	183.9	105.9	102.4	100.0	95.2	92.2	84.1	83.0	85.7	84.8	84.0	1.0	-4.2	-2.6
Libya	..	..	..	..	..	..	..	..	..	..	..	..	..	..
Morocco	100.8	98.8	89.3	100.0	102.2	105.8	118.3	115.3	111.9	115.1	120.0	-1.8	0.8	3.2
Tunisia	121.7	99.2	100.9	100.0	102.9	99.8	98.9	99.7	99.9	99.3	98.8	0.2	-1.5	-0.3
ALL AFRICA	177.7	98.1	98.3	100.0	105.7	102.0	92.5	96.2	110.9	108.3	110.5	1.2	-3.2	1.2

Note: 2002 data are preliminary (see page 2).

5-18. Forest products exports

	Thousands of cubic meters											Average annual percentage growth		
	1980	1987	1988	1989	1990	1991	1992	1993	1994	1995	1996	75-84	85-94	95-MR
SUB-SAHARAN AFRICA	8,169	6,803	8,821	7,032	6,931	6,824	7,170	4,764	4,364	3,788	4,289	149.9	-3.3	..
excluding South Africa	7,413	5,283	6,044	5,855	5,794	5,632	5,478	4,339	3,960	3,300	3,748	149.8	-3.1	
excl. S.Africa & Nigeria	7,402	5,266	6,028	5,844	5,757	5,583	5,444	3,908	3,672	3,030	3,499	150.2	-3.7	
Angola	..	0	0	3	0	..	2	..	..	..	..	..	35.0	
Benin	..	..	..	..	..	0	0	..	..	..	..	..	..	
Botswana	..	..	..	..	..	..	..	..	..	..	..	..	..	
Burkina Faso	..	..	..	..	..	..	..	..	..	..	..	..	..	
Burundi	..	..	..	..	..	..	..	..	..	..	..	..	..	
Cameroon	934	521	652	539	837	1,049	816	..	..	..	..	151.6	4.4	
Cape Verde	..	..	..	..	..	..	..	..	..	..	..	..	..	
Central African Republic	177	74	80	113	67	37	36	..	..	..	..	150.6	-13.6	
Chad	..	..	..	..	..	..	..	..	..	..	..	..	..	
Comoros	..	..	..	..	1	..	0	..	..	..	..	..	..	
Congo, Dem. Rep. of	116	147	163	143	142	172	136	113	101	74	91	171.2	-3.3	
Congo, Rep. of	385	643	941	937	816	609	530	..	..	..	..	163.8	9.7	
Côte d'Ivoire	3,394	1,175	1,138	1,084	1,127	967	878	..	..	..	..	150.4	-11.5	
Djibouti	..	..	..	..	..	..	..	..	..	..	..	..	..	
Equatorial Guinea	16	133	133	142	129	126	143	400	380	..	5	218.1	13.5	
Eritrea	..	..	..	..	..	..	..	..	..	..	..	..	..	
Ethiopia														
Gabon	1,150	1,353	1,343	1,460	1,244	1,392	1,447	1,685	1,729	1,359	1,632	154.9	2.6	
Gambia, The	..	..	..	..	..	0	0	..	..	..	..	..	..	
Ghana	183	514	531	371	361	390	426	936	735	754	1,018	107.8	13.8	
Guinea	..	8	8	8	13	15	17	45	45	45	45	112.1	16.4	
Guinea-Bissau	6	5	4	4	6	12	9	5	5	6	8	117.7	15.0	
Kenya	33	4	4	3	4	3	0	82	94	95	27	138.6	8.6	
Lesotho	..	..	..	..	..	..	..	..	..	..	..	..	..	
Liberia	524	255	701	729	663	429	642	149	145	206	225	147.3	-1.0	
Madagascar	0	2	1	2	3	26	6	6	10	8	4	111.7	35.7	
Malawi	..	..	1	0	0	0	1	1	1	1	1	153.8	-8.8	
Mali	..	..	..	..	..	0	..	..	..	..	..	..	..	
Mauritania	..	..	..	..	1	..	..	..	..	..	..	..	..	
Mauritius	..	..	..	..	..	..	2	..	..	..	..	..	..	
Mozambique	31	5	10	2	5	4	1	149	137	140	158	68.8	28.7	
Namibia	..	..	..	..	..	..	..	..	..	..	..	..	..	
Niger	..	..	..	..	..	..	..	..	..	..	..	..	..	
Nigeria	11	17	16	11	37	49	34	431	288	269	248	143.7	16.5	
Rwanda	..	..	..	..	..	0	..	..	..	..	..	..	..	
São Tomé and Principe	..	..	..	..	0	..	..	0	..	..	..	..	..	
Senegal	..	..	..	..	..	..	..	..	..	..	..	..	..	
Seychelles	..	..	..	..	0	..	..	..	..	..	..	..	..	
Sierra Leone	..	1	1	0	0	0	0	..	..	..	..	..	-26.0	
Somalia								48						
South Africa	756	1,520	2,777	1,177	1,137	1,191	1,692	425	405	488	541	150.9	-4.1	
Sudan	..	..	..	..	..	0	..	..	..	..	..	..	..	
Swaziland	421	355	293	285	254	254	254	241	239	299	270	163.6	-7.8	
Tanzania	5	5	6	3	25	14	8	40	40	37	9	115.7	24.2	
Togo	..	..	..	..	0	..	..	0	0	1	0	..	..	
Uganda	0	..	..	..	..	..	..	9	11	7	7	45.4	..	
Zambia	..	..	..	..	0	0	..	..	..	..	..	..	..	
Zimbabwe	26	65	17	17	56	83	89	..	..	..	..	214.2	10.3	
NORTH AFRICA	88	94	117	95	95	77	105	78	84	71	60	160.0	0.4	..
Algeria	..	..	..	..	1	..	..	..	..	..	..	..	..	
Egypt, Arab Rep.	..	..	..	..	0	0	..	3	6	0	..	..	..	
Libya	..	..	..	..	..	0	0	..	..	..	..	..	..	
Morocco	74	85	102	88	84	70	98	43	48	50	39	169.1	-3.2	
Tunisia	14	10	16	7	10	8	7	32	29	20	21	135.1	9.7	
ALL AFRICA	8,258	6,897	8,938	7,127	7,026	6,901	7,275	4,842	4,448	3,859	4,349	150.0	-3.3	..

5-19. Petroleum exports

	Thousands of metric tons											Average annual percentage growth		
	1980	1992	1993	1994	1995	1996	1997	1998	1999	2000	2001	75-84	85-94	95-MR
SUB-SAHARAN AFRICA	118,522	138,295	147,611	146,069	148,560	163,548	174,930	178,213	172,584	187,664	182,983	-4.5	5.3	3.5
excluding South Africa	118,522	138,217	147,308	145,873	148,476	163,546	174,089	177,557	171,159	187,492	182,805	-4.5	5.3	3.5
excl. S.Africa & Nigeria	21,791	55,211	55,114	56,615	61,159	67,009	70,526	73,462	73,492	78,933	75,629	3.8	6.9	4.4
Angola	6,334	25,706	23,497	25,315	28,654	31,441	33,410	35,108	35,171	37,853	35,089	-0.2	11.1	5.0
Benin	..	138	157	131	97	84	65	62	45	38	40	..	8.8	-16.3
Botswana	..	..	..	..	..	..	..	..	..	..	..	..	..	..
Burkina Faso	..	..	..	..	..	..	..	..	..	..	..	..	..	..
Burundi	..	..	..	..	..	..	..	..	..	..	..	..	..	..
Cameroon	3,407	6,097	6,091	5,278	5,014	5,354	5,532	6,200	5,503	5,797	5,528	81.5	-2.8	1.5
Cape Verde	..	..	..	..	..	..	..	..	..	..	..	..	..	..
Central African Republic	..	..	..	..	..	..	..	..	..	..	..	..	..	..
Chad	..	..	..	..	..	..	..	..	..	..	..	..	..	..
Comoros	..	..	..	..	..	..	..	..	..	..	..	..	..	..
Congo, Dem. Rep. of	859	1,027	1,019	1,141	1,138	1,133	1,136	1,138	1,182	1,224	1,167	0.3	-3.1	0.8
Congo, Rep. of	3,432	8,358	9,201	8,725	9,047	10,272	11,809	13,125	14,087	13,589	12,550	12.2	5.6	6.9
Côte d'Ivoire	122	95	126	315	137	1,049	719	514	476	430	356	..	0.2	4.7
Djibouti	..	..	..	..	..	..	..	..	..	..	..	..	..	..
Equatorial Guinea	..	..	..	..	..	..	..	..	..	..	..	..	..	..
Eritrea	..	..	..	..	..	..	..	..	..	..	..	..	..	..
Ethiopia	..	..	..	..	..	..	..	..	..	..	..	..	..	..
Gabon	7,637	13,790	15,023	15,710	17,072	17,676	17,855	17,315	15,326	13,261	13,063	-4.5	9.6	-3.5
Gambia, The	..	..	..	..	..	..	..	..	..	..	..	..	..	..
Ghana	..	..	..	..	..	..	..	..	..	..	..	..	..	..
Guinea	..	..	..	..	..	..	..	..	..	..	..	..	..	..
Guinea-Bissau	..	..	..	..	..	..	..	..	..	..	..	..	..	..
Kenya	..	..	..	..	..	..	..	..	..	..	..	..	..	..
Lesotho	..	..	..	..	..	..	..	..	..	..	..	..	..	..
Liberia	..	..	..	..	..	..	..	..	..	..	..	..	..	..
Madagascar	..	..	..	..	..	..	..	..	..	..	..	..	..	..
Malawi	..	..	..	..	..	..	..	..	..	..	..	..	..	..
Mali	..	..	..	..	..	..	..	..	..	..	..	..	..	..
Mauritania	..	..	..	..	..	..	..	..	..	..	..	..	..	..
Mauritius	..	..	..	..	..	..	..	..	..	..	..	..	..	..
Mozambique	..	..	..	..	..	..	..	..	..	..	..	..	..	..
Namibia	..	..	..	..	..	..	..	..	..	..	..	..	..	..
Niger	..	..	..	..	..	..	..	..	..	..	..	..	..	..
Nigeria	96,731	83,006	92,194	89,258	87,317	96,537	103,563	104,095	97,667	108,559	107,176	-6.8	4.4	2.9
Rwanda	..	..	..	..	..	..	..	..	..	..	..	..	..	..
São Tomé and Principe	..	..	..	..	..	..	..	..	..	..	..	..	..	..
Senegal	..	..	..	..	..	..	..	..	..	..	..	..	..	..
Seychelles	..	..	..	..	..	..	..	..	..	..	..	..	..	..
Sierra Leone	..	..	..	..	..	..	..	..	..	..	..	..	..	..
Somalia	..	..	..	..	..	..	..	..	..	..	..	..	..	..
South Africa	..	78	303	196	84	2	841	656	1,425	172	178	..	..	30.5
Sudan	..	..	..	..	..	..	..	..	1,702	6,741	7,836	..	..	..
Swaziland	..	..	..	..	..	..	..	..	..	..	..	..	..	..
Tanzania	..	..	..	..	..	..	..	..	..	..	..	..	..	..
Togo	..	..	..	..	..	..	..	..	..	..	..	..	..	..
Uganda	..	..	..	..	..	..	..	..	..	..	..	..	..	..
Zambia	..	..	..	..	..	..	..	..	..	..	..	..	..	..
Zimbabwe	..	..	..	..	..	..	..	..	..	..	..	..	..	..
NORTH AFRICA	146,129	115,283	111,512	100,666	99,750	102,320	98,236	100,246	92,090	99,543	98,824	-3.6	1.5	-0.5
Algeria	39,182	32,299	33,246	33,254	33,108	36,722	35,499	37,040	36,802	39,652	38,556	-5.4	1.7	2.4
Egypt, Arab Rep.	17,146	20,412	19,924	8,480	8,503	6,836	6,241	2,836	2,865	7,190	7,058	20.7	-5.8	-6.4
Libya	85,054	58,463	54,893	55,661	54,573	55,365	53,633	57,443	49,067	49,725	50,392	-6.4	4.3	-1.7
Morocco	..	..	..	..	..	..	..	..	..	..	..	..	..	..
Tunisia	4,747	4,109	3,449	3,271	3,566	3,397	2,863	2,927	3,356	2,976	2,818	-0.5	-1.4	-2.3
ALL AFRICA	264,651	253,578	259,123	246,735	248,310	265,868	273,166	278,459	264,674	287,207	281,807	-4.0	3.5	2.0

5-20. Copper exports

	1980	1989	1990	1991	1992	1993	1994	1995	1996	1997	1998	75-84	85-94	95-MR
	Thousands of metric tons											*Average annual percentage growth*		
SUB-SAHARAN AFRICA	1,286	1,074	973	792	714	598	495	418	392	393	316	5.2	-8.6	-9.1
excluding South Africa	1,164	958	883	688	581	517	421	339	318	322	248	4.6	-9.3	-10.5
excl. S.Africa & Nigeria	1,164	958	883	688	581	517	421	339	318	322	248	4.6	-9.3	-10.5
Angola	0	0	0	0	0	0	0	0	0	0	0	..	..	..
Benin	0	0	0	0	0	0	0	0	0	0	0	..	..	..
Botswana	20	19	19	20	19	22	20	18	23	18	20	..	0.2	0.3
Burkina Faso	0	0	0	0	0	0	0	0	0	0	0	..	..	..
Burundi	0	0	0	0	0	0	0	0	0	0	0	..	..	..
Cameroon	0	0	0	0	0	0	0	0	0	0	0	..	..	..
Cape Verde	0	0	0	0	0	0	0	0	0	0	0	..	..	..
Central African Republic	0	0	0	0	0	0	0	0	0	0	0	..	..	..
Chad	0	0	0	0	0	0	0	0	0	0	0	..	..	..
Comoros	0	0	0	0	0	0	0	0	0	0	0	..	..	..
Congo, Dem. Rep. of	461	439	374	252	116	28	14	5	0	0	0	16.8	-27.6	..
Congo, Rep. of	1	0	0	0	0	0	0	0	0	0	0	..	..	..
Côte d'Ivoire	0	0	0	0	0	0	0	0	0	0	0	..	..	..
Djibouti	0	0	0	0	0	0	0	0	0	0	0	..	..	..
Equatorial Guinea	0	0	0	0	0	0	0	0	0	0	0	..	..	..
Eritrea	0	0	0	0	0	0	0	0	0	0	0	..	..	..
Ethiopia	0	0	0	0	0	0	0	0	0	0	0	..	..	..
Gabon	0	0	0	0	0	0	0	0	0	0	0	..	..	..
Gambia, The	0	0	0	0	0	0	0	0	0	0	0	..	..	..
Ghana	0	0	0	0	0	0	0	0	0	0	0	..	..	..
Guinea	0	0	0	0	0	0	0	0	0	0	0	..	..	..
Guinea-Bissau	0	0	0	0	0	0	0	0	0	0	0	..	..	..
Kenya	0	0	0	0	0	0	0	0	0	0	0	..	..	..
Lesotho	0	0	0	0	0	0	0	0	0	0	0	..	..	..
Liberia	0	0	0	0	0	0	0	0	0	0	0	..	..	..
Madagascar	0	0	0	0	0	0	0	0	0	0	0	..	..	..
Malawi	0	0	0	0	0	0	0	0	0	0	0	..	..	..
Mali	0	0	0	0	0	0	0	0	0	0	0	..	..	..
Mauritania	1	0	0	0	0	0	0	0	0	0	0	..	..	..
Mauritius	0	0	0	0	0	0	0	0	0	0	0	..	..	..
Mozambique	0	0	0	0	0	0	0	0	0	0	0	..	..	..
Namibia	41	33	30	34	35	30	26	25	18	0	0	1.9	-5.2	..
Niger	0	0	0	0	0	0	0	0	0	0	0	..	..	..
Nigeria	0	0	0	0	0	0	0	0	0	0	0	..	..	..
Rwanda	0	0	0	0	0	0	0	0	0	0	0	..	..	..
São Tomé and Principe	0	0	0	0	0	0	0	0	0	0	0	..	..	..
Senegal	0	0	0	0	0	0	0	0	0	0	0	..	..	..
Seychelles	0	0	0	0	0	0	0	0	0	0	0	..	..	..
Sierra Leone	0	0	0	0	0	0	0	0	0	0	0	..	..	..
Somalia	0	0	0	0	0	0	0	0	0	0	0	..	..	..
South Africa	121	115	90	104	132	81	74	79	74	71	68	13.2	-3.2	-2.8
Sudan	0	0	0	0	0	0	0	0	0	0	0	..	..	..
Swaziland	0	0	0	0	0	0	0	0	0	0	0	..	..	..
Tanzania	0	0	0	0	0	0	0	0	0	0	0	..	..	..
Togo	0	0	0	0	0	0	0	0	0	0	0	..	..	..
Uganda	0	0	0	0	0	0	0	0	0	0	0	..	..	..
Zambia	617	456	460	382	412	437	361	292	276	304	228	-1.8	-3.0	-8.4
Zimbabwe	23	10	0	0	0	0	0	0	0	0	0	3.8	-16.6	..
NORTH AFRICA	6	12	16	16	17	13	19	16	16	0	0	..	-3.3	..
Algeria	0	0	0	0	0	0	0	0	0	0	0	..	..	..
Egypt, Arab Rep.	0	0	0	0	0	0	0	0	0	0	0	..	..	..
Libya	0	0	0	0	0	0	0	0	0	0	0	..	..	..
Morocco	6	12	16	16	17	13	19	16	16	0	0	..	-3.2	..
Tunisia	0	0	0	0	0	0	0	0	0	0	0	..	..	..
ALL AFRICA	1,292	1,086	989	807	730	611	514	434	408	393	316	5.4	-8.4	-10.1

5-21. Iron exports

	1980	1987	1988	1989	1990	1991	1992	1993	1994	1995	1996	75-84	85-94	95-MR
	Thousands of metric tons											*Average annual percentage growth*		
SUB-SAHARAN AFRICA	28,215	20,447	22,981	24,956	21,057	17,509	15,778	18,986	19,465	21,397	19,545	..	-3.0	..
excluding South Africa	17,482	14,903	15,734	15,780	9,988	7,474	6,114	6,276	6,722	7,196	7,000	..	-11.5	..
excl. S.Africa & Nigeria	17,482	14,903	15,734	15,780	9,988	7,474	6,114	6,276	6,722	7,196	7,000	..	-11.5	..
Angola	0	0	0	0	0	0	0	0	0	0	0	..	..	..
Benin	0	0	0	0	0	0	0	0	0	0	0	..	..	..
Botswana	0	0	0	0	0	0	0	0	0	0	0	..	..	..
Burkina Faso	0	0	0	0	0	0	0	0	0	0	0	..	..	..
Burundi	0	0	0	0	0	0	0	0	0	0	0	..	..	..
Cameroon	0	0	0	0	0	0	0	0	0	0	0	..	..	..
Cape Verde	0	0	0	0	0	0	0	0	0	0	0	..	..	..
Central African Republic	0	0	0	0	0	0	0	0	0	0	0	..	..	..
Chad	0	0	0	0	0	0	0	0	0	0	0	..	..	..
Comoros	0	0	0	0	0	0	0	0	0	0	0	..	..	..
Congo, Dem. Rep. of	0	0	0	0	0	0	0	0	0	0	0	..	..	..
Congo, Rep. of	0	0	0	0	0	0	0	0	0	0	0	..	..	..
Côte d'Ivoire	0	0	0	0	0	0	0	0	0	0	0	..	..	..
Djibouti	0	0	0	0	0	0	0	0	0	0	0	..	..	..
Equatorial Guinea	0	0	0	0	0	0	0	0	0	0	0	..	..	..
Eritrea	0	0	0	0	0	0	0	0	0	0	0	..	..	..
Ethiopia	0	0	0	0	0	0	0	0	0	0	0	..	..	..
Gabon	0	0	0	0	0	0	0	0	0	0	0	..	..	..
Gambia, The	0	0	0	0	0	0	0	0	0	0	0	..	..	..
Ghana	0	0	0	0	0	0	0	0	0	0	0	..	..	..
Guinea	0	0	0	0	0	0	0	0	0	0	0	..	..	..
Guinea-Bissau	0	0	0	0	0	0	0	0	0	0	0	..	..	..
Kenya	0	0	0	0	0	0	0	0	0	0	0	..	..	..
Lesotho	0	0	0	0	0	0	0	0	0	0	0	..	..	..
Liberia	11,695	9,052	9,231	8,540	2,607	670	853	0	0	0	0	..	-30.0	..
Madagascar	0	0	0	0	0	0	0	0	0	0	0	..	..	..
Malawi	0	0	0	0	0	0	0	0	0	0	0	..	..	..
Mali	0	0	0	0	0	0	0	0	0	0	0	..	..	..
Mauritania	5,673	5,851	6,503	7,240	7,381	6,804	5,261	6,276	6,722	7,196	7,000	..	0.6	..
Mauritius	0	0	0	0	0	0	0	0	0	0	0	..	..	..
Mozambique	0	0	0	0	0	0	0	0	0	0	0	..	..	..
Namibia	0	0	0	0	0	0	0	0	0	0	0	..	..	..
Niger	0	0	0	0	0	0	0	0	0	0	0	..	..	..
Nigeria	0	0	0	0	0	0	0	0	0	0	0	..	..	..
Rwanda	0	0	0	0	0	0	0	0	0	0	0	..	..	..
São Tomé and Principe	0	0	0	0	0	0	0	0	0	0	0	..	..	..
Senegal	0	0	0	0	0	0	0	0	0	0	0	..	..	..
Seychelles	0	0	0	0	0	0	0	0	0	0	0	..	..	..
Sierra Leone	0	0	0	0	0	0	0	0	0	0	0	..	..	..
Somalia	0	0	0	0	0	0	0	0	0	0	0	..	..	..
South Africa	10,733	5,544	7,247	9,176	11,069	10,035	9,664	12,710	12,743	14,201	12,545	..	8.2	..
Sudan	0	0	0	0	0	0	0	0	0	0	0	..	..	..
Swaziland	114	0	0	0	0	0	0	0	0	0	0	..	..	..
Tanzania	0	0	0	0	0	0	0	0	0	0	0	..	..	..
Togo	0	0	0	0	0	0	0	0	0	0	0	..	..	..
Uganda	0	0	0	0	0	0	0	0	0	0	0	..	..	..
Zambia	0	0	0	0	0	0	0	0	0	0	0	..	..	..
Zimbabwe	0	0	0	0	0	0	0	0	0	0	0	..	..	..
NORTH AFRICA	784	6	48	62	47	50	55	58	42	21	4	..	4.9	..
Algeria	699	6	0	10	9	10	20	25	25	5	4	..	-6.7	..
Egypt, Arab Rep.	0	0	0	0	0	0	0	0	0	0	0	..	..	..
Libya	0	0	0	0	0	0	0	0	0	0	0	..	..	..
Morocco	85	0	48	52	38	40	35	33	17	16	0	..	-13.6	..
Tunisia	0	0	0	0	0	0	0	0	0	0	0	..	..	..
ALL AFRICA	28,999	20,453	23,029	25,018	21,104	17,559	15,833	19,044	19,507	21,418	19,549	..	-3.1	..

5-22. Phosphates exports

	Thousands of metric tons											Average annual percentage growth		
	1980	1988	1989	1990	1991	1992	1993	1994	1995	1996	1997	75-84	85-94	95-MR
SUB-SAHARAN AFRICA	4,277	5,983	5,877	4,995	5,544	4,617	3,747	4,154	4,919	4,496	4,290	0.4	-0.9	..
excluding South Africa	4,274	4,715	4,783	3,778	4,378	3,272	2,550	2,881	3,511	3,522	2,990	-0.6	-3.2	..
excl. S.Africa & Nigeria	4,274	4,715	4,783	3,778	4,378	3,272	2,550	2,881	3,511	3,522	2,990	-0.6	-3.2	..
Angola	0	0	0	0	0	0	0	0	0	0	0	..	..	..
Benin	0	0	0	0	0	0	0	0	0	0	0	..	..	..
Botswana	0	0	0	0	0	0	0	0	0	0	0	..	..	..
Burkina Faso	0	0	0	0	0	0	0	0	0	0	0	..	..	..
Burundi	0	0	0	0	0	0	0	0	0	0	0	..	..	..
Cameroon	0	0	0	0	0	0	0	0	0	0	0	..	..	..
Cape Verde	0	0	0	0	0	0	0	0	0	0	0	..	..	..
Central African Republic	0	0	0	0	0	0	0	0	0	0	0	..	..	..
Chad	0	0	0	0	0	0	0	0	0	0	0	..	..	..
Comoros	0	0	0	0	0	0	0	0	0	0	0	..	..	..
Congo, Dem. Rep. of	0	0	0	0	0	0	0	0	0	0	0	..	..	..
Congo, Rep. of	0	0	0	0	0	0	0	0	0	0	0	..	..	..
Côte d'Ivoire	0	0	0	0	0	0	0	0	0	0	0	..	..	..
Djibouti	0	0	0	0	0	0	0	0	0	0	0	..	..	..
Equatorial Guinea	0	0	0	0	0	0	0	0	0	0	0	..	..	..
Eritrea	0	0	0	0	0	0	0	0	0	0	0	..	..	..
Ethiopia	0	0	0	0	0	0	0	0	0	0	0	..	..	..
Gabon	0	0	0	0	0	0	0	0	0	0	0	..	..	..
Gambia, The	0	0	0	0	0	0	0	0	0	0	0	..	..	..
Ghana	0	0	0	0	0	0	0	0	0	0	0	..	..	..
Guinea	0	0	0	0	0	0	0	0	0	0	0	..	..	..
Guinea-Bissau	0	0	0	0	0	0	0	0	0	0	0	..	..	..
Kenya	0	0	0	0	0	0	0	0	0	0	0	..	..	..
Lesotho	0	0	0	0	0	0	0	0	0	0	0	..	..	..
Liberia	0	0	0	0	0	0	0	0	0	0	0	..	..	..
Madagascar	0	0	0	0	0	0	0	0	0	0	0	..	..	..
Malawi	0	0	0	0	0	0	0	0	0	0	0	..	..	..
Mali	0	0	0	0	0	0	0	0	0	0	0	..	..	..
Mauritania	0	0	0	0	0	0	0	0	0	0	0	..	..	..
Mauritius	0	0	0	0	0	0	0	0	0	0	0	..	..	..
Mozambique	0	0	0	0	0	0	0	0	0	0	0	..	..	..
Namibia	0	0	0	0	0	0	0	0	0	0	0	..	..	..
Niger	0	0	0	0	0	0	0	0	0	0	0	..	..	..
Nigeria	0	0	0	0	0	0	0	0	0	0	0	..	..	..
Rwanda	0	0	0	0	0	0	0	0	0	0	0	..	..	..
São Tomé and Principe	0	0	0	0	0	0	0	0	0	0	0	..	..	..
Senegal	1,378	1,847	1,435	1,356	1,304	1,187	983	648	859	836	598	-3.9	-5.0	..
Seychelles	0	0	0	0	0	0	0	0	0	0	0	..	..	..
Sierra Leone	0	0	0	0	0	0	0	0	0	0	0	..	..	..
Somalia	0	0	0	0	0	0	0	0	0	0	0	..	..	..
South Africa	4	1,268	1,094	1,217	1,166	1,344	1,197	1,273	1,408	974	1,300	39.6	8.6	..
Sudan	0	0	0	0	0	0	0	0	0	0	0	..	..	..
Swaziland	0	0	0	0	0	0	0	0	0	0	0	..	..	..
Tanzania	0	0	0	0	0	0	0	0	0	0	0	..	..	..
Togo	2,896	2,868	3,347	2,422	3,074	2,086	1,567	2,234	2,652	2,686	2,392	1.9	-2.6	..
Uganda	0	0	0	0	0	0	0	0	0	0	0	..	..	..
Zambia	0	0	0	0	0	0	0	0	0	0	0	..	..	..
Zimbabwe	0	0	0	0	0	0	0	0	0	0	0	..	..	..
NORTH AFRICA	18,932	16,560	14,700	13,297	10,537	11,068	10,096	11,523	11,466	12,422	13,390	-1.1	-5.3	..
Algeria	768	877	970	735	804	800	449	575	671	993	474	5.6	-2.3	..
Egypt, Arab Rep.	258	268	246	297	164	180	134	114	48	65	..	12.4	-4.3	..
Libya	0	0	0	0	0	0	0	0	0	0	0	..	..	..
Morocco	16,457	14,260	12,407	11,672	9,143	9,132	8,398	9,527	9,420	10,141	11,669	-0.8	-5.9	..
Tunisia	1,449	1,156	1,077	593	426	956	1,114	1,308	1,327	1,224	1,247	-6.9	-2.6	..
ALL AFRICA	23,210	22,543	20,576	18,292	16,080	15,684	13,843	15,678	16,385	16,918	17,680	-0.8	-4.2	..

5-23. Cocoa exports

	Thousands of metric tons											Average annual percentage growth		
	1980	1992	1993	1994	1995	1996	1997	1998	1999	2000	2001	75-84	85-94	95-MR
SUB-SAHARAN AFRICA	870	1,190	1,469	1,271	1,342	1,995	1,688	1,659	1,952	1,956	1,695	0.4	3.2	4.6
excluding South Africa	869	1,180	1,456	1,260	1,334	1,985	1,678	1,650	1,944	1,949	1,686	0.4	3.1	4.7
excl. S.Africa & Nigeria	719	1,069	1,296	1,113	1,195	1,803	1,531	1,515	1,736	1,803	1,511	1.0	3.6	5.0
Angola	0	0	0	0	0	0	0	0	0	0	0	-20.0	..	..
Benin	5	0	0	0	0	0	0	0	0	0	0	6.2	-70.3	..
Botswana	0	0	0	0	0	0	0	0	0	0	0	..	25.8	8.5
Burkina Faso	0	0	0	0	0	0	0	0	0	0	0	..	..	..
Burundi	0	0	0	0	0	0	0	0	0	0	0	..	..	..
Cameroon	105	68	112	82	120	142	110	118	127	101	137	0.1	-2.3	3.0
Cape Verde	0	0	0	0	0	0	0	0	0	0	0	..	..	..
Central African Republic	0	0	0	0	0	0	0	0	0	0	0	-21.8	..	..
Chad	0	0	0	0	0	0	0	0	0	0	0	..	..	..
Comoros	0	0	0	0	0	0	0	0	0	0	0	-14.3	..	..
Congo, Dem. Rep. of	4	3	3	6	2	3	3	3	2	2	2	-0.2	-1.7	-12.7
Congo, Rep. of	2	0	0	0	0	1	1	1	1	1	1	-5.1	-21.7	17.0
Côte d'Ivoire	332	724	872	744	795	1,138	1,090	1,020	1,253	1,257	1,095	9.1	5.3	6.4
Djibouti	0	0	0	0	0	0	0	0	0	0	0	..	..	..
Equatorial Guinea	7	5	3	3	3	6	4	6	3	4	4	-0.2	-9.2	1.2
Eritrea	0	0	0	0	0	0	0	0	0	0	0	..	..	..
Ethiopia	0	0	0	0	0	0	0	0	0	0	0	..	..	..
Gabon	4	2	1	1	1	1	1	1	1	1	0	-4.2	-3.0	-11.5
Gambia, The	0	0	0	0	0	0	0	0	0	0	0	..	..	..
Ghana	218	243	278	252	253	478	288	333	319	405	246	-7.7	4.4	1.3
Guinea	4	2	4	4	3	6	7	8	0	2	3	4.3	-2.6	-3.5
Guinea-Bissau	0	0	0	0	0	0	0	0	0	0	0	..	..	..
Kenya	0	1	1	1	0	0	0	0	0	0	0	-8.2	64.2	-10.8
Lesotho	0	0	0	0	0	0	0	0	0	0	0	..	..	..
Liberia	4	0	0	0	0	1	1	2	2	3	1	9.1	-25.5	46.1
Madagascar	2	3	4	3	2	2	1	1	1	4	3	5.8	5.1	1.5
Malawi	0	0	0	0	0	0	0	0	0	0	0	-21.2	..	..
Mali	0	0	0	0	0	0	0	0	0	0	0	..	..	..
Mauritania	0	0	0	0	0	0	0	0	0	0	0	..	..	..
Mauritius	0	0	0	0	0	0	0	0	0	0	0	..	..	29.2
Mozambique	0	0	0	0	0	0	0	0	0	0	0	..	..	..
Namibia	0	0	0	0	0	0	0	0	0	0	0	..	..	..
Niger	0	0	0	0	0	0	0	0	0	0	0	..	..	..
Nigeria	151	111	161	148	139	182	147	135	208	145	175	-2.6	0.1	2.1
Rwanda	0	0	0	0	0	0	0	0	0	0	0	..	..	..
São Tomé and Principe	7	4	4	3	5	4	3	3	4	4	3	-5.6	-1.1	-2.0
Senegal	0	0	0	0	0	0	0	0	0	0	0	65.7	-3.6	6.6
Seychelles	0	0	0	0	0	0	0	0	0	0	0	..	..	-27.3
Sierra Leone	8	5	4	3	3	4	3	3	3	2	2	6.0	-9.8	-7.5
Somalia	0	0	0	0	0	0	0	0	0	0	0	..	..	..
South Africa	0	10	13	11	8	10	10	9	8	7	9	-8.5	36.1	-3.1
Sudan	0	0	0	0	0	0	0	0	0	0	0	..	..	..
Swaziland	0	0	0	0	0	0	6	8	7	10	4	..	..	-3.6
Tanzania	1	2	2	2	3	3	3	2	3	2	2	9.0	5.5	-3.4
Togo	15	6	5	6	4	11	10	5	8	6	6	-1.7	-9.6	-1.0
Uganda	0	1	1	1	1	1	1	2	2	2	1	2.5	12.6	11.0
Zambia	0	0	0	0	0	0	0	0	0	0	0	..	..	..
Zimbabwe	0	0	0	0	0	0	0	0	0	0	0	-14.6	22.9	-6.7
NORTH AFRICA	0	1	0	0	1	1	1	1	1	1	2	6.1	11.9	11.3
Algeria	0	0	0	0	0	0	0	0	0	0	1	..	..	16.8
Egypt, Arab Rep.	0	0	0	0	0	1	1	0	1	0	0	-22.9	41.1	-1.3
Libya	0	0	0	0	0	0	0	0	0	0	0	..	..	..
Morocco	0	0	0	0	0	0	0	0	0	0	0	..	21.1	-12.8
Tunisia	0	0	0	0	0	0	0	0	0	0	0	..	-3.9	30.0
ALL AFRICA	870	1,191	1,469	1,272	1,343	1,996	1,689	1,659	1,953	1,957	1,697	0.4	3.2	4.6

5-24. Coffee exports

	Thousands of metric tons											Average annual percentage growth		
	1980	*1993*	*1994*	*1995*	*1996*	*1997*	*1998*	*1999*	*2000*	*2001*	*2002*	*75-84*	*85-94*	*95-MR*
SUB-SAHARAN AFRICA	819	829	759	787	945	898	849	797	926	674	647	-2.3	-1.0	-2.1
excluding South Africa	818	829	758	786	944	894	843	795	924	673	645	-2.4	-1.0	-2.1
excl. S.Africa & Nigeria	816	828	758	785	943	893	843	795	924	673	645	-2.4	-1.0	-2.1
Angola	47	2	0	2	3	3	3	3	3	0	0	-17.7	-30.1	30.0
Benin	0	0	0	0	0	0	0	0	0	0	0	18.1	-19.5	-27.3
Botswana	0	0	0	0	0	0	0	0	0	0	0	3.8	-5.6	20.3
Burkina Faso	..	..	..	..	..	..	..	..	..	..	..	..	..	..
Burundi	19	23	29	29	13	25	42	24	22	19	18	3.0	-0.6	-3.6
Cameroon	92	67	54	63	74	59	53	86	89	71	48	0.0	-4.1	0.9
Cape Verde	0	0	0	0	0	0	0	0	0	0	0	..	..	..
Central African Republic	11	8	8	14	5	12	12	12	6	4	6	2.2	-5.8	-7.5
Chad	..	..	..	..	..	..	..	..	..	..	..	..	..	..
Comoros	0	0	0	0	0	0	0	0	0	0	0	-17.4	..	..
Congo, Dem. Rep. of	74	55	63	60	49	23	38	23	29	10	5	0.3	-1.9	-24.2
Congo, Rep. of	2	0	0	2	1	0	0	0	0	0	0	8.4	-34.0	-7.4
Côte d'Ivoire	207	226	122	135	145	233	215	106	308	216	144	-2.6	-2.0	4.8
Djibouti	..	..	..	..	..	..	..	..	..	..	..	..	..	..
Equatorial Guinea	0	0	0	0	0	0	0	0	0	0	0	-10.7	-24.2	-4.6
Eritrea	..	..	..	..	..	..	..	..	..	..	..	..	..	..
Ethiopia	..	70	89	77	110	119	115	109	119	80	119	..	..	2.3
Gabon	1	0	0	0	0	0	0	0	0	0	0	26.9	-19.4	-30.2
Gambia, The	0	0	0	0	0	0	0	0	0	0	0	..	..	..
Ghana	0	3	1	2	1	3	6	6	5	2	1	-21.1	12.7	8.9
Guinea	3	6	12	19	9	18	14	9	12	12	6	0.4	29.7	-7.3
Guinea-Bissau	..	..	..	..	..	..	..	..	..	..	..	..	..	..
Kenya	80	88	80	89	115	68	51	70	87	62	17	2.9	-2.9	-12.3
Lesotho	..	..	..	..	..	..	..	..	..	..	..	..	..	..
Liberia	13	0	0	0	0	0	0	1	0	0	0	6.3	-19.0	..
Madagascar	69	51	37	35	40	26	30	13	5	1	4	-2.5	-0.9	-32.7
Malawi	0	6	5	5	5	4	4	4	3	4	3	25.2	10.1	-5.9
Mali	0	0	0	0	0	0	0	0	0	0	0	..	..	..
Mauritania	..	..	..	..	..	..	..	..	..	..	..	..	..	..
Mauritius	0	0	0	0	0	0	0	0	0	0	0	..	..	..
Mozambique	0	0	0	0	0	0	0	0	0	0	0	..	..	..
Namibia	0	0	0	0	0	0	0	0	0	0	0	..	..	23.0
Niger	0	0	0	0	0	0	0	0	0	0	0	..	..	..
Nigeria	2	1	0	1	1	1	1	0	0	0	0	-1.8	8.4	-11.3
Rwanda	22	30	2	8	2	10	1	18	13	18	20	1.4	-13.2	30.9
São Tomé and Principe	0	0	0	0	0	0	0	0	0	0	0	-9.5	-8.1	28.0
Senegal	1	0	0	0	0	0	0	0	0	0	0	0.9	-2.5	..
Seychelles	0	0	0	0	0	0	0	0	0	0	0	..	..	..
Sierra Leone	10	3	4	5	2	3	3	1	2	1	3	-0.7	-2.4	-7.9
Somalia	..	..	..	..	..	..	..	..	..	..	..	..	..	..
South Africa	0	0	0	1	1	4	6	2	2	1	1	24.9	11.7	9.1
Sudan	0	0	0	0	0	0	0	0	0	0	0	..	..	..
Swaziland	0	0	0	0	0	0	0	0	0	0	0	..	..	165.8
Tanzania	43	59	37	48	62	41	39	45	54	48	36	0.8	0.3	-0.4
Togo	9	13	9	13	5	19	8	19	13	8	5	-6.2	9.0	-3.9
Uganda	110	114	202	169	289	211	199	236	143	110	201	-2.8	0.1	-4.3
Zambia	0	0	0	0	2	2	2	2	4	5	5	..	16.1	45.2
Zimbabwe	3	4	4	10	11	12	8	7	6	1	4	13.2	-7.6	-12.4
NORTH AFRICA	0	0	0	0	0	0	0	0	0	0	0	-34.0	10.3	19.1
Algeria	0	0	0	0	0	0	0	0	0	0	0	..	..	..
Egypt, Arab Rep.	0	0	0	0	0	0	0	0	0	0	0	..	-29.4	10.8
Libya	..	..	..	..	..	..	..	..	..	..	..	..	..	..
Morocco	0	0	0	0	0	0	0	0	0	0	0	..	..	27.1
Tunisia	0	0	0	0	0	0	0	0	0	0	0	..	6.4	4.3
ALL AFRICA	819	829	759	787	945	898	850	797	926	674	647	-2.4	-1.0	-2.1

Note: 2002 data are preliminary (see page 2).

5-25. Cotton exports

					Thousands of metric tons							Average annual percentage growth		
	1980	1993	1994	1995	1996	1997	1998	1999	2000	2001	2002	75-84	85-94	95-MR
SUB-SAHARAN AFRICA	459	697	706	793	854	962	979	965	1,023	818	861	1.2	2.2	2.1
excluding South Africa	459	697	706	793	853	958	972	960	1,017	814	860	1.3	2.2	2.1
excl. S.Africa & Nigeria	459	694	703	791	831	926	963	952	1,017	794	849	1.3	2.2	2.0
Angola	0	0	0	0	0	0	0	0	0	0	0	-27.7	10.4	..
Benin	8	60	74	99	89	112	128	163	134	108	146	-0.6	11.8	7.2
Botswana	0	1	1	1	1	1	1	2	0	0	0	..	..	-8.0
Burkina Faso	28	62	48	62	64	89	139	114	109	113	0	10.8	6.7	14.0
Burundi	1	2	2	1	0	0	0	0	0	0	0	-0.4	18.9	..
Cameroon	26	51	59	54	66	51	61	73	73	89	100	15.1	10.5	7.2
Cape Verde	0	0	0	0	0	0	0	0	0	0	0	..	..	..
Central African Republic	14	8	5	12	15	9	15	10	10	9	12	-4.0	-6.6	2.5
Chad	35	40	32	62	50	72	68	60	63	47	47	-2.4	1.9	1.6
Comoros	0	0	0	0	0	0	0	0	0	0	0	..	..	..
Congo, Dem. Rep. of	2	0	1	1	1	0	0	0	0	0	0	..	..	-35.9
Congo, Rep. of	0	0	0	0	0	0	0	0	0	0	0	..	..	..
Côte d'Ivoire	39	96	100	88	75	94	122	131	161	113	138	14.7	6.1	6.7
Djibouti	0	0	0	0	0	0	0	0	0	0	0	..	..	..
Equatorial Guinea	0	0	0	0	0	0	0	0	0	0	0	..	..	..
Eritrea	0	0	0	0	0	0	0	0	0	0	0		..	..
Ethiopia	0	0	0	8	1	0	0	0	4	4	2	..	..	19.8
Gabon	0	0	0	0	0	0	0	0	0	0	0	..	..	..
Gambia, The	0	1	1	1	1	0	0	0	0	0	0	..	13.0	-23.5
Ghana	0	2	7	1	0	0	1	7	10	2	3	..	..	27.4
Guinea	0	10	6	4	4	2	2	9	4	1	0	..	45.9	-17.4
Guinea-Bissau	0	1	1	1	1	1	1	1	1	3	4	..	2.9	23.1
Kenya	4	8	7	1	0	0	0	0	0	0	1	-18.6	50.8	-23.8
Lesotho	0	0	0	0	0	0	0	0	0	0	0	..	..	..
Liberia	0	0	0	0	0	0	0	0	0	0	0	..	..	..
Madagascar	1	0	1	1	1	0	0	0	0	0	0	22.2	-13.7	-23.3
Malawi	3	0	0	0	0	9	5	3	7	4	6	-20.5	-26.3	-4.2
Mali	53	133	90	105	130	140	160	138	164	83	121	9.9	9.0	1.5
Mauritania	0	0	0	0	0	0	0	0	0	0	0	..	..	..
Mauritius	0	0	0	0	0	0	0	0	0	0	0	..	..	..
Mozambique	6	13	16	13	16	16	17	10	10	15	20	-8.0	18.0	-0.2
Namibia	0	0	0	0	0	0	0	0	0	0	0	..	..	..
Niger	0	1	0	5	2	2	1	2	2	1	1	-12.4	7.6	0.9
Nigeria	0	3	3	2	22	32	9	7	0	20	11	..	59.8	2.0
Rwanda	0	0	0	0	0	0	0	0	0	0	0	..	..	..
São Tomé and Principe	0	0	0	0	0	0	0	0	0	0	0	..	..	..
Senegal	6	20	15	9	11	15	14	5	7	7	15	2.1	7.5	-4.8
Seychelles	0	0	0	0	0	0	0	0	0	0	0	..	..	..
Sierra Leone	0	0	0	0	0	0	0	0	0	0	0	..	..	..
Somalia	0	0	0	0	0	0	0	0	0	0	0	..	..	..
South Africa	0	0	0	0	0	4	7	5	6	5	1	-30.6	25.4	81.7
Sudan	132	48	78	96	104	75	63	30	43	40	71	0.0	-11.5	-9.1
Swaziland	4	7	4	3	4	2	0	0	0	1	0	4.8	14.0	-40.2
Tanzania	31	61	60	71	82	69	23	30	30	30	31	-3.9	9.0	-12.7
Togo	5	42	43	61	56	48	45	45	30	48	30	27.3	10.4	-5.6
Uganda	2	8	4	6	10	10	5	14	14	3	5	-21.5	-0.1	-0.7
Zambia	5	1	1	1	5	17	12	25	3	5	13	15.9	-10.7	26.6
Zimbabwe	54	18	47	27	44	91	78	80	140	69	83	4.2	-10.8	12.9
NORTH AFRICA	167	20	114	68	23	42	67	112	63	82	161	0.1	-17.7	8.5
Algeria	0	0	0	0	0	0	0	0	0	0	0	..	..	..
Egypt, Arab Rep.	164	18	113	67	23	42	66	112	63	82	161	0.2	-18.4	8.6
Libya	0	0	0	0	0	0	0	0	0	0	0	..	..	..
Morocco	3	2	1	0	0	0	1	0	0	0	0	3.4	-15.6	-8.9
Tunisia	0	0	0	0	0	0	0	0	0	0	0	..	..	-25.8
ALL AFRICA	627	718	820	861	877	1,004	1,046	1,077	1,087	900	1,022	0.9	0.1	2.6

Note: 2002 data are preliminary (see page 2).

5-26. Groundnut exports

					Thousands of metric tons							Average annual percentage growth		
	1980	*1993*	*1994*	*1995*	*1996*	*1997*	*1998*	*1999*	*2000*	*2001*	*2002*	*75-84*	*85-94*	*95-MR*
SUB-SAHARAN AFRICA	605	276	398	281	392	381	392	301	370	395	379	-8.9	-0.7	0.8
excluding South Africa	560	249	338	245	353	323	359	275	339	352	323	-8.7	-1.2	1.1
excl. S.Africa & Nigeria	559	249	331	244	349	301	346	270	339	350	320	-8.2	-1.3	1.3
Angola	1	0	0	0	0	0	0	0	0	0	0	-4.9	..	..
Benin	2	0	0	0	0	1	0	0	0	0	0	-27.0	..	-25.2
Botswana	0	0	0	0	0	0	0	0	0	0	0	-10.2	-4.8	12.6
Burkina Faso	1	0	2	0	1	3	1	1	2	0	0	-43.9	10.3	-8.9
Burundi	0	0	0	0	0	0	0	0	0	0	0	..	..	..
Cameroon	1	0	0	0	0	0	0	0	1	0	1	-39.5	-10.0	30.0
Cape Verde	0	0	0	0	0	0	0	0	0	0	0	..	..	..
Central African Republic	0	0	1	1	0	1	1	1	1	0	0	..	..	-46.4
Chad	0	1	2	0	1	0	0	1	7	1	1	..	..	2.9
Comoros	..	..	..	..	..	..	..	..	..	..	..	..	..	..
Congo, Dem. Rep. of	0	0	0	0	0	0	0	0	0	0	0	..	..	..
Congo, Rep. of	0	0	0	0	0	0	0	0	0	0	0	-10.6	..	..
Côte d'Ivoire	0	0	0	1	0	0	0	1	1	0	0	-8.4	..	7.6
Djibouti	..	..	..	..	..	..	..	..	..	..	..	..	..	..
Equatorial Guinea	..	..	..	..	..	..	..	..	..	..	..	..	..	..
Eritrea	..	..	..	..	..	..	..	..	..	..	..	..	..	..
Ethiopia	..	0	0	0	0	0	0	0	0	0	0	..	..	-4.7
Gabon	0	0	0	0	0	0	0	0	0	0	0	..	..	..
Gambia, The	67	28	26	38	32	38	30	20	33	40	59	-7.7	-4.6	4.8
Ghana	2	0	0	0	0	0	0	0	1	0	1	..	..	63.8
Guinea	0	0	0	0	0	0	0	0	0	0	0	..	..	..
Guinea-Bissau	8	0	0	0	0	0	0	0	0	0	0	-4.4	-26.1	-48.0
Kenya	0	1	0	0	0	0	0	0	0	0	0	-24.6	42.7	3.5
Lesotho	..	..	..	..	..	..	..	..	..	..	..	..	..	..
Liberia	..	..	..	..	..	..	..	..	..	..	..	..	..	..
Madagascar	4	0	0	0	0	1	0	0	1	0	0	-44.9	26.8	-2.3
Malawi	28	0	1	1	1	3	4	1	0	1	1	-17.8	-35.1	-7.6
Mali	15	12	17	16	15	15	12	13	11	7	10	-11.7	6.6	-7.8
Mauritania	0	0	0	0	0	0	0	0	0	0	0	..	..	..
Mauritius	0	0	0	0	0	0	0	0	0	0	0	..	8.5	10.5
Mozambique	10	0	0	1	0	0	0	0	0	0	0	-8.5	-21.0	-16.8
Namibia	0	0	0	0	0	0	0	0	0	0	0	..	..	-6.7
Niger	1	0	0	1	2	3	4	2	2	1	1	-38.0	11.2	32.8
Nigeria	1	0	7	1	4	22	13	5	0	2	3	-37.9	46.0	-12.8
Rwanda	0	0	0	0	0	0	0	0	0	0	0	..	..	..
São Tomé and Principe	..	..	..	..	..	..	..	..	..	..	..	..	..	..
Senegal	175	119	164	98	207	88	103	155	238	260	195	-9.1	-1.6	7.7
Seychelles	..	..	..	..	..	..	..	..	..	..	..	..	..	..
Sierra Leone	..	..	..	..	..	..	..	..	..	..	..	..	..	..
Somalia	0	0	0	0	0	0	0	0	0	0	0	..	..	..
South Africa	45	27	59	36	38	58	33	26	31	43	56	-12.5	6.4	-1.7
Sudan	238	84	110	82	84	140	160	63	29	33	30	-6.0	3.7	-16.4
Swaziland	0	0	0	0	0	3	11	8	7	3	4	..	..	-8.6
Tanzania	1	0	0	0	1	1	1	1	2	2	8	..	280.1	54.5
Togo	0	0	0	0	2	0	0	0	0	0	6	-36.2	-18.2	31.8
Uganda	0	1	0	0	0	0	0	0	0	0	0	..	..	-21.0
Zambia	0	0	0	0	0	1	0	1	0	0	1	-26.0	14.6	33.2
Zimbabwe	3	3	7	3	1	5	15	2	3	0	0	-19.6	28.8	-23.2
NORTH AFRICA	13	21	16	15	10	19	24	14	26	29	13	-7.3	23.3	4.2
Algeria	0	0	0	0	0	0	0	0	0	0	0	..	..	..
Egypt, Arab Rep.	13	12	9	10	6	11	15	4	3	4	11	-7.3	14.0	-6.1
Libya	0	8	4	5	5	8	9	9	23	25	1	..	..	5.6
Morocco	0	0	0	0	0	0	0	0	0	0	0	..	..	..
Tunisia	0	0	3	0	0	0	0	0	0	0	0	..	..	..
ALL AFRICA	618	297	414	297	402	401	416	315	396	425	391	-8.9	-0.3	1.0

Note: 2002 data are preliminary (see page 2).

5-27. Oil palm products exports

	Thousands of metric tons											Average annual percentage growth		
	1980	*1993*	*1994*	*1995*	*1996*	*1997*	*1998*	*1999*	*2000*	*2001*	*2002*	*75-84*	*85-94*	*95-MR*
SUB-SAHARAN AFRICA	280	319	252	197	228	187	210	186	324	211	192	-12.2	4.6	-0.3
excluding South Africa	280	317	249	197	227	186	208	185	323	204	190	-12.2	4.5	-0.4
excl. S.Africa & Nigeria	184	315	242	185	210	176	197	171	160	190	180	-9.3	8.9	-2.8
Angola	..	..	..	..	..	..	..	..	..	..	..	..	..	..
Benin	13	3	12	13	8	16	19	18	14	17	17	-12.5	0.1	5.4
Botswana	0	0	0	0	0	0	0	0	0	0	0	..	..	2.9
Burkina Faso	0	0	0	0	0	0	0	0	0	0	1	..	..	..
Burundi	0	0	0	1	1	0	0	0	0	0	0	..	..	-43.8
Cameroon	21	27	30	8	41	13	15	11	12	11	4	-7.7	3.5	-14.5
Cape Verde	..	..	..	..	..	..	..	..	..	..	..	..	..	..
Central African Republic	0	0	0	0	0	0	0	0	0	0	0	..	..	-0.5
Chad	..	..	..	..	..	..	..	..	..	..	..	..	..	..
Comoros	0	0	0	0	0	0	0	0	0	0	0	..	..	..
Congo, Dem. Rep. of	10	1	3	6	1	1	1	0	0	0	0	-23.7	-14.6	-39.0
Congo, Rep. of	0	0	0	0	0	0	0	0	0	0	0	-17.6	..	..
Côte d'Ivoire	99	207	153	121	103	76	102	98	72	86	97	-7.9	11.7	-5.3
Djibouti	0	0	0	0	0	0	0	0	0	0	1	..	..	..
Equatorial Guinea	0	0	0	0	0	0	0	0	0	0	0	..	..	..
Eritrea	..	..	..	..	..	..	..	..	..	..	..	..	..	..
Ethiopia	..	..	..	..	..	..	..	..	..	..	..	..	..	..
Gabon	0	1	0	3	6	9	3	6	6	6	2	..	-1.8	-3.7
Gambia, The	1	0	0	0	0	0	0	0	0	0	0	-19.8	..	..
Ghana	0	9	11	12	21	19	10	11	14	38	30	..	21.2	10.7
Guinea	15	7	1	0	4	5	1	0	0	0	0	-3.6	-0.3	-37.7
Guinea-Bissau	6	2	3	1	3	1	2	2	3	2	2	2.0	-7.6	5.6
Kenya	0	53	14	13	11	26	31	12	1	4	2	-52.7	326.3	-25.8
Lesotho	..	..	..	..	..	..	..	..	..	..	..	..	..	..
Liberia	6	5	5	5	5	5	6	6	6	6	0	24.9	2.1	-21.3
Madagascar	0	0	0	0	0	0	0	0	0	0	0	..	..	30.4
Malawi	..	..	..	..	..	..	..	..	..	..	..	..	..	..
Mali	..	..	..	..	..	..	..	..	..	..	..	..	..	..
Mauritania	..	..	..	..	..	..	..	..	..	..	..	..	..	..
Mauritius	0	0	0	0	0	0	0	0	0	0	0	..	..	-19.8
Mozambique	..	..	..	..	..	..	..	..	..	..	..	..	..	..
Namibia	0	0	0	0	0	0	0	0	0	0	0	..	..	..
Niger	0	0	0	0	0	0	0	0	0	0	0	..	..	-12.8
Nigeria	96	2	6	11	17	10	11	14	163	14	11	-16.9	-28.8	13.3
Rwanda	..	..	..	..	..	..	..	..	..	..	..	..	..	..
São Tomé and Principe	0	0	0	0	0	0	0	0	0	0	0	-19.1	..	..
Senegal	0	0	0	0	0	2	2	2	27	1	1	-55.4	13.2	64.1
Seychelles	0	0	0	0	0	0	0	0	0	0	0	..	..	..
Sierra Leone	1	0	11	0	0	0	0	0	0	0	0	-11.4	-23.8	-16.6
Somalia	..	..	..	..	..	..	..	..	..	..	..	..	..	..
South Africa	0	2	3	0	1	1	3	1	2	7	2	..	79.1	13.3
Sudan	..	..	..	..	..	..	..	..	..	..	..	..	..	..
Swaziland	0	0	0	0	0	0	0	0	0	0	0	..	..	..
Tanzania	1	0	0	0	0	1	2	2	3	15	6	..	..	57.5
Togo	10	0	0	0	0	0	0	0	0	4	14	-13.6	-11.2	102.5
Uganda	0	0	0	1	5	2	3	2	1	0	1	..	..	-2.2
Zambia	0	0	0	0	0	0	0	1	0	0	0	..	..	..
Zimbabwe	0	0	0	0	0	0	0	0	0	0	0	..	..	..
NORTH AFRICA	0	0	0	0	0	0	1	1	1	1	5	..	..	50.8
Algeria	..	..	..	..	..	..	..	..	..	..	..	..	..	..
Egypt, Arab Rep.	0	0	0	0	0	0	0	0	0	0	0	..	..	-1.9
Libya	0	0	0	0	0	0	1	1	1	1	1	..	..	0.0
Morocco	0	0	0	0	0	0	0	0	0	0	3	..	..	61.6
Tunisia	0	0	0	0	0	0	0	0	0	0	1	..	..	38.9
ALL AFRICA	280	320	252	197	228	187	211	187	325	212	197	-12.2	4.6	-0.1

Note: 2002 data are preliminary (see page 2).

5-28. Sisal exports

	Thousands of metric tons											Average annual percentage growth		
	1980	1993	1994	1995	1996	1997	1998	1999	2000	2001	2002	75-84	85-94	95-MR
SUB-SAHARAN AFRICA	109	42	41	47	41	36	34	33	35	32	22	-9.6	-5.7	-6.5
excluding South Africa	109	42	41	47	41	36	34	33	35	32	22	-9.7	-5.5	-6.5
excl. S.Africa & Nigeria	109	42	41	47	41	36	34	33	35	32	22	-9.7	-5.5	-6.5
Angola	3	0	0	0	0	0	0	0	0	0	0	-30.8	..	..
Benin	0	0	0	0	0	0	0	0	0	0	0	..	..	..
Botswana	0	0	0	0	0	0	0	0	0	0	0	..	..	..
Burkina Faso	0	0	0	0	0	0	0	0	0	0	0	..	..	..
Burundi	0	0	0	0	0	0	0	0	0	0	0		..	..
Cameroon	0	0	0	0	0	0	0	0	0	0	0	..	..	..
Cape Verde	0	0	0	0	0	0	0	0	0	0	0	..	..	..
Central African Republic	0	0	0	0	0	0	0	0	0	0	0	..	..	..
Chad	0	0	0	0	0	0	0	0	0	0	0	..	..	..
Comoros	0	0	0	0	0	0	0	0	0	0	0	..	..	..
Congo, Dem. Rep. of	0	0	0	0	0	0	0	0	0	0	0	..	..	..
Congo, Rep. of	0	0	0	0	0	0	0	0	0	0	0	..	..	..
Côte d'Ivoire	0	0	0	0	0	0	0	0	0	0	0	..	..	-4.9
Djibouti	0	0	0	0	0	0	0	0	0	0	0	..	..	..
Equatorial Guinea	0	0	0	0	0	0	0	0	0	0	0	..	..	..
Eritrea	0	0	0	0	0	0	0	0	0	0	0	..	..	..
Ethiopia	0	0	0	0	0	0	0	0	0	0	0	..	..	..
Gabon	0	0	0	0	0	0	0	0	0	0	0	..	..	..
Gambia, The	0	0	0	0	0	0	0	0	0	0	0	..	..	..
Ghana	0	0	0	0	0	0	0	0	0	0	0	..	..	..
Guinea	0	0	0	0	0	0	0	0	0	0	0	..	..	..
Guinea-Bissau	0	0	0	0	0	0	0	0	0	0	0	..	..	..
Kenya	40	27	26	25	22	19	18	17	17	18	9	-1.3	-3.2	-9.1
Lesotho	0	0	0	0	0	0	0	0	0	0	0	..	..	..
Liberia	0	0	0	0	0	0	0	0	0	0	0	..	..	..
Madagascar	10	9	8	10	10	4	3	5	5	0	0	-5.9	-1.6	-13.9
Malawi	0	0	0	0	0	0	0	0	0	0	0	..	..	..
Mali	0	0	0	0	0	0	0	0	0	0	0	..	..	..
Mauritania	0	0	0	0	0	0	0	0	0	0	0	..	..	..
Mauritius	0	0	0	0	0	0	0	0	0	0	0	..	..	..
Mozambique	7	0	0	0	0	0	0	0	0	0	0	-14.5	-11.3	-19.3
Namibia	0	0	0	0	0	0	0	0	0	0	0	..	..	..
Niger	0	0	0	0	0	0	0	0	0	0	0	..	..	..
Nigeria	0	0	0	0	0	0	0	0	0	0	0	..	..	..
Rwanda	0	0	0	0	0	0	0	0	0	0	0	..	..	..
São Tomé and Principe	0	0	0	0	0	0	0	0	0	0	0	..	..	..
Senegal	0	0	0	0	0	0	0	0	0	0	0	38.6	..	..
Seychelles	0	0	0	0	0	0	0	0	0	0	0	..	..	..
Sierra Leone	0	0	0	0	0	0	0	0	0	0	0	..	..	..
Somalia	0	0	0	0	0	0	0	0	0	0	0	..	..	..
South Africa	0	0	0	0	0	0	0	0	0	0	0	-4.4	-38.0	27.7
Sudan	0	0	0	0	0	0	0	0	0	0	0	..	..	..
Swaziland	0	0	0	0	0	0	0	0	0	0	0	..	..	..
Tanzania	48	5	7	11	9	13	14	12	13	14	13	-12.1	-14.6	6.1
Togo	0	0	0	0	0	0	0	0	0	0	0	..	..	..
Uganda	0	0	0	0	0	0	0	0	0	0	0	..	..	..
Zambia	0	0	0	0	0	0	0	0	0	0	0	..	..	..
Zimbabwe	0	0	0	0	0	0	0	0	0	0	0	..	..	..
NORTH AFRICA	0	0	0	0	0	0	0	0	0	0	0	..	-0.5	32.2
Algeria	0	0	0	0	0	0	0	0	0	0	0	..	..	..
Egypt, Arab Rep.	0	0	0	0	0	0	0	0	0	0	0	..	..	42.7
Libya	0	0	0	0	0	0	0	0	0	0	0	..	..	..
Morocco	0	0	0	0	0	0	0	0	0	0	0	..	..	36.8
Tunisia	0	0	0	0	0	0	0	0	0	0	0	..	..	-2.2
ALL AFRICA	109	42	41	47	41	36	34	33	35	32	22	-9.6	-5.7	-6.4

Note: 2002 data are preliminary (see page 2).

External Sector

5-29. Tea exports

	Thousands of metric tons											Average annual percentage growth		
	1980	1993	1994	1995	1996	1997	1998	1999	2000	2001	2002	75-84	85-94	95-MR
SUB-SAHARAN AFRICA	182	298	263	337	340	312	388	357	383	324	235	3.8	3.3	-0.3
excluding South Africa	180	297	262	335	339	311	385	353	372	318	224	3.7	3.3	-0.8
excl. S.Africa & Nigeria	180	297	262	335	339	311	385	353	372	317	223	3.7	3.3	-0.8
Angola	0	0	0	0	0	0	0	0	0	0	0	..	..	..
Benin	0	0	0	0	0	0	0	0	0	0	0	..	..	..
Botswana	0	0	0	0	0	0	0	0	0	0	0	21.8	0.0	28.4
Burkina Faso	0	0	0	0	0	0	0	0	0	0	2	-6.7	..	..
Burundi	1	5	7	7	4	6	6	2	3	9	1	12.3	6.4	-15.6
Cameroon	1	0	0	0	0	0	0	0	0	0	0	23.2	-19.0	..
Cape Verde	0	0	0	0	0	0	0	0	0	0	0	..	..	..
Central African Republic	0	0	0	0	0	0	0	0	0	0	0	..	..	..
Chad	0	0	0	0	0	0	0	0	0	0	0	..	..	..
Comoros	0	0	0	0	0	0	0	0	0	0	0	..	..	..
Congo, Dem. Rep. of	1	2	2	1	2	1	1	1	1	1	0	-8.5	-5.6	-19.3
Congo, Rep. of	0	0	0	0	0	0	0	0	0	0	0	..	..	..
Côte d'Ivoire	0	0	0	0	0	0	0	0	0	0	0	..	..	..
Djibouti	0	0	0	0	0	0	2	0	0	0	1	..	..	..
Equatorial Guinea	0	0	0	0	0	0	0	0	0	0	0	..	..	..
Eritrea	0	0	0	0	0	0	0	0	0	0	0		..	..
Ethiopia	0	0	0	0	0	0	0	0	1	0	0	..	..	3.0
Gabon	0	0	0	0	0	0	0	0	0	0	0	..	..	..
Gambia, The	0	0	0	0	0	0	0	0	0	0	0	..	..	-27.1
Ghana	0	0	0	0	0	0	0	0	0	0	0	..	..	72.1
Guinea	0	0	0	0	0	0	0	0	0	0	0	..	..	..
Guinea-Bissau	0	0	0	0	0	0	0	0	0	0	0	..	..	..
Kenya	84	199	177	259	262	199	264	246	217	207	88	6.7	4.9	-5.8
Lesotho	0	0	0	0	0	0	0	0	0	0	0	..	..	..
Liberia	0	0	0	0	0	0	0	0	0	0	0	..	..	..
Madagascar	0	0	0	0	0	0	0	0	0	0	0	..	10.3	14.2
Malawi	31	35	35	32	32	40	41	30	70	32	37	3.8	-0.4	2.4
Mali	0	0	0	0	0	0	0	0	0	0	1	..	..	..
Mauritania	0	0	0	0	0	0	0	0	0	0	0	..	..	..
Mauritius	4	4	4	3	1	0	0	0	0	0	0	8.2	-5.3	-49.2
Mozambique	30	0	0	0	0	0	0	0	0	1	2	-0.2	-23.2	17.0
Namibia	0	0	0	0	0	0	0	0	0	0	0	..	..	-9.3
Niger	0	0	0	0	0	0	0	0	0	0	1	..	..	23.3
Nigeria	0	0	0	0	0	0	0	0	0	1	1	..	..	50.5
Rwanda	7	12	5	3	3	13	15	12	12	18	15	8.5	-0.5	23.7
São Tomé and Principe	0	0	0	0	0	0	0	0	0	0	0	..	..	..
Senegal	0	0	0	0	0	0	0	0	0	0	0	-8.6	..	..
Seychelles	0	0	0	0	0	0	0	0	0	0	0	-7.6	..	-9.4
Sierra Leone	0	0	0	0	0	0	0	0	0	0	0	..	..	..
Somalia	0	0	0	0	0	0	0	0	0	0	0	..	..	..
South Africa	2	1	1	1	1	1	3	5	10	6	11	44.8	16.3	42.5
Sudan	0	0	0	0	0	0	0	0	0	0	0	..	..	..
Swaziland	0	0	0	0	0	0	0	0	0	0	0	..	..	45.3
Tanzania	13	20	22	22	22	19	21	22	23	23	24	2.6	8.0	1.4
Togo	0	0	0	0	0	0	0	0	0	0	0	..	..	..
Uganda	1	10	0	0	0	17	23	22	26	18	30	-28.0	22.1	6.8
Zambia	0	0	0	0	0	0	0	1	1	1	1	..	..	71.2
Zimbabwe	6	8	10	9	12	13	11	16	17	6	19	10.5	-2.6	4.1
NORTH AFRICA	0	0	0	0	0	0	0	0	1	1	2	..	21.8	22.0
Algeria	0	0	0	0	0	0	0	0	0	0	0	..	..	..
Egypt, Arab Rep.	0	0	0	0	0	0	0	0	1	1	1	..	52.7	28.7
Libya	0	0	0	0	0	0	0	0	0	0	0	..	..	-19.8
Morocco	0	0	0	0	0	0	0	0	0	0	0	..	-1.6	50.6
Tunisia	0	0	0	0	0	0	0	0	0	0	0	..	..	-32.5
ALL AFRICA	182	298	263	337	340	312	388	358	384	325	237	3.8	3.3	-0.2

Note: 2002 data are preliminary (see page 2).

5-30. Sugar exports

	Thousands of metric tons											Average annual percentage growth		
	1980	1993	1994	1995	1996	1997	1998	1999	2000	2001	2002	75-84	85-94	95-MR
SUB-SAHARAN AFRICA	2,148	1,292	1,742	1,590	2,358	2,663	2,878	2,597	3,556	3,146	2,666	0.8	-4.6	7.9
excluding South Africa	1,362	1,150	1,424	1,201	1,525	1,658	1,646	1,459	2,082	1,607	1,502	3.1	-1.1	2.7
excl. S.Africa & Nigeria	1,362	1,150	1,424	1,201	1,525	1,658	1,646	1,459	2,081	1,596	1,492	3.1	-1.1	2.6
Angola	0	0	0	0	0	0	0	0	0	0	0	..	..	..
Benin	0	0	0	0	0	0	0	0	0	0	0	..	..	..
Botswana	0	0	0	0	1	1	0	1	0	1	1	-14.0	28.8	23.8
Burkina Faso	2	0	0	0	0	0	0	0	3	8	13	91.6	..	..
Burundi	0	0	0	0	4	0	1	2	5	3	5	..	..	155.3
Cameroon	9	1	0	1	7	1	1	1	0	0	0	42.1	-35.6	6.1
Cape Verde	0	0	0	0	0	0	0	0	0	0	0	..	..	..
Central African Republic	0	0	0	0	0	0	0	0	0	0	0	..	..	4.8
Chad	0	0	0	0	0	0	0	0	0	0	0	..	..	..
Comoros	0	0	0	0	0	0	0	0	0	0	0	..	..	..
Congo, Dem. Rep. of	0	0	0	0	0	0	0	0	0	0	0	..	..	..
Congo, Rep. of	0	18	11	14	7	37	21	25	33	49	40	-1.3	-3.7	21.9
Côte d'Ivoire	11	39	33	12	28	41	12	25	71	53	19	142.4	2.9	6.2
Djibouti	0	0	0	0	0	0	10	0	0	0	2	..	..	..
Equatorial Guinea	0	0	0	0	0	0	0	0	0	0	0	..	..	..
Eritrea	0	0	0	0	0	0	0	0	0	0	0	..	..	..
Ethiopia	0	15	5	0	0	0	0	1	65	50	81	..	..	46.0
Gabon	2	0	0	0	0	0	0	0	0	0	0	9.3	..	..
Gambia, The	0	35	0	0	0	0	0	0	0	0	0	..	..	..
Ghana	0	0	0	0	1	0	0	2	4	0	0	..	..	7.5
Guinea	0	0	0	0	0	0	0	0	0	0	0	..	..	..
Guinea-Bissau	0	0	0	0	0	0	0	0	0	0	0	..	..	..
Kenya	56	50	112	13	55	31	2	5	4	8	37	19.0	148.8	-19.4
Lesotho	0	0	0	0	0	0	0	0	0	0	0	..	..	..
Liberia	0	0	0	0	0	0	0	0	0	0	0	8.1	..	..
Madagascar	26	11	24	15	7	1	1	7	1	2	1	-1.1	-3.5	-30.2
Malawi	92	26	34	66	55	30	72	48	48	58	83	13.9	-13.4	5.8
Mali	0	0	0	0	0	0	0	0	0	0	0	..	..	..
Mauritania	0	0	0	0	0	0	0	0	0	0	0	..	..	..
Mauritius	618	535	519	524	773	575	602	534	424	599	571	-0.7	-0.7	-0.8
Mozambique	64	0	52	54	25	59	20	20	69	15	95	-12.8	13.3	-0.8
Namibia	0	0	0	0	0	10	23	5	5	4	6	..	..	-21.5
Niger	0	0	0	0	0	0	1	0	2	1	12	..	..	76.7
Nigeria	0	0	0	0	0	0	0	0	1	11	9	..	-57.9	133.8
Rwanda	0	0	0	0	0	0	0	0	0	0	0	..	..	..
São Tomé and Principe	0	0	0	0	0	0	0	0	0	0	0	..	..	..
Senegal	0	0	0	0	0	0	0	0	0	0	0	-34.3	-38.1	36.3
Seychelles	0	0	0	0	0	0	0	0	0	0	0	..	..	..
Sierra Leone	0	0	0	0	0	0	0	0	0	0	0	..	..	..
Somalia	0	0	0	0	0	0	0	0	0	0	0	..	..	..
South Africa	786	141	318	390	833	1,005	1,233	1,138	1,474	1,538	1,165	-2.7	-13.8	19.3
Sudan	0	39	136	20	49	145	217	103	114	109	22	..	..	-1.4
Swaziland	300	363	279	275	241	466	345	395	859	302	216	9.2	-1.7	2.7
Tanzania	13	11	11	11	12	4	18	25	16	46	25	33.4	0.4	18.3
Togo	0	0	0	0	0	0	0	0	3	6	6	..	..	76.4
Uganda	0	0	1	1	0	1	1	5	2	1	1	..	..	13.8
Zambia	0	8	7	36	69	35	89	90	76	101	104	60.8	-4.5	28.4
Zimbabwe	169	0	201	160	192	219	207	165	278	179	150	3.9	-28.8	-0.6
NORTH AFRICA	23	1	7	6	4	1	2	0	0	36	21	-29.0	9.5	4.7
Algeria	0	0	0	0	0	0	0	0	0	0	0	..	..	..
Egypt, Arab Rep.	10	1	7	6	4	0	2	0	0	35	20	-12.4	31.6	-5.0
Libya	0	0	0	0	0	0	0	0	0	0	0	..	..	..
Morocco	0	0	0	0	0	0	0	0	0	0	0	..	-20.0	-14.3
Tunisia	13	0	0	0	0	0	0	0	0	1	0	-28.6	-42.9	119.4
ALL AFRICA	2,171	1,293	1,749	1,596	2,362	2,663	2,880	2,598	3,556	3,181	2,687	0.4	-4.5	7.9

Note: 2002 data are preliminary (see page 2).

5-31. Tobacco exports

	Hundreds of metric tons											Average annual percentage growth		
	1980	1993	1994	1995	1996	1997	1998	1999	2000	2001	2002	75-84	85-94	95-MR
SUB-SAHARAN AFRICA	1,777	3,221	4,439	3,150	3,699	3,495	3,788	3,178	3,319	3,998	3,206	3.0	8.6	-1.5
excluding South Africa	1,705	3,128	4,269	3,039	3,611	3,374	3,643	3,019	3,175	3,632	3,017	3.2	8.8	-2.0
excl. S.Africa & Nigeria	1,705	3,125	4,265	3,037	3,602	3,371	3,641	3,018	3,175	3,632	3,017	3.2	8.8	-2.0
Angola	16	0	0	0	0	0	0	0	0	0	0	-4.7	..	..
Benin	0	0	0	0	0	0	0	0	0	0	0	-36.9	..	..
Botswana	1	0	0	0	1	1	1	0	0	0	0	32.5	-10.3	-1.6
Burkina Faso	0	0	0	0	0	0	0	2	0	0	5	..	..	41.0
Burundi	0	10	4	0	2	0	1	0	0	4	0	..	23.1	-15.4
Cameroon	21	6	1	3	0	1	3	1	2	3	1	-7.9	-14.1	0.0
Cape Verde	0	0	0	0	0	0	0	0	0	0	0			
Central African Republic	8	1	1	2	1	1	1	1	2	0	4	-8.6	-18.9	-1.3
Chad	0	0	0	0	0	0	0	0	0	0	0	..	..	..
Comoros	0	0	0	0	0	0	0	0	0	0	0	..	..	..
Congo, Dem. Rep. of	0	40	30	14	15	12	3	1	2	10	59	..	..	-8.7
Congo, Rep. of	1	0	0	0	0	0	0	0	0	0	4	-23.6	..	..
Côte d'Ivoire	0	0	0	2	1	2	2	3	3	1	1	-2.6	..	-2.9
Djibouti	0	0	0	0	0	0	0	0	0	0	0	..	..	..
Equatorial Guinea	0	0	0	0	0	0	0	0	0	0	0	..	..	..
Eritrea	0	0	0	0	0	0	0	0	0	0	0		..	..
Ethiopia	0	0	0	0	0	0	0	0	0	0	0	..		
Gabon	0	0	0	0	0	0	0	0	0	0	0			
Gambia, The	0	0	0	1	0	0	0	0	0	0	0	..	..	..
Ghana	0	3	5	2	7	4	2	3	2	3	2	-33.6	18.8	-8.2
Guinea	0	0	0	0	0	0	1	0	0	1	0	..	..	17.9
Guinea-Bissau	0	0	0	0	0	0	0	0	0	0	0	..	..	..
Kenya	0	56	29	30	96	51	50	44	53	122	108	9.8	31.9	14.6
Lesotho	0	0	0	0	0	0	0	0	0	0	0	..	..	..
Liberia	0	0	0	0	0	0	0	0	0	0	0	3.3	..	..
Madagascar	1	0	0	4	4	1	0	0	0	0	0	-11.2	-33.7	-10.7
Malawi	611	957	983	980	1,121	1,168	1,296	956	903	930	1,146	8.4	6.0	-0.3
Mali	0	0	0	0	0	0	0	0	0	0	1	-53.9	..	..
Mauritania	0	0	0	0	0	0	0	0	0	0	0	..	..	..
Mauritius	0	0	0	0	0	0	0	0	0	0	0	..	..	..
Mozambique	0	0	0	0	0	0	0	0	0	0	83	..	..	..
Namibia	0	0	0	0	0	0	0	0	0	0	0	..	..	51.3
Niger	3	0	1	4	6	5	4	1	11	1	1	39.9	..	-6.6
Nigeria	0	2	4	2	9	3	2	2	0	0	0	..	46.3	-36.1
Rwanda	0	0	0	0	0	0	0	0	0	0	0	..	..	..
São Tomé and Principe	0	0	0	0	0	0	0	0	0	0	0		..	..
Senegal	0	1	1	1	1	2	2	4	8	1	1	..	14.6	13.8
Seychelles	0	0	0	0	0	0	0	0	0	0	0	..	..	..
Sierra Leone	0	2	2	2	2	2	2	1	5	5	0	..	13.6	10.2
Somalia	0	0	0	0	0	0	0	0	0	0	0	..	..	..
South Africa	72	94	169	112	88	121	145	159	143	365	188	-1.8	5.0	9.1
Sudan	0	0	0	0	0	0	0	0	1	0	0	..	..	7.3
Swaziland	2	1	1	1	1	0	0	0	0	0	0	-17.4	-7.1	-31.8
Tanzania	83	106	154	171	249	355	214	263	195	191	241	-7.4	8.2	2.3
Togo	0	0	0	0	0	0	0	0	0	0	0	4.7	..	..
Uganda	3	41	34	51	21	83	81	47	153	72	229	-8.6	33.1	22.3
Zambia	26	58	30	9	34	35	38	51	64	76	73	-13.6	9.8	21.3
Zimbabwe	930	1,843	2,989	1,760	2,042	1,650	1,941	1,639	1,771	2,211	1,055	3.9	9.9	-6.1
NORTH AFRICA	15	7	9	12	4	6	5	3	16	18	3	6.5	-3.1	-1.8
Algeria	0	0	0	0	0	0	0	0	0	0	0	..	..	..
Egypt, Arab Rep.	0	0	0	0	0	0	0	0	14	14	0	..	..	64.3
Libya	0	0	0	0	0	0	0	0	0	0	0	..	..	..
Morocco	0	3	1	0	0	0	0	0	0	0	1	..	..	-7.6
Tunisia	15	4	8	12	4	6	5	3	2	4	2	26.9	-5.5	-17.7
ALL AFRICA	1,792	3,228	4,448	3,162	3,703	3,502	3,793	3,181	3,334	4,016	3,209	3.0	8.5	-1.5

Note: 2002 data are preliminary (see page 2).

5-32. Meat exports

	Hundreds of metric tons											Average annual percentage growth		
	1980	1993	1994	1995	1996	1997	1998	1999	2000	2001	2002	75-84	85-94	95-MR
SUB-SAHARAN AFRICA	1,436	1,281	1,154	1,418	1,322	1,151	1,413	1,127	1,180	1,094	1,289	-6.8	0.6	-1.0
excluding South Africa	895	1,133	1,070	1,114	980	1,010	1,220	935	960	869	1,035	-7.2	1.1	-1.7
excl. S.Africa & Nigeria	895	1,133	1,070	1,114	980	1,010	1,220	935	960	869	1,035	-7.2	1.1	-1.7
Angola	0	0	0	0	0	0	0	0	0	0	0	..	..	..
Benin	0	0	1	0	0	0	0	1	9	143	301	..	..	110.8
Botswana	249	279	250	241	201	228	262	215	212	274	133	-0.8	-3.2	-3.4
Burkina Faso	3	0	0	0	0	0	1	0	0	0	1	-4.6	-36.7	13.2
Burundi	0	0	0	0	0	0	0	0	0	0	0	..	..	..
Cameroon	0	0	0	0	0	0	0	0	0	0	0	-53.6	-27.6	34.0
Cape Verde	0	0	0	0	0	0	0	0	0	0	0	..	..	..
Central African Republic	20	0	0	0	0	0	0	0	0	0	0	-19.8	..	..
Chad	0	2	2	2	2	8	9	5	2	3	3	-37.5	16.9	3.9
Comoros	0	0	0	0	1	0	0	0	0	0	0	..	..	..
Congo, Dem. Rep. of	0	0	0	0	0	0	0	0	0	0	0	..	..	..
Congo, Rep. of	0	0	1	0	0	0	0	0	0	0	2	..	..	3.2
Côte d'Ivoire	2	0	0	0	0	1	0	3	4	3	1	11.9	..	42.4
Djibouti	0	0	0	0	0	0	0	0	0	0	0	..	..	..
Equatorial Guinea	0	0	0	0	0	0	0	0	0	0	0	..	..	..
Eritrea	0	0	0	0	0	0	0	0	0	0	0	..	..	..
Ethiopia	0	0	2	6	6	18	25	19	12	2	12	..	..	10.0
Gabon	0	0	0	0	0	0	0	0	0	0	0	..	..	30.0
Gambia, The	0	0	0	0	0	0	0	0	0	0	0	..	..	..
Ghana	0	0	0	0	0	0	0	0	2	1	8	..	..	86.1
Guinea	0	0	0	0	0	0	0	0	0	0	0	..	..	..
Guinea-Bissau	0	0	0	0	0	0	0	0	0	0	0	..	..	..
Kenya	16	10	11	8	12	12	12	12	7	11	6	-11.6	-5.3	-3.4
Lesotho	0	0	0	0	0	0	0	0	0	0	0	..	..	..
Liberia	0	0	0	0	0	0	0	0	0	0	0	..	..	..
Madagascar	72	22	30	49	24	8	1	0	1	0	0	-16.0	16.4	-61.8
Malawi	0	0	0	0	0	0	0	0	0	0	0	..	..	..
Mali	0	0	0	0	0	0	0	0	0	0	0	-24.4	..	..
Mauritania	0	0	0	0	0	0	0	0	0	0	0	..	..	..
Mauritius	0	32	65	69	45	52	32	11	5	0	1	13.7	43.7	-49.3
Mozambique	0	0	0	0	0	0	0	0	0	0	0	9.6	..	..
Namibia	306	438	459	425	391	402	540	339	337	338	316	5.1	8.3	-4.3
Niger	0	0	0	0	0	0	0	1	1	0	0	-20.1	..	70.0
Nigeria	0	0	0	0	0	0	0	0	0	0	0	..	..	..
Rwanda	0	0	0	0	0	0	0	0	0	0	0	..	..	..
São Tomé and Principe	0	0	0	0	0	0	0	0	0	0	0	..	..	..
Senegal	3	1	1	0	0	1	1	1	1	1	1	3.1	-11.5	5.3
Seychelles	0	0	0	0	0	0	0	0	0	0	0	..	..	..
Sierra Leone	0	0	0	0	0	0	0	0	0	0	0	..	..	..
Somalia	10	0	0	0	0	0	0	0	0	0	0	-40.8	..	..
South Africa	542	148	84	304	342	141	193	192	220	226	255	-7.0	-2.6	5.0
Sudan	0	61	40	65	134	118	146	96	86	65	84	-12.0	..	3.0
Swaziland	35	10	10	9	10	16	21	22	75	7	27	-5.1	-8.1	13.9
Tanzania	2	0	0	0	0	1	2	4	3	9	1	-37.0	..	9.4
Togo	0	0	0	0	0	0	1	0	3	6	14	..	-22.5	98.7
Uganda	0	0	0	1	0	0	0	0	0	0	0	..	..	-14.6
Zambia	0	1	1	0	0	2	1	1	1	0	1	-11.8	30.6	0.2
Zimbabwe	175	275	195	238	151	143	164	205	200	5	122	-16.5	-4.0	-19.1
NORTH AFRICA	34	39	24	17	13	19	20	18	17	18	20	-2.2	37.0	-0.1
Algeria	0	0	0	0	0	0	0	0	0	0	0	-58.2	..	-41.3
Egypt, Arab Rep.	1	37	21	14	10	14	11	7	8	8	11	-0.4	60.0	-8.3
Libya	0	0	0	0	0	0	0	0	0	0	0	..	..	..
Morocco	32	1	2	2	2	3	3	5	3	2	1	-2.5	-6.4	1.6
Tunisia	1	1	2	1	1	2	5	6	6	7	8	-6.5	4.1	31.8
ALL AFRICA	1,471	1,320	1,178	1,435	1,335	1,170	1,432	1,146	1,197	1,112	1,309	-6.7	1.0	-1.0

Note: 2002 data are preliminary (see page 2).

5-33. Manufactured goods exports

| | Millions of U.S. dollars (current prices) | | | | | | | | | | Annual average | | |
	1980	1993	1994	1995	1996	1997	1998	1999	2000	2001	2002	75-84	85-94	95-MR
SUB-SAHARAN AFRICA	6,464	15,564	17,479	22,243	22,607	23,863	22,539	22,653	25,144	24,077	25,017	5,107	12,870	23,518
excluding South Africa	767	4,205	4,799	6,094	6,376	6,016	5,816	5,681	6,122	5,853	6,100	687	3,708	6,007
excl. S.Africa & Nigeria	767	4,165	4,752	6,023	6,329	5,977	5,676	5,654	5,984	5,906	5,774	687	3,674	5,916
Angola	..	63	72	78	105	101	62	75	132	93	95	..	76	93
Benin	..	0	0	0	0	0	0	0	0	0	0	0	0	0
Botswana	..	48	144	336	299	368	305	198	111	30	30	..	96	210
Burkina Faso	..	..	..	..	..	..	..	..	..	..	..	..	..	..
Burundi	1	9	5	7	4	1	0	1	1	1	1	3	7	2
Cameroon	96	227	204	259	302	291	423	399	381	351	392	81	246	350
Cape Verde	..	1	2	6	0	0	0	0	0	0	0	..	1	1
Central African Republic	..	0	0	0	0	0	0	0	0	0	0	..	0	0
Chad	..	0	..	..	..	..	..	..	..	..	..	5	3	..
Comoros	..	0	0	0	0	0	0	0	0	0	0	0	0	0
Congo, Dem. Rep. of	..	93	140	225	305	..	..	..	97	129	130	..	173	177
Congo, Rep. of	0	20	13	23	17	16	10	12	12	12	13	6	32	14
Côte d'Ivoire	..	956	1,012	1,294	1,287	1,182	1,244	1,222	1,205	1,182	1,424	672	935	1,255
Djibouti	..	..	..	26	27	29	39	46	46	50	55	..	..	40
Equatorial Guinea	..	0	0	0	0	0	0	0	0	0	0	0	0	0
Eritrea	..	16	21	31	41	20	6	8	4	6	7	..	12	15
Ethiopia	..	40	52	76	61	75	56	37	42	86	67	85	70	62
Gabon	..	0	0	0	0	0	0	0	0	0	0	0	0	0
Gambia, The	..	..	..	..	..	..	..	..	..	..	..	..	..	..
Ghana	..	..	..	..	..	..	..	..	..	..	..	..	..	..
Guinea	..	0	0	0	0	0	0	0	0	0	..	..	0	0
Guinea-Bissau	..	..	..	..	..	..	..	..	..	..	..	..	..	..
Kenya	177	241	378	467	454	455	440	409	367	432	467	128	194	436
Lesotho	..	..	..	..	..	..	..	27	7	6	51	..	..	23
Liberia	..	..	..	..	..	..	..	..	..	..	..	..	..	..
Madagascar	..	175	191	296	318	346	356	398	608	572	119	42	109	377
Malawi	..	32	39	49	69	74	63	56	56	60	60	..	35	61
Mali	..	..	..	..	..	..	..	..	..	..	..	..	..	..
Mauritania	..	..	..	..	..	..	..	..	..	..	..	0	..	..
Mauritius	108	861	887	1,004	1,104	1,098	1,034	1,135	1,171	1,177	1,101	117	606	1,103
Mozambique	..	7	3	5	8	20	14	14	14	13	13	0	9	13
Namibia	158	256	302	320	343	223	237	249	331	266	271	169	251	280
Niger	..	0	0	0	0	0	0	..	..	..	..	0	0	0
Nigeria	..	40	47	70	47	40	140	27	138	-54	325	..	49	92
Rwanda	..	7	2	4	5	18	10	16	42	48	27	4	4	21
São Tomé and Principe	..	..	..	..	..	..	..	..	..	..	..	..	..	..
Senegal	136	164	201	254	250	254	258	242	241	250	250	171	173	250
Seychelles	..	11	17	19	35	60	80	102	116	147	169	0	9	91
Sierra Leone	..	0	0	0	0	0	0	0	0	0	0	0	0	0
Somalia	..	..	..	..	..	..	..	..	..	..	..	..	..	..
South Africa	5,697	11,359	12,680	16,149	16,231	17,847	16,723	16,972	19,022	18,224	18,917	4,420	9,162	17,511
Sudan	..	..	..	..	..	..	..	..	110	109	93	31	26	104
Swaziland	..	56	52	66	80	82	81	79	62	2	2	..	26	57
Tanzania	91	52	77	109	123	111	30	22	34	56	66	54	61	69
Togo	..	75	60	86	78	74	78	79	65	73	79	66	102	76
Uganda	..	..	..	..	..	..	..	..	..	..	..	..	..	..
Zambia	..	103	129	155	168	180	194	189	163	203	213	101	64	183
Zimbabwe	..	652	750	829	846	900	655	640	567	552	579	319	581	696
NORTH AFRICA	1,292	6,332	7,178	9,189	8,761	8,824	9,693	10,271	10,927	11,432	12,213	1,039	4,613	10,164
Algeria	..	68	28	30	31	40	42	46	81	124	133	7	132	66
Egypt, Arab Rep.	..	1,167	1,127	1,655	1,314	1,302	1,685	2,080	2,845	3,187	3,321	..	1,103	2,174
Libya	..	..	..	..	..	..	..	..	..	..	..	..	..	..
Morocco	387	2,710	3,010	3,754	3,673	3,802	3,932	4,087	3,997	3,822	3,966	320	1,841	3,879
Tunisia	905	2,387	3,012	3,750	3,742	3,680	4,033	4,058	4,005	4,300	4,792	718	1,758	4,045
ALL AFRICA	7,756	21,896	24,657	31,432	31,368	32,687	32,232	32,924	36,071	35,509	37,230	6,146	17,484	33,682

Note: 2002 data are preliminary (see page 2).

5-34. Manufactured goods exports, growth

	Percentage											Average annual percentage growth		
	1980	1993	1994	1995	1996	1997	1998	1999	2000	2001	2002	75-84	85-94	95-MR
SUB-SAHARAN AFRICA	1.7	2.3	12.2	20.3	9.4	8.4	0.0	3.8	15.4	2.9	-9.4	-0.1	10.2	6.1
excluding South Africa	388.6	2.9	17.9	7.6	8.8	4.6	-0.6	-1.0	9.2	-1.4	-25.2	37.4	17.4	1.1
excl. S.Africa & Nigeria	388.6	2.8	17.9	7.3	9.2	4.7	-2.3	0.8	7.5	1.3	-25.8	37.4	17.3	1.2
Angola	..	28.4	11.7	-4.6	4.7	-0.6	-20.1	8.2	1.8	-8.0	-4.9	..	-3.3	-3.3
Benin	..	..	..	..	..	..	..	..	..	..	..	..	..	..
Botswana	..	..	189.3	120.8	-6.2	32.0	-14.0	-34.8	-42.7	-71.7	-4.0	..	..	-21.6
Burkina Faso	..	..	..	..	..	..	..	..	..	..	..	..	..	..
Burundi	..	-19.2	-39.1	19.1	-36.3	-87.7	3.0	2.2	6.2	6.1	6.2	..	-2.9	-27.9
Cameroon	21.3	-0.4	-4.6	-5.5	21.1	5.6	2.7	20.0	5.0	8.0	3.4	13.0	2.3	8.3
Cape Verde	..	..	..	..	..	..	..	..	..	..	..	..	..	..
Central African Republic	..	..	..	..	..	..	..	..	..	..	..	..	..	..
Chad	..	-4.5	..	..	..	..	..	..	..	..	..	..	5.7	..
Comoros	..	..	..	..	..	..	..	100.0	50.0	..	..	..	..	..
Congo, Dem. Rep. of	..	..	..	..	..	..	..	..	..	..	..	..	..	..
Congo, Rep. of	..	-33.3	0.0	0.0	0.0	0.0	0.0	0.0	0.0	0.0	0.0	..	-5.4	0.0
Côte d'Ivoire	..	-7.3	19.7	1.2	5.2	-2.7	13.7	-5.4	7.3	3.8	12.3	..	1.8	3.8
Djibouti	..	..	..	..	-0.2	1.1	31.4	14.9	-2.9	5.6	6.3	..	..	8.8
Equatorial Guinea	..	..	..	..	..	..	..	..	..	..	..	..	..	..
Eritrea	..	1,326.3	30.9	45.8	29.5	-51.6	-70.7	26.5	-54.2	..	..	..	..	-31.2
Ethiopia	..	44.9	66.6	2.0	-23.0	16.2	-16.1	-26.2	43.4	42.8	-11.8	..	-7.4	0.1
Gabon	..	..	..	..	..	..	..	..	..	..	..	..	..	..
Gambia, The	..	..	..	..	..	..	..	..	..	..	..	..	..	..
Ghana	..	..	..	..	..	..	..	..	..	..	..	..	..	..
Guinea	..	..	..	..	..	..	..	..	..	..	..	..	..	..
Guinea-Bissau	..	..	..	..	..	..	..	..	..	..	..	..	..	..
Kenya	..	16.4	68.3	11.9	0.5	8.9	-1.6	-5.2	-5.9	20.8	5.3	..	12.7	2.6
Lesotho	..	..	..	..	..	..	..	..	-73.2	-4.7	0.5	..	..	..
Liberia	..	..	..	..	..	..	..	..	..	..	..	..	..	..
Madagascar	..	9.7	5.4	46.5	13.2	17.0	6.7	12.2	55.9	-4.6	-79.4	..	13.8	5.1
Malawi	..	..	..	..	..	..	..	..	..	..	..	..	..	..
Mali	..	..	..	..	..	..	..	..	..	..	..	..	..	..
Mauritania	..	..	..	..	..	..	..	..	..	..	..	..	..	..
Mauritius	..	4.8	0.8	8.1	9.5	5.8	-0.4	12.0	4.3	4.0	..	..	5.6	6.0
Mozambique	..	-47.1	-55.2	44.4	66.9	158.0	-24.4	-0.2	2.7	-6.9	4.5	..	179.7	19.5
Namibia	..	-19.4	13.7	-2.1	9.8	-33.3	9.2	7.6	36.2	-17.4	4.3	..	0.2	0.3
Niger	..	..	..	..	..	..	..	..	..	..	..	..	..	..
Nigeria	..	11.6	14.4	38.3	-30.6	-10.0	260.3	-81.2	406.2	-137.7	..	..	0.5	10.2
Rwanda	..	-25.9	-38.8	175.0	-15.5	2.8	-46.9	61.9	93.7	14.2	-35.5	..	-19.5	11.9
São Tomé and Principe	..	..	..	..	..	..	..	..	..	..	..	..	..	..
Senegal	..	12.7	-1.5	18.1	-8.3	27.3	1.7	-7.0	-1.8	5.2	-0.1	..	-2.9	3.1
Seychelles	..	-9.6	64.8	-14.5	103.7	60.9	4.9	60.0	19.9	6.0	1.5	..	16.5	30.4
Sierra Leone	..	..	..	..	..	..	..	..	..	..	..	..	..	..
Somalia	..	..	..	..	..	..	..	..	..	..	..	..	..	..
South Africa	-4.2	2.1	10.5	24.6	9.6	9.5	0.2	5.1	17.0	3.9	-5.9	-1.6	8.7	7.4
Sudan	..	..	..	..	..	..	..	..	..	..	..	..	..	..
Swaziland	..	113.9	-10.4	40.3	27.5	10.2	2.6	-1.5	-18.8	-96.7	1.1	..	..	-30.2
Tanzania	..	-19.0	48.1	41.8	12.5	-9.4	-73.2	-27.9	59.1	64.3	17.3	..	..	-10.7
Togo	..	192.4	-22.7	88.5	-94.3	1,063.5	29.6	32.8	..	..	..	..	..	..
Uganda	..	..	..	..	..	..	..	..	..	..	..	..	..	..
Zambia	..	65.8	19.9	13.7	14.3	14.8	12.0	-2.2	-12.0	26.1	4.4	..	746.2	7.3
Zimbabwe	..	8.8	20.2	-4.6	5.1	14.9	-25.1	0.2	-9.1	2.2	0.8	..	3.2	-3.5
NORTH AFRICA	..	-5.2	11.7	11.0	-9.1	8.4	18.6	12.8	-34.0	-49.7	6.0	..	21.7	-7.9
Algeria	..	..	..	..	..	..	..	..	..	..	..	..	..	..
Egypt, Arab Rep.	..	-21.9	-5.5	40.1	-20.9	-15.0	69.5	25.9	39.2	..	..	..	3.6	16.1
Libya	..	..	..	..	..	..	..	..	..	..	..	..	..	..
Morocco	..	4.3	1.1	0.6	-0.8	11.6	-3.2	13.9	-3.3	3.3	6.0	..	..	3.5
Tunisia	..	-4.0	34.9	8.5	-10.0	16.4	21.0	5.7	..	..	..	..	8.4	8.1
ALL AFRICA	1.7	0.2	12.1	17.9	4.9	8.4	4.0	6.0	2.6	-5.9	-8.1	0.7	12.5	3.7

Note: 2002 data are preliminary (see page 2).

5-35. Food Imports

	Millions of U.S. dollars (current prices)											Annual average		
	1980	1993	1994	1995	1996	1997	1998	1999	2000	2001	2002	75-84	85-94	95-MR
SUB-SAHARAN AFRICA	4,815	5,440	5,682	7,068	6,897	7,371	7,355	6,828	6,742	7,270	7,330	3,250	4,930	7,108
excluding South Africa	4,391	4,665	4,653	5,757	5,609	5,919	6,144	5,787	5,766	6,352	6,347	2,787	4,261	5,960
excl. S.Africa & Nigeria	1,230	3,894	3,916	4,697	4,680	4,699	4,747	4,271	4,194	4,562	4,430	881	3,438	4,535
Angola	..	203	215	205	275	365	..	..	..	..	..	..	232	282
Benin	..	113	85	134	136	130	138	145	137	143	..	80	120	138
Botswana	..	315	288	305	292	297	306	305	247	231	216	..	288	275
Burkina Faso	..	0	0	70	86	71	111	..	..	..	..	..	58	84
Burundi	18	19	30	29	11	11	10	11	11	12	12	19	16	13
Cameroon	82	161	189	123	138	155	173	169	162	181	203	70	160	163
Cape Verde	..	53	65	79	75	78	50	53	55	58	61	..	46	64
Central African Republic	..	25	23	29	22	20	23	23	18	14	15	20	27	20
Chad	..	6	25	22	21	18	4	4	..	..	..	..	13	14
Comoros	..	10	9	18	12	20	18	18	9	12	12	8	9	15
Congo, Dem. Rep. of	..	..	..	..	..	..	..	..	..	..	..	..	..	..
Congo, Rep. of	0	36	15	16	18	19	20	21	23	24	26	10	26	21
Côte d'Ivoire	435	431	317	523	496	529	634	560	433	543	597	389	429	539
Djibouti	..	..	..	70	67	69	72	75	78	81	85	..	..	75
Equatorial Guinea	..	..	..	..	..	..	..	..	..	..	..	..	..	..
Eritrea	..	32	69	68	85	83	62	92	117	154	105	..	45	96
Ethiopia	..	167	126	181	103	17	28	100	116	110	209	126	171	108
Gabon	..	166	166	181	191	189	166	138	142	149	158	142	156	164
Gambia, The	..	52	46	55	50	57	82	64	63	72	76	..	26	65
Ghana	..	..	..	..	..	..	..	..	..	..	..	39	45	..
Guinea	..	53	76	77	76	77	79	82	87	93	..	..	27	82
Guinea-Bissau	..	25	17	26	25	31	17	31	34	30	45	16	18	30
Kenya	109	75	79	96	136	158	162	156	182	207	146	89	89	155
Lesotho	..	..	..	..	..	..	..	..	..	..	73	..	..	73
Liberia	..	..	..	..	..	..	..	..	..	..	..	..	..	..
Madagascar	89	51	79	67	60	49	54	46	77	84	61	87	48	62
Malawi	..	5	65	82	43	32	77	32	30	34	41	..	16	46
Mali	103	97	86	111	113	111	123	105	111	118	..	113	95	113
Mauritania	..	104	95	128	103	117	103	98	120	113	106	76	112	111
Mauritius	143	219	235	287	330	350	320	339	299	291	316	137	169	317
Mozambique	..	..	..	44	29	30	32	47	87	72	99	..	..	55
Namibia	..	286	301	331	333	352	319	299	306	283	293	..	282	314
Niger	..	22	16	18	19	27	36	..	..	..	..	..	28	25
Nigeria	3,161	771	738	1,060	929	1,219	1,397	1,516	1,573	1,790	1,917	1,906	823	1,425
Rwanda	..	59	218	56	51	54	57	35	47	52	55	27	53	51
São Tomé and Principe	..	7	7	7	6	5	5	5	5	5	6	8	7	5
Senegal	210	348	293	364	353	289	350	359	304	359	335	246	294	339
Seychelles	..	46	42	42	58	75	80	81	81	102	112	17	32	79
Sierra Leone	..	57	52	66	110	41	36	28	66	72	68	39	50	61
Somalia	..	..	..	..	..	..	..	..	..	..	..	..	..	..
South Africa	424	774	1,029	1,311	1,288	1,453	1,210	1,041	976	917	983	462	669	1,147
Sudan	..	205	181	215	232	243	264	276	340	416	441	219	200	303
Swaziland	42	135	136	202	173	171	156	187	167	132	128	32	82	165
Tanzania	..	58	97	97	54	57	169	200	176	169	147	96	70	134
Togo	..	82	75	96	149	209	212	..	..	..	..	118	129	166
Uganda	..	..	..	..	..	..	..	..	..	..	..	..	..	..
Zambia	..	50	55	98	25	12	108	..	9	10	11	24	50	39
Zimbabwe	..	121	43	78	119	84	90	88	54	135	170	77	102	102
NORTH AFRICA	3,100	5,364	5,541	7,766	7,034	7,192	7,746	6,142	5,735	6,319	6,737	2,484	4,772	6,834
Algeria	1,992	2,092	2,206	2,762	2,601	2,544	2,657	2,609	2,465	2,704	2,958	1,558	2,096	2,662
Egypt, Arab Rep.	..	1,878	1,982	2,760	2,513	2,885	3,194	1,799	1,395	1,473	1,469	..	1,995	2,186
Libya	..	..	..	..	..	..	..	..	..	..	..	..	..	..
Morocco	720	978	817	1,373	1,298	1,072	1,191	1,177	1,338	1,370	1,459	594	643	1,285
Tunisia	388	417	537	871	622	691	705	557	538	772	851	333	436	701
ALL AFRICA	7,915	10,804	11,224	14,834	13,931	14,563	15,101	12,970	12,478	13,589	14,067	5,733	9,702	13,942

Note: 2002 data are preliminary (see page 2).

5-36. Food imports, growth

					Percentage							Average annual percentage growth		
	1980	*1993*	*1994*	*1995*	*1996*	*1997*	*1998*	*1999*	*2000*	*2001*	*2002*	*75-84*	*85-94*	*95-MR*
SUB-SAHARAN AFRICA	42.6	-5.5	0.2	22.1	0.1	7.7	-25.2	-4.1	-1.6	4.0	-2.6	11.3	1.4	-3.0
excluding South Africa	58.9	-3.5	-6.6	20.3	-2.5	6.2	-30.3	-1.8	-2.1	7.7	-6.6	20.5	0.7	-4.3
excl. S.Africa & Nigeria	58.0	-3.6	-5.2	17.6	1.6	-1.4	-7.9	-1.8	-2.1	7.7	-6.6	20.5	5.1	-0.5
Angola	..	-12.6	2.5	-13.2	34.2	47.1	..	..	..	..	..	..	-5.4	..
Benin	..	..	..	..	..	..	..	..	..	..	..	..	..	..
Botswana	..	..	-11.8	0.0	0.7	9.3	7.0	0.0	-17.4	-1.8	-10.2	..	..	-1.2
Burkina Faso	..	..	..	..	..	..	..	..	..	..	..	..	..	..
Burundi	..	75.5	61.3	-4.0	-62.2	2.8	-9.6	4.0	4.6	4.6	4.6	..	8.1	-10.2
Cameroon	0.8	-17.2	9.5	-27.6	-3.8	20.6	9.5	-10.1	1.6	9.8	9.0	-0.9	9.8	1.9
Cape Verde	..	-27.7	11.9	12.5	-8.4	11.0	-35.0	3.5	3.1	5.4	4.5	..	11.4	-3.8
Central African Republic	..	-16.9	-11.4	19.4	-26.5	-7.7	9.4	-3.9	-21.1	-25.4	4.5	..	-4.6	-9.0
Chad	..	500.0	25.0	-12.8	-0.3	-1.9	2.8	1.2	..	..	..	..	-10.6	-1.7
Comoros	..	-12.6	32.7	77.9	-30.5	1.0	1.5	2.0	..	..	..	..	4.3	0.8
Congo, Dem. Rep. of	..	..	..	62.8	50.1	..	..	..	..	..	..	..	..	..
Congo, Rep. of	..	32.2	10.9	-1.1	-0.7	9.6	7.6	3.0	3.5	3.2	3.4	..	-2.7	4.1
Côte d'Ivoire	..	13.0	-26.1	52.6	1.5	7.1	5.0	4.0	-2.0	1.0	5.5	..	-8.8	5.8
Djibouti	..	..	..	..	-7.3	-1.5	0.9	1.5	-0.1	2.3	2.4	..	..	0.1
Equatorial Guinea	..	..	..	..	..	..	..	..	..	..	..	..	..	..
Eritrea	..	..	..	..	..	..	..	..	..	..	..	..	..	..
Ethiopia	..	..	..	..	..	..	..	..	..	..	..	..	..	..
Gabon	..	..	..	..	..	..	..	..	..	..	..	..	..	..
Gambia, The	..	-3.5	-12.8	15.5	-12.3	9.1	41.0	-23.6	-2.6	11.0	3.4	..	41.6	3.1
Ghana	..	5.5	4.2	5.4	7.7	-0.7	7.3	6.0	4.1	6.0	6.3	..	3.3	5.1
Guinea	..	12.8	38.7	-7.4	0.0	-2.0	5.3	5.8	5.2	5.0	..	..	25.8	2.1
Guinea-Bissau	..	-21.4	-15.6	61.3	-7.9	20.2	-44.9	87.3	11.4	-9.6	54.7	..	9.8	9.3
Kenya	37.5	29.4	-2.3	3.9	49.4	20.2	1.5	9.9	27.6	8.5	-29.7	9.7	-10.4	12.5
Lesotho	..	..	..	..	..	..	..	..	..	..	..	..	..	..
Liberia	..	..	..	..	..	..	..	..	..	..	..	..	..	..
Madagascar	..	-17.5	53.4	-26.2	-19.9	-8.8	22.0	-22.2	-9.1	20.5	-10.6	..	-1.7	-6.6
Malawi	..	-90.5	967.9	23.5	-47.9	-30.5	56.2	-8.6	-1.7	83.0	41.1	..	53.2	3.4
Mali	2.1	1.9	-8.7	13.3	11.3	7.5	11.4	-10.2	23.5	8.3	..	6.7	-4.4	8.0
Mauritania	..	-22.4	-5.1	-19.4	4.6	-6.1	11.9	-9.0	52.0	-7.3	-7.4	..	-0.9	3.4
Mauritius	..	..	..	..	..	..	..	..	..	..	..	..	..	..
Mozambique	..	..	..	..	-40.9	4.3	..	..	..	..	..	..	..	..
Namibia	..	-2.5	-2.7	10.0	-5.0	0.0	-14.4	-11.3	-3.0	-12.5	-2.3	..	..	-6.5
Niger	..	..	..	..	..	..	..	..	..	..	..	..	..	..
Nigeria	59.2	-3.0	-11.7	31.3	-17.1	39.8	..	..	..	..	..	20.0	-7.8	..
Rwanda	..	0.9	5.1	8.1	12.2	-10.8	-12.7	-3.8	-6.6	9.1	-0.2	..	-2.9	-2.7
São Tomé and Principe	..	23.6	-14.2	2.9	-24.9	-14.6	25.7	-17.2	-4.7	5.1	27.1	..	0.8	-3.3
Senegal	..	0.7	-34.3	10.6	-9.7	4.4	27.2	-1.9	-19.6	24.8	-5.9	..	2.1	2.8
Seychelles	..	27.2	-16.4	3.1	36.9	29.3	23.5	21.0	-7.1	49.6	20.3	..	5.4	21.2
Sierra Leone	..	5.4	-11.6	16.3	64.9	-60.1	-5.5	-25.8	131.1	11.3	-4.9	..	..	0.6
Somalia	..	..	..	..	..	..	..	..	..	..	..	..	-2.0	..
South Africa	-8.9	-12.6	26.0	27.0	6.9	11.3	-13.1	-8.3	-0.7	-3.2	6.1	-1.5	4.3	0.1
Sudan	..	..	..	..	..	..	..	3.1	20.4	19.9	..	..	10.1	..
Swaziland	..	21.4	0.4	52.1	-14.9	-1.7	-9.3	43.5	-9.3	-19.8	-1.6	..	..	0.9
Tanzania	..	..	..	..	-64.1	..	..	..	..	..	..	..	..	..
Togo	..	..	..	..	..	..	..	..	..	..	..	..	0.9	..
Uganda	..	..	..	..	..	..	..	..	..	..	..	..	..	..
Zambia	..	-80.3	0.7	64.0	-75.9	-47.3	864.4	..	..	10.6	9.2	..	15.4	-18.5
Zimbabwe	..	-51.0	-65.7	71.9	59.4	-26.4	13.5	0.8	-40.8	135.9	19.9	..	19.3	10.6
NORTH AFRICA	..	-5.2	-8.6	11.0	-12.3	2.7	16.5	-49.6	-14.4	-62.9	2.3	..	9.8	-20.6
Algeria	..	-10.5	7.5	-12.0	-7.0	-10.6	12.4	..	..	..	..	..	2.5	-5.6
Egypt, Arab Rep.	..	-4.8	2.0	27.8	-15.3	14.1	21.1	-35.3	-13.3	..	..	..	-1.9	-2.7
Libya	..	..	..	..	..	..	..	..	..	..	..	..	..	..
Morocco	..	2.9	-56.5	35.5	-6.9	-1.3	16.4	0.7	17.8	-2.4	2.3	..	..	6.2
Tunisia	..	2.3	21.1	35.2	-30.8	18.3	6.3	-9.7	..	..	..	..	-6.6	0.2
ALL AFRICA	42.6	-5.3	-5.0	15.8	-6.7	5.1	-4.4	-31.7	-7.4	-23.7	-1.6	14.0	5.4	-10.1

Note: 2002 data are preliminary (see page 2).

5-37. Nonfood consumer goods imports

	Millions of U.S. dollars (current prices)											Annual average		
	1980	1993	1994	1995	1996	1997	1998	1999	2000	2001	2002	75-84	85-94	95-MR
SUB-SAHARAN AFRICA	4,164	8,347	8,682	10,575	10,603	11,636	10,091	10,151	10,240	10,542	9,830	2,937	7,221	10,458
excluding South Africa	1,849	5,391	5,374	6,753	6,532	7,270	5,985	6,310	6,017	6,540	5,580	1,212	4,822	6,373
excl. S.Africa & Nigeria	1,849	5,391	5,374	6,753	6,532	7,270	5,985	6,310	6,017	6,540	5,580	1,212	4,822	6,373
Angola	..	778	712	1,069	1,119	1,263	..	..	..	..	..	..	536	1,150
Benin	..	121	92	144	146	140	148	156	147	153	..	..	103	148
Botswana	..	451	459	511	475	539	559	632	512	479	448	..	427	519
Burkina Faso	..	0	0	170	192	176	160	..	..	..	..	..	119	175
Burundi	53	33	28	28	8	19	49	-4	10	10	30	43	38	19
Cameroon	136	89	76	64	74	179	244	402	432	428	685	222	178	313
Cape Verde	..	57	65	85	91	81	45	48	49	51	52	..	51	63
Central African Republic	..	26	29	11	32	51	15	-13	-31	-27	-25	30	39	2
Chad	..	131	-86	22	-56	-60	-9	-21	..	..	..	..	89	-25
Comoros	..	41	36	35	28	22	17	17	15	21	24	25	35	22
Congo, Dem. Rep. of	..	..	..	..	..	..	..	..	..	..	..	..	..	..
Congo, Rep. of	0	3	5	5	7	9	28	36	82	99	119	26	107	48
Côte d'Ivoire	629	491	454	743	675	669	766	681	420	466	513	466	469	617
Djibouti	..	..	..	35	34	34	36	38	39	41	43	..	..	37
Equatorial Guinea	..	25	22	29	50	43	39	49	49	51	53	21	27	45
Eritrea	..	109	95	28	59	3	3	2	1	2	3	..	134	13
Ethiopia	..	167	165	159	207	259	252	329	310	358	379	116	155	282
Gabon	..	241	71	77	78	79	67	61	65	68	72	330	217	71
Gambia, The	..	29	26	34	30	34	36	40	39	45	47	..	12	38
Ghana	..	..	..	..	..	..	..	..	..	..	..	80	165	..
Guinea	..	318	320	389	313	355	378	405	436	467	..	..	296	392
Guinea-Bissau	..	5	6	7	7	9	9	10	10	9	8	11	9	9
Kenya	524	519	808	614	637	882	920	832	831	1,070	915	307	608	838
Lesotho	..	..	..	..	..	..	..	..	..	..	110	..	..	110
Liberia	..	..	..	..	..	..	..	..	..	..	..	..	..	..
Madagascar	..	209	236	299	309	353	387	417	479	571	291	89	140	388
Malawi	..	54	39	31	45	58	30	44	33	35	58	..	45	42
Mali	181	188	176	159	182	168	154	147	165	191	..	163	129	167
Mauritania	..	16	12	18	17	23	22	25	-15	18	39	23	28	18
Mauritius	46	159	163	186	204	179	181	188	188	181	108	36	106	177
Mozambique	..	..	..	140	137	137	147	216	175	120	130	..	..	150
Namibia	..	176	185	204	205	217	196	184	189	175	180	..	174	194
Niger	..	92	117	112	154	130	147	..	..	..	..	..	103	136
Nigeria	..	..	..	..	..	..	..	..	..	..	..	..	..	..
Rwanda	..	88	158	69	71	120	105	133	91	122	114	31	70	103
São Tomé and Principe	..	11	9	7	8	6	6	..	..	..	..	15	9	6
Senegal	151	192	186	215	203	202	196	201	186	212	197	139	186	201
Seychelles	..	39	33	65	75	80	87	75	64	61	77	8	23	73
Sierra Leone	..	19	16	11	11	4	7	6	19	142	121	18	25	40
Somalia	..	..	..	..	..	..	..	..	..	..	..	..	..	..
South Africa	2,316	2,956	3,308	3,822	4,071	4,365	4,106	3,841	4,223	4,002	4,250	1,725	2,399	4,085
Sudan	..	8	15	160	-11	87	38	365	391	313	148	120	69	186
Swaziland	127	78	46	32	39	41	37	47	43	23	22	86	64	36
Tanzania	..	293	237	355	268	323	272	357	376	362	367	71	171	335
Togo	..	16	22	27	29	28	14	..	..	..	..	61	55	24
Uganda	..	..	..	..	..	..	..	..	..	..	..	..	..	..
Zambia	..	..	167	199	200	125	121	128	125	139	176	..	167	152
Zimbabwe	..	119	173	205	183	203	77	76	93	84	77	303	162	125
NORTH AFRICA	2,714	6,125	7,969	7,761	5,877	7,122	7,454	8,469	11,000	7,696	10,582	2,083	5,105	8,245
Algeria	1,785	1,373	2,027	1,757	1,037	1,095	1,314	1,422	1,386	1,507	1,683	1,333	1,885	1,400
Egypt, Arab Rep.	..	1,448	2,159	1,531	121	1,167	785	1,621	4,087	435	2,734	..	1,155	1,560
Libya	..	..	..	..	..	..	..	..	..	..	..	..	..	..
Morocco	334	1,366	1,525	1,853	2,037	2,134	2,418	2,481	2,701	2,649	2,816	288	977	2,386
Tunisia	595	1,938	2,258	2,621	2,683	2,726	2,937	2,945	2,825	3,105	3,350	462	1,318	2,899
ALL AFRICA	6,878	14,472	16,651	18,336	16,480	18,757	17,545	18,620	21,240	18,238	20,412	5,019	12,326	18,704

Note: 2002 data are preliminary (see page 2).

5-38. Nonfood consumer goods imports, growth

	1980	1993	1994	1995	1996	1997	1998	1999	2000	2001	2002	75-84	85-94	95-MR
						Percentage							*Average annual percentage growth*	
SUB-SAHARAN AFRICA	19.8	8.2	5.6	9.6	16.0	9.5	-13.3	-2.0	9.8	2.5	-3.6	4.9	8.0	2.5
excluding South Africa	-1.2	6.3	1.3	9.5	14.9	11.5	-22.2	0.1	9.3	4.2	-12.2	34.3	11.6	0.6
excl. S.Africa & Nigeria	-1.2	6.3	1.3	9.5	14.9	11.5	-22.2	0.1	9.3	4.2	-12.2	34.3	11.6	0.6
Angola	..	-19.0	-11.5	36.7	4.7	25.1	..	..	..	..	..	..	25.8	..
Benin	..	..	..	..	..	..	..	..	..	..	..	..	..	..
Botswana	..	..	-1.8	5.1	-2.2	22.0	7.7	13.4	-17.4	-1.8	-10.2	..	..	2.6
Burkina Faso	..	..	..	..	..	..	..	..	..	..	..	..	..	..
Burundi	..	-33.2	-46.6	0.2	-101.6	-5,796.8	259.1	-130.0	-120.4	-0.8	735.0	..	-10.6	-9.9
Cameroon	-40.2	-25.5	69.5	-22.2	40.4	21.7	16.6	3.4	5.0	5.0	5.0	-3.7	6.3	10.5
Cape Verde	..	-4.5	-6.5	20.1	14.7	-8.7	-44.4	1.5	1.9	1.9	2.8	..	7.9	-7.1
Central African Republic	..	-1.4	8.2	-64.1	166.4	66.9	-72.7	-186.3	133.1	-16.1	-9.8	..	-9.7	-1.6
Chad	..	-20.4	-96.4	-4,951.8	43.3	-6.9	27.8	72.3	..	..	..	..	-31.0	..
Comoros	..	-9.5	27.5	-11.0	20.0	1.0	1.5	2.0	..	..	..	..	2.0	3.4
Congo, Dem. Rep. of	..	..	..	..	..	..	..	..	..	..	..	..	..	..
Congo, Rep. of	..	32.2	10.9	-1.1	140.8	-22.9	-22.1	8.7	-3.1	-6.4	8.7	..	3.2	2.8
Côte d'Ivoire	..	-8.2	-8.4	48.7	5.0	4.7	4.5	4.0	-2.0	1.0	5.0	..	-1.3	5.6
Djibouti	..	..	..	..	-7.1	-1.5	0.9	2.4	-0.1	1.3	1.4	..	..	0.1
Equatorial Guinea	..	13.5	-8.5	18.6	71.3	57.6	157.1	-59.7	-27.2	-8.5	0.1	..	4.9	9.5
Eritrea	..	..	..	..	..	..	..	..	..	..	..	..	..	..
Ethiopia	..	..	..	..	..	..	..	..	..	..	..	..	..	..
Gabon	..	..	..	..	..	..	..	..	..	..	..	..	..	..
Gambia, The	..	-8.3	-12.3	25.2	-15.2	11.0	3.5	6.7	-2.6	11.0	3.4	..	114.9	3.9
Ghana	..	69.6	-30.7	4.8	10.3	0.9	7.3	6.1	4.1	6.0	6.3	..	15.5	5.6
Guinea	..	6.2	-3.0	10.6	-20.2	18.6	4.0	4.4	4.8	4.8	..	..	2.4	3.3
Guinea-Bissau	..	-36.5	15.8	13.8	10.9	12.2	2.8	9.3	9.2	-9.0	-4.9	..	-2.0	5.8
Kenya	..	..	..	..	..	..	..	..	..	..	..	..	..	..
Lesotho	..	..	..	..	..	..	..	..	..	..	..	..	..	..
Liberia	..	..	..	..	..	..	..	..	..	..	..	..	..	..
Madagascar	..	10.7	9.1	19.4	8.7	22.9	13.8	8.2	17.3	20.9	-49.3	..	6.8	9.2
Malawi	..	-5.4	-32.3	-35.3	66.0	45.9	-19.2	-8.9	18.0	6.8	41.1	..	-1.1	9.5
Mali	2.5	7.7	-9.5	-19.0	17.8	10.4	-119.4	-455.4	148.9	-40.3	..	-3.4	7.5	4.6
Mauritania	..	-46.9	-12.1	23.2	7.7	-7.1	4.3	-42.3	679.9	46.3	-95.7	..	-12.2	7.2
Mauritius	..	..	..	..	..	..	..	..	..	..	..	..	..	..
Mozambique	..	..	..	..	0.4	4.3	..	..	..	..	..	..	..	..
Namibia	..	-3.6	1.6	1.6	3.0	8.5	-7.1	-3.8	5.2	-5.1	5.9	..	..	0.3
Niger	..	..	..	..	..	..	..	..	..	..	..	..	..	..
Nigeria	..	..	..	..	..	..	..	..	..	..	..	..	..	..
Rwanda	..	-6.3	3.3	-45.0	-83.6	552.5	15.0	55.2	-67.5	54.1	-98.2	..	7.5	-22.8
São Tomé and Principe	..	13.3	-20.2	-31.9	17.6	5.1	-57.9	152.8	27.8	-48.6	-2.7	..	-1.9	-3.1
Senegal	..	-8.8	-33.8	2.7	-12.1	27.2	2.0	-2.0	-12.1	20.4	-6.4	..	-0.2	2.1
Seychelles	..	47.0	-25.4	101.5	22.7	3.8	17.6	-13.7	-25.3	7.9	39.1	..	15.3	6.8
Sierra Leone	..	34.3	-17.7	-38.2	4.1	-58.2	66.6	-8.0	189.4	647.6	-14.1	..	..	34.6
Somalia	..	..	..	..	..	..	..	..	..	..	..	..	1.4	..
South Africa	28.2	11.0	11.8	9.9	17.5	7.0	-1.7	-4.2	10.4	0.7	5.9	-0.1	4.7	4.6
Sudan	..	..	..	..	..	..	..	842.7	4.5	-21.7	..	..	..	..
Swaziland	..	33.7	-41.0	-28.4	20.7	4.1	-10.6	47.6	-4.0	-43.8	1.8	..	..	-2.0
Tanzania	..	..	..	..	13.1	..	..	..	..	..	..	..	..	..
Togo	..	..	..	..	..	..	..	..	..	..	..	..	7.9	..
Uganda	..	..	..	..	..	..	..	..	..	..	..	..	..	..
Zambia	..	..	..	12.5	5.7	-32.6	-0.1	6.6	-0.2	12.7	25.5	..	..	-0.6
Zimbabwe	..	2.2	40.9	11.7	-6.2	15.5	-59.5	0.8	25.3	-5.4	-11.7	..	-7.0	-10.3
NORTH AFRICA	..	15.6	28.7	-2.8	-16.0	18.0	4.1	23.9	-0.3	-54.4	5.0	..	5.4	-4.3
Algeria	..	-9.3	73.2	17.3	-16.7	-27.0	5.5	..	..	..	..	..	-11.3	-10.1
Egypt, Arab Rep.	..	78.6	44.1	-34.9	-92.6	858.0	-26.3	336.0	53.6	..	..	..	21.1	24.1
Libya	..	..	..	..	..	..	..	..	..	..	..	..	..	..
Morocco	..	0.9	6.8	18.0	28.3	13.8	13.2	5.1	12.7	9.0	5.0	..	..	12.7
Tunisia	..	8.3	11.6	3.1	0.3	8.0	6.8	1.9	..	..	..	..	8.6	4.3
ALL AFRICA	19.8	11.1	15.0	4.0	2.5	12.5	-6.9	8.6	5.1	-22.6	-1.3	8.2	6.8	0.1

Note: 2002 data are preliminary (see page 2).

External Sector

5-39. Fuel imports

	Millions of U.S. dollars (current prices)											Annual average		
	1980	1993	1994	1995	1996	1997	1998	1999	2000	2001	2002	75-84	85-94	95-MR
SUB-SAHARAN AFRICA	4,587	4,327	4,394	5,189	5,815	5,941	5,295	5,557	7,619	6,981	8,625	2,818	3,967	6,378
excluding South Africa	2,698	3,376	3,346	3,858	4,612	4,757	4,345	4,421	5,889	5,405	7,165	1,675	3,043	5,057
excl. S.Africa & Nigeria	2,358	3,330	3,260	3,740	4,522	4,614	4,222	4,269	5,730	5,233	4,863	1,405	2,986	4,649
Angola	..	0	0	0	0	0	..	..	..	..	..	..	0	0
Benin	..	39	27	43	54	48	64	56	66	55	60	34	31	56
Botswana	..	133	93	98	110	127	125	107	87	81	76	..	110	101
Burkina Faso	..	99	45	52	73	69	72	81	91	93	102	..	72	79
Burundi	25	24	29	27	18	14	14	19	20	21	22	30	27	19
Cameroon	187	7	7	139	151	136	149	12	24	63	58	96	11	91
Cape Verde	..	6	5	10	9	9	7	11	20	26	26	..	7	15
Central African Republic	..	15	11	17	13	15	14	13	16	17	18	17	17	16
Chad	..	4	13	14	22	21	21	21	21	27	27	20	21	22
Comoros	..	6	6	8	4	4	4	5	7	10	11	5	5	7
Congo, Dem. Rep. of	..	..	..	..	..	..	..	..	49	43	43	..	..	45
Congo, Rep. of	0	162	367	187	215	225	216	221	229	237	246	2	100	222
Côte d'Ivoire	557	459	396	470	651	508	448	534	841	670	534	433	424	582
Djibouti	..	..	..	14	14	14	11	11	12	12	13	..	..	13
Equatorial Guinea	..	3	3	3	5	11	11	13	13	14	14	5	5	11
Eritrea	..	1	2	8	6	7	6	4	5	3	5	..	2	6
Ethiopia	..	198	222	169	148	147	143	111	250	292	268	183	138	191
Gabon	..	11	161	173	221	217	216	162	177	187	199	44	37	194
Gambia, The	..	28	30	45	40	29	23	25	25	28	30	..	17	31
Ghana	..	158	176	194	266	240	220	342	533	257	275	168	165	291
Guinea	..	73	69	82	87	90	86	93	99	107	..	..	63	92
Guinea-Bissau	..	3	6	8	9	9	6	7	10	9	14	9	7	9
Kenya	852	407	333	401	448	519	532	527	850	721	741	456	374	592
Lesotho	..	..	..	..	..	..	..	..	..	..	110	..	..	110
Liberia	..	..	..	..	..	..	..	..	..	..	..	..	..	..
Madagascar	159	85	72	81	106	117	101	124	212	168	217	123	71	141
Malawi	..	40	25	49	59	79	56	66	75	68	97	..	41	69
Mali	120	74	52	85	102	105	88	112	166	147	..	99	70	115
Mauritania	..	37	36	51	43	69	50	61	99	95	108	43	37	72
Mauritius	84	126	116	123	146	169	159	135	151	236	184	85	99	163
Mozambique	..	..	..	68	78	78	84	124	44	41	43	..	..	70
Namibia	..	79	83	91	92	97	88	82	84	78	81	..	78	86
Niger	..	23	20	35	32	28	23	..	..	..	..	..	21	30
Nigeria	340	46	86	118	89	143	123	152	159	173	2,302	270	57	407
Rwanda	..	35	24	22	27	37	35	46	94	73	74	49	44	51
São Tomé and Principe	..	2	2	3	4	4	3	4	4	4	3	..	1	3
Senegal	276	124	142	138	176	191	156	209	341	317	284	272	157	226
Seychelles	..	34	32	30	43	50	36	43	74	70	60	26	29	51
Sierra Leone	..	22	29	24	23	15	25	21	29	36	38	45	26	26
Somalia	..	..	..	..	..	..	..	..	..	..	..	..	..	..
South Africa	1,889	951	1,047	1,331	1,203	1,184	949	1,136	1,729	1,575	1,461	1,143	924	1,321
Sudan	..	230	178	194	306	299	256	184	108	130	131	351	239	201
Swaziland	99	91	42	78	136	150	153	143	140	97	94	57	77	124
Tanzania	..	101	124	186	189	194	129	104	95	106	..	247	161	143
Togo	..	26	22	41	34	42	38	..	..	..	..	33	29	39
Uganda	..	58	55	64	90	92	84	108	143	170	154	91	69	113
Zambia	..	47	56	41	51	87	42	115	177	220	247	144	78	122
Zimbabwe	..	260	150	176	222	250	229	216	250	202	161	213	171	213
NORTH AFRICA	2,065	2,820	2,270	2,554	2,856	3,934	3,616	3,222	5,424	5,775	5,078	1,237	2,300	4,057
Algeria	259	141	150	115	110	132	110	127	106	112	113	149	162	116
Egypt, Arab Rep.	..	1,267	542	721	854	1,909	2,188	1,228	2,451	3,233	2,497	..	1,040	1,885
Libya	..	..	..	..	..	..	..	..	..	..	..	..	..	..
Morocco	1,006	957	1,113	1,177	1,285	1,296	922	1,326	2,039	2,026	2,086	745	924	1,520
Tunisia	799	455	466	541	607	597	396	541	827	403	383	387	382	537
ALL AFRICA	6,652	7,147	6,664	7,743	8,671	9,874	8,911	8,779	13,042	12,756	13,703	4,054	6,267	10,435

Note: 2002 data are preliminary (see page 2).

5-40. Fuel imports, growth

	1980	1993	1994	1995	1996	1997	1998	1999	2000	2001	2002	75-84	85-94	95-MR
	Percentage											*Average annual percentage growth*		
SUB-SAHARAN AFRICA	35.1	25.9	-4.5	15.3	-2.8	5.5	3.7	1.7	1.4	-0.2	-2.7	5.7	1.2	2.3
excluding South Africa	43.6	22.7	-21.9	16.2	9.0	15.6	15.1	-2.8	-4.5	0.3	-8.3	11.9	3.2	4.9
excl. S.Africa & Nigeria	75.8	23.1	-24.0	15.7	11.3	14.0	20.2	-2.8	-4.5	0.3	-8.3	20.9	3.4	5.7
Angola	..	-25.0	-33.3	-50.0	..	..	..	..	..	..	..	..	..	..
Benin	..	..	..	..	..	..	..	..	..	..	..	..	..	..
Botswana	..	..	-32.5	-0.5	18.0	24.1	2.2	-14.1	-17.4	-1.8	-10.2	..	..	-0.8
Burkina Faso	..	..	..	..	..	..	..	..	..	..	..	..	..	..
Burundi	..	2.4	29.0	-15.1	-42.3	-19.8	50.0	20.0	-3.8	2.9	4.0	..	0.9	-1.0
Cameroon	9.7	379.3	-38.3	40.6	-12.9	101.9	-4.4	-44.7	255.0	10.0	10.0	-42.7	-0.1	23.8
Cape Verde	..	-10.2	-15.1	91.5	-9.9	-1.1	-18.2	13.5	12.0	4.8	5.2	..	1.0	4.4
Central African Republic	..	-5.9	-28.1	46.2	-25.4	18.6	-12.5	-9.0	15.4	6.8	1.5	..	-3.2	0.9
Chad	..	-21.0	190.0	35.4	20.5	9.3	124.3	135.4	..	..	..	..	-16.1	51.5
Comoros	..	-5.7	42.0	13.8	-47.9	2.0	2.5	2.9	..	..	..	..	2.0	-10.9
Congo, Dem. Rep. of	..	..	..	..	..	..	..	..	..	..	..	..	..	..
Congo, Rep. of	..	32.2	10.9	-1.1	-3.6	12.7	9.4	2.1	3.1	3.2	3.5	..	0.2	4.3
Côte d'Ivoire	..	1.8	27.1	9.8	9.5	6.2	4.8	3.5	-5.7	-2.0	1.3	..	-1.4	3.0
Djibouti	..	..	..	..	-7.2	-1.7	-25.8	2.4	-0.5	1.3	2.4	..	..	-5.3
Equatorial Guinea	..	-2.4	-4.5	15.8	23.9	126.9	5.3	24.7	1.9	3.9	-1.2	..	-2.2	23.3
Eritrea	..	..	..	..	..	..	..	..	..	..	..	..	..	..
Ethiopia	..	119.9	..	..	..	..	..	..	..	..	..	..	5.3	..
Gabon	..	..	..	..	..	..	..	..	..	..	..	..	..	..
Gambia, The	..	1.3	4.1	45.1	-13.5	-29.4	-21.7	3.7	-2.6	11.0	3.4	..	23.7	-6.6
Ghana	..	3.2	19.0	3.9	9.9	17.9	22.7	11.9	4.4	6.0	5.7	..	3.3	11.4
Guinea	..	14.1	0.1	10.2	11.1	1.5	7.7	5.4	6.5	6.1	..	..	2.9	6.5
Guinea-Bissau	..	-39.3	137.1	44.3	14.9	4.0	-33.1	15.0	47.3	-8.2	53.8	..	-2.1	8.3
Kenya	89.1	7.6	-14.7	8.6	17.5	20.7	33.6	-14.5	14.6	-3.1	0.0	19.6	3.5	9.6
Lesotho	..	..	..	..	..	..	..	..	..	..	..	..	..	..
Liberia	..	..	..	..	..	..	..	..	..	..	..	..	..	..
Madagascar	..	33.7	-14.4	3.8	11.6	16.9	27.3	-12.2	8.7	1.5	-25.9	..	2.1	5.3
Malawi	..	-2.8	-33.5	78.2	2.7	41.8	31.5	1.2	19.7	-6.1	41.1	..	-3.3	20.2
Mali	3.0	-14.1	12.9	28.3	14.8	20.2	70.0	-10.6	-6.6	3.1	..	0.7	4.0	15.9
Mauritania	..	17.2	-2.6	158.8	3.3	-6.1	15.0	17.1	-23.9	10.3	40.5	..	1.4	10.6
Mauritius	..	..	..	..	..	..	..	..	..	..	..	..	..	..
Mozambique	..	..	..	..	7.8	-62.5	..	..	..	..	..	..	..	..
Namibia	..	8.5	11.7	1.7	-15.5	-11.1	-23.8	-21.1	-13.8	-22.2	-13.2	..	..	-16.6
Niger	..	..	..	..	..	..	..	..	..	..	..	..	..	..
Nigeria	-35.3	5.3	98.6	26.6	-36.1	70.8	..	..	..	..	..	-10.6	-1.8	..
Rwanda	..	-8.2	-5.4	8.0	3.5	26.4	60.5	-14.5	-3.4	3.1	32.0	..	-8.7	12.1
São Tomé and Principe	..	-21.7	-1.9	36.5	6.2	40.8	-12.3	17.2	-35.0	4.4	16.6	..	..	3.5
Senegal	..	-8.9	-37.7	-13.3	18.9	38.4	-14.5	28.2	55.1	-1.8	-9.6	..	-4.7	14.1
Seychelles	..	8.2	-3.4	-8.6	37.6	16.1	5.9	2.2	10.2	9.8	-9.8	..	6.1	8.9
Sierra Leone	..	-0.6	27.3	-25.5	-1.1	-28.4	69.4	-18.4	38.1	24.3	5.1	..	..	6.2
Somalia	..	..	..	..	..	..	..	..	..	..	..	..	-11.2	..
South Africa	33.1	28.3	8.0	14.8	-9.1	-0.9	-4.7	5.7	6.2	-0.5	1.4	4.0	0.1	0.7
Sudan	..	..	..	..	..	..	..	-29.1	-42.6	17.9	..	-15.0	..	..
Swaziland	..	-10.0	-49.9	39.0	87.0	18.3	9.4	-32.4	-36.8	-55.3	-37.4	..	..	-11.7
Tanzania	..	..	..	..	-5.2	..	..	..	..	..	..	..	..	..
Togo	..	..	..	..	..	..	..	..	..	..	..	..	8.4	..
Uganda	..	..	..	..	..	..	..	..	..	..	..	..	..	..
Zambia	..	0.1	25.2	-31.7	4.6	82.1	-29.5	98.0	-0.4	44.3	9.0	..	-4.4	18.9
Zimbabwe	..	42.3	-39.1	8.5	6.3	19.4	34.8	-31.3	-25.5	-8.4	-5.6	..	7.9	-3.1
NORTH AFRICA	..	13.3	-8.3	5.9	-5.2	26.2	27.2	-15.6	0.8	-43.4	4.0	..	23.4	-1.8
Algeria	..	-13.6	5.9	1.3	-12.8	-9.9	30.0	..	..	..	..	..	-0.6	-1.7
Egypt, Arab Rep.	..	41.4	-53.2	31.9	4.1	80.0	65.9	-41.9	34.2	..	..	..	-6.6	22.9
Libya	..	..	..	..	..	..	..	..	..	..	..	..	..	..
Morocco	..	-4.4	31.2	-3.8	-9.5	4.4	0.8	24.8	4.7	13.6	4.0	..	..	5.6
Tunisia	..	16.5	9.8	7.1	-4.7	5.8	-12.0	25.5	..	..	..	..	4.2	1.7
ALL AFRICA	35.1	21.5	-5.8	12.3	-3.5	11.6	11.5	-4.9	1.2	-14.6	-1.2	6.1	5.0	1.2

Note: 2002 data are preliminary (see page 2).

5-41. Primary intermediate goods imports

| | Millions of U.S. dollars (current prices) | | | | | | | | | | | Annual average | | |
	1980	1993	1994	1995	1996	1997	1998	1999	2000	2001	2002	75-84	85-94	95-MR
SUB-SAHARAN AFRICA	3,846	3,286	3,710	4,999	4,771	4,754	4,197	4,154	5,089	4,506	5,167	2,485	3,354	4,705
excluding South Africa	119	1,388	1,757	2,349	2,490	2,411	2,192	2,067	2,079	1,790	2,376	160	1,477	2,219
excl. S.Africa & Nigeria	119	1,388	1,757	2,349	2,490	2,411	2,192	2,067	2,079	1,790	2,376	160	1,477	2,219
Angola	..	89	129	157	0	0	..	..	..	..	..	..	251	52
Benin	..	..	..	..	..	..	..	..	..	..	..			
Botswana	..	163	159	177	176	205	211	203	164	154	144	..	127	179
Burkina Faso	..	0	0	42	42	40	68	..	..	..	..	..	15	48
Burundi	0	0	0	0	0	0	0	0	0	0	0	0	0	0
Cameroon	55	61	60	69	77	94	76	69	70	71	72	61	72	75
Cape Verde	..	..	..	..	16	16	17	18	21	29	36	..	..	22
Central African Republic	..	40	44	58	44	39	45	54	56	59	63	..	52	52
Chad	..	0	0	0	0	0	0	0	..	..	..	..	0	0
Comoros	..	4	4	4	2	0	0	0	0	0	0	2	3	1
Congo, Dem. Rep. of	..	..	..	..	..	..	..	..	..	..	..			..
Congo, Rep. of	0	28	72	78	98	89	101	108	117	126	135	0	22	107
Côte d'Ivoire	..	..	..	..	..	..	..	..	..	..	..	..	..	..
Djibouti	..	..	..	7	7	7	7	7	8	8	8	..	..	7
Equatorial Guinea	..	..	..	..	..	..	..	..	..	..	..	..	..	..
Eritrea	..	5	7	10	17	9	6	9	6	4	5	..	4	8
Ethiopia	..	21	15	21	29	27	28	27	20	24	30	35	25	26
Gabon	..	10	10	10	10	11	5	5	5	6	6	..	10	7
Gambia, The	..	2	2	3	6	3	2	3	3	4	4	..	27	4
Ghana	..	..	..	..	..	..	..	..	..	..	..	..	..	
Guinea	..	0	0	0	0	0	0	0	0	0	..	..	0	0
Guinea-Bissau	..	..	..	..	12	15	4	19	19	18	18	..	..	15
Kenya	..	47	51	74	66	76	105	82	84	102	81	42	51	84
Lesotho	..	..	..	..	..	..	..	..	..	..	183	..	..	183
Liberia	..	..	..	..	..	..	..	..	..	..	..	..	..	
Madagascar	..	..	..	..	..	..	..	..	..	..	81	..	..	81
Malawi	..	81	58	46	67	87	46	66	50	53	83	..	96	62
Mali	..	..	..	..	..	..	..	..	..	..	..	..	..	..
Mauritania	..	0	0	0	0	0	0	0	0	0	0	..	0	0
Mauritius	0	0	0	0	0	0	0	0	0	0	215	0	0	27
Mozambique	..	..	..	124	140	140	151	221	169	172	185	..	..	163
Namibia	..	153	161	178	178	189	171	160	164	152	157	..	151	168
Niger	..	..	..	..	..	..	..	..	..	..	..	..	..	..
Nigeria	..	..	..	..	..	..	..	..	..	..	..	..	..	..
Rwanda	..	0	0	0	0	0	0	0	0	0	0	0	0	0
São Tomé and Principe	..	0	0	0	0	0	0	0	0	0	0	..	0	0
Senegal	..	..	96	118	119	108	129	134	112	118	160	..	96	125
Seychelles	..	0	0	0	0	0	0	0	0	0	0	..	0	0
Sierra Leone	..	13	11	18	29	14	12	12	20	20	23	..	12	19
Somalia	..	..	..	..	..	..	..	..	..	..	..	..	..	..
South Africa	3,728	1,898	1,952	2,650	2,281	2,344	2,005	2,087	3,011	2,716	2,791	2,325	1,878	2,486
Sudan	..	113	117	134	234	192	157	114	221	160	207	172	155	177
Swaziland	64	132	197	283	236	194	200	213	170	155	150	41	81	200
Tanzania	..	116	113	255	381	284	123	207	200	..	..	134	212	241
Togo	..	..	..	..	..	..	..	..	..	..	..	..	..	..
Uganda	..	..	..	..	..	..	..	..	..	..	..	..	..	..
Zambia	..	20	72	80	80	50	54	2	13	15	16	..	45	39
Zimbabwe	..	292	379	404	424	522	476	332	386	344	316	39	233	400
NORTH AFRICA	1,106	1,601	1,818	1,903	1,432	1,391	1,402	1,368	1,345	1,938	2,075	930	1,522	1,607
Algeria	606	942	999	831	539	520	603	607	580	516	565	535	799	595
Egypt, Arab Rep.	..	..	..	..	..	..	..	..	..	..	..	..	..	..
Libya	..	..	..	..	..	..	..	..	..	..	..	..	..	..
Morocco	501	659	819	1,072	893	871	799	761	765	755	801	395	723	840
Tunisia	..	..	..	..	..	..	..	..	..	668	709	..	..	689
ALL AFRICA	4,953	4,887	5,528	6,902	6,204	6,146	5,599	5,522	6,435	6,444	7,242	3,415	4,876	6,312

Note: 2002 data are preliminary (see page 2).

5-42. Primary intermediate goods imports, growth

	Percentage											Average annual percentage growth		
	1980	1993	1994	1995	1996	1997	1998	1999	2000	2001	2002	75-84	85-94	95-MR
SUB-SAHARAN AFRICA	17.7	-11.9	12.3	25.4	-4.3	6.8	-6.4	-3.2	26.0	-3.8	2.2	-3.3	4.2	3.6
excluding South Africa	17.2	-4.1	22.9	20.1	-8.6	9.9	-5.1	-13.5	-1.2	-1.8	-0.3	33.5	16.0	-2.1
excl. S.Africa & Nigeria	17.2	-4.1	22.9	20.1	-8.6	9.9	-5.1	-13.5	-1.2	-1.8	-0.3	33.5	16.0	-2.1
Angola	..	-58.0	40.2	10.8	..	..	..	..	..	..	..	..	-9.4	..
Benin	..	..	..	..	..	..	..	..	..	..	..	..	..	..
Botswana	..	..	-5.9	5.1	4.6	25.2	6.9	-3.5	-17.4	-1.8	-10.2	..	..	1.0
Burkina Faso	..	..	..	..	..	..	..	..	..	..	..	..	..	..
Burundi	..	..	..	..	..	..	..	..	..	..	..	..	..	..
Cameroon	17.2	-16.5	-19.4	2.6	-8.7	12.6	-7.3	-4.0	1.3	2.0	2.0	15.3	-1.1	-0.5
Cape Verde	..	..	..	..	..	..	..	..	..	..	..	..	..	..
Central African Republic	..	-25.0	8.5	19.4	-26.5	-7.7	9.4	17.5	-0.2	3.5	3.6	..	-6.4	1.2
Chad	..	..	..	..	..	..	..	..	..	..	..	..	..	..
Comoros	..	16.6	64.2	-1.4	-46.7	..	..	..	..	..	..	..	7.2	..
Congo, Dem. Rep. of	..	..	..	..	..	..	..	..	..	..	..	..	..	..
Congo, Rep. of	..	..	..	..	..	..	..	..	..	..	..	..	..	..
Côte d'Ivoire	..	..	..	..	..	..	..	..	..	..	..	..	..	..
Djibouti	..	..	..	..	-6.6	-2.3	1.9	2.4	1.8	2.0	1.9	..	..	0.7
Equatorial Guinea	..	..	..	..	..	..	..	..	..	..	..	..	..	..
Eritrea	..	..	..	..	..	..	..	..	..	..	..	..	..	..
Ethiopia	..	..	..	..	..	..	..	..	..	..	..	..	..	..
Gabon	..	..	..	..	..	..	..	..	..	..	..	..	..	..
Gambia, The	..	-13.1	-10.3	53.0	98.7	-57.0	-22.8	38.4	-2.6	11.0	3.4	..	-45.5	0.3
Ghana	..	..	..	..	..	..	..	..	..	..	..	..	..	..
Guinea	..	..	..	..	..	..	..	..	..	..	..	..	..	..
Guinea-Bissau	..	..	..	..	..	..	..	..	..	..	..	..	..	..
Kenya	..	-24.5	-1.0	34.4	-13.6	6.5	46.6	-11.9	1.1	6.0	-21.4	..	1.0	4.8
Lesotho	..	..	..	..	..	..	..	..	..	..	..	..	..	..
Liberia	..	..	..	..	..	..	..	..	..	..	..	..	..	..
Madagascar	..	..	..	..	..	..	..	..	..	..	..	..	..	..
Malawi	..	-5.4	-32.3	-35.3	66.0	45.9	-19.2	-8.9	18.0	6.8	41.1	..	-14.4	9.5
Mali	..	..	..	..	..	..	..	..	..	..	..	..	..	..
Mauritania	..	..	..	..	..	..	..	..	..	..	..	..	..	..
Mauritius	..	..	..	..	..	..	..	..	..	..	..	..	..	..
Mozambique	..	..	..	..	6.1	4.3	..	..	..	..	..	..	..	..
Namibia	..	-3.6	1.6	1.6	3.0	8.5	-7.1	-3.8	5.2	-5.1	5.9	..	..	0.3
Niger	..	..	..	..	..	..	..	..	..	..	..	..	..	..
Nigeria	..	..	..	..	..	..	..	..	..	..	..	..	..	..
Rwanda	..	..	..	..	..	..	..	..	..	..	..	..	..	..
São Tomé and Principe	..	..	..	..	..	..	..	..	..	..	..	..	..	..
Senegal	..	..	..	9.2	-6.5	16.5	25.0	-0.7	-20.5	10.9	37.5	..	..	5.7
Seychelles	..	..	..	..	-12.0	27.7	-30.4	-1.9	-69.5	51.1	123.9	..	..	-12.2
Sierra Leone	..	-6.4	-14.1	52.7	54.4	-45.4	-8.3	-7.1	64.8	-1.9	19.0	..	..	4.7
Somalia	..	..	..	..	..	..	..	..	..	..	..	..	..	..
South Africa	17.7	-16.4	5.3	29.5	-1.3	4.8	-7.2	4.0	42.0	-4.6	3.2	-3.9	0.3	6.8
Sudan	..	..	..	..	..	..	..	-28.5	89.8	-29.3	..	..	..	..
Swaziland	..	12.3	43.6	59.0	-12.3	-11.6	7.1	7.6	-17.4	-5.6	0.4	..	..	-1.4
Tanzania	..	..	..	..	43.8	..	..	..	..	..	..	..	..	..
Togo	..	..	..	..	..	..	..	..	..	..	..	..	..	..
Uganda	..	..	..	..	..	..	..	..	..	..	..	..	..	..
Zambia	..	-52.3	222.6	0.1	-13.5	-37.5	5.1	-95.8	559.3	22.8	9.5	..	6.5	-25.5
Zimbabwe	..	1.1	25.6	0.2	10.4	28.2	-2.9	-28.8	11.6	-5.2	-10.1	..	21.1	-0.9
NORTH AFRICA	..	-11.6	19.4	6.0	-9.4	0.2	5.1	-9.7	1.1	-13.6	15.0	..	11.3	-2.2
Algeria	..	-13.6	10.1	1.3	-10.8	-10.6	25.6	..	..	..	..	..	-4.2	-1.9
Egypt, Arab Rep.	..	..	..	..	..	..	..	..	..	..	..	..	..	..
Libya	..	..	..	..	..	..	..	..	..	..	..	..	..	..
Morocco	..	-10.7	24.1	8.1	-8.8	4.7	-2.1	30.8	1.1	-13.6	15.0	..	..	3.7
Tunisia	..	..	..	..	..	..	..	..	..	..	..	..	..	..
ALL AFRICA	17.7	-11.8	14.6	18.8	-5.8	4.9	-3.2	-5.2	18.9	-6.2	5.1	-2.2	6.1	1.9

Note: 2002 data are preliminary (see page 2).

5-43. Manufactured goods imports

| | Millions of U.S. dollars (current prices) | | | | | | | | | | | Annual average | | |
	1980	1993	1994	1995	1996	1997	1998	1999	2000	2001	2002	75-84	85-94	95-MR
SUB-SAHARAN AFRICA	9,423	14,105	15,881	19,863	20,732	21,592	20,683	18,840	19,705	19,149	20,645	7,123	12,042	20,151
excluding South Africa	1,003	3,358	3,455	4,374	5,127	5,393	5,259	4,717	4,526	4,908	5,637	688	3,010	4,993
excl. S.Africa & Nigeria	1,003	3,358	3,455	4,374	5,127	5,393	5,259	4,717	4,526	4,908	5,637	688	3,010	4,993
Angola	..	72	71	94	343	400	..	..	..	..	..	..	129	279
Benin	..	..	..	..	..	..	..	..	..	..	..	206	..	..
Botswana	..	179	153	166	152	241	249	189	153	143	134	..	454	178
Burkina Faso	..	..	..	..	..	..	..	..	..	..	..	..	..	..
Burundi	40	57	55	62	38	33	35	41	44	48	51	46	54	44
Cameroon	605	378	370	363	398	385	407	424	438	458	483	511	502	420
Cape Verde	..	..	..	..	10	10	12	13	14	16	16	..	..	13
Central African Republic	..	..	..	..	..	..	..	..	..	..	..	..	..	..
Chad	..	156	136	92	108	109	82	81	..	..	..	..	111	95
Comoros	..	2	2	2	2	3	3	3	3	4	4	0	2	3
Congo, Dem. Rep. of	..	61	45	52	82	..	..	..	..	..	..	..	55	67
Congo, Rep. of	0	141	86	94	118	141	148	156	164	172	180	14	128	147
Côte d'Ivoire	..	..	..	..	..	..	..	..	..	..	..	..	..	..
Djibouti	..	..	..	28	27	26	37	39	40	41	43	..	..	35
Equatorial Guinea	..	..	..	..	..	..	..	..	..	..	..	..	..	..
Eritrea	..	63	102	117	177	94	87	78	76	75	88	..	69	99
Ethiopia	..	95	129	183	200	332	321	312	205	284	288	117	131	266
Gabon	..	89	30	32	286	289	388	401	422	443	468	..	82	341
Gambia, The	..	46	36	34	29	16	21	22	22	25	27	..	44	25
Ghana	..	..	..	..	..	..	..	..	..	..	..	..	..	..
Guinea	..	196	151	173	159	174	194	215	227	247	..	..	172	198
Guinea-Bissau	..	..	..	..	5	6	2	8	8	8	8	..	..	6
Kenya	..	229	268	487	443	465	413	402	361	437	421	186	272	429
Lesotho	..	..	..	..	..	..	..	..	..	..	110	..	..	110
Liberia	..	..	..	..	..	..	..	..	..	..	..	..	..	..
Madagascar	..	..	..	..	..	..	..	..	..	..	20	..	..	20
Malawi	..	214	176	122	169	230	106	160	153	159	199	..	107	162
Mali	193	136	122	150	150	148	159	189	209	216	..	174	116	174
Mauritania	..	133	113	138	200	97	148	86	54	86	109	..	118	115
Mauritius	0	0	0	0	0	0	0	0	0	0	644	0	0	81
Mozambique	..	..	..	185	229	221	237	348	277	262	281	..	..	255
Namibia	..	200	210	232	233	246	223	209	214	198	205	..	197	220
Niger	..	..	..	..	..	..	..	..	..	..	..	..	..	..
Nigeria	..	..	..	..	..	..	..	..	..	..	..	..	..	..
Rwanda	..	91	23	41	55	71	66	48	43	44	45	82	93	52
São Tomé and Principe	..	0	0	0	0	0	0	0	0	0	0	..	0	0
Senegal	..	..	289	354	356	324	387	402	336	353	481	..	289	374
Seychelles	..	0	0	26	30	37	34	42	35	37	43	..	0	35
Sierra Leone	..	15	15	7	15	6	8	6	9	11	14	..	17	9
Somalia	..	..	..	..	..	..	..	..	..	..	..	..	..	..
South Africa	8,420	10,747	12,426	15,489	15,605	16,200	15,424	14,124	15,179	14,240	15,008	6,434	9,031	15,159
Sudan	..	311	255	307	324	339	636	276	354	547	695	160	162	435
Swaziland	165	211	229	321	277	296	291	261	289	245	238	91	147	277
Tanzania	..	12	10	15	17	27	18	15	14	..	..	6	11	18
Togo	..	60	48	80	72	63	75	..	..	..	..	67	81	72
Uganda	..	..	..	..	..	..	..	..	..	..	..	..	..	..
Zambia	..	..	40	54	55	116	108	103	105	116	129	..	40	98
Zimbabwe	..	212	290	364	369	447	365	189	257	232	213	166	214	304
NORTH AFRICA	3,492	3,882	4,342	4,740	4,035	3,774	4,108	3,892	3,930	6,005	6,492	3,057	3,600	4,622
Algeria	2,593	2,212	2,347	2,390	1,788	1,564	1,732	1,665	1,681	1,828	1,956	2,341	2,150	1,826
Egypt, Arab Rep.	..	..	..	..	..	..	..	..	..	..	..	..	..	..
Libya	..	..	..	..	..	..	..	..	..	..	..	..	..	..
Morocco	899	1,670	1,994	2,350	2,247	2,210	2,376	2,227	2,249	2,358	2,528	716	1,450	2,318
Tunisia	..	..	..	..	..	..	..	..	..	1,819	2,008	..	..	1,913
ALL AFRICA	12,915	17,987	20,223	24,602	24,767	25,366	24,791	22,732	23,635	25,153	27,137	10,179	15,641	24,773

Note: 2002 data are preliminary (see page 2).

5-44. Manufactured goods imports, growth

	Percentage										Average annual percentage growth		
	1980	*1993*	*1994*	*1995*	*1996*	*1997*	*1998*	*1999*	*2000*	*2001*	*2002*	*75-84*	*85-94*	*95-MR*
SUB-SAHARAN AFRICA	11.2	8.5	15.4	20.2	14.5	7.8	-0.6	-8.4	4.2	-0.1	3.9	-2.1	4.9	3.3
excluding South Africa	18.5	9.4	5.0	25.0	10.4	15.3	-14.4	-8.1	-2.8	3.4	-5.2	30.2	5.4	0.4
excl. S.Africa & Nigeria	18.5	9.4	5.0	25.0	10.4	15.3	-14.4	-8.1	-2.8	3.4	-5.2	30.2	5.4	0.4
Angola	..	-43.9	-5.0	20.5	264.7	29.4	..	..	..	..	..	..	-9.2	..
Benin	..	..	..	..	..	..	..	..	..	..	..	..	..	..
Botswana	..	..	-17.5	2.5	-3.7	70.4	7.3	-23.9	-17.4	-1.8	-10.2	..	..	0.6
Burkina Faso	..	..	..	..	..	..	..	..	..	..	..	..	..	..
Burundi	..	1.9	-6.4	4.3	-36.1	-7.9	9.0	15.7	6.1	6.1	2.3	..	-1.7	-0.6
Cameroon	16.5	31.5	-12.3	10.6	2.4	0.8	8.1	2.3	10.0	5.2	5.2	-3.9	-0.2	5.2
Cape Verde	..	..	..	..	..	..	..	..	..	..	..	..	..	..
Central African Republic	..	..	..	..	..	..	..	..	..	..	..	..	..	..
Chad	..	-13.0	27.0	21.5	18.3	-0.6	7.0	3.6	..	..	..	..	-3.0	8.9
Comoros	..	-1.4	24.3	3.3	6.7	2.0	2.0	2.0	..	..	..	..	6.6	3.3
Congo, Dem. Rep. of	..	..	..	..	..	..	..	..	..	..	..	..	..	..
Congo, Rep. of	..	32.2	10.9	-1.1	35.9	35.9	-31.0	8.5	4.6	4.5	4.0	..	1.3	4.8
Côte d'Ivoire	..	..	..	..	..	..	..	..	..	..	..	..	..	..
Djibouti	..	..	..	..	-7.3	-4.5	33.9	2.4	-0.1	1.3	1.4	..	..	4.8
Equatorial Guinea	..	..	..	..	..	..	..	..	..	..	..	..	..	..
Eritrea	..	..	..	..	..	..	..	..	..	..	..	..	..	..
Ethiopia	..	..	..	..	..	..	..	..	..	..	..	..	..	..
Gabon	..	..	..	..	..	..	..	..	..	..	..	..	..	..
Gambia, The	..	4.5	-22.2	-9.6	-17.2	-47.4	26.8	6.0	-2.6	11.0	3.4	..	-4.6	-6.3
Ghana	..	..	..	..	..	..	..	..	..	..	..	..	..	..
Guinea	..	-2.0	-25.6	3.2	-7.5	8.1	9.4	7.9	2.9	6.2	..	..	1.7	4.6
Guinea-Bissau	..	..	..	..	..	..	..	..	..	..	..	..	..	..
Kenya	..	-5.8	13.4	64.7	-7.8	-4.4	-9.5	-5.0	-19.6	11.7	-6.6	..	-3.9	-3.2
Lesotho	..	..	..	..	..	..	..	..	..	..	..	..	..	..
Liberia	..	..	..	..	..	..	..	..	..	..	..	..	..	..
Madagascar	..	..	..	..	..	..	..	..	..	..	..	..	..	..
Malawi	..	-3.9	-18.3	-42.3	60.6	48.2	-18.4	-8.9	17.0	5.6	41.1	..	32.0	8.5
Mali	4.5	-5.0	-13.6	10.2	3.5	4.7	3.8	18.4	8.4	3.0	..	4.6	3.8	7.5
Mauritania	..	-2.2	-6.3	-20.3	-3.8	0.8	26.6	-23.3	-50.5	55.5	22.3	..	0.7	-6.2
Mauritius	..	..	..	..	..	..	..	..	..	..	..	..	..	..
Mozambique	..	..	..	..	16.1	-3.3	..	..	..	..	..	..	..	..
Namibia	..	-3.6	1.6	1.6	3.0	8.5	-7.1	-3.8	5.2	-5.1	5.9	..	..	0.3
Niger	..	..	..	..	..	..	..	..	..	..	..	..	..	..
Nigeria	..	..	..	..	..	..	..	..	..	..	..	..	..	..
Rwanda	..	-6.3	3.3	62.1	36.6	39.3	-5.3	-25.5	-4.1	9.0	8.0	..	-5.8	7.2
São Tomé and Principe	..	..	..	..	..	..	..	..	..	..	..	..	..	..
Senegal	..	..	..	9.2	-6.5	16.5	25.0	-0.7	-20.5	10.9	37.5	..	..	5.7
Seychelles	..	..	..	..	26.1	21.4	-1.5	23.1	-25.6	17.2	29.1	..	..	7.8
Sierra Leone	..	-14.2	-2.4	-59.6	120.8	-54.9	47.5	-33.2	43.4	33.8	19.0	..	..	1.0
Somalia	..	..	..	..	..	..	..	..	..	..	..	..	..	..
South Africa	10.1	8.2	18.4	19.0	15.5	5.9	3.3	-8.5	5.8	-0.8	5.9	-3.7	4.9	4.0
Sudan	..	..	..	..	..	..	..	-57.1	25.3	50.9	..	..	..	..
Swaziland	..	24.0	4.9	54.7	-9.3	14.9	2.1	-9.4	14.6	-12.2	0.4	..	..	3.2
Tanzania	..	..	..	..	-29.3	..	..	..	..	..	..	..	..	..
Togo	..	..	..	..	..	..	..	..	..	..	..	..	..	..
Uganda	..	..	..	..	..	..	..	..	..	..	..	..	..	..
Zambia	..	..	..	61.4	51.5	125.2	-0.1	-11.2	4.7	11.5	10.1	..	..	23.1
Zimbabwe	..	-13.7	32.5	18.1	6.4	26.2	-13.1	-47.0	39.4	-5.4	-11.7	..	3.0	-4.0
NORTH AFRICA	..	-9.2	2.9	0.3	-6.6	0.5	9.7	-33.9	-3.6	6.7	8.0	..	3.6	-5.2
Algeria	..	-13.6	6.7	1.3	-11.1	-10.6	5.5	..	..	..	..	..	-7.1	-5.4
Egypt, Arab Rep.	..	..	..	..	..	..	..	..	..	..	..	..	..	..
Libya	..	..	..	..	..	..	..	..	..	..	..	..	..	..
Morocco	..	-5.5	0.0	-0.6	-2.8	9.0	12.3	5.2	-3.6	6.7	8.0	..	..	4.5
Tunisia	..	..	..	..	..	..	..	..	..	..	..	..	..	..
ALL AFRICA	11.2	4.0	12.7	16.2	10.8	6.8	0.8	-12.2	3.3	0.6	4.3	-0.6	4.5	2.0

Note: 2002 data are preliminary (see page 2).

5-45. Capital goods imports

	Millions of U.S. dollars (current prices)											Annual average		
	1980	1993	1994	1995	1996	1997	1998	1999	2000	2001	2002	75-84	85-94	95-MR
SUB-SAHARAN AFRICA	6,087	11,591	12,475	15,971	17,022	16,851	16,690	14,986	14,560	14,307	14,494	4,120	10,208	15,610
excluding South Africa	2,862	8,043	8,024	10,612	11,403	10,998	10,758	10,107	9,603	9,567	9,534	1,747	7,114	10,323
excl. S.Africa & Nigeria	2,862	8,043	8,024	10,612	11,403	10,998	10,758	10,107	9,603	9,567	9,534	1,747	7,114	10,323
Angola	..	322	327	327	303	354	..	..	..	..	..	..	284	328
Benin	..	207	156	246	249	239	253	266	250	262	..	..	152	252
Botswana	..	542	485	657	521	850	875	760	616	576	538	..	576	674
Burkina Faso	..	114	81	151	169	155	194	203	173	157	179	..	113	173
Burundi	33	78	81	88	49	45	49	52	59	66	68	45	74	59
Cameroon	388	325	314	315	362	399	403	407	412	416	421	359	420	392
Cape Verde	..	71	98	121	114	117	95	99	106	106	109	..	66	108
Central African Republic	..	53	43	63	14	20	54	62	82	88	94	73	62	59
Chad	..	125	124	126	149	158	174	154	..	..	..	52	87	152
Comoros	..	..	..	..	..	13	11	14	4	5	6	..	..	9
Congo, Dem. Rep. of	..	464	553	788	862	..	..	..	..	..	..	..	567	825
Congo, Rep. of	0	203	113	336	1,105	510	371	321	525	496	528	20	217	524
Côte d'Ivoire	1,102	417	410	584	576	621	709	720	471	492	596	663	467	596
Djibouti	..	..	..	54	53	54	77	81	96	101	103	..	..	77
Equatorial Guinea	..	24	42	64	192	300	384	205	108	83	82	10	25	177
Eritrea	..	62	114	173	162	161	141	122	80	91	115	..	62	131
Ethiopia	..	404	257	350	458	528	586	679	710	487	523	449	379	540
Gabon	..	320	320	339	355	388	343	311	327	344	363	188	292	346
Gambia, The	..	48	39	37	32	37	43	40	40	45	48	..	21	40
Ghana	..	..	..	..	..	..	..	..	..	..	..	200	201	..
Guinea	..	92	72	88	78	83	85	106	120	132	..	..	79	99
Guinea-Bissau	..	14	15	15	10	18	26	-10	4	7	10	12	16	10
Kenya	409	329	503	995	869	844	896	680	724	639	754	287	481	800
Lesotho	..	..	..	..	..	..	..	..	..	..	134	..	..	134
Liberia	..	..	..	..	..	..	..	..	..	..	..	..	..	..
Madagascar	333	140	143	141	164	146	139	140	167	164	92	160	131	144
Malawi	..	272	199	164	259	326	250	305	223	217	317	..	170	258
Mali	225	182	193	246	226	221	231	252	257	280	..	214	169	245
Mauritania	..	114	73	93	72	79	64	59	78	61	56	85	105	70
Mauritius	89	378	381	529	412	493	548	498	653	465	456	72	283	507
Mozambique	..	..	..	166	170	154	166	243	410	396	525	..	..	279
Namibia	..	443	466	514	516	545	494	463	475	439	454	..	437	487
Niger	..	80	67	87	56	68	87	..	..	..	..	..	100	74
Nigeria	..	..	..	..	..	..	..	..	..	..	..	..	..	..
Rwanda	..	72	36	50	54	62	60	55	53	51	53	50	71	55
São Tomé and Principe	..	11	12	12	7	7	8	11	12	13	14	1	11	11
Senegal	158	159	154	180	193	192	214	243	234	242	317	137	158	227
Seychelles	..	60	48	70	172	98	147	193	87	204	126	16	41	137
Sierra Leone	..	23	27	11	24	12	9	5	18	22	26	54	35	16
Somalia	..	..	..	..	..	..	..	..	..	..	..	..	..	..
South Africa	3,225	3,547	4,451	5,359	5,619	5,854	5,933	4,879	4,957	4,741	4,960	2,373	3,093	5,288
Sudan	..	202	189	210	254	261	348	358	324	551	621	348	273	366
Swaziland	126	172	213	249	286	302	329	290	303	197	191	95	146	268
Tanzania	..	628	597	602	461	503	733	693	638	755	813	458	534	650
Togo	..	58	41	75	105	101	97	..	..	..	..	51	92	95
Uganda	..	..	..	..	..	..	..	..	..	..	..	..	..	..
Zambia	..	328	296	396	361	388	284	253	284	460	325	118	282	344
Zimbabwe	..	508	743	901	930	1,148	784	773	480	458	476	345	525	744
NORTH AFRICA	4,871	7,841	7,905	9,775	10,634	10,607	12,193	13,795	13,108	14,066	15,775	4,580	6,809	12,494
Algeria	3,324	1,835	2,118	2,934	3,023	2,831	2,907	3,155	2,983	4,128	4,985	3,054	2,304	3,368
Egypt, Arab Rep.	..	2,545	2,349	3,108	4,101	4,114	4,801	5,575	5,639	5,583	5,999	..	2,500	4,865
Libya	..	..	..	..	..	..	..	..	..	..	..	..	..	..
Morocco	806	1,946	2,003	2,186	1,948	1,939	2,567	2,833	2,388	2,237	2,393	808	1,477	2,311
Tunisia	742	1,515	1,434	1,547	1,562	1,724	1,918	2,233	2,099	2,118	2,398	719	1,028	1,950
ALL AFRICA	10,958	19,432	20,380	25,745	27,656	27,458	28,883	28,781	27,668	28,373	30,269	8,700	17,016	28,104

Note: 2002 data are preliminary (see page 2).

5-46. Capital goods imports, growth

					Percentage							Average annual percentage growth		
	1980	1993	1994	1995	1996	1997	1998	1999	2000	2001	2002	75-84	85-94	95-MR
SUB-SAHARAN AFRICA	32.6	5.5	12.7	20.5	14.5	7.9	-0.2	-8.1	1.2	3.7	-0.3	3.7	5.0	3.1
excluding South Africa	22.4	1.9	2.7	23.7	11.3	8.0	-6.8	-1.3	-3.9	4.9	-4.5	17.7	5.9	2.1
excl. S.Africa & Nigeria	22.4	1.9	2.7	23.7	11.3	8.0	-6.8	-1.3	-3.9	4.9	-4.5	17.7	5.9	2.1
Angola	..	-10.5	-1.7	-9.0	-7.3	29.4	..	..	..	..	..	..	1.9	..
Benin	..	..	..	..	..	..	..	..	..	..	..	..	..	..
Botswana	..	..	-13.6	27.9	-16.6	75.3	6.9	-12.9	-17.4	-1.8	-10.2	..	..	3.0
Burkina Faso	..	..	..	..	..	..	..	..	..	..	..	..	..	..
Burundi	..	6.9	0.2	-3.3	-42.7	2.8	12.0	7.0	10.9	10.9	2.7	..	-0.5	-0.3
Cameroon	-7.4	2.3	-15.3	13.2	21.9	6.3	6.0	4.0	45.0	5.0	5.9	-5.6	2.1	13.0
Cape Verde	..	-27.7	36.1	21.4	-8.3	0.1	-21.2	4.3	5.8	-0.6	1.4	..	10.8	-2.1
Central African Republic	..	-17.2	-21.1	34.1	-79.1	47.6	162.6	11.9	28.5	4.6	4.7	..	-4.8	12.9
Chad	..	-8.0	-2.0	29.6	18.9	5.9	0.4	1.1	..	..	..	..	-8.5	9.9
Comoros	..	..	..	..	..	..	..	..	..	..	..	..	..	..
Congo, Dem. Rep. of	..	..	..	..	..	..	..	..	..	..	..	..	..	..
Congo, Rep. of	..	32.2	10.9	-1.1	199.4	-58.4	19.1	2.6	1.2	1.2	1.2	..	-1.1	3.3
Côte d'Ivoire	..	-13.5	-2.6	29.4	23.7	8.5	7.5	8.0	6.5	7.5	7.5	..	2.2	10.7
Djibouti	..	..	..	..	-4.9	-2.5	37.1	3.0	14.6	1.7	-0.3	..	..	8.4
Equatorial Guinea	..	-4.3	67.5	39.0	189.2	62.3	22.4	-48.3	-48.7	-25.5	-2.9	..	9.1	0.6
Eritrea	..	..	..	..	..	..	..	..	..	..	..	..	..	..
Ethiopia	..	..	..	..	..	..	..	..	..	..	..	..	..	..
Gabon	..	..	..	..	..	..	..	..	..	..	..	..	..	..
Gambia, The	..	-1.0	-20.8	-7.9	-15.7	11.1	13.2	-8.6	-2.6	11.0	3.4	..	74.5	0.6
Ghana	..	14.7	6.0	9.1	24.8	-17.1	13.8	9.8	7.6	8.5	8.0	..	4.7	6.9
Guinea	..	-0.5	-24.3	9.4	5.2	7.2	23.5	21.2	11.1	7.1	..	..	2.7	13.0
Guinea-Bissau	..	-40.9	26.2	13.8	-37.4	74.0	38.2	-138.9	-140.2	100.0	38.1	..	8.0	-9.5
Kenya	8.0	-22.9	48.6	79.0	-11.4	-11.5	-16.7	-3.7	5.5	-12.5	14.4	10.9	-2.8	-2.9
Lesotho	..	..	..	..	..	..	..	..	..	..	..	..	..	..
Liberia	..	..	..	..	..	..	..	..	..	..	..	..	..	..
Madagascar	..	13.9	-2.1	-9.9	20.1	-3.3	2.8	5.5	10.6	10.8	-20.6	..	2.3	3.5
Malawi	..	-1.8	-28.7	-20.4	59.8	29.5	-8.1	1.6	-46.6	-4.5	-0.1	..	15.9	-3.2
Mali	3.0	-5.0	2.2	15.5	-8.0	8.9	8.7	9.0	0.1	8.1	..	-1.1	2.0	5.5
Mauritania	..	-4.9	-31.0	46.9	-26.3	-15.9	-0.1	-24.0	56.5	-22.2	-8.3	..	-7.1	-4.8
Mauritius	..	..	..	..	..	..	..	..	..	..	..	..	..	..
Mozambique	..	..	..	..	-11.9	-9.6	..	..	..	..	..	..	..	..
Namibia	..	-3.6	1.6	1.6	3.0	8.5	-7.1	-3.8	5.2	-5.1	5.9	..	..	0.3
Niger	..	..	..	..	..	..	..	..	..	..	..	..	..	..
Nigeria	..	..	..	..	..	..	..	..	..	..	..	..	..	..
Rwanda	..	-6.3	3.3	25.8	11.5	23.3	-0.8	6.1	1.6	8.0	6.4	..	-0.3	8.7
São Tomé and Principe	..	20.8	3.9	-6.4	-38.0	0.2	51.7	5.6	7.1	7.9	4.9	..	2.1	4.2
Senegal	..	-8.7	-34.0	4.5	-0.4	27.6	16.8	8.6	-8.5	9.2	31.9	..	-1.2	9.9
Seychelles	..	56.4	-19.5	43.9	164.2	-44.3	62.0	30.8	-60.2	162.3	-31.8	..	13.8	13.2
Sierra Leone	..	-3.2	16.1	-61.4	106.6	-47.0	-21.1	-46.8	273.4	19.6	19.0	..	..	1.2
Somalia	..	..	..	..	..	..	..	..	..	..	..	..	6.9	..
South Africa	37.4	11.1	27.2	16.8	18.4	7.9	7.5	-14.9	7.2	2.4	4.3	-0.3	4.0	4.3
Sudan	..	..	..	..	..	..	..	1.5	-11.7	66.4	..	..	20.1	..
Swaziland	..	-11.9	19.8	29.3	20.8	13.5	13.1	-11.0	8.2	-32.7	0.4	..	..	2.6
Tanzania	..	..	..	..	-22.7	..	..	..	..	..	..	..	..	..
Togo	..	..	..	..	..	..	..	..	..	..	..	..	7.2	..
Uganda	..	..	..	..	..	..	..	..	..	..	..	..	..	..
Zambia	..	-6.6	-12.9	26.3	-4.0	15.4	-24.0	-10.7	14.6	64.5	-29.7	..	5.6	2.3
Zimbabwe	..	-17.3	41.4	14.0	8.5	28.5	-27.2	0.8	-36.2	0.0	0.0	..	5.1	-6.1
NORTH AFRICA	..	-6.9	-11.8	15.6	8.4	6.7	30.1	-15.2	-13.1	-72.2	8.0	..	5.0	-11.3
Algeria	..	-10.5	7.6	7.0	8.9	-1.0	25.3	..	..	..	..	..	-8.3	8.5
Egypt, Arab Rep.	..	-4.7	-9.6	26.2	31.5	6.6	23.4	18.4	2.9	..	..	..	0.9	18.0
Libya	..	..	..	..	..	..	..	..	..	..	..	..	..	..
Morocco	..	-19.7	-23.3	24.7	-21.6	11.1	66.9	-7.3	3.3	-8.9	8.0	..	..	7.7
Tunisia	..	20.7	-23.7	-4.2	-1.0	17.1	10.3	17.2	..	..	..	..	2.7	8.0
ALL AFRICA	32.6	-0.7	1.3	18.5	12.1	7.5	11.2	-11.2	-4.8	-25.6	0.9	7.3	5.0	-0.8

Note: 2002 data are preliminary (see page 2).

5-47. Direction of trade matrix, imports, 1992

		Importers																	*Percentage of total imports*		
Exporters		DZA	AGO	BEN	BWA	BFA	BDI	CMR	CPV	CAF	TCD	COM	ZAR	COG	CIV	DJI	EGY	GNQ	ERI	ETH	GAB
Algeria	DZA	**	0.0	0.0	0.0	0.0	0.0	0.2	0.0	0.0	0.0	0.0	0.0	0.3	0.0	0.0	0.8	0.0	..	0.0	0.1
Angola	AGO	0.0	**	0.0	0.0	0.0	0.0	0.0	0.3	0.0	0.0	0.0	0.0	0.6	0.1	0.0	0.0	0.0	..	0	0.1
Benin	BEN	0.0	0.0	**	0.0	0.0	0.0	0.0	0.0	0.0	0.0	0.0	0.0	0.0	0.2	0.0	0.0	0.0	..	0.0	0
Bostwana	BWA	..	..	..	**	..	..	..	..	..	..	..	..	..	..	..	..	..	..	..	..
Burkina Faso	BFA	0.0	0.0	2.6	0.0	**	0.0	0.1	0.0	0.0	0.0	0.0	0.0	0.0	2.5	0.0	0.0	0.0	..	0.0	0.0
Burundi	BDI	0.0	0.0	0.0	0.0	0.0	**	0.0	0.0	0.0	0.0	0.0	0.1	0.0	0.0	0.2	0.0	0.0	..	0.0	0.0
Cameroon	CMR	0.0	0.0	0.0	0.0	0.0	0.0	**	0.0	0.0	0.0	0.0	0.0	0.3	0.0	0.0	0.0	0.0	..	0.0	0.0
Cape Verde	CPV	0.0	0.0	0.0	0.0	0.0	0.0	0.0	**	0.0	0.0	0.0	0.0	0.0	0.6	0.0	0.0	0.0	..	0.0	0.0
Central African Republic	CAF	0.0	0.0	0.0	0.0	0.0	0.0	0.6	0.0	**	0.6	0.0	0.2	0	0.0	0.0	0.0	0.0	..	0.0	0.0
Chad	TCD	0.0	0.0	0.0	0.0	0.0	0.0	0.0	0.0	0.1	**	0.0	0.0	0.0	0	0.0	0.0	0.0	..	0.0	0.0
Comoros	COM	0.0	0.0	0.0	0.0	0.0	0.0	0.0	0.0	0.0	0.0	**	0.0	0.0	0.0	0	0.0	0.0	..	0.0	0.0
Congo, Dem. Rep. of	ZAR	0.0	0.0	0.0	0.0	0.0	2.3	0.0	0.0	1.8	0.0	0.0	**	0.2	0.6	0.0	0	0.0	..	0.0	0.0
Congo, Rep. of	COG	0.0	0.0	1.1	0.0	0.0	0.0	0.0	0.0	0.0	0.0	0.0	0.2	**	0.1	0.0	0.0	0.0	..	0.0	0.1
Côte d'Ivoire	CIV	0.0	0.0	1.4	0.0	0.1	0.1	0.0	0.0	1.5	0.0	0.0	0.1	0.0	**	0.0	0.0	16.2	..	0.0	0.1
Djibouti	DJI	0.0	0.0	0.0	0.0	0.0	0.0	0.0	0.0	0.0	0.0	0.0	0.0	0.0	0.0	**	0.1	0.0	..	6.7	0.0
Egypt, Arab Rep.	EGY	0.0	0.0	0.0	0.0	0.1	0.0	0.0	0.0	0.0	0.0	0.4	0.5	0.0	0.0	0.4	**	0	..	0.1	0.0
Equatorial Guinea	GNQ	0.0	0.0	0.0	0.0	0.0	0.0	0.0	0.0	0.0	0.0	0.0	0.0	0.0	0.1	0.0	0.0	**	..	0.0	0.0
Eritrea	ERI	..	..	..	..	..	..	..	..	..	..	..	..	..	..	..	..	..	**	..	..
Ethiopia	ETH	0.0	0.0	0.0	0.0	0.0	0.0	0.0	0.0	0.0	0.0	0.0	0.0	0.0	0.0	44.1	0.0	0.0	..	**	0.0
Gabon	GAB	0.0	0.0	0.2	0.0	0.0	0.0	1.7	0.0	0.0	0.0	0.0	0.1	0.0	0.4	0.0	0.0	0.0	..	0.0	**
Gambia, The	GMB	0.0	0.0	0.0	0.0	0.0	0.0	0.0	0.0	0.0	0.0	0.0	0.0	0.0	0.4	0.0	0.0	0.0	..	0.0	0.0
Ghana	GHA	0.0	0.0	0.0	0.0	0.0	0.0	0.4	0.1	0.0	0.0	0.0	0.0	0.0	0.7	0.0	0.0	0.0	..	0.5	0.0
Guinea	GIN	0.0	0.0	0.0	0.0	0.0	0.0	0.4	0.0	0.0	0.0	0.0	0.0	0.0	3.0	0.0	0.0	0.0	..	0.0	0.0
Guinea-Bissau	GNB	0.0	0.0	0.0	0.0	0.0	0.0	0.0	1.8	0.0	0.0	0.0	0.0	0.0	0.2	0.0	0.0	0.0	..	0.0	0.0
Kenya	KEN	0.0	0.0	0.0	0.0	0.0	0.6	0.0	0.0	0.0	0.0	0.1	0.1	0.0	0.0	0.0	0.0	0.0	..	0.0	0.0
Lesotho	LSO	..	..	..	..	..	..	..	..	..	..	..	..	..	..	..	..	..	..	..	..
Liberia	LBR	0.1	0.0	0.0	0.0	0.0	0.0	0.0	0.0	0.0	0.0	0.0	0.0	0.0	0.8	0.0	0.2	0.0	..	0.0	0.0
Libya	LBY	0.0	0.0	0.0	0.0	0.0	0.0	0.0	0.0	0.0	0.0	0.0	0.0	0.0	0.0	0.0	1.0	0.5	..	0.0	0.0
Madagascar	MDG	0.0	0.0	0.0	0.0	0.0	0.0	0.0	0.0	0.0	0.0	0.0	0.0	0.0	0.0	0.0	0.0	0.0	..	0.0	0.0
Malawi	MWI	0.0	0.0	0.0	1.4	0.0	0.0	0.0	0.0	0.0	0.0	0.0	0.0	0.0	0.0	0.0	0.0	0.0	..	0.0	0.0
Mali	MLI	0.0	0.0	0.3	0.0	0.1	0.0	0.0	0.0	0.0	0.0	0.0	0.0	0.0	4.1	0.0	0.0	0.0	..	0.0	0.0
Mauritania	MRT	0.1	0.0	0.0	0.0	0.0	0.0	0.0	0.0	0.0	0.0	0.0	0.0	0.0	0.6	0.0	0.0	0.0	..	0.0	0.0
Mauritius	MUS	0.0	0.0	0.0	0.0	0.4	0.0	0.0	0.0	0.0	0.0	0.0	0.0	0.0	0.2	0.4	0.0	0.0	..	0.0	0.0
Morocco	MAR	0.8	0.0	14.4	0.0	0.1	0.0	3.9	0.0	46.3	4.5	0.0	0.0	0.8	0.8	0.0	0.2	0.2	..	0.0	0.9
Mozambique	MOZ	0.0	0.0	0.0	0.2	0.0	0.0	0.0	0.0	0.0	0.0	0.0	0.0	0.0	0.0	0.0	0.0	0.0	..	0.0	0.0
Namibia	NAM	..	..	..	..	..	..	..	..	..	..	..	..	..	..	..	..	..	..	..	..
Niger	NER	0.1	0.0	2.7	0.0	0.5	0.0	0.0	0.0	0.0	0.0	0.0	0.0	0.0	1.0	0.0	0.0	0.0	..	0.0	0.0
Nigeria	NGA	0.0	0.0	3.6	0.0	0.1	0.0	0.6	0.0	0.0	2.6	0.0	0.0	0.3	3.7	0.0	0.1	0.0	..	0.0	0.0
Reunion	REU	0.0	0.0	0.0	3.7	0.0	0.0	0.0	0.0	0.0	0.0	0.0	0.0	0.0	0.0	0.0	0.0	0.0	..	0.0	0.0
Rwanda	RWA	0.0	0.0	0.0	0.0	0.0	3.1	0.0	0.0	0.0	0.0	0.0	0.1	0.0	0.0	0.0	0.0	0.0	..	0.0	0.0
São Tomé and Principe	STP	0.0	0.0	0.0	0.0	0.0	0.0	0.0	0.0	0.0	0.0	0.0	0.0	0.0	0.0	0.0	0.0	0.0	..	0.0	0.0
Senegal	SEN	0.0	0.4	0.1	0.0	0.0	0.0	0.2	0.0	0.0	0.0	0.0	0.0	0.0	2.5	0.0	0.0	0.0	..	0.0	0.7
Seychelles	SYC	0.0	0.0	0.0	0.0	0.0	0.0	0.0	0.0	0.0	0.0	0.0	0.0	0.0	0.0	0.0	0.0	0.0	..	0.0	0.0
Sierra Leone	SLE	0.0	0.0	0.0	0.0	0.0	0.0	0.0	0.0	0.0	0.0	0.0	0.0	0.0	0.9	0.0	0.0	0.0	..	0.0	0.0
Somalia	SOM	0.0	0.0	0.0	0.0	0.0	0.0	0.0	0.0	0.0	0.0	0.0	0.0	0.0	0.0	26.7	0.0	0.0	..	0.0	0.0
South Africa	ZAF	0.0	0.0	0.0	0.0	0.0	0.0	0.4	2.9	0.0	4.6	0.0	0.3	0.1	1.5	0.0	0.0	0.0	..	0.0	0.1
Sudan	SDN	0.0	0.0	0.0	0.0	0.0	0.0	0.0	0.0	1.9	0.2	0.0	0.0	0.0	0.0	0.0	0.8	0.0	..	0.0	0.0
Swaziland	SWZ	..	..	..	..	..	..	..	..	..	..	..	..	..	..	..	..	..	..	..	..
Tanzania	TZA	0.0	0.0	0.0	0.2	0.0	0.7	0.0	0.0	0.0	0.0	0.0	0.0	0.0	0.1	0.0	0.0	0.0	..	0.0	0.0
Togo	TGO	0.0	0.0	1.7	0.0	0.5	0.0	0.0	0.0	0.0	0.0	0.0	0.0	0.1	1.0	0.0	0.0	0.0	..	0.0	0.1
Tunisia	TUN	1.3	0.0	0.0	0.0	0.0	0.0	0.2	0.0	0.0	0.0	0.0	0.1	0.0	0.9	0.0	0.4	0.0	..	0.0	0.0
Uganda	UGA	0.0	0.0	0.0	0.0	0.0	0.3	0.0	0.0	0.0	0.0	0.0	0.0	0.0	0.0	0.0	0.0	0.0	..	0.0	0.0
Zambia	ZMB	0.0	0.0	0.0	1.4	0.0	0.3	0.0	0.0	0.0	0.0	0.0	0.1	0.0	0.0	0.0	1.2	0.0	..	0.0	0.0
Zimbabwe	ZWE	0.0	0.0	0.0	10.1	0.0	0.0	0.0	0.0	0.0	0.0	0.0	0.0	0.0	0.0	0.0	0.0	0.0	..	0.0	0.0
Sub-Saharan Africa	SSA	0.3	0.5	13.8	17.1	1.6	7.3	4.6	5.1	5.4	8.0	0.1	1.4	1.5	25.5	71.5	2.5	16.3	..	0.6	1.1
European Community	EU	74.1	32.0	47.8	38.1	14.0	78.7	80.5	47.9	45.7	71.4	54.5	63.6	59.2	58.7	3.0	52.8	78.9	..	48.7	40.4
Canada	CAN	0.7	0.0	0.0	0.2	0.0	0.1	0.1	0.0	0.0	0.0	1.4	3.5	0.0	0.6	0.0	0.8	0.0	..	2.0	0.0
United States	USA	14.0	62.7	7.7	4.1	0.0	7.5	5.0	0.8	0.4	0.4	34.9	18.5	35.9	6.3	0.0	7.5	0.2	..	4.3	39.1
North America	NNA	14.8	62.7	7.7	4.3	0.0	7.6	5.1	0.8	0.4	0.4	36.3	21.9	35.9	6.9	0.0	8.4	0.2	..	6.2	39.1
Rest of World	ROW	10.8	4.7	30.7	40.5	84.4	6.4	9.8	46.2	48.6	20.3	9.0	13.1	3.4	8.9	25.5	36.3	4.7	..	44.4	19.4
World	WLD	100.0	100.0	100.0	100.0	100.0	100.0	100.0	100.0	100.0	100.0	100.0	100.0	100.0	100.0	100.0	100.0	100.0	..	100.0	100.0

Note: ** means "not applicable."

South Africa's data for 1992 is taken from partner countries' data.

Source: International Monetary Fund's Direction of Trade database.

(Table continues on the following page.)

5-47. Direction of trade matrix, imports, 1992 (continued)

Exporters		GMB	GHA	GIN	GNB	KEN	LSO	LBR	LBY	MDG	MWI	MLI	MRT	MUS	MAR	MOZ	NAM	NER	NGA	REU	RWA	STP
Algeria	DZA	0.0	0.0	0.0	0.0	0.0	0.0	0.0	0.0	0.0	0.0	0.0	0.0	0.0	1.6	0.0	0.0	0.0	0.0	0.0	0.0	0.0
Angola	AGO	0.0	0.5	0.0	0.0	0.0	0.0	0.0	0.0	0.0	0.0	0.0	0.0	0.0	0.2	0.0	0.0	0.0	0.0	0.0	0.0	0.0
Benin	BEN	0.0	0.0	0.0	0.0	0.0	0.0	0.0	0.0	0.1	0.0	0.0	0.7	0.0	0.0	0.0	0.0	0.0	0.0	0.0	0.0	0.0
Bostwana	BWA	..	..	..	..	..	..	..	..	..	..	..	..	..	..	..	..	..	..	..	..	..
Burkina Faso	BFA	0.0	0.4	0.0	0.0	0.0	0.0	0.0	0.0	0.0	0.0	0.8	0.4	0.0	0.0	0.0	0.0	0.1	0.1	0.0	0.0	0.0
Burundi	BDI	0.0	0.0	0.0	0.0	0.5	0.0	0.0	0.0	0.0	0.0	0.0	0.0	0.0	0.0	0.0	0.0	0.0	0.0	0.0	0.1	0.0
Cameroon	CMR	0.0	0.0	3.5	0.0	0.0	0.0	0.0	0.0	0.0	0.0	0.0	0.0	0.0	0.1	0.0	0.0	0.0	0.1	0.0	0.0	0.0
Cape Verde	CPV	0.0	0.0	0.0	0.0	0.0	0.0	0.0	0.0	0.0	0.0	0.0	0.0	0.0	0.0	0.0	0.0	0.0	0.0	0.0	0.0	0.0
Central African Republic	CAF	0.0	0.0	0.0	0.0	0.0	0.0	0.0	0.0	0.0	0.0	0.0	0.0	0.0	0.0	0.0	0.1	0.0	0.0	0.0	0.0	0.0
Chad	TCD	0.0	0.0	0.0	0.0	0.0	0.0	0.0	0.0	0.0	0.0	0.0	0.0	0.0	0.0	0.0	0.0	0.0	0.1	0.0	0.0	0.0
Comoros	COM	0.0	0.0	0.0	0.0	0.3	0.0	0.0	0.0	0.4	0.0	0.0	0.0	0.2	0.0	0.0	0.0	0.0	0.0	1.2	0.0	0.0
Congo, Dem. Rep. of	ZAR	0.0	0.0	0.0	0.0	0.6	0.0	0.0	0.0	0.0	0.3	0.0	0.0	0.0	0.1	0.0	0.0	0.0	0.3	0.0	0.2	0.0
Congo, Rep. of	COG	0.0	0.0	0.0	0.0	0.0	0.0	0.0	0.0	0.0	0.0	2.5	1.1	0.0	0.1	0.1	0.0	0.0	0.0	0.0	0.0	0.0
Côte d'Ivoire	CIV	0.0	0.1	0.8	16.6	0.1	0.0	0.0	0.0	0.0	0.0	3.7	6.0	0.0	0.1	0.0	0.0	0.3	3.1	0.0	0.0	0.0
Djibouti	DJI	0.0	0.0	0.0	0.0	0.3	0.0	0.0	0.0	0.0	0.0	0.0	0.0	0.0	0.0	0.0	0.0	0.0	0.0	0.2	0.0	0.0
Egypt, Arab Rep.	EGY	0.0	0.4	0.0	0.0	3.6	0.0	0.0	0.5	0.0	0.8	0.0	0.3	0.0	0.0	0.0	0.0	0.0	0.0	0.0	0.0	0.0
Equatorial Guinea	GNQ	0.0	0.0	0.0	0.0	0.0	0.0	0.0	0.0	0.0	0.0	0.0	0.0	0.0	0.0	0.0	0.0	0.0	0.0	0.0	0.0	0.0
Eritrea	ERI	..	..	..	..	..	..	..	..	..	..	..	..	..	..	..	..	..	..	..	..	..
Ethiopia	ETH	0.0	0.0	0.0	0.0	1.6	0.0	0.0	0.0	0.0	0.0	0.0	0.0	0.0	0.0	0.0	0.0	0.0	0.0	0.0	0.0	0.0
Gabon	GAB	0.0	0.0	0.0	0.0	0.0	0.0	0.0	0.0	0.0	0.1	0.0	0.0	0.0	0.1	0.0	0.0	0.0	0.2	0.0	0.0	0.0
Gambia, The	GMB	**	0.0	0.0	0.5	0.0	0.0	0.0	0.0	0.0	0.0	0.0	0.0	0.0	0.0	0.0	0.0	0.0	0.0	0.0	0.0	0.0
Ghana	GHA	0.1	**	0.0	0.0	0.0	0.0	0.0	0.0	0.0	0.0	0.0	0.1	0.0	0.0	0.3	0.0	0.0	2.2	0.0	0.0	0.0
Guinea	GIN	0.0	0.0	**	0.3	0.0	0.0	0.0	0.0	0.0	0.0	0.0	0.0	0.0	0.1	0.0	0.0	0.0	0.1	0.0	0.0	0.0
Guinea-Bissau	GNB	0.1	0.0	0.0	**	0.0	0.0	0.0	0.0	0.0	0.0	0.0	0.0	0.0	0.0	0.0	0.0	0.0	0.0	0.0	0.0	0.0
Kenya	KEN	0.0	0.0	0.0	0.0	**	0.0	0.8	0.0	0.0	0.0	0.0	0.0	0.1	0.1	0.0	0.0	0.0	0.0	0.0	0.0	0.0
Lesotho	LSO	..	..	..	..	..	**	..	..	..	..	..	..	..	..	..	..	..	..	..	..	..
Liberia	LBR	0.0	0.0	0.0	0.0	0.0	0.0	**	0.0	0.0	0.0	0.0	0.8	0.0	0.0	0.0	0.0	0.0	0.0	0.0	0.0	0.0
Libya	LBY	0.0	0.0	0.0	0.0	0.0	0.0	0.0	**	0.0	0.0	0.0	0.0	0.0	2.4	0.0	0.0	0.0	0.0	0.0	0.0	0.0
Madagascar	MDG	0.0	0.0	0.0	0.0	0.1	0.0	0.0	0.0	**	0.0	0.0	0.0	0.3	0.0	1.3	0.0	0.0	0.0	0.2	0.0	0.0
Malawi	MWI	0.0	0.0	0.0	0.0	0.1	0.2	0.0	0.0	0.0	**	0.0	0.0	0.0	0.0	0.0	0.1	0.0	0.0	0.0	0.0	0.0
Mali	MLI	0.0	0.0	0.0	0.0	0.0	0.0	0.0	0.0	0.0	0.0	**	0.0	0.0	0.1	0.0	0.0	0.1	0.0	0.0	0.0	0.0
Mauritania	MRT	0.0	0.0	0.0	0.0	0.0	0.0	0.0	0.0	0.0	0.1	0.0	**	0.0	0.1	0.0	0.0	0.0	0.0	0.0	0.0	0.0
Mauritius	MUS	0.0	0.0	0.0	0.0	1.6	0.0	0.0	0.0	3.5	0.1	0.0	0.0	**	0.0	0.0	0.0	0.0	0.2	0.0	0.0	0.0
Morocco	MAR	0.0	0.0	0.2	0.0	0.0	0.0	0.0	0.9	0.2	0.0	0.4	0.0	0.0	**	0.4	0.0	0.3	0.0	0.0	0.0	0.0
Mozambique	MOZ	0.0	0.0	0.0	0.0	0.0	0.1	0.0	0.0	0.0	0.8	0.0	0.0	0.0	0.0	**	0.4	0.0	0.0	0.0	0.0	0.0
Namibia	NAM	..	..	..	..	..	..	..	..	..	..	..	..	..	..	..	**	..	..	..	..	..
Niger	NER	0.0	0.3	0.0	0.0	0.0	0.0	0.0	0.0	0.0	0.0	0.2	0.1	0.0	0.0	0.0	0.0	**	0.4	0.0	0.0	0.0
Nigeria	NGA	0.0	4.0	0.1	0.0	0.3	0.0	0.0	0.0	0.0	0.0	0.7	0.0	0.0	0.2	0.0	2.9	2.7	**	0.0	0.0	0.0
Reunion	REU	0.0	0.0	0.0	0.0	0.9	0.0	0.0	0.0	4.3	0.0	0.0	0.0	2.0	0.0	0.0	0.0	0.0	0.0	**	0.0	0.0
Rwanda	RWA	0.0	0.0	0.0	0.0	1.9	0.0	0.0	0.0	0.0	0.0	0.0	0.0	0.0	0.0	0.0	0.0	0.0	0.0	0.0	**	0.0
São Tomé and Principe	STP	0.0	0.0	0.0	0.0	0.0	0.0	0.0	0.0	0.0	0.0	0.0	0.0	0.0	0.0	0.0	0.0	0.0	0.0	0.0	0.0	**
Senegal	SEN	0.8	0.0	0.1	0.1	0.0	0.0	0.0	0.0	0.0	0.1	0.7	0.0	0.0	0.1	0.0	0.0	0.0	0.6	0.0	0.0	0.0
Seychelles	SYC	0.0	0.0	0.0	0.0	0.2	0.0	0.8	0.0	0.0	0.0	0.0	0.0	0.2	0.0	0.0	0.0	0.0	0.0	0.0	0.0	0.0
Sierra Leone	SLE	0.0	0.0	0.0	0.0	0.0	0.0	0.1	0.0	0.0	0.1	0.0	0.0	0.0	0.0	0.0	0.0	0.0	0.1	0.0	0.0	0.0
Somalia	SOM	0.0	0.0	0.0	0.0	2.2	0.0	0.0	0.0	0.0	0.0	0.0	0.0	0.0	0.0	0.0	0.0	0.0	0.0	0.0	0.0	0.0
South Africa	ZAF	0.0	0.0	0.0	0.0	0.4	0.0	0.6	0.0	0.5	9.6	1.1	0.0	0.8	0.0	6.0	0.0	0.0	0.0	0.8	0.0	0.0
Sudan	SDN	0.0	0.0	0.0	0.0	0.9	0.0	0.0	1.7	0.0	0.0	0.0	0.0	0.0	0.0	0.0	0.0	0.0	0.0	0.0	0.0	0.0
Swaziland	SWZ	..	..	..	..	..	..	..	..	..	..	..	..	..	..	..	..	..	..	..	..	..
Tanzania	TZA	0.0	0.0	0.0	0.0	3.3	0.0	0.0	0.0	0.1	0.2	0.0	0.0	0.1	0.0	0.02	0.0	0.0	0.0	0.0	0.0	0.0
Togo	TGO	0.0	8.6	0.0	0.6	0.0	0.0	0.0	0.0	0.0	0.0	0.1	0.7	0.0	0.1	0.0	0.0	0.2	0.1	0.0	0.0	0.0
Tunisia	TUN	0.0	0.0	0.0	0.0	0.0	0.0	0.0	0.5	0.4	0.0	1.6	0.0	0.0	1.3	0.0	0.0	0.0	0.0	0.0	0.0	0.0
Uganda	UGA	0.0	0.0	0.0	0.0	5.4	0.0	0.0	0.0	0.0	0.0	0.0	0.0	0.0	0.0	0.0	0.0	0.0	0.0	0.0	0.0	0.0
Zambia	ZMB	0.0	0.0	0.0	0.0	0.4	0.5	0.0	0.0	0.0	0.5	0.0	0.0	0.1	0.0	0.1	0.4	0.0	0.0	0.0	0.0	0.0
Zimbabwe	ZWE	0.0	0.0	0.0	0.0	0.3	0.2	0.0	0.0	0.0	0.5	0.4	0.1	0.4	0.0	1.7	0.3	0.1	0.0	0.0	0.0	0.0
Sub-Saharan Africa	SSA	1.1	14.0	4.6	18.2	21.3	1.0	0.8	1.7	9.0	12.3	10.2	10.2	4.1	1.7	9.6	4.1	3.5	7.4	2.4	0.4	0.0
European Community	EU	79.0	60.1	36.0	52.6	48.0	36.9	75.3	83.3	56.9	48.3	45.6	52.0	81.7	69.9	34.6	73.0	88.8	41.3	96.3	89.5	80.2
Canada	CAN	0.0	0.4	0.9	0.0	0.8	2.3	0.1	0.0	1.4	0.2	2.2	0.1	0.9	1.1	1.9	6.5	4.3	3.1	0.0	0.2	0.0
United States	USA	0.4	8.9	12.2	0.0	5.4	57.0	1.6	0.0	13.3	13.0	0.7	4.7	10.0	3.3	7.1	8.5	1.5	38.9	0.1	2.4	5.3
North America	NNA	0.5	9.3	13.1	0.0	6.2	59.3	1.7	0.0	14.7	13.3	2.9	4.7	10.9	4.4	9.0	15.1	5.8	42.1	0.1	2.6	5.3
Rest of World	ROW	19.4	16.6	46.3	29.3	24.5	2.7	22.2	15.0	19.4	26.2	41.4	33.1	3.3	24.0	46.8	7.8	1.8	9.2	1.2	7.5	14.4
World	WLD	100.0	100.0	100.0	100.0	100.0	100.0	100.0	100.0	100.0	100.0	100.0	100.0	100.0	100.0	100.0	100.0	100.0	100.0	100.0	100.0	100.0

Note: ** means "not applicable."

South Africa's data for 1992 is taken from partner countries' data.

Source: International Monetary Fund's Direction of Trade database.

(Table continues on the following page.)

External Sector

5-47. Direction of trade matrix, imports, 1992 (continued)

	Exporters	Importers SEN	SYC	SLE	SOM	ZAF	SDN	SWZ	TZA	TGO	TUN	UGA	ZMB	ZWE	Percentage of total imports SSA	EU	CAN	USA	NNA	ROW	WLD
Algeria	DZA	0.0	0.0	0.7	0.0	0.0	0.2	0.0	0.0	0.1	2.9	0.0	0.0	0.0	0.0	0.4	0.1	0.2	0.2	0.1	0.2
Angola	AGO	0.8	0.0	0.0	0.0	0.8	0.0	0.0	0.0	0.0	0.0	0.0	0.0	0.3	0.3	0.1	0.0	0.0	0.0	0.0	0.1
Benin	BEN	1.6	0.0	0.0	0.0	0.0	0.0	0.0	0.0	0.1	0.1	0.0	0.0	0.0	0.0	0.0	0.0	0.0	0.0	0.0	0.0
Bostwana	BWA	..	..	..	..	..	..	..	..	..	..	..	..	..	..	..	..	..	..	..	..
Burkina Faso	BFA	1.2	0.0	0.0	0.0	0.0	0.0	0.0	0.0	7.2	0.0	0.0	0.0	0.1	0.2	0.0	0.0	0.0	0.0	0.0	0.0
Burundi	BDI	0.0	0.0	0.0	0.0	0.0	0.0	0.0	3.8	0.0	0.0	0.0	0.5	0.1	0.1	0.0	0.0	0.0	0.0	0.0	0.0
Cameroon	CMR	1.3	0.0	0.0	0.0	0.0	0.0	0.0	0.0	0.0	0.3	0.0	0.0	0.0	0.1	0.0	0.0	0.0	0.0	0.0	0.0
Cape Verde	CPV	0.0	0.0	0.0	0.0	0.0	0.0	0.0	0.0	0.0	0.0	0.0	0.0	0.0	0.0	0.0	0.0	0.0	0.0	0.0	0.0
Central African Republic	CAF	0.1	0.0	0.0	0.0	0.0	0.0	0.0	0.0	0.0	0.0	0.0	0.0	0.0	0.0	0.0	0.0	0.0	0.0	0.0	0.0
Chad	TCD	0.1	0.0	0.0	0.0	0.0	0.0	0.0	0.0	0.0	0.0	0.0	0.0	0.0	0.0	0.0	0.0	0.0	0.0	0.0	0.0
Comoros	COM	0.0	0.0	0.0	0.0	0.1	0.0	0.0	0.0	0.0	0.0	0.0	0.0	0.0	0.0	0.0	0.0	0.0	0.0	0.0	0.0
Congo, Dem. Rep. of	ZAR	0.0	0.0	0.0	0.0	0.6	0.0	0.0	0.2	0.0	0.0	0.0	0.4	0.2	0.3	0.0	0.0	0.0	0.0	0.0	0.0
Congo, Rep. of	COG	0.9	0.0	0.0	0.0	0.0	0.0	0.1	0.0	0.5	0.0	0.0	0.0	0.0	0.1	0.0	0.0	0.0	0.0	0.0	0.0
Côte d'Ivoire	CIV	3.0	0.0	0.7	0.0	0.1	0.0	0.3	0.0	0.2	0.1	0.0	0.0	0.4	0.9	0.1	0.0	0.0	0.0	0.0	0.1
Djibouti	DJI	0.0	0.0	0.0	0.1	0.0	0.0	0.0	0.1	0.0	0.0	0.0	0.0	0.0	0.0	0.0	0.0	0.0	0.0	0.0	0.0
Egypt, Arab Rep.	EGY	0.0	0.0	0.0	0.5	0.0	6.2	0.0	0.3	0.0	0.1	1.1	0.0	0.4	0.2	0.2	0.1	0.3	0.2	0.2	0.2
Equatorial Guinea	GNQ	0.0	0.0	0.0	0.0	0.0	0.0	0.0	0.0	0.0	0.0	0.0	0.0	0.0	0.0	0.0	0.0	0.0	0.0	0.0	0.0
Eritrea	ERI	..	..	..	..	..	..	..	..	..	..	..	..	..	..	..	..	..	..	..	..
Ethiopia	ETH	0.0	0.0	0.0	0.0	0.0	0.0	0.0	0.0	0.0	0.0	0.0	0.0	0.0	0.0	0.0	0.0	0.0	0.0	0.0	0.0
Gabon	GAB	0.6	0.0	0.0	0.0	0.0	0.0	0.0	0.0	0.3	0.0	0.0	0.0	0.0	0.1	0.0	0.0	0.0	0.0	0.0	0.0
Gambia, The	GMB	1.9	0.0	0.0	0.0	0.0	0.0	0.0	0.0	0.0	0.0	0.0	0.0	0.0	0.0	0.0	0.0	0.0	0.0	0.0	0.0
Ghana	GHA	0.1	0.1	0.0	0.0	0.0	0.0	0.0	0.0	2.6	1.1	0.0	0.0	0.5	0.6	0.1	0.0	0.0	0.0	0.0	0.1
Guinea	GIN	2.9	0.0	0.0	0.3	0.0	0.0	0.0	0.0	0.1	0.0	0.0	0.0	0.0	0.2	0.0	0.0	0.0	0.0	0.0	0.0
Guinea-Bissau	GNB	0.5	0.0	0.0	0.0	0.0	0.0	0.0	0.0	0.0	0.0	0.0	0.0	0.0	0.0	0.0	0.0	0.0	0.0	0.0	0.0
Kenya	KEN	0.0	0.0	0.0	0.1	0.0	0.4	1.9	1.8	0.1	0.0	2.4	0.7	0.9	0.1	0.0	0.0	0.0	0.0	0.1	0.0
Lesotho	LSO	..	..	..	..	..	..	..	..	..	..	..	..	..	..	..	..	..	..	..	..
Liberia	LBR	0.1	0.0	0.0	0.0	0.0	0.0	0.0	0.0	0.0	0.0	0.0	0.0	0.0	0.0	0.1	0.0	0.0	0.0	0.3	0.1
Libya	LBY	0.0	0.0	0.0	0.0	0.0	1.4	0.0	0.0	0.0	7.2	0.0	0.0	0.2	0.0	0.2	0.1	0.0	0.0	0.1	0.1
Madagascar	MDG	0.0	0.7	0.0	0.0	0.1	0.0	0.1	0.2	0.0	0.0	0.0	0.0	0.1	0.1	0.0	0.0	0.0	0.0	0.0	0.0
Malawi	MWI	0.0	0.0	0.0	0.0	1.5	0.0	0.5	0.4	0.0	0.0	0.0	0.4	2.6	0.5	0.0	0.0	0.0	0.0	0.0	0.0
Mali	MLI	6.4	0.0	0.0	0.0	0.0	0.0	0.0	0.0	0.4	0.0	0.0	0.0	0.0	0.3	0.0	0.0	0.0	0.0	0.0	0.0
Mauritania	MRT	0.7	0.0	0.0	0.0	0.0	0.0	0.0	0.0	0.0	0.0	0.0	0.0	0.0	0.0	0.0	0.0	0.0	0.0	0.0	0.0
Mauritius	MUS	0.0	1.1	0.0	0.0	1.2	0.0	0.6	0.2	0.0	0.0	0.0	0.0	0.2	0.4	0.0	0.0	0.0	0.0	0.0	0.0
Morocco	MAR	0.0	0.0	0.1	0.0	0.0	0.0	0.0	0.0	1.6	1.2	0.0	0.0	0.2	0.4	0.3	0.1	0.1	0.1	0.2	0.2
Mozambique	MOZ	0.0	0.0	0.0	0.0	1.5	0.0	4.4	0.2	0.0	0.0	0.0	0.0	2.0	0.5	0.0	0.0	0.0	0.0	0.0	0.0
Namibia	NAM	..	..	..	..	..	..	..	..	..	..	..	..	..	..	..	..	..	..	..	..
Niger	NER	0.0	0.0	0.0	0.0	0.0	0.0	0.0	0.0	0.3	0.0	0.0	0.0	0.0	0.2	0.0	0.0	0.0	0.0	0.0	0.0
Nigeria	NGA	0.7	0.0	0.0	0.0	0.0	0.0	0.0	0.0	5.6	0.0	0.0	0.0	0.0	0.4	0.3	0.0	0.2	0.2	0.2	0.2
Reunion	REU	0.0	0.0	0.0	0.0	0.3	0.0	0.0	0.0	0.0	0.0	0.0	0.0	0.0	0.2	0.1	0.0	0.0	0.0	0.0	0.1
Rwanda	RWA	0.0	0.0	0.0	0.0	0.0	0.0	0.0	4.6	0.0	0.0	0.3	0.0	0.0	0.1	0.0	0.0	0.0	0.0	0.0	0.0
São Tomé and Principe	STP	0.0	0.0	0.0	0.0	0.0	0.0	0.0	0.0	0.0	0.0	0.0	0.0	0.0	0.0	0.0	0.0	0.0	0.0	0.0	0.0
Senegal	SEN	**	0.0	0.0	0.0	0.0	0.0	0.1	0.0	0.0	0.0	0.0	0.0	0.0	0.3	0.0	0.0	0.0	0.0	0.0	0.0
Seychelles	SYC	0.0	**	0.0	0.0	0.2	0.0	0.0	0.0	0.0	0.0	0.0	0.0	0.0	0.1	0.0	0.0	0.0	0.0	0.0	0.0
Sierra Leone	SLE	0.3	0.0	**	0.0	0.0	0.0	0.0	0.0	0.0	0.0	0.0	0.0	0.0	0.1	0.0	0.0	0.0	0.0	0.0	0.0
Somalia	SOM	0.0	0.0	0.0	**	0.0	0.1	0.0	0.3	0.0	0.0	0.0	0.0	0.0	0.1	0.0	0.0	0.0	0.0	0.0	0.0
South Africa	ZAF	0.0	0.3	0.0	0.0	**	0.0	0.0	0.7	3.3	0.0	0.0	0.4	10.1	0.6	0.4	0.1	0.5	0.4	0.2	0.4
Sudan	SDN	0.0	0.0	0.0	0.0	0.0	**	0.0	0.6	0.0	0.1	0.1	0.0	0.1	0.1	0.0	0.0	0.0	0.0	0.0	0.0
Swaziland	SWZ	..	..	..	..	..	..	**	..	..	..	..	..	..	..	..	..	..	..	..	..
Tanzania	TZA	0.0	0.0	0.0	0.4	0.1	0.0	0.6	**	0.0	0.0	0.5	0.1	0.2	0.1	0.0	0.0	0.0	0.0	0.1	0.0
Togo	TGO	0.5	0.0	0.0	0.0	0.0	0.0	0.0	0.0	**	0.1	0.0	0.0	0.0	0.3	0.0	0.0	0.0	0.0	0.0	0.0
Tunisia	TUN	0.4	0.0	0.0	0.0	0.0	1.0	0.0	0.0	0.0	**	0.0	0.0	0.3	0.1	0.3	0.0	0.1	0.1	0.1	0.2
Uganda	UGA	0.0	0.0	0.0	0.1	0.0	0.0	0.0	1.1	0.0	0.0	**	0.0	0.3	0.1	0.0	0.0	0.0	0.0	0.0	0.0
Zambia	ZMB	0.0	0.0	0.0	0.0	1.3	0.0	0.6	0.6	0.0	0.0	0.0	**	3.2	0.5	0.0	0.0	0.0	0.0	0.0	0.0
Zimbabwe	ZWE	0.0	0.1	0.0	0.0	3.1	0.0	3.6	1.2	0.0	0.0	0.0	1.1	**	1.0	0.0	0.0	0.0	0.0	0.0	0.1
Sub-Saharan Africa	SSA	23.7	2.3	0.7	1.0	11.0	0.5	13.0	15.7	20.8	1.8	3.4	3.7	21.5	9.1	1.9	0.2	1.1	0.9	1.3	1.6
European Community	EU	47.8	32.1	74.0	11.4	48.6	33.3	34.9	43.0	30.5	76.7	70.8	23.0	38.2	48.1	65.9	8.8	24.7	21.1	26.6	42.1
Canada	CAN	1.1	0.4	1.5	0.0	0.7	0.0	3.7	0.5	12.5	0.0	1.3	0.0	0.2	1.3	0.9	**	18.1	14.1	2.2	3.5
United States	USA	1.7	0.9	17.0	1.7	10.2	3.3	5.3	2.4	3.0	1.2	6.9	5.5	6.7	20.4	6.6	73.3	**	16.4	20.6	14.2
North America	NNA	2.8	1.3	18.4	1.7	10.9	3.3	9.0	2.9	15.5	1.2	8.2	5.9	7.0	21.7	7.5	73.3	18.1	30.5	22.7	17.7
Rest of World	ROW	25.7	64.3	6.9	85.9	29.4	62.9	43.1	38.4	33.2	20.2	17.5	67.4	33.3	21.1	24.8	17.6	56.0	47.5	49.3	38.6
World	WLD	100.0	100.0	100.0	100.0	100.0	100.0	100.0	100.0	100.0	100.0	100.0	100.0	100.0	100.0	100.0	100.0	100.0	100.0	100.0	100.0

Note: ** means "not applicable."

South Africa's data for 1992 is taken from partner countries' data.

Source: International Monetary Fund's Direction of Trade database.

5-48. Direction of trade matrix, imports, 1997

| | | *Importers* | | | | | | | | | | | | | | | | | | |
Exporters		DZA	AGO	BEN	BWA	BFA	BDI	CMR	CPV	CAF	TCD	COM	ZAR	COG	CIV	DJI	EGY	GNQ	ERI	ETH	GAB
Algeria	DZA	**	0.0	0.1	0.0	0.0	0.0	0.4	0.0	0.0	0.0	0.0	0.0	0.0	1.2	0.0	0.4	0.0	..	1.1	0.0
Angola	AGO	0.0	**	0.0	0.0	0.0	0.4	0.1	0.0	0.0	0.0	0.0	0.0	0.4	0.0	0.0	0.0	0.0	..	0	0.0
Benin	BEN	0.0	0.0	**	0.0	0.0	0.0	0.6	0.0	0.0	0.0	0.0	0.0	0.0	0.6	0.0	0.0	0.0	..	0.0	0
Bostwana	BWA	..	..	..	**	..	..	..	..	..	..	..	..	..	..	..	..	..	..	..	..
Burkina Faso	BFA	0.0	0.0	0.2	0.0	**	0.0	0.2	0.0	0.0	0.0	0.0	0.0	0.0	1.9	0.0	0.0	0.0	..	0.0	0.0
Burundi	BDI	0.0	0.0	0.0	0.0	0.0	**	0.0	0.0	0.0	0.0	0.0	0.0	0.0	0.0	0.0	0.0	0.0	..	0.0	0.0
Cameroon	CMR	0.0	0.2	0.0	0.0	0.0	0.0	**	0.0	0.0	0.7	0.0	0.0	0.1	1.1	0.0	0.0	8.6	..	0.0	0.1
Cape Verde	CPV	0.0	0.0	0.0	0.0	0.0	0.0	0.0	**	0.0	0.0	0.0	0.0	0.0	0.0	0.0	0.0	0.0	..	0.0	0.0
Central African Republic	CAF	0.0	0.0	0.0	0.0	0.0	0.0	0.8	0.0	**	1.1	0.0	0.1	0	0.0	0.0	0.0	0.0	..	0.0	0.0
Chad	TCD	0.0	0.0	0.0	0.0	0.0	0.0	0.5	0.0	0.1	**	0.0	0.0	0	0.0	0.0	0.0	0.0	..	0.0	0.0
Comoros	COM	0.0	0.0	0.0	0.0	0.0	0.0	0.0	0.0	0.0	0.0	**	0.0	0.0	0.0	0	0.0	0.0	..	0.0	0.0
Congo, Dem. Rep. of	ZAR	0.0	0.0	0.0	0.0	0.0	0.0	0.1	0.0	1.0	0.0	0.0	**	0.4	0.0	0.0	0	0.0	..	0.0	0.2
Congo, Rep. of	COG	0.0	0.1	0.0	0.0	0.0	0.2	0.6	0.0	0.2	0.0	0.0	0.1	**	0.0	0.0	0.0	0.0	..	0.0	0.2
Côte d'Ivoire	CIV	0.0	0.0	0.1	0.0	0.1	0.0	0.3	0.2	0.0	0.0	0.0	0.0	0.0	**	0.0	0.0	0.0	..	0.0	0.0
Djibouti	DJI	0.0	0.0	0.0	0.0	0.0	0.0	0.0	0.0	0.0	0.0	0.0	0.0	0.0	0.0	**	0.0	0.0	..	7.7	0.0
Egypt, Arab Rep.	EGY	0.0	0.0	0.0	0.0	0.0	0.0	0.0	0.6	3.9	0.1	0.0	0.0	0.0	0.0	0.0	**	0	..	2.8	0.0
Equatorial Guinea	GNQ	0.0	0.0	0.0	0.0	0.0	0.0	1.1	0.0	0.0	0.0	0.0	0.0	0.0	0.0	0.0	0.0	**	..	0.0	0.0
Eritrea	ERI	..	..	..	..	..	..	..	..	..	..	..	..	..	..	..	..	..	**	..	..
Ethiopia	ETH	0.0	0.0	0.0	0.0	0.0	0.0	0.0	0.0	0.0	0.0	0.0	0.0	0.0	0.0	5.3	0.0	0.0	..	**	0.0
Gabon	GAB	0.0	0.0	0.0	0.0	0.0	0.0	2.0	0.0	0.0	0.0	0.0	0.0	0.1	2.2	0.0	0.0	0.0	..	0.0	**
Gambia, The	GMB	0.0	0.0	0.0	0.0	0.0	0.0	0.0	0.2	0.0	0.0	0.0	0.0	0.0	0.2	0.0	0.0	0.0	..	0.0	0.0
Ghana	GHA	0.0	0.0	0.1	0.0	4.0	0.0	0.0	0.0	0.0	0.0	0.0	0.0	0.0	3.7	0.0	0.0	0.0	..	0.0	0.0
Guinea	GIN	0.0	0.0	0.0	0.0	0.0	0.0	0.0	0.0	0.0	0.0	0.0	0.0	0.1	0.8	0.0	0.0	0.0	..	0.0	0.1
Guinea-Bissau	GNB	0.0	0.0	0.0	0.0	0.0	0.0	0.0	0.1	0.0	0.0	0.0	0.0	0.0	0.0	0.0	0.0	0.0	..	0.0	0.0
Kenya	KEN	0.0	0.0	0.0	0.1	0.0	0.0	0.0	0.0	0.0	0.0	0.0	0.2	0.0	0.0	0.1	0.1	0.0	..	1.6	0.0
Lesotho	LSO	..	..	..	..	..	..	..	..	..	..	..	..	..	..	..	..	..	..	..	..
Liberia	LBR	0.0	0.0	0.0	0.0	0.0	0.0	0.0	0.0	0.0	0.0	0.0	0.0	0.0	0.3	0.0	0.0	0.0	..	0.0	0.0
Libya	LBY	0.0	0.0	0.0	0.0	0.0	0.0	0.0	0.0	0.0	0.0	0.0	0.0	0.0	0.0	0.0	1.2	0.1	..	0.1	0.0
Madagascar	MDG	0.0	0.0	0.0	0.0	0.0	0.0	0.0	0.0	0.0	0.0	0.0	0.0	0.0	0.0	0.0	0.0	0.0	..	0.0	0.0
Malawi	MWI	0.0	0.0	0.0	0.0	0.0	0.0	0.0	0.0	0.0	0.0	0.0	0.0	0.0	0.0	0.0	0.0	0.0	..	0.0	0.0
Mali	MLI	0.0	0.0	0.5	0.0	1.4	0.0	0.7	0.0	0.0	0.0	0.0	0.0	0.0	4.8	0.0	0.0	0.0	..	0.0	0.0
Mauritania	MRT	0.4	0.0	0.0	0.0	0.0	0.0	0.0	0.0	0.0	0.0	0.0	0.0	0.0	0.1	0.0	0.0	0.0	..	0.0	0.0
Mauritius	MUS	0.0	0.0	0.0	0.0	4.4	0.0	0.0	0.0	0.0	0.0	0.0	0.0	0.0	0.0	0.0	0.0	0.0	..	0.0	0.0
Morocco	MAR	0.7	0.0	7.6	0.0	1.8	0.0	0.3	0.0	0.3	1.5	0.0	0.1	0.2	0.6	0.0	0.3	0.0	..	0.1	0.6
Mozambique	MOZ	0.0	0.0	0.0	0.3	0.0	0.0	0.0	0.0	0.0	0.0	0.0	0.0	0.0	0.0	0.0	0.0	0.0	..	0.0	0.0
Namibia	NAM	..	..	..	..	..	..	..	..	..	..	..	..	..	..	..	..	..	..	..	..
Niger	NER	0.0	0.0	1.2	0.0	1.4	0.0	0.0	0.0	0.0	0.0	0.0	0.0	0.0	0.7	0.0	0.0	0.0	..	0.0	0.0
Nigeria	NGA	0.0	0.0	0.5	0.0	0.0	0.0	0.3	0.0	0.0	2.1	0.0	0.4	0.0	0.9	0.0	0.0	0.0	..	0.0	0.0
Reunion	REU	0.0	0.0	0.0	0.0	0.0	0.0	0.0	0.0	0.0	0.0	0.0	0.0	0.0	0.0	0.0	0.0	0.0	..	0.0	0.0
Rwanda	RWA	0.0	0.0	0.0	0.0	0.0	0.5	0.0	0.0	0.0	0.0	0.0	0.3	0.0	0.0	0.0	0.0	0.0	..	0.0	0.0
São Tomé and Principe	STP	0.0	0.0	0.0	0.0	0.0	0.0	0.0	0.2	0.0	0.0	0.0	0.0	0.0	0.0	0.0	0.0	0.0	..	0.0	0.0
Senegal	SEN	0.1	0.0	0.0	0.0	0.0	0.0	0.4	0.0	0.0	0.0	0.0	0.0	0.0	0.7	0.0	0.0	0.0	..	0.0	0.0
Seychelles	SYC	0.0	0.0	0.0	0.0	0.0	0.0	0.0	0.0	0.0	0.0	0.0	0.0	0.0	0.0	0.0	0.0	0.0	..	0.0	0.0
Sierra Leone	SLE	0.0	0.0	0.0	0.0	0.0	0.0	0.0	0.0	0.0	0.0	0.0	0.0	0.0	0.6	0.0	0.0	0.0	..	0.0	0.0
Somalia	SOM	0.0	0.0	0.0	0.0	0.0	0.0	0.0	0.0	0.0	0.0	0.0	0.0	0.0	0.0	56.5	0.0	0.0	..	0.0	0.0
South Africa	ZAF	0.0	0.9	0.5	0.0	0.1	0.6	0.1	0.0	0.0	0.2	0.0	7.1	0.1	0.6	0.0	0.6	0.0	..	0.1	0.2
Sudan	SDN	0.0	0.0	0.0	0.0	0.0	0.0	0.0	0.0	0.2	0.2	0.0	0.0	0.0	0.0	0.0	0.4	0.0	..	0.0	0.0
Swaziland	SWZ	..	..	..	..	..	..	..	..	..	..	..	..	..	..	..	..	..	..	..	..
Tanzania	TZA	0.0	0.0	0.0	0.1	0.0	0.1	0.0	0.0	0.0	0.0	0.0	0.0	0.0	0.0	0.0	0.0	0.0	..	0.0	0.0
Togo	TGO	0.0	0.0	1.2	0.0	0.8	0.0	0.3	0.0	0.0	0.0	0.0	0.0	0.0	0.5	0.0	0.0	0.0	..	0.0	0.0
Tunisia	TUN	0.4	0.0	0.4	0.0	0.9	0.0	0.7	30.1	3.6	5.1	11.9	0.1	0.0	0.5	0.0	0.6	0.0	..	0.3	0.1
Uganda	UGA	0.0	0.0	0.0	0.0	0.0	0.0	0.0	0.0	0.0	0.0	0.0	0.0	0.0	0.0	0.0	0.0	0.0	..	0.3	0.0
Zambia	ZMB	0.0	0.0	0.0	0.9	0.0	0.0	0.0	0.0	0.0	0.0	0.0	0.0	0.0	0.0	0.0	0.1	0.0	..	0.0	0.0
Zimbabwe	ZWE	0.0	0.0	0.0	14.4	0.0	0.0	0.0	0.0	0.0	0.0	0.0	0.0	0.0	0.0	0.0	0.0	0.0	..	0.1	0.0
Sub-Saharan Africa	SSA	0.6	1.2	4.6	15.8	12.3	1.8	7.5	0.7	1.5	4.3	0.0	7.9	1.2	19.7	62.1	1.5	8.7	..	2.1	1.0
European Community	EU	61.3	14.1	24.7	50.2	41.9	70.7	73.9	62.2	76.9	61.9	64.2	60.4	31.9	54.1	7.7	50.4	31.5	..	49.1	11.7
Canada	CAN	3.1	0.0	0.0	0.3	0.0	0.1	0.3	0.2	0.1	0.0	0.2	0.6	0.2	1.1	0.0	0.4	0.0	..	1.3	0.0
United States	USA	17.2	62.1	3.1	6.1	0.5	15.9	2.6	1.5	0.8	2.0	18.2	21.8	20.4	6.8	0.0	10.9	8.3	..	11.4	64.8
North America	NNA	20.3	62.1	3.1	6.4	0.5	16.0	2.9	1.7	0.9	2.1	18.4	22.4	20.6	7.9	0.0	11.3	8.4	..	12.7	64.8
Rest of World	ROW	17.8	22.5	67.6	27.6	45.3	11.5	15.7	35.4	20.7	31.7	17.3	9.3	46.3	18.3	30.2	36.8	51.5	..	36.1	22.5
World	WLD	100.0	100.0	100.0	100.0	100.0	100.0	100.0	100.0	100.0	100.0	100.0	100.0	100.0	100.0	100.0	100.0	100.0	..	100.0	100.0

Note: ** means "not applicable."

South Africa's data for 1997 is taken from partner countries' data.

Source: International Monetary Fund's Direction of Trade database.

(Table continues on the following page.)

5-48. Direction of trade matrix, imports, 1997 (continued)

Exporters		GMB	GHA	GIN	GNB	KEN	LSO	LBR	LBY	MDG	MWI	MLI	MRT	MUS	MAR	MOZ	NAM	NER	NGA	REU	RWA	STP
Algeria	DZA	0.0	0.0	0.2	0.0	0.0	0.0	0.0	0.0	2.0	0.0	0.3	0.0	0.0	0.1	0.0	0.0	0.2	0.0	..	0.0	0.0
Angola	AGO	0.0	0.8	0.0	0.0	0.0	0.0	0.0	0.0	0.0	0.0	0.0	0.0	0.0	0.1	0.2	0.0	0.0	0.0	..	0.0	0.0
Benin	BEN	0.0	1.2	0.0	0.0	0.0	0.0	0.0	0.0	0.0	0.0	0.0	0.0	0.0	0.0	0.0	0.0	0.0	0.0	..	0.0	0.0
Bostwana	BWA	..	..	..	..	..	..	..	..	..	..	..	..	..	..	..	..	..	..	..	..	..
Burkina Faso	BFA	0.0	0.3	0.0	0.0	0.0	0.0	0.0	0.0	0.0	0.0	0.5	0.0	0.0	0.0	0.0	0.0	0.2	0.1	..	0.0	0.0
Burundi	BDI	0.0	0.0	0.0	0.0	0.2	0.0	0.0	0.0	0.0	0.0	0.0	0.0	0.0	0.0	27.6	0.0	15.2	0.0	..	0.9	0.0
Cameroon	CMR	0.0	0.0	4.0	0.6	0.1	0.0	0.0	0.0	0.0	0.0	0.0	0.9	0.0	0.1	0.0	0.2	0.0	0.5	..	0.0	0.0
Cape Verde	CPV	0.2	0.0	0.0	0.2	0.0	0.0	0.0	0.0	0.0	0.0	0.0	0.0	0.0	0.0	0.1	0.0	0.0	0.0	..	0.0	0.0
Central African Republic	CAF	0.0	0.0	0.0	0.0	0.0	0.0	0.0	0.0	0.0	0.0	0.0	0.0	0.0	0.0	0.0	0.1	0.0	0.0	..	0.0	0.0
Chad	TCD	0.0	0.0	0.0	0.0	0.0	0.0	0.0	0.0	0.0	0.0	0.0	0.0	0.0	0.0	0.0	0.0	0.0	0.1	..	0.0	0.0
Comoros	COM	0.0	0.0	0.0	0.0	0.2	0.0	0.0	0.0	0.1	0.0	0.0	0.0	0.0	0.0	0.0	0.0	0.0	0.0	..	0.0	0.0
Congo, Dem. Rep. of	ZAR	0.0	0.0	0.0	0.0	1.9	0.0	0.0	0.0	0.0	0.1	0.0	0.0	0.0	0.0	0.0	0.0	0.0	0.4	..	0.8	0.0
Congo, Rep. of	COG	0.0	0.5	0.0	0.0	0.1	0.0	0.0	0.0	0.0	0.0	0.0	0.9	0.0	0.1	0.0	0.0	0.0	0.0	..	0.0	0.0
Côte d'Ivoire	CIV	0.0	0.1	0.8	0.0	0.0	0.0	0.0	0.0	0.0	0.0	1.0	2.5	0.0	0.1	0.0	0.0	0.0	2.4	..	0.0	0.0
Djibouti	DJI	0.0	0.0	0.0	0.0	0.2	0.0	0.0	0.0	0.0	0.0	0.0	0.0	0.0	0.0	0.0	0.0	0.0	0.0	..	0.0	0.0
Egypt, Arab Rep.	EGY	0.0	0.1	0.0	0.0	3.4	0.0	0.0	0.7	0.0	2.2	0.1	0.3	0.0	0.1	0.0	0.0	0.0	0.0	..	0.0	0.0
Equatorial Guinea	GNQ	0.0	0.0	0.0	0.0	0.0	0.0	0.0	0.0	0.0	0.0	0.0	0.1	0.0	0.0	0.0	0.0	0.0	0.0	..	0.0	0.0
Eritrea	ERI	..	..	..	..	..	..	..	..	..	..	..	..	..	..	..	..	..	..	..	..	..
Ethiopia	ETH	0.0	0.0	0.0	0.0	1.0	0.0	0.0	0.0	0.0	0.0	0.0	0.0	0.0	0.0	0.0	0.0	0.0	0.0	..	0.0	0.0
Gabon	GAB	0.0	0.0	0.0	0.0	0.0	0.0	0.0	0.0	0.0	0.1	0.0	0.1	0.0	0.3	0.0	0.0	0.0	0.0	..	0.0	0.1
Gambia, The	GMB	**	0.0	0.0	0.1	0.0	0.0	0.0	0.0	0.0	0.1	0.0	0.0	0.0	0.0	0.0	0.0	0.0	0.0	..	0.0	0.0
Ghana	GHA	0.1	**	0.0	0.0	0.0	0.0	0.0	0.0	0.0	0.0	0.0	0.2	0.0	0.1	0.0	0.0	2.1	2.6	..	0.0	0.0
Guinea	GIN	0.7	0.0	**	0.0	0.0	0.0	0.0	0.0	0.0	0.0	0.0	0.0	0.0	0.0	0.0	0.0	0.0	0.0	..	0.0	0.0
Guinea-Bissau	GNB	0.1	0.0	0.0	**	0.0	0.0	0.0	0.0	0.0	0.0	0.0	0.0	0.0	0.0	0.0	0.0	0.0	0.0	..	0.0	0.0
Kenya	KEN	0.0	0.0	0.0	0.0	**	0.0	0.0	0.0	0.0	0.0	0.0	0.0	0.3	0.0	0.7	0.0	0.0	0.0	..	2.9	0.0
Lesotho	LSO	..	..	..	..	..	**	..	..	..	..	..	..	..	..	..	..	..	..	..	..	..
Liberia	LBR	0.0	0.0	0.7	0.0	0.0	0.0	**	0.0	0.0	0.0	0.0	1.5	0.0	0.0	0.0	0.0	0.0	0.0	..	0.0	0.0
Libya	LBY	0.0	0.0	0.0	0.0	0.0	0.0	0.0	**	0.0	0.0	0.0	0.0	0.0	1.8	0.0	0.0	0.0	0.0	..	0.0	0.0
Madagascar	MDG	0.0	0.0	0.0	0.0	0.1	0.0	0.0	0.0	**	0.0	0.0	0.0	0.3	0.0	0.0	0.0	0.0	0.0	..	0.0	0.0
Malawi	MWI	0.0	0.0	0.0	0.0	0.3	0.0	0.0	0.0	0.0	**	0.0	0.0	0.2	0.0	6.3	0.0	0.0	0.0	..	0.0	0.0
Mali	MLI	0.0	0.0	0.0	0.0	0.0	0.0	0.0	0.0	0.0	0.0	**	0.1	0.0	0.1	0.0	0.0	0.1	0.0	..	0.0	0.0
Mauritania	MRT	0.0	0.0	0.0	0.0	0.0	0.0	0.0	0.0	0.0	0.0	0.0	**	0.0	0.1	0.0	0.0	0.0	0.0	..	0.0	0.0
Mauritius	MUS	0.0	0.0	0.0	0.0	0.5	0.0	0.0	0.0	4.6	0.6	0.0	0.0	**	0.0	0.0	0.0	0.0	0.0	..	0.0	0.0
Morocco	MAR	0.0	0.2	1.5	0.0	0.0	0.0	0.0	0.3	0.1	0.4	1.6	0.1	0.0	**	0.6	0.0	0.0	1.1	..	0.0	0.0
Mozambique	MOZ	0.0	0.0	0.0	0.0	0.0	0.0	0.0	0.0	0.0	0.5	0.0	0.0	0.0	0.0	**	0.2	0.0	0.0	..	0.0	0.0
Namibia	NAM	..	..	..	..	..	..	..	..	..	..	..	..	..	..	..	**	..	..	..	..	..
Niger	NER	0.0	0.2	0.0	0.0	0.0	0.0	0.0	0.0	0.0	0.0	0.1	0.0	0.0	0.0	0.0	0.0	**	0.2	..	0.0	0.0
Nigeria	NGA	0.0	4.1	0.5	0.0	0.1	0.0	0.0	0.0	0.0	0.0	0.7	0.0	0.0	0.1	0.0	1.7	12.7	**	..	0.1	0.0
Reunion	REU	0.0	0.0	0.0	0.0	0.0	0.0	0.0	0.0	0.0	0.0	0.0	0.0	0.0	0.0	0.0	0.0	0.0	0.0	**	0.0	0.0
Rwanda	RWA	0.0	0.0	0.0	0.0	2.9	0.0	0.0	0.0	0.0	0.0	0.0	0.0	0.1	0.0	0.0	0.0	0.0	0.0	..	**	0.0
São Tomé and Principe	STP	0.0	0.0	0.0	0.0	0.0	0.0	0.0	0.0	0.0	0.0	0.0	0.0	0.0	0.0	0.0	0.0	0.0	0.0	..	0.0	**
Senegal	SEN	0.0	0.1	0.0	0.0	0.0	0.0	0.0	0.0	0.0	0.0	0.1	0.0	0.0	0.1	0.0	0.0	0.0	0.5	..	0.0	0.0
Seychelles	SYC	0.0	0.0	0.0	0.0	0.3	0.0	0.0	0.0	0.1	0.0	0.0	0.0	0.4	0.0	0.0	0.0	0.0	0.0	..	0.0	0.0
Sierra Leone	SLE	0.0	0.0	0.0	0.0	0.0	0.0	0.2	0.0	0.0	0.0	0.0	0.0	0.0	0.0	0.0	0.0	0.0	0.1	..	0.0	0.0
Somalia	SOM	0.0	0.0	0.0	0.0	1.6	0.0	0.0	0.0	0.0	0.0	0.0	0.0	0.0	0.0	0.0	0.0	0.0	0.0	..	0.0	0.0
South Africa	ZAF	0.0	0.2	0.0	0.2	0.8	0.0	1.1	0.0	0.4	14.5	1.1	0.0	0.4	0.1	11.3	0.0	0.0	1.0	..	0.5	0.0
Sudan	SDN	0.0	0.0	0.0	0.0	1.6	0.0	0.0	2.5	0.0	0.0	0.0	0.0	0.0	0.0	0.0	0.0	0.0	0.0	..	0.0	0.0
Swaziland	SWZ	..	..	..	..	..	..	..	..	..	..	..	..	..	..	..	..	..	..	..	..	..
Tanzania	TZA	0.0	0.0	0.0	0.0	4.1	0.1	0.0	0.0	0.0	0.5	0.1	0.0	0.0	0.0	1.5	0.0	0.0	0.0	..	0.7	0.0
Togo	TGO	0.0	0.6	0.2	0.0	0.0	0.0	0.0	0.0	0.0	0.0	0.0	3.1	0.0	0.0	0.3	0.0	0.1	0.1	..	0.0	0.0
Tunisia	TUN	2.2	0.1	0.3	0.2	0.0	0.1	0.0	2.0	0.3	0.2	1.8	0.2	0.0	0.7	0.7	0.0	0.0	0.0	..	0.0	0.0
Uganda	UGA	0.0	0.0	0.0	0.0	13.9	0.0	0.0	0.0	0.0	0.2	0.0	0.0	0.0	0.0	0.0	0.0	0.0	0.0	..	0.0	0.0
Zambia	ZMB	0.0	0.0	0.0	0.0	0.1	0.0	0.0	0.0	0.0	0.5	0.0	0.0	0.1	0.0	0.1	0.3	0.0	0.0	..	0.0	0.0
Zimbabwe	ZWE	0.1	0.0	0.0	0.0	0.7	0.1	0.0	0.0	0.0	2.6	0.1	0.0	0.9	0.0	6.9	2.1	0.0	0.0	..	0.0	8.9
Sub-Saharan Africa	SSA	1.3	8.3	6.0	1.3	30.6	0.3	1.4	2.6	5.3	19.9	3.6	9.5	2.8	1.4	27.6	4.5	15.2	8.0	..	5.8	9.0
European Community	EU	83.6	58.7	40.2	19.9	43.1	30.3	55.3	82.7	70.4	37.4	33.0	60.9	74.6	69.9	39.4	67.3	13.4	28.1	..	70.7	73.7
Canada	CAN	0.1	0.6	2.0	0.2	0.6	3.7	0.0	0.0	0.7	0.4	3.4	0.0	0.7	0.7	0.3	3.2	2.1	2.3	..	0.2	0.3
United States	USA	1.6	10.0	12.7	0.1	5.4	52.7	0.6	0.0	9.6	14.8	1.3	0.1	15.3	4.2	10.0	16.5	13.2	37.1	..	3.9	1.8
North America	NNA	1.6	10.6	14.8	0.3	6.0	56.4	0.6	0.0	10.3	15.1	4.7	0.1	16.1	4.9	10.3	19.7	15.4	39.4	..	4.1	2.1
Rest of World	ROW	13.5	22.4	39.1	78.5	20.3	13.0	42.7	14.7	14.0	27.5	58.7	29.5	6.5	23.8	22.7	8.5	56.0	24.5	..	19.5	15.3
World	WLD	100.0	100.0	100.0	100.0	100.0	100.0	100.0	100.0	100.0	100.0	100.0	100.0	100.0	100.0	100.0	100.0	100.0	100.0	..	100.0	100.0

Importers   *Percentage of total imports*

Note: ** means "not applicable."

South Africa's data for 1997 is taken from partner countries' data.

Source: International Monetary Fund's Direction of Trade database.

(Table continues on the following page.)

5-48. Direction of trade matrix, imports, 1997 (continued)

Exporters		SEN	SYC	SLE	SOM	ZAF	SDN	SWZ	TZA	TGO	TUN	UGA	ZMB	ZWE	SSA	EU	CAN	USA	NNA	ROW	WLD
						Percentage of total imports															
Algeria	DZA	0.2	0.0	0.0	0.0	0.1	0.0	0.2	0.0	0.2	0.3	0.3	0.0	0.0	0.1	0.3	0.2	0.1	0.1	0.1	0.2
Angola	AGO	0.0	0.0	0.0	0.0	0.7	0.0	0.0	0.0	0.0	0.0	0.0	0.1	0.4	0.3	0.1	0.0	0.0	0.0	0.0	0.0
Benin	BEN	1.8	0.0	0.0	0.0	0.0	0.0	0.0	0.0	1.2	0.1	0.0	0.0	0.0	0.1	0.0	0.0	0.0	0.0	0.0	0.0
Bostwana	BWA	..	..	..	..	..	..	..	..	..	..	..	..	..	..	..	..	..	..	..	..
Burkina Faso	BFA	1.2	0.0	0.0	0.0	0.0	0.0	0.0	0.0	2.2	0.0	0.0	0.0	0.0	0.2	0.0	0.0	0.0	0.0	0.0	0.0
Burundi	BDI	0.0	0.0	0.0	0.0	0.0	0.0	0.0	0.4	0.0	0.0	0.0	0.6	0.1	0.0	0.0	0.0	0.0	0.0	0.0	0.0
Cameroon	CMR	2.2	0.0	0.0	0.0	0.0	0.0	0.1	0.0	0.0	0.2	0.0	0.0	0.0	0.3	0.0	0.0	0.0	0.0	0.0	0.0
Cape Verde	CPV	0.3	0.0	0.0	0.0	0.0	0.0	0.0	0.0	0.0	0.0	0.0	0.0	0.0	0.0	0.0	0.0	0.0	0.0	0.0	0.0
Central African Republic	CAF	0.0	0.0	0.0	0.0	0.0	0.0	0.0	0.0	0.0	0.0	0.0	0.0	0.0	0.0	0.0	0.0	0.0	0.0	0.0	0.0
Chad	TCD	0.4	0.0	0.0	0.0	0.0	0.0	0.0	0.0	0.0	0.0	0.0	0.0	0.0	0.0	0.0	0.0	0.0	0.0	0.0	0.0
Comoros	COM	0.0	0.0	0.0	0.0	0.0	0.0	0.0	0.0	0.0	0.0	0.0	0.0	0.0	0.0	0.0	0.0	0.0	0.0	0.0	0.0
Congo, Dem. Rep. of	ZAR	0.1	0.0	0.0	0.0	0.7	0.0	0.0	1.4	0.0	0.0	0.0	2.6	0.5	0.5	0.0	0.0	0.0	0.0	0.0	0.0
Congo, Rep. of	COG	0.6	0.0	0.0	0.0	0.1	0.0	0.0	0.0	0.0	0.0	0.0	0.7	0.3	0.1	0.0	0.0	0.0	0.0	0.0	0.0
Côte d'Ivoire	CIV	3.0	0.0	0.0	0.0	0.1	0.0	0.0	0.0	0.5	0.1	0.0	0.0	0.0	0.6	0.1	0.0	0.0	0.0	0.0	0.0
Djibouti	DJI	0.1	0.0	0.0	0.2	0.0	0.0	0.0	0.0	0.0	0.0	0.0	0.0	0.0	0.1	0.0	0.0	0.0	0.0	0.0	0.0
Egypt, Arab Rep.	EGY	0.0	0.0	0.0	0.1	0.0	4.1	0.0	0.2	0.0	0.2	0.1	0.0	0.3	0.2	0.3	0.0	0.2	0.2	0.2	0.2
Equatorial Guinea	GNQ	0.0	0.0	0.0	0.0	0.0	0.0	0.0	0.0	0.0	0.1	0.0	0.0	0.0	0.0	0.0	0.0	0.0	0.0	0.0	0.0
Eritrea	ERI	..	..	..	..	..	..	..	..	..	..	..	..	..	..	..	..	..	..	..	..
Ethiopia	ETH	0.0	0.0	0.0	0.0	0.0	0.1	0.0	0.0	0.0	0.0	0.0	0.0	0.0	0.0	0.0	0.0	0.0	0.0	0.0	0.0
Gabon	GAB	1.8	0.0	0.0	0.0	0.1	0.0	0.0	0.0	0.2	0.1	0.0	0.0	0.0	0.2	0.0	0.0	0.0	0.0	0.0	0.0
Gambia, The	GMB	0.6	0.0	0.1	0.0	0.0	0.0	0.0	0.0	0.0	0.0	0.0	0.0	0.0	0.0	0.0	0.0	0.0	0.0	0.0	0.0
Ghana	GHA	0.3	0.0	0.0	0.0	0.3	0.0	0.0	0.1	0.4	0.1	0.0	0.0	0.1	0.9	0.1	0.0	0.0	0.0	0.0	0.1
Guinea	GIN	1.2	0.0	0.1	0.0	0.1	0.0	0.0	0.0	0.1	0.0	0.0	0.0	0.0	0.1	0.0	0.0	0.0	0.0	0.0	0.0
Guinea-Bissau	GNB	1.4	0.0	0.0	0.0	0.0	0.0	0.0	0.0	0.0	0.0	0.0	0.0	0.0	0.0	0.0	0.0	0.0	0.0	0.0	0.0
Kenya	KEN	0.0	0.1	0.0	0.0	1.2	1.0	0.1	2.1	0.0	0.0	1.2	0.2	0.0	0.5	0.1	0.0	0.0	0.0	0.1	0.1
Lesotho	LSO	..	..	..	..	..	..	..	..	..	..	..	..	..	..	..	..	..	..	..	..
Liberia	LBR	0.0	0.0	0.0	0.0	0.0	0.0	0.0	0.0	0.0	0.0	0.0	0.0	0.0	0.0	0.0	0.0	0.0	0.0	0.1	0.1
Libya	LBY	0.0	0.0	0.0	0.0	0.0	1.3	0.0	0.0	0.0	4.3	0.0	0.0	0.1	0.0	0.2	0.1	0.0	0.0	0.1	0.1
Madagascar	MDG	0.0	1.5	0.0	0.0	0.2	0.0	0.0	0.1	0.0	0.0	0.0	0.0	0.0	0.1	0.0	0.0	0.0	0.0	0.0	0.0
Malawi	MWI	0.0	0.0	0.0	0.0	0.9	0.0	0.0	0.9	0.0	0.0	0.0	1.9	3.8	0.5	0.0	0.0	0.0	0.0	0.0	0.0
Mali	MLI	6.3	0.0	0.0	0.0	0.1	0.0	0.0	0.1	0.1	0.0	0.0	0.0	0.0	0.3	0.0	0.0	0.0	0.0	0.0	0.0
Mauritania	MRT	2.4	0.0	0.0	0.0	0.0	0.0	0.0	0.0	0.0	0.0	0.0	0.0	0.0	0.0	0.0	0.0	0.0	0.0	0.0	0.0
Mauritius	MUS	0.0	0.2	0.0	0.0	0.9	0.0	1.5	0.1	0.0	0.0	0.0	0.0	0.2	0.4	0.0	0.0	0.0	0.0	0.0	0.0
Morocco	MAR	0.3	0.0	0.9	0.0	0.3	0.0	0.0	0.1	0.5	0.7	0.0	0.0	0.2	0.5	0.2	0.1	0.1	0.1	0.1	0.2
Mozambique	MOZ	0.0	0.0	0.0	0.0	2.2	0.0	5.0	0.0	0.0	0.0	0.0	0.0	0.8	0.8	0.0	0.0	0.0	0.0	0.0	0.0
Namibia	NAM	..	..	..	..	..	..	..	..	..	..	..	..	..	..	..	..	..	..	..	..
Niger	NER	0.4	0.0	0.0	0.0	0.0	0.0	0.0	0.0	0.9	0.0	0.0	0.0	0.0	0.1	0.0	0.0	0.0	0.0	0.0	0.0
Nigeria	NGA	0.4	0.0	0.0	0.0	0.2	0.0	0.1	0.0	0.1	0.0	0.0	0.0	0.1	0.3	0.2	0.0	0.1	0.1	0.1	0.1
Reunion	REU	0.0	0.0	0.0	0.0	0.0	0.0	0.0	0.0	0.0	0.0	0.0	0.0	0.0	0.0	0.0	0.0	0.0	0.0	0.0	0.0
Rwanda	RWA	0.0	0.0	0.0	0.0	0.0	0.0	0.0	1.0	0.0	0.0	0.2	0.1	0.0	0.1	0.0	0.0	0.0	0.0	0.0	0.0
São Tomé and Principe	STP	0.0	0.0	0.0	0.0	0.0	0.0	0.0	0.0	0.0	0.0	0.0	0.0	0.0	0.0	0.0	0.0	0.0	0.0	0.0	0.0
Senegal	SEN	**	0.0	0.0	0.0	0.0	0.0	0.0	0.0	0.1	0.0	0.0	0.0	0.0	0.2	0.0	0.0	0.0	0.0	0.0	0.0
Seychelles	SYC	0.0	**	0.0	0.0	0.2	0.0	0.0	0.0	0.0	0.0	0.0	0.0	0.1	0.1	0.0	0.0	0.0	0.0	0.0	0.0
Sierra Leone	SLE	0.1	0.0	**	0.0	0.0	0.0	0.0	0.0	0.0	0.0	0.0	0.0	0.0	0.1	0.0	0.0	0.0	0.0	0.0	0.0
Somalia	SOM	0.0	0.0	0.0	**	0.0	0.1	0.0	0.0	0.0	0.0	0.0	0.0	0.0	0.0	0.0	0.0	0.0	0.0	0.0	0.0
South Africa	ZAF	0.3	1.3	0.0	0.0	**	0.1	0.0	1.2	6.2	0.1	0.1	4.0	12.8	1.0	0.6	0.1	0.4	0.3	0.4	0.4
Sudan	SDN	0.0	0.0	0.0	0.0	0.0	**	0.0	0.2	0.0	0.0	0.0	0.0	0.2	0.1	0.0	0.0	0.0	0.0	0.0	0.0
Swaziland	SWZ	..	..	..	..	..	..	**	..	..	..	..	..	..	..	..	..	..	..	..	..
Tanzania	TZA	0.0	0.0	0.0	0.0	0.4	0.0	2.7	**	0.0	0.0	0.8	0.4	0.2	0.3	0.0	0.0	0.0	0.0	0.0	0.0
Togo	TGO	0.8	0.0	0.0	0.0	0.0	0.0	0.0	0.0	**	0.0	0.0	0.0	0.0	0.1	0.0	0.0	0.0	0.0	0.0	0.0
Tunisia	TUN	0.8	0.6	0.0	0.0	0.0	0.8	0.3	0.0	0.0	**	0.3	0.0	0.2	0.1	0.3	0.0	0.0	0.0	0.1	0.2
Uganda	UGA	0.0	0.0	0.0	0.2	0.1	0.0	0.0	1.1	0.0	0.0	**	0.0	0.1	0.4	0.0	0.0	0.0	0.0	0.0	0.0
Zambia	ZMB	0.0	0.0	0.0	0.0	1.0	0.0	1.8	0.3	0.0	0.0	0.0	**	2.6	0.4	0.0	0.0	0.0	0.0	0.0	0.0
Zimbabwe	ZWE	0.0	0.0	0.0	0.0	4.6	0.0	3.6	2.1	0.0	0.0	0.0	2.4	**	1.8	0.0	0.0	0.0	0.0	0.0	0.1
Sub-Saharan Africa	SSA	25.8	3.2	0.3	0.3	14.2	1.3	14.9	11.2	12.1	0.9	2.3	13.2	22.3	10.8	1.5	0.3	0.8	0.7	1.1	1.3
European Community	EU	52.7	75.4	81.7	15.6	34.4	34.2	42.0	36.9	22.0	82.6	72.7	26.4	40.6	36.9	59.5	6.7	21.6	18.2	23.3	35.3
Canada	CAN	0.4	1.2	3.9	0.0	1.3	0.0	1.4	0.3	12.8	0.1	1.2	2.3	1.0	1.3	1.1	**	19.1	14.8	1.8	3.8
United States	USA	1.1	2.4	9.1	0.1	8.8	2.3	15.3	4.0	3.1	1.2	5.8	5.1	6.5	19.8	8.3	77.7	**	17.5	21.3	16.1
North America	NNA	1.5	3.6	13.0	0.1	10.1	2.3	16.7	4.3	15.9	1.3	7.0	7.4	7.4	21.1	9.4	77.7	19.1	32.2	23.1	19.9
Rest of World	ROW	20.0	17.8	5.1	83.9	41.3	62.2	26.5	47.7	50.0	15.2	18.0	53.0	29.7	31.2	29.6	15.4	58.5	48.8	52.5	43.5
World	WLD	100.0	100.0	100.0	100.0	100.0	100.0	100.0	100.0	100.0	100.0	100.0	100.0	100.0	100.0	100.0	100.0	100.0	100.0	100.0	100.0

Note: ** means "not applicable."

South Africa's data for 1997 is taken from partner countries' data.

Source: International Monetary Fund's Direction of Trade database.

5-49. Direction of trade matrix, imports, 2002

		Importers								*Percentage of total imports*											
Exporters		DZA	AGO	BEN	BWA	BFA	BDI	CMR	CPV	CAF	TCD	COM	ZAR	COG	CIV	DJI	EGY	GNQ	ERI	ETH	GAB
Algeria	DZA	**	0.0	0.0	0.0	0.4	0.0	0.1	0.0	0.1	0.0	0.0	0.0	0.0	1.1	0.0	0.9	0.0	..	0.3	0.0
Angola	AGO	0.0	**	0.0	0.0	0.0	0.0	0.8	0.1	0.0	0.0	0.0	0.0	0.6	0.0	0.0	0.0	0.0	..	0	0.1
Benin	BEN	0.1	0.0	**	0.0	0.1	0.0	0.1	0.0	0.0	0.1	0.0	0.0	0.0	0.7	0.0	0.0	0.0	..	0.0	0
Bostwana	BWA	..	..	..	**	..	..	..	..	..	..	..	..	..	..	..	..	..	..	..	..
Burkina Faso	BFA	0.0	0.0	0.6	0.0	**	0.0	0.0	0.0	0.0	0.0	0.0	0.0	0.0	2.9	0.0	0.0	0.0	..	0.0	0.0
Burundi	BDI	0.0	0.0	0.0	0.0	0.0	**	0.0	0.0	0.0	0.0	0.0	0.1	0.0	0.0	0.1	0.0	0.0	..	0.0	0.0
Cameroon	CMR	0.0	0.0	0.2	0.0	0.0	0.0	**	0.0	0.0	0.2	0.0	0.0	0.3	0.4	0.0	0.1	2.2	..	0.0	0.1
Cape Verde	CPV	0.0	0.0	0.0	0.0	0.0	0.0	0.0	**	0.0	0.0	0.0	0.0	0.0	0.0	0.0	0.0	0.0	..	0.0	0.0
Central African Republic	CAF	0.0	0.0	0.0	0.0	0.0	0.0	0.3	0.0	**	3.7	0.0	0.1	0	0.0	0.0	0.0	0.0	..	0.0	0.0
Chad	TCD	0.0	0.0	0.6	0.0	0.0	0.0	0.7	0.0	0.1	**	0.0	0.0	0	0	0.0	0.0	0.0	..	0.0	0.0
Comoros	COM	0.0	0.0	0.0	0.0	0.0	0.0	0.0	0.0	0.0	0.0	**	0.0	0.0	0.0	0	0.0	0.0	..	0.0	0.0
Congo, Dem. Rep. of	ZAR	0.0	0.0	0.0	0.0	0.0	0.6	1.6	0.0	1.7	0.0	0.0	**	0.6	0.0	0.0	0	0.0	..	0.0	0.4
Congo, Rep. of	COG	0.0	0.1	0.1	0.0	0.0	0.4	1.1	0.0	0.2	0.0	0.0	0.1	**	0.0	0.0	0.0	0.0	..	0.0	0.3
Côte d'Ivoire	CIV	0.0	0.0	0.2	0.0	0.5	0.0	0.2	0.0	0.0	0.0	0.0	0.0	0.0	**	0.0	0.0	0.0	..	0.0	0.0
Djibouti	DJI	0.0	0.0	0.0	0.0	0.0	0.0	0.0	0.0	0.0	0.0	0.0	0.0	0.0	0.0	**	0.0	0.0	..	13.5	0.0
Egypt, Arab Rep.	EGY	0.8	0.0	0.0	0.0	0.0	0.0	0.0	0.0	0.0	0.3	0.0	0.0	0.0	0.0	0.0	**	0	..	0.8	0.0
Equatorial Guinea	GNQ	0.0	0.0	0.0	0.0	0.0	0.0	0.6	0.0	0.0	0.0	0.0	0.0	0.0	0.0	0.0	0.0	**	..	0.0	0.1
Eritrea	ERI	..	..	..	..	..	..	..	..	..	..	..	..	..	..	..	..	..	**	..	..
Ethiopia	ETH	0.0	0.0	0.0	0.0	0.0	0.0	0.0	0.0	0.0	0.0	0.0	0.0	0.0	0.0	5.9	0.0	0.0	..	**	0.0
Gabon	GAB	0.0	0.0	0.1	0.0	0.0	0.0	0.9	0.0	0.0	0.0	0.0	0.0	0.1	0.4	0.0	0.0	0.0	..	0.0	**
Gambia, The	GMB	0.0	0.0	0.0	0.0	0.0	0.0	0.0	0.0	0.0	0.0	0.0	0.0	0.0	0.3	0.0	0.0	0.0	..	0.0	0.0
Ghana	GHA	0.0	0.0	0.0	0.0	7.6	0.0	0.0	0.0	0.0	0.1	0.0	0.0	0.0	3.9	0.0	0.1	0.0	..	0.0	0.0
Guinea	GIN	0.0	0.0	0.0	0.0	0.0	0.0	0.0	0.0	0.0	0.0	0.0	0.0	0.0	1.9	0.0	0.0	0.0	..	0.0	0.1
Guinea-Bissau	GNB	0.0	0.0	0.0	0.0	0.0	0.0	0.0	0.0	0.0	0.0	0.0	0.0	0.0	0.0	0.0	0.0	0.0	..	0.0	0.0
Kenya	KEN	0.0	0.0	0.0	0.0	0.0	10.3	0.0	0.0	0.0	0.0	0.0	0.0	0.0	0.0	0.0	0.4	0.0	..	0.3	0.0
Lesotho	LSO	..	..	..	..	..	..	..	..	..	..	..	..	..	..	..	..	..	..	..	..
Liberia	LBR	0.0	0.0	0.0	0.0	0.0	0.0	0.0	0.0	0.0	0.0	0.0	0.0	0.0	0.7	0.0	0.0	0.0	..	0.0	0.0
Libya	LBY	0.0	0.0	0.0	0.0	0.0	0.0	0.0	0.0	0.0	0.0	0.0	0.0	0.0	0.0	0.0	0.8	0.0	..	0.0	0.0
Madagascar	MDG	0.0	0.0	0.0	0.0	0.0	0.0	0.0	0.0	0.0	0.0	0.1	0.0	0.0	0.0	0.0	0.0	0.0	..	0.0	0.0
Malawi	MWI	0.0	0.0	0.0	0.0	0.0	0.0	0.0	0.0	0.0	0.0	0.0	0.0	0.0	0.0	0.0	0.0	0.0	..	0.0	0.0
Mali	MLI	0.0	0.0	0.4	0.0	2.7	0.0	0.0	0.0	0.0	0.0	0.0	0.0	0.0	4.8	0.0	0.0	0.0	..	0.0	0.0
Mauritania	MRT	0.1	0.0	0.0	0.0	0.0	0.0	0.0	0.3	0.0	0.0	0.0	0.0	0.0	0.1	0.0	0.0	0.0	..	0.0	0.0
Mauritius	MUS	0.0	0.0	0.5	0.0	0.6	0.0	0.1	0.0	0.2	0.0	0.2	0.0	0.0	0.0	0.0	0.1	0.0	..	0.0	0.0
Morocco	MAR	0.7	0.0	3.4	0.0	3.1	0.0	0.5	0.0	0.2	4.9	0.0	0.0	0.2	0.3	0.0	0.8	0.2	..	0.4	0.7
Mozambique	MOZ	0.0	0.0	0.0	0.0	0.0	0.0	0.0	0.0	0.0	0.0	0.0	0.0	0.0	0.0	0.0	0.0	0.0	..	0.0	0.0
Namibia	NAM	..	..	..	..	..	..	..	..	..	..	..	..	..	..	..	..	..	..	..	..
Niger	NER	0.0	0.0	4.4	0.0	3.2	0.0	0.0	0.0	0.0	0.0	0.0	0.0	0.0	1.2	0.0	0.0	0.0	..	0.0	0.0
Nigeria	NGA	0.0	0.0	0.3	0.0	0.0	0.0	0.7	0.0	0.0	5.8	0.0	0.0	0.0	1.1	0.0	0.1	0.0	..	0.0	0.0
Reunion	REU	0.0	0.0	0.0	0.0	0.0	0.0	0.0	0.0	0.0	0.0	0.0	0.0	0.0	0.0	0.0	0.0	0.0	..	0.0	0.0
Rwanda	RWA	0.0	0.0	0.0	0.0	0.0	8.6	0.0	0.0	0.0	0.0	0.0	0.5	0.0	0.0	0.0	0.0	0.0	..	0.1	0.0
São Tomé and Principe	STP	0.0	0.0	0.0	0.0	0.0	0.0	0.0	0.0	0.0	0.0	0.0	0.0	0.0	0.0	0.0	0.0	0.0	..	0.0	0.0
Senegal	SEN	0.0	0.1	0.3	0.0	0.1	0.0	0.3	0.2	0.0	0.0	0.0	0.0	0.4	1.1	0.0	0.2	0.0	..	0.0	0.2
Seychelles	SYC	0.0	0.0	0.0	0.0	0.0	0.0	0.0	0.0	0.0	0.0	0.0	0.0	0.0	0.0	0.0	0.0	0.0	..	0.0	0.0
Sierra Leone	SLE	0.0	0.0	0.0	0.0	0.0	0.0	0.0	0.0	0.0	0.0	0.0	0.0	0.0	0.5	0.0	0.0	0.0	..	0.0	0.0
Somalia	SOM	0.0	0.0	0.0	0.0	0.0	0.0	0.0	0.0	0.0	0.0	0.0	0.0	0.0	0.0	75.2	0.0	0.0	..	0.0	0.0
South Africa	ZAF	0.0	0.1	1.0	0.0	0.0	0.5	0.1	0.0	0.1	0.0	0.0	0.1	0.1	0.3	0.0	0.2	0.0	..	0.2	2.2
Sudan	SDN	0.0	0.0	0.0	0.0	0.0	0.0	0.0	0.0	0.3	0.7	0.0	0.0	0.0	0.0	0.0	0.6	0.0	..	0.1	0.0
Swaziland	SWZ	..	..	..	..	..	..	..	..	..	..	..	..	..	..	..	..	..	..	..	..
Tanzania	TZA	0.0	0.0	0.0	0.0	0.0	0.0	0.0	0.0	0.0	0.0	0.0	0.0	0.0	0.0	0.0	0.1	0.0	..	0.1	0.0
Togo	TGO	0.0	0.0	1.6	0.0	0.6	0.0	0.0	0.0	0.0	0.0	0.0	0.0	0.0	0.4	0.0	0.0	0.0	..	0.0	0.0
Tunisia	TUN	0.4	0.0	0.0	0.0	0.5	0.0	0.4	0.0	0.3	0.0	0.0	0.0	0.0	0.4	0.0	0.7	0.0	..	0.0	0.2
Uganda	UGA	0.0	0.0	0.0	0.0	0.0	3.2	0.0	0.0	0.0	0.0	0.0	0.0	0.0	0.0	0.0	0.0	0.0	..	0.0	0.0
Zambia	ZMB	0.0	0.0	0.0	0.4	0.0	0.0	0.0	0.0	0.0	0.0	0.0	0.0	0.0	0.0	0.3	0.0	0.0	..	0.0	0.0
Zimbabwe	ZWE	0.0	0.0	0.0	2.1	0.0	0.0	0.0	0.0	0.0	0.0	0.0	6.7	0.0	0.0	0.0	0.0	0.0	..	0.0	0.0
Sub-Saharan Africa	SSA	0.3	0.4	10.3	2.5	15.5	23.6	7.5	0.7	2.6	10.6	0.3	7.6	2.3	20.8	81.6	2.1	2.2	..	0.9	3.6
European Community	EU	64.3	26.8	27.1	91.0	32.6	58.7	71.0	87.3	87.7	59.9	64.9	75.7	23.2	51.5	3.3	45.8	36.4	..	48.1	18.6
Canada	CAN	5.8	0.0	0.0	0.0	0.0	1.0	0.4	0.1	0.1	0.0	0.5	0.0	0.0	1.0	0.3	0.6	10.6	..	0.8	0.1
United States	USA	12.2	41.1	0.4	1.7	1.9	2.6	8.9	8.1	1.1	8.5	17.7	13.5	10.2	7.9	1.4	21.1	28.3	..	5.4	55.1
North America	NNA	17.9	41.1	0.4	1.8	1.9	3.6	9.2	8.1	1.3	8.6	18.2	13.5	10.2	8.9	1.8	21.7	38.9	..	6.3	55.1
Rest of World	ROW	17.5	31.6	62.2	4.7	50.0	14.1	12.2	3.9	8.4	20.9	16.5	3.2	64.3	18.8	13.3	30.5	22.4	..	44.8	22.7
World	WLD	100.0	100.0	100.0	100.0	100.0	100.0	100.0	100.0	100.0	100.0	100.0	100.0	100.0	100.0	100.0	100.0	100.0	..	100.0	100.0

Note: ** means "not applicable."

South Africa's data for 2002 is taken from partner countries' data.

Source: International Monetary Fund's Direction of Trade database.

(Table continues on the following page.)

5-49. Direction of trade matrix, imports, 2002 (continued)

| | | Importers | | | | | | | | | | | | | | | | | | | | |
| | | *Percentage of total imports* | | | | | | | | | | | | | | | | | | | | |
Exporters		GMB	GHA	GIN	GNB	KEN	LSO	LBR	LBY	MDG	MWI	MLI	MRT	MUS	MAR	MOZ	NAM	NER	NGA	REU	RWA	STP
Algeria	DZA	0.0	0.0	0.0	0.0	0.1	0.0	0.0	0.0	0.0	0.7	0.0	0.9	0.0	0.2	0.0	0.0	0.0	0.0	..	0.0	0.0
Angola	AGO	0.0	1.2	0.0	0.0	0.0	0.0	0.0	0.0	0.0	0.0	0.0	0.0	0.0	0.1	0.1	0.0	0.0	0.0	..	0.0	0.0
Benin	BEN	0.2	1.9	0.0	0.0	0.0	0.0	0.0	0.0	0.0	0.0	0.0	0.0	0.0	0.0	0.0	0.0	2.1	0.1	..	0.0	0.0
Bostwana	BWA	..	..	..	..	..	..	..	..	..	..	..	..	..	..	..	..	..	..	..	..	..
Burkina Faso	BFA	0.0	0.5	0.0	0.0	0.0	0.0	0.0	0.2	0.0	0.0	1.5	0.1	0.0	0.1	0.0	0.0	0.4	0.1	..	0.0	0.0
Burundi	BDI	0.0	0.0	0.0	0.0	0.4	0.0	0.0	0.0	0.0	0.1	0.0	0.0	0.0	0.0	0.0	0.0	0.0	0.0	..	0.4	0.0
Cameroon	CMR	0.0	0.0	4.0	0.9	0.0	0.0	0.0	0.0	0.0	0.0	0.0	2.9	0.0	0.0	0.0	0.0	0.0	1.5	..	0.0	0.0
Cape Verde	CPV	0.0	0.0	0.0	0.0	0.0	0.0	0.0	0.0	0.0	0.0	0.0	0.0	0.0	0.0	0.0	0.0	0.0	0.0	..	0.0	0.0
Central African Republic	CAF	0.0	0.0	0.0	0.0	0.0	0.0	0.0	0.0	0.0	0.0	0.0	0.0	0.0	0.0	0.0	0.0	0.0	0.0	..	0.0	0.0
Chad	TCD	0.0	0.0	0.0	0.0	0.0	0.0	0.0	0.0	0.0	0.0	0.0	0.0	0.0	0.0	0.0	0.0	0.1	0.1	..	0.0	0.0
Comoros	COM	0.0	0.0	0.0	0.0	0.2	0.0	0.0	0.0	0.2	0.0	0.0	0.0	0.2	0.0	0.0	0.0	0.0	0.0	..	0.0	0.0
Congo, Dem. Rep. of	ZAR	0.0	0.0	0.0	0.0	1.9	0.0	0.0	0.0	0.0	0.3	0.0	0.0	0.0	0.0	0.0	0.0	0.0	0.5	..	1.0	0.0
Congo, Rep. of	COG	0.0	0.7	0.0	0.0	0.1	0.0	0.0	0.0	0.0	0.0	0.0	1.3	0.0	0.1	0.4	0.0	0.0	0.0	..	0.0	0.0
Côte d'Ivoire	CIV	0.0	0.5	1.2	0.6	0.0	0.0	0.2	0.0	0.0	0.0	1.4	3.8	0.0	0.1	0.0	0.0	1.0	2.7	..	0.0	0.0
Djibouti	DJI	0.0	0.0	0.0	0.0	0.2	0.0	0.0	0.0	0.0	0.0	0.0	0.0	0.0	0.0	0.0	0.0	0.0	0.0	..	0.0	0.0
Egypt, Arab Rep.	EGY	0.0	0.1	0.0	0.0	4.2	0.0	0.0	0.4	0.0	6.2	0.3	0.4	0.0	0.3	0.0	0.0	0.0	0.0	..	0.0	0.1
Equatorial Guinea	GNQ	0.0	0.0	0.0	0.0	0.0	0.0	0.0	0.0	0.0	0.0	0.0	0.1	0.0	0.1	0.0	0.0	0.0	0.0	..	0.0	0.0
Eritrea	ERI	..		..	..	..	..	..	..	..	..	..	..	..	..	..	..	..	..	..	..	..
Ethiopia	ETH	0.0	0.0	0.0	0.0	1.0	0.0	0.0	0.0	0.0	0.0	0.0	0.0	0.0	0.0	0.0	0.0	0.0	0.0	..	0.0	0.0
Gabon	GAB	0.0	0.0	0.0	0.0	0.0	0.0	0.0	0.0	0.0	0.1	0.0	0.1	0.2	0.1	0.0	0.0	0.0	0.1	..	0.0	0.1
Gambia, The	GMB	**	0.1	0.0	0.1	0.0	0.0	0.0	0.0	0.0	0.0	0.0	0.0	0.0	0.0	0.0	0.0	0.0	0.0	..	0.0	0.0
Ghana	GHA	0.7	**	0.0	0.0	0.0	0.0	0.0	0.0	0.0	0.0	0.0	0.4	0.0	0.1	0.0	0.0	2.3	3.7	..	0.0	0.0
Guinea	GIN	0.1	0.0	**	0.6	0.0	0.0	0.0	0.0	0.0	0.0	0.0	0.0	0.0	0.0	0.0	0.0	0.0	0.0	..	0.0	0.0
Guinea-Bissau	GNB	1.2	0.0	0.0	**	0.0	0.0	0.0	0.0	0.0	0.0	0.0	0.0	0.0	0.0	0.0	0.0	0.0	0.0	..	0.0	0.0
Kenya	KEN	0.0	0.0	0.0	0.0	**	0.0	1.0	0.0	0.2	0.0	0.0	0.0	0.4	0.0	0.0	0.0	0.0	0.0	..	0.2	0.0
Lesotho	LSO	..	..	..	..	..	**	..	..	..	..	..	..	..	..	..	..	..	..		..	
Liberia	LBR	0.0	0.0	0.2	0.0	0.0	0.0	**	0.0	0.0	0.0	0.0	2.4	0.0	0.0	0.0	0.0	0.0	0.0	..	0.0	0.0
Libya	LBY	0.0	0.0	0.0	0.0	0.0	0.0	0.0	**	0.0	0.0	0.0	0.0	0.0	0.7	0.0	0.0	0.4	0.0	..	0.0	0.0
Madagascar	MDG	0.0	0.0	0.0	0.0	0.3	0.0	0.0	0.0	**	0.1	0.0	0.0	0.8	0.0	0.0	0.0	0.0	0.1	..	0.0	0.0
Malawi	MWI	0.0	0.0	0.0	0.0	0.4	0.0	0.0	0.0	0.0	**	0.0	0.0	0.1	0.0	1.4	0.0	0.0	0.0	..	0.0	0.0
Mali	MLI	0.1	0.0	0.1	0.0	0.0	0.0	0.0	0.0	0.0	0.0	**	0.1	0.0	0.2	0.0	0.0	0.1	0.0	..	0.0	0.0
Mauritania	MRT	0.4	0.0	0.0	0.0	0.0	0.0	0.0	0.0	0.0	0.0	0.0	**	0.0	0.2	0.0	0.0	0.0	0.0	..	0.0	0.0
Mauritius	MUS	0.0	0.0	0.0	0.0	0.1	0.0	0.0	0.0	2.5	0.0	4.2	0.2	**	0.0	0.9	0.1	0.0	0.0	..	0.0	0.0
Morocco	MAR	0.0	0.1	1.0	0.0	0.0	0.0	0.1	0.7	0.1	0.2	1.2	0.0	0.1	**	0.0	0.0	0.0	0.0	..	0.0	0.0
Mozambique	MOZ	0.0	0.0	0.0	0.0	0.0	0.0	0.0	0.0	0.0	0.6	0.0	0.0	0.0	0.0	**	0.0	0.0	0.0	..	0.0	0.0
Namibia	NAM	..	..	..	..	..	..	..	..	..	..	..	..	..	..	..	**	..	..	..	..	..
Niger	NER	0.0	0.5	0.0	0.0	0.0	0.0	0.0	0.0	0.0	0.0	0.3	0.0	0.0	0.0	0.0	0.0	**	0.2	..	0.0	0.0
Nigeria	NGA	0.0	5.2	0.0	0.0	0.1	0.0	0.0	0.0	0.0	0.0	1.8	0.0	0.0	0.2	0.0	0.7	35.1	**	..	0.1	0.0
Reunion	REU	0.0	0.0	0.0	0.0	0.0	0.0	0.0	0.0	0.0	0.0	0.0	0.0	0.0	0.0	0.0	0.0	0.0	0.0	**	0.0	0.0
Rwanda	RWA	0.0	0.0	0.0	0.0	2.9	0.0	0.0	0.0	0.0	0.0	0.0	0.0	0.1	0.0	0.0	0.0	0.0	0.0	..	**	0.0
São Tomé and Principe	STP	0.0	0.0	0.0	0.0	0.0	0.0	0.0	0.0	0.0	0.0	0.0	0.0	0.0	0.0	0.0	0.0	0.0	0.0	..	0.0	**
Senegal	SEN	0.6	0.4	0.1	0.0	0.0	0.0	0.3	0.0	0.0	0.0	0.0	0.0	0.0	0.2	0.0	0.0	0.0	0.9	..	0.0	0.0
Seychelles	SYC	0.0	0.0	0.1	0.0	0.2	0.0	0.0	0.0	0.1	0.0	0.0	0.0	0.8	0.0	0.0	0.0	0.0	0.0	..	0.0	0.0
Sierra Leone	SLE	0.1	0.0	0.1	0.0	0.0	0.0	0.3	0.0	0.0	0.1	0.0	0.0	0.0	0.0	0.0	0.0	0.0	0.1	..	0.0	0.0
Somalia	SOM	0.0	0.0	0.0	0.0	2.0	0.0	0.0	0.0	0.0	0.0	0.0	0.0	0.0	0.0	0.0	0.0	0.0	0.0	..	0.0	0.0
South Africa	ZAF	0.3	0.4	0.0	0.0	0.4	0.0	0.1	0.0	0.4	10.3	0.5	0.0	0.5	0.1	4.4	0.0	5.6	1.8	..	0.3	0.0
Sudan	SDN	0.0	0.0	0.0	0.0	2.9	0.0	0.0	0.0	0.0	0.0	0.0	0.0	0.0	0.0	0.0	0.0	0.0	0.0	..	0.0	0.0
Swaziland	SWZ	..	..	..	..	..	..	..	..	..	..	..	..	..	..	..	..	..	..	..	..	..
Tanzania	TZA	0.2	0.0	0.0	0.0	3.9	0.0	0.0	0.0	0.0	0.3	0.0	0.0	0.1	0.0	0.0	0.1	0.5	0.0	..	RWA	0.0
Togo	TGO	0.0	0.5	0.0	0.0	0.0	0.0	0.0	0.0	0.0	0.0	0.0	1.4	0.0	0.0	0.0	0.0	0.4	0.0	..	0.0	0.0
Tunisia	TUN	0.1	0.0	0.0	0.0	0.0	0.0	0.0	2.7	0.0	0.0	2.0	0.1	0.0	0.6	0.0	0.0	0.0	0.0	..	0.0	0.0
Uganda	UGA	0.0	0.0	0.0	0.0	18.9	0.0	0.0	0.0	0.0	0.5	0.0	0.0	0.1	0.0	0.0	0.0	0.0	0.0	..	0.0	0.0
Zambia	ZMB	0.1	0.0	0.0	0.0	0.1	0.0	0.0	0.0	0.0	0.7	0.0	0.0	0.0	0.0	0.0	0.2	0.0	0.0	..	0.0	0.1
Zimbabwe	ZWE	0.0	0.0	0.0	0.0	0.1	0.0	0.0	0.0	0.0	0.7	0.1	0.0	0.4	0.0	5.1	0.6	0.0	0.0	..	0.0	0.2
Sub-Saharan Africa	SSA	4.2	11.8	5.9	2.3	36.0	0.0	1.9	0.2	3.5	13.9	9.9	12.9	3.9	1.8	12.4	1.6	47.6	11.9	..	2.0	0.4
European Community	EU	76.3	56.3	44.5	7.9	32.5	2.6	74.8	82.2	59.4	34.3	37.4	67.0	72.9	67.5	72.7	81.5	46.2	25.5	..	31.9	69.8
Canada	CAN	0.1	1.7	3.1	0.0	0.4	1.0	0.1	0.0	0.4	0.3	1.2	0.1	0.5	0.7	0.0	1.8	0.6	0.8	..	0.4	10.8
United States	USA	1.0	7.5	9.2	0.0	8.3	96.0	4.0	0.0	25.8	17.3	1.6	0.2	17.2	4.7	1.1	7.3	0.6	33.3	..	2.4	3.4
North America	NNA	1.1	9.2	12.3	0.0	8.7	97.0	4.1	0.0	26.2	17.6	2.8	0.2	17.8	5.4	1.1	9.1	1.2	34.1	..	2.9	14.2
Rest of World	ROW	18.4	22.6	37.4	89.8	22.8	0.3	19.2	17.6	10.9	34.2	49.9	19.8	5.4	25.3	13.8	7.8	5.1	28.5	..	63.3	15.6
World	WLD	100.0	100.0	100.0	100.0	100.0	100.0	100.0	100.0	100.0	100.0	100.0	100.0	100.0	100.0	100.0	100.0	100.0	100.0	..	100.0	100.0

Note: ** means "not applicable."

South Africa's data for 2002 is taken from partner countries' data.

Source: International Monetary Fund's Direction of Trade database.

(Table continues on the following page.)

5-49. Direction of trade matrix, imports, 2002 (continued)

		Importers														EU	CAN	USA	NNA	ROW	WLD
Exporters		SEN	SYC	SLE	SOM	ZAF	SDN	SWZ	TZA	TGO	TUN	UGA	ZMB	ZWE	SSA	EU	CAN	USA	NNA	ROW	WLD
Algeria	DZA	0.1	0.1	0.0	0.1	0.0	0.0	0.0	0.3	0.1	1.4	0.4	0.0	0.1	0.1	0.3	0.1	0.2	0.1	0.1	0.2
Angola	AGO	0.0	0.0	0.0	0.0	1.1	0.0	0.0	0.1	0.0	0.0	0.0	0.1	0.1	0.4	0.1	0.0	0.1	0.0	0.0	0.0
Benin	BEN	2.4	0.0	0.0	0.0	0.0	0.0	0.3	0.0	13.2	0.0	0.0	0.0	0.0	0.2	0.0	0.0	0.0	0.0	0.0	0.0
Bostwana	BWA	..	..	..	..	..	..	..	..	..	..	..	..	..	..	..	..	..	..	..	..
Burkina Faso	BFA	0.7	0.0	0.0	0.0	0.0	0.0	0.0	0.0	8.1	0.1	0.0	0.0	0.0	0.2	0.0	0.0	0.0	0.00	0.0	0.0
Burundi	BDI	0.0	0.0	0.0	0.0	0.0	0.0	0.0	1.0	0.0	0.0	0.0	0.1	0.3	0.0	0.0	0.0	0.0	0.0	0.0	0.0
Cameroon	CMR	0.8	0.0	0.0	0.0	0.1	0.0	0.0	0.0	0.6	0.0	0.0	0.0	0.1	0.5	0.1	0.0	0.0	0.0	0.0	0.0
Cape Verde	CPV	0.6	0.0	0.0	0.0	0.0	0.0	0.0	0.0	0.0	0.0	0.0	0.0	0.0	0.0	0.0	0.0	0.0	0.0	0.0	0.0
Central African Republic	CAF	0.1	0.0	0.0	0.0	0.0	0.0	0.0	0.0	0.0	0.0	0.0	0.0	0.0	0.0	0.0	0.0	0.0	0.0	0.0	0.0
Chad	TCD	0.1	0.0	0.0	0.0	0.0	0.0	0.0	0.0	0.5	0.0	0.0	0.0	0.0	0.0	0.0	0.0	0.0	0.0	0.0	0.0
Comoros	COM	0.0	0.0	0.0	0.0	0.0	0.0	0.0	0.0	0.0	0.0	0.0	0.0	0.0	0.0	0.0	0.0	0.0	0.0	0.0	0.0
Congo, Dem. Rep. of	ZAR	0.1	0.0	0.0	0.0	0.6	0.0	0.0	2.2	0.0	0.0	0.0	0.0	0.2	0.4	0.0	0.0	0.0	0.0	0.0	0.0
Congo, Rep. of	COG	1.0	0.0	0.0	0.0	0.1	0.0	0.0	0.0	0.4	0.1	0.0	0.0	0.0	0.1	0.0	0.0	0.0	0.0	0.0	0.0
Côte d'Ivoire	CIV	3.7	0.0	0.2	0.0	0.2	0.0	0.0	0.0	0.1	0.2	0.0	0.0	0.0	0.7	0.1	0.0	0.0	0.0	0.0	0.0
Djibouti	DJI	0.0	0.0	0.0	0.7	0.0	0.0	0.0	0.0	0.0	0.0	0.0	0.0	0.0	0.1	0.0	0.0	0.0	0.0	0.0	0.0
Egypt, Arab Rep.	EGY	0.0	0.0	0.0	0.8	0.1	3.4	0.0	0.2	0.8	0.4	0.8	6.6	0.1	0.3	0.3	0.0	0.4	0.3	0.3	0.3
Equatorial Guinea	GNQ	0.0	0.0	0.0	0.0	0.0	0.0	0.0	0.0	0.0	0.0	0.0	0.0	0.0	0.0	0.0	0.0	0.0	0.0	0.0	0.0
Eritrea	ERI	..	..	..	..	..	..	..	..	..	..	..	..	..	..	..	..	..	..	..	..
Ethiopia	ETH	0.0	0.0	0.0	0.0	0.1	0.1	0.0	0.1	0.0	0.0	0.0	0.0	0.0	0.1	0.0	0.0	0.0	0.0	0.0	0.0
Gabon	GAB	0.9	0.0	0.0	0.0	0.1	0.0	0.0	0.0	0.2	0.0	0.0	0.0	0.0	0.1	0.0	0.0	0.0	0.0	0.0	0.0
Gambia, The	GMB	3.7	0.0	0.3	0.0	0.0	0.0	0.0	0.0	0.0	0.0	0.0	0.0	0.0	0.1	0.0	0.0	0.0	0.0	0.0	0.0
Ghana	GHA	0.6	0.0	0.0	0.2	0.3	0.0	0.0	0.0	17.6	0.0	0.0	1.1	0.1	1.1	0.0	0.0	0.0	0.0	0.0	0.0
Guinea	GIN	1.8	0.0	0.0	0.0	0.0	0.0	0.0	0.0	0.0	0.0	0.0	0.0	0.0	0.1	0.0	0.0	0.0	0.0	0.0	0.0
Guinea-Bissau	GNB	2.2	0.0	0.0	0.0	0.0	0.0	0.0	0.0	0.0	0.0	0.0	0.0	0.0	0.0	0.0	0.0	0.0	0.0	0.0	0.0
Kenya	KEN	0.0	0.0	0.0	0.1	0.8	0.1	0.0	4.9	0.0	0.0	0.4	0.8	0.3	0.4	0.0	0.0	0.0	0.0	0.1	0.0
Lesotho	LSO	..	..	..	..	..	..	..	..	..	..	..	..	..	..	..	..	..	..	..	..
Liberia	LBR	0.3	0.0	0.0	0.0	0.0	0.0	0.0	0.0	0.1	0.0	0.0	0.0	0.0	0.1	0.1	0.0	0.0	0.0	0.1	0.1
Libya	LBY	0.0	0.0	0.0	0.0	0.0	0.0	0.0	0.0	0.0	4.8	0.0	0.0	0.0	0.0	0.1	0.0	0.0	0.0	0.1	0.1
Madagascar	MDG	0.0	0.9	0.0	0.0	0.1	0.0	0.3	0.1	0.0	0.0	0.0	0.0	0.0	0.1	0.0	0.0	0.0	0.0	0.0	0.0
Malawi	MWI	0.0	0.0	0.0	0.0	0.8	0.0	0.0	2.5	0.0	0.0	0.0	10.7	0.7	0.4	0.0	0.0	0.0	0.0	0.0	0.0
Mali	MLI	9.4	0.0	0.0	0.0	0.1	0.0	0.0	0.1	0.6	0.0	0.0	0.0	0.0	0.4	0.0	0.0	0.0	0.0	0.0	0.0
Mauritania	MRT	3.3	0.0	0.0	0.0	0.0	0.0	0.0	0.0	0.0	0.0	0.0	0.0	0.0	0.1	0.0	0.0	0.0	0.0	0.0	0.0
Mauritius	MUS	0.0	9.3	0.0	0.0	0.8	0.0	1.7	0.0	0.0	0.0	0.0	1.0	0.2	0.4	0.0	0.0	0.0	0.0	0.0	0.0
Morocco	MAR	0.3	0.0	0.9	0.0	0.4	0.0	0.0	0.1	1.4	0.7	0.4	0.0	0.1	0.2	0.3	0.0	0.1	0.1	0.1	0.2
Mozambique	MOZ	0.0	0.0	0.0	0.0	1.2	0.0	0.5	0.1	0.0	0.0	0.0	0.0	0.7	0.4	0.0	0.0	0.0	0.0	0.0	0.0
Namibia	NAM	..	..	..	..	..	..	..	..	..	..	..	..	..	..	..	..	..	..	..	..
Niger	NER	0.0	0.0	0.0	0.0	0.0	0.0	0.0	0.0	4.0	0.1	0.0	0.0	0.0	0.1	0.0	0.0	0.0	0.0	0.0	0.0
Nigeria	NGA	0.5	0.0	0.0	0.0	1.0	0.0	0.1	0.1	1.4	0.0	0.0	0.0	0.2	0.6	0.2	0.0	0.2	0.1	0.2	0.2
Reunion	REU	0.0	0.0	0.0	0.0	0.0	0.0	0.0	0.0	0.0	0.0	0.0	0.0	0.0	0.0	0.0	0.0	0.0	0.0	0.0	0.0
Rwanda	RWA	0.0	0.0	0.0	0.0	0.0	0.0	0.0	0.5	0.0	0.0	0.7	0.5	0.0	0.1	0.0	0.0	0.0	0.0	0.0	0.0
São Tomé and Principe	STP	0.0	0.0	0.0	0.0	0.0	0.0	0.0	0.0	0.0	0.0	0.0	0.0	0.0	0.0	0.0	0.0	0.0	0.0	0.0	0.0
Senegal	SEN	**	0.0	0.1	0.0	0.1	0.0	0.0	0.1	0.2	0.1	0.0	0.0	0.1	0.3	0.0	0.0	0.0	0.0	0.0	0.0
Seychelles	SYC	0.0	**	0.0	0.0	0.1	0.0	0.1	0.0	0.0	0.0	0.0	0.0	0.0	0.1	0.0	0.0	0.0	0.0	0.0	0.0
Sierra Leone	SLE	0.4	0.0	**	0.0	0.0	0.0	0.0	0.2	0.0	0.0	0.0	0.0	0.0	0.1	0.0	0.0	0.0	0.0	0.0	0.0
Somalia	SOM	0.0	0.0	0.0	**	0.0	0.0	0.0	0.1	0.0	0.0	0.0	0.0	0.0	0.1	0.0	0.0	0.0	0.0	0.0	0.0
South Africa	ZAF	0.0	0.3	1.7	0.0	**	0.0	0.0	1.1	1.3	0.1	0.5	10.2	13.5	0.9	0.5	0.1	0.4	0.3	0.3	0.4
Sudan	SDN	0.0	0.0	0.0	0.0	0.1	**	0.0	0.0	0.0	0.0	0.1	0.0	0.1	0.1	0.0	0.0	0.0	0.0	0.0	0.0
Swaziland	SWZ	..	..	..	..	..	..	**	..	..	..	..	..	..	..	..	..	..	..	..	..
Tanzania	TZA	0.0	0.0	0.0	0.0	0.6	0.0	3.5	**	0.0	0.0	0.7	0.6	0.1	0.3	0.0	0.0	0.0	0.0	0.0	0.0
Togo	TGO	1.0	0.0	0.0	0.0	0.0	0.0	0.0	0.0	**	0.0	0.0	0.0	0.0	0.1	0.0	0.0	0.0	0.0	0.0	0.0
Tunisia	TUN	0.3	0.0	0.0	0.0	0.0	0.3	0.2	0.0	0.5	**	0.3	0.0	0.0	0.1	0.3	0.0	0.0	0.0	0.1	0.1
Uganda	UGA	0.0	0.0	0.0	0.9	0.2	0.0	0.0	0.8	0.0	0.0	**	0.3	0.0	0.5	0.0	0.0	0.0	0.0	0.0	0.0
Zambia	ZMB	0.0	0.0	0.0	0.0	1.9	0.0	1.3	2.4	0.0	0.0	0.0	**	0.9	0.7	0.0	0.0	0.0	0.0	0.0	0.0
Zimbabwe	ZWE	0.0	0.0	0.0	0.0	2.5	0.0	2.6	0.2	0.0	0.0	0.0	2.2	**	1.1	0.0	0.0	0.0	0.0	0.0	0.0
Sub-Saharan Africa	SSA	33.8	10.5	2.4	1.3	13.2	0.3	10.4	16.6	48.4	1.0	2.6	27.5	17.5	11.2	1.5	0.2	0.9	0.7	1.1	1.3
European Community	EU	39.6	66.5	86.1	3.5	41.5	9.6	27.8	38.3	19.0	80.4	65.0	16.0	38.6	39.6	59.5	6.1	22.5	18.3	22.9	35.1
Canada	CAN	0.1	0.2	1.7	0.3	1.0	0.0	0.4	0.3	0.1	0.2	0.1	0.1	0.5	0.9	1.2	**	20.3	15.1	2.0	3.7
United States	USA	0.4	7.7	3.8	0.5	12.8	0.1	27.5	3.3	1.0	1.4	4.8	1.2	7.4	19.1	10.2	82.0	**	21.1	22.9	18.2
North America	NNA	0.5	7.8	5.5	0.8	13.8	0.1	27.9	3.7	1.1	1.5	4.9	1.3	7.8	20.0	11.3	82.0	20.3	36.2	24.9	21.9
Rest of World	ROW	26.1	15.2	6.0	94.4	31.5	90.0	33.9	41.5	31.4	17.1	27.5	55.2	36.1	29.2	27.6	11.7	56.2	44.8	51.2	41.7
World	WLD	100.0	100.0	100.0	100.0	100.0	100.0	100.0	100.0	100.0	100.0	100.0	100.0	100.0	100.0	100.0	100.0	100.0	100.0	100.0	100.0

Note: ** means "not applicable."

South Africa's data for 2002 is taken from partner countries' data.

Source: International Monetary Fund's Direction of Trade database.

5-50. Direction of trade matrix, exports, 1992

		Importers																	*Percentage of total exports*		
	Exporters	DZA	AGO	BEN	BWA	BFA	BDI	CMR	CPV	CAF	TCD	COM	ZAR	COG	CIV	DJI	EGY	GNQ	ERI	ETH	GAB
Algeria	DZA	**	0.0	0.0	0.0	0.0	0.0	0.0	0.0	0.0	0.0	0.0	0.0	0.0	0.0	0.0	0.0	0.0	..	0.0	0.0
Angola	AGO	0.0	**	0.0	0.0	0.0	0.0	0.0	0.8	0.0	0.0	0.0	0.0	0.1	0.0	0.0	0.0	0.0	..	0	0.0
Benin	BEN	0.0	0.0	**	0.0	0.3	0.0	0.0	0.7	0.0	0.0	0.0	0.0	0.1	0.1	0.0	0.0	0.0	..	0.0	0
Bostwana	BWA	..	..	..	**	..	..	..	..	..	..	..	..	..	..	..	..	..	..	..	..
Burkina Faso	BFA	0.0	0.0	0.0	0.0	**	0.0	0.0	0.0	0.0	0.0	0.0	0.0	0.0	0.8	0.0	0.0	0.0	..	0.0	0.0
Burundi	BDI	0.0	0.0	0.0	0.0	0.0	**	0.0	0.0	0.0	0.0	0.0	0.3	0.0	0.0	0.0	0.0	0.0	..	0.0	0.0
Cameroon	CMR	0.0	0.0	0.0	0.0	0.0	0.0	**	0.0	0.0	0.0	0.0	0.0	0.0	0.3	0.0	0.0	0.0	..	0.0	3.4
Cape Verde	CPV	0.0	0.0	0.0	0.0	0.0	0.0	0.0	**	0.0	0.0	0.0	0.0	0.0	0.0	0.0	0.0	0.0	..	0.0	0.0
Central African Republic	CAF	0.0	0.0	0.0	0.0	0.0	0.0	0.0	0.0	**	0.2	0.0	0.5	0	0.0	0.0	0.0	0.0	..	0.0	0.0
Chad	TCD	0.0	0.0	0.0	0.0	0.0	0.0	0.0	0.0	0.4	**	0.0	0.0	0.0	0	0.0	0.0	0.0	..	0.0	0.0
Comoros	COM	0.0	0.0	0.0	0.0	0.0	0.0	0.0	0.0	0.0	0.0	**	0.0	0.0	0	0.0	0.0	0.0	..	0.0	0.0
Congo, Dem. Rep. of	ZAR	0.0	0.0	0.1	0.0	0.0	0.7	0.0	0.0	2.0	0.0	0.0	**	0.4	0.1	0.0	0	0.0	..	0.0	0.1
Congo, Rep. of	COG	0.2	0.3	0.0	0.0	0.0	0.0	0.0	0.0	0.0	0.0	0.0	0.5	**	0.0	0.0	0.0	0.0	..	0.0	0.0
Côte d'Ivoire	CIV	0.0	0.1	4.0	0.0	30.3	0.2	0.0	10.2	10.4	0.7	0.0	2.2	1.2	**	0.0	0.0	5.3	..	0.0	1.3
Djibouti	DJI	0.0	0.0	0.0	0.0	0.0	0.1	0.0	0.0	0.0	0.0	0.0	0.0	0.0	0.0	**	0.0	0.0	..	3.7	0.0
Egypt, Arab Rep.	EGY	0.4	0.0	0.0	0.0	0.0	0.0	0.1	0.0	0.1	0.0	0.0	0.2	0.0	0.0	0.7	**	0	..	0.2	0.0
Equatorial Guinea	GNQ	0.0	0.0	0.0	0.0	0.0	0.0	0.0	0.0	0.0	0.0	0.0	0.0	0.0	0.3	0.0	0.0	**	..	0.0	0.0
Eritrea	ERI	..	..	..	..	..	..	..	..	..	..	..	..	..	..	..	..	..	**	..	..
Ethiopia	ETH	0.0	0.0	0.0	0.0	0.0	0.0	0.0	0.0	0.0	0.0	0.0	0.0	0.0	0.0	3.0	0.0	0.0	..	**	0.0
Gabon	GAB	0.0	0.0	0.1	0.0	0.0	0.0	0.0	0.0	0.9	0.0	0.0	0.0	0.0	0.1	0.0	0.0	0.0	..	0.0	**
Gambia, The	GMB	0.0	0.0	0.0	0.0	0.0	0.0	0.0	0.0	0.0	0.0	0.0	0.0	0.0	0.0	0.0	0.0	0.0	..	0.0	0.0
Ghana	GHA	0.0	0.2	0.0	0.0	0.0	0.0	0.0	0.0	0.0	0.0	0.0	0.0	0.0	3.1	0.0	0.0	0.0	..	0.1	0.0
Guinea	GIN	0.0	0.0	0.0	0.0	0.0	0.0	2.8	0.0	0.0	0.0	0.0	0.0	0.0	0.3	0.0	0.0	0.0	..	0.0	0.0
Guinea-Bissau	GNB	0.0	0.0	0.0	0.0	0.0	0.0	0.0	0.0	0.0	0.0	0.0	0.0	0.0	0.1	0.0	0.0	0.0	..	0.0	0.0
Kenya	KEN	0.0	0.0	0.0	0.0	0.0	3.8	0.0	0.0	0.0	0.0	4.0	1.0	0.0	0.0	0.8	0.3	0.0	..	1.0	0.0
Lesotho	LSO	..	..	..	..	..	..	..	..	..	..	..	..	..	..	..	..	..	..	..	..
Liberia	LBR	0.0	0.0	0.0	0.0	0.0	0.0	0.0	0.0	0.0	0.0	0.0	0.0	0.0	0.0	0.0	0.0	0.0	..	0.0	0.0
Libya	LBY	0.0	0.0	0.0	0.0	0.0	0.0	0.0	0.0	0.0	0.0	0.0	0.0	0.0	0.0	0.0	0.4	0.0	..	0.0	0.0
Madagascar	MDG	0.0	0.0	0.0	0.0	0.0	0.0	0.0	0.0	0.0	0.0	1.4	0.0	0.0	0.0	0.0	0.0	0.0	..	0.0	0.0
Malawi	MWI	0.0	0.0	0.0	1.0	0.0	0.0	0.0	0.0	0.0	0.0	0.0	0.3	0.0	0.0	0.0	0.0	0.0	..	0.0	0.0
Mali	MLI	0.0	0.0	0.0	0.0	0.4	0.0	0.0	0.0	0.0	0.0	0.0	0.0	0.8	0.4	0.0	0.0	0.0	..	0.0	0.0
Mauritania	MRT	0.0	0.0	0.6	0.0	0.4	0.0	0.0	0.0	0.0	0.0	0.0	0.0	0.7	1.2	0.0	0.0	0.3	..	0.0	0.0
Mauritius	MUS	0.0	0.0	0.0	0.0	0.0	0.0	0.0	0.0	0.0	0.0	1.9	0.0	0.0	0.0	0.0	0.0	0.0	..	0.0	0.0
Morocco	MAR	1.0	0.4	0.3	0.0	0.2	0.4	0.7	0.0	0.5	0.0	0.5	0.4	0.7	0.3	0.0	0.0	1.2	..	0.2	0.9
Mozambique	MOZ	0.0	0.0	0.0	0.0	0.0	0.0	0.0	0.0	0.0	0.0	0.0	0.0	0.0	0.0	0.0	0.0	0.0	..	0.0	0.0
Namibia	NAM	..	..	..	..	..	..	..	..	..	..	..	..	..	..	..	..	..	..	..	..
Niger	NER	0.0	0.0	0.5	0.0	0.2	0.0	0.0	0.0	0.0	0.2	0.0	0.0	0.0	0.1	0.0	0.0	0.0	..	0.0	0.0
Nigeria	NGA	0.0	0.0	1.5	0.0	2.9	0.0	0.6	0.0	0.1	7.1	0.1	5.6	0.4	17.6	0.0	0.0	0.0	..	0.0	2.7
Reunion	REU	0.0	0.0	0.0	0.0	0.0	0.0	0.0	0.0	0.0	0.0	1.6	0.0	0.0	0.0	0.1	0.0	0.0	..	0.0	0.0
Rwanda	RWA	0.0	0.0	0.0	0.0	0.0	0.1	0.0	0.0	0.0	0.0	0.0	0.0	0.0	0.0	0.0	0.0	0.0	..	0.0	0.0
São Tomé and Principe	STP	0.0	0.0	0.0	0.0	0.0	0.0	0.0	0.0	0.0	0.0	0.0	0.0	0.0	0.0	0.0	0.0	0.0	..	0.0	0.0
Senegal	SEN	0.0	0.2	1.2	0.0	0.6	0.0	2.3	0.0	0.2	0.4	0.0	0.0	0.7	0.0	0.0	0.0	0.0	..	0.0	0.4
Seychelles	SYC	0.0	0.0	0.0	0.0	0.0	0.0	0.0	0.0	0.0	0.0	0.0	0.0	0.0	0.0	0.0	0.0	0.0	..	0.0	0.0
Sierra Leone	SLE	0.0	0.0	0.0	0.0	0.0	0.0	0.0	0.0	0.0	0.0	0.0	0.0	0.0	0.0	0.0	0.0	0.0	..	0.0	0.0
Somalia	SOM	0.0	0.0	0.0	0.0	0.0	0.0	0.0	0.0	0.0	0.0	0.0	0.0	0.0	0.0	0.0	0.0	0.0	..	0.0	0.0
South Africa	ZAF	0.0	5.8	0.0	0.0	0.0	0.0	0.0	0.0	0.2	0.0	11.5	0.0	0.9	0.6	0.0	0.0	0.0	..	0.0	0.6
Sudan	SDN	0.0	0.0	0.0	0.0	0.0	0.0	0.0	0.0	0.0	0.0	0.0	0.0	0.0	0.0	0.0	0.2	0.0	..	0.0	0.0
Swaziland	SWZ	..	..	..	..	..	..	..	..	..	..	..	..	..	..	..	..	..	..	..	..
Tanzania	TZA	0.0	0.0	0.0	0.3	0.0	10.3	0.0	0.0	0.0	0.0	0.0	0.3	0.0	0.0	0.1	0.0	0.0	..	0.0	0.0
Togo	TGO	0.0	0.0	0.1	0.0	3.4	0.0	0.0	0.0	0.1	0.0	0.0	0.0	0.2	0.0	0.0	0.0	0.0	..	0.0	0.1
Tunisia	TUN	1.3	0.0	0.5	0.0	0.0	0.0	0.7	0.0	0.0	0.0	0.0	0.0	0.0	0.2	0.0	0.1	0.0	..	0.5	0.0
Uganda	UGA	0.0	0.0	0.0	0.0	0.0	0.0	0.0	0.0	0.0	0.0	0.0	0.0	0.0	0.0	0.0	0.0	0.0	..	0.0	0.0
Zambia	ZMB	0.0	0.0	0.0	0.8	0.0	0.6	0.0	0.0	0.0	0.0	0.0	0.7	0.0	0.0	0.0	0.0	0.0	..	0.0	0.0
Zimbabwe	ZWE	0.0	0.2	0.0	24.2	0.0	0.5	0.0	0.1	0.0	0.0	0.0	0.5	0.0	0.0	0.0	0.0	0.0	..	0.0	0.0
Sub-Saharan Africa	SSA	0.3	6.9	8.1	26.3	38.5	16.3	5.8	11.8	14.4	8.7	20.5	12.1	5.5	25.2	4.0	0.6	5.7	..	1.1	8.7
European Community	EU	72.1	74.5	52.6	32.6	46.4	58.4	70.1	72.6	73.3	80.1	63.1	52.2	63.3	56.3	45.1	39.2	69.1	..	42.8	69.0
Canada	CAN	1.6	0.2	0.2	1.0	1.1	0.2	1.4	0.0	0.1	0.1	0.0	0.9	0.1	0.2	0.1	0.7	0.0	..	0.9	0.7
United States	USA	9.2	6.5	4.8	17.3	2.9	5.7	4.8	2.5	0.8	4.2	0.6	4.5	8.7	4.0	2.5	24.7	19.2	..	21.8	6.5
North America	NNA	10.9	6.7	5.0	18.3	4.0	5.9	6.2	2.5	0.9	4.2	0.6	5.3	8.8	4.2	2.6	25.4	19.2	..	22.8	7.2
Rest of World	ROW	16.7	11.9	34.3	22.7	11.0	19.5	17.8	13.0	11.4	6.9	15.8	30.3	22.5	14.3	48.2	34.7	6.0	..	33.4	15.1
World	WLD	100.0	100.0	100.0	100.0	100.0	100.0	100.0	100.0	100.0	100.0	100.0	100.0	100.0	100.0	100.0	100.0	100.0	..	100.0	100.0

Note: ** means "not applicable."

South Africa's data for 1992 is taken from partner countries' data.

Source: International Monetary Fund's Direction of Trade database.

(Table continues on the following page.)

5-50. Direction of trade matrix, exports, 1992 (continued)

Importers / Exporters		GMB	GHA	GIN	GNB	KEN	LSO	LBR	LBY	MDG	MWI	MLI	MRT	MUS	MAR	MOZ	NAM	NER	NGA	REU	RWA	STP
Algeria	DZA	0.0	0.0	0.1	0.0	0.0	0.0	0.2	0.1	0.0	0.0	0.0	3.0	0.0	1.8	0.0	0.0	0.0	0.0	0.0	0.0	0.0
Angola	AGO	0.0	0.0	0.0	0.0	0.0	0.0	0.0	0.0	0.0	0.0	0.0	0.0	0.0	0.0	0.0	0.0	0.0	0.0	0.0	0.0	0.0
Benin	BEN	0.0	0.0	0.0	0.0	0.0	0.0	0.0	0.0	0.4	0.0	0.1	0.0	0.0	0.1	0.0	0.0	0.2	0.0	0.0	0.0	0.0
Bostwana	BWA	..	..	..	..	..	..	..	..	..	..	..	..	..	..	..	..	..	..	..	..	..
Burkina Faso	BFA	0.0	0.1	0.0	0.0	0.0	0.0	0.0	0.0	0.0	0.0	0.1	0.0	0.0	0.0	0.0	0.0	0.1	0.0	0.0	0.0	0.0
Burundi	BDI	0.0	0.0	0.0	0.0	0.2	0.0	0.0	0.0	0.0	0.0	0.0	0.0	0.0	0.0	0.0	0.0	0.0	0.0	0.0	2.7	0.0
Cameroon	CMR	0.0	0.0	0.9	0.0	0.0	0.0	0.0	0.0	0.0	0.0	0.0	0.0	0.0	0.6	0.0	0.0	0.0	0.1	0.0	0.0	0.0
Cape Verde	CPV	0.0	0.0	0.0	0.2	0.0	0.0	0.0	0.0	0.0	0.0	0.0	0.0	0.0	0.0	0.0	0.0	0.0	0.0	0.0	0.0	0.0
Central African Republic	CAF	0.0	0.0	0.0	0.0	0.0	0.0	0.0	0.0	0.0	0.0	0.0	0.0	0.0	0.0	0.0	0.0	0.0	0.0	0.0	0.0	0.0
Chad	TCD	0.0	0.0	0.0	0.0	0.0	0.0	0.0	0.0	0.0	0.0	0.0	0.0	0.0	0.0	0.0	0.0	0.0	0.0	0.0	0.0	0.0
Comoros	COM	0.0	0.0	0.0	0.0	0.0	0.0	0.0	0.0	0.0	0.0	0.0	0.0	0.0	0.0	0.0	0.0	0.0	0.0	0.0	0.0	0.0
Congo, Dem. Rep. of	ZAR	0.0	0.0	0.0	0.0	0.0	0.0	0.0	0.0	0.0	0.0	0.0	0.0	0.0	0.0	0.0	0.0	0.0	0.0	0.0	0.9	0.0
Congo, Rep. of	COG	0.0	0.0	0.0	0.0	0.0	0.0	0.0	0.0	0.0	0.0	0.0	0.0	0.0	0.1	0.0	0.0	0.0	0.1	0.1	0.0	0.0
Côte d'Ivoire	CIV	3.6	3.9	11.7	4.7	0.0	0.0	0.4	0.0	0.0	0.0	23.4	3.1	0.8	0.2	0.3	0.0	9.0	1.3	0.0	0.0	0.0
Djibouti	DJI	0.0	0.0	0.0	0.0	0.0	0.0	0.0	0.0	0.0	0.0	0.0	0.0	0.0	0.0	0.0	0.0	0.0	0.0	0.0	0.0	0.0
Egypt, Arab Rep.	EGY	0.0	0.0	0.0	0.1	0.1	0.0	0.3	1.2	0.0	0.2	0.0	0.0	0.0	0.1	0.1	0.0	0.0	0.0	0.0	0.0	0.0
Equatorial Guinea	GNQ	0.0	0.0	0.0	0.0	0.0	0.0	0.0	0.0	0.0	0.0	0.0	0.0	0.0	0.0	0.0	0.0	0.0	0.0	0.0	0.0	0.0
Eritrea	ERI	..	..	..	..	..	..	..	..	..	..	..	..	..	..	..	..	..	..	..	..	..
Ethiopia	ETH	0.0	0.0	0.0	0.0	0.0	0.0	0.0	0.0	0.0	0.0	0.0	0.0	0.0	0.0	0.0	0.0	0.0	0.0	0.0	0.0	0.0
Gabon	GAB	0.0	0.0	0.0	0.0	0.0	0.0	0.0	0.0	0.1	0.0	0.0	0.1	0.0	0.3	0.0	0.0	0.0	0.0	0.0	0.0	0.1
Gambia, The	GMB	**	0.0	1.0	0.3	0.0	0.0	0.0	0.0	0.0	0.0	0.0	0.0	0.0	0.0	0.0	0.0	0.0	0.0	0.0	0.0	0.0
Ghana	GHA	0.0	**	0.0	0.0	0.0	0.0	0.0	0.0	0.0	0.0	0.0	0.0	0.0	0.0	0.0	0.0	0.0	0.5	0.0	0.0	0.0
Guinea	GIN	0.0	0.0	**	0.1	0.0	0.0	0.0	0.0	0.0	0.0	0.0	0.0	0.0	0.0	0.0	0.0	0.0	0.0	0.0	0.0	0.0
Guinea-Bissau	GNB	0.0	0.0	0.0	**	0.0	0.0	0.0	0.0	0.0	0.0	0.0	0.0	0.0	0.0	0.0	0.0	0.0	0.0	0.0	0.0	0.0
Kenya	KEN	0.0	0.0	0.0	0.0	**	0.0	0.0	0.0	0.2	0.2	0.0	0.0	0.5	0.0	0.0	0.0	0.0	0.0	0.2	6.4	0.0
Lesotho	LSO	..	..	..	..	..	**	..	..	..	..	..	..	..	..	..	..	..	..	..	..	..
Liberia	LBR	0.0	0.0	0.0	0.0	0.0	0.0	**	0.0	0.0	0.0	0.0	0.0	0.0	0.0	0.0	0.0	0.0	0.0	0.0	0.0	0.0
Libya	LBY	0.0	0.0	0.0	0.0	0.0	0.0	0.0	**	0.0	0.0	0.0	0.1	0.0	1.2	0.0	0.0	0.0	0.0	0.0	0.0	0.0
Madagascar	MDG	0.0	0.0	0.0	0.0	0.1	0.0	0.0	0.0	**	0.0	0.0	0.0	0.6	0.0	0.0	0.0	0.0	0.0	0.6	0.0	0.0
Malawi	MWI	0.0	0.0	0.0	0.0	0.0	0.0	0.0	0.0	0.0	**	0.0	0.0	0.0	0.0	0.3	0.0	0.0	0.0	0.0	0.0	0.0
Mali	MLI	0.0	0.0	0.0	0.0	0.0	0.0	0.0	0.0	0.0	0.0	**	0.0	0.0	0.0	0.0	0.0	0.1	0.0	0.0	0.0	0.0
Mauritania	MRT	0.0	0.0	0.0	0.0	0.0	0.0	0.1	0.0	0.0	0.0	0.0	**	0.0	0.0	0.0	0.0	0.0	0.0	0.0	0.0	0.0
Mauritius	MUS	0.0	0.0	0.0	0.0	0.1	0.0	0.0	0.0	3.3	0.0	0.0	0.0	**	0.0	0.0	0.0	0.0	0.0	1.4	1.0	0.0
Morocco	MAR	0.1	0.1	1.0	0.1	0.1	0.0	0.0	2.8	0.2	0.0	1.1	1.3	0.1	**	0.0	0.0	0.1	0.1	0.1	0.0	0.0
Mozambique	MOZ	0.0	0.0	0.0	0.0	0.0	0.0	0.0	0.0	0.0	0.0	0.0	0.0	0.1	0.0	**	0.0	0.0	0.0	0.0	0.0	0.0
Namibia	NAM	..	..	..	..	..	..	..	..	..	..	..	..	..	..	..	**	..	..	..	..	..
Niger	NER	0.0	0.1	0.0	0.0	0.0	0.0	0.0	0.0	0.0	0.0	0.2	0.0	0.0	0.0	0.0	0.0	**	0.7	0.0	0.0	0.0
Nigeria	NGA	0.1	16.7	2.0	0.0	0.0	0.0	0.0	0.0	0.6	0.0	0.1	0.0	0.0	0.0	0.0	0.0	0.9	**	0.0	0.0	0.0
Reunion	REU	0.0	0.0	0.0	0.0	0.0	0.0	0.0	0.0	1.3	0.0	0.0	0.0	0.2	0.0	0.0	0.0	0.0	0.0	**	0.0	0.0
Rwanda	RWA	0.0	0.0	0.0	0.0	0.0	0.0	0.0	0.0	0.0	0.0	0.0	0.0	0.0	0.0	0.0	0.0	0.0	0.0	0.0	**	0.0
São Tomé and Principe	STP	0.0	0.0	0.0	0.0	0.0	0.0	0.0	0.0	0.0	0.0	0.0	0.0	0.0	0.0	0.0	0.0	0.0	0.0	0.0	0.0	**
Senegal	SEN	3.3	0.0	2.4	3.1	0.0	0.0	0.0	0.0	0.0	0.0	7.8	0.8	0.0	0.0	0.0	0.0	0.2	0.1	0.0	0.0	0.0
Seychelles	SYC	0.0	0.0	0.0	0.0	0.0	0.0	0.0	0.0	0.0	0.0	0.0	0.0	0.1	0.0	0.0	0.0	0.0	0.0	0.0	0.0	0.0
Sierra Leone	SLE	0.0	0.0	0.0	0.0	0.0	0.0	0.0	0.0	0.0	0.0	0.0	0.0	0.0	0.0	0.0	0.0	0.0	0.0	0.0	0.0	0.0
Somalia	SOM	0.0	0.0	0.0	0.0	0.0	0.0	0.0	0.0	0.0	0.0	0.0	0.0	0.0	0.0	0.0	0.0	0.0	0.0	0.0	0.0	0.0
South Africa	ZAF	0.4	0.1	0.6	0.0	0.0	0.0	0.0	0.0	5.9	44.1	0.1	0.0	15.8	0.0	25.4	0.0	0.0	0.0	2.6	0.5	4.8
Sudan	SDN	0.0	0.0	0.0	0.0	0.1	0.0	0.0	0.1	0.0	0.0	0.0	0.0	0.0	0.0	0.0	0.0	0.0	0.0	0.0	0.0	0.0
Swaziland	SWZ	..	..	..	..	..	..	..	..	..	..	..	..	..	..	..	..	..	..	..	..	..
Tanzania	TZA	0.0	0.0	0.0	0.0	0.4	0.0	0.0	0.0	0.2	0.2	0.0	0.0	0.1	0.0	0.1	0.0	0.0	0.0	0.0	10.2	0.0
Togo	TGO	0.0	0.3	0.0	0.0	0.0	0.0	0.0	0.0	0.0	0.0	0.2	0.0	0.0	0.0	0.0	0.0	1.2	0.2	0.0	0.0	0.0
Tunisia	TUN	0.0	0.4	0.0	0.0	0.1	0.0	0.0	3.9	0.0	0.0	0.0	0.0	0.0	0.6	0.0	0.0	0.0	0.0	0.0	0.0	0.0
Uganda	UGA	0.0	0.0	0.0	0.0	0.2	0.0	0.0	0.0	0.0	0.0	0.0	0.0	0.0	0.0	0.0	0.0	0.0	0.0	0.0	0.3	0.0
Zambia	ZMB	0.0	0.0	0.0	0.0	1.4	0.0	0.0	0.0	0.0	0.8	0.0	0.0	0.0	0.0	0.0	0.4	0.0	0.0	0.0	0.0	0.0
Zimbabwe	ZWE	0.0	0.2	0.0	0.0	0.9	0.7	0.0	0.1	0.0	6.6	0.0	0.0	0.2	0.0	4.1	1.3	0.0	0.0	0.0	0.0	0.1
Sub-Saharan Africa	SSA	7.6	21.5	18.6	8.3	3.4	0.8	0.5	0.3	12.2	52.0	32.0	4.1	18.4	1.6	30.3	1.7	11.8	3.1	5.0	21.9	5.0
European Community	EU	42.1	43.9	49.1	55.6	39.5	54.3	22.3	62.7	56.4	24.8	49.7	59.7	36.8	64.5	28.2	68.7	66.1	51.6	84.0	50.8	65.0
Canada	CAN	0.0	1.3	0.2	0.0	1.0	0.0	0.0	1.4	0.2	0.4	1.0	0.2	0.1	1.3	1.6	0.8	0.3	0.5	0.0	1.2	0.4
United States	USA	2.9	7.4	7.8	1.3	6.5	4.4	0.6	0.0	1.4	2.2	2.2	11.5	1.6	6.4	14.5	20.9	4.3	11.6	0.2	1.3	8.1
North America	NNA	2.9	8.7	8.0	1.3	7.5	4.5	0.6	1.4	1.6	2.6	3.2	11.7	1.7	7.7	16.1	21.6	4.6	12.1	0.2	2.5	8.5
Rest of World	ROW	47.4	26.0	24.3	34.9	49.5	40.5	76.6	35.7	29.8	20.5	15.1	24.6	43.1	26.1	25.5	8.0	17.5	33.2	10.9	24.8	21.5
World	WLD	100.0	100.0	100.0	100.0	100.0	100.0	100.0	100.0	100.0	100.0	100.0	100.0	100.0	100.0	100.0	100.0	100.0	100.0	100.0	100.0	100.0

Note: ** means "not applicable."
South Africa's data for 1992 is taken from partner countries' data.
Source: International Monetary Fund's Direction of Trade database.

(Table continues on the following page.)

5-50. Direction of trade matrix, exports, 1992 (continued)

Percentage of total exports

	Exporters	SEN	SYC	SLE	SOM	ZAF	SDN	SWZ	TZA	TGO	TUN	UGA	ZMB	ZWE	SSA	EU	CAN	USA	NNA	ROW	WLD
Algeria	DZA	0.1	0.0	0.0	0.0	0.0	0.0	0.0	0.0	0.0	1.3	0.0	0.0	0.0	0.0	0.5	0.0	0.3	0.2	0.1	0.3
Angola	AGO	1.2	0.0	0.0	0.0	0.0	0.0	0.0	0.0	0.1	0.0	0.0	0.0	0.0	0.0	0.1	0.0	0.4	0.3	0.0	0.1
Benin	BEN	0.0	0.0	0.0	0.0	0.0	0.0	0.0	0.0	0.2	0.0	0.0	0.0	0.0	0.0	0.0	0.0	0.0	0.0	0.0	0.0
Bostwana	BWA	..	..	..	..	..	..	..	..	..	..	..	..	..	..	..	..	..	..	..	..
Burkina Faso	BFA	0.0	0.0	0.0	0.0	0.0	0.0	0.0	0.0	0.3	0.0	0.0	0.0	0.0	0.0	0.0	0.0	0.0	0.0	0.0	0.0
Burundi	BDI	0.0	0.0	0.0	0.0	0.0	0.0	0.0	0.1	0.0	0.0	0.1	0.0	0.1	0.0	0.0	0.0	0.0	0.0	0.0	0.0
Cameroon	CMR	0.2	0.0	0.0	0.0	0.1	0.0	0.0	0.0	0.0	0.0	0.0	0.0	0.0	0.1	0.1	0.0	0.0	0.0	0.0	0.0
Cape Verde	CPV	0.0	0.0	0.0	0.0	0.0	0.0	0.0	0.0	0.0	0.0	0.0	0.0	0.0	0.0	0.0	0.0	0.0	0.0	0.0	0.0
Central African Republic	CAF	0.0	0.0	0.0	0.0	0.0	0.3	0.0	0.0	0.0	0.0	0.0	0.0	0.0	0.0	0.0	0.0	0.0	0.0	0.0	0.0
Chad	TCD	0.0	0.0	0.0	0.0	0.0	0.0	0.0	0.0	0.0	0.0	0.0	0.0	0.0	0.0	0.0	0.0	0.0	0.0	0.0	0.0
Comoros	COM	0.0	0.0	0.0	0.0	0.0	0.0	0.0	0.0	0.0	0.0	0.0	0.0	0.0	0.0	0.0	0.0	0.0	0.0	0.0	0.0
Congo, Dem. Rep. of	ZAR	0.0	0.0	0.0	0.0	0.0	0.0	0.0	0.0	0.0	0.0	0.0	0.2	0.0	0.0	0.1	0.0	0.0	0.0	0.0	0.0
Congo, Rep. of	COG	0.0	0.0	0.0	0.0	0.0	0.0	0.0	0.0	0.1	0.0	0.0	0.0	0.0	0.0	0.0	0.0	0.1	0.1	0.0	0.0
Côte d'Ivoire	CIV	7.2	0.0	12.3	0.0	0.4	0.0	0.0	0.2	3.6	0.3	0.0	0.0	0.0	1.5	0.1	0.0	0.0	0.0	0.0	0.1
Djibouti	DJI	0.0	0.0	0.0	13.1	0.0	0.0	0.0	0.0	0.0	0.0	0.0	0.0	0.0	0.1	0.0	0.0	0.0	0.0	0.0	0.0
Egypt, Arab Rep.	EGY	0.0	0.0	0.0	0.0	0.0	3.9	0.0	0.0	0.0	0.3	0.1	0.0	0.0	0.1	0.1	0.0	0.1	0.0	0.1	0.1
Equatorial Guinea	GNQ	0.0	0.0	0.0	0.0	0.0	0.0	0.0	0.0	0.0	0.0	0.0	0.0	0.0	0.0	0.0	0.0	0.0	0.0	0.0	0.0
Eritrea	ERI	..	..	..	..	..	..	..	..	..	..	..	..	..	..	..	..	..	..	..	..
Ethiopia	ETH	0.0	0.0	0.0	0.0	0.0	0.0	0.0	0.0	0.0	0.0	0.0	0.0	0.0	0.0	0.0	0.0	0.0	0.0	0.0	0.0
Gabon	GAB	1.2	0.0	0.0	0.0	0.0	0.0	0.0	0.0	0.4	0.0	0.0	0.0	0.0	0.0	0.1	0.0	0.2	0.1	0.0	0.1
Gambia, The	GMB	0.1	0.0	0.0	0.0	0.0	0.0	0.0	0.0	0.0	0.0	0.0	0.0	0.0	0.0	0.0	0.0	0.0	0.0	0.0	0.0
Ghana	GHA	0.0	0.0	0.0	0.0	0.0	0.0	0.0	0.0	10.8	0.0	0.0	0.0	0.0	0.3	0.0	0.0	0.0	0.0	0.0	0.0
Guinea	GIN	0.0	0.0	0.0	0.0	0.0	0.0	0.0	0.0	0.0	0.0	0.0	0.0	0.0	0.1	0.0	0.0	0.0	0.0	0.0	0.0
Guinea-Bissau	GNB	0.0	0.0	0.0	0.0	0.0	0.0	0.0	0.0	0.0	0.0	0.0	0.0	0.0	0.0	0.0	0.0	0.0	0.0	0.0	0.0
Kenya	KEN	0.0	0.5	0.0	15.2	0.0	1.1	0.0	3.2	0.0	0.0	19.9	0.3	0.2	0.4	0.0	0.0	0.0	0.0	0.0	0.0
Lesotho	LSO	..	..	..	..	..	..	..	..	..	..	..	..	..	..	..	..	..	..	..	..
Liberia	LBR	0.0	0.0	0.2	0.0	0.0	0.0	0.0	0.0	0.0	0.0	0.0	0.0	0.0	0.0	0.0	0.0	0.0	0.0	0.0	0.0
Libya	LBY	0.0	0.0	0.0	0.0	0.0	14.5	0.0	0.0	0.0	0.8	0.0	0.0	0.0	0.3	0.5	0.0	0.0	0.0	0.1	0.3
Madagascar	MDG	0.1	0.0	0.0	0.0	0.0	0.0	0.0	0.0	0.0	0.0	0.0	0.0	0.0	0.0	0.0	0.0	0.0	0.0	0.0	0.0
Malawi	MWI	0.0	0.0	0.2	0.0	0.3	0.0	0.0	0.2	0.0	0.0	0.0	0.2	0.2	0.1	0.0	0.0	0.0	0.0	0.0	0.0
Mali	MLI	0.1	0.0	0.0	0.0	0.0	0.0	0.0	0.0	0.0	0.1	0.0	0.0	0.1	0.0	0.0	0.0	0.0	0.0	0.0	0.0
Mauritania	MRT	0.0	0.0	0.0	0.0	0.0	0.0	0.0	0.0	0.4	0.0	0.0	0.0	0.0	0.1	0.0	0.0	0.0	0.0	0.0	0.0
Mauritius	MUS	0.0	1.6	0.0	0.0	0.1	0.0	0.0	0.0	0.0	0.0	0.0	0.0	0.2	0.1	0.1	0.0	0.0	0.0	0.0	0.0
Morocco	MAR	0.5	0.0	0.2	0.0	0.0	0.1	0.0	0.0	0.4	0.8	0.0	0.0	0.0	0.2	0.2	0.0	0.0	0.0	0.1	0.1
Mozambique	MOZ	0.0	0.0	0.0	0.0	0.1	0.0	0.0	0.0	0.0	0.0	0.0	0.0	0.5	0.0	0.0	0.0	0.0	0.0	0.0	0.0
Namibia	NAM	..	..	..	..	..	..	..	..	..	..	..	..	..	..	..	..	..	..	..	..
Niger	NER	0.0	0.0	0.0	0.0	0.0	0.0	0.0	0.0	0.2	0.0	0.0	0.0	0.0	0.1	0.0	0.0	0.0	0.0	0.0	0.0
Nigeria	NGA	5.7	0.0	3.1	0.0	0.0	0.0	0.0	0.0	0.3	0.0	0.0	0.1	0.1	1.5	0.3	0.3	0.9	0.8	0.1	0.3
Reunion	REU	0.0	0.1	0.0	0.0	0.0	0.0	0.0	0.0	0.0	0.0	0.0	0.0	0.0	0.0	0.0	0.0	0.0	0.0	0.0	0.0
Rwanda	RWA	0.0	0.0	0.0	0.0	0.0	0.0	0.0	0.0	0.0	0.0	0.0	0.0	0.0	0.0	0.0	0.0	0.0	0.0	0.0	0.0
São Tomé and Principe	STP	0.0	0.0	0.0	0.0	0.0	0.0	0.0	0.0	0.0	0.0	0.0	0.0	0.0	0.0	0.0	0.0	0.0	0.0	0.0	0.0
Senegal	SEN	**	0.0	0.8	0.0	0.0	0.0	0.0	0.0	0.4	0.0	0.0	0.0	0.0	0.2	0.0	0.0	0.0	0.0	0.0	0.0
Seychelles	SYC	0.0	**	0.0	0.0	0.0	0.0	0.0	0.0	0.0	0.0	0.0	0.0	0.0	0.0	0.0	0.0	0.0	0.0	0.0	0.0
Sierra Leone	SLE	0.0	0.0	**	0.0	0.0	0.0	0.0	0.0	0.0	0.0	0.0	0.0	0.0	0.0	0.0	0.0	0.0	0.0	0.0	0.0
Somalia	SOM	0.0	0.0	0.0	**	0.0	0.0	0.0	0.0	0.0	0.0	0.0	0.0	0.0	0.0	0.0	0.0	0.0	0.0	0.0	0.0
South Africa	ZAF	0.0	16.3	0.0	0.0	**	0.7	0.0	0.8	0.5	0.0	0.3	21.9	35.0	3.1	0.5	0.1	0.3	0.3	0.4	0.5
Sudan	SDN	0.0	0.0	0.0	0.1	0.0	**	0.0	0.0	0.0	0.1	0.0	0.0	0.0	0.0	0.0	0.0	0.0	0.0	0.0	0.0
Swaziland	SWZ	..	..	..	..	..	..	**	..	..	..	..	..	..	..	..	..	..	..	..	..
Tanzania	TZA	0.0	0.0	0.0	0.7	0.0	0.2	0.0	**	0.0	0.0	1.3	0.3	0.4	0.1	0.0	0.0	0.0	0.0	0.0	0.0
Togo	TGO	0.0	0.0	0.0	0.0	0.1	0.0	0.0	0.0	**	0.0	0.0	0.0	0.0	0.1	0.0	0.0	0.0	0.0	0.0	0.0
Tunisia	TUN	0.1	0.0	0.0	0.0	0.0	0.2	0.0	0.0	0.2	**	0.0	0.0	0.0	0.1	0.2	0.0	0.0	0.0	0.1	0.1
Uganda	UGA	0.0	0.0	0.0	0.0	0.0	0.0	0.0	0.1	0.0	0.0	**	0.0	0.0	0.0	0.0	0.0	0.0	0.0	0.0	0.0
Zambia	ZMB	0.0	0.0	0.0	0.0	0.0	0.0	0.3	0.1	0.0	0.0	0.0	**	1.5	0.1	0.0	0.0	0.0	0.0	0.0	0.0
Zimbabwe	ZWE	0.0	0.6	0.0	0.0	1.2	0.1	1.9	0.2	0.0	0.0	1.1	4.7	**	0.7	0.0	0.0	0.0	0.0	0.0	0.0
Sub-Saharan Africa	SSA	16.0	19.1	16.6	16.0	2.5	2.5	2.2	4.9	17.4	0.6	22.8	27.7	38.3	9.2	1.6	0.5	2.1	1.8	0.9	1.5
European Community	EU	57.8	32.5	48.6	29.0	50.5	33.5	31.3	37.7	39.6	78.1	38.5	30.4	33.2	48.4	66.2	9.7	19.1	17.3	26.4	42.0
Canada	CAN	1.4	0.0	0.2	0.6	0.6	0.4	0.6	0.9	0.6	0.6	2.1	0.9	1.0	0.6	0.6	**	19.3	15.7	1.4	3.6
United States	USA	6.4	1.3	13.2	10.7	17.4	4.5	5.6	2.5	2.3	3.9	4.2	6.7	9.3	9.1	6.8	72.7	**	13.6	16.9	11.9
North America	NNA	7.8	1.3	13.4	11.4	18.0	5.0	6.2	3.4	2.9	4.6	6.3	7.5	10.3	9.6	7.4	72.7	19.3	29.3	18.3	15.5
Rest of World	ROW	18.5	47.1	21.4	43.7	28.9	59.0	60.3	54.0	40.2	16.7	32.3	34.5	18.2	32.8	24.7	17.1	59.5	51.6	54.4	41.0
World	WLD	100.0	100.0	100.0	100.0	100.0	100.0	100.0	100.0	100.0	100.0	100.0	100.0	100.0	100.0	100.0	100.0	100.0	100.0	100.0	100.0

Note: ** means "not applicable."

South Africa's data for 1992 is taken from partner countries' data.

Source: International Monetary Fund's Direction of Trade database.

5-51. Direction of trade matrix, exports, 1997

| | | Importers | | | | | | | | | | | | | | | | | | *Percentage of total exports* |
Exporters		DZA	AGO	BEN	BWA	BFA	BDI	CMR	CPV	CAF	TCD	COM	ZAR	COG	CIV	DJI	EGY	GNQ	ERI	ETH	GAB
Algeria	DZA	**	0.0	0.0	0.0	0.0	0.0	0.0	0.0	0.0	0.0	0.0	0.0	0.0	0.0	0.0	0.0	0.0	..	0.0	0.0
Angola	AGO	0.0	**	0.0	0.0	0.0	0.0	0.6	0.0	0.0	0.0	0.0	0.0	0.5	0.0	0.0	0.0	0.0	..	0	0.0
Benin	BEN	0.0	0.0	**	0.0	0.1	0.0	0.1	0.0	0.1	0.0	0.0	0.0	0.0	0.1	0.0	0.0	0.0	..	0.0	0
Bostwana	BWA	..	..	..	**	..	..	..	..	..	..	..	..	..	..	..	..	..	..	..	..
Burkina Faso	BFA	0.0	0.0	0.1	0.0	**	0.0	0.0	0.0	0.0	0.0	0.0	0.0	0.0	0.8	0.0	0.0	0.0	..	0.0	0.0
Burundi	BDI	0.0	0.0	0.0	0.0	0.0	**	0.0	0.0	0.0	0.0	0.0	0.0	0.0	0.0	0.0	0.0	0.0	..	0.0	0.0
Cameroon	CMR	0.0	0.0	0.2	0.0	0.0	0.0	**	0.0	14.6	9.6	0.0	0.2	1.8	0.3	0.0	0.0	13.3	..	0.0	4.0
Cape Verde	CPV	0.0	0.0	0.0	0.0	0.0	0.0	0.0	**	0.0	0.0	0.0	0.0	0.0	0.0	0.0	0.0	0.0	..	0.0	0.0
Central African Republic	CAF	0.0	0.0	0.0	0.0	0.0	0.0	0.2	0.0	**	0.1	0.0	0.2	0	0.0	0.0	0.0	0.0	..	0.0	0.0
Chad	TCD	0.0	0.0	0.0	0.0	0.0	0.0	0.1	0.0	1.2	**	0.0	0.0	0.0	0	0.0	0.0	0.0	..	0.0	0.0
Comoros	COM	0.0	0.0	0.0	0.0	0.0	0.0	0.0	0.0	0.0	0.0	**	0.0	0.0	0.0	0	0.0	0.0	..	0.0	0.0
Congo, Dem. Rep. of	ZAR	0.0	0.0	0.0	0.0	0.0	0.4	0.0	0.1	0.9	0.0	0.0	**	0.1	0.0	0.0	0	0.0	..	0.0	0.0
Congo, Rep. of	COG	0.0	0.3	0.0	0.0	0.0	0.0	0.1	0.0	0.0	0.0	0.0	0.9	**	0.0	0.0	0.0	0.0	..	0.0	0.1
Côte d'Ivoire	CIV	0.3	0.0	5.3	0.0	25.4	0.0	3.7	1.2	0.0	0.0	0.0	0.0	0.0	**	0.0	0.0	0.0	..	0.0	8.3
Djibouti	DJI	0.0	0.0	0.0	0.0	0.0	0.1	0.0	0.0	0.0	0.0	0.0	0.0	0.0	0.0	**	0.0	0.0	..	0.4	0.0
Egypt, Arab Rep.	EGY	0.1	0.0	0.0	0.0	0.0	0.1	0.0	0.0	0.0	0.3	0.0	0.1	0.0	0.1	0.3	**	0	..	0.2	0.0
Equatorial Guinea	GNQ	0.0	0.0	0.0	0.0	0.0	0.0	2.2	0.0	0.0	0.0	0.0	0.0	0.0	0.0	0.0	0.0	**	..	0.0	0.0
Eritrea	ERI	..	..	..	..	..	..	..	..	..	..	..	..	..	..	..	..	..	**	..	..
Ethiopia	ETH	0.0	0.0	0.0	0.0	0.0	0.0	0.0	0.0	0.0	0.0	0.0	0.0	0.0	0.0	12.8	0.0	0.0	..	**	0.0
Gabon	GAB	0.0	0.0	0.3	0.0	0.0	0.0	0.1	0.0	0.0	0.0	0.0	0.8	0.8	0.0	0.0	0.0	0.7	..	0.0	**
Gambia, The	GMB	0.0	0.0	0.0	0.0	0.0	0.0	0.0	0.0	0.0	0.0	0.0	0.0	0.0	0.0	0.0	0.0	0.0	..	0.0	0.0
Ghana	GHA	0.0	0.5	1.9	0.0	0.9	0.0	0.0	0.0	0.0	0.0	0.0	0.0	1.0	0.0	0.0	0.0	0.0	..	0.0	0.0
Guinea	GIN	0.0	0.0	0.0	0.0	0.0	0.0	1.8	0.1	0.0	0.0	0.0	0.0	0.0	0.0	0.0	0.0	0.0	..	0.0	0.0
Guinea-Bissau	GNB	0.0	0.0	0.0	0.0	0.0	0.0	0.0	0.1	0.0	0.0	0.0	0.0	0.0	0.0	0.0	0.0	0.0	..	0.0	0.0
Kenya	KEN	0.0	0.0	0.0	0.0	0.1	6.3	0.1	0.0	0.0	0.0	2.2	4.2	0.2	0.0	1.0	0.3	0.1	..	2.6	0.0
Lesotho	LSO	..	..	..	..	..	..	..	..	..	..	..	..	..	..	..	..	..	..	..	..
Liberia	LBR	0.0	0.0	0.0	0.0	0.0	0.0	0.0	0.0	0.0	0.0	0.0	0.0	0.0	0.0	0.0	0.0	0.0	..	0.0	0.0
Libya	LBY	0.0	0.0	0.0	0.0	0.0	0.0	0.0	0.0	0.0	0.0	0.0	0.0	0.0	0.0	0.0	0.4	0.0	..	0.0	0.0
Madagascar	MDG	0.0	0.0	0.0	0.0	0.0	0.0	0.0	0.0	0.0	0.0	0.5	0.0	0.0	0.0	0.0	0.0	0.0	..	0.0	0.0
Malawi	MWI	0.0	0.0	0.0	0.0	0.0	0.0	0.0	0.0	0.0	0.0	0.0	0.1	0.0	0.0	0.0	0.1	0.0	..	0.0	0.0
Mali	MLI	0.0	0.0	0.0	0.0	0.3	0.0	0.0	0.0	0.0	0.0	0.0	0.0	0.0	0.1	0.0	0.0	0.0	..	0.0	0.0
Mauritania	MRT	0.0	0.0	0.0	0.0	0.1	0.0	0.4	0.0	0.0	0.0	0.0	0.0	0.6	0.5	0.0	0.0	0.2	..	0.0	0.0
Mauritius	MUS	0.0	0.0	0.0	0.0	0.0	0.0	0.0	0.0	0.0	0.0	0.8	0.0	0.0	0.0	0.0	0.0	0.0	..	0.0	0.0
Morocco	MAR	0.0	0.3	0.4	0.0	0.2	0.0	0.2	0.1	0.1	0.1	0.3	0.3	0.8	0.8	0.0	0.1	0.8	..	0.0	1.7
Mozambique	MOZ	0.0	0.0	0.0	0.0	0.0	0.0	0.0	0.0	0.0	0.0	0.0	0.0	0.0	0.0	0.0	0.0	0.0	..	0.0	0.0
Namibia	NAM	..	..	..	..	..	..	..	..	..	..	..	..	..	..	..	..	..	..	..	..
Niger	NER	0.0	0.0	0.3	0.0	0.3	0.0	0.0	0.0	0.0	0.0	0.0	0.0	0.0	0.3	0.0	0.0	0.0	..	0.0	0.0
Nigeria	NGA	0.0	0.0	0.8	0.0	2.7	0.0	6.4	0.2	0.7	11.7	0.0	7.1	0.3	15.1	0.0	0.0	0.0	..	0.0	0.6
Reunion	REU	0.0	0.0	0.0	0.0	0.0	0.0	0.0	0.0	0.0	0.0	0.0	0.0	0.0	0.0	0.0	0.0	0.0	..	0.0	0.0
Rwanda	RWA	0.0	0.0	0.0	0.0	0.0	1.2	0.0	0.0	0.0	0.0	0.0	0.1	0.0	0.0	0.0	0.0	0.0	..	0.0	0.0
São Tomé and Principe	STP	0.0	0.0	0.0	0.0	0.0	0.0	0.0	0.0	0.0	0.0	0.0	0.0	0.0	0.0	0.0	0.0	0.0	..	0.0	0.0
Senegal	SEN	0.0	0.0	1.7	0.0	1.0	0.0	0.9	2.1	0.0	2.2	0.0	0.0	0.5	1.1	0.1	0.0	0.1	..	0.0	1.0
Seychelles	SYC	0.0	0.0	0.0	0.0	0.0	0.0	0.0	0.0	0.0	0.0	0.0	0.0	0.0	0.0	0.0	0.0	0.0	..	0.0	0.0
Sierra Leone	SLE	0.0	0.0	0.0	0.0	0.0	0.0	0.0	0.0	0.0	0.0	0.0	0.0	0.0	0.0	0.0	0.0	0.0	..	0.0	0.0
Somalia	SOM	0.0	0.0	0.0	0.0	0.0	0.0	0.0	0.0	0.0	0.0	0.0	0.0	0.0	0.0	0.1	0.0	0.0	..	0.0	0.0
South Africa	ZAF	0.3	9.1	0.4	0.0	0.6	6.7	0.9	2.4	0.2	0.2	4.3	0.0	4.8	0.8	0.2	0.1	0.0	..	0.2	2.2
Sudan	SDN	0.0	0.0	0.0	0.0	0.0	0.0	0.0	0.0	0.0	0.0	0.0	0.0	0.0	0.0	0.0	0.1	0.0	..	0.0	0.0
Swaziland	SWZ	..	..	..	..	..	..	..	..	..	..	..	..	..	..	..	..	..	..	..	..
Tanzania	TZA	0.0	0.0	0.0	0.0	0.0	1.2	0.0	0.0	0.0	0.0	0.0	1.0	0.0	0.0	0.0	0.0	0.0	..	0.3	0.0
Togo	TGO	0.0	0.0	1.0	0.0	0.9	0.0	0.0	0.0	0.0	0.0	0.0	0.0	0.0	0.0	0.0	0.0	0.0	..	0.0	0.1
Tunisia	TUN	0.5	0.1	0.6	0.0	0.5	0.2	0.6	1.3	1.0	0.1	0.0	0.0	0.0	0.4	0.0	0.1	2.2	..	0.0	0.3
Uganda	UGA	0.0	0.0	0.0	0.0	0.0	0.0	0.0	0.0	0.0	0.0	0.0	0.0	0.0	0.0	0.0	0.0	0.0	..	0.0	0.0
Zambia	ZMB	0.0	0.0	0.0	0.6	0.0	2.1	0.0	0.0	0.0	0.0	0.0	2.9	0.9	0.0	0.0	0.0	0.0	..	0.0	0.0
Zimbabwe	ZWE	0.0	0.3	0.0	19.0	0.0	1.4	0.2	0.0	0.0	0.0	0.0	1.1	0.8	0.0	0.0	0.0	0.0	..	0.0	0.0
Sub-Saharan Africa	SSA	0.7	10.4	11.9	19.7	32.5	19.2	17.8	6.3	17.8	23.8	7.7	18.7	12.6	19.1	14.1	0.7	14.4	..	3.2	16.3
European Community	EU	61.3	52.1	45.3	25.4	48.1	64.5	59.5	68.4	55.5	61.0	71.3	34.3	61.4	56.2	41.9	39.6	52.3	..	40.9	60.5
Canada	CAN	5.3	0.3	0.9	5.1	0.2	0.0	0.2	0.5	0.2	0.2	0.0	0.6	0.3	0.2	0.2	0.7	0.0	..	0.4	0.6
United States	USA	8.7	12.2	5.4	8.7	3.8	0.7	8.8	9.3	3.2	2.6	0.2	4.2	9.9	5.8	2.1	20.1	25.8	..	9.0	7.6
North America	NNA	14.0	12.6	6.2	13.8	4.0	0.7	9.0	9.8	3.3	2.8	0.2	4.8	10.2	6.0	2.3	20.7	25.8	..	9.3	8.2
Rest of World	ROW	24.1	24.9	36.5	41.2	15.4	15.6	13.7	15.5	23.4	12.3	20.8	42.2	15.8	18.7	41.7	39.0	7.5	..	46.5	15.0
World	WLD	100.0	100.0	100.0	100.0	100.0	100.0	100.0	100.0	100.0	100.0	100.0	100.0	100.0	100.0	100.0	100.0	100.0	..	100.0	100.0

Note: ** means "not applicable."
South Africa's data for 1997 is taken from partner countries' data.
Source: International Monetary Fund's Direction of Trade database.

(Table continues on the following page.)

5-51. Direction of trade matrix, exports, 1997 (continued)

Importer	Exporters	GMB	GHA	GIN	GNB	KEN	LSO	LBR	LBY	MDG	MWI	MLI	MRT	MUS	MAR	MOZ	NAM	NER	NGA	REU	RWA
Algeria	DZA	0.0	0.0	0.0	0.0	0.0	0.0	0.0	0.1	0.0	0.0	0.0	9.4	0.0	1.0	0.0	0.0	0.2	0.0	..	0.0
Angola	AGO	0.0	0.0	0.0	0.0	0.0	0.0	0.0	0.0	0.0	0.0	0.0	0.0	0.0	0.0	0.0	0.0	0.0	0.0	..	0.0
Benin	BEN	0.0	0.0	0.0	0.0	0.0	0.0	0.0	0.0	0.0	0.0	0.2	0.0	0.0	0.2	0.0	0.0	1.1	0.0	..	0.0
Bostwana	BWA	..	..	..	..	..	..	..	..	..	..	..	..	..	..	..	..	..	..	..	..
Burkina Faso	BFA	0.0	0.2	0.0	0.0	0.0	0.0	0.0	0.0	0.0	0.0	0.3	0.0	0.1	0.0	0.0	0.0	0.8	0.0	..	0.0
Burundi	BDI	0.0	0.0	0.0	0.0	0.0	0.0	0.0	0.0	0.0	0.0	0.0	0.0	0.0	0.0	0.0	0.0	0.0	0.0	..	0.1
Cameroon	CMR	0.0	0.0	0.1	0.1	0.0	0.0	0.0	0.0	0.0	0.0	0.0	0.0	0.0	0.1	0.0	0.0	0.0	0.1	..	0.0
Cape Verde	CPV	0.0	0.0	0.0	0.0	0.0	0.0	0.0	0.0	0.0	0.0	0.0	0.0	0.0	0.0	0.0	0.0	0.0	0.0	..	0.0
Central African Republic	CAF	0.0	0.0	0.0	0.0	0.0	0.0	0.0	0.0	0.0	0.0	0.0	0.0	0.0	0.0	0.0	0.0	0.0	0.0	..	0.0
Chad	TCD	0.0	0.0	0.0	0.0	0.0	0.0	0.0	0.0	0.0	0.0	0.0	0.0	0.0	0.0	0.0	0.0	0.0	0.0	..	0.0
Comoros	COM	0.0	0.0	0.0	0.0	0.0	0.0	0.0	0.0	0.0	0.0	0.0	0.0	0.0	0.0	0.0	0.0	0.0	0.0	..	0.0
Congo, Dem. Rep. of	ZAR	0.0	0.0	0.0	0.0	0.1	0.0	0.0	0.0	0.0	0.0	0.0	0.0	0.0	0.0	0.0	0.0	0.0	0.0	..	1.6
Congo, Rep. of	COG	0.0	0.0	0.4	0.0	0.0	0.0	0.0	0.0	0.0	0.0	0.0	0.0	0.0	0.1	0.0	0.0	0.0	0.0	..	0.0
Côte d'Ivoire	CIV	4.3	5.1	8.8	1.0	0.0	0.0	0.3	0.0	0.0	0.0	27.8	0.9	0.0	0.3	0.0	0.0	13.1	0.6	..	0.0
Djibouti	DJI	0.0	0.0	0.0	0.0	0.0	0.0	0.0	0.0	0.0	0.0	0.0	0.0	0.0	0.0	0.0	0.0	0.0	0.0	..	0.0
Egypt, Arab Rep.	EGY	0.0	0.0	0.0	0.0	0.1	0.0	0.0	1.4	0.0	0.0	0.0	0.0	0.0	0.1	0.0	0.0	0.0	0.0	..	0.0
Equatorial Guinea	GNQ	0.0	0.0	0.0	0.0	0.0	0.0	0.0	0.0	0.0	0.0	0.0	0.0	0.0	0.0	0.0	0.0	0.0	0.0	..	0.0
Eritrea	ERI	..	..	..	..	..	..	..	..	..	..	..	..	..	..	..	..	..	..	..	..
Ethiopia	ETH	0.0	0.0	0.0	0.0	0.5	0.0	0.0	0.0	0.0	0.0	0.0	0.0	0.0	0.0	0.0	0.0	0.0	0.0	..	0.0
Gabon	GAB	0.0	0.0	0.4	0.0	0.0	0.0	0.0	0.0	0.0	0.0	0.0	0.0	0.0	0.2	0.0	0.0	0.0	0.0	..	0.0
Gambia, The	GMB	**	0.0	0.0	0.1	0.0	0.0	0.0	0.0	0.0	0.0	0.0	0.0	0.0	0.0	0.0	0.0	0.0	0.0	..	0.0
Ghana	GHA	0.0	**	0.0	0.0	0.0	0.0	0.0	0.0	0.0	0.0	0.0	0.0	0.0	0.0	0.0	0.0	1.1	0.9	..	0.0
Guinea	GIN	0.0	0.0	**	0.0	0.0	0.0	0.2	0.0	0.0	0.0	0.0	0.0	0.0	0.0	0.0	0.0	0.0	0.1	..	0.0
Guinea-Bissau	GNB	0.0	0.0	0.0	**	0.0	0.0	0.0	0.0	0.0	0.0	0.0	0.0	0.0	0.0	0.0	0.0	0.0	0.0	..	0.0
Kenya	KEN	0.2	0.0	0.0	0.0	**	0.2	0.0	0.0	0.4	1.0	0.0	0.0	0.7	0.0	0.1	0.0	0.0	0.0	..	22.4
Lesotho	LSO	..	..	..	..	..	**	..	..	..	..	..	..	..	..	..	..	..	..	..	..
Liberia	LBR	0.0	0.0	0.0	0.0	0.0	0.0	**	0.0	0.0	0.0	0.0	0.0	0.0	0.0	0.0	0.0	0.0	0.0	..	0.0
Libya	LBY	0.0	0.0	0.0	0.0	0.0	0.0	0.0	**	0.0	0.0	0.0	0.1	0.0	0.3	0.0	0.0	0.2	0.0	..	0.0
Madagascar	MDG	0.0	0.0	0.0	0.0	0.0	0.0	0.0	0.0	**	0.0	0.0	0.0	0.6	0.0	0.0	0.0	0.0	0.0	..	0.0
Malawi	MWI	0.2	0.0	0.0	0.1	0.0	0.0	0.0	0.0	0.0	**	0.0	0.0	0.2	0.0	0.3	0.0	0.0	0.0	..	0.0
Mali	MLI	0.0	0.0	0.0	0.0	0.0	0.0	0.0	0.0	0.0	0.0	**	0.0	0.0	0.1	0.0	0.0	0.1	0.0	..	0.0
Mauritania	MRT	0.0	0.0	0.0	0.0	0.0	0.0	0.0	0.2	0.0	0.0	0.1	**	0.0	0.0	0.0	0.0	0.0	0.0	..	0.0
Mauritius	MUS	0.0	0.0	0.0	0.0	0.1	0.0	0.0	0.0	8.0	0.6	0.0	0.0	**	0.0	0.0	0.0	0.0	0.0	..	0.6
Morocco	MAR	0.5	0.2	1.1	0.0	0.0	0.0	0.0	2.6	0.1	0.0	1.1	1.8	0.1	**	0.0	0.0	0.3	0.1	..	0.0
Mozambique	MOZ	0.0	0.0	0.0	0.0	0.1	0.0	0.0	0.0	0.0	3.3	0.0	0.0	0.1	0.0	**	0.1	0.0	0.0	..	0.0
Namibia	NAM	..	..	..	..	..	..	..	..	..	..	..	..	..	..	..	**	..	..	..	..
Niger	NER	0.0	0.2	0.0	0.0	0.0	0.0	0.0	0.0	0.0	0.0	0.0	0.0	0.0	0.0	0.0	0.0	**	0.6	..	0.0
Nigeria	NGA	0.4	14.2	0.4	0.0	0.0	0.0	0.0	0.0	0.0	0.0	0.1	0.0	0.0	2.1	0.0	0.0	8.2	**	..	0.0
Reunion	REU	0.0	0.0	0.0	0.0	0.0	0.0	0.0	0.0	0.0	0.0	0.0	0.0	0.0	0.0	0.0	0.0	0.0	0.0	**	0.0
Rwanda	RWA	0.0	0.0	0.0	0.0	0.1	0.0	0.0	0.0	0.0	0.0	0.0	0.0	0.0	0.0	0.0	0.0	0.0	0.0	..	**
São Tomé and Principe	STP	0.0	0.0	0.0	0.0	0.0	0.0	0.0	0.0	0.0	0.0	0.0	0.0	0.0	0.0	0.0	0.0	0.0	0.0	..	0.0
Senegal	SEN	4.2	0.1	1.3	11.5	0.0	0.0	0.0	0.0	0.0	0.0	5.2	2.7	0.0	0.0	0.0	0.0	0.3	0.0	..	0.0
Seychelles	SYC	0.0	0.0	0.0	0.0	0.0	0.0	0.0	0.0	0.0	0.0	0.0	0.0	0.0	0.0	0.0	0.0	0.0	0.0	..	0.0
Sierra Leone	SLE	0.0	0.0	0.0	0.0	0.0	0.0	0.0	0.0	0.0	0.0	0.0	0.0	0.0	0.0	0.0	0.0	0.0	0.0	..	0.0
Somalia	SOM	0.0	0.0	0.0	0.0	0.0	0.0	0.0	0.0	0.0	0.0	0.0	0.0	0.0	0.0	0.0	0.0	0.0	0.0	..	0.0
South Africa	ZAF	0.3	3.1	2.1	0.4	11.5	0.0	0.3	0.1	7.7	48.8	2.3	0.4	13.9	1.0	59.8	0.0	0.2	0.8	..	2.1
Sudan	SDN	0.0	0.0	0.0	0.0	0.2	0.0	0.0	0.1	0.0	0.0	0.0	0.0	0.0	0.0	0.0	0.0	0.0	0.0	..	0.0
Swaziland	SWZ	..	..	..	..	..	..	..	..	..	..	..	..	..	..	..	..	..	..	..	..
Tanzania	TZA	0.0	0.0	0.0	0.0	0.8	0.0	0.0	0.0	0.0	1.0	0.0	0.0	0.1	0.0	0.0	0.0	0.0	0.0	..	2.4
Togo	TGO	0.0	0.0	0.0	0.0	0.0	0.0	0.0	0.0	0.0	0.0	0.1	0.0	0.0	0.0	0.0	0.0	0.6	0.0	..	0.0
Tunisia	TUN	0.4	0.1	0.0	0.1	0.0	0.0	0.0	4.5	0.0	0.0	0.2	0.3	0.0	0.5	0.2	0.0	0.6	0.0	..	0.0
Uganda	UGA	0.0	0.0	0.0	0.0	0.2	0.0	0.0	0.0	0.0	0.0	0.0	0.0	0.0	0.0	0.0	0.0	0.0	0.0	..	0.5
Zambia	ZMB	0.0	0.0	0.0	0.0	0.0	0.0	0.0	0.0	0.0	3.5	0.0	0.0	0.0	0.0	0.0	1.1	0.0	0.0	..	0.5
Zimbabwe	ZWE	0.0	0.1	0.0	0.0	0.6	0.5	0.0	0.0	0.0	14.2	0.0	0.0	0.1	0.0	6.5	9.1	0.0	0.0	..	0.2
Sub-Saharan Africa	SSA	9.7	23.1	13.6	13.3	14.2	0.7	1.1	0.3	16.1	72.5	36.2	4.1	15.8	4.1	66.8	10.3	25.5	3.3	..	30.5
European Community	EU	39.6	42.2	49.2	43.9	31.4	27.7	17.8	62.1	50.1	13.1	48.0	56.8	37.3	65.7	10.3	44.3	50.6	46.9	..	34.6
Canada	CAN	0.0	1.3	0.8	0.3	0.4	0.1	0.0	3.0	0.1	1.0	0.9	0.1	0.2	1.5	1.4	0.2	2.3	0.7	..	1.0
United States	USA	3.3	10.4	11.5	3.6	7.0	3.2	1.2	0.0	1.6	3.2	3.6	3.3	1.6	4.9	4.2	11.9	7.6	12.8	..	13.3
North America	NNA	3.4	11.6	12.2	3.9	7.4	3.3	1.3	3.0	1.7	4.2	4.5	3.4	1.8	6.4	5.6	12.1	10.0	13.5	..	14.4
Rest of World	ROW	47.3	23.1	24.9	38.9	46.9	68.3	79.8	34.7	32.1	10.2	11.3	35.7	45.1	23.8	17.3	33.3	13.9	36.3	..	20.5
World	WLD	100.0	100.0	100.0	100.0	100.0	100.0	100.0	100.0	100.0	100.0	100.0	100.0	100.0	100.0	100.0	100.0	100.0	100.0	..	100.0

Note: ** means "not applicable."

South Africa's data for 1997 is taken from partner countries' data.

Source: International Monetary Fund's Direction of Trade database.

5-51. Direction of trade matrix, exports, 1997

Importer / Exporters		STP	SEN	SYC	SLE	SOM	ZAF	SDN	SWZ	TZA	TGO	TUN	UGA	ZMB	ZWE	SSA	EU	CAN	USA	NNA	ROW	WLD
Algeria	DZA	0.0	0.7	0.0	0.0	0.0	0.0	0.3	0.0	0.0	0.0	0.8	0.0	0.0	0.0	0.1	0.4	0.2	0.3	0.3	0.1	0.2
Angola	AGO	0.0	0.0	0.0	0.0	0.0	0.2	0.0	0.0	0.0	0.0	0.0	0.0	0.0	0.0	0.1	0.0	0.0	0.3	0.3	0.0	0.1
Benin	BEN	0.0	0.0	0.0	0.0	0.2	0.0	0.0	0.0	0.0	0.2	0.0	0.0	0.0	0.0	0.0	0.0	0.0	0.0	0.0	0.0	0.0
Bostwana	BWA	..	..	..	..	..	..	..	..	..	..	..	..	..	..	..	..	..	..	..	..	..
Burkina Faso	BFA	0.0	0.0	0.0	0.0	0.0	0.0	0.0	0.0	0.0	0.4	0.0	0.0	0.0	0.0	0.1	0.0	0.0	0.0	0.0	0.0	0.0
Burundi	BDI	0.0	0.0	0.0	0.0	0.0	0.0	0.0	0.0	0.0	0.0	0.0	0.0	0.0	0.0	0.0	0.0	0.0	0.0	0.0	0.0	0.0
Cameroon	CMR	0.0	0.5	0.0	0.0	0.0	0.0	0.0	0.0	0.0	0.2	0.1	0.0	0.0	0.0	0.2	0.1	0.0	0.0	0.0	0.0	0.0
Cape Verde	CPV	0.1	0.0	0.0	0.0	0.0	0.0	0.0	0.0	0.0	0.0	0.0	0.0	0.0	0.0	0.0	0.0	0.0	0.0	0.0	0.0	0.0
Central African Republic	CAF	0.0	0.0	0.0	0.0	0.0	0.0	0.0	0.0	0.0	0.0	0.0	0.0	0.0	0.0	0.0	0.0	0.0	0.0	0.0	0.0	0.0
Chad	TCD	0.0	0.0	0.0	0.0	0.0	0.0	0.0	0.0	0.0	0.0	0.1	0.0	0.0	0.0	0.0	0.0	0.0	0.0	0.0	0.0	0.0
Comoros	COM	0.0	0.0	0.0	0.0	0.0	0.0	0.0	0.0	0.0	0.0	0.0	0.0	0.0	0.0	0.0	0.0	0.0	0.0	0.0	0.0	0.0
Congo, Dem. Rep. of	ZAR	0.0	0.0	0.0	0.0	0.0	0.4	0.0	0.0	0.0	0.0	0.0	0.0	0.0	0.0	0.2	0.0	0.0	0.0	0.0	0.0	0.0
Congo, Rep. of	COG	0.0	0.0	0.0	0.0	0.0	0.0	0.0	0.0	0.0	0.0	0.0	0.0	0.0	0.0	0.0	0.0	0.0	0.1	0.0	0.0	0.0
Côte d'Ivoire	CIV	0.0	3.3	0.0	11.3	0.0	0.1	0.0	0.0	0.0	9.4	0.2	0.0	0.0	0.0	1.4	0.1	0.0	0.0	0.0	0.0	0.1
Djibouti	DJI	0.0	0.0	0.0	0.0	24.4	0.0	0.0	0.0	0.0	0.0	0.0	0.0	0.0	0.0	0.1	0.0	0.0	0.0	0.0	0.0	0.0
Egypt, Arab Rep.	EGY	0.0	0.1	0.0	0.2	0.2	0.2	1.8	0.0	0.1	0.0	0.2	0.1	0.2	0.0	0.1	0.1	0.0	0.1	0.0	0.1	0.1
Equatorial Guinea	GNQ	0.0	0.0	0.0	0.0	0.0	0.0	0.0	0.0	0.0	0.0	0.0	0.0	0.0	0.0	0.0	0.0	0.0	0.0	0.0	0.0	0.0
Eritrea	ERI	..	..	..	..	..	..	..	..	..	..	..	..	..	..	..	..	..	..	..	..	..
Ethiopia	ETH	0.0	0.0	0.0	0.0	0.0	0.0	0.0	0.0	0.0	0.0	0.0	0.2	0.0	0.0	0.0	0.0	0.0	0.0	0.0	0.0	0.0
Gabon	GAB	2.1	0.1	0.0	0.0	0.0	0.0	0.0	0.0	0.0	0.0	0.0	0.0	0.0	0.0	0.0	0.0	0.0	0.2	0.2	0.0	0.1
Gambia, The	GMB	0.0	0.0	0.0	0.0	0.0	0.0	0.0	0.0	0.0	0.0	0.0	0.0	0.0	0.0	0.0	0.0	0.0	0.0	0.0	0.0	0.0
Ghana	GHA	0.0	0.1	0.0	0.0	0.0	0.0	0.0	0.0	0.0	1.3	0.0	0.0	0.0	0.0	0.2	0.0	0.0	0.0	0.0	0.0	0.0
Guinea	GIN	0.0	0.0	0.0	0.0	0.0	0.0	0.0	0.0	0.0	0.0	0.0	0.0	0.0	0.0	0.1	0.0	0.0	0.0	0.0	0.0	0.0
Guinea-Bissau	GNB	0.0	0.0	0.0	0.0	0.0	0.0	0.0	0.0	0.0	0.0	0.0	0.0	0.0	0.0	0.0	0.0	0.0	0.0	0.0	0.0	0.0
Kenya	KEN	0.0	0.1	1.3	0.1	13.6	0.1	2.3	0.1	13.7	0.0	0.0	37.5	0.4	0.3	1.1	0.0	0.0	0.0	0.0	0.0	0.0
Lesotho	LSO	..	..	..	..	..	..	..	..	..	..	..	..	..	..	..	..	..	..	..	..	..
Liberia	LBR	0.0	0.0	0.0	0.4	0.0	0.0	0.0	0.0	0.0	0.0	0.0	0.0	0.0	0.0	0.0	0.0	0.0	0.0	0.0	0.0	0.0
Libya	LBY	0.0	0.0	0.0	0.0	0.0	0.0	18.7	0.0	0.0	0.0	2.6	0.0	0.0	0.0	0.4	0.4	0.0	0.0	0.0	0.1	0.2
Madagascar	MDG	0.0	0.0	0.1	0.0	0.0	0.0	0.0	0.0	0.0	0.0	0.0	0.0	0.0	0.0	0.0	0.0	0.0	0.0	0.0	0.0	0.0
Malawi	MWI	0.0	0.0	0.0	0.1	0.0	0.4	0.0	0.0	0.1	0.0	0.0	0.2	0.3	0.6	0.2	0.0	0.0	0.0	0.0	0.0	0.0
Mali	MLI	0.0	0.0	0.0	0.0	0.0	0.0	0.0	0.0	0.0	0.0	0.1	0.0	0.0	0.0	0.0	0.0	0.0	0.0	0.0	0.0	0.0
Mauritania	MRT	0.0	0.0	0.0	0.0	0.0	0.0	0.0	0.0	0.0	2.3	0.0	0.0	0.0	0.0	0.1	0.0	0.0	0.0	0.0	0.0	0.0
Mauritius	MUS	0.0	0.0	1.2	0.0	0.0	0.0	0.0	0.1	0.1	0.0	0.0	0.0	0.0	0.5	0.1	0.1	0.0	0.0	0.0	0.0	0.0
Morocco	MAR	0.0	0.8	0.0	0.2	0.0	0.0	0.0	0.0	0.0	0.3	0.5	0.0	0.0	0.0	0.2	0.1	0.0	0.0	0.0	0.1	0.1
Mozambique	MOZ	0.0	0.0	0.0	0.0	0.0	0.1	0.0	0.3	0.0	0.0	0.0	0.0	0.0	0.4	0.1	0.0	0.0	0.0	0.0	0.0	0.0
Namibia	NAM	..	..	..	..	..	..	..	..	..	..	..	..	..	..	..	..	..	..	..	..	..
Niger	NER	0.0	0.0	0.0	0.0	0.0	0.0	0.0	0.0	0.0	0.0	0.0	0.0	0.0	0.0	0.1	0.0	0.0	0.0	0.0	0.0	0.0
Nigeria	NGA	0.0	5.7	0.0	4.6	0.0	0.7	0.0	0.0	0.0	1.7	0.0	0.0	0.0	0.0	1.9	0.2	0.2	0.7	0.6	0.2	0.3
Reunion	REU	0.0	0.0	0.0	0.0	0.0	0.0	0.0	0.0	0.0	0.0	0.0	0.0	0.0	0.0	0.0	0.0	0.0	0.0	0.0	0.0	0.0
Rwanda	RWA	0.0	0.0	0.0	0.0	0.0	0.0	0.0	0.0	0.0	0.0	0.0	0.0	0.0	0.0	0.0	0.0	0.0	0.0	0.0	0.0	0.0
São Tomé and Principe	STP	**	0.0	0.0	0.0	0.0	0.0	0.0	0.0	0.0	0.0	0.0	0.0	0.0	0.0	0.0	0.0	0.0	0.0	0.0	0.0	0.0
Senegal	SEN	0.0	**	0.0	0.2	0.0	0.0	0.0	0.0	0.0	0.5	0.0	0.0	0.0	0.0	0.2	0.0	0.0	0.0	0.0	0.0	0.0
Seychelles	SYC	0.0	0.0	**	0.0	0.0	0.0	0.0	0.0	0.0	0.0	0.0	0.0	0.0	0.0	0.0	0.0	0.0	0.0	0.0	0.0	0.0
Sierra Leone	SLE	0.0	0.0	0.0	**	0.0	0.0	0.0	0.0	0.0	0.0	0.0	0.0	0.0	0.0	0.0	0.0	0.0	0.0	0.0	0.0	0.0
Somalia	SOM	0.0	0.0	0.0	0.0	**	0.0	0.0	0.0	0.0	0.0	0.0	0.0	0.0	0.0	0.0	0.0	0.0	0.0	0.0	0.0	0.0
South Africa	ZAF	7.2	0.2	15.7	3.7	0.0	**	0.4	0.0	6.1	0.8	0.0	5.1	32.6	57.6	5.6	0.5	0.2	0.3	0.3	0.5	0.5
Sudan	SDN	0.0	0.0	0.0	0.0	0.2	0.0	**	0.0	0.0	0.0	0.1	0.0	0.0	0.0	0.0	0.0	0.0	0.0	0.0	0.0	0.0
Swaziland	SWZ	..	..	..	..	..	..	..	**	..	..	..	..	..	..	..	..	..	..	..	..	..
Tanzania	TZA	0.0	0.0	0.0	0.0	0.0	0.0	0.1	0.3	**	0.0	0.0	1.0	0.2	0.7	0.1	0.0	0.0	0.0	0.0	0.0	0.0
Togo	TGO	0.4	0.0	0.0	0.0	0.0	0.1	0.0	0.0	0.0	**	0.0	0.0	0.0	0.0	0.1	0.0	0.0	0.0	0.0	0.0	0.0
Tunisia	TUN	0.0	0.5	0.0	0.0	0.0	0.0	0.0	0.0	0.0	0.2	**	0.0	0.0	0.0	0.1	0.2	0.0	0.0	0.0	0.1	0.1
Uganda	UGA	0.0	0.0	0.0	0.0	0.0	0.0	0.0	0.0	0.3	0.0	0.0	**	0.0	0.0	0.0	0.0	0.0	0.0	0.0	0.0	0.0
Zambia	ZMB	0.0	0.0	0.0	0.0	0.0	0.2	0.0	0.6	0.3	0.0	0.0	0.0	**	1.3	0.2	0.0	0.0	0.0	0.0	0.0	0.0
Zimbabwe	ZWE	0.1	0.0	0.9	0.0	0.0	1.2	0.3	1.8	0.8	0.0	0.0	0.3	12.3	**	1.1	0.0	0.0	0.0	0.0	0.0	0.0
Sub-Saharan Africa	SSA	10.0	9.9	19.2	20.5	14.0	3.7	3.2	3.2	21.4	16.9	0.7	44.4	45.9	61.5	13.2	1.5	0.5	1.8	1.6	1.1	1.5
European Community	EU	24.6	64.2	38.6	51.9	7.1	44.6	28.3	28.2	26.3	39.4	78.0	28.9	17.7	20.9	41.4	64.2	8.1	18.4	16.5	25.8	37.9
Canada	CAN	0.1	0.9	0.1	0.6	0.3	1.0	0.7	0.1	0.5	0.4	0.6	0.7	0.5	0.5	0.7	0.5	**	20.5	16.8	1.0	3.9
United States	USA	34.5	3.7	2.1	7.2	1.2	12.2	2.7	7.0	3.7	3.6	3.3	4.8	3.1	3.5	8.6	7.2	77.3	**	14.2	16.1	12.4
North America	NNA	34.6	4.6	2.2	7.8	1.5	13.2	3.4	7.1	4.2	4.0	4.0	5.5	3.6	4.0	9.4	7.7	77.3	20.5	31.0	17.1	16.3
Rest of World	ROW	30.8	21.3	40.0	19.8	77.4	38.5	65.1	61.5	48.0	39.7	17.3	21.2	32.8	13.7	36.0	26.6	14.1	59.3	51.0	56.1	44.4
World	WLD	100.0	100.0	100.0	100.0	100.0	100.0	100.0	100.0	100.0	100.0	100.0	100.0	100.0	100.0	100.0	100.0	100.0	100.0	100.0	100.0	100.0

Percentage of total exports

(Table continues on the following page.) Note: ** means "not applicable."

South Africa's data for 1997 is taken from partner countries' data.

Source: International Monetary Fund's Direction of Trade database.

5-52. Direction of trade matrix, exports, 2002

		Importers																		*Percentage of total exports*	
Exporters		DZA	AGO	BEN	BWA	BFA	BDI	CMR	CPV	CAF	TCD	COM	ZAR	COG	CIV	DJI	EGY	GNQ	ERI	ETH	GAB
Algeria	DZA	**	0.0	1.8	0.0	0.0	6.4	0.0	2.7	0.0	0.0	0.0	0.0	0.0	0.0	0.0	0.9	0.0	..	0.0	0.5
Angola	AGO	0.0	**	0.0	0.0	0.0	0.0	0.1	0.2	0.0	0.0	0.0	0.0	0.7	0.0	0.0	0.0	0.0	..	0	0.1
Benin	BEN	0.0	0.0	**	0.0	0.2	0.0	0.0	0.0	0.0	0.3	0.0	0.0	0.0	0.0	0.0	0.0	0.0	..	0.0	0
Bostwana	BWA	..	..	..	**	..	..	..	..	..	..	..	..	..	..	..	..	..	..	..	..
Burkina Faso	BFA	0.0	0.0	0.0	0.0	**	0.0	0.0	0.0	0.0	0.0	0.0	0.0	0.0	0.0	0.0	0.0	0.0	..	0.0	0.0
Burundi	BDI	0.0	0.0	0.0	0.0	0.0	**	0.0	0.0	0.0	0.0	0.0	0.0	0.0	0.0	0.0	0.0	0.0	..	0.0	0.0
Cameroon	CMR	0.0	0.6	0.1	0.0	0.0	0.0	**	0.0	6.3	3.1	0.0	3.4	2.3	0.1	0.0	0.0	2.8	..	0.0	1.7
Cape Verde	CPV	0.0	0.0	0.0	0.0	0.0	0.0	0.0	**	0.0	0.0	0.0	0.0	0.0	0.0	0.0	0.0	0.0	..	0.0	0.0
Central African Republic	CAF	0.0	0.0	0.0	0.0	0.0	0.0	0.0	0.0	**	0.1	0.0	0.3	0	0.0	0.0	0.0	0.0	..	0.0	0.0
Chad	TCD	0.0	0.0	0.0	0.0	0.0	0.0	0.0	0.0	2.6	**	0.0	0.0	0.0	0	0.0	0.0	0.0	..	0.0	0.0
Comoros	COM	0.0	0.0	0.0	0.0	0.0	0.0	0.0	0.0	0.0	0.0	**	0.0	0.0	0.0	0	0.0	0.0	..	0.0	0.0
Congo, Dem. Rep. of	ZAR	0.0	0.0	0.0	0.0	0.0	0.7	0.0	0.0	1.9	0.0	0.0	**	0.2	0.0	0.0	0	0.0	..	0.0	0.0
Congo, Rep. of	COG	0.0	0.4	0.0	0.0	0.0	0.0	0.2	0.0	0.0	0.0	0.0	1.3	**	0.0	0.0	0.0	0.0	..	0.0	0.2
Côte d'Ivoire	CIV	0.4	0.0	2.4	0.0	24.3	0.0	1.6	3.2	0.0	0.0	0.0	0.0	0.0	**	0.0	0.0	0.0	..	0.0	1.9
Djibouti	DJI	0.0	0.0	0.0	0.0	0.0	0.1	0.0	0.0	0.0	0.0	0.0	0.0	0.0	0.0	**	0.0	0.0	..	0.7	0.0
Egypt, Arab Rep.	EGY	0.4	0.0	0.0	0.0	0.0	0.1	0.1	0.0	0.0	0.0	0.0	0.2	0.0	0.2	0.0	**	0	..	0.2	0.0
Equatorial Guinea	GNQ	0.0	0.0	0.0	0.0	0.0	0.0	2.0	0.0	0.0	0.0	0.0	0.0	0.0	0.0	0.0	0.0	**	..	0.0	0.0
Eritrea	ERI	..	..	..	..	..	..	..	..	..	..	..	..	..	..	..	..	..	**	..	..
Ethiopia	ETH	0.0	0.0	0.0	0.0	0.0	0.0	0.0	0.0	0.0	0.0	0.0	0.0	0.0	0.0	11.0	0.0	0.0	..	**	0.0
Gabon	GAB	0.0	0.0	0.0	0.0	0.0	0.0	0.2	0.0	0.0	0.0	0.0	1.2	1.0	0.0	0.0	0.0	0.4	..	0.0	**
Gambia, The	GMB	0.0	0.0	0.0	0.0	0.0	0.0	0.0	0.0	0.0	0.0	0.0	0.0	0.0	0.0	0.0	0.0	0.0	..	0.0	0.0
Ghana	GHA	0.0	0.7	2.1	0.0	1.4	0.0	0.0	0.0	0.0	0.0	0.0	0.0	1.2	0.3	0.0	0.0	0.0	..	0.0	0.0
Guinea	GIN	0.0	0.0	0.0	0.0	0.0	0.0	4.1	0.0	0.0	0.0	0.0	0.0	0.0	0.0	0.0	0.0	0.0	..	0.0	0.0
Guinea-Bissau	GNB	0.0	0.0	0.0	0.0	0.0	0.0	0.1	0.0	0.0	0.0	0.0	0.0	0.0	0.0	0.0	0.0	0.0	..	0.0	0.0
Kenya	KEN	0.0	0.0	0.0	0.0	0.0	8.7	0.0	0.0	0.0	0.0	5.6	4.9	0.2	0.0	0.6	0.6	0.0	..	3.2	0.0
Lesotho	LSO	..	..	..	..	..	..	..	..	..	..	..	..	..	..	..	..	..	..	..	..
Liberia	LBR	0.0	0.0	0.0	0.0	0.0	0.0	0.0	0.0	0.0	0.0	0.0	0.0	0.0	0.1	0.0	0.0	0.0	..	0.0	0.0
Libya	LBY	0.0	0.0	0.0	0.0	2.9	0.0	0.0	0.0	0.0	0.0	0.0	0.0	0.0	0.0	0.0	0.2	0.0	..	0.0	0.0
Madagascar	MDG	0.0	0.0	0.0	0.0	0.0	0.0	0.0	0.0	0.0	0.0	2.0	0.0	0.0	0.0	0.0	0.0	0.0	..	0.0	0.0
Malawi	MWI	0.0	0.0	0.0	0.0	0.0	0.5	0.0	0.0	0.0	0.0	0.0	0.1	0.0	0.0	0.0	0.1	0.0	..	0.0	0.0
Mali	MLI	0.0	0.0	0.0	0.0	0.4	0.0	0.0	0.0	0.0	0.0	0.0	0.0	0.0	0.1	0.0	0.0	0.0	..	0.0	0.0
Mauritania	MRT	0.0	0.0	0.0	0.0	0.1	0.0	0.8	0.0	0.0	0.0	0.0	0.0	0.8	0.8	0.0	0.0	0.1	..	0.0	0.0
Mauritius	MUS	0.0	0.0	0.0	0.2	0.1	0.4	0.0	0.0	0.0	0.0	3.8	0.0	0.0	0.0	0.0	0.0	0.0	..	0.0	0.3
Morocco	MAR	0.1	0.3	0.2	0.0	0.8	0.0	0.3	0.2	0.2	0.0	0.9	0.3	1.0	0.6	0.1	0.2	1.2	..	0.0	0.8
Mozambique	MOZ	0.0	0.0	0.0	0.1	0.0	0.0	0.0	0.0	0.0	0.0	0.0	0.0	0.3	0.0	0.0	0.0	0.0	..	0.0	0.0
Namibia	NAM	..	..	..	..	..	..	..	..	..	..	..	..	..	..	..	..	..	..	..	..
Niger	NER	0.0	0.0	0.2	0.0	0.1	0.0	0.0	0.0	0.0	0.0	0.0	0.0	0.0	0.1	0.0	0.0	0.0	..	0.0	0.0
Nigeria	NGA	0.0	0.0	0.8	0.0	3.6	0.0	12.6	0.0	1.3	5.0	0.0	10.8	0.4	18.8	0.0	0.0	0.0	..	0.0	0.9
Reunion	REU	0.0	0.0	0.0	0.0	0.0	0.0	0.0	0.0	0.0	0.0	0.0	0.0	0.0	0.0	0.0	0.0	0.0	..	0.0	0.0
Rwanda	RWA	0.0	0.0	0.0	0.0	0.0	0.5	0.0	0.0	0.0	0.0	0.0	0.1	0.0	0.0	0.0	0.0	0.0	..	0.0	0.0
São Tomé and Principe	STP	0.0	0.0	0.0	0.0	0.0	0.0	0.0	0.0	0.0	0.0	0.0	0.0	0.0	0.0	0.0	0.0	0.0	..	0.0	0.0
Senegal	SEN	0.0	0.0	1.6	0.0	1.2	0.0	0.4	2.0	0.7	0.1	0.0	0.1	1.1	1.3	0.0	0.0	0.1	..	0.0	0.8
Seychelles	SYC	0.0	0.0	0.0	0.0	0.0	0.0	0.0	0.0	0.0	0.0	0.0	0.0	0.0	0.0	0.0	0.0	0.0	..	0.0	0.0
Sierra Leone	SLE	0.0	0.0	0.0	0.0	0.0	0.0	0.0	0.0	0.0	0.0	0.0	0.0	0.0	0.0	0.0	0.0	0.0	..	0.0	0.0
Somalia	SOM	0.0	0.0	0.0	0.0	0.0	0.0	0.0	0.0	0.0	0.0	0.0	0.0	0.0	0.0	0.1	0.0	0.0	..	0.0	0.0
South Africa	ZAF	0.3	12.8	1.0	0.0	0.4	4.0	1.9	0.5	0.6	0.2	16.6	19.4	4.2	1.9	1.1	0.1	0.9	..	1.6	2.0
Sudan	SDN	0.0	0.0	0.0	0.0	0.0	0.0	0.0	0.0	0.0	0.0	0.0	0.0	0.0	0.0	0.0	0.4	0.0	..	0.2	0.0
Swaziland	SWZ	..	..	..	..	..	..	..	..	..	..	..	..	..	..	..	..	..	..	..	..
Tanzania	TZA	0.0	0.1	0.0	0.0	0.0	6.6	0.0	0.0	0.0	0.0	0.4	1.8	0.0	0.0	0.0	0.0	0.0	..	0.0	0.0
Togo	TGO	0.0	0.0	2.9	0.0	4.5	0.0	0.0	0.0	0.0	0.4	0.0	0.0	0.1	0.0	0.0	0.0	0.0	..	0.0	0.1
Tunisia	TUN	0.7	0.0	0.2	0.0	1.1	0.0	0.1	0.0	0.0	0.1	0.1	0.0	0.4	0.5	0.2	0.1	0.1	..	0.0	0.2
Uganda	UGA	0.0	0.0	0.0	0.0	0.0	0.0	0.0	0.0	0.0	0.0	0.0	0.0	0.0	0.0	0.0	0.0	0.0	..	0.0	0.0
Zambia	ZMB	0.0	0.0	0.0	1.4	0.0	0.7	0.0	0.0	0.0	0.0	0.0	0.0	0.0	0.0	0.0	0.3	0.0	..	0.0	0.0
Zimbabwe	ZWE	0.0	0.0	0.0	5.5	0.0	0.3	0.0	0.0	0.0	0.0	0.0	0.3	0.0	0.0	0.0	0.1	0.0	..	0.0	0.0
Sub-Saharan Africa	SSA	0.9	14.6	11.1	7.1	36.4	22.3	24.0	5.9	13.6	9.2	28.4	43.8	12.5	23.7	12.7	1.6	4.3	..	5.2	8.1
European Community	EU	62.3	47.6	37.6	56.3	46.4	39.0	52.4	80.9	65.3	49.2	44.7	40.1	55.7	47.6	25.7	35.8	52.8	..	31.6	74.4
Canada	CAN	2.2	0.2	0.2	0.7	0.2	0.4	0.4	0.0	0.3	0.2	0.0	0.8	0.3	0.5	0.1	0.7	0.3	..	0.3	0.4
United States	USA	8.1	13.5	2.5	13.1	3.4	1.5	7.8	3.4	7.2	31.0	0.1	3.2	5.9	3.1	9.6	17.1	27.6	..	5.5	6.4
North America	NNA	10.3	13.7	2.8	13.8	3.6	2.0	8.3	3.4	7.5	31.2	0.1	4.0	6.1	3.6	9.7	17.7	27.9	..	5.8	6.8
Rest of World	ROW	26.6	24.1	48.6	22.8	13.6	36.8	15.4	9.8	13.5	10.4	26.7	12.1	25.6	25.1	51.9	44.9	15.0	..	57.3	10.7
World	WLD	100.0	100.0	100.0	100.0	100.0	100.0	100.0	100.0	100.0	100.0	100.0	100.0	100.0	100.0	100.0	100.0	100.0	..	100.0	100.0

Note: ** means "not applicable."

South Africa's data for 1997 is taken from partner countries' data.

Source: International Monetary Fund's Direction of Trade database.

(Table continues on the following page.)

5-52. Direction of trade matrix, exports, 2002 (continued)

		Importers												Percentage of total exports								
Exporters		GMB	GHA	GIN	GNB	KEN	LSO	LBR	LBY	MDG	MWI	MLI	MRT	MUS	MAR	MOZ	NAM	NER	NGA	REU	RWA	STP
Algeria	DZA	0.0	0.0	0.0	0.0	0.0	0.0	0.0	0.2	0.0	0.0	0.0	1.4	0.0	1.2	0.0	0.0	0.0	0.0	..	0.0	0.0
Angola	AGO	0.0	0.1	0.0	0.0	0.0	0.0	0.0	0.0	0.0	0.0	0.0	0.0	0.0	0.0	0.0	0.0	0.0	0.0	..	0.0	0.0
Benin	BEN	0.0	0.0	0.0	0.0	0.0	0.0	0.0	0.0	0.0	0.0	0.1	0.0	0.1	0.1	0.0	0.0	1.9	0.0	..	0.0	0.0
Bostwana	BWA	..	..	..	..	..	..	..	..	..	..	..	..	..	..	..	..	..	..	..	..	..
Burkina Faso	BFA	0.0	0.4	0.0	0.0	0.0	0.0	0.0	0.0	0.0	0.0	0.4	0.0	0.0	0.0	0.0	0.0	0.9	0.0	..	0.0	0.0
Burundi	BDI	0.0	0.0	0.0	0.0	0.1	0.0	0.0	0.0	0.0	0.0	0.0	0.0	0.0	0.0	0.0	0.0	0.0	0.0	..	1.1	0.0
Cameroon	CMR	0.0	0.0	0.0	0.0	0.0	0.0	0.0	0.0	0.0	0.0	0.0	0.0	0.1	0.1	0.0	0.0	0.0	0.1	..	0.0	0.0
Cape Verde	CPV	0.0	0.0	0.0	0.0	0.0	0.0	0.0	0.0	0.0	0.0	0.0	0.0	0.0	0.0	0.0	0.0	0.0	0.0	..	0.0	0.0
Central African Republic	CAF	0.0	0.0	0.0	0.0	0.0	0.0	0.0	0.0	0.0	0.0	0.0	0.0	0.0	0.0	0.0	0.0	0.0	0.0	..	0.0	0.0
Chad	TCD	0.0	0.0	0.0	0.0	0.0	0.0	0.0	0.0	0.0	0.0	0.0	0.0	0.0	0.0	0.0	0.0	0.0	0.0	..	0.0	0.0
Comoros	COM	0.0	0.0	0.0	0.0	0.0	0.0	0.0	0.0	0.0	0.0	0.0	0.0	0.0	0.0	0.0	0.0	0.0	0.0	..	0.0	0.0
Congo, Dem. Rep. of	ZAR	0.0	0.0	0.0	0.0	0.0	0.0	0.0	0.0	0.0	0.0	0.0	0.0	0.0	0.0	0.0	0.0	0.0	0.0	..	3.1	0.0
Congo, Rep. of	COG	0.0	0.0	0.0	0.0	0.0	0.0	0.0	0.0	0.0	0.0	0.0	0.0	0.0	0.0	0.0	0.0	0.0	0.0	..	0.0	0.0
Côte d'Ivoire	CIV	3.6	6.0	7.7	0.5	0.0	0.0	0.7	0.0	0.0	0.0	26.4	0.8	0.0	0.1	0.0	0.0	11.4	0.5	..	0.0	0.0
Djibouti	DJI	0.0	0.0	0.0	0.0	0.0	0.0	0.0	0.0	0.0	0.0	0.0	0.0	0.0	0.0	0.0	0.0	0.0	0.0	..	0.0	0.0
Egypt, Arab Rep.	EGY	0.4	0.1	0.3	0.0	0.7	0.0	0.0	1.0	0.3	0.0	0.1	0.2	0.5	0.2	0.0	0.0	0.0	0.1	..	0.0	0.0
Equatorial Guinea	GNQ	0.0	0.0	0.0	0.0	0.0	0.0	0.0	0.0	0.0	0.0	0.0	0.0	0.0	0.0	0.0	0.0	0.0	0.0	..	0.0	0.0
Eritrea	ERI	..	..	..	..	..	..	..	..	..	..	..	..	..	..	..	..	..	..	..	..	..
Ethiopia	ETH	0.0	0.0	0.0	0.0	0.2	0.0	0.0	0.0	0.0	0.0	0.0	0.0	0.0	0.0	0.0	0.0	0.0	0.0	..	0.3	0.0
Gabon	GAB	0.0	0.0	0.5	0.0	0.0	0.0	0.0	0.0	0.0	0.0	0.0	0.0	0.0	0.2	0.0	0.0	0.0	0.0	..	0.0	2.1
Gambia, The	GMB	**	0.0	0.0	0.3	0.0	0.0	0.0	0.0	0.0	0.0	0.0	0.0	0.0	0.0	0.0	0.0	0.0	0.0	..	0.0	0.0
Ghana	GHA	0.2	0	0.0	0.0	0.0	0.0	0.0	0.0	0.0	0.0	0.0	0.0	0.0	0.0	0.0	0.0	1.5	0.7	..	0.0	0.0
Guinea	GIN	0.0	0.0	0	0.2	0.0	0.0	0.0	0.0	0.0	0.0	0.1	0.0	0.0	0.0	0.0	0.0	0.0	0.0	..	0.0	0.0
Guinea-Bissau	GNB	0.0	0.0	0.1	0	0.0	0.0	0.0	0.0	0.0	0.0	0.0	0.0	0.0	0.0	0.0	0.0	0.0	0.0	..	0.0	0.0
Kenya	KEN	0.0	0.0	0.0	0.0	0	0.0	0.0	0.0	0.8	1.5	0.1	0.0	0.1	0.0	0.0	0.0	0.0	0.0	..	29.1	0.0
Lesotho	LSO	..	..	..	..	..	..	..	..	..	..	..	..	..	..	..	..	..	..	..	..	..
Liberia	LBR	0.0	0.0	0.0	0.0	0.3	0.0	0	0.0	0.0	0.0	0.0	0.0	0.0	0.0	0.0	0.0	0.0	0.0	..	0.0	0.0
Libya	LBY	0.0	0.0	0.0	0.0	0.0	0.0	0.0	0	0.0	0.0	0.0	0.0	0.0	0.6	0.0	0.0	0.1	0.0	..	0.0	0.0
Madagascar	MDG	0.0	0.0	0.0	0.0	0.1	0.0	0.0	0.0	**	0.0	0.0	0.0	0.8	0.0	0.0	0.0	0.0	0.0	..	0.0	0.0
Malawi	MWI	0.0	0.0	0.0	0.2	0.0	0.0	0.0	0.0	0.0	**	0.0	0.0	0.0	0.0	0.2	0.0	0.0	0.0	..	0.0	0.0
Mali	MLI	0.0	0.0	0.0	0.0	0.0	0.0	0.0	0.0	0.0	0.0	**	0.0	0.3	0.0	0.0	0.0	0.1	0.0	..	0.0	0.0
Mauritania	MRT	0.0	0.1	0.0	0.0	0.0	0.0	0.3	0.0	0.0	0.0	0.1	**	0.0	0.0	0.0	0.0	0.0	0.0	..	0.0	0.0
Mauritius	MUS	0.0	0.0	0.0	0.0	0.2	0.0	0.0	0.0	9.5	0.3	0.0	0.0	**	0.0	0.1	0.0	0.0	0.0	..	0.4	0.0
Morocco	MAR	1.1	0.1	1.1	0.8	0.0	0.0	0.1	1.2	0.1	0.0	1.7	2.5	0.1	**	0.0	0.0	0.2	0.2	..	0.0	0.0
Mozambique	MOZ	0.0	0.0	0.0	0.0	0.0	0.0	0.0	0.0	0.0	1.9	0.0	0.0	0.0	0.0	**	0.0	0.0	0.0	..	0.0	0.0
Namibia	NAM	..	..	..	..	..	..	..	..	..	..	..	..	..	..	..	**	..	..	..	..	..
Niger	NER	0.0	0.1	0.0	0.0	0.0	0.0	0.0	0.0	0.0	0.0	0.0	0.0	0.0	0.0	0.0	0.0	**	0.5	..	0.0	0.0
Nigeria	NGA	0.1	21.1	0.2	0.0	0.0	0.0	0.0	0.0	1.7	0.0	0.1	0.0	0.0	0.1	0.0	0.0	5.6	**	..	0.0	0.0
Reunion	REU	0.0	0.0	0.0	0.0	0.0	0.0	0.0	0.0	0.0	0.0	0.0	0.0	0.0	0.0	0.0	0.0	0.0	0.0	**	0.0	0.0
Rwanda	RWA	0.0	0.0	0.0	0.0	0.0	0.0	0.0	0.0	0.0	0.0	0.0	0.0	0.0	0.0	0.0	0.0	0.0	0.0	..	**	0.0
São Tomé and Principe	STP	0.0	0.0	0.0	0.0	0.0	0.0	0.0	0.0	0.0	0.0	0.0	0.0	0.0	0.0	0.0	0.0	0.0	0.0	..	0.0	**
Senegal	SEN	9.2	0.2	2.1	21.5	0.0	0.0	0.1	0.0	0.0	0.0	10.0	4.0	0.0	0.0	0.0	0.0	0.1	0.0	..	0.0	0.0
Seychelles	SYC	0.0	0.0	0.0	0.0	0.0	0.0	0.0	0.0	0.4	0.0	0.0	0.0	1.5	0.0	0.0	0.0	0.0	0.0	..	0.0	0.0
Sierra Leone	SLE	0.0	0.0	0.0	0.0	0.0	0.0	0.0	0.0	0.0	0.0	0.0	0.0	0.0	0.0	0.0	0.0	0.0	0.0	..	0.0	0.0
Somalia	SOM	0.0	0.0	0.0	0.0	0.0	0.0	0.0	0.0	0.0	0.0	0.0	0.0	0.0	0.0	0.0	0.0	0.0	0.0	..	0.0	0.0
South Africa	ZAF	0.9	3.4	1.6	0.2	7.5	0.0	0.0	0.0	5.9	45.1	2.3	1.4	13.8	0.9	43.2	0.0	1.3	2.5	..	4.0	2.1
Sudan	SDN	0.0	0.0	0.0	0.0	0.1	0.0	0.0	0.0	0.0	0.0	0.0	0.0	0.0	0.0	0.0	0.0	0.0	0.0	..	0.0	0.0
Swaziland	SWZ	..	..	..	..	..	..	..	..	..	..	..	..	..	..	..	..	..	..	..	..	..
Tanzania	TZA	0.0	0.0	0.0	0.0	1.1	0.0	0.0	0.0	0.1	3.2	0.1	0.0	0.0	0.0	0.1	0.0	0.1	0.0	..	1.8	0.0
Togo	TGO	0.0	1.8	0.2	0.0	0.0	0.0	0.0	0.0	0.0	0.0	0.2	0.0	0.0	0.0	0.0	0.0	2.6	0.0	..	0.0	0.1
Tunisia	TUN	0.2	0.1	0.2	0.0	0.0	0.0	0.0	6.5	0.1	0.0	0.4	0.3	0.0	0.4	0.0	0.0	2.2	0.0	..	0.0	0.0
Uganda	UGA	0.0	0.0	0.0	0.0	0.0	0.0	0.0	0.0	0.0	0.0	0.0	0.0	0.0	0.0	0.0	0.0	0.0	0.0	..	1.0	0.0
Zambia	ZMB	0.0	0.2	0.0	0.0	0.2	0.0	0.0	0.0	0.0	12.5	0.0	0.0	0.3	0.0	0.0	0.4	0.0	0.0	..	1.5	0.0
Zimbabwe	ZWE	0.0	0.0	0.0	0.0	0.1	0.6	0.0	0.0	0.0	1.7	0.0	0.0	0.1	0.0	0.6	0.7	0.0	0.0	..	0.0	0.0
Sub-Saharan Africa	SSA	14.1	33.5	12.3	23.0	10.0	0.7	1.2	0.0	18.6	66.3	39.9	6.2	17.3	1.7	44.2	1.1	25.6	4.4	..	42.3	4.2
European Community	EU	31.1	32.5	52.3	41.2	26.6	6.1	27.7	60.5	35.6	12.1	42.7	51.6	34.8	61.9	19.8	50.5	41.8	42.8	..	36.0	85.0
Canada	CAN	0.1	1.5	0.5	0.0	0.4	0.0	0.0	0.6	0.1	0.7	0.2	0.3	0.1	1.0	0.6	0.2	0.3	0.4	..	0.5	0.0
United States	USA	2.6	6.5	8.0	2.6	8.4	1.2	0.6	0.4	2.1	5.5	1.3	3.1	1.4	4.8	6.4	18.4	8.7	9.2	..	4.7	3.5
North America	NNA	2.7	8.0	8.5	2.6	8.8	1.2	0.6	1.0	2.2	6.2	1.6	3.4	1.5	5.8	7.0	18.6	9.0	9.7	..	5.2	3.5
Rest of World	ROW	52.1	26.1	26.8	33.2	54.6	92.1	70.5	38.5	43.6	15.5	15.8	38.7	46.4	30.6	29.0	29.8	23.6	43.1	..	16.5	7.3
World	WLD	100.0	100.0	100.0	100.0	100.0	100.0	100.0	100.0	100.0	100.0	100.0	100.0	100.0	100.0	100.0	100.0	100.0	100.0	..	100.0	100.0

Note: ** means "not applicable."

South Africa's data for 1997 is taken from partner countries' data.

Source: International Monetary Fund's Direction of Trade database.

(Table continues on the following page.)

5-52. Direction of trade matrix, exports, 2002

	Exporters	*Importers* SEN	SYC	SLE	SOM	ZAF	SDN	SWZ	TZA	TGO	TUN	UGA	ZMB	ZWE	SSA	*Percentage of total exports* EU	CAN	USA	NNA	ROW	WLD
Algeria	DZA	0.1	0.0	0.0	0.0	0.0	0.0	0.0	0.0	0.0	0.9	0.0	0.0	0.0	0.1	0.5	0.4	0.2	0.3	0.1	0.3
Angola	AGO	0.5	0.0	0.0	0.0	0.0	0.0	0.0	0.0	0.0	0.0	0.0	0.0	0.0	0.0	0.1	0.0	0.3	0.2	0.1	0.1
Benin	BEN	0.0	0.0	0.0	0.0	0.0	0.0	0.0	0.0	0.4	0.0	0.0	0.0	0.0	0.0	0.0	0.0	0.0	0.0	0.0	0.0
Bostwana	BWA	..	..	..	..	..	..	..	..	..	..	..	..	..	..	..	..	..	..	..	..
Burkina Faso	BFA	0.0	0.0	0.0	0.0	0.0	0.0	0.0	0.0	0.1	0.0	0.0	0.0	0.0	0.0	0.0	0.0	0.0	0.0	0.0	0.0
Burundi	BDI	0.0	0.0	0.0	0.0	0.0	0.0	0.0	0.0	0.0	0.0	0.1	0.0	0.0	0.0	0.0	0.0	0.0	0.0	0.0	0.0
Cameroon	CMR	0.3	0.0	0.0	0.0	0.0	0.0	0.0	0.0	0.4	0.1	0.0	0.0	0.0	0.2	0.1	0.0	0.0	0.0	0.0	0.0
Cape Verde	CPV	0.0	0.0	0.0	0.0	0.0	0.0	0.0	0.0	0.0	0.0	0.0	0.0	0.0	0.0	0.0	0.0	0.0	0.0	0.0	0.0
Central African Republic	CAF	0.0	0.0	0.0	0.0	0.0	0.0	0.0	0.0	0.0	0.0	0.0	0.0	0.0	0.0	0.0	0.0	0.0	0.0	0.0	0.0
Chad	TCD	0.0	0.0	0.0	0.0	0.0	0.0	0.0	0.0	0.0	0.0	0.0	0.0	0.0	0.0	0.0	0.0	0.0	0.0	0.0	0.0
Comoros	COM	0.0	0.0	0.0	0.0	0.0	0.0	0.0	0.0	0.0	0.0	0.0	0.0	0.0	0.0	0.0	0.0	0.0	0.0	0.0	0.0
Congo, Dem. Rep. of	ZAR	0.0	0.0	0.0	0.0	0.0	0.0	0.0	0.0	0.0	0.0	0.0	0.0	6.6	0.1	0.0	0.0	0.0	0.0	0.0	0.0
Congo, Rep. of	COG	0.3	0.0	0.0	0.0	0.0	0.0	0.0	0.0	0.0	0.0	0.0	0.0	0.0	0.0	0.0	0.0	0.0	0.0	0.0	0.0
Côte d'Ivoire	CIV	2.5	0.0	5.0	0.0	0.1	0.0	0.0	0.0	10.1	0.2	0.0	0.0	0.0	1.2	0.1	0.0	0.0	0.0	0.0	0.1
Djibouti	DJI	0.0	0.0	0.0	35.1	0.0	0.0	0.0	0.0	0.0	0.0	0.0	0.0	0.0	0.1	0.0	0.0	0.0	0.0	0.0	0.0
Egypt, Arab Rep.	EGY	0.5	0.0	0.5	0.0	0.0	1.8	0.0	0.3	0.0	0.5	0.1	0.1	0.0	0.2	0.1	0.0	0.1	0.1	0.1	0.1
Equatorial Guinea	GNQ	0.0	0.0	0.0	0.0	0.0	0.0	0.0	0.0	0.0	0.0	0.0	0.0	0.0	0.0	0.0	0.1	0.0	0.1	0.0	0.0
Eritrea	ERI	..	..	..	..	..	..	..	..	..	..	..	..	..	..	..	..	..	..	..	..
Ethiopia	ETH	0.0	0.0	0.0	0.0	0.0	0.0	0.0	0.0	0.0	0.0	0.0	0.0	0.0	0.0	0.0	0.0	0.0	0.0	0.0	0.0
Gabon	GAB	0.3	0.0	0.0	0.0	0.3	0.0	0.0	0.0	0.1	0.1	0.0	0.0	0.0	0.1	0.0	0.0	0.1	0.1	0.0	0.0
Gambia, The	GMB	0.0	0.0	0.0	0.0	0.0	0.0	0.0	0.0	0.0	0.0	0.0	0.0	0.0	0.0	0.0	0.0	0.0	0.0	0.0	0.0
Ghana	GHA	0.3	0.0	0.0	0.0	0.0	0.0	0.0	0.0	0.8	0.0	0.0	0.0	0.0	0.2	0.0	0.0	0.0	0.0	0.0	0.0
Guinea	GIN	0.0	0.2	0.3	0.0	0.0	0.0	0.0	0.0	0.0	0.0	0.0	0.0	0.0	0.1	0.0	0.0	0.0	0.0	0.0	0.0
Guinea-Bissau	GNB	0.0	0.0	0.0	0.0	0.0	0.0	0.0	0.0	0.0	0.0	0.0	0.0	0.0	0.0	0.0	0.0	0.0	0.0	0.0	0.0
Kenya	KEN	0.0	1.0	0.0	15.9	0.0	3.2	0.0	5.6	0.0	0.0	46.5	0.3	0.1	1.0	0.0	0.0	0.0	0.0	0.0	0.0
Lesotho	LSO	..	..	..	..	..	..	..	..	..	..	..	..	..	..	..	..	..	..	..	..
Liberia	LBR	0.1	0.0	0.3	0.0	0.0	0.0	0.0	0.0	0.0	0.0	0.0	0.0	0.0	0.0	0.0	0.0	0.0	0.0	0.0	0.0
Libya	LBY	0.0	0.0	0.0	0.0	0.0	0.1	0.0	0.0	0.0	2.9	0.0	0.0	0.0	0.0	0.3	0.0	0.0	0.0	0.1	0.2
Madagascar	MDG	0.0	0.2	0.0	0.0	0.0	0.0	0.0	0.0	0.0	0.0	0.0	0.0	0.0	0.0	0.0	0.0	0.0	0.0	0.0	0.0
Malawi	MWI	0.0	0.0	0.1	0.0	0.2	0.0	0.0	0.1	0.0	0.0	0.2	0.3	0.2	0.1	0.0	0.0	0.0	0.0	0.0	0.0
Mali	MLI	0.0	0.0	0.0	0.0	0.0	0.0	0.0	0.0	0.0	0.0	0.0	0.0	0.0	0.0	0.0	0.0	0.0	0.0	0.0	0.0
Mauritania	MRT	0.0	0.0	0.0	0.0	0.0	0.0	0.0	0.0	0.8	0.0	0.0	0.0	0.0	0.1	0.0	0.0	0.0	0.0	0.0	0.0
Mauritius	MUS	0.0	3.9	0.0	0.0	0.1	0.0	0.0	0.2	0.0	0.0	0.1	0.1	0.5	0.2	0.0	0.0	0.0	0.0	0.0	0.0
Morocco	MAR	0.7	0.0	0.4	0.0	0.0	0.0	0.0	0.0	0.3	0.6	0.0	0.0	0.0	0.2	0.2	0.0	0.0	0.0	0.1	0.1
Mozambique	MOZ	0.0	0.0	0.0	0.0	0.5	0.0	0.5	0.0	0.0	0.0	0.0	0.0	2.7	0.2	0.0	0.0	0.0	0.0	0.0	0.0
Namibia	NAM	..	..	..	..	..	..	..	..	..	..	..	..	..	..	..	..	..	..	..	..
Niger	NER	0.0	0.0	0.0	0.0	0.0	0.0	0.0	0.0	0.1	0.0	0.0	0.0	0.0	0.1	0.0	0.0	0.0	0.0	0.0	0.0
Nigeria	NGA	7.8	0.0	3.4	0.0	1.3	0.0	0.0	0.0	0.5	0.0	0.0	0.0	0.0	2.5	0.2	0.1	0.5	0.4	0.2	0.3
Reunion	REU	0.0	0.0	0.0	0.0	0.0	0.0	0.0	0.0	0.0	0.0	0.0	0.0	0.0	0.0	0.0	0.0	0.0	0.0	0.0	0.0
Rwanda	RWA	0.0	0.0	0.0	0.0	0.0	0.0	0.0	0.0	0.0	0.0	0.0	0.0	0.0	0.0	0.0	0.0	0.0	0.0	0.0	0.0
São Tomé and Principe	STP	0.0	0.0	0.0	0.0	0.0	0.0	0.0	0.0	0.0	0.0	0.0	0.0	0.0	0.0	0.0	0.0	0.0	0.0	0.0	0.0
Senegal	SEN	**	0.0	0.8	0.0	0.0	0.0	0.0	0.0	0.9	0.0	0.0	0.0	0.0	0.4	0.0	0.0	0.0	0.0	0.0	0.0
Seychelles	SYC	0.0	**	0.0	0.0	0.0	0.0	0.0	0.0	0.0	0.0	0.0	0.0	0.0	0.0	0.0	0.0	0.0	0.0	0.0	0.0
Sierra Leone	SLE	0.0	0.0	**	0.0	0.0	0.0	0.0	0.0	0.0	0.0	0.0	0.0	0.0	0.0	0.0	0.0	0.0	0.0	0.0	0.0
Somalia	SOM	0.0	0.0	0.0	**	0.0	0.0	0.0	0.0	0.0	0.0	0.1	0.0	0.0	0.0	0.0	0.0	0.0	0.0	0.0	0.0
South Africa	ZAF	1.1	11.0	1.3	0.1	**	1.6	0.0	13.6	0.6	0.0	6.6	63.5	52.5	5.3	0.4	0.1	0.0	0.0	0.3	0.3
Sudan	SDN	0.0	0.0	0.0	0.3	0.0	**	0.0	0.0	0.0	0.1	0.0	0.0	0.0	0.0	0.0	0.0	0.0	0.0	0.1	0.0
Swaziland	SWZ	..	..	..	..	..	..	**	..	..	..	..	..	..	..	..	..	..	..	..	..
Tanzania	TZA	0.0	0.1	0.3	0.1	0.1	0.0	0.4	**	0.0	0.0	0.6	1.9	0.1	0.2	0.0	0.0	0.0	0.0	0.0	0.0
Togo	TGO	0.0	0.0	0.0	0.0	0.0	0.0	0.0	0.0	**	0.0	0.0	0.0	0.0	0.2	0.0	0.0	0.0	0.0	0.0	0.0
Tunisia	TUN	0.6	0.0	0.0	0.0	0.0	0.0	0.0	0.0	0.2	**	0.0	0.0	0.0	0.1	0.2	0.0	0.0	0.0	0.0	0.1
Uganda	UGA	0.0	0.0	0.0	0.0	0.0	0.0	0.0	0.2	0.0	0.0	**	0.0	0.0	0.0	0.0	0.0	0.0	0.0	0.0	0.0
Zambia	ZMB	0.0	0.0	0.0	0.0	0.3	0.0	0.7	0.3	0.0	0.0	0.2	**	1.0	0.2	0.0	0.0	0.0	0.0	0.0	0.0
Zimbabwe	ZWE	0.0	0.0	0.0	0.0	0.8	0.1	0.0	0.1	0.0	0.0	0.1	1.3	**	0.3	0.0	0.0	0.0	0.0	0.1	0.0
Sub-Saharan Africa	SSA	13.5	16.4	11.6	16.5	3.7	5.0	1.6	20.2	14.7	0.6	54.5	67.6	63.8	13.0	1.3	0.3	1.1	1.0	1.0	1.3
European Community	EU	56.2	44.7	65.5	10.6	45.5	25.9	18.2	23.3	44.2	78.1	20.8	11.3	12.5	40.5	63.8	9.6	20.1	18.4	25.1	37.9
Canada	CAN	0.3	0.3	0.7	0.0	0.6	1.7	0.2	0.7	1.0	0.9	0.3	0.5	0.2	0.5	0.5	0	19.6	16.4	0.8	3.9
United States	USA	3.8	2.4	5.8	2.2	9.7	0.5	11.5	4.0	1.5	2.1	2.5	3.9	3.4	7.2	6.2	73.4	0	11.9	14.4	10.8
North America	NNA	4.1	2.7	6.6	2.3	10.3	2.2	11.7	4.7	2.5	3.1	2.8	4.5	3.7	7.7	6.6	73.4	19.6	28.3	15.2	14.8
Rest of World	ROW	26.1	36.2	16.2	70.7	40.5	66.9	68.6	51.9	38.6	18.2	21.9	16.6	20.0	38.8	28.2	16.7	59.2	52.3	58.8	46.1
World	WLD	100.0	100.0	100.0	100.0	100.0	100.0	100.0	100.0	100.0	100.0	100.0	100.0	100.0	100.0	100.0	100.0	100.0	100.0	100.0	100.0

Note: ** means "not applicable."

South Africa's data for 1997 is taken from partner countries' data.

Source: International Monetary Fund's Direction of Trade database.

5-53. Direction of trade matrix, current U.S. dollars, 1992

		Importers																			*Millions of current U.S. dollars*
Exporters		DZA	AGO	BEN	BWA	BFA	BDI	CMR	CPV	CAF	TCD	COM	ZAR	COG	CIV	DJI	EGY	GNQ	ERI	ETH	GAB
Algeria	DZA	**	0	0	0	0	0	0	0	0	0	0	0	0	0	0	1	0	0	0	0
Angola	AGO	0	**	0	0	0	0	0	1	0	0	0	0	1	0	0	0	0	0	0	0
Benin	BEN	0	0	**	0	1	0	0	1	0	0	0	0	1	2	0	0	0	0	0	0
Bostwana	BWA	..	..	..	**	..	..	..	..	..	..	..	..	..	..	..	..	..	..	..	..
Burkina Faso	BFA	0	0	0	0	**	0	0	0	0	0	0	0	0	18	0	0	0	0	0	0
Burundi	BDI	0	0	0	0	0	**	0	0	0	0	0	3	0	0	0	0	0	0	0	0
Cameroon	CMR	0	0	0	0	0	0	**	0	0	0	0	0	0	7	0	0	0	0	0	28
Cape Verde	CPV	0	0	0	0	0	0	0	**	0	0	0	0	0	0	0	0	0	0	0	0
Central African Republic	CAF	0	0	0	0	0	0	0	0	**	0	0	4	0	0	0	0	0	0	0	0
Chad	TCD	0	0	0	0	0	0	0	0	0	**	0	0	0	0	0	0	0	0	0	0
Comoros	COM	0	0	0	0	0	0	0	0	0	0	**	0	0	0	0	0	0	0	0	0
Congo, Dem. Rep. of	ZAR	0	0	0	0	0	1	0	0	2	0	0	**	3	2	0	6	0	0	0	1
Congo, Rep. of	COG	16	8	0	0	0	0	0	0	0	0	0	3	**	0	0	0	0	0	0	0
Côte d'Ivoire	CIV	1	3	23	0	137	0	0	17	12	1	0	16	8	**	0	0	3	0	0	11
Djibouti	DJI	0	0	0	0	0	0	0	0	0	0	0	0	0	0	**	0	0	0	42	0
Egypt, Arab Rep.	EGY	28	1	0	0	0	0	1	0	0	0	0	1	0	1	3	**	0	0	2	0
Equatorial Guinea	GNQ	0	0	0	0	0	0	0	0	0	0	0	0	0	7	0	0	**	0	0	0
Eritrea	ERI	..	..	..	..	..	..	..	..	..	..	..	..	..	..	..	..	..	**	..	..
Ethiopia	ETH	0	0	0	0	0	0	0	0	0	0	0	0	0	0	13	0	0	0	**	0
Gabon	GAB	1	0	0	0	0	0	0	0	1	0	0	0	0	1	0	1	0	0	0	**
Gambia, The	GMB	0	0	0	0	0	0	0	0	0	0	0	0	0	0	0	0	0	0	0	0
Ghana	GHA	0	5	0	0	0	0	0	0	0	0	0	0	0	67	0	0	0	0	1	0
Guinea	GIN	0	0	0	0	0	0	33	0	0	0	0	0	0	8	0	0	0	0	0	0
Guinea-Bissau	GNB	0	0	0	0	0	0	0	0	0	0	0	0	0	2	0	0	0	0	0	0
Kenya	KEN	0	0	0	0	0	6	0	0	0	0	4	8	0	0	3	41	0	0	11	0
Lesotho	LSO	..	..	..	..	..	..	..	..	..	..	..	..	..	..	..	..	..	..	..	..
Liberia	LBR	0	0	0	0	0	0	0	0	0	0	0	0	0	0	0	0	0	0	0	0
Libya	LBY	2	0	0	0	0	0	0	0	0	0	0	0	0	0	0	46	0	0	0	0
Madagascar	MDG	0	0	0	0	0	0	0	0	0	0	1	0	0	0	0	0	0	0	0	0
Malawi	MWI	0	0	0	3	0	0	0	0	0	0	0	2	0	0	0	3	0	0	0	0
Mali	MLI	0	0	0	0	2	0	0	0	0	0	0	0	5	8	0	0	0	0	0	0
Mauritania	MRT	0	0	3	0	2	0	0	0	0	0	0	0	5	27	0	2	0	0	0	0
Mauritius	MUS	0	0	0	0	0	0	0	0	0	0	2	0	0	0	0	0	0	0	0	0
Morocco	MAR	72	8	2	0	1	1	8	0	1	0	1	3	5	6	0	2	1	0	3	8
Mozambique	MOZ	0	0	0	0	0	0	0	0	0	0	0	0	0	0	0	0	0	0	0	0
Namibia	NAM	..	..	..	..	..	..	..	..	..	..	..	..	..	..	..	..	..	..	..	..
Niger	NER	1	0	3	0	1	0	0	0	0	0	0	0	0	3	0	0	0	0	0	0
Nigeria	NGA	1	0	9	0	13	0	7	0	0	9	0	42	3	386	0	0	0	0	0	23
Reunion	REU	0	0	0	0	0	0	0	0	0	0	2	0	0	0	0	0	0	0	0	0
Rwanda	RWA	0	0	0	0	0	0	0	0	0	0	0	0	0	0	0	0	0	0	0	0
São Tomé and Principe	STP	0	0	0	0	0	0	0	0	0	0	0	0	0	0	0	0	0	0	0	0
Senegal	SEN	0	5	6	0	3	0	27	0	0	1	0	0	5	0	0	0	0	0	0	4
Seychelles	SYC	0	0	0	0	0	0	0	0	0	0	0	0	0	0	0	0	0	0	0	0
Sierra Leone	SLE	0	0	0	0	0	0	0	0	0	0	0	0	0	0	0	0	0	0	0	0
Somalia	SOM	0	0	0	0	0	0	0	0	0	0	0	0	0	0	0	1	0	0	0	0
South Africa	ZAF	3	141	0	0	0	0	1	0	0	0	12	0	6	13	0	1	0	0	0	5
Sudan	SDN	1	0	0	0	0	0	0	0	0	0	0	0	0	0	0	20	0	0	0	0
Swaziland	SWZ	..	..	..	..	..	..	..	..	..	..	..	..	..	..	..	..	..	..	..	..
Tanzania	TZA	0	0	0	1	0	17	0	0	0	0	0	2	0	0	0	1	0	0	0	0
Togo	TGO	0	0	0	0	15	0	0	0	0	0	0	0	1	0	0	0	0	0	0	1
Tunisia	TUN	98	0	3	0	0	0	8	0	0	0	0	0	0	4	0	7	0	0	6	0
Uganda	UGA	0	0	0	0	0	0	0	0	0	0	0	0	0	0	0	2	0	0	0	0
Zambia	ZMB	0	0	0	2	0	1	0	0	0	0	0	5	0	0	0	0	0	0	0	0
Zimbabwe	ZWE	0	4	0	65	0	1	0	0	0	0	0	3	0	0	0	0	0	0	0	0
Sub-Saharan Africa	SSA	25	167	46	71	175	27	69	19	16	11	22	89	38	552	17	80	3	0	12	74
European Community	EU	5,282	1,803	296	88	211	98	825	118	82	102	67	384	437	1,233	189	4,903	39	0	490	582
Canada	CAN	119	5	1	3	5	0	16	0	0	0	0	6	1	5	0	86	0	0	11	6
United States	USA	677	158	27	47	13	10	57	4	1	5	1	33	60	87	11	3,087	11	0	250	55
North America	NNA	796	163	28	49	18	10	73	4	1	5	1	39	61	93	11	3,173	11	0	260	61
Rest of World	ROW	1,225	288	193	61	50	33	210	21	13	9	17	223	156	314	202	4,340	3	0	382	127
World	WLD	7,327	2,421	563	269	453	168	1,176	163	112	128	106	735	691	2,192	419	12,496	57	0	1,144	844

Note: ** means "not applicable."

South Africa's data for 1992 is taken from partner countries' data.

Source: International Monetary Fund's Direction of Trade database.

(Table continues on the following page.)

5-53. Direction of trade matrix, current U.S. dollars, 1992 (continued)

Exporters (Importers)		GMB	GHA	GIN	GNB	KEN	LSO	LBR	LBY	MDG	MWI	MLI	MRT	MUS	MAR	MOZ	NAM	NER	NGA	REU	RWA	STP
Algeria	DZA	0	0	1	0	0	0	10	3	0	0	0	16	0	137	0	0	0	0	0	0	0
Angola	AGO	0	0	0	0	0	0	0	0	0	0	0	0	0	0	0	0	0	0	0	0	0
Benin	BEN	0	0	0	0	0	0	0	0	2	0	0	0	0	10	0	0	1	3	0	0	0
Bostwana	BWA	..	..	..	..	..	..	..	..	..	..	..	..	..	..	..	..	..	..	..	..	..
Burkina Faso	BFA	0	1	0	0	0	0	0	0	0	0	1	0	0	0	0	0	0	0	0	0	0
Burundi	BDI	0	0	0	0	4	0	0	0	0	0	0	0	0	0	0	0	0	0	0	6	0
Cameroon	CMR	0	0	7	0	0	0	0	0	0	0	0	0	0	45	0	0	0	10	0	0	0
Cape Verde	CPV	0	0	0	0	0	0	0	0	0	0	0	0	0	0	0	0	0	0	0	0	0
Central African Republic	CAF	0	0	0	0	0	0	0	0	0	0	0	0	0	0	0	0	0	0	0	0	0
Chad	TCD	0	0	0	0	0	0	0	0	0	0	0	0	0	4	0	0	0	2	0	0	0
Comoros	COM	0	0	0	0	0	0	0	0	0	0	0	0	0	0	0	0	0	0	0	0	0
Congo, Dem. Rep. of	ZAR	0	0	0	0	1	0	0	0	0	0	0	0	0	0	0	0	0	0	0	2	0
Congo, Rep. of	COG	0	0	0	0	0	0	0	0	0	0	0	0	0	11	0	0	0	4	3	0	0
Côte d'Ivoire	CIV	13	64	90	5	0	0	23	1	0	0	121	17	11	18	3	0	27	111	0	0	0
Djibouti	DJI	0	0	0	0	0	0	0	0	0	0	0	0	0	0	0	0	0	0	0	0	0
Egypt, Arab Rep.	EGY	0	0	0	0	2	0	14	58	0	1	0	0	0	6	1	0	0	3	0	0	0
Equatorial Guinea	GNQ	0	0	0	0	0	0	0	0	0	0	0	0	0	0	0	0	0	0	0	0	0
Eritrea	ERI	..	..	..	..	..	..	..	..	..	..	..	..	..	..	..	..	..	..	..	..	..
Ethiopia	ETH	0	0	0	0	0	0	0	0	0	0	0	0	0	0	0	0	0	0	0	0	0
Gabon	GAB	0	0	0	0	0	0	0	0	0	0	0	0	0	20	0	0	0	1	0	0	0
Gambia, The	GMB	**	0	8	0	0	0	0	0	0	0	0	0	0	0	0	0	0	0	0	0	0
Ghana	GHA	0	**	0	0	0	0	0	0	0	0	0	0	0	1	0	0	0	42	0	0	0
Guinea	GIN	0	0	**	0	0	0	0	0	0	0	0	0	0	2	0	0	0	1	0	0	0
Guinea-Bissau	GNB	0	0	0	**	0	0	0	0	0	0	0	0	0	0	0	0	0	0	0	0	0
Kenya	KEN	0	0	0	0	**	0	0	0	1	1	0	0	6	0	0	0	0	4	3	13	0
Lesotho	LSO	..	..	..	..	..	**	..	..	..	..	..	..	..	..	..	..	..	..	..	..	..
Liberia	LBR	0	0	0	0	0	0	**	0	0	0	0	0	0	0	0	0	0	0	0	0	0
Libya	LBY	0	0	0	0	0	0	0	**	0	0	0	1	0	93	0	0	0	0	0	0	0
Madagascar	MDG	0	0	0	0	1	0	0	0	**	0	0	0	8	0	0	0	0	0	13	0	0
Malawi	MWI	0	0	0	0	0	0	0	0	0	**	0	0	0	0	3	0	0	0	0	0	0
Mali	MLI	0	0	0	0	0	0	0	0	0	0	**	0	0	1	0	0	0	2	0	0	0
Mauritania	MRT	0	1	0	0	0	0	3	0	0	0	0	**	0	0	0	0	0	0	0	0	0
Mauritius	MUS	0	0	0	0	2	0	0	0	14	0	0	0	**	0	0	0	0	0	29	2	0
Morocco	MAR	0	1	8	0	1	0	0	131	1	0	6	7	2	**	0	0	0	12	2	0	0
Mozambique	MOZ	0	0	0	0	0	0	0	0	0	0	0	0	1	0	**	0	0	0	0	0	0
Namibia	NAM	..	..	..	..	..	..	..	..	..	..	..	..	..	..	..	**	..	..	..	..	..
Niger	NER	0	2	0	0	0	0	0	2	0	0	1	0	0	0	0	0	**	60	0	0	0
Nigeria	NGA	0	277	15	0	0	0	1	0	3	0	0	0	0	4	0	0	3	**	0	0	0
Reunion	REU	0	0	0	0	0	0	0	0	6	0	0	0	3	0	0	0	0	0	**	0	0
Rwanda	RWA	0	0	0	0	0	0	0	0	0	0	0	0	0	0	0	0	0	0	0	**	0
São Tomé and Principe	STP	0	0	0	0	0	0	0	0	0	0	0	0	0	0	0	0	0	0	0	0	**
Senegal	SEN	12	0	18	3	0	0	0	0	0	0	40	4	0	0	0	0	1	5	0	0	0
Seychelles	SYC	0	0	0	0	0	0	0	0	0	0	0	0	1	0	0	0	0	0	0	0	0
Sierra Leone	SLE	0	0	0	0	0	0	0	0	0	0	0	0	0	0	0	0	0	0	0	0	0
Somalia	SOM	0	0	0	0	0	0	0	0	0	0	0	0	0	0	0	0	0	0	0	0	0
South Africa	ZAF	1	1	4	0	0	0	0	2	25	269	1	0	210	1	262	0	0	2	53	1	2
Sudan	SDN	0	0	0	0	1	0	0	5	0	0	0	0	0	0	0	0	0	0	0	0	0
Swaziland	SWZ	..	..	..	..	..	..	..	..	..	..	..	..	..	..	..	..	..	..	..	..	..
Tanzania	TZA	0	0	0	0	8	0	0	0	1	1	0	0	1	0	1	0	0	0	0	21	0
Togo	TGO	0	6	0	0	0	0	0	0	0	0	1	0	0	3	0	0	4	21	0	0	0
Tunisia	TUN	0	7	0	0	2	0	0	181	0	0	0	0	0	46	0	0	0	1	0	0	0
Uganda	UGA	0	0	0	0	4	0	0	0	0	0	0	0	0	0	0	0	0	0	0	1	0
Zambia	ZMB	0	0	0	0	26	0	0	0	0	5	0	0	0	0	0	1	0	0	0	0	0
Zimbabwe	ZWE	0	3	0	0	17	1	0	4	0	41	0	0	3	1	42	2	0	1	0	0	0
Sub-Saharan Africa	SSA	27	356	144	9	66	1	28	13	53	317	166	22	246	122	312	3	35	270	102	45	2
European Community	EU	148	729	380	58	753	39	1,176	2,938	244	151	258	318	490	4,969	290	113	196	4,438	1,720	105	21
Canada	CAN	0	21	1	0	20	0	1	64	1	2	5	1	1	103	16	1	1	40	0	2	0
United States	USA	10	124	61	1	124	3	31	0	6	14	11	61	21	493	150	34	13	1,001	3	3	3
North America	NNA	10	144	62	1	144	3	32	64	7	16	17	62	22	596	166	35	14	1,041	3	5	3
Rest of World	ROW	167	431	187	36	944	29	4,044	1,671	129	125	79	131	574	2,012	262	13	52	2,860	223	51	7
World	WLD	353	1,661	773	104	1,906	72	5,280	4,687	432	610	519	532	1,332	7,700	1,030	164	296	8,608	2,048	206	32

Note: ** means "not applicable."

South Africa's data for 1992 is taken from partner countries' data.

Source: International Monetary Fund's Direction of Trade database.

(Table continues on the following page.)

5-53. Direction of trade matrix, current U.S. dollars, 1992

Exporters		Importers SEN	SYC	SLE	SOM	Millions of current U.S. dollars ZAF	SDN	SWZ	TZA	TGO	TUN	UGA	ZMB	ZWE	SSA	Millions of current US dollars EU	CAN	USA	NNA	ROW	WLD
Algeria	DZA	1	0	0	0	0	0	0	0	0	78	0	0	0	28	8,386	33	1,553	1,587	1,136	11,137
Angola	AGO	14	0	0	0	0	0	0	0	1	0	0	0	0	19	1,131	0	2,214	2,215	162	3,527
Benin	BEN	0	0	0	0	0	0	0	0	2	0	0	0	..	14	28	0	0	0	23	65
Bostwana	BWA	..	..	..		..		..		..		..	..	..		..		..		..	
Burkina Faso	BFA	0	0	0	0	0	0	0	0	2	0	0	0	0	22	14	0	0	0	39	76
Burundi	BDI	0	0	0	0	0	0	0	1	0	0	0	0	2	15	25	0	6	6	29	74
Cameroon	CMR	2	0	0	0	8	0	0	0	0	2	0	0	0	62	1,370	0	106	106	303	1,840
Cape Verde	CPV	0	0	0	0	0	0	0	0	0	0	0	0	0	1	5	0	0	0	0	6
Central African Republic	CAF	0	0	0	0	0	4	0	0	0	0	0	0	0	8	73	0	0	0	26	107
Chad	TCD	0	0	0	0	4	0	0	0	0	0	0	0	0	7	55	0	0	0	15	77
Comoros	COM	0	0	0	0	0	0	0	0	0	0	0	0	0	0	15	0	10	10	2	27
Congo, Dem. Rep. of	ZAR	0	0	0	0	4	0	0	0	0	1	0	2	0	18	811	44	235	279	377	1,486
Congo, Rep. of	COG	0	0	0	0	1	0	0	0	1	0	0	0	0	21	514	0	517	517	135	1,187
Côte d'Ivoire	CIV	89	0	26	0	50	0	0	3	30	17	0	0	0	917	1,619	1	124	125	330	2,991
Djibouti	DJI	0	0	0	26	0	0	0	0	0	0	0	0	0	68	3	0	0	0	24	96
Egypt, Arab Rep.	EGY	0	0	0	0	2	46	0	0	0	20	0	0	0	75	1,211	6	286	293	1,471	3,050
Equatorial Guinea	GNQ	0	0	0	0	0	0	0	0	0	0	0	0	0	7	34	0	0	0	2	43
Eritrea	ERI	..	..	..		..		..		..		..	..			..		..		..	
Ethiopia	ETH	0	0	0	0	0	0	0	0	0	0	0	0	0	0	75	0	7	7	104	187
Gabon	GAB	15	0	0	0	1	0	0	0	3	1	0	0	0	24	916	0	894	894	452	2,286
Gambia, The	GMB	2	0	0	0	0	0	0	0	0	0	0	0	0	11	176	0	1	1	44	232
Ghana	GHA	0	0	0	0	0	0	0	0	90	0	0	0	0	206	375	4	32	37	620	1,237
Guinea	GIN	1	0	0	0	0	0	0	0	0	0	0	0	0	43	342	8	114	122	67	573
Guinea-Bissau	GNB	0	0	0	0	0	0	0	0	0	0	0	0	0	2	7	0	0	0	4	13
Kenya	KEN	0	1	0	30	6	12	0	44	0	0	72	3	3	231	447	7	40	47	613	1,337
Lesotho	LSO	..	..			..									..	..		..		..	
Liberia	LBR	0	0	0	0	5	0	0	0	0	0	0	0	0	6	587	1	12	13	173	781
Libya	LBY	1	0	0	0	0	168	0	0	0	47	0	0	0	170	8,251	0	0	0	1,521	9,942
Madagascar	MDG	1	0	0	0	2	0	0	0	0	1	0	0	0	29	134	1	42	42	63	268
Malawi	MWI	0	0	0	0	47	0	0	2	0	0	0	2	2	64	215	1	58	59	172	510
Mali	MLI	1	0	0	0	3	0	0	0	0	3	0	0	1	22	97	5	1	6	91	216
Mauritania	MRT	0	0	0	0	0	0	0	0	3	0	0	0	0	45	230	0	21	21	152	448
Mauritius	MUS	0	3	0	0	10	0	0	1	0	0	0	0	4	67	1,015	10	161	172	48	1,301
Morocco	MAR	6	0	0	0	0	1	0	0	4	50	0	0	0	98	2,582	24	149	173	1,552	4,405
Mozambique	MOZ	0	0	0	0	18	0	0	0	0	0	0	0	8	28	67	0	19	19	21	134
Namibia	NAM	..	..	..		..		..		..		..	..		..	..		..		..	
Niger	NER	0	0	0	0	0	0	0	0	2	0	0	0	0	74	144	0	0	0	53	271
Nigeria	NGA	71	0	6	0	1	0	0	0	2	0	0	1	1	874	5,110	387	4,818	5,204	1,182	12,370
Reunion	REU	0	0	0	0	1	0	0	0	0	0	0	0	0	12	176	0	0	0	20	209
Rwanda	RWA	0	0	0	0	0	0	0	0	0	0	0	0	0	1	167	0	4	5	25	197
São Tomé and Principe	STP	0	0	0	0	0	0	0	0	0	0	0	0	0	0	4	0	0	0	1	5
Senegal	SEN	**	0	2	0	0	0	0	0	3	3	0	0	0	140	296	0	3	3	303	741
Seychelles	SYC	0	**	0	0	0	0	0	0	0	0	0	0	0	2	15	0	0	0	1	18
Sierra Leone	SLE	0	0	**	0	0	0	0	0	0	0	0	0	0	0	70	0	46	46	34	150
Somalia	SOM	0	0	0	**	0	0	0	0	0	0	0	0	2	1	15	0	2	2	112	130
South Africa	ZAF	0	28	0	0	**	8	0	11	4	0	1	224	537	1,823	8,538	122	1,795	1,916	5,279	17,556
Sudan	SDN	0	0	0	0	0	**	0	0	0	3	0	0	0	2	107	0	11	11	201	320
Swaziland	SWZ	..	..	..		..		**		..		..			..	..		..		..	
Tanzania	TZA	0	0	0	1	4	3	0	**	0	0	5	3	6	74	197	2	11	13	190	474
Togo	TGO	0	0	0	0	8	0	0	0	**	0	0	0	0	57	64	26	6	33	101	256
Tunisia	TUN	1	0	0	0	0	3	0	0	2	**	0	0	0	37	3,140	1	34	35	832	4,044
Uganda	UGA	0	0	0	0	0	0	0	0	0	0	**	0	0	6	127	2	12	15	31	179
Zambia	ZMB	0	0	0	0	5	0	0	1	0	0	0	**	23	70	182	3	5	8	492	752
Zimbabwe	ZWE	0	1	0	0	171	2	1	3	0	1	4	48	**	415	436	4	81	84	323	1,257
Sub-Saharan Africa	SSA	199	32	35	31	351	29	1	68	145	33	83	283	588	5,436	26,024	632	11,408	12,040	12,414	55,914
European Community	EU	719	55	103	57	7,038	389	20	517	329	4,617	140	311	510	28,669	1,049,442	11,970	102,538	114,508	380,185	1,572,804
Canada	CAN	17	0	0	1	85	5	0	13	5	38	8	9	15	334	9,732	0	103,860	103,860	19,520	133,447
United States	USA	80	2	28	21	2,425	53	4	34	19	232	15	68	143	5,382	107,739	90,156	0	90,156	244,033	447,310
North America	NNA	97	2	29	22	2,510	58	4	47	24	270	23	77	159	5,716	117,471	90,156	103,860	194,016	263,554	580,757
Rest of World	ROW	230	80	45	85	4,032	686	39	741	334	990	117	353	279	19,464	392,104	21,253	320,318	341,571	784,207	1,537,346
World	WLD	1,244	169	212	195	13,932	1,162	64	1,372	831	5,910	363	1,023	1,536	59,285	1,585,040	124,012	538,124	662,135	1,440,361	3,746,821

Note: ** means "not applicable."

South Africa's data for 1992 is taken from partner countries' data.

Source: International Monetary Fund's Direction of Trade database.

5-54. Direction of trade matrix, current U.S. dollars, 1997

		Importers																		Millions of current U.S. dollars	
	Exporters	DZA	AGO	BEN	BWA	BFA	BDI	CMR	CPV	CAF	TCD	COM	ZAR	COG	CIV	DJI	EGY	GNQ	ERI	ETH	GAB
Algeria	DZA	**	0	0	0	0	0	0	0	0	0	0	0	0	0	0	5	0	0	0	0
Angola	AGO	0	**	0	0	0	0	8	0	0	0	0	0	4	0	0	0	0	0	0	0
Benin	BEN	0	0	**	0	0	0	1	0	0	0	0	0	0	2	0	0	0	0	0	0
Bostwana	BWA	..	..	..	**	..	..	..	..	..	..	..	..	..	..	..	..	..	..	..	..
Burkina Faso	BFA	0	0	1	0	**	0	0	0	0	0	0	0	0	20	0	0	0	0	0	0
Burundi	BDI	0	0	0	0	0	**	0	0	0	0	0	0	0	0	0	0	0	0	0	0
Cameroon	CMR	0	1	2	0	0	0	**	0	17	12	0	2	14	7	0	0	24	0	0	44
Cape Verde	CPV	0	0	0	0	0	0	0	**	0	0	0	0	0	0	0	0	0	0	0	0
Central African Republic	CAF	0	0	0	0	0	0	3	0	**	0	0	2	0	0	0	0	0	0	0	0
Chad	TCD	0	0	0	0	0	0	1	0	1	**	0	0	0	0	0	0	0	0	0	0
Comoros	COM	0	0	0	0	0	0	0	0	0	0	**	0	0	0	0	0	0	0	0	0
Congo, Dem. Rep. of	ZAR	0	0	0	0	0	0	0	0	1	0	0	**	1	0	0	0	0	0	0	0
Congo, Rep. of	COG	0	8	0	0	0	0	1	0	0	0	0	8	**	0	0	0	0	0	0	1
Côte d'Ivoire	CIV	22	0	51	0	124	0	51	1	0	0	0	0	0	**	0	0	0	0	0	91
Djibouti	DJI	0	0	0	0	0	0	0	0	0	0	0	0	0	0	**	0	0	0	5	0
Egypt, Arab Rep.	EGY	7	1	0	0	0	0	0	0	0	0	0	1	0	2	1	**	0	0	2	0
Equatorial Guinea	GNQ	0	0	0	0	0	0	31	0	0	0	0	0	0	0	0	0	**	0	0	0
Eritrea	ERI	..	..	..	..	..	..	..	..	..	..	..	..	..	..	..	..	..	**	..	..
Ethiopia	ETH	0	0	0	0	0	0	0	0	0	0	0	0	0	0	45	9	0	0	**	0
Gabon	GAB	0	1	3	0	0	0	2	0	0	0	0	7	6	0	0	0	1	0	0	**
Gambia, The	GMB	0	0	0	0	0	0	0	0	0	0	0	0	0	0	0	0	0	0	0	0
Ghana	GHA	0	11	18	0	5	0	0	0	0	0	0	0	8	1	0	1	0	0	0	0
Guinea	GIN	0	0	0	0	0	0	24	0	0	0	0	0	0	0	0	0	0	0	0	0
Guinea-Bissau	GNB	0	0	0	0	0	0	0	0	0	0	0	0	0	0	0	0	0	0	0	0
Kenya	KEN	1	0	0	0	0	5	1	0	0	0	3	38	2	0	3	52	0	1	35	0
Lesotho	LSO	..	..	..	..	..	..	..	..	..	..	..	..	..	..	..	..	..	..	..	..
Liberia	LBR	0	0	0	0	0	0	0	0	0	0	0	0	0	0	0	0	0	0	0	0
Libya	LBY	2	0	0	0	0	0	0	0	0	0	0	0	0	0	0	68	0	0	0	0
Madagascar	MDG	2	0	0	0	0	0	0	0	0	0	1	0	0	0	0	0	0	0	0	0
Malawi	MWI	0	0	0	0	0	0	0	0	0	0	0	1	0	0	0	12	0	0	0	0
Mali	MLI	1	0	0	0	1	0	0	0	0	0	0	0	0	3	0	0	0	0	0	0
Mauritania	MRT	0	0	0	0	0	0	5	0	0	0	0	0	5	14	0	2	0	0	0	0
Mauritius	MUS	0	0	0	0	0	0	0	0	0	0	1	0	0	0	0	0	0	0	0	0
Morocco	MAR	3	6	4	0	1	0	3	0	0	0	0	3	6	22	0	12	2	0	0	18
Mozambique	MOZ	0	1	0	0	0	0	0	0	0	0	0	0	0	0	0	0	0	0	0	0
Namibia	NAM	..	..	..	..	..	..	..	..	..	..	..	..	..	..	..	..	..	..	..	..
Niger	NER	0	0	3	0	1	0	0	0	0	0	0	0	0	8	0	0	0	0	0	0
Nigeria	NGA	1	0	8	0	13	0	88	0	1	14	0	64	2	390	0	2	0	0	0	6
Reunion	REU	0	0	0	0	0	0	0	0	0	0	0	0	0	0	0	0	0	0	0	0
Rwanda	RWA	0	0	0	0	0	1	0	0	0	0	0	1	0	0	0	0	0	0	0	0
São Tomé and Principe	STP	0	0	0	0	0	0	0	0	0	0	0	0	0	0	0	0	0	0	0	0
Senegal	SEN	0	0	16	0	5	0	13	2	0	3	0	0	4	29	0	0	0	0	0	11
Seychelles	SYC	0	0	0	0	0	0	0	0	0	0	0	0	0	0	0	0	0	0	0	0
Sierra Leone	SLE	0	0	0	0	0	0	0	0	0	0	0	0	0	0	0	0	0	0	0	0
Somalia	SOM	0	0	0	0	0	0	0	0	0	0	0	0	0	0	0	0	0	0	0	0
South Africa	ZAF	21	209	4	0	3	5	13	3	0	0	6	0	36	20	1	15	0	0	3	24
Sudan	SDN	0	0	0	0	0	0	0	0	0	0	0	0	0	0	0	21	0	0	0	0
Swaziland	SWZ	..	..	..	..	..	..	..	..	..	..	..	..	..	..	..	..	..	..	..	..
Tanzania	TZA	0	0	0	0	0	1	0	0	0	0	0	9	0	0	0	1	0	0	4	0
Togo	TGO	1	0	10	0	5	0	0	0	0	0	0	0	0	0	0	0	0	0	0	1
Tunisia	TUN	36	1	5	0	2	0	9	1	1	0	0	0	0	10	0	27	4	0	1	3
Uganda	UGA	2	0	0	0	0	0	0	0	0	0	0	0	0	0	0	1	0	0	0	0
Zambia	ZMB	0	1	0	3	0	2	0	0	0	0	0	27	7	0	0	7	0	0	0	0
Zimbabwe	ZWE	1	7	0	94	0	1	2	0	0	0	0	10	6	0	0	5	0	0	0	0
Sub-Saharan Africa	SSA	53	240	115	97	158	14	245	7	21	29	11	169	95	495	49	127	26	1	43	181
European Community	EU	4,910	1,197	437	125	234	46	822	73	65	74	105	310	467	1,455	146	7,571	96	0	552	670
Canada	CAN	422	8	8	25	1	0	2	1	0	0	0	6	2	5	1	129	0	0	5	7
United States	USA	695	281	52	43	18	1	122	10	4	3	0	38	75	151	7	3,840	47	16	121	84
North America	NNA	1,117	288	60	68	19	1	124	10	4	3	0	44	77	156	8	3,969	47	16	126	91
Rest of World	ROW	1,926	572	352	203	75	11	189	16	27	15	31	382	120	484	145	7,475	14	-18	627	166
World	WLD	8,006	2,297	964	494	487	72	1,381	106	117	121	148	904	761	2,590	349	19,142	183	0	1,348	1,107

Note: ** means "not applicable."

South Africa's data for 1997 is taken from partner countries' data.

Source: International Monetary Fund's Direction of Trade database.

(Table continues on the following page.)

5-54. Direction of trade matrix, current U.S. dollars, 1997 (continued)

Importers — Millions of current U.S. dollars

Exporters		GMB	GHA	GIN	GNB	KEN	LSO	LBR	LBY	MDG	MWI	MLI	MRT	MUS	MAR	MOZ	NAM	NER	NGA	REU	RWA	STP
Algeria	DZA	0	0	0	0	0	0	0	3	0	0	0	51	0	93	0	0	1	1	0	0	0
Angola	AGO	0	1	0	0	0	0	0	0	0	0	0	0	0	0	0	0	0	0	0	0	0
Benin	BEN	0	0	0	0	0	0	0	0	0	0	1	0	0	16	0	0	4	1	0	0	0
Bostwana	BWA	..	..	..	..	..	..	..	..	..	..	..	..	..	..	..	..	..	..	..	..	..
Burkina Faso	BFA	0	6	0	0	0	0	0	0	0	0	2	0	3	0	0	0	3	0	0	0	0
Burundi	BDI	0	0	0	0	0	0	0	0	0	0	0	0	0	0	0	0	0	0	0	0	0
Cameroon	CMR	0	0	1	0	0	0	0	0	0	0	0	0	0	5	0	0	0	7	0	0	0
Cape Verde	CPV	0	0	0	0	0	0	0	0	0	0	0	0	0	0	0	0	0	0	0	0	0
Central African Republic	CAF	0	0	0	0	0	0	0	0	0	0	0	0	0	0	0	0	0	0	0	0	0
Chad	TCD	0	0	0	0	0	0	0	0	0	0	0	0	0	2	0	0	0	3	0	0	0
Comoros	COM	0	0	0	0	0	0	0	0	0	0	0	0	0	0	0	0	0	0	0	0	0
Congo, Dem. Rep. of	ZAR	0	0	0	0	3	0	0	0	0	0	0	0	0	1	0	0	0	0	0	4	0
Congo, Rep. of	COG	0	0	3	0	0	0	0	0	0	0	0	0	0	5	0	0	0	0	0	0	0
Côte d'Ivoire	CIV	12	154	64	1	0	0	12	0	0	0	202	5	0	25	0	0	43	37	0	0	0
Djibouti	DJI	0	0	0	0	0	0	0	0	0	0	0	0	0	0	0	0	0	0	0	0	0
Egypt, Arab Rep.	EGY	0	0	0	0	3	0	0	70	0	0	0	0	0	11	0	0	0	2	0	0	0
Equatorial Guinea	GNQ	0	0	0	0	0	0	0	0	0	0	0	0	0	0	0	0	0	0	0	0	0
Eritrea	ERI	..	..	..	..	..	..	..	..	..	..	..	..	..	..	..	..	..	..	..	..	..
Ethiopia	ETH	0	0	0	..	15	0	0	..	0	0	0	0	0	0	0	0	0	0	0	0	0
Gabon	GAB	0	0	3	0	0	0	0	0	0	0	0	0	0	21	0	0	0	0	0	0	1
Gambia, The	GMB	**	0	0	0	0	0	0	0	0	0	0	0	0	0	0	0	0	0	0	0	0
Ghana	GHA	0	**	0	0	0	0	0	0	0	0	0	0	0	2	0	0	4	59	0	0	0
Guinea	GIN	0	0	**	0	0	0	6	0	0	0	0	0	0	3	0	0	0	5	0	0	0
Guinea-Bissau	GNB	0	0	0	**	0	0	0	0	0	0	0	0	0	0	0	0	0	0	0	0	0
Kenya	KEN	0	0	0	0	**	0	0	0	3	6	0	0	14	0	2	0	0	3	0	59	0
Lesotho	LSO	..	..	..	..	..	**	..	..	..	..	..	..	..	..	..	..	..	..	..	..	..
Liberia	LBR	0	0	0	0	0	0	**	0	0	0	0	0	0	0	0	0	0	0	0	0	0
Libya	LBY	0	0	0	0	0	0	0	**	0	0	0	1	0	30	0	0	1	0	0	0	0
Madagascar	MDG	0	0	0	0	0	0	0	0	**	0	0	0	11	0	0	0	0	0	0	0	0
Malawi	MWI	1	0	0	0	0	0	0	0	0	**	0	0	3	2	3	0	0	0	0	0	0
Mali	MLI	0	0	0	0	0	0	0	0	0	0	**	0	0	5	0	0	0	2	0	0	0
Mauritania	MRT	0	1	0	0	0	0	8	0	0	0	0	**	0	1	0	0	0	0	0	0	0
Mauritius	MUS	0	0	0	0	4	0	0	0	57	3	0	0	**	0	0	0	0	0	0	2	0
Morocco	MAR	1	5	8	0	0	0	1	130	1	0	8	10	1	**	0	0	1	5	0	0	0
Mozambique	MOZ	0	0	0	0	2	0	0	0	0	18	0	0	1	0	**	0	0	0	0	0	0
Namibia	NAM	..	..	..	..	..	..	..	..	..	..	..	..	..	..	..	**	..	..	..	..	..
Niger	NER	0	6	0	0	0	0	0	0	0	0	0	0	0	0	0	0	**	36	0	0	0
Nigeria	NGA	1	430	3	0	1	0	1	0	0	0	1	0	0	188	0	0	27	**	0	0	0
Reunion	REU	0	0	0	0	0	0	0	0	0	0	0	0	0	0	0	0	0	0	**	0	0
Rwanda	RWA	0	0	0	0	3	0	0	0	0	0	0	0	0	0	0	0	0	0	0	**	0
São Tomé and Principe	STP	0	0	0	0	0	0	0	0	0	0	0	0	0	0	0	0	0	0	0	0	**
Senegal	SEN	12	2	9	8	0	0	0	0	0	0	38	15	0	1	0	0	1	3	0	0	0
Seychelles	SYC	0	0	0	0	0	0	0	0	0	0	0	0	0	0	0	0	0	0	0	0	0
Sierra Leone	SLE	0	0	0	0	0	0	0	0	0	0	0	0	0	0	0	0	0	0	0	0	0
Somalia	SOM	0	0	0	0	0	0	0	0	0	0	0	0	0	0	0	0	0	0	0	0	0
South Africa	ZAF	1	93	15	0	370	0	11	4	55	271	17	2	273	87	647	0	1	49	0	6	3
Sudan	SDN	0	0	0	0	5	0	0	7	0	0	0	0	0	0	0	0	0	0	0	0	0
Swaziland	SWZ	..	..	..	..	..	..	..	..	..	..	..	..	..	..	..	..	..	..	..	..	..
Tanzania	TZA	0	1	0	0	25	0	0	0	0	6	0	0	1	0	0	0	0	0	0	6	0
Togo	TGO	0	1	0	0	0	0	0	0	0	0	0	0	0	1	0	0	2	0	0	0	0
Tunisia	TUN	1	4	0	0	0	0	0	227	0	0	1	2	0	41	2	0	2	1	0	0	0
Uganda	UGA	0	0	0	0	7	0	0	0	0	0	0	0	0	0	0	0	0	0	0	1	0
Zambia	ZMB	0	0	0	0	1	0	0	0	0	20	0	0	1	0	0	2	0	0	0	1	0
Zimbabwe	ZWE	0	3	0	0	20	0	0	1	0	79	0	0	2	0	71	20	0	3	0	1	0
Sub-Saharan Africa	SSA	28	701	99	10	458	1	38	13	116	402	263	22	309	366	723	22	84	209	0	80	4
European Community	EU	115	1,280	356	31	1,011	21	613	3,138	360	73	349	310	733	5,870	112	95	167	2,986	0	91	9
Canada	CAN	0	39	6	0	14	0	1	150	1	5	7	0	5	130	15	0	8	47	0	3	0
United States	USA	10	314	83	3	226	2	43	0	12	18	26	18	31	438	46	26	25	814	0	35	13
North America	NNA	10	354	89	3	239	3	44	150	12	23	33	19	36	568	61	26	33	861	0	38	13
Rest of World	ROW	137	701	180	28	1,512	51	2,749	1,751	231	57	82	195	884	2,127	187	71	46	2,314	0	54	12
World	WLD	290	3,036	723	72	3,221	75	3,444	5,052	719	555	726	546	1,962	8,931	1,082	214	330	6,370	0	263	38

Note: ** means "not applicable."

South Africa's data for 1997 is taken from partner countries' data.

Source: International Monetary Fund's Direction of Trade database.

(Table continues on the following page.)

5-54. Direction of trade matrix, current U.S. dollars, 1997

		Importers													*Millions of current U.S. dollars*					
Exporters		SEN	SYC	SLE	SOM	ZAF	SDN	SWZ	TZA	TGO	TUN	UGA	ZMB	ZWE	SSA	EU	CAN	USA	NNA	ROW	WLD
Algeria	DZA	10	0	0	0	0	4	0	0	0	59	0	0	0	68	8,718	464	2,194	2,658	2,287	13,731
Angola	AGO	0	0	0	0	45	0	0	0	0	0	0	0	0	58	609	0	2,696	2,696	947	4,310
Benin	BEN	0	0	0	0	2	0	0	0	2	0	0	0	0	14	41	0	0	0	130	185
Bostwana	BWA	..	..	..	..	..	..	..	..	..	..	..	..	..	..	..	..	..	..	..	..
Burkina Faso	BFA	0	0	0	0	0	0	0	0	3	0	0	0	0	38	63	0	3	4	89	194
Burundi	BDI	0	0	0	0	1	0	0	0	0	0	0	0	0	1	57	0	1	1	29	87
Cameroon	CMR	7	0	0	0	3	0	0	0	1	8	0	0	0	144	1,402	0	14	14	299	1,858
Cape Verde	CPV	0	0	0	0	0	0	0	0	0	0	0	0	0	0	13	0	1	1	0	14
Central African Republic	CAF	0	0	0	0	0	0	0	0	0	0	0	0	0	6	92	0	0	0	0	98
Chad	TCD	0	0	0	0	0	0	0	0	0	7	0	0	0	6	43	0	3	3	42	93
Comoros	COM	0	0	0	0	0	0	0	0	0	0	0	0	0	0	4	0	1	1	1	6
Congo, Dem. Rep. of	ZAR	0	0	0	0	99	0	0	0	0	1	0	0	0	109	767	7	277	284	118	1,278
Congo, Rep. of	COG	0	0	0	0	1	0	0	0	0	1	0	0	1	24	696	5	456	462	1,078	2,259
Côte d'Ivoire	CIV	46	0	25	0	26	0	0	0	67	14	0	0	0	1,012	2,209	10	310	320	609	4,150
Djibouti	DJI	0	0	0	58	0	0	0	0	0	0	0	0	0	64	8	0	0	0	31	102
Egypt, Arab Rep.	EGY	1	0	0	0	40	25	0	1	0	19	1	2	0	84	1,621	6	447	453	1,749	3,908
Equatorial Guinea	GNQ	0	0	0	0	0	0	0	0	0	0	0	0	0	31	108	0	30	30	186	355
Eritrea	ERI	..	..	..	..	..	..	..	..	..	..	..	..	..	..	..	..	..	..	..	..
Ethiopia	ETH	0	0	0	0	0	0	0	0	0	0	2	0	0	17	254	3	67	70	251	592
Gabon	GAB	1	0	0	0	8	0	0	0	0	3	0	0	0	34	391	0	2,135	2,135	920	3,479
Gambia, The	GMB	1	0	0	0	0	0	0	0	0	0	0	0	0	1	10	0	1	1	3	15
Ghana	GHA	1	0	0	0	4	0	0	0	9	2	0	0	0	120	852	9	145	154	422	1,547
Guinea	GIN	0	0	0	0	0	0	0	0	0	0	0	0	0	36	400	20	148	168	36	640
Guinea-Bissau	GNB	0	0	0	0	0	0	0	0	0	0	0	0	0	1	10	0	0	0	41	52
Kenya	KEN	1	4	0	32	17	32	0	237	0	1	278	4	7	785	673	10	57	68	423	1,948
Lesotho	LSO	..	..	..	..	..	..	..	..	..	..	..	..	..	..	..	..	..	..	..	..
Liberia	LBR	0	0	1	0	10	0	0	0	0	0	0	0	0	11	448	0	5	5	341	805
Libya	LBY	0	0	0	0	0	261	0	0	0	194	0	0	0	263	7,899	0	0	0	1,414	9,576
Madagascar	MDG	0	0	0	0	3	0	0	0	0	0	0	0	0	15	147	1	11	11	50	224
Malawi	MWI	0	0	0	0	87	0	0	3	0	1	1	3	14	116	192	2	80	82	148	537
Mali	MLI	0	0	0	0	3	0	0	0	0	5	0	0	0	11	84	10	4	14	176	284
Mauritania	MRT	0	0	0	0	0	0	0	0	16	1	0	0	0	51	313	0	0	0	163	527
Mauritius	MUS	0	4	0	0	7	0	0	1	0	0	0	0	12	91	1,181	9	227	237	87	1,595
Morocco	MAR	11	0	1	0	4	0	0	1	2	40	0	0	0	127	2,839	30	165	195	1,966	5,127
Mozambique	MOZ	0	0	0	0	36	0	0	0	0	0	0	0	10	69	85	1	26	27	43	223
Namibia	NAM	..	..	..	..	..	..	..	..	..	..	..	..	..	..	..	..	..	..	..	..
Niger	NER	0	0	0	0	0	0	0	0	0	0	0	0	0	55	102	0	1	1	35	192
Nigeria	NGA	80	0	10	0	182	0	0	0	12	0	0	0	1	1,338	4,641	377	6,107	6,484	4,061	16,525
Reunion	REU	0	0	0	0	0	0	0	0	0	0	0	0	0	0	0	0	0	0	0	0
Rwanda	RWA	0	0	0	0	1	0	0	1	0	0	0	0	0	5	66	0	4	4	42	118
São Tomé and Príncipe	STP	0	0	0	0	0	0	0	0	0	0	0	0	1	1	7	0	0	0	1	9
Senegal	SEN	**	0	0	0	2	0	0	0	4	1	0	0	0	178	301	0	2	2	213	694
Seychelles	SYC	0	**	0	0	1	0	0	0	0	0	0	0	0	2	62	0	0	0	5	68
Sierra Leone	SLE	0	0	**	0	0	0	0	0	0	0	0	0	0	0	10	0	0	0	7	17
Somalia	SOM	0	0	0	**	0	0	0	0	0	0	0	0	0	1	25	0	0	0	132	157
South Africa	ZAF	2	46	8	0	**	6	0	106	6	3	38	308	1,364	4,020	10,264	393	2,616	3,009	12,560	29,853
Sudan	SDN	0	0	0	1	0	**	0	0	0	4	0	0	0	7	174	0	12	12	317	510
Swaziland	SWZ	..	..	..	..	..	..	**	..	..	..	..	..	..	..	..	..	..	..	..	..
Tanzania	TZA	0	0	0	0	8	2	0	**	0	0	7	2	17	91	229	1	12	12	287	619
Togo	TGO	0	0	0	0	21	0	0	0	**	0	0	0	0	41	45	29	0	29	121	236
Tunisia	TUN	7	0	0	0	7	1	0	0	1	**	0	0	0	68	4,408	8	36	44	1,243	5,763
Uganda	UGA	0	0	0	0	0	0	0	5	0	2	**	0	0	15	430	7	36	43	112	600
Zambia	ZMB	0	0	0	0	44	0	0	5	0	0	0	**	30	144	311	0	75	75	525	1,055
Zimbabwe	ZWE	0	2	0	0	293	4	1	13	0	0	2	116	**	752	763	6	122	128	503	2,146
Sub-Saharan Africa	SSA	139	56	44	33	906	45	2	372	121	54	329	433	1,456	9,451	28,569	902	15,684	16,586	25,550	80,156
European Community	EU	898	112	113	17	11,001	396	20	457	281	5,888	214	167	494	29,610	1,265,037	15,719	158,570	174,289	625,043	2,093,980
Canada	CAN	13	0	1	1	254	10	0	9	3	48	5	4	12	534	10,556	**	177,317	177,317	24,612	213,020
United States	USA	52	6	16	3	3,000	37	5	65	26	251	35	30	82	6,165	141,412	150,124	**	150,124	389,880	687,581
North America	NNA	65	6	17	4	3,254	47	5	74	29	299	41	34	94	6,700	151,968	150,124	177,317	327,441	414,492	900,602
Rest of World	ROW	298	116	43	183	9,511	912	45	833	283	1,307	157	310	324	25,773	523,747	27,382	512,144	539,526	1,361,656	2,450,702
World	WLD	1,399	291	217	237	24,672	1,400	73	1,736	713	7,549	741	944	2,367	71,534	1,969,321	194,128	863,715	1,057,843	2,426,742	5,525,440

Note: ** means "not applicable."

South Africa's data for 1997 is taken from partner countries' data.

Source: International Monetary Fund's Direction of Trade database.

5-55. Direction of trade matrix, current U.S. dollars, 2002

Importers — *Millions of current U.S. dollars*

Exporters		DZA	AGO	BEN	BWA	BFA	BDI	CMR	CPV	CAF	TCD	COM	ZAR	COG	CIV	DJI	EGY	GNQ	ERI	ETH	GAB
Algeria	DZA	**	0	25	0	0	7	0	8	0	0	0	0	0	0	0	156	0	0	0	5
Angola	AGO	0	**	0	0	0	0	2	0	0	0	0	0	6	0	0	0	0	0	0	1
Benin	BEN	0	0	**	0	1	0	0	0	0	1	0	0	0	0	0	0	0	0	0	0
Bostwana	BWA	0	0	0	**	0	0	0	0	0	0	0	0	0	0	0	0	0	0	0	0
Burkina Faso	BFA	1	0	0	0	**	0	0	0	0	0	0	0	0	1	0	0	0	0	0	0
Burundi	BDI	0	0	0	0	0	**	0	0	0	0	0	0	0	0	0	0	0	0	0	0
Cameroon	CMR	1	16	1	0	0	0	**	0	6	13	0	29	20	3	0	0	11	0	0	17
Cape Verde	CPV	0	0	0	0	0	0	0	**	0	0	0	0	0	0	0	0	0	0	0	0
Central African Republic	CAF	0	0	0	0	0	0	0	0	**	0	0	3	0	0	0	0	0	0	0	0
Chad	TCD	0	0	0	0	0	0	0	0	2	**	0	0	0	0	0	0	0	0	0	0
Comoros	COM	0	0	0	0	0	0	0	0	0	0	**	0	0	0	0	0	0	0	0	0
Congo, Dem. Rep. of	ZAR	0	0	0	0	0	1	0	0	2	0	0	**	2	0	0	0	0	0	0	0
Congo, Rep. of	COG	1	11	0	0	0	0	5	0	0	0	0	11	**	0	0	0	0	0	0	2
Côte d'Ivoire	CIV	50	0	33	0	133	0	33	9	0	0	0	0	0	**	0	0	0	0	0	19
Djibouti	DJI	0	0	0	0	0	0	0	0	0	0	0	0	0	0	**	0	0	0	7	0
Egypt, Arab Rep.	EGY	53	1	0	0	0	0	3	0	0	0	0	2	0	5	0	**	0	0	3	0
Equatorial Guinea	GNQ	0	0	0	0	0	0	39	0	0	0	0	0	0	0	0	0	**	0	0	0
Eritrea	ERI	0	0	0	0	0	0	0	0	0	0	0	0	0	0	0	0	0	**	0	0
Ethiopia	ETH	2	0	0	0	0	0	0	0	0	0	0	0	0	0	64	4	0	0	**	0
Gabon	GAB	1	1	0	0	0	0	3	0	0	0	0	10	9	0	0	0	2	0	0	**
Gambia, The	GMB	0	0	0	0	0	0	0	0	0	0	0	0	0	0	0	0	0	0	0	0
Ghana	GHA	0	18	29	0	8	0	1	0	0	0	0	0	11	7	0	1	0	0	0	0
Guinea	GIN	0	0	0	0	0	0	81	0	0	0	0	0	0	0	0	0	0	0	0	0
Guinea-Bissau	GNB	0	0	0	0	0	0	1	0	0	0	0	0	0	1	0	0	0	0	0	0
Kenya	KEN	2	0	0	0	0	9	0	0	0	0	5	43	1	0	3	94	0	5	35	0
Lesotho	LSO	0	0	0	0	0	0	0	0	0	0	0	0	0	0	0	0	0	0	0	0
Liberia	LBR	0	0	0	0	0	0	0	0	0	0	0	0	0	2	0	0	0	0	0	0
Libya	LBY	2	0	0	0	16	0	0	0	0	0	0	0	0	0	0	38	0	0	0	0
Madagascar	MDG	0	0	0	0	0	0	0	0	0	0	2	0	0	0	0	0	0	0	0	0
Malawi	MWI	3	0	0	0	0	0	0	0	0	0	0	1	0	0	0	25	0	0	0	0
Mali	MLI	0	0	0	0	2	0	0	0	0	0	0	0	0	2	0	1	0	0	0	0
Mauritania	MRT	5	0	0	0	0	0	15	0	0	0	0	0	7	20	0	2	1	0	0	0
Mauritius	MUS	0	0	0	0	1	0	0	0	0	0	3	0	0	0	0	1	0	0	0	3
Morocco	MAR	16	7	3	0	5	0	6	1	0	0	1	3	9	16	0	26	5	0	0	9
Mozambique	MOZ	0	0	0	0	0	0	0	0	0	0	0	0	3	0	0	0	0	0	0	0
Namibia	NAM	0	0	0	0	0	0	0	0	0	0	0	0	0	0	0	0	0	0	0	0
Niger	NER	0	0	3	0	1	0	0	0	0	0	0	0	0	1	0	0	0	0	0	0
Nigeria	NGA	2	0	11	0	20	0	250	0	1	21	0	94	4	462	0	0	0	0	0	9
Reunion	REU	0	0	0	0	0	0	0	0	0	0	0	0	0	0	0	0	0	0	0	0
Rwanda	RWA	0	0	0	0	0	0	0	0	0	0	0	1	0	0	0	0	0	0	0	0
São Tomé and Principe	STP	0	0	0	0	0	0	0	0	0	0	0	0	0	0	0	0	0	0	0	0
Senegal	SEN	0	0	22	0	6	0	7	6	1	1	0	1	9	33	0	0	0	0	0	8
Seychelles	SYC	0	0	0	0	0	0	0	0	0	0	0	0	0	0	0	0	0	0	0	0
Sierra Leone	SLE	0	0	0	0	0	0	0	0	0	0	0	0	0	0	0	0	0	0	0	0
Somalia	SOM	0	0	0	0	0	0	0	0	0	0	0	0	0	0	0	0	0	0	0	0
South Africa	ZAF	32	353	14	0	2	4	38	1	1	1	14	168	37	48	6	19	4	2	18	21
Sudan	SDN	1	0	0	0	0	0	0	0	0	0	0	0	0	0	0	63	0	0	3	0
Swaziland	SWZ	0	0	0	0	0	0	0	0	0	0	0	0	0	0	0	0	0	0	0	0
Tanzania	TZA	0	1	0	0	0	7	0	0	0	0	0	16	0	0	0	2	0	0	0	0
Togo	TGO	0	0	40	0	25	0	1	0	0	1	0	0	1	1	0	0	0	0	0	1
Tunisia	TUN	86	0	3	0	6	0	2	0	0	1	0	0	4	11	1	25	0	1	0	2
Uganda	UGA	1	0	0	0	0	0	0	0	0	0	0	0	0	0	0	3	0	0	0	0
Zambia	ZMB	0	0	0	3	0	1	0	0	0	0	0	0	0	0	0	42	0	0	0	0
Zimbabwe	ZWE	1	1	0	13	0	0	0	0	0	0	0	3	0	0	0	16	0	0	0	0
Sub-Saharan Africa	SSA	104	404	154	17	199	24	477	17	12	38	24	381	112	583	74	273	17	8	57	82
European Community	EU	7,589	1,313	524	136	254	41	1,041	230	59	202	37	349	498	1,174	150	6,011	208	0	347	755
Canada	CAN	265	4	3	2	1	0	9	0	0	1	0	7	3	13	1	112	1	0	4	4
United States	USA	985	373	35	32	19	2	156	10	7	127	0	28	52	76	56	2,866	109	29	60	65
North America	NNA	1,250	377	39	33	20	2	165	10	7	128	0	35	55	89	57	2,978	110	29	64	69
Rest of World	ROW	3,248	665	678	55	74	39	305	28	12	43	22	106	229	619	304	7,543	59	-37	630	109
World	WLD	12,191	2,759	1,395	242	547	106	1,988	285	90	411	84	870	894	2,465	585	16,806	394	0	1,098	1,015

Note: ** means "not applicable."

South Africa's data for 2002 is taken from partner countries' data.

Source: International Monetary Fund's Direction of Trade database.

(Table continues on the following page.)

5-55. Direction of trade matrix, current U.S. dollars, 2002 (continued)

		Importers																				
												Millions of current U.S. dollars										
Exporters		GMB	GHA	GIN	GNB	KEN	LSO	LBR	LBY	MDG	MWI	MLI	MRT	MUS	MAR	MOZ	NAM	NER	NGA	REU	RWA	STP
Algeria	DZA	0	0	0	0	0	0	0	9	0	0	0	10	0	141	0	0	0	3	0	0	0
Angola	AGO	0	2	0	0	0	0	0	0	0	0	0	0	0	0	0	0	0	0	0	0	0
Benin	BEN	0	0	0	0	0	0	0	0	0	0	1	0	1	7	0	0	9	1	0	0	0
Bostwana	BWA	0	0	0	0	0	0	0	0	0	0	0	0	0	0	0	0	0	0	0	0	0
Burkina Faso	BFA	0	11	0	0	0	0	0	0	0	0	4	0	1	4	0	0	4	0	0	0	0
Burundi	BDI	0	0	0	0	3	0	0	0	0	0	0	0	0	0	0	0	0	0	0	2	0
Cameroon	CMR	0	0	0	0	0	0	0	0	0	0	0	0	2	9	0	0	0	14	0	0	0
Cape Verde	CPV	0	0	0	0	0	0	0	0	0	0	0	0	0	0	0	0	0	0	0	0	0
Central African Republic	CAF	0	0	0	0	0	0	0	0	0	0	0	0	0	0	0	0	0	0	0	0	0
Chad	TCD	0	0	0	0	0	0	0	0	0	0	0	0	0	3	0	0	0	4	0	0	0
Comoros	COM	0	0	0	0	0	0	0	0	0	0	0	0	0	0	0	0	0	0	0	0	0
Congo, Dem. Rep. of	ZAR	0	0	0	0	0	0	0	0	0	0	0	0	0	0	0	0	0	0	0	7	0
Congo, Rep. of	COG	0	0	0	0	0	0	0	0	0	0	0	0	1	4	0	0	0	0	0	0	0
Côte d'Ivoire	CIV	13	179	60	0	0	0	34	0	0	0	221	6	1	13	0	0	54	53	0	0	0
Djibouti	DJI	0	0	0	0	0	0	0	0	0	0	0	0	0	0	0	0	0	0	0	0	0
Egypt, Arab Rep.	EGY	1	4	3	0	22	0	0	47	2	0	1	2	9	28	0	0	0	7	0	0	0
Equatorial Guinea	GNQ	0	0	0	0	0	0	0	0	0	0	0	0	0	3	0	0	0	0	0	0	0
Eritrea	ERI	0	0	0	0	0	0	0	0	0	0	0	0	0	0	0	0	0	0	0	0	0
Ethiopia	ETH	0	0	0	0	5	0	0	0	0	0	0	0	0	2	0	0	0	0	0	1	0
Gabon	GAB	0	0	4	0	0	0	0	0	0	0	0	0	0	20	0	0	0	0	0	0	1
Gambia, The	GMB	**	0	0	0	0	0	0	0	0	0	0	0	0	0	0	0	0	0	0	0	0
Ghana	GHA	1	**	0	0	0	0	0	0	0	0	0	0	0	1	0	0	7	80	0	0	0
Guinea	GIN	0	0	**	0	0	0	2	0	0	0	1	0	0	1	0	0	0	0	0	0	0
Guinea-Bissau	GNB	0	0	1	**	0	0	0	0	0	0	0	0	0	0	0	0	0	0	0	0	0
Kenya	KEN	0	0	0	0	**	0	0	0	6	8	1	0	2	0	1	0	0	3	0	64	0
Lesotho	LSO	0	0	0	0	0	**	0	0	0	0	0	0	0	0	0	0	0	0	0	0	0
Liberia	LBR	0	1	0	0	11	0	**	0	0	0	0	0	0	1	0	0	0	0	0	0	0
Libya	LBY	0	0	0	0	0	0	0	**	0	0	0	0	0	67	0	0	0	3	0	0	0
Madagascar	MDG	0	0	0	0	2	0	0	0	**	0	0	0	16	1	0	0	0	0	0	0	0
Malawi	MWI	0	0	0	0	0	0	0	0	0	**	0	0	0	1	3	0	0	0	0	0	0
Mali	MLI	0	0	0	0	0	0	0	0	0	0	**	0	7	2	0	0	1	3	0	0	0
Mauritania	MRT	0	2	0	0	0	0	13	0	0	0	1	**	1	0	0	0	0	0	0	0	0
Mauritius	MUS	0	0	0	0	7	0	0	0	68	2	0	0	**	1	2	0	0	0	0	1	0
Morocco	MAR	4	4	8	1	1	0	3	60	1	0	14	18	3	**	0	0	1	18	0	0	0
Mozambique	MOZ	0	0	0	0	0	0	0	0	0	10	0	0	0	0	**	0	0	0	0	0	0
Namibia	NAM	0	0	0	0	0	0	0	0	0	0	0	0	0	0	0	**	0	0	0	0	0
Niger	NER	0	3	0	0	0	0	0	1	0	0	0	0	0	0	0	0	**	52	0	0	0
Nigeria	NGA	0	625	1	0	2	0	2	0	13	0	1	0	0	6	0	0	26	**	0	0	0
Reunion	REU	0	0	0	0	0	0	0	0	0	0	0	0	0	0	0	0	0	0	**	0	0
Rwanda	RWA	0	0	0	0	0	0	0	0	0	0	0	0	0	0	0	0	0	0	0	**	0
São Tomé and Principe	STP	0	0	0	0	0	0	0	0	0	0	0	0	0	0	0	0	0	0	0	0	**
Senegal	SEN	34	5	17	20	0	0	3	0	0	0	84	29	0	3	0	0	1	4	0	0	0
Seychelles	SYC	0	0	0	0	0	0	0	0	3	0	0	0	30	0	0	0	0	0	0	0	0
Sierra Leone	SLE	0	0	0	0	0	0	0	0	0	0	0	0	0	1	0	0	0	0	0	0	0
Somalia	SOM	0	0	0	0	0	0	0	0	0	0	0	0	0	0	0	0	0	0	0	0	0
South Africa	ZAF	3	102	12	0	243	0	2	0	43	247	19	10	279	111	657	0	6	283	0	9	1
Sudan	SDN	0	0	0	0	2	0	0	0	0	0	0	0	0	0	0	0	0	0	0	0	0
Swaziland	SWZ	0	0	0	0	0	0	0	0	0	0	0	0	0	0	0	0	0	0	0	0	0
Tanzania	TZA	0	0	0	0	35	0	0	0	1	18	1	0	0	0	2	0	0	1	0	4	0
Togo	TGO	0	54	2	0	0	0	0	0	0	0	2	0	0	2	0	0	12	4	0	0	0
Tunisia	TUN	1	3	2	0	1	0	0	317	1	0	3	2	0	47	0	0	10	2	0	0	0
Uganda	UGA	0	0	0	0	1	0	0	0	0	0	0	0	0	1	0	0	0	0	0	2	0
Zambia	ZMB	0	7	0	0	5	0	0	0	0	68	0	0	7	0	0	1	0	0	0	3	0
Zimbabwe	ZWE	0	1	0	0	4	1	0	0	0	9	0	0	2	0	9	2	0	2	0	0	0
Sub-Saharan Africa	SSA	52	992	97	21	321	1	55	1	134	363	334	45	350	200	673	3	120	506	0	92	2
European Community	EU	114	962	411	38	859	10	1,272	2,963	257	66	358	374	702	7,230	300	159	196	4,895	0	78	47
Canada	CAN	0	44	4	0	13	0	1	29	1	4	2	2	2	112	8	1	1	51	0	1	0
United States	USA	10	193	63	2	271	2	28	18	15	30	11	23	27	566	98	58	41	1,057	0	10	2
North America	NNA	10	236	67	2	285	2	29	47	16	34	13	25	30	678	106	58	42	1,108	0	11	2
Rest of World	ROW	191	774	210	31	1,759	156	3,235	1,885	315	85	133	280	937	3,570	441	94	111	4,938	0	36	4
World	WLD	366	2,965	784	93	3,223	169	4,591	4,896	722	548	838	724	2,018	11,677	1,520	315	470	11,446	0	218	55

Note: ** means "not applicable."

South Africa's data for 2002 is taken from partner countries' data.

Source: International Monetary Fund's Direction of Trade database.

(Table continues on the following page.)

5-55. Direction of trade matrix, current U.S. dollars, 2002

Importers — *Millions of current U.S. dollars*

Exporters		SEN	SYC	SLE	SOM	ZAF	SDN	SWZ	TZA	TGO	TUN	UGA	ZMB	ZWE	SSA	EU	CAN	USA	NNA	ROW	WLD
Algeria	DZA	2	0	0	0	0	0	0	0	0	84	0	0	0	60	11,842	929	2,633	3,562	3,063	18,528
Angola	AGO	9	0	0	0	11	0	0	0	0	0	0	0	0	31	1,941	0	2,978	2,978	2,291	7,240
Benin	BEN	0	0	0	0	2	0	0	0	3	0	0	0	0	21	54	0	1	1	124	199
Bostwana	BWA	0	0	0	0	0	0	0	0	0	0	0	0	0	0	0	0	0	0	0	0
Burkina Faso	BFA	0	0	0	0	0	0	0	0	1	1	0	0	0	21	45	0	3	3	102	171
Burundi	BDI	0	0	0	0	0	0	0	0	0	0	1	0	0	7	16	0	1	1	5	28
Cameroon	CMR	6	0	0	0	1	0	0	0	4	7	0	0	0	144	1,335	7	167	174	248	1,900
Cape Verde	CPV	0	0	0	0	0	0	0	0	0	0	0	0	0	0	19	0	2	2	1	21
Central African Republic	CAF	0	0	0	0	0	0	0	0	0	1	0	0	0	4	150	0	2	2	14	171
Chad	TCD	0	0	0	0	0	0	0	0	0	0	0	0	0	7	39	0	6	6	14	66
Comoros	COM	0	0	0	0	0	0	0	0	0	0	0	0	0	0	18	0	5	5	5	28
Congo, Dem. Rep. of	ZAR	0	0	0	0	2	0	0	0	0	0	0	0	95	108	1,069	0	190	190	49	1,416
Congo, Rep. of	COG	7	0	0	0	3	0	0	0	0	1	0	0	0	40	436	1	191	192	1,265	1,934
Côte d'Ivoire	CIV	50	0	22	0	15	0	0	0	92	17	0	0	0	1,027	2,366	45	363	408	1,246	5,046
Djibouti	DJI	0	0	0	96	0	0	0	0	0	0	0	0	0	104	4	0	2	2	17	127
Egypt, Arab Rep.	EGY	10	0	2	0	10	36	0	5	0	43	1	1	1	132	2,799	37	1,288	1,325	2,687	6,943
Equatorial Guinea	GNQ	0	0	0	0	0	0	0	0	0	0	0	0	0	40	648	188	503	692	398	1,777
Eritrea	ERI	0	0	0	0	0	0	0	0	0	0	0	0	0	0	0	0	0	0	0	0
Ethiopia	ETH	0	0	0	0	1	0	0	1	0	0	0	0	0	8	228	4	26	30	308	573
Gabon	GAB	6	0	0	0	67	0	0	0	1	6	0	0	0	104	512	2	1,514	1,516	906	3,037
Gambia, The	GMB	0	0	0	0	0	0	0	0	0	0	0	0	0	1	21	0	0	0	5	27
Ghana	GHA	6	0	0	0	7	0	0	0	7	0	0	0	0	183	873	26	117	143	501	1,700
Guinea	GIN	1	1	1	0	0	0	0	0	0	0	0	0	0	87	373	26	77	103	308	871
Guinea-Bissau	GNB	0	0	0	0	0	0	0	0	0	0	0	0	0	3	9	0	0	0	108	120
Kenya	KEN	0	3	0	43	10	64	0	87	0	0	419	3	2	817	720	8	184	192	534	2,263
Lesotho	LSO	0	0	0	0	0	0	0	0	0	0	0	0	0	0	0	0	0	0	0	0
Liberia	LBR	3	0	1	0	1	0	0	0	0	0	0	0	0	19	808	1	43	44	207	1,079
Libya	LBY	0	0	0	0	0	2	0	0	0	262	0	0	0	22	8,115	0	0	0	1,743	9,879
Madagascar	MDG	0	1	0	0	1	0	0	0	0	0	0	0	0	21	278	13	98	112	84	495
Malawi	MWI	0	0	0	0	45	0	0	1	0	0	2	3	3	60	137	1	69	70	141	408
Mali	MLI	0	0	0	0	1	0	0	0	0	3	0	0	0	16	59	2	2	4	85	165
Mauritania	MRT	0	0	0	0	0	0	0	0	8	0	0	0	0	69	358	0	1	1	113	542
Mauritius	MUS	0	13	0	0	19	0	0	3	0	1	1	1	7	133	1,099	8	344	352	123	1,707
Morocco	MAR	15	0	2	0	5	0	0	0	2	52	0	0	0	164	5,487	55	386	441	2,170	8,262
Mozambique	MOZ	0	0	0	0	120	0	0	0	0	0	0	0	39	174	416	0	11	11	81	682
Namibia	NAM	0	0	0	0	0	0	0	0	0	0	0	0	0	0	0	0	0	0	0	0
Niger	NER	0	0	0	0	0	0	0	0	1	0	0	0	0	61	67	0	0	0	28	156
Nigeria	NGA	155	0	15	0	342	1	0	1	5	0	0	0	0	2,061	4,324	130	5,654	5,783	4,913	17,081
Reunion	REU	0	0	0	0	0	0	0	0	0	0	0	0	0	0	0	6	1	0	0	8
Rwanda	RWA	0	0	0	0	0	0	0	0	0	0	0	0	0	2	39	1	3	4	118	164
São Tomé and Principe	STP	0	0	0	0	0	0	0	0	0	0	0	0	0	0	6	1	0	1	1	8
Senegal	SEN	**	0	3	0	1	0	0	0	9	3	0	0	0	304	325	1	2	4	316	949
Seychelles	SYC	0	**	0	0	1	0	0	0	0	0	0	0	0	34	216	1	25	25	49	325
Sierra Leone	SLE	0	0	**	0	2	0	0	0	0	0	0	0	0	2	81	2	4	5	10	98
Somalia	SOM	0	0	0	**	0	0	0	0	0	0	1	0	0	1	2	0	0	0	81	85
South Africa	ZAF	22	37	6	0	**	32	0	210	5	4	60	575	757	4,346	9,795	185	5	190	7,081	21,413
Sudan	SDN	0	0	0	1	0	**	0	0	0	5	0	0	0	6	180	0	1	2	1,686	1,873
Swaziland	SWZ	0	0	0	0	0	0	**	0	0	0	0	0	0	0	0	0	0	0	0	0
Tanzania	TZA	0	0	1	0	17	0	0	**	0	0	5	17	1	130	476	1	14	15	328	949
Togo	TGO	1	0	0	0	4	0	0	0	**	2	0	0	0	149	58	0	3	3	90	301
Tunisia	TUN	11	0	0	0	5	0	0	0	2	**	0	0	0	73	5,395	4	54	58	1,273	6,799
Uganda	UGA	0	0	0	0	2	0	0	2	0	1	**	0	0	9	210	0	16	16	89	324
Zambia	ZMB	0	0	0	0	71	0	1	4	0	0	2	**	14	188	102	1	7	8	351	649
Zimbabwe	ZWE	1	0	0	0	200	1	0	2	0	0	0	12	**	266	518	6	99	105	1,592	2,481
Sub-Saharan Africa	SSA	268	55	50	45	948	99	2	313	135	52	492	613	920	10,706	30,426	662	12,730	13,391	25,998	80,522
European Community	EU	1,115	150	284	29	11,798	515	18	361	405	7,140	188	102	181	33,416	1,484,103	21,041	226,641	247,682	664,960	2,430,161
Canada	CAN	7	1	3	0	158	33	0	11	9	87	3	5	3	421	10,540	**	221,292	221,292	20,128	252,381
United States	USA	75	8	25	6	2,525	11	12	62	14	195	23	36	49	5,966	144,085	160,799	**	160,799	382,274	693,123
North America	NNA	82	9	29	6	2,684	44	12	73	23	282	26	41	53	6,386	154,624	160,799	221,292	382,092	402,402	945,504
Rest of World	ROW	518	121	70	193	10,518	1,332	69	805	354	1,668	198	150	288	31,981	656,635	36,497	668,402	704,899	1,558,228	2,951,742
World	WLD	1,983	336	433	273	25,948	1,990	100	1,552	916	9,142	903	905	1,442	82,490	2,325,788	218,999	1,129,065	1,348,064	2,651,588	6,407,930

Note: ** means "not applicable."

South Africa's data for 2002 is taken from partner countries' data.

Source: International Monetary Fund's Direction of Trade database.

Figure 5-1. Terms of trade gains and losses, average 1993-2002*

(annual average percentage change)

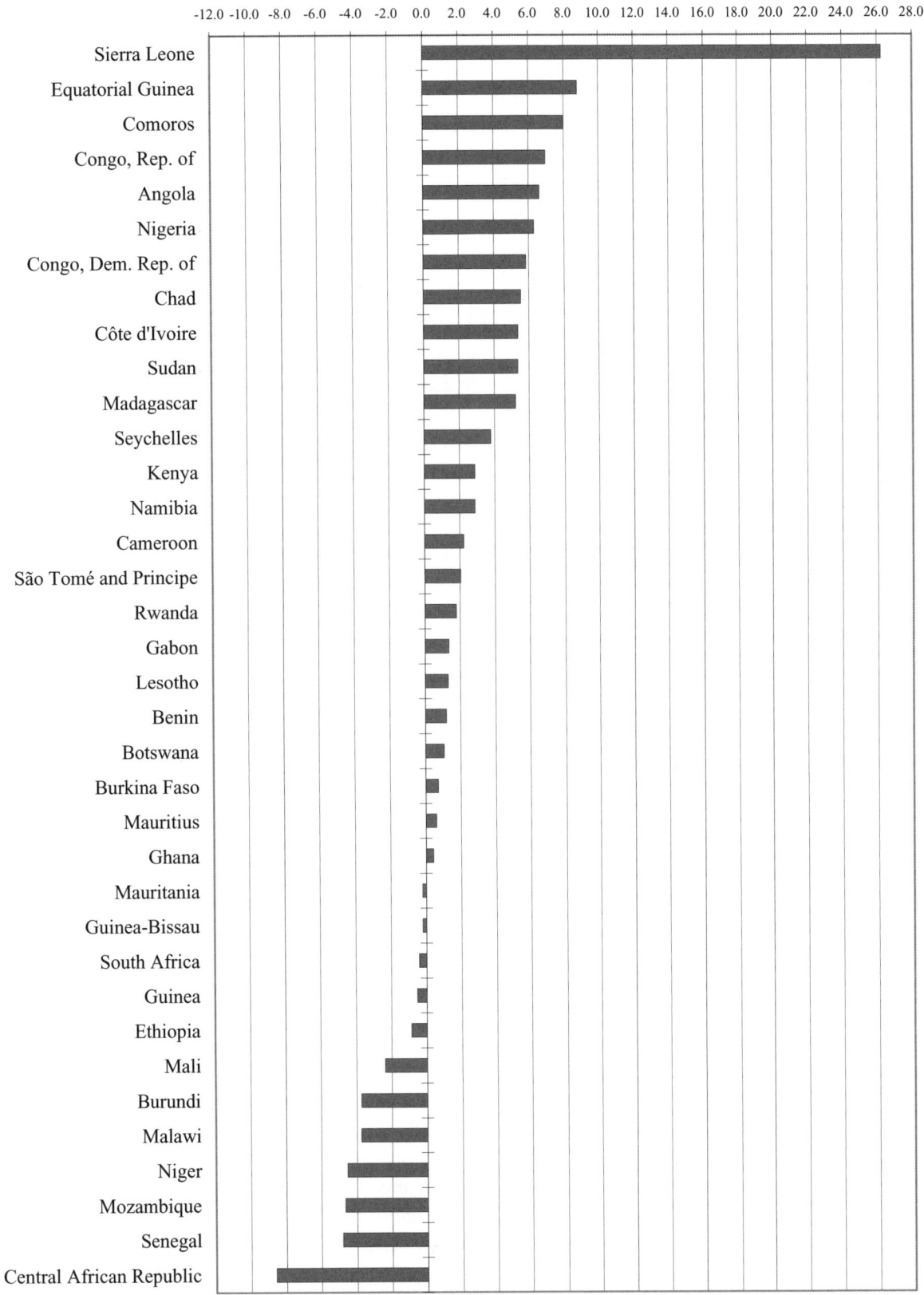

* Or most recent year available.

Technical notes

Tables

Tables 5-1 and 5-2. Merchandise exports and merchandise imports, f.o.b. Merchandise exports and imports (World Bank country desks) are both valued f.o.b. and comprise all transactions involving a change of ownership of goods, including nonmonetary gold, between residents of a country and the rest of the world. These transactions include those in which ownership changes even though goods do not cross customs borders. The few types of goods not covered by the merchandise account include travelers' purchases abroad, which are included in travel, and purchases of goods by diplomatic and military personnel, which are classified under other official goods, services, and income.

Tables 5-3 and 5-4. Exports and imports of total services. Service exports and imports (World Bank country desks) include total nonfactor and factor services, based on transactions involving ownership changes as explained above for goods. Nonfactor services comprise shipment, passenger and other transport services, and travel, as well as current account transactions not separately reported (that is, not classified as merchandise, nonfactor services, or transfers). These include transactions with nonresidents by government agencies and their personnel abroad, as well as transactions by private residents with foreign governments and government personnel stationed in the reporting country. Factor services comprise services of labor and capital, thus covering income from direct investment abroad, interest, dividends, and property and labor income. Net interest is recorded on an accrual basis; that is, interest obligations are included whether payments are made or not.

Table 5-5. Net private transfers. Net private transfers (World Bank country desks) are inflows (from private sources to either private or public recipients) less outflows from private sources to either private or public recipients that carry no provisions for repayments. They include workers' remittances; transfers by migrants; gifts, dowries, and inheritances; and alimony and other support remittances.

Table 5-6. Net official current transfers. Net official transfers (World Bank country desks) are the official sources counterpart of Table 5-5. They include transfers on both current and capital accounts, including government grants of real resources and financial items such as subsidies to current budgets, grants of technical assistance, and government contributions to international organizations for administrative expenses.

Table 5-7. Current account balance, excluding net capital grants. Current account balance (World Bank country desks), as presented here, is the difference between exports of goods and all services plus inflows of unrequited current transfers (official and private) and imports of goods and all services plus outflows of unrequited transfers to the rest of the world. Other common presentations exclude or include both current and capital official transfers. Data in previous volumes included both.

Table 5-8. Current account balance, excluding net capital grants, as a percentage of GDP. It is defined as the ratio of figures presented in Table 5-7 to GDP in current prices (Table 2-5).

Table 5-9. Net capital grants. These grants (World Bank country desks) are unrequited transfers, often used to finance balance of payments deficits.

Table 5-10. Net foreign direct investment. Net foreign direct investment (World Bank country desks) is the net amount invested or reinvested by nonresidents to acquire a lasting interest in enterprises in which they exercise significant managerial control. Investment includes equity capital, reinvested earnings, and other capital. The net figures subtract the value of direct investment abroad by residents of the reporting country.

Table 5-11. Net long-term borrowing. Net long-term borrowing is calculated as disbursements less the repayment of principal (amortization) of public, publicly guaranteed, and private nonguaranteed borrowings that have an original or extended maturity of more than one year and that are repayable in foreign currencies, goods, or services. These data are as reported in the World Bank's Debtor Reporting System (DRS) and are in accord with the data on external debt discussed in Chapter 6.

Table 5-12. Other capital flows. Other capital flows comprise the net balance of inflows and outflows of capital not elsewhere included. It covers, for example, changes in the stock of short-term debt, arrears, and other liabilities (all adjusted for valuation changes resulting from exchange rate changes and other factors), and errors and omissions. This table incorporates corrections to data in *ADI 1992*.

Table 5-13. Use of reserves. This table (World Bank country desks) shows the variation from year to year of the net balance of international reserve assets and is valued throughout at year-end London prices (for example, US$37.37 an ounce in 1980 and US$484.10 an ounce in 1987). Positive numbers represent a decrease or use of reserves; negative numbers represent an increase in reserves. This table incorporates corrections to data in *ADI 1996*.

Table 5-14. Import coverage ratio of reserves. This ratio gives the number of months, at current import levels, that can adequately be covered by available foreign exchange reserves (World Bank country desks). It is obtained by dividing the stock of reserves by imports divided by 12.

Tables 5-15 and 5-16. Export and import unit values. The indexes for total export and import unit values (World Bank country desks) are based on exports and imports of goods and nonfactor services from the national accounts. These indexes are calculated by dividing the values of exports and imports expressed in current U.S. dollars (Tables 2-14 and 2-15) by the volume of exports (f.o.b.) and imports (c.i.f.) expressed in constant 1995 U.S. dollars (Tables 2-16 and 2-17). Because of the way these trade unit value indexes are calculated (Paasche indexes, with changing weights), they reflect the composition of exports and imports in each year and may not give a reliable trend in unit values when trade composition changes dramatically. By contrast, this index reflects more accurately shifts in a country's actual composition of trade than would an index using weights based on trade shares in a single year. Data may differ from those in *ADI 1992* and *ADI 1994/95* because a different source was used for this volume.

Table 5-17. Terms of trade. Terms of trade measure the relative movement of export and import prices. This series is calculated as the ratio of a country's export unit values or prices (Table 5-15) to its import unit values or prices (Table 5-16). It shows changes over a base year (1995) in the level of export unit values as a percentage of import unit values. Data may differ from those in *ADI 1992* and *ADI 1994/95* because a different source was used for this volume.

Table 5-18. Forest products exports. Exports of forest production (FAO data) are given as an aggregate including all wood from trees and forests (coniferous and nonconiferous), whether in natural form or partially processed (UN Standard International

Trade Classification [SITC] 245, 246, and 247); sawwood and sleepers (SITC 248); and wood-based panels and fiberwood, compressed or noncompressed (SITC 634 and 641).

Table 5-19. Petroleum exports. This table contains the volumes of crude petroleum exported (World Bank, International Energy Agency [IEA]). Data may differ from *ADI 1992* and *ADI 1994/95* because a different source was used for this volume.

Table 5-20. Copper exports. The table presents the unweighted sum of the metal content weights of copper ore and concentrate and of unrefined plus refined copper, metal, and alloys, unwrought (World Bank, Metals and Minerals Database [METMIN]). Data may differ from *ADI 1992* and *ADI 1994/95* because a different source was used for this volume.

Table 5-21. Iron exports. These are exports measured in metal content weight of iron ore (World Bank, METMIN).

Table 5-22. Phosphates exports. These are the volume of phosphates exports, expressed as the weight of mineral content in phosphate rock (World Bank, METMIN).

Table 5-23. Cocoa exports. Cocoa exports include cocoa beans, cocoa powder and cake, cocoa paste, cocoa butter, and chocolate products not elsewhere specified (FAO data).

Table 5-24. Coffee exports. Coffee exports are shown for green and roasted beans (FAO data).

Table 5-25. Cotton exports. Cotton exports refer to cotton lint only (FAO data).

Table 5-26. Groundnut exports. Groundnut exports include the weight of groundnuts in shelled equivalent (using a conversion factor of 70 percent), groundnut oil, and groundnut cake (FAO data).

Table 5-27. Palm oil products exports. Exports of palm oil products consist of palm oil and palm kernels (FAO data).

Table 5-28. Sisal exports. Only sisal fiber exports are included (FAO data).

Table 5-29. Tea exports. Tea exports figures are for processed tea (FAO data).

Table 5-30. Sugar exports. Sugar exports are shown in terms of raw sugar equivalent. The conversion factor to express refined sugar in raw sugar equivalent is 1.087 for all countries (FAO data).

Table 5-31. Tobacco exports. Only tobacco leaves are included (FAO data).

Table 5-32. Meat exports. Meat exports are defined as fresh, chilled, or frozen meat (SITC category 011) (FAO data).

Tables 5-33 and 5-34. Manufactured goods exports. Data reported in these tables follow the classification of manufacturing industries as reported in the UN *International Standard Industrial Classification of All Economic Activities* (ISIC), Revision 2 (World Bank country desks). Table 5-33 is expressed in current prices; Table 5-34 shows growth.

Tables 5-35 and 5-36. Food imports. Data refer to the sum of food, beverages, tobacco, oilseeds and oleaginous fruits, animal and vegetable oils, and fats (SITC sections 0, 1, and 4 and division 22) (World Bank country desks). Table 5-35 is expressed in current prices; Table 5-36 shows growth.

Tables 5-37 and 5-38. Nonfood consumer goods imports. Data reported in these tables show consumer goods imports other than food. Data are calculated as total merchandise imports less food, fuel, intermediate goods, and capital goods imports (World Bank country desks). Table 5-37 is expressed in current prices; Table 5-38 shows growth.

Tables 5-39 and 5-40. Fuel imports. Figures are defined as SITC section 3 (sum of Canada, Mexico, and United States) (World Bank country desks). Table 5-39 presents data in current prices; Table 5-40 shows growth.

Tables 5-41 and 5-42. Primary intermediate goods imports. Data on these tables comprise minerals, ores, and metals imports (the sum of SITC divisions 27, 28, and 68, and item 522.56) and agricultural raw materials imports (the sum of SITC section 2, less divisions 22, 27, and 28, and groups 233, 244, 266, and 267). Synthetics are excluded (World Bank country desks). Table 41 presents data in current prices; Table 42 shows growth.

Tables 5-43 and 5-44. Manufactured goods imports. Data reported on these tables follow the classification of manufacturing industries as reported in the UN International Standard Industrial Classification of All Economic Activities (ISIC), Revision 2 (World Bank country desks). Table 5-43 presents data in current prices; Table 5-44 shows growth.

Tables 5-45 and 5-46. Capital goods imports. Data shown here are for machinery and transport equipment (SITC section 7) (World Bank country desks). Table 5-45 presents data in current prices; Table 5-46 shows growth.

Tables 5-47, 5-48, and 5-49. Direction of trade matrix, imports. These tables show, for each importing country, the percentage of the value of its total imports that originates from each of the exporting countries for 1992, 1997, and 2002, respectively. They are calculated from Tables 5-53 to 5-55, below.

In these tables data posted under South Africa are for the Southern African Customs Union, which comprises Botswana, Lesotho, Namibia, South Africa, and Swaziland.

Tables 5-50, 5-51, and 5-52. Direction of trade matrix, exports. As with the foregoing, for each exporter, these tables show the percentage of the value of total exports, f.o.b., that goes to each of its trade partners for 1992, 1997, and 2002, respectively. These are calculated from Tables 5-53 to 5-55, below.

In these tables data posted under South Africa are for the Southern African Customs Union, which comprises Botswana, Lesotho, Namibia, South Africa, and Swaziland.

Tables 5-53, 5-54, and 5-55. Direction of trade matrix, current U.S. dollars. These are the value of trade in goods and services to or from the countries indicated. Matrices are shown for 1992, 1997, and 2002. They form the basis for the calculations in the previous six tables. Data for South Africa are for the Southern African Customs Union, which comprises Botswana, Lesotho, Namibia, South Africa, and Swaziland. The source of the data is the International Monetary Fund's Direction of Trade database. IMF staff have estimated some of these numbers in order to have a consistent time series.

Figure

The following indicator has been used to derive the figures in this chapter.

Figure 5-1. Terms of trade gains or losses (Table 5-17).

Methodology used for regional aggregations and period averages in Chapter 5

Table	Aggregations[a]					Period averages[b]	
	(1)	(3)	(4)	(6)	(9)	(2)	(3)
5-1		X					X
5-2		X					X
5-3		X					X
5-4		X					X
5-5	X					X	
5-6	X					X	
5-7	X					X	
5-8				X		X	
5-9	X					X	
5-10	X					X	
5-11	X					X	
5-12	X					X	
5-13	X					X	
5-14				X		X	
5-15			X			X	
5-16			X			X	
5-17			X			X	
5-18	X						X
5-19	X						X
5-20	X						X
5-21	X						X
5-22	X						X
5-23	X						X
5-24	X						X
5-25	X						X
5-26	X						X
5-27	X						X
5-28	X						X
5-29	X						X
5-30	X						X
5-31	X						X
5-32	X					X	
5-33	X					X	
5-34					X		X
5-35	X					X	
5-36					X		X
5-37	X					X	
5-38					X		X
5-39	X					X	
5-40					X		X
5-41	X					X	
5-42					X		X
5-43	X					X	
5-44					X		X
5-45	X					X	
5-46					X		X
5-47	X						
5-48	X						
5-49	X						
5-50	X						
5-51	X						
5-52	X						
5-53	X						
5-54	X						
5-55	X						

Note: Regional aggregations are shown in the rows for Sub-Saharan Africa, North Africa, and All Africa. Period averages are shown in the last three columns. This table shows only the methodologies used in this chapter.

a. Regional aggregations: (1) simple total; (2) simple total of the first indicator divided by the simple total of the second indicator (same country coverage); (3) simple total of the gap-filled indicator; (4) simple total of the gap-filled main indicator divided by the simple total of the gap-filled secondary indicator; (5) simple total of the first gap-filled main indicator less the simple total of the second gap-filled main indicator, all divided by the simple total of the secondary indicator; (6) weighted total (by population); (7) median; (8) no aggregation; (9) simple arithmetic mean.

b. Period averages: (1) arithmetic mean (using the same series as shown in the table; i.e., ratio if the rest of the table is shown as ratio, level if the rest of the table is shown as level, growth rate if the rest is shown as growth rate); (2) least-squares growth rate (using main indicator); (3) least-squares growth rate (using main indicator in constant terms, with the rest of the table in current terms).

6

External Debt and Related Flows

The tables in this chapter provide a consistent presentation of the structure and terms of external debt and debt servicing. No data are presented on debt owed to domestic lenders. The aggregates and ratios provide various measures of a country's external debt situation. These measures include the size of debt and its servicing requirements, the amount of debt relative to GDP, the ratio of debt-servicing payments to exports, and the interest rate and terms of the stock of debt (including grace period, maturity, and grant element).

These tables follow the presentation in the *Global Development Finance (GDF—*formerly *World Debt Tables)* and therefore show IMF purchases, repurchases, charges, and net purchases separately from long- and short-term lending, repayments, interests, or net lending. While IMF purchases and repurchases are not strictly lending (they are swaps of currency), they do add to, or subtract from, the resources available for consumption or investment and do impose a liability against future income streams. For this reason, IMF transactions are included here.

Data on debt and related flows are drawn largely from the World Bank's Debtor Reporting System (DRS), to which member countries submit detailed accounts on the annual status, transactions, and terms of debt and related flows. World Bank and IMF staff estimates based on other sources of data supplement

DRS data, especially for recent years, on debt not guaranteed by debtor governments and on short-term debt. The figures in this chapter are based mostly on data supplied by debtor countries. Other data series on debt, on which the World Bank may base some of its estimates, are maintained by the Organisation for Economic Co-operation and Development (OECD) and the Bank for International Settlements (BIS) from data provided by creditor governments and agencies. No figures are given for Libya and Namibia, which do not report debt information to the DRS. However, totals do include estimates for these countries.

The following definitions apply throughout the chapter. Long-term loans have an original or extended maturity of more than one year, while the maturity on short-term loans is one year or less. Official and private refer to the source of the foreign loans. Official loans are from multilateral organizations (excluding the IMF) and from foreign governments; these loans are either made directly to the government of the borrowing country or guaranteed by it, or its agencies, when made to a third party. Private loans are from the private sector, including foreign parent companies and their affiliates, suppliers, financial markets (such as commercial banks), and other sources. These private loans may or may not be guaranteed by creditor or debtor governments and agencies. *Public and publicly guaranteed* loans, as defined by the DRS, refer to loans from both official and private foreign sources that are made to, or guaranteed by, the debtor government or its agencies. Almost all loans from foreign official sources are public or publicly guaranteed. Some loans from foreign private sources are made to, or guaranteed by, the debtor government or its agencies (these are labeled *private guaranteed* by the DRS). Some loans from foreign private sources are not public or publicly guaranteed (these are labeled *private nonguaranteed* by the DRS).

Concessional loans carry a grant element of 25 percent or more (based on a standard 10 percent discount rate), which is consistent with the Development Assistance Committee (DAC) of the OECD definition of ODA (see Chapter 12). Nonconcessional loans carry a grant element of less than 25 percent. In this chapter, private loans are shown separately from official nonconcessional loans.

Additional information, definitions, and methodology are available in the *Global Development Finance 2001* (formerly *World Debt Tables*) (World Bank).

6-1. Gross disbursements: official concessional long-term loans

	Millions of U.S. dollars (current prices)											Annual average		
	1980	1993	1994	1995	1996	1997	1998	1999	2000	2001	2002	75-84	85-94	95-MR
SUB-SAHARAN AFRICA	2,547	4,872	4,870	4,726	4,208	3,975	3,513	3,313	3,365	3,461	4,116	2,637	4,593	3,835
excluding South Africa	2,547	4,872	4,870	4,726	4,208	3,975	3,513	3,313	3,365	3,461	4,116	2,637	4,593	3,835
excl. S.Africa & Nigeria	2,499	4,805	4,793	4,627	4,114	3,878	3,368	3,232	3,297	3,442	4,070	2,612	4,549	3,753
Angola	0	31	73	63	43	36	80	68	34	15	21	0	31	45
Benin	35	79	101	96	104	49	50	70	30	113	67	33	79	73
Botswana	9	49	37	57	15	13	12	9	23	7	2	11	26	17
Burkina Faso	41	131	105	110	102	70	90	108	87	125	131	36	95	103
Burundi	38	76	52	45	34	19	30	20	36	12	36	32	88	29
Cameroon	143	311	372	118	155	220	161	171	216	103	94	118	184	155
Cape Verde	0	6	28	16	17	20	32	57	29	40	30	3	11	30
Central African Republic	19	50	44	32	27	5	3	6	16	0	1	15	67	11
Chad	5	58	69	58	97	80	43	86	33	39	97	16	59	67
Comoros	13	8	12	10	10	6	4	1	3	12	12	11	12	7
Congo, Dem. Rep. of	131	58	1	0	3	0	0	8	0	0	415	127	163	53
Congo, Rep. of	49	8	194	14	2	3	0	0	0	38	2	61	72	7
Côte d'Ivoire	42	473	767	548	395	150	312	141	131	10	211	62	259	237
Djibouti	1	26	26	18	24	12	5	3	8	12	28	7	29	14
Equatorial Guinea	4	10	4	2	2	3	1	4	2	0	2	3	13	2
Eritrea	0	0	27	7	5	32	64	98	50	104	84	0	3	55
Ethiopia	70	348	211	199	223	95	115	206	180	522	574	395	334	264
Gabon	16	19	53	64	27	96	13	21	0	0	14	11	40	29
Gambia, The	27	22	22	23	58	24	16	21	21	23	52	13	27	30
Ghana	114	342	324	407	392	404	416	317	320	323	192	66	287	346
Guinea	56	228	125	123	84	173	118	76	60	91	48	57	176	97
Guinea-Bissau	49	23	26	21	28	30	15	2	14	6	6	16	32	15
Kenya	160	309	197	507	257	146	153	129	295	142	83	117	261	214
Lesotho	7	28	43	28	24	29	28	28	28	20	30	11	35	27
Liberia	39	33	0	0	0	0	0	0	0	0	0	34	13	0
Madagascar	153	104	72	88	116	214	102	125	140	132	181	95	151	137
Malawi	45	187	107	211	161	162	147	128	115	117	72	44	115	139
Mali	75	79	120	188	153	127	96	121	99	114	143	73	137	130
Mauritania	96	142	111	101	114	80	53	47	107	74	107	82	100	85
Mauritius	16	42	25	22	12	30	13	19	26	21	17	14	42	20
Mozambique	0	173	221	219	272	239	220	128	123	121	245	63	213	196
Namibia	..	..	..	..	..	..	..	..	..	..	..	..	..	..
Niger	59	68	70	28	41	85	85	62	71	78	119	40	88	71
Nigeria	49	67	77	99	94	97	145	81	68	20	46	25	44	81
Rwanda	27	61	22	54	62	70	88	82	40	64	85	27	71	68
São Tomé and Principe	8	15	15	13	11	5	7	12	6	7	4	4	15	8
Senegal	113	85	98	150	181	199	190	67	121	179	224	88	215	164
Seychelles	6	4	1	2	4	6	6	8	15	1	4	3	5	6
Sierra Leone	33	96	61	94	73	40	34	14	77	83	66	18	33	60
Somalia	74	0	0	0	0	0	0	0	0	0	0	101	47	0
South Africa	0	0	0	0	0	0	0	0	0	0	0	0	0	0
Sudan	270	95	10	27	2	0	0	0	0	0	0	313	152	4
Swaziland	7	1	14	13	5	4	4	11	2	10	10	8	8	7
Tanzania	159	191	230	201	198	245	195	251	203	172	188	186	223	207
Togo	35	17	41	26	99	57	58	38	25	33	13	37	61	44
Uganda	13	328	265	219	211	270	170	171	217	338	170	33	198	220
Zambia	243	205	218	309	205	210	59	194	245	142	167	100	158	191
Zimbabwe	1	190	183	97	66	120	81	111	52	-1	25	29	121	69
NORTH AFRICA	2,079	1,691	1,631	1,660	1,569	1,189	956	1,115	888	763	654	1,746	1,345	1,099
Algeria	79	352	388	645	387	212	145	341	182	106	85	78	176	263
Egypt, Arab Rep.	1,064	578	463	360	430	389	371	181	154	86	95	1,085	608	258
Libya	..	..	..	..	..	..	..	..	..	..	..	..	..	..
Morocco	731	534	504	477	589	450	297	303	180	201	216	406	342	339
Tunisia	204	227	277	178	164	138	144	290	372	371	258	177	219	239
ALL AFRICA	4,626	6,563	6,501	6,386	5,777	5,164	4,469	4,428	4,253	4,224	4,770	4,383	5,938	4,934

6-2. Gross disbursements: official nonconcessional long-term loans

	Millions of U.S. dollars (current prices)											Annual average		
	1980	*1993*	*1994*	*1995*	*1996*	*1997*	*1998*	*1999*	*2000*	*2001*	*2002*	*75-84*	*85-94*	*95-MR*
SUB-SAHARAN AFRICA	1,691	1,664	1,445	1,194	1,066	970	743	546	507	344	290	1,434	1,942	707
excluding South Africa	1,691	1,664	1,445	1,194	1,066	970	743	509	416	340	283	1,434	1,942	690
excl. S.Africa & Nigeria	1,618	1,188	923	861	852	752	612	415	331	293	249	1,254	1,414	545
Angola	0	5	0	56	11	0	1	0	0	1	0	0	40	9
Benin	24	2	4	5	5	1	11	3	0	0	0	8	6	3
Botswana	16	32	22	10	12	8	11	3	1	1	0	15	42	6
Burkina Faso	18	7	2	2	1	1	0	0	1	14	3	11	11	3
Burundi	1	1	1	0	1	0	0	0	0	0	4	3	5	1
Cameroon	108	84	68	44	21	25	16	18	17	31	1	71	167	21
Cape Verde	0	5	1	1	1	0	23	7	0	0	0	5	2	4
Central African Republic	6	0	0	1	0	1	0	0	0	0	0	3	5	0
Chad	0	1	0	0	2	0	0	0	0	9	0	2	9	1
Comoros	0	0	0	0	0	0	0	0	0	0	0	1	1	0
Congo, Dem. Rep. of	70	0	0	0	0	0	0	0	0	0	0	61	71	0
Congo, Rep. of	60	0	137	1	2	21	0	0	0	0	0	38	42	3
Côte d'Ivoire	189	151	151	121	70	34	77	50	18	2	12	178	265	48
Djibouti	4	0	0	0	0	0	0	0	0	1	3	1	0	0
Equatorial Guinea	11	0	0	0	0	0	0	0	0	0	0	3	1	0
Eritrea	0	0	0	0	2	1	3	11	1	0	0	0	0	2
Ethiopia	7	21	21	33	49	54	17	24	4	10	23	11	48	27
Gabon	19	71	79	157	62	30	22	6	9	4	16	36	76	38
Gambia, The	2	3	1	0	0	0	0	0	0	0	0	2	2	0
Ghana	106	26	21	21	123	37	22	13	30	39	35	38	44	40
Guinea	9	47	44	47	42	39	24	19	10	4	2	12	24	23
Guinea-Bissau	6	0	3	0	1	0	0	0	0	0	0	3	5	0
Kenya	73	20	46	38	69	14	14	9	12	29	2	100	94	23
Lesotho	1	41	19	27	20	15	8	9	40	4	3	3	15	16
Liberia	26	0	0	0	0	0	0	0	0	0	0	23	5	0
Madagascar	59	19	10	1	21	103	0	4	11	8	5	49	33	19
Malawi	60	6	4	4	1	5	9	13	3	0	0	26	14	4
Mali	10	5	1	5	3	0	0	0	1	0	0	5	4	1
Mauritania	16	25	28	11	16	9	3	2	8	1	6	24	30	7
Mauritius	20	23	11	17	37	45	37	29	22	5	112	18	29	38
Mozambique	0	9	8	11	10	20	3	2	2	13	6	0	14	8
Namibia	..	..	..	..	..	..	..	..	..	..	..	..	..	..
Niger	33	33	4	0	1	0	0	0	5	0	0	27	8	1
Nigeria	73	476	522	334	214	218	131	94	85	47	34	180	528	145
Rwanda	0	0	0	0	0	2	0	0	0	0	0	0	0	0
São Tomé and Principe	2	0	0	0	0	0	0	5	3	1	0	2	1	1
Senegal	74	68	34	7	0	1	15	4	7	7	6	63	35	6
Seychelles	6	5	8	7	7	5	8	3	1	0	0	2	4	4
Sierra Leone	9	3	3	1	2	0	13	2	0	0	0	4	2	2
Somalia	13	0	0	0	0	0	0	0	0	0	0	19	1	0
South Africa	0	0	0	0	0	0	0	38	91	4	7	0	0	17
Sudan	297	6	2	24	15	5	0	0	0	0	0	138	14	5
Swaziland	20	7	1	4	23	18	27	22	14	12	3	15	6	15
Tanzania	86	4	18	20	5	7	21	2	0	2	1	81	23	7
Togo	12	2	0	0	2	0	11	0	0	0	0	15	3	2
Uganda	5	62	3	11	14	21	4	3	2	2	1	15	32	7
Zambia	68	25	42	18	19	12	5	7	6	10	3	91	54	10
Zimbabwe	77	370	130	137	172	209	210	113	79	34	0	31	127	119
NORTH AFRICA	1,690	3,064	2,822	2,717	2,836	2,274	1,587	1,681	1,465	1,435	1,417	1,769	3,171	1,926
Algeria	487	812	1,134	947	1,191	993	606	389	608	343	339	489	961	677
Egypt, Arab Rep.	840	453	471	242	220	242	88	50	81	108	183	702	631	152
Libya	..	..	..	..	..	..	..	..	..	..	..	..	..	..
Morocco	135	785	635	1,095	904	509	578	740	449	341	390	229	713	626
Tunisia	119	614	583	433	521	518	315	502	328	644	506	131	439	471
ALL AFRICA	3,382	4,728	4,267	3,912	3,902	3,243	2,330	2,227	1,973	1,778	1,707	3,203	5,113	2,634

6-3. Gross disbursements: private long-term loans

	Millions of U.S. dollars (current prices)											Annual average		
	1980	1993	1994	1995	1996	1997	1998	1999	2000	2001	2002	75-84	85-94	95-MR
SUB-SAHARAN AFRICA	6,290	1,969	4,664	5,202	4,306	6,586	3,474	4,306	4,872	5,090	5,095	4,372	2,748	4,866
excluding South Africa	6,290	1,969	1,146	1,654	2,015	1,956	1,428	1,611	1,352	1,491	1,069	4,372	2,396	1,572
excl. S.Africa & Nigeria	4,660	1,969	1,146	1,654	2,015	1,956	1,428	1,611	1,352	1,491	1,069	2,973	1,957	1,572
Angola	..	649	344	431	723	1,154	709	875	1,011	1,047	801	..	472	844
Benin	4	0	0	0	0	0	0	0	0	0	0	44	0	0
Botswana	3	30	0	0	0	0	0	11	4	0	0	6	5	2
Burkina Faso	6	0	0	0	0	0	0	0	0	0	0	8	1	0
Burundi	0	0	0	0	0	0	1	0	3	2	0	5	1	1
Cameroon	364	104	8	0	25	14	10	56	39	0	0	230	228	18
Cape Verde	..	0	0	4	5	2	0	0	0	11	4	0	0	3
Central African Republic	0	0	0	0	0	0	0	0	0	0	0	2	0	0
Chad	0	0	0	0	0	0	0	0	0	0	0	5	0	0
Comoros	0	0	0	0	0	0	0	0	0	0	0	0	0	0
Congo, Dem. Rep. of	263	0	0	0	0	0	0	0	0	0	0	176	8	0
Congo, Rep. of	412	451	1	0	0	0	0	0	0	0	0	207	212	0
Côte d'Ivoire	1,508	190	317	75	411	52	56	56	0	0	0	791	230	81
Djibouti	5	0	0	0	0	0	0	0	0	0	0	1	0	0
Equatorial Guinea	5	0	0	0	0	0	0	0	0	0	0	3	0	0
Eritrea	..	..	0	0	0	0	0	0	0	0	0	..	0	0
Ethiopia	33	10	4	0	22	30	10	1	2	0	0	45	93	8
Gabon	135	3	2	0	0	20	10	33	21	13	41	174	93	17
Gambia, The	22	0	0	0	0	0	0	1	0	0	0	5	0	0
Ghana	0	77	123	178	384	208	164	67	45	212	21	12	76	160
Guinea	57	11	0	0	17	20	7	0	0	0	0	29	8	5
Guinea-Bissau	21	0	0	0	0	0	0	0	0	0	0	5	3	0
Kenya	387	87	6	132	42	25	152	127	85	5	136	224	237	88
Lesotho	5	3	2	16	33	24	29	15	2	2	0	4	6	15
Liberia	11	0	0	0	0	0	0	0	0	0	0	23	0	0
Madagascar	163	0	0	1	0	0	0	0	0	0	0	64	5	0
Malawi	48	1	10	0	0	1	0	1	0	0	0	29	7	0
Mali	10	0	0	0	0	0	0	0	0	0	0	6	0	0
Mauritania	14	0	0	0	25	0	0	0	0	0	4	24	2	4
Mauritius	61	39	150	369	91	118	11	97	85	45	43	28	62	107
Mozambique	..	8	4	36	0	6	0	0	0	0	0	201	30	5
Namibia	..	..	..	..	..	..	..	..	..	..	..	..	..	..
Niger	190	0	0	0	0	0	0	0	0	0	0	91	27	0
Nigeria	1,630	0	0	0	0	0	0	0	0	0	0	1,399	439	0
Rwanda	0	0	0	0	0	0	0	0	0	0	0	3	1	0
São Tomé and Principe	0	0	0	0	0	0	0	0	0	0	0	1	0	0
Senegal	141	1	1	1	0	21	2	1	1	58	12	74	18	12
Seychelles	0	8	9	0	1	0	10	0	0	10	8	2	8	4
Sierra Leone	42	0	0	0	0	0	0	0	0	0	0	24	1	0
Somalia	27	0	0	0	0	0	0	0	0	0	0	25	1	0
South Africa	..	..	3,518	3,549	2,291	4,630	2,046	2,695	3,520	3,599	4,026	..	3,518	3,294
Sudan	145	0	0	0	0	0	0	0	0	0	0	100	0	0
Swaziland	0	0	0	0	0	33	0	0	0	14	0	3	2	6
Tanzania	122	45	17	42	6	0	0	7	5	1	0	63	36	8
Togo	50	0	0	0	0	0	0	0	0	0	0	63	0	0
Uganda	65	18	0	0	0	0	0	0	0	4	0	36	37	1
Zambia	289	11	35	25	13	50	20	50	10	60	0	154	48	28
Zimbabwe	55	172	115	338	209	167	225	180	40	7	0	167	180	146
NORTH AFRICA	5,204	6,594	4,569	3,810	2,583	2,245	2,070	2,252	2,626	3,838	3,208	4,921	6,406	2,829
Algeria	2,832	5,363	3,268	2,092	1,308	438	399	394	425	583	1,112	2,743	4,578	844
Egypt, Arab Rep.	776	168	260	40	33	265	289	353	352	1,722	221	780	882	409
Libya	..	..	..	..	..	..	..	..	..	..	..	..	..	..
Morocco	1,308	783	769	788	437	549	809	641	1,009	648	845	956	569	716
Tunisia	288	281	199	777	648	824	190	639	840	885	1,030	306	310	729
ALL AFRICA	11,494	8,563	9,233	9,012	6,889	8,831	5,544	6,558	7,498	8,928	8,303	9,293	9,154	7,695

6-4. Disbursements: long-term loans and IMF purchases

	Millions of U.S. dollars (current prices)											Annual average		
	1980	*1993*	*1994*	*1995*	*1996*	*1997*	*1998*	*1999*	*2000*	*2001*	*2002*	*75-84*	*85-94*	*95-MR*
SUB-SAHARAN AFRICA	11,745	9,652	11,896	14,117	10,233	12,054	8,534	8,681	9,244	9,439	10,731	9,410	10,071	10,379
excluding South Africa	11,745	8,794	8,378	10,568	7,942	7,424	6,489	5,949	5,633	5,836	6,698	9,410	9,633	7,067
excl. S.Africa & Nigeria	9,993	8,250	7,780	10,135	7,633	7,110	6,213	5,774	5,480	5,770	6,618	7,806	8,622	6,842
Angola	..	685	417	550	778	1,190	790	943	1,045	1,063	822	..	589	898
Benin	71	103	130	115	128	57	62	83	39	124	72	86	92	85
Botswana	27	111	59	67	27	21	23	22	28	7	2	33	73	25
Burkina Faso	70	151	132	139	112	89	108	125	96	161	148	56	111	122
Burundi	45	77	53	45	35	19	31	20	39	14	53	44	100	32
Cameroon	626	499	478	175	230	296	260	306	340	154	136	427	595	237
Cape Verde	0	10	29	21	24	22	55	63	29	52	38	11	13	38
Central African Republic	40	50	59	33	27	6	15	17	16	11	1	27	78	16
Chad	5	58	83	70	123	92	54	98	47	66	115	26	74	83
Comoros	13	8	14	10	10	6	4	1	3	12	12	12	12	7
Congo, Dem. Rep. of	603	58	1	0	3	0	0	8	0	0	959	482	306	121
Congo, Rep. of	526	459	350	15	24	24	10	0	14	38	2	310	329	16
Côte d'Ivoire	1,777	813	1,405	924	1,014	236	613	247	148	12	299	1,114	819	437
Djibouti	10	26	26	18	28	14	8	8	11	17	37	9	29	18
Equatorial Guinea	38	14	7	2	2	3	1	4	2	0	2	12	17	2
Eritrea	..	..	27	7	7	33	67	108	51	104	84	..	27	58
Ethiopia	119	409	256	232	315	179	162	231	185	576	642	470	486	315
Gabon	171	93	198	279	121	168	46	59	47	17	71	222	230	101
Gambia, The	56	26	23	23	58	24	21	26	30	31	56	26	34	34
Ghana	249	509	468	648	940	649	713	457	429	641	316	183	506	599
Guinea	129	286	182	200	143	265	180	106	70	122	66	103	218	144
Guinea-Bissau	75	23	28	24	31	36	18	5	22	6	6	24	40	19
Kenya	714	447	281	677	404	185	318	265	437	176	220	515	657	335
Lesotho	15	82	69	70	76	68	65	53	69	35	43	19	60	60
Liberia	109	33	0	0	0	0	0	0	0	0	0	113	19	0
Madagascar	444	123	82	90	156	336	102	147	200	169	201	234	209	175
Malawi	190	194	147	227	184	178	173	152	126	117	94	120	151	156
Mali	109	98	164	238	186	156	111	144	109	137	152	95	156	154
Mauritania	155	179	163	133	176	108	55	57	123	98	133	141	146	110
Mauritius	143	105	186	409	140	193	60	145	132	71	172	87	139	165
Mozambique	..	211	254	267	300	300	258	158	184	145	262	834	278	234
Namibia	..	..	..	..	..	..	..	..	..	..	..	..	..	..
Niger	290	100	89	28	56	111	111	62	87	89	140	164	135	86
Nigeria	1,753	544	598	433	308	314	276	175	153	67	81	1,603	1,011	226
Rwanda	34	61	22	68	62	92	104	111	65	76	85	31	73	83
São Tomé and Principe	10	15	15	13	11	5	7	16	11	8	4	8	16	9
Senegal	395	153	201	241	216	270	255	92	148	273	253	261	316	218
Seychelles	12	18	18	8	12	11	23	11	16	11	12	12	17	13
Sierra Leone	104	100	200	115	90	47	62	36	91	143	102	63	52	86
Somalia	135	0	0	0	0	0	0	0	0	0	0	158	56	0
South Africa	0	858	3,518	3,549	2,291	4,630	2,046	2,733	3,611	3,603	4,033	0	438	3,312
Sudan	921	101	12	51	17	5	0	0	0	0	0	655	166	9
Swaziland	29	8	15	18	28	55	31	33	16	36	13	29	16	29
Tanzania	433	240	265	262	246	336	264	341	261	226	241	353	309	272
Togo	119	19	56	59	101	72	84	38	25	33	13	124	76	53
Uganda	161	409	320	285	288	351	224	209	231	355	172	135	311	264
Zambia	690	241	294	2,606	236	286	84	264	287	308	341	482	272	551
Zimbabwe	132	799	504	652	447	496	570	437	171	40	25	257	464	355
NORTH AFRICA	9,313	11,348	9,864	8,661	7,731	6,172	4,956	5,354	4,979	6,036	5,279	8,661	11,274	6,146
Algeria	3,398	6,526	5,631	4,157	3,629	2,107	1,494	1,429	1,215	1,031	1,536	3,310	5,891	2,075
Egypt, Arab Rep.	2,743	1,199	1,193	642	683	896	749	584	586	1,915	498	2,627	2,156	819
Libya	..	..	..	..	..	..	..	..	..	..	..	..	..	..
Morocco	2,452	2,102	1,908	2,361	1,929	1,508	1,683	1,685	1,638	1,189	1,451	1,753	1,712	1,681
Tunisia	611	1,122	1,059	1,389	1,333	1,480	648	1,430	1,540	1,900	1,794	616	1,021	1,439
ALL AFRICA	21,059	21,000	21,760	22,778	17,964	18,226	13,491	14,035	14,223	15,475	16,010	18,070	21,345	16,525

Note: In 1995, Zambia was able to clear its arrears to the IMF after completing a three-year Rights Arrangement Program.

6-5. Amortization: official concessional long-term loans

	Millions of U.S. dollars (current prices)											Annual average		
	1980	*1993*	*1994*	*1995*	*1996*	*1997*	*1998*	*1999*	*2000*	*2001*	*2002*	*75-84*	*85-94*	*95-MR*
SUB-SAHARAN AFRICA	243	770	715	873	889	1,031	1,729	1,633	1,295	1,308	1,228	237	594	1,248
excluding South Africa	243	770	715	873	889	1,031	1,729	1,633	1,295	1,308	1,228	237	594	1,248
excl. S.Africa & Nigeria	229	609	714	871	888	959	1,409	1,631	1,290	1,290	1,190	224	571	1,191
Angola	0	2	9	3	8	8	363	406	217	303	5	0	3	164
Benin	1	12	12	15	14	18	19	22	34	20	25	2	7	21
Botswana	0	13	13	11	15	30	15	18	19	16	20	1	7	18
Burkina Faso	4	11	18	20	23	25	27	30	21	15	22	2	10	23
Burundi	1	15	16	14	6	8	9	12	9	12	12	1	13	10
Cameroon	13	37	12	12	14	49	75	47	60	53	77	12	23	48
Cape Verde	0	2	3	4	3	7	6	4	7	6	9	0	2	6
Central African Republic	0	1	5	2	2	4	10	6	7	9	0	1	2	5
Chad	3	1	6	2	7	6	7	12	12	14	11	1	3	9
Comoros	0	2	2	0	1	1	1	2	1	1	4	0	1	1
Congo, Dem. Rep. of	3	4	0	0	0	0	0	0	0	0	167	5	7	21
Congo, Rep. of	11	1	8	7	22	0	0	0	1	5	2	10	3	5
Côte d'Ivoire	18	78	56	65	81	68	106	216	131	70	95	15	55	104
Djibouti	2	6	9	9	9	5	3	6	8	7	7	1	6	7
Equatorial Guinea	0	0	0	0	1	1	1	1	1	1	1	0	0	1
Eritrea	0	0	0	0	0	0	0	0	0	0	2	0	0	0
Ethiopia	7	16	19	25	35	26	38	48	37	76	24	9	35	39
Gabon	4	7	8	12	9	39	28	45	16	80	69	5	7	37
Gambia, The	0	8	9	8	9	10	12	9	10	7	10	1	7	9
Ghana	14	30	53	50	54	52	81	96	107	62	38	20	35	67
Guinea	44	16	26	86	44	29	31	43	38	45	64	36	37	47
Guinea-Bissau	0	1	2	4	3	5	6	3	3	6	7	0	3	4
Kenya	6	39	67	69	75	66	67	87	75	86	125	8	34	81
Lesotho	0	9	6	11	11	12	10	11	13	31	13	1	4	14
Liberia	1	1	1	0	0	0	0	0	0	0	0	4	2	0
Madagascar	18	12	13	10	21	55	39	40	59	26	27	19	14	35
Malawi	2	9	10	16	19	21	19	15	18	16	8	2	7	17
Mali	4	23	39	45	42	38	40	58	46	43	43	4	20	44
Mauritania	3	40	33	37	37	39	41	36	29	26	26	3	28	34
Mauritius	2	23	22	25	27	47	23	23	23	28	31	2	16	28
Mozambique	0	12	17	24	29	33	24	21	23	31	18	1	15	25
Namibia	..	..	..	..	..	..	..	..	..	..	..	..	..	..
Niger	16	12	6	6	8	18	12	11	12	7	8	5	7	10
Nigeria	14	162	1	2	1	72	321	3	5	17	38	13	22	57
Rwanda	0	11	2	11	8	9	8	10	11	10	12	1	7	10
São Tomé and Principe	0	0	0	1	1	1	1	2	2	2	3	0	1	1
Senegal	7	31	68	72	64	47	89	89	85	79	78	5	37	75
Seychelles	0	4	3	4	2	2	4	5	2	1	1	0	2	3
Sierra Leone	2	3	9	7	6	6	10	3	6	5	6	3	4	6
Somalia	2	0	0	0	0	0	0	0	0	0	0	2	1	0
South Africa	0	0	0	0	0	0	0	0	0	0	0	0	0	0
Sudan	14	5	3	9	0	0	0	0	2	1	0	16	26	2
Swaziland	1	7	7	8	10	8	7	6	8	6	5	1	5	7
Tanzania	19	38	40	38	54	35	48	63	55	50	31	14	35	47
Togo	2	4	4	7	15	13	13	16	10	11	1	8	5	11
Uganda	2	16	23	22	23	37	41	42	18	11	25	2	10	27
Zambia	3	10	21	47	34	33	27	15	40	13	61	2	5	34
Zimbabwe	2	38	35	58	47	51	48	52	13	4	0	1	19	34
NORTH AFRICA	294	576	737	699	775	866	1,099	1,166	1,364	1,502	1,670	264	469	1,143
Algeria	73	84	62	54	110	128	175	234	273	288	290	72	90	194
Egypt, Arab Rep.	119	56	68	151	225	289	434	461	580	625	697	111	124	433
Libya	..	..	..	..	..	..	..	..	..	..	..	..	..	..
Morocco	62	281	341	287	225	237	265	262	288	370	457	41	113	299
Tunisia	41	154	266	207	216	211	225	209	223	219	226	39	142	217
ALL AFRICA	537	1,346	1,452	1,572	1,664	1,896	2,828	2,799	2,659	2,810	2,898	501	1,062	2,391

6-6. Amortization: official nonconcessional long-term loans

	Millions of U.S. dollars (current prices)											Annual average		
	1980	1993	1994	1995	1996	1997	1998	1999	2000	2001	2002	75-84	85-94	95-MR
SUB-SAHARAN AFRICA	423	1,428	1,906	2,117	2,445	1,953	1,782	1,836	2,032	2,331	1,460	336	1,412	1,995
excluding South Africa	423	1,428	1,906	2,117	2,445	1,953	1,782	1,836	2,032	2,331	1,457	336	1,412	1,994
excl. S.Africa & Nigeria	392	1,100	1,476	1,650	1,718	1,442	1,354	1,380	1,122	818	989	301	1,038	1,309
Angola	0	21	25	21	26	40	71	28	52	35	46	0	27	40
Benin	1	6	9	10	11	10	10	14	7	3	3	2	6	8
Botswana	6	43	46	47	49	39	34	33	26	21	22	3	33	34
Burkina Faso	4	9	9	9	7	7	6	9	5	4	6	2	6	6
Burundi	1	3	5	3	6	4	4	2	0	0	0	0	4	2
Cameroon	16	98	117	133	178	175	146	111	99	37	76	18	73	119
Cape Verde	0	2	3	2	2	3	8	11	2	2	3	0	2	4
Central African Republic	0	1	2	0	0	0	2	1	0	0	0	1	3	1
Chad	0	4	2	1	3	7	5	3	3	1	2	0	1	3
Comoros	0	0	0	0	0	0	0	0	0	0	0	0	1	0
Congo, Dem. Rep. of	100	0	0	0	0	0	0	0	0	0	82	36	33	10
Congo, Rep. of	10	0	119	25	104	53	7	0	4	49	7	11	27	31
Côte d'Ivoire	37	216	299	414	429	261	248	268	152	123	227	30	160	265
Djibouti	1	0	0	0	0	0	0	0	0	0	1	0	0	0
Equatorial Guinea	1	1	0	0	2	0	0	0	0	0	0	1	1	0
Eritrea	0	0	0	0	0	0	0	0	1	1	1	0	0	0
Ethiopia	4	13	13	19	26	18	18	28	25	22	26	6	23	23
Gabon	15	24	55	78	71	104	67	187	144	142	134	14	27	116
Gambia, The	0	6	6	7	5	3	2	2	3	2	3	0	3	3
Ghana	22	36	45	62	45	55	56	54	62	32	30	15	29	49
Guinea	20	17	12	20	14	21	46	23	52	14	25	9	19	27
Guinea-Bissau	0	0	1	4	3	1	1	0	7	8	2	0	1	3
Kenya	25	139	183	201	199	170	190	185	117	123	57	22	123	155
Lesotho	0	6	6	7	5	8	10	10	14	9	28	1	5	11
Liberia	2	12	13	0	0	0	0	0	0	0	0	6	6	0
Madagascar	1	14	14	9	18	43	18	23	14	6	10	8	28	18
Malawi	3	21	23	27	18	15	14	12	11	5	4	5	26	13
Mali	0	3	14	11	5	4	5	6	4	4	4	0	4	5
Mauritania	1	36	24	32	36	22	19	22	16	13	13	6	29	21
Mauritius	4	34	36	36	31	31	30	30	33	33	42	4	27	33
Mozambique	0	15	35	34	25	12	11	8	3	10	4	0	12	13
Namibia	..	..	..	..	..	..	..	..	..	..	..	..	..	..
Niger	2	20	8	1	1	2	0	1	0	6	1	5	10	2
Nigeria	31	328	429	468	727	510	428	456	910	1,513	469	34	375	685
Rwanda	0	0	0	0	1	1	1	1	2	0	0	0	0	1
São Tomé and Principe	1	1	1	0	1	0	1	1	1	0	1	1	1	0
Senegal	12	19	47	55	41	42	48	33	35	24	35	8	43	39
Seychelles	0	3	3	3	3	5	5	6	2	1	0	0	3	3
Sierra Leone	2	2	9	22	41	1	4	3	3	5	7	2	4	11
Somalia	5	0	0	0	0	0	0	0	0	0	0	3	1	0
South Africa	0	0	0	0	0	0	0	0	0	0	3	0	0	0
Sudan	32	4	0	6	0	0	1	6	2	1	0	24	10	2
Swaziland	4	9	12	8	10	8	6	11	6	8	6	3	13	8
Tanzania	7	49	45	62	69	33	33	20	46	31	15	8	48	39
Togo	8	2	2	0	6	9	4	7	0	0	0	8	18	3
Uganda	9	61	49	38	25	22	24	18	8	7	6	6	30	18
Zambia	34	80	105	132	83	75	53	36	39	19	65	28	71	63
Zimbabwe	3	71	81	109	121	139	142	170	125	21	1	5	46	103
NORTH AFRICA	287	2,558	2,954	2,827	2,399	2,965	2,633	2,462	2,164	2,326	2,912	533	2,365	2,586
Algeria	171	1,080	598	618	560	917	801	884	782	992	1,206	157	882	845
Egypt, Arab Rep.	32	336	306	391	348	352	274	258	283	281	326	54	406	314
Libya	..	..	..	..	..	..	..	..	..	..	..	..	..	..
Morocco	52	806	1,128	1,351	1,115	1,305	1,047	876	641	621	884	57	527	980
Tunisia	32	312	342	432	376	373	386	444	458	432	496	44	233	425
ALL AFRICA	711	3,987	4,859	4,944	4,844	4,917	4,415	4,298	4,195	4,657	4,372	868	3,778	4,580

6-7. Amortization: private long-term loans

| | Millions of U.S. dollars (current prices) | | | | | | | | | | | Annual average | | |
	1980	1993	1994	1995	1996	1997	1998	1999	2000	2001	2002	75-84	85-94	95-MR
SUB-SAHARAN AFRICA	2,123	1,271	3,954	4,087	5,501	7,007	4,757	4,926	5,120	5,020	5,562	1,845	2,506	5,247
excluding South Africa	2,123	1,271	1,959	2,017	2,731	2,326	2,315	2,082	2,511	1,848	1,969	1,845	2,307	2,225
excl. S.Africa & Nigeria	1,926	1,182	1,644	1,568	2,041	2,069	2,291	1,936	2,334	1,664	1,327	1,305	1,608	1,904
Angola	..	39	120	308	619	768	850	836	1,262	1,001	692	..	104	792
Benin	3	0	0	0	0	0	0	0	0	0	0	4	4	0
Botswana	0	1	2	6	9	5	5	1	7	2	2	2	6	5
Burkina Faso	2	0	0	0	0	0	0	0	0	0	0	2	3	0
Burundi	3	1	1	1	1	0	0	0	0	0	2	2	5	1
Cameroon	85	98	67	65	49	39	54	108	90	91	49	76	196	68
Cape Verde	..	0	0	0	0	1	2	1	2	3	3	0	0	1
Central African Republic	1	0	0	0	0	0	0	0	0	0	0	1	1	0
Chad	0	1	0	0	0	0	0	1	1	1	1	1	1	0
Comoros	0	0	0	0	0	0	0	0	0	0	0	0	0	0
Congo, Dem. Rep. of	90	0	0	0	0	0	0	0	0	0	0	42	19	0
Congo, Rep. of	12	75	157	50	15	0	0	0	0	0	0	62	199	8
Côte d'Ivoire	667	242	356	60	302	487	316	339	159	110	114	350	262	236
Djibouti	0	0	0	0	0	0	0	0	0	0	0	1	1	0
Equatorial Guinea	0	0	0	0	0	0	0	0	0	0	0	1	0	0
Eritrea	..	..	0	0	0	0	0	0	0	0	0	..	0	0
Ethiopia	7	37	36	48	231	8	8	13	10	10	4	10	60	41
Gabon	260	4	33	75	51	25	17	24	27	40	25	149	38	36
Gambia, The	0	4	4	0	0	0	0	0	1	0	0	1	3	0
Ghana	42	52	66	85	105	124	110	118	103	57	44	11	58	93
Guinea	11	8	9	15	0	40	17	0	0	0	0	8	10	9
Guinea-Bissau	3	0	0	0	0	0	0	0	0	0	0	1	0	0
Kenya	165	127	287	295	237	146	153	195	153	136	147	161	181	183
Lesotho	3	6	5	4	3	3	4	7	7	7	8	2	5	5
Liberia	12	0	0	0	0	0	0	0	0	0	0	9	0	0
Madagascar	23	8	5	5	5	2	1	1	0	2	0	10	19	2
Malawi	28	13	14	23	4	3	1	0	0	0	0	17	15	4
Mali	2	1	1	0	0	0	0	0	0	0	0	1	2	0
Mauritania	13	0	0	0	0	2	2	2	2	3	0	21	3	1
Mauritius	14	26	45	93	50	58	101	54	346	73	114	17	32	111
Mozambique	..	10	5	13	6	5	4	10	31	30	25	0	13	15
Namibia	..	..	..	..	..	..	..	..	..	..	..	..	..	..
Niger	40	24	24	24	24	14	24	2	2	6	8	40	35	13
Nigeria	197	89	316	448	690	258	25	146	177	184	642	540	698	321
Rwanda	2	0	0	0	0	0	0	0	0	0	0	1	2	0
São Tomé and Principe	0	0	0	0	0	0	0	0	0	0	0	0	0	0
Senegal	137	4	10	27	11	7	17	7	3	17	11	46	37	12
Seychelles	0	5	4	9	5	3	5	6	4	5	10	0	5	6
Sierra Leone	29	0	0	28	0	0	0	0	0	0	0	16	1	4
Somalia	0	0	0	0	0	0	0	0	0	0	0	3	0	0
South Africa	..	..	1,995	2,070	2,770	4,680	2,442	2,844	2,609	3,172	3,593	..	1,995	3,023
Sudan	7	0	0	0	0	0	0	0	0	0	0	16	1	0
Swaziland	3	2	2	0	0	0	0	0	0	0	0	2	3	0
Tanzania	23	11	16	27	22	22	17	24	21	22	26	18	17	23
Togo	9	0	0	0	0	6	0	0	0	0	0	16	5	1
Uganda	21	32	15	9	7	1	2	2	1	1	1	15	25	3
Zambia	175	51	60	62	39	57	52	8	19	6	12	111	52	32
Zimbabwe	34	301	256	234	246	244	525	170	84	39	29	58	219	196
NORTH AFRICA	3,139	7,527	4,185	2,843	2,807	2,137	2,872	3,714	3,231	2,555	2,822	2,399	5,710	2,873
Algeria	2,284	5,816	2,698	1,577	1,297	975	1,727	1,905	1,667	1,543	1,155	1,646	4,225	1,481
Egypt, Arab Rep.	192	579	544	352	454	302	255	488	237	207	218	238	750	314
Libya	..	..	..	..	..	..	..	..	..	..	..	..	..	..
Morocco	477	754	624	630	617	457	457	845	700	586	1,244	325	353	692
Tunisia	186	378	320	285	268	241	208	248	628	219	206	157	362	288
ALL AFRICA	5,262	8,798	8,139	6,930	8,308	9,144	7,629	8,640	8,351	7,575	8,384	4,244	8,217	8,120

6-8. Amortization: long-term loans and IMF repurchases

				Millions of U.S. dollars (current prices)									*Annual average*		
	1980	1993	1994	1995	1996	1997	1998	1999	2000	2001	2002	75-84	85-94	95-MR
SUB-SAHARAN AFRICA	3,173	3,924	7,041	9,450	9,431	11,056	9,372	8,959	8,911	9,139	9,011	2,703	5,386	9,416
excluding South Africa	3,173	3,924	5,046	7,379	6,662	5,953	6,513	6,115	6,302	5,966	5,415	2,703	5,186	6,288
excl. S.Africa & Nigeria	2,931	3,345	4,300	6,461	5,244	5,113	5,740	5,510	5,211	4,252	4,267	2,115	4,091	5,225
Angola	..	63	153	332	652	816	1,285	1,270	1,530	1,338	743	..	153	996
Benin	6	18	21	26	27	32	35	45	51	32	37	7	19	36
Botswana	6	56	61	64	73	74	53	52	52	39	45	6	46	57
Burkina Faso	11	20	27	29	31	33	35	44	33	25	35	7	20	33
Burundi	4	23	28	27	21	20	21	21	14	16	17	5	25	20
Cameroon	131	280	202	216	246	275	291	284	267	183	201	112	307	245
Cape Verde	0	4	6	6	5	10	16	16	11	10	14	1	4	11
Central African Republic	7	3	13	10	8	12	25	12	8	9	0	6	13	11
Chad	5	8	10	10	16	24	23	21	16	17	19	4	7	18
Comoros	0	2	2	0	1	1	2	2	1	2	4	0	1	2
Congo, Dem. Rep. of	277	4	5	1	37	0	1	1	0	0	637	123	172	85
Congo, Rep. of	41	77	287	84	140	56	18	4	5	56	17	86	233	47
Côte d'Ivoire	722	585	787	625	860	838	670	832	481	369	522	405	596	650
Djibouti	2	6	9	9	9	5	3	7	11	9	10	2	7	8
Equatorial Guinea	2	1	1	1	3	4	4	4	4	4	3	2	4	3
Eritrea	..	..	0	0	0	0	0	0	1	1	3	..	0	0
Ethiopia	17	66	68	91	292	52	68	98	84	120	65	30	135	109
Gabon	279	71	119	216	137	172	135	281	196	273	240	169	85	206
Gambia, The	0	21	24	22	22	20	20	15	14	10	13	4	19	17
Ghana	106	184	245	304	329	395	387	344	310	216	116	57	232	300
Guinea	76	44	54	129	67	100	104	73	98	68	99	56	73	92
Guinea-Bissau	3	1	4	9	7	6	7	4	10	13	10	2	5	8
Kenya	205	367	552	605	571	449	473	527	387	369	348	217	424	466
Lesotho	3	20	18	25	22	27	29	33	39	51	52	4	16	35
Liberia	18	13	15	0	0	0	1	1	1	1	0	23	10	0
Madagascar	44	48	43	38	60	118	72	76	79	35	39	43	97	65
Malawi	35	49	53	76	56	55	60	50	38	25	20	30	69	47
Mali	9	35	63	62	54	49	55	75	66	62	65	8	42	61
Mauritania	26	82	63	79	82	70	69	70	53	47	44	35	72	64
Mauritius	19	83	103	154	108	136	153	107	402	133	186	30	103	172
Mozambique	..	44	67	85	92	64	64	57	57	71	53	12	42	68
Namibia	..	..	..	..	..	..	..	..	..	..	..	..	..	..
Niger	58	66	48	41	44	49	50	20	16	20	19	50	66	32
Nigeria	242	579	746	918	1,418	840	773	605	1,091	1,715	1,148	588	1,095	1,063
Rwanda	3	11	2	11	10	13	11	20	24	12	14	3	11	14
São Tomé and Principe	1	1	1	1	2	2	2	3	2	2	3	1	1	2
Senegal	165	81	154	195	160	158	215	161	144	143	147	67	168	165
Seychelles	0	12	10	16	10	10	13	17	8	7	11	1	10	11
Sierra Leone	50	13	99	60	50	7	14	19	35	85	14	28	23	35
Somalia	11	0	0	0	0	0	0	0	0	0	0	9	10	0
South Africa	0	0	1,995	2,070	2,769	5,103	2,859	2,844	2,609	3,172	3,596	0	199	3,128
Sudan	131	9	3	54	36	42	59	44	59	54	22	90	37	46
Swaziland	8	17	20	16	21	16	13	17	15	14	11	6	23	15
Tanzania	81	104	116	146	166	121	136	136	132	106	77	59	116	128
Togo	19	14	13	18	32	40	29	32	20	22	10	33	42	25
Uganda	45	119	111	97	105	117	121	97	48	32	50	35	116	83
Zambia	269	211	206	2,067	156	165	132	59	98	80	199	193	167	369
Zimbabwe	40	410	372	401	423	459	763	454	292	73	33	67	324	362
NORTH AFRICA	3,942	11,151	8,244	6,750	6,297	6,387	7,089	7,811	6,891	6,555	7,702	3,276	8,908	6,935
Algeria	2,529	7,309	3,553	2,419	2,102	2,370	3,139	3,382	2,815	2,964	2,948	1,875	5,266	2,767
Egypt, Arab Rep.	446	971	939	989	1,112	959	964	1,207	1,100	1,113	1,241	450	1,324	1,085
Libya	..	..	..	..	..	..	..	..	..	..	..	..	..	..
Morocco	678	1,997	2,244	2,369	2,004	2,003	1,769	1,982	1,629	1,577	2,584	454	1,215	1,990
Tunisia	290	850	928	939	907	875	868	951	1,348	901	928	243	765	965
ALL AFRICA	7,115	15,075	15,285	16,200	15,728	17,442	16,461	16,769	15,802	15,693	16,713	5,979	14,293	16,351

Note: In 1995, Zambia was able to clear its arrears to the IMF after completing a three-year Rights Arrangement Program.

6-9. Interest payments: official concessional long-term loans

	Millions of U.S. dollars (current prices)											Annual average		
	1980	1993	1994	1995	1996	1997	1998	1999	2000	2001	2002	75-84	85-94	95-MR
SUB-SAHARAN AFRICA	237	760	599	614	793	737	930	761	602	544	720	172	516	713
excluding South Africa	237	760	599	614	793	737	930	761	602	544	720	172	516	713
excl. S.Africa & Nigeria	229	503	597	613	790	669	794	756	596	525	711	164	418	682
Angola	0	3	7	7	3	6	4	2	6	3	3	0	2	4
Benin	1	8	9	10	9	11	12	13	11	10	17	1	6	12
Botswana	1	6	3	3	9	7	6	5	5	5	6	1	3	6
Burkina Faso	2	6	7	9	11	13	13	15	10	9	13	2	6	12
Burundi	1	9	10	9	6	7	7	6	5	5	5	1	8	6
Cameroon	15	24	19	54	36	61	62	55	66	36	45	13	24	52
Cape Verde	0	1	2	2	1	2	2	2	3	3	5	0	1	3
Central African Republic	0	2	6	3	3	2	5	4	4	4	0	0	4	3
Chad	0	4	5	3	7	5	6	6	6	4	8	0	3	6
Comoros	0	1	1	1	1	1	0	1	1	1	1	0	1	1
Congo, Dem. Rep. of	47	7	0	0	0	0	0	0	0	0	102	11	11	13
Congo, Rep. of	12	4	93	9	35	1	1	0	1	4	2	6	17	7
Côte d'Ivoire	14	30	32	47	77	75	145	118	57	47	55	13	21	78
Djibouti	1	2	2	2	3	2	2	2	2	1	2	1	2	2
Equatorial Guinea	0	0	1	0	1	1	1	1	1	1	1	0	0	1
Eritrea	0	0	0	0	0	0	4	3	2	5	6	0	0	3
Ethiopia	7	12	16	19	19	21	25	30	31	47	28	7	19	28
Gabon	3	4	15	40	39	36	24	27	9	43	23	2	6	30
Gambia, The	0	4	4	3	3	5	5	5	5	3	5	0	3	4
Ghana	11	36	37	28	50	42	63	57	50	34	32	13	24	44
Guinea	12	23	27	29	22	23	24	25	22	20	22	10	18	23
Guinea-Bissau	0	2	2	3	3	3	4	5	2	5	4	0	2	4
Kenya	9	39	47	59	56	46	48	47	30	36	49	10	30	46
Lesotho	0	5	4	5	5	5	5	5	9	6	4	0	3	5
Liberia	2	1	0	0	0	0	0	0	0	0	0	2	1	0
Madagascar	4	14	11	11	12	42	36	34	17	15	19	7	13	23
Malawi	4	13	13	19	17	18	16	13	15	12	14	4	9	15
Mali	2	38	19	19	57	18	16	19	16	14	21	3	15	22
Mauritania	8	20	22	18	18	19	18	15	13	14	12	8	14	16
Mauritius	1	16	17	18	17	15	15	14	12	11	11	1	10	14
Mozambique	0	31	16	19	25	27	23	32	16	7	13	0	16	20
Namibia	..	..	..	..	..	..	..	..	..	..	..	..	..	..
Niger	2	7	6	7	5	8	7	7	7	5	7	2	6	7
Nigeria	9	256	2	2	3	68	136	5	6	20	9	8	99	31
Rwanda	1	4	2	8	6	7	6	8	8	5	7	1	5	7
São Tomé and Principe	0	1	1	1	1	2	1	1	1	1	2	0	1	1
Senegal	7	7	25	22	80	30	37	34	39	34	42	4	26	40
Seychelles	0	1	1	2	1	1	1	1	1	0	1	0	1	1
Sierra Leone	0	3	4	5	4	4	5	3	4	4	4	1	2	4
Somalia	2	0	0	0	0	0	0	0	0	0	0	2	2	0
South Africa	0	0	0	0	0	0	0	0	0	0	0	0	0	0
Sudan	28	6	0	1	0	0	0	0	2	1	0	13	12	0
Swaziland	1	2	2	2	3	2	2	2	2	1	1	0	2	2
Tanzania	15	49	28	28	55	27	76	51	38	28	50	14	21	44
Togo	1	6	5	5	13	8	8	7	5	6	0	1	6	6
Uganda	1	13	18	23	25	25	20	19	16	10	22	1	9	20
Zambia	14	22	36	32	29	20	23	41	41	23	49	5	14	32
Zimbabwe	1	19	23	26	23	22	20	21	8	4	1	2	15	16
NORTH AFRICA	289	672	783	909	948	775	778	783	714	814	1,096	237	395	852
Algeria	35	26	55	89	144	117	124	128	124	117	102	32	25	118
Egypt, Arab Rep.	153	423	469	570	553	416	380	380	372	359	332	121	223	420
Libya	..	..	..	..	..	..	..	..	..	..	..	..	..	..
Morocco	70	145	152	161	166	164	199	203	149	266	590	55	73	237
Tunisia	30	78	107	89	84	78	75	72	69	72	72	29	74	76
ALL AFRICA	526	1,432	1,382	1,523	1,740	1,513	1,708	1,545	1,316	1,358	1,817	409	912	1,565

6-10. Interest payments: official nonconcessional long-term loans

	Millions of U.S. dollars (current prices)											*Annual average*		
	1980	*1993*	*1994*	*1995*	*1996*	*1997*	*1998*	*1999*	*2000*	*2001*	*2002*	*75-84*	*85-94*	*95-MR*
SUB-SAHARAN AFRICA	452	1,185	1,426	1,403	1,873	1,352	1,123	1,159	1,216	1,060	756	383	1,487	1,243
excluding South Africa	452	1,185	1,426	1,403	1,873	1,352	1,123	1,159	1,215	1,048	753	383	1,487	1,241
excl. S.Africa & Nigeria	398	871	1,091	1,081	1,361	1,054	884	919	705	437	602	324	955	880
Angola	0	5	3	5	24	15	11	6	30	6	7	0	8	13
Benin	1	4	10	11	7	7	9	7	3	4	6	1	4	7
Botswana	5	26	26	22	61	18	15	14	9	7	9	5	26	19
Burkina Faso	2	10	8	9	4	3	3	2	1	1	2	2	7	3
Burundi	0	3	3	2	3	2	1	1	0	0	0	0	4	1
Cameroon	27	104	114	98	184	112	97	124	132	69	76	22	77	111
Cape Verde	0	1	1	1	1	1	1	1	1	1	1	1	2	1
Central African Republic	0	1	2	0	0	0	1	1	0	0	0	1	3	0
Chad	0	4	2	1	6	4	5	4	3	1	1	0	1	3
Comoros	0	0	0	0	0	0	0	0	0	0	0	0	0	0
Congo, Dem. Rep. of	59	1	0	0	0	0	0	0	0	0	62	33	48	8
Congo, Rep. of	13	0	85	11	141	40	6	0	6	22	1	8	26	28
Côte d'Ivoire	64	188	236	206	252	194	224	194	132	66	129	48	184	175
Djibouti	0	0	0	0	0	0	0	0	0	0	0	0	0	0
Equatorial Guinea	0	0	0	0	0	0	0	0	0	0	0	0	1	0
Eritrea	0	0	0	0	0	0	0	0	0	0	0	0	0	0
Ethiopia	8	9	15	13	19	21	20	21	17	11	13	6	10	17
Gabon	17	25	59	133	180	192	110	194	109	113	129	11	55	145
Gambia, The	0	2	2	2	1	1	1	1	1	1	1	0	2	1
Ghana	13	31	24	24	27	36	26	23	24	8	13	10	23	22
Guinea	9	13	12	14	21	19	19	19	19	10	11	7	13	16
Guinea-Bissau	0	0	1	2	1	0	0	0	8	4	0	0	1	2
Kenya	45	87	114	108	106	71	61	41	25	18	15	37	99	56
Lesotho	0	6	7	8	7	9	8	7	8	5	5	1	4	7
Liberia	5	8	0	0	0	0	0	0	0	0	0	6	4	0
Madagascar	3	10	7	4	5	51	15	42	11	13	10	6	37	19
Malawi	6	12	10	16	9	7	6	4	3	1	2	8	16	6
Mali	1	2	5	4	3	2	2	2	1	1	1	1	2	2
Mauritania	1	23	16	14	11	14	12	12	6	7	5	4	16	10
Mauritius	6	19	18	17	16	14	13	12	11	10	9	5	20	13
Mozambique	0	40	36	52	21	14	5	0	3	0	1	0	15	12
Namibia	..	..	..	..	..	..	..	..	..	..	..	..	..	..
Niger	5	7	3	0	1	2	2	3	2	0	0	5	11	1
Nigeria	54	314	335	322	512	297	240	240	510	611	151	59	532	360
Rwanda	0	0	0	0	0	0	0	0	0	0	0	0	0	0
São Tomé and Principe	0	0	0	0	0	0	0	0	0	1	1	0	0	0
Senegal	15	14	36	43	36	44	51	23	18	18	23	13	44	32
Seychelles	0	2	2	3	2	3	3	3	1	0	0	0	2	2
Sierra Leone	2	10	17	16	9	3	6	3	5	5	4	2	4	6
Somalia	0	0	0	0	3	0	0	0	0	0	0	0	1	0
South Africa	0	0	0	0	0	0	0	0	1	12	3	0	0	2
Sudan	16	2	0	2	0	0	2	7	1	0	0	13	5	1
Swaziland	6	4	4	3	9	5	5	10	9	8	6	4	7	7
Tanzania	19	49	33	49	35	10	25	10	14	10	8	15	28	20
Togo	11	1	1	2	11	5	2	1	0	0	0	8	19	3
Uganda	1	14	14	9	13	13	4	8	5	0	1	2	13	7
Zambia	39	54	75	83	39	33	25	31	35	11	50	31	59	38
Zimbabwe	1	79	90	95	95	93	85	89	56	8	2	6	53	65
NORTH AFRICA	401	1,848	2,039	2,367	2,651	2,299	2,310	2,034	1,834	1,682	1,649	420	1,507	2,103
Algeria	124	343	346	734	1,108	1,009	1,073	1,061	1,007	894	863	104	307	969
Egypt, Arab Rep.	68	463	542	552	427	278	258	250	201	216	234	162	468	302
Libya	..	..	..	..	..	..	..	..	..	..	..	..	..	..
Morocco	66	780	865	762	723	639	580	466	401	383	336	66	528	536
Tunisia	44	231	256	279	286	261	253	258	226	189	216	37	168	246
ALL AFRICA	853	3,033	3,465	3,770	4,524	3,650	3,433	3,193	3,050	2,742	2,405	803	2,993	3,346

6-11. Interest payments: private long-term loans

	Millions of U.S. dollars (current prices)											Annual average		
	1980	1993	1994	1995	1996	1997	1998	1999	2000	2001	2002	75-84	85-94	95-MR
SUB-SAHARAN AFRICA	1,694	753	1,947	1,969	2,158	1,576	1,753	1,575	1,512	1,370	1,328	1,259	1,558	1,655
excluding South Africa	1,694	753	1,330	1,114	1,235	726	861	761	771	522	472	1,259	1,496	808
excl. S.Africa & Nigeria	1,228	461	591	579	707	548	716	588	597	349	308	850	797	549
Angola	..	18	41	67	266	127	187	105	114	102	91	..	55	132
Benin	1	0	0	0	0	0	0	0	0	0	0	3	3	0
Botswana	1	1	1	3	9	2	2	2	1	1	0	1	3	2
Burkina Faso	3	0	0	0	0	0	0	0	0	0	0	1	0	0
Burundi	1	0	0	0	0	0	0	0	0	0	0	1	1	0
Cameroon	78	26	21	21	14	16	19	22	17	12	8	56	69	16
Cape Verde	..	0	0	0	0	1	1	0	1	0	1	0	0	1
Central African Republic	0	0	0	0	0	0	0	0	0	0	0	1	0	0
Chad	0	0	0	0	0	0	0	0	0	0	0	0	0	0
Comoros	0	0	0	0	0	0	0	0	0	0	0	0	0	0
Congo, Dem. Rep. of	99	0	0	0	0	0	0	0	0	0	0	61	22	0
Congo, Rep. of	13	17	50	40	3	0	0	0	0	0	0	36	50	5
Côte d'Ivoire	513	163	159	138	145	145	246	231	273	102	96	343	267	172
Djibouti	0	0	0	0	0	0	0	0	0	0	0	0	0	0
Equatorial Guinea	0	0	0	0	0	0	0	0	0	0	0	0	0	0
Eritrea	..	..	0	0	0	0	0	0	0	0	0	..	0	0
Ethiopia	2	3	9	29	15	4	3	5	4	3	1	4	20	8
Gabon	100	6	29	44	12	10	8	9	7	10	6	52	26	13
Gambia, The	0	0	0	0	0	0	0	0	0	0	0	0	1	0
Ghana	7	17	21	8	31	48	63	57	42	28	31	4	17	38
Guinea	2	1	2	1	0	3	0	0	0	0	0	2	2	1
Guinea-Bissau	1	0	0	0	0	0	0	0	0	0	0	0	0	0
Kenya	110	82	129	95	79	67	48	45	43	30	21	69	90	53
Lesotho	1	1	1	3	4	6	9	10	7	6	6	1	1	6
Liberia	16	0	0	0	0	0	0	0	0	0	0	5	0	0
Madagascar	19	1	1	1	2	0	0	0	0	1	1	12	9	1
Malawi	25	2	2	4	2	1	0	0	0	0	0	13	6	1
Mali	1	0	0	0	0	0	0	0	0	0	0	1	0	0
Mauritania	4	0	0	0	0	2	2	2	2	2	0	3	1	1
Mauritius	15	8	11	21	38	34	35	31	29	17	15	11	11	27
Mozambique	..	4	2	4	1	1	8	8	0	0	0	3	5	3
Namibia	..	..	..	..	..	..	..	..	..	..	..	..	..	..
Niger	58	7	6	6	5	3	2	0	0	1	1	30	18	2
Nigeria	466	292	739	535	528	178	145	173	174	173	164	409	699	259
Rwanda	0	0	0	0	0	0	0	0	0	0	0	0	0	0
São Tomé and Principe	0	0	0	0	0	0	0	0	0	0	0	0	0	0
Senegal	46	2	2	4	2	1	1	1	0	4	2	22	15	2
Seychelles	0	2	3	2	1	1	2	1	1	1	2	0	2	1
Sierra Leone	11	4	5	0	0	0	0	0	0	0	0	7	4	0
Somalia	0	0	0	0	0	0	0	0	0	0	0	1	0	0
South Africa	..	..	617	855	923	850	892	814	741	849	856	..	617	848
Sudan	5	0	0	0	0	0	0	0	0	0	0	15	4	0
Swaziland	2	0	0	0	0	0	7	7	6	3	1	1	1	3
Tanzania	13	5	1	5	6	3	3	12	3	2	3	9	3	4
Togo	8	0	0	0	0	0	0	0	0	0	0	7	3	0
Uganda	1	3	1	2	0	0	2	0	0	2	2	2	4	1
Zambia	63	15	15	9	8	12	7	5	4	3	3	43	21	6
Zimbabwe	9	72	79	74	65	59	60	32	43	21	16	30	81	46
NORTH AFRICA	2,118	1,972	1,678	1,603	1,457	1,268	1,184	1,190	1,060	880	727	1,389	2,154	1,171
Algeria	1,280	1,338	1,098	918	770	817	682	532	421	323	203	837	1,321	583
Egypt, Arab Rep.	129	170	137	130	97	71	69	54	47	114	162	128	240	93
Libya	..	..	..	..	..	..	..	..	..	..	..	..	..	..
Morocco	515	354	345	437	447	233	241	402	398	276	152	319	464	323
Tunisia	154	109	99	118	137	140	168	173	194	167	210	88	129	163
ALL AFRICA	3,812	2,724	3,625	3,572	3,615	2,844	2,937	2,766	2,572	2,251	2,055	2,648	3,712	2,826

6-12. Interest payments: long-term loans and IMF charges

	Millions of U.S. dollars (current prices)											*Annual average*		
	1980	*1993*	*1994*	*1995*	*1996*	*1997*	*1998*	*1999*	*2000*	*2001*	*2002*	*75-84*	*85-94*	*95-MR*
SUB-SAHARAN AFRICA	2,487	2,835	4,141	4,546	4,947	3,766	3,871	3,553	3,373	3,010	2,947	1,943	3,834	3,752
excluding South Africa	2,487	2,835	3,486	3,641	3,985	2,883	2,964	2,738	2,630	2,150	2,088	1,943	3,769	2,885
excl. S.Africa & Nigeria	1,958	1,973	2,411	2,782	2,941	2,339	2,443	2,320	1,940	1,346	1,764	1,467	2,439	2,234
Angola	..	26	51	79	293	148	202	114	149	110	101	..	72	150
Benin	3	13	19	22	17	19	22	21	14	15	23	5	14	19
Botswana	7	33	30	27	78	28	23	21	15	12	15	7	33	27
Burkina Faso	6	16	15	18	16	16	16	18	12	10	16	5	14	15
Burundi	3	12	13	11	9	9	8	6	5	5	5	2	13	7
Cameroon	121	157	156	175	237	191	181	204	217	118	132	92	174	182
Cape Verde	0	2	3	3	3	4	4	3	5	4	7	1	3	4
Central African Republic	1	4	9	5	4	3	7	5	4	4	0	3	9	4
Chad	1	8	8	5	14	11	11	11	9	6	10	1	5	10
Comoros	0	1	1	1	1	1	0	1	1	1	1	0	1	1
Congo, Dem. Rep. of	220	10	2	16	5	0	0	2	0	0	276	118	114	38
Congo, Rep. of	38	21	228	62	181	41	7	1	7	27	4	50	93	41
Côte d'Ivoire	590	399	437	398	478	416	618	547	465	218	283	417	507	428
Djibouti	1	2	2	2	3	2	2	2	3	2	2	1	3	2
Equatorial Guinea	0	1	1	1	1	1	1	1	1	1	1	0	1	1
Eritrea	..	..	0	0	0	1	4	3	3	5	6	..	0	3
Ethiopia	19	24	40	61	54	46	49	56	52	62	42	20	52	53
Gabon	120	41	106	223	236	244	148	235	128	170	160	66	93	193
Gambia, The	1	6	6	5	5	6	6	6	6	4	6	2	7	5
Ghana	35	97	93	69	115	131	154	138	117	71	78	30	97	109
Guinea	24	37	41	44	44	45	44	45	42	30	33	20	35	41
Guinea-Bissau	1	2	4	6	4	3	5	5	10	10	4	1	3	6
Kenya	171	212	292	263	243	185	158	133	98	84	85	126	242	156
Lesotho	2	12	11	16	16	20	22	22	23	18	15	2	8	19
Liberia	24	9	0	2	2	0	0	2	0	0	1	17	7	1
Madagascar	28	27	20	17	19	93	51	77	29	29	31	29	68	43
Malawi	37	28	26	40	29	27	23	17	18	13	16	28	37	23
Mali	4	42	25	23	60	21	19	22	18	16	23	5	22	25
Mauritania	15	43	38	33	30	36	33	29	21	23	18	16	33	28
Mauritius	26	42	45	56	71	63	62	56	52	38	35	24	48	54
Mozambique	..	76	55	76	48	42	36	42	20	9	15	5	37	36
Namibia	..	..	..	..	..	..	..	..	..	..	..	..	..	..
Niger	65	23	16	14	11	14	11	11	9	7	9	37	39	11
Nigeria	529	862	1,075	859	1,043	544	521	418	690	804	324	476	1,330	650
Rwanda	2	5	2	8	7	8	7	9	10	6	7	1	6	8
São Tomé and Principe	0	1	1	1	1	2	1	1	1	2	3	0	1	2
Senegal	70	26	66	72	122	78	91	59	59	57	67	45	98	76
Seychelles	0	5	6	7	5	5	6	6	3	1	2	1	5	4
Sierra Leone	16	18	64	21	14	8	12	7	11	11	9	12	16	12
Somalia	2	0	0	1	3	0	0	1	0	0	0	5	6	1
South Africa	0	0	656	905	962	884	908	815	743	860	859	0	66	867
Sudan	63	11	1	15	12	15	3	13	2	2	1	57	30	8
Swaziland	9	6	6	5	12	7	14	19	17	11	8	5	10	12
Tanzania	54	103	62	83	97	42	104	75	56	41	63	41	56	70
Togo	19	9	6	8	24	14	10	9	5	6	1	17	32	10
Uganda	7	32	35	36	40	40	28	30	23	14	27	13	39	30
Zambia	141	151	167	544	86	71	60	83	85	42	107	102	129	135
Zimbabwe	10	179	203	209	194	184	175	152	118	35	19	41	159	136
NORTH AFRICA	2,838	4,593	4,569	4,980	5,147	4,445	4,378	4,235	3,704	3,453	3,515	2,083	4,170	4,232
Algeria	1,440	1,749	1,530	1,810	2,097	2,036	1,977	1,799	1,644	1,410	1,211	972	1,682	1,748
Egypt, Arab Rep.	367	1,068	1,157	1,261	1,081	764	707	684	620	688	728	422	941	817
Libya	..	..	..	..	..	..	..	..	..	..	..	..	..	..
Morocco	663	1,310	1,375	1,367	1,338	1,037	1,020	1,071	948	926	1,077	466	1,126	1,098
Tunisia	229	436	477	503	519	488	503	507	492	429	498	155	385	492
ALL AFRICA	5,325	7,428	8,711	9,526	10,094	8,211	8,249	7,788	7,076	6,463	6,462	4,026	8,005	7,984

6-13. Total external debt service payments: long-term loans and IMF credits

	Millions of U.S. dollars (current prices)											Annual average		
	1980	1993	1994	1995	1996	1997	1998	1999	2000	2001	2002	75-84	85-94	95-MR
SUB-SAHARAN AFRICA	5,660	6,759	11,182	13,995	14,379	14,822	13,243	12,512	12,338	12,218	11,959	4,645	9,220	13,183
excluding South Africa	5,660	6,759	8,532	11,020	10,647	8,835	9,477	8,853	8,986	8,185	7,504	4,645	8,955	9,188
excl. S.Africa & Nigeria	4,889	5,318	6,710	9,243	8,185	7,452	8,183	7,830	7,205	5,666	6,032	3,582	6,530	7,474
Angola	0	89	204	411	945	965	1,487	1,384	1,680	1,448	844	0	135	1,145
Benin	9	31	40	48	44	51	56	65	66	47	60	13	33	55
Botswana	13	89	92	91	151	102	76	73	67	51	60	13	78	84
Burkina Faso	17	36	42	47	47	49	51	61	46	35	51	11	34	48
Burundi	7	35	40	38	30	29	29	27	19	21	21	8	38	27
Cameroon	252	436	358	391	483	466	471	487	484	301	333	203	481	427
Cape Verde	0	6	9	9	8	14	19	20	16	13	21	1	7	15
Central African Republic	8	7	21	15	12	15	32	17	13	13	1	9	22	15
Chad	6	16	18	15	30	35	34	32	25	23	29	5	11	28
Comoros	0	2	3	1	1	2	2	3	2	2	5	1	3	2
Congo, Dem. Rep. of	497	15	6	18	42	0	1	3	0	0	913	241	286	122
Congo, Rep. of	78	98	515	146	321	96	25	5	13	83	21	136	326	89
Côte d'Ivoire	1,312	984	1,224	1,023	1,338	1,254	1,288	1,379	946	587	805	822	1,103	1,078
Djibouti	3	9	11	11	12	7	5	10	13	11	12	3	10	10
Equatorial Guinea	2	1	2	2	4	5	5	4	5	4	3	3	5	4
Eritrea	0	0	0	0	0	1	4	3	3	6	9	0	0	3
Ethiopia	36	90	107	153	346	99	117	154	136	182	108	51	187	162
Gabon	399	112	225	439	373	415	283	515	325	443	400	235	178	399
Gambia, The	1	27	30	27	27	26	25	20	20	13	19	5	26	22
Ghana	141	281	339	374	444	526	541	481	427	287	194	87	329	409
Guinea	100	81	94	173	110	145	147	118	140	98	133	76	108	133
Guinea-Bissau	4	3	7	15	11	9	12	9	20	23	14	2	8	14
Kenya	376	579	844	869	814	634	631	661	485	452	433	343	666	622
Lesotho	5	33	30	41	38	48	52	55	62	69	67	6	24	54
Liberia	43	22	15	2	2	0	1	3	1	1	1	41	16	1
Madagascar	72	75	63	55	79	211	123	153	108	64	70	72	164	108
Malawi	71	78	79	116	85	82	83	67	56	38	35	58	106	70
Mali	13	77	87	85	115	70	74	98	85	78	88	13	64	86
Mauritania	40	124	102	112	112	105	102	98	74	70	62	51	105	92
Mauritius	44	125	148	210	179	199	215	163	453	171	221	54	150	226
Mozambique	0	119	123	161	140	107	100	99	77	80	68	2	79	104
Namibia	..	..	..	..	..	..	..	..	..	..	..	..	..	..
Niger	122	88	64	55	56	62	61	31	24	28	28	87	104	43
Nigeria	772	1,441	1,822	1,777	2,461	1,383	1,294	1,023	1,781	2,519	1,472	1,064	2,425	1,714
Rwanda	4	16	3	20	17	21	19	30	34	18	22	4	17	22
São Tomé and Principe	1	2	3	2	3	3	4	4	3	4	6	1	2	4
Senegal	235	107	220	267	282	237	306	221	202	199	214	112	265	241
Seychelles	0	17	16	23	15	14	20	22	10	8	13	1	15	16
Sierra Leone	66	31	163	82	65	15	25	26	46	95	23	39	39	47
Somalia	13	0	0	1	3	0	0	1	0	0	0	14	17	1
South Africa	0	0	2,650	2,976	3,732	5,987	3,766	3,659	3,352	4,033	4,455	0	265	3,995
Sudan	194	20	3	69	48	58	61	57	61	56	24	147	67	54
Swaziland	17	23	26	21	32	23	28	35	31	25	19	12	33	27
Tanzania	135	207	179	229	263	163	240	211	188	147	140	100	172	198
Togo	38	23	19	26	56	54	39	41	25	28	11	50	74	35
Uganda	52	151	146	133	145	157	149	126	71	46	77	48	155	113
Zambia	410	362	374	2,611	242	236	193	141	183	122	307	295	296	504
Zimbabwe	50	590	574	610	617	642	938	605	410	107	52	107	483	498
NORTH AFRICA	6,780	15,745	12,814	11,730	11,444	10,832	11,467	12,046	11,055	10,547	11,217	5,359	13,078	11,292
Algeria	3,968	9,058	5,083	4,228	4,199	4,406	5,117	5,181	4,459	4,374	4,160	2,848	6,948	4,515
Egypt, Arab Rep.	813	2,040	2,096	2,250	2,193	1,723	1,671	1,890	1,719	1,801	1,969	871	2,265	1,902
Libya	..	..	..	..	..	..	..	..	..	..	..	..	..	..
Morocco	1,341	3,307	3,619	3,736	3,342	3,039	2,789	3,053	2,577	2,502	3,662	921	2,341	3,087
Tunisia	518	1,285	1,405	1,442	1,426	1,364	1,371	1,458	1,840	1,330	1,426	398	1,150	1,457
ALL AFRICA	12,440	22,504	23,996	25,726	25,823	25,653	24,710	24,558	23,392	22,764	23,176	10,004	22,298	24,475

Note: In 1995, Zambia was able to clear its arrears to the IMF after completing a three-year Rights Arrangement Program.

6-14. Interest payments: short-term loans

	Millions of U.S. dollars (current prices)											Annual average		
	1980	1993	1994	1995	1996	1997	1998	1999	2000	2001	2002	75-84	85-94	95-MR
SUB-SAHARAN AFRICA	1,025	523	631	819	885	1,053	1,158	1,160	1,101	650	476	537	631	913
excluding South Africa	1,025	523	379	404	380	498	536	529	592	327	239	537	606	438
excl. S.Africa & Nigeria	646	473	329	348	333	465	499	489	528	304	221	301	501	398
Angola	0	66	55	53	49	46	45	45	26	22	19	0	30	38
Benin	11	1	1	2	2	4	5	5	5	3	3	5	5	3
Botswana	2	0	0	0	0	1	0	1	1	1	0	0	0	1
Burkina Faso	5	2	2	2	2	3	3	3	1	3	2	2	4	2
Burundi	2	1	1	1	0	0	1	2	3	2	2	1	1	1
Cameroon	28	30	24	39	24	40	55	59	72	34	25	17	43	43
Cape Verde	0	0	0	1	0	0	0	1	0	1	1	0	0	0
Central African Republic	2	2	2	1	1	1	1	2	1	0	0	1	2	1
Chad	0	1	0	1	0	1	1	1	1	1	1	0	1	1
Comoros	0	0	0	0	0	0	0	0	1	0	0	0	0	0
Congo, Dem. Rep. of	45	13	9	8	7	12	18	18	25	18	14	18	21	15
Congo, Rep. of	31	30	20	35	18	16	16	20	30	9	3	12	40	19
Côte d'Ivoire	95	110	20	23	37	105	96	70	74	34	26	47	97	58
Djibouti	1	2	1	1	0	1	0	0	0	0	0	1	2	0
Equatorial Guinea	1	0	1	0	0	1	2	1	0	0	0	1	0	1
Eritrea	0	0	0	0	0	0	0	0	0	1	0	0	0	0
Ethiopia	9	5	4	1	1	1	1	2	1	1	1	4	6	1
Gabon	33	45	43	17	11	18	25	23	28	12	10	13	38	18
Gambia, The	3	1	2	1	1	1	1	1	1	1	1	1	1	1
Ghana	18	22	26	28	36	29	38	38	38	27	17	12	16	31
Guinea	9	3	3	5	3	10	12	11	15	8	3	4	4	8
Guinea-Bissau	1	0	0	0	1	1	0	0	1	1	0	1	2	0
Kenya	58	53	38	36	30	30	39	40	41	26	20	24	47	33
Lesotho	1	0	0	0	0	0	0	0	0	0	0	0	0	0
Liberia	11	0	0	0	0	0	0	0	0	0	0	4	1	0
Madagascar	29	3	2	3	4	1	2	6	9	4	4	9	4	4
Malawi	16	1	1	3	4	3	1	2	3	1	1	5	4	2
Mali	3	2	1	2	2	15	8	8	8	3	2	2	3	6
Mauritania	7	4	4	5	4	8	8	7	10	5	3	5	7	6
Mauritius	8	4	10	16	19	23	27	27	32	31	30	3	4	26
Mozambique	0	3	1	1	1	3	4	6	11	10	8	0	7	5
Namibia	..	..	..	..	..	..	..	..	..	..	..	..	..	..
Niger	19	2	2	1	1	2	1	1	1	1	0	7	6	1
Nigeria	379	50	50	56	48	33	38	41	64	24	18	236	105	40
Rwanda	3	6	1	1	1	2	2	2	2	1	0	1	4	1
São Tomé and Principe	0	1	0	0	0	0	0	0	1	0	0	0	0	0
Senegal	24	15	14	14	7	11	15	17	15	6	5	13	20	11
Seychelles	37	1	1	1	1	1	1	2	4	3	2	5	2	2
Sierra Leone	0	0	0	1	1	1	0	1	0	0	1	0	0	1
Somalia	0	0	0	0	0	0	0	0	0	0	0	0	0	0
South Africa	0	0	251	415	504	555	622	631	509	322	236	0	25	474
Sudan	70	0	0	0	0	0	0	0	0	0	0	39	22	0
Swaziland	2	0	0	0	0	8	2	2	4	2	1	1	1	2
Tanzania	26	4	5	4	6	6	7	8	10	6	6	12	12	7
Togo	14	4	4	3	2	2	2	4	5	5	2	6	5	3
Uganda	5	3	3	2	3	4	4	5	4	4	2	2	3	3
Zambia	0	1	2	1	9	10	10	8	3	3	2	0	1	6
Zimbabwe	15	33	28	35	44	44	43	41	42	16	6	22	32	34
NORTH AFRICA	869	385	333	316	321	522	438	445	297	241	144	589	624	340
Algeria	116	36	33	22	13	13	15	10	10	9	7	150	118	12
Egypt, Arab Rep.	422	164	130	132	133	262	227	231	113	150	97	246	274	168
Libya	..	..	..	..	..	..	..	..	..	..	..	..	..	..
Morocco	105	18	18	24	40	100	106	102	112	54	29	57	45	71
Tunisia	26	67	52	38	39	49	60	77	61	29	11	9	33	46
ALL AFRICA	1,895	908	964	1,135	1,205	1,575	1,596	1,604	1,398	891	620	1,126	1,255	1,253

6-15. Net flows: long- and short-term loans, including IMF

	Millions of U.S. dollars (current prices)											Annual average		
	1980	1993	1994	1995	1996	1997	1998	1999	2000	2001	2002	75-84	85-94	95-MR
SUB-SAHARAN AFRICA	10,026	4,991	2,547	7,653	3,172	4,494	-1,385	-958	-795	-1,746	-51	7,731	5,512	1,298
excluding South Africa	10,026	4,991	1,023	4,240	2,491	4,871	-1,088	-260	-1,981	-979	467	7,731	5,359	970
excl. S.Africa & Nigeria	7,245	4,519	1,683	4,799	3,826	5,534	-809	125	-1,284	518	1,968	5,981	4,856	1,834
Angola	..	294	305	-90	76	418	-314	-530	-734	-279	-119	..	598	-196
Benin	42	87	112	105	101	114	-24	74	-61	105	30	82	70	55
Botswana	8	55	-2	4	-44	-19	-63	-18	-28	-27	-47	28	27	-30
Burkina Faso	56	109	117	124	81	72	66	127	44	115	106	49	91	92
Burundi	40	45	25	26	4	3	10	46	17	13	35	39	75	19
Cameroon	538	137	306	119	-186	679	67	-80	-32	-268	-252	342	298	6
Cape Verde	..	6	25	35	-5	13	39	60	11	49	30	18	9	29
Central African Republic	31	54	32	25	14	-4	-13	25	-14	-5	1	21	66	4
Chad	-8	51	72	61	109	77	27	78	29	47	96	22	68	65
Comoros	13	7	11	11	7	9	-1	4	4	4	11	12	11	6
Congo, Dem. Rep. of	278	0	-140	61	-91	242	-13	13	20	2	244	368	121	60
Congo, Rep. of	541	310	97	166	-451	96	-66	154	-52	-341	159	230	114	-42
Côte d'Ivoire	1,257	726	-1,002	935	2,117	413	-1,064	-904	-617	-518	-362	741	385	0
Djibouti	9	36	-10	13	18	11	3	-1	-2	8	27	9	20	10
Equatorial Guinea	41	13	17	-8	0	19	12	-21	-12	-2	1	10	12	-1
Eritrea	..	..	27	7	7	33	67	103	61	110	93	..	27	60
Ethiopia	94	314	188	133	21	130	93	134	90	454	583	441	347	205
Gabon	-122	19	-18	14	-84	260	-172	-112	-344	-270	-248	72	154	-120
Gambia, The	58	26	-20	-8	44	-5	4	19	21	21	54	26	14	19
Ghana	75	373	326	414	660	275	369	105	-16	400	235	128	308	305
Guinea	23	228	120	98	72	403	-43	68	-41	14	-31	49	144	67
Guinea-Bissau	73	19	27	13	30	27	7	0	23	-10	-8	27	32	10
Kenya	718	153	-336	78	-251	-13	-148	-328	90	-375	3	318	256	-118
Lesotho	20	62	51	46	54	41	35	20	31	-17	-10	16	44	25
Liberia	95	10	-14	0	11	-21	3	1	-5	-5	0	91	9	-2
Madagascar	476	65	22	59	60	210	100	165	45	130	158	195	109	116
Malawi	154	107	95	183	181	48	112	127	86	70	146	88	78	119
Mali	99	62	92	200	135	293	-33	71	-11	30	184	91	110	109
Mauritania	139	85	96	68	103	158	-84	-11	60	64	51	111	73	51
Mauritius	104	22	260	312	110	134	-16	38	-75	43	6	56	61	69
Mozambique	..	99	189	193	197	335	192	215	63	181	64	822	230	180
Namibia	..	..	..	..	..	..	..	..	..	..	..	..	..	..
Niger	286	26	27	-9	14	98	33	45	64	54	118	115	65	52
Nigeria	2,780	472	-660	-559	-1,334	-663	-279	-385	-696	-1,497	-1,501	1,750	503	-864
Rwanda	36	50	-11	53	52	114	79	95	25	62	80	31	60	70
São Tomé and Principe	7	15	8	13	5	5	5	20	9	5	6	7	15	8
Senegal	246	70	-29	74	-14	143	100	-34	-157	185	198	210	144	62
Seychelles	-390	-3	6	-17	-2	9	33	-6	50	16	1	-78	7	11
Sierra Leone	54	86	102	55	38	24	56	13	57	65	84	35	29	49
Somalia	138	0	0	0	0	-7	5	0	-7	2	9	153	44	0
South Africa	..	..	1,524	3,412	681	-377	-297	-698	1,186	-767	-518	..	1,524	328
Sudan	839	91	9	0	-119	-157	-14	-191	-97	-183	-26	640	102	-98
Swaziland	29	-8	-4	6	-1	195	-113	41	12	30	-8	22	-7	20
Tanzania	405	112	169	94	148	226	138	214	173	39	205	341	173	155
Togo	108	-57	56	39	72	12	52	87	-43	25	22	94	34	33
Uganda	130	244	223	184	206	244	106	119	176	324	122	100	196	185
Zambia	360	29	88	435	169	-84	25	85	159	325	70	305	137	148
Zimbabwe	148	283	28	437	142	213	-402	-38	-354	-174	-150	220	156	-41
NORTH AFRICA	6,015	-1,698	1,679	2,261	2,953	1,105	-2,323	-1,995	-3,162	-1,391	-2,482	6,095	1,898	-629
Algeria	1,261	-875	2,014	1,361	1,597	-428	-1,622	-1,943	-1,574	-1,956	-1,504	1,442	513	-759
Egypt, Arab Rep.	2,465	-286	182	92	-453	581	1,056	-588	-702	71	-647	2,598	547	-74
Libya	..	..	..	..	..	..	..	..	..	..	..	..	..	..
Morocco	1,814	31	-423	-30	1,156	221	-406	-124	-448	-278	-1,114	1,395	462	-128
Tunisia	267	221	448	654	692	568	-719	976	-438	771	783	382	350	411
ALL AFRICA	16,040	3,293	4,225	9,914	6,125	5,599	-3,708	-2,952	-3,957	-3,138	-2,533	13,827	7,410	669

6-16. Net flows: long-term loans, including IMF

					Millions of U.S. dollars (current prices)							*Annual average*		
	1980	*1993*	*1994*	*1995*	*1996*	*1997*	*1998*	*1999*	*2000*	*2001*	*2002*	*75-84*	*85-94*	*95-MR*
SUB-SAHARAN AFRICA	8,573	4,869	4,856	4,666	802	998	-838	-314	228	305	1,720	6,707	4,600	946
excluding South Africa	8,573	4,869	3,332	3,188	1,280	1,472	-25	-166	-686	-126	1,283	6,707	4,447	778
excl. S.Africa & Nigeria	7,062	4,904	3,480	3,674	2,390	1,997	472	264	252	1,522	2,351	5,692	4,531	1,615
Angola	0	623	263	218	126	374	-494	-327	-486	-275	79	0	262	-98
Benin	66	85	109	89	101	24	27	38	-12	91	35	79	73	49
Botswana	21	55	-2	3	-46	-53	-31	-31	-24	-32	-43	27	27	-32
Burkina Faso	59	131	105	110	82	56	73	81	63	135	113	50	90	89
Burundi	41	54	25	18	14	-1	9	-1	26	-3	36	39	76	12
Cameroon	495	219	276	-41	-16	21	-30	22	73	-29	-65	315	288	-8
Cape Verde	0	6	23	16	19	11	39	47	18	42	23	7	9	27
Central African Republic	33	46	47	23	19	-5	-11	5	8	2	1	21	65	5
Chad	0	50	74	60	107	68	31	76	31	48	96	22	67	65
Comoros	13	6	12	9	9	4	3	-2	2	10	8	11	11	5
Congo, Dem. Rep. of	326	53	-3	-1	-33	0	-1	7	0	0	322	359	134	37
Congo, Rep. of	485	383	63	-69	-116	-32	-8	-4	9	-18	-15	224	97	-32
Côte d'Ivoire	1,055	229	618	299	154	-602	-57	-585	-333	-357	-223	709	223	-213
Djibouti	8	19	17	9	19	9	5	1	1	8	27	8	22	10
Equatorial Guinea	36	13	6	1	-1	-2	-3	0	-2	-3	-1	10	13	-1
Eritrea	0	0	27	7	7	33	67	108	50	103	81	0	3	57
Ethiopia	102	343	188	141	23	127	94	133	101	456	577	440	351	206
Gabon	-109	22	79	62	-16	-4	-89	-221	-149	-256	-169	53	145	-105
Gambia, The	55	5	-1	1	36	4	1	12	15	22	43	22	15	17
Ghana	143	326	223	343	610	254	327	113	120	425	200	126	275	299
Guinea	54	242	128	71	76	165	77	33	-29	53	-33	47	144	52
Guinea-Bissau	72	22	25	14	25	30	11	1	13	-8	-4	23	35	10
Kenya	509	80	-271	72	-167	-264	-155	-262	50	-192	-127	298	233	-131
Lesotho	12	62	51	46	54	41	35	20	31	-17	-10	15	44	25
Liberia	91	20	-15	0	0	0	-1	-1	-1	-1	0	89	9	0
Madagascar	401	75	39	51	96	218	30	71	121	134	162	191	112	111
Malawi	156	145	94	151	128	123	113	102	88	91	75	90	82	109
Mali	100	63	101	176	132	107	55	69	42	76	87	87	114	93
Mauritania	129	97	100	55	94	39	-13	-12	70	51	88	107	74	46
Mauritius	124	22	83	255	32	57	-93	38	-269	-62	-14	56	36	-7
Mozambique	0	168	187	182	208	236	194	101	128	73	209	82	236	166
Namibia	..	..	..	..	..	..	..	..	..	..	..	..	..	..
Niger	233	35	41	-13	12	62	61	42	72	68	122	114	69	53
Nigeria	1,510	-35	-148	-486	-1,110	-525	-497	-430	-938	-1,648	-1,068	1,015	-84	-838
Rwanda	31	50	20	56	52	80	93	91	41	64	71	28	62	69
São Tomé and Principe	9	14	14	12	10	3	4	13	9	7	1	6	15	7
Senegal	230	72	47	46	56	112	40	-70	4	131	106	195	148	53
Seychelles	12	6	8	-7	2	2	10	-5	8	4	1	5	7	2
Sierra Leone	54	86	102	55	40	40	49	17	56	58	89	35	29	50
Somalia	125	0	0	0	0	0	0	0	0	0	0	149	46	0
South Africa	0	0	1,524	1,478	-478	-473	-813	-148	914	431	437	0	152	168
Sudan	790	91	9	-3	-18	-38	-59	-44	-59	-54	-22	565	129	-37
Swaziland	22	-9	-5	2	8	39	17	16	1	22	2	22	-7	13
Tanzania	352	136	149	116	80	215	128	204	129	120	164	294	193	144
Togo	101	5	43	41	69	32	56	6	6	11	3	91	34	28
Uganda	116	289	209	188	183	233	103	112	182	323	122	100	195	181
Zambia	421	29	88	539	80	121	-49	206	190	228	142	289	105	182
Zimbabwe	93	389	132	250	24	37	-193	-17	-121	-33	-8	190	141	-8
NORTH AFRICA	5,371	197	1,620	1,911	1,434	-215	-2,133	-2,457	-1,947	-659	-2,423	5,385	2,366	-811
Algeria	869	-782	2,078	1,739	1,527	-263	-1,646	-1,953	-1,600	-1,933	-1,413	1,435	625	-693
Egypt, Arab Rep.	2,297	227	254	-347	-430	-63	-215	-622	-513	803	-743	2,177	832	-266
Libya	..	..	..	..	..	..	..	..	..	..	..	..	..	..
Morocco	1,774	105	-336	-8	-75	-495	-85	-298	10	-388	-1,133	1,299	497	-309
Tunisia	321	272	131	450	426	605	-220	479	192	999	866	373	256	474
ALL AFRICA	13,944	5,067	6,476	6,577	2,236	784	-2,971	-2,771	-1,719	-354	-703	12,092	6,966	135

6-17. Net transfers: long- and short-term loans, including IMF

	Millions of U.S. dollars (current prices)											Annual average		
	1980	1993	1994	1995	1996	1997	1998	1999	2000	2001	2002	75-84	85-94	95-MR
SUB-SAHARAN AFRICA	6,513	2,491	-2,225	2,288	-2,660	-325	-5,996	-5,558	-5,293	-5,809	-4,231	5,251	1,132	-3,448
excluding South Africa	6,513	1,633	-2,842	196	-1,874	1,490	-4,586	-3,451	-5,316	-3,859	-2,617	5,251	985	-2,502
excl. S.Africa & Nigeria	4,642	2,073	-1,057	1,669	551	2,729	-3,748	-2,608	-3,865	-1,535	-775	4,214	1,917	-948
Angola	0	202	200	-222	-266	224	-562	-689	-909	-411	-239	0	286	-384
Benin	27	73	92	81	82	91	-45	48	-78	87	4	72	51	34
Botswana	0	22	-33	-24	-122	-48	-86	-40	-45	-39	-63	20	-6	-58
Burkina Faso	45	91	100	104	64	53	32	95	30	88	82	43	73	68
Burundi	36	32	12	15	-5	-6	2	38	9	11	19	36	60	10
Cameroon	389	-50	126	-95	-447	447	-226	-386	-372	-438	-450	234	81	-246
Cape Verde	0	4	21	30	-8	9	35	56	6	45	19	7	6	24
Central African Republic	28	49	21	19	9	-8	-19	13	-19	-19	0	17	56	-3
Chad	-9	42	63	55	95	65	4	56	6	25	74	21	63	47
Comoros	13	7	10	11	6	9	-2	4	2	3	11	11	9	5
Congo, Dem. Rep. of	13	-23	-151	38	-103	229	-31	-5	-4	-16	-201	232	-13	-12
Congo, Rep. of	473	258	-152	69	-650	39	-76	144	-104	-391	141	168	-19	-103
Côte d'Ivoire	572	217	-1,459	514	1,602	-109	-1,764	-1,410	-1,094	-761	-735	277	-218	-470
Djibouti	7	31	-13	11	15	9	-3	-8	-6	4	21	8	15	5
Equatorial Guinea	40	12	15	-9	-1	17	13	-20	-11	-1	1	9	10	-1
Eritrea	0	0	27	7	7	33	64	100	58	104	87	0	3	57
Ethiopia	67	285	144	70	-35	83	23	101	50	359	507	417	289	145
Gabon	-275	-67	-167	-226	-331	-2	-343	-369	-530	-463	-428	-7	22	-337
Gambia, The	55	18	-27	-14	38	-12	2	11	13	17	43	23	6	12
Ghana	22	253	207	317	509	115	176	-94	-208	266	61	86	195	143
Guinea	-11	188	76	49	25	348	-121	2	-98	-54	-86	25	106	8
Guinea-Bissau	71	17	23	7	26	23	2	-5	12	-20	-8	26	27	5
Kenya	489	-112	-665	-222	-525	-228	-344	-485	-83	-486	-104	168	-33	-309
Lesotho	18	49	39	30	38	20	12	-2	8	-44	-34	13	36	3
Liberia	60	1	-14	-2	10	-21	3	-1	-5	-5	-1	69	1	-3
Madagascar	419	35	0	39	37	116	60	75	-38	70	111	157	37	59
Malawi	101	78	69	141	148	18	87	109	75	53	130	55	38	95
Mali	92	19	67	175	73	257	-60	59	-19	8	169	84	85	83
Mauritania	117	39	54	30	69	114	-126	-45	36	20	20	90	33	15
Mauritius	70	-24	204	241	21	47	-105	-46	-159	-26	-59	30	9	-11
Mozambique	0	20	133	116	148	290	177	153	-27	152	35	82	186	130
Namibia	..	..	..	..	..	..	..	..	..	..	..	..	..	..
Niger	202	1	9	-24	2	83	9	40	46	36	90	70	20	35
Nigeria	1,872	-440	-1,785	-1,474	-2,425	-1,239	-838	-843	-1,451	-2,325	-1,842	1,038	-932	-1,555
Rwanda	31	39	-14	44	45	104	52	54	0	45	74	28	51	52
São Tomé and Principe	7	13	7	12	3	4	4	19	7	5	5	6	14	7
Senegal	151	28	-110	-13	-143	53	-7	-110	-234	128	124	151	27	-25
Seychelles	-427	-10	-2	-25	-7	4	26	-14	44	12	-2	-44	0	5
Sierra Leone	39	68	37	32	22	16	29	6	45	39	-3	23	13	23
Somalia	135	0	0	-1	-3	-7	5	-1	-7	2	9	148	38	0
South Africa	0	858	617	2,092	-786	-1,816	-1,410	-2,107	23	-1,950	-1,614	0	147	-946
Sudan	707	81	9	-15	-131	-173	41	-166	-45	-133	-5	544	51	-78
Swaziland	18	-15	-10	1	-13	180	-129	21	-9	17	-18	16	-18	6
Tanzania	324	5	102	8	45	179	69	160	65	-58	90	288	105	70
Togo	74	-70	47	28	45	-4	37	84	-45	24	28	70	-4	25
Uganda	118	209	185	146	163	201	73	50	146	288	71	84	154	142
Zambia	219	-124	-81	-111	74	-165	-45	-5	70	140	-194	203	8	-29
Zimbabwe	122	70	-202	193	-96	-15	-620	-230	-444	-216	-171	158	-36	-200
NORTH AFRICA	2,307	-6,676	-3,224	-3,036	-2,513	-3,862	-7,460	-6,674	-7,162	-4,914	-5,844	3,424	-2,896	-5,183
Algeria	-294	-2,660	450	-471	-513	-2,477	-3,984	-3,753	-3,228	-3,235	-2,425	320	-1,287	-2,511
Egypt, Arab Rep.	1,676	-1,518	-1,105	-1,302	-1,666	-445	122	-1,503	-1,435	-767	-1,472	1,930	-667	-1,059
Libya	..	..	..	..	..	..	..	..	..	..	..	..	..	..
Morocco	1,046	-1,298	-1,816	-1,421	-222	-916	-1,533	-1,296	-1,508	-1,257	-2,221	872	-709	-1,297
Tunisia	12	-282	-81	113	134	30	-1,232	393	-991	345	273	218	-69	-117
ALL AFRICA	8,820	-4,186	-5,449	-748	-5,173	-4,187	-13,456	-12,233	-12,455	-10,723	-10,075	8,675	-1,764	-8,631

6-18. Net transfers: long-term loans, including IMF

				Millions of U.S. dollars (current prices)								*Annual average*		
	1980	*1993*	*1994*	*1995*	*1996*	*1997*	*1998*	*1999*	*2000*	*2001*	*2002*	*75-84*	*85-94*	*95-MR*
SUB-SAHARAN AFRICA	6,085	2,892	715	121	-4,146	-2,768	-4,290	-3,755	-3,152	-3,111	-1,985	4,764	851	-2,886
excluding South Africa	6,085	2,034	-153	-452	-2,705	-1,411	-2,987	-2,828	-3,412	-2,682	-1,562	4,764	678	-2,255
excl. S.Africa & Nigeria	5,104	2,931	1,070	892	-552	-342	-1,969	-1,981	-1,784	-229	-171	4,225	2,093	-767
Angola	0	597	213	139	-167	226	-697	-441	-635	-385	-22	0	219	-248
Benin	63	72	91	67	84	6	11	17	-25	76	12	74	59	31
Botswana	15	22	-33	-24	-124	-81	-53	-51	-39	-44	-58	20	-5	-59
Burkina Faso	53	115	90	92	66	40	42	52	50	111	91	45	77	68
Burundi	38	41	12	7	5	-10	2	-7	21	-3	22	36	62	5
Cameroon	374	63	121	-216	-253	-170	-268	-225	-195	-165	-238	223	114	-216
Cape Verde	0	4	20	13	16	7	35	44	13	38	14	7	6	22
Central African Republic	32	43	38	18	15	-8	-16	-7	4	-13	0	18	57	-1
Chad	-1	42	66	55	93	57	9	54	8	27	74	21	63	47
Comoros	13	6	11	9	8	4	2	-2	1	9	8	11	10	5
Congo, Dem. Rep. of	106	43	-5	-18	-39	0	0	6	0	0	-109	241	20	-20
Congo, Rep. of	448	362	-166	-131	-296	-73	-2	6	-13	-58	-29	174	3	-74
Côte d'Ivoire	465	-171	181	-99	-324	-1,018	-662	-1,021	-737	-567	-569	292	-284	-624
Djibouti	7	17	15	7	16	7	0	-5	-3	4	21	7	20	6
Equatorial Guinea	36	12	5	0	-3	-3	-1	2	-1	-1	0	9	11	-1
Eritrea	..	..	27	7	7	33	64	105	48	98	75	..	27	55
Ethiopia	83	319	148	79	-31	81	25	101	62	362	501	419	299	147
Gabon	-228	-19	-27	-160	-252	-247	-236	-455	-308	-438	-339	-13	52	-305
Gambia, The	54	-2	-7	-4	31	-2	0	5	9	18	33	21	8	11
Ghana	108	228	130	274	496	123	173	-48	-34	318	44	96	177	168
Guinea	30	204	88	27	32	119	10	-23	-70	-7	-85	27	109	0
Guinea-Bissau	71	20	21	9	21	27	6	-4	3	-17	-4	22	32	5
Kenya	338	-132	-563	-192	-410	-449	-312	-379	-82	-277	-215	172	-9	-290
Lesotho	10	50	39	30	38	21	12	-2	8	-44	-34	13	36	4
Liberia	67	11	-15	-2	-2	0	0	-2	0	0	-1	72	3	-1
Madagascar	373	48	19	35	77	125	-7	-12	47	77	118	162	45	58
Malawi	119	117	68	111	99	96	90	85	80	75	59	63	45	87
Mali	96	22	76	153	72	86	36	65	42	56	74	82	92	73
Mauritania	115	55	62	22	63	3	-47	-39	56	13	60	90	41	16
Mauritius	98	-21	37	199	-39	-7	-155	-19	-321	-100	-49	33	-12	-61
Mozambique	0	92	132	106	160	193	182	46	48	55	189	82	199	122
Namibia	..	..	..	..	..	..	..	..	..	..	..	..	..	..
Niger	168	12	25	-26	1	49	38	37	54	51	93	77	31	37
Nigeria	981	-897	-1,223	-1,344	-2,153	-1,069	-1,018	-848	-1,628	-2,452	-1,391	540	-1,415	-1,488
Rwanda	29	45	19	48	45	72	68	52	18	48	66	27	57	52
São Tomé and Principe	9	13	12	11	8	2	3	12	8	7	1	6	14	7
Senegal	160	46	-19	-26	-66	34	-52	-129	-57	80	37	150	50	-22
Seychelles	12	0	2	-14	-3	-3	3	-11	5	3	-1	5	2	-3
Sierra Leone	39	68	37	33	25	32	21	10	44	32	2	23	13	25
Somalia	122	0	0	-1	-3	0	0	-1	0	0	0	144	40	-1
South Africa	0	858	868	573	-1,441	-1,357	-1,304	-926	260	-430	-422	0	173	-631
Sudan	727	81	9	-18	-31	-53	-4	-19	-7	-3	-2	509	99	-17
Swaziland	13	-16	-10	-3	-4	32	3	-2	-16	10	-6	17	-17	2
Tanzania	297	33	87	33	-17	173	67	159	31	31	55	253	137	66
Togo	81	-3	37	33	45	18	42	7	10	16	12	74	2	23
Uganda	109	257	174	152	143	193	74	48	155	290	73	87	156	141
Zambia	280	-122	-80	-6	-6	50	-109	123	103	46	-120	187	-24	10
Zimbabwe	82	209	-71	42	-170	-147	-368	-167	-169	-58	-24	150	-18	-133
NORTH AFRICA	2,533	-4,396	-2,950	-3,070	-3,712	-4,659	-6,832	-6,692	-5,616	-3,799	-5,640	3,302	-1,804	-5,003
Algeria	-570	-2,531	548	-71	-570	-2,299	-3,993	-3,752	-3,245	-3,202	-2,327	463	-1,057	-2,432
Egypt, Arab Rep.	1,930	-841	-903	-1,608	-1,509	-827	-922	-1,306	-1,133	114	-1,471	1,755	-109	-1,083
Libya	..	..	..	..	..	..	..	..	..	..	..	..	..	..
Morocco	1,111	-1,206	-1,712	-1,375	-1,413	-1,531	-1,106	-1,368	-938	-1,313	-2,211	833	-629	-1,407
Tunisia	92	-163	-346	-53	-93	116	-674	-27	-300	601	368	218	-129	-8
ALL AFRICA	8,618	-1,504	-2,235	-2,949	-7,858	-7,427	-11,122	-10,447	-8,768	-6,911	-7,625	8,066	-953	-7,888

6-19. Long-term debt: official concessional

	Millions of U.S. dollars (current prices)											Annual average		
	1980	*1993*	*1994*	*1995*	*1996*	*1997*	*1998*	*1999*	*2000*	*2001*	*2002*	*75-84*	*85-94*	*95-MR*
SUB-SAHARAN AFRICA	16,381	69,849	76,133	81,098	83,098	83,334	89,799	84,327	82,647	80,151	88,550	16,406	54,740	84,125
excluding South Africa	16,381	69,849	76,133	81,098	83,098	83,334	89,799	84,327	82,647	80,151	88,550	16,406	54,740	84,125
excl. S.Africa & Nigeria	15,942	68,755	74,844	79,721	81,744	82,012	88,217	82,603	81,190	78,813	87,078	16,038	54,048	82,672
Angola	..	1,315	1,405	1,490	2,152	2,212	2,386	2,004	1,791	1,581	1,658	..	1,231	1,909
Benin	166	1,165	1,270	1,253	1,293	1,265	1,333	1,359	1,343	1,413	1,585	166	828	1,356
Botswana	59	272	305	352	335	302	311	298	290	268	296	86	185	306
Burkina Faso	221	916	912	1,008	1,092	1,083	1,219	1,301	1,162	1,250	1,344	177	644	1,182
Burundi	104	946	1,012	1,047	1,041	989	1,048	1,023	1,003	950	1,062	107	731	1,020
Cameroon	873	2,484	3,503	4,156	4,203	4,278	4,603	4,307	4,248	4,211	4,494	690	1,870	4,312
Cape Verde	..	107	133	147	154	162	193	256	268	304	346	32	92	229
Central African Republic	59	674	723	765	768	724	745	741	714	678	745	64	492	735
Chad	171	592	674	692	760	803	872	927	903	895	1,051	141	379	863
Comoros	43	167	181	192	196	195	203	197	193	210	231	44	160	202
Congo, Dem. Rep. of	862	3,265	3,453	3,563	3,412	3,175	3,471	3,311	3,139	3,014	3,807	829	2,648	3,362
Congo, Rep. of	404	1,690	1,884	1,984	2,002	1,854	1,886	1,730	1,648	1,627	1,800	373	1,331	1,816
Côte d'Ivoire	438	3,696	3,882	4,563	4,806	4,503	4,943	4,418	4,126	3,880	4,526	411	2,643	4,471
Djibouti	15	229	253	267	278	252	263	248	237	235	295	19	167	259
Equatorial Guinea	32	139	142	148	145	139	144	142	137	132	143	31	107	141
Eritrea	..	..	29	37	42	73	140	236	281	379	480	..	29	208
Ethiopia	562	8,185	8,483	8,715	8,693	8,632	8,810	4,798	4,811	5,056	5,815	1,352	6,930	6,916
Gabon	113	408	579	708	748	898	953	825	1,366	1,282	1,312	87	349	1,011
Gambia, The	68	310	336	361	394	388	417	418	421	421	491	59	239	414
Ghana	775	2,845	3,290	3,693	3,966	4,043	4,584	4,784	4,714	4,631	5,176	683	2,018	4,449
Guinea	678	2,157	2,329	2,457	2,426	2,479	2,649	2,618	2,536	2,485	2,614	734	1,622	2,533
Guinea-Bissau	87	475	534	565	675	666	698	668	607	569	607	63	344	632
Kenya	684	3,090	3,394	3,859	3,931	3,742	4,083	4,115	4,092	4,107	4,450	650	2,307	4,047
Lesotho	44	382	440	470	468	435	448	454	448	427	472	48	273	453
Liberia	211	599	622	635	610	585	599	582	568	556	582	221	568	590
Madagascar	467	1,952	2,118	2,242	2,132	2,681	2,913	2,918	2,875	2,763	3,065	499	1,594	2,698
Malawi	258	1,502	1,681	1,897	1,946	1,973	2,184	2,475	2,452	2,407	2,606	275	1,049	2,242
Mali	613	2,693	2,464	2,660	2,688	2,636	2,654	2,639	2,502	2,477	2,455	592	2,074	2,589
Mauritania	526	1,525	1,602	1,692	1,743	1,705	1,721	1,789	1,821	1,734	1,818	507	1,294	1,753
Mauritius	65	384	417	441	403	345	354	316	299	274	294	65	298	341
Mozambique	..	2,864	3,239	2,936	3,204	3,185	4,055	3,515	3,482	2,063	2,377	764	2,277	3,102
Namibia	..	..	..	..	..	..	..	..	..	..	..	..	..	..
Niger	155	937	967	1,006	1,021	1,039	1,153	1,207	1,217	1,225	1,440	173	752	1,163
Nigeria	439	1,094	1,290	1,377	1,354	1,322	1,582	1,724	1,457	1,339	1,472	368	692	1,453
Rwanda	141	835	903	961	977	985	1,114	1,158	1,145	1,162	1,303	126	636	1,101
São Tomé and Principe	20	158	177	221	218	219	236	284	278	277	289	20	104	253
Senegal	400	2,111	2,104	2,268	2,313	2,416	2,800	2,709	2,615	2,634	2,987	412	1,820	2,593
Seychelles	19	67	69	69	69	69	72	72	84	82	98	22	63	77
Sierra Leone	176	493	591	701	737	732	783	778	815	940	1,065	157	345	819
Somalia	546	1,546	1,576	1,596	1,557	1,503	1,531	1,516	1,487	1,461	1,513	564	1,432	1,520
South Africa	..	..	0	0	0	0	0	0	0	0	0	..	0	0
Sudan	1,730	4,671	4,775	4,838	4,750	4,636	4,704	4,654	4,569	4,503	4,634	1,697	4,173	4,661
Swaziland	82	124	141	153	140	126	127	124	113	113	127	60	126	128
Tanzania	2,692	4,018	4,373	4,455	4,483	5,111	5,524	5,859	5,542	5,254	5,717	2,556	3,442	5,243
Togo	318	811	892	912	971	961	1,052	1,046	1,005	987	1,090	228	626	1,003
Uganda	254	2,130	2,456	2,766	2,876	2,973	3,137	2,824	2,910	3,053	3,424	222	1,343	2,995
Zambia	797	2,616	3,087	3,294	3,502	3,488	3,648	3,532	3,578	3,557	3,920	672	2,055	3,565
Zimbabwe	15	1,209	1,443	1,464	1,407	1,356	1,456	1,427	1,358	1,288	1,477	81	875	1,404
NORTH AFRICA	13,488	27,883	30,907	33,098	37,199	35,125	36,285	35,188	32,995	31,145	32,607	11,996	24,582	34,205
Algeria	1,269	1,318	2,054	3,076	3,287	3,145	3,303	3,415	3,101	2,696	2,759	1,031	924	3,098
Egypt, Arab Rep.	8,116	18,082	19,643	20,414	24,110	22,669	23,550	22,623	21,204	20,094	21,174	7,117	15,009	21,980
Libya	..	..	..	..	..	..	..	..	..	..	..	..	..	..
Morocco	2,717	5,572	6,128	6,570	6,966	6,773	6,935	6,566	6,098	5,760	5,797	2,597	6,043	6,433
Tunisia	1,386	2,910	3,082	3,039	2,836	2,539	2,497	2,584	2,591	2,595	2,877	1,251	2,605	2,695
ALL AFRICA	29,869	97,732	107,041	114,196	120,296	118,459	126,084	119,515	115,642	111,297	121,157	28,402	79,322	118,331

6-20. Long-term debt: official nonconcessional

	Millions of U.S. dollars (current prices)											*Annual average*		
	1980	*1993*	*1994*	*1995*	*1996*	*1997*	*1998*	*1999*	*2000*	*2001*	*2002*	*75-84*	*85-94*	*95-MR*
SUB-SAHARAN AFRICA	9,282	50,307	54,968	56,672	52,656	47,671	48,634	43,941	51,951	48,540	48,076	8,289	42,931	49,768
excluding South Africa	9,282	50,307	54,968	56,672	52,656	47,671	48,634	43,910	51,807	48,418	47,947	8,289	42,931	49,714
excl. S.Africa & Nigeria	8,728	33,155	36,447	37,557	35,365	31,981	32,547	28,984	26,689	23,823	23,881	7,556	29,622	30,103
Angola	0	608	688	736	716	658	1,016	976	912	860	1,232	0	379	888
Benin	50	203	213	226	150	128	135	111	100	94	101	30	145	131
Botswana	64	336	334	308	250	205	190	155	120	92	151	69	323	184
Burkina Faso	39	148	130	131	71	59	65	51	47	58	55	34	126	67
Burundi	6	49	48	47	40	33	30	25	24	23	30	9	55	31
Cameroon	364	2,539	2,774	2,996	3,018	2,935	3,142	2,968	2,846	2,574	2,576	298	1,691	2,882
Cape Verde	0	31	31	32	30	26	38	42	39	22	19	12	32	31
Central African Republic	40	78	62	71	68	64	63	52	49	46	201	37	93	77
Chad	34	116	78	137	134	115	115	101	91	83	84	24	57	108
Comoros	0	7	8	8	9	8	9	9	9	8	9	2	11	8
Congo, Dem. Rep. of	1,747	4,679	4,981	5,195	5,002	4,620	4,845	4,447	4,245	4,084	3,434	1,327	4,316	4,484
Congo, Rep. of	200	1,192	1,949	2,059	1,797	1,598	1,551	1,422	1,346	1,251	1,385	158	1,110	1,551
Côte d'Ivoire	809	4,906	4,760	4,654	3,981	3,403	3,359	2,837	2,543	2,331	2,226	694	3,997	3,167
Djibouti	7	2	2	2	1	1	1	1	1	1	5	4	4	2
Equatorial Guinea	14	61	62	65	61	56	58	52	50	48	52	13	64	55
Eritrea	0	0	0	0	2	3	7	17	17	16	16	0	0	10
Ethiopia	76	399	433	464	437	442	456	437	399	375	401	82	300	426
Gabon	203	1,929	2,848	3,069	3,081	2,637	2,755	2,337	1,964	1,664	1,766	173	1,486	2,409
Gambia, The	5	35	32	24	18	13	17	13	15	12	11	5	35	15
Ghana	259	435	427	400	442	395	375	327	275	453	420	181	374	386
Guinea	183	398	460	448	458	454	448	414	375	330	330	149	410	407
Guinea-Bissau	10	212	200	202	180	172	176	165	108	58	55	15	180	140
Kenya	523	1,060	1,445	1,358	1,150	965	848	668	478	309	291	490	1,283	758
Lesotho	2	97	116	137	134	131	120	116	133	91	76	5	58	117
Liberia	148	303	306	319	301	285	295	275	276	266	287	131	307	288
Madagascar	105	1,277	1,333	1,380	1,344	1,149	1,152	1,411	1,382	958	979	251	1,397	1,219
Malawi	184	177	170	157	126	106	106	102	85	67	72	132	230	103
Mali	15	89	79	77	75	66	179	168	163	160	32	13	61	115
Mauritania	57	393	415	426	401	350	308	341	303	211	161	74	381	313
Mauritius	89	241	233	223	212	209	227	225	201	166	298	74	253	220
Mozambique	0	1,832	1,888	2,227	2,127	2,008	1,893	1,105	1,045	140	146	36	1,250	1,336
Namibia	..	..	..	..	..	..	..	..	..	..	..	..	..	..
Niger	101	273	285	309	295	270	284	244	242	183	164	90	293	249
Nigeria	554	17,153	18,521	19,115	17,291	15,689	16,087	14,926	25,117	24,595	24,066	733	13,309	19,611
Rwanda	1	1	1	7	6	7	4	2	1	0	0	1	1	3
São Tomé and Principe	3	23	23	11	8	7	7	6	16	17	19	5	22	11
Senegal	253	829	840	868	816	699	484	454	391	337	340	272	863	549
Seychelles	6	29	36	40	40	37	42	39	36	34	36	6	27	38
Sierra Leone	71	305	296	265	218	201	220	198	185	179	194	51	208	207
Somalia	21	316	323	329	325	315	320	310	305	302	313	60	312	315
South Africa	0	0	0	0	0	0	0	31	145	122	129	0	0	53
Sudan	1,564	2,870	2,990	3,083	3,026	2,886	2,962	2,851	2,760	2,698	2,861	1,201	2,754	2,891
Swaziland	79	63	56	56	66	70	94	100	99	96	115	57	91	87
Tanzania	348	1,388	1,360	1,345	1,228	692	673	604	504	411	393	341	1,482	731
Togo	236	267	287	322	289	253	274	239	225	216	247	180	359	258
Uganda	37	354	320	212	197	318	176	139	123	225	228	63	332	202
Zambia	688	1,462	1,854	1,793	1,697	1,600	1,572	946	839	807	787	621	1,782	1,255
Zimbabwe	86	1,144	1,273	1,345	1,321	1,295	1,421	1,293	1,169	1,153	1,279	86	688	1,284
NORTH AFRICA	9,190	29,203	33,752	38,525	35,336	33,635	34,772	32,824	30,784	30,468	27,105	9,205	29,183	32,931
Algeria	2,226	5,188	8,874	12,602	14,894	15,120	16,142	15,066	14,356	13,463	13,496	1,739	4,956	14,392
Egypt, Arab Rep	4,507	7,471	8,234	8,543	3,581	3,234	3,370	3,088	2,766	3,260	3,478	4,824	11,744	3,915
Libya	..	..	..	..	..	..	..	..	..	..	..	..	..	..
Morocco	802	9,979	10,175	10,356	9,553	8,169	8,097	7,409	6,745	6,189	6,108	983	7,658	7,828
Tunisia	575	3,338	3,804	4,361	4,644	4,447	4,562	3,830	3,458	3,535	4,023	518	2,396	4,108
ALL AFRICA	18,472	79,510	88,720	95,197	87,992	81,305	83,406	76,765	82,735	79,008	75,181	17,494	72,114	82,699

6-21. Long-term debt: private

| | *Millions of U.S. dollars (current prices)* | | | | | | | | | | | *Annual average* | | |
	1980	1993	1994	1995	1996	1997	1998	1999	2000	2001	2002	75-84	85-94	95-MR
SUB-SAHARAN AFRICA	20,830	33,129	46,859	48,585	44,766	41,750	40,467	38,857	37,182	36,464	37,909	17,403	36,804	40,747
excluding South Africa	20,830	33,129	33,824	33,813	30,431	27,820	27,159	25,796	22,019	20,891	20,397	17,403	35,501	26,041
excl. S.Africa & Nigeria	16,454	24,633	25,370	25,864	23,345	21,905	21,098	19,838	18,358	17,426	17,730	12,907	23,123	20,695
Angola	..	6,781	7,031	7,318	6,511	5,813	5,700	5,734	5,383	5,390	5,992	..	6,131	5,980
Benin	118	4	4	4	4	3	4	3	3	3	3	142	151	3
Botswana	8	48	50	47	36	28	24	32	28	19	17	15	38	29
Burkina Faso	20	4	4	5	4	4	4	4	3	3	1	18	23	3
Burundi	8	3	2	2	1	1	1	1	4	5	4	10	13	2
Cameroon	1,014	1,397	1,189	1,186	1,069	751	658	727	647	382	348	727	1,447	721
Cape Verde	..	2	2	6	12	12	10	9	8	16	20	0	3	12
Central African Republic	48	21	18	18	14	14	33	33	33	33	34	40	22	26
Chad	54	6	6	2	17	17	17	16	15	14	13	42	19	14
Comoros	0	0	0	0	0	0	0	0	0	0	0	0	0	0
Congo, Dem. Rep. of	1,462	836	860	878	861	834	899	504	496	488	150	1,393	870	639
Congo, Rep. of	652	1,232	941	913	866	832	814	782	764	753	789	546	1,213	814
Côte d'Ivoire	5,091	5,125	5,210	5,345	4,429	4,592	4,330	4,039	3,876	3,764	3,617	3,507	5,442	4,249
Djibouti	5	0	0	0	0	0	0	0	0	0	6	3	2	1
Equatorial Guinea	7	15	16	17	16	14	15	13	12	12	14	9	17	14
Eritrea	..	..	0	0	0	0	0	0	0	0	0	..	0	0
Ethiopia	49	704	652	594	354	350	348	127	117	100	98	103	631	261
Gabon	955	596	268	199	143	131	125	129	118	88	153	766	713	136
Gambia, The	24	5	1	0	0	0	0	1	2	1	1	16	17	1
Ghana	131	345	419	525	799	851	919	840	755	811	786	132	313	786
Guinea	159	104	98	82	98	76	30	29	29	29	29	133	116	50
Guinea-Bissau	36	25	28	32	1	1	1	1	1	0	0	17	37	4
Kenya	1,286	1,700	1,207	1,089	866	701	846	757	670	443	446	898	1,505	727
Lesotho	11	24	22	35	61	77	93	91	76	58	63	9	24	69
Liberia	156	200	208	208	199	192	199	205	197	189	196	115	192	198
Madagascar	346	87	86	84	77	45	41	40	39	73	93	256	191	61
Malawi	192	50	49	28	24	21	20	19	18	10	10	128	67	19
Mali	36	4	2	2	0	0	0	0	0	0	0	30	22	0
Mauritania	131	19	9	8	25	24	22	20	19	4	6	118	93	16
Mauritius	165	275	448	751	783	787	702	733	453	411	319	94	232	617
Mozambique	..	162	1,743	1,815	1,872	1,930	1,770	1,759	1,728	1,553	1,516	232	713	1,743
Namibia	..	..	..	..	..	..	..	..	..	..	..	..	..	..
Niger	432	182	157	133	110	96	72	70	68	62	54	267	298	83
Nigeria	4,376	8,496	8,455	7,949	7,086	5,915	6,061	5,958	3,661	3,466	2,668	4,496	12,377	5,345
Rwanda	8	1	2	2	2	1	1	1	1	1	1	7	6	1
São Tomé and Principe	0	1	1	0	0	0	0	0	0	0	0	1	2	0
Senegal	461	156	153	127	53	66	33	23	21	61	46	301	243	54
Seychelles	0	35	43	36	30	25	31	24	12	16	15	4	29	24
Sierra Leone	157	522	509	92	92	91	91	90	6	2	2	168	424	58
Somalia	28	34	36	37	36	34	35	34	33	32	34	86	47	34
South Africa	..	..	13,035	14,772	14,335	13,930	13,309	13,061	15,163	15,573	17,512	..	13,035	14,707
Sudan	854	1,949	2,131	2,355	2,090	1,973	2,055	1,843	1,813	1,782	2,044	872	1,893	1,994
Swaziland	24	2	1	0	0	31	26	24	20	22	31	14	9	19
Tanzania	341	422	420	465	437	302	288	271	234	115	91	263	468	275
Togo	415	50	51	52	50	0	0	0	0	0	0	247	57	13
Uganda	244	115	93	87	81	80	66	26	24	37	38	149	261	55
Zambia	726	333	259	224	193	183	141	106	96	149	139	671	460	154
Zimbabwe	594	1,051	935	1,052	1,009	906	618	605	539	495	513	561	1,112	717
NORTH AFRICA	22,372	28,984	27,885	26,469	23,127	20,932	20,341	19,771	16,945	17,066	17,873	17,349	31,892	20,315
Algeria	13,545	18,588	17,509	15,625	13,104	10,447	9,036	7,414	5,875	4,706	5,107	9,882	18,166	8,914
Egypt, Arab Rep.	2,070	2,915	2,520	2,066	1,484	1,206	1,258	1,039	1,112	2,605	2,630	2,132	5,426	1,675
Libya	..	..	..	..	..	..	..	..	..	..	..	..	..	..
Morocco	4,969	5,949	6,300	6,646	6,313	6,458	6,851	6,991	6,318	5,690	5,009	3,841	6,403	6,284
Tunisia	1,429	1,372	1,319	1,817	2,086	2,531	2,622	3,853	3,639	4,066	5,128	1,069	1,647	3,218
ALL AFRICA	43,202	62,113	74,744	75,054	67,893	62,682	60,809	58,628	54,126	53,530	55,782	34,752	68,696	61,063

6-22. Total external debt

	Millions of U.S. dollars (current prices)											*Annual average*		
	1980	*1993*	*1994*	*1995*	*1996*	*1997*	*1998*	*1999*	*2000*	*2001*	*2002*	*75-84*	*85-94*	*95-MR*
SUB-SAHARAN AFRICA	60,696	188,509	221,491	235,713	231,576	221,074	228,766	215,308	211,445	202,872	210,685	54,506	161,811	219,680
excluding South Africa	60,696	188,509	199,820	210,355	205,526	195,801	204,014	191,401	186,584	178,822	185,645	54,506	159,644	194,769
excl. S.Africa & Nigeria	51,774	157,773	166,728	176,262	174,120	167,346	173,719	162,274	155,230	147,780	155,169	45,991	130,700	163,987
Angola	..	10,586	11,295	11,502	10,548	9,950	10,786	10,301	9,410	9,296	10,134	..	9,473	10,241
Benin	424	1,447	1,589	1,614	1,593	1,627	1,651	1,687	1,602	1,672	1,843	408	1,243	1,661
Botswana	136	664	700	717	626	575	532	504	453	400	480	175	551	536
Burkina Faso	330	1,119	1,135	1,274	1,302	1,304	1,459	1,579	1,409	1,492	1,580	269	864	1,425
Burundi	166	1,062	1,123	1,158	1,127	1,066	1,119	1,131	1,103	1,070	1,204	153	856	1,122
Cameroon	2,588	7,371	8,255	9,425	9,622	9,371	9,957	9,476	9,277	8,367	8,502	1,976	5,873	9,250
Cape Verde	..	148	176	214	202	207	247	327	327	361	414	62	132	287
Central African Republic	195	875	888	946	933	883	919	909	858	822	1,066	181	686	917
Chad	284	768	828	900	994	1,023	1,091	1,141	1,115	1,104	1,281	227	509	1,081
Comoros	44	189	202	214	218	219	227	228	232	243	270	48	183	231
Congo, Dem. Rep. of	4,773	11,273	12,322	13,239	12,830	12,337	13,203	12,048	11,692	11,519	8,726	4,319	9,563	11,949
Congo, Rep. of	1,526	5,081	5,413	6,004	5,241	5,071	5,119	5,033	4,887	4,491	5,152	1,227	4,429	5,125
Côte d'Ivoire	7,462	19,071	17,395	18,899	19,524	15,609	14,852	13,170	12,138	11,618	11,816	5,644	15,329	14,703
Djibouti	32	264	263	282	296	274	288	275	262	263	335	33	201	284
Equatorial Guinea	76	264	288	292	282	283	306	271	248	239	260	71	223	273
Eritrea	..	..	29	37	44	76	151	253	311	414	528	..	29	227
Ethiopia	824	9,703	10,063	10,308	10,078	10,077	10,347	5,544	5,483	5,697	6,523	1,656	8,111	8,007
Gabon	1,514	3,861	4,171	4,360	4,310	4,278	4,425	3,979	3,912	3,413	3,533	1,231	3,205	4,026
Gambia, The	137	426	423	426	452	425	460	465	483	487	573	116	351	471
Ghana	1,402	4,834	5,416	5,888	6,402	6,313	6,933	6,979	6,625	6,734	7,338	1,313	3,762	6,652
Guinea	1,134	2,848	3,110	3,242	3,240	3,519	3,546	3,522	3,388	3,254	3,401	1,119	2,343	3,389
Guinea-Bissau	140	787	852	898	937	921	966	934	804	668	699	110	617	853
Kenya	3,387	7,115	7,128	7,313	6,811	6,456	6,808	6,450	6,159	5,562	6,031	2,646	6,193	6,449
Lesotho	72	542	623	684	701	674	688	682	671	594	637	69	375	667
Liberia	686	1,957	2,056	2,154	2,107	2,012	2,103	2,077	2,032	2,164	2,324	620	1,749	2,122
Madagascar	1,248	3,805	4,096	4,322	4,146	4,109	4,394	4,755	4,701	4,160	4,518	1,187	3,576	4,388
Malawi	830	1,826	2,025	2,243	2,315	2,229	2,444	2,751	2,716	2,604	2,912	659	1,510	2,527
Mali	727	2,903	2,695	2,958	3,007	3,152	3,205	3,189	2,974	2,911	2,803	699	2,296	3,025
Mauritania	840	2,174	2,260	2,396	2,457	2,495	2,392	2,534	2,489	2,296	2,309	805	2,011	2,421
Mauritius	467	1,008	1,382	1,757	1,818	1,837	1,856	1,847	1,720	1,723	1,803	359	931	1,795
Mozambique	..	5,212	7,272	7,458	7,566	7,632	8,289	6,965	7,038	4,449	4,609	1,438	4,600	6,751
Namibia	..	..	..	..	..	..	..	..	..	..	..	..	..	..
Niger	863	1,542	1,510	1,572	1,522	1,556	1,650	1,668	1,686	1,589	1,797	640	1,519	1,630
Nigeria	8,921	30,736	33,092	34,093	31,407	28,455	30,294	29,128	31,355	31,042	30,476	8,515	28,943	30,781
Rwanda	190	909	952	1,029	1,043	1,111	1,226	1,292	1,271	1,283	1,435	158	694	1,211
São Tomé and Principe	24	210	223	245	234	237	257	320	315	313	333	28	142	282
Senegal	1,473	3,764	3,658	3,870	3,690	3,687	3,883	3,766	3,428	3,482	3,918	1,269	3,537	3,715
Seychelles	84	157	171	159	148	149	187	175	215	231	253	59	153	190
Sierra Leone	470	1,557	1,558	1,250	1,242	1,200	1,314	1,298	1,229	1,295	1,448	443	1,172	1,284
Somalia	660	2,501	2,616	2,678	2,643	2,561	2,635	2,606	2,561	2,563	2,688	785	2,208	2,617
South Africa	..	..	21,671	25,358	26,050	25,272	24,753	23,907	24,861	24,050	25,041	..	21,671	24,911
Sudan	5,177	15,837	16,918	17,603	16,972	16,326	16,843	16,132	15,741	15,414	16,389	4,807	13,292	16,428
Swaziland	206	196	206	220	208	385	275	301	295	303	342	146	240	291
Tanzania	5,324	6,790	7,250	7,425	7,386	7,199	7,669	8,066	7,394	6,678	7,244	4,883	6,514	7,383
Togo	1,122	1,294	1,456	1,476	1,488	1,346	1,472	1,521	1,432	1,406	1,581	757	1,237	1,465
Uganda	687	3,028	3,371	3,575	3,677	3,878	3,912	3,492	3,503	3,743	4,100	610	2,335	3,735
Zambia	3,244	6,485	6,816	6,966	7,069	6,669	6,879	5,868	5,731	5,671	5,969	2,954	6,380	6,353
Zimbabwe	786	4,285	4,524	5,007	4,976	4,919	4,669	4,440	3,911	3,726	4,066	982	3,291	4,464
NORTH AFRICA	53,980	91,634	98,719	104,744	104,194	99,450	101,248	97,481	85,809	82,097	84,776	46,727	96,424	94,975
Algeria	19,365	26,267	30,233	33,042	33,645	30,892	30,678	27,997	25,272	22,581	22,800	14,323	25,913	28,363
Egypt, Arab Rep.	19,131	30,675	32,523	33,499	31,538	30,102	32,440	31,045	29,187	29,331	30,750	18,167	37,207	30,986
Libya	..	..	..	..	..	..	..	..	..	..	..	..	..	..
Morocco	9,722	22,099	22,972	23,821	24,269	23,549	23,714	22,982	20,721	19,308	18,601	8,641	21,365	22,121
Tunisia	3,527	8,694	9,614	10,820	11,379	11,230	10,850	11,880	10,629	10,877	12,625	3,002	7,421	11,286
ALL AFRICA	114,676	280,142	320,211	340,456	335,770	320,523	330,014	312,790	297,254	284,969	295,461	101,233	258,235	314,655

6-23. Structure of external debt

| | Bilateral | | | | Multilateral | | | | Private | | Short-term | | IMF | |
| | Concessional | | Nonconcessional | | Concessional | | Nonconcessional | | | | | | | |
	1980	2002	1980	2002	1980	2002	1980	2002	1980	2002	1980	2002	1980	2002
SUB-SAHARAN AFRICA	12,445	35,700	5,683	39,798	3,936	52,850	3,599	8,277	20,830	37,909	11,170	29,121	3,033	7,030
excluding South Africa	12,445	35,700	5,683	39,798	3,936	52,850	3,599	8,148	20,830	20,397	11,170	21,721	3,033	7,030
excluding South Africa & Nigeria	12,044	35,060	5,663	17,792	3,899	52,018	3,066	6,088	16,454	17,730	7,617	19,451	3,033	7,030
Angola	..	1,366	0	1,211	..	292	0	21	..	5,992	..	1,252	..	0
Benin	82	458	31	84	84	1,127	20	18	118	3	73	80	16	73
Botswana	28	130	12	0	32	166	53	151	8	17	4	16	0	0
Burkina Faso	89	133	30	20	133	1,211	9	35	20	1	35	55	15	127
Burundi	49	139	1	4	55	922	5	26	8	4	12	96	36	13
Cameroon	663	3,417	142	2,231	210	1,077	222	344	1,014	348	278	778	59	307
Cape Verde	..	73	0	13	..	273	0	6	..	20	..	25	0	3
Central African Republic	17	172	28	189	42	573	12	12	48	34	25	53	24	33
Chad	97	88	34	49	75	963	0	35	54	13	12	26	14	107
Congo, Rep. of	21	51	0	0	21	180	0	9	0	0	1	30	0	1
Congo, Dem. Rep. of	667	1,937	1,620	2,889	194	1,870	127	545	1,462	150	329	764	373	571
Congo, Rep. of	355	1,533	132	1,083	49	267	69	302	652	789	247	1,145	22	33
Côte d'Ivoire	369	2,553	355	1,159	69	1,973	454	1,066	5,091	3,617	1,059	956	65	491
Djibouti	14	101	5	2	1	194	1	3	5	6	6	10	0	21
Equatorial Guinea	30	53	13	45	2	90	1	8	7	14	7	50	16	1
Eritrea	..	167	0	10	..	313	0	7	..	0	..	31	..	0
Ethiopia	281	2,140	18	208	282	3,675	58	193	49	98	57	66	79	143
Gabon	103	1,284	173	1,395	10	28	30	371	955	153	228	235	15	67
Gambia, The	33	106	0	4	36	385	5	8	24	1	23	37	16	32
Ghana	637	1,203	119	309	139	3,973	140	111	131	786	131	593	105	363
Guinea	615	1,064	116	172	63	1,551	67	158	159	29	80	289	35	139
Guinea-Bissau	58	225	5	47	29	383	5	8	36	0	5	14	1	23
Kenya	414	1,644	159	130	270	2,806	364	162	1,286	446	640	756	254	88
Lesotho	4	41	2	13	40	431	0	63	11	63	8	4	6	22
Liberia	179	385	50	77	33	197	98	211	156	196	81	956	89	304
Madagascar	319	997	71	918	148	2,068	34	61	346	93	244	231	87	150
Malawi	111	408	112	7	147	2,198	72	65	192	10	116	130	80	95
Mali	451	725	6	19	163	1,730	9	14	36	0	24	151	39	166
Mauritania	420	760	38	83	106	1,057	18	78	131	6	65	212	62	113
Mauritius	39	231	37	84	25	63	53	214	165	319	47	892	102	0
Mozambique	..	924	0	106	..	1,453	0	40	..	1,516	..	371	..	200
Namibia	..	..	..	..	..	..	..	..	..	..	..	..	..	..
Niger	42	238	70	149	112	1,202	30	15	432	54	159	33	16	106
Nigeria	401	640	21	22,006	37	831	533	2,060	4,376	2,668	3,553	2,270	0	0
Rwanda	51	148	1	0	91	1,155	0	0	8	1	26	46	14	85
São Tomé and Principe	9	109	4	15	11	180	0	5	0	0	0	23	0	3
Senegal	221	929	169	218	179	2,058	84	122	461	46	219	293	140	253
Seychelles	16	72	4	6	3	26	2	31	0	15	59	103	0	0
Sierra Leone	138	365	47	173	39	701	23	22	157	2	7	16	59	169
Somalia	400	803	9	296	147	710	13	18	28	34	47	676	18	152
South Africa	..	0	0	0	..	0	0	129	..	17,512	..	7,400	0	0
Sudan	1,361	2,839	1,298	2,665	368	1,794	266	196	854	2,044	598	6,277	431	573
Swaziland	65	56	34	17	17	71	45	99	24	31	15	68	6	0
Tanzania	2,388	2,179	89	361	305	3,537	259	33	341	91	1,771	643	171	400
Togo	228	283	210	231	90	807	26	17	415	0	120	192	33	52
Uganda	191	327	21	169	63	3,096	16	60	244	38	63	153	89	257
Zambia	778	1,297	314	659	19	2,623	374	128	726	139	586	108	447	1,015
Zimbabwe	15	910	83	277	0	567	3	1,002	594	513	90	517	0	280
NORTH AFRICA	11,435	28,328	7,177	13,786	2,053	4,280	2,013	13,319	22,372	17,873	8,063	5,861	868	1,330
Algeria	1,255	2,387	1,956	10,029	14	372	270	3,468	13,545	5,107	2,325	108	0	1,330
Egypt, Arab Rep.	6,231	18,858	3,767	1,924	1,885	2,316	741	1,554	2,070	2,630	4,027	3,468	411	0
Libya	..	..	..	..	..	..	..	..	..	..	..	..	..	..
Morocco	2,638	4,818	158	1,391	79	979	644	4,717	4,969	5,009	778	1,688	457	0
Tunisia	1,311	2,264	218	443	75	613	357	3,580	1,429	5,128	136	598	0	0
ALL AFRICA	23,880	64,028	12,860	53,585	5,989	57,129	5,612	21,596	43,202	55,782	19,233	34,982	3,901	8,360

Millions of U.S. dollars (current prices)

6-24. Structure of external debt service payments

	Millions of U.S. dollars (current prices)													
	Bilateral				Multilateral				Private		Short-term		IMF	
	Concessional		Nonconcessional		Concessional		Nonconcessional							
	1980	2002	1980	2002	1980	2002	1980	2002	1980	2002	1980	2002	1980	2002
SUB-SAHARAN AFRICA	422	915	451	747	59	1,033	425	1,468	3,818	6,890	1,025	476	487	905
excluding South Africa	422	915	451	747	59	1,033	425	1,462	3,818	2,441	1,025	239	487	905
excluding South Africa & Nigeria	400	887	436	557	58	1,015	354	1,033	3,154	1,635	646	221	487	905
Angola	..	3	0	50	..	5	0	4	..	784	0	19	..	0
Benin	1	15	1	5	1	27	1	3	4	0	11	3	0	10
Botswana	1	15	1	0	0	11	10	30	1	3	2	0	0	0
Burkina Faso	3	5	4	1	3	30	2	7	5	0	5	2	0	9
Burundi	1	0	0	0	0	16	1	0	4	2	2	2	1	3
Cameroon	25	98	18	49	4	24	24	103	163	57	28	25	19	2
Cape Verde	..	4	0	1	..	9	0	3	..	4	0	1	0	0
Central African Republic	0	0	0	0	0	0	0	0	1	0	2	0	7	0
Chad	1	3	0	1	2	16	0	2	0	1	0	1	3	5
Congo, Rep. of	0	1	0	0	0	4	0	0	0	0	0	0	0	0
Congo, Dem. Rep. of	48	0	136	0	2	269	22	143	189	0	45	14	101	501
Congo, Rep. of	22	0	13	0	1	4	11	8	25	0	31	3	8	9
Côte d'Ivoire	29	115	55	18	3	35	46	338	1,180	211	95	26	0	89
Djibouti	2	5	1	0	0	4	0	1	0	0	1	0	0	3
Equatorial Guinea	0	0	1	0	0	2	0	0	0	0	1	0	0	1
Eritrea	..	4	0	0	..	4	0	1	..	0	0	0	..	0
Ethiopia	11	12	1	3	2	39	10	37	9	5	9	1	2	12
Gabon	6	91	28	219	0	0	4	44	359	31	33	10	1	15
Gambia, The	0	7	0	2	0	8	0	2	0	0	3	1	1	0
Ghana	24	23	22	7	1	46	13	36	48	75	18	17	33	6
Guinea	55	49	7	3	0	37	21	33	14	0	9	3	2	11
Guinea-Bissau	0	7	0	0	0	4	0	2	4	0	1	0	0	2
Kenya	13	104	22	32	2	70	47	40	274	168	58	20	17	19
Lesotho	0	4	0	2	0	13	0	30	4	14	1	0	0	4
Liberia	3	0	0	0	0	0	7	0	27	0	11	0	5	1
Madagascar	21	16	2	9	1	30	3	11	42	1	29	4	3	2
Malawi	4	0	7	0	2	22	3	5	53	0	16	1	3	8
Mali	4	22	0	2	1	41	0	3	3	0	3	2	4	19
Mauritania	8	17	0	0	3	22	2	17	17	0	7	3	11	6
Mauritius	2	37	4	14	0	5	6	37	29	128	8	30	3	0
Mozambique	..	13	0	1	..	19	0	4	..	25	0	8	..	6
Namibia	..	..	..	..	..	..	..	..	..	..	..	..	..	..
Niger	3	2	5	0	16	13	2	1	98	9	19	0	0	3
Nigeria	22	29	15	190	1	18	70	429	663	806	379	18	0	0
Rwanda	0	7	0	0	1	12	0	0	3	0	3	0	0	3
São Tomé and Principe	0	1	1	1	0	4	0	0	0	0	0	0	0	0
Senegal	13	73	19	29	1	47	8	30	183	13	24	5	12	24
Seychelles	0	1	0	0	0	0	0	0	0	11	37	2	0	0
Sierra Leone	2	2	2	10	0	8	2	1	41	0	0	1	19	2
Somalia	3	0	0	0	1	0	5	0	0	0	0	0	4	0
South Africa	..	0	0	0	..	0	0	6	..	4,449	0	236	0	0
Sudan	37	0	30	0	5	1	18	0	12	0	70	0	92	23
Swaziland	2	4	6	0	0	2	4	12	5	1	2	1	0	0
Tanzania	32	38	2	16	2	43	23	8	36	29	26	6	39	7
Togo	2	0	17	0	1	1	2	0	16	0	14	2	0	10
Uganda	3	5	8	1	1	42	2	5	22	3	5	2	16	20
Zambia	16	83	21	82	0	28	51	33	238	15	0	2	84	67
Zimbabwe	3	1	0	1	0	0	3	1	43	46	15	6	0	3
NORTH AFRICA	571	2,407	428	1,716	11	360	261	2,845	5,256	3,549	869	144	253	341
Algeria	107	319	226	1,196	2	73	69	873	3,564	1,358	116	7	0	341
Egypt, Arab Rep.	265	901	50	224	7	128	51	337	320	380	422	97	121	0
Libya	..	..	..	..	..	..	..	..	..	..	..	..	..	..
Morocco	130	949	24	192	1	98	94	1,028	992	1,396	105	29	100	0
Tunisia	70	238	28	103	1	61	47	608	340	416	26	11	33	0
ALL AFRICA	994	3,322	879	2,463	70	1,393	685	4,314	9,074	10,439	1,895	620	739	1,245

Note: In 1995, Zambia was able to clear its arrears to the IMF after completing a three-year Rights Arrangement Program.

6-25. Average terms of new commitments in 2002

	Concessional terms				Nonconcessional terms				Structure of financing (percentage of total)	
	Interest (percent)	Grace period (years)	Maturity (years)	Grant element (percent)	Interest (percent)	Grace period (years)	Maturity (years)	Grant element (percent)	Con-cessional loans	Noncon-cessional loans
SUB-SAHARAN AFRICA	1.1	9.0	35.9	72.7	3.9	1.5	9.5	20.7	98.5	1.5
excluding South Africa	1.1	9.0	35.9	72.7	3.9	1.5	9.5	20.7	98.5	1.5
excl. S. Africa & Nigeria	1.1	9.0	35.8	72.9	3.9	1.5	9.5	20.7	98.5	1.5
Angola	0.8	10.1	49.6	83.0	..	..	..	..	100.0	..
Benin	1.0	9.6	39.6	77.4	..	..	..	..	100.0	..
Botswana	0.0	10.3	19.2	74.6	..	..	..	..	100.0	..
Burkina Faso	1.4	8.2	33.9	70.3	3.0	0.3	7.8	21.5	98.6	1.4
Burundi	0.8	10.3	39.8	80.6	..	..	..	..	100.0	..
Cameroon	0.9	8.9	33.2	73.8	..	..	..	..	100.0	..
Cape Verde	0.9	10.3	42.9	80.2	..	..	..	..	100.0	..
Central African Republic	..	..	..	..	..	..	..	..	..	..
Chad	0.8	9.7	38.5	78.3	..	..	..	..	100.0	..
Comoros	..	..	..	..	..	..	..	..	..	..
Congo, Democratic Rep. of	0.8	10.3	39.8	80.7	..	..	..	..	100.0	..
Congo, Republic of	0.8	9.8	39.3	80.1	..	..	..	..	100.0	..
Côte d'Ivoire	0.8	9.9	42.1	80.9	..	..	..	..	100.0	..
Djibouti	..	..	..	..	..	..	..	..	..	..
Equatorial Guinea	..	..	..	..	..	..	..	..	..	..
Eritrea	1.0	9.1	36.6	75.7	..	..	..	..	100.0	..
Ethiopia	1.1	9.9	39.6	76.8	..	..	..	..	100.0	..
Gabon	4.3	4.3	10.4	27.1	..	..	..	..	100.0	..
Gambia, The	1.9	8.3	31.0	64.8	..	..	..	..	100.0	..
Ghana	0.8	10.3	49.8	83.2	1.4	1.2	5.7	23.3	90.3	9.7
Guinea	0.8	10.3	47.7	82.7	..	..	..	..	100.0	..
Guinea-Bissau	0.8	10.1	41.4	80.9	..	..	..	..	100.0	..
Kenya	0.9	8.0	31.1	69.8	..	..	..	..	100.0 ..	
Lesotho	1.0	9.4	45.0	77.8	..	..	..	..	100.0	..
Liberia	..	..	..	..	..	..	..	..	..	..
Madagascar	0.8	10.2	40.6	80.7	..	..	..	..	100.0	..
Malawi	0.8	9.7	47.8	81.8	..	..	..	..	100.0	..
Mali	0.9	8.5	39.2	75.5	..	..	..	..	100.0	..
Mauritania	1.8	7.3	26.5	61.9	..	..	..	..	100.0	..
Mauritius	2.6	3.5	11.8	34.6	4.5	0.5	10.0	20.0	93.0	7.0
Mozambique	0.9	9.2	35.8	76.0	..	..	..	..	100.0	..
Namibia	..	..	..	..	..	..	..	..	..	..
Niger	1.3	8.2	33.7	70.0	..	..	..	..	100.0	..
Nigeria	1.2	8.2	38.0	67.7	..	..	..	..	100.0	..
Rwanda	0.8	10.3	39.8	80.6	..	..	..	..	100.0	..
São Tomé and Principe	0.9	7.8	20.8	63.6	..	..	..	..	100.0	..
Senegal	1.6	10.0	36.1	71.2	6.0	3.1	12.1	19.1	95.5	4.5
Seychelles	2.6	5.4	22.5	52.0	5.0	3.0	12.0	24.1	78.2	21.8
Sierra Leone	1.1	8.1	38.2	74.1	6.0	1.7	15.2	20.0	91.8	8.2
Somalia	..	..	..	..	..	..	..	..	..	..
South Africa	..	..	..	..	..	..	..	..	..	..
Sudan	..	..	..	..	..	..	..	..	..	..
Swaziland	..	..	..	..	..	..	..	..	..	..
Tanzania	0.6	9.8	38.8	80.0	..	..	..	..	100.0	..
Togo	..	..	..	..	..	..	..	..	..	..
Uganda	0.7	9.7	39.2	78.9	1.6	0.9	3.9	16.9	98.3	1.7
Zambia	0.8	10.0	39.5	80.3	..	..	..	..	100.0	..
Zimbabwe	2.1	9.5	27.7	63.4	..	..	..	..	100.0	..
NORTH AFRICA	2.7	5.0	17.0	44.2	5.1	1.6	8.5	13.5	84.7	15.3
Algeria	2.7	7.0	17.5	48.3	7.0	0.2	6.9	7.8	95.6	4.4
Egypt, Arab Republic	2.2	4.0	14.8	43.2	2.3	1.5	2.2	12.2	62.8	37.2
Libya	..	..	..	..	..	..	..	..	..	..
Morocco	2.8	4.8	19.0	45.5	6.0	3.0	16.5	20.5	80.5	19.5
Tunisia	3.2	4.3	16.7	39.8	..	..	..	..	100.0	..
ALL AFRICA	1.3	8.6	34.0	69.9	4.3	1.5	9.2	18.5	97.2	2.8

Note: No data indicates no commitment for the year 2002. Commitments are for offical long-term loans, only.

6-26. External debt and debt service ratios, 2002

	Debt-GDP ratio		Total external debt per capita (U. S. dollars)	Percentage of debt disbursed	Debt-export ratio		Present value of debt-export ratio, 2002	Debt service-export ratio (Ex post)
	Concessional	*Non-concessional*			*Concessional*	*Non-concessional*		
SUB-SAHARAN AFRICA	27	38	307	89	78	107	142	11
excluding South Africa	41	45	289	89	117	128	182	10
excl. S. Africa & Nigeria	51	39	305	88	147	115	178	11
Angola	15	11	772	89	19	98	114	10
Benin	59	4	281	81	342	56	..	14
Botswana	6	3	280	93	10	6	14	2
Burkina Faso	43	2	134	74	406	71	140	16
Burundi	148	4	170	88	1,621	218	1,146	36
Cameroon	48	27	539	91	174	155	187	14
Cape Verde	54	3	903	61	123	24	95	8
Central African Republic	71	19	279	92	576	248	592	1
Chad	52	4	154	76	419	92	244	12
Congo, Rep. of	94	3	461	96	317	53	263	7
Congo, Dem. Rep. of	67	60	169	96	314	406	694	77
Congo, Rep. of	60	46	1,409	95	74	137	200	1
Côte d'Ivoire	39	19	716	92	81	131	169	15
Djibouti	..	0	484	84	..	..	..	..
Equatorial Guinea	7	2	540	88	5	4	8	0
Eritrea	75	3	123	21	141	14	90	3
Ethiopia	96	7	97	91	597	73	408	11
Gabon	26	36	2,687	90	39	65	103	12
Gambia, The	138	3	412	85	185	31	111	7
Ghana	84	7	362	83	195	82	147	8
Guinea	81	10	439	85	335	101	184	17
Guinea-Bissau	299	27	483	91	1,036	157	778	25
Kenya	36	2	192	83	134	48	135	14
Lesotho	66	11	359	78	73	26	67	10
Liberia	..	..	705	99	..	..	..	..
Madagascar	70	22	275	89	405	192	185	10
Malawi	137	4	271	81	520	61	175	7
Mali	79	1	246	82	210	30	106	8
Mauritania	185	16	829	90	442	120	139	16
Mauritius	6	7	1,488	78	10	50	58	8
Mozambique	66	4	250	82	194	182	73	6
Namibia	..	..	..	..	..	..	..	..
Niger	66	8	157	80	382	95	135	7
Nigeria	3	55	230	94	9	179	194	9
Rwanda	75	0	176	80	923	93	488	16
São Tomé and Principe	575	38	2,165	83	1,480	230	575	31
Senegal	59	7	399	81	168	52	135	12
Seychelles	14	5	3,008	73	18	28	46	3
Sierra Leone	136	25	277	96	746	268	502	16
Somalia	..	..	288	89	..	..	..	..
South Africa	0	0	552	89	0	65	65	12
Sudan	34	21	500	94	230	584	787	1
Swaziland	11	10	314	73	10	18	27	2
Tanzania	61	4	206	83	349	93	107	9
Togo	79	18	332	86	217	98	232	3
Uganda	59	4	167	87	471	93	174	11
Zambia	106	21	583	92	354	185	387	28
Zimbabwe	18	15	313	75	73	127	192	3
NORTH AFRICA	16	25	618	89	47	75	113	16
Algeria	5	23	728	82	12	90	98	19
Egypt, Arab Rep.	23	4	463	94	93	42	118	9
Libya	..	..	..	..	..	..	..	..
Morocco	15	16	628	89	43	95	126	27
Tunisia	13	18	1,291	73	27	91	117	13
ALL AFRICA	23	33	358	89	66	95	131	13

Figure 6-1. Debt service ratio (ex post), 2002

(percentage of exports of goods and services)

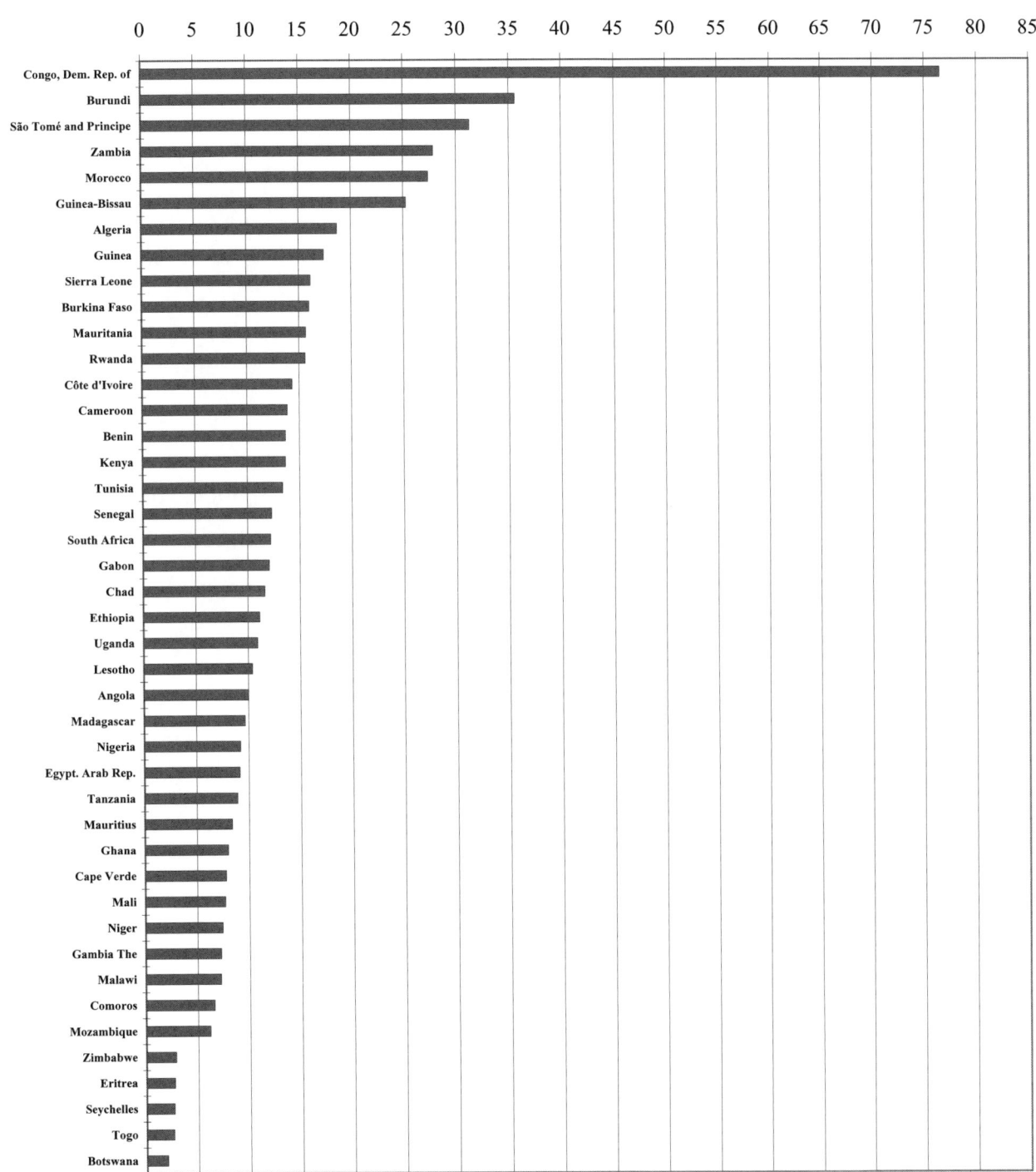

Figure 6-2. Debt to GDP ratio, 2002*

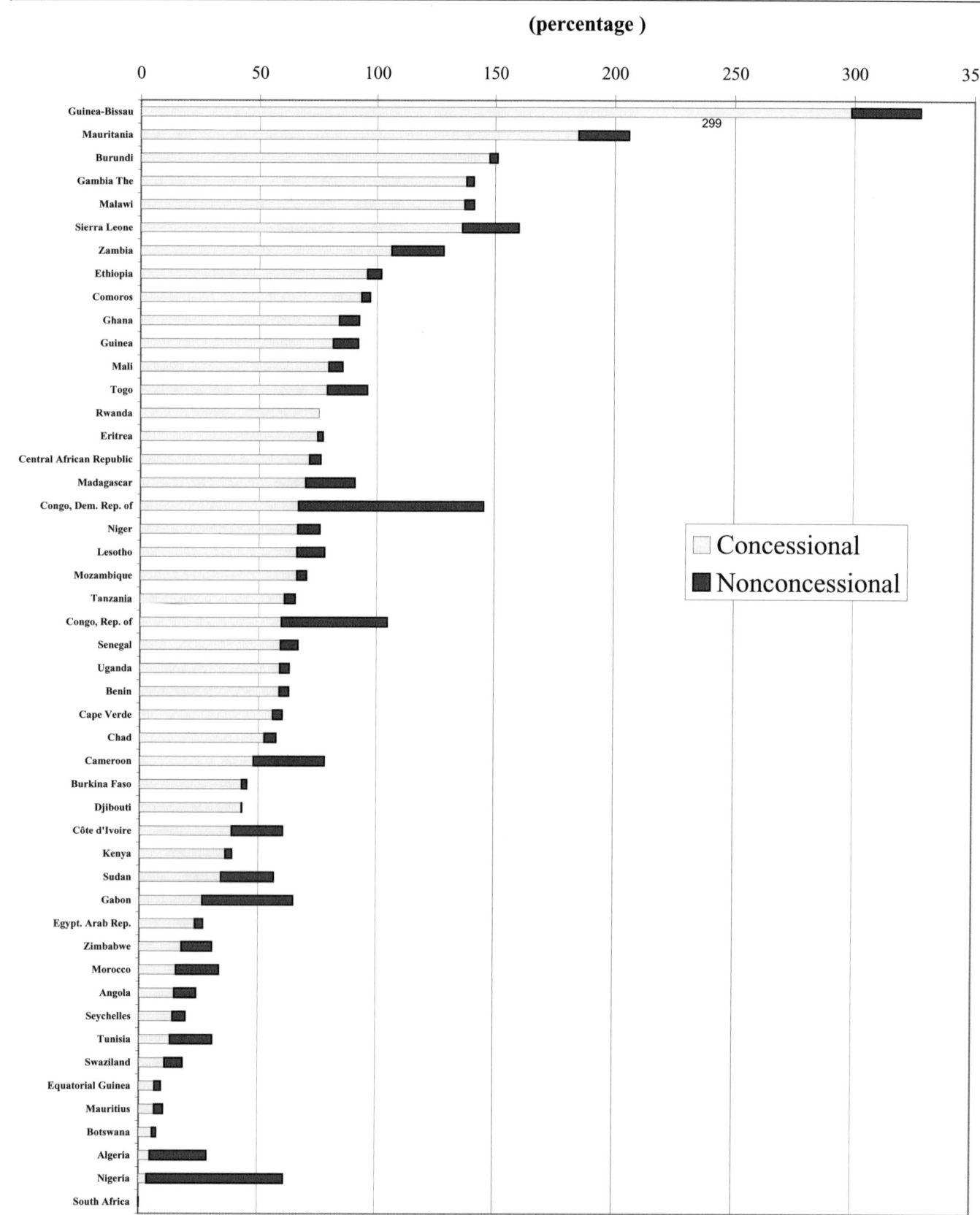

(percentage)

* Sorted by concessional debt.

Technical notes

Tables

Tables 6-1, 6-2, and 6-3. Gross disbursements: official concessional, official nonconcessional, and private long-term loans. Gross disbursements are from commitments of long-term external loans by official concessional, official nonconcessional, and private sources, respectively (World Bank, DRS).

Table 6-4. Disbursements: long-term loans and IMF purchases. This is the sum of Tables 6-1 through 6-3, plus IMF purchases.

Tables 6-5, 6-6, and 6-7. Amortization: official concessional, official nonconcessional, and private long-term loans. Amortization is the actual repayment of principal made in foreign currencies, goods, or services on outstanding long-term official concessional, official nonconcessional, and private long-term loans as described above (World Bank, DRS).

Table 6-8. Amortization: long-term loans and IMF repurchases. This is the sum of Tables 6-5 to 6-7, plus repurchases of drawings from the IMF.

Tables 6-9, 6-10, and 6-11. Interest payments: official concessional, official nonconcessional, and private long-term loans. These are actual payments made in foreign currencies, goods, and services to various lenders described above on interest obligations, including IMF charges on drawings due on disbursed debt and on commitment charges due on undisbursed debt (where information is available), that is, on long-term official concessional, official nonconcessional, and private loans (World Bank, DRS).

Table 6-12. Interest payments: long-term loans and IMF charges. This is the sum of Tables 6-9 through 6-11, plus IMF charges on drawings.

Table 6-13. Total external debt service payments: long-term loans and IMF credit. Total external debt service payments include the sum of amortization on long-term loans and IMF credit and interest payments on long-term loans and IMF credit (World Bank, DRS).

Table 6-14. Interest payments: short-term loans. These are estimated for the respective year based on the estimated year-end stock of short-term debt (which may include interest arrears on long-term debt) and the annual average six-month London interbank offered rate (LIBOR) on notes denominated in U.S. dollars as reported in the *IFS* (with no adjustment for spreads). Actual payments may be different because the LIBOR only approximates actual interest rates on short-term loans, and because not all interest due on short-term loans is actually paid (World Bank, DRS).

Table 6-15. Net flows: long- and short-term loans, including IMF. These flows represent all disbursements of long- and short-term loans net of all repayments of principal on long- and short-term loans and IMF credit (World Bank, DRS).

Table 6-16. Net flows: long-term loans, including IMF. Net flows of long-term loans are as defined above for Table 6-15, but excluding short-term loans (World Bank, DRS).

Table 6-17. Net transfers: long- and short-term loans, including IMF. Net transfers are net flows (Table 6-15) less interest payments (Tables 6-12 and 6-14).

Table 6-18. Net transfers: long-term loans, including IMF. Net transfers include long-term loans and IMF credit only (Table 6-16 less Table 6-12).

Tables 6-19, 6-20, and 6-21. Long-term debt: official concessional, official nonconcessional, and private. This series reflects the total debt outstanding and disbursed of official concessional, official nonconcessional, and private loans (World Bank, DRS). The time series reflects changes in the valuation of year-end debt stocks (because of U.S. dollar exchange rate fluctuation) and debt cancellation, as well as net disbursements. Therefore, changes in debt stocks from year to year cannot be used as a measure of net borrowing or vice versa.

Table 6-22. Total external debt. When Tables 6-19 to 6-21 are supplemented with IMF credit and estimates of total short-term debt (which includes interest in arrears on public and publicly guaranteed long-term loans), they sum up to total external debt (World Bank, DRS).

Table 6-23. Structure of external debt. This table summarizes debt structure for 1980 and 2002 (World Bank, DRS). The columns cover the type of creditor and concessionality. The private debt shown includes both the private guaranteed (by an entity of the debtor government) and the private nonguaranteed debt. For each year, all components shown add up to the totals in Table 6-22.

Table 6-24. Structure of external debt service payments. This summary table compares debt service payments for all types of creditors in 1980 and 2002 (World Bank, DRS). Debt service payments on short-term loans are excluded, to be consistent with Table 6-13. Debt service payments are actual repayments of principal (amortization) and actual payments of interest. The column headings have the same definitions as given above for Table 6-23.

Table 6-25. Average terms of new commitments, 2002. This table presents the average interest rates, grace periods, maturities, and grant elements shown separately for official concessional and nonconcessional long-term loans (excluding private financing); short-term loans are excluded (World Bank, DRS). Grant elements are calculated using a standard 10 percent discount rate. The indicators are weighted averages (based on amount of commitments) across all loans in each category.

Table 6-26. External debt and debt service ratios, 2002. This table includes the ratio of debt outstanding and disbursed to GDP; per capita debt; the ratio of debt outstanding and disbursed to debt outstanding, including undisbursed; the ratio of debt outstanding and disbursed and the ratio of the present value of debt to exports of goods and all services, including receipts of workers' remittances; and the ratio of total debt service paid to exports of goods and all services, more commonly called the debt service ratio (World Bank, DRS). Ratios are shown separately for concessional debt and for all nonconcessional (including private) debt. Both the stock of external debt and debt service payments include short- and long-term loans and IMF credit, except for the ratio of debt outstanding to debt outstanding including undisbursed, which is calculated for public and publicly guaranteed debt only. The data for exports of goods and all services, plus receipts of workers' remittances, are taken from balance of payments data in Chapter 5. The present value of debt is the sum of all future payments discounted to the present (usually with a commercial discount rate similar to LIBOR). The debt service ratio is shown for the ex post category, showing the amount paid after debt relief and/or arrears.

Figures

The following indicators have been used to derive the figures in this chapter.

Figure 6-1. Debt service ratio (Table 6-26).

Figure 6-2. Debt to GDP ratio (Table 6-26).

Methodology used for regional aggregations and period averages in Chapter 6

Table	Aggregations[a]			Period averages[b]
	(1)	*(2)*	*(6)*	*(1)*
6-1	x			x
6-2	x			x
6-3	x			x
6-4	x			x
6-5	x			x
6-6	x			x
6-7	x			x
6-8	x			x
6-9	x			x
6-10	x			x
6-11	x			x
6-12	x			x
6-13	x			x
6-14	x			x
6-15	x			x
6-16	x			x
6-17	x			x
6-18	x			x
6-19	x			x
6-20	x			x
6-21	x			x
6-22	x			
6-23	x			
6-24	x			
6-25			x	
6-26		x		

Note: Regional aggregations are shown in the rows for Sub-Saharan Africa, North Africa, and All Africa. Period averages are shown in the last three columns. This table shows only the methodologies used in this chapter.

   a. Regional aggregations: (1) simple total; (2) simple total of the first indicator divided by the simple total of the second indicator (same country coverage); (3) simple total of the gap-filled indicator; (4) simple total of the gap-filled main indicator divided by the simple total of the gap-filled secondary indicator; (5) simple total of the first gap-filled main indicator less the simple total of the second gap-filled main indicator, all divided by the simple total of the secondary indicator; (6) weighted total (by population); (7) median; (8) no aggregation; (9) simple arithmetic mean.

   b. Period averages: (1) arithmetic mean (using the same series as shown in the table; i.e., ratio if the rest of the table is shown as ratio, level if the rest of the table is shown as level, growth rate if the rest is shown as growth rate); (2) least-squares growth rate (using main indicator); (3) least-squares growth rate (using main indicator in constant terms, with the rest of the table in current terms).

7

Government Finance

The data in this chapter pertain to consolidated government (except when not available) instead of to central government operations, which were reported in previous volumes.

Definitions have been taken from the IMF's *Government Finance Statistics (GFS)*. For this volume, data are taken from country desks. When not available from country desks, data are taken from *GFS* and supplemented with data from IMF and World Bank staff reports, or from other national government sources. Data from various sources have been harmonized to produce a consistent and comparable time series.

The focus of this chapter is on the principal financial transactions of government—taxing, borrowing, spending, and lending—rather than on the production and consumption of goods and services, the use of labor, or other government activities. Spending covers both current and capital transactions.

The data comprise major government finance indicators—fiscal deficit or surplus, expenditure and lending minus repayments, revenue, grants, and domestic and foreign financing—expressed as a percentage of GDP. The chapter also includes information on the major components of revenue and expenditure by economic category, shown as percentages of total revenue and as a percentage of expenditure and lending minus repayments, respectively.

Measures of fiscal deficit or surplus are among the single most important indicators of government fiscal performance. The measure is usually calculated as the difference between total revenue (including grants) and total expenditure (including lending minus repayments). As such, it measures government net financing requirements. *GFS* methodology recommends grouping grants receipts with revenue because they can be spent without incurring an obligation for future payments but lists them separately because grants can sometimes be treated as financing items. Financing includes all government borrowing from others (at home and abroad) minus amortization (government repayment of its borrowing from others and changes in cash balances). Other measures of fiscal balance include the fiscal deficit or surplus without capital grants, which measures the government's ability to operate without foreign capital transfers, and the fiscal deficit or surplus, excluding interest payments from expenditure, referred to as the primary deficit or surplus.

Revenue is divided between taxes—unrequited compulsory payments to government—and nontax revenue. It includes only non-repayable receipts other than grants. Tax revenue is also classified according to the base upon which the tax is levied (for example, income and profits).

Expenditure is classified by economic category (such as wages, purchases, and interest payments). Lending minus repayments—government lending less repayment of past government lending—is grouped with expenditure, except in certain cases (see the technical notes at the end of this chapter).

The economic classification of expenditures (for example, on wages) is presented as a percentage of total expenditure and lending minus repayments, because lending minus repayments is itself a separate economic classification.

No attempt was made to reconcile *GFS* data in this chapter with the System of National Accounts (SNA). The fundamental difference between the two systems is that *GFS* focuses on government financial transactions, whereas the SNA considers government transactions as part of total demand and value added. (For further discussion, see World Bank 1988b, box 2.1, p. 45.) Indicators calculated as ratios to GDP use GDP at purchaser values or market prices (see technical notes to Chapter 1). Because GDP at purchaser values includes import duties (and GDP at market prices includes indirect taxes), ratios for revenues tend to understate tax burdens, especially where such taxes are an important source of government revenue.

Fiscal year data are compared with the calendar year GDP data that correspond either to the second half of the fiscal year or to the calendar year in which most of the fiscal year falls. Fiscal years do not correspond to calendar years in Botswana, Cameroon, Egypt, Ethiopia, The Gambia, and Ghana (before 1982), and Kenya, Lesotho, Liberia, Malawi, Mauritius, Niger, Nigeria, Senegal, Sierra Leone, Sudan, Swaziland, Tanzania, Uganda, and Zimbabwe (after 1985).

Government Finance

7-1. Government deficit/surplus (including grants)

					Percentage of GDP							Annual average		
	1980	*1993*	*1994*	*1995*	*1996*	*1997*	*1998*	*1999*	*2000*	*2001*	*2002*	*75-84*	*85-94*	*95-MR*
SUB-SAHARAN AFRICA	..	-2.1	-4.8	-3.2	-3.1	-3.2	-3.5	-2.8	-2.0	-1.9	-2.6	-4.5	-4.5	-2.8
excluding South Africa		5.1	-3.5	-1.5	-1.2	-2.0	-4.2	-3.5	-2.0	-2.1	-3.9	..	-3.9	-2.5
excl. S.Africa & Nigeria	..	5.1	-4.6	-3.8	-3.2	-2.6	-3.2	-2.8	-3.7	-2.3	-3.5	..	-4.0	-3.1
Angola	..	-21.7	-20.1	-37.5	-16.1	-22.0	-7.9	-16.4	-6.3	0.6	-6.2	..	-20.3	-14.0
Benin	..	-2.9	-4.4	-4.6	-0.4	0.3	2.1	1.9	-1.8	-1.5	-2.2	..	-5.9	-0.8
Botswana	..	11.0	6.6	4.6	4.7	5.8	2.7	-2.1	7.5	6.3	-3.1	10.4	10.0	3.3
Burkina Faso	..	-4.1	-3.1	-3.5	-0.5	-2.9	-2.9	-3.6	-3.9	-4.0	-4.7	..	-3.4	-3.2
Burundi	9.8	-3.7	-2.2	-2.2	-7.4	-4.1	-4.7	-6.4	-0.8	-0.9	-0.8	9.5	-3.3	-3.4
Cameroon	0.4	-6.3	-9.2	-3.2	-1.7	-1.2	-1.7	-3.2	1.4	1.5	1.6	0.5	-6.4	-0.8
Cape Verde	..	-9.3	-14.0	-19.1	-17.2	-6.0	0.4	-9.9	-19.1	-5.2	-0.9	-7.2	-6.7	-9.6
Central African Republic	..	-8.2	-10.0	-5.1	-3.4	-2.3	-0.8	-1.9	-2.0	-0.2	0.3	..	-8.8	-1.9
Chad	..	-8.6	-4.7	-4.4	-5.1	-3.9	-2.6	-6.0	-7.6	-6.2	-5.9	..	-6.1	-5.2
Comoros	..	-2.0	-13.8	-6.2	-5.2	-2.1	-3.5	-0.8	-2.5	-3.6	-6.2	0.0	-5.8	-3.8
Congo, Dem. Rep. of	..	..	..	..	-4.2	-5.8	-6.2	-5.0	-5.3	-1.5	-2.0	..	..	-4.3
Congo, Rep. of	..	-12.6	-13.2	-8.2	-10.5	-8.9	-20.0	-5.9	1.1	-0.7	-8.1	7.1	-9.9	-7.6
Côte d'Ivoire	..	-11.2	-5.9	-3.1	-1.4	-1.4	-1.5	-2.0	-1.3	0.9	-1.6	..	-8.8	-1.4
Djibouti	..	-13.0	-8.4	-8.0	-3.9	-4.3	0.9	-2.2	-1.8	..	..	..	-11.0	-3.2
Equatorial Guinea	..	..	-5.7	-6.3	-6.3	1.5	-5.7	0.1	9.1	12.1	16.2	..	-5.7	2.6
Eritrea	..	14.2	6.5	-12.2	-9.3	0.1	-29.9	-48.3	-28.3	-14.2	-20.5	..	8.7	-20.3
Ethiopia	..	-5.9	-7.7	-3.9	-5.6	-1.4	-3.1	-7.1	-11.6	-5.4	-9.2	-5.9	-6.6	-5.9
Gabon	..	-5.7	-1.6	3.2	2.7	2.5	-14.4	-1.4	0.6	2.2	3.6	-36.9	-5.4	-0.1
Gambia, The	..	1.3	-1.1	-6.3	-10.0	-6.5	-2.4	-3.5	-1.4	-6.3	-4.8	-14.7	2.1	-5.2
Ghana	..	-3.1	-8.9	-6.4	-9.5	-9.4	-6.5	-8.2	-7.9	-10.1	-4.0	-2.3	-2.9	-7.8
Guinea	..	-3.7	-3.6	-2.7	-3.0	-2.8	-0.3	-3.0	0.3	-4.4	-5.9	..	-3.7	-2.7
Guinea-Bissau	0.0	-13.0	-8.4	-1.4	-12.2	-5.0	-16.4	-10.1	-10.9	-11.7	-12.0	-8.3	-13.9	-10.0
Kenya	-7.0	-1.2	0.2	-1.4	0.3	-1.8	-0.7	18.4	2.9	7.7	1.3	-5.9	-3.8	3.3
Lesotho	..	-1.5	4.3	5.0	4.5	2.3	-1.8	-13.2	-5.0	0.1	-2.3	-5.4	-7.5	-1.3
Liberia	..	..	..	..	..	..	..	..	..	..	..	..	..	..
Madagascar	..	-7.6	-8.7	-5.3	-8.1	-2.4	-5.8	-2.8	-2.8	-4.3	-5.5	1.7	-2.4	-4.6
Malawi	-11.6	-6.1	-17.4	-4.7	-3.7	-5.5	-6.6	-4.5	-4.9	-7.6	-7.7	-8.3	-7.1	-5.6
Mali	-14.9	-4.1	-4.6	-3.1	-0.9	-2.1	-3.3	-3.5	-4.0	-5.1	-5.5	-11.9	-4.6	-3.4
Mauritania	..	-7.4	-0.5	1.2	7.4	5.1	3.6	4.7	-1.7	-1.8	10.2	..	-7.3	3.6
Mauritius	-10.9	-1.9	-2.4	-3.6	-7.2	-7.4	-3.9	-3.4	-3.8	-5.7	-6.0	-10.5	-2.5	-5.1
Mozambique	-2.1	-3.6	-5.3	-3.2	-2.9	-2.6	-2.4	-1.5	-6.0	-6.6	-7.9	-8.6	-6.1	-4.1
Namibia	..	-4.9	-2.0	-3.3	-5.3	-3.8	-3.8	-2.5	-1.1	-3.7	-4.1	-5.3	-0.7	-3.4
Niger	..	-3.8	-6.7	-2.7	-0.2	-2.7	-4.2	-5.1	-2.7	-2.4	-5.3	-4.9	-5.0	-3.2
Nigeria	..	..	1.9	9.9	9.1	1.0	-9.3	-7.1	6.8	-1.5	-5.8	..	1.9	0.4
Rwanda	..	-8.2	-11.5	-2.4	-5.8	-2.5	-3.0	-4.0	0.7	-1.3	-2.4	..	-7.6	-2.6
São Tomé and Principe	..	-33.6	-43.0	-37.6	-32.3	-26.7	-24.9	-23.2	-16.6	-22.0	-25.9	..	-19.6	-26.1
Senegal	-4.6	-3.1	-1.9	0.0	-0.1	0.5	-0.3	-1.4	0.1	-2.0	-1.3	-6.8	-1.8	-0.6
Seychelles	..	-11.3	3.4	1.8	-19.0	-15.7	-27.0	-6.9	-12.8	-10.7	-19.4	..	-3.7	-13.7
Sierra Leone	..	-7.4	-5.5	-9.2	-5.1	-7.0	-10.4	-9.5	-9.3	-11.4	-10.0	..	-14.3	-9.0
Somalia	..	..	..	..	..	..	..	..	..	..	..	..	..	..
South Africa	-18.0	-8.9	-6.2	-5.2	-5.4	-4.5	-2.6	-2.0	-2.0	-1.6	-1.2	-6.5	-5.1	-3.1
Sudan	..	137.3	-1.1	-0.7	-1.1	-0.6	-0.5	-0.7	-0.6	-0.9	-0.7	..	16.4	-0.7
Swaziland	..	-4.5	-5.2	-1.7	-1.2	1.8	1.0	-1.0	-1.5	-2.6	-4.2	..	-1.5	-1.2
Tanzania	..	-1.4	1.6	-3.4	-1.9	1.8	0.2	0.4	-1.2	-1.5	-1.4	-9.4	-1.0	-0.9
Togo	..	-15.5	-11.5	-6.4	-4.5	0.8	-5.2	-3.4	-5.4	-2.1	-1.6	-2.1	-6.0	-3.5
Uganda	..	-3.2	-3.8	-2.6	-1.9	-1.4	-0.5	-1.3	-9.7	-2.2	-5.7	-2.1	-4.0	-3.1
Zambia	..	-5.6	-6.5	-4.3	-0.5	-0.2	-3.2	-2.4	-5.0	-7.2	-5.6	..	-8.4	-3.6
Zimbabwe	7.6	-6.1	-6.7	-10.1	-7.7	-7.6	-2.5	-9.6	-21.4	-11.3	-12.1	8.0	-7.1	-10.3
NORTH AFRICA	..	-4.4	-2.6	-2.1	-0.6	-0.5	-2.2	-2.8	0.2	-0.3	-1.0	..	-5.7	-1.2
Algeria	-8.4	-8.6	-4.4	-1.4	2.9	2.4	-3.9	-0.5	9.9	6.4	5.3	-9.5	-5.5	2.6
Egypt, Arab Rep.	..	-2.3	-0.9	-0.3	-0.7	-0.3	-0.5	-3.6	-3.3	-4.5	-4.3	..	-9.1	-2.2
Libya	..	..	..	..	..	..	..	..	..	..	..	..	..	..
Morocco	-10.9	-2.9	-3.8	-5.4	-3.5	-3.4	-2.7	-4.7	-6.2	-0.8	-3.4	-0.8	-3.9	-3.7
Tunisia	0.9	-2.8	-2.1	-4.2	-4.9	-3.9	-2.5	-2.2	-2.9	-2.7	-2.5	-1.7	-2.7	-3.2
ALL AFRICA	..	-3.0	-4.0	-2.8	-2.3	-2.3	-3.0	-2.8	-1.3	-1.3	-2.1	..	-5.1	-2.2

Note: 2002 data are preliminary. Nigeria: from 1992 accounts are for consolidated budget; since 1994, ratios are distorted as off. exch. rate used by the Gov. for oil exports oil value added is significantly over-valued.

7-2. Government deficit/surplus (excluding grants)

					Percentage of GDP							Annual average		
	1980	*1993*	*1994*	*1995*	*1996*	*1997*	*1998*	*1999*	*2000*	*2001*	*2002*	*75-84*	*85-94*	*95-MR*
SUB-SAHARAN AFRICA	..	-4.1	-6.2	-4.4	-4.2	-4.2	-4.6	-4.0	-3.1	-3.1	-3.8	-5.3	-5.7	-3.9
excluding South Africa	..	1.0	-6.2	-3.7	-3.1	-3.9	-6.2	-5.7	-4.0	-4.5	-6.0	..	-6.6	-4.6
excl. S.Africa & Nigeria	..	1.0	-7.8	-6.4	-5.5	-4.9	-5.6	-5.4	-6.1	-5.1	-6.0	..	-6.6	-5.6
Angola	..	-21.7	-20.1	-37.5	-19.3	-24.4	-11.3	-35.7	-8.6	-3.7	-9.0	..	-20.3	-18.7
Benin	..	-6.8	-7.0	-7.3	-4.3	-4.2	-1.0	-1.6	-3.5	-4.2	-3.3	..	-10.9	-3.7
Botswana	..	9.8	5.2	4.1	4.4	5.4	2.1	-2.7	7.1	6.1	-3.3	7.8	8.4	2.9
Burkina Faso	..	-8.8	-9.9	-9.8	-8.2	-9.3	-9.2	-11.7	-11.1	-11.3	-10.2	..	-8.1	-10.1
Burundi	6.1	-12.7	-4.7	-5.8	-9.7	-7.1	-5.6	-9.2	-4.1	-3.5	-1.7	5.4	-7.8	-5.8
Cameroon	0.4	-6.3	-9.4	-3.3	-1.7	-1.2	-2.0	-3.4	1.4	1.0	1.3	0.5	-6.4	-1.0
Cape Verde	..	-24.6	-29.2	-27.8	-22.2	-16.1	-14.1	-14.8	-25.2	-11.0	-9.3	-45.0	-22.2	-17.5
Central African Republic	..	-13.5	-15.0	-11.4	-5.0	-6.3	-8.6	-8.7	-9.3	-7.9	-7.8	..	-13.7	-8.1
Chad	..	-13.2	-14.2	-11.9	-11.2	-10.3	-7.5	-10.7	-13.1	-11.8	-12.8	..	-14.1	-11.2
Comoros	..	-11.3	-23.8	-17.9	-14.1	-11.1	-10.7	-7.4	-5.7	-6.0	-7.7	-19.1	-20.4	-10.1
Congo, Dem. Rep. of	..	..	..	..	-4.2	-5.8	-6.2	-5.0	-5.3	-1.5	-2.3	..	..	-4.4
Congo, Rep. of	..	-12.6	-14.3	-9.2	-10.9	-9.0	-20.3	-6.3	0.8	-0.9	-8.3	6.2	-10.2	-8.0
Côte d'Ivoire	..	-11.7	-6.5	-4.4	-2.7	-2.7	-2.8	-3.0	-1.9	0.3	-2.1	..	-9.0	-2.4
Djibouti	..	-21.8	-13.4	-10.0	-5.7	-8.1	-7.9	-9.6	-10.4	..	..	..	-19.8	-8.6
Equatorial Guinea	..	..	-9.9	-8.9	-7.2	0.8	-6.4	-0.2	8.9	11.9	16.1	..	-9.9	1.9
Eritrea	..	-27.2	-31.7	-37.0	-31.0	-11.5	-47.7	-62.6	-64.3	-49.3	-45.1	..	-23.4	-43.6
Ethiopia	..	-7.6	-11.1	-7.3	-8.5	-5.1	-5.6	-10.5	-13.8	-10.2	-13.9	-8.0	-9.7	-9.4
Gabon	..	-6.0	-2.0	3.2	2.7	2.5	-14.4	-1.4	0.6	2.2	3.6	-37.3	-5.8	-0.1
Gambia, The	..	-2.4	-4.2	-8.7	-12.2	-7.8	-4.4	-4.9	-3.6	-9.8	-9.4	-14.7	-7.3	-7.6
Ghana	..	-9.8	-12.4	-10.0	-12.1	-11.7	-10.3	-9.8	-10.0	-14.6	-8.1	-3.1	-6.4	-10.8
Guinea	..	-7.3	-7.1	-6.7	-6.2	-5.9	-3.2	-5.3	-2.0	-7.8	-8.2	..	-7.2	-5.7
Guinea-Bissau	0.0	-29.9	-23.1	-17.7	-21.2	-17.8	-19.6	-14.4	-25.0	-26.2	-18.1	-10.1	-34.0	-20.0
Kenya	-9.5	-4.3	-2.6	-2.7	-0.9	-3.2	-2.2	17.1	1.8	3.9	-0.4	-7.6	-6.1	1.7
Lesotho	..	-1.5	0.7	0.3	-0.3	-1.6	-4.5	-15.5	-7.2	-2.5	-5.8	-8.9	-8.9	-4.6
Liberia	..	..	..	..	..	..	..	..	..	..	..	..	..	..
Madagascar	..	-11.0	-11.7	-8.2	-12.3	-7.7	-9.3	-6.4	-6.4	-8.2	-7.7	1.0	-4.7	-8.3
Malawi	-15.9	-8.8	-29.5	-12.7	-8.3	-9.0	-12.8	-11.0	-14.2	-14.6	-14.5	-11.1	-11.4	-12.1
Mali	-35.4	-9.6	-14.6	-10.7	-8.1	-7.9	-9.2	-8.8	-9.1	-9.5	-9.4	-38.2	-10.9	-9.1
Mauritania	..	-9.6	-3.1	-0.8	5.2	4.3	2.2	2.1	-4.9	-5.7	6.0	..	-11.0	1.1
Mauritius	-10.9	-2.1	-2.6	-4.0	-7.5	-7.4	-4.1	-3.5	-4.0	-5.9	-6.2	-10.8	-3.0	-5.3
Mozambique	-3.9	-15.5	-19.2	-13.0	-9.9	-11.9	-10.5	-13.2	-14.0	-21.4	-19.7	-10.4	-14.8	-14.2
Namibia	..	-5.6	-2.4	-3.6	-5.6	-4.0	-3.9	-2.7	-1.3	-4.0	-4.4	-18.2	-6.0	-3.7
Niger	..	-9.4	-12.5	-7.4	-5.1	-7.3	-8.6	-9.0	-7.5	-7.1	-6.5	-8.3	-9.8	-7.3
Nigeria	..	..	1.9	9.9	9.1	1.0	-9.3	-7.1	6.8	-1.5	-5.8	..	1.9	0.4
Rwanda	..	-14.6	-12.4	-13.7	-13.2	-9.2	-8.3	-9.7	-8.9	-9.5	-11.0	..	-12.7	-10.4
São Tomé and Principe	..	-50.3	-60.5	-60.9	-55.8	-54.5	-34.6	-50.1	-44.5	-60.1	-54.7	..	-37.0	-51.9
Senegal	-5.3	-4.2	-6.1	-3.2	-4.4	-2.0	-3.3	-3.5	-2.0	-3.9	-3.1	-7.7	-3.4	-3.2
Seychelles	..	-12.9	2.7	1.3	-19.5	-16.0	-27.5	-7.6	-13.7	-11.1	-20.0	..	-5.1	-14.3
Sierra Leone	..	-7.4	-5.5	-9.2	-7.1	-7.5	-13.0	-16.9	-18.5	-18.6	-20.5	..	-14.7	-13.9
Somalia	..	..	..	..	..	..	..	..	..	..	..	..	..	..
South Africa	-18.0	-8.9	-6.2	-5.2	-5.4	-4.5	-2.7	-2.1	-2.0	-1.6	-1.2	-6.5	-5.1	-3.1
Sudan	..	120.0	-2.8	-1.4	-1.5	-0.8	-0.7	-0.8	-0.8	-1.0	-0.9	..	12.6	-1.0
Swaziland	..	-5.4	-5.9	-1.9	-1.5	1.6	0.5	-2.2	-2.6	-3.8	-5.5	..	-2.4	-1.9
Tanzania	..	-4.8	-1.7	-5.2	-3.9	-1.4	-2.6	-3.4	-5.4	-5.0	-5.7	-12.2	-3.9	-4.1
Togo	..	-15.8	-12.9	-7.7	-5.1	-0.6	-6.5	-5.1	-5.9	-2.6	-2.9	-5.6	-8.3	-4.5
Uganda	..	-11.3	-10.3	-6.9	-5.9	-5.8	-5.8	-6.3	-15.5	-8.9	-12.8	-2.7	-7.3	-8.5
Zambia	..	-13.6	-11.8	-9.5	-6.6	-5.3	-9.8	-10.3	-10.7	-13.0	-13.9	..	-12.7	-9.9
Zimbabwe	6.9	-8.1	-8.6	-11.9	-9.0	-8.6	-4.2	-10.6	-22.5	-11.6	-12.9	7.0	-8.4	-11.4
NORTH AFRICA	..	-4.9	-3.2	-2.5	-0.9	-0.8	-2.4	-3.0	0.0	-0.5	-1.2	..	-6.7	-1.4
Algeria	-8.4	-8.6	-4.4	-1.4	2.9	2.4	-3.9	-0.6	9.9	6.0	5.0	-9.5	-5.5	2.5
Egypt, Arab Rep.	..	-3.5	-2.1	-1.2	-1.3	-0.9	-1.0	-4.2	-3.6	-4.6	-4.5	..	-11.2	-2.7
Libya	..	..	..	..	..	..	..	..	..	..	..	..	..	..
Morocco	-11.3	-3.3	-4.0	-5.4	-3.5	-3.4	-2.7	-4.7	-6.2	-0.8	-3.4	-2.6	-4.7	-3.8
Tunisia	0.9	-2.8	-2.5	-4.5	-5.1	-4.2	-2.8	-2.6	-3.3	-3.0	-2.8	-1.7	-2.7	-3.5
ALL AFRICA	..	-4.4	-5.1	-3.7	-3.0	-3.0	-3.8	-3.7	-2.0	-2.2	-2.9	..	-6.1	-3.1

Note: 2002 data are preliminary. Nigeria: from 1992 accounts are for consolidated budget; since 1994, ratios are distorted as off. exch. rate used by the Gov. for oil exports oil value added is significantly over-valued.

7-3. Government primary deficit/surplus (-/+)

					Percentage of GDP							Annual average		
	1980	1993	1994	1995	1996	1997	1998	1999	2000	2001	2002	75-84	85-94	95-MR
SUB-SAHARAN AFRICA	..	..	..	..	..	..	..	..	..	..	..	..	..	..
excluding South Africa		-0.6	5.0	2.8	2.6	1.3	-0.7	0.7	2.2	1.5	-0.2	..	-0.1	1.3
excl. S.Africa & Nigeria		-0.6	4.4	0.4	0.8	0.8	0.4	0.7	0.0	0.8	-0.5	..	-0.9	0.4
Angola	..	-12.2	219.0	-26.6	-4.5	-16.5	-1.0	-7.3	-0.7	5.3	-3.0	..	7.7	-6.8
Benin	..	-0.2	-1.2	-1.8	2.1	2.0	3.1	2.8	-0.9	-0.6	-1.4	..	-2.9	0.7
Botswana	..	11.0	6.6	4.6	4.7	5.8	2.7	-2.1	7.5	6.3	-3.1	..	4.8	3.3
Burkina Faso	..	-2.7	-1.7	-2.1	0.3	-2.1	-2.1	-2.8	-3.0	-3.1	-4.0	..	-2.1	-2.4
Burundi	10.1	-2.2	-0.7	-0.4	-5.6	-2.1	-2.3	-3.2	2.2	1.7	1.9	10.1	-1.2	-1.0
Cameroon	0.7	-1.5	-2.2	3.2	5.0	4.9	4.0	2.0	5.7	5.0	4.5	1.6	-3.4	4.3
Cape Verde		-2.9	-13.0	-15.9	-13.6	-2.1	3.9	-8.6	-16.9	-3.1	1.7	-7.2	-4.4	-6.8
Central African Republic	..	-6.1	-7.6	-2.8	-1.5	-0.9	0.5	-0.5	-0.1	1.2	1.7	..	-6.9	-0.3
Chad	..	-7.4	-3.5	-3.4	-4.0	-2.9	-1.7	-5.1	-6.5	-5.4	-5.1	..	-5.5	-4.3
Comoros	..	-1.1	-12.6	-5.2	-4.3	-1.1	-2.4	0.2	-1.6	-4.8	-7.4	-22.0	-6.5	-3.3
Congo, Dem. Rep. of	..	..	..	..	-1.2	-3.3	-2.4	-2.9	-3.5	-0.3	1.1	..	..	-1.8
Congo, Rep. of	..	-5.2	-1.1	5.9	2.1	4.2	-6.1	5.7	8.1	6.7	0.3	7.1	-2.9	3.4
Côte d'Ivoire	..	-3.0	1.3	3.2	3.8	3.0	2.3	1.9	2.7	4.2	1.7	..	-0.6	2.8
Djibouti	..	-12.5	-8.1	-7.4	-3.2	-3.8	1.3	-1.8	-1.0	..	..	..	-10.6	-2.7
Equatorial Guinea	..	..	1.4	-0.4	-2.4	2.9	-4.1	1.4	9.3	12.3	16.4	..	1.4	4.4
Eritrea	..	-6.6	-13.0	-23.9	-8.5	1.1	-28.7	-46.4	-25.4	-10.7	-16.6	..	-7.5	-19.9
Ethiopia	..	-3.9	-4.3	-1.4	-3.2	0.8	-1.1	-5.1	-9.3	-3.4	-7.3	-5.0	-5.0	-3.7
Gabon	..	1.3	5.1	11.3	8.6	8.3	-7.1	5.8	6.1	7.2	7.8	-34.5	0.1	6.0
Gambia, The	..	5.1	2.6	-2.5	-5.6	-1.3	2.9	1.5	3.2	-1.5	0.4	..	6.1	-0.4
Ghana	..	0.4	-4.4	-2.1	-4.4	-3.1	-1.4	-2.6	-0.4	-2.3	2.1	-1.1	-0.9	-1.8
Guinea	..	-2.4	-2.0	-1.3	-1.7	-1.2	1.1	-1.5	2.0	-2.5	-4.0	..	-1.5	-1.1
Guinea-Bissau	0.0	-7.2	-3.0	5.2	-5.6	0.4	-9.6	-9.2	-5.1	-3.3	-7.1	-3.2	-9.4	-4.3
Kenya	-3.5	13.1	11.5	5.4	7.4	3.8	4.7	23.8	6.8	10.7	4.1	-2.1	3.9	8.4
Lesotho	..	1.0	6.2	6.7	6.1	4.1	0.6	-10.1	-1.0	3.4	0.6	..	-6.3	1.3
Liberia	..	..	..	..	..	..	..	..	..	..	..	..	..	..
Madagascar	..	-3.5	-3.3	-0.2	-3.4	0.6	-3.1	-0.7	-0.5	-2.4	-3.3	3.2	0.1	-1.6
Malawi	-8.3	-3.0	-12.4	1.7	1.6	-2.1	-2.7	-1.1	-0.4	-2.2	-2.0	-5.2	-2.2	-0.9
Mali	-10.5	-2.5	-2.1	-1.7	0.2	-1.1	-2.6	-2.6	-3.0	-4.4	-4.6	-7.7	-2.8	-2.5
Mauritania	..	-3.3	2.4	4.4	10.6	8.0	7.1	8.3	1.5	1.3	13.0	..	-4.2	6.8
Mauritius	..	0.9	0.3	-0.6	-4.1	-3.9	-0.1	0.1	-0.4	-1.3	-2.6	-4.6	1.8	-1.6
Mozambique	-2.1	-1.1	-4.2	-1.6	-1.4	-1.3	-1.4	-0.8	-5.8	-5.9	-6.4	-8.5	-4.7	-3.1
Namibia	..	-4.3	-1.1	-2.2	-3.8	-1.9	-1.3	-0.1	1.1	-1.6	-1.6	-2.4	1.0	-1.4
Niger	..	-2.1	-4.4	-0.4	1.4	-1.2	-2.6	-3.6	-1.0	-0.6	-3.8	-2.8	-2.6	-1.5
Nigeria	..	..	7.5	13.6	11.4	3.5	-6.3	0.8	13.4	4.6	1.2	..	7.5	5.3
Rwanda	..	-6.1	-7.0	0.0	-4.1	-1.2	-2.0	-3.2	1.6	-0.5	-1.4	..	-5.4	-1.4
São Tomé and Principe	..	-22.2	-32.0	-25.5	-22.3	-15.4	-12.5	-11.9	-10.0	-13.1	-16.9	..	-10.9	-16.0
Senegal	-2.5	-0.8	1.6	2.9	2.3	2.8	1.0	0.0	1.6	-1.1	-0.2	-4.3	1.1	1.2
Seychelles	..	-3.4	11.8	12.3	-8.8	-5.7	-16.8	2.2	-5.4	-3.4	-10.8	..	4.3	-4.6
Sierra Leone	..	-3.4	-3.0	-7.3	-3.0	-4.9	-5.6	-3.7	-3.0	-6.5	-3.6	..	-8.5	-4.7
Somalia	..	..	..	..	..	..	..	..	..	..	..	..	..	..
South Africa	..	..	..	..	..	..	..	..	..	..	..	..	..	..
Sudan	..	..	..	..	..	..	0.2	0.1	0.7	..	..	..	..	0.4
Swaziland	..	-3.8	-4.6	-1.1	-0.5	2.5	1.7	-0.2	-0.8	-1.8	-3.0	..	-0.8	-0.4
Tanzania	..	-2.5	0.5	-0.4	1.1	4.2	2.3	1.9	0.5	0.1	-0.1	-7.0	-0.2	1.2
Togo	..	-11.2	-6.0	-2.8	-1.8	3.1	-2.6	-0.9	-3.2	-0.1	0.4	4.0	-1.6	-1.0
Uganda	..	-1.4	-2.3	-1.6	-0.9	-0.4	0.5	-0.4	-8.6	-1.1	-4.3	-0.1	-2.7	-2.1
Zambia	..	6.7	5.2	3.8	4.2	3.9	0.1	0.5	-1.9	-4.7	-1.6	..	1.3	0.5
Zimbabwe	-2.2	0.1	0.0	-0.7	0.7	-0.4	7.4	0.7	-4.2	-1.2	..	-3.2	-1.9	0.3
NORTH AFRICA	..	1.1	3.4	3.3	4.7	4.5	2.5	..	4.8	4.4	3.3	..	0.3	3.9
Algeria	..	-6.3	-1.6	1.7	6.4	6.3	0.1	..	14.0	10.6	8.6	..	0.3	6.8
Egypt, Arab Rep.	..	6.1	8.6	6.9	6.2	5.7	4.8	1.8	2.0	0.9	1.1	-22.6	-6.8	3.7
Libya	..	..	..	..	..	..	..	..	..	..	..	..	..	..
Morocco	-8.5	3.0	1.9	0.6	1.9	2.1	2.4	0.8	-1.0	4.0	1.3	2.3	2.0	1.5
Tunisia	2.5	0.7	1.6	-0.2	-0.6	-0.4	0.6	1.1	0.4	0.2	0.1	0.1	0.4	0.2
ALL AFRICA	..	..	..	..	..	..	..	..	..	..	..	..	..	..

Note: 2002 data are preliminary. Nigeria: from 1992 accounts are for consolidated budget; since 1994, ratios are distorted as off. exch. rate used by the Gov. for oil exports oil value added is significantly overvalued.

Government Finance

7-4. Government expenditure and lending minus repayments

	1980	1993	1994	1995	1996	1997	1998	1999	2000	2001	2002	75-84	85-94	95-MR
					Percentage of GDP								*Annual average*	
SUB-SAHARAN AFRICA	..	31.5	29.2	27.8	27.0	27.4	25.6	26.6	26.6	27.4	27.2	27.1	29.0	27.0
excluding South Africa	..	27.2	24.9	23.0	21.6	22.8	24.5	26.8	27.4	28.5	28.4	..	27.5	25.4
excl. S.Africa & Nigeria	..	27.2	26.6	25.1	23.7	23.6	24.4	25.0	25.2	24.3	25.0	25.8	27.6	24.5
Angola	..	60.7	62.1	67.6	64.1	64.7	42.8	82.6	60.4	46.3	47.9	..	52.5	59.5
Benin	..	17.8	19.8	22.1	19.5	18.6	16.3	17.6	20.1	20.3	20.2	..	19.6	19.3
Botswana	..	38.9	37.3	32.8	33.9	33.9	37.5	40.0	38.7	38.9	42.7	35.8	36.2	37.3
Burkina Faso	..	19.8	20.3	20.1	19.5	21.3	22.2	25.4	23.0	22.4	22.1	..	19.0	22.0
Burundi	11.9	30.1	24.7	25.9	27.4	22.2	23.6	28.7	25.0	25.1	20.8	12.6	25.5	24.8
Cameroon	16.0	20.0	19.3	16.2	16.0	16.3	17.9	18.9	17.4	18.8	17.9	10.6	22.6	17.4
Cape Verde	..	48.0	52.6	51.7	42.9	40.4	36.4	41.1	46.0	31.6	31.8	67.4	41.2	40.2
Central African Republic	..	21.2	22.4	20.6	11.0	14.0	17.7	17.9	18.9	18.7	19.7	..	22.0	17.3
Chad	..	20.2	19.1	18.1	18.5	18.1	14.9	19.0	20.5	18.0	20.0	..	20.2	18.4
Comoros	..	25.1	38.3	31.1	26.5	24.9	22.1	19.2	15.8	22.0	26.8	36.8	34.1	23.6
Congo, Dem. Rep. of	..	..	..	..	9.6	10.9	12.2	9.5	9.8	7.4	10.0	..	..	9.9
Congo, Rep. of	..	36.7	36.7	32.8	38.4	37.5	42.9	32.8	25.5	31.6	35.5	28.4	35.3	34.6
Côte d'Ivoire	..	28.3	24.9	24.5	22.5	22.1	21.2	19.5	18.2	16.6	19.6	..	31.0	20.5
Djibouti	..	50.1	43.0	38.7	34.7	35.4	33.3	33.1	32.7	..	..	..	48.0	34.6
Equatorial Guinea	..	55.9	27.1	24.6	24.9	16.6	30.0	16.0	8.6	5.0	5.2	..	43.8	16.3
Eritrea	..	63.7	62.0	73.3	62.4	52.5	78.5	94.5	98.6	75.1	70.6	..	53.1	75.7
Ethiopia	..	19.6	25.0	24.7	26.9	24.2	24.3	30.1	32.6	29.8	34.1	25.4	26.5	28.3
Gabon	..	28.6	25.5	26.3	23.0	28.8	46.2	27.0	21.5	23.0	20.8	36.9	32.1	27.1
Gambia, The	..	25.4	25.1	27.2	31.1	26.9	23.2	22.7	22.1	26.0	26.3	35.9	28.9	25.7
Ghana	18.7	29.0	31.2	30.4	29.7	29.0	28.6	26.2	27.7	32.7	26.1	13.1	21.4	28.8
Guinea	..	18.5	17.3	17.7	16.5	17.4	14.4	16.1	12.9	19.1	20.2	..	20.7	16.8
Guinea-Bissau	0.0	40.3	35.5	30.4	33.7	33.1	25.1	25.8	41.9	42.1	33.7	10.8	47.2	33.2
Kenya	34.3	35.3	31.1	29.3	28.2	26.9	28.0	26.6	22.2	26.3	23.8	27.2	30.3	26.4
Lesotho	..	45.2	46.4	47.6	48.3	48.1	49.1	56.4	49.9	44.1	45.3	37.6	46.3	48.6
Liberia	..	..	..	..	..	..	..	..	..	..	..	..	..	..
Madagascar	..	21.9	20.4	16.9	21.7	17.4	19.9	17.8	18.1	18.4	15.6	13.4	16.8	18.2
Malawi	35.7	26.0	49.0	31.0	23.3	24.2	29.5	29.1	31.6	33.1	33.1	29.2	32.2	29.4
Mali	108.2	23.4	27.2	23.5	23.5	23.9	25.0	26.1	23.9	24.6	25.9	106.8	25.8	24.6
Mauritania	..	36.8	27.7	24.8	24.0	22.7	25.0	25.8	30.4	25.5	31.6	..	35.5	26.2
Mauritius	32.9	23.1	23.5	23.3	24.6	27.0	23.6	24.0	24.6	23.9	24.4	32.5	25.1	24.4
Mozambique	17.4	29.5	30.9	24.4	20.5	23.5	21.8	25.1	27.3	34.7	33.8	26.5	26.9	26.4
Namibia	..	36.7	32.4	34.4	35.3	35.9	35.7	36.1	34.3	35.9	36.4	41.6	37.0	35.5
Niger	..	16.7	18.6	14.7	12.9	15.7	17.8	17.8	16.7	16.7	17.1	19.2	19.2	16.2
Nigeria	..	..	16.6	12.7	10.6	19.0	25.5	36.4	38.6	50.2	46.0	..	16.6	29.9
Rwanda	..	23.7	16.0	20.5	22.5	19.6	18.9	19.6	18.7	20.9	23.2	..	21.4	20.5
São Tomé and Principe	..	68.3	73.8	77.5	69.3	70.1	59.6	69.5	66.0	81.6	79.5	..	57.2	71.6
Senegal	27.4	20.8	21.0	19.6	21.0	19.0	20.1	20.9	20.0	21.7	22.0	26.8	20.7	20.5
Seychelles	..	64.3	50.6	47.1	61.7	57.7	64.7	48.4	49.5	46.0	56.6	..	53.3	54.0
Sierra Leone	..	21.3	17.3	18.0	16.9	13.0	20.1	22.0	28.7	30.1	32.4	..	25.4	22.7
Somalia	..	..	..	..	..	..	..	..	..	..	..	..	..	..
South Africa	24.1	35.5	34.0	33.0	33.3	32.6	26.9	26.4	25.8	26.0	25.9	26.4	30.6	28.7
Sudan	..	19.1	17.9	8.0	7.4	7.4	8.0	8.5	12.1	12.8	14.1	30.9	27.9	9.8
Swaziland	..	32.3	32.9	29.7	30.1	27.7	28.8	31.4	30.3	30.7	31.2	..	31.1	30.0
Tanzania	..	17.7	15.6	16.2	15.8	13.6	13.7	14.1	16.1	16.3	17.2	30.9	17.9	15.4
Togo	40.5	26.7	25.1	22.6	20.0	18.0	22.7	19.5	19.2	16.3	17.5	34.9	29.0	19.5
Uganda	..	18.6	18.6	16.7	16.2	16.8	16.4	18.0	26.8	19.8	25.1	13.7	14.1	19.5
Zambia	38.1	29.4	31.9	29.3	27.3	25.2	28.6	28.1	30.1	32.1	31.8	35.1	32.0	29.1
Zimbabwe	4.2	34.8	33.1	38.6	34.5	37.4	35.7	39.5	49.9	34.9	36.5	11.4	34.9	38.4
NORTH AFRICA	..	33.1	31.9	30.3	29.2	29.1	28.9	30.1	29.4	31.3	30.8	..	33.7	29.9
Algeria	46.2	36.1	33.5	31.6	29.2	31.2	31.7	30.5	29.4	35.4	35.9	47.8	35.5	31.9
Egypt, Arab Rep.	..	33.2	32.2	28.6	27.8	26.1	25.3	28.4	27.2	27.8	27.5	..	38.1	27.3
Libya	..	..	..	..	..	..	..	..	..	..	..	..	..	..
Morocco	32.2	29.8	28.2	29.3	28.1	29.8	30.0	31.9	32.4	31.4	29.2	24.6	27.7	30.3
Tunisia	27.9	30.7	33.8	34.5	35.5	32.6	32.0	31.5	31.9	32.0	31.2	32.3	31.5	32.6
ALL AFRICA	..	32.1	30.2	28.6	27.7	27.9	26.7	27.8	27.6	28.7	28.5	30.3	30.9	28.0

Note: 2002 data are preliminary. Nigeria: from 1992 accounts are for consolidated budget; since 1994, ratios are distorted as off. exch. rate used by the Gov. for oil exports oil value added is significantly over-valued.

Government Finance

7-5. Government interest payments

				Percentage of GDP								*Annual average*		
	1980	1993	1994	1995	1996	1997	1998	1999	2000	2001	2002	75-84	85-94	95-MR
SUB-SAHARAN AFRICA	..	..	..	..	..	..	..	..	..	..	..	..	..	..
excluding South Africa	..	5.2	8.9	4.3	3.8	3.4	3.5	4.2	4.1	3.7	4.0	3.4	5.1	3.9
excl. S.Africa & Nigeria	..	4.6	9.6	4.5	4.1	3.6	3.5	3.4	3.7	3.2	3.4	3.2	4.3	3.7
Angola	..	9.4	12.1	10.9	11.6	5.6	6.9	9.1	5.6	4.7	3.2	..	5.4	7.2
Benin	..	2.7	3.2	2.8	2.4	1.7	1.0	0.9	0.9	0.9	0.8	..	2.5	1.4
Botswana	..	0.0	0.0	0.0	0.0	0.0	0.0	0.0	0.0	0.0	0.0	..	0.0	0.0
Burkina Faso	..	1.4	1.4	1.3	0.8	0.8	0.8	0.8	0.9	0.9	0.8	0.6	1.1	0.9
Burundi	0.2	1.5	1.5	1.8	1.8	2.0	2.4	3.2	3.1	2.6	2.7	0.7	1.8	2.4
Cameroon	0.3	4.8	7.0	6.4	6.7	6.1	5.7	5.2	4.4	3.6	2.9	0.6	3.0	5.1
Cape Verde	..	1.2	1.0	3.2	3.6	3.9	3.6	1.3	2.2	2.1	2.6	0.0	1.1	2.8
Central African Republic	..	2.1	2.4	2.3	1.9	1.3	1.3	1.4	1.9	1.4	1.4	..	1.6	1.6
Chad	..	1.2	1.2	1.0	1.0	1.0	0.8	0.9	1.0	0.8	0.9	..	0.6	0.9
Comoros	..	0.9	1.2	0.9	1.0	1.0	1.1	1.0	0.9	0.9	0.8	0.0	0.7	0.9
Congo, Dem. Rep. of	..	..	..	..	3.0	2.6	3.8	2.1	1.8	1.3	3.1	..	..	2.5
Congo, Rep. of	..	7.4	12.1	14.1	12.6	13.1	13.9	11.6	6.9	7.4	8.4	0.0	7.0	11.0
Côte d'Ivoire	0.0	8.2	7.2	6.3	5.2	4.4	3.8	3.9	4.1	3.3	3.3	1.6	8.2	4.3
Djibouti	..	0.4	0.3	0.6	0.7	0.5	0.3	0.3	0.7	..	..	..	0.4	0.5
Equatorial Guinea	..	7.6	7.1	5.9	3.9	1.4	1.7	1.4	0.3	0.2	0.2	..	6.5	1.9
Eritrea	..	0.0	0.1	0.5	0.8	1.0	1.2	1.9	2.8	3.5	3.9	..	0.0	1.9
Ethiopia	..	2.0	3.4	2.5	2.4	2.2	1.9	2.1	2.3	2.0	1.9	0.9	1.6	2.2
Gabon	..	7.0	6.7	8.1	5.9	5.8	7.3	7.2	5.5	5.0	4.3	2.4	5.6	6.1
Gambia, The	..	3.8	3.7	3.8	4.4	5.1	5.3	5.0	4.6	4.8	5.2	..	4.0	4.8
Ghana	..	3.5	4.4	4.2	5.1	6.3	5.1	5.6	7.5	7.8	6.1	1.3	2.1	6.0
Guinea	..	1.3	1.6	1.4	1.3	1.6	1.4	1.6	1.7	1.9	1.9	..	2.2	1.6
Guinea-Bissau	0.0	5.8	5.4	6.7	6.6	5.5	6.8	0.9	5.7	8.4	4.9	0.1	4.4	5.7
Kenya	3.5	14.3	11.2	6.8	7.0	5.6	5.5	5.4	3.9	3.0	2.8	3.7	7.8	5.0
Lesotho	..	2.4	1.9	1.7	1.6	1.8	2.4	3.0	4.0	3.3	2.9	..	3.8	2.6
Liberia	..	..	..	..	..	..	..	..	..	..	..	..	..	..
Madagascar	..	4.0	5.4	5.1	4.7	3.0	2.7	2.1	2.3	2.0	2.2	1.0	2.5	3.0
Malawi	3.2	3.1	5.1	6.4	5.3	3.4	3.8	3.4	4.4	5.4	5.7	4.2	4.8	4.7
Mali	4.4	1.6	2.4	1.4	1.1	1.0	0.8	1.0	0.9	0.8	0.9	5.9	1.8	1.0
Mauritania	..	4.1	2.9	3.2	3.2	3.0	3.5	3.6	3.1	3.1	2.8	..	3.1	3.2
Mauritius	..	2.8	2.7	3.0	3.2	3.4	3.7	3.5	3.4	4.4	3.3	5.8	4.3	3.5
Mozambique	0.0	2.5	1.1	1.6	1.4	1.3	1.0	0.6	0.2	0.7	1.5	0.0	1.4	1.0
Namibia	..	0.6	0.9	1.1	1.5	1.9	2.4	2.4	2.2	2.1	2.5	2.8	1.8	2.0
Niger	..	1.7	2.3	2.3	1.7	1.5	1.6	1.6	1.7	1.8	1.5	2.1	2.4	1.7
Nigeria	1.4	8.2	5.6	3.7	2.3	2.4	3.1	7.9	6.5	6.1	7.0	1.7	8.5	4.9
Rwanda	0.2	2.1	4.5	2.3	1.6	1.2	0.9	0.8	0.9	0.8	1.0	0.4	1.6	1.2
São Tomé and Principe	..	11.5	11.0	12.0	10.0	11.3	12.4	11.3	6.6	8.9	9.0	..	8.7	10.2
Senegal	2.0	2.3	3.5	2.9	2.4	2.3	1.3	1.5	1.5	0.9	1.1	2.5	2.9	1.7
Seychelles	1.8	7.9	8.3	10.5	10.2	10.0	10.2	9.1	7.4	7.3	8.6	1.9	7.3	9.2
Sierra Leone	2.0	4.0	2.4	1.9	2.1	2.1	4.8	5.8	6.3	4.9	6.4	2.3	5.9	4.3
Somalia	..	..	..	..	..	..	..	..	..	..	..	..	..	..
South Africa	..	..	..	..	..	..	..	..	..	..	..	..	..	..
Sudan	..	..	..	..	..	..	0.7	0.8	1.3	..	..	..	..	1.0
Swaziland	..	0.6	0.6	0.6	0.7	0.6	0.7	0.8	0.7	0.9	1.2	..	0.7	0.8
Tanzania	..	2.3	2.2	3.0	3.0	2.4	2.1	1.5	1.7	1.6	1.3	2.4	2.2	2.1
Togo	..	4.3	5.5	3.5	2.8	2.3	2.6	2.5	2.2	1.9	2.0	7.2	4.4	2.5
Uganda	..	1.8	1.4	1.0	1.0	0.9	1.0	0.9	1.1	1.1	1.4	2.0	1.3	1.1
Zambia	4.1	12.3	11.6	8.1	4.8	4.1	3.4	2.8	3.0	2.5	4.1	4.2	9.6	4.1
Zimbabwe	1.2	6.2	6.7	9.4	8.5	7.1	9.9	10.3	17.2	10.2	14.2	2.6	5.2	10.8
NORTH AFRICA	..	5.6	6.0	5.4	5.3	5.0	4.6	..	4.7	4.6	4.3	..	4.7	4.9
Algeria	..	2.3	2.8	3.1	3.5	4.0	4.0	..	4.0	4.2	3.3	..	2.1	3.7
Egypt, Arab Rep.	..	8.5	9.4	7.3	7.0	6.0	5.3	5.4	5.3	5.4	5.4	0.0	5.0	5.9
Libya	..	..	..	..	..	..	..	..	..	..	..	..	..	..
Morocco	2.4	5.9	5.7	6.0	5.4	5.4	5.2	5.5	5.3	4.8	4.6	4.1	5.9	5.3
Tunisia	1.6	3.5	3.7	4.0	4.3	3.4	3.1	3.4	3.3	2.9	2.7	1.8	3.0	3.4
ALL AFRICA	..	..	..	..	..	..	..	..	..	..	..	..	..	..

Note: 2002 data are preliminary. Nigeria: from 1992 accounts are for consolidated budget; since 1994, ratios are distorted as off. exch. rate used by the Gov. for oil exports oil value added is significantly over-valued.

7-6. Government revenue (excluding grants)

					Percentage of GDP							*Annual average*		
	1980	1993	1994	1995	1996	1997	1998	1999	2000	2001	2002	75-84	85-94	95-MR
SUB-SAHARAN AFRICA	..	27.2	23.0	23.4	22.8	23.2	21.1	22.6	23.6	24.2	23.5	21.4	22.9	23.0
excluding South Africa	..	27.7	18.8	19.4	18.5	18.9	18.4	21.2	23.4	24.0	22.5	..	20.4	20.8
excl. S.Africa & Nigeria	..	28.2	18.8	18.7	18.3	18.7	18.8	19.6	19.1	19.3	19.0	19.4	20.9	18.9
Angola	..	39.1	42.1	30.1	44.8	40.3	31.6	46.8	51.7	42.5	39.0	..	32.2	40.9
Benin	..	11.0	12.8	14.8	15.2	14.5	15.3	16.0	16.6	16.2	16.9	14.2	8.7	15.7
Botswana	..	48.7	42.5	36.9	38.3	39.3	39.6	37.3	45.8	44.9	39.5	43.5	44.7	40.2
Burkina Faso	..	11.0	10.3	10.3	11.3	11.9	13.1	13.7	11.8	11.2	11.9	8.6	10.1	11.9
Burundi	18.1	17.4	20.1	20.1	17.7	15.1	18.0	19.5	20.9	21.6	19.1	18.0	17.6	19.0
Cameroon	16.3	13.7	9.9	12.9	14.3	15.1	15.9	15.5	18.8	19.8	19.2	11.1	16.2	16.4
Cape Verde	..	23.5	23.4	23.9	20.7	24.3	22.4	26.4	20.8	20.6	22.5	22.4	18.0	22.7
Central African Republic	..	7.7	7.5	9.2	6.1	7.7	9.1	9.2	9.7	10.8	12.0	..	8.8	9.2
Chad	..	7.0	4.9	6.2	7.3	7.8	7.4	8.3	7.4	6.2	7.1	3.6	5.8	7.2
Comoros	..	13.8	14.5	13.2	12.3	13.8	11.4	11.7	10.1	16.0	19.1	17.6	13.7	13.5
Congo, Dem. Rep. of	..	..	..	..	5.4	5.0	6.0	4.5	4.5	5.9	7.7	..	..	5.6
Congo, Rep. of	..	24.1	22.4	23.6	27.5	28.5	22.6	26.5	26.3	30.7	27.2	34.6	25.1	26.6
Côte d'Ivoire	..	16.6	18.3	20.1	19.8	19.4	18.4	16.4	16.4	17.0	17.5	30.2	22.1	18.1
Djibouti	..	28.4	29.5	28.7	28.9	27.3	25.3	23.5	22.3	..	..	..	28.3	26.0
Equatorial Guinea	..	..	17.3	15.7	17.7	17.4	23.6	15.8	17.6	16.9	21.2	..	17.3	18.2
Eritrea	..	36.5	30.3	36.4	31.4	40.9	30.7	31.9	34.3	25.8	25.5	..	29.7	32.1
Ethiopia	..	12.0	13.9	17.4	18.4	19.0	18.7	19.6	18.8	19.6	20.2	17.4	16.8	19.0
Gabon	..	22.6	23.5	29.5	25.7	31.3	31.8	25.6	22.1	25.2	24.4	-0.3	26.3	27.0
Gambia, The	..	23.0	20.9	18.5	18.8	19.1	18.8	17.9	18.5	16.2	16.9	21.2	21.6	18.1
Ghana	..	19.2	18.7	20.4	17.6	17.3	18.3	16.4	17.7	18.1	18.0	8.0	14.9	18.0
Guinea	..	11.2	10.2	11.0	10.3	11.5	11.2	10.8	10.9	11.3	12.0	..	13.5	11.1
Guinea-Bissau	0.0	10.4	12.4	12.7	12.5	15.3	5.4	11.4	16.9	15.9	15.6	0.7	13.2	13.2
Kenya	24.8	31.0	28.5	26.6	27.3	23.7	25.8	43.7	24.0	30.2	23.3	19.6	24.2	28.1
Lesotho	..	43.7	47.0	48.0	48.0	46.5	44.6	40.9	42.7	41.6	39.5	31.7	37.4	44.0
Liberia	..	..	..	..	..	..	..	..	..	..	..	..	..	..
Madagascar	..	10.8	8.8	8.8	9.4	9.7	10.6	11.4	11.7	10.1	8.0	14.4	12.2	10.0
Malawi	19.8	17.1	19.5	18.3	15.1	15.2	16.8	18.1	17.4	18.4	18.6	18.1	20.8	17.2
Mali	72.8	13.8	12.7	12.9	15.4	16.0	15.8	17.3	14.7	15.2	16.5	68.6	14.9	15.5
Mauritania	..	27.2	24.7	24.0	29.2	27.0	27.1	27.9	25.6	19.8	37.5	..	24.5	27.3
Mauritius	22.0	21.0	20.8	19.3	17.1	19.6	19.5	20.5	20.7	18.0	18.2	21.8	22.1	19.1
Mozambique	13.4	14.0	11.8	11.3	10.6	11.6	11.3	12.0	13.2	13.3	14.2	16.1	12.0	12.2
Namibia	0.0	31.1	30.0	30.8	29.7	31.9	31.8	33.4	33.0	31.9	32.0	14.0	31.1	31.8
Niger	..	7.3	6.0	7.2	7.8	8.4	9.1	8.8	9.3	9.6	10.6	11.0	9.4	8.9
Nigeria	..	25.5	18.5	22.6	19.7	20.0	16.2	29.3	45.4	48.7	40.2	..	18.6	30.3
Rwanda	..	9.1	3.6	6.8	9.3	10.4	10.6	9.9	9.7	11.4	12.3	9.0	9.6	10.1
São Tomé and Principe	..	18.0	13.3	16.5	13.4	15.6	25.0	19.3	21.5	21.5	24.8	..	20.2	19.7
Senegal	22.1	16.6	14.9	16.4	16.6	16.9	16.8	17.3	18.1	17.8	18.9	19.1	17.2	17.4
Seychelles	..	51.4	53.3	48.4	42.2	41.6	37.2	40.8	35.7	34.9	36.5	40.2	47.6	39.7
Sierra Leone	..	13.9	11.8	8.9	9.8	5.4	7.1	5.1	10.2	11.4	11.9	..	10.7	8.7
Somalia	..	..	..	..	..	..	..	..	..	..	..	..	..	..
South Africa	6.0	26.6	27.8	27.8	27.9	28.1	24.2	24.3	23.8	24.4	24.6	19.9	25.5	25.7
Sudan	..	..	15.1	6.6	6.0	6.6	7.3	7.6	11.3	11.8	13.2	..	16.4	8.8
Swaziland	..	26.8	27.0	27.7	28.6	29.3	29.3	29.2	27.7	26.9	25.7	..	28.7	28.1
Tanzania	..	12.9	13.9	11.0	11.9	12.2	11.1	10.7	10.6	11.4	11.5	18.6	14.0	11.3
Togo	..	10.9	12.2	14.9	14.9	17.4	16.1	14.4	13.3	13.8	14.6	28.1	20.7	14.9
Uganda	..	7.3	8.3	9.8	10.2	11.0	10.7	11.7	11.3	10.9	12.3	11.1	6.8	11.0
Zambia	..	15.9	20.1	19.8	20.7	19.9	18.8	17.7	19.4	19.1	17.9	..	19.4	19.2
Zimbabwe	11.1	26.8	24.5	26.7	25.5	28.7	31.4	28.9	27.4	23.3	23.6	18.5	26.6	26.9
NORTH AFRICA	..	28.2	28.7	27.8	28.3	28.3	26.5	27.0	29.4	30.8	29.5	..	27.0	28.4
Algeria	37.9	27.5	29.1	30.2	32.2	33.5	27.8	29.9	39.3	41.3	40.9	38.3	30.0	34.4
Egypt, Arab Rep.	..	29.7	30.0	27.3	26.5	25.2	24.3	24.2	23.6	23.2	23.0	..	26.9	24.6
Libya	..	..	..	..	..	..	..	..	..	..	..	..	..	..
Morocco	20.9	26.6	24.2	23.9	24.6	26.4	27.3	27.2	26.2	30.6	25.8	22.0	22.9	26.5
Tunisia	28.8	27.8	31.3	30.0	30.3	28.4	29.1	28.9	28.6	29.0	28.5	30.6	28.8	29.1
ALL AFRICA	..	27.5	25.0	24.9	24.7	24.9	22.9	24.1	25.6	26.5	25.5	24.1	24.4	24.9

Note: 2002 data are preliminary. Nigeria: from 1992 accounts are for consolidated budget; since 1994, ratios are distorted as off. exch. rate used by the Gov. for oil exports oil value added is significantly over-valued.

Government Finance

7-7. Grants to government

	Percentage of GDP											Annual average		
	1980	*1993*	*1994*	*1995*	*1996*	*1997*	*1998*	*1999*	*2000*	*2001*	*2002*	*75-84*	*85-94*	*95-MR*
SUB-SAHARAN AFRICA	0.4	1.8	1.3	1.1	1.0	1.0	1.1	1.2	1.1	1.3	1.1	0.5	1.1	1.1
excluding South Africa	0.7	3.3	2.5	2.1	1.9	1.9	2.0	2.2	2.0	2.3	2.1	0.9	2.0	2.1
excl. S.Africa & Nigeria	0.9	3.9	3.0	2.5	2.3	2.2	2.4	2.6	2.4	2.8	2.5	1.1	2.4	2.5
Angola	..	0.0	0.0	0.0	3.2	2.4	3.3	19.4	2.3	4.3	2.8	..	0.0	4.7
Benin	0.0	3.9	2.6	2.7	3.9	4.5	3.1	3.5	1.7	2.6	1.1	1.1	4.5	2.9
Botswana	0.0	1.2	1.4	0.5	0.3	0.5	0.6	0.6	0.4	0.2	0.2	0.3	1.6	0.4
Burkina Faso	0.0	4.7	6.9	6.4	7.7	6.4	6.3	8.2	7.3	7.3	5.4	0.7	4.8	6.9
Burundi	3.7	9.1	2.4	3.6	2.2	3.1	0.9	2.8	3.3	2.6	0.9	2.0	4.5	2.4
Cameroon	0.0	0.0	0.1	0.0	0.0	0.0	0.3	0.2	0.0	0.5	0.3	0.0	0.0	0.2
Cape Verde	0.0	15.3	15.2	8.7	5.0	10.1	14.4	4.9	6.1	5.8	8.4	3.8	16.2	7.9
Central African Republic	4.4	5.3	4.9	6.3	1.5	4.0	7.8	6.8	7.3	7.8	8.1	1.6	5.0	6.2
Chad	0.0	4.6	9.5	7.5	6.2	6.4	5.0	4.7	5.6	5.6	6.9	0.8	8.1	6.0
Comoros	0.0	9.2	10.0	11.7	8.9	9.0	7.3	6.6	3.2	2.4	1.5	3.8	14.6	6.3
Congo, Dem. Rep. of	0.0	0.0	0.0	0.0	0.0	0.0	0.0	0.0	0.0	0.0	0.4	0.0	0.0	0.0
Congo, Rep. of	0.0	0.0	1.1	1.0	0.3	0.1	0.3	0.4	0.3	0.2	0.2	0.2	0.2	0.4
Côte d'Ivoire	0.0	0.5	0.6	1.3	1.3	1.3	1.3	1.0	0.5	0.5	0.5	0.0	0.2	1.0
Djibouti	..	8.8	5.0	2.0	1.8	3.8	8.8	7.4	8.6	..	..	..	2.9	5.4
Equatorial Guinea	..	19.3	4.2	2.6	0.9	0.7	0.7	0.2	0.1	0.2	0.1	0.0	12.2	0.7
Eritrea	..	41.4	38.2	24.7	21.7	11.6	17.8	14.3	36.0	35.1	24.6	..	32.1	23.2
Ethiopia	..	1.7	3.5	3.3	2.9	3.7	2.5	3.4	2.3	4.8	4.7	2.1	3.1	3.5
Gabon	0.0	0.3	0.4	0.0	0.0	0.0	0.0	0.0	0.0	0.0	0.0	0.0	0.4	0.0
Gambia, The	0.0	3.7	3.1	2.4	2.2	1.3	2.0	1.3	2.3	3.5	4.6	0.0	9.4	2.4
Ghana	0.1	6.8	3.5	3.6	2.6	2.3	3.8	1.7	2.1	4.4	4.1	0.1	3.5	3.1
Guinea	..	3.6	3.5	4.0	3.2	3.1	2.9	2.3	2.3	3.4	2.3	..	3.4	2.9
Guinea-Bissau	0.0	16.9	14.7	16.3	9.0	12.8	3.2	4.3	14.1	14.5	6.1	1.8	20.1	10.0
Kenya	2.5	3.1	2.8	1.3	1.3	1.4	1.4	1.3	1.1	3.8	1.7	1.1	2.3	1.7
Lesotho	0.0	0.0	3.6	4.7	4.8	3.9	2.7	2.3	2.1	2.6	3.6	1.0	1.3	3.3
Liberia	0.0	..	..	..	..	..	..	..	..	..	..	0.0	0.0	..
Madagascar	0.0	3.5	3.0	2.9	4.2	5.3	3.5	3.6	3.6	3.9	2.2	0.2	2.3	3.6
Malawi	4.3	2.8	12.1	8.0	4.5	3.5	6.2	6.5	9.3	7.1	6.8	2.2	4.3	6.5
Mali	20.5	5.5	10.0	7.5	7.2	5.8	5.9	5.3	5.2	4.3	4.0	26.3	6.2	5.6
Mauritania	0.0	2.2	2.6	2.0	2.2	0.8	1.4	2.6	3.2	3.9	4.2	0.0	3.7	2.5
Mauritius	0.0	0.1	0.2	0.4	0.3	0.1	0.2	0.1	0.1	0.2	0.2	0.2	0.5	0.2
Mozambique	1.8	11.9	13.8	9.8	7.0	9.3	8.1	11.7	8.0	14.8	11.8	1.9	8.7	10.1
Namibia	0.0	0.6	0.4	0.3	0.3	0.1	0.2	0.2	0.2	0.3	0.3	7.8	5.3	0.3
Niger	0.0	5.6	5.8	4.7	4.9	4.6	4.4	3.9	4.8	4.7	1.2	0.3	4.9	4.1
Nigeria	0.0	0.0	0.0	0.0	0.0	0.0	0.0	0.0	0.0	0.0	0.0	0.0	0.0	0.0
Rwanda	0.0	6.4	0.9	11.3	7.4	6.8	5.3	5.7	9.6	8.2	8.6	1.6	4.3	7.9
São Tomé and Principe	0.0	16.6	17.5	23.4	23.5	27.8	9.7	27.0	27.9	38.1	28.8	0.0	15.6	25.8
Senegal	0.7	1.1	4.2	3.3	4.3	2.6	3.0	2.1	2.1	1.8	1.8	0.5	1.6	2.6
Seychelles	0.0	1.6	0.8	0.6	0.5	0.3	0.4	0.7	0.9	0.4	0.7	1.0	1.8	0.5
Sierra Leone	1.0	0.0	0.0	0.0	2.0	0.6	2.6	7.4	9.2	7.2	10.5	0.4	0.4	4.9
Somalia	0.0	..	..	..	..	..	..	..	..	..	..	0.0	0.0	..
South Africa	0.0	0.0	0.0	0.0	0.0	0.0	0.1	0.0	0.0	0.0	0.0	0.0	0.0	0.0
Sudan	0.0	17.3	1.6	0.7	0.3	0.2	0.2	0.1	0.2	0.1	0.3	0.0	1.9	0.3
Swaziland	0.0	1.0	0.7	0.3	0.3	0.3	0.5	1.1	1.2	1.1	1.2	0.0	0.4	0.8
Tanzania	..	3.4	3.3	1.8	2.0	3.2	2.8	3.7	4.2	3.5	4.2	2.8	3.0	3.2
Togo	1.5	0.3	1.4	1.4	0.5	1.4	1.3	1.6	0.5	0.5	1.3	1.4	2.4	1.1
Uganda	0.0	8.1	6.5	4.4	4.1	4.4	5.3	5.0	5.8	6.7	7.1	0.1	3.2	5.4
Zambia	0.0	8.0	5.3	5.2	6.1	5.1	6.6	8.0	5.7	5.7	8.3	0.0	4.3	6.3
Zimbabwe	0.7	2.0	1.9	1.8	1.3	1.1	1.7	1.0	1.1	0.3	0.8	0.5	1.3	1.1
NORTH AFRICA	0.1	0.5	0.6	0.4	0.2	0.3	0.2	0.3	0.2	0.2	0.2	0.3	0.8	0.3
Algeria	0.0	0.0	0.0	0.0	0.0	0.0	0.0	0.1	0.0	0.4	0.3	0.0	0.0	0.1
Egypt, Arab Rep.	0.0	1.2	1.3	0.9	0.6	0.6	0.5	0.6	0.4	0.2	0.2	0.0	1.6	0.5
Libya	0.0	..	..	..	..	..	..	..	..	..	..	0.0	0.0	..
Morocco	0.5	0.3	0.2	0.1	0.0	0.0	0.0	0.0	0.0	0.0	0.0	1.7	0.8	0.0
Tunisia	0.0	0.0	0.4	0.3	0.2	0.3	0.4	0.3	0.4	0.3	0.2	0.0	0.0	0.3
ALL AFRICA	0.3	1.3	1.1	0.9	0.8	0.8	0.8	0.9	0.8	0.9	0.8	0.4	1.0	0.8

Note: 2002 data are preliminary. Nigeria: from 1992 accounts are for consolidated budget; since 1994, ratios are distorted as off. exch. rate used by the Gov. for oil exports oil value added is significantly over-valued.

7-8. Foreign financing

					Percentage of GDP							*Annual average*		
	1980	*1993*	*1994*	*1995*	*1996*	*1997*	*1998*	*1999*	*2000*	*2001*	*2002*	*75-84*	*85-94*	*95-MR*
SUB-SAHARAN AFRICA	1.0	1.3	2.0	0.8	1.2	0.9	0.3	0.1	0.0	1.5	1.3	1.1	1.3	0.8
excluding South Africa	..	2.4	3.5	1.3	2.0	1.4	0.5	-0.5	-0.3	0.6	0.9	1.7	2.6	0.7
excl. S.Africa & Nigeria	..	3.8	5.0	2.1	2.7	1.4	0.9	0.5	0.4	1.5	1.7	2.2	3.5	1.4
Angola	..	-8.7	7.3	17.0	-8.8	7.0	-12.8	2.1	-4.8	-4.9	-4.9	..	0.8	-1.3
Benin	..	6.9	10.3	8.3	7.6	0.6	0.8	1.1	1.6	3.3	1.9	..	12.3	3.2
Botswana	..	0.7	0.2	-0.2	-0.1	0.5	0.3	-0.1	-0.3	-0.6	-0.6	..	0.2	-0.2
Burkina Faso	..	8.7	9.4	11.6	10.0	8.5	-2.6	-3.7	-3.0	-1.6	-1.7	2.6	4.2	2.2
Burundi	3.3	10.6	7.4	2.9	3.0	1.6	2.6	1.7	0.5	1.2	-1.1	5.6	8.9	1.5
Cameroon	2.2	0.1	20.5	0.1	8.2	-4.0	9.0	3.3	1.3	2.0	5.8	1.6	5.1	3.2
Cape Verde	..	3.2	..	..	..	..	6.5	8.2	3.8	3.5	3.7	11.5	3.5	5.1
Central African Republic	0.4	0.3	2.3	0.6	-1.6	-1.6	-1.6	-1.9	-1.9	-1.7	-1.8	1.0	1.5	-1.4
Chad	..	2.8	2.6	2.8	6.7	5.6	2.6	5.4	3.3	3.7	5.3	0.5	3.7	4.4
Comoros		2.3	4.8	4.1	3.5	2.7	1.8	1.5	-2.6	3.8	3.8	0.0	1.3	2.3
Congo, Dem. Rep. of	..	..	..	..	..	..	..	..	..	..	..	..	..	..
Congo, Rep. of	11.2	8.1	5.4	-14.1	32.2	11.0	-13.3	-12.2	-10.4	-4.2	-0.7	5.7	8.8	-1.5
Côte d'Ivoire	7.9	7.1	10.1	3.8	2.6	0.7	0.8	0.2	2.2	0.4	1.2	6.9	7.5	1.5
Djibouti	..	3.4	2.5	1.6	3.4	1.4	0.7	2.0	3.7	..	..	..	2.5	2.1
Equatorial Guinea	..	0.6	-8.5	-8.0	-0.4	-0.7	-0.9	-0.6	-0.1	-0.1	-0.3	..	-1.9	-1.4
Eritrea	..	0.1	4.7	1.2	1.2	4.2	3.7	8.8	8.7	13.6	10.2	..	1.6	6.5
Ethiopia	..	2.7	6.0	3.7	3.8	1.6	1.3	3.6	2.0	4.3	9.5	2.6	2.9	3.7
Gabon	..	-5.1	-3.2	-5.7	-3.1	-4.9	-6.2	-6.9	-2.7	-0.9	-1.5	..	1.6	-4.0
Gambia, The	0.0	2.0	0.7	2.9	6.6	4.1	1.2	0.6	-0.8	-1.4	0.7	1.3	4.3	1.7
Ghana	0.9	6.2	4.5	4.3	3.7	4.6	3.1	2.2	0.5	3.8	-1.6	0.7	3.6	2.6
Guinea	..	3.1	-0.3	1.7	1.2	4.1	1.8	2.4	1.5	4.1	1.8	..	2.9	2.3
Guinea-Bissau	0.0	14.0	9.9	3.3	9.0	20.8	7.8	-0.1	7.4	11.0	4.8	0.0	8.0	8.0
Kenya	0.3	1.2	-0.5	-0.7	0.1	-1.0	-1.1	-1.6	-2.8	1.4	-1.1	0.2	1.1	-0.9
Lesotho	..	9.8	8.1	9.4	11.6	11.3	6.8	4.8	7.3	7.1	6.5	-0.5	8.3	8.1
Liberia	..	..	..	..	..	..	..	..	..	..	..	..	..	..
Madagascar	5.6	2.9	1.7	1.9	5.0	3.8	1.9	1.2	2.7	2.1	3.6	4.1	3.0	2.8
Malawi	4.0	4.4	12.9	1.8	4.9	3.4	9.0	3.1	4.3	3.5	-0.1	4.8	4.8	3.7
Mali	15.2	3.4	7.8	7.4	6.1	3.4	3.8	3.8	3.0	3.4	4.1	20.5	6.8	4.4
Mauritania	..	23.5	6.8	2.7	3.4	0.1	-3.2	-2.0	-0.1	-1.2	-0.4	0.0	6.4	-0.1
Mauritius	5.7	-0.6	-0.2	-0.6	3.2	0.2	-0.3	-1.1	-0.5	-2.9	0.8	3.0	-0.5	-0.1
Mozambique	2.1	2.6	5.9	3.8	4.2	5.8	4.6	1.8	3.5	3.9	6.3	3.7	4.1	4.3
Namibia	..	0.6	0.4	0.7	0.8	1.0	0.7	-0.7	-0.5	-0.4	-0.3	0.0	0.1	0.2
Niger	..	-0.1	12.5	-0.6	4.1	3.5	4.3	..	..	..	..	5.4	4.2	2.8
Nigeria	0.5	-4.7	-3.7	-2.9	-2.1	1.4	-1.4	-5.6	-3.7	-3.9	-2.9	0.6	-1.4	-2.6
Rwanda	-0.3	3.0	-1.4	2.2	2.5	2.1	6.3	3.3	1.6	5.4	4.2	0.9	3.0	3.4
São Tomé and Principe	..	23.4	29.8	29.6	24.9	26.7	5.3	16.9	37.6	7.5	-8.1	..	18.0	17.5
Senegal	2.7	0.6	9.2	3.4	1.7	1.8	1.8	0.8	0.5	1.6	3.2	4.0	3.0	1.9
Seychelles	..	0.9	-1.5	-1.8	1.8	0.0	..	..	..	..	..	6.6	1.5	0.0
Sierra Leone	7.8	8.6	4.9	6.9	3.7	1.4	1.4	-1.2	6.1	42.0	8.7	5.0	1.0	8.6
Somalia	..	..	..	..	..	..	..	..	..	..	..	..	..	..
South Africa	-0.1	0.0	0.4	0.4	0.2	0.5	0.0	0.8	0.4	2.6	1.7	0.1	0.0	0.8
Sudan	..	17.3	1.6	0.7	0.3	0.2	0.2	0.3	0.4	0.2	0.3	..	9.5	0.3
Swaziland	..	-0.6	-0.9	0.0	0.3	0.5	2.1	-0.4	-0.5	0.7	1.5	..	-0.6	0.5
Tanzania	..	1.7	2.1	0.8	-1.1	-0.4	0.9	0.4	1.4	1.1	1.3	1.5	1.0	0.6
Togo	..	0.8	4.9	11.7	5.9	5.4	4.3	2.0	2.3	1.5	-0.1	..	4.4	4.1
Uganda	..	5.2	5.5	4.5	3.4	3.2	2.8	3.3	3.2	2.8	5.0	0.4	3.3	3.5
Zambia	..	6.4	4.1	4.1	2.3	..	..	..	-1.0	-1.1	0.0	..	4.4	0.8
Zimbabwe	0.4	2.0	0.5	0.2	0.2	0.3	-2.6	-1.1	-2.5	..	..	1.8	1.9	-0.9
NORTH AFRICA	..	0.1	1.9	2.0	0.8	0.1	-0.8	-1.4	-1.7	-0.4	-0.7	1.4	1.1	-0.3
Algeria	-0.1	1.7	8.3	7.6	4.1	2.3	-0.3	-2.3	-2.4	-1.3	-1.4	-0.1	1.1	0.8
Egypt, Arab Rep.	..	-1.0	-1.0	-1.1	-1.2	-1.2	-1.0	-1.2	-1.2	-0.9	-1.0	3.7	2.7	-1.1
Libya	..	..	..	..	..	..	..	..	..	..	..	..	..	..
Morocco	4.8	-0.7	-1.8	-0.8	-1.5	-1.9	-1.7	-2.0	-1.8	-1.4	-1.7	4.0	-2.9	-1.6
Tunisia	..	1.2	1.4	2.9	2.8	2.4	0.0	1.4	..	5.9	4.2	2.4	2.2	2.8
ALL AFRICA	..	0.9	2.0	1.2	1.0	0.7	-0.1	-0.4	-0.5	0.9	0.6	1.1	1.2	0.4

Note: 2002 data are preliminary. Nigeria: from 1992 accounts are for consolidated budget; since 1994, ratios are distorted as off. exch. rate used by the Gov. for oil exports oil value added is significantly over-valued.

7-9. Taxes on income and profits

	Percentage of total revenue											Annual average		
	1980	1993	1994	1995	1996	1997	1998	1999	2000	2001	2002	75-84	85-94	95-MR
SUB-SAHARAN AFRICA	..	33.2	33.5	33.7	34.3	36.1	41.7	40.6	41.6	42.0	42.4	41.7	36.5	39.1
excluding South Africa	..	19.7	21.8	22.3	22.5	24.5	27.0	25.0	27.1	27.3	27.8	..	21.3	25.4
excl. S.Africa & Nigeria	..	23.7	26.2	26.8	26.9	27.2	27.6	26.8	28.0	27.9	28.6	23.3	25.9	27.5
Angola	..	66.4	72.9	91.7	93.3	90.6	84.0	92.5	93.4	87.8	85.7	..	55.3	89.9
Benin	..	29.6	30.9	28.5	26.9	23.5	23.6	21.1	20.7	22.5	24.0	26.3	29.8	23.8
Botswana	..	48.0	54.8	57.2	52.6	58.2	59.4	55.1	63.4	65.6	64.7	12.1	35.8	59.5
Burkina Faso	..	18.9	18.7	23.4	24.7	21.9	20.2	22.7	28.0	24.6	23.8	19.7	19.7	23.7
Burundi	18.9	27.3	18.3	19.1	22.3	23.8	26.1	24.4	19.6	24.9	21.6	21.0	20.4	22.7
Cameroon	21.7	10.9	12.6	10.9	10.0	13.5	15.7	20.8	16.7	19.3	21.0	26.9	35.2	16.0
Cape Verde	..	22.2	25.1	24.4	29.4	24.8	25.7	24.6	29.5	36.2	37.4	29.5	22.8	29.0
Central African Republic	..	23.0	24.4	20.6	24.3	19.4	14.0	19.9	21.2	21.1	21.3	..	23.6	20.2
Chad	..	23.5	28.7	38.9	37.6	32.7	30.5	32.2	33.3	39.4	45.7	7.6	21.6	36.3
Comoros	..	9.0	12.4	12.2	9.6	11.2	14.7	17.3	17.2	10.8	18.5	0.0	12.7	13.9
Congo, Dem. Rep. of	..	..	..	..	17.2	25.0	29.9	17.5	26.0	23.6	26.6	..	..	23.7
Congo, Rep. of	..	51.3	67.7	49.1	61.0	78.7	53.6	72.1	78.0	70.5	70.9	15.1	43.2	66.7
Côte d'Ivoire	..	19.4	14.9	18.3	20.5	22.9	23.6	25.3	27.1	24.4	23.3	15.8	19.0	23.2
Djibouti	..	38.7	38.5	37.2	41.0	39.2	39.2	37.4	39.8	38.6	37.5	..	38.7	38.7
Equatorial Guinea	..	..	19.6	20.5	52.9	61.7	76.6	77.4	83.4	87.1	88.3	..	19.6	68.5
Eritrea	..	20.1	31.9	25.2	27.4	22.1	30.3	27.4	22.5	28.8	24.1	..	21.7	26.0
Ethiopia	24.3	23.1	24.0	22.2	25.2	24.1	22.3	21.1	23.6	25.9	29.8	24.8	28.2	24.3
Gabon	..	12.8	10.7	10.5	10.6	10.1	13.0	17.0	13.7	14.1	14.0	..	15.9	12.9
Gambia, The	..	16.2	17.7	19.4	19.9	21.1	22.3	23.0	22.5	25.3	26.5	14.2	14.4	22.5
Ghana	..	14.8	17.5	17.4	21.7	24.8	24.0	27.3	29.3	30.8	31.7	18.7	19.9	25.9
Guinea	..	6.9	8.8	9.1	10.9	9.7	9.7	11.2	9.8	11.6	12.4	..	3.9	10.6
Guinea-Bissau	..	7.2	6.7	7.9	7.8	8.3	15.2	5.7	4.0	7.8	9.0	21.9	8.3	8.2
Kenya	27.8	31.7	35.2	34.9	33.3	32.4	31.3	17.0	28.4	20.9	24.7	27.0	30.6	27.9
Lesotho	..	14.3	15.3	16.3	15.1	15.0	17.1	18.1	17.9	20.1	21.6	14.2	13.1	17.6
Liberia	..	..	..	..	..	..	..	..	..	..	..	..	..	..
Madagascar	..	14.9	18.8	14.2	16.9	18.9	15.7	14.9	15.2	19.6	23.1	15.3	12.8	17.3
Malawi	83.8	32.9	32.3	31.7	40.3	38.0	40.7	40.0	41.5	42.1	39.8	83.4	57.0	39.3
Mali	15.2	13.1	15.2	18.4	18.5	18.0	21.0	16.0	17.2	21.9	19.9	17.4	13.2	18.9
Mauritania	..	24.8	24.5	25.3	17.3	19.2	18.5	18.3	18.6	22.1	12.1	..	26.6	18.9
Mauritius	19.2	19.3	17.7	20.3	22.7	19.9	19.2	18.4	17.5	19.4	19.6	25.4	17.7	19.6
Mozambique	12.4	14.3	17.3	16.6	18.2	19.0	18.1	14.0	13.7	16.0	17.5	15.5	18.9	16.6
Namibia	..	31.1	29.0	27.4	28.8	34.1	33.8	32.5	32.0	35.9	38.7	18.1	31.2	32.9
Niger	..	33.7	30.0	30.5	25.4	21.1	21.8	24.0	20.0	23.0	22.1	22.0	27.9	23.5
Nigeria	..	..	..	..	..	10.0	23.9	15.6	22.5	24.2	23.5	..	..	20.0
Rwanda	..	24.8	25.8	12.5	26.2	25.1	27.7	24.8	27.0	28.4	30.1	26.0	24.7	25.2
São Tomé and Principe	..	8.9	10.7	14.1	21.1	29.3	16.4	18.5	20.9	26.7	30.1	..	9.7	22.1
Senegal	26.2	23.4	21.1	21.9	21.6	21.8	23.3	21.2	22.9	21.7	21.4	25.7	23.5	22.0
Seychelles	..	26.8	29.6	27.2	18.6	17.8	18.9	22.1	25.7	26.3	25.9	22.6	20.9	22.8
Sierra Leone	..	21.7	21.4	15.9	17.0	13.2	17.9	35.7	29.3	32.0	32.2	..	24.4	24.1
Somalia	..	..	..	..	..	..	..	..	..	..	..	..	..	..
South Africa	58.2	48.2	46.6	46.5	48.0	49.8	58.8	58.7	58.5	59.2	59.4	59.2	52.5	54.9
Sudan	..	2.9	26.4	28.7	28.3	20.4	19.9	17.6	11.5	11.2	8.8	..	17.6	18.3
Swaziland	..	33.5	32.1	28.1	28.5	26.8	26.1	27.2	25.6	24.5	24.7	..	33.0	26.4
Tanzania	..	30.9	31.2	41.1	37.4	34.7	39.6	34.3	37.8	29.6	30.7	33.6	29.6	35.6
Togo	..	30.9	40.1	41.4	30.5	22.6	22.3	25.6	23.1	19.1	21.3	35.0	33.5	25.7
Uganda	..	14.5	14.6	14.7	13.2	14.0	15.6	17.9	18.0	20.7	22.6	6.7	10.1	17.1
Zambia	..	28.6	28.7	28.9	30.0	32.0	35.2	36.5	32.5	38.0	42.7	..	27.8	34.5
Zimbabwe	0.0	48.7	47.7	45.9	45.7	47.6	48.0	48.9	50.4	48.2	47.6	8.6	46.1	47.8
NORTH AFRICA	..	19.1	19.8	19.7	20.2	20.8	22.6	20.6	21.4	20.4	20.9	..	18.9	20.8
Algeria	11.0	10.9	9.9	8.9	8.2	8.8	11.4	7.6	5.2	4.7	4.9	12.0	15.1	7.5
Egypt, Arab Rep.	..	23.8	22.9	21.8	22.5	22.6	22.5	21.2	24.6	25.4	24.9	..	20.7	23.2
Libya	..	..	..	..	..	..	..	..	..	..	..	..	..	..
Morocco	22.8	23.2	22.5	24.0	25.5	25.8	30.5	28.6	28.9	23.3	26.7	22.7	23.8	26.7
Tunisia	16.1	17.2	31.0	33.3	35.1	38.1	38.9	38.7	40.5	40.4	39.4	15.6	16.4	38.1
ALL AFRICA	..	28.3	28.7	28.8	29.5	30.9	35.1	33.7	34.7	34.6	35.0	34.4	30.7	32.8

Note: 2002 data are preliminary (see page 2). Total revenue does not include grants. Nigeria's fiscal data are for consolidated government starting from 1992.

7-10. Taxes on international trade and transactions

	1980	1993	1994	1995	1996	1997	1998	1999	2000	2001	2002	75-84	85-94	95-MR
		Percentage of total revenue										*Annual average*		
SUB-SAHARAN AFRICA	..	10.6	12.5	13.2	13.9	14.4	14.8	13.9	13.1	13.6	13.6	8.2	10.9	13.8
excluding South Africa	..	17.5	20.9	22.1	22.8	23.8	24.6	22.9	21.1	22.2	22.3	..	17.3	22.7
excl. S.Africa & Nigeria	..	21.1	25.1	26.6	27.2	26.2	26.6	25.6	24.1	24.8	24.8	16.0	21.0	25.7
Angola	..	6.5	4.6	4.9	4.3	4.8	7.0	2.8	2.7	4.9	5.5	..	4.2	4.6
Benin	..	50.8	39.6	40.6	40.9	45.5	43.3	45.5	47.6	47.4	45.8	52.7	59.2	44.6
Botswana	..	..	..	..	..	..	..	..	..	..	..	22.3	13.3	..
Burkina Faso	..	36.4	54.0	48.4	28.2	27.6	25.7	23.4	17.4	17.2	16.3	35.3	42.7	25.5
Burundi	30.5	21.0	26.6	25.4	15.5	17.5	25.8	21.7	22.3	21.8	15.2	22.5	25.6	20.7
Cameroon	..	16.6	18.3	19.5	19.3	17.0	17.1	16.5	12.9	13.0	12.5	..	17.0	16.0
Cape Verde	..	41.2	40.5	41.6	45.7	36.2	41.1	34.7	47.9	45.8	43.3	..	43.5	42.0
Central African Republic	..	33.0	32.5	42.5	38.7	38.1	44.7	38.0	38.4	35.8	36.2	..	35.5	39.0
Chad	..	13.6	19.4	27.1	31.1	30.3	36.0	29.5	29.9	35.7	32.1	..	20.8	31.5
Comoros	..	36.6	36.0	32.3	35.2	43.1	33.2	31.7	57.8	53.9	49.4	..	38.9	42.1
Congo, Dem. Rep. of	..	..	..	..	24.6	23.2	25.0	16.9	32.8	34.4	35.9	..	..	27.6
Congo, Rep. of	..	20.0	13.9	19.2	16.3	9.1	13.4	5.6	5.2	6.9	6.7	0.0	11.0	10.3
Côte d'Ivoire	..	26.3	39.0	38.9	39.6	36.5	34.4	34.4	31.6	33.9	36.4	..	31.9	36.2
Djibouti	..	22.0	24.7	24.7	22.2	21.3	37.6	40.7	39.7	38.9	37.5	..	22.1	32.8
Equatorial Guinea	..	..	26.9	30.8	19.0	18.8	8.0	8.2	5.3	3.8	3.2	..	26.9	12.1
Eritrea	..	21.8	20.1	16.7	19.5	14.8	15.8	13.9	12.9	20.6	26.9	..	22.5	17.6
Ethiopia	34.7	22.6	32.9	27.4	26.0	27.4	26.7	24.2	25.5	31.4	31.6	33.5	19.6	27.5
Gabon	..	21.1	16.0	17.6	19.6	17.7	19.6	25.6	20.1	20.8	24.1	..	19.4	20.6
Gambia, The	..	44.3	37.6	49.4	61.8	0.0	0.0	56.3	57.6	53.5	49.7	..	50.1	41.0
Ghana	..	16.3	28.2	22.7	27.3	25.8	27.5	23.3	20.5	22.7	22.7	..	29.7	24.1
Guinea	..	14.6	15.7	14.4	14.1	15.5	14.5	15.6	20.0	17.0	18.2	..	9.9	16.2
Guinea-Bissau	..	11.8	12.7	19.5	14.1	36.7	34.8	44.3	26.6	33.6	40.7	..	11.4	31.3
Kenya	16.0	12.3	14.6	30.6	30.3	30.8	30.0	17.6	29.8	21.4	23.7	18.0	12.5	26.8
Lesotho	..	57.2	58.6	54.8	50.4	51.6	48.8	50.3	44.8	49.5	49.2	57.9	55.9	49.9
Liberia	..	..	..	..	..	..	..	..	..	..	..	..	..	..
Madagascar	..	38.6	41.9	53.7	49.3	54.3	55.3	55.5	51.9	47.9	43.4	26.9	39.2	51.4
Malawi	..	15.5	19.9	25.3	22.9	21.9	16.1	14.1	12.9	10.7	10.2	..	27.7	16.8
Mali	51.6	45.3	44.4	46.1	45.8	48.7	52.9	49.3	51.1	48.3	44.9	46.8	33.6	48.4
Mauritania	..	33.7	32.4	22.5	16.5	12.0	10.9	9.6	9.6	12.0	6.2	..	32.7	12.4
Mauritius	52.0	45.6	41.8	38.8	38.8	33.9	33.7	28.2	29.7	28.2	22.7	46.2	49.8	31.8
Mozambique	18.5	25.5	21.8	24.0	19.9	17.6	17.6	16.9	17.0	15.6	15.4	11.7	18.2	18.0
Namibia	..	..	..	..	..	..	..	..	..	..	..	..	..	..
Niger	..	41.3	41.5	43.2	46.7	47.7	50.9	46.8	49.3	48.6	48.5	36.9	37.0	47.7
Nigeria	..	..	..	..	..	11.6	14.0	9.3	5.9	8.4	9.3	..	..	9.8
Rwanda	..	27.8	35.8	38.5	29.2	31.8	23.9	17.3	16.9	16.2	16.5	54.7	37.8	23.8
São Tomé and Principe	..	28.2	30.8	24.1	25.5	21.0	18.6	31.0	22.7	21.7	21.0	..	28.5	23.2
Senegal	..	27.6	26.3	26.5	29.4	25.2	24.1	21.0	12.9	17.8	17.6	..	27.0	21.8
Seychelles	..	37.7	30.5	41.6	43.8	44.6	48.3	42.5	25.0	24.6	25.7	..	44.9	37.0
Sierra Leone	..	39.2	38.1	45.7	48.7	39.4	54.7	66.0	54.0	55.4	50.7	..	42.7	51.8
Somalia	..	..	..	..	..	..	..	..	..	..	..	..	..	..
South Africa	12.9	2.9	3.0	3.2	3.6	3.4	3.4	3.4	3.7	3.6	3.5	5.8	4.1	3.5
Sudan	..	2.8	26.3	29.0	43.9	39.1	44.2	41.0	21.3	19.5	23.6	..	14.6	32.7
Swaziland	..	..	..	..	..	..	..	..	..	..	..	..	..	..
Tanzania	..	14.2	15.7	27.6	27.0	30.5	29.2	31.7	28.5	39.1	38.6	17.4	18.7	31.5
Togo	..	35.3	40.8	37.4	40.7	37.4	42.6	41.9	42.5	44.2	41.9	35.2	36.2	41.1
Uganda	..	50.8	53.0	48.6	50.6	51.4	47.7	44.1	42.9	43.0	38.2	58.1	54.4	45.8
Zambia	..	33.3	30.8	27.4	29.7	28.2	25.2	25.5	30.6	33.0	28.8	..	31.5	28.5
Zimbabwe	..	..	..	..	..	..	..	14.0	9.7	13.2	14.2	..	..	12.8
NORTH AFRICA	..	12.4	13.1	13.9	12.7	11.6	12.0	12.2	10.1	9.8	10.3	..	12.8	11.6
Algeria	4.8	9.4	11.0	12.2	10.2	7.9	9.7	8.5	5.5	7.5	8.6	6.0	7.4	8.8
Egypt, Arab Rep.	..	10.7	11.6	12.6	13.0	12.6	13.1	15.1	11.8	12.0	11.7	..	12.8	12.7
Libya	..	..	..	..	..	..	..	..	..	..	..	..	..	..
Morocco	22.8	19.0	17.7	17.6	15.2	14.9	13.6	13.5	13.8	10.8	11.9	27.4	18.1	13.9
Tunisia	10.2	14.9	15.6	16.0	13.5	12.4	11.4	10.2	9.9	6.8	6.9	12.9	15.6	10.9
ALL AFRICA	..	11.2	12.7	13.4	13.5	13.4	13.8	13.3	12.1	12.3	12.5	9.1	11.4	13.0

Note: 2002 data are preliminary (see page 2). Total revenue does not include grants. Nigeria's fiscal data are for consolidated government starting from 1992.

7-11. Indirect taxes

	1980	1993	1994	1995	1996	1997	1998	1999	2000	2001	2002	75-84	85-94	95-MR
					Percentage of total revenue								*Annual average*	
SUB-SAHARAN AFRICA	..	41.0	43.3	56.1	42.5	62.0	46.5	44.5	44.0	44.5	44.5	43.9	41.7	48.1
excluding South Africa	..	43.3	46.7	71.3	46.2	83.2	52.8	49.2	47.9	49.1	49.2	..	45.1	56.1
excl. S.Africa & Nigeria	..	52.0	56.1	85.7	55.1	96.0	57.2	55.5	55.2	55.9	56.0	55.7	54.9	64.6
Angola	..	31.9	25.5	7.3	6.2	8.6	14.7	6.9	6.2	11.5	13.2	..	24.5	9.3
Benin	..	72.0	55.6	54.3	56.0	63.8	63.1	64.4	67.2	65.5	64.8	67.4	77.1	62.4
Botswana	..	24.7	22.4	20.5	18.6	18.2	20.6	23.2	21.1	19.7	19.2	70.8	41.3	20.1
Burkina Faso	..	51.2	71.2	66.8	65.6	67.4	69.7	68.3	61.9	66.2	66.5	61.9	62.6	66.6
Burundi	53.8	59.6	64.4	63.3	50.4	60.7	61.6	64.9	68.1	58.1	67.7	50.3	60.3	61.9
Cameroon	61.6	52.7	59.5	61.0	58.9	79.1	76.4	72.9	77.8	76.4	75.4	40.4	45.6	72.2
Cape Verde	..	47.3	45.9	46.6	51.8	40.4	46.6	38.5	59.3	53.2	51.7	45.4	49.0	48.5
Central African Republic	..	70.4	66.4	75.1	74.8	74.8	75.2	68.1	68.9	65.9	67.0	..	69.6	71.2
Chad	..	54.0	67.5	49.7	49.7	55.0	54.9	49.7	60.3	63.7	53.2	71.0	66.3	54.5
Comoros	..	78.5	76.3	74.0	78.1	82.1	70.7	69.7	71.1	63.9	58.7	62.7	69.8	71.0
Congo, Dem. Rep. of	..	..	..	..	45.5	45.5	51.6	39.3	48.6	49.2	65.7	..	..	49.3
Congo, Rep. of	..	45.7	30.7	41.7	35.7	20.1	43.5	25.5	20.5	27.1	27.4	13.8	38.4	30.2
Côte d'Ivoire	..	64.6	65.2	63.0	64.0	60.9	58.6	65.0	60.3	63.0	63.5	48.6	60.0	62.3
Djibouti	..	55.9	56.6	55.7	51.5	50.5	48.3	54.8	54.5	53.2	51.4	..	56.0	52.5
Equatorial Guinea	..	..	61.2	62.4	35.1	32.2	19.4	18.1	11.2	8.2	6.7	..	61.2	24.2
Eritrea	..	37.9	34.5	27.9	32.5	25.3	27.5	26.4	24.1	35.5	43.0	..	40.1	30.3
Ethiopia	58.6	46.0	54.1	43.4	42.6	43.8	40.8	36.8	39.9	44.4	45.9	54.0	42.2	42.2
Gabon	..	37.0	26.7	26.1	25.3	24.2	27.5	37.2	30.1	30.2	30.6	..	45.3	28.9
Gambia, The	..	74.0	70.7	70.6	71.2	68.3	68.1	65.1	64.9	60.9	60.1	75.9	77.2	66.1
Ghana	..	53.7	68.7	54.5	63.9	59.9	62.2	63.5	62.5	64.2	65.4	63.8	63.7	62.0
Guinea	..	86.2	84.1	84.6	82.6	83.5	83.7	82.5	81.2	78.9	78.2	..	89.4	81.9
Guinea-Bissau	..	41.3	48.5	46.8	47.0	43.8	53.0	24.1	49.8	50.9	46.6	..	44.9	45.2
Kenya	56.3	55.2	53.5	50.3	50.0	50.8	49.4	29.7	51.2	40.2	46.2	57.9	54.8	46.0
Lesotho	..	72.9	72.7	68.6	62.9	64.0	61.4	62.7	57.8	62.5	63.4	63.6	74.7	62.9
Liberia	..	..	..	..	..	..	..	..	..	..	..	..	..	..
Madagascar	..	60.6	68.9	80.8	73.3	75.4	74.3	80.3	80.3	76.3	72.8	50.6	62.1	76.7
Malawi	0.0	46.4	55.5	56.5	52.2	54.5	50.2	46.9	50.2	49.2	48.0	0.0	26.1	51.0
Mali	71.7	66.9	68.0	64.6	65.3	66.9	74.7	74.1	78.1	74.3	71.3	67.3	55.4	71.2
Mauritania	..	45.3	48.1	45.8	41.3	38.9	39.2	38.2	38.4	47.7	25.7	..	48.3	39.4
Mauritius	69.2	71.4	71.2	65.7	68.3	65.4	66.6	66.0	70.8	70.3	66.6	63.4	72.5	67.5
Mozambique	65.7	76.7	71.3	74.7	73.6	72.6	74.7	78.4	77.4	72.7	70.6	53.8	64.9	74.3
Namibia	..	62.1	58.9	61.7	60.5	56.8	56.6	59.0	60.3	56.3	52.0	72.2	56.9	57.9
Niger	..	56.1	59.1	60.9	61.4	64.9	64.9	67.8	66.7	68.0	67.8	65.3	54.6	65.3
Nigeria	..	..	..	..	..	17.0	30.0	16.6	10.2	13.7	14.2	..	..	17.0
Rwanda	..	67.5	73.5	81.4	65.8	69.5	67.1	70.1	68.2	63.8	63.3	86.9	75.1	68.7
São Tomé and Principe	..	63.4	64.5	45.1	46.0	38.6	35.7	65.2	60.0	59.8	53.7	..	49.2	50.5
Senegal	67.7	73.0	67.8	68.3	72.1	71.0	72.1	75.7	72.7	74.0	73.2	67.8	61.7	72.4
Seychelles	..	56.7	48.7	44.0	46.7	48.9	53.1	46.3	49.4	50.4	49.0	49.1	54.0	48.5
Sierra Leone	..	69.0	70.7	76.9	78.4	73.2	76.8	91.3	73.8	85.0	85.6	..	73.9	80.1
Somalia	..	..	..	..	..	..	..	..	..	..	..	..	..	..
South Africa	103.6	38.5	39.5	39.1	38.1	37.4	39.1	38.9	39.6	39.2	38.9	39.0	38.1	38.8
Sudan	..	5.0	45.3	50.3	56.3	62.1	60.7	57.0	31.8	39.8	36.6	..	37.6	49.3
Swaziland	..	60.2	63.8	68.9	68.0	67.1	65.8	65.8	69.0	69.2	70.1	..	59.7	68.0
Tanzania	..	35.0	37.8	49.5	48.2	55.2	51.9	55.1	51.8	59.4	59.3	59.6	51.9	53.8
Togo	..	49.8	50.4	50.0	57.2	53.4	63.3	65.7	67.0	65.8	64.5	43.4	48.3	60.9
Uganda	..	77.5	78.5	77.7	80.7	80.1	78.5	75.5	73.9	74.4	69.5	86.8	81.4	76.3
Zambia	..	68.0	64.4	62.7	62.1	62.6	61.5	61.0	56.6	58.7	55.1	..	66.1	60.0
Zimbabwe	0.0	39.1	40.3	42.7	44.6	44.2	44.6	42.7	43.3	45.9	46.5	9.2	42.4	44.3
NORTH AFRICA	..	41.3	41.2	43.3	41.2	40.8	42.2	42.0	38.2	58.7	60.9	..	42.3	45.9
Algeria	25.3	28.5	27.7	29.9	27.0	25.1	31.2	25.6	16.9	90.3	90.1	29.6	32.0	42.0
Egypt, Arab Rep.	..	34.7	36.8	39.7	40.3	40.2	42.2	44.4	41.1	43.0	43.1	..	34.1	41.7
Libya	..	..	..	..	..	..	..	..	..	..	..	..	..	..
Morocco	66.8	64.2	65.4	66.5	60.9	60.5	54.4	57.2	57.8	46.6	56.9	63.7	67.0	57.6
Tunisia	42.3	58.2	49.1	50.2	47.4	49.9	50.5	50.7	50.5	50.0	51.0	42.6	54.7	50.0
ALL AFRICA	..	41.1	42.6	51.6	42.0	54.7	45.0	43.6	42.0	49.4	50.1	44.4	42.1	47.3

Note: 2002 data are preliminary (see page 2). Total revenue does not include grants. Nigeria's fiscal data are for consolidated government starting from 1992.

7-12. Nontax revenue (excluding grants)

				Percentage of total revenue								*Annual average*		
	1980	1993	1994	1995	1996	1997	1998	1999	2000	2001	2002	75-84	85-94	95-MR
SUB-SAHARAN AFRICA	..	12.7	12.8	14.0	13.6	19.5	11.6	13.7	14.6	13.1	12.5	13.2	11.2	14.1
excluding South Africa	..	12.6	12.0	14.1	13.6	25.5	19.8	23.5	25.4	23.0	21.8	..	13.8	20.8
excl. S.Africa & Nigeria	..	15.2	14.5	16.9	16.3	16.4	14.8	14.9	17.5	16.1	14.0	19.5	16.7	15.9
Angola	..	1.8	1.6	1.0	0.5	0.8	1.4	0.6	0.4	0.8	1.1	..	20.1	0.8
Benin	..	18.1	13.7	17.6	17.0	12.7	13.4	14.5	12.1	12.1	11.2	6.3	27.2	13.8
Botswana	..	27.2	22.8	22.2	28.7	23.6	20.0	21.7	15.5	14.7	16.1	17.0	22.9	20.3
Burkina Faso	..	26.8	8.3	8.4	6.9	7.7	7.2	6.7	7.5	6.4	7.1	19.9	16.3	7.2
Burundi	6.7	33.0	9.4	11.6	14.7	17.1	8.5	4.7	4.7	13.8	9.0	8.5	20.0	10.5
Cameroon	16.7	10.5	7.5	8.2	9.3	7.4	7.9	6.3	5.6	4.4	3.6	32.7	14.6	6.6
Cape Verde	..	58.9	60.6	37.5	27.6	8.8	26.9	11.9	11.2	10.6	10.9	25.1	83.5	18.2
Central African Republic	..	6.6	9.2	4.3	0.9	5.7	10.7	12.0	9.9	12.9	11.7	..	6.8	8.5
Chad	..	35.2	59.4	43.7	39.8	21.9	31.4	19.7	16.3	17.2	11.7	21.4	26.3	25.2
Comoros	..	12.6	11.3	13.7	12.3	6.7	14.6	13.0	11.7	12.5	12.6	0.0	19.6	12.2
Congo, Dem. Rep. of	..	..	..	..	37.3	29.5	18.5	43.2	25.4	27.2	7.7	..	..	27.0
Congo, Rep. of	..	2.9	6.3	9.2	3.2	1.2	2.9	2.4	1.4	2.4	1.8	68.5	18.5	3.1
Côte d'Ivoire	..	16.0	19.9	21.8	18.8	19.5	21.4	12.8	14.4	13.8	16.5	33.6	20.4	17.4
Djibouti	..	5.4	5.0	7.2	7.5	10.4	..	..	..	..	..	..	5.4	8.3
Equatorial Guinea	..	..	19.2	21.4	12.0	6.0	4.1	5.5	5.8	5.1	5.0	..	19.2	8.1
Eritrea	..	42.1	33.6	46.8	40.0	52.6	35.4	31.6	38.1	26.8	31.6	..	38.3	37.9
Ethiopia	17.2	30.9	21.9	34.4	32.2	27.6	33.1	33.7	29.9	25.9	23.7	21.2	29.7	30.1
Gabon	..	4.8	3.1	2.9	4.6	4.3	6.7	4.6	56.1	55.7	..	..	4.4	19.3
Gambia, The	..	18.6	16.4	9.8	8.9	10.6	9.7	12.0	12.6	13.7	13.4	9.5	29.1	11.3
Ghana	..	31.5	13.8	28.2	14.4	15.2	13.8	9.2	8.2	5.0	2.9	17.5	16.4	12.1
Guinea	..	6.8	7.1	6.3	6.5	6.8	6.6	6.3	9.0	9.4	9.3	..	6.7	7.5
Guinea-Bissau	..	65.6	50.6	98.5	53.7	85.8	90.9	75.9	94.8	77.2	52.9	248.0	105.7	78.7
Kenya	15.3	13.1	11.4	14.8	16.7	16.9	19.3	12.5	13.4	10.5	16.0	14.7	14.1	15.0
Lesotho	..	12.9	12.0	15.2	22.0	20.9	21.5	19.2	24.3	17.4	15.0	21.9	12.7	19.5
Liberia	..	..	..	..	..	..	..	..	..	..	..	..	..	..
Madagascar	..	21.0	15.5	7.5	17.2	49.0	15.6	17.6	16.4	18.2	14.5	13.4	17.5	19.5
Malawi	16.2	20.7	12.2	11.7	7.5	7.5	9.0	13.1	8.2	8.7	12.2	16.6	17.0	9.8
Mali	12.9	20.1	15.4	16.2	16.1	14.5	4.3	9.9	4.8	3.8	8.8	15.0	31.2	9.8
Mauritania	..	27.9	25.9	24.0	38.9	39.6	39.4	41.8	43.1	30.2	62.2	..	20.4	39.9
Mauritius	11.5	9.3	9.9	11.5	5.4	14.7	14.2	13.2	9.5	10.3	13.8	11.2	9.7	11.6
Mozambique	21.8	8.9	11.4	8.7	8.2	8.4	7.1	7.6	8.9	11.3	11.8	30.7	16.2	9.0
Namibia	..	6.8	12.1	10.8	10.6	9.1	9.5	8.5	7.7	8.1	9.3	9.7	11.9	9.2
Niger	..	47.8	46.3	30.1	41.2	34.0	37.1	19.2	24.9	24.0	21.8	12.7	28.8	29.0
Nigeria	..	..	..	..	..	73.0	46.1	67.8	66.3	58.4	62.2	..	..	62.3
Rwanda	..	77.8	25.7	172.1	87.7	70.5	55.1	63.1	103.8	79.6	76.5	12.5	35.0	88.5
São Tomé and Principe	..	27.7	31.2	63.9	43.7	38.6	25.4	39.0	25.7	13.5	16.3	..	76.4	33.2
Senegal	6.0	3.6	11.2	9.8	6.3	7.2	4.6	3.1	4.4	4.3	5.3	6.5	14.9	5.6
Seychelles	..	8.6	21.7	28.7	34.6	33.3	27.9	31.6	24.9	23.2	25.1	28.3	20.8	28.7
Sierra Leone	..	9.3	7.9	7.2	21.9	23.9	39.0	78.3	75.1	38.9	64.6	..	1.7	43.6
Somalia	..	..	..	..	..	..	..	..	..	..	..	..	..	..
South Africa	44.3	12.8	13.6	13.9	13.6	12.6	2.1	2.4	1.7	1.7	1.6	14.7	8.5	6.2
Sudan	..	1.9	25.6	21.0	15.4	24.2	19.4	26.0	51.8	48.4	51.2	..	25.2	32.2
Swaziland	..	6.3	4.1	3.0	3.5	6.1	8.0	7.0	5.5	6.3	5.2	..	7.3	5.6
Tanzania	..	8.0	6.9	9.5	14.4	10.1	8.6	10.6	10.4	11.0	10.0	6.8	8.2	10.6
Togo	..	17.4	8.3	7.7	11.0	8.4	9.1	8.5	9.9	15.1	14.2	22.2	17.8	10.5
Uganda	..	8.0	6.9	7.7	6.1	5.9	5.9	6.6	8.1	4.9	7.8	6.6	8.5	6.6
Zambia	..	3.4	6.8	8.4	8.0	5.4	3.4	2.6	1.1	2.4	2.1	..	6.1	4.2
Zimbabwe	0.0	12.2	12.0	11.4	9.7	8.2	7.4	4.9	6.3	5.9	..	2.2	11.5	7.7
NORTH AFRICA	..	19.6	18.9	17.2	17.6	16.9	16.3	15.5	13.7	14.2	14.3	..	17.8	15.7
Algeria	2.6	2.8	3.1	1.5	1.8	2.2	2.4	4.6	1.0	4.4	4.4	6.0	7.5	2.8
Egypt, Arab Rep.	..	35.0	34.3	33.5	32.0	31.4	29.3	26.1	25.2	26.0	26.6	..	30.0	28.8
Libya	..	..	..	..	..	..	..	..	..	..	..	..	..	..
Morocco	10.4	12.6	12.1	9.5	13.6	13.7	15.1	14.2	13.3	9.1	8.5	11.6	9.2	12.1
Tunisia	24.8	23.8	19.8	16.4	17.2	11.8	10.5	10.5	8.9	8.5	8.8	25.8	23.9	11.6
ALL AFRICA	..	15.1	14.9	15.1	15.0	18.6	13.2	14.3	14.3	13.5	13.1	13.2	13.3	14.6

Note: 2002 data are preliminary (see page 2). Nigeria's fiscal data are for consolidated government starting from 1992.

7-13. Government expenditure: wages and salaries

	Percentage of total expenditure and lending minus repayments											*Annual average*		
	1980	*1993*	*1994*	*1995*	*1996*	*1997*	*1998*	*1999*	*2000*	*2001*	*2002*	*75-84*	*85-94*	*95-MR*
SUB-SAHARAN AFRICA	..	29.4	27.1	27.4	27.0	27.6	31.2	31.3	30.6	30.2	30.7	20.8	20.7	29.5
excluding South Africa	..	25.1	21.1	21.6	21.8	22.7	22.8	23.4	22.9	23.0	24.2	..	22.7	22.8
excl. S.Africa & Nigeria	..	25.1	23.2	23.5	23.4	25.4	25.6	25.8	24.1	25.1	25.8	19.6	22.9	24.8
Angola	..	21.5	8.7	11.1	10.8	15.6	21.0	5.0	9.6	15.4	21.9	..	38.1	13.8
Benin	..	35.5	27.8	24.3	26.4	26.5	28.7	25.6	23.2	22.9	23.7	..	34.7	25.2
Botswana	..	..	23.6	26.1	23.3	22.6	23.1	23.7	23.4	22.9	22.3	..	23.6	23.4
Burkina Faso	..	29.0	26.2	24.9	23.4	20.9	19.7	18.8	20.8	21.5	21.4	..	31.3	21.4
Burundi	49.1	23.7	30.0	28.0	28.7	32.2	29.3	26.0	27.7	28.0	33.0	49.0	26.6	29.1
Cameroon	31.4	43.7	31.4	29.1	25.8	26.5	27.7	26.9	28.9	29.5	32.9	24.8	34.0	28.4
Cape Verde	..	22.1	19.2	20.2	24.1	23.8	25.4	24.1	21.9	29.5	29.6	0.0	20.1	24.8
Central African Republic	..	29.5	24.2	22.5	41.8	32.6	24.2	23.3	21.1	20.4	19.2	..	27.7	25.6
Chad	..	27.1	28.0	28.6	20.3	19.4	20.6	19.0	19.7	20.1	17.6	..	20.7	20.6
Comoros	..	30.8	23.2	28.6	35.4	37.0	34.1	32.6	35.4	36.2	30.0	0.0	17.3	33.6
Congo, Dem. Rep. of	..	..	..	..	6.8	35.6	43.8	42.1	22.2	20.4	19.8	..	..	27.3
Congo, Rep. of	..	48.8	36.3	32.1	21.2	20.5	20.8	21.2	18.3	18.3	16.1	0.0	37.3	21.0
Côte d'Ivoire	..	35.6	28.6	25.8	27.9	27.0	26.0	28.3	32.6	37.0	32.9	..	30.9	29.7
Djibouti	..	48.0	56.4	61.6	60.3	62.2	49.3	47.1	46.1	44.3	43.3	..	50.3	51.8
Equatorial Guinea	..	10.8	16.4	17.9	17.3	15.3	11.3	17.6	15.6	21.9	21.5	..	13.7	17.3
Eritrea	..	15.0	22.7	24.0	29.0	27.3	19.9	17.5	21.6	20.2	23.2	..	18.8	22.8
Ethiopia	26.1	28.3	24.8	22.6	20.6	22.2	21.3	19.7	20.4	22.3	21.4	25.8	25.3	21.3
Gabon	..	34.0	27.9	27.4	27.3	21.4	16.1	29.8	25.8	26.4	27.3	16.2	28.7	25.2
Gambia, The	..	21.1	23.3	21.8	20.3	24.0	27.5	27.0	28.6	21.6	21.1	..	20.1	24.0
Ghana	..	20.2	18.3	18.3	18.2	18.4	19.4	21.5	18.9	18.6	32.5	17.6	23.7	20.7
Guinea	..	24.2	25.1	23.9	27.1	23.9	28.4	25.2	15.7	19.0	18.4	..	19.3	22.7
Guinea-Bissau	..	8.1	7.5	9.2	9.5	9.4	18.8	19.3	16.3	17.9	22.0	10.4	10.9	15.3
Kenya	16.8	23.7	25.8	31.4	30.7	28.7	32.0	32.0	37.3	29.3	33.7	19.2	23.6	31.9
Lesotho	..	29.6	31.4	31.2	29.8	30.5	33.5	26.6	30.3	33.5	31.1	32.1	29.8	30.8
Liberia	..	..	..	..	..	..	..	..	..	..	..	..	..	..
Madagascar	..	17.0	16.4	18.8	14.5	21.3	20.4	24.0	21.9	24.4	29.3	40.5	27.5	21.8
Malawi	14.3	21.6	18.3	22.7	19.6	23.5	17.4	16.7	15.9	17.4	20.9	16.4	17.5	19.2
Mali	16.5	23.0	16.7	16.6	16.1	16.4	15.9	15.8	17.6	17.2	16.1	19.8	23.1	16.5
Mauritania	..	15.4	19.0	20.3	20.3	21.2	19.3	18.6	16.1	18.6	15.4	..	17.6	18.7
Mauritius	28.1	28.9	31.7	32.2	29.1	26.1	29.4	30.0	27.9	27.4	26.3	29.0	29.5	28.5
Mozambique	25.8	10.4	7.9	9.6	10.8	15.4	20.5	23.0	24.6	20.0	21.5	19.2	11.0	18.2
Namibia	..	..	..	..	..	..	..	..	..	..	..	..	..	..
Niger	..	38.3	29.4	36.1	25.5	26.1	20.7	22.8	24.2	21.2	21.4	18.8	27.0	24.8
Nigeria	..	..	10.8	12.2	13.7	8.2	7.8	11.1	16.9	12.0	15.8	..	10.8	12.2
Rwanda	..	24.1	25.0	19.5	20.1	26.2	24.6	27.2	27.8	24.6	21.2	..	24.6	23.9
São Tomé and Principe	..	7.8	7.0	4.3	6.0	8.4	11.3	10.9	11.8	9.6	9.8	..	10.8	9.0
Senegal	39.7	41.4	35.1	35.9	32.7	33.1	29.0	27.3	28.2	24.2	25.8	38.8	41.3	29.5
Seychelles	..	20.9	26.9	31.5	25.4	24.9	23.2	29.8	28.6	30.6	24.1	..	25.2	27.3
Sierra Leone	..	18.5	20.9	17.3	27.4	25.4	23.8	27.5	23.4	25.0	26.8	..	10.8	24.6
Somalia	..	..	..	..	..	..	..	..	..	..	..	..	..	..
South Africa	17.2	33.4	33.7	33.8	33.1	33.4	41.0	40.4	39.5	38.6	38.3	17.7	27.4	37.2
Sudan	..	18.3	14.5	13.5	28.1	31.2	33.5	35.4	27.6	32.8	32.8	..	8.8	29.4
Swaziland	..	..	..	..	..	..	..	..	..	..	..	..	..	..
Tanzania	..	19.0	21.7	22.8	26.2	31.2	28.6	24.4	24.4	23.0	22.0	20.9	20.8	25.3
Togo	..	41.2	36.0	35.5	35.8	36.2	31.1	34.5	34.2	36.7	32.7	27.1	30.9	34.6
Uganda	..	8.7	10.3	15.1	16.9	20.3	20.7	23.3	15.6	22.0	21.4	10.9	10.3	19.4
Zambia	..	17.7	16.1	20.2	20.5	25.1	19.0	19.2	17.7	21.1	25.2	..	20.8	21.0
Zimbabwe	..	29.5	29.1	29.2	32.0	35.5	35.5	34.3	30.6	38.1	34.0	68.2	30.0	33.6
NORTH AFRICA	..	26.3	27.3	27.9	28.0	28.9	29.8	29.4	28.0	31.7	32.4	..	27.0	29.5
Algeria	15.5	27.3	29.1	28.5	28.4	27.3	29.3	28.8	23.9	33.7	34.5	15.3	28.5	29.3
Egypt, Arab Rep.	..	18.8	19.7	21.5	22.0	23.0	24.1	22.7	24.0	24.3	24.8	..	17.3	23.3
Libya	..	..	..	..	..	..	..	..	..	..	..	..	..	..
Morocco	33.1	34.4	37.5	38.1	38.1	39.7	39.1	38.7	37.0	40.2	41.2	32.0	36.5	39.0
Tunisia	34.7	35.5	30.1	30.3	29.1	34.1	35.1	37.4	36.8	36.5	37.2	31.4	33.9	34.6
ALL AFRICA	..	28.2	27.1	27.5	27.3	28.0	30.7	30.6	29.7	30.7	31.3	21.8	22.8	29.5

Note: 2002 data are preliminary (see page 2). Nigeria's fiscal data are for consolidated government starting from 1992.

7-14. Government expenditure: trends in real wages and salaries

					Index 1987 = 100								*Annual average*	
	1980	*1993*	*1994*	*1995*	*1996*	*1997*	*1998*	*1999*	*2000*	*2001*	*2002*	*75-84*	*85-94*	*95-MR*
SUB-SAHARAN AFRICA	..	181	173	138	137	130	136	146	165	154	203	..	157	151
excluding South Africa	..	176	167	127	129	127	131	145	157	144	170	..	153	141
excl. S.Africa & Nigeria	..	127	120	86	83	85	93	106	110	98	121	..	116	98
Angola	..	..	..	..	..	..	..	..	..	..	..	..	..	..
Benin	..	..	..	..	..	..	..	..	..	..	..	..	..	..
Botswana	..	..	..	..	..	..	..	..	..	..	..	..	..	..
Burkina Faso	..	119	106	105	103	106	107	124	134	141	145	..	112	120
Burundi	..	126	117	102	96	82	83	88	80	87	101	99	111	90
Cameroon	..	100	56	48	45	48	57	60	65	74	83	71	96	60
Cape Verde	..	154	163	175	179	174	180	211	232	230	243	..	119	203
Central African Republic	..	100	90	76	71	74	75	78	75	73	72	..	100	74
Chad	..	193	212	207	152	144	131	152	172	170	178	..	152	163
Comoros	..	..	..	..	..	..	..	..	..	..	..	..	..	..
Congo, Dem. Rep. of	..	..	..	..	..	..	..	..	..	..	..	..	..	..
Congo, Rep. of	..	161	108	84	73	..	..	..	..	..	..	..	119	..
Côte d'Ivoire	..	80	66	61	67	68	66	67	69	71	75	0	92	68
Djibouti	..	..	..	..	..	..	..	..	..	..	..	..	..	..
Equatorial Guinea	..	131	113	118	176	220	266	414	332	363	401	..	113	286
Eritrea	..	..	..	..	..	..	..	..	..	..	..	..	..	..
Ethiopia	74	81	90	88	103	107	108	125	152	169	175	81	95	128
Gabon	..	168	137	134	138	141	144	156	140	..	..	..	122	142
Gambia, The	..	..	..	..	..	..	..	..	..	..	..	..	..	..
Ghana	..	24	25	23	22	21	22	24	24	29	45	..	51	26
Guinea	..	247	246	248	269	262	263	270	143	265	283	..	207	250
Guinea-Bissau	..	95	85	93	110	103	112	137	192	194	179	..	105	140
Kenya	..	75	78	102	100	95	114	110	104	102	114	80	87	105
Lesotho	..	..	..	..	..	..	..	..	..	..	..	..	..	..
Liberia	..	..	..	..	..	..	..	..	..	..	..	..	..	..
Madagascar	..	86	80	75	74	93	108	119	111	133	118	122	94	104
Malawi	..	117	157	142	114	145	131	127	129	139	..	92	103	133
Mali	..	..	..	..	..	..	..	..	..	..	..	..	..	..
Mauritania	..	97	97	95	97	100	105	107	117	125	128	..	100	109
Mauritius	110	140	167	172	170	178	184	197	197	196	198	91	128	186
Mozambique	..	187	158	154	152	282	403	560	633	752	808	..	144	468
Namibia	..	..	..	..	..	..	..	..	..	..	..	..	..	..
Niger	..	172	149	141	90	116	113	130	129	121	129	..	129	121
Nigeria	..	295	229	183	189	196	218	506	899	814	964	..	190	496
Rwanda	..	100	..	..	..	..	..	..	..	..	..	..	100	..
São Tomé and Principe	..	57	78	65	91	154	165	189	194	199	201	..	76	157
Senegal	..	114	97	95	96	93	92	95	99	97	107	115	108	97
Seychelles	..	..	..	..	..	..	..	..	..	..	..	..	..	..
Sierra Leone	..	234	231	191	283	169	228	247	305	374	493	415	152	286
Somalia	..	..	..	..	..	..	..	..	..	..	..	..	..	..
South Africa	..	..	..	..	..	..	..	..	..	..	..	..	..	..
Sudan	..	74	51	37	59	68	89	108	..	..	..	..	52	72
Swaziland	..	..	..	..	..	..	..	..	..	..	..	..	..	..
Tanzania	..	146	148	164	190	209	204	190	233	239	254	136	121	210
Togo	..	112	103	94	92	90	92	92	88	82	79	98	105	89
Uganda	..	396	486	719	828	1,051	1,184	1,485	1,583	1,801	2,286	..	237	1,367
Zambia	..	..	..	..	..	..	..	..	..	..	..	..	..	..
Zimbabwe	..	106	108	113	126	152	147	154	169	130	..	83	113	142
NORTH AFRICA	..	116	126	125	132	142	148	159	161	180	183	..	111	154
Algeria	56	115	113	107	108	112	117	123	124	221	239	57	104	144
Egypt, Arab Rep.	..	105	109	107	112	117	124	138	151	163	174	..	101	136
Libya	..	..	..	..	..	..	..	..	..	..	..	..	..	..
Morocco	36	121	134	134	141	154	161	169	165	189	187	61	117	163
Tunisia	..	130	125	130	139	158	167	188	195	206	217	96	111	175
ALL AFRICA	..	171	166	138	137	130	136	146	165	154	201	..	151	151

Note: 2002 data are preliminary (see page 2). Nigeria's fiscal data are for consolidated government starting from 1992.

Government Finance

7-15. Government expenditure: other goods and services

	1980	1993	1994	1995	1996	1997	1998	1999	2000	2001	2002	75-84	85-94	95-MR
				Percentage of total expenditure and lending minus repayments								*Annual average*		
SUB-SAHARAN AFRICA	..	-6.9	25.0	23.6	24.7	25.8	17.4	17.5	20.2	18.7	18.6	-7.2	2.5	20.8
excluding South Africa	..	21.6	24.8	21.7	21.4	23.0	21.9	21.5	25.7	23.5	22.5	..	20.3	22.6
excl. S.Africa & Nigeria	..	21.6	20.1	22.5	22.6	23.0	22.1	22.1	21.1	21.6	20.7	18.2	19.8	22.0
Angola	..	43.1	41.0	55.0	9.2	27.6	41.7	33.0	44.2	35.9	40.4	..	26.4	35.9
Benin	..	8.4	6.3	5.2	7.6	6.9	7.5	7.1	6.0	5.8	5.7	..	7.5	6.5
Botswana	..	..	22.9	26.1	24.8	25.8	31.4	32.3	33.1	35.6	34.4	..	22.9	30.4
Burkina Faso	..	10.7	12.0	10.8	9.8	8.7	9.4	8.6	9.4	8.9	13.0	..	9.2	9.8
Burundi	28.0	20.4	21.3	24.0	20.9	33.2	27.0	30.1	31.0	25.7	28.2	22.6	17.2	27.5
Cameroon	22.9	10.7	7.5	15.8	16.0	16.1	14.5	16.3	18.9	20.7	24.4	20.3	12.7	17.8
Cape Verde	..	1.8	1.6	1.5	1.6	3.3	1.8	2.6	1.6	2.6	2.5	23.4	5.0	2.2
Central African Republic	..	11.5	13.9	10.0	12.6	15.7	10.3	11.4	10.5	11.3	12.0	..	12.1	11.7
Chad	..	26.3	14.4	11.7	22.1	19.2	22.3	25.2	18.5	22.4	20.9	..	22.3	20.3
Comoros	..	26.4	20.3	22.6	17.7	14.3	14.8	23.5	24.2	33.6	42.8	0.0	12.9	24.2
Congo, Dem. Rep. of	..	..	..	..	43.8	36.1	23.7	22.6	11.6	15.1	5.9	..	..	22.7
Congo, Rep. of	..	9.1	8.1	7.7	6.2	30.3	29.2	19.2	19.1	15.1	21.6	24.5	9.8	18.6
Côte d'Ivoire	..	22.2	21.7	22.4	23.5	23.5	21.3	26.1	22.4	26.8	25.2	..	27.3	23.9
Djibouti	..	29.2	24.2	22.0	19.0	14.9	21.4	32.6	31.1	31.5	31.4	..	27.5	25.5
Equatorial Guinea	..	10.1	20.3	25.2	23.8	30.6	16.0	23.9	43.1	22.7	22.2	..	15.6	25.9
Eritrea	..	44.1	49.2	42.7	40.5	26.1	45.2	40.3	50.3	58.3	44.0	..	54.8	43.4
Ethiopia	31.8	14.0	14.8	16.7	15.2	15.9	27.3	36.3	43.1	24.3	23.3	31.9	21.4	25.3
Gabon	..	19.4	19.2	17.3	21.1	24.5	36.8	21.9	20.9	21.6	22.3	13.8	20.6	23.3
Gambia, The	..	25.5	25.1	18.9	19.7	17.9	16.0	18.5	-0.1	22.8	17.9	..	21.9	16.5
Ghana	..	12.6	10.5	8.1	7.2	6.9	7.5	9.0	9.3	5.6	11.4	34.5	13.6	8.1
Guinea	..	13.9	13.2	11.3	11.7	11.7	14.0	11.6	13.9	11.8	16.3	..	20.8	12.8
Guinea-Bissau	..	9.4	12.6	11.9	10.0	11.8	18.4	22.4	17.0	12.0	16.1	0.0	12.9	14.9
Kenya	27.6	19.6	10.8	7.8	9.8	11.3	4.9	4.9	-0.2	4.8	3.1	30.1	24.1	5.8
Lesotho	..	24.9	22.9	23.3	15.3	13.6	19.0	28.6	31.6	26.4	28.3	19.9	22.3	23.3
Liberia	..	..	..	..	..	..	..	..	..	..	..	..	..	..
Madagascar	..	16.6	15.8	6.4	30.5	23.6	18.9	16.4	15.7	21.0	22.7	-11.5	3.7	19.4
Malawi	0.0	37.3	41.4	29.1	31.6	36.6	23.7	28.0	24.4	21.1	25.7	0.0	22.4	27.5
Mali	13.0	10.2	10.6	12.2	11.7	13.0	6.5	6.2	6.9	6.8	5.9	15.8	6.5	8.6
Mauritania	..	14.4	17.6	20.1	20.0	21.8	20.8	22.5	25.9	27.5	32.4	..	12.5	23.9
Mauritius	8.3	9.7	9.6	9.4	9.5	9.4	8.7	8.8	8.5	9.2	8.9	7.6	8.7	9.0
Mozambique	44.2	29.3	33.8	22.4	28.3	23.6	27.3	14.8	13.4	11.0	11.0	36.0	32.6	19.0
Namibia	..	..	..	..	..	..	..	..	..	..	..	..	..	..
Niger	..	15.3	18.8	17.9	21.3	22.9	24.3	25.3	22.1	22.5	20.5	13.8	16.0	22.1
Nigeria	..	..	48.1	17.7	15.1	23.1	20.9	18.5	49.6	33.0	31.7	..	48.1	26.2
Rwanda	..	24.8	26.4	25.0	26.3	20.3	26.7	27.5	26.7	29.8	28.4	..	26.8	26.3
São Tomé and Principe	..	3.7	5.0	4.6	5.0	5.0	5.5	5.5	6.6	8.0	9.5	..	9.6	6.2
Senegal	22.9	11.9	11.8	11.5	12.3	10.8	13.0	13.0	15.6	17.8	13.0	17.9	14.7	13.4
Seychelles	..	25.1	30.6	19.6	13.6	17.1	11.5	13.4	11.4	13.5	15.0	..	29.7	14.4
Sierra Leone	..	31.2	35.4	51.6	28.7	44.1	19.3	23.6	25.2	31.5	36.6	..	36.5	32.6
Somalia	..	..	..	..	..	..	..	..	..	..	..	..	..	..
South Africa	..	..	25.1	25.7	28.5	28.9	12.2	12.8	13.7	13.2	14.1	..	25.1	18.6
Sudan	..	19.6	21.2	53.7	44.8	47.8	38.4	33.1	30.6	30.2	21.1	..	20.4	37.5
Swaziland	..	..	..	..	..	..	..	..	..	..	..	..	..	..
Tanzania	..	30.7	30.4	28.9	24.2	23.7	21.1	26.0	23.4	28.4	31.4	30.5	32.3	25.9
Togo	..	19.0	16.3	18.9	22.9	21.1	22.6	22.4	21.9	20.4	24.2	-27.1	-3.7	21.8
Uganda	..	26.6	29.7	33.9	33.1	33.8	32.2	31.0	21.3	29.4	28.5	35.0	39.0	30.4
Zambia	..	20.3	22.3	22.5	21.2	18.3	20.3	15.2	9.9	19.0	11.3	..	20.3	17.2
Zimbabwe	..	19.4	18.1	16.9	16.5	14.1	13.2	14.6	17.9	17.1	12.4	-5.1	16.9	15.3
NORTH AFRICA	..	11.7	10.7	11.1	11.2	11.6	11.8	10.6	10.9	11.9	11.4	..	10.7	11.3
Algeria	2.9	4.0	3.6	4.7	4.6	5.1	5.4	5.5	4.6	6.5	6.8	2.9	2.8	5.4
Egypt, Arab Rep.	..	15.3	15.5	16.1	15.9	16.3	16.3	13.8	15.0	15.2	15.5	..	14.5	15.5
Libya	..	..	..	..	..	..	..	..	..	..	..	..	..	..
Morocco	17.6	16.9	14.3	13.7	14.5	15.7	16.0	15.2	14.6	16.7	13.1	40.9	14.7	14.9
Tunisia	13.1	10.7	6.5	6.1	6.9	5.9	5.7	5.0	6.3	6.1	6.6	11.7	11.1	6.1
ALL AFRICA	..	0.0	20.0	19.2	20.1	20.9	15.5	15.1	17.0	16.4	16.1	-1.3	5.3	17.5

Note: 2002 data are preliminary (see page 2). Nigeria's fiscal data are for consolidated government starting from 1992.

7-16. Government expenditure: interest payments

	Percentage of total expenditure and lending minus repayments											Annual average		
	1980	1993	1994	1995	1996	1997	1998	1999	2000	2001	2002	75-84	85-94	95-MR
SUB-SAHARAN AFRICA	..	7.3	13.6	10.0	9.6	7.9	7.7	8.3	8.0	6.8	7.3	3.6	7.0	8.2
excluding South Africa	..	15.1	25.8	19.0	17.9	14.6	14.2	15.4	14.9	12.6	13.5	..	14.6	15.3
excl. S.Africa & Nigeria	..	15.1	24.1	17.0	17.2	15.0	14.7	14.1	14.6	12.6	13.2	11.0	14.4	14.8
Angola	..	15.5	..	16.1	18.2	8.6	16.2	11.1	9.3	10.2	6.7	..	8.5	12.0
Benin	..	15.0	15.9	12.6	12.4	9.0	6.2	5.2	4.4	4.3	4.1	..	15.5	7.3
Botswana	..	0.0	0.0	0.0	0.0	0.0	0.0	0.0	0.0	0.0	0.0	..	0.0	0.0
Burkina Faso	..	6.9	6.9	6.6	4.2	3.6	3.5	3.1	3.9	3.8	3.5	..	6.6	4.0
Burundi	2.0	5.0	6.0	6.9	6.7	8.9	10.2	11.2	12.3	10.3	12.8	5.3	7.5	9.9
Cameroon	2.0	24.1	36.5	39.5	41.8	37.2	32.0	27.6	25.1	18.9	16.3	2.9	14.0	29.8
Cape Verde	..	2.5	1.9	6.2	8.4	9.6	9.8	3.2	4.7	6.8	8.3	0.0	3.1	7.1
Central African Republic	..	9.9	10.8	11.1	17.2	9.6	7.6	7.8	10.2	7.4	7.1	..	8.0	9.7
Chad	..	5.8	6.1	5.6	5.6	5.3	5.5	4.8	5.1	4.2	4.3	..	3.1	5.0
Comoros	..	3.7	3.1	3.0	3.6	4.1	4.9	5.2	5.6	3.9	2.9	0.0	2.2	4.1
Congo, Dem. Rep. of	..	..	..	..	31.1	23.5	31.1	22.6	18.7	17.0	30.9	..	..	25.0
Congo, Rep. of	..	20.1	33.0	43.0	33.0	35.0	32.4	35.4	27.2	23.5	23.7	0.0	19.2	31.6
Côte d'Ivoire	..	29.0	29.1	25.6	23.1	20.0	17.9	19.9	22.4	19.9	16.6	..	26.7	20.7
Djibouti	..	0.8	0.8	1.5	2.0	1.4	1.0	0.9	2.3	2.5	2.7	..	0.9	1.8
Equatorial Guinea	..	13.7	26.0	24.0	15.6	8.7	5.5	8.5	3.4	4.1	3.5	..	16.9	9.2
Eritrea	..	0.1	0.2	0.6	1.3	1.9	1.6	2.0	2.9	4.6	5.5	..	0.1	2.5
Ethiopia	3.0	10.2	13.5	10.0	9.0	9.2	8.0	6.8	7.0	6.7	5.7	3.2	6.4	7.8
Gabon	..	24.4	26.4	30.9	25.6	20.1	15.9	26.8	25.4	21.7	20.5	6.6	19.0	23.3
Gambia, The	..	14.8	14.8	14.1	14.2	19.1	23.0	22.2	20.8	18.5	19.8	..	13.8	19.0
Ghana	..	12.0	14.2	13.9	17.2	21.7	17.9	21.3	27.0	24.0	23.5	11.4	9.4	20.8
Guinea	..	7.2	9.0	8.1	8.1	9.4	10.0	9.6	12.8	10.0	9.2	..	10.7	9.7
Guinea-Bissau	..	14.3	15.2	21.9	19.7	16.6	27.3	3.4	13.7	19.9	14.4	1.1	9.8	17.1
Kenya	10.1	40.6	36.2	23.3	24.9	20.7	19.6	20.3	17.4	11.6	11.8	13.9	25.1	18.7
Lesotho	..	5.4	4.2	3.6	3.3	3.7	4.9	5.4	8.1	7.5	6.3	..	7.5	5.3
Liberia	..	..	..	..	..	..	..	..	..	..	..	..	..	..
Madagascar	..	18.3	26.4	30.1	21.6	17.5	13.7	11.8	12.9	10.8	14.0	11.2	14.5	16.5
Malawi	9.1	11.9	10.3	20.5	22.9	14.1	12.9	11.7	14.1	16.3	17.2	12.9	14.9	16.2
Mali	4.1	6.9	9.0	6.1	4.8	4.1	3.1	3.7	3.9	3.1	3.3	4.8	7.2	4.0
Mauritania	..	11.1	10.4	13.0	13.4	13.0	14.0	13.9	10.2	12.1	8.9	..	9.0	12.3
Mauritius	..	12.2	11.7	13.0	12.8	12.7	15.8	14.6	13.9	18.5	13.6	18.0	16.9	14.4
Mozambique	0.0	8.6	3.6	6.6	7.0	5.7	4.5	2.5	0.7	1.9	4.4	0.1	5.0	4.2
Namibia	..	1.7	2.8	3.2	4.2	5.4	6.8	6.6	5.9	6.8	6.8	6.8	4.7	5.6
Niger	..	10.2	12.3	16.0	12.8	9.7	8.8	8.9	10.1	10.7	8.7	11.1	12.2	10.7
Nigeria	..	..	33.9	28.9	21.8	12.8	12.0	21.7	16.9	12.2	15.2	..	33.9	17.7
Rwanda	..	9.1	27.9	11.3	7.2	6.2	4.9	4.2	4.9	3.9	4.3	..	11.5	5.9
São Tomé and Principe	..	16.8	14.9	15.6	14.4	16.1	20.8	16.3	10.0	10.9	11.4	..	18.6	14.4
Senegal	7.5	10.9	16.8	14.7	11.2	12.1	6.3	7.0	7.3	4.1	5.2	9.4	14.1	8.5
Seychelles	..	12.3	16.5	22.3	16.5	17.4	15.8	18.8	15.0	15.9	15.2	..	15.2	17.1
Sierra Leone	..	18.9	14.0	10.5	12.5	16.3	23.9	26.4	21.9	16.3	19.7	..	23.7	18.5
Somalia	..	..	..	..	..	..	..	..	..	..	..	..	..	..
South Africa	..	..	..	..	..	..	..	..	..	..	..	..	..	..
Sudan	..	..	..	..	..	..	9.1	9.8	10.9	..	..	..	..	9.9
Swaziland	..	2.0	1.8	2.1	2.2	2.3	2.3	2.6	2.3	2.8	3.9	..	2.3	2.6
Tanzania	..	12.9	14.4	18.4	18.9	17.4	15.2	10.6	10.9	9.6	7.8	8.0	12.7	13.6
Togo	..	16.2	22.0	15.6	13.8	12.6	11.6	13.0	11.7	11.8	11.4	20.9	15.0	12.7
Uganda	..	9.7	7.8	5.9	6.0	5.6	6.1	5.1	4.0	5.7	5.5	14.4	8.6	5.5
Zambia	10.9	41.8	36.5	27.7	17.4	16.4	11.8	10.1	10.1	7.9	12.8	12.2	29.7	14.3
Zimbabwe	27.7	17.9	20.4	24.2	24.5	19.1	27.8	26.0	34.4	29.1	38.9	24.8	14.9	28.0
NORTH AFRICA	..	17.1	19.1	18.2	18.5	17.6	16.5	12.0	16.1	15.2	14.5	..	13.0	16.1
Algeria	..	6.4	8.2	9.9	11.9	12.7	12.6	..	13.8	11.9	9.3	..	6.6	11.7
Egypt, Arab Rep.	..	25.5	29.3	25.4	25.1	23.1	21.1	19.1	19.4	19.4	19.5	..	15.8	21.5
Libya	..	..	..	..	..	..	..	..	..	..	..	..	..	..
Morocco	7.4	19.8	20.1	20.3	19.3	18.2	17.2	17.1	16.2	15.3	15.9	20.2	21.5	17.4
Tunisia	5.8	11.5	11.0	11.7	12.2	10.6	9.6	10.7	10.2	9.0	8.5	5.5	9.6	10.3
ALL AFRICA	..	10.9	15.5	12.9	12.7	11.2	10.7	9.6	10.8	9.6	9.7	5.3	8.8	10.9

Note: 2002 data are preliminary (see page 2). Nigeria's fiscal data are for consolidated government starting from 1992.

7-17. Government expenditure: subsidies and current transfers

		Percentage of total expenditure and lending minus repayments										*Annual average*		
	1980	1993	1994	1995	1996	1997	1998	1999	2000	2001	2002	75-84	85-94	95-MR
SUB-SAHARAN AFRICA	..	1.0	2.8	2.4	2.2	2.3	1.2	1.1	1.5	1.9	1.3	1.7	1.3	1.7
excluding South Africa	..	2.1	1.3	1.4	1.3	1.7	2.3	2.1	2.7	3.5	2.5	..	2.3	2.2
excl. S.Africa & Nigeria	..	2.1	1.5	1.7	1.6	2.0	2.7	2.5	3.2	4.2	3.0	2.7	2.3	2.6
Angola	..	9.1	0.0	0.0	0.0	0.0	0.0	0.0	1.9	7.4	0.0	..	5.5	1.2
Benin	..	..	..	..	..	..	..	..	..	..	..	..	..	..
Botswana	..	0.8	0.8	1.0	1.3	1.2	1.5	1.6	1.1	1.6	2.0	..	0.9	1.4
Burkina Faso	..	..	..	..	..	..	..	..	..	..	..	..	..	..
Burundi	10.9	5.7	7.5	6.7	5.9	7.6	7.6	7.0	6.5	6.1	8.7	10.1	6.3	7.0
Cameroon	11.1	0.0	0.0	0.0	0.0	4.2	4.8	5.4	5.7	7.2	5.2	8.6	0.0	4.1
Cape Verde	..	9.0	9.8	11.2	9.4	3.4	4.7	20.5	22.3	2.3	4.0	1.2	3.9	9.7
Central African Republic	..	..	..	..	..	..	..	..	..	..	..	..	..	..
Chad	..	0.0	0.0	0.0	0.0	0.0	0.0	0.0	0.0	0.0	0.0	..	0.0	0.0
Comoros	..	0.0	0.0	0.0	0.0	0.0	0.0	0.0	0.0	0.0	0.0	0.0	0.0	0.0
Congo, Dem. Rep. of	..	..	..	..	0.5	0.3	0.7	0.3	6.9	4.3	3.4	..	..	2.3
Congo, Rep. of	..	0.0	0.0	0.0	0.0	0.0	0.0	0.0	0.0	0.0	0.0	0.0	1.4	0.0
Côte d'Ivoire	..	3.0	3.7	3.9	2.9	3.6	3.5	4.0	6.5	5.0	4.7	..	3.8	4.3
Djibouti	..	3.6	3.6	-9.2	-1.2	-1.7	-2.8	2.7	2.8	2.8	2.8	..	3.6	-0.5
Equatorial Guinea	..	3.5	4.4	4.4	4.0	4.1	9.0	4.7	6.7	9.4	9.3	..	4.9	6.4
Eritrea	..	0.0	0.0	0.0	0.0	0.0	0.0	0.0	0.0	0.0	0.0	..	0.0	0.0
Ethiopia	5.8	0.1	1.2	1.8	1.7	1.3	0.0	0.0	0.0	0.0	0.0	2.3	1.3	0.6
Gabon	..	0.0	0.0	0.0	0.0	0.0	0.0	0.0	0.0	0.0	0.0	0.0	0.0	0.0
Gambia, The	..	0.6	0.1	0.0	0.0	0.0	0.0	0.0	0.0	0.0	0.0	..	3.6	0.0
Ghana	..	0.0	0.0	7.9	5.6	4.9	9.3	5.3	5.9	6.3	0.0	..	0.0	5.7
Guinea	..	3.6	4.3	6.2	6.0	7.5	8.3	9.1	2.3	21.7	17.4	..	5.4	9.8
Guinea-Bissau	..	0.0	0.0	0.0	0.0	0.0	0.0	0.0	0.0	0.0	0.0	0.0	0.0	0.0
Kenya	0.1	0.0	0.0	0.0	0.0	0.0	0.0	0.0	0.1	0.1	0.1	0.2	1.0	0.0
Lesotho	..	0.0	0.0	0.0	0.0	0.0	0.0	0.0	0.0	0.0	0.0	..	0.0	0.0
Liberia	..	..	..	..	..	..	..	..	..	..	..	..	..	..
Madagascar	..	..	..	..	..	..	..	..	0.0	..	0.0	..	..	0.0
Malawi	0.0	5.1	9.8	3.1	2.0	1.5	12.9	3.0	2.6	5.2	3.7	0.0	1.5	4.3
Mali	6.0	2.7	1.6	1.3	1.4	1.2	5.7	5.6	10.8	12.8	11.1	3.7	1.9	6.2
Mauritania	..	..	..	..	..	..	..	..	..	..	..	..	..	..
Mauritius	0.0	4.6	1.7	1.5	2.7	3.7	3.3	3.0	2.8	2.7	2.4	0.0	1.4	2.8
Mozambique	1.4	1.2	0.9	1.3	1.2	1.0	1.0	0.5	0.4	0.3	0.2	7.1	8.2	0.7
Namibia	..	0.0	0.0	0.0	0.0	0.0	0.0	0.0	0.0	0.0	0.0	0.0	0.0	0.0
Niger	..	12.9	6.6	4.4	6.0	7.6	5.2	5.1	11.2	11.8	11.6	9.4	7.4	7.9
Nigeria	..	..	0.0	0.0	0.0	0.0	0.0	0.0	0.0	0.0	..	..	0.0	0.0
Rwanda	..	5.0	3.8	4.8	3.3	5.7	7.9	9.1	8.4	9.6	10.6	..	8.5	7.4
São Tomé and Principe	..	..	..	..	..	..	..	..	..	..	..	..	..	..
Senegal	13.9	13.9	9.2	6.6	5.7	8.6	6.4	7.8	12.3	23.5	17.2	12.1	10.1	11.0
Seychelles	..	4.6	6.3	0.1	0.0	0.0	0.0	0.1	0.2	0.2	0.2	..	5.9	0.1
Sierra Leone	..	0.0	0.0	0.0	0.0	0.0	0.0	0.0	0.0	0.0	0.0	..	0.9	0.0
Somalia	..	..	..	..	..	..	..	..	..	..	..	..	..	..
South Africa	..	..	4.5	3.5	3.2	3.0	0.0	0.0	0.0	0.0	0.0	..	4.5	1.2
Sudan	..	..	..	..	..	..	5.1	3.3	2.5	3.4	..	..	..	3.6
Swaziland	..	3.3	2.6	6.6	18.0	15.6	15.0	17.4	18.4	15.6	14.0	..	2.7	15.1
Tanzania	..	0.0	0.0	0.0	0.0	0.0	0.0	0.0	0.0	0.0	0.0	0.0	0.0	0.0
Togo	..	4.6	9.0	6.6	5.4	7.0	6.4	9.4	9.8	11.0	10.1	2.3	3.2	8.2
Uganda	..	0.0	0.0	0.0	0.0	0.0	0.0	0.0	0.0	0.0	0.0	0.0	0.0	0.0
Zambia	13.7	0.6	0.0	0.0	0.0	0.2	0.9	0.8	2.9	0.8	0.9	9.9	8.5	0.8
Zimbabwe	29.3	4.9	1.4	0.5	0.3	0.1	0.0	0.0	0.0	0.0	0.0	23.2	7.1	0.1
NORTH AFRICA	..	9.2	6.6	5.7	5.9	4.9	4.7	4.4	4.9	9.8	9.7	..	7.8	6.3
Algeria	..	13.6	9.4	6.2	4.4	2.1	2.2	2.0	1.9	21.8	21.5	..	4.9	7.8
Egypt, Arab Rep.	..	7.7	5.8	6.6	6.8	6.2	5.9	5.2	5.9	6.0	6.0	..	10.2	6.1
Libya	..	..	..	..	..	..	..	..	..	..	..	..	..	..
Morocco	6.0	2.6	4.1	3.3	6.0	6.4	6.0	7.4	8.2	3.4	3.3	7.5	3.2	5.5
Tunisia	15.1	13.9	6.0	5.9	6.2	5.6	4.8	3.0	3.5	2.4	2.4	20.3	15.9	4.2
ALL AFRICA	..	4.0	4.1	3.6	3.5	3.2	2.4	2.3	2.6	4.6	4.2	2.8	3.5	3.3

Note: 2002 data are preliminary (see page 2). Nigeria's fiscal data are for consolidated government starting from 1992.

7-18. Government expenditure: capital and net lending

					Percentage of total expenditure and lending minus repayments								*Annual average*		
	1980	*1993*	*1994*	*1995*	*1996*	*1997*	*1998*	*1999*	*2000*	*2001*	*2002*	*75-84*	*85-94*	*95-MR*
SUB-SAHARAN AFRICA	..	18.3	19.5	19.5	19.8	20.0	20.3	18.8	15.6	16.2	16.4	22.0	18.0	18.3
excluding South Africa	..	24.8	28.4	28.7	29.5	30.4	31.7	29.8	24.2	23.6	23.2	..	26.5	27.6
excl. S.Africa & Nigeria	..	24.8	25.8	26.1	25.6	25.5	26.4	26.2	25.7	24.2	24.0	29.7	26.2	25.5
Angola	..	10.7	5.7	10.3	20.3	7.2	13.8	15.6	10.5	12.9	14.3	..	13.8	13.1
Benin	..	26.8	32.9	36.6	32.9	36.3	36.3	37.7	38.1	38.4	31.8	..	27.1	36.0
Botswana	..	40.9	37.4	31.6	32.8	33.6	32.7	31.1	30.3	26.6	26.8	43.3	44.7	30.7
Burkina Faso	..	34.4	40.8	45.9	51.3	56.5	56.2	58.9	54.3	52.2	47.3	..	38.2	52.8
Burundi	113.6	43.4	32.6	30.3	35.8	18.0	25.8	25.7	22.5	29.9	17.3	119.7	51.9	25.7
Cameroon	32.6	13.8	17.3	7.1	5.9	10.8	16.8	19.5	15.4	18.0	14.6	40.3	31.1	13.5
Cape Verde	..	58.7	60.9	52.4	47.8	44.7	43.7	35.4	26.1	33.2	35.3	67.8	52.6	39.8
Central African Republic	..	41.1	46.0	50.2	21.9	37.5	54.2	50.9	52.4	55.3	56.4	..	42.1	47.3
Chad	..	38.0	47.5	50.4	49.1	53.8	51.1	50.8	50.8	50.2	50.4	..	50.9	50.8
Comoros	..	15.6	32.1	20.5	21.8	24.0	35.0	28.0	21.6	20.1	17.7	0.0	41.1	23.6
Congo, Dem. Rep. of	..	..	..	..	..	..	..	..	4.1	1.5	9.3	..	..	5.0
Congo, Rep. of	..	4.6	7.6	9.1	33.6	9.2	11.1	18.7	27.3	31.8	24.6	61.7	16.1	20.7
Côte d'Ivoire	..	10.3	17.0	20.9	21.8	24.6	28.5	21.8	15.3	11.0	13.0	..	11.4	19.6
Djibouti	..	16.4	12.9	9.4	11.3	12.1	20.0	9.4	9.9	11.2	12.3	..	15.9	11.9
Equatorial Guinea	..	49.5	32.9	18.0	9.6	20.9	36.4	43.8	31.3	41.9	43.5	..	43.7	30.7
Eritrea	..	29.2	22.4	21.4	31.6	44.3	33.3	40.0	12.0	23.4	24.1	..	21.3	28.8
Ethiopia	20.9	34.2	38.0	37.7	45.2	42.6	34.0	28.2	21.0	32.8	34.7	24.5	31.2	34.5
Gabon	..	17.7	22.1	20.9	22.8	31.7	29.2	8.9	24.9	27.0	26.4	58.1	27.1	24.0
Gambia, The	..	29.9	27.4	35.4	36.9	29.3	22.2	20.7	17.3	22.2	29.5	36.5	31.6	26.7
Ghana	17.8	38.3	42.7	46.1	44.8	42.9	39.6	37.2	33.1	39.1	23.4	14.5	39.5	38.3
Guinea	..	49.4	46.3	48.6	45.1	47.6	39.3	44.5	55.3	37.5	38.6	..	43.0	44.5
Guinea-Bissau	..	64.4	59.1	49.6	53.0	53.8	24.7	41.7	25.3	37.8	31.4	32.0	62.6	39.7
Kenya	29.5	10.8	10.8	21.1	18.8	15.7	17.0	18.2	10.7	14.1	10.8	23.5	16.3	15.8
Lesotho	..	33.0	31.4	32.8	40.6	38.3	24.4	29.1	20.8	20.2	20.6	37.9	30.2	28.3
Liberia	..	..	..	..	..	..	..	..	..	..	..	..	..	..
Madagascar	..	35.9	32.2	36.2	32.5	37.5	47.1	47.7	49.4	43.8	33.9	39.9	39.8	41.0
Malawi	48.8	20.3	17.2	21.4	19.9	19.3	26.9	32.9	35.8	26.4	22.4	38.0	24.1	25.6
Mali	53.0	50.4	50.4	53.5	56.2	51.4	56.4	54.2	52.0	48.7	49.2	47.9	56.9	52.7
Mauritania	..	41.3	32.9	27.6	27.8	25.8	29.2	29.3	42.1	35.1	37.9	..	28.2	31.8
Mauritius	27.2	20.3	18.2	15.9	18.7	22.1	12.9	12.1	15.9	10.3	16.6	21.8	19.0	15.6
Mozambique	44.0	49.3	51.1	57.3	55.1	55.8	47.6	49.7	50.7	57.7	54.0	40.1	43.3	53.5
Namibia	..	15.3	12.3	13.2	13.1	14.5	12.6	13.0	14.4	15.3	17.2	21.2	16.2	14.2
Niger	..	21.5	28.6	27.1	29.6	30.6	31.9	30.6	29.5	33.9	37.7	46.9	34.6	31.4
Nigeria	..	..	41.1	41.3	49.4	55.8	59.4	48.6	16.6	20.6	18.8	..	41.1	38.8
Rwanda	..	32.1	16.6	39.4	41.3	41.6	36.0	32.3	31.9	31.6	29.4	..	27.9	35.5
São Tomé and Principe	..	52.3	57.9	69.1	60.7	60.3	51.8	60.9	63.4	55.4	55.0	..	50.5	59.6
Senegal	17.6	20.3	25.0	27.8	37.2	34.4	43.7	42.4	34.0	29.5	38.1	16.4	16.4	35.9
Seychelles	..	22.8	11.0	10.7	18.9	19.5	27.9	22.3	24.6	14.1	18.5	..	19.9	19.6
Sierra Leone	..	25.2	21.8	13.4	19.6	11.3	24.6	11.2	21.1	10.4	10.5	..	22.8	15.3
Somalia	..	..	..	..	..	..	..	..	..	..	..	..	..	..
South Africa	25.8	12.3	9.6	9.2	8.4	7.8	6.9	6.0	5.6	7.6	8.5	23.6	10.3	7.5
Sudan	..	15.9	17.6	15.1	7.2	7.7	9.1	14.2	21.3	19.6	23.6	30.6	14.8	14.7
Swaziland	..	25.4	24.7	23.8	18.1	17.1	23.0	21.7	20.5	25.1	24.7	..	26.1	21.8
Tanzania	..	21.2	20.8	17.6	20.4	17.3	25.8	27.4	30.8	21.4	18.7	26.2	19.8	22.4
Togo	..	8.8	9.1	15.5	13.9	11.2	19.2	17.7	15.0	15.6	14.7	..	17.2	15.4
Uganda	..	55.0	52.2	45.1	44.1	40.2	41.0	40.5	53.0	36.3	40.2	39.7	42.1	42.6
Zambia	10.5	10.7	12.5	17.5	32.0	30.1	39.4	44.9	46.9	38.8	38.9	11.6	8.1	36.1
Zimbabwe	43.1	16.8	17.6	14.5	12.7	12.3	6.7	14.2	5.2	2.8	4.7	42.7	16.9	9.1
NORTH AFRICA	..	24.5	22.4	22.0	20.7	20.7	21.4	22.8	24.4	22.0	22.4	..	29.1	22.1
Algeria	63.3	31.3	31.0	29.4	26.6	25.2	24.8	19.9	27.3	23.6	25.5	61.6	38.3	25.3
Egypt, Arab Rep.	..	20.9	18.1	18.2	18.7	20.0	21.3	28.9	25.2	21.8	21.0	..	32.3	21.9
Libya	..	..	..	..	..	..	..	..	..	..	..	..	..	..
Morocco	33.4	20.5	18.4	18.8	16.0	14.5	16.2	15.9	18.4	18.6	19.3	65.0	19.1	17.2
Tunisia	28.9	25.6	21.1	20.9	20.7	22.4	21.9	21.4	24.5	24.4	24.4	27.7	23.2	22.6
ALL AFRICA	..	20.6	20.5	20.3	20.1	20.2	20.7	20.1	18.6	18.2	18.4	26.6	22.4	19.6

Note: 2002 data are preliminary (see page 2). Nigeria's fiscal data are for consolidated government starting from 1992.

7-19. Government expenditure: trends in real defense spending

	Index 1980=100											Annual average		
	1980	1993	1994	1995	1996	1997	1998	1999	2000	2001	2002	75-84	85-94	95-MR
SUB-SAHARAN AFRICA	100.0	42.2	161.9	38.7	43.1	46.0	71.1	124.3	182.5	113.2	97.4	88.4	102.8	89.5
excluding South Africa	100.0	42.2	161.9	38.7	43.1	46.0	71.1	124.3	182.5	113.2	97.4	88.4	102.8	89.5
excl. S.Africa & Nigeria	100.0	42.2	161.9	38.7	43.1	46.0	71.1	124.3	182.5	113.2	97.4	88.4	102.8	89.5
Angola	..	..	..	..	..	..	..	..	..	..	..	..	..	..
Benin	..	..	..	..	..	..	..	..	..	..	..	..	..	..
Botswana	..	..	..	..	..	..	..	..	..	..	..	..	..	..
Burkina Faso	100.0	..	293.0	..	..	..	..	..	..	..	..	100.0	192.6	..
Burundi	..	..	..	..	..	..	..	..	..	..	..	..	..	..
Cameroon	..	..	..	..	..	..	..	..	..	..	..	..	..	..
Cape Verde	..	..	..	..	..	..	..	..	..	..	..	..	..	..
Central African Republic	100.0	..	249.4	..	..	..	..	..	..	..	..	100.0	164.2	..
Chad	..	..	..	..	..	..	..	..	..	..	..	..	..	..
Comoros	..	..	..	..	..	..	..	..	..	..	..	..	..	..
Congo, Dem. Rep. of	..	..	..	..	..	..	..	..	..	..	..	..	..	..
Congo, Rep. of	..	..	..	..	..	..	..	..	..	..	..	..	..	..
Côte d'Ivoire	..	..	..	..	..	..	..	..	..	..	..	..	..	..
Djibouti	..	..	..	..	..	..	..	..	..	..	..	..	..	..
Equatorial Guinea	..	..	..	..	..	..	..	..	..	..	..	..	..	..
Eritrea	..	..	..	..	..	..	..	..	..	..	..	..	..	..
Ethiopia	100.0	40.9	37.0	37.4	41.3	45.2	99.6	204.7	319.7	168.8	131.2	97.5	101.7	131.0
Gabon	..	..	..	..	..	..	..	..	..	..	..	..	..	..
Gambia, The	..	..	..	..	..	..	..	..	..	..	..	..	..	..
Ghana	..	..	..	..	..	..	..	..	..	..	..	..	..	..
Guinea	..	..	..	..	..	..	..	..	..	..	..	..	..	..
Guinea-Bissau	..	..	..	..	..	..	..	..	..	..	..	..	..	..
Kenya	100.0	43.5	36.2	39.9	45.0	46.8	42.6	43.9	45.3	57.7	63.7	77.5	71.1	48.1
Lesotho	..	..	..	..	..	..	..	..	..	..	..	..	..	..
Liberia	..	..	..	..	..	..	..	..	..	..	..	..	..	..
Madagascar	100.0	..	..	..	..	..	..	..	..	..	..	100.0	..	..
Malawi	..	..	..	..	..	..	..	..	..	..	..	..	..	..
Mali	..	..	..	..	..	..	..	..	..	..	..	..	..	..
Mauritania	..	..	..	..	..	..	..	..	..	..	..	..	..	..
Mauritius	..	..	..	..	..	..	..	..	..	..	..	..	..	..
Mozambique	..	..	..	..	..	..	..	..	..	..	..	..	..	..
Namibia	..	..	..	..	..	..	..	..	..	..	..	..	..	..
Niger	100.0	..	187.4	..	..	..	..	..	..	..	..	100.0	168.7	..
Nigeria	..	..	..	..	..	..	..	..	..	..	..	..	..	..
Rwanda	..	..	..	..	..	..	..	..	..	..	..	..	..	..
São Tomé and Principe	..	..	..	..	..	..	..	..	..	..	..	..	..	..
Senegal	..	..	..	..	..	..	..	..	..	..	..	..	..	..
Seychelles	..	..	..	..	..	..	..	..	..	..	..	..	..	..
Sierra Leone	..	..	..	..	..	..	..	..	..	..	..	..	..	..
Somalia	..	..	..	..	..	..	..	..	..	..	..	..	..	..
South Africa	..	..	..	..	..	..	..	..	..	..	..	..	..	..
Sudan	..	..	..	..	..	..	..	..	..	..	..	..	..	..
Swaziland	100.0	..	..	..	..	..	..	..	..	..	..	100.0	79.7	..
Tanzania	..	..	..	..	..	..	..	..	..	..	..	..	..	..
Togo	100.0	..	136.5	..	..	..	..	..	..	..	..	100.0	138.9	..
Uganda	..	..	..	..	..	..	..	..	..	..	..	..	..	..
Zambia	..	..	..	..	..	..	..	..	..	..	..	..	..	..
Zimbabwe	..	..	..	..	..	..	..	..	..	..	..	..	..	..
NORTH AFRICA	100.0	..	181.3	..	..	..	..	..	..	..	..	100.0	136.0	..
Algeria	100.0	..	267.0	..	..	..	..	..	..	..	..	100.0	175.4	..
Egypt, Arab Rep.	100.0	..	..	..	..	..	..	..	..	..	..	100.0	85.1	..
Libya	100.0	..	..	..	..	..	..	..	..	..	..	100.0	231.8	..
Morocco	100.0	..	95.5	..	..	..	..	..	..	..	..	100.0	88.0	..
Tunisia	..	..	..	..	..	..	..	..	..	..	..	..	..	..
ALL AFRICA	100.0	42.2	161.9	38.7	43.1	46.0	71.1	124.3	182.5	113.2	97.4	88.4	102.5	89.5

Note: Note: 2002 data are preliminary (see page 2). Nigeria's fiscal data are for federal level only. Nigeria's fiscal data are for consolidated government starting from 1992.

7-20. Government expenditure: real per capita education spending

	Constant 1995 U.S. dollars											Annual average		
	1980	*1993*	*1994*	*1995*	*1996*	*1997*	*1998*	*1999*	*2000*	*2001*	*2002*	*75-84*	*85-94*	*95-MR*
SUB-SAHARAN AFRICA	..	..	..	..	..	..	..	..	..	..	..	..	..	..
excluding South Africa	..	..	..	..	..	..	..	..	..	..	..	..	..	..
excl. S.Africa & Nigeria	..	..	..	..	..	..	..	11.5	10.5	..	..	..	..	10.96
Angola	..	..	..	..	..	..	..	..	..	..	..	..	..	..
Benin	..	..	..	..	12.2	10.1	10.1	10.6	12.0	15.6	19.2	11.71	..	12.83
Botswana	..	240.4	245.1	267.6	310.5	..	..	..	..	..	..	..	208.05	289.08
Burkina Faso	3.5	6.4	..	8.8	9.7	9.7	11.0	..	..	..	..	3.47	5.31	9.79
Burundi	..	3.5	3.1	2.4	1.8	1.1	1.4	..	..	..	..	..	3.55	1.69
Cameroon	..	..	..	..	..	..	..	..	..	..	..	..	..	..
Cape Verde	..	..	..	..	..	..	..	..	127.6	128.8	127.2	..	..	127.86
Central African Republic	..	..	..	..	..	..	..	..	..	..	..	15.51	..	..
Chad	..	4.4	3.5	3.2	3.1	3.6	3.3	3.9	4.0	4.6	4.2	..	3.97	3.73
Comoros	..	..	..	..	18.3	17.7	14.9	9.8	9.5	9.4	9.6	..	..	12.75
Congo, Dem. Rep. of	..	..	..	..	..	..	..	..	..	..	..	..	..	..
Congo, Rep. of	..	..	..	..	..	..	..	..	..	..	..	0.00	0.00	..
Côte d'Ivoire	..	50.8	36.5	34.1	32.9	34.3	36.3	39.9	45.3	44.4	43.4	..	38.78	38.84
Djibouti	..	..	..	..	..	..	..	..	..	..	..	..	..	..
Equatorial Guinea	..	..	..	..	..	..	..	..	..	..	..	..	..	..
Eritrea	..	3.7	3.7	5.8	4.9	8.4	8.9	8.9	11.3	15.0	17.5	..	3.14	10.09
Ethiopia	..	2.6	3.5	3.4	4.0	4.0	3.7	3.9	3.6	4.8	5.5	2.87	2.83	4.11
Gabon	..	..	..	..	..	..	..	..	..	..	..	..	..	..
Gambia, The	..	10.9	11.2	11.4	11.8	12.4	10.3	10.2	11.0	15.2	13.6	..	10.79	11.99
Ghana	..	..	14.6	14.1	15.3	13.8	15.0	0.0	0.0	0.0	0.0	..	14.56	7.28
Guinea	..	..	12.2	12.9	15.9	14.3	10.8	11.7	11.3	11.6	12.1	..	12.25	12.58
Guinea-Bissau	..	1.8	4.7	6.8	6.8	6.7	2.4	6.4	4.1	3.7	5.5	0.00	2.81	5.31
Kenya	19.5	22.2	20.6	21.9	21.3	21.9	23.1	21.6	19.7	18.3	18.2	15.53	21.59	20.74
Lesotho	..	50.6	61.8	69.5	70.0	71.0	78.1	75.5	71.8	61.2	62.2	..	43.87	69.91
Liberia	..	..	..	..	..	..	..	..	..	..	..	..	..	..
Madagascar	..	..	..	..	..	5.3	6.0	7.2	7.3	..	..	..	..	6.45
Malawi	..	..	..	..	..	..	..	..	..	..	..	..	..	..
Mali	..	..	..	7.9	8.0	7.8	8.8	11.4	8.9	9.3	..	6.66	6.44	8.87
Mauritania	..	..	..	..	2.4	24.4	23.7	24.9	26.9	25.6	27.2	..	..	22.16
Mauritius	..	..	..	..	..	..	..	..	..	..	..	..	..	..
Mozambique	..	3.0	2.7	2.8	2.8	3.3	4.6	6.7	10.6	14.5	..	3.21	2.65	6.47
Namibia	..	..	..	..	..	..	..	..	..	..	..	..	..	..
Niger	11.0	..	..	..	..	..	..	..	..	..	..	8.40	..	..
Nigeria	..	..	..	..	..	..	..	..	..	..	..	..	..	..
Rwanda	..	..	..	4.0	4.1	4.4	6.9	7.5	8.3	9.8	..	..	..	6.43
São Tomé and Principe	..	..	..	..	..	24.2	15.1	..	..	..	..	..	..	19.65
Senegal	..	23.1	19.4	20.6	22.5	21.3	23.2	24.1	23.8	27.0	40.7	..	21.23	25.39
Seychelles	..	..	..	..	..	..	..	..	..	..	..	..	..	..
Sierra Leone	..	..	..	..	..	..	..	..	2.4	3.5	5.4	..	..	3.74
Somalia	..	..	..	..	..	..	..	..	..	..	..	..	..	..
South Africa	..	..	..	..	..	..	..	..	..	..	..	..	..	..
Sudan	..	..	..	..	..	..	2.1	1.2	4.7	5.3	..	..	..	3.34
Swaziland	76.9	..	..	..	..	..	..	..	..	..	..	64.23	74.99	..
Tanzania	..	..	..	..	..	..	..	3.9	4.8	6.0	5.8	..	..	5.13
Togo	..	..	..	..	..	..	..	..	..	..	..	21.20	19.61	..
Uganda	..	..	4.9	6.2	5.8	8.1	8.9	11.2	12.3	13.0	16.1	..	4.91	10.20
Zambia	..	9.1	8.5	6.0	11.5	12.3	9.7	10.8	9.5	..	..	..	10.54	9.96
Zimbabwe	..	..	..	..	..	..	83.6	54.3	..	..	..	..	..	68.99
NORTH AFRICA	45.3	58.4	61.2	61.0	..	..	..	..	..	..	..	46.78	54.30	61.01
Algeria	..	..	..	..	..	..	..	..	..	..	..	..	..	..
Egypt, Arab Rep.	29.9	43.5	48.2	48.2	..	..	..	..	..	..	..	32.48	41.64	48.19
Libya	..	..	..	..	..	..	..	..	..	..	..	..	..	..
Morocco	63.8	72.7	72.0	69.0	..	..	..	..	..	..	..	61.86	65.76	68.97
Tunisia	88.3	112.4	113.9	120.8	128.9	..	..	..	..	..	..	92.78	101.90	124.85
ALL AFRICA	..	..	..	..	..	..	..	..	..	..	..	..	..	..

Note: Note: 2002 data are preliminary (see page 2). Nigeria's fiscal data are for consolidated government starting from 1992.

Figure 7-1. Government deficit as percentage of GDP, 1993-2002*

(percentage)

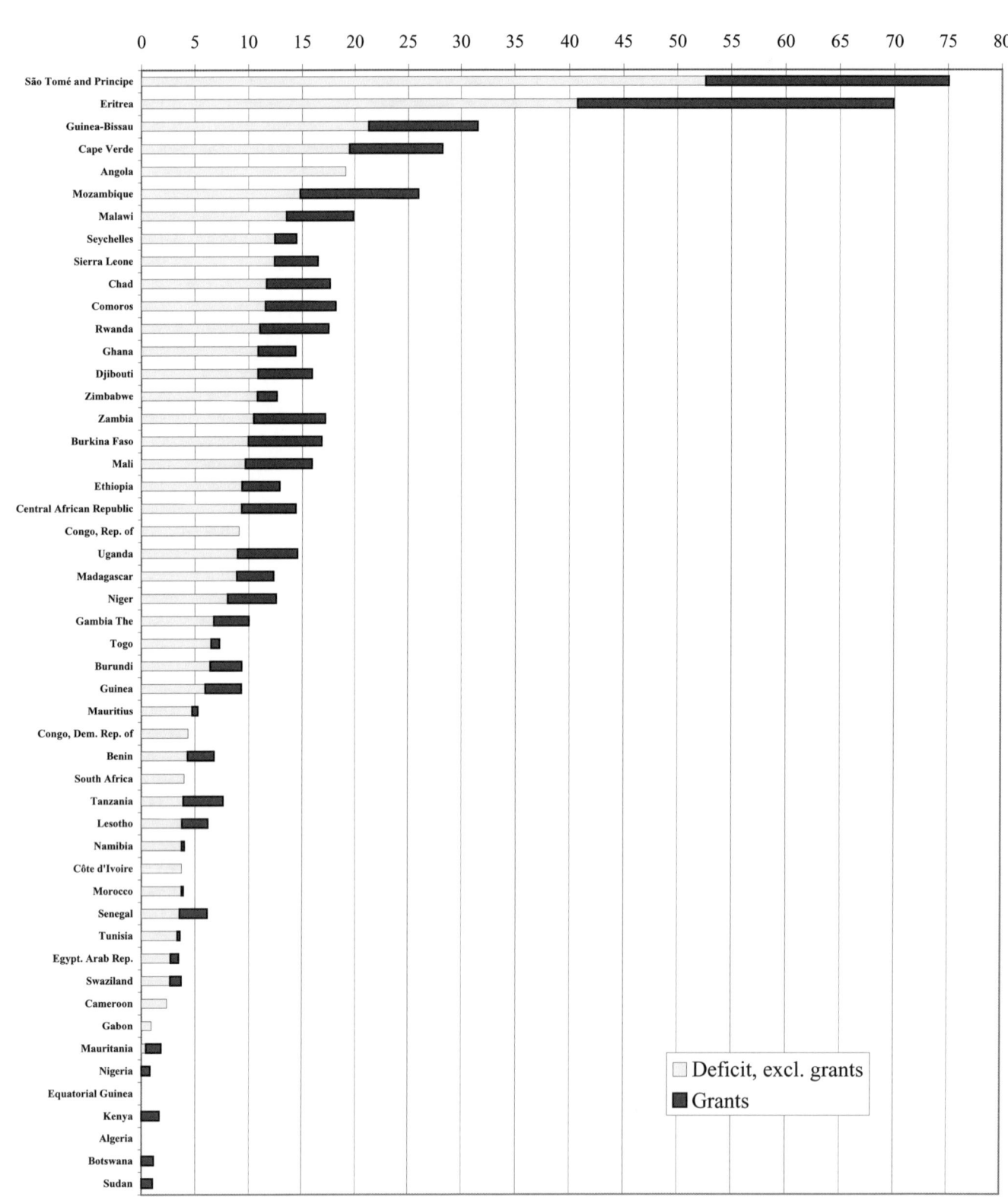

* Or most recent year available.

Technical notes

Tables

Table 7-1. Government deficit/surplus (including grants). Overall surplus/deficit is the difference between total revenue plus grants (as defined in *GFS*, line A-I) and total expenditures and lending minus repayments (as defined in *GFS*, line C-I). It represents the net financing requirement of the consolidated government. This indicator is shown as a percentage of current GDP in national currency (World Bank country desks).

Table 7-2. Government deficit/surplus (excluding grants). This is calculated as above, except that capital grants are excluded from receipts (as defined in *GFS*, line A-II less line C-I). It is a measure of the ability of a government to fund its activities from its own resources. Because some budgetary grants may be tied to certain expenditures that would not otherwise be incurred, excluding grants may overstate the deficit or understate the surplus if no account is taken of the expenditures dependent on these grants. This indicator is shown as a percentage of current GDP in national currency (World Bank country desks).

Table 7-3. Government primary deficit/surplus (–/ +). The primary deficit or surplus is the government deficit or surplus including grants (as presented in Table 7-1) excluding interest expenditures on both domestic and foreign debt (Table 7-5). In countries with large government interest payments, this ratio may provide a more reliable indicator for monitoring fiscal stabilization efforts. This indicator is shown as a percentage of current GDP in national currency (World Bank country desks).

Table 7-4. Government expenditure and lending minus repayments. Total expenditure and lending minus repayments (as defined in *GFS*, line C-I) represents the government's total outlays for current or capital purposes. Expenditure includes all nonrepayable payments by the government. Lending minus repayments comprises government transactions in debt and equity claims upon others, acquired for purposes of public policy rather than for managing government liquidity or earning a return. It consists of gross lending and acquisition of financial equity minus repayments of past government lending and government sales of equities. (This definition differs from the concept of lending minus repayments adopted in the SNA, which is gross government lending minus repayments of past government lending minus net government borrowing.) In determining a government's deficit or surplus, lending minus repayments is grouped with expenditures rather than with financing. This indicator is shown as a percentage of current GDP in national currency (World Bank country desks).

Table 7-5. Government interest payments. Government interest payments (as defined in *GFS*, line C2) include interest on all borrowings, both domestic and foreign, but exclude commission charges paid for assistance in placement of debt (which would be classified as expenditure for the payment of goods and services). This indicator is shown as a percentage of current GDP in national currency (World Bank country desks).

Table 7-6. Government revenue (excluding grants). Government revenue less grants (as defined in *GFS* line A-II) refers to current revenues (tax and nontax) and capital revenues, such as proceeds from the sale of real assets, including land. It does not include grant receipts from other governments or international organizations. This indicator is shown as a percentage of current GDP in national currency (World Bank country desks).

Table 7-7. Grants to government. These are unrequited, nonrepayable, noncompulsory government receipts from other governments or international institutions (as defined in *GFS*, line A-II). Grants of goods and services in kind are excluded. This indicator is shown as a percentage of current GDP in national currency (World Bank country desks).

Table 7-8. Foreign financing. This includes all government financing transactions except grants (as defined in *GFS*, line D-III) with nonresident individuals, enterprises, governments, international organizations, and other entities. It may be affected by trading in outstanding government securities between residents and nonresidents. The data also reflect changes resulting from transactions, but not revaluations, in government holdings of foreign exchange, deposits in nonresident financial institutions, and securities issued by nonresident entities held by government for liquidity purposes (reserves). This indicator is shown as a percentage of current GDP in national currency (World Bank country desks).

Table 7-9. Taxes on income and profits. These taxes (as defined in *GFS*, line A1) are levied on the actual or presumptive net income of individuals and profits of enterprises. Also included are taxes levied on capital gains that are realized on land sales, securities, and other assets. This indicator is shown as a percentage of total revenue (as defined in *GFS*, line A-II) (World Bank country desks).

Table 7-10. Taxes on international trade and transactions. These taxes include import duties, export duties, profits of export or import monopolies remitted to government, and monopoly profits of monetary authorities made in foreign exchange transactions, as well as taxes levied on the sale of foreign exchange (as defined in *GFS*, line A6). This indicator is shown as a percentage of total revenue (as defined in *GFS*, line A-II) (World Bank country desks).

Table 7-11. Indirect taxes. These are sales and excise taxes and duties (as defined in GFS line A-IV less A1). This indicator is shown as a percentage of total revenue (as defined in GFS line A-II) (World Bank country desks).

Table 7-12. Nontax revenues (excluding grants). This is all nonrepayable government receipts, other than compulsory unrequited receipts (taxes) and revenue from capital sales or government grants, plus all fines and penalties other than for noncompliance with taxes (as defined in *GFS*, line A-V). For some mineral-exporting countries in Africa, this category is quite large, since royalties on the extraction of minerals, such as petroleum in Egypt and Nigeria and bauxite in Guinea, make up significant portions of total government revenues. This indicator is shown as a percentage of total revenue (as defined in *GFS*, line A-II) (World Bank country desks).

Table 7-13. Government expenditure: wages and salaries. These expenditures are payments in cash, but not in kind, to employees in return for services, before withholding taxes and employee contributions to social security and pension funds are deducted (as defined in GFS line C1.1). Included are basic wages and salaries; pay for overtime, weekends, and nights; cost of living allowances; local allowances and expatriation allowances; and similar compensation. Reimbursement to employees for expenses incurred as part of their employment are excluded. This indicator is shown as a percentage of total expenditure and lending minus repayments (as defined in GFS line C-I) (World Bank country desks).

Table 7-14. Government expenditure: trends in real wages and salaries. This includes expenditures on wages and salaries as discussed above (as defined in *GFS*, line C1.1), deflated by the CPI. For most countries the trend is shown in index numbers beginning with 100 in 1987 (World Bank country desks).

Table 7-15. Government expenditure: other goods and services. These expenditures include disbursements for all goods and services (except fixed capital assets and wages and salaries) bought on the market, goods and services to be used to produce fixed capital assets, strategic or emergency stocks, stocks held by market regulatory organizations, and land and intangible assets. This category encompasses purchases of materials, office supplies, fuel and lighting, travel services, and payment of rent, as well as payments in kind to certain civil servants (as defined in *GFS*, line C1.3). This indicator is presented as a percentage of total expenditure and lending minus repayments (as defined in *GFS*, lines C-I) (World Bank country desks).

Table 7-16. Government expenditure: interest payments. These are payments for the use of all borrowed money, excluding commission charges paid for assistance in placing debt, which would be classified as expenditures for payment of other goods and services (as defined in *GFS*, line C2). This indicator is presented as a percentage of total expenditure and lending minus repayments (as defined in *GFS*, line C-I) (World Bank country desks).

Table 7-17. Government expenditure: subsidies and current transfers. These expenditures are all unrequited, nonrepayable government payments for current purposes (as defined in *GFS*, line C3). Transfers for capital purposes (that is, to permit the recipient to acquire capital assets) and transfers in kind are excluded. This indicator is presented as a percentage of total expenditure and lending minus repayments (as defined in *GFS*, line C-I) (World Bank country desks).

Table 7-18. Government expenditure: capital and net lending. This represents payments for acquiring land, buildings, and other nonfinancial assets to be used for more than one year in the process of production, including transfers for capital assets as well as net lending (as defined in *GFS*, line C-IV plus C-V). This indicator is presented as a percentage of total expenditure and lending minus repayments (as defined in *GFS*, line C-I) (World Bank country desks).

Table 7-19. Government expenditure: trends in real defense spending. Real defense spending has been calculated by deflating defense spending in current prices national currency (IMF, as defined in *GFS*, line B2) by the national GDP deflator (Table 3-1). The results are presented in the form of 1980 base indexes.

Table 7-20. Government expenditure: real per capita education spending. This table presents education spending (IMF, as defined in *GFS*, line B4) deflated by the national GDP deflator (Table 3-1) and divided by total population (Table 1-2). The result is converted into 1995 U.S. dollars by using the 1995 local currency/U.S. dollar conversion factor (Table 3-6).

Figure

The following indicators have been used to derive the figure in this chapter.

Figure 7-1. Government deficit/surplus (Tables 7-1 and 7-2).

Methodology used for regional aggregations and period averages in Chapter 7

Table	Aggregations[a]		Period averages[b]
	(6)	(7)	(1)
7-1	X		X
7-2	X		X
7-3	X		X
7-4	X		X
7-5	X		X
7-6	X		X
7-7	X		X
7-8	X		X
7-9	X		X
7-10	X		X
7-11	X		X
7-12	X		X
7-13	X		X
7-14		X	X
7-15	X		X
7-16	X		X
7-17	X		X
7-18	X		X
7-19		X	X
7-20	X		X

Note: Regional aggregations are shown in the rows for Sub-Saharan Africa, North Africa, and All Africa. Period averages are shown in the last three columns. This table shows only the methodologies used in this chapter. For aggregation purposes, all data used in this chapter were converted to U.S. dollars, using the conversion factors shown in Table 3-6.

a. Regional aggregations: (1) simple total; (2) simple total of the first indicator divided by the simple total of the second indicator (same country coverage); (3) simple total of the gap-filled indicator; (4) simple total of the gap-filled main indicator divided by the simple total of the gap-filled secondary indicator; (5) simple total of the first gap-filled main indicator less the simple total of the second gap-filled main indicator, all divided by the simple total of the secondary indicator; (6) weighted total (by population); (7) median; (8) no aggregation; (9) simple arithmetic mean.

b. Period averages: (1) arithmetic mean (using the same series as shown in the table; i.e., ratio if the rest of the table is shown as ratio, level if the rest of the table is shown as level, growth rate if the rest is shown as growth rate); (2) least-squares growth rate (using main indicator); (3) least-squares growth rate (using main indicator in constant terms, with the rest of the table in current terms).

8

Agriculture

Agriculture is one of Africa's most important sectors. African agriculture has two major components: food production and export commodities. Food production, including meat, is the livelihood for most Africans. Export crops provide many African countries with their main source of foreign exchange and thus the capacity to import, invest, and develop. The information in this chapter provides a basis for assessing recent trends in producer prices, aggregate agricultural production and trade, cereal imports, and food aid in Africa.

The data in presented are estimates based on a variety of sources whose quality and reliability vary from country to country and from year to year. Furthermore, production and export data are probably underestimated for two reasons. First, it is difficult to estimate production levels of staple food crops, especially roots and tubers, when much of the output is consumed directly by farmers, rather than marketed. Second, parallel market activity, including trade, may not be fully accounted for.

8-1. Nominal producer prices

								Local currency per kilogram									
	Category	1980	1986	1987	1988	1989	1990	1991	1992	1993	1994	1995	1996	1997	1998	1999	2000	2001
ALGERIA																		
Wheat (hard)	F1	1.2	2.2	2.2	2.7	3.7	4.6	5.4	10.3	10.3	10.3	19.0	..	..	..	..	..	..
Citrus (oranges)	F2	0.8	1.6	1.7	2.3	2.8	4.2	5.0	..	..	..	..	..	..	..	..	..	..
Dates	F3	4.5	11.3	11.5	12.0	12.5	13.0	15.0	..	..	..	..	..	..	..	..	..	..
Barley	NT1	0.8	1.4	1.7	1.7	2.3	2.3	2.3	4.7	4.7	6.0	14.0	..	..	..	..	..	..
Potatoes	NT2	1.3	2.6	2.8	2.7	3.0	3.3	3.3	6.5	6.5	6.5	10.0	..	..	..	..	..	..
ANGOLA																		
Coffee	X1	..	67.0	67.0	67.0	67.0	135.0	158.0	..	..	..	..	..	..	..	..	..	..
Maize	F1	4.5	10.0	10.0	11.5	11.5	11.5	100.0	..	..	..	..	..	..	..	..	..	..
Millet	F2	4.0	10.0	10.0	10.0	10.0	10.0	100.0	..	..	..	..	..	..	..	..	..	..
Wheat	F3	4.5	17.5	17.5	17.5	17.5	17.5	200.0	..	..	..	..	..	..	..	..	..	..
Cassava	NT1	2.1	5.0	5.0	7.7	7.7	7.7	150.0	..	..	..	..	..	..	..	..	..	..
Sweet potatoes	NT2	..	..	..	..	..	..	..	..	..	..	..	..	..	..	..	..	..
BENIN																		
Cotton (seed cotton)	X1	65.0	110.0	100.0	105.0	95.0	100.0	100.0	100.0	94.8	..	..	..	..	..	..	..	..
Palm kernels	X2	40.0	20.0	20.0	30.0	30.0	30.0	35.0	35.0	..	..	..	..	..	..	..	..	..
Maize	F1	40.0	65.0	68.0	64.0	55.0	85.0	58.0	62.0	53.0	..	..	..	..	..	..	..	..
Sorghum	F2	46.0	65.0	72.0	67.0	60.0	60.0	63.0	65.0	55.0	..	..	..	..	..	..	..	..
Cassava	NT1	30.0	15.0	20.0	16.0	16.0	16.0	17.0	17.5	18.2	..	..	..	..	..	..	..	..
Yams	NT2	32.0	50.0	58.0	49.0	49.0	49.0	49.0	50.0	52.0	..	..	..	..	..	..	..	..
BOTSWANA																		
Groundnuts (in shell)	X1	0.2	0.7	0.7	0.7	0.7	0.7	1.1	1.0	1.4	..	..	..	..	..	..	..	..
Sorghum	F1	0.1	0.3	0.3	0.3	0.3	0.3	0.3	0.4	0.4	..	..	..	..	..	..	..	..
Maize	F2	0.1	0.3	0.3	0.3	0.3	0.3	0.3	0.3	0.4	..	..	..	..	..	..	..	..
BURKINA FASO1/																		
Cotton (seed cotton)	X1	55.0	97.2	89.7	94.4	94.6	95.0	95.0	95.0	95.0	95.0	95.0	95.0	95.0	95.0	110.8	110.8	110.8
Groundnuts (in shell)	X2	54.0	50.0	60.0	55.0	60.0	60.0	60.0	103.2	83.2	78.2	111.5	156.4	159.7	193.0	179.0	155.0	169.0
Sesame seed	X3	70.0	80.0	55.0	65.0	85.0	80.0	80.0	199.0	199.0	199.0	199.0	199.0	199.0	199.0	274.0	288.0	217.0
Sorghum	F1	45.0	40.0	45.0	40.0	45.0	60.0	60.0	62.0	50.0	47.0	67.0	94.0	96.0	116.0	91.0	69.0	108.0
Millet	F2	45.0	40.0	45.0	40.0	45.0	60.0	60.0	65.0	56.0	55.0	76.0	110.0	106.0	129.0	99.0	75.0	120.0
Maize	F3	45.0	45.0	55.0	45.0	50.0	65.0	60.0	62.0	52.0	48.0	74.0	96.0	97.0	105.0	80.0	66.0	100.0
BURUNDI1/																		
Coffee (green)	X1	..	..	..	..	..	..	..	437.5	450.0	450.0	600.0	725.0	825.0	1050.0	1125.0	1125.0	1125.0
Tea	X2	100.0	145.0	150.0	156.2	162.2	167.9	173.2	26.0	26.0	26.0	33.0	35.0	35.0	35.0	65.0	75.0	75.0
Cotton (seed cotton)	X3	36.1	51.9	52.6	55.3	57.8	60.2	62.4	50.0	55.0	60.0	65.0	75.0	85.0	95.0	100.0	120.0	135.0
Maize	F1	25.0	37.6	39.4	42.3	45.1	47.7	50.2	50.0	60.0	50.0	52.0	80.0	150.0	160.0	135.9	182.3	182.5
Sorghum	F2	20.0	26.2	27.0	28.1	29.3	30.6	32.0	43.0	49.0	79.0	82.0	150.0	200.0	140.0	199.9	270.0	244.7
Rice	F3	25.0	32.1	33.6	35.1	36.7	38.3	40.0	44.0	50.0	60.0	68.0	78.0	100.0	135.0	135.0	200.0	200.0
Millet	F4	20.0	26.4	27.3	28.4	29.6	31.0	32.4	33.1	39.7	33.1	34.4	52.9	99.2	105.8	89.9	120.5	120.7
Bananas	NT1	6.0	7.6	7.8	8.1	8.4	8.7	9.0	46.0	51.0	89.4	100.8	93.7	129.5	121.1	156.0	274.3	288.0
Cassava	NT1	10.9	9.3	9.7	10.0	10.2	10.4	10.7	30.0	50.0	70.0	52.0	100.0	155.0	200.0	133.9	208.0	193.8
CAMEROON1/																		
Coffee (Arabica)	X1	..	..	..	..	..	..	..	125.0	125.0	400.0	450.0	450.0	425.0	425.0	425.0	350.0	380.9
Cocoa (grade 1, superior)	X2	300.0	420.0	420.0	42.0	250.0	220.0	200.0	200.0	200.0	225.0	480.0	320.0	350.0	650.0	575.0	450.0	489.7
Cotton (seed cotton)	X3	70.0	130.0	130.0	140.0	95.0	95.0	95.0	95.0	85.0	130.0	135.0	160.0	160.0	175.0	175.0	170.0	185.0
Maize	F1	60.0	83.2	76.8	82.4	57.0	51.7	55.0	75.0	68.3	61.6	76.0	95.0	100.0	101.0	120.0	116.6	126.9
Sorghum	F2	40.0	38.9	60.6	47.2	43.0	77.9	80.0	73.0	66.5	60.0	80.0	60.0	90.0	120.0	230.0	223.4	243.1
Millet	F3	40.0	38.9	60.6	47.2	43.0	77.9	80.0	116.8	106.4	96.0	128.0	96.0	144.0	192.0	368.0	357.5	389.0
Rice	F4	105.0	91.0	64.7	77.5	82.7	53.5	60.0	54.0	54.0	57.0	68.0	95.0	98.0	98.0	106.0	103.0	112.1
Cassava	NT1	19.0	48.0	46.6	41.7	41.0	41.0	41.0	50.0	45.2	24.0	36.0	37.0	43.5	45.0	45.0	42.6	46.3
Plantains	NT2	25.0	45.3	46.7	47.3	50.0	54.0	58.0	58.0	58.0	65.3	52.0	55.0	50.0	53.0	53.0	41.5	45.1
CENTRAL AFRICAN REPUBLIC																		
Coffee (Robusta, cherries)	X1	120.0	135.0	135.0	190.0	110.0	80.0	40.0	40.0	120.0	120.0	240.0	..	..	..	..	..	..
Cotton (seed cotton)	X2	60.0	100.0	100.0	100.0	100.0	80.0	68.5	60.0	60.0	87.0	117.0	..	..	..	..	..	..
Sorghum	F1	30.0	103.5	128.3	107.7	92.5	95.0	97.0	..	..	136.7	168.9	..	..	..	..	..	..
Maize	F2	40.0	65.3	67.7	104.3	111.6	94.9	99.0	..	..	136.0	271.0	..	..	..	..	..	..
Groundnuts (unshelled)	F3	70.0	150.0	165.0	171.7	175.0	180.0	185.0	..	..	217.6	526.3	..	..	..	..	..	..
Cassava	NT1	30.0	76.2	89.5	57.5	103.7	105.0	107.0	..	..	119.2	176.6	..	..	..	..	..	..
Yams	NT2	25.0	107.1	91.0	124.5	86.6	90.0	120.0	..	..	..	222.5	..	..	..	..	..	..
CHAD																		
Cotton (seed cotton)	X1	80.0	99.0	99.0	97.0	88.0	88.0	88.0	77.0	89.0	..	..	..	..	..	..	..	..
Millet	F2	31.0	31.0	31.0	48.0	47.0	52.0	62.0	41.0	41.0	..	..	..	..	..	..	..	..
Groundnuts	F3	64.9	57.0	46.0	44.0	46.0	48.0	70.0	67.0	77.0	..	..	..	..	..	..	..	..

(Table continues on the following page.)

8-1. Nominal producer prices (continued)

	Category	|	1980	1986	1987	1988	1989	1990	1991	1992	1993	1994	1995	1996	1997	1998	1999	2000	2001
COMOROS																			
Vanilla	X1		1,150.0	1,100.0	1,110.0	1,137.6	1,149.1	1,156.2	1,168.3	..	..	..	..	..	..	..	..	..	..
Cloves	X2		1,250.0	1,505.0	1,506.0	1,582.8	1,626.7	1,645.4	1,659.6	..	..	..	..	..	..	..	..	..	..
Maize	X3		30.2	34.1	34.3	34.8	35.2	35.5	35.8	..	..	..	..	..	..	..	..	..	..
Cocoa beans	X4		233.0	273.6	273.9	283.5	288.6	291.4	293.3	..	..	..	..	..	..	..	..	..	..
Bananas	F1		50.0	73.8	74.0	76.9	79.1	80.5	81.3	..	..	..	..	..	..	..	..	..	..
Cassava	NT1		40.0	48.5	48.7	49.7	50.5	51.1	51.5	..	..	..	..	..	..	..	..	..	..
CONGO, DEMOCRATIC REPUBLIC OF																			
Coffee (Arabica, green beans)	X1		4.0	42.6	69.3	107.5	166.9	440.5	13837.3	..	..	..	..	..	..	..	..	..	..
Palm oil	X2		2.1	23.0	37.6	59.4	93.8	247.7	7778.7	..	..	..	..	..	..	..	..	..	..
Rubber (natural)	X3		2.1	75.8	102.3	260.9	407.0	1074.4	2836.3	..	..	..	..	..	..	..	..	..	..
Cocoa (beans)	X4		..	30.0	50.0	..	..	..	..	..	..	..	..	..	..	..	..	..	..
Maize	F1		1.2	7.5	10.1	25.8	40.3	106.4	280.8	..	..	..	..	..	..	..	..	..	..
Rice (paddy)	F2		2.0	11.5	17.0	28.7	45.2	119.4	315.2	..	..	..	..	..	..	..	..	..	..
Cassava	NT1		1.3	3.0	3.9	8.4	13.2	34.7	1090.8	..	..	..	..	..	..	..	..	..	..
Plantains	NT2		2.9	8.3	11.2	28.5	44.4	117.2	309.4	..	..	..	..	..	..	..	..	..	..
CONGO, REPUBLIC OF1/																			
Coffee	X1		146.0	215.0	215.0	115.0	115.0	119.0	115.0	115.0	115.0	115.0	115.0	115.0	115.0	200.0	839.6	215.0	210.0
Cocoa	X2		134.8	190.0	240.0	108.0	108.0	88.0	88.0	88.0	88.0	88.0	88.0	100.0	102.0	150.0	787.3	190.0	195.0
Maize	F1		43.0	73.0	85.0	60.0	60.0	60.0	60.0	100.0	100.0	100.0	100.0	125.0	125.0	160.0	179.7	187.0	170.6
Cassava	NT1		100.0	180.0	200.0	200.0	250.0	250.0	300.0	300.0	300.0	300.0	300.0	300.0	355.0	410.0	579.2	539.0	492.4
Plantains	NT2		67.5	180.0	250.0	250.0	300.0	400.0	500.0	90.3	90.3	90.3	86.0	90.0	100.0	110.0	115.8	110.0	103.6
COTE D'IVOIRE1/																			
Coffee (Robusta, green)	X1		310.6	399.5	400.0	400.0	404.0	419.0	390.0	232.0	200.0	530.0	700.0	700.0	560.0	560.0	470.0	380.0	421.0
Cocoa (beans)	X2		300.0	400.0	400.0	400.0	400.0	200.0	200.0	200.0	200.0	315.0	320.0	320.0	430.0	430.0	397.0	364.0	691.0
Palm oil	X3		..	..	..	213.8	213.8	213.8	213.8	190.0	190.0	225.0	225.0	160.7	164.6	128.6	123.2	160.7	160.7
Rice (paddy)	F1		50.0	84.0	84.0	60.0	60.0	60.0	60.0	60.0	75.0	75.0	110.0	110.0	150.0	166.7	166.7	170.8	175.0
Maize	F2		68.0	76.0	45.0	45.0	45.0	45.0	45.0	62.0	62.0	75.0	68.0	68.0	80.0	88.9	88.9	91.1	93.3
Cassava	NT1		49.0	46.0	46.0	46.0	46.0	46.0	46.0	46.0	46.0	53.7	81.8	86.9	92.0	102.2	102.2	104.8	107.3
Yams	NT2		59.0	99.9	100.0	100.0	100.0	100.0	100.0	100.0	100.0	116.7	177.8	188.9	200.0	222.2	222.2	227.8	233.3
EGYPT1/																			
Cotton	X1		0.3	0.6	0.7	0.9	1.3	1.7	2.0	2.4	2.4	2.1	2.7	3.2	3.2	3.2	2.6	2.6	2.6
Rice (96% humidity)	X2		0.1	0.2	0.2	0.3	0.4	0.4	0.4	0.5	0.5	0.6	0.7	0.7	0.7	0.7	0.7	0.6	0.6
Wheat (94% humidity)	F1		0.1	0.2	0.2	0.2	0.4	0.5	0.5	0.5	0.5	0.5	0.6	0.6	0.7	0.7	0.7	0.7	0.7
Sugarcane	F2		0.0	0.0	0.0	0.0	0.1	0.1	0.1	0.1	0.1	0.1	0.1	0.1	0.1	0.1	0.1	0.1	0.1
Broadbeans	NT1		0.2	0.5	0.6	0.6	0.6	0.7	0.9	1.1	1.0	1.0	1.0	1.1	1.2	1.2	1.3	1.3	1.3
EQUATORIAL GUINEA																			
Cocoa (first grade dried beans)	X1		..	..	..	..	..	..	..	250.0	320.0	325.0	400.0	500.0	450.0	500.0	500.0	400.0	500.0
Coffee (Robusta, cherry)	X2		..	..	..	..	..	..	..	..	..	..	..	..	..	..	..	..	..
Cassava	NT1		..	..	..	..	..	..	..	29.7	38.0	38.6	47.5	59.4	53.4	59.4	59.4	47.5	59.4
Plantains	NT2		..	..	..	..	..	..	..	36.9	47.3	48.0	59.1	73.9	66.5	73.9	73.9	59.1	73.9
ETHIOPIA																			
Coffee (Arabica, beans)	X1		2.7	3.7	4.1	4.2	4.2	4.2	3.1	3.1	..	..	..	..	..	..	..	..	..
Sesame seed	X2		..	1.1	1.1	1.3	1.3	1.4	1.7	..	..	..	..	..	..	..	..	..	..
Sorghum (mixed)	F1		..	0.5	0.4	0.5	0.5	0.5	0.8	0.8	..	..	..	..	..	..	..	..	..
Maize	F2		..	0.5	0.4	0.4	0.5	0.4	0.6	0.7	..	..	..	..	..	..	..	..	..
Barley (non-white mixed)	NT1		..	0.5	0.4	0.5	0.5	0.5	0.7	0.9	..	..	..	..	..	..	..	..	..
GABON																			
Cocoa (first quality)	X1		320.0	430.0	430.0	370.0	210.0	224.0	224.0	260.0	..	..	..	..	..	..	..	..	..
Coffee (merchant, processed)	X2		180.0	..	260.0	130.0	130.0	..	150.0	147.0	..	..	..	..	..	..	..	..	..
Maize	F1		54.5	77.9	77.9	67.0	67.0	71.7	71.7	..	..	..	..	..	..	..	..	..	..
Cassava	NT1		139.5	171.4	171.4	147.4	147.4	157.7	157.7	..	..	..	..	..	..	..	..	..	..
Yams	NT3		124.5	145.6	145.6	125.3	125.3	134.0	134.0	..	..	..	..	..	..	..	..	..	..
GAMBIA, THE																			
Groundnuts (unshelled)	X1		0.5	1.8	1.5	1.1	1.5	1.8	1.8	..	..	..	..	..	..	..	..	..	..
Cotton (seed cotton)	X2		0.5	1.3	1.5	1.6	1.8	1.9	1.9	2.0	2.0	2.2	2.2	..	..	..	..	..	..
Palm kernels	X3		0.3	0.3	..	..	..	..	..	..	..	..	..	..	..	..	..	..	..
Millet	F1		0.5	1.1	1.2	1.2	1.5	1.9	1.9	..	..	..	..	..	..	..	..	..	..
Rice (paddy)	F2		0.8	1.7	2.1	2.1	3.4	2.8	2.7	..	..	..	..	..	..	..	..	..	..
Maize	F3		0.8	1.1	1.2	1.2	1.4	2.1	1.9	..	..	..	..	..	..	..	..	..	..
Sorghum	F4		0.3	0.9	1.0	1.0	1.2	1.5	1.9	..	..	..	..	..	..	..	..	..	..

Local currency per kilogram

(Table continues on the following page.)

8-1. Nominal producer prices (continued)

	Category	1980	1986	1987	1988	1989	1990	1991	1992	1993	1994	1995	1996	1997	1998	1999	2000	2001
GHANA																		
Cocoa	X1	4.0	80.3	101.3	153.8	160.0	230.0	250.0	280.0	300.0	330.0	204.9	..	..	..	..	..	..
Maize	F1	4.1	25.0	42.0	48.0	35.8	86.9	69.5	83.5	93.7	95.0	82.0	..	..	..	..	..	..
Millet	F2	5.3	24.2	36.0	83.3	89.7	77.9	113.5	141.4	149.9	160.0	87.8	..	..	..	..	..	..
Groundnuts	F3	8.4	92.0	160.0	202.0	389.0	400.0	493.0	508.0	800.0	896.0	121.4	..	..	..	..	..	..
Cassava	NT1	1.5	8.8	10.8	12.9	10.0	10.0	15.8	22.5	25.3	26.0	29.4	..	..	..	..	..	..
Plantains	NT2	1.9	15.0	18.6	43.0	45.9	27.8	26.8	35.5	91.4	93.0	39.0	..	..	..	..	..	..
GUINEA																		
Coffee (Robusta)	X1	49.0	400.0	400.0	..	..	..	..	..	..	..	..	..	..	..	..	..	..
Palm kernels	X2	6.0	60.0	60.0	..	..	..	..	..	..	..	..	..	..	..	..	..	..
Rice (paddy)	F1	9.0	85.7	100.0	130.0	150.0	168.0	166.0	170.0	230.0	230.0	230.0	..	..	..	..	..	..
Maize	F2	7.0	74.3	74.3	83.6	83.6	130.0	144.0	147.0	198.0	198.0	198.0	..	..	..	..	..	..
Groundnuts (unshelled)	F3	11.0	100.0	150.0	200.0	250.0	213.0	217.0	293.0	293.0	293.0	293.0	..	..	..	..	..	..
Cassava	NT1	5.0	40.0	40.0	45.0	45.0	77.0	81.0	83.0	112.0	112.0	112.0	..	..	..	..	..	..
Plantains	NT2	4.5	80.0	80.0	110.0	170.0	200.0	200.0	210.0	240.0	240.0	240.0	..	..	..	..	..	..
GUINEA-BISSAU																		
Cashew nuts	X1	8.0	38.5	125.0	230.0	350.0	450.0	550.0	1000.0	3500.0	4000.0	..	..	..	..	..	..	..
Groundnuts (unshelled, grade 1)	X2	7.5	32.5	40.0	80.0	140.0	225.0	275.0	500.0	1000.0	1500.0	..	..	..	..	..	..	..
Palm kernels	X3	..	..	..	..	..	..	..	..	..	..	..	..	..	..	..	..	..
Rice (paddy, grade 1)	F1	8.5	37.5	50.0	85.0	180.0	225.0	400.0	650.0	1100.0	1600.0	..	..	..	..	..	..	..
Sorghum	F2	6.0	32.8	43.7	74.3	157.4	284.3	350.0	437.0	738.5	1070.0	..	..	..	..	..	..	..
Maize (grade 1)	F3	4.3	32.8	43.7	74.3	157.4	284.3	350.0	437.5	740.0	1070.0	..	..	..	..	..	..	..
KENYA																		
Coffee (Arabica, washed bean, grade 1-6)	X1	26.4	54.8	34.1	43.0	43.1	36.4	46.5	49.4	98.9	..	..	..	..	..	..	..	..
Tea	X2	15.9	33.8	25.0	26.8	27.2	35.2	38.5	47.5	92.4	..	..	..	..	..	..	..	..
Sugar (cane)	X3	0.1	0.3	0.3	0.4	0.4	0.5	0.5	0.6	0.8	..	..	..	..	..	..	..	..
Sisal	X4	4.2	7.4	7.1	7.4	8.9	9.2	9.4	9.8	9.9	..	..	..	..	..	..	..	..
Maize	F1	1.0	2.1	2.1	2.2	2.7	2.6	3.1	4.7	8.1	..	..	..	..	..	..	..	..
Wheat	F2	1.6	2.9	3.0	3.2	3.4	4.5	5.0	5.6	5.7	..	..	..	..	..	..	..	..
LESOTHO																		
Wheat	X1	0.2	0.4	0.5	0.5	0.6	..	..	0.8	..	..	..	..	..	..	..	..	..
Beans	X2	0.5	1.1	1.3	1.3	1.4	..	..	..	..	..	..	..	..	..	..	..	..
Peas	X3	0.4	0.9	0.9	1.1	1.2	1.2	..	..	..	..	..	..	..	..	..	..	..
Maize	X4	0.1	0.3	0.3	0.4	0.4	0.4	0.5	0.6	0.6	0.6	..	..	..	..	..	..	..
Sorghum	F1	0.2	0.2	0.3	0.3	0.3	0.3	..	0.5	0.6	..	..	..	..	..	..	..	..
LIBERIA																		
Rubber (nonspec. coagul.)	X1	0.8	1.0	1.0	1.0	1.5	1.5	1.6	1700.0	1800.0	1900.0	0.0	..	..	..	..	..	..
Coffee (Robusta)	X2	2.1	1.6	1.6	..	..	..	..	..	..	..	..	..	..	..	..	..	..
Cocoa (fair average quality)	X3	2.1	2.3	2.3	2.4	3.0	3.1	3.2	3.3	3.4	3.6	3.8	..	..	..	..	..	..
Rice	F1	0.3	0.3	0.3	0.3	0.6	0.6	0.6	0.7	0.7	0.7	0.0	..	..	..	..	..	..
Cassava	NT1	0.0	0.1	0.1	0.1	0.2	0.2	0.2	0.2	0.2	0.2	0.2	..	..	..	..	..	..
LIBYA																		
Wheat	F1	0.1	0.2	0.2	0.3	0.3	0.3	0.3	..	..	..	..	..	..	..	..	..	..
Olives	F2	0.1	0.1	0.1	0.1	0.1	0.1	0.1	..	..	..	..	..	..	..	..	..	..
Oranges	F3	0.1	0.2	0.2	0.2	0.3	0.3	0.3	..	..	..	..	..	..	..	..	..	..
Barley	NT1	0.1	0.2	0.2	0.2	0.2	0.2	0.2	..	..	..	..	..	..	..	..	..	..
MADAGASCAR1/																		
Coffee (Robusta)	X1	215.0	600.0	800.0	950.0	950.0	950.0	1000.0	500.0	500.0	8200.0	6000.0	4570.0	5000.0	6500.0	5500.0	2650.0	2793.1
Vanilla (green)	X2	600.0	1100.0	1200.0	1700.0	2000.0	2000.0	2000.0	5000.0	5000.0	8450.0	10000.0	5150.0	10500.0	10500.0	25000.0	66250.0	69827.5
Cloves	X3	395.0	525.0	600.0	600.0	600.0	600.0	600.0	766.0	900.0	1800.0	1850.0	1900.0	1550.0	9000.0	23000.0	24875.0	26218.2
Rice (paddy)	F1	42.5	100.0	127.5	180.0	250.0	250.0	274.0	350.0	470.0	648.0	725.0	728.0	858.0	1070.0	1100.0	1290.0	1359.7
Cassava	NT1	7.0	55.0	55.0	70.0	80.0	100.0	124.0	210.0	200.0	410.0	594.0	586.0	537.0	995.0	525.0	536.0	565.0
Sweet potatoes	NT2	30.0	50.0	60.0	60.0	60.0	100.0	116.0	267.0	347.0	463.0	547.0	751.0	875.0	1171.0	890.0	908.7	957.8
MALAWI1/																		
Tobacco (flue-cured)	X1	0.4	1.0	1.0	1.1	1.7	2.5	2.8	2.8	2.8	3.4	4.5	8.7	13.7	14.9	24.8	32.3	55.6
Tobacco (Northen division dark-fired, G2)	X1	0.4	1.0	1.0	1.1	1.7	2.5	2.8	2.8	2.8	3.4	4.5	8.7	13.7	14.9	24.8	32.3	55.6
Tea (dry leaves)	X2	0.7	1.0	1.0	1.5	1.6	2.0	2.0	2.5	2.5	3.0	5.0	9.7	15.3	16.7	27.8	36.1	62.3
Groundnuts (in shell)	X3	0.3	0.5	0.6	0.6	0.6	0.8	0.7	0.9	1.1	1.6	2.5	4.9	7.6	8.3	13.9	18.1	31.1
Cotton (seed cotton)	X4	0.3	0.5	0.5	0.7	0.8	0.8	0.8	0.9	0.9	1.0	2.5	4.9	7.6	8.3	13.9	18.1	31.1
Maize	F1	0.1	0.1	0.1	0.2	0.2	0.3	0.3	0.3	0.4	0.5	0.7	1.4	2.2	2.4	4.0	5.2	9.0
Sorghum	F2	0.1	0.2	0.1	0.1	0.2	0.2	0.4	0.6	0.7	0.8	1.1	2.1	3.4	3.7	6.1	7.9	13.7
Rice (paddy, grade 1)	F3	0.1	0.2	0.2	0.3	0.3	0.4	0.4	0.5	0.9	1.5	1.8	3.5	5.5	6.0	10.0	13.0	22.4
Cassava	NT1	0.0	0.1	0.1	0.1	0.1	0.1	0.1	0.2	0.2	0.3	0.3	0.6	1.0	1.1	1.8	2.4	4.1

(Table continues on the following page.)

8-1. Nominal producer prices (continued)

	Category	1980	1986	1987	1988	1989	1990	1991	1992	1993	1994	1995	1996	1997	1998	1999	2000	2001
MALI1/																		
Cotton (seed cotton)	X1	55.0	85.0	85.0	85.0	85.0	85.0	85.0	95.0	85.0	97.5	130.0	155.0	155.0	170.0	185.0	150.0	170.0
Groundnuts (unshelled)	X2	40.0	70.0	60.0	62.0	63.0	64.0	65.0	179.0	179.0	162.0	180.0	249.0	223.2	249.2	268.8	172.1	229.9
Millet	F1	35.0	55.0	55.0	58.0	60.0	77.0	41.5	45.0	45.0	51.0	97.0	77.0	93.9	124.2	88.4	60.6	80.9
Rice (paddy)	F2	37.5	70.0	70.0	70.0	70.0	70.0	70.0	66.0	85.0	87.0	118.0	105.0	110.0	110.0	110.0	110.0	110.0
Sorghum	F3	35.0	55.0	55.0	58.0	60.0	61.0	41.0	45.0	38.0	59.0	99.0	77.0	94.1	126.4	86.2	62.2	55.0
Maize	F4	35.0	55.0	55.0	58.0	60.0	54.0	35.0	38.0	33.0	55.0	83.0	69.0	107.0	141.3	115.3	76.7	102.4
MAURITANIA																		
Sorghum	F1	11.0	15.4	15.4	16.0	16.0	16.0	16.5	16.5	16.8	17.0	17.2	..	..	..	..	..	..
Millet	F2	11.0	15.4	15.4	16.0	16.0	16.0	16.5	16.5	16.8	17.0	17.2	..	..	..	..	..	..
Rice (paddy)	F3	10.0	14.0	14.0	15.0	15.0	15.0	16.0	16.0	16.3	16.6	0.0	..	..	..	..	..	..
Maize	F4	15.0	15.0	15.0	16.0	16.0	16.0	17.0	17.0	17.3	17.6	17.9	..	..	..	..	..	..
MAURITIUS																		
Sugarcane	X1	0.2	0.3	0.3	0.3	0.3	0.4	0.4	0.4	0.4	0.4	0.4	..	..	..	..	..	..
Tea	X2	11.0	9.2	7.4	10.3	10.4	13.5	13.4	16.8	16.4	17.0	15.3	..	..	..	..	..	..
Maize (12% moisture)	F1	2.0	4.3	4.3	4.8	4.8	4.8	4.8	5.0	5.0	5.0	5.5	..	..	..	..	..	..
Rice (paddy, 14% moisture)	F2	1.4	4.9	4.9	5.0	7.0	8.0	8.0	8.5	8.5	8.5	12.3	..	..	..	..	..	..
Potatoes	NT1	2.2	1.9	2.5	2.5	2.8	3.1	3.7	4.1	4.7	5.0	4.8	..	..	..	..	..	..
Onions	NT2	4.2	4.2	4.8	5.8	5.7	7.1	7.8	7.7	7.6	8.0	9.7	..	..	..	..	..	..
MOROCCO1/																		
Citrus (oranges)	X1	1.3	1.6	1.6	1.7	1.8	1.9	2.0	2.2	2.7	2.3	2.2	2.9	1.2	1.2	1.8	1.5	1.4
Cotton	X3	3.2	6.0	6.0	6.0	6.7	6.7	6.7	5.7	5.7	6.2	6.5	6.5	6.5	6.5	6.5	6.5	6.5
Wheat (hard)	F1	1.5	2.2	2.2	2.1	2.3	2.5	2.5	2.7	2.7	2.4	2.9	2.3	2.5	2.5	2.5	2.6	2.5
Sugarbeet (16.5% sugar)	F2	0.1	0.2	0.2	0.2	0.2	0.2	0.3	0.3	0.3	0.3	0.3	0.3	0.3	0.3	0.3	0.3	0.3
Barley	NT1	1.3	1.3	1.3	1.2	1.3	1.5	1.5	2.0	2.0	1.2	2.0	1.4	1.7	1.8	1.9	2.3	2.2
MOZAMBIQUE																		
Cashew nuts	X1	7.5	13.2	86.0	232.0	325.0	358.0	..	..	..	..	..	..	..	..	..	..	..
Cotton (seed, prime grade)	X2	11.0	16.0	65.0	175.0	246.0	270.0	..	..	..	..	..	..	..	..	..	..	..
Tea	X3	25.6	45.0	140.0	378.0	529.0	582.0	..	..	..	..	..	..	..	..	..	..	..
Maize	F1	3.2	10.0	30.0	81.0	113.4	124.7	124.7	..	..	..	..	..	..	..	..	..	..
Rice	F2	6.2	16.0	48.0	130.0	181.4	199.6	199.6	..	..	..	..	..	..	..	..	..	..
Cassava	NT1	2.0	6.0	15.0	40.0	56.0	62.0	62.0	..	..	..	..	..	..	..	..	..	..
NAMIBIA																		
Wheat	F1	0.2	0.4	0.4	0.4	0.5	0.6	0.6	0.7	0.7	0.7	..	..	..	..	..	..	..
Maize (white)	F2	0.1	0.3	0.3	0.4	0.4	0.4	0.5	0.5	0.6	0.7	..	..	..	..	..	..	..
NIGER																		
Cowpeas	X1	45.0	80.0	80.0	80.0	85.0	90.0	95.0	100.0	100.0	100.4	102.0	..	..	..	..	..	..
Cotton (unginned, top grade)	X2	62.0	120.0	120.0	120.0	130.0	110.0	70.0	70.0	77.0	77.0	137.3	..	..	..	..	..	..
Groundnuts (in shell)	X3	50.0	130.0	130.0	130.0	132.0	133.0	134.0	135.0	140.0	143.8	146.4	..	..	..	..	..	..
Millet	F1	50.0	80.0	87.6	93.5	98.3	100.7	102.7	105.2	108.1	111.1	114.6	..	..	..	..	..	..
Sorghum (red)	F2	50.0	80.0	87.2	93.5	99.5	103.1	106.4	110.0	113.8	117.5	121.9	..	..	..	..	..	..
NIGERIA1/																		
Cocoa (bean)	X1	1.3	3.5	7.5	11.0	10.1	8.5	10.2	12.7	25.3	61.2	73.4	80.2	89.7	79.6	85.8	83.8	107.3
Palm kernels	X2	0.2	0.4	0.9	1.0	1.3	1.2	2.5	5.7	10.6	14.4	31.7	22.2	16.6	21.0	19.1	20.0	25.6
Cotton (seed cotton)	X3	0.4	1.0	4.0	4.5	2.4	2.6	4.2	3.8	5.0	45.0	45.2	37.8	35.8	33.0	40.2	35.0	44.8
Groundnuts (in shell)	X4	0.4	1.0	2.3	2.3	4.8	4.3	6.3	6.8	15.2	13.5	20.1	24.1	17.8	21.5	28.1	28.0	35.8
Sorghum	F1	0.2	0.6	0.8	1.6	2.0	1.7	3.6	4.7	7.0	5.3	18.6	14.8	19.2	22.6	18.4	19.4	24.8
Millet	F2	0.2	0.6	0.6	1.3	2.1	1.7	3.4	5.7	6.6	6.2	9.1	15.7	19.7	25.4	17.9	18.8	24.0
Maize	F3	0.2	0.5	0.6	1.6	2.7	2.1	3.3	5.5	7.5	5.6	14.5	17.6	23.3	26.3	19.2	20.2	25.8
Rice (paddy)	F4	0.3	1.0	2.3	3.8	6.3	6.3	7.5	12.6	18.8	12.3	14.3	25.8	25.3	32.0	27.0	28.4	36.4
Yams	NT1	0.4	1.0	0.9	2.0	2.4	2.3	2.6	5.9	11.7	14.4	18.7	23.7	26.7	28.5	30.3	31.8	40.8
Cassava (gari)	NT2	0.3	0.3	0.4	0.8	1.2	2.2	2.1	2.3	4.6	4.5	6.6	10.6	11.9	11.5	13.6	14.3	18.3
RWANDA																		
Coffee	X1	120.0	122.5	125.0	125.0	125.0	99.7	107.4	115.0	..	..	427.0	..	..	..	..	..	..
Tea	X2	75.0	75.0	75.0	75.0	75.0	75.0	75.0	80.0	180.0	180.0	180.0	..	..	..	..	..	..
Beans (dry)	F1	20.3	22.3	28.6	30.5	38.4	37.9	40.8	40.2	90.0	90.0	90.0	..	..	..	..	..	..
Sorghum	F2	12.7	20.2	20.2	19.3	23.3	24.5	29.3	33.6	141.0	141.0	141.0	..	..	..	..	..	..
Maize	F3	11.9	15.6	15.4	13.6	24.7	26.9	32.4	29.0	45.0	45.0	45.0	..	..	..	..	..	..
Bananas	NT1	0.0	0.0	0.0	10.6	10.7	12.7	15.9	14.9	..	..	..	..	..	..	..	..	..
Sweet potatoes	NT2	5.7	6.1	6.2	5.5	9.4	9.8	9.9	6.8	24.0	24.0	24.0	..	..	..	..	..	..
SAO TOME & PRINCIPE																		
Cocoa	X1	16.5	24.0	25.0	26.0	27.0	28.0	29.0	30.0	..	..	..	..	..	..	..	..	..
Maize	F1	1.9	2.5	2.6	2.6	2.7	2.7	2.8	2.8	..	..	..	..	..	..	..	..	..
Cassava	NT1	2.1	2.7	2.7	2.8	2.8	2.9	2.9	3.0	..	..	..	..	..	..	..	..	..

Local currency per kilogram

(Table continues on the following page.)

8-1. Nominal producer prices (continued)

	Category	Local currency per kilogram																
		1980	1986	1987	1988	1989	1990	1991	1992	1993	1994	1995	1996	1997	1998	1999	2000	2001
SENEGAL																		
Groundnuts (in shell)	X1	50.0	90.0	90.0	70.0	70.0	70.0	70.0	70.0	100.0	120.0	125.0	..	..	..	..	..	..
Cotton (seed cotton, first quality)	X2	60.0	100.0	100.0	100.0	100.0	100.0	100.0	100.0	115.0	150.0	170.0	..	..	..	..	..	..
Millet	F1	40.0	70.0	70.0	70.0	70.0	70.0	70.0	70.0	70.0	70.0	70.0	..	..	..	..	..	..
Rice (paddy)	F2	41.5	85.0	85.0	85.0	85.0	85.0	85.0	85.0	90.0	..	..	..	..	..	..	..	..
Maize	F3	37.0	70.0	70.0	70.0	70.0	70.0	70.0	70.0	70.0	70.0	70.0	..	..	..	..	..	..
Sorghum	F4	40.0	70.0	70.0	70.0	70.0	70.0	70.0	70.0	70.0	70.0	70.0	..	..	..	..	..	..
SIERRA LEONE																		
Cocoa	X1	2.1	17.8	2.1	30.2	40.0	51.0	61.0	..	..	..	..	..	..	..	..	..	..
Coffee (Robusta)	X2	..	..	2.0	25.0	40.3	..	..	..	..	..	..	..	..	..	..	..	..
Palm kernels	X3	..	..	0.2	..	..	..	..	..	..	..	..	..	..	..	..	..	..
Rice (paddy)	F1	0.4	2.8	0.4	2.8	7.4	22.2	29.0	37.0	44.4	..	..	..	..	..	..	..	..
Cassava	NT1	0.3	4.9	0.3	14.5	19.0	24.0	29.0	..	..	..	..	..	..	..	..	..	..
SOMALIA																		
Bananas	X1	1.1	6.9	7.7	8.5	9.1	9.5	10.0	..	..	..	..	..	..	..	..	..	..
Maize	F1	5.5	21.4	34.5	30.0	32.1	33.4	35.4	..	..	..	..	..	..	..	..	..	..
Sorghum	F2	5.8	18.9	22.7	25.0	26.7	37.0	39.0	..	..	..	..	..	..	..	..	..	..
Sesame (seed)	NT1	25.2	61.6	76.4	84.0	89.7	93.5	99.1	..	..	..	..	..	..	..	..	..	..
SOUTH AFRICA																		
Maize	X1	0.1	0.2	0.3	0.3	0.3	0.3	0.4	0.5	0.4	0.4	0.6	..	..	..	..	..	..
Wheat	X2	0.2	0.4	0.4	0.4	0.5	0.5	0.6	0.7	0.8	0.8	0.8	..	..	..	..	..	..
Sugar cane	X3	0.0	0.0	0.0	0.0	..	0.1	0.1	0.1	0.1	0.1	0.0	..	..	..	..	..	..
Sorghum	F1	0.1	0.2	0.2	0.2	0.2	0.2	0.3	0.5	0.5	0.4	0.4	..	..	..	..	..	..
Barley	F2	0.2	0.3	0.3	0.3	0.4	0.5	0.5	0.6	0.7	0.7	0.7	..	..	..	..	..	..
SUDAN1/																		
Cotton (seed cotton, long-staple, grade 1)	X1	0.4	1.8	2.5	4.3	4.8	6.7	14.1	37.2	84.9	12.6	39.2	53.0	82.9	127.0	166.3	154.7	121.7
Groundnuts (El-Obeid, in shell)	X2	0.2	1.1	1.2	1.8	4.4	23.5	21.1	2.3	3.5	5.2	12.1	102.1	31.0	41.9	40.0	87.0	56.2
Sesame (El-Obeid, mixed)	X3	0.3	1.3	1.6	5.0	6.5	12.7	30.9	4.2	5.5	10.5	37.3	56.7	59.9	91.9	120.3	111.9	88.0
Gum arabic (El-Obeid)	X4	0.0	6.8	9.0	9.4	10.2	10.3	18.9	3.5	19.3	44.6	72.6	60.9	55.6	92.0	106.6	116.7	106.9
Sorghum	F1	0.1	0.2	0.8	0.9	1.9	11.4	6.6	1.2	1.1	3.7	5.4	12.0	30.7	22.8	21.4	42.6	49.7
Wheat	F2	0.2	0.7	1.0	2.3	2.9	5.7	8.3	0.9	1.3	6.7	8.3	25.0	33.3	55.1	63.9	69.9	64.1
SWAZILAND																		
Sugarcane (sucrose)	X1	0.0	0.0	0.0	0.0	0.0	..	..	..	..	..	..	..	..	..	..	..	..
Citrus	X2	0.2	0.4	0.2	0.4	0.4	..	..	..	..	..	..	..	..	..	..	..	..
Pineapple	X3	0.0	0.3	0.2	0.2	0.3	0.4	0.5	0.5	0.5	0.6	0.6	..	..	..	..	..	..
Cotton (seed cotton)	X4	0.5	0.9	0.9	1.1	1.1	..	..	..	..	..	..	..	..	..	..	..	..
Maize	F1	0.1	0.3	0.3	0.3	0.4	..	..	..	..	..	..	..	..	..	..	..	..
TANZANIA																		
Coffee (Arabica) (parchment)	X1	9.0	50.8	66.0	90.0	..	..	..	..	..	..	..	..	..	..	..	..	..
Cotton (seed cotton, AR)	X2	3.2	16.9	19.5	22.4	28.0	41.0	45.0	..	..	..	..	..	..	..	..	..	..
Tea (green leaves)	X3	1.5	7.6	9.9	13.4	17.0	20.4	24.9	..	..	..	..	..	..	..	..	..	..
Maize	F1	1.0	6.3	8.2	9.0	11.0	13.0	15.9	..	..	..	..	..	..	..	..	..	..
Sorghum	F2	1.0	4.8	6.0	6.2	7.8	9.4	11.4	..	..	..	..	..	..	..	..	..	..
Rice (paddy)	F3	1.8	9.6	14.4	17.3	19.0	26.0	31.7	..	..	..	..	..	..	..	..	..	..
Millet	F4	1.5	4.8	6.0	6.6	7.3	8.7	10.6	..	..	..	..	..	..	..	..	..	..
Cassava (grade 1, Makopa)	NT1	0.7	3.6	4.5	5.0	5.5	6.5	8.0	..	..	..	..	..	..	..	..	..	..
TOGO1/																		
Coffee (Robusta)	X1	200.0	365.0	400.0	350.0	175.0	175.0	175.0	185.0	140.0	350.0	650.0	750.0	891.6	1033.1	1067.9	1003.3	1298.2
Cocoa	X2	220.0	330.0	360.0	300.0	225.0	250.0	250.0	250.0	225.0	300.0	550.0	450.0	534.9	619.9	640.7	602.0	682.6
Cotton (seed cotton)	X3	52.0	105.0	105.0	95.0	95.0	100.0	100.0	100.0	90.0	110.0	145.0	180.0	214.0	247.9	256.3	240.8	267.6
Maize	F1	68.4	73.0	72.0	79.0	60.0	61.0	58.0	73.0	43.0	62.0	95.0	112.0	132.0	102.0	83.0	86.0	93.7
Sorghum	F2	68.0	76.0	66.0	98.0	69.0	68.0	67.0	92.0	64.0	68.0	123.0	160.0	146.0	145.0	148.0	100.0	109.4
Millet	F3	66.7	59.0	61.0	87.0	72.0	58.0	75.0	87.0	61.0	52.0	119.0	153.0	147.5	142.0	122.0	87.0	94.6
Cassava	NT1	20.3	30.0	32.0	26.0	30.0	23.0	28.0	29.0	30.0	31.0	36.0	37.0	53.0	64.0	49.0	47.0	50.4
Yams	NT2	48.5	61.0	63.0	63.0	68.0	68.0	66.0	66.0	63.0	59.0	69.0	94.0	105.0	105.0	91.0	93.0	97.4
TUNISIA																		
Olives	X1	0.1	0.1	0.2	0.2	0.2	0.2	0.3	0.3	0.3	0.3	0.3	..	..	..	..	..	..
Citrus (oranges)	X2	0.1	0.1	0.2	0.2	0.2	0.3	0.3	..	..	..	..	..	..	..	..	..	..
Wheat	F1	0.1	0.2	0.2	0.2	0.2	0.2	0.2	0.3	0.3	0.3	0.3	..	..	..	..	..	..
Barley	NT1	0.1	0.1	0.1	0.1	0.1	0.2	0.2	0.2	0.2	0.2	0.2	..	..	..	..	..	..

(Table continues on the following page.)

8-1. Nominal producer prices

| | | Local currency per kilogram | | | | | | | | | | | | | | | |
	Category	1980	1986	1987	1988	1989	1990	1991	1992	1993	1994	1995	1996	1997	1998	1999	2000	2001
UGANDA																		
Coffee	X1	0.1	8.5	24.0	44.5	60.0	97.5	210.0	190.0	..	..	..	..	..	..	..	..	..
Cotton (seed cotton)	X2	0.2	4.0	19.0	56.0	105.0	175.0	286.7	340.0	..	..	..	..	..	..	..	..	..
Tea (green leaf)	X3	0.0	5.0	10.0	20.0	35.0	38.3	45.0	70.0	..	..	..	..	..	..	..	..	..
Millet	F1	0.2	7.4	17.6	30.7	109.6	134.8	142.6	294.3	..	..	..	..	..	..	..	..	..
Maize	F2	0.1	4.6	11.3	26.0	82.9	72.0	80.0	225.0	..	..	..	..	..	..	..	..	..
Sorghum	F3	0.1	5.4	18.3	30.5	84.6	104.0	115.3	237.3	..	..	..	..	..	..	..	..	..
Cassava	NT1	0.1	2.3	9.3	22.5	35.5	39.5	76.0	163.0	..	..	..	..	..	..	..	..	..
Plantains	NT2	0.1	3.9	7.5	13.6	46.9	51.2	64.5	156.7	..	..	..	..	..	..	..	..	..
ZAMBIA																		
Cotton (seed cotton)	X1	0.5	1.0	1.6	3.0	3.6	9.7	..	..	..	..	..	..	..	..	..	..	..
Tobacco (Virginia)	X2	1.6	5.1	6.3	14.0	14.4	60.0	94.5	..	..	..	..	..	..	..	..	..	..
Sunflower (seeds)	X3	0.3	0.8	1.4	1.8	3.2	6.4	11.4	..	..	..	..	..	..	..	..	..	..
Maize	F1	0.1	0.6	0.9	0.9	1.2	3.2	5.6	..	..	..	..	..	..	..	..	..	..
Wheat	F2	0.2	1.0	1.2	2.1	..	5.4	8.6	..	..	..	..	..	..	..	..	..	..
Cassava	NT1	..	0.6	0.7	1.0	1.4	3.2	5.4	..	..	..	..	..	..	..	..	..	..
ZIMBABWE																		
Tobacco	X1	0.8	3.1	2.2	3.9	4.0	6.5	11.6	8.1	6.5	..	..	..	..	..	..	..	..
Cotton (seed cotton)	X2	0.4	0.8	0.8	0.9	1.1	1.4	1.6	1.4	2.6	..	..	..	..	..	..	..	..
Sugarcane	X3	0.0	..	..	..	..	..	..	..	..	..	..	..	..	..	..	..	..
Maize	X4	0.1	0.2	0.2	0.2	0.2	0.2	0.3	0.6	0.9	..	..	..	..	..	..	..	..
Wheat	F1	0.2	0.3	0.3	0.4	0.4	0.5	0.5	1.0	1.5	..	..	..	..	..	..	..	..

Notes: The categories of crops are defined in the technical notes.

Categories are mutually exclusive, and ordering is intended to reflect relative importance of these crops as of 1986-88. In many cases official markets operate simultaneously with parallel or open market activites. Where a large majority of marketed production is believed to pass through the official channels, the official price is also reported as the farmgate price. In most cases, only very rough estimates of the share of marketed production passing through each channel are available.

The CPI is based in 1987 rescaled from price index based in 1980.

For each country one to four export crops (X1,...,X4) are presented in order of importance, in terms of value of total production.

Similarly, up to three traded food crops (F1,...,F3) and two nontraded staples (NT1,NT2) are included.

1/ Data was updated for only 10 countries by FAO

Agriculture

8-2. Food price index

	Index (average 1995 = 100)											Average annual percentage growth		
	1980	1992	1993	1994	1995	1996	1997	1998	1999	2000	2001	75-84	85-94	95-MR
SUB-SAHARAN AFRICA	15	70	76	90	100	108	121	127	127	133	134	..	9.9	5.8
excluding South Africa	15	69	73	90	100	109	121	128	127	133	133	..	8.6	5.7
excl. S.Africa & Nigeria	22	70	76	90	100	108	121	127	127	132	131	..	8.3	5.6
Angola	..	16	..	..	100	3,954	7,968	..	..	..	..	..	..	..
Benin	..	62	62	84	100	114	118	126	126	..	..	..	-0.4	8.2
Botswana	..	73	83	90	100	113	125	133	142	148	152	..	11.4	7.9
Burkina Faso	69	80	76	89	100	115	123	132	124	117	127	..	-0.6	4.3
Burundi	30	61	71	83	100	..	..	..	..	..	..	..	6.6	..
Cameroon	..	..	..	92	100	103	110	114	115	118	126	..	..	4.1
Cape Verde	..	85	88	90	100	105	116	121	126	..	..	..	7.1	7.0
Central African Republic	..	68	65	81	100	106	107	104	100	104	..	..	-1.0	2.7
Chad	..	73	63	95	100	114	124	128	112	121	..	..	-2.9	3.9
Comoros	..	..	..	..	..	..	..	..	..	..	..	..	..	..
Congo, Dem. Rep. of	..	..	..	..	..	..	..	..	..	..	..	..	..	..
Congo, Rep. of	42	59	63	94	100	107	119	133	140	132	130	..	0.4	5.6
Côte d'Ivoire	..	..	..	..	..	..	..	..	..	..	..	..	..	..
Djibouti	..	..	..	..	..	..	..	..	..	..	..	..	..	..
Equatorial Guinea	..	..	..	..	..	..	..	..	..	..	..	..	..	..
Eritrea	..	..	..	..	..	..	..	..	..	..	..	..	..	..
Ethiopia	34	80	81	89	100	95	50	51	56	55	47	..	8.0	-10.2
Gabon	48	70	71	93	100	101	107	111	110	110	116	..	0.5	2.8
Gambia, The	14	86	93	92	100	101	103	106	110	111	110	..	14.6	2.5
Ghana	1	39	49	62	100	136	164	199	216	242	298	..	23.3	22.5
Guinea	..	79	88	93	100	101	..	..	..	..	..	..	17.1	..
Guinea-Bissau	..	..	..	..	..	..	..	..	..	..	..	..	..	..
Kenya	12	54	78	102	100	108	125	130	132	136	..	..	16.1	5.9
Lesotho	15	76	84	89	100	111	..	..	..	..	..	..	14.2	..
Liberia	..	..	..	..	..	..	..	..	..	..	..	..	..	..
Madagascar	7	44	47	66	100	119	124	131	147	168	..	..	13.9	14.0
Malawi	5	30	37	52	100	145	157	201	287	344	412	..	20.3	31.5
Mali	..	..	..	..	..	..	..	..	..	..	..	..	..	..
Mauritania	..	82	90	93	100	107	112	122	126	131	..	..	2.1	6.0
Mauritius	33	76	86	94	100	105	111	120	127	129	134	..	7.1	5.3
Mozambique	..	..	..	..	..	..	..	..	..	..	..	..	..	..
Namibia	..	74	79	90	100	107	115	118	125	133	149	..	13.8	6.8
Niger	73	75	83	91	100	110	121	134	127	131	131	..	-2.5	5.4
Nigeria	2	25	40	58	100	130	141	151	152	156	199	..	28.7	14.5
Rwanda	..	55	67	82	100	122	149	178	152	153	162	..	7.3	9.6
São Tomé and Principe	..	..	..	..	..	..	..	..	..	..	..	..	..	..
Senegal	43	67	66	91	100	102	104	106	106	105	110	..	1.0	2.1
Seychelles	75	105	108	100	100	97	99	102	101	102	107	..	1.9	0.8
Sierra Leone	..	..	..	..	..	..	..	..	..	..	..	..	..	..
Somalia	..	..	..	..	..	..	..	..	..	..	..	..	..	..
South Africa	12	76	81	92	100	106	116	123	129	139	147	..	16.7	6.9
Sudan	..	..	..	..	..	..	..	..	..	..	..	..	..	..
Swaziland	13	62	70	83	100	113	129	136	160	146	155	..	13.6	9.1
Tanzania	2	46	57	75	100	120	141	162	176	188	200	..	30.5	14.4
Togo	77	99	98	129	100	106	121	117	..	..	..	..	0.2	-0.1
Uganda	..	86	83	96	100	107	115	123	132	133	129	..	..	5.2
Zambia	0	17	50	75	100	146	176	219	272	331	..	..	96.7	27.8
Zimbabwe	6	45	62	78	100	127	149	208	349	520	854	..	21.1	40.1
NORTH AFRICA	34	79	85	92	100	106	110	114	119	123	125	..	8.8	4.3
Algeria	11	44	55	78	100	122	128	136	138	135	141	..	16.0	7.5
Egypt, Arab Rep.	..	77	83	91	100	108	112	116	124	127	128	..	16.8	5.0
Libya	..	..	..	..	..	..	..	..	..	..	..	..	..	..
Morocco	35	81	87	93	100	101	100	103	102	103	102	..	5.1	1.1
Tunisia	34	86	89	92	100	104	108	111	114	119	121	..	6.7	3.7
ALL AFRICA	15	73	78	90	100	108	119	125	127	132	131	..	9.6	5.6

8-3. Food production index

	Index (average 1989-91 = 100)											Average annual percentage growth		
	1980	1993	1994	1995	1996	1997	1998	1999	2000	2001	2002	75-84	85-94	95-MR
SUB-SAHARAN AFRICA	77	112	116	117	124	124	131	135	137	140	140	0.9	3.5	2.6
excluding South Africa	76	114	117	120	126	126	133	138	139	142	142	0.9	3.6	2.7
excl. S.Africa & Nigeria	81	108	110	113	119	117	125	129	130	135	133	1.0	2.4	2.7
Angola	91	109	126	124	129	129	150	143	161	179	177	-0.7	2.3	5.2
Benin	66	113	119	128	136	148	152	162	170	170	182	3.3	3.9	5.3
Botswana	73	103	95	112	106	95	91	79	84	93	93	0.7	0.8	-2.1
Burkina Faso	59	129	120	127	140	126	149	154	132	172	170	2.4	5.0	4.1
Burundi	79	106	89	96	96	97	91	92	87	96	96	0.3	1.7	0.1
Cameroon	80	110	114	119	125	122	126	137	140	138	137	0.6	2.6	2.6
Cape Verde	63	119	94	124	111	114	129	163	144	143	145	1.5	6.0	5.2
Central African Republic	80	109	112	115	129	125	130	133	148	144	148	2.0	3.1	3.6
Chad	82	96	114	118	121	136	159	144	137	161	156	1.3	4.2	4.2
Comoros	82	110	118	115	120	119	125	129	132	135	136	0.7	3.8	2.3
Congo, Dem. Rep. of	73	105	107	93	92	90	92	90	88	86	85	2.3	2.7	-2.1
Congo, Rep. of	83	102	109	114	118	119	117	126	128	130	133	2.2	0.7	2.4
Côte d'Ivoire	70	106	107	123	131	131	133	140	146	137	127	4.1	2.7	2.2
Djibouti	53	77	83	85	87	88	88	90	89	89	89	11.0	0.5	0.8
Equatorial Guinea	71	102	104	108	111	111	108	117	116	113	113	0.0	4.1	1.0
Eritrea	..	85	117	108	104	104	150	135	117	124	108	..	..	1.0
Ethiopia	..	107	106	119	139	140	128	137	146	160	152	..	..	4.1
Gabon	80	101	103	105	108	110	113	114	117	117	117	3.0	2.2	1.7
Gambia, The	71	87	91	88	70	90	86	126	139	152	91	-1.1	-2.0	5.8
Ghana	69	125	120	138	149	144	157	167	171	175	198	-1.6	5.0	5.4
Guinea	95	119	124	130	134	141	147	153	153	162	170	0.9	3.4	3.9
Guinea-Bissau	66	106	108	112	116	125	129	136	142	144	141	3.3	2.4	3.9
Kenya	65	95	106	104	105	108	113	118	117	125	124	2.2	3.3	2.5
Lesotho	95	101	109	87	110	108	96	97	109	96	130	0.9	-0.2	1.4
Liberia	..	..	..	..	..	..	..	..	..	..	..	..	..	..
Madagascar	85	106	104	108	110	112	111	114	113	117	117	1.1	1.4	1.4
Malawi	91	112	88	106	123	114	141	160	184	191	147	1.7	-0.4	8.7
Mali	75	105	111	110	113	111	121	128	124	126	136	3.2	3.5	2.6
Mauritania	87	95	97	102	108	106	107	107	110	108	107	2.8	1.7	1.1
Mauritius	78	104	99	106	108	116	111	86	106	118	103	-0.3	1.0	0.3
Mozambique	101	92	90	108	122	130	139	141	125	129	129	-1.4	-0.7	3.5
Namibia	109	104	111	105	116	83	95	100	105	92	93	-2.6	3.1	-1.8
Niger	100	97	119	110	123	102	153	139	128	150	142	2.7	5.0	3.5
Nigeria	58	124	128	132	139	143	149	154	156	153	159	0.6	7.4	2.7
Rwanda	84	83	58	66	76	78	85	90	111	111	131	4.1	-2.1	10.0
São Tomé and Principe	112	127	134	124	143	160	180	187	191	198	198	-2.5	1.7	6.4
Senegal	59	101	104	116	107	101	101	138	136	130	101	-3.6	2.6	1.8
Seychelles	132	93	115	143	139	143	128	135	135	131	134	-0.2	-2.8	0.4
Sierra Leone	85	92	98	92	97	102	95	85	79	86	87	0.8	0.4	-2.0
Somalia	..	..	..	..	..	..	..	..	..	..	..	..	..	..
South Africa	89	97	102	88	105	106	100	107	113	108	112	0.6	1.6	1.9
Sudan	103	117	139	141	155	157	163	160	162	175	166	1.3	2.9	2.5
Swaziland	82	95	98	89	100	86	89	93	101	101	98	3.3	0.4	0.8
Tanzania	73	97	96	105	106	93	107	108	113	113	112	3.5	1.0	1.9
Togo	77	116	113	112	133	136	129	140	131	131	132	1.2	3.2	1.9
Uganda	66	109	106	111	102	105	117	128	132	139	139	-1.7	3.8	4.2
Zambia	74	116	103	93	114	105	99	112	110	103	109	-1.4	0.9	0.9
Zimbabwe	78	92	101	75	103	107	94	104	118	112	96	-1.9	-0.1	2.1
NORTH AFRICA	72	115	116	118	143	131	141	146	146	148	148	1.7	4.1	3.1
Algeria	71	114	105	121	144	115	131	135	128	142	139	0.4	4.0	2.6
Egypt, Arab Rep.	69	114	114	126	137	142	143	152	159	157	158	2.1	4.2	4.0
Libya	82	103	110	120	127	132	139	138	134	133	135	5.0	2.2	2.2
Morocco	58	83	108	74	114	97	113	105	97	104	111	2.0	4.3	1.5
Tunisia	73	116	84	82	143	98	125	136	133	115	97	0.5	3.8	3.0
ALL AFRICA	76	113	116	117	128	125	133	137	139	141	141	1.0	3.6	2.7

8-4. Nonfood production index

	Index (average 1989-91 = 100)											Average annual percentage growth		
	1980	1993	1994	1995	1996	1997	1998	1999	2000	2001	2002	75-84	85-94	95-MR
SUB-SAHARAN AFRICA	80	96	98	99	109	112	105	106	97	107	101	1.8	0.6	0.1
excluding South Africa	77	96	99	100	110	114	106	107	98	108	102	2.1	0.9	0.1
excl. S.Africa & Nigeria	80	96	99	99	109	112	105	106	97	107	101	1.9	0.7	0.1
Angola	209	95	85	90	90	94	94	89	94	91	87	-19.4	-3.3	0.2
Benin	12	195	174	219	280	261	253	208	257	238	238	8.1	12.9	1.9
Botswana	100	100	100	100	100	81	75	77	95	95	81	0.0	0.0	-1.9
Burkina Faso	35	92	95	91	125	205	194	171	155	162	227	8.9	4.9	9.5
Burundi	59	87	114	80	76	58	60	88	64	64	59	5.3	1.5	-5.3
Cameroon	86	88	98	112	126	100	127	127	131	134	118	3.5	-0.5	2.7
Cape Verde	94	21	21	21	21	21	21	21	21	21	21	-3.0	-17.2	0.0
Central African Republic	89	60	94	89	132	125	105	107	83	84	97	-0.5	-4.0	-1.9
Chad	51	60	99	99	138	166	103	119	94	113	97	-4.4	4.0	-1.3
Comoros	53	106	82	88	76	76	71	68	62	58	58	-5.0	2.5	-5.1
Congo, Dem. Rep. of	105	92	90	87	79	77	65	59	54	49	46	0.6	-2.7	-8.7
Congo, Rep. of	156	91	92	94	90	78	61	82	84	86	89	0.0	-3.5	-0.9
Côte d'Ivoire	77	76	80	83	82	114	138	141	146	114	116	0.2	2.4	6.6
Djibouti	..	..	..	..	..	..	..	..	..	..	..	..	..	..
Equatorial Guinea	92	85	78	70	63	54	52	55	55	55	55	2.2	-3.1	-3.8
Eritrea	..	96	99	98	99	99	99	99	98	102	102	..	..	0.3
Ethiopia	..	89	101	109	116	110	109	104	108	110	112	..	..	0.4
Gabon	36	93	124	142	209	284	307	307	307	307	311	19.5	3.3	12.1
Gambia, The	55	157	135	84	79	51	16	14	8	7	15	22.5	8.8	-31.2
Ghana	86	243	180	188	248	254	321	261	271	285	285	-6.0	17.0	5.6
Guinea	48	120	117	112	96	105	127	146	177	179	179	0.9	14.6	8.1
Guinea-Bissau	111	83	75	109	109	100	100	126	126	126	126	25.0	-8.3	5.2
Kenya	62	99	99	115	119	103	119	111	113	97	121	6.1	2.4	0.4
Lesotho	87	176	176	180	116	123	85	85	92	92	92	2.0	5.4	-8.7
Liberia	..	..	..	..	..	..	..	..	..	..	..	..	..	..
Madagascar	90	91	89	83	84	77	80	83	74	79	80	-1.0	-1.3	-1.2
Malawi	59	120	93	120	132	141	115	94	101	85	77	6.3	4.2	-4.4
Mali	38	92	117	154	172	197	198	179	92	209	224	5.1	7.8	3.7
Mauritania	..	..	..	..	..	..	..	..	..	..	..	..	..	..
Mauritius	84	105	92	73	51	38	33	34	29	32	33	5.0	-3.7	-12.3
Mozambique	251	117	124	120	124	160	192	193	177	244	249	-6.7	3.8	10.2
Namibia	276	96	123	115	109	121	119	135	135	135	135	-6.7	-2.9	2.4
Niger	84	140	178	275	204	220	181	540	478	298	50	-5.3	1.0	-3.7
Nigeria	41	85	86	101	116	122	126	129	130	131	133	-8.0	13.3	4.8
Rwanda	61	90	25	65	63	73	76	80	80	92	86	6.4	-6.3	11.7
São Tomé and Principe	321	107	118	91	113	241	193	311	96	107	107	1.1	-3.6	0.1
Senegal	47	129	78	85	105	105	31	32	58	98	93	1.0	2.2	-2.1
Seychelles	21	121	121	111	110	133	123	116	121	114	114	7.6	11.6	-0.2
Sierra Leone	44	96	106	97	97	114	98	60	60	66	66	11.2	2.2	-7.4
Somalia	..	..	..	..	..	..	..	..	..	..	..	..	..	..
South Africa	107	69	73	66	66	60	64	68	61	67	66	0.7	-3.2	-0.7
Sudan	90	76	85	105	115	102	95	93	94	108	100	-1.8	-6.2	0.4
Swaziland	65	41	31	19	41	66	49	60	61	61	61	-3.4	-2.5	12.3
Tanzania	100	106	92	121	129	120	106	101	100	127	127	-2.2	1.8	1.3
Togo	34	100	121	106	140	150	172	130	124	149	169	5.1	10.0	3.3
Uganda	82	107	141	131	199	160	162	195	145	172	172	-5.8	1.1	2.0
Zambia	49	118	92	50	86	126	121	284	132	137	138	5.1	2.7	11.1
Zimbabwe	77	117	106	104	129	137	153	129	154	140	107	2.1	1.9	2.0
NORTH AFRICA	84	97	92	91	95	100	94	81	80	103	103	4.1	-0.2	0.5
Algeria	84	103	98	96	91	91	94	75	80	83	86	5.1	-0.4	-2.3
Egypt, Arab Rep.	171	135	86	85	114	114	80	81	79	104	104	0.6	-2.8	0.5
Libya	105	97	94	100	108	110	99	113	113	114	114	0.2	-0.1	2.2
Morocco	46	89	92	91	95	100	104	95	102	103	103	0.9	1.7	1.5
Tunisia	73	87	74	75	74	74	75	72	76	75	77	3.8	0.2	0.3
ALL AFRICA	82	96	95	98	109	110	103	101	96	104	102	2.4	0.4	0.2

8-5. Food production per capita index

	Index (average 1989-91 = 100)											Average annual percentage growth		
	1980	1993	1994	1995	1996	1997	1998	1999	2000	2001	2002	75-84	85-94	95-MR
SUB-SAHARAN AFRICA	107	97	95	98	98	96	99	101	97	98	95	-1.6	-0.4	0.0
excluding South Africa	106	97	96	98	98	97	99	102	98	99	95	-1.7	-0.4	0.1
excl. S.Africa & Nigeria	107	97	95	98	98	96	99	101	97	98	95	-1.7	-0.4	0.0
Angola	123	99	110	104	105	103	116	107	118	127	122	-3.6	-0.7	2.2
Benin	89	102	104	109	112	119	119	123	126	123	128	0.5	0.7	2.5
Botswana	100	95	85	97	91	79	75	65	68	74	74	-2.7	-2.2	-3.6
Burkina Faso	77	119	108	112	120	106	123	124	103	131	126	0.0	2.1	1.6
Burundi	107	101	83	89	89	88	83	83	77	83	81	-2.3	-0.7	-1.1
Cameroon	107	101	102	104	107	102	103	110	109	105	103	-2.3	-0.2	0.3
Cape Verde	74	112	86	111	97	97	108	133	115	111	111	0.5	3.9	2.8
Central African Republic	102	101	101	101	111	105	107	107	117	112	113	-0.5	0.8	1.5
Chad	106	88	102	102	102	110	125	110	101	115	108	-0.7	1.3	1.0
Comoros	112	101	105	99	101	97	99	99	99	98	95	-3.0	0.8	-0.7
Congo, Dem. Rep. of	101	93	91	77	74	71	70	67	64	61	58	-0.7	-0.9	-4.7
Congo, Rep. of	111	93	96	98	98	96	92	96	95	93	93	-0.7	-2.3	-0.6
Côte d'Ivoire	104	97	96	107	112	110	109	113	115	105	96	-0.5	-0.6	0.0
Djibouti	83	72	77	78	77	76	74	72	70	69	68	4.6	-4.4	-1.8
Equatorial Guinea	116	95	94	96	95	93	88	93	89	85	82	-2.2	1.5	-1.7
Eritrea	..	84	115	104	99	97	136	118	99	101	83	..	..	-2.0
Ethiopia	..	97	94	102	116	114	102	106	110	118	110	..	..	1.5
Gabon	109	93	92	91	91	90	91	89	89	87	84	0.0	-0.8	-0.9
Gambia, The	103	78	78	73	56	70	65	92	99	105	61	-4.1	-5.9	2.6
Ghana	96	116	108	121	127	121	129	134	134	134	149	-4.2	2.1	3.1
Guinea	125	107	108	109	110	113	115	118	116	121	125	-1.8	0.3	1.8
Guinea-Bissau	82	98	97	98	100	105	106	110	112	111	106	0.1	0.0	1.7
Kenya	93	87	94	90	88	89	90	93	90	94	92	-1.6	-0.1	0.2
Lesotho	117	94	100	78	97	93	81	81	90	78	105	-1.3	-2.3	-0.2
Liberia	..	..	..	..	..	..	..	..	..	..	..	..	..	..
Madagascar	113	98	93	93	92	91	88	88	85	85	83	-1.6	-1.4	-1.6
Malawi	138	107	83	99	113	103	123	136	153	155	117	-1.4	-4.1	6.2
Mali	96	98	101	97	97	93	99	102	96	95	99	1.0	0.9	-0.1
Mauritania	112	88	87	89	92	87	85	82	82	78	75	0.3	-0.8	-2.0
Mauritius	86	101	95	100	101	108	103	79	97	106	92	-1.7	0.1	-0.6
Mozambique	118	83	78	91	100	104	108	108	93	95	93	-3.9	-2.4	1.2
Namibia	151	95	98	91	98	69	77	80	82	71	70	-4.4	-0.7	-3.8
Niger	137	88	105	93	101	81	117	102	91	103	94	-0.4	1.7	-0.1
Nigeria	78	114	114	115	117	117	119	120	118	113	114	-2.4	4.3	-0.1
Rwanda	108	101	76	89	97	91	88	85	97	93	107	1.0	-1.3	2.5
São Tomé and Principe	137	120	124	113	128	141	155	159	159	162	159	-5.0	-0.3	4.5
Senegal	78	94	94	102	92	85	82	110	105	99	75	-6.3	-0.1	-0.8
Seychelles	146	88	108	133	127	129	115	119	117	113	112	-1.3	-4.1	-1.0
Sierra Leone	106	91	97	91	96	100	92	81	72	76	74	-1.2	-1.2	-4.0
Somalia	..	..	..	..	..	..	..	..	..	..	..	..	..	..
South Africa	111	91	94	80	93	93	87	91	95	90	92	-1.8	-0.5	0.4
Sudan	132	109	126	125	135	134	136	131	130	137	127	-1.7	0.6	0.3
Swaziland	112	90	92	81	90	76	76	79	84	83	79	0.4	-2.4	-1.0
Tanzania	101	87	83	89	87	74	84	82	84	82	80	0.4	-2.3	-0.7
Togo	106	109	104	101	116	115	105	110	100	97	96	-1.4	0.5	-1.3
Uganda	92	100	94	95	85	85	92	97	98	100	97	-4.6	0.4	1.2
Zambia	101	106	92	81	97	87	80	89	84	78	81	-4.5	-0.2	-1.5
Zimbabwe	111	85	92	66	90	91	79	86	96	89	75	-5.1	-3.1	0.2
NORTH AFRICA	93	107	100	109	122	99	112	115	110	106	105	-1.4	1.5	0.1
Algeria	94	107	96	109	127	99	112	113	105	114	110	-2.8	1.5	0.7
Egypt, Arab Rep.	88	107	106	114	122	124	123	128	132	128	127	-0.3	1.8	2.1
Libya	116	97	102	109	112	115	118	115	110	106	105	0.4	-0.2	0.0
Morocco	74	78	100	67	101	84	96	88	80	84	88	-0.4	2.0	-0.4
Tunisia	93	109	78	75	129	88	110	119	115	99	82	-2.0	1.7	1.8
ALL AFRICA	106	97	96	98	100	97	102	102	99	99	95	-1.3	-0.3	0.1

8-6. Volume of food output, by major food crop

		1980	1990	1993	1994	1995	1996	1997	1998	1999	2000	2001	2002	2003	Average annual* percentage growth 75-84	85-89	90-MR
ALGERIA																	
	Wheat	1,080	1,152	1,837	1,017	714	1,500	2,983	662	2,280	1,470	760	2,039	1,502	0.1	0.7	0.2
	Citrus	454	268	362	361	376	323	334	351	418	454	433	470	473	-0.4	0.1	0.2
	Dates	208	210	261	262	317	285	361	303	387	428	366	437	437	0.6	0.5	0.3
	Barley	457	790	1,398	408	234	585	1,800	191	700	510	163	575	550	0.5	1.1	-0.2
	Potatoes	501	1,001	1,158	1,065	716	1,200	1,150	948	1,100	996	1,208	967	1,000	0.2	1.3	0.0
ANGOLA																	
	Maize	300	204	320	275	201	211	398	370	505	428	395	429	430	-0.4	0.2	0.3
	Millet	40	63	75	40	60	61	102	62	89	102	105	148	100	-0.4	0.4	0.3
	Cassava	1,150	1,600	1,861	1,861	2,379	2,550	2,500	2,326	3,211	3,130	4,433	5,394	5,400	-0.2	0.4	0.5
	Sweet potatoes	162	165	180	185	180	185	188	189	190	182	224	353	355	0.0	0.0	0.2
BENIN																	
	Palm oil	25	20	14	14	9	13	15	9	15	15	15	15	15	0.0	-0.6	-0.1
	Maize	307	424	460	483	492	576	556	701	662	783	750	686	622	0.4	-0.4	0.2
	Sorghum	63	106	110	106	113	117	110	120	138	126	155	165	195	-0.3	0.6	0.2
	Cassava	735	977	1,041	1,147	1,146	1,238	1,457	1,918	1,989	2,113	2,350	2,703	2,452	0.1	-0.2	0.4
	Yam	699	1,010	1,125	1,185	1,250	1,286	1,346	1,408	1,584	1,647	1,742	1,701	1,875	0.3	0.3	0.2
BOTSWANA																	
	Onions ,dry	1	1	1	1	1	1	1	1	1	1	1	1	1	-7.8	0.0	0.0
	Sorghum	4	53	16	38	37	38	78	17	9	13	11	15	15	-1.6	2.7	-0.5
	Maize	2	20	3	3	11	2	25	12	1	5	9	10	10	-2.0	0.6	-0.1
	Millet	1	2	1	2	4	1	8	2	1	1	1	1	1	-1.1	-1.0	-0.1
BURKINA FASO																	
	Groundnuts	78	131	143	206	203	181	221	152	215	283	169	301	324	0.2	0.6	0.3
	Sorghum	653	991	1,292	1,281	973	1,266	1,254	943	1,203	1,178	1,016	1,372	1,373	0.1	0.6	0.1
	Millet	378	649	784	899	831	734	811	604	973	945	726	1,009	995	0.3	1.0	0.1
	Maize	99	257	343	271	350	212	294	366	378	469	423	606	653	0.7	1.2	0.3
	Rice	47	42	47	54	61	84	112	90	89	94	103	110	89	0.2	-1.3	0.4
BURUNDI																	
	Maize	9	13	14	13	11	14	11	17	11	10	9	10	11	0.1	0.3	-0.1
	Sorghum	55	66	67	65	45	66	66	68	67	60	61	69	73	1.1	0.4	0.0
	Rice	9	40	40	40	38	27	42	65	41	59	52	61	63	0.4	1.8	0.2
	Millet	9	13	14	13	11	14	11	17	11	10	9	11	11	0.1	0.3	-0.1
	Bananas	1,185	1,524	1,626	1,586	1,487	1,421	1,544	1,543	1,399	1,511	1,514	1,549	1,603	-0.1	0.5	0.0
	Cassava	385	569	598	584	527	501	549	603	622	617	657	713	750	0.1	0.4	0.1
CAMEROON																	
	Maize	408	387	531	507	524	618	750	760	793	785	741	739	825	-0.1	-0.3	0.3
	Sorghum	310	343	380	390	350	460	439	400	500	272	420	505	525	0.3	-0.2	0.1
	Millets	104	65	55	60	50	66	71	70	65	60	52	50	50	0.3	-0.8	-0.1
	Rice	49	62	53	29	36	35	36	37	53	67	61	62	51	0.9	-0.3	0.1
	Cassava	950	1,210	1,636	1,648	1,715	1,780	1,848	1,918	1,966	1,889	1,918	1,947	1,950	0.3	0.1	0.1
	Plantains	1,017	1,136	1,038	1,120	1,211	1,250	1,290	1,326	1,359	1,157	1,164	1,187	1,200	0.3	-0.5	0.1
CENTRAL AFRICAN REP																	
	Sorghum	37	37	21	20	21	22	26	28	29	45	48	107	113	0.1	-0.1	0.4
	Maize	34	62	59	58	63	71	76	83	88	95	101	107	113	0.1	0.7	0.3
	Groundnuts	122	103	71	72	79	86	91	88	102	110	116	122	128	0.2	-0.5	0.2
	Cassava	940	516	580	575	518	492	526	579	608	559	560	562	563	0.0	-0.7	0.0
	Yam	150	200	260	260	280	320	340	340	360	360	380	380	350	0.0	0.1	0.2
CHAD																	
	Sorghum	237	237	387	243	481	437	353	427	514	457	392	497	481	-0.4	0.5	0.3
	Millet	231	179	293	212	320	228	258	248	357	361	259	398	357	-0.3	1.1	0.2
	Groundnuts	94	152	224	190	207	293	305	352	471	372	359	448	450	0.0	0.4	0.5
COMOROS																	
	Bananas	32	50	52	52	57	56	57	53	57	58	59	60	60	0.2	0.7	0.1
	Cassava	34	45	51	52	48	49	50	51	52	53	53	54	55	-0.2	0.8	0.1
CONGO																	
	Maize	17	21	5	5	5	8	8	9	10	6	6	7	7	-0.4	0.9	-0.1
	Cassava	600	699	600	632	723	747	772	780	739	812	828	845	862	0.2	0.2	0.1
	Plantains	40	62	73	75	78	77	76	76	71	68	70	71	71	0.5	0.3	0.0
COTE D'IVOIRE																	
	Palm oil	131	193	281	274	276	268	297	249	269	264	278	205	276	0.3	0.5	0.1
	Rice	534	635	660	676	701	764	1,139	1,287	1,197	1,208	1,231	1,212	818	0.1	0.7	0.3
	Maize	275	484	514	517	536	552	569	574	573	815	693	573	625	0.5	-0.1	0.1
	Cassava	1,112	1,349	1,502	1,509	1,564	1,608	1,653	1,699	1,692	1,681	1,691	1,688	1,700	0.3	0.3	0.1
	Yams	2,068	2,474	2,758	2,771	2,824	2,869	2,924	2,987	2,921	2,944	2,950	2,938	3,000	0.2	0.1	0.1

(Table continues on the following page.)

8-6. Volume of food output, by major food crop (continued)

						Thousands of metric tons								*Average annual* *percentage growth*		
	1980	1990	1993	1994	1995	1996	1997	1998	1999	2000	2001	2002	2003	75-84	85-89	90-MR
EGYPT																
Rice	2,511	2,679	3,910	4,161	4,583	4,788	4,895	5,480	4,474	5,817	6,000	5,227	5,600	0.1	0.0	0.3
Wheat	1,856	3,182	4,618	4,833	4,437	5,722	5,735	5,849	6,093	6,347	6,564	6,255	6,183	0.1	0.8	0.2
Sugarcane	8,791	11,213	11,708	12,412	13,822	14,105	13,958	13,726	14,353	15,254	15,706	15,572	15,000	0.1	-0.2	0.1
Dry Broadbeans	237	460	382	438	357	392	442	476	523	307	354	439	440	-0.2	0.3	0.0
EQUATORIAL GUINEA																
Cassava	31	44	47	47	47	47	48	45	43	45	45	45	45	0.0	0.2	0.0
Sweet Potatoes	20	30	35	35	35	35	36	35	34	36	36	36	36	0.0	0.3	0.1
ETHIOPIA																
Sorghum	0	0	0	628	703	1,141	1,808	2,040	1,083	1,334	1,188	1,541	1,566	..	..	0.3
Maize	0	0	0	1,456	1,396	1,990	3,164	2,987	2,344	2,832	2,683	3,298	2,968	..	..	0.3
Barley	0	0	0	787	875	986	1,125	953	983	962	804	1,017	1,093	..	..	0.1
Sugarcane	0	0	0	1,700	1,200	1,200	1,582	1,490	1,650	2,086	2,177	2,232	2,232	..	..	0.3
GABON																
Oil palm	2	3	7	8	8	7	7	7	6	6	6	6	6	-0.1	0.8	0.1
Maize	10	20	25	27	30	29	28	28	25	25	26	33	31	0.3	1.3	0.1
Cassava	239	212	230	207	197	202	214	221	227	224	228	230	230	0.3	0.0	0.0
Yam	76	100	120	110	125	130	135	140	145	150	155	155	155	0.4	0.1	0.2
Plantains	163	235	253	238	244	237	258	263	274	265	270	270	270	0.4	0.1	0.1
GAMBIA, THE																
Groundnuts	67	130	55	77	81	75	46	78	73	123	138	151	72	-0.4	0.1	0.1
Palm oil	3	3	3	3	3	3	3	3	3	3	3	3	3	0.0	0.0	0.0
Millet	9	51	46	52	53	54	61	66	65	81	95	105	85	0.3	1.0	0.3
Rice	29	21	19	12	20	19	18	13	19	32	34	33	20	0.8	-0.6	0.1
Maize	7	14	18	24	13	14	10	8	13	20	22	29	19	0.7	1.0	0.1
Sorghum	3	11	12	9	9	12	14	13	10	18	25	33	15	0.4	-0.3	0.3
GHANA																
Maize	380	715	731	961	940	1,034	1,008	996	1,035	1,014	1,013	938	1,400	0.1	1.3	0.2
Millet	149	180	133	198	168	201	193	144	172	160	169	134	159	-0.2	0.8	0.1
Groundnuts	107	200	100	140	176	168	162	154	212	193	209	258	520	0.1	0.9	0.3
Cassava	1,759	3,320	5,662	5,973	6,025	6,611	7,111	7,000	7,172	7,845	8,107	8,966	9,731	0.1	0.7	0.4
Plantains	784	1,040	1,082	1,322	1,475	1,638	1,823	1,818	1,913	2,046	1,933	2,074	2,279	-0.3	0.3	0.3
GUINEA																
Palm oil	40	40	40	48	50	50	55	55	50	50	50	50	50	0.1	0.0	0.1
Rice	348	358	512	531	544	631	673	716	764	816	739	789	843	0.0	-0.5	0.3
Maize	80	68	88	85	83	79	82	85	89	92	95	99	103	0.3	-0.4	0.1
Groundnuts	82	59	139	128	126	132	145	158	174	191	206	226	248	0.1	-0.6	0.5
Cassava	475	317	512	550	525	601	667	776	812	900	925	1,026	1,138	-0.3	-1.0	0.5
Plantains	350	370	405	410	420	425	435	430	429	429	430	430	430	0.2	0.1	0.1
GUINEA-BISSAU																
Groundnuts	35	16	16	18	18	17	17	18	18	19	19	19	19	-0.1	-0.6	0.1
Palm kernels	10	10	7	7	7	7	7	8	8	8	8	8	8	0.2	0.1	0.0
Rice	40	110	124	126	131	133	120	100	87	80	106	85	80	0.1	0.2	-0.1
Sorghum	15	9	11	14	14	16	22	12	11	15	21	15	14	1.3	-0.9	0.1
Maize	8	10	10	13	14	15	9	15	15	25	26	28	23	0.8	0.0	0.3
KENYA																
Sugarcane	3,678	4,825	4,180	4,370	3,800	4,550	4,650	4,450	4,661	4,416	3,942	3,551	4,502	0.8	0.1	0.0
Maize	1,755	2,631	2,430	2,089	3,060	2,699	2,160	2,214	2,400	2,322	2,160	2,776	2,340	-0.3	0.5	0.0
Wheat	207	244	126	150	297	313	290	227	263	212	204	252	234	0.3	0.1	0.1
LESOTHO																
Wheat	34	30	12	8	12	11	30	34	29	15	51	18	51	-0.9	0.6	0.3
Dry Beans	8	10	1	2	3	5	6	14	8	9	8	11	8	-0.9	1.6	0.3
Dry Peas	7	1	2	1	1	1	4	3	5	3	6	3	3	-0.3	-1.6	0.4
Maize	125	137	61	92	149	63	188	142	119	125	158	103	150	0.3	0.5	0.1
Sorghum	69	31	19	52	61	7	36	29	23	33	45	38	46	0.2	0.1	0.2
LIBERIA																
Rice	249	294	110	65	50	56	94	168	209	196	183	145	110	0.1	0.0	0.0
Cassava	300	446	280	245	250	175	213	282	307	361	441	480	480	0.1	0.9	0.1
LIBYA																
Wheat	110	185	125	126	120	117	124	156	140	130	125	130	125	1.0	-0.4	-0.1
Olives	100	65	100	120	140	168	186	190	200	275	165	150	150	0.7	-1.9	0.4
MADAGASCAR																
Rice Paddy	2,045	2,380	2,450	2,550	2,357	2,450	2,500	2,558	2,447	2,570	2,480	2,662	2,671	0.0	0.0	0.0
Cassava	1,570	2,277	2,280	2,350	2,360	2,400	2,353	2,418	2,412	2,461	2,463	2,510	2,511	0.3	0.1	0.0
Sweet potatoes	365	483	452	500	560	450	500	510	510	520	513	525	526	0.0	0.0	0.0

(Table continues on the following page.)

8-6. Volume of food output, by major food crop (continued)

					Thousands of metric tons									*Average annual* percentage growth*		
	1980	1990	1993	1994	1995	1996	1997	1998	1999	2000	2001	2002	2003	75-84	85-89	90-MR
MALAWI																
Groundnuts	170	62	26	55	31	32	40	69	97	125	117	148	158	0.0	0.9	0.4
Maize	1,393	1,510	657	2,034	1,040	1,661	1,793	1,226	1,772	2,479	2,501	1,589	1,557	0.1	-0.3	0.1
Sorghum	20	20	4	22	17	45	55	40	41	41	37	37	39	-2.4	0.8	0.4
Cassava	288	155	129	216	250	328	535	714	830	895	2,757	3,313	1,540	0.1	-0.3	1.1
MALI																
Groundnuts	146	157	127	149	215	157	134	144	152	191	193	196	257	-0.5	0.7	0.1
Millet	429	842	582	708	898	707	739	641	814	819	759	793	1,034	0.2	0.5	0.0
Rice	240	338	410	428	469	476	627	576	718	727	743	933	926	-0.1	0.9	0.4
Sorghum	317	731	602	777	746	712	541	560	600	689	565	517	951	0.3	0.4	0.0
Maize	76	225	193	283	322	266	294	343	393	620	215	299	321	-0.2	0.7	0.2
MAURITANIA																
Sorghum	21	111	50	92	147	157	145	58	73	95	85	53	29	0.2	2.9	-0.1
Millet	2	14	2	4	7	8	8	3	3	6	4	59	77	0.2	3.2	0.7
Rice	9	55	51	65	45	53	67	81	102	86	76	59	77	1.6	2.0	0.2
Maize	5	3	3	7	6	4	14	12	11	5	14	6	5	0.5	-2.8	0.4
MAURITIUS																
Sugarcane	6,313	5,436	5,781	5,402	4,813	5,159	5,260	5,787	5,781	3,883	5,110	5,792	4,874	-0.1	0.4	-0.1
Potatoes	8	20	19	14	18	16	11	18	15	15	14	16	13	0.1	0.0	-0.1
Dry Onions	2	3	3	4	5	6	6	5	7	9	11	11	7	0.8	-0.4	0.5
MOROCCO																
Citrus	927	1,441	1,111	1,227	1,320	999	1,394	1,231	1,599	1,316	1,426	988	1,152	0.2	-0.1	0.0
Wheat	1,796	3,927	1,562	1,573	5,523	1,091	5,916	2,316	4,378	2,154	1,381	3,316	3,359	0.1	0.2	0.0
Sugarbeet	2,175	2,877	2,754	3,062	3,144	2,717	2,750	2,613	2,783	3,168	2,774	3,029	2,986	0.4	0.1	0.0
Barley	1,888	2,999	1,081	1,027	3,720	608	3,831	1,324	1,970	1,474	467	1,155	1,669	0.2	0.1	-0.2
MOZAMBIQUE																
Cashew nuts	66	50	54	24	23	33	67	43	52	59	58	58	58	-1.0	0.5	0.2
Maize	400	330	132	533	489	734	947	1,042	1,124	1,246	1,019	1,143	1,236	-0.3	-0.6	0.6
Rice	70	95	33	66	101	113	139	180	191	186	151	167	167	0.0	0.1	0.4
Cassava	3,500	3,700	3,239	3,511	3,352	4,178	4,734	5,337	5,639	5,353	5,362	5,400	5,400	0.1	0.0	0.2
NAMIBIA																
Wheat	1	4	3	6	6	6	6	6	5	4	3	6	7	0.9	0.8	0.0
Maize	30	24	11	26	41	18	19	49	18	19	32	28	29	0.2	-3.9	0.0
NIGER																
Cowpeas	304	319	402	168	525	184	295	199	787	436	269	350	350	0.7	-0.4	0.2
Groundnuts	88	26	57	26	67	103	196	88	112	104	113	129	100	0.2	-0.5	0.8
Sorghum	351	422	387	289	393	266	408	290	503	476	371	656	700	0.5	0.5	0.2
Millet	1,255	1,333	1,788	1,658	1,968	1,769	1,761	1,352	2,391	2,296	1,679	2,414	2,500	0.4	-0.1	0.2
NIGERIA																
Groundnuts	507	1,017	1,297	1,323	1,453	1,579	2,278	2,531	2,534	2,894	2,901	2,683	2,699	-0.3	0.3	0.4
Palm oil	650	700	792	825	837	860	776	810	845	896	899	903	905	0.2	0.8	0.1
Sorghum	2,797	4,831	5,909	6,051	6,197	6,997	7,084	7,297	7,516	7,520	7,711	7,081	7,704	0.0	0.6	0.2
Millet	2,366	4,770	4,501	4,602	4,757	5,563	5,681	5,902	5,956	5,960	6,105	5,530	6,100	-0.3	0.5	0.1
Maize	488	5,008	5,840	6,290	6,902	6,931	5,667	5,254	5,127	5,476	4,107	4,620	4,934	-0.2	3.0	-0.1
Rice	750	3,303	3,260	3,065	2,427	2,920	3,122	3,268	3,275	3,277	3,298	2,752	3,192	1.4	0.8	0.1
Yam	5,256	9,609	19,781	21,632	23,153	22,818	23,201	23,972	24,768	25,873	26,201	26,374	26,849	-0.3	0.0	0.3
Cassava	12,000	17,404	29,184	30,128	31,005	31,404	31,418	32,050	32,695	32,697	32,010	32,586	34,476	0.1	0.6	0.2
RWANDA																
Sorghum	163	147	113	128	55	77	102	122	121	108	155	175	194	0.3	0.1	0.0
Maize	83	95	98	87	67	56	67	83	59	55	63	81	92	0.3	-0.3	-0.2
Plantains	2,023	3,020	3,547	2,136	1,489	2,002	2,105	2,248	2,625	2,897	2,212	1,784	2,785	0.2	0.1	-0.1
Sweet potatoes	868	772	1,055	997	739	551	665	742	751	863	1,033	1,156	1,292	0.5	0.1	0.1
SENEGAL																
Groundnuts	676	844	578	628	678	791	646	545	579	1,014	1,062	944	501	0.1	1.2	0.0
Millet	424	639	446	654	548	667	601	426	428	675	600	470	415	0.3	1.8	0.2
Rice	97	168	177	193	162	155	149	174	124	240	202	244	178	0.4	0.2	0.1
Maize	46	131	115	138	108	107	89	60	44	66	79	106	98	0.4	0.9	-0.2
Sorghum	96	127	117	99	123	127	133	118	120	147	144	140	144	0.4	0.9	0.1
SIERRA LEONE																
Palm oil	45	49	48	47	50	45	48	51	40	36	36	36	36	0.2	0.1	-0.1
Palm kernels	33	33	31	33	32	29	31	32	26	22	22	23	23	-0.3	-0.2	-0.2
Rice	500	518	479	486	405	356	392	411	328	247	199	230	250	-0.1	-0.1	-0.3
Cassava	90	118	117	106	244	219	281	310	289	240	241	260	260	0.1	0.2	0.4

(Table continues on the following page.)

8-6. Volume of food output, by major food crop (continued)

	1980	1990	1993	1994	1995	1996	1997	1998	1999	2000	2001	2002	2003	75-84	85-89	90-MR
						Thousands of metric tons									*Average annual* percentage growth*	
SOMALIA																
Bananas	72	105	70	55	43	50	55	55	48	50	55	60	60	-0.5	0.7	-0.2
Maize	108	299	101	79	150	146	142	128	150	143	155	145	201	0.3	0.2	-0.1
Sorghum	140	334	92	80	252	136	145	153	79	130	160	110	173	0.4	0.9	-0.2
Sesame	41	50	15	22	22	25	23	24	21	22	23	25	25	0.4	0.5	-0.2
SOUTH AFRICA																
Maize	8,475	12,481	3,277	9,997	13,275	4,866	10,171	10,136	7,693	7,946	11,431	7,748	10,049	0.4	1.1	0.0
Wheat	2,087	2,010	1,324	1,984	1,840	1,977	2,712	2,429	1,892	1,733	2,428	2,504	2,293	0.0	0.9	0.0
Sugarcane	18,412	18,587	12,955	11,244	15,683	16,714	20,951	22,155	22,930	21,223	23,876	21,157	22,928	0.0	0.5	0.1
Sorghum	377	511	118	515	520	291	536	433	358	224	473	206	257	0.4	1.7	-0.2
Barley	141	291	265	230	275	300	176	182	204	92	116	157	180	0.6	1.3	-0.2
SUDAN																
Groundnuts	858	218	380	428	714	738	815	1,104	776	1,047	947	990	1,267	-0.3	0.2	0.7
Sesame	222	140	266	175	170	313	416	281	262	329	282	262	269	-0.3	0.6	0.4
Sorghum	1,461	1,536	4,042	2,386	3,648	2,450	4,179	2,870	4,284	2,347	2,666	4,470	2,800	0.0	-0.3	0.1
Wheat	165	247	838	453	475	448	527	642	585	172	214	303	247	-0.3	-0.4	-0.1
SWAZILAND																
Sugarcane	2,196	3,797	3,885	3,647	3,786	3,440	3,846	3,694	3,887	4,323	3,885	4,000	4,000	0.6	0.1	0.0
Citrus (oranges)	43	25	35	23	48	29	33	33	31	35	36	36	36	-0.1	-0.3	0.0
Maize	65	133	54	73	99	76	151	108	125	113	85	82	85	-0.2	0.7	0.0
TANZANIA																
Maize	1,720	3,128	2,226	2,282	2,159	2,874	2,648	1,831	2,685	2,452	2,551	2,698	2,701	0.3	0.6	0.0
Sorghum	695	537	587	719	478	839	872	499	563	561	664	736	700	0.9	0.7	0.1
Rice	262	718	392	641	614	623	807	550	849	778	782	514	514	-0.1	1.3	0.0
Millet	460	300	263	210	218	342	585	347	236	194	219	207	300	0.9	-0.1	0.0
Cassava	5,644	6,896	7,112	6,833	7,209	5,969	5,994	5,704	7,033	7,182	7,120	6,884	6,888	0.3	-0.3	0.0
TOGO																
Maize	159	287	278	393	348	290	388	452	350	494	482	464	510	0.4	0.1	0.2
Sorghum	87	153	112	126	110	172	156	152	137	142	151	142	169	0.4	-0.1	0.1
Millet	49	97	75	75	58	74	55	49	41	39	37	41	52	-1.4	0.2	-0.2
Cassava	433	409	452	389	532	602	548	596	579	694	701	652	728	0.1	-0.2	0.2
Yam	483	405	368	530	484	531	605	683	696	666	563	549	575	0.3	-0.1	0.2
TUNISIA																
Olive oil	85	130	120	210	70	60	310	90	180	225	110	95	30	-0.5	-0.6	-0.1
Citrus	183	305	226	338	255	235	260	261	279	261	276	306	312	0.5	0.8	0.0
Wheat	680	420	1,584	1,413	503	531	2,018	885	1,354	1,390	842	1,118	422	0.2	2.0	0.1
Barley	270	200	570	478	145	80	835	160	303	420	241	233	90	0.8	1.9	0.0
UGANDA																
Millet	481	610	634	610	610	632	440	502	642	606	534	584	590	-0.3	0.5	0.0
Maize	453	624	657	804	850	913	759	740	924	1,053	1,096	1,174	1,200	-0.4	0.0	0.3
Sorghum	316	347	375	383	390	399	298	294	420	413	361	423	430	-0.2	0.0	0.1
Cassava	1,294	3,568	2,896	3,139	2,080	2,224	2,245	2,291	3,204	4,875	4,966	5,265	5,300	-0.3	0.0	0.2
Plantains	6,090	7,469	7,806	8,222	8,500	9,012	9,144	9,303	9,318	8,949	9,428	9,732	9,888	-0.4	0.2	0.1
ZAIRE																
Palm oil	170	178	181	182	171	196	186	168	169	168	168	167	170	-0.1	0.2	0.0
Maize	582	960	1,053	1,130	1,184	1,008	1,101	1,167	1,215	1,199	1,184	1,169	1,154	0.3	0.5	0.1
Rice	227	370	403	430	426	366	348	322	363	350	338	326	315	0.2	0.4	-0.1
Cassava	12,566	18,000	19,780	18,890	19,102	16,870	16,887	16,402	17,060	16,500	15,959	15,436	14,929	0.1	0.3	-0.1
Plantains	1,496	1,950	2,117	2,186	2,262	1,394	1,349	1,145	1,143	1,154	1,178	1,216	1,250	0.1	0.2	-0.3
ZAMBIA																
Sunflower seeds	13	15	1	15	10	14	26	7	6	6	19	602	602	0.8	-1.8	0.8
Maize	878	1,845	483	1,598	1,021	738	1,409	960	638	822	882	602	602	-0.5	0.3	-0.3
Wheat	7	47	54	69	61	38	58	71	64	69	75	75	75	2.4	1.9	0.2
Cassava	295	600	682	744	744	744	744	702	817	971	815	950	950	0.4	0.4	0.2
ZIMBABWE																
Sugarcane	2,555	3,671	125	538	3,420	3,773	2,826	4,651	4,811	4,657	4,228	4,700	4,700	0.3	-0.2	0.4
Maize	1,142	2,019	362	2,012	2,326	840	2,609	2,192	1,418	1,520	2,108	1,467	1,000	0.1	0.1	-0.1
Wheat	162	284	58	276	239	83	280	300	280	320	250	250	150	0.5	1.3	0.0

Notes: Crops shown represent same major food crops as in Table 8-1, Nominal producer prices, excluding beverages (coffee, tea, cocoa), cotton, and tobacco.

The following commodities are in their least-processed form unless otherwise indicated:

Groundnuts, unshelled	Citrus, total for country
Rice, paddy	Sesame, seeds
Sunflower, seeds	

For South Africa, barley production is for white areas only.

Countries excluded from listing: Cape Verde, Djibouti, Eritrea, São Tomé and Principe, and Seychelles.

* The standard World Bank least square methodology was used to compute the annual percentage growth.

8-7. Value of agricultural exports

	Millions of U.S. dollars (current prices)											Average annual percentage growth		
	1980	1988	1989	1990	1991	1992	1993	1994	1995	1996	1997	75-84	85-94	95-MR
SUB-SAHARAN AFRICA	12,212	10,099	10,711	10,358	9,563	9,258	9,317	11,506	13,108	14,312	13,368	1.8	0.3	5.5
excluding South Africa	9,695	8,582	8,699	8,440	7,725	7,467	7,738	9,389	10,823	11,823	10,904	2.0	-0.6	5.5
excl. S.Africa & Nigeria	9,249	8,141	8,444	8,210	7,511	7,277	7,462	9,062	10,420	11,281	10,383	2.4	-0.5	5.0
Angola	172	22	16	6	5	5	3	1	5	6	6	-12.8	-34.7	61.6
Benin	55	44	79	84	86	93	83	115	201	188	198	3.0	3.8	16.9
Botswana	51	74	79	79	90	91	96	97	132	115	115	5.2	3.5	3.8
Burkina Faso	80	87	66	116	94	86	93	80	141	123	119	5.3	4.4	11.2
Burundi	64	127	73	69	88	67	53	113	96	32	82	8.8	-4.2	-18.8
Cameroon	699	510	661	563	341	364	245	393	565	624	504	2.6	-5.2	8.9
Cape Verde	0	0	0	0	0	0	0	0	0	0	0	17.7	0.0	-3.0
Central African Republic	60	54	69	45	46	33	36	37	51	28	33	6.8	-4.8	-8.5
Chad	115	112	114	134	136	127	84	118	145	127	135	13.2	-1.3	2.8
Comoros	7	18	13	11	20	16	18	8	7	4	4	8.6	3.0	-23.3
Congo, Dem. Rep. of	235	165	182	141	78	83	53	93	135	102	95	-1.7	-14.7	-2.1
Congo, Rep. of	13	10	7	15	14	17	9	7	11	16	15	-1.7	-3.5	28.8
Côte d'Ivoire	2,009	1,735	1,807	1,615	1,532	1,434	1,605	1,557	2,216	2,421	2,001	7.0	-3.8	8.8
Djibouti	0	0	0	0	0	0	0	0	0	0	0	96.6	-1.9	5.6
Equatorial Guinea	12	12	8	8	6	6	3	4	4	7	4	-4.0	-15.4	9.6
Eritrea	..	..	..	..	..	..	4	4	2	2	2	..	..	-11.0
Ethiopia	..	..	..	..	..	..	193	362	409	426	526	..	..	12.3
Gabon	14	8	7	3	6	7	4	5	8	10	10	13.3	-6.1	27.9
Gambia, The	28	13	10	14	12	11	15	15	16	16	12	-5.0	-5.3	-7.7
Ghana	744	482	426	413	369	319	302	358	393	638	616	-5.1	-3.4	23.5
Guinea	33	32	31	27	23	31	43	45	61	43	48	5.3	7.0	-1.2
Guinea-Bissau	6	13	10	13	16	4	14	32	21	22	22	9.0	5.7	-11.0
Kenya	693	735	669	687	641	812	975	1,044	1,153	1,165	1,157	6.5	2.4	3.2
Lesotho	16	25	21	13	12	13	12	13	12	9	9	7.0	-2.4	-15.3
Liberia	151	119	135	23	27	23	32	24	13	13	20	5.7	-18.7	-6.1
Madagascar	334	180	206	176	157	143	133	237	200	138	92	2.6	-4.7	-27.6
Malawi	251	274	249	376	462	371	286	288	389	383	359	9.2	3.4	6.7
Mali	192	208	240	251	267	266	251	239	270	312	271	12.3	3.7	5.3
Mauritania	39	33	34	44	47	48	49	31	38	40	40	7.3	3.0	9.4
Mauritius	302	356	346	379	365	402	367	367	420	501	405	-1.1	5.8	4.8
Mozambique	157	47	44	41	45	53	26	64	67	50	50	-8.0	0.5	-10.0
Namibia	188	161	170	147	180	200	185	201	199	202	201	-8.0	9.5	0.0
Niger	86	50	54	62	65	55	48	48	45	45	45	8.4	-2.3	-1.8
Nigeria	446	440	255	230	214	189	275	327	403	542	522	-4.4	-3.5	18.6
Rwanda	66	99	113	95	85	60	52	14	42	39	38	5.5	-11.6	34.3
São Tomé and Principe	19	6	5	4	4	4	4	5	2	3	3	0.1	-7.0	-10.8
Senegal	115	153	204	219	135	126	91	126	115	87	58	-5.6	-0.4	-23.0
Seychelles	3	1	1	1	1	1	1	1	2	2	2	-1.8	-2.3	10.3
Sierra Leone	59	31	21	18	24	11	9	21	15	16	14	-0.3	-13.4	-10.6
Somalia	125	76	75	74	41	62	60	68	75	76	76	4.9	-3.3	3.6
South Africa	2,517	1,517	2,012	1,918	1,838	1,792	1,580	2,118	2,284	2,489	2,464	0.6	5.4	5.5
Sudan	553	507	662	550	381	367	455	471	501	565	556	1.9	-0.4	6.3
Swaziland	211	272	253	347	339	306	265	283	291	311	300	6.7	9.9	2.4
Tanzania	406	289	299	279	243	281	303	379	431	496	400	-0.2	0.8	3.1
Togo	77	100	92	120	101	125	75	76	127	133	128	5.4	0.7	17.7
Uganda	344	284	280	173	167	134	180	425	469	491	405	1.1	-6.7	-1.0
Zambia	13	13	20	24	29	36	27	16	32	46	50	-8.1	7.7	46.7
Zimbabwe	453	608	592	750	731	584	617	1,177	895	1,207	1,157	4.4	5.9	2.5
NORTH AFRICA	1,544	1,310	1,296	1,406	1,591	1,396	1,313	1,708	1,892	1,876	1,895	-2.1	2.2	3.1
Algeria	120	30	35	50	54	76	97	35	108	137	91	-12.7	4.9	36.5
Egypt, Arab Rep.	677	514	532	427	391	401	360	553	536	521	442	-1.9	-6.0	-6.7
Libya	0	0	0	0	0	0	0	0	0	0	0	-58.1	66.1	20.6
Morocco	606	572	520	647	670	581	509	598	780	896	832	0.4	5.8	11.9
Tunisia	140	193	208	282	477	338	347	523	468	322	530	-2.7	13.7	-3.2
ALL AFRICA	13,756	11,408	12,007	11,764	11,154	10,654	10,630	13,214	15,000	16,188	15,263	1.2	0.5	5.2

8-8. Cereal production

	Thousands of metric tons											Average annual percentage growth		
	1980	*1993*	*1994*	*1995*	*1996*	*1997*	*1998*	*1999*	*2000*	*2001*	*2002*	*75-84*	*85-94*	*95-MR*
SUB-SAHARAN AFRICA	49,742	78,183	83,993	76,641	90,618	85,754	86,186	86,575	87,836	88,009	89,939	-0.6	3.9	1.1
excluding South Africa	36,369	65,391	68,026	69,150	76,970	72,524	75,995	76,541	73,338	77,331	77,089	0.0	4.4	1.3
excl. S.Africa & Nigeria	28,581	45,300	47,653	46,638	55,305	50,671	53,955	54,136	51,968	57,217	55,000	-0.3	3.6	1.9
Angola	435	322	285	296	525	457	621	550	520	597	550	-6.0	-0.2	8.5
Benin	346	625	645	734	714	877	867	974	993	943	926	3.0	3.2	5.1
Botswana	44	43	52	42	111	31	12	20	22	27	27	-20.5	12.9	-12.2
Burkina Faso	1,048	2,527	2,232	2,308	2,482	2,014	2,657	2,700	2,286	3,109	3,119	0.3	6.3	4.0
Burundi	217	300	225	269	273	305	261	265	245	273	282	3.9	1.1	1.0
Cameroon	892	986	961	1,180	1,296	1,267	1,412	1,185	1,275	1,356	1,452	-1.6	2.8	3.3
Cape Verde	9	12	8	8	10	5	5	36	24	20	5	2.1	11.4	7.7
Central African Republic	100	94	101	113	126	138	148	173	184	195	198	1.4	-3.4	9.3
Chad	573	617	1,175	907	878	986	1,312	1,231	930	1,321	1,212	-5.2	6.8	2.7
Comoros	18	21	21	21	21	21	21	21	21	21	21	1.4	2.7	0.2
Congo, Dem. Rep. of	889	1,655	1,708	1,475	1,557	1,584	1,675	1,648	1,623	1,600	1,574	3.9	4.8	0.1
Congo, Rep. of	12	7	7	9	10	10	11	7	8	8	8	-6.2	-12.3	-0.8
Côte d'Ivoire	860	1,286	1,331	1,409	1,793	1,961	1,873	2,121	2,039	1,901	1,554	2.6	2.3	3.1
Djibouti	0	0	0	0	0	0	0	0	0	0	0	..	6.1	0.0
Equatorial Guinea	..	..	..	..	..	..	..	..	..	..	..	..	..	..
Eritrea	..	87	259	123	83	95	458	319	121	208	60	..	..	-3.8
Ethiopia	..	5,295	5,245	6,740	9,379	9,473	7,197	8,379	8,005	9,578	9,112	..	..	4.8
Gabon	11	27	31	29	29	28	26	26	27	34	32	5.7	7.0	0.6
Gambia, The	70	97	95	98	103	100	106	151	176	200	139	7.0	-0.1	8.9
Ghana	674	1,645	1,594	1,797	1,770	1,669	1,788	1,686	1,711	1,627	2,155	-0.6	5.3	1.4
Guinea	725	711	718	825	876	927	982	1,042	973	1,031	1,094	1.2	0.8	4.6
Guinea-Bissau	93	181	190	201	175	140	139	145	178	160	145	8.3	1.8	-2.8
Kenya	2,233	2,530	3,663	3,275	2,714	2,711	2,962	2,802	2,591	3,285	2,790	-2.3	2.3	-1.9
Lesotho	194	153	223	81	256	206	171	174	255	160	248	-4.8	-0.2	3.8
Liberia	243	65	50	56	94	168	209	196	183	145	110	2.2	-17.0	13.3
Madagascar	2,238	2,724	2,517	2,642	2,685	2,742	2,610	2,756	2,660	2,853	2,862	0.5	1.5	1.2
Malawi	1,252	2,137	1,109	1,778	1,943	1,349	1,904	2,636	2,631	1,742	1,711	0.6	-1.1	5.0
Mali	968	2,228	2,457	2,189	2,219	2,138	2,548	2,894	2,310	2,572	3,257	0.5	5.3	3.4
Mauritania	47	169	207	222	234	154	189	194	180	124	113	1.8	6.5	-7.2
Mauritius	1	2	1	0	0	0	0	0	1	0	0	-0.9	-14.3	-4.7
Mozambique	663	765	791	1,127	1,379	1,531	1,688	1,822	1,473	1,687	1,768	-1.0	-2.3	8.2
Namibia	74	75	116	66	89	185	70	74	121	107	95	3.7	0.4	0.5
Niger	1,775	2,024	2,430	2,096	2,232	1,719	2,973	2,853	2,127	3,161	3,289	3.2	5.6	4.9
Nigeria	7,788	20,091	20,373	22,513	21,665	21,853	22,040	22,405	21,370	20,114	22,089	1.3	6.2	0.0
Rwanda	273	234	131	143	183	223	194	179	240	284	318	4.4	-5.3	10.4
São Tomé and Principe	0	4	4	4	5	4	1	1	2	3	3	1.5	23.4	-9.5
Senegal	676	1,086	943	1,059	976	781	717	1,131	1,026	962	835	-1.6	0.6	-0.5
Seychelles	..	..	..	..	..	..	..	..	..	..	..	..	..	..
Sierra Leone	551	542	466	408	444	467	373	280	222	257	280	-1.0	-0.5	-8.5
Somalia	267	165	405	285	290	284	232	276	318	260	379	8.2	-8.9	-0.6
South Africa	13,373	12,792	15,967	7,491	13,648	13,230	10,191	10,035	14,498	10,679	12,850	-3.3	1.3	0.1
Sudan	2,701	3,102	5,146	3,305	5,202	4,209	5,583	3,066	3,436	5,415	3,741	-3.5	6.7	-1.6
Swaziland	105	75	101	79	152	110	126	114	86	83	86	-4.2	-7.2	-2.6
Tanzania	2,961	3,917	3,534	4,759	5,001	3,309	4,450	4,073	4,312	4,247	4,296	5.8	0.6	0.6
Togo	296	633	572	591	687	748	624	759	737	715	804	4.1	4.5	3.5
Uganda	1,078	1,880	1,936	2,030	1,588	1,625	2,085	2,178	2,112	2,309	2,344	-4.5	7.2	3.4
Zambia	984	1,756	1,188	870	1,573	1,137	798	1,003	1,050	745	745	-6.3	0.1	-5.3
Zimbabwe	1,989	2,498	2,780	987	3,146	2,784	1,878	1,996	2,537	1,896	1,262	-4.1	-2.7	-3.2
NORTH AFRICA	16,445	21,339	26,450	20,798	34,592	24,311	29,512	27,308	24,351	28,154	27,267	-0.3	4.5	0.7
Algeria	2,419	1,454	965	2,140	4,902	870	3,026	2,021	935	2,659	2,089	-2.5	-2.0	2.1
Egypt, Arab Rep.	8,100	14,961	15,012	16,097	16,542	18,071	17,964	19,401	20,106	19,310	19,164	1.0	7.2	3.4
Libya	215	180	165	146	160	207	213	214	218	220	215	4.2	-4.1	5.0
Morocco	4,515	2,818	9,639	1,783	10,104	4,098	6,632	3,846	2,002	4,607	5,283	-2.2	0.4	-4.7
Tunisia	1,197	1,927	670	631	2,884	1,065	1,676	1,826	1,091	1,359	516	0.5	3.2	-0.2
ALL AFRICA	66,187	99,523	110,443	97,439	125,210	110,065	115,698	113,883	112,187	116,164	117,205	-0.5	4.1	1.0

8-9. Crop production index

	Index (average 1989-91 = 100)										Average annual percentage growth		
	1980	*1993*	*1994*	*1995*	*1996*	*1997*	*1998*	*1999*	*2000*	*2001*	*2002*	*75-84*	*85-94*	*95-MR*
SUB-SAHARAN AFRICA	76	111	117	117	128	127	134	137	137	141	140	-0.4	3.6	2.5
excluding South Africa	76	113	118	121	131	129	137	140	139	144	144	-0.4	3.7	2.6
excl. S.Africa & Nigeria	82	106	111	113	123	120	129	130	129	137	134	-0.3	2.2	2.6
Angola	107	108	137	132	134	128	158	145	176	207	204	-6.5	2.3	6.2
Benin	52	127	129	146	163	172	174	178	194	191	202	3.2	6.7	5.1
Botswana	91	87	97	81	134	84	72	81	84	93	92	-6.4	3.7	-1.2
Burkina Faso	55	131	117	122	139	133	163	163	129	182	190	2.2	5.1	5.5
Burundi	77	105	90	96	96	96	90	93	87	96	95	0.8	1.6	0.0
Cameroon	87	108	114	123	132	123	132	142	145	141	138	0.3	1.7	2.6
Cape Verde	94	77	70	70	91	80	85	129	114	114	117	2.2	-0.2	7.7
Central African Republic	103	97	107	112	125	127	131	134	133	134	142	0.0	0.5	3.2
Chad	70	86	120	123	133	151	173	153	139	177	166	-1.2	4.6	4.2
Comoros	78	111	118	115	120	120	126	129	133	136	137	0.8	4.3	2.3
Congo, Dem. Rep. of	74	105	107	92	91	88	89	87	85	83	81	2.4	2.6	-2.5
Congo, Rep. of	86	100	108	114	119	119	115	124	126	128	129	1.8	0.3	2.1
Côte d'Ivoire	71	99	101	115	123	128	135	141	147	132	123	3.3	2.5	2.8
Djibouti	66	105	108	110	112	116	117	121	122	123	123	29.6	2.8	1.8
Equatorial Guinea	77	97	97	98	98	96	93	101	99	97	97	0.6	2.1	0.1
Eritrea	..	93	158	133	110	109	210	169	126	141	99	..	..	-1.6
Ethiopia	..	109	110	128	153	154	135	145	153	170	159	..	..	3.8
Gabon	79	100	103	106	109	113	117	117	121	122	122	4.6	2.6	2.2
Gambia, The	66	86	89	84	63	87	83	130	147	163	89	-1.0	-2.6	7.0
Ghana	68	130	123	144	156	152	167	177	179	183	208	-2.5	5.7	5.5
Guinea	92	119	123	126	129	136	143	150	151	159	166	0.9	3.8	4.0
Guinea-Bissau	63	104	107	112	116	126	130	140	147	149	146	3.7	2.1	4.6
Kenya	68	99	113	116	116	111	124	124	116	124	130	1.6	3.4	1.4
Lesotho	94	88	120	70	136	131	111	113	144	111	189	-4.2	1.3	5.4
Liberia	..	..	..	..	..	..	..	..	..	..	..	..	..	..
Madagascar	85	106	100	102	104	106	104	108	106	110	110	0.3	1.2	1.0
Malawi	84	115	88	112	127	124	138	148	169	170	129	2.0	0.7	6.1
Mali	51	100	115	118	124	129	141	146	109	149	173	0.1	6.2	3.8
Mauritania	61	117	142	153	156	144	140	123	136	129	114	2.4	5.0	-3.0
Mauritius	80	101	92	100	98	106	104	75	96	108	91	0.1	-0.4	-0.4
Mozambique	111	93	91	113	130	141	155	156	136	143	144	-2.3	-0.6	4.6
Namibia	80	88	104	93	104	135	105	111	126	127	127	1.9	0.8	3.3
Niger	92	90	127	104	128	93	174	151	131	164	148	2.1	6.0	4.3
Nigeria	51	125	129	135	142	146	151	157	156	153	159	-0.9	9.2	2.5
Rwanda	82	82	51	64	73	76	82	87	108	109	129	4.3	-2.9	11.0
São Tomé and Principe	117	127	134	123	144	162	183	191	193	201	201	-2.7	1.4	6.6
Senegal	57	95	94	109	97	87	83	133	130	122	82	-5.1	1.3	1.3
Seychelles	190	87	103	118	124	116	107	100	82	80	86	-2.8	-6.7	-4.7
Sierra Leone	81	91	98	90	95	102	92	78	70	77	79	1.0	0.3	-3.6
Somalia	..	..	..	..	..	..	..	..	..	..	..	..	..	..
South Africa	92	93	106	81	109	108	99	107	116	105	109	-0.5	1.2	1.7
Sudan	122	110	150	144	177	169	169	156	157	183	158	-2.4	0.4	1.0
Swaziland	74	77	84	71	87	88	87	95	84	86	86	3.6	-1.0	1.1
Tanzania	78	92	90	100	108	90	104	103	107	108	108	2.9	0.0	1.9
Togo	71	115	118	116	142	146	143	142	132	138	144	1.8	4.1	1.9
Uganda	65	108	108	112	109	108	120	133	133	141	143	-3.2	3.4	4.1
Zambia	65	115	94	79	109	97	87	114	100	89	100	-2.5	1.9	0.9
Zimbabwe	76	100	106	78	120	126	118	113	134	121	87	-0.6	0.1	1.1
NORTH AFRICA	78	113	110	110	146	124	136	141	137	141	140	1.0	3.4	2.8
Algeria	81	110	93	114	154	104	129	135	114	138	132	-1.6	2.5	2.8
Egypt, Arab Rep.	77	116	112	123	135	138	136	148	156	154	155	2.1	3.7	4.0
Libya	79	104	108	116	121	127	128	130	132	128	128	4.1	1.8	2.0
Morocco	59	74	110	62	122	91	112	95	83	93	100	0.6	3.2	0.1
Tunisia	75	114	73	68	144	87	114	128	121	99	74	0.6	3.5	2.1
ALL AFRICA	77	111	115	116	132	126	134	138	137	141	140	-0.1	3.5	2.6

8-10. Fertilizer use

				Thousands of metric tons							Average annual percentage growth		
	1980	1991	1992	1993	1994	1995	1996	1997	1998	1999	2000	75-84	85-94	95-MR
SUB-SAHARAN AFRICA	1,973	1,927	1,917	2,169	1,957	1,834	2,100	2,006	2,009	2,074	1,983	4.4	0.9	0.9
excluding South Africa	909	1,186	1,184	1,326	1,204	1,067	1,296	1,245	1,226	1,297	1,225	5.3	2.7	1.4
excl. S.Africa & Nigeria	735	757	744	865	908	884	1,122	1,107	1,062	1,114	1,039	2.4	1.4	2.9
Angola	17	7	9	8	10	8	6	2	3	3	1	-0.5	-3.7	-25.3
Benin	1	12	15	17	17	36	31	39	38	57	35	7.5	7.3	12.5
Botswana	1	1	1	1	1	2	3	4	4	5	5	-5.7	2.9	24.9
Burkina Faso	4	21	21	21	23	24	24	43	50	43	34	23.4	6.6	11.7
Burundi	1	2	5	4	3	3	3	1	4	4	4	11.4	5.2	4.3
Cameroon	32	18	21	22	30	30	34	39	40	48	48	12.9	-8.6	9.3
Cape Verde	0	0	0	0	0	0	0	0	0	0	0	-0.6	..	..
Central African Republic	1	1	1	1	0	0	0	0	1	1	1	-11.1	-7.3	16.0
Chad	1	9	10	5	7	9	12	8	17	18	18	-4.9	2.3	17.5
Comoros	0	0	0	0	0	0	0	0	0	0	0	..	..	0.0
Congo, Dem. Rep. of	8	8	2	4	10	9	6	0	3	1	1	0.1	-1.2	-38.0
Congo, Rep. of	1	1	2	2	2	2	4	4	5	5	5	4.0	-5.1	19.4
Côte d'Ivoire	53	39	37	54	65	66	71	110	90	71	73	1.4	5.0	2.6
Djibouti	1	0	0	0	0	0	0	0	0	0	0	-44.2	..	..
Equatorial Guinea	0	0	0	0	0	0	0	0	0	0	0	0.0	..	..
Eritrea	..	..	..	1	1	2	5	6	7	11	11	..	..	45.3
Ethiopia	..	..	..	76	116	134	178	132	164	168	157	..	..	4.7
Gabon	0	1	1	0	0	0	0	0	0	0	0	28.9	-19.7	-2.4
Gambia, The	2	1	1	1	1	1	1	1	3	1	1	7.9	-15.4	5.9
Ghana	12	8	10	8	8	10	17	21	15	15	12	-0.9	-2.0	7.8
Guinea	0	2	1	2	4	5	4	2	3	3	3	-15.8	22.5	-6.4
Guinea-Bissau	0	1	0	0	0	0	0	0	1	1	2	9.8	-9.7	34.6
Kenya	62	113	102	100	130	78	161	134	127	150	141	6.1	1.5	4.8
Lesotho	5	6	6	6	5	6	6	6	6	5	6	18.1	4.5	-0.8
Liberia	3	0	0	0	0	0	0	0	0	0	0	-11.1	-6.7	..
Madagascar	9	9	8	11	11	13	17	10	9	8	9	3.1	2.8	-7.6
Malawi	33	70	74	74	21	44	58	57	50	50	33	12.4	2.5	5.2
Mali	14	15	27	25	25	27	27	48	46	50	52	14.3	-0.6	15.1
Mauritania	1	5	7	5	4	4	5	2	2	2	0	-9.6	22.8	-15.8
Mauritius	27	28	27	26	29	32	38	33	33	35	36	0.7	-0.1	2.4
Mozambique	28	5	5	3	6	8	8	7	8	8	14	6.5	1.1	9.3
Namibia	0	0	0	0	0	0	0	0	0	0	0	..	..	..
Niger	3	1	1	2	6	10	9	1	1	4	5	23.0	-2.5	-17.9
Nigeria	174	429	440	461	296	183	174	138	164	183	187	23.8	5.9	-5.0
Rwanda	0	2	1	1	0	0	0	0	0	0	0	11.8	-1.7	-2.8
São Tomé and Principe	..	..	..	..	..	..	..	..	..	..	..	..	..	..
Senegal	19	17	17	24	26	16	22	23	27	41	45	-8.9	1.3	14.3
Seychelles	0	0	0	0	0	0	0	0	0	0	0	..	..	..
Sierra Leone	2	1	1	3	3	3	3	3	0	0	0	-3.5	1.4	-48.0
Somalia	1	0	0	0	0	0	1	1	1	1	1	7.3	8.1	0.0
South Africa	1,064	740	733	843	752	767	804	761	783	777	758	3.6	-1.6	0.1
Sudan	81	56	60	53	58	52	95	77	38	39	38	-1.5	-0.2	-9.6
Swaziland	20	12	12	12	5	5	4	5	6	6	6	4.0	-1.7	3.5
Tanzania	36	50	48	36	36	27	31	40	30	21	22	-1.0	0.2	-6.8
Togo	3	12	12	10	11	16	18	17	17	17	20	8.6	2.6	6.5
Uganda	1	1	1	2	2	1	1	1	4	4	5	-16.2	18.7	28.5
Zambia	79	62	85	85	59	55	51	57	37	34	30	2.2	-0.4	-11.1
Zimbabwe	173	164	114	159	171	145	168	175	175	185	165	2.0	0.0	1.6
NORTH AFRICA	1,221	1,527	1,456	1,660	1,421	1,621	1,645	1,661	1,768	1,847	1,892	6.5	-1.0	4.4
Algeria	236	92	97	131	119	46	38	97	108	93	92	1.6	-9.4	6.1
Egypt, Arab Rep.	664	963	877	988	843	1,126	1,158	1,079	1,171	1,197	1,270	7.5	-0.1	5.0
Libya	53	85	86	111	75	89	62	62	51	87	57	14.2	0.2	-3.8
Morocco	207	289	291	334	295	282	290	327	325	359	362	5.4	0.7	4.4
Tunisia	62	99	105	95	89	77	97	97	114	112	111	6.3	-0.2	5.8
ALL AFRICA	3,194	3,454	3,373	3,829	3,378	3,455	3,744	3,667	3,777	3,921	3,876	5.3	0.0	2.4

8-11. Fertilizer imports

	Thousands of metric tons										Average annual percentage growth		
	1980	1992	1993	1994	1995	1996	1997	1998	1999	2000	2001	75-84	85-94	95-MR
SUB-SAHARAN AFRICA	971	1,154	1,273	1,218	1,005	1,429	1,424	1,407	1,448	1,691	1,708	6.1	1.8	6.1
excluding South Africa	742	950	1,074	1,019	820	1,207	1,155	1,123	1,139	1,178	1,265	7.1	1.7	3.8
excl. S.Africa & Nigeria	565	710	793	729	797	1,130	1,064	995	1,041	991	1,044	4.2	1.4	4.0
Angola	17	9	8	10	8	6	2	5	2	1	0	-0.2	-4.3	-26.7
Benin	1	16	18	17	36	30	39	38	57	35	31	6.7	7.2	7.4
Botswana	1	1	1	1	3	4	4	4	5	5	5	-5.7	2.9	19.0
Burkina Faso	5	21	21	23	24	31	44	50	43	34	33	23.7	6.2	6.2
Burundi	1	6	5	3	3	3	1	4	4	4	4	11.9	6.4	5.2
Cameroon	32	21	22	47	32	34	39	40	50	46	53	13.1	-8.1	4.5
Cape Verde	0	0	0	0	0	0	0	0	0	0	0	-0.6	..	..
Central African Republic	1	1	1	0	0	0	0	1	1	1	1	-11.1	-7.3	14.1
Chad	1	10	5	8	8	24	8	17	18	18	18	-4.9	2.9	11.6
Comoros	0	0	0	0	0	0	0	0	0	0	0	..	..	0.0
Congo, Dem. Rep. of	8	2	4	10	9	6	0	3	1	1	2	0.1	-1.2	-31.8
Congo, Rep. of	1	2	2	3	3	4	4	5	5	5	5	34.9	-0.7	9.0
Côte d'Ivoire	45	68	52	79	87	75	181	135	107	103	90	6.9	1.9	3.0
Djibouti	1	0	0	0	0	0	0	0	0	0	0	-44.2	..	..
Equatorial Guinea	0	0	0	0	0	0	0	0	0	0	0	0.0	..	..
Eritrea	..	..	1	2	2	6	6	7	11	11	10	..	..	32.7
Ethiopia	..	..	115	35	149	251	93	166	168	157	207	..	..	15.4
Gabon	0	1	0	0	0	0	0	0	0	0	0	27.6	-19.7	-1.7
Gambia, The	2	1	1	1	1	1	1	3	1	1	1	7.9	-15.8	1.4
Ghana	12	11	7	8	10	17	22	15	15	12	10	-0.3	-2.7	2.7
Guinea	0	1	2	4	5	4	2	3	3	3	3	-16.0	22.5	-4.8
Guinea-Bissau	0	0	0	0	0	0	0	1	1	2	2	9.8	-9.7	39.1
Kenya	62	102	100	131	78	161	134	127	149	153	145	4.9	2.1	4.6
Lesotho	5	6	6	6	6	7	6	6	6	8	11	18.1	4.6	7.5
Liberia	3	0	0	0	0	0	0	0	0	0	0	-11.1	-6.7	..
Madagascar	9	8	11	11	13	17	10	9	8	9	7	3.1	2.8	-8.5
Malawi	33	68	74	21	44	58	57	50	50	50	23	13.9	1.2	0.7
Mali	14	27	25	25	27	27	48	46	50	44	42	14.3	-0.7	9.7
Mauritania	1	9	7	4	4	5	2	2	2	0	2	-9.6	26.6	-12.0
Mauritius	17	28	22	24	24	38	36	24	23	27	27	-0.3	0.1	-0.4
Mozambique	20	5	3	6	9	8	7	8	8	16	27	23.8	-2.3	16.9
Namibia	0	0	0	0	0	0	0	0	0	0	0	..	..	..
Niger	3	1	2	5	8	9	1	1	4	5	5	23.0	-3.6	-4.8
Nigeria	177	240	281	290	24	77	92	128	98	188	221	22.7	2.5	11.9
Rwanda	0	1	1	0	0	0	0	0	0	0	0	11.8	-4.8	-2.4
São Tomé and Principe	..	..	..	..	..	..	..	..	..	..	..	..	..	..
Senegal	16	27	35	14	18	16	34	26	36	31	35	-8.2	6.3	14.4
Seychelles	0	0	0	0	0	0	0	0	0	0	0	..	..	..
Sierra Leone	2	2	3	3	3	3	3	0	0	0	0	-4.1	2.1	-40.7
Somalia	2	0	0	0	0	1	1	1	1	1	1	0.9	16.9	0.0
South Africa	229	204	198	199	185	222	269	284	310	513	444	2.6	2.4	15.0
Sudan	81	60	53	60	50	95	77	38	57	52	81	2.4	-3.2	0.0
Swaziland	18	12	12	5	5	4	5	6	6	6	7	1.2	-1.9	5.2
Tanzania	20	40	42	31	27	35	39	31	21	22	23	3.7	2.2	-5.6
Togo	3	12	13	13	14	22	17	17	17	20	19	7.6	3.0	4.6
Uganda	1	1	2	2	1	1	1	4	4	7	7	-13.1	18.7	34.4
Zambia	69	86	68	53	52	47	53	34	31	31	40	1.6	1.4	-7.1
Zimbabwe	56	44	49	63	34	81	87	70	77	71	70	5.4	2.6	4.9
NORTH AFRICA	588	344	332	312	381	287	434	473	466	453	429	-2.7	-4.3	5.7
Algeria	189	19	26	52	19	51	90	90	93	102	105	-1.8	-14.9	20.0
Egypt, Arab Rep.	182	107	59	13	76	33	87	131	101	70	84	-11.8	-13.3	21.5
Libya	53	87	107	73	102	62	62	42	60	32	33	11.7	2.0	-13.3
Morocco	133	126	136	167	177	137	189	195	207	242	200	2.9	0.2	5.0
Tunisia	30	6	4	7	7	4	7	15	5	8	7	-8.3	4.2	2.2
ALL AFRICA	1,559	1,498	1,605	1,530	1,386	1,716	1,858	1,880	1,914	2,144	2,137	3.0	0.1	6.0

8-12. Area under permanent crops

	Thousands of hectares											Average annual percentage growth		
	1980	1991	1992	1993	1994	1995	1996	1997	1998	1999	2000	75-84	85-94	95-MR
SUB-SAHARAN AFRICA	123,663	134,344	135,566	149,757	150,549	152,912	153,462	154,296	155,075	155,330	155,692	0.7	1.5	0.5
excluding South Africa	111,223	120,614	121,546	135,447	135,949	137,997	138,587	139,486	140,284	140,577	140,939	0.9	1.5	0.6
excl. S.Africa & Nigeria	83,373	90,814	91,624	105,403	105,784	107,626	109,887	111,286	112,084	112,377	112,739	1.0	1.8	1.1
Angola	2,900	2,950	3,000	3,000	3,000	3,000	3,000	3,000	3,000	3,000	3,000	0.0	0.4	0.0
Benin	1,500	1,620	1,630	1,650	1,680	1,710	1,750	1,800	1,850	1,900	1,950	1.7	0.6	2.6
Botswana	402	417	415	407	397	343	343	343	343	343	370	0.1	0.1	-0.8
Burkina Faso	2,745	3,495	3,470	3,450	3,381	3,400	3,500	3,600	3,700	3,750	3,800	1.8	1.9	2.2
Burundi	930	930	930	930	920	920	920	910	900	900	900	0.0	0.0	-0.5
Cameroon	5,910	5,950	5,960	5,960	5,960	5,960	5,960	5,960	5,960	5,960	5,960	0.8	0.1	0.0
Cape Verde	38	41	41	41	40	39	39	39	39	39	39	0.0	0.9	-0.3
Central African Republic	1,870	1,920	1,930	1,930	1,930	1,930	1,930	1,930	1,930	1,930	1,930	0.5	0.1	0.0
Chad	3,137	3,322	3,342	3,370	3,390	3,420	3,470	3,500	3,520	3,520	3,520	0.5	0.9	0.7
Comoros	75	78	78	78	78	78	78	78	78	78	78	0.0	0.3	0.0
Congo, Dem. Rep. of	6,620	6,680	6,700	6,700	6,700	6,700	6,700	6,700	6,700	6,700	6,700	0.2	0.0	0.0
Congo, Rep. of	138	156	155	160	163	165	167	170	173	175	175	1.5	1.1	1.3
Côte d'Ivoire	1,955	2,450	2,600	2,902	2,905	2,920	2,930	2,950	2,950	2,950	2,950	1.9	2.1	0.3
Djibouti	..	..	..	..	..	..	..	..	..	..	..	..	..	..
Equatorial Guinea	130	130	130	130	130	130	130	130	130	130	130	0.0	0.0	0.0
Eritrea	..	..	..	498	437	438	369	391	498	498	498	..	..	3.4
Ethiopia	..	..	..	10,000	9,822	9,850	9,850	9,900	9,950	10,000	10,000	..	..	0.3
Gabon	290	295	295	295	295	325	325	325	325	325	325	2.5	0.2	1.0
Gambia, The	155	191	157	156	175	180	185	195	205	220	230	1.0	-0.1	4.8
Ghana	1,900	2,800	2,800	2,800	2,800	2,800	2,800	3,600	3,600	3,600	3,609	2.5	2.1	5.6
Guinea	702	735	755	785	820	883	885	885	885	885	885	0.4	1.0	0.8
Guinea-Bissau	255	300	300	300	300	300	300	300	300	300	300	1.0	0.4	0.0
Kenya	3,800	4,000	4,000	4,000	4,000	4,000	4,000	4,000	4,000	4,000	4,000	0.4	0.2	0.0
Lesotho	292	319	332	330	325	320	322	325	325	325	325	-2.3	1.0	0.1
Liberia	371	390	390	370	370	370	370	370	380	380	380	0.4	-0.2	0.6
Madagascar	2,540	2,750	2,780	2,800	2,800	2,800	2,800	2,820	2,850	2,900	2,900	1.8	0.7	0.7
Malawi	1,518	1,823	1,830	1,837	1,845	1,875	1,900	1,950	2,000	2,050	2,100	3.0	0.5	2.2
Mali	2,010	2,063	2,163	3,060	3,160	3,379	4,606	4,606	4,606	4,606	4,630	1.0	3.8	6.5
Mauritania	210	410	420	431	470	498	488	488	488	488	488	4.0	5.0	0.3
Mauritius	100	100	100	100	100	100	100	100	100	100	100	0.0	0.0	0.0
Mozambique	2,870	3,500	3,520	3,520	3,570	3,650	3,750	3,900	4,000	3,950	3,900	0.7	1.4	1.8
Namibia	655	660	660	698	747	816	816	816	816	816	816	0.1	0.8	1.0
Niger	3,544	3,595	3,990	4,090	4,090	4,190	4,190	4,190	4,490	4,490	4,490	4.3	1.6	1.8
Nigeria	27,850	29,800	29,922	30,044	30,165	30,371	28,700	28,200	28,200	28,200	28,200	0.3	0.6	-1.3
Rwanda	760	880	880	850	700	700	750	800	820	866	900	2.0	-0.4	4.6
São Tomé and Principe	1	2	2	2	3	3	4	4	4	4	4	0.0	5.1	5.3
Senegal	2,341	2,323	2,320	2,318	2,331	2,230	2,250	2,254	2,263	2,313	2,362	0.0	-0.1	0.4
Seychelles	1	1	1	1	1	1	1	1	1	1	1	0.0	0.0	0.0
Sierra Leone	450	486	486	486	485	485	485	484	484	484	490	1.1	0.3	0.1
Somalia	984	1,022	1,023	1,024	1,030	1,035	1,039	1,043	1,043	1,043	1,043	0.5	0.2	0.2
South Africa	12,440	13,730	14,020	14,310	14,600	14,915	14,875	14,810	14,791	14,753	14,753	-0.2	1.8	0.0
Sudan	12,360	13,000	12,900	14,618	15,000	16,157	16,672	16,600	16,500	16,380	16,233	0.4	1.5	0.9
Swaziland	185	183	179	178	178	178	178	178	178	178	178	-0.9	1.4	0.0
Tanzania	3,100	3,550	3,600	3,650	3,700	3,748	3,750	3,750	3,750	3,750	4,000	4.8	1.1	0.8
Togo	1,950	2,100	2,100	2,200	2,200	2,200	2,300	2,330	2,410	2,510	2,510	1.2	1.0	2.6
Uganda	4,080	5,020	5,040	5,040	5,060	5,060	5,060	5,060	5,060	5,060	5,060	1.5	0.4	0.0
Zambia	5,094	5,249	5,254	5,254	5,254	5,260	5,260	5,260	5,260	5,260	5,260	0.4	0.2	0.0
Zimbabwe	2,505	2,928	2,966	3,004	3,042	3,080	3,165	3,251	3,220	3,220	3,220	0.8	1.4	1.0
NORTH AFRICA	21,635	22,962	23,668	23,951	23,996	23,969	24,310	24,337	24,222	24,049	23,991	-0.1	1.0	0.0
Algeria	6,875	7,260	7,562	7,533	7,477	7,519	7,521	7,650	7,661	7,673	7,675	0.0	0.9	0.5
Egypt, Arab Rep.	2,286	2,267	2,449	2,617	2,740	2,817	2,820	2,834	2,834	2,834	2,825	-1.8	1.4	0.4
Libya	1,753	1,810	1,815	1,815	1,825	1,870	2,028	2,028	1,815	1,815	1,815	0.2	0.2	-0.7
Morocco	7,530	8,717	8,934	8,999	9,124	8,921	9,096	8,980	9,033	8,818	8,767	0.8	1.7	-0.5
Tunisia	3,191	2,908	2,908	2,987	2,830	2,842	2,845	2,845	2,879	2,909	2,909	-1.1	-0.7	0.5
ALL AFRICA	145,298	157,306	159,234	173,708	174,545	176,881	177,772	178,633	179,297	179,379	179,683	0.6	1.5	0.4

8-13. Agricultural yields by major crop

						Thousands of hectograms per hectare									*Average annual* percentage growth		
	1980	1991	1992	1993	1994	1995	1996	1997	1998	1999	2000	2001	2002	2003	75-84	85-89	90-MR
ALGERIA																	
Wheat	7.3	10.8	9.9	8.1	8.0	8.9	13.1	8.0	8.8	10.7	9.2	11.1	10.7	19.2	3.7	2.0	2.8
Citrus	262.9	87.2	92.5	87.1	91.4	80.2	86.1	87.2	101.8	111.3	104.6	112.8	114.6	114.6	-2.2	2.1	2.0
Dates	30.0	25.5	31.2	31.0	37.2	32.8	37.3	31.4	39.5	42.7	36.5	43.7	43.7	43.7	3.7	3.6	3.0
Barley	8.4	11.6	9.0	6.3	6.5	7.1	14.0	7.2	7.5	10.9	7.6	11.1	13.7	15.0	7.1	0.9	2.7
Potatoes	77.7	90.7	107.9	111.2	95.1	136.8	134.6	141.0	160.3	153.5	166.1	147.0	151.5	151.5	1.3	-2.0	2.9
ANGOLA																	
Coffee (green)	2.2	0.5	0.5	0.5	0.3	0.4	0.3	0.3	0.4	0.4	0.4	0.3	0.3	0.3	-12.2	-5.5	-2.1
Maize	6.0	4.0	3.8	2.6	2.5	3.5	7.0	6.0	7.4	6.4	5.7	6.1	6.1	6.1	-3.5	4.8	4.4
Millet	7.1	4.8	4.8	2.7	5.4	5.1	4.8	3.8	5.0	5.3	5.3	6.3	5.0	5.0	-3.5	0.8	0.4
Wheat	5.8	8.0	8.0	8.6	10.0	16.7	16.7	16.7	17.1	17.4	17.4	16.7	16.7	16.7	-6.3	-1.3	4.4
Cassava	33.8	40.3	42.3	42.3	58.6	51.0	48.1	44.2	55.7	59.8	83.0	94.1	93.9	93.9	-0.9	-1.5	4.5
Sweet potatoes	91.7	89.5	90.0	88.1	85.7	88.1	85.5	85.9	86.4	82.9	34.9	44.5	44.4	44.4	0.2	0.1	-3.0
BENIN																	
Seed cotton	6.6	11.7	12.0	17.9	13.9	13.3	12.0	10.1	9.7	10.1	10.6	11.0	11.7	11.8	0.2	-2.2	-0.5
Maize	7.4	9.3	9.8	9.8	10.2	11.7	10.8	12.0	11.1	12.5	11.5	11.0	8.8	12.5	0.1	-4.1	1.1
Sorghum	6.3	7.8	7.7	7.6	7.8	8.2	7.6	8.1	8.2	8.2	8.8	9.1	10.1	9.4	-0.8	0.0	1.1
Cassava	65.9	83.0	83.8	84.9	81.5	78.4	87.2	103.3	105.0	104.5	107.1	112.6	92.7	92.0	-1.3	-2.5	1.3
Yams	97.2	114.0	106.0	107.7	108.4	109.7	103.0	107.9	109.5	113.3	111.8	109.2	107.1	102.9	-0.9	-1.5	-0.1
BOTSWANA																	
Sorghum	2.2	3.7	2.9	2.9	2.2	2.1	2.6	2.1	1.8	1.9	1.1	1.9	1.9	1.9	-11.8	-12.7	-3.1
Maize	2.5	4.0	1.9	1.4	1.7	1.2	2.5	3.9	1.4	2.5	1.1	1.2	1.2	1.2	-11.7	10.2	-4.3
Millet	1.6	1.8	1.3	1.4	3.6	1.0	3.7	2.5	1.7	1.9	1.7	1.8	1.8	1.8	-5.7	-22.3	0.1
BURKINA FASO																	
Seed cotton	8.3	10.0	10.0	9.6	8.9	10.3	10.1	12.4	9.7	12.1	10.2	11.4	10.7	14.3	10.1	-2.6	0.9
Groundnuts	5.1	5.6	6.2	9.5	8.4	6.6	10.4	6.5	10.0	10.4	7.1	9.1	9.4	9.4	4.5	-3.5	2.3
Sorghum	5.7	9.1	9.4	11.0	7.8	8.8	9.1	6.8	8.5	8.9	8.3	9.3	9.3	9.5	2.5	-1.8	1.0
Millet	4.9	7.0	6.5	7.0	6.3	7.2	7.5	5.2	7.8	7.4	6.4	7.6	7.2	8.1	4.0	-2.2	1.7
Maize	9.0	16.9	15.2	13.7	16.0	11.4	15.5	15.2	13.9	16.2	17.5	18.1	17.4	17.0	1.7	-4.9	1.8
BURUNDI																	
Coffee	6.3	9.0	9.3	8.2	9.4	7.3	7.9	7.0	6.1	9.7	7.4	8.8	20.0	20.0	0.5	2.2	2.2
Tea	4.0	8.8	10.7	9.0	10.4	9.8	7.5	5.6	8.9	9.2	8.4	9.9	7.4	7.4	-4.5	2.9	0.2
Maize	10.8	13.9	14.2	14.3	12.3	12.8	13.1	12.6	11.5	11.2	10.5	10.8	10.9	10.9	0.3	-0.9	-1.3
Sorghum	10.0	11.2	11.5	11.3	9.9	13.2	13.2	12.4	12.5	12.0	12.2	12.6	12.9	12.9	0.1	1.5	1.0
Rice, paddy	23.5	30.9	31.1	30.9	29.4	26.8	27.9	32.6	29.9	32.6	30.4	32.1	32.6	32.6	3.2	-6.3	-0.2
Millet	10.0	11.2	11.0	10.3	11.1	14.4	11.3	16.7	11.1	11.2	10.5	10.0	11.6	11.6	0.5	-0.4	-0.1
Bananas	..	..	..	..	..	..	..	..	..	..	..	..	..	..	..	..	..
Cassava	90.9	89.8	92.0	89.9	87.9	83.5	85.8	86.2	88.8	88.2	90.0	89.1	91.5	91.5	0.0	0.6	0.1
CAMEROON																	
Coffee	3.0	4.0	2.6	2.5	3.0	3.0	3.9	1.8	3.8	3.3	2.9	2.4	2.6	2.6	3.6	-7.8	-1.1
Cocoa	2.6	3.0	2.9	2.9	3.1	3.7	3.5	3.5	3.5	3.1	3.3	3.3	3.4	3.4	0.3	-0.5	0.5
Seed cotton	12.9	12.7	12.7	12.3	10.8	10.3	11.7	10.9	11.3	10.9	10.3	9.9	10.0	9.5	11.4	-3.4	-1.4
Maize	8.3	19.8	14.0	11.3	11.6	15.5	18.8	20.3	18.9	25.9	24.6	24.4	23.6	23.6	0.4	-0.7	1.6
Sorghum	8.7	7.7	7.6	7.6	7.3	8.7	8.3	8.9	11.1	11.2	12.0	12.0	12.0	12.0	1.4	-5.5	2.4
Millet	7.6	10.5	10.0	10.3	10.0	10.2	10.1	10.0	10.0	10.0	10.1	10.0	10.1	10.0	1.3	-6.2	-0.2
Rice	23.4	36.4	35.0	29.0	36.2	35.3	31.4	33.6	35.5	33.1	30.1	30.2	25.5	27.5	10.2	-2.7	-2.3
Cassava	59.0	162.2	136.3	131.8	127.0	118.7	115.5	106.6	90.0	136.6	133.0	134.3	134.5	134.5	0.2	0.9	-0.8
Plantains	..	..	..	..	..	..	..	..	..	..	..	..	..	..	..	..	..
CENTRAL AFRICAN REPUBLIC																	
Coffee	3.6	6.9	5.0	4.1	8.2	4.7	7.2	6.0	4.8	4.5	5.2	4.9	5.2	5.2	1.0	-2.5	-1.2
Seed cotton	3.4	5.1	6.0	6.6	6.6	7.6	7.3	7.3	7.0	3.9	5.3	6.4	5.7	5.7	3.8	3.5	-0.2
Sorghum	6.5	10.1	12.6	11.6	8.0	7.3	7.8	8.4	8.8	9.6	9.9	10.1	9.6	9.6	-1.5	-8.5	-0.7
Maize	3.8	8.1	9.0	9.0	8.5	8.5	8.5	9.2	9.8	10.6	10.6	10.7	9.8	9.8	-1.1	-3.1	0.9
Groundnuts	10.1	8.6	9.8	9.8	9.4	9.4	9.3	8.8	10.2	11.0	10.9	11.1	11.0	11.0	3.0	-2.3	0.7
Cassava	30.7	33.6	34.5	34.5	31.0	28.9	29.2	30.5	30.4	29.4	29.5	29.6	29.6	29.6	0.4	-0.3	-0.4
Yams	60.0	65.7	68.4	65.0	66.7	66.7	68.0	68.0	67.9	67.9	67.9	67.9	60.3	60.3	0.2	-0.6	-0.1
CHAD																	
Seed cotton	5.1	6.2	6.3	6.1	7.7	7.6	7.9	6.8	5.4	5.9	6.4	6.3	6.1	6.1	4.3	3.3	-0.8
Sorghum	5.1	5.7	7.4	4.9	7.8	6.5	6.0	5.8	7.2	7.1	6.0	6.3	6.9	8.0	1.2	-1.4	0.9
Millet	4.7	4.0	5.2	4.2	4.9	3.6	4.1	3.8	4.5	4.6	3.3	4.7	5.1	6.1	2.1	-2.5	1.1
Groundnuts	5.7	10.2	8.1	7.1	7.5	9.2	9.6	8.8	11.2	9.7	8.2	9.4	9.4	9.4	1.0	-5.5	0.9
COMOROS																	
Bananas	..	..	..	..	..	..	..	..	..	..	..	..	..	..	..	..	..
Cassava	48.5	53.0	56.6	57.9	53.6	53.3	54.0	53.9	54.1	54.8	59.3	54.1	55.0	55.0	-1.7	1.0	0.5

(Table continues on the following page.)

8-13. Agricultural yields by major crop (continued)

	1980	1991	1992	1993	1994	1995	1996	1997	1998	1999	2000	2001	2002	2003	75-84	85-89	90-MR
CONGO																	
Coffee	8.0	4.0	4.2	4.3	4.4	4.6	4.7	4.2	2.7	3.0	3.0	3.0	3.0	3.0	2.3	-6.4	-2.2
Cocoa beans	5.6	3.8	3.9	3.9	4.0	4.0	3.1	3.2	3.3	3.0	3.0	3.0	3.0	3.0	0.6	1.5	-1.1
Maize	8.1	6.8	7.1	7.3	7.6	8.0	8.5	8.9	9.8	8.0	8.0	8.0	8.1	7.8	-0.4	-2.2	0.8
Cassava	68.8	73.7	73.9	65.6	76.1	78.6	81.3	82.1	77.7	90.0	90.0	90.0	90.0	91.8	2.2	0.5	1.6
Plantains	..	..	..	..	..	..	..	..	..	..	..	..	..	..	..	..	..
COTE D'IVOIRE																	
Coffee	2.4	2.0	3.2	1.7	1.8	2.1	2.1	3.4	3.9	3.8	4.1	3.1	1.7	1.7	-6.7	1.6	1.1
Cocoa	5.0	5.4	5.6	5.5	5.4	5.7	5.7	5.6	5.7	5.6	5.9	5.5	4.5	4.5	0.7	0.1	-0.4
Oil Palm, fruit	..	..	..	..	..	..	..	..	..	..	..	..	..	..	..	..	..
Rice	11.7	10.5	10.2	13.4	11.2	11.8	23.6	26.7	24.8	23.7	24.1	23.8	16.0	16.0	1.1	0.1	3.4
Maize	8.1	7.3	7.8	7.8	7.9	8.1	8.2	8.2	8.2	11.6	9.9	8.2	9.1	9.1	2.2	0.5	1.5
Cassava	52.3	52.7	50.1	49.5	50.5	51.9	55.6	53.1	56.4	56.0	52.8	52.8	53.1	53.1	3.1	-0.3	0.0
Yams	90.7	96.3	89.0	88.0	89.6	89.7	88.6	87.9	85.9	84.1	84.3	83.9	85.7	85.7	1.5	0.1	-0.7
EGYPT																	
Seed cotton	26.9	22.8	27.6	29.2	22.4	21.4	24.8	25.5	18.9	22.8	25.4	27.1	27.6	27.6	4.2	2.4	0.9
Rice, paddy	58.3	74.6	76.5	77.2	79.1	81.4	82.9	84.2	86.4	88.8	91.0	92.8	91.4	94.3	1.4	-1.0	1.6
Wheat	31.2	48.2	52.5	53.0	50.0	54.2	56.4	56.0	59.9	63.5	63.4	63.6	60.1	61.5	-0.8	0.4	1.3
Sugarcane	812.5	1,036.4	1,029.1	1,061.7	1,093.4	1,095.3	1,107.4	1,122.5	1,172.0	1,181.7	1,172.2	1,188.1	1,136.4	909.1	..	-5.0	0.6
Dry Broadbeans	20.7	34.0	21.4	35.1	22.7	31.7	32.0	31.9	32.3	22.9	31.1	31.4	31.4	31.4	-0.5	-0.9	0.0
EQUATORIAL GUINEA																	
Cocoa	1.1	1.0	0.7	0.5	0.6	1.1	0.7	1.0	0.7	0.9	0.8	0.7	0.7	0.7	-1.6	2.5	-1.7
Coffee (green)	3.4	3.7	3.7	3.7	3.7	3.7	3.6	3.6	3.6	3.7	3.7	3.7	3.7	3.7	-0.4	0.0	-0.1
Cassava	24.6	25.6	26.1	26.1	26.1	26.1	25.3	25.0	25.3	25.0	25.0	25.0	25.0	25.0	-0.4	0.0	-0.4
ETHIOPIA																	
Coffee (green)	2.4	4.1	3.9	4.3	4.3	2.7	3.7	2.6	2.4	2.4	2.4	2.4	3.6	3.6	..	0.4	-2.1
Sorghum	..	..	..	..	..	..	..	..	..	..	..	..	..	..	..	..	..
Maize	16.6	16.9	17.6	17.9	18.6	19.1	19.0	17.8	16.1	16.4	16.2	16.7	16.3	16.3	..	0.9	0.0
Barley	..	..	..	..	..	..	..	..	..	..	..	..	..	..	..	..	..
GABON																	
Coffee (green)	2.4	4.1	3.9	4.3	4.3	2.7	3.7	2.6	2.4	2.4	2.4	2.4	3.6	3.6	7.5	0.4	-2.1
Sugarcane	497.5	517.0	488.9	542.0	568.6	569.5	528.6	519.9	546.8	506.8	591.2	587.5	587.5	587.5	15.6	0.3	0.5
Maize	16.6	16.9	17.6	17.9	18.6	19.1	19.0	17.8	16.1	16.4	16.2	16.7	16.3	16.3	1.8	0.9	0.0
Cassava	50.0	51.6	51.1	49.3	45.8	47.0	49.8	49.1	50.4	49.8	50.7	51.1	51.1	51.1	-0.1	-0.1	0.0
Taro (cocoyam)	58.8	57.8	57.6	60.4	61.7	59.6	60.0	60.5	61.1	61.6	62.1	62.1	62.1	62.1	0.0	1.4	0.4
Yams	56.4	64.7	66.7	64.7	69.4	68.4	67.5	70.0	72.5	75.0	70.5	70.5	70.5	70.5	1.1	0.3	0.7
GAMBIA,THE																	
Groundnuts	8.7	10.5	8.5	12.1	10.8	9.6	7.1	11.1	10.4	12.4	11.7	12.6	7.9	7.9	-0.7	0.5	-0.5
Seed cotton	6.9	6.3	7.5	9.4	5.9	4.2	4.7	4.4	3.0	7.3	5.1	4.0	3.6	3.6	4.1	-0.2	-2.7
Oil Palm, fruit	..	..	..	..	..	..	..	..	..	..	..	..	..	..	..	..	..
Millet	8.7	10.3	11.2	10.3	10.6	9.8	11.0	9.0	9.6	11.2	11.0	11.3	9.2	10.9	-0.4	0.8	0.3
Rice, paddy	19.7	15.3	17.3	14.6	15.4	12.3	10.7	10.2	13.4	21.7	22.1	23.3	20.5	20.5	8.8	-1.8	1.9
Maize	10.7	11.8	15.1	16.3	12.6	12.9	12.2	11.7	14.3	15.9	16.1	18.2	10.9	14.7	3.2	-2.3	0.8
Sorghum	8.0	9.6	9.5	11.0	10.6	8.5	10.8	9.6	8.1	11.1	12.7	16.6	9.5	15.6	1.1	-5.1	2.0
GHANA																	
Cocoa	2.3	3.4	4.3	3.6	4.2	4.0	3.8	3.0	3.0	3.3	2.9	2.5	3.0	3.0	-0.4	-6.2	-1.4
Maize	8.7	15.3	12.0	15.1	14.9	15.0	15.2	15.3	14.9	14.6	14.6	13.2	14.9	10.1	-0.9	-4.6	-0.1
Millet	5.9	5.4	6.4	9.7	8.8	9.8	10.2	8.4	9.5	8.6	8.1	7.0	8.0	7.6	0.9	1.5	1.4
Groundnuts	17.0	6.7	7.7	8.8	9.4	9.3	9.0	8.7	10.9	10.4	9.6	10.2	13.5	13.5	-0.7	-3.5	0.8
Cassava	80.8	106.6	102.6	112.3	115.8	119.9	120.4	118.8	113.9	122.5	122.8	123.4	122.5	122.5	1.2	-0.5	2.0
Plantains	..	..	..	..	..	..	..	..	..	..	..	..	..	..	..	..	..
GUINEA																	
Coffee (green)	3.2	5.2	5.3	5.2	5.5	5.1	4.1	4.0	4.2	4.2	4.1	4.1	4.1	4.1	-0.2	-4.0	-0.3
Oil Palm, fruit	..	..	..	..	..	..	..	..	..	..	..	..	..	..	..	..	..
Rice, paddy	9.0	13.8	13.3	13.8	13.8	14.4	14.7	14.9	15.2	15.5	15.5	15.8	16.1	16.1	0.2	-2.9	2.0
Maize	10.0	10.4	10.7	10.4	10.3	9.7	9.9	10.1	10.4	10.6	10.8	11.1	11.3	10.0	-1.8	0.1	0.4
Groundnuts	6.6	8.8	10.1	8.8	9.2	9.1	9.5	9.8	10.3	10.7	11.2	11.7	12.2	12.0	0.1	-0.7	2.7
Cassava	70.0	74.9	71.7	75.5	71.9	63.0	61.2	63.3	58.0	56.3	53.8	52.2	50.7	51.1	0.0	-0.5	-2.1
GUINEA-BISSAU																	
Groundnuts	3.5	7.8	10.1	10.0	11.7	11.0	11.0	11.6	11.3	11.9	11.9	11.9	11.9	11.9	-1.8	-6.5	1.4
Rice, paddy	7.0	20.1	19.0	19.7	20.1	19.1	18.4	16.7	14.5	11.8	14.2	12.3	11.8	11.8	-2.4	-1.4	-2.9
Sorghum	6.4	10.3	8.6	9.0	9.2	9.3	9.1	8.3	7.5	9.7	7.8	8.0	7.1	7.5	-1.9	-4.7	-1.5
Millet	7.2	12.2	8.6	8.6	7.7	9.1	8.6	3.2	8.0	7.8	7.8	8.3	8.2	6.9	0.8	-4.3	-1.5
Maize	10.0	11.4	9.5	9.3	9.3	10.0	9.4	10.0	10.0	9.9	10.3	9.7	9.1	8.0	0.6	-4.4	-1.0

Thousands of hectograms per hectare — *Average annual* percentage growth*

(Table continues on the following page.)

8-13. Agricultural yields by major crop (continued)

						Thousands of hectograms per hectare									Average annual* percentage growth		
	1980	1991	1992	1993	1994	1995	1996	1997	1998	1999	2000	2001	2002	2003	75-84	85-89	90-MR
KENYA																	
Coffee (green)	8.9	5.6	5.5	4.7	5.0	5.9	5.5	3.9	3.0	4.0	5.9	3.0	2.8	2.8	-1.7	-3.1	-4.2
Tea	11.7	20.2	18.5	20.1	19.0	21.7	22.6	19.4	24.8	20.0	18.2	21.9	20.5	20.7	2.0	-1.2	0.4
Sugarcane	1,211.8	960.7	877.7	841.3	662.1	810.4	815.8	794.6	930.2	771.4	688.6	742.9	834.9	818.2	4.8	-2.7	-1.6
Sisal	9.9	11.4	11.4	11.7	11.3	13.2	13.4	13.4	9.0	7.0	7.5	7.5	10.3	10.0	-0.2	0.5	-1.7
Maize	12.0	15.9	17.3	16.0	20.4	19.6	14.5	14.7	16.0	14.8	14.4	16.9	15.6	15.3	-0.9	-3.5	-0.5
Wheat	21.6	18.6	12.6	9.7	19.2	19.6	18.5	14.5	17.7	16.5	15.5	19.4	17.7	16.8	3.2	-4.6	0.7
LESOTHO																	
Wheat	9.7	2.0	8.6	7.3	4.2	6.2	13.3	11.8	11.6	12.3	17.2	10.5	16.7	16.7	1.9	0.7	5.6
Dry Peas	7.8	0.7	5.6	5.4	3.1	2.9	9.2	3.5	5.8	7.8	5.9	7.7	7.7	7.7	4.9	-6.5	5.6
Dry Beans	5.2	3.4	2.9	10.7	3.2	12.4	6.3	10.4	8.4	8.0	6.4	10.5	6.7	6.7	4.0	-4.9	1.3
Maize	9.6	5.4	5.8	8.9	8.6	8.1	12.5	9.9	9.5	9.4	8.5	7.9	8.3	8.3	2.8	-5.7	0.3
Sorghum	9.7	5.4	6.1	13.0	8.8	8.0	8.6	8.1	7.6	11.1	8.6	13.8	8.7	8.7	2.7	-8.6	1.7
LIBERIA																	
Rubber	7.6	9.5	10.7	10.0	6.7	9.3	10.0	9.9	9.4	10.0	10.0	9.7	9.4	9.4	-1.1	-0.2	-0.5
Coffee (green)	4.6	1.0	1.9	2.0	2.0	2.0	2.0	2.0	2.0	2.0	2.0	2.0	2.0	2.0	-1.1	-1.6	1.4
Cocoa	2.3	1.0	0.9	0.8	0.9	1.3	1.3	1.2	1.3	1.3	1.3	1.0	1.5	1.5	-1.2	-3.3	0.3
Rice, paddy	12.3	9.1	9.2	10.8	11.1	11.2	12.5	12.5	12.9	12.8	12.8	11.2	9.2	9.2	0.4	0.4	0.0
Cassava	66.7	64.3	66.7	61.3	62.5	60.3	65.0	65.2	65.3	65.1	65.7	66.2	66.2	66.2	1.5	-0.5	-0.6
LIBYA																	
Wheat	5.2	12.4	11.9	8.4	7.7	7.3	7.3	10.1	8.8	7.9	7.6	7.9	7.6	7.6	2.3	0.3	-1.7
MADAGASCAR																	
Coffee	3.7	3.8	3.7	3.7	4.2	3.5	3.5	2.9	3.1	3.4	3.0	3.3	3.3	3.3	-1.3	-0.8	-0.6
Vanilla	0.4	0.6	0.4	0.7	0.6	0.6	0.6	0.6	0.7	0.7	0.6	0.6	0.6	0.6	-6.6	7.6	-0.7
Cloves	1.7	1.8	1.4	2.1	1.8	1.7	1.7	1.8	1.7	1.9	2.0	1.9	1.9	1.9	-7.7	-1.6	2.1
Rice	17.6	20.5	20.9	20.8	20.7	21.3	21.9	21.7	20.3	21.3	20.5	22.0	22.0	21.2	-1.1	0.2	0.3
Cassava	60.8	66.5	67.1	67.7	67.4	68.9	67.4	67.5	67.0	70.0	70.0	71.3	71.3	71.4	-1.2	0.6	0.4
Sweet potatoes	48.6	50.3	53.1	51.1	53.8	59.1	58.1	56.0	54.3	56.5	56.3	57.6	55.6	55.8	-2.9	-0.6	0.4
MALAWI																	
Tobacco leaves	8.6	9.7	9.7	10.0	12.5	12.2	12.4	13.8	10.9	7.3	8.3	7.2	5.7	5.7	2.7	-1.0	-1.9
Tea	17.1	21.9	15.4	21.3	18.7	18.2	19.8	23.4	21.5	22.3	24.6	24.5	25.3	25.0	2.0	-4.2	0.8
Groundnuts	7.1	8.2	4.0	9.0	3.2	3.6	5.6	6.9	6.9	7.3	6.9	8.1	7.7	7.7	-0.8	0.4	0.5
Seed cotton	6.9	6.3	7.5	9.4	5.9	4.2	4.7	4.4	3.0	7.3	5.1	4.0	3.6	3.6	4.1	-0.2	-2.7
Maize	12.2	11.4	4.8	15.3	9.2	13.5	14.4	9.9	13.7	18.1	17.4	11.0	10.5	12.8	0.0	-2.1	1.2
Sorghum	6.7	6.0	1.4	4.9	3.1	7.3	7.2	4.7	6.1	7.0	6.7	6.8	7.2	7.5	-4.0	-7.1	1.5
Cassava	58.4	23.4	20.1	28.8	34.7	34.7	45.9	56.7	54.6	53.9	152.5	166.9	149.6	149.6	-0.6	2.4	10.0
MALI																	
Seed cotton	10.6	13.3	13.6	12.8	11.5	12.1	10.7	10.5	10.3	9.5	10.7	10.7	11.5	11.5	3.8	0.0	-1.4
Groundnuts	8.9	10.9	7.5	7.8	8.4	9.4	9.8	9.5	8.8	7.7	9.7	7.3	8.2	8.2	0.5	-7.4	-0.9
Millet	6.2	8.3	5.9	5.4	6.4	5.5	7.9	7.3	8.9	8.8	7.0	5.5	8.3	6.5	6.1	-0.7	0.2
Rice, paddy	9.7	17.3	17.6	17.4	16.5	15.5	19.1	17.6	22.0	22.4	21.1	20.0	20.5	20.5	1.0	0.7	2.1
Sorghum	8.0	10.9	6.4	7.5	7.6	8.3	10.0	9.8	9.7	9.4	8.4	7.4	9.3	6.4	6.7	0.4	-0.4
Maize	11.1	13.8	10.1	11.0	11.3	13.0	15.8	17.0	16.4	14.5	13.3	11.5	8.7	10.1	9.2	-1.3	-0.7
MAURITANIA																	
Sorghum	3.2	4.5	5.0	5.9	5.8	6.4	6.9	4.1	4.7	5.4	5.2	3.3	3.6	5.0	-2.9	1.4	-1.5
Rice	32.0	28.1	39.9	32.9	27.4	39.4	38.3	37.2	40.6	39.7	42.4	45.3	45.6	45.6	1.7	1.4	1.2
Millet	2.3	2.7	2.6	2.6	2.9	3.6	3.4	1.4	1.6	3.5	3.0	3.2	1.1	0.8	4.3	-6.7	-3.7
Maize	6.5	6.0	7.7	12.3	5.0	8.0	5.9	8.6	8.4	7.6	9.1	10.0	5.6	9.7	4.9	-8.6	0.6
MAURITIUS																	
Sugarcane	576.8	740.0	770.0	729.7	659.2	716.6	732.6	794.9	781.2	535.5	699.4	791.3	674.5	674.5	-1.7	1.3	-0.5
Potatoes	165.6	197.4	192.1	200.9	175.7	198.5	195.9	215.8	176.0	239.8	222.6	209.9	220.1	220.1	1.8	0.7	0.5
Onions	107.6	137.7	151.4	164.6	176.0	184.4	177.9	171.3	220.6	287.8	359.2	328.8	299.0	299.0	2.0	-2.8	4.9
MOROCCO																	
Wheat	10.6	18.7	7.0	6.8	18.1	5.5	18.4	9.3	14.2	8.0	4.8	12.3	12.8	17.2	5.9	-10.5	-0.2
Sugarbeet	353.5	438.7	528.6	490.6	499.8	467.7	487.1	415.4	569.2	521.9	512.7	573.6	502.7	572.7	2.7	-1.5	1.0
Barley	10.3	13.8	4.8	4.8	14.4	3.9	15.8	6.6	8.1	7.1	2.1	5.4	8.3	11.4	4.9	-15.6	-1.2
MOZAMBIQUE																	
Seed cotton	4.9	5.3	5.8	6.1	6.6	6.0	6.8	4.4	4.6	4.8	4.7	4.8	4.7	4.7	3.1	4.1	2.3
Tea	10.3	7.7	5.1	8.4	10.0	4.9	8.4	7.5	7.5	8.0	18.6	18.6	18.6	18.6	0.7	9.3	6.2
Maize	5.4	3.2	1.6	6.3	5.2	6.8	9.4	9.0	9.0	10.8	9.4	9.0	9.5	9.6	-6.2	-4.9	6.2
Rice, paddy	8.3	5.3	3.0	6.2	8.3	8.7	9.7	10.9	10.6	10.0	9.6	9.6	9.6	9.6	-2.0	-1.2	2.0
Cassava	41.4	38.0	33.3	41.7	36.9	42.4	47.7	53.8	55.6	55.9	57.9	58.1	58.1	58.1	0.0	0.5	2.0

(Table continues on the following page.)

8-13. Agricultural yields by major crop (continued)

							Thousands of hectograms per hectare									Average annual* percentage growth		
	1980	1991	1992	1993	1994	1995	1996	1997	1998	1999	2000	2001	2002	2003	75-84	85-89	90-MR
NAMIBIA																	
Wheat	25.0	59.0	51.9	43.8	52.5	55.2	43.8	46.4	49.3	55.5	56.4	80.0	85.0	88.9	4.5	-2.5	3.1
Maize	12.3	12.0	2.4	7.8	11.5	8.8	6.8	15.7	6.6	5.3	7.2	13.3	13.9	14.3	0.4	-10.7	-0.3
NIGER																	
Cowpeas	2.4	1.5	1.0	0.5	1.8	0.5	1.0	0.6	2.1	1.1	1.1	1.2	1.2	1.2	5.0	-9.4	1.0
Groundnuts	6.7	3.4	3.3	2.3	4.5	3.8	4.7	3.8	4.9	4.1	3.1	8.2	4.3	4.3	2.5	-2.5	3.6
Millet	4.4	4.2	3.6	3.5	4.0	3.4	3.5	3.0	4.5	4.3	3.3	4.6	4.8	4.8	1.7	-7.4	0.8
Sorghum	4.8	2.1	1.5	1.3	2.0	1.4	1.9	1.5	2.2	2.3	1.7	2.5	2.7	3.1	0.6	-5.7	1.4
NIGERIA																	
Cocoa	2.2	3.7	4.0	4.2	4.3	2.6	4.4	4.3	5.0	3.0	3.5	3.5	3.3	3.3	-3.5	-7.6	-0.2
Oil Palm, fruit	..	..	..	..	..	..	..	..	..	..	..	..	..	..	..	..	..
Seed cotton	1.8	4.8	5.3	5.3	5.3	5.8	6.7	8.1	7.3	7.4	7.4	7.4	6.6	6.6	-9.7	-6.0	1.9
Groundnuts	8.4	12.1	12.4	11.8	9.2	8.9	10.1	11.2	9.7	10.9	10.9	9.8	9.7	9.7	4.6	-3.7	-1.9
Sorghum	11.2	9.7	10.8	10.8	10.8	11.5	11.4	11.1	11.3	11.3	11.2	10.2	10.9	11.5	8.3	0.0	0.5
Millet	8.3	9.0	10.3	9.5	9.5	10.9	10.6	10.8	10.6	10.6	10.5	9.4	9.9	12.9	5.8	0.4	0.1
Maize	13.2	11.3	11.2	11.8	12.7	12.7	13.3	12.5	13.2	13.8	10.3	11.4	11.0	14.0	6.3	-2.6	-0.1
Rice, paddy	19.8	19.5	19.6	19.6	14.2	16.3	17.5	16.0	16.0	15.0	15.0	12.5	10.2	10.2	6.2	3.6	-2.9
Yams	105.4	103.5	113.5	113.5	114.0	107.7	106.8	110.5	94.4	95.5	95.6	90.5	89.0	89.0	1.1	-6.1	-0.8
Cassava	95.8	101.9	105.9	105.9	105.9	106.7	106.6	118.8	107.5	106.4	105.6	95.0	99.8	99.8	0.1	-1.4	-0.5
RWANDA																	
Coffee (green)	6.9	5.2	6.8	5.2	2.8	11.0	7.6	7.4	5.7	7.0	6.0	6.6	6.9	7.5	2.5	3.0	0.1
Tea	7.4	11.3	10.9	11.2	4.6	6.0	8.2	12.7	13.5	12.9	11.8	13.9	11.9	11.9	-4.9	-1.4	0.6
Sorghum	12.4	12.8	7.5	12.8	6.9	11.5	13.6	11.2	10.5	8.3	8.9	9.4	11.3	11.3	0.9	2.4	-0.5
Maize	11.8	11.6	12.3	17.4	16.8	11.2	11.1	10.9	8.2	7.6	7.0	7.7	8.8	8.8	1.1	0.1	-2.7
Plantains	..	..	..	..	..	..	..	..	..	..	..	..	..	..	..	..	..
Sweet potatoes	76.3	50.0	50.2	49.9	50.0	50.0	51.1	49.7	50.5	47.9	59.1	60.0	66.1	66.1	2.7	2.6	0.8
SENEGAL																	
Groundnuts	4.9	8.3	6.0	8.5	7.6	9.4	7.0	6.9	10.4	11.1	9.7	9.6	6.0	10.0	3.0	2.8	0.5
Seed cotton	6.9	11.5	10.6	8.9	8.4	9.0	7.6	7.5	2.4	6.8	9.2	10.9	9.6	9.7	-3.3	3.8	-1.8
Millet	4.7	6.7	5.8	6.7	5.9	7.5	6.2	5.2	5.6	6.7	7.1	5.9	5.1	5.5	3.5	4.0	-0.4
Rice, paddy	9.6	23.5	24.1	24.8	20.9	22.5	20.2	23.3	27.2	25.0	23.5	27.7	23.6	23.6	3.4	-1.2	0.6
Maize	7.3	11.3	10.9	12.7	10.1	10.9	10.4	9.7	8.3	9.4	11.1	12.0	9.2	9.6	-3.5	0.1	-1.1
Sorghum	7.7	7.8	8.9	7.8	8.7	8.6	8.9	7.7	5.9	6.4	8.7	8.0	7.2	7.7	3.3	-0.7	-1.0
SIERRA LEONE																	
Cocoa	4.0	3.8	2.7	2.7	3.7	3.7	3.7	3.7	3.7	3.6	3.6	3.6	3.6	3.6	-0.2	-0.8	-0.4
Coffee (green)	12.7	22.6	23.0	23.0	18.5	17.9	17.9	21.9	18.6	11.0	11.0	10.6	10.6	10.6	0.3	-1.6	-4.4
Palm oil	..	..	..	..	..	..	..	..	..	..	..	..	..	..	..	..	..
Rice, paddy	12.5	13.5	13.5	12.7	12.3	13.0	13.5	13.0	11.5	11.6	10.9	12.4	12.5	12.5	-1.1	-0.7	-0.4
Cassava	38.0	54.0	53.3	45.8	58.7	58.5	58.6	49.9	51.6	51.8	51.8	55.3	55.3	55.3	-3.5	-3.7	0.3
SOMALIA																	
Bananas	..	..	..	..	..	..	..	..	..	..	..	..	..	..	..	..	..
Maize	10.1	10.0	10.1	9.9	4.1	7.3	7.1	6.4	7.5	7.2	8.4	7.8	9.6	8.2	-1.4	-3.0	-2.0
Sorghum	3.1	4.1	3.1	2.9	4.1	3.4	3.2	3.1	2.9	3.3	3.6	3.1	4.7	3.5	1.7	-2.2	-1.4
Sesame	4.6	4.1	3.8	3.1	3.0	3.4	3.3	3.4	3.0	3.1	3.3	3.4	3.4	3.4	-3.0	-1.6	-1.4
SOUTH AFRICA																	
Maize	24.2	22.6	7.9	22.8	28.5	13.8	27.0	25.2	21.6	22.3	30.0	24.0	30.0	29.0	6.3	-5.1	1.8
Wheat	9.0	14.9	17.7	18.5	17.6	14.5	21.0	17.6	25.3	24.1	28.4	26.1	24.4	17.8	-0.3	3.0	3.2
Sugarcane	661.4	727.4	471.6	422.9	582.4	612.0	699.2	747.0	724.8	672.1	741.7	657.0	705.5	633.9	-2.1	2.4	0.1
Sorghum	26.9	18.2	6.2	21.6	22.9	16.1	30.8	26.9	27.3	22.6	33.2	22.8	34.1	30.0	6.3	-0.7	2.8
Barley	8.8	12.6	19.2	19.8	22.9	24.0	13.9	13.8	18.2	9.1	16.1	19.8	25.0	18.8	8.3	7.6	-0.5
SUDAN																	
Seed cotton	8.2	12.6	14.6	11.4	12.1	14.1	12.4	10.2	13.4	12.3	8.6	13.7	12.0	15.0	1.5	3.9	-0.2
Groundnuts	8.0	7.8	7.0	5.5	8.0	6.8	8.6	7.2	5.6	6.9	6.5	6.5	6.7	6.3	-1.6	-2.9	0.3
Sesame	2.6	1.8	2.0	1.4	1.3	2.1	2.2	1.8	1.9	1.5	1.5	1.4	1.7	1.4	0.2	5.3	-0.4
Sorghum	7.1	7.0	6.5	5.1	5.7	4.9	6.4	4.4	6.8	5.2	6.4	7.8	5.8	7.9	-3.1	-11.2	1.2
Wheat	12.1	14.8	22.1	13.8	13.3	16.1	17.7	19.5	22.9	12.1	23.3	25.2	21.4	24.2	-2.0	0.1	1.9
SWAZILAND																	
Sugarcane	1,077.2	985.3	971.2	911.8	946.5	908.4	986.0	953.9	1,009.7	1,080.8	1,064.3	1,081.1	1,081.1	1,081.1	0.3	0.0	0.4
Seed cotton	10.2	14.8	4.5	9.5	8.8	8.8	13.3	7.9	7.3	6.6	8.0	7.9	7.9	7.9	-1.3	3.1	-1.9
Maize	13.6	17.3	9.4	12.2	17.6	12.7	24.5	17.8	19.2	17.4	15.4	14.9	15.5	15.5	-1.1	-0.6	1.5

(Table continues on the following page.)

8-13. Agricultural yields by major crop (continued)

							Thousands of hectograms per hectare								*Average annual* percentage growth		
	1980	*1991*	*1992*	*1993*	*1994*	*1995*	*1996*	*1997*	*1998*	*1999*	*2000*	*2001*	*2002*	*2003*	*75-84*	*85-89*	*90-MR*
TANZANIA																	
Coffee	4.2	3.9	4.2	4.4	2.8	3.5	4.2	4.0	3.5	4.0	4.0	4.5	4.5	4.5	-0.3	4.0	0.2
Seed cotton	4.5	5.3	7.1	3.1	3.8	6.8	5.8	4.7	4.6	5.4	5.8	5.8	5.2	4.8	-3.0	1.8	1.1
Tea	10.9	10.4	11.8	12.0	13.2	13.1	13.0	13.4	11.8	13.2	12.4	13.4	13.4	13.4	2.8	3.4	0.1
Maize	12.3	12.6	11.7	12.5	13.4	16.3	16.2	11.7	12.9	13.9	14.6	17.1	17.1	15.4	3.0	1.7	0.9
Rice	11.9	16.9	12.8	18.1	17.4	15.8	15.7	12.5	13.0	16.4	15.1	12.8	12.8	12.8	-4.8	-1.5	-1.4
Sorghum	6.9	10.2	8.6	11.2	7.2	12.2	13.1	8.0	9.5	8.5	10.4	11.9	11.5	10.3	10.6	1.3	0.1
Millet	7.6	7.8	8.5	6.5	6.4	11.3	12.4	9.8	8.8	9.9	8.7	10.3	12.0	10.8	6.5	4.6	0.9
Cassava	107.3	123.5	104.0	104.0	104.0	102.1	101.9	86.0	94.4	109.5	87.9	104.2	104.2	104.2	5.9	-0.1	-0.3
TOGO																	
Coffee (green)	4.9	6.6	1.6	2.8	2.4	2.5	4.6	2.2	4.1	3.5	3.2	1.5	3.7	3.5	2.5	-1.2	-3.1
Cocoa	4.5	1.5	2.0	2.3	1.8	2.8	6.6	2.7	5.7	3.3	3.1	3.0	2.9	3.2	-3.6	4.1	3.4
Seed cotton	7.7	11.9	12.5	12.4	13.9	10.6	13.6	9.7	8.9	8.7	8.3	8.3	9.1	9.9	11.9	5.6	-1.2
Maize	9.2	9.1	10.1	11.6	9.3	8.6	9.4	10.7	8.7	12.0	12.0	11.4	11.5	11.5	1.8	-3.3	0.5
Sorghum	7.5	7.4	7.8	6.4	5.4	8.7	6.3	7.3	6.7	8.0	8.3	7.7	7.7	7.7	1.3	-2.9	0.4
Millet	2.6	3.7	5.6	5.0	3.7	6.7	4.7	5.2	4.5	4.7	4.7	5.2	5.3	5.3	-7.1	2.4	0.0
Cassava	103.3	77.9	68.9	68.6	58.8	59.2	56.9	62.3	62.2	60.6	56.5	59.8	60.6	60.3	-10.9	1.6	-1.2
Yams	86.6	90.3	83.3	103.4	98.2	85.8	87.2	109.9	99.1	109.2	110.0	101.8	104.5	103.4	-0.7	-2.8	0.4
TUNISIA																	
Wheat	10.2	17.0	17.0	13.7	10.7	12.8	16.2	11.1	14.2	14.2	11.7	20.0	14.1	38.5	3.8	12.9	3.2
Barley	7.7	13.1	12.0	9.3	5.9	6.6	11.9	5.2	11.6	9.0	6.5	11.7	9.2	35.2	3.3	20.8	3.6
UGANDA																	
Coffee (green)	6.0	5.5	4.2	5.5	7.5	6.9	10.3	8.1	7.7	9.2	4.8	7.5	7.5	7.5	-1.9	1.0	1.9
Seed cotton	0.4	2.0	1.3	3.0	3.3	3.3	4.5	2.8	2.6	2.6	2.7	2.7	2.7	2.7	-13.0	-1.1	2.2
Millet	16.5	15.0	16.0	15.1	14.8	16.0	11.0	12.7	16.0	16.1	13.9	15.0	15.1	15.0	4.2	1.1	-0.1
Maize	11.1	13.5	15.0	16.0	15.1	16.0	13.0	12.4	15.0	17.3	17.4	18.0	18.2	18.2	0.4	-1.1	1.3
Sorghum	17.9	14.8	15.0	15.0	15.0	15.0	11.0	10.7	15.0	15.0	12.9	15.0	15.4	15.2	3.3	1.3	0.1
Cassava	68.6	83.0	80.0	85.1	65.0	67.0	67.0	67.0	90.0	130.0	123.8	135.0	135.9	135.9	1.2	0.3	2.4
Plantains	..	..	..	..	..	..	..	..	..	..	..	..	..	..	..	..	..
ZAIRE																	
Coffee (green)	3.7	3.3	3.2	3.6	3.5	3.7	3.2	3.7	3.7	3.7	3.7	3.7	3.7	4.0	-0.9	0.9	0.5
Palm oil	..	..	..	..	..	..	..	..	..	..	..	..	..	..	..	..	..
Maize	8.0	8.1	8.1	8.3	8.3	7.9	8.0	8.2	8.3	8.0	8.0	8.0	8.0	7.6	1.4	1.2	-0.1
Rice	8.0	8.0	7.3	7.2	7.3	7.4	7.5	7.6	7.6	7.6	7.6	7.6	7.6	7.6	0.4	0.3	-0.3
Cassava	70.0	80.0	80.0	78.1	77.2	81.4	81.1	81.1	81.1	81.1	81.1	81.1	81.1	81.1	0.2	-0.3	0.1
Plantains	..	..	..	..	..	..	..	..	..	..	..	..	..	..	..	..	..
ZAMBIA																	
Seed cotton	5.0	6.6	4.3	6.3	6.5	4.7	5.6	14.3	13.2	13.3	11.3	11.3	11.3	11.3	-5.0	-4.3	3.9
Tobacco leaves	10.4	17.8	4.4	5.1	9.6	12.4	10.5	10.8	10.9	10.7	10.0	10.7	10.7	10.7	1.2	11.3	1.0
Sunflower	9.2	2.9	0.5	3.9	6.3	4.2	5.5	3.6	3.6	4.6	5.3	5.4	5.6	5.6	0.6	6.9	3.4
Maize	16.9	17.1	7.3	25.2	15.0	14.2	20.9	14.8	12.5	13.8	15.0	14.6	14.0	15.5	4.3	-6.4	-1.2
Wheat	40.7	43.8	41.0	50.7	52.7	48.7	55.8	66.2	56.7	69.8	62.1	62.0	62.0	64.5	5.6	-5.1	2.1
Cassava	61.8	62.0	62.0	62.0	62.0	62.0	62.0	62.0	62.0	57.1	49.4	57.6	57.6	57.6	0.0	0.0	-0.4
ZIMBABWE																	
Tobacco leaves	19.5	24.9	24.3	21.9	24.6	24.2	24.2	22.0	26.3	21.2	25.1	24.6	21.6	21.6	2.0	1.2	0.1
Seed cotton	17.5	7.8	2.7	8.6	7.8	4.6	9.2	10.2	9.2	9.2	8.8	8.5	4.9	4.9	1.3	-3.4	-1.1
Sugarcane	1,031.2	1,027.2	89.3	597.8	1,072.5	1,109.7	905.1	1,081.6	962.2	1,083.0	983.1	1,119.0	1,119.0	1,119.0	3.0	-0.8	1.9
Maize	13.4	14.4	4.1	16.3	16.6	6.0	17.0	13.4	11.6	10.5	14.9	12.0	7.2	6.2	-1.7	-14.4	-2.5
Wheat	49.7	56.4	48.3	70.3	56.1	20.8	54.9	51.7	53.8	56.1	53.9	56.2	40.0	29.4	2.5	0.0	-1.1

Notes: The following commodities are in their least-processed form unless otherwise indicated:

   Cotton, Seed cotton

   Groundnuts, unshelled

   Coffee, green or roasted

   Rice, paddy

   Cloves, whole

   Cocoa, beans

   Tobacco, leaves

   Sunflower, seeds

   1 hectogram = 100 grams = 3.527 oz.

Countries excluded from listing: Cape Verde, Djibouti, Sao Tome and Principe, and Seychelles.

For livestock "yield", see Table 8.6 (Food output by major crops).

* The standard World Bank least square methodology was used to compute the annual percentage growth.

8-14. Incidence of drought

	1991	1992	1993	1994	1995	1996	1997	1998	1999	2000	2001	2002	2003
				D=Significant shortage of rain									
SUB-SAHARAN AFRICA	..	..	..	..	..	..	..	..	..	..	..	..	..
excluding South Africa	..	..	..	..	..	..	..	..	..	..	..	..	..
excluding South Africa & Nigeria	..	..	..	..	..	..	..	..	..	..	..	..	..
Angola	..	..	..	..	..	..	..	..	..	..	..	..	..
Benin	..	..	..	..	..	..	..	..	..	..	..	..	..
Botswana	..	D	..	..	D	..	..	..	..	..	..	..	..
Burkina Faso	..	..	..	..	..	..	D	..	..	D	..	..	..
Burundi	..	..	..	..	..	..	..	D	D	D	..	..	..
Cameroon	..	..	..	..	..	D	D	..	..	..	..	..	..
Cape Verde	..	..	D	D	..	..	D	D	D	D	D	D	D
Central African Republic	..	..	..	..	..	..	..	..	..	..	..	..	..
Chad	..	..	D	..	D	D	D	..	D	D	..	..	..
Comoros	..	..	..	..	..	..	..	..	..	..	..	..	..
Congo, Democratic Rep. of	..	..	..	..	..	..	..	..	..	..	..	..	..
Congo, Republic of	..	..	..	..	..	..	..	..	..	..	..	..	..
Côte d'Ivoire	..	..	..	..	..	..	D	..	..	..	..	..	..
Djibouti	..	..	..	..	..	..	..	..	D	D	..	..	..
Equatorial Guinea	..	..	..	..	..	..	..	..	..	..	..	..	..
Eritrea	..	..	..	..	..	D	D	..	D	D	D	D	D
Ethiopia	D	D	..	D	..	..	D	..	D	D	D	D	D
Gabon	..	..	..	..	..	..	..	..	..	..	..	..	..
Gambia, The	..	..	..	..	..	..	..	..	..	..	..	..	..
Ghana	..	..	..	..	..	..	..	D	..	D	..	..	..
Guinea	..	..	..	..	..	..	..	..	..	..	..	..	..
Guinea-Bissau	..	..	..	..	..	..	..	..	..	..	..	..	..
Kenya	..	D	D	..	..	..	D	D	D	D	D	D	D
Lesotho	..	D	..	..	D	..	..	..	..	..	..	..	..
Liberia	..	..	..	..	..	..	..	..	..	..	..	..	..
Madagascar	..	..	..	..	..	..	..	..	D	D	D	D	D
Malawi	..	D	..	D	D	..	D	D	..	..	..	D	..
Mali	..	..	..	..	..	..	..	..	..	..	..	..	..
Mauritania	..	..	..	..	..	..	..	..	..	..	D	D	D
Mauritius	..	..	..	..	..	..	..	..	..	..	..	..	..
Mozambique	..	D	..	..	D	..	..	D	..	..	D	D	D
Namibia	..	D	..	..	D	..	..	..	..	..	..	..	..
Niger	..	..	..	..	D	D	D	..	..	D	..	..	..
Nigeria	..	..	..	..	..	..	..	..	..	..	..	..	..
Rwanda	..	..	..	..	D	D	..	D	D	D	..	..	..
São Tomé and Principe	..	..	..	..	..	..	..	..	..	..	..	..	..
Senegal	..	..	..	..	..	..	..	..	..	..	..	..	..
Seychelles	..	..	..	..	..	..	..	..	..	..	..	..	..
Sierra Leone	..	..	..	..	..	..	..	..	..	..	..	..	..
Somalia	..	..	..	..	..	..	..	D	..	..	D	D	D
South Africa	..	D	..	..	D	..	D	..	..	..	..	..	..
Sudan	..	..	..	..	D	..	D	..	..	D	D	D	D
Swaziland	..	D	..	..	D	..	..	..	..	..	D	D	D
Tanzania	..	D	..	..	..	..	D	D	D	D	..	D	D
Togo	..	..	..	..	..	..	..	..	..	D	..	..	..
Uganda	..	..	..	..	..	..	D	..	D	D	D	D	D
Zambia	..	D	..	D	D	..	D	D	..	..	D	D	D
Zimbabwe	..	D	..	D	D	..	..	..	..	..	D	D	D
NORTH AFRICA	..	..	..	..	..	..	..	..	..	..	..	..	..
Algeria	..	..	D	D	D	..	D	..	D	D	..	..	..
Egypt, Arab Republic	..	..	..	..	..	..	..	..	..	..	..	..	..
Libya	..	..	..	..	..	..	..	..	..	..	..	..	..
Morocco	..	..	..	..	D	..	D	..	D	D	..	..	..
Tunisia	..	..	..	..	D	..	..	..	..	..	..	..	..
ALL AFRICA	..	..	..	..	..	..	..	..	..	..	..	..	..

238

Figure 8-1. Food price index, 2001*

(Index, average 1995 = 100)

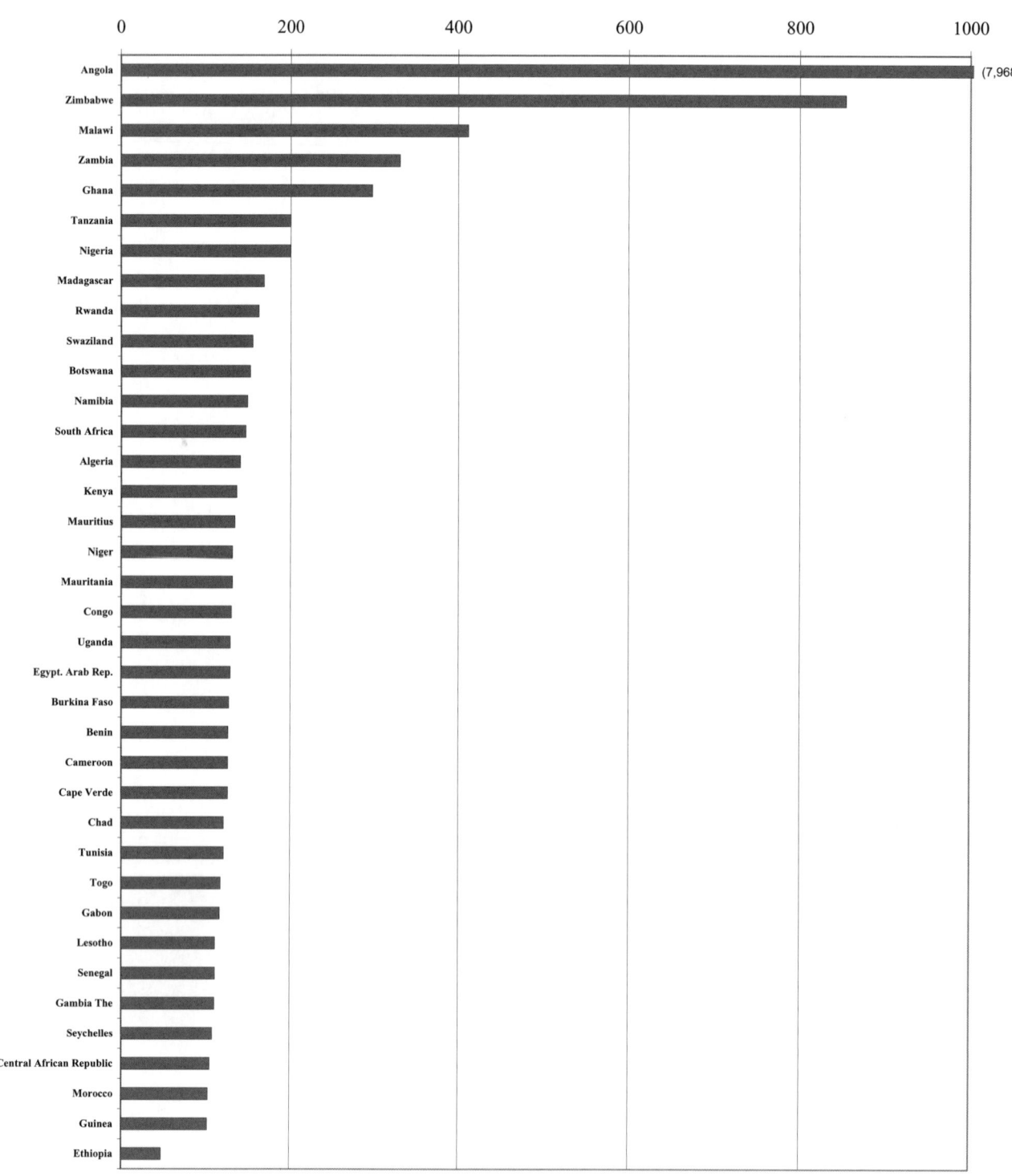

* Or most recent year available.

Figure 8-2. Food production per capita index, 2002*

(Index, average 1989-91 = 100)

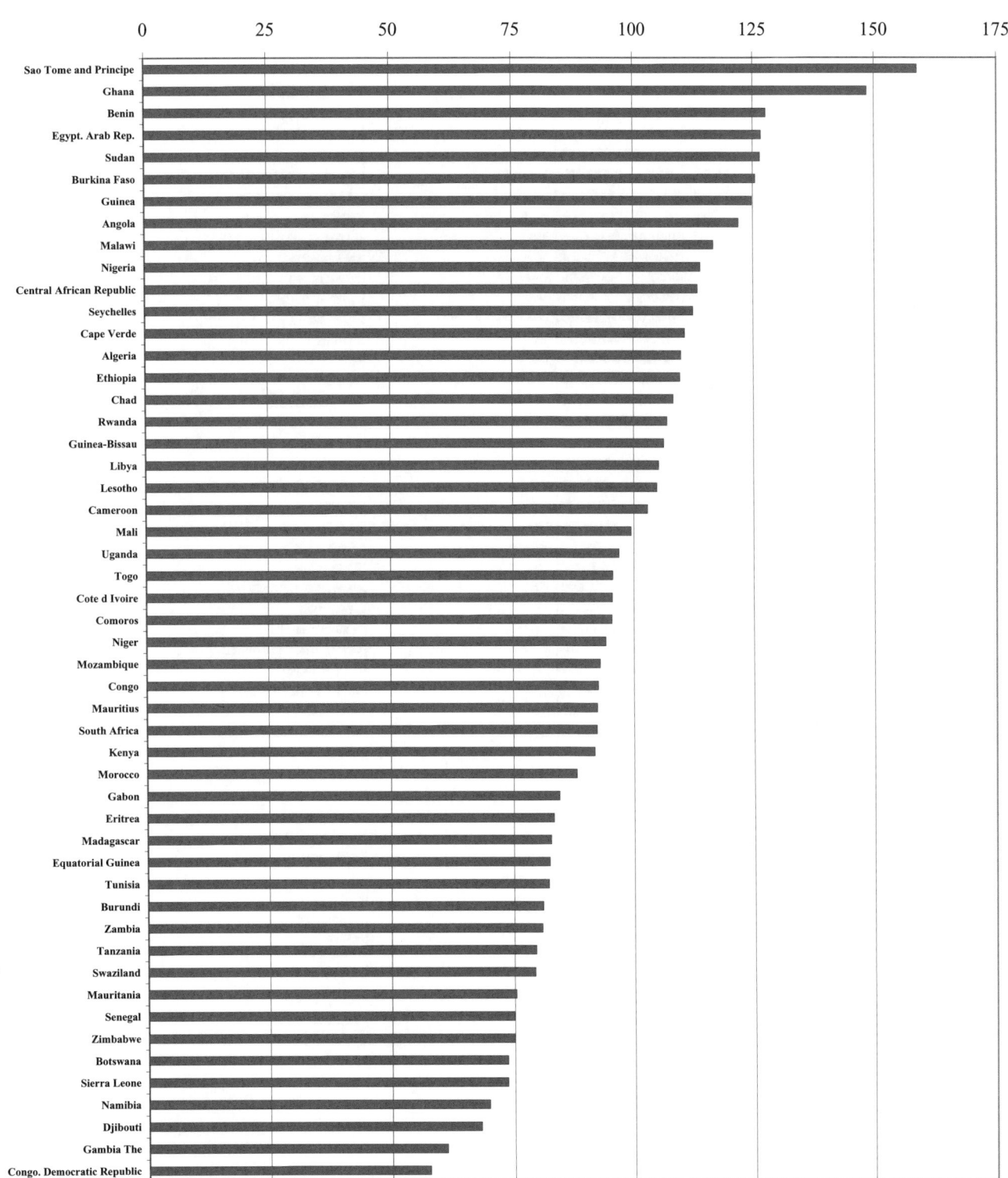

* Or most recent year available.

Figure 8-3. Food and nonfood production index, 2002*

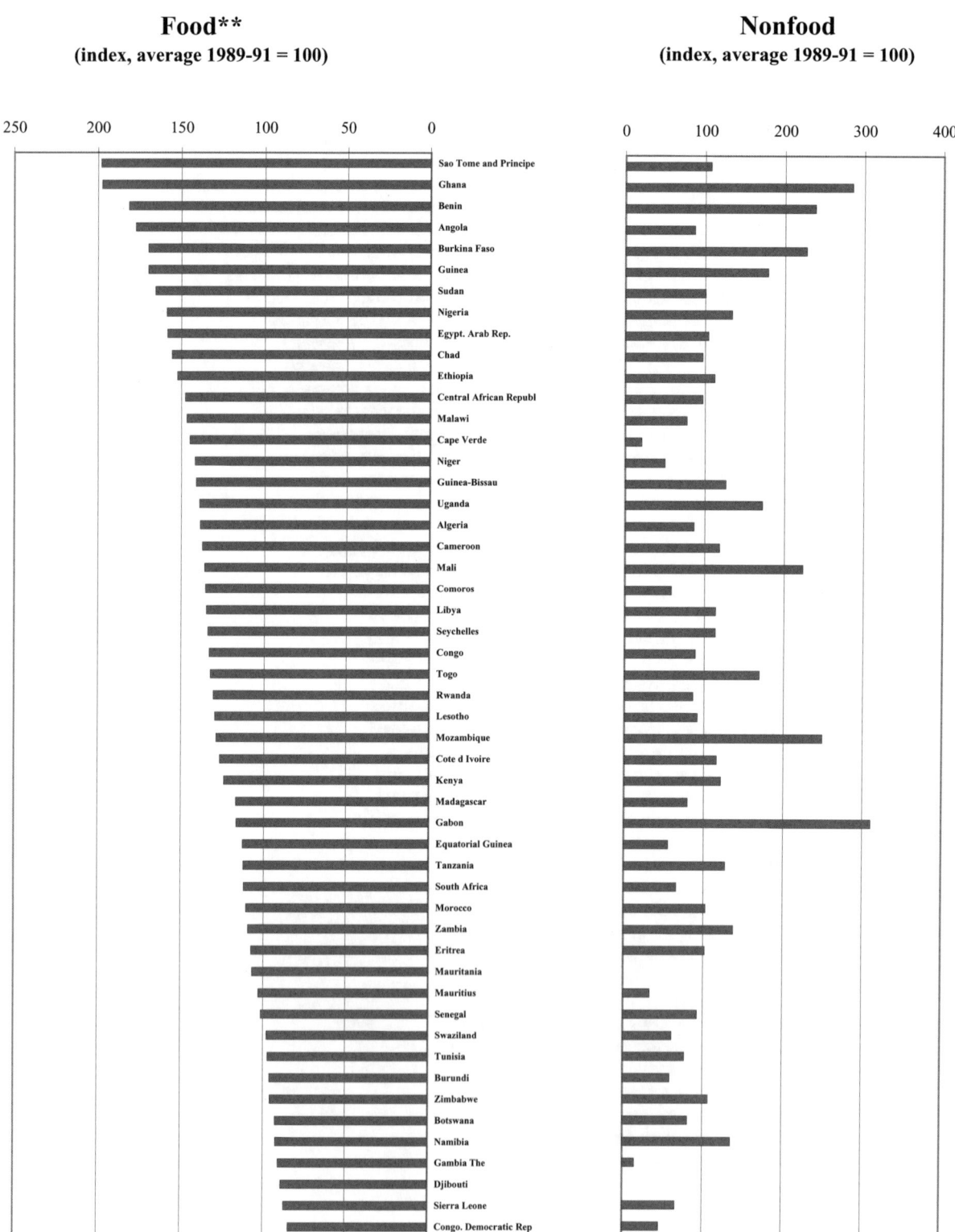

Food**
(index, average 1989-91 = 100)

Nonfood
(index, average 1989-91 = 100)

* Or most recent year available.
** Sorted by food production.

Figure 8-4. Agriculture exports, 1997*

Millions of U.S. dollars

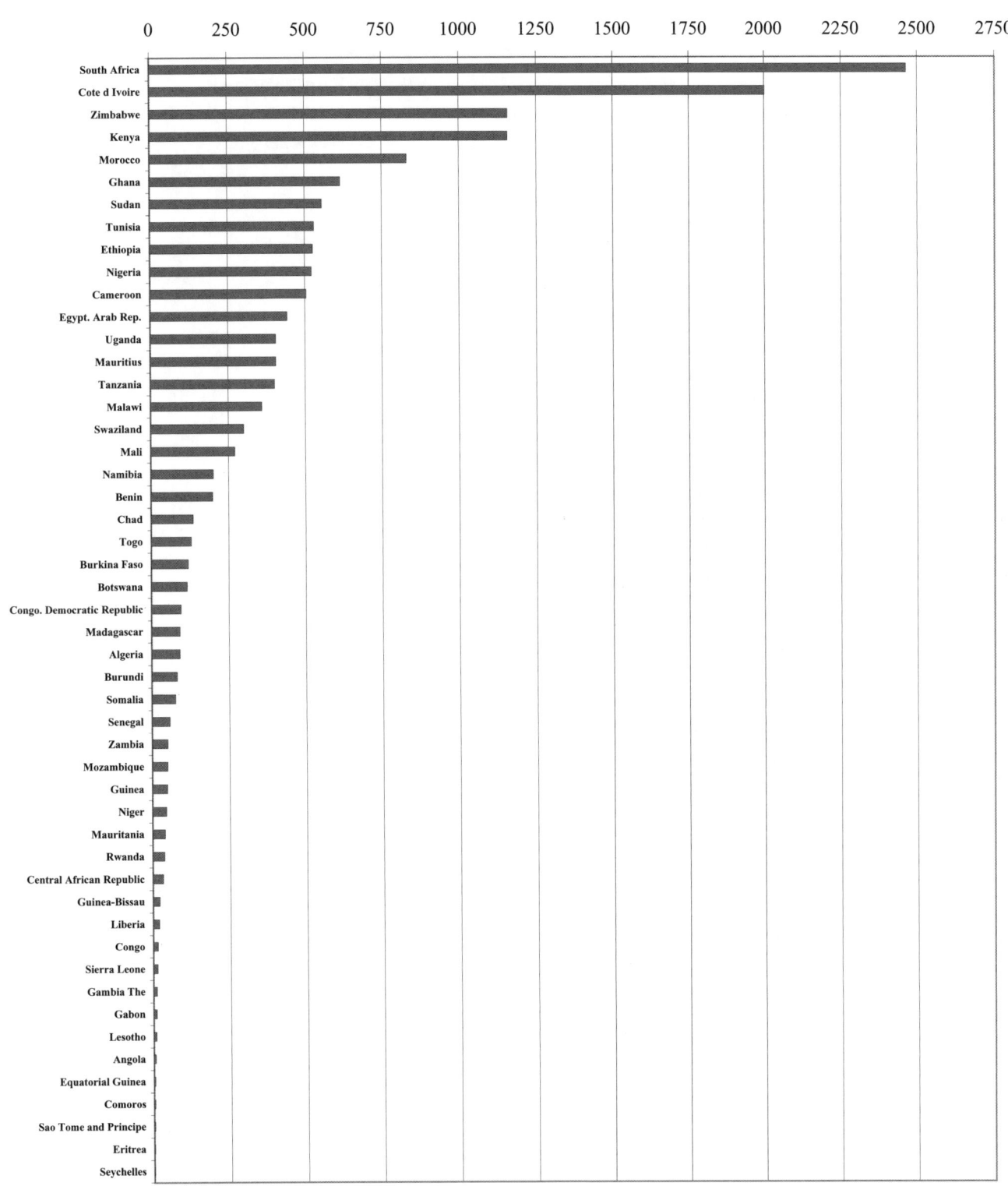

* Or most recent year available.

242

Figure 8-5. Drought, 1980-2003

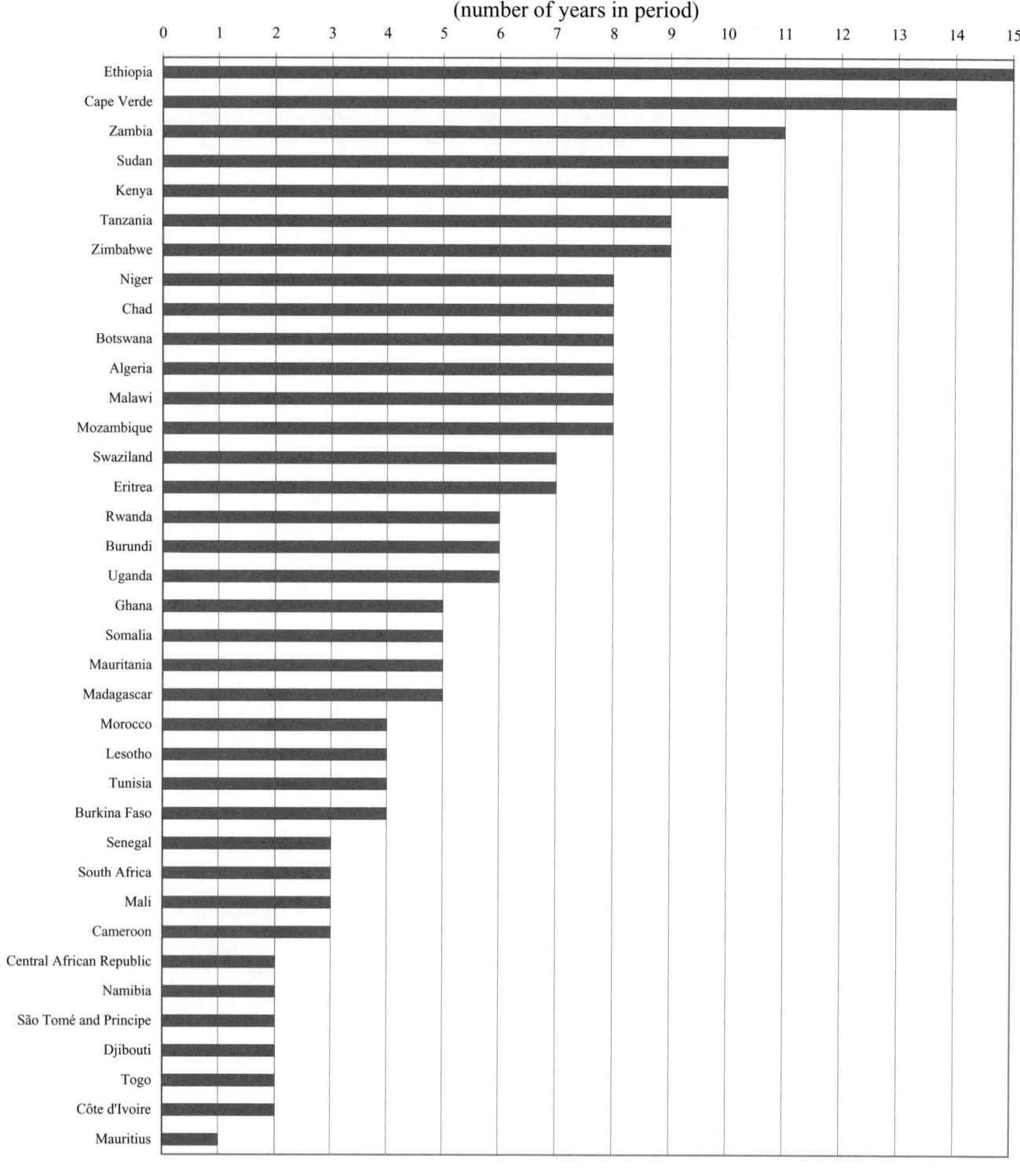

Technical notes

Tables

Table 8-1. Nominal producer prices. Data on nominal producer prices are compiled from FAO. In general, the figures reflect the average annual price received by farmers in the most important producing regions. But given the wide regional and seasonal variation and the lack of precision in recording specifics about prices quoted, the data should be interpreted only as a rough indication of price levels for an entire country during an entire year.

The data do not differentiate between official producer prices and farmgate prices. In most cases they are the same.

Crop years for most countries span parts of two calendar years; planting takes place in the first calendar year, while harvest and marketing take place at the end of the first year and beginning of the second year. For consistency, producer prices are listed corresponding to the calendar year during which planting decisions are made. For example, producer prices for the crop year 1987/88 are listed as 1987.

For each country, up to four export crops and five food crops are included, which represent the most important commodities for that country in terms of value of total production during the early 1980s. The food crops include up to three cereals of "traded" grains (those commonly imported or exported) and up to two "nontraded" staples—generally roots and tubers— which are not normally imported or exported by African countries. In the table, these categories of crops are designated by the following symbols: X1 through X4 for export crops; F1 through F3 for traded food crops; and NT1 and NT2 for nontraded staple food crops. The categorization is consistent across countries, but the numbering of crops within categories in each country depends on which crops are most important.

Where commodities may be marketed in several different forms, the form is generally specified (for instance, shelled or unshelled groundnuts). When not specified, the form of the commodity is the most common (for instance, shelled and dried maize). Where commodities are graded, an average grade has been used unless otherwise specified.

Table 8-2. Food price index. This is a subindex of the consumer price index. It reflects the cost to the average consumer of acquiring a fixed basket of food (IMF, *IFS*).

Table 8-3. Food production index. This index is based on 169 commodities that provide calories when consumed (FAO data). Some of these (such as cottonseed, cocoa, and vanilla) are not, however, a significant part of African diets, but are produced primarily for export.

Table 8-4. Nonfood production index. Data in this table are derived from 29 products that are not considered nutritious, including coffee, rubber, cotton lint, and tobacco leaves (FAO data).

Table 8-5. Food production per capita index. These data are derived as the ratio of the food production index (Table 8-3) to estimated total midyear population figures (Table 1-2).

Table 8-6. Volume of food output, by major food crop. The table covers, with only a few differences, the same major food crops as presented in Table 8-1, excluding beverages (coffee, tea, cocoa), cotton, and tobacco. Also included are figures for livestock, which represent the combined total number of cattle, sheep, goats, pigs, horses, asses, mules, and rabbits (FAO data).

Table 8-7. Value of agricultural exports. The value of agricultural exports is expressed in current U.S. dollars at f.o.b. prices (FAO data).

Table 8-8. Cereal production. This refers to crops harvested for dry grain only. Cereal crops harvested for hay or harvested green for food, feed, or silage and those used for grazing are excluded (FAO data).

Table 8-9. Crop production index. This table shows agricultural production for each year relative to the base period 1989–91. It includes all crops except fodder crops (FAO data).

Tables 8-10 and 8-11. Fertilizer use and imports. Figures are in metric tons and represent the aggregate of nitrogenous, phosphate, and potash fertilizers (FAO database for the *Fertilizer Yearbook*).

Table 8-12. Area under permanent crops. Data in this table reflect land under permanent crops as defined and reported by FAO.

Table 8-13. Agricultural yields, by major crop. This table closely follows the selection of commodities in Table 8-1. Units are in thousands of hectograms (which are equivalent to hundreds of kilograms) per hectare. Most of the data come from the database for the FAO's *Production Yearbook*, with additional information from World Bank agricultural sector reports.

Table 8-14. Incidence of drought. This is the only indicator in this chapter based on subjective considerations. Data on rainfall levels from other sources are usually presented to suit different purposes, without considering seasonal and regional characteristics of the producing regions. A low rainfall level might not harm agricultural production if it did not adversely affect the regions where the main crops are produced, whereas an average rainfall level might be associated with difficulties in the producing regions—due to delay, for example. Therefore, simply presenting the annual rainfall levels would not necessarily enrich the agricultural data.

For each country, a binary classification was thus created. A "D" was assigned to a country if a significant shortage of rain unfavorably affected its agricultural production. For normal or average rainfall, the standard sign was given, as in the cases of insufficient information or "not applicable." (Specialists who work on the relevant countries were surveyed, as well as World Bank agricultural and environmental experts. In addition, the Famine Early Warning System Project of the U.S. Agency for International Development provided information for 1993–94 for about half of the countries listed.) FAO's Global Information and Early Waning System on Food and Agriculture provided information for 1999–2003.

Figures

The following indicators have been used to derive the figures in this chapter.

Figure 8-1. Food price index (Table 8-2).

Figure 8-2. Food production per capita index (Table 8-5).

Figure 8-3. Food production index (Table 8-3); nonfood production index (Table 8-4).

Figure 8-4. Agriculture exports (Table 8-7).

Figure 8-5. Drought (Table 8-14).

Methodology used for regional aggregations and period averages in Chapter 8

Table	Aggregations [a] (1)	(6)	(7)	(8)	Period averages [b] (2)
8-1				x	
8-2			x		x
8-3		x			x
8-4			x		
8-5			x		x
8-6				x	x
8-7	x				x
8-8	x				x
8-9		x			x
8-10	x				x
8-11	x				x
8-12	x				x
8-13				x	x
8-14				x	

Note: Regional aggregations are shown in the rows for Sub-Saharan Africa, North Africa, and All Africa. Period averages are shown in the last three columns. This table shows only the methodologies used in this chapter.

a. Regional aggregations: (1) simple total; (2) simple total of the first indicator divided by the simple total of the second indicator (same country coverage); (3) simple total of the gap-filled indicator; (4) simple total of the gap-filled main indicator divided by the simple total of the gap-filled secondary indicator; (5) simple total of the first gap-filled main indicator less the simple total of the second gap-filled main indicator, all divided by the simple total of the secondary indicator; (6) weighted total (by population); (7) median; (8) no aggregation; (9) simple arithmetic mean.

b. Period averages: (1) arithmetic mean (using the same series as shown in the table; i.e., ratio if the rest of the table is shown as ratio, level if the rest of the table is shown as level, growth rate if the rest is shown as growth rate); (2) least-squares growth rate (using main indicator); (3) least-squares growth rate (using main indicator in constant terms, with the rest of the table in current terms).

9

Power, Communications and Transportation

An adequate and reliable supply of power is a vital ingredient for the economic development of African countries. This chapter provides data on the power, communications, and transportation sectors of the economy. Data are from the International Energy Agency's (IEA's) *Energy Statistics and Balances of Non-OECD Countries,* and from the United Nations Statistics Division's *Energy Statistics Yearbook.*

Telecommunications, computers, and the Internet are also essential ingredients of a modern economy. In this chapter, telephone main lines represent the supply side of the system, which in Africa is well short of demand. In fact, waiting time for telephone lines is longer in Africa than in any other region. Because of the growing importance of computers on development, a new table on computers and the Internet was added. Data on telecommunications are from the International Telecommunications Union's (ITU's) *World Telecommunication Development Report* (2003), *Challenges to the Network: Internet for Development* (1999), and the *World Telecommunication Development Report* (2003b). The data on Internet hosts are from the Internet Software Consortium (www.isc.com).

In addition to power and communications, countries must have a solid transportation sector to underpin expansion of their economies and ensure support to the activities of households, producers, and government. This chapter presents data on vehicle use, roads, and railway traffic. Data are from World Bank databases, the International World Road Federation's *World Road Statistics,* and Eurostat (europa.eu.int/comm/eurostat). The air transport data are from the International Civil Aviation Organization's (ICAD's) *Civil Aviation Statistics of the World* and ICAO staff estimates.

9-1. Electric power consumption per capita

	kWh											Annual average		
	1980	1991	1992	1993	1994	1995	1996	1997	1998	1999	2000	75-84	85-94	95-MR
SUB-SAHARAN AFRICA	425.4	432.6	416.0	430.8	419.8	430.6	436.9	439.5	444.6	443.0	441.6	405.3	437.0	439.4
excluding South Africa	132.9	118.8	119.8	122.9	118.0	119.7	122.2	118.6	109.8	113.0	113.2	127.8	125.5	116.1
excl. S.Africa & Nigeria	156.9	132.6	132.6	133.3	129.0	132.9	136.1	131.1	..	..	..	151.3	140.6	133.4
Angola	66.8	63.0	61.9	60.1	58.4	56.9	59.0	80.3	85.2	83.8	88.2	72.7	62.4	75.6
Benin	29.8	38.9	41.2	41.7	42.1	45.0	42.7	51.8	48.7	56.8	63.6	29.5	37.6	51.4
Botswana	..	..	..	..	..	..	..	..	..	..	..	..	..	..
Burkina Faso	..	..	..	..	..	..	..	..	..	..	..	..	..	..
Burundi	..	..	..	..	..	..	..	..	..	..	..	..	..	..
Cameroon	154.3	195.3	192.0	194.6	170.9	164.0	170.3	180.8	178.3	184.2	182.8	178.4	202.4	176.7
Cape Verde	..	..	..	..	..	..	..	..	..	..	..	..	..	..
Central African Republic	..	..	..	..	..	..	..	..	..	..	..	..	..	..
Chad	..	..	..	..	..	..	..	..	..	..	..	..	..	..
Comoros	..	..	..	..	..	..	..	..	..	..	..	..	..	..
Congo, Dem. Rep. of	147.8	58.7	60.5	66.4	47.2	47.1	44.9	43.5	42.3	43.2	40.2	139.5	97.6	43.5
Congo, Rep. of	83.3	168.8	160.3	136.6	129.2	129.1	129.6	104.8	81.1	50.8	86.1	81.4	149.4	96.9
Côte d'Ivoire	191.6	149.6	81.4	139.6	140.3	170.5	174.3	181.3	..	..	..	166.4	149.3	175.4
Djibouti	..	..	..	..	..	..	..	..	..	..	..	..	..	..
Equatorial Guinea	..	..	..	..	..	..	..	..	..	..	..	..	..	..
Eritrea	..	..	..	..	..	..	..	..	..	..	..	..	..	..
Ethiopia	16.2	17.7	17.9	20.1	20.8	21.7	22.3	22.2	22.2	21.4	22.1	16.3	18.4	22.0
Gabon	617.1	806.4	783.1	765.0	769.9	750.5	754.2	762.6	757.3	701.0	696.7	604.8	876.3	737.0
Gambia, The	..	..	..	..	..	..	..	..	..	..	..	..	..	..
Ghana	423.6	303.2	316.2	322.9	299.6	334.8	362.8	281.2	199.4	246.7	288.3	335.9	283.3	285.5
Guinea	..	..	..	..	..	..	..	..	..	..	..	..	..	..
Guinea-Bissau	..	..	..	..	..	..	..	..	..	..	..	..	..	..
Kenya	92.5	117.5	118.1	121.3	123.2	125.1	128.1	126.2	127.4	118.0	105.9	90.1	112.9	121.8
Lesotho	..	..	..	..	..	..	..	..	..	..	..	..	..	..
Liberia	..	..	..	..	..	..	..	..	..	..	..	..	..	..
Madagascar	..	..	..	..	..	..	..	..	..	..	..	..	..	..
Malawi	..	..	..	..	..	..	..	..	..	..	..	..	..	..
Mali	..	..	..	..	..	..	..	..	..	..	..	..	..	..
Mauritania	..	..	..	..	..	..	..	..	..	..	..	..	..	..
Mauritius	..	..	..	..	..	..	..	..	..	..	..	..	..	..
Mozambique	34.0	48.3	46.2	46.2	41.3	44.1	40.7	46.8	54.1	53.0	52.6	42.4	38.1	48.6
Namibia	..	..	..	..	..	..	..	..	..	..	..	..	..	..
Niger	..	..	..	..	..	..	..	..	..	..	..	..	..	..
Nigeria	68.2	81.6	85.5	95.3	88.8	84.8	85.3	85.4	81.9	79.8	80.9	64.6	85.3	83.0
Rwanda	..	..	..	..	..	..	..	..	..	..	..	..	..	..
São Tomé and Principe	..	..	..	..	..	..	..	..	..	..	..	..	..	..
Senegal	96.4	98.5	105.7	101.0	107.1	106.5	108.1	114.6	119.0	114.5	120.6	92.7	99.8	113.9
Seychelles	..	..	..	..	..	..	..	..	..	..	..	..	..	..
Sierra Leone	..	..	..	..	..	..	..	..	..	..	..	..	..	..
Somalia	..	..	..	..	..	..	..	..	..	..	..	..	..	..
South Africa	3,212.9	3,618.2	3,447.4	3,581.3	3,530.7	3,659.8	3,723.2	3,800.2	3,831.9	3,775.5	3,745.2	3,037.2	3,563.1	3,756.0
Sudan	34.2	49.1	49.2	47.2	48.8	48.0	48.7	45.8	44.6	66.6	66.2	36.0	48.3	53.3
Swaziland	..	..	..	..	..	..	..	..	..	..	..	..	..	..
Tanzania	36.8	54.4	53.2	51.4	50.7	54.7	58.8	54.3	53.5	54.1	55.6	35.4	46.9	55.2
Togo	..	..	..	..	..	..	..	..	..	..	..	..	..	..
Uganda	..	..	..	..	..	..	..	..	..	..	..	..	..	..
Zambia	1,015.7	730.0	726.0	723.4	712.4	691.0	668.6	620.9	568.0	574.2	556.3	1,058.2	810.5	613.2
Zimbabwe	973.2	789.8	858.1	751.9	788.8	814.7	858.9	850.8	872.3	883.3	845.2	939.3	853.3	854.2
NORTH AFRICA	362.8	696.7	710.8	713.4	732.6	744.5	756.9	782.3	815.2	845.9	894.9	352.0	657.1	806.6
Algeria	265.3	492.5	521.9	507.9	509.0	516.9	526.3	523.2	550.0	584.6	611.9	259.8	452.3	552.2
Egypt, Arab Rep.	379.9	707.1	710.3	726.3	742.7	762.0	781.2	819.9	860.3	899.7	976.0	377.8	660.6	849.8
Libya	1,588.2	3,814.6	3,773.6	3,714.0	3,816.5	3,785.5	3,772.4	3,831.3	3,853.7	3,875.8	3,921.4	1,503.4	3,727.2	3,840.0
Morocco	222.8	355.4	380.9	377.1	398.1	403.7	408.4	422.7	443.0	430.3	447.2	212.1	334.7	425.9
Tunisia	379.2	617.3	651.4	674.1	718.3	734.4	744.8	783.0	824.0	910.9	938.9	323.7	590.9	822.7
ALL AFRICA	410.8	492.1	482.0	494.2	489.4	500.0	507.1	514.3	527.1	532.3	541.7	392.7	486.8	520.4

9-2. Energy production and use

	Energy production (KT oil equivalent)		Commercial energy use (KT oil equivalent)		Electric power transmission and distribution losses (% of output)	
	1980	2001	1980	2000	1980	2001
SUB-SAHARAN AFRICA	320,598	556,627	208,143	341,194	..	..
excluding South Africa	247,429	411,340	142,726	233,599	..	..
excl. S. Africa & Nigeria	98,950	204,316	89,880	143,431	..	..
Angola	11,301	43,559	4,437	7,667	25	15
Benin	1,212	1,483	1,363	2,362	220	70
Botswana	..	..	..	..	..	..
Burkina Faso	..	..	..	..	..	..
Burundi	..	..	..	..	..	..
Cameroon	6,707	12,485	3,676	6,355	7	26
Cape Verde	..	..	..	..	..	..
Central African Republic	..	..	..	..	..	..
Chad	..	..	..	..	..	..
Comoros	..	..	..	..	..	..
Congo, Dem. Rep. of	8,697	15,707	8,706	14,888	8	4
Congo, Rep. of	4,024	13,668	862	895	9	65
Côte d'Ivoire	2,419	6,177	3,662	6,928	7	..
Djibouti	..	..	..	..	..	..
Equatorial Guinea	..	..	..	..	..	..
Eritrea	..	..	..	..	..	..
Ethiopia	10,575	18,000	11,145	18,732	8	10
Gabon	9,441	14,788	1,493	1,563	1	18
Gambia, The	..	..	..	..	..	..
Ghana	3,305	5,995	4,063	7,720	5	15
Guinea	..	..	..	..	..	..
Guinea-Bissau	..	..	..	..	..	..
Kenya	7,891	12,644	9,791	15,482	16	21
Lesotho	..	..	..	..	..	..
Liberia	..	..	..	..	..	..
Madagascar	..	..	..	..	..	..
Malawi	..	..	..	..	..	..
Mali	..	..	..	..	..	..
Mauritania	..	..	..	..	..	..
Mauritius	..	..	..	..	..	..
Mozambique	7,413	7,560	8,074	7,126	39	3
Namibia	..	294	..	1,031	..	..
Niger	..	..	..	..	..	..
Nigeria	148,479	207,024	52,846	90,169	36	38
Rwanda	..	..	..	..	..	..
São Tomé and Principe	..	..	..	..	..	..
Senegal	1,046	1,765	1,919	3,086	10	19
Seychelles	..	..	..	..	..	..
Sierra Leone	..	..	..	..	..	..
Somalia	..	..	..	..	..	..
South Africa	73,169	145,287	65,417	107,595	8	8
Sudan	7,089	21,551	8,406	16,216	14	15
Swaziland	..	..	..	..	..	..
Tanzania	7,296	13,001	10,280	15,386	14	25
Togo	562	1,056	715	1,530	..	..
Uganda	..	..	..	..	..	..
Zambia	4,179	6,052	4,719	6,244	7	3
Zimbabwe	5,793	8,531	6,570	10,219	9	21
NORTH AFRICA	205,685	285,463	44,033	110,101	..	..
Algeria	67,103	144,330	12,185	29,060	11	16
Egypt, Arab Rep.	34,168	59,301	15,970	46,423	13	12
Libya	96,550	74,363	7,193	16,438	..	..
Morocco	877	583	4,778	10,293	10	7
Tunisia	6,987	6,886	3,907	7,888	12	11
ALL AFRICA	526,283	842,090	252,176	451,296	..	..

9-3. Telephone, radio, and television availability, 1996-02

	Telephones				Radios	Television sets
	Mainlines (per 1,000 people)	Waiting list (thousands)	Average cost of call US$ per three minutes	Mobile phones (per 1,000 people)	(per 1,000 people)	(per 1,000 people)
SUB-SAHARAN AFRICA	15	192	..	37	198	69
excluding South Africa	8	190	..	18	188	62
excl. S. Africa & Nigeria	9	200	..	20	185	51
Angola	6	17	0.09	9	74	52
Benin	9	4	0.28	32	441	12
Botswana	87	13	0.02	241	150	44
Burkina Faso	5	1	0.10	8	433	79
Burundi	3	1	0.02	7	220	31
Cameroon	7	3	0.06	43	163	75
Cape Verde	160	4	0.04	98	181	101
Central African Republic	2	0	0.43	3	80	6
Chad	2	0	0.11	4	236	2
Comoros	13	4	0.14	0	174	4
Congo, Dem. Rep. of	0	..	..	11	386	2
Congo, Rep. of	7	..	..	67	123	13
Côte d'Ivoire	20	1	0.22	62	183	61
Djibouti	15	0	0.20	23	87	78
Equatorial Guinea	17	4	0.05	63	427	116
Eritrea	9	10	0.03	0	464	50
Ethiopia	5	2	0.02	1	189	6
Gabon	25	9	0.22	215	501	308
Gambia, The	28	8	0.03	73	396	15
Ghana	13	7	0.03	21	710	53
Guinea	3	0	0.08	12	52	47
Guinea-Bissau	9	4	0.15	0	204	36
Kenya	10	4	0.07	42	221	26
Lesotho	13	10	0.11	42	53	35
Liberia	2	1	..	1	274	25
Madagascar	4	0	0.07	10	216	25
Malawi	7	2	0.06	8	499	4
Mali	5	..	0.07	5	180	33
Mauritania	12	19	0.13	92	149	99
Mauritius	270	11	0.04	289	379	299
Mozambique	5	1	0.08	14	44	14
Namibia	65	1	0.03	80	141	269
Niger	2	..	0.10	1	121	10
Nigeria	6	0	..	13	200	103
Rwanda	3	1	0.09	14	85	0
São Tomé and Principe	41	4	0.17	13	318	93
Senegal	22	1	0.10	55	126	78
Seychelles	269	22	0.14	553	543	202
Sierra Leone	5	5	0.03	13	259	13
Somalia	10	..	..	3	60	14
South Africa	107	1	0.09	304	338	177
Sudan	21	14	0.03	6	466	386
Swaziland	34	15	0.04	61	162	34
Tanzania	5	0	0.12	19	406	45
Togo	10	6	0.10	35	265	123
Uganda	2	0	0.21	16	127	18
Zambia	8	1	0.09	13	175	51
Zimbabwe	25	14	0.04	30	362	56
NORTH AFRICA	84	44	..	81	282	188
Algeria	61	24	0.02	13	244	114
Egypt, Arab Rep.	8	1	0.09	13	175	229
Libya	25	14	0.04	30	362	137
Morocco	61	24	0.02	13	244	167
Tunisia	110	3	0.02	67	339	207
ALL AFRICA	26	268	..	45	213	89

9-4. Personal computers and Internet use

	Personal computers (per 1,000 people)		Internet hosts (per 10,000 people)		Internet users (thousands)	
	2001	2002	1999	2000	2001	2002
SUB-SAHARAN AFRICA	10.2	11.9	2.36	3.18	4,542	6,223
excluding South Africa	5.4	7.0	0.15	0.32	1,652	3,123
excl. S. Africa & Nigeria	5.0	7.0	0.19	0.41	1,537	2,703
Angola	1.3	1.9	0.00	0.01	20	41
Benin	1.7	2.2	0.04	0.04	25	50
Botswana	38.7	40.7	5.79	13.99	50	..
Burkina Faso	1.5	1.6	0.19	0.19	19	25
Burundi	0.7	0.7	0.00	0.00	6	8
Cameroon	3.9	5.7	0.00	0.01	45	60
Cape Verde	68.6	79.7	0.02	0.05	12	16
Central African Republic	1.9	2.0	0.00	0.02	3	5
Chad	1.6	1.7	0.00	0.01	4	15
Comoros	5.5	5.5	0.57	0.72	3	3
Congo, Dem. Rep. of	..	..	0.00	0.00	6	50
Congo, Rep. of	3.9	3.9	0.00	0.01	1	5
Côte d'Ivoire	7.2	9.3	0.24	0.37	70	90
Djibouti	10.9	15.2	0.00	0.65	3	5
Equatorial Guinea	5.3	6.9	0.00	0.00	1	2
Eritrea	1.8	2.5	0.01	0.02	6	9
Ethiopia	1.1	1.5	0.01	0.01	25	50
Gabon	15.8	19.2	0.02	0.21	17	25
Gambia, The	12.7	13.8	0.02	0.12	18	25
Ghana	3.3	3.8	0.06	0.06	40	170
Guinea	4.2	5.5	0.00	0.00	15	35
Guinea-Bissau	..	..	0.13	0.11	4	5
Kenya	5.6	6.4	0.19	0.32	200	400
Lesotho	..	..	0.08	0.42	5	21
Liberia	..	..	0.00	0.00	1	..
Madagascar	2.6	4.4	0.12	0.36	35	55
Malawi	1.3	1.3	0.00	0.00	20	27
Mali	1.3	1.4	0.01	0.05	20	25
Mauritania	10.3	10.8	0.00	0.20	7	10
Mauritius	108.3	116.5	4.55	27.68	158	120
Mozambique	4.0	4.5	0.09	0.10	30	..
Namibia	54.7	70.9	11.61	19.57	45	50
Niger	0.5	0.6	0.03	0.12	12	15
Nigeria	6.8	7.1	0.00	0.01	115	420
Rwanda	..	..	0.00	0.47	20	25
São Tomé and Principe	..	..	17.32	45.00	9	11
Senegal	18.4	19.8	0.28	0.51	100	105
Seychelles	146.5	160.8	0.12	0.49	9	12
Sierra Leone	..	..	0.14	0.16	7	8
Somalia	..	..	0.00	0.00	1	89
South Africa	69.6	72.6	33.36	43.12	2,890	3,100
Sudan	3.6	6.1	0.00	0.00	56	84
Swaziland	15.7	24.2	6.28	7.07	14	20
Tanzania	3.6	4.2	0.05	0.16	60	80
Togo	25.3	30.8	0.18	0.35	150	200
Uganda	2.9	3.3	0.06	0.07	60	100
Zambia	7.1	7.5	0.48	0.86	25	52
Zimbabwe	17.4	51.6	1.14	2.50	100	500
NORTH AFRICA	14.0	17.4	0.19	0.47	1,620	3,731
Algeria	7.1	7.7	0.01	0.01	200	500
Egypt, Arab Rep.	15.5	16.6	0.28	0.85	600	1,900
Libya	..	23.4	0.00	0.02	20	125
Morocco	13.7	23.6	0.28	0.33	400	700
Tunisia	26.4	30.7	0.06	0.10	400	506
ALL AFRICA	10.9	12.9	1.99	2.71	6,162	9,954

9-5. Vehicle ownership

	Units per 1000 people											Annual average		
	1980	*1990*	*1991*	*1992*	*1993*	*1994*	*1995*	*1996*	*1997*	*1998*	*1999*	*75-84*	*85-94*	*95-MR*
SUB-SAHARAN AFRICA	..	21	23	23	24	22	23	23	..	..	..	..	..	23
excluding South Africa	..	9	14	14	15	14	15	15	..	..	..	..	..	15
excl. S.Africa & Nigeria	..	9	10	10	11	12	12	12	..	..	..	..	..	12
Angola	..	18	19	19	19	19	20	20	..	..	..	..	..	20
Benin	..	3	4	5	6	6	7	8	..	..	..	..	..	7
Botswana	27	18	23	28	32	35	62	48	51	59	68	27	..	58
Burkina Faso	..	4	4	5	5	5	5	6	..	..	..	..	..	5
Burundi	..	0	..	..	..	..	..	..	..	..	..	..	..	..
Cameroon	8	10	10	10	11	11	12	12	..	..	..	8	..	12
Cape Verde	..	9	9	9	9	10	10	10	..	..	..	..	..	10
Central African Republic	8	1	1	0	1	1	0	0	0	..	..	8	..	0
Chad	..	2	3	3	3	3	4	4	..	..	..	..	..	4
Comoros	..	13	15	17	18	23	24	28	..	..	..	..	..	26
Congo, Dem. Rep. of	..	22	25	28	28	29	30	31	..	..	..	..	..	30
Congo, Rep. of	..	18	19	19	20	19	20	20	..	..	..	..	..	20
Côte d'Ivoire	24	24	24	25	27	29	30	32	..	..	..	24	..	31
Djibouti	..	15	16	16	16	17	18	19	..	..	..	..	..	18
Equatorial Guinea	..	3	4	4	4	5	5	5	..	..	..	..	..	5
Eritrea	..	1	1	1	1	1	2	2	..	..	..	..	..	2
Ethiopia	2	1	1	1	1	1	1	1	1	1	..	2	1	1
Gabon	..	32	33	35	36	35	37	37	..	..	..	..	..	37
Gambia, The	..	13	13	13	13	15	15	15	..	..	..	..	..	15
Ghana	..	..	..	..	..	8	8	8	..	..	..	..	..	8
Guinea	..	4	4	5	5	5	5	5	..	..	..	..	..	5
Guinea-Bissau	..	7	7	7	8	10	10	12	..	..	..	..	..	11
Kenya	8	12	13	13	13	13	13	13	..	..	..	8	12	13
Lesotho	10	11	12	13	14	17	18	20	..	..	..	10	..	19
Liberia	1	14	14	14	14	15	14	15	..	..	..	1	..	14
Madagascar	..	6	5	5	5	7	7	8	..	..	..	..	..	8
Malawi	5	4	5	5	5	5	6	6	..	..	..	5	..	6
Mali	..	3	4	4	4	4	4	5	..	..	..	..	..	4
Mauritania	..	10	10	10	10	12	12	13	..	..	..	..	..	12
Mauritius	44	59	63	68	71	75	79	83	88	93	98	44	54	88
Mozambique	..	4	5	5	5	3	2	1	..	..	..	..	..	1
Namibia	..	71	83	73	78	81	81	84	..	..	..	..	..	83
Niger	6	6	6	6	6	6	6	6	..	..	..	6	5	6
Nigeria	4	..	30	29	29	22	25	24	..	..	..	4	..	24
Rwanda	2	2	3	3	3	5	5	5	..	..	..	2	1	5
São Tomé and Principe	..	36	37	37	38	40	40	41	..	..	..	..	..	41
Senegal	19	11	11	12	13	13	13	14	..	..	..	19	..	14
Seychelles	..	104	104	105	107	116	114	119	118	..	..	..	..	117
Sierra Leone	..	10	10	11	10	11	9	6	..	..	..	..	10	7
Somalia	..	2	2	2	2	1	1	1	..	..	..	..	..	1
South Africa	133	139	140	139	136	141	139	142	..	..	143	133	160	142
Sudan	..	9	9	10	10	11	11	12	..	..	..	..	..	11
Swaziland	52	66	71	68	65	62	66	68	67	70	..	52	63	68
Tanzania	3	5	4	5	5	5	5	5	..	..	..	3	..	5
Togo	..	24	25	26	26	26	28	28	..	..	..	..	1	28
Uganda	1	2	3	3	3	3	4	4	5	5	5	1	..	5
Zambia	..	14	16	18	20	22	24	26	..	..	..	..	..	25
Zimbabwe	..	..	..	..	32	32	31	30	..	..	..	..	..	31
NORTH AFRICA	..	33	34	34	35	46	49	49	..	..	..	..	38	49
Algeria	..	..	..	..	..	55	54	53	..	..	..	..	54	53
Egypt, Arab Rep.	..	29	29	29	28	29	29	30	..	..	..	..	26	30
Libya	..	..	..	..	..	165	240	241	..	..	..	..	..	240
Morocco	..	37	38	41	43	47	48	48	49	51	52	..	..	50
Tunisia	38	48	49	51	52	59	59	64	..	..	..	38	62	62
ALL AFRICA	..	23	25	25	25	27	28	28	..	..	..	..	..	28

9-6. Road-to-population ratio

	Road 1000 km/1 million people											Annual average		
	1980	1985	1989	1990	1991	1992	1993	1994	1995	1996	1997	75-84	85-94	95-MR
SUB-SAHARAN AFRICA	3.3	3.0	..	2.5	..	..	2.5	2.4	2.9	2.4	..	3.3	2.6	2.6
excluding South Africa	3.1	2.8	..	2.2	..	..	2.5	2.4	2.5	2.4	..	3.1	2.5	2.4
excl. S.Africa & Nigeria	3.5	3.2	..	2.5	..	..	2.8	2.6	2.6	2.6	..	3.5	2.8	2.6
Angola	10.3	8.7	..	7.8	..	7.3	7.1	6.9	6.7	6.5	6.3	11.0	7.5	6.5
Benin	2.1	1.9	1.3	1.8	1.2	1.2	1.3	1.3	1.2	1.2	..	2.1	1.4	1.2
Botswana	9.1	7.6	..	7.0	..	..	13.1	12.6	12.2	12.0	..	11.7	10.5	12.1
Burkina Faso	1.1	1.1	..	..	..	1.4	1.1	1.1	1.3	1.2	..	1.7	1.2	1.2
Burundi	1.2	0.6	..	1.2	..	2.5	2.5	2.4	2.4	2.3	..	1.8	1.8	2.3
Cameroon	7.1	6.4	..	6.0	..	..	2.7	2.6	2.6	..	..	6.5	4.6	2.6
Cape Verde	..	..	..	..	..	..	3.0	2.9	2.9	2.8	..	..	3.0	2.8
Central African Republic	9.8	7.6	8.2	8.0	7.9	7.7	7.5	7.3	7.1	7.0	..	9.7	7.7	7.0
Chad	6.0	5.3	..	4.6	..	..	5.0	4.9	4.9	4.8	..	6.6	4.9	4.8
Comoros	..	..	..	..	..	..	1.8	1.8	1.8	1.8	..	2.3	1.8	1.8
Congo, Dem. Rep. of	5.2	4.5	..	..	3.8	3.6	3.6	3.6	3.5	3.4	..	5.3	3.8	3.5
Congo, Rep. of	4.7	4.1	..	..	4.9	4.8	4.6	4.5	4.4	4.2	..	5.1	4.6	4.3
Côte d'Ivoire	5.0	4.8	..	4.2	..	..	3.8	3.7	3.6	3.5	..	5.6	4.1	3.6
Djibouti	..	8.2	6.5	5.9	5.7	..	5.3	5.1	5.0	4.8	..	8.2	6.4	4.9
Equatorial Guinea	..	..	..	..	..	..	7.1	7.1	7.0	7.0	..	5.2	7.1	7.0
Eritrea	..	..	..	..	..	..	1.1	1.1	1.1	1.1	..	..	1.1	1.1
Ethiopia	1.0	0.9	0.4	0.5	0.5	..	0.5	0.5	0.5	0.5	..	0.9	0.6	0.5
Gabon	10.2	9.4	..	..	7.6	7.4	7.2	7.1	6.9	6.7	..	10.9	7.7	6.8
Gambia, The	3.4	4.1	..	2.6	..	..	2.4	2.4	2.4	2.3	..	3.0	2.9	2.4
Ghana	2.9	2.7	2.5	2.5	..	..	2.3	2.2	2.1	2.1	..	2.8	2.4	2.1
Guinea	5.4	5.8	..	..	..	2.6	0.0	4.7	4.6	4.5	..	4.2	3.3	4.6
Guinea-Bissau	..	..	..	..	..	..	3.8	3.7	3.7	3.6	..	4.7	3.8	3.6
Kenya	3.1	3.3	2.7	2.6	2.6	..	2.5	2.4	2.4	2.3	..	3.2	2.7	2.4
Lesotho	3.1	2.8	..	..	..	3.3	3.3	3.2	3.0	3.0	..	2.8	3.2	3.0
Liberia	2.9	2.4	..	2.4	..	..	3.8	3.8	3.8	3.8	..	3.9	3.3	3.8
Madagascar	5.7	4.9	1.3	..	2.9	2.8	4.0	3.9	3.7	3.6	..	4.8	3.7	3.7
Malawi	1.7	1.6	1.4	3.2	..	..	1.6	1.6	1.6	1.5	1.7	1.9	1.9	1.6
Mali	2.0	1.8	1.7	1.7	1.7	..	1.6	1.5	1.5	1.5	..	2.1	1.7	1.5
Mauritania	4.5	4.0	..	3.6	..	..	3.4	3.4	3.3	3.2	..	4.5	3.6	3.3
Mauritius	1.8	1.8	1.7	1.7	1.7	..	1.8	1.7	1.7	1.7	1.7	2.2	1.7	1.7
Mozambique	2.9	2.6	1.9	2.5	..	..	1.9	1.9	1.9	1.9	..	3.3	2.0	1.9
Namibia	..	..	..	27.5	..	..	39.9	39.4	38.4	37.5	36.5	..	35.6	37.5
Niger	2.8	2.8	..	1.5	..	..	1.6	1.1	1.1	1.1	..	2.4	2.1	1.1
Nigeria	1.5	1.3	..	1.2	..	..	1.6	1.6	1.7	1.7	..	1.5	1.4	1.7
Rwanda	2.1	2.0	1.8	1.9	..	..	1.8	2.7	2.6	2.6	..	1.7	2.0	2.6
São Tomé and Principe	..	..	..	..	..	..	2.4	2.3	2.3	2.4	..	..	2.4	2.4
Senegal	2.5	2.2	..	2.0	..	..	1.8	1.8	1.8	1.7	..	2.4	2.0	1.7
Seychelles	..	..	..	..	..	..	3.6	3.5	3.6	3.7	..	..	3.5	3.6
Sierra Leone	2.4	2.3	..	..	..	2.8	2.7	2.7	2.5	2.4	2.4	2.5	2.6	2.4
Somalia	2.6	3.2	..	3.0	..	..	2.8	2.9	3.0	2.9	..	3.3	3.0	3.0
South Africa	6.7	5.9	5.3	5.3	5.1	..	..	..	8.5	..	..	7.1	5.4	8.5
Sudan	0.5	0.4	..	0.4	..	..	0.4	0.4	0.4	0.4	..	0.7	0.4	0.4
Swaziland	5.8	5.1	3.8	3.6	3.5	3.6	3.3	3.3	4.1	4.1	..	5.1	3.8	4.1
Tanzania	2.5	3.8	..	..	2.1	2.1	3.1	3.1	3.0	2.9	..	2.5	2.8	2.9
Togo	2.8	2.4	..	2.2	2.1	2.1	2.0	2.0	1.9	1.9	..	2.8	2.2	1.9
Uganda	2.1	1.9	..	1.7	..	1.6	..	..	..	..	..	2.1	1.7	..
Zambia	6.3	5.6	5.0	4.8	4.7	4.5	4.4	4.4	7.5	7.4	7.2	6.4	4.9	7.4
Zimbabwe	11.8	9.0	..	..	..	8.4	8.3	1.7	1.6	1.6	..	11.8	6.9	1.6
NORTH AFRICA	2.1	2.0	1.6	..	1.9	1.6	2.5	..	..	..	..	2.1	1.8	..
Algeria	3.9	3.6	..	..	3.5	3.6	3.7	3.6	3.7	3.6	..	4.1	3.6	3.6
Egypt, Arab Rep.	0.7	0.7	0.9	0.9	0.9	0.9	0.8	..	..	..	..	0.7	0.8	..
Libya	..	..	..	..	..	..	17.2	17.2	17.2	5.1	..	..	17.2	11.1
Morocco	3.0	2.7	2.5	..	2.4	1.1	2.4	2.3	2.3	2.3	2.1	2.9	2.3	2.2
Tunisia	3.7	3.6	3.7	..	..	..	2.4	2.5	2.5	2.5	..	3.4	3.3	2.5
ALL AFRICA	3.1	2.9	..	2.3	..	..	2.5	2.6	3.0	2.5	..	3.1	2.6	2.7

9-7. Paved primary roads

	Percentage of roads									Percentage in good condition
	1992	1993	1994	1995	1996	1997	1998	1999	2000	1989
SUB-SAHARAN AFRICA	17.0	17.0	18.0	16.2	16.0	16.6	15.0	13.5	16.2	39
excluding South Africa	17.0	17.0	18.0	16.0	15.7	16.5	14.0	13.3	12.1	39
excl. S. Africa & Nigeria	16.5	16.4	17.1	15.8	15.3	16.3	13.8	13.0	12.1	41
Angola	25.0	25.0	25.0	25.0	25.0	25.0	25.0	25.0	..	..
Benin	20.0	20.0	20.0	20.0	20.0	20.0	20.0	20.0	..	13
Botswana	19.9	21.1	22.2	48.0	52.0	54.0	56.0	55.0	..	94
Burkina Faso	17.6	18.2	18.7	16.0	16.0	16.0	16.0	16.0	..	70
Burundi	..	..	..	..	..	..	7.1	7.1	..	75
Cameroon	11.3	11.7	12.1	12.5	12.5	12.5	12.5	12.5	..	25
Cape Verde	78.0	78.0	78.0	78.0	78.0	78.0	78.0	78.0	..	14
Central African Republic	..	..	2.1	2.1	2.1	2.4	2.7	..	..	30
Chad	0.8	0.8	0.8	0.8	0.8	0.8	0.8	0.8	..	..
Comoros	72.1	73.5	75.0	76.5	..	..	76.5	76.5	..	43
Congo, Dem. Rep. of	..	..	..	..	..	..	..	..	..	20
Congo, Rep. of	9.7	9.7	9.7	9.7	9.7	9.7	9.7	9.7	..	50
Côte d'Ivoire	9.1	9.2	9.4	9.6	9.7	9.7	9.7	9.7	..	75
Djibouti	12.6	12.6	12.6	12.6	12.6	12.6	12.6	12.6	..	51
Equatorial Guinea	..	..	..	..	..	..	..	..	..	27
Eritrea	20.2	20.6	21.0	21.4	21.8	21.8	21.8	21.8	..	..
Ethiopia	15.0	15.0	15.0	15.5	15.3	..	14.0	13.3	12.0	47
Gabon	8.2	8.2	8.2	8.2	9.9	..	9.9	9.9	9.9	30
Gambia, The	33.3	34.0	34.6	35.3	35.4	35.4	35.4	35.4	..	22
Ghana	23.5	23.9	24.4	24.9	24.1	..	..	29.6	..	28
Guinea	15.5	15.8	16.1	16.4	16.5	16.5	16.5	16.5	..	50
Guinea-Bissau	9.1	9.4	9.8	10.2	10.3	10.3	10.3	10.3	..	39
Kenya	13.8	14.3	13.6	13.8	12.1	12.1	12.1	12.1	12.1	32
Lesotho	16.0	15.0	15.0	17.9	17.9	16.8	17.3	18.3	..	53
Liberia	5.7	5.9	6.0	6.1	6.2	6.2	6.2	6.2	..	85
Madagascar	15.4	11.5	18.7	11.5	11.6	..	..	11.6	..	56
Malawi	17.0	18.0	18.0	18.0	20.0	20.0	19.0	18.5	..	56
Mali	11.3	11.5	11.8	12.0	12.1	12.1	12.1	12.1	..	70
Mauritania	11.1	11.1	11.1	11.2	11.3	11.3	11.3	11.3	..	58
Mauritius	93.0	93.0	93.0	93.0	95.0	95.0	96.0	96.0	97.0	95
Mozambique	17.5	17.8	18.2	18.6	18.7	18.7	18.7	18.7	..	19
Namibia	10.9	7.3	7.9	7.9	11.4	13.2	13.5	13.6	..	..
Niger	..	..	7.9	7.9	7.9	7.9	7.9	7.9	..	67
Nigeria	30.0	30.0	21.3	18.8	18.8	30.9	30.9	30.9	..	34
Rwanda	9.4	9.6	9.7	9.9	9.1	..	..	8.3	..	41
São Tomé and Principe	64.1	65.4	66.7	68.0	68.1	68.1	68.1	68.1	..	..
Senegal	28.3	28.3	28.4	28.5	29.3	29.3	29.3	29.3	29.3	28
Seychelles	59.1	60.3	61.5	62.8	80.3	84.5	..	..	..	..
Sierra Leone	11.0	11.0	11.0	8.0	8.0	8.0	8.0	7.9	..	62
Somalia	11.5	11.8	11.8	11.8	11.8	11.8	11.8	11.8	..	52
South Africa	..	..	..	41.5	19.7	19.7	19.7	20.3	20.3	..
Sudan	33.7	34.5	35.4	36.2	36.3	36.3	36.3	36.3	..	27
Swaziland	58.6	59.8	28.2	..	..	..	..	..	..	35
Tanzania	37.0	4.2	4.2	4.2	4.2	4.2	4.2	4.2	..	39
Togo	31.0	31.6	31.6	31.6	31.6	31.6	31.6	31.6	..	75
Uganda	..	..	..	..	..	..	..	6.7	..	10
Zambia	17.3	17.6	18.0	..	..	..	..	..	..	40
Zimbabwe	16.0	17.0	54.9	48.0	47.4	47.4	47.4	47.4	..	70
NORTH AFRICA	66.0	66.7	68.0	68.9	73.5	73.5	66.3	63.8	60.6	..
Algeria	66.0	66.7	68.0	68.9	68.9	68.9	68.9	68.9	..	..
Egypt, Arab Rep.	73.0	72.0	75.0	78.0	78.1	78.1	78.1	78.1	..	..
Libya	53.8	54.9	56.0	57.1	..	..	..	57.2	..	..
Morocco	49.5	49.6	50.2	50.2	50.2	52.3	52.3	56.3	56.4	..
Tunisia	74.6	76.0	77.4	78.8	78.9	78.9	63.7	63.8	64.8	..
ALL AFRICA	17.6	17.9	18.5	18.6	17.9	18.9	16.9	16.5	24.8	39

9-8. Rail goods traffic-to-$PPP GDP ratio

	Ton-km per million of $PPP GDP											Annual average		
	1980	*1991*	*1992*	*1993*	*1994*	*1995*	*1996*	*1997*	*1998*	*1999*	*2000*	*75-84*	*85-94*	*95-MR*
SUB-SAHARAN AFRICA	..	..	..	..	..	..	..	..	..	..	..	..	..	..
excluding South Africa	..	..	..	..	..	..	..	..	..	..	..	..	..	..
excl. S.Africa & Nigeria	..	..	..	..	..	..	..	..	..	..	..	..	..	..
Angola	..	..	..	..	..	..	..	..	..	..	..	..	..	..
Benin	..	..	..	..	..	..	..	..	..	..	..	..	..	..
Botswana	..	..	..	..	..	..	..	..	..	..	..	..	..	..
Burkina Faso	..	..	..	..	..	..	..	..	..	..	..	..	..	..
Burundi	..	..	..	..	..	..	..	..	..	..	..	..	..	..
Cameroon	58,578	37,115	39,867	34,509	44,068	44,481	31,391	42,797	..	27,499	..	62,253	42,342	36,542
Cape Verde	..	..	..	..	..	..	..	..	..	..	..	..	..	..
Central African Republic	..	..	..	..	..	..	..	..	..	..	..	..	..	..
Chad	..	..	..	..	..	..	..	..	..	..	..	..	..	..
Comoros	..	..	..	..	..	..	..	..	..	..	..	..	..	..
Congo, Dem. Rep. of	58,007	..	..	..	4,555	..	..	..	11,696	11,087	..	53,668	32,326	11,391
Congo, Rep. of	..	296,135	179,667	134,689	119,302	..	..	..	..	..	..	384,767	275,945	..
Côte d'Ivoire	59,026	15,407	14,624	8,985	9,330	15,102	..	22,200	..	..	..	50,304	21,536	18,651
Djibouti	..	..	..	..	..	..	..	..	..	..	..	..	..	..
Equatorial Guinea	..	..	..	..	..	..	..	..	..	..	..	..	..	..
Eritrea	..	..	..	..	..	..	..	..	..	..	..	..	..	..
Ethiopia	..	2,084	..	..	..	..	..	..	..	..	..	8,140	3,736	..
Gabon	9,357	..	55,788	63,218	60,605	77,236	..	69,175	..	232,714	..	19,905	51,726	126,375
Gambia, The	..	..	..	..	..	..	..	..	..	..	..	..	..	..
Ghana	10,688	..	..	..	..	..	..	..	..	..	..	8,437	6,647	..
Guinea	..	..	..	..	..	..	..	..	..	..	..	..	..	..
Guinea-Bissau	..	..	..	..	..	..	..	..	..	..	..	..	..	..
Kenya	228,599	77,679	61,485	51,628	50,979	..	..	46,661	..	38,184	..	194,251	86,917	42,422
Lesotho	..	..	..	..	..	..	..	..	..	..	..	..	..	..
Liberia	..	..	..	..	..	..	..	..	..	..	..	..	..	..
Madagascar	..	..	..	..	..	..	..	..	..	..	..	..	..	..
Malawi	108,535	18,755	14,461	11,958	12,000	12,658	11,604	9,342	12,657	13,104	14,226	83,708	21,869	12,265
Mali	42,443	55,264	50,002	..	..	..	..	36,727	..	30,270	..	45,133	56,937	33,499
Mauritania	..	..	..	..	..	..	..	..	..	..	..	..	..	..
Mauritius	..	..	..	..	..	..	..	..	..	..	..	..	..	..
Mozambique	..	..	..	..	..	..	..	..	..	..	..	..	..	..
Namibia	..	198,455	175,589	143,372	130,936	125,908	..	..	..	..	..	..	185,067	125,908
Niger	..	..	..	..	..	..	..	..	..	..	..	..	..	..
Nigeria	19,776	..	624	..	..	..	..	5,108	..	535	..	28,554	6,491	2,821
Rwanda	..	..	..	..	..	..	..	..	..	..	..	..	..	..
São Tomé and Principe	..	..	..	..	..	..	..	..	..	..	..	..	..	..
Senegal	71,312	56,054	52,463	43,094	40,223	..	..	38,879	..	33,909	..	64,133	60,403	36,394
Seychelles	..	..	..	..	..	..	..	..	..	..	..	..	..	..
Sierra Leone	..	..	..	..	..	..	..	..	..	..	..	..	..	..
Somalia	..	..	..	..	..	..	..	..	..	..	..	..	..	..
South Africa	559,834	321,801	303,062	301,898	294,706	282,739	..	..	..	..	..	480,692	337,064	282,739
Sudan	164,304	25,012	..	..	..	42,322	..	39,371	..	35,022	..	103,972	39,539	38,905
Swaziland	..	..	..	..	..	..	..	..	..	..	..	..	..	..
Tanzania	..	83,057	77,370	101,516	86,523	99,952	85,595	75,831	63,373	74,763	..	..	82,982	79,903
Togo	..	..	..	..	..	..	..	..	..	..	..	..	..	..
Uganda	..	10,407	8,257	8,634	12,278	12,164	..	4,692	4,854	7,837	..	11,415	9,258	7,387
Zambia	358,572	163,175	152,984	151,817	99,966	67,482	76,551	66,328	66,946	76,543	..	328,423	191,871	70,770
Zimbabwe	678,501	216,350	237,952	224,907	159,252	168,771	161,390	150,952	..	..	..	535,919	275,939	160,371
NORTH AFRICA	..	..	..	..	..	..	..	..	..	..	..	..	..	..
Algeria	41,816	23,407	20,756	19,171	18,748	..	..	..	..	13,277	..	38,741	25,198	13,277
Egypt, Arab Rep.	40,900	24,845	21,276	24,659	26,836	..	22,731	21,715	21,195	16,787	..	37,472	26,080	20,607
Libya	..	..	..	..	..	..	..	..	..	..	..	..	..	..
Morocco	121,509	58,740	66,923	58,167	55,187	57,128	..	54,247	51,289	49,884	..	115,525	73,422	53,137
Tunisia	113,751	55,235	54,069	51,171	54,070	53,765	..	47,862	46,606	43,327	..	98,578	66,966	47,890
ALL AFRICA	..	..	..	..	..	..	..	..	..	..	..	..	..	..

9-9. Rail load-to-locomotive ratio

	Million rail ton-km/locomotive											Annual average		
	1980	1988	1989	1990	1991	1992	1993	1994	1995	1996	1997	75-84	85-94	95-MR
SUB-SAHARAN AFRICA	..	..	..	20.5	18.5	16.8	..	19.1	..	..	..	14.9	17.2	..
excluding South Africa	..	..	..	..	..	..	..	..	..	..	..	..	..	..
excl. S.Africa & Nigeria	..	..	..	..	..	..	..	..	..	..	..	..	..	..
Angola	..	..	..	..	..	..	..	..	..	..	..	..	..	..
Benin	..	..	..	..	..	..	..	..	..	..	..	..	..	..
Botswana	..	..	..	..	..	..	..	..	..	..	19.9	..	..	19.9
Burkina Faso	..	..	..	..	..	..	..	..	..	18.0	24.9	..	..	21.4
Burundi	..	..	..	..	..	..	..	..	..	..	..	..	..	..
Cameroon	10.9	6.5	9.0	10.1	8.9	9.6	8.6	12.4	13.3	10.0	14.2	9.8	9.2	12.5
Cape Verde	..	..	..	..	..	..	..	..	..	..	..	..	..	..
Central African Republic	..	..	..	..	..	..	..	..	..	..	..	..	..	..
Chad	..	..	..	..	..	..	..	..	..	..	..	..	..	..
Comoros	..	..	..	..	..	..	..	..	..	..	..	..	..	..
Congo, Dem. Rep. of	11.7	10.9	..	11.2	..	..	..	1.0	..	..	1.7	12.0	9.7	1.7
Congo, Rep. of	..	..	..	..	14.8	9.4	..	5.8	..	..	3.0	11.3	9.7	3.0
Côte d'Ivoire	12.8	..	..	8.0	6.7	6.8	4.5	4.5	5.7	..	17.4	12.3	8.4	11.5
Djibouti	..	..	..	..	..	..	..	..	..	..	..	..	..	..
Equatorial Guinea	..	..	..	..	..	..	..	..	..	..	..	..	..	..
Eritrea	..	..	..	..	..	..	..	..	..	..	..	..	..	..
Ethiopia	..	..	6.1	..	2.3	..	..	..	..	..	..	..	4.2	..
Gabon	2.1	7.4	6.1	..	..	4.8	5.2	5.3	7.6	..	30.8	4.2	6.0	19.2
Gambia, The	..	..	..	..	..	..	..	..	..	..	..	..	..	..
Ghana	..	..	..	3.3	..	..	..	..	..	..	..	..	2.4	..
Guinea	..	..	..	..	..	..	..	..	..	..	..	..	..	..
Guinea-Bissau	..	..	..	..	..	..	..	..	..	..	..	..	..	..
Kenya	6.9	..	9.2	8.8	9.0	..	..	..	..	..	..	9.2	8.7	..
Lesotho	..	..	..	..	..	..	..	..	..	..	..	..	..	..
Liberia	..	..	..	..	..	..	..	..	..	..	..	..	..	..
Madagascar	..	..	..	..	..	..	..	..	..	..	..	..	..	..
Malawi	..	1.4	1.4	1.4	1.5	1.1	1.0	0.9	1.1	..	..	3.5	1.5	1.1
Mali	..	6.7	7.8	7.8	7.8	7.9	..	..	..	..	11.2	6.6	8.6	11.2
Mauritania	..	..	..	..	..	..	..	..	..	..	..	..	..	..
Mauritius	..	..	..	..	..	..	..	..	..	..	..	..	..	..
Mozambique	..	..	..	..	..	..	..	..	..	..	5.9	..	..	5.9
Namibia	..	..	..	27.7	21.4	22.3	19.9	20.3	21.6	..	..	..	22.3	21.6
Niger	..	..	..	..	..	..	..	..	..	..	..	..	..	..
Nigeria	3.8	..	..	..	..	0.3	..	0.0	..	..	..	5.0	1.6	..
Rwanda	..	..	..	..	..	..	..	..	..	..	..	..	..	..
São Tomé and Principe	..	..	..	..	..	..	..	..	..	..	..	..	..	..
Senegal	13.3	18.4	16.7	20.9	18.0	16.4	14.6	16.1	..	..	..	14.3	17.6	..
Seychelles	..	..	..	..	..	..	..	..	..	..	..	..	..	..
Sierra Leone	..	..	..	..	..	..	..	..	..	10.8	15.4	..	..	13.1
Somalia	..	..	..	..	..	..	..	..	..	..	..	..	..	..
South Africa	..	19.9	23.2	25.4	23.6	22.6	25.8	26.4	26.9	..	..	18.2	22.6	26.9
Sudan	8.0	..	..	..	4.5	..	..	..	11.1	14.2	12.3	7.0	4.7	12.5
Swaziland	..	..	..	..	..	..	..	..	..	..	..	..	..	..
Tanzania	..	..	8.4	..	11.7	11.4	13.9	12.2	14.9	..	17.4	7.7	10.9	16.1
Togo	..	..	..	..	..	..	..	..	..	..	..	..	..	..
Uganda	..	2.1	1.9	3.1	2.7	2.0	2.3	3.5	4.1	..	8.3	..	2.1	6.2
Zambia	16.1	23.0	22.7	7.5	15.4	14.6	15.1	9.9	6.8	..	7.2	17.2	16.8	7.0
Zimbabwe	21.7	19.3	..	13.6	14.0	16.0	17.5	27.9	27.5	..	..	20.7	18.8	27.5
NORTH AFRICA	9.9	..	..	10.2	10.6	9.7	10.3	10.4	..	..	10.3	9.9	10.3	10.3
Algeria	9.8	15.6	13.3	12.2	12.5	10.7	11.1	10.8	..	..	7.7	10.9	12.5	7.7
Egypt, Arab Rep.	3.9	..	..	3.7	6.1	3.6	4.9	4.9	..	..	5.1	3.7	4.4	5.1
Libya	..	..	..	..	..	..	..	..	..	..	..	..	..	..
Morocco	19.5	24.2	18.7	20.4	17.3	19.6	17.4	19.2	19.8	..	22.3	19.1	19.5	21.0
Tunisia	13.9	10.8	10.5	9.3	9.3	10.3	14.0	12.7	13.4	..	13.5	12.7	10.7	13.4
ALL AFRICA	..	..	..	16.0	15.2	13.9	16.4	15.5	..	..	..	12.9	14.8	..

9-10. Air transport

	Aircraft departures (thousands)		Passengers carried (thousands)		Air freight (million tons per km)	
	2000	2001	2000	2001	2000	2001
SUB-SAHARAN AFRICA	355	342	17,909	17,069	..	..
excluding South Africa	244	220	9,908	9,120	..	..
excl. S. Africa & Nigeria	231	211	9,401	8,591	..	..
Angola	4	4	235	193	61	51
Benin	2	1	77	46	12	7
Botswana	7	7	164	168	0	0
Burkina Faso	3	2	144	100	12	7
Burundi	..	..	..	..	..	..
Cameroon	6	5	312	247	51	42
Cape Verde	13	9	264	243	1	0
Central African Republic	2	1	77	46	12	7
Chad	2	1	77	46	12	7
Comoros	..	..	..	..	..	..
Congo, Dem. Rep. of	..	..	..	..	..	..
Congo, Rep. of	6	5	128	95	12	7
Côte d'Ivoire	2	1	108	46	12	7
Djibouti	..	..	..	..	..	..
Equatorial Guinea	..	..	..	..	..	..
Eritrea	..	..	..	..	..	..
Ethiopia	27	28	945	1,028	78	79
Gabon	7	8	447	374	58	49
Gambia, The	..	..	..	..	..	..
Ghana	5	6	314	301	40	33
Guinea	..	..	..	..	..	..
Guinea-Bissau	..	..	..	..	..	..
Kenya	29	25	1,555	1,418	77	93
Lesotho	..	..	..	..	..	..
Liberia	..	..	..	..	..	..
Madagascar	22	21	667	624	33	34
Malawi	5	5	116	113	1	1
Mali	2	1	77	46	12	7
Mauritania	4	2	185	156	13	7
Mauritius	12	13	949	997	183	175
Mozambique	7	7	260	264	7	7
Namibia	5	6	247	212	76	73
Niger	2	1	77	46	12	7
Nigeria	13	8	507	529	9	3
Rwanda	..	..	..	..	..	..
São Tomé and Principe	1	1	35	35	0	0
Senegal	1	0	20	6	..	..
Seychelles	19	20	394	420	20	22
Sierra Leone	0	0	19	14	9	6
Somalia	..	..	..	..	..	..
South Africa	110	122	8,001	7,948	688	747
Sudan	8	8	414	415	37	33
Swaziland	3	2	90	90	0	0
Tanzania	6	5	193	171	3	3
Togo	2	1	77	46	12	7
Uganda	0	0	39	41	21	21
Zambia	6	5	90	49	1	..
Zimbabwe	14	13	606	495	159	158
NORTH AFRICA	158	155	13,699	13,818	..	..
Algeria	40	44	2,998	3,240	13	19
Egypt, Arab Rep.	47	41	4,522	4,389	278	239
Libya	6	6	601	583	0	0
Morocco	45	44	3,671	3,681	63	63
Tunisia	20	19	1,908	1,926	21	20
ALL AFRICA	513	497	31,608	30,887	..	..

Technical notes

Tables

Table 9-1. Electric power consumption per capita. This table refers to per capita electricity consumption, which means the production of power plants and combined heat and power plants, less distribution losses, and own use by heat and power plants (IEA and UN *Energy Statistics Yearbook*).

Table 9-2. Energy production and use, 1980 and 2000. This table presents three indicators. *Energy production* refers to commercial forms of primary energy—petroleum (crude oil, natural gas liquids, and oil from nonconventional sources), natural gas, solid fuels, and primary electricity—all converted into oil equivalent (IEA and UN *Energy Statistics Yearbook*). *Commercial energy use* is indigenous production plus imports and stock changes, minus exports and international marine bunkers (IEA and UN *Energy Statistics Yearbook*). *Electric power transmission and distribution losses* include losses in transmission between sources of supply and points of distribution and in the distribution to consumers, including pilferage. Production less transmission and distribution losses, own use, and transformation losses is equal to end-use electricity consumption (IEA and UN *Energy Statistics Yearbook*).

Table 9-3. Telephone, radio, and television availability, 1995–2002. This table presents data for six communication indicators. Telephone main lines (ITU) refer to telephone lines connecting a customer's equipment to the public-switched telephone network, where main line is normally identified by a unique number. Mainlines are presented for every 1,000 people (Table 1.2). *Waiting list* shows the number of applications (in thousands) for a connection to a main line that have been held up by a lack of technical capacity (ITU). *Cost of local call* is the cost of a three-minute call within the same exchange area using the subscriber's equipment (that is, not from a public phone) (ITU). *Mobile phones* refer to users of portable telephones who subscribe to an automatic public mobile telephone service using cellular technology that provides access to the public switched-telephone network, per 1,000 people (Table 1.2)(ITU). *Radios* are the estimated number of radio receivers in use for broadcast to the general public, per 1,000 people (Table 1.2) (*UNESCO Statistical Yearbook*). *Television sets* are the estimated number of television sets in use, per 1,000 people (Table 1.2) (ITU).

Table 9-4. Personal computers and Internet use. *Personal computers* are self-contained computers designed to be be used by a single individual. *Internet hosts* are computers with active Internet Protocol (IP) addresses connected to the Internet. All hosts without a country code identification are assumed to be located in the United States. *Internet users* are people with access to the worldwide network. The data on personal computers and Internet users are from the ITU. They are reported in the ITU's *World Telecommunication Development Report* (2003), and the *World Telecommunication Indicators Database* (2003b). The data on Internet hosts are from the Internet Software Consortium (www.isc.org).

Table 9-5. Vehicle ownership. Vehicles (International Road Federation) include all forms of road transportation, except buses. They are expressed as the number of vehicles per 1,000 people (Table 1.2).

Table 9-6. Road-to-population ratio. This table presents the ratio of 1,000 kilometers of paved or unpaved road (International Road Federation) per 1 million people (Table 1.2).

Table 9-7. Paved primary roads. This table presents paved primary roads, that is, those that have been sealed with asphalt or similar road-bonding material (International Road Federation) as a ratio to total roads and then shows the percentage that is in good condition (World Bank data).

Table 9-8. Rail goods traffic-to-$PPP GDP ratio. This measures the tonnage of goods per million dollars of GDP measured in purchasing power parity (PPP) terms (World Bank data).

Table 9-9. Rail load-to-locomotive ratio. This is the volume of rail-transported goods (measured in millions of metric tons per kilometers traveled) per single locomotive (World Bank data).

Table 9-10. Air transport. *Aircraft departures* are the number of domestic and international takeoffs of air carriers registered in the country. *Passengers carried* include both domestic and international aircraft passengers of air carriers registered in the country. *Air freight* is the sum of the metric tons of freight, express, and diplomatic bags carried on each flight stage (the operation of an aircraft from takeoff to its next landing) multiplied by the stage distance for air carriers registered in the country. The air transport data are from the International Civil Aviation Organization's (ICAO's) *Civil Aviation Statistics of the World* and ICAO staff estimates.

Methodology used for regional aggregations and period averages in Chapter 9

Table	Aggregations[a]				Period averages[b]
	(1)	(6)	(7)	(8)	(1)
9-1		x			x
9-2					
Columns 1-4	x				
Columns 5-6				x	
9-3					
Columns 1-2, 4-6		x			
Column 3				x	
9-4					
Columns 1-2		x			
Column 3	x				
9-5		x	x		x
9-6		x	x		x
9-7					
Columns 1-8				x	
Column 9		x			
9-8				x	x
9-9		x	x		x
9-10	x				

Note: Regional aggregations are shown in the rows for Sub-Saharan Africa, North Africa, and All Africa. Period averages are shown in the last three columns. This table shows only the methodologies used in this chapter.

  a. Regional aggregations: (1) simple total; (2) simple total of the first indicator divided by the simple total of the second indicator (same country coverage); (3) simple total of the gap-filled indicator; (4) simple total of the gap-filled main indicator divided by the simple total of the gap-filled secondary indicator; (5) simple total of the first gap-filled main indicator less the simple total of the second gap-filled main indicator, all divided by the simple total of the secondary indicator; (6) weighted total (by population); (7) median; (8) no aggregation; (9) simple arithmetic mean.

  b. Period averages: (1) arithmetic mean (using the same series as shown in the table; i.e., ratio if the rest of the table is shown as ratio, level if the rest of the table is shown as level, growth rate if the rest is shown as growth rate); (2) least-squares growth rate (using main indicator); (3) least-squares growth rate (using main indicator in constant terms, with the rest of the table in current terms).

10

Privatization of Public Enterprises

In the past, the dominance of the public enterprise sector in most African economies warranted the collection and publication of the sector's performance. With its diminishing size and importance due to privatization, it is no longer informative to produce such data. Instead, as privatization programs advance to maturity, it will become important to track the performance of private sector businesses. In the meantime, measurement of the level of privatization activity is a useful gauge of the decreasing role of governments in commercial business; conversely, it indicates how much of state-owned commercial activity has been transferred to the private sector. To the extent that data are available, it is also possible to measure how privatization has, over time, contributed to government revenues and mobilized savings and investment. However, this measurement is by no means precise or easy to obtain, partly because of incomplete and inconsistent data but also because of redefinitions of the public enterprise sector. For example, some enterprises, notably those formerly in a monopolistic position, are being split in order to separate their commercial, social, developmental, and regulatory activities. In some cases, separate operating divisions or geographically distinct assets are sold separately. And in yet other cases, commercial and semi-commercial activities are being separated out from government ministries and other agencies to become redefined as "commercial enterprises." These include, for example, business centers, media, and some training institutes. So, the public enterprise sector, as defined several years ago, has changed. Nevertheless, the well over 3,500 privatization transactions that were reported across Africa up to the end of 2002 have brought about fundamental changes:

- The fiscal burden of public enterprises has been reduced or eliminated.
- Privatization receipts have contributed to a reduction in fiscal deficits.
- Privatization has attracted foreign direct investment both to acquire enterprises and for post-privatization investment in those businesses.
- The process has stimulated private sector development by making investment opportunities available, spurring capital market development, and contributing to a more competitive business environment.
- Because it is a politically sensitive subject, the process has highlighted the need for transparency and public accountability.

The tables presented in this chapter summarize data contained in the World Bank's Africa Privatization Database, which is accessible through the Internet:

www4.worldbank.org/afr/database/
afrpriv/p1query.cfm

10-1. Summary of privatization of public enterprises

	Total number of trans-actions	Total sales value (US$m)	Transactions completed Before 1998	1998	1999	2000	2001	2002	Transactions by sector Agriculture production & process	Financial	Manu-facturing	Services
SUB-SAHARAN AFRICA	3,486	6,686	2,777	141	76	72	7	7	826	180	1,603	877
excluding South Africa	3,475	4,477	2,771	140	76	70	7	7	826	180	1,598	871
excl. S. Africa & Nigeria	3,394	4,270	2,690	141	76	72	7	7	826	180	1,575	860
Angola	57	..	56	..	..	1	..	..	20	1	35	1
Benin	57	63	43	..	3	1	..	..	8	1	27	21
Botswana	..											
Burkina Faso	31	9	15	..	5	1	..	..	7	3	9	12
Burundi	46	12	44	..	..	..	..	..	24	4	8	10
Cameroon	58	72	44	3	..	..	..	..	26	4	9	19
Cape Verde	70	172	43	3	5	9	2	2	8	4	27	31
Central African Republic	52	..	34	1	1	..	..	..	13	8	13	18
Chad	44	6	30	..	2	2	..	..	12	7	9	16
Comoros	..	..	..	..	..	..	..	..	..	..	..	..
Congo, Dem. Rep. of	21	..	21	..	..	..	..	..	3	1	7	10
Congo, Rep. of	105	50	61	..	..	3	..	..	28	9	32	36
Côte d'Ivoire	134	810	83	11	6	3	..	..	46	5	41	42
Djibouti	..											
Equatorial Guinea	..											
Eritrea	..		..	..	..				..		..	
Ethiopia	164	..	125	18	10	11	..	..	23	..	118	23
Gabon	29	..	1	1	1	2	2	2	8	1	8	12
Gambia, The	39	10	30	1	..	1	..	..	8	6	14	11
Ghana	233	667	216	4	8	4	..	..	44	8	146	35
Guinea	122	9	115	..	..	..	..	..	11	7	91	13
Guinea-Bissau	58	1	30	1	..	..	1	1	14	1	21	22
Kenya	188	248	184	4	..	..	..	..	72	12	66	38
Lesotho	24	128	9	4	5	1	2	2	3	4	8	9
Liberia	..		..	..	..				..		..	
Madagascar	138	43	83	..	1	1	..	..	51	4	49	34
Malawi	91	57	44	1	..	1	..	..	34	13	25	19
Mali	87	32	59	1	1	8	..	..	13	5	36	33
Mauritania	56	10	35	..	2	6	..	..	21	6	14	15
Mauritius	..	..	..	..	..	..			..	..	..	..
Mozambique	579	217	579	..	..	..	..	..	75	2	389	113
Namibia	..	..	..	..					..	..	..	..
Niger	41	3	34	..	..	..	..	..	2	3	29	7
Nigeria	81	207	81	..	..	..	..	..	23	24	23	11
Rwanda	21	..	1	..	..	..	..	..	9	1	6	5
São Tomé and Principe	9	..	9	..	..	..	..	..	..	..	7	2
Senegal	71	326	51	4	1	1	..	..	7	11	18	35
Seychelles	..	..										
Sierra Leone	9	..	8	..	..	..	..	..	..	..	3	6
Somalia	..		..						..		..	..
South Africa	11	2,209	6	1	..	2	..	..	..	..	5	6
Sudan	32	..	32	..	..	..	..	..	11	1	9	11
Swaziland	..		..	..	..				..	..	..	..
Tanzania	283	246	194	64	23	1	..	..	98	3	149	33
Togo	78	39	53	3	1	3	..	..	11	9	26	32
Uganda	108	198	82	..	..	10	..	..	20	5	44	39
Zambia	253	686	236	16	1	..	..	..	69	6	81	97
Zimbabwe	6	156	6	..	..	..	..	..	4	1	1	..
NORTH AFRICA	186	595	27	30	40	1	..	..	13	..	58	53
Algeria	..	..										
Egypt, Arab Rep.	59	307	10	8	31	..	..	..	5	..	34	8
Libya	..	..	..						..		..	..
Morocco	64	259	17	16	6	1	..	..	4	..	10	28
Tunisia	63	29	..	6	3	..	..	..	4	..	14	17
ALL AFRICA	3,672	7,280	2,804	171	116	73	..	..	839	..	1,661	930

10-2. Divestiture methods employed (to end 2002)

	Sales of shares				Sale of assets			Other methods							
	Com-petitive sale	Direct Sale	Pre-emption rights	Public flotation	Liqui-dation	Compet-itive sale	Direct sale	Debt/Equity swaps	Leases	Joint ventures	Mgmt./employee buyouts	Mgmt. con-tracts	Trustees	Restit-ution	Other
SUB-SAHARAN AFRICA	931	82	176	100	628	634	39	11	130	42	81	57	20	48	121
excluding South Africa	925	82	176	100	628	634	39	11	130	42	81	57	20	48	121
excl. S. Africa & Nigeria	920	82	176	100	628	634	39	11	130	42	81	57	20	48	121
Angola	..	..	..	..	..	56	..	..	..	..	..	..	..	..	..
Benin	1	2	..	..	22	12	3	..	2	..	..	2	..	1	4
Botswana	..	..	..	..	..	..	..	..	..	..	..	..	..	..	..
Burkina Faso	8	3	..	..	2	..	..	..	..	..	..	1	1	..	4
Burundi	12	3	..	..	13	7	..	..	..	..	1	10	..	..	..
Cameroon	20	..	..	..	17	..	..	..	..	..	..	..	..	..	9
Cape Verde	20	2	5	..	11	1	1	..	..	7	6	1	1	..	6
Central African Republic	..	..	..	..	26	..	..	..	1	1	..	1	..	..	7
Chad	13	2	..	..	11	..	..	..	..	..	..	6	..	..	4
Comoros	..	..	..	..	..	..	..	..	..	..	..	..	..	..	..
Congo, Dem. Rep. of	1	..	..	..	15	..	..	..	..	..	..	5	..	..	..
Congo, Rep. of	1	..	..	..	53	..	..	..	..	..	..	2	..	..	8
Côte d'Ivoire	15	2	23	22	2	23	8	..	3	1	..	..	..	..	4
Djibouti	..	..	..	..	..	..	..	..	..	..	..	..	..	..	..
Equatorial Guinea	..	..	..	..	..	..	..	..	..	..	..	..	..	..	..
Eritrea	..	..	..	..	..	..	..	..	..	..	..	..	..	..	..
Ethiopia	..	..	..	..	..	118	..	..	..	..	45	..	..	..	..
Gabon	..	..	..	..	3	..	..	..	..	..	..	1	..	..	6
Gambia, The	13	7	..	..	3	1	..	..	5	..	1	..	..	..	1
Ghana	8	11	19	13	56	76	12	2	5	13	..	1	..	12	5
Guinea	41	1	..	..	67	1	..	..	3	..	..	2	..	..	1
Guinea-Bissau	8	2	..	..	9	2	..	..	2	1	..	7	..	..	..
Kenya	13	..	96	16	36	17	4	1	..	..	1	1	..	..	3
Lesotho	6	2	..	..	7	1	..	..	1	..	..	1	..	..	3
Liberia	..	..	..	..	..	..	..	..	..	..	..	..	..	..	..
Madagascar	6	14	..	..	29	16	6	..	1	1	..	3	..	7	3
Malawi	22	5	..	2	..	13	..	..	..	..	..	..	3	..	1
Mali	14	1	..	..	31	10	..	..	1	..	..	1	3	..	13
Mauritania	25	..	..	..	17	3	..	..	..	..	..	1	3	..	7
Mauritius	..	..	..	..	..	..	..	..	..	..	..	..	..	..	..
Mozambique	509	..	..	..	..	22	..	..	37	10	..	1	..	..	..
Namibia	..	..	..	..	..	..	..	..	..	..	..	..	..	..	..
Niger	13	..	..	..	17	..	..	..	..	..	..	2	..	..	3
Nigeria	5	5	..	37	2	29	..	..	..	..	1	..	2	..	..
Rwanda	..	..	..	..	2	..	..	..	..	..	..	..	..	..	3
São Tomé and Principe	..	1	..	..	6	..	..	..	..	..	1	1	..	..	..
Senegal	25	1	1	1	23	1	..	1	3	1	..	1	..	..	2
Seychelles	..	..	..	..	..	..	..	..	..	..	..	..	..	..	..
Sierra Leone	..	..	..	..	1	..	..	..	..	..	..	..	..	..	..
Somalia	..	..	..	..	..	..	..	..	..	..	..	..	..	..	..
South Africa	6	..	..	..	..	1	..	..	..	..	..	..	..	..	..
Sudan	7	..	..	..	..	15	..	5	1	..	..	..	..	..	4
Swaziland	..	..	..	..	..	..	..	..	..	..	..	..	..	..	..
Tanzania	61	4	13	1	84	70	3	1	25	3	6	3	2	2	5
Togo	8	7	..	..	20	13	1	..	6	..	..	3	..	..	2
Uganda	13	..	5	1	21	23	..	1	1	3	2	..	5	10	12
Zambia	35	6	14	4	22	103	1	..	33	1	17	..	..	16	1
Zimbabwe	2	1	..	3	..	..	..	..	..	..	..	..	..	..	..
NORTH AFRICA	..	..	..	..	..	..	..	..	..	..	..	..	..	..	..
Algeria	..	..	..	..	..	..	..	..	..	..	..	..	..	..	..
Egypt, Arab. Rep.	..	..	..	..	..	..	..	..	..	..	..	..	..	..	..
Libya	..	..	..	..	..	..	..	..	..	..	..	..	..	..	..
Morocco	..	..	..	..	..	..	..	..	..	..	..	..	..	..	..
Tunisia	..	..	..	..	..	..	..	..	..	..	..	..	..	..	..
ALL AFRICA	931	82	176	100	628	634	39	11	130	42	81	57	20	48	121

10-3. Progress in privatization: ownership and control changes*

	Transfer of majority owner-ship to private shareholders	Government retention of majority ownership	Government retention of minority interest	Sales of minority government interest	Total share transactions	Total asset sales and liquidation	Other transactions	Total trans-actions
SUB-SAHARAN AFRICA	2,300	211	381	387	1,289	1,301	510	3,486
excluding South Africa	2,297	209	381	387	1,283	1,300	510	3,475
excl. S. Africa & Nigeria	2,242	208	381	387	1,236	1,269	510	3,394
Angola	57	..	1	..	..	56	..	57
Benin	42	3	2	1	3	37	9	57
Botswana	..	..	..	..	..	..	..	..
Burkina Faso	11	..	11	2	11	2	6	31
Burundi	33	..	1	11	15	20	11	46
Cameroon	45	1	1	..	20	17	9	58
Cape Verde	33	2	20	14	27	13	21	70
Central African Republic	28	2	2	1	..	26	10	52
Chad	18	5	6	4	15	11	10	44
Comoros	..	..	..	..	..	..	..	..
Congo, Dem. Rep. of	16	5	..	..	1	15	5	21
Congo, Rep. of	60	1	1	..	1	53	10	105
Côte d'Ivoire	51	9	29	29	62	33	8	134
Djibouti	..	..	..	..	..	..	..	..
Equatorial Guinea	..	..	..	..	..	..	..	..
Eritrea	..	..	..	..	..	..	..	..
Ethiopia	10	..	..	154	..	118	45	164
Gabon	1	1	..	..	..	3	7	29
Gambia, The	16	5	..	6	20	4	7	39
Ghana	183	12	27	24	51	144	38	233
Guinea	107	9	18	..	42	68	6	122
Guinea-Bissau	22	8	1	..	10	11	10	58
Kenya	77	3	53	61	125	57	6	188
Lesotho	13	3	2	1	8	8	5	24
Liberia	..	..	..	..	..	..	..	..
Madagascar	81	4	17	..	20	51	15	138
Malawi	39	..	7	5	29	13	4	91
Mali	55	1	9	3	15	41	18	87
Mauritania	29	3	7	18	25	20	11	56
Mauritius	..	..	..	..	..	..	..	..
Mozambique	536	42	75	..	509	22	48	579
Namibia	..	..	..	..	..	..	..	..
Niger	29	2	3	2	13	17	5	41
Nigeria	55	1	8	23	47	31	3	81
Rwanda	..	..	..	..	..	2	3	21
São Tomé and Principe	8	1	..	..	1	6	2	9
Senegal	39	8	11	5	28	24	8	71
Seychelles	..	..	..	..	..	..	..	..
Sierra Leone	..	9	..	..	..	1	..	9
Somalia	..	..	..	..	..	..	..	..
South Africa	3	2	..	..	6	1	..	11
Sudan	31	1	3	..	7	15	10	32
Swaziland	..	..	..	..	..	..	..	..
Tanzania	235	29	35	3	79	157	47	283
Togo	39	8	1	9	15	34	11	78
Uganda	78	1	5	7	19	44	34	108
Zambia	215	30	21	4	59	126	68	253
Zimbabwe	5	..	4	..	6	..	..	6
NORTH AFRICA	..	..	..	..	..	..	..	..
Algeria	..	..	..	..	..	..	..	..
Egypt, Arab Rep.	..	..	..	..	..	..	..	..
Libya	..	..	..	..	..	..	..	..
Morocco	..	..	..	..	..	..	..	..
Tunisia	..	..	..	..	..	..	..	..
ALL AFRICA	..	..	..	..	..	..	..	..

* Data reflected to end-2002.

Technical notes

Tables

Table 10-1. Summary of privatization of public enterprises. For purposes of monitoring and reporting on privatization activity, all reported transactions involving a sale of assets or shares (however small) or the formal yielding of management control (as through a management contract) are included in the World Bank's Africa Privatization Database. Hence, in the table, *privatization* is used generically to include (a) the sale or disposal of some or all of the assets of public enterprises, (b) the sale of government-owned shares in enterprises, (c) the reduction in equity percentage held by a government through share dilutions or through transfer of enterprise assets to a new joint venture, (d) liquidations, (e) leases, and (f) management contracts. Sometimes, the process of privatizing an enterprise involves several consecutive transactions (for example, a sale of a block of shares to a core investor and a subsequent initial public offering). The table summarizes the data contained in the Africa Privatization Database, which originate from national privatization agencies and other sources. The data are frequently updated, and changes to previous entries occur as more information becomes available. There are a few instances where previously reported privatizations are removed from the database because a transaction has been nullified on account of non-fulfillment of contractual conditions on the part of one of the parties. For financial data, the term *sale value* is preferred since the use of the term *proceeds* might imply the value of amounts actually paid. In practice, some deals are structured so that new investors may acquire assets or shares on deferred terms. Also, it should be noted that (a) in the cases of some subsidiary companies, the cash proceeds are not paid to government but instead go to the parent company; and (b) for official liquidations, the proceeds are paid to the liquidator who first applies them toward settling enterprise debts.

During the revision of the Africa Privatization Database, the data in the category "Other" from previous ADI versions were reallocated across the Financial, Manufacturing, and Services sectors. Simultaneously, data in "Trade" were incorporated into "Industry." The improvement resulted in a lower total number of transactions, but the data quality is improved.

Table 10-2. Divestiture methods employed (to end 2002). The table shows the various privatization methods employed in each country. The methods employed could not be confirmed for all transactions. *Direct sales* refers to a transaction which was negotiated directly with one party and which was not the outcome of a competitive bidding process. However, in some cases a direct sale was concluded (on a non-competitive basis) as a result of a failure of an earlier competitive bidding process. *Preemptive right* refers to transactions whereby a government has sold shares to an existing private shareholder (or shareholders) who exercised preemptive rights to acquire those shares in accordance with specific provisions of the company's charter (Articles of Association). In some cases, the charter specified the amount to be paid per share or the formula for calculating that amount; in other cases it has been the subject of negotiation. *Joint ventures* refer to the type of transaction whereby a government concluded a deal (usually with a foreign investor) involving the formation of a new company in which the government's equity contribution was in the form of the major assets or all assets of a public enterprise. The remaining shell company would then be maintained only as a book company or would be liquidated; if it were liquidated it would not be included as a liquidation since this would be double counting. Transactions labled *Trustees* refer to privatizations achieved by transference of shares of a public enterprise to a trustee for onward sale—at a later date or over a period—to the public or to selected segments of the public. *Restitutions* are those transactions whereby a company has been handed back to a previous owner from whom the company had been expropriated. *Other sales* includes sundry methods, such as enterprises donated by governments to local communities, but principally comprises transactions where the method of privatization was not reported.

Table 10-3. Progress in privatization: ownership and control changes (2002). This table presents the inferred outcome of privatization transactions on the ownership and control of enterprises or their assets.

Ownership changes are important in indicating the effect that privatization transactions may or may not have on the enterprises and in indicating the extent of a government's willingness and/or ability to exit from equity participation in commercial activity. Although a government's influence is not necessarily restricted by its equity participation, it is generally assumed that once a government owns less than 50 percent of the voting shares of a company, that company is "private" and the private shareholders (except in the instance of exercise of golden share rights) have management control of the company. Ownership control is usually unaffected when government continues to be a majority shareholder or sells a minority interest. Concessions, leases, and management contracts are assumed not to have affected ownership rights but to have transferred management control to the private sector for a defined period. The table shows the number of reported transactions where governments have (a) fully sold wholly- or majority-owned enterprises, (b) sold shares and transferred ownership control but retained a minority equity interest, (c) sold shares but retained ownership control, (d) sold a proportion of a minority stake, and (e) conducted other transactions where management control has been ceded.

Methodology used for regional aggregations and period averages in Chapter 10

| Table | Aggregations [a] | | Period averages [b] |
	(1)	(2)	(1)
10-1	x		
10-2	x		
10-3	x		

Note: Regional aggregations are shown in the rows for Sub-Saharan Africa, North Africa, and All Africa. Period averages are shown in the last three columns. This table shows only the methodologies used in this chapter.

a. Regional aggregations: (1) simple total; (2) simple total of the first indicator divided by the simple total of the second indicator (same country coverage); (3) simple total of the gap-filled indicator; (4) simple total of the gap-filled main indicator divided by the simple total of the gap-filled secondary indicator; (5) simple total of the first gap-filled main indicator less the simple total of the second gap-filled main indicator, all divided by the simple total of the secondary indicator; (6) weighted total (by population); (7) median; (8) no aggregation; (9) simple arithmetic mean.

b. Period averages: (1) arithmetic mean (using the same series as shown in the table; i.e., ratio if the rest of the table is shown as ratio, level if the rest of the table is shown as level, growth rate if the rest is shown as growth rate); (2) least-squares growth rate (using main indicator); (3) least-squares growth rate (using main indicator in constant terms, with the rest of the table in current terms).

11

Labor Force and Employment

This chapter presents data on the level and structure of the labor force. The distribution of the labor force into various industrial activities is also given, as well as the participation rates of the population in economic activities. Information is also presented on average wages in different sectors.

The treatment of statistics on public sector employment is not consistent among countries. The scope covered often varies. While some countries include the education and health sectors, others leave them out. Staff of local, regional, and state or provincial governments are likewise treated differently.

The stipulations on wages take different forms among African countries. While some countries have a minimum wage per hour worked, others stipulate a minimum monthly wage for a worker. To permit some measure of comparability, we have computed and reported the monthly average earnings per wage earner. These earnings are further converted to U.S. dollars at the *Atlas* exchange rate. These data should be used with caution because some countries have more than one minimum wage rate based on the industry and the occupation within the industry as well as on the region of the country concerned.

The definition of labor force or economically active population is that used by the International Labor Organization (ILO), which follows the UN System of National Accounts (SNA). The labor force is measured by dividing economically active persons into two categories: employed and unemployed. Caution in the use of the data is necessary because, as pointed out in the ILO's *World Labour Report 1* (1987), many persons do not clearly come within one of these categories or the other. Many are visibly underemployed in that they work less than full time. Others work full time but earn less than a subsistence income. Some of the unemployed may even be voluntarily idle.

The comparability of the data is further hampered by the fact that practices vary among countries as regards the treatment of such groups as armed forces, inmates of institutions, persons living on reservations, persons seeking their first job, seasonal workers, and persons engaged in part-time economic activities. In some countries, all or part of these groups are included among the economically active, while in others they are treated as inactive. In addition, the extent to which family workers, particularly females, who assist in family enterprises are included among the enumerated economically active population varies considerably from country to country. Further, in some countries the statistics of the economically active relate only to employed and unemployed persons above a specified age, while in others there is no such age provision.

The reference period is also an important factor of difference, especially in regard to the classification of the labor force according to industry. In some countries, such classification refers to the actual position of each individual on the day of the census or survey date, while in others the data recorded refer to the usual position of each person, generally without reference to any given period of time.

The sources for the tables in this chapter are various issues of the ILO's *Yearbook of Labour Statistics*, and electronic ILO files kept in World Bank SIMA.

11-1. Number and gender structure of the labor force

	Total labor force (thousands)			Percentage of total labor force that is female		
	1980	*1990*	*2002*	*1980*	*1990*	*2002*
SUB-SAHARAN AFRICA	171,980	224,619	305,169	42.0	41.7	42.0
excluding South Africa	161,634	211,021	287,763	42.4	42.0	42.3
excl. S. Africa & Nigeria	132,114	172,559	234,835	43.8	43.5	43.5
Angola	3,491	4,484	6,409	47.0	46.5	46.2
Benin	1,657	2,114	2,995	47.0	48.3	48.3
Botswana	395	556	766	50.1	46.8	45.1
Burkina Faso	3,802	4,590	5,801	47.6	46.8	46.5
Burundi	2,269	2,934	3,886	50.2	49.1	48.6
Cameroon	3,649	4,671	6,353	36.8	37.0	38.2
Cape Verde	94	127	192	34.0	38.9	38.8
Central African Republic	1,215	1,447	1,848	..	..	..
Chad	2,233	2,783	3,953	43.4	44.0	44.8
Comoros	152	193	270	43.1	42.9	42.2
Congo, Dem. Rep. of	11,961	15,717	22,299	44.5	43.9	43.3
Congo, Rep. of	703	933	1,323	42.4	43.2	43.5
Côte d'Ivoire	3,280	4,465	6,777	32.2	32.4	33.6
Djibouti	..	..	..	..	..	..
Equatorial Guinea	96	150	202	35.1	35.6	35.7
Eritrea	1,218	1,584	2,172	47.4	47.5	47.4
Ethiopia	16,924	22,806	28,947	42.3	40.9	41.0
Gabon	363	455	585	45.0	44.2	44.8
Gambia, The	330	470	697	44.8	44.6	45.2
Ghana	5,088	7,063	9,606	51.0	50.9	50.4
Guinea	2,293	2,821	3,671	47.1	47.5	47.2
Guinea-Bissau	382	453	588	39.9	40.1	40.5
Kenya	7,829	11,184	16,296	46.0	45.9	46.1
Lesotho	571	676	865	37.9	36.5	37.0
Liberia	790	989	1,319	38.4	39.1	39.6
Madagascar	4,323	5,453	7,796	45.2	45.0	44.7
Malawi	3,112	4,189	5,166	50.6	49.5	48.4
Mali	3,393	4,254	5,545	46.7	46.6	46.1
Mauritania	746	904	1,309	45.0	44.3	43.5
Mauritius	343	432	525	25.7	30.3	33.0
Mozambique	6,686	7,492	9,588	49.0	48.4	48.4
Namibia	429	571	753	40.1	40.4	41.0
Niger	2,803	3,746	5,440	44.6	44.1	44.3
Nigeria	29,519	38,462	52,928	36.2	35.4	36.7
Rwanda	2,639	3,628	4,827	49.1	49.0	48.7
São Tomé and Principe	..	..	..	..	..	..
Senegal	2,542	3,269	4,489	42.2	42.4	42.6
Seychelles	..	..	..	..	..	..
Sierra Leone	1,248	1,490	1,961	35.5	35.5	37.1
Somalia	2,968	3,170	4,023	43.4	43.3	43.4
South Africa	10,347	13,598	17,406	35.1	36.9	37.9
Sudan	7,070	9,207	13,053	26.9	27.1	30.0
Swaziland	202	262	404	33.5	37.0	37.8
Tanzania	9,508	13,122	18,136	49.8	49.6	49.0
Togo	1,099	1,447	1,982	39.3	39.8	40.0
Uganda	6,617	8,319	11,485	47.9	47.8	47.6
Zambia	2,398	3,184	4,488	45.4	45.7	44.6
Zimbabwe	3,204	4,755	6,045	44.4	44.2	44.5
NORTH AFRICA	29,265	38,446	54,504	27.2	27.6	31.3
Algeria	4,848	7,046	10,953	21.4	21.1	29.0
Egypt, Arab Rep.	14,319	18,313	25,905	26.5	27.0	31.0
Libya	943	1,235	1,592	18.6	18.2	24.0
Morocco	6,968	8,987	12,093	33.5	34.6	34.9
Tunisia	2,187	2,865	3,961	28.9	29.1	32.1
ALL AFRICA	201,245	263,065	359,673	39.8	39.6	40.4

11-2. Children under 14 working in the labor force

	As percentage of population age 10 to 14			
	1970	1980	1990	2002
SUB-SAHARAN AFRICA	36.2	34.5	32.2	29.9
excluding South Africa	39.0	37.0	34.5	31.8
excl. S.Africa & Nigeria	40.9	39.2	36.2	33.5
Angola	31.4	29.7	28.1	25.7
Benin	34.4	30.3	28.6	26.1
Botswana	32.3	25.9	19.4	13.5
Burkina Faso	75.1	70.9	58.7	40.4
Burundi	50.8	50.0	49.4	48.3
Cameroon	38.9	33.9	27.5	22.0
Cape Verde	17.3	16.0	14.7	13.3
Central African Republic	45.0	39.4	33.8	28.6
Chad	41.9	41.6	40.0	36.0
Comoros	45.8	44.7	40.9	36.9
Congo, Dem. Rep. of	36.5	33.2	30.5	28.3
Congo, Rep. of	28.3	27.5	26.6	25.2
Côte d'Ivoire	34.6	28.4	22.3	18.0
Djibouti	..	..	..	..
Equatorial Guinea	42.7	40.4	35.8	31.3
Eritrea	46.1	43.8	40.8	37.9
Ethiopia	48.5	46.3	43.5	40.6
Gabon	35.6	29.1	22.7	12.4
Gambia, The	45.9	44.4	40.2	32.7
Ghana	16.3	16.2	14.6	11.5
Guinea	43.3	41.2	37.0	29.9
Guinea-Bissau	45.2	43.4	40.4	36.0
Kenya	45.0	45.0	43.4	38.3
Lesotho	30.9	27.7	23.5	20.2
Liberia	31.1	25.7	21.8	14.1
Madagascar	41.7	40.2	37.6	33.5
Malawi	50.7	45.2	38.9	30.0
Mali	62.5	61.2	57.9	49.8
Mauritania	33.3	29.6	25.8	21.4
Mauritius	5.8	4.8	4.0	1.4
Mozambique	40.7	39.5	35.2	31.9
Namibia	40.2	33.6	26.0	15.6
Niger	48.8	47.8	46.8	42.9
Nigeria	30.8	29.2	27.6	23.2
Rwanda	43.3	42.5	42.1	41.2
São Tomé and Principe	..	..	..	..
Senegal	46.9	42.9	35.4	25.7
Seychelles	..	..	..	..
Sierra Leone	21.7	19.4	17.1	13.4
Somalia	39.9	37.7	34.5	30.7
South Africa	2.7	0.9	0.0	0.0
Sudan	34.1	33.3	31.4	26.6
Swaziland	19.1	17.2	15.3	11.6
Tanzania	45.6	42.8	42.1	35.9
Togo	40.4	36.1	30.4	26.2
Uganda	50.4	48.8	46.8	43.2
Zambia	21.1	19.0	16.9	15.4
Zimbabwe	41.1	36.7	31.8	26.1
NORTH AFRICA	12.7	15.1	8.8	5.8
Algeria	11.4	7.1	3.3	0.0
Egypt, Arab Rep.	23.6	18.3	13.2	8.3
Libya	12.8	8.7	0.5	0.0
Morocco	21.5	20.9	10.6	0.5
Tunisia	12.2	5.8	0.0	0.0
ALL AFRICA	31.3	30.9	28.0	25.8

11-3. Unpaid family workers as share of active workers

| | Percentage of unpaid family workers in economically active workers | | |
| | *(most recent year available between 1980-2001)* | | |
	Female	*Male*	*Total*
SUB-SAHARAN AFRICA	..	..	..
excluding South Africa	..	..	..
excl. S.Africa & Nigeria	..	..	..
Angola	..	..	..
Benin	..	..	..
Botswana	41.8	36.0	77.7
Burkina Faso	..	..	..
Burundi	..	..	..
Cameroon	32.7	9.2	41.9
Cape Verde	..	..	..
Central African Republic	..	..	..
Chad	..	..	..
Comoros	..	..	..
Congo, Dem. Rep. of	..	..	..
Congo, Rep. of	..	..	..
Côte d'Ivoire	..	..	..
Djibouti	..	..	..
Equatorial Guinea	..	..	..
Eritrea	..	..	..
Ethiopia	..	..	..
Gabon	..	..	..
Gambia, The	..	..	..
Ghana	..	..	..
Guinea	..	..	..
Guinea-Bissau	..	..	..
Kenya	..	..	..
Lesotho	..	..	..
Liberia	..	..	..
Madagascar	..	..	..
Malawi	..	..	..
Mali	..	..	..
Mauritania	..	..	..
Mauritius	..	..	..
Mozambique	..	..	..
Namibia	..	..	..
Niger	..	..	..
Nigeria	14.9	8.6	23.5
Rwanda	..	..	..
São Tomé and Principe	..	..	..
Senegal	..	..	..
Seychelles	0.4	0.2	0.6
Sierra Leone	..	..	..
Somalia	..	..	..
South Africa	..	..	..
Sudan	..	..	..
Swaziland	..	..	..
Tanzania	..	..	..
Togo	..	..	..
Uganda	..	..	..
Zambia	..	..	..
Zimbabwe	..	..	..
NORTH AFRICA	..	6.9	13.4
Algeria	..	5.6	6.2
Egypt, Arab Rep.	1.9	15.0	16.9
Libya	..	..	..
Morocco	..	..	..
Tunisia	18.5	5.1	23.6
ALL AFRICA	..	..	..

11-4. Industrial structure of the labor force

	Percentage of labor force working in								
	Agriculture			Industry			Services		
	1980	1990	1995-2000	1980	1990	1995-2000	1980	1990	1995-2000
SUB-SAHARAN AFRICA	..	..	..	..	..	..	..	..	..
excluding South Africa	..	..	..	..	..	..	..	..	..
excl. S.Africa & Nigeria	68	64	..	12	12	..	20	24	..
Angola	76	75	..	8	8	..	16	17	..
Benin	67	64	..	7	8	..	26	28	..
Botswana	5	3	..	33	31	..	62	66	..
Burkina Faso	92	92	..	3	2	..	5	6	..
Burundi	..	..	..	..	..	..	..	..	..
Cameroon	73	70	..	8	9	..	19	22	..
Cape Verde	36	31	..	31	29	..	33	40	..
Central African Republic	85	80	..	3	4	..	12	16	..
Chad	88	83	..	3	4	..	9	13	..
Comoros	81	77	..	8	9	..	12	13	..
Congo, Dem. Rep. of	72	68	..	12	13	..	16	19	..
Congo, Rep. of	58	49	..	13	15	..	29	37	..
Côte d'Ivoire	65	60	..	8	10	..	27	31	..
Djibouti	..	..	..	..	..	..	..	..	..
Equatorial Guinea	78	75	..	5	5	..	17	20	..
Eritrea	83	81	..	5	5	..	12	15	..
Ethiopia	..	..	89	..	..	2	..	..	10
Gabon	66	52	..	12	16	..	22	33	..
Gambia, The	84	82	..	7	8	..	9	11	..
Ghana	..	..	..	..	..	..	..	..	..
Guinea	91	87	..	1	2	..	8	11	..
Guinea-Bissau	87	85	..	2	2	..	11	13	..
Kenya	23	19	19	22	20	20	55	61	62
Lesotho	40	40	..	34	28	..	26	32	..
Liberia	77	72	..	6	6	..	18	22	..
Madagascar	82	78	..	6	7	..	13	15	..
Malawi	..	..	..	..	..	..	..	..	..
Mali	89	86	..	2	2	..	9	12	..
Mauritania	71	55	55	7	10	8	22	34	37
Mauritius	29	16	15	25	44	40	43	38	46
Mozambique	84	83	..	8	8	..	8	9	..
Namibia	47	53	38	16	18	14	37	29	47
Niger	6	8	..	67	49	..	26	44	..
Nigeria	..	..	3	..	..	22	..	..	75
Rwanda	93	92	..	3	3	..	4	5	..
São Tomé and Principe	..	..	..	..	..	..	..	..	..
Senegal	81	77	..	6	8	..	13	16	..
Seychelles	..	..	..	..	..	..	..	..	..
Sierra Leone	70	67	..	14	15	..	16	17	..
Somalia	78	75	..	7	8	..	15	16	..
South Africa	..	..	..	..	..	..	..	..	..
Sudan	72	70	..	8	9	..	20	22	..
Swaziland	40	24	..	26	26	..	35	50	..
Tanzania	..	..	..	..	..	..	..	..	..
Togo	69	66	..	10	10	..	22	24	..
Uganda	..	..	..	..	..	..	..	..	..
Zambia	76	75	..	8	8	..	16	17	..
Zimbabwe	32	24	..	27	28	..	40	48	..
NORTH AFRICA	40	27	22	23	27	26	36	46	52
Algeria	36	26	..	27	31	..	37	43	..
Egypt, Arab Rep.	42	39	30	20	21	22	36	40	48
Libya	25	11	..	24	23	..	51	66	..
Morocco	..	4	6	..	36	33	..	60	61
Tunisia	39	..	..	30	..	..	31	..	..
ALL AFRICA	..	..	..	..	..	..	..	..	..

Note: Figures may not add up to 100% because of rounding.

11-5. Industrial structure of economically active population

	Agriculture				Industry				Services			
	Male		Female		Male		Female		Male		Female	
	1980	2001*	1980	2001*	1980	2001*	1980	2001*	1980	2001*	1980	2001*
SUB-SAHARAN AFRICA	..	..	..	..	..	..	..	..	..	..	..	..
excluding South Africa	..	..	..	..	..	..	..	..	..	..	..	..
excl. S.Africa & Nigeria	62	58	78	73	15	15	4	5	23	26	18	22
Angola	67	65	87	86	13	14	1	2	20	21	11	13
Benin	66	62	69	65	10	12	4	4	24	27	27	30
Botswana	6	3	3	2	41	38	8	18	53	60	89	80
Burkina Faso	92	91	93	94	3	2	2	2	5	7	5	5
Burundi	88	86	98	98	4	4	1	1	9	10	1	1
Cameroon	65	62	87	83	11	12	2	3	24	26	11	14
Cape Verde	34	30	39	33	38	38	18	16	28	33	42	51
Central African Republic	79	74	90	87	5	6	1	0	15	20	9	13
Chad	82	77	95	91	6	7	0	1	12	16	4	8
Comoros	70	68	93	90	12	13	3	5	17	20	4	5
Congo, Dem. Rep. of	62	58	84	81	18	20	4	5	20	23	12	14
Congo, Rep. of	42	33	81	69	20	23	2	4	38	44	17	27
Côte d'Ivoire	60	54	75	72	10	12	5	6	30	34	20	22
Djibouti	..	3	..	0	..	11	..	1	..	78	..	88
Equatorial Guinea	71	66	91	91	7	7	3	2	23	27	6	8
Eritrea	79	77	88	85	7	8	2	2	14	16	11	13
Ethiopia	..	89	..	88	..	2	..	2	..	9	..	11
Gabon	59	46	74	59	18	21	6	10	24	33	21	32
Gambia, The	78	74	93	92	10	12	3	2	13	14	5	6
Ghana	..	66	..	59	..	10	..	10	..	23	..	32
Guinea	86	83	97	92	2	3	1	1	12	15	3	7
Guinea-Bissau	81	78	98	96	3	3	0	1	17	19	3	3
Kenya	23	20	25	16	24	23	9	10	53	57	65	75
Lesotho	26	29	64	59	52	41	5	5	22	30	31	36
Liberia	69	65	89	84	9	9	1	1	22	26	10	16
Madagascar	73	70	93	88	9	10	2	3	19	20	5	9
Malawi	..	50	..	73	..	25	..	7	..	25	..	20
Mali	86	83	92	89	2	2	1	2	12	15	7	9
Mauritania	65	49	79	63	11	16	2	4	25	35	19	34
Mauritius	29	15	30	13	19	39	40	43	47	46	31	45
Mozambique	72	70	97	96	14	15	1	1	14	15	2	3
Namibia	52	38	42	39	22	19	10	8	27	43	47	52
Niger	7	8	6	5	69	51	29	24	25	41	66	71
Nigeria	..	4	..	2	..	30	..	11	..	67	..	87
Rwanda	88	86	98	98	5	6	1	1	7	8	1	2
São Tomé and Principe	..	..	..	..	..	..	..	..	..	..	..	..
Senegal	74	70	90	86	9	10	2	4	17	20	8	11
Seychelles	..	..	..	..	..	..	..	..	..	..	..	..
Sierra Leone	63	60	82	81	20	22	4	4	17	18	14	16
Somalia	69	66	90	87	12	13	2	2	19	21	8	11
South Africa	18	16	16	10	45	42	16	15	37	42	68	76
Sudan	66	64	88	84	9	10	4	5	24	26	8	11
Swaziland	40	..	38	..	29	..	14	..	30	..	48	..
Tanzania	..	78	..	90	..	7	..	1	..	15	..	8
Togo	70	66	67	65	12	12	7	7	19	22	26	29
Uganda	..	91	..	91	..	4	..	6	..	5	..	3
Zambia	69	68	85	83	13	13	3	3	19	19	13	14
Zimbabwe	29	23	50	38	31	32	8	10	40	46	42	52
NORTH AFRICA	38	21	27	24	25	27	13	21	36	51	54	54
Algeria	27	18	69	57	33	38	6	7	40	45	25	36
Egypt, Arab Rep.	45	29	10	35	21	25	13	9	33	46	69	56
Libya	16	7	63	28	29	27	3	5	55	66	34	68
Morocco	..	6	..	6	..	32	..	40	..	63	..	54
Tunisia	33	22	53	20	30	32	32	40	37	44	16	38
ALL AFRICA	..	..	..	..	..	..	..	..	..	..	..	..

Percentage of population economically active

* Or most recent available data.

11-6. Wages in agriculture

	Monthly earnings in current U.S. dollars										
	1980	*1993*	*1994*	*1995*	*1996*	*1997*	*1998*	*1999*	*2000*	*2001*	*2002*
SUB-SAHARAN AFRICA	..	..	..	..	..	..	..	..	..	..	..
excluding South Africa	..	..	..	..	..	..	..	..	..	..	..
excl. S.Africa & Nigeria	..	..	..	..	..	..	..	..	..	..	..
Angola	..	..	..	..	..	..	..	..	..	..	..
Benin	..	..	..	..	..	..	..	..	..	..	..
Botswana	..	..	..	..	..	..	86	83	92	73	..
Burkina Faso	..	..	..	..	..	..	..	..	..	..	..
Burundi	..	..	..	..	..	..	..	..	..	..	..
Cameroon	..	..	..	..	..	..	..	..	..	..	..
Cape Verde	..	..	..	..	..	..	..	..	..	..	..
Central African Republic	..	..	..	..	..	..	..	..	..	..	..
Chad	..	..	..	..	..	..	..	..	..	..	..
Comoros	..	..	..	..	..	..	..	..	..	..	..
Congo, Dem. Rep. of	..	..	..	..	..	..	..	..	..	..	..
Congo, Rep. of	..	..	..	..	..	..	..	..	..	..	..
Côte d'Ivoire	..	..	..	..	..	..	..	..	..	..	..
Djibouti	..	..	..	..	..	..	..	..	..	..	..
Equatorial Guinea	..	..	..	..	..	..	..	..	..	..	..
Eritrea	..	..	..	..	..	..	..	..	..	..	..
Ethiopia	..	..	..	..	..	..	..	..	..	..	..
Gabon	..	..	..	..	..	..	..	..	..	..	..
Gambia, The	..	..	..	..	..	..	..	..	..	..	..
Ghana	34	..	..	..	..	..	..	..	..	..	..
Guinea	..	..	..	..	..	..	..	..	..	..	..
Guinea-Bissau	..	..	..	..	..	..	..	..	..	..	..
Kenya	59	..	..	..	..	..	..	..	..	..	..
Lesotho	..	..	..	..	..	..	..	..	..	..	..
Liberia	..	..	..	..	..	..	..	..	..	..	..
Madagascar	..	..	..	..	..	..	..	..	..	..	..
Malawi	20	..	..	..	..	..	..	..	..	..	..
Mali	..	..	..	..	..	..	..	..	..	..	..
Mauritania	..	..	..	..	..	..	..	..	..	..	..
Mauritius	..	..	..	..	..	..	..	235	252	260	..
Mozambique	..	..	..	..	..	..	..	..	..	..	..
Namibia	..	..	..	..	..	..	..	..	..	..	..
Niger	..	..	..	..	..	..	..	..	..	..	..
Nigeria	..	..	..	..	..	..	..	..	..	..	..
Rwanda	..	..	..	..	..	..	..	..	..	..	..
São Tomé and Principe	..	..	..	..	..	..	..	..	..	..	..
Senegal	..	..	..	..	..	..	..	..	..	..	..
Seychelles	139	..	..	..	..	..	..	..	..	..	..
Sierra Leone	..	..	..	..	..	..	..	..	..	..	..
Somalia	..	..	..	..	..	..	..	..	..	..	..
South Africa	..	..	..	..	..	..	..	..	..	..	..
Sudan	..	..	..	..	..	..	..	..	..	..	..
Swaziland	..	512	550	482	496	700	..	..	..	..	..
Tanzania	..	..	..	..	..	..	..	..	..	..	..
Togo	..	..	..	..	..	..	..	..	..	..	..
Uganda	..	..	..	..	..	..	..	..	..	..	..
Zambia	112	..	..	..	..	..	..	..	..	..	..
Zimbabwe	..	38	35	34	40	44	30	27	33	60	..
NORTH AFRICA	..	..	..	..	..	..	..	..	..	..	..
Algeria	..	..	..	..	..	..	..	..	..	..	..
Egypt, Arab Rep.	..	..	..	..	85	84	104	113	110	79	..
Libya	..	..	..	..	..	..	..	..	..	..	..
Morocco	..	..	..	..	..	..	..	..	..	..	..
Tunisia	..	..	..	..	..	..	..	..	..	..	..
ALL AFRICA	..	..	..	..	..	..	..	..	..	..	..

11-7. Wages in manufacturing

	Monthly earnings in current U.S. dollars										
	1980	*1993*	*1994*	*1995*	*1996*	*1997*	*1998*	*1999*	*2000*	*2001*	*2002*
SUB-SAHARAN AFRICA	..	..	..	..	..	..	..	..	..	..	..
excluding South Africa	..	..	..	..	..	..	..	..	..	..	..
excl. S.Africa & Nigeria	..	..	..	..	..	..	..	..	..	..	..
Angola	..	..	..	..	..	..	..	..	..	..	..
Benin	..	..	..	..	..	..	..	..	..	..	..
Botswana	..	..	..	..	..	..	164	170	153	153	..
Burkina Faso	..	..	..	..	..	..	..	..	..	..	..
Burundi	..	..	..	..	..	..	..	..	..	..	..
Cameroon	..	..	..	..	..	..	..	..	..	..	..
Cape Verde	..	..	..	..	..	..	..	..	..	..	..
Central African Republic	..	..	..	..	..	..	..	..	..	..	..
Chad	..	..	..	..	..	..	..	..	..	..	..
Comoros	..	..	..	..	..	..	..	..	..	..	..
Congo, Dem. Rep. of	..	..	..	..	..	..	..	..	..	..	..
Congo, Rep. of	..	..	..	..	..	..	..	..	..	..	..
Côte d'Ivoire	..	..	..	..	..	..	..	..	..	..	..
Djibouti	..	..	..	..	..	..	..	..	..	..	..
Equatorial Guinea	..	..	..	..	..	..	..	..	..	..	..
Eritrea	..	..	..	..	75	..	..	..	..	..	..
Ethiopia	..	..	..	..	..	..	..	..	..	..	..
Gabon	..	..	..	..	..	..	..	..	..	..	..
Gambia, The	..	110	109	..	..	..	91	..	..	..	..
Ghana	57	..	..	..	..	..	..	..	..	..	..
Guinea	..	115	133	131	152	..	..	..	..	..	..
Guinea-Bissau	..	..	..	..	..	..	..	..	..	..	..
Kenya	169	..	..	..	..	..	..	..	..	..	..
Lesotho	..	..	..	..	..	..	..	..	..	..	..
Liberia	..	..	..	..	..	..	..	..	..	..	..
Madagascar	..	..	..	..	..	..	..	..	..	..	..
Malawi	75	..	..	..	..	..	..	..	..	..	..
Mali	..	..	..	..	..	..	..	..	..	..	..
Mauritania	..	..	..	..	..	..	..	..	..	..	..
Mauritius	..	..	..	..	..	..	..	204	211	201	205
Mozambique	..	..	..	..	..	..	..	..	..	..	..
Namibia	..	..	..	..	..	..	..	..	..	..	..
Niger	..	..	..	..	..	..	..	..	..	..	..
Nigeria	..	..	..	..	..	..	..	..	..	..	..
Rwanda	..	..	..	..	..	..	..	..	..	..	..
São Tomé and Principe	..	..	..	..	..	..	..	..	..	..	..
Senegal	..	..	..	..	..	..	..	..	..	..	..
Seychelles	212	..	..	..	..	..	..	..	..	..	..
Sierra Leone	..	..	..	..	..	..	..	..	..	..	..
Somalia	..	..	..	..	..	..	..	..	..	..	..
South Africa	475	..	..	..	..	..	..	..	..	..	..
Sudan	..	..	..	..	..	..	..	..	..	..	..
Swaziland	571	..	..	..	..	..	..	..	..	..	..
Tanzania	..	..	..	..	..	..	..	..	..	..	..
Togo	..	..	..	..	..	..	..	..	..	..	..
Uganda	..	..	..	..	..	..	..	..	..	..	..
Zambia	..	..	..	..	..	..	..	..	..	..	..
Zimbabwe	..	185	171	196	206	216	138	123	165	233	..
NORTH AFRICA	..	..	..	..	..	..	..	..	..	..	..
Algeria	..	343	255	220	225	..	..	..	..	..	..
Egypt, Arab Rep.	..	..	..	..	118	131	136	153	155	147	..
Libya	..	..	..	..	..	..	..	..	..	..	..
Morocco	..	..	..	..	..	..	..	..	..	..	..
Tunisia	..	..	..	..	..	..	..	..	..	..	..
ALL AFRICA	..	..	..	..	..	..	..	..	..	..	..

11-8. Wages in mining and quarrying

	Monthly earnings in current U.S. dollars										
	1980	*1993*	*1994*	*1995*	*1996*	*1997*	*1998*	*1999*	*2000*	*2001*	*2002*
SUB-SAHARAN AFRICA	..	..	..	..	..	..	..	..	..	..	..
excluding South Africa	..	..	..	..	..	..	..	..	..	..	..
excl. S.Africa & Nigeria	..	..	..	..	..	..	..	..	..	..	..
Angola	..	..	..	..	..	..	..	..	..	..	..
Benin											
Botswana							..	528	486	540	547	..
Burkina Faso	..	..	..	..	..	..	..	..	..	..	..
Burundi	..	..	..	..	..	..	..	..	..	..	..
Cameroon	..	..	..	..	..	..	..	..	..	..	..
Cape Verde	..	..	..	..	..	..	..	..	..	..	..
Central African Republic	..	..	..	..	..	..	..	..	..	..	..
Chad	..	..	..	..	..	..	..	..	..	..	..
Comoros	..	..	..	..	..	..	..	..	..	..	..
Congo, Dem. Rep. of	..	..	..	..	..	..	..	..	..	..	..
Congo, Rep. of	..	..	..	..	..	..	..	..	..	..	..
Côte d'Ivoire	..	..	..	..	..	..	..	..	..	..	..
Djibouti	..	..	..	..	..	..	..	..	..	..	..
Equatorial Guinea	..	..	..	..	..	..	..	..	..	..	..
Eritrea	..	..	..	..	63	..	..	..	..	..	..
Ethiopia	..	..	..	..	..	..	..	..	..	..	..
Gabon	..	..	..	..	..	..	..	..	..	..	..
Gambia, The	..	..	..	..	..	..	..	..	..	..	..
Ghana	64	..	..	..	..	..	..	..	..	..	..
Guinea	..	..	..	..	..	..	..	..	..	..	..
Guinea-Bissau	..	..	..	..	..	..	..	..	..	..	..
Kenya	157	..	..	..	..	..	..	..	..	..	..
Lesotho	..	..	..	..	..	..	..	..	..	..	..
Liberia	..	..	..	..	..	..	..	..	..	..	..
Madagascar	..	..	..	..	..	..	..	..	..	..	..
Malawi	36	..	..	..	..	..	..	..	..	..	..
Mali	..	..	..	..	..	..	..	..	..	..	..
Mauritania	..	..	..	..	..	..	..	..	..	..	..
Mauritius	..	..	..	..	..	..	..	144	148	160	172
Mozambique	..	..	..	..	..	..	..	..	..	..	..
Namibia	..	..	..	..	..	..	..	..	..	..	..
Niger	..	..	..	..	..	..	..	..	..	..	..
Nigeria	..	..	..	..	..	..	..	..	..	..	..
Rwanda	..	..	..	..	..	..	..	..	..	..	..
São Tomé and Principe	..	..	..	..	..	..	..	..	..	..	..
Senegal	..	..	..	..	..	..	..	..	..	..	..
Seychelles	212	..	..	..	..	..	..	..	..	..	..
Sierra Leone	..	..	..	..	..	..	..	..	..	..	..
Somalia	..	..	..	..	..	..	..	..	..	..	..
South Africa	330	..	..	..	..	..	..	..	..	..	..
Sudan	..	..	..	..	..	..	..	..	..	..	..
Swaziland	822	..	..	..	..	..	..	..	..	..	..
Tanzania	..	..	..	..	..	..	..	..	..	..	..
Togo	..	..	..	..	..	..	..	..	..	..	..
Uganda	..	..	..	..	..	..	..	..	..	..	..
Zambia	358	..	..	..	..	..	..	..	..	..	..
Zimbabwe	..	154	144	165	180	207	147	128	160	221	..
NORTH AFRICA	..	..	..	..	..	..	..	..	..	..	..
Algeria	..	498	312	253	261	..	..	..	..	..	..
Egypt, Arab Rep.					229	266	324	332	521	382	..
Libya	..	..	..	..	..	..	..	..	..	..	..
Morocco	..	..	..	..	..	..	..	..	..	..	..
Tunisia	..	..	..	..	..	..	..	..	..	..	..
ALL AFRICA	..	..	..	..	..	..	..	..	..	..	..

11-9. Wages in construction

	Monthly earnings in current U.S. dollars										
	1980	*1993*	*1994*	*1995*	*1996*	*1997*	*1998*	*1999*	*2000*	*2001*	*2002*
SUB-SAHARAN AFRICA	..	..	..	..	..	..	..	..	..	..	..
excluding South Africa	..	..	..	..	..	..	..	..	..	..	..
excl. S.Africa & Nigeria	..	..	..	..	..	..	..	..	..	..	..
Angola	..	..	..	..	..	..	..	..	..	..	..
Benin	..	..	..	..	..	..	..	..	..	..	..
Botswana	..	..	..	..	..	..	178	168	175	166	..
Burkina Faso	..	..	..	..	..	..	..	..	..	..	..
Burundi	..	..	..	..	..	..	..	..	..	..	..
Cameroon	..	..	..	..	..	..	..	..	..	..	..
Cape Verde	..	..	..	..	..	..	..	..	..	..	..
Central African Republic	..	..	..	..	..	..	..	..	..	..	..
Chad	..	..	..	..	..	..	..	..	..	..	..
Comoros	..	..	..	..	..	..	..	..	..	..	..
Congo, Dem. Rep. of	..	..	..	..	..	..	..	..	..	..	..
Congo, Rep. of	..	..	..	..	..	..	..	..	..	..	..
Côte d'Ivoire	..	..	..	..	..	..	..	..	..	..	..
Djibouti	..	..	..	..	..	..	..	..	..	..	..
Equatorial Guinea	..	..	..	..	..	..	..	..	..	..	..
Eritrea	..	..	..	..	..	..	..	..	..	..	..
Ethiopia	..	..	..	..	..	..	..	..	..	..	..
Gabon	..	..	..	..	..	..	..	..	..	..	..
Gambia, The	..	123	98	..	..	..	162	..	..	..	..
Ghana	37	..	..	..	..	..	..	..	..	..	..
Guinea	..	135	132	177	174	..	..	..	..	..	..
Guinea-Bissau	..	..	..	..	..	..	..	..	..	..	..
Kenya	133	..	..	..	..	..	..	..	..	..	..
Lesotho	..	..	..	..	..	..	..	..	..	..	..
Liberia	..	..	..	..	..	..	..	..	..	..	..
Madagascar	..	..	..	..	..	..	..	..	..	..	..
Malawi	60	..	..	..	..	..	..	..	..	..	..
Mali	..	..	..	..	..	..	..	..	..	..	..
Mauritania	..	..	..	..	..	..	..	..	..	..	..
Mauritius	..	..	..	..	..	..	..	311	333	308	310
Mozambique	..	..	..	..	..	..	..	..	..	..	..
Namibia	..	..	..	..	..	..	..	..	..	..	..
Niger	..	..	..	..	..	..	..	..	..	..	..
Nigeria	..	..	..	..	..	..	..	..	..	..	..
Rwanda	..	..	..	..	..	..	..	..	..	..	..
São Tomé and Principe	..	..	..	..	..	..	..	..	..	..	..
Senegal	..	..	..	..	..	..	..	..	..	..	..
Seychelles	..	..	..	..	..	..	..	..	..	..	..
Sierra Leone	..	..	..	..	..	..	..	..	..	..	..
Somalia	..	..	..	..	..	..	..	..	..	..	..
South Africa	371	..	..	..	..	..	..	..	..	..	..
Sudan	..	..	..	..	..	..	..	..	..	..	..
Swaziland	525	..	..	..	..	..	..	..	..	..	..
Tanzania	..	..	..	..	..	..	..	..	..	..	..
Togo	..	..	..	..	..	..	..	..	..	..	..
Uganda	..	..	..	..	..	..	..	..	..	..	..
Zambia	172	..	..	..	..	..	..	..	..	..	..
Zimbabwe	..	88	82	106	115	140	93	74	134	159	..
NORTH AFRICA	..	..	..	..	..	..	..	..	..	..	..
Algeria	..	315	270	235	242	..	..	..	..	..	..
Egypt, Arab Rep.	..	..	..	..	127	118	96	144	238	170	..
Libya	..	..	..	..	..	..	..	..	..	..	..
Morocco	..	..	..	..	..	..	..	..	..	..	..
Tunisia	..	..	..	..	..	..	..	..	..	..	..
ALL AFRICA	..	..	..	..	..	..	..	..	..	..	..

11-10. Wages in transport, storage, and communication

	Monthly earnings in current U.S. dollars										
	1980	*1993*	*1994*	*1995*	*1996*	*1997*	*1998*	*1999*	*2000*	*2001*	*2002*
SUB-SAHARAN AFRICA	..	..	..	..	..	..	..	..	..	..	..
excluding South Africa	..	..	..	..	..	..	..	..	..	..	..
excl. S.Africa & Nigeria	..	..	..	..	..	..	..	..	..	..	..
Angola	..	..	..	..	..	..	..	..	..	..	..
Benin	..	..	..	..	..	..	..	..	..	..	..
Botswana	..	..	..	..	..	..	503	501	524	475	..
Burkina Faso	..	..	..	..	..	..	..	..	..	..	..
Burundi	..	..	..	..	..	..	..	..	..	..	..
Cameroon	..	..	..	..	..	..	..	..	..	..	..
Cape Verde	..	..	..	..	..	..	..	..	..	..	..
Central African Republic	..	..	..	..	..	..	..	..	..	..	..
Chad	..	..	..	..	..	..	..	..	..	..	..
Comoros	..	..	..	..	..	..	..	..	..	..	..
Congo, Dem. Rep. of	..	..	..	..	..	..	..	..	..	..	..
Congo, Rep. of	..	..	..	..	..	..	..	..	..	..	..
Côte d'Ivoire	..	..	..	..	..	..	..	..	..	..	..
Djibouti	..	..	..	..	..	..	..	..	..	..	..
Equatorial Guinea	..	..	..	..	..	..	..	..	..	..	..
Eritrea	..	..	..	..	..	..	..	..	..	..	..
Ethiopia	..	..	..	..	..	..	..	..	..	..	..
Gabon	..	..	..	..	..	..	..	..	..	..	..
Gambia, The	..	154	116	..	..	..	194	..	..	..	..
Ghana	55	..	..	..	..	..	..	..	..	..	..
Guinea	..	..	119	121	124	..	..	..	..	..	..
Guinea-Bissau	..	..	..	..	..	..	..	..	..	..	..
Kenya	237	..	..	..	..	..	..	..	..	..	..
Lesotho	..	..	..	..	..	..	..	..	..	..	..
Liberia	..	..	..	..	..	..	..	..	..	..	..
Madagascar	..	..	..	..	..	..	..	..	..	..	..
Malawi	99	..	..	..	..	..	..	..	..	..	..
Mali	..	..	..	..	..	..	..	..	..	..	..
Mauritania	..	..	..	..	..	..	..	..	..	..	..
Mauritius	..	..	..	..	..	..	..	398	438	411	426
Mozambique	..	..	..	..	..	..	..	..	..	..	..
Namibia	..	..	..	..	..	..	..	..	..	..	..
Niger	..	..	..	..	..	..	..	..	..	..	..
Nigeria	..	..	..	..	..	..	..	..	..	..	..
Rwanda	..	..	..	..	..	..	..	..	..	..	..
São Tomé and Principe	..	..	..	..	..	..	..	..	..	..	..
Senegal	..	..	..	..	..	..	..	..	..	..	..
Seychelles	299	..	..	..	..	..	..	..	..	..	..
Sierra Leone	..	..	..	..	..	..	..	..	..	..	..
Somalia	..	..	..	..	..	..	..	..	..	..	..
South Africa	..	..	..	..	..	..	1,042	872	812	714	..
Sudan	..	..	..	..	..	..	..	..	..	..	..
Swaziland	520	..	..	..	..	..	..	..	..	..	..
Tanzania	..	..	..	..	..	..	..	..	..	..	..
Togo	..	..	..	..	..	..	..	..	..	..	..
Uganda	..	..	..	..	..	..	..	..	..	..	..
Zambia	153	..	..	..	..	..	..	..	..	..	..
Zimbabwe	..	244	223	243	249	273	192	185	280	323	..
NORTH AFRICA	..	..	..	..	..	..	..	..	..	..	..
Algeria	..	338	260	232	231	..	..	..	..	..	..
Egypt, Arab Rep.	..	..	..	..	142	128	185	167	171	206	..
Libya	..	..	..	..	..	..	..	..	..	..	..
Morocco	..	..	..	..	..	..	..	..	..	..	..
Tunisia	..	..	..	..	..	..	..	..	..	..	..
ALL AFRICA	..	..	..	..	..	..	..	..	..	..	..

11-11. Wages in community, social, and personal services

					Monthly earnings in current U.S. dollars						
	1980	1993	1994	1995	1996	1997	1998	1999	2000	2001	2002
SUB-SAHARAN AFRICA	..	..	..	..	..	..	..	..	..	..	..
excluding South Africa	..	..	..	..	..	..	..	..	..	..	..
excl. S.Africa & Nigeria	..	..	..	..	..	..	..	..	..	..	..
Angola	..	..	..	..	..	..	..	..	..	..	..
Benin	..	..	..	..	..	..	..	..	..	..	..
Botswana	..	..	..	..	..	..	192	175	238	233	..
Burkina Faso	..	..	..	..	..	..	..	..	..	..	..
Burundi	..	..	..	..	..	..	..	..	..	..	..
Cameroon	..	..	..	..	..	..	..	..	..	..	..
Cape Verde	..	..	..	..	..	..	..	..	..	..	..
Central African Republic	..	..	..	..	..	..	..	..	..	..	..
Chad	..	..	..	..	..	..	..	..	..	..	..
Comoros	..	..	..	..	..	..	..	..	..	..	..
Congo, Dem. Rep. of	..	..	..	..	..	..	..	..	..	..	..
Congo, Rep. of	..	..	..	..	..	..	..	..	..	..	..
Côte d'Ivoire	..	..	..	..	..	..	..	..	..	..	..
Djibouti	..	..	..	..	..	..	..	..	..	..	..
Equatorial Guinea	..	..	..	..	..	..	..	..	..	..	..
Eritrea	..	..	..	..	90	..	..	..	..	..	..
Ethiopia	..	..	..	..	..	..	..	..	..	..	..
Gabon	..	..	..	..	..	..	..	..	..	..	..
Gambia, The	..	104	128	..	..	..	125	..	..	..	..
Ghana	..	..	..	..	..	..	..	..	..	..	..
Guinea	..	..	..	..	..	..	..	..	..	..	..
Guinea-Bissau	..	..	..	..	..	..	..	..	..	..	..
Kenya	..	..	78	99	108	75	..	..	..	..	..
Lesotho	..	..	..	..	..	..	..	..	..	..	..
Liberia	..	..	..	..	..	..	..	..	..	..	..
Madagascar	..	..	..	..	..	..	..	..	..	..	..
Malawi	..	43	23	12	..	..	..	..	..	..	..
Mali	..	..	..	..	..	..	..	..	..	..	..
Mauritania	..	..	..	..	..	..	..	..	..	..	..
Mauritius	..	..	..	..	..	..	..	312	303	281	266
Mozambique	..	..	..	..	..	..	..	..	..	..	..
Namibia	..	..	..	..	..	..	..	..	..	..	..
Niger	..	..	..	..	..	..	..	..	..	..	..
Nigeria	..	..	..	..	..	..	..	..	..	..	..
Rwanda	..	..	..	..	..	..	..	..	..	..	..
São Tomé and Principe	..	..	..	..	..	..	..	..	..	..	..
Senegal	..	..	..	..	..	..	..	..	..	..	..
Seychelles	..	554	575	612	620	637	637	622	599	584	..
Sierra Leone	..	..	..	..	..	..	..	..	..	..	..
Somalia	..	..	..	..	..	..	..	..	..	..	..
South Africa	..	..	..	..	..	..	915	922	875	776	..
Sudan	..	..	..	..	..	..	..	..	..	..	..
Swaziland	..	238	455	352	352	388	..	..	..	..	..
Tanzania	..	..	..	..	..	..	..	..	..	..	..
Togo	..	..	..	..	..	..	..	..	..	..	..
Uganda	..	..	..	..	..	..	..	..	..	..	..
Zambia	..	..	..	..	..	..	..	..	..	..	..
Zimbabwe	..	128	119	130	178	233	150	135	237	267	..
NORTH AFRICA	..	..	..	..	..	..	..	..	..	..	..
Algeria	..	281	203	202	187	..	..	..	..	..	..
Egypt, Arab Rep.	..	..	..	..	186	72	..	..	..	..	..
Libya	..	..	..	..	..	..	..	..	..	..	..
Morocco	..	..	..	..	..	..	..	..	..	..	..
Tunisia	..	..	..	..	..	..	..	..	..	..	..
ALL AFRICA	..	..	..	..	..	..	..	..	..	..	..

Technical notes

Tables

Table 11-1. Number and gender structure of the labor force. The date presented here (ILO data) provide the total number of persons in the labor force and the percentage that is female. *Labor force* refers to "economically active" persons, including the armed forces and the unemployed but excluding housewives and students. The *economically active* population comprises all persons who furnish the labor to produce economic goods and services, as defined by the SNA, during a specified period. The production of economic goods and services should include all production and processing of primary products, whether for the market, for barter, or for own consumption; the production of all other goods and services for the market; and, for households that produce such goods and services for the markets, the corresponding production for own consumption.

Table 11-2. Children under 14 working in the labor force. This table (ILO data) shows the percentage of children between the ages of 10 to 14 who participate in the labor force.

Table 11-3. Unpaid family workers as share of active workers. This table (ILO data) shows the percentage of family members—male and female—who are active workers but receive no compensation for their services.

Table 11-4. Industrial structure of the labor force. The industrial structure of the labor force can often indicate the relative level of development of the economy. This table (ILO data) shows the distribution of the labor force among the various sectors of economic activities. The agriculture sector includes farming, animal husbandry, hunting, forestry, and fishing. The industry sector includes mining and quarrying, manufacturing, construction and public works, electricity, water, and gas. All other branches of activity are included in services.

Table 11-5. Industrial structure of economically active population. This is the percentage of the economically active population working in agriculture, industry, or services. Data are shown for males and females (ILO data).

Table 11-6. Wages in agriculture. Data are from the ILO *Yearbook of Labour Statistics* (1988, 1993, 1994, 1995, 1998, and 2003) and show the monthly earnings at the average wage converted to U.S. dollars at the official exchange rates in the countries concerned. Earnings here are limited to wages and salaries of employees, unless otherwise specified. They include remuneration for time not worked, such as for annual vacation, other paid leave or holidays, bonuses and gratuities, and housing and family allowances paid by the employer. They exclude employers' contributions to social security and pension schemes and the benefits received by employees under these schemes, as well as severance and termination pay.

These earnings do *not* reflect workers' disposable or net earnings since they include gross wages before deductions, such as taxes or social security contributions.

International comparisons of wages in agriculture should be interpreted with caution because of the wide variety of coverage variations, mainly as a result of the form of remuneration, the nature of the work, and the length of the working day.

Data for Botswana are for nationals only. Data for Egypt are for establishments with 10 or more persons employed. Data for Kenya include the value of payments in kind. Data for Malawi include forestry and fishing. Data for the Seychelles exclude hunting. Data for Swaziland are for skilled male workers. Data for Zimbabwe refer to all persons engaged.

The following countries' data are based upon ISIC Revision 2: Ghana, Guinea, Kenya, Malawi, Namibia, South Africa, Sudan, Swaziland, and Zimbabwe.

The following countries' data are based upon ISIC Revision 3: Algeria, Botswana, Egypt, Eritrea, The Gambia, Mauritius, and the Seychelles.

Figures for Egypt were converted from weekly to monthly earnings using a rate of 4.3 weeks per month. Figures for Tunisia were converted from daily to monthly using a rate of 22 days per month.

Table 11-7. Wages in manufacturing. Data are from ILO *Yearbook of Labor Statistics* (1988, 1993, 1994, 1995, 1998, and 2003). Refer to the definitions in Table 11-6.

Data for Botswana are for nationals only. Data for Egypt are for establishments with 10 or more persons employed. Data for The Gambia were collected in enterprises with five or more employees, and the survey results are influenced by a low response rate. Data for Kenya include the value of payments in kind. Data for Swaziland are for skilled male workers. Data for Zimbabwe refer to all persons engaged.

Figures for Egypt were converted from weekly to monthly earnings using a rate of 4.3 weeks per month.

Table 11-8. Wages in mining and quarrying. Data are from the ILO *Yearbook of Labour Statistics* (1988, 1993, 1994, 1995, 1998, and 2003). Refer to the definitions in Table 11-6.

Data for Botswana are for nationals only. Data for Egypt are for establishments with 10 or more persons employed. Data for Kenya include the value of payments in kind. Data for the Seychelles include con-

struction. Data for Swaziland are for skilled male workers. Data for Zimbabwe refer to all persons engaged.

Figures for Egypt were converted from weekly to monthly earnings using a rate of 4.3 weeks per month.

Table 11-9. Wages in construction. Data are from ILO *Yearbook of Labor Statistics* (1988, 1993, 1994, 1995, 1998, and 2003). Refer to the definitions in Table 11-6.

Data for Botswana are for nationals only. Data for Egypt are for establishments with 10 or more persons employed. Data for The Gambia were collected in enterprises with five or more employees, and the survey results are influenced by a low response rate. Data for Kenya include the value of payments in kind. Data for Swaziland are for skilled male workers. Data for Zimbabwe refer to all persons engaged.

Figures for Egypt were converted from weekly to monthly earnings using a rate of 4.3 weeks per month.

Table 11-10. Wages in transport, storage, and communications. Data are from the ILO *Yearbook of Labour Statistics* (1988, 1993, 1994, 1995, 1998, and 2003). Refer to the definitions in Table 11-6.

Data for Botswana are for nationals only. Data for Egypt are for establishments with 10 or more persons employed. Data for the Gambia were collected in enterprises with five or more employees, and the survey results are influenced by a low response rate. Data for Kenya include the value of payments in kind. Data for Swaziland are for skilled male workers. Data for Zimbabwe refer to all persons engaged.

Figures for Egypt were converted from weekly to monthly earnings using a rate of 4.3 weeks per month.

Table 11-11. Wages in community, social, and personal services. Data are from the ILO *Yearbook of Labour Statistics* (1988, 1993, 1994, 1995, 1998, and 2003). Refer to the definitions in Table 11-6. This sector comprises public administration and defense; sanitary and similar services; educational services; research and scientific institutes; medical, dental, and other health services; welfare institutions; business, professional, and labor associations; and other social and community services.

Data for Botswana are for nationals only. Data for Egypt are for establishments with 10 or more persons employed. Data for The Gambia were collected in enterprises with five or more employees, and the survey results are influenced by a low response rate.

Data for Kenya include the value of payments in kind. Data for Swaziland are for skilled male workers. Data for Zimbabwe refer to all persons engaged.

Figures for Egypt were converted from weekly to monthly earnings using a rate of 4.3 weeks per month.

Methodology used for regional aggregations and period averages in Chapter 11

	Aggregations [a]		
Table	(1)	(6)	(8)
11-1			
Columns 1-3	x		
Columns 4-6		x	
11-2		x	
11-3			x
11-4		x	
11-5		x	
11-6			x
11-7			x
11-8			x
11-9			x
11-10			x
11-11			x

Note: Regional aggregations are shown in the rows for Sub-Saharan Africa, North Africa, and All Africa. Period averages are shown in the last three columns. This table shows only the methodologies used in this chapter.

   a. Regional aggregations: (1) simple total; (2) simple total of the first indicator divided by the simple total of the second indicator (same country coverage); (3) simple total of the gap-filled indicator; (4) simple total of the gap-filled main indicator divided by the simple total of the gap-filled secondary indicator; (5) simple total of the first gap-filled main indicator less the simple total of the second gap-filled main indicator, all divided by the simple total of the secondary indicator; (6) weighted total (by population); (7) median; (8) no aggregation; (9) simple arithmetic mean.

12

Aid Flows

Official development assistance (ODA) consists of concessional financial flows that aim to promote economic development and welfare. ODA disbursements from bilateral and multilateral sources became increasingly important to Africa in the second half of the 1980s. For many countries, the foreign savings made available through ODA flows are equivalent to a sizable share of GDP and to the bulk of their domestic investment. Thus, monitoring aid flows is of special importance because of their significance to the economic performance of the region.

The tables in this chapter show data on net ODA flows and their relative importance to key economic and demographic indicators in recipient countries, real growth in net ODA flows to Sub-Saharan Africa from major donors or donor groups, and the share of each donor's worldwide aid portfolio allocated to Sub-Saharan Africa.

These flows are concessional in character and contain a grant element of at least 25 percent (based on a standard 10 percent discount rate). Net ODA disbursements equal gross ODA disbursements less principal repayments (amortization) of previous ODA loans.

ODA includes both grants (inflows of unrequited transfers from official sources) for current and capital expenditures and disbursements of concessional loans. However, because of different sources and definitions of data, ODA flows shown in this chapter will not necessarily equal those that could be calculated by adding net disbursements of official concessional long-term loans (Table 6-1 less Table 6-4) and net official transfers (Tables 5-6 and 5-9). For example, one of the reasons for differences is that the flows shown here include "off-shore" disbursements of grants, primarily for technical cooperation, which are generally excluded from transfers as recorded in the balance of payments (Tables 5-6 and 5-9). Other reasons include possible differences in the timing of the recording of disbursements and in the recording of multilateral ODA.

The data on net ODA disbursements are taken from the most recent electronic version of the OECD's *Geographic Distribution of Aid Flows to Developing Countries.* The tables include only those flows for which the recipient is specified in creditor reports.

To determine growth rates (based on constant price series), import price deflators (from the World Bank) have been used to deflate the current price series, regardless of the type of donor, to indicate the volume of imports that aid can finance over time.

12-1. Net aid from all donors, nominal

	Millions of U.S. dollars (current prices)											Annual average		
	1980	1993	1994	1995	1996	1997	1998	1999	2000	2001	2002	75-84	85-94	95-MR
SUB-SAHARAN AFRICA	7,760	17,594	19,437	18,877	16,519	14,958	14,752	13,240	13,446	14,012	19,359	6,230	15,707	15,645
excluding South Africa	7,760	17,319	19,142	18,488	16,155	14,461	14,238	12,699	12,959	13,583	18,702	6,230	15,650	15,161
excl. S.Africa & Nigeria	7,724	17,029	18,952	18,276	15,965	14,261	14,035	12,547	12,774	13,398	18,388	6,186	15,461	14,956
Angola	53	290	449	418	473	355	335	388	307	289	421	51	232	373
Benin	90	288	256	280	288	221	205	211	239	274	220	72	214	242
Botswana	106	130	86	90	75	122	106	61	31	29	38	83	127	69
Burkina Faso	212	467	434	491	420	368	400	398	336	392	473	165	340	410
Burundi	117	217	312	288	111	56	67	74	93	137	172	96	230	125
Cameroon	265	545	731	444	412	499	499	435	380	404	632	187	426	463
Cape Verde	64	117	122	117	117	111	130	137	94	77	92	42	102	109
Central African Republic	111	173	168	169	170	91	120	118	75	67	60	80	176	109
Chad	35	225	213	236	296	228	168	188	131	187	233	79	232	208
Comoros	43	49	39	42	39	27	35	21	19	27	32	30	49	30
Congo, Dem. Rep. of	428	179	246	196	166	158	125	132	184	263	807	317	475	254
Congo, Rep. of	92	123	362	125	429	270	66	142	33	75	420	82	145	195
Côte d'Ivoire	210	764	1,594	1,213	965	446	967	448	352	170	1,069	136	579	704
Djibouti	73	134	129	105	97	85	81	75	71	58	78	60	115	81
Equatorial Guinea	9	53	30	34	31	24	22	20	21	13	20	7	46	23
Eritrea	..	67	157	149	159	123	167	149	176	281	230	..	112	179
Ethiopia	212	1,090	1,071	883	818	579	660	643	693	1,116	1,307	208	914	837
Gabon	56	101	181	144	127	39	45	48	12	9	72	50	109	62
Gambia, The	55	85	70	47	37	39	39	34	49	54	61	38	91	45
Ghana	192	624	548	651	651	494	702	609	600	653	653	136	549	627
Guinea	90	408	359	417	299	381	359	238	153	280	250	68	302	297
Guinea-Bissau	59	94	175	119	181	124	96	52	80	59	59	49	108	96
Kenya	397	910	678	734	597	448	415	310	512	463	393	319	791	484
Lesotho	94	144	116	114	104	92	61	31	37	56	76	72	121	71
Liberia	98	123	64	124	173	76	72	94	68	39	52	77	97	87
Madagascar	230	363	289	301	357	834	481	359	322	366	373	148	334	424
Malawi	143	498	471	435	492	344	435	447	446	404	377	115	400	422
Mali	267	363	441	541	491	429	347	355	360	354	472	194	416	419
Mauritania	176	325	267	230	272	238	165	219	212	268	355	177	232	245
Mauritius	33	26	14	23	20	43	42	42	20	22	24	36	50	29
Mozambique	169	1,179	1,200	1,064	888	948	1,040	805	877	933	2,058	141	904	1,077
Namibia	..	154	138	192	188	166	181	179	153	110	135	0	86	163
Niger	170	344	377	274	255	333	292	187	211	257	298	165	352	263
Nigeria	36	290	190	212	190	200	204	152	185	185	314	44	189	205
Rwanda	155	356	716	702	467	230	350	373	322	299	356	131	319	387
São Tomé and Principe	4	47	50	84	47	33	28	28	35	38	26	7	37	40
Senegal	263	500	640	666	580	423	501	535	423	413	449	254	611	499
Seychelles	22	20	13	13	19	17	24	13	18	14	8	16	23	16
Sierra Leone	91	208	276	206	184	119	106	74	182	345	353	51	121	196
Somalia	433	893	537	189	88	81	80	115	104	150	194	283	507	125
South Africa	..	275	295	389	364	496	514	541	488	428	657	..	285	485
Sudan	623	454	412	242	220	139	209	243	225	185	351	540	779	227
Swaziland	50	55	58	58	33	28	35	29	13	29	25	33	45	31
Tanzania	679	950	966	877	877	945	1,000	990	1,022	1,271	1,233	513	949	1,027
Togo	91	97	125	192	157	125	128	71	70	44	51	81	172	105
Uganda	114	610	752	835	676	813	647	590	819	793	638	85	494	727
Zambia	318	872	718	2,034	610	610	349	624	795	349	641	204	604	751
Zimbabwe	164	498	560	492	371	336	261	245	178	164	201	114	388	281
NORTH AFRICA	2,719	3,596	3,765	2,961	3,347	2,922	3,084	2,723	2,222	2,367	2,798	2,694	3,940	2,803
Algeria	183	225	294	298	308	250	421	138	201	185	361	140	202	270
Egypt, Arab Rep.	1,385	2,387	2,682	2,016	2,200	1,985	1,955	1,582	1,328	1,257	1,286	1,774	2,731	1,701
Libya	17	4	4	6	8	7	7	7	15	10	10	9	10	9
Morocco	899	712	631	495	650	464	530	679	419	519	636	537	704	549
Tunisia	232	226	105	75	127	194	150	253	223	378	475	223	273	234
ALL AFRICA	10,479	21,190	23,202	21,838	19,867	17,879	17,836	15,963	15,669	16,378	22,157	8,924	19,647	18,448

Note: Regional aggregates for aid include data for economies not specified elsewhere. Thus, the sum of countries may not add up to the regional totals.

12-2. Net aid from DAC donors, nominal

	Millions of U.S. dollars (current prices)											Annual average		
	1980	1993	1994	1995	1996	1997	1998	1999	2000	2001	2002	75-84	85-94	95-MR
SUB-SAHARAN AFRICA	4,642	10,816	11,338	10,707	10,054	9,277	9,133	8,380	8,606	8,260	11,587	3,695	9,778	9,500
excluding South Africa	4,642	10,633	11,124	10,389	9,742	8,862	8,712	7,994	8,252	7,947	11,211	3,695	9,738	9,139
excl. S.Africa & Nigeria	4,625	10,562	11,077	10,316	9,695	8,810	8,678	7,941	8,168	7,840	10,996	3,668	9,627	9,055
Angola	36	150	223	242	294	227	214	252	189	179	286	30	136	236
Benin	36	148	142	177	165	148	144	119	191	144	140	36	119	154
Botswana	83	80	57	54	68	56	73	41	24	24	37	63	97	47
Burkina Faso	151	255	265	252	269	218	227	232	228	221	230	112	221	235
Burundi	60	126	108	108	68	38	44	52	41	55	85	50	109	61
Cameroon	171	528	397	346	280	330	303	254	213	275	436	130	324	305
Cape Verde	39	81	82	77	77	68	85	89	70	49	43	28	70	70
Central African Republic	75	117	94	122	121	61	57	59	53	48	40	52	98	70
Chad	20	146	104	127	122	96	75	64	53	73	67	44	131	85
Comoros	13	29	18	22	22	15	19	13	11	10	11	11	27	15
Congo, Dem. Rep. of	317	99	97	118	106	105	80	87	103	143	351	221	302	137
Congo, Rep. of	55	116	253	105	395	260	60	121	23	30	41	49	123	129
Côte d'Ivoire	152	708	820	727	449	233	490	366	250	159	831	105	398	438
Djibouti	32	94	94	80	71	62	62	55	42	28	37	35	76	55
Equatorial Guinea	1	28	17	22	23	18	18	15	18	13	14	4	27	18
Eritrea	..	48	96	95	128	81	98	80	112	151	121	..	72	108
Ethiopia	91	417	567	526	448	374	365	325	379	367	489	86	448	409
Gabon	49	97	161	136	113	30	37	34	12	8	49	42	99	53
Gambia, The	17	50	38	25	17	17	13	15	15	13	18	16	50	16
Ghana	107	312	332	359	349	292	375	356	376	396	406	75	263	363
Guinea	33	185	186	220	135	126	148	111	93	120	126	20	154	135
Guinea-Bissau	34	56	124	77	125	59	65	32	42	30	26	29	60	57
Kenya	277	426	401	459	346	301	276	254	293	270	288	244	508	311
Lesotho	64	74	45	62	49	45	33	26	22	29	30	44	66	37
Liberia	60	25	35	31	112	31	31	45	24	16	27	53	46	40
Madagascar	91	228	190	195	230	549	334	192	139	138	126	77	202	238
Malawi	76	159	251	221	264	174	204	228	269	196	225	63	171	223
Mali	131	221	243	285	298	257	236	237	300	209	257	104	253	260
Mauritania	54	196	128	126	99	97	64	89	82	81	147	45	124	98
Mauritius	25	27	8	11	1	3	20	5	12	8	4	23	42	8
Mozambique	115	813	733	698	552	622	713	593	624	720	1,661	104	645	773
Namibia	..	123	113	148	136	123	129	117	97	77	85	0	55	114
Niger	105	254	261	194	163	181	145	120	106	114	114	97	234	142
Nigeria	17	71	47	73	47	52	34	53	84	108	215	27	111	83
Rwanda	97	201	487	339	252	179	209	181	175	149	199	83	193	210
São Tomé and Principe	1	28	26	62	29	21	18	19	18	22	19	2	18	26
Senegal	182	364	475	399	392	292	289	416	288	224	243	157	408	318
Seychelles	18	7	7	11	8	6	17	5	3	8	4	14	16	8
Sierra Leone	57	106	54	60	67	41	53	60	116	167	225	28	59	99
Somalia	139	688	438	119	40	46	42	76	56	88	102	93	350	71
South Africa	..	183	214	319	312	415	421	386	354	313	375	..	199	362
Sudan	272	164	174	131	118	86	150	159	90	108	232	211	381	134
Swaziland	33	33	27	38	21	16	17	15	3	4	7	22	26	15
Tanzania	524	650	570	587	605	569	769	613	779	944	903	383	673	721
Togo	52	77	63	118	97	76	66	47	52	28	39	46	102	65
Uganda	42	348	344	423	370	439	384	357	578	386	466	31	203	425
Zambia	234	511	434	439	354	367	257	340	486	274	360	156	427	360
Zimbabwe	112	310	280	348	281	222	216	219	193	149	178	86	291	226
NORTH AFRICA	1,663	2,510	2,949	2,397	2,650	1,990	1,994	1,837	1,680	1,663	1,643	1,437	3,005	1,982
Algeria	118	142	248	275	267	193	148	86	66	25	123	116	153	148
Egypt, Arab Rep.	1,187	1,816	2,302	1,691	1,934	1,497	1,472	1,298	1,139	1,090	1,124	959	2,209	1,406
Libya	10	2	2	3	2	2	4	3	12	4	4	4	4	4
Morocco	188	422	318	347	391	215	251	333	293	342	219	189	445	299
Tunisia	158	125	71	56	44	70	102	102	150	184	145	160	186	107
ALL AFRICA	6,305	13,327	14,287	13,104	12,704	11,267	11,127	10,217	10,286	9,924	13,230	5,132	12,783	11,483

Note: Regional aggregates for aid include data for economies not specified elsewhere. Thus, the sum of countries may not add up to the regional totals.

12-3. Net aid from non-DAC bilateral donors, nominal

	Millions of U.S. dollars (current prices)											Annual average		
	1980	1993	1994	1995	1996	1997	1998	1999	2000	2001	2002	75-84	85-94	95-MR
SUB-SAHARAN AFRICA	688	127	122	138	148	185	134	144	210	169	376	628	299	188
excluding South Africa	688	127	121	135	142	185	133	142	208	168	375	628	299	186
excl. S.Africa & Nigeria	688	116	121	135	141	184	133	140	208	166	373	628	296	185
Angola	1	3	0	0	0	0	0	0	6	1	1	1	2	1
Benin	2	0	4	7	6	0	1	2	1	1	2	1	2	3
Botswana	..	7	1	0	2	3	3	1	1	1	2	8	2	2
Burkina Faso	0	1	1	8	6	3	6	9	4	14	45	2	5	12
Burundi	4	2	3	3	1	0	1	0	0	0	0	4	4	1
Cameroon	23	1	0	2	2	2	2	3	3	3	1	9	2	2
Cape Verde	2	1	1	0	3	0	0	0	0	0	1	1	1	1
Central African Republic	2	3	2	3	5	0	0	..	0	0	0	1	3	1
Chad	..	3	1	1	3	5	5	7	1	0	2	4	1	3
Comoros	16	0	0	0	0	0	0	..	0	2	5	7	1	1
Congo, Dem. Rep. of	5	0	0	0	3	9	2	0	0	0	0	5	16	2
Congo, Rep. of	15	0	0	0	0	..	0	0	0	0	0	11	0	0
Côte d'Ivoire	..	0	1	1	0	1	1	2	1	0	0	0	0	1
Djibouti	33	11	12	3	5	5	2	1	10	0	2	24	18	3
Equatorial Guinea	..	..	..	0	0	0	0	..	0	1	0	1	1	0
Eritrea	..	1	12	5	3	17	32	19	9	3	13	..	6	12
Ethiopia	..	1	0	1	1	7	13	15	15	28	34	14	10	14
Gabon	..	0	0	1	2	3	1	0	0	0	0	5	3	1
Gambia, The	7	2	2	1	2	2	1	1	2	2	3	5	1	2
Ghana	25	2	4	6	1	13	3	4	2	3	5	11	5	5
Guinea	0	4	2	6	20	34	24	18	3	1	6	11	6	14
Guinea-Bissau	1	4	3	3	4	0	0	..	0	0	0	3	4	1
Kenya	..	3	3	5	3	2	1	3	5	5	10	7	5	4
Lesotho	0	3	1	0	4	7	1	1	1	1	1	1	1	2
Liberia	9	1	1	1	2	1	0	0	..	0	0	5	1	1
Madagascar	48	0	0	0	0	0	0	0	1	1	1	18	1	1
Malawi	..	3	4	3	0	1	1	5	6	11	10	0	4	5
Mali	33	4	11	14	8	6	5	0	1	13	54	17	12	13
Mauritania	86	6	10	16	11	13	7	5	0	1	2	83	19	7
Mauritius	..	0	1	1	1	10	1	0	1	7	1	2	2	3
Mozambique	20	4	3	2	3	1	2	2	0	4	2	5	3	2
Namibia	..	0	1	0	0	1	1	1	1	1	2	..	1	1
Niger	2	2	5	1	1	10	1	1	0	1	3	17	4	2
Nigeria	..	11	0	0	1	0	1	3	0	1	2	0	3	1
Rwanda	1	2	3	0	1	1	0	0	0	0	0	2	5	0
São Tomé and Principe	..	0	0	0	0	0	0	..	..	0	0	..	0	0
Senegal	2	14	2	13	11	9	1	4	5	1	11	21	19	7
Seychelles	..	1	0	0	3	5	1	2	7	0	0	1	1	2
Sierra Leone	4	0	0	1	4	1	3	0	0	2	3	3	2	2
Somalia	128	14	0	0	0	1	0	0	0	14	44	81	16	8
South Africa	..	..	1	3	6	0	1	2	2	1	1	..	1	2
Sudan	158	3	3	4	1	0	1	26	99	10	51	183	79	24
Swaziland	..	3	2	3	3	2	4	0	0	3	4	..	2	2
Tanzania	27	0	6	5	2	3	3	1	3	5	4	12	3	3
Togo	0	0	0	0	2	1	1	3	1	4	3	2	3	2
Uganda	1	1	13	12	9	3	0	1	6	2	5	7	16	5
Zambia	23	0	0	0	0	0	1	0	0	1	2	22	0	1
Zimbabwe	5	1	3	3	3	3	1	0	1	4	0	10	3	2
NORTH AFRICA	745	407	141	171	125	164	294	144	132	151	353	818	566	192
Algeria	49	1	2	12	7	12	19	31	71	54	143	12	16	44
Egypt, Arab Rep.	2	380	95	117	54	100	214	73	54	61	31	471	376	88
Libya	..	0	0	0	0	0	0	0	0	1	1	..	0	0
Morocco	645	18	29	20	26	32	30	29	4	34	135	300	149	39
Tunisia	49	9	15	22	38	20	31	11	1	1	43	35	25	21
ALL AFRICA	1,433	534	263	309	273	349	428	289	342	320	729	1,446	865	380

Note: Regional aggregates for aid include data for economies not specified elsewhere. Thus, sum of countries may not add up to the regional totals.

12-4. Net aid from multilateral donors, nominal

	Millions of U.S. dollars (current prices)											Annual average		
	1980	1993	1994	1995	1996	1997	1998	1999	2000	2001	2002	75-84	85-94	95-MR
SUB-SAHARAN AFRICA	2,430	6,697	8,052	8,125	6,394	5,564	5,539	4,734	4,715	5,640	7,424	1,916	5,668	6,017
excluding South Africa	2,430	6,605	7,972	8,058	6,347	5,483	5,446	4,580	4,583	5,526	7,143	1,916	5,651	5,896
excl. S.Africa & Nigeria	2,412	6,397	7,829	7,918	6,204	5,335	5,277	4,484	4,483	5,447	7,043	1,899	5,576	5,774
Angola	16	137	226	176	179	128	121	136	112	110	136	20	95	137
Benin	53	140	111	96	118	73	63	93	49	128	78	34	94	87
Botswana	23	43	28	35	8	69	36	21	8	4	3	17	30	23
Burkina Faso	61	212	168	231	144	147	167	157	104	158	198	52	115	163
Burundi	54	94	207	182	44	18	24	22	52	83	87	42	118	64
Cameroon	71	16	334	97	134	171	198	184	169	132	195	51	102	160
Cape Verde	23	36	40	40	36	43	45	48	25	29	50	13	31	40
Central African Republic	34	54	72	43	45	30	63	59	22	19	20	27	76	38
Chad	15	76	109	109	171	126	88	116	77	114	164	33	100	121
Comoros	13	20	21	20	17	12	16	8	8	16	17	12	21	14
Congo, Dem. Rep. of	106	79	148	78	57	44	43	45	81	119	455	93	166	115
Congo, Rep. of	22	7	109	20	35	10	6	20	10	46	378	23	23	66
Côte d'Ivoire	58	55	773	486	515	213	477	81	101	11	237	31	181	265
Djibouti	9	29	23	22	21	19	17	19	20	30	39	9	21	23
Equatorial Guinea	8	25	13	12	8	6	4	6	3	1	7	4	19	6
Eritrea	..	18	49	49	29	26	38	50	55	127	97	..	34	59
Ethiopia	120	671	504	357	369	198	282	303	298	721	784	111	457	414
Gabon	7	4	20	9	15	11	9	13	23	17	22	5	8	15
Gambia, The	31	37	34	23	22	23	25	19	32	38	40	17	41	28
Ghana	59	309	220	298	303	189	325	250	222	254	241	55	285	260
Guinea	57	228	174	191	143	222	187	109	58	160	118	36	143	148
Guinea-Bissau	24	34	48	39	52	66	31	20	39	29	34	18	44	39
Kenya	120	487	280	270	248	145	138	53	214	188	95	71	281	169
Lesotho	31	68	70	52	51	40	30	7	16	28	48	27	54	34
Liberia	29	97	28	91	58	44	41	49	44	24	26	21	51	47
Madagascar	91	135	99	106	127	284	148	166	185	229	248	59	134	187
Malawi	68	336	216	211	228	171	230	214	171	198	142	52	224	196
Mali	103	146	209	270	201	178	117	117	61	132	162	73	154	155
Mauritania	36	135	150	120	185	154	108	125	129	188	210	49	95	152
Mauritius	8	1	7	14	22	30	23	37	7	6	20	12	8	20
Mozambique	34	363	464	364	333	328	330	213	253	208	394	34	256	303
Namibia	..	31	25	44	51	42	51	60	55	31	48	..	31	48
Niger	64	88	111	80	91	141	146	66	105	142	181	50	114	119
Nigeria	18	208	143	140	143	149	170	96	100	79	101	17	75	122
Rwanda	57	152	226	363	213	50	141	193	146	150	157	46	121	177
São Tomé and Principe	3	18	24	23	19	12	10	8	17	16	7	5	19	14
Senegal	79	122	164	254	177	122	211	115	140	189	195	78	184	175
Seychelles	3	12	6	2	8	6	6	6	8	5	4	2	6	6
Sierra Leone	30	102	222	146	113	76	51	13	67	176	125	21	59	96
Somalia	166	191	99	70	49	34	38	39	47	47	47	109	143	46
South Africa	..	92	80	67	46	81	92	153	132	114	281	..	86	121
Sudan	192	287	235	108	101	52	59	58	36	68	68	147	318	69
Swaziland	17	19	28	18	10	10	14	14	10	22	14	12	17	14
Tanzania	128	300	389	286	274	373	228	376	246	333	333	118	274	306
Togo	39	19	62	74	62	51	61	21	16	12	9	34	68	38
Uganda	70	261	394	400	297	371	263	232	236	405	167	49	275	296
Zambia	62	361	284	1,594	255	243	93	283	309	74	279	37	178	391
Zimbabwe	47	189	283	147	93	116	46	25	14	19	22	28	97	60
NORTH AFRICA	311	696	705	462	648	808	857	762	419	552	802	459	387	664
Algeria	17	82	44	34	35	45	253	21	64	107	95	15	33	82
Egypt, Arab Rep.	196	192	285	208	212	389	268	211	136	105	131	363	158	207
Libya	7	2	2	3	6	5	3	4	3	5	5	6	6	4
Morocco	66	273	285	128	233	217	249	316	130	142	283	48	111	212
Tunisia	25	109	49	41	121	144	78	161	72	193	288	28	69	137
ALL AFRICA	2,741	7,393	8,757	8,587	7,042	6,372	6,396	5,496	5,133	6,192	8,226	2,374	6,056	6,680

Note: Regional aggregates for aid include data for economies not specified elsewhere. Thus, the sum of countries may not add up to the regional totals.

12-5. Net aid from all donors, real

	Millions of U.S. dollars (constant 2001 prices)											Average annual percentage growth		
	1980	*1993*	*1994*	*1995*	*1996*	*1997*	*1998*	*1999*	*2000*	*2001*	*2002*	*75-84*	*85-94*	*95-MR*
SUB-SAHARAN AFRICA	11,858	16,434	17,571	15,293	13,599	13,427	13,455	12,107	13,126	14,012	18,401	7.3	1.4	-0.4
excluding South Africa	11,858	16,161	17,286	14,948	13,284	12,973	12,984	11,612	12,645	13,583	17,785	7.3	1.2	-0.6
excl. S.Africa & Nigeria	11,805	15,889	17,111	14,776	13,122	12,789	12,795	11,472	12,464	13,398	17,482	7.6	1.1	-0.7
Angola	75	273	415	348	387	317	306	357	300	289	402	40.6	9.2	-1.8
Benin	137	261	225	217	234	197	185	191	235	274	209	2.7	6.1	0.6
Botswana	160	124	80	76	62	107	98	55	30	29	36	5.5	-6.2	-12.8
Burkina Faso	316	424	378	383	331	323	354	358	329	392	448	4.2	1.9	1.4
Burundi	174	200	277	234	90	50	61	70	91	137	163	10.3	0.0	-5.5
Cameroon	384	474	629	334	319	430	445	389	371	404	600	2.1	9.2	1.0
Cape Verde	97	108	108	92	94	99	116	123	92	77	88	14.4	-1.6	-1.9
Central African Republic	153	153	146	128	134	79	105	104	72	67	58	6.9	-3.5	-10.5
Chad	55	205	185	184	235	199	147	169	128	187	221	-4.1	-1.9	-1.0
Comoros	65	44	34	32	31	23	31	19	18	27	31	4.0	-7.0	-3.4
Congo, Dem. Rep. of	626	163	216	149	130	138	112	120	180	263	766	2.8	-11.1	12.9
Congo, Rep. of	129	106	309	94	333	224	56	126	33	75	403	3.3	1.2	-7.7
Côte d'Ivoire	288	661	1,379	933	778	392	877	399	343	170	1,012	0.0	18.7	-12.4
Djibouti	109	121	110	80	76	74	72	66	68	58	75	6.6	-3.8	-4.7
Equatorial Guinea	15	48	26	26	24	22	20	18	21	13	19	18.3	3.3	-6.4
Eritrea	..	65	144	121	132	112	156	137	174	281	220	..	..	8.6
Ethiopia	326	1,040	980	738	684	524	600	595	680	1,116	1,252	5.5	2.5	4.0
Gabon	74	87	150	109	95	33	38	42	12	9	68	3.0	-1.0	-21.7
Gambia, The	88	81	63	39	32	36	35	31	48	54	59	14.2	-3.4	2.1
Ghana	305	588	494	531	548	452	665	561	578	653	621	6.7	4.5	3.2
Guinea	142	374	320	329	247	342	329	215	149	280	240	16.7	6.5	-5.1
Guinea-Bissau	85	88	160	94	148	112	88	47	80	59	56	17.5	1.5	-12.0
Kenya	619	851	605	587	496	403	382	285	494	463	376	10.0	1.2	-4.8
Lesotho	148	136	106	95	87	82	56	28	36	56	73	11.5	-2.5	-9.3
Liberia	173	118	61	104	140	70	66	91	67	39	50	18.0	-5.6	-7.9
Madagascar	362	330	253	239	293	726	431	325	313	366	356	8.5	-0.7	3.4
Malawi	232	471	430	373	432	314	403	409	434	404	360	5.7	7.4	-0.3
Mali	413	338	392	430	395	383	315	324	354	354	450	4.8	-4.6	-0.7
Mauritania	277	289	229	176	216	209	146	194	205	268	334	0.4	-3.6	4.4
Mauritius	48	22	12	19	16	38	36	37	20	22	22	0.8	-11.1	5.6
Mozambique	249	1,114	1,096	877	740	859	947	735	864	933	1,937	42.0	9.9	4.5
Namibia	..	143	123	148	151	147	160	160	149	110	127	..	35.9	-1.1
Niger	253	311	325	220	201	293	260	167	205	257	285	-0.8	-2.3	-0.9
Nigeria	53	273	175	172	162	184	189	141	180	185	303	-11.6	17.6	4.0
Rwanda	231	328	690	602	385	203	319	344	315	299	338	5.9	4.8	-7.7
São Tomé and Principe	6	43	44	68	39	29	25	25	35	38	24	15.7	11.7	-7.3
Senegal	392	456	550	517	473	372	443	476	412	413	430	7.2	-2.0	-2.8
Seychelles	32	18	12	10	15	15	22	12	18	14	7	-0.8	-8.6	-1.4
Sierra Leone	154	195	249	170	158	109	99	70	178	345	336	15.4	5.6	5.3
Somalia	709	948	568	169	72	72	73	106	103	150	183	10.4	-1.5	-6.1
South Africa	..	273	285	345	315	454	471	495	481	428	616	..	..	8.1
Sudan	993	430	380	197	184	126	193	232	220	185	336	10.7	-12.7	0.5
Swaziland	82	56	53	50	28	26	34	26	12	29	24	1.1	2.0	-10.3
Tanzania	1,016	888	868	701	729	842	910	902	978	1,271	1,164	8.6	0.4	6.2
Togo	135	87	110	149	126	111	115	64	68	44	48	4.6	-5.3	-13.5
Uganda	182	586	691	691	570	734	597	543	802	793	603	20.2	10.5	0.4
Zambia	492	812	653	1,663	514	563	321	569	776	349	612	10.4	5.4	-6.6
Zimbabwe	259	466	513	404	306	302	241	224	168	164	193	63.1	3.1	-12.7
NORTH AFRICA	4,542	3,480	3,436	2,453	2,809	2,607	2,828	2,497	2,184	2,367	2,678	-5.2	1.5	-2.7
Algeria	260	202	251	221	231	211	356	122	197	185	341	-5.8	-1.9	-0.3
Egypt, Arab Rep.	2,511	2,399	2,506	1,749	1,944	1,822	1,866	1,505	1,322	1,257	1,251	-8.0	2.8	-7.6
Libya	26	3	4	5	7	6	6	7	15	10	10	-9.0	-7.5	13.8
Morocco	1,408	640	548	374	498	391	456	591	403	519	600	7.6	0.4	2.2
Tunisia	332	198	85	50	88	160	124	217	210	378	449	-3.9	-7.0	28.0
ALL AFRICA	16,400	19,914	21,007	17,746	16,408	16,034	16,282	14,604	15,309	16,378	21,078	3.1	1.5	-0.8

Note: Regional aggregates for aid include data for economies not specified elsewhere. Thus, the sum of countries may not add up to the regional totals.

12-6. Net aid from DAC donors, real

| | Millions of U.S. dollars (constant 2001 prices) | | | | | | | | | | | Average annual percentage growth | | |
	1980	1993	1994	1995	1996	1997	1998	1999	2000	2001	2002	75-84	85-94	95-MR
SUB-SAHARAN AFRICA	6,776	10,097	10,318	8,723	8,260	8,371	8,346	7,702	8,427	8,260	10,987	7.9	1.3	0.1
excluding South Africa	6,776	9,908	10,104	8,432	7,987	7,986	7,955	7,344	8,079	7,947	10,632	7.9	1.2	-0.1
excl. S.Africa & Nigeria	6,752	9,836	10,057	8,373	7,947	7,938	7,926	7,295	7,995	7,840	10,424	8.3	1.1	-0.2
Angola	48	143	212	208	242	205	199	234	186	179	274	42.9	6.0	0.3
Benin	48	130	122	134	132	132	130	108	189	144	133	2.8	6.7	1.8
Botswana	123	78	54	49	57	52	70	38	22	24	35	3.8	-5.7	-9.5
Burkina Faso	216	227	227	192	207	190	197	207	224	221	217	7.2	0.9	0.8
Burundi	81	114	94	89	54	34	39	50	40	55	80	11.6	-1.0	-3.8
Cameroon	232	459	331	256	210	277	264	224	209	275	414	5.1	7.1	1.5
Cape Verde	55	74	72	60	62	61	75	79	69	49	41	28.1	-0.5	-3.9
Central African Republic	95	100	80	90	93	53	50	52	50	48	38	10.0	-3.3	-9.7
Chad	30	130	87	96	90	81	63	56	53	73	63	-2.9	-1.6	-5.8
Comoros	17	25	15	16	16	13	16	11	11	10	10	1.0	-5.7	-6.4
Congo, Dem. Rep. of	446	88	82	86	81	90	70	78	101	143	330	2.0	-14.0	13.1
Congo, Rep. of	70	99	210	79	304	215	50	107	23	30	39	4.0	2.4	-22.8
Côte d'Ivoire	193	610	683	539	348	200	434	323	245	159	784	3.6	14.9	-5.4
Djibouti	42	84	79	59	54	53	55	48	40	28	35	0.6	-0.2	-9.7
Equatorial Guinea	2	24	14	17	18	16	16	13	18	13	13	124.0	4.6	-2.3
Eritrea	..	47	89	78	106	74	92	74	112	151	115	..	..	5.4
Ethiopia	130	409	529	450	374	340	334	306	376	367	469	-0.3	-0.1	-2.0
Gabon	63	83	133	102	84	26	32	30	11	8	47	4.7	0.4	-23.0
Gambia, The	26	49	35	22	15	16	12	12	14	13	17	14.1	-4.5	-7.6
Ghana	167	297	299	296	297	270	361	328	361	396	385	2.7	8.9	4.2
Guinea	49	164	166	172	112	112	137	101	90	120	122	17.7	7.1	-4.6
Guinea-Bissau	44	52	114	60	101	54	60	29	42	30	24	41.3	4.7	-16.3
Kenya	424	396	356	366	287	272	256	234	282	270	276	8.9	-3.0	-3.4
Lesotho	98	70	43	54	42	40	30	23	22	29	28	12.4	-5.5	-8.5
Liberia	112	26	36	29	89	30	30	46	24	16	26	23.4	-14.8	-8.6
Madagascar	135	204	163	154	188	472	298	174	135	138	120	13.2	0.2	-5.2
Malawi	122	152	232	202	242	161	194	212	262	196	215	-1.7	7.1	0.0
Mali	191	206	215	225	235	230	214	217	296	209	244	7.1	-5.7	1.1
Mauritania	79	169	105	93	77	85	58	79	78	81	138	12.2	-1.8	1.1
Mauritius	35	23	6	9	0	3	18	5	12	8	3	3.8	-11.7	8.9
Mozambique	161	771	677	583	459	566	648	544	618	720	1,560	44.9	8.4	7.8
Namibia	..	114	100	113	110	110	114	105	94	77	80	..	40.7	-3.9
Niger	147	228	222	156	126	157	126	107	103	114	110	0.4	-0.6	-7.3
Nigeria	24	72	47	59	41	49	29	49	84	108	208	-16.8	11.1	16.6
Rwanda	135	184	485	307	207	160	189	168	173	149	188	6.3	5.7	-9.9
São Tomé and Principe	2	26	23	50	23	19	16	17	18	22	18	37.6	19.5	-6.6
Senegal	259	329	403	304	317	255	253	369	280	224	233	10.0	-0.2	-4.8
Seychelles	27	6	7	9	6	5	15	4	3	8	4	-2.6	-11.4	-6.9
Sierra Leone	98	100	49	52	60	40	50	58	113	167	213	17.0	3.0	20.1
Somalia	230	756	479	113	32	42	38	72	56	88	96	29.8	2.3	-8.8
South Africa	..	189	214	290	273	384	391	358	348	313	354	..	..	4.5
Sudan	422	157	167	107	100	79	139	155	89	108	222	23.8	-15.6	2.7
Swaziland	54	36	26	34	18	16	18	14	2	4	7	-0.1	-0.1	-23.8
Tanzania	764	607	513	468	501	505	697	558	742	944	848	7.3	-2.0	8.7
Togo	72	68	54	89	75	66	58	42	50	28	37	4.5	-3.2	-9.8
Uganda	65	340	324	361	315	396	355	332	569	386	439	27.2	16.7	4.1
Zambia	355	476	398	369	300	344	237	311	477	274	345	7.8	3.2	-1.1
Zimbabwe	174	290	263	290	234	200	201	201	182	149	171	57.3	-0.9	-6.8
NORTH AFRICA	2,825	2,470	2,713	2,008	2,256	1,795	1,876	1,713	1,652	1,663	1,592	8.9	0.0	-5.5
Algeria	154	125	211	204	198	161	124	74	65	25	114	-3.6	-2.2	-17.8
Egypt, Arab Rep.	2,189	1,861	2,167	1,489	1,726	1,390	1,432	1,250	1,137	1,090	1,098	17.8	0.9	-7.4
Libya	15	2	1	2	1	1	3	3	12	4	4	-11.3	-13.4	19.7
Morocco	252	374	272	259	295	176	216	287	278	342	208	2.8	-1.5	0.2
Tunisia	211	106	55	36	26	55	86	86	139	184	141	-2.4	-8.9	22.9
ALL AFRICA	9,601	12,567	13,031	10,731	10,516	10,166	10,222	9,415	10,079	9,924	12,579	8.1	1.1	-0.9

Note: Regional aggregates for aid include data for economies not specified elsewhere. Thus, the sum of countries may not add up to the regional totals.

12-7. Net aid from non-DAC bilateral donors, real

	Millions of U.S. dollars (constant 2001 prices)										Average annual percentage growth		
	1980	1993	1994	1995	1996	1997	1998	1999	2000	2001	2002	75-84	85-94	95-MR
SUB-SAHARAN AFRICA	1,117	115	110	110	124	167	126	133	202	169	361	6.2	-23.4	11.9
excluding South Africa	1,117	115	110	108	119	166	125	131	200	168	361	6.2	-23.4	12.2
excl. S.Africa & Nigeria	1,117	106	110	108	119	166	124	129	200	166	359	6.2	-23.7	12.1
Angola	1	3	0	0	0	0	0	0	5	1	1	..	-13.5	50.1
Benin	3	0	3	6	5	0	1	1	1	1	2	-13.7	-12.5	-6.0
Botswana	..	7	1	0	1	3	2	1	1	1	2	..	-8.7	7.9
Burkina Faso	0	1	1	6	5	3	6	9	4	14	43	0.3	-22.4	32.6
Burundi	6	2	3	2	1	0	1	0	0	0	0	28.4	-23.8	-42.4
Cameroon	37	1	0	1	1	2	2	3	3	3	0	-9.0	-25.1	12.8
Cape Verde	3	0	0	0	2	0	0	0	0	0	1	-2.7	-21.1	11.6
Central African Republic	3	2	2	3	4	0	0	..	0	0	0	-16.7	7.7	-44.6
Chad	..	3	1	1	3	4	5	6	1	0	2	-27.6	27.1	-1.3
Comoros	27	0	0	0	0	0	0	..	0	2	5	7.7	-35.2	66.7
Congo, Dem. Rep. of	8	0	0	0	2	8	2	0	0	0	0	-64.4	18.4	-12.5
Congo, Rep. of	24	0	0	0	0	..	0	0	0	0	0	11.8	-39.9	13.8
Côte d'Ivoire	..	0	0	0	0	0	1	2	1	0	0	..	20.0	3.1
Djibouti	53	10	11	3	4	4	2	1	9	0	2	-12.3	-19.8	-22.5
Equatorial Guinea	..	..	..	0	0	0	0	..	0	1	0	..	68.2	48.6
Eritrea	..	1	11	4	3	15	30	17	9	3	12	..	..	2.8
Ethiopia	..	1	0	0	0	6	12	14	15	28	33	6.8	-17.2	89.9
Gabon	..	0	0	1	2	2	1	0	0	0	0	-21.5	-27.7	-30.8
Gambia, The	12	2	2	1	1	1	0	1	2	2	3	-2.7	11.4	7.0
Ghana	41	1	4	5	1	11	2	4	2	3	5	50.0	-14.6	1.4
Guinea	0	4	2	5	17	31	22	16	2	1	6	0.3	-22.2	-7.2
Guinea-Bissau	2	4	3	3	4	0	0	..	0	0	0	-6.4	-11.8	-50.1
Kenya	..	3	3	4	2	1	1	3	5	5	10	174.2	-21.8	15.7
Lesotho	0	2	1	0	3	6	1	1	1	1	1	83.9	-8.6	17.4
Liberia	15	1	1	1	2	1	0	0	..	0	0	-69.5	28.9	-52.5
Madagascar	78	0	0	0	0	0	0	0	1	1	1	20.2	-40.3	43.0
Malawi	..	3	4	2	0	1	1	4	6	11	9	..	70.5	33.7
Mali	53	4	10	11	7	5	5	0	1	13	52	3.7	-17.5	0.7
Mauritania	140	5	9	13	10	12	6	5	0	1	2	-5.8	-27.2	-32.4
Mauritius	..	0	1	1	1	9	1	0	1	7	1	..	-23.4	-3.0
Mozambique	33	3	2	2	2	1	2	1	0	4	2	52.2	-17.5	-5.2
Namibia	..	0	1	0	0	1	1	1	1	1	2	..	..	30.1
Niger	3	2	5	1	1	9	1	1	0	1	3	16.4	-19.2	-13.4
Nigeria	..	9	0	0	0	0	1	3	0	1	2	..	25.3	35.4
Rwanda	2	2	3	0	1	0	0	0	0	0	0	-12.6	-20.7	-27.4
São Tomé and Principe	..	0	0	0	0	0	0	..	..	0	0			-6.3
Senegal	3	14	1	10	9	9	1	4	5	1	10	18.2	-26.9	-5.3
Seychelles	..	1	0	0	3	4	1	2	6	0	0	..	-22.8	-15.6
Sierra Leone	7	0	0	1	4	1	2	0	0	2	3	3.7	-40.1	10.2
Somalia	208	12	0	0	0	1	0	0	0	14	43	-12.2	-25.2	90.0
South Africa	..	..	1	2	5	0	1	2	2	1	1	..	..	-2.4
Sudan	257	2	2	3	0	0	1	24	96	10	49	0.8	-41.6	69.4
Swaziland	..	3	2	2	2	1	4	0	0	3	4	..	15.6	-7.1
Tanzania	45	0	6	4	2	2	3	1	3	5	3	46.0	-19.6	-2.5
Togo	0	0	0	0	2	1	1	3	1	4	3	-7.3	-31.6	39.6
Uganda	2	1	11	9	7	3	0	1	5	2	5	-14.5	24.3	-15.2
Zambia	37	0	0	0	0	0	1	0	0	1	2	19.2	..	39.9
Zimbabwe	8	1	2	3	2	2	0	0	1	4	0	15.7	-3.2	-20.5
NORTH AFRICA	1,210	385	127	139	106	149	275	133	126	151	340	-24.8	3.0	7.6
Algeria	79	1	2	10	6	11	18	29	69	54	138	-28.0	-3.0	58.9
Egypt, Arab Rep.	3	359	86	95	46	91	201	68	52	61	29	-45.8	25.5	-9.0
Libya	..	0	0	0	0	0	0	0	0	1	1	..	..	35.9
Morocco	1,048	17	26	16	22	29	28	27	4	34	130	16.4	-15.4	9.1
Tunisia	80	8	13	18	32	18	28	10	0	1	41	-9.1	-6.8	-24.0
ALL AFRICA	2,327	500	237	250	230	316	401	266	329	320	701	-10.3	-12.1	9.8

Note: Regional aggregates for aid include data for economies not specified elsewhere. Thus, the sum of countries may not add up to the regional totals.

12-8. Net aid from multilateral donors, real

	Millions of U.S. dollars (constant 2001 prices)											Average annual percentage growth		
	1980	1993	1994	1995	1996	1997	1998	1999	2000	2001	2002	75-84	85-94	95-MR
SUB-SAHARAN AFRICA	3,966	6,265	7,213	6,536	5,278	4,952	5,033	4,288	4,578	5,640	7,079	6.8	3.8	-1.6
excluding South Africa	3,966	6,181	7,143	6,483	5,241	4,882	4,954	4,153	4,447	5,526	6,818	6.8	3.7	-1.9
excl. S.Africa & Nigeria	3,936	5,990	7,015	6,370	5,119	4,747	4,794	4,064	4,351	5,447	6,721	6.9	3.5	-1.9
Angola	26	127	202	140	145	112	107	123	109	110	129	42.8	14.2	-4.9
Benin	86	131	100	78	98	64	56	85	47	128	74	2.3	5.5	-1.4
Botswana	37	40	25	28	7	59	31	18	8	4	3	6.6	-6.5	-23.8
Burkina Faso	100	197	150	185	119	130	151	142	102	158	188	-0.2	4.8	0.4
Burundi	88	88	186	147	37	17	22	20	50	83	83	8.1	2.7	-6.7
Cameroon	116	15	298	76	110	154	183	168	164	132	186	-4.6	11.6	1.1
Cape Verde	38	33	35	32	30	38	41	44	24	29	48	3.3	-2.9	0.9
Central African Republic	55	50	64	34	37	26	55	53	22	19	19	2.9	-4.0	-11.0
Chad	25	72	97	87	142	113	80	107	74	114	156	-3.0	-2.7	2.3
Comoros	22	18	19	16	14	11	14	7	8	16	16	22.5	-6.4	-3.7
Congo, Dem. Rep. of	172	75	134	62	46	40	39	41	79	119	436	4.8	-7.5	13.8
Congo, Rep. of	36	6	99	16	29	9	6	19	10	46	364	-3.0	-2.4	12.4
Côte d'Ivoire	95	51	695	393	430	191	443	74	98	11	228	-11.6	32.0	-27.3
Djibouti	14	28	21	18	18	17	15	17	19	30	37	35.1	-5.4	7.0
Equatorial Guinea	13	24	12	10	6	6	3	5	3	1	6	29.1	1.6	-18.4
Eritrea	..	17	45	39	24	23	35	46	53	127	93	..	..	15.7
Ethiopia	197	630	450	287	310	177	254	275	290	721	751	9.0	5.0	8.9
Gabon	11	3	17	7	12	10	7	12	23	17	21	4.0	-8.6	8.4
Gambia, The	51	35	30	19	18	21	22	17	31	38	39	14.1	-1.3	7.0
Ghana	97	290	198	240	251	170	302	229	215	254	231	13.1	0.4	1.3
Guinea	93	214	156	152	117	199	171	98	56	160	112	29.9	9.5	-5.4
Guinea-Bissau	39	32	43	31	43	58	28	18	38	29	32	19.5	-2.0	-4.6
Kenya	195	458	252	217	207	130	126	48	207	188	90	11.8	13.6	-8.8
Lesotho	50	63	62	41	42	35	27	6	16	28	46	9.5	1.4	-9.7
Liberia	47	91	24	74	49	39	36	45	43	24	24	8.0	5.7	-5.8
Madagascar	149	126	89	85	105	254	132	151	179	229	237	3.0	-2.7	13.2
Malawi	111	316	194	169	190	154	209	193	166	198	135	16.8	7.4	-1.7
Mali	169	136	187	216	167	159	106	107	59	132	154	1.5	-0.4	-7.6
Mauritania	59	125	134	96	149	135	94	111	127	188	198	1.1	2.9	5.2
Mauritius	13	1	6	11	17	26	19	32	7	6	18	-6.6	-8.8	1.9
Mozambique	56	340	417	292	279	294	301	192	247	208	375	38.4	14.1	-3.5
Namibia	..	29	22	35	41	36	44	53	54	31	45	..	31.3	6.1
Niger	104	81	99	63	74	126	132	60	102	142	173	-6.2	-5.1	7.9
Nigeria	30	192	128	114	122	136	160	89	96	79	97	-0.7	22.7	-5.1
Rwanda	94	142	203	295	177	43	130	176	143	150	150	6.0	3.8	-3.7
São Tomé and Principe	4	17	21	18	16	11	9	8	17	16	6	12.9	6.8	-8.5
Senegal	129	114	146	203	147	108	189	103	136	189	186	1.3	-0.8	1.0
Seychelles	6	11	5	2	6	5	5	5	8	5	4	25.7	-1.1	4.2
Sierra Leone	49	95	199	117	94	68	46	12	65	176	120	10.8	9.6	-5.3
Somalia	271	179	89	56	40	29	34	35	46	47	45	11.4	-9.6	-4.6
South Africa	..	84	70	52	36	69	79	135	131	114	261	..	..	19.8
Sudan	314	270	212	87	84	46	53	53	35	68	64	8.8	-4.0	-11.2
Swaziland	29	17	25	14	8	9	12	13	10	22	14	4.4	4.2	-0.6
Tanzania	208	281	349	230	230	335	210	343	238	333	319	11.9	6.5	1.4
Togo	63	18	55	60	52	46	57	19	16	12	9	5.0	-7.4	-22.9
Uganda	114	245	355	321	248	334	242	211	228	405	159	24.6	6.1	-5.1
Zambia	101	336	255	1,294	214	219	85	257	298	74	265	19.5	10.5	-11.9
Zimbabwe	77	177	252	117	75	104	41	23	13	19	21	128.5	14.0	-28.7
NORTH AFRICA	506	642	622	362	512	700	734	670	414	552	746	-4.1	9.3	2.6
Algeria	28	76	38	27	28	39	215	19	63	107	89	-11.2	5.5	15.0
Egypt, Arab Rep.	319	179	253	165	172	341	234	187	133	105	123	-2.9	4.1	-8.5
Libya	11	2	2	2	5	5	3	4	3	5	4	-3.9	-3.0	6.7
Morocco	108	250	251	99	181	185	211	277	129	142	262	7.3	26.6	1.7
Tunisia	41	101	43	32	94	123	67	141	71	193	267	-4.0	2.8	22.8
ALL AFRICA	4,472	6,907	7,835	6,898	5,790	5,652	5,767	4,958	4,992	6,192	7,824	4.6	4.1	-1.3

Note: Regional aggregates for aid include data for economies not specified elsewhere. Thus, the sum of countries may not add up to the regional totals.

12-9. Net aid from all donors as share of recipient GDP

					Percentage of GDP								*Annual average*		
	1980	1993	1994	1995	1996	1997	1998	1999	2000	2001	2002	75-84	85-94	95-MR
SUB-SAHARAN AFRICA	4.1	5.8	6.8	5.8	4.9	4.3	4.6	4.1	4.1	4.4	6.0	4.3	8.3	4.8
excluding South Africa	4.1	10.5	13.1	10.9	8.5	7.4	7.5	6.6	6.5	6.6	8.7	4.3	9.4	7.8
excl. S.Africa & Nigeria	6.7	11.9	15.5	12.9	10.3	8.9	9.0	8.1	8.2	8.3	10.7	6.3	11.0	9.6
Angola	..	5.5	11.1	8.3	6.3	4.6	5.2	6.4	3.5	3.0	3.7	..	3.6	5.1
Benin	6.4	13.7	17.1	14.0	13.1	10.2	8.8	8.8	10.6	11.5	8.2	7.0	13.2	10.6
Botswana	10.0	3.1	2.0	1.9	1.6	2.3	2.2	1.2	0.6	0.6	0.7	10.7	5.0	1.4
Burkina Faso	11.0	19.9	22.0	19.9	15.1	14.1	14.3	14.2	12.9	14.1	15.1	11.0	14.3	15.0
Burundi	12.8	23.1	33.7	28.8	12.3	5.9	7.7	10.4	13.7	19.9	23.9	11.9	21.4	15.3
Cameroon	3.9	4.6	9.3	5.6	4.5	5.5	5.7	4.7	4.3	4.8	6.7	3.6	4.0	5.2
Cape Verde	60.3	32.3	29.6	23.9	23.2	22.0	24.1	23.4	17.7	13.5	14.3	47.2	36.5	20.3
Central African Republic	13.9	13.3	19.7	15.0	15.9	9.1	11.5	11.2	7.9	6.9	5.7	12.8	14.5	10.4
Chad	3.4	15.4	18.1	16.4	18.4	15.1	9.6	12.2	9.4	11.2	11.6	8.6	16.4	13.0
Comoros	35.1	17.6	20.9	18.0	17.1	12.9	16.3	9.6	9.2	12.5	13.1	36.9	24.3	13.6
Congo, Dem. Rep. of	3.0	1.7	4.2	3.5	2.9	2.6	2.0	2.8	3.8	5.1	14.1	2.6	5.7	4.6
Congo, Rep. of	5.4	6.4	20.5	5.9	16.9	11.6	3.4	6.0	1.0	2.7	13.9	6.4	6.7	7.7
Côte d'Ivoire	2.1	6.9	19.2	11.0	7.9	3.8	7.6	3.6	3.3	1.6	9.1	2.0	5.7	6.0
Djibouti	..	28.5	26.4	21.1	19.6	17.0	15.7	14.0	12.9	..	..	..	27.0	16.7
Equatorial Guinea	..	34.8	23.7	20.5	11.9	4.9	4.8	2.3	1.6	0.7	0.9	1.1	36.8	6.0
Eritrea	..	14.3	29.6	25.4	23.0	18.0	22.5	20.4	27.5	39.7	35.9	..	21.9	26.5
Ethiopia	..	17.4	19.3	15.3	13.6	9.1	10.1	9.9	10.6	17.1	21.6	5.1	12.2	13.4
Gabon	1.3	2.3	4.3	2.9	2.2	0.7	1.0	1.1	0.2	0.2	1.4	1.6	2.5	1.2
Gambia, The	22.6	23.2	19.2	12.2	9.5	9.5	9.3	7.8	11.7	13.7	17.0	19.6	32.9	11.3
Ghana	4.3	10.5	10.1	10.1	9.4	7.2	9.4	7.9	12.1	12.3	10.6	3.6	9.7	9.9
Guinea	..	12.5	10.5	11.3	7.7	10.1	10.0	6.9	4.9	9.2	7.8	..	11.6	8.5
Guinea-Bissau	53.7	39.9	74.2	46.7	66.8	46.3	46.6	23.4	37.3	29.7	29.2	37.3	53.6	40.7
Kenya	5.5	18.3	9.5	8.1	6.4	4.2	3.7	2.9	4.9	4.1	3.2	5.5	10.7	4.7
Lesotho	21.9	17.7	13.9	12.2	11.0	9.0	6.9	3.4	4.3	7.3	10.7	22.5	22.3	8.1
Liberia	8.8	..	..	..	..	..	..	..	..	..	..	7.4	6.9	..
Madagascar	5.7	10.8	9.7	9.5	8.9	23.5	12.9	9.6	8.3	8.1	8.5	4.6	11.8	11.2
Malawi	11.6	24.0	39.8	30.4	20.2	13.6	25.0	24.7	26.2	23.9	19.8	11.1	25.2	23.0
Mali	15.0	13.6	25.0	22.0	18.8	17.3	13.4	13.8	14.7	13.4	15.3	15.0	20.6	16.1
Mauritania	24.8	34.4	26.0	21.6	24.4	21.7	16.4	22.8	22.6	26.6	36.1	27.8	24.5	24.0
Mauritius	2.9	0.8	0.4	0.6	0.5	1.0	1.0	1.0	0.5	0.5	0.5	3.7	2.5	0.7
Mozambique	4.8	59.5	55.1	46.1	31.3	27.9	26.9	20.2	23.8	27.1	57.2	5.8	40.0	32.6
Namibia	..	5.4	4.2	5.5	5.4	4.6	5.3	5.3	4.4	3.5	4.7	0.0	3.3	4.8
Niger	6.8	21.4	24.1	14.6	12.8	18.0	14.0	9.3	11.7	13.2	13.7	9.9	17.7	13.4
Nigeria	0.1	1.4	0.8	0.8	0.5	0.6	0.6	0.4	0.4	0.4	0.7	0.1	0.8	0.6
Rwanda	13.4	18.1	95.0	54.3	33.8	12.4	17.6	19.3	17.8	17.5	20.6	12.5	21.3	24.2
São Tomé and Principe	8.4	98.0	101.0	185.2	105.7	76.0	68.8	58.7	75.2	81.6	51.8	15.9	73.1	87.9
Senegal	8.8	9.2	17.6	14.9	12.5	9.7	10.8	11.3	9.7	8.9	8.9	10.5	13.2	10.8
Seychelles	14.7	4.1	2.6	2.6	3.8	3.0	4.0	2.1	3.0	2.2	1.1	14.5	7.7	2.7
Sierra Leone	8.3	27.0	27.7	22.2	19.6	14.0	15.8	11.0	28.7	46.1	45.1	5.0	15.4	25.3
Somalia	71.8	..	..	..	..	..	..	..	..	..	..	42.1	48.0	..
South Africa	..	0.2	0.2	0.3	0.3	0.3	0.4	0.4	0.4	0.4	0.6	..	0.2	0.4
Sudan	9.2	7.6	6.3	2.5	2.6	1.3	2.0	2.3	2.0	1.5	2.6	7.5	8.5	2.1
Swaziland	9.2	5.1	5.1	4.3	2.5	2.0	2.6	2.1	0.9	2.3	2.1	7.9	5.9	2.3
Tanzania	..	22.3	21.4	16.7	13.5	12.3	11.9	11.5	11.3	13.6	13.1	11.4	21.6	13.0
Togo	8.0	7.8	12.8	14.7	10.7	8.3	9.1	5.0	5.7	3.5	3.7	10.0	13.2	7.6
Uganda	9.1	18.9	18.8	14.5	11.2	13.0	9.9	9.9	13.9	14.1	11.0	4.3	12.8	12.2
Zambia	8.2	26.6	21.5	58.5	18.6	15.6	10.8	19.9	24.6	9.6	17.3	6.3	20.4	21.9
Zimbabwe	2.5	7.6	8.1	6.9	4.3	4.0	4.6	4.5	2.5	1.8	2.4	1.6	5.5	3.9
NORTH AFRICA	2.1	2.6	2.7	1.9	2.0	1.7	1.7	1.4	1.1	1.1	1.3	3.1	2.8	1.5
Algeria	0.4	0.5	0.7	0.7	0.7	0.5	0.9	0.3	0.4	0.3	0.6	0.5	0.4	0.5
Egypt, Arab Rep.	6.0	5.1	5.2	3.4	3.3	2.6	2.4	1.8	1.3	1.3	1.4	10.3	6.7	2.2
Libya	0.0	..	..	..	..	..	..	..	..	..	..	0.0	0.0	..
Morocco	4.8	2.7	2.1	1.5	1.8	1.4	1.5	1.9	1.3	1.5	1.7	3.8	3.1	1.6
Tunisia	2.7	1.5	0.7	0.4	0.6	1.0	0.8	1.2	1.1	1.9	2.2	3.5	2.4	1.2
ALL AFRICA	3.2	4.8	5.4	4.6	3.9	3.4	3.5	3.1	2.9	3.1	4.2	3.7	5.9	3.6

Note: Regional aggregates for aid include data for economies not specified elsewhere.

Aid Flows

12-10. Net aid from DAC donors as share of recipient GDP

	Percentage of GDP											Annual average		
	1980	1993	1994	1995	1996	1997	1998	1999	2000	2001	2002	75-84	85-94	95-MR
SUB-SAHARAN AFRICA	2.4	3.5	3.9	3.3	3.0	2.7	2.8	2.6	2.6	2.6	3.6	2.5	5.2	2.9
excluding South Africa	2.4	6.4	7.5	6.1	5.1	4.5	4.6	4.2	4.2	3.9	5.2	2.5	5.8	4.7
excl. S.Africa & Nigeria	4.0	7.3	9.0	7.3	6.3	5.5	5.5	5.1	5.3	4.9	6.4	3.7	6.8	5.8
Angola	..	2.8	5.5	4.8	3.9	3.0	3.3	4.1	2.1	1.9	2.5	..	2.1	3.2
Benin	2.5	7.0	9.5	8.8	7.5	6.9	6.2	5.0	8.4	6.1	5.2	3.6	7.3	6.8
Botswana	7.9	1.9	1.3	1.1	1.4	1.1	1.5	0.8	0.4	0.5	0.7	8.2	3.7	0.9
Burkina Faso	7.8	10.9	13.4	10.2	9.7	8.4	8.1	8.3	8.8	7.9	7.4	7.4	9.2	8.6
Burundi	6.5	13.4	11.7	10.8	7.5	4.0	5.1	7.3	6.0	7.9	11.8	6.3	10.1	7.6
Cameroon	2.5	4.4	5.1	4.3	3.1	3.6	3.5	2.8	2.4	3.2	4.7	2.5	3.0	3.4
Cape Verde	36.5	22.4	19.8	15.7	15.4	13.4	15.8	15.2	13.1	8.6	6.7	30.6	24.7	13.0
Central African Republic	9.4	9.0	11.0	10.9	11.3	6.1	5.4	5.6	5.6	5.0	3.8	8.2	8.1	6.7
Chad	2.0	10.0	8.8	8.8	7.6	6.4	4.3	4.2	3.8	4.4	3.3	4.7	9.3	5.4
Comoros	10.9	10.4	9.6	9.4	9.5	7.2	8.6	5.9	5.3	4.4	4.5	14.0	13.0	6.8
Congo, Dem. Rep. of	2.2	0.9	1.7	2.1	1.8	1.7	1.3	1.8	2.1	2.8	6.2	1.8	3.5	2.5
Congo, Rep. of	3.2	6.1	14.3	5.0	15.5	11.2	3.1	5.2	0.7	1.1	1.4	3.8	5.6	5.4
Côte d'Ivoire	1.5	6.4	9.9	6.6	3.7	2.0	3.8	2.9	2.4	1.5	7.1	1.5	3.8	3.7
Djibouti	..	19.9	19.3	16.0	14.3	12.4	12.1	10.3	7.6	..	..	..	17.9	12.1
Equatorial Guinea	..	18.2	13.1	13.2	9.0	3.6	4.0	1.7	1.4	0.7	0.6	..	21.3	4.3
Eritrea	..	10.3	18.0	16.1	18.4	11.8	13.1	11.1	17.5	21.4	18.8	..	14.1	16.0
Ethiopia	..	6.7	10.2	9.1	7.5	5.9	5.6	5.0	5.8	5.6	8.1	1.9	6.0	6.6
Gabon	1.1	2.2	3.8	2.7	2.0	0.6	0.8	0.8	0.2	0.2	1.0	1.3	2.3	1.0
Gambia, The	6.8	13.6	10.5	6.6	4.4	4.2	3.2	3.1	3.5	3.4	4.9	8.7	18.3	4.2
Ghana	2.4	5.2	6.1	5.6	5.0	4.2	5.0	4.6	7.6	7.5	6.6	2.0	4.6	5.8
Guinea	..	5.6	5.4	6.0	3.5	3.3	4.1	3.2	3.0	4.0	3.9	..	6.0	3.9
Guinea-Bissau	31.1	23.8	52.4	30.3	46.1	21.8	31.5	14.3	19.3	15.2	12.7	21.9	29.4	23.9
Kenya	3.8	8.6	5.6	5.1	3.7	2.8	2.5	2.4	2.8	2.4	2.3	4.3	6.8	3.0
Lesotho	14.8	9.1	5.4	6.6	5.2	4.4	3.7	2.8	2.5	3.8	4.2	13.7	12.5	4.1
Liberia	5.4	..	..	..	..	..	..	..	..	..	..	5.1	4.8	
Madagascar	2.2	6.8	6.4	6.2	5.8	15.5	8.9	5.2	3.6	3.0	2.9	2.4	7.1	6.4
Malawi	6.1	7.7	21.2	15.5	10.9	6.9	11.7	12.6	15.8	11.6	11.8	6.3	11.2	12.1
Mali	7.3	8.3	13.8	11.6	11.4	10.4	9.1	9.2	12.3	7.9	8.3	8.0	12.6	10.0
Mauritania	7.6	20.8	12.5	11.8	8.9	8.8	6.3	9.3	8.8	8.1	14.9	6.7	13.0	9.6
Mauritius	2.2	0.8	0.2	0.3	0.0	0.1	0.5	0.1	0.3	0.2	0.1	2.4	2.1	0.2
Mozambique	3.3	41.0	33.7	30.2	19.4	18.3	18.4	14.9	16.9	21.0	46.2	4.3	28.5	23.2
Namibia	..	4.3	3.5	4.2	3.9	3.4	3.8	3.5	2.8	2.4	2.9	0.0	2.1	3.4
Niger	4.2	15.8	16.7	10.3	8.2	9.8	7.0	6.0	5.9	5.8	5.3	5.9	11.9	7.3
Nigeria	0.0	0.3	0.2	0.3	0.1	0.1	0.1	0.1	0.2	0.3	0.5	0.1	0.4	0.2
Rwanda	8.3	10.2	64.7	26.2	18.2	9.6	10.5	9.3	9.7	8.7	11.5	7.9	13.3	13.0
São Tomé and Principe	2.6	59.5	53.2	135.2	64.3	48.2	44.4	40.7	38.1	46.7	38.3	4.6	35.7	57.0
Senegal	6.1	6.7	13.0	8.9	8.5	6.7	6.2	8.8	6.6	4.9	4.8	6.5	8.8	6.9
Seychelles	12.4	1.4	1.5	2.2	1.6	1.1	2.8	0.8	0.5	1.3	0.5	13.0	5.6	1.4
Sierra Leone	5.2	13.7	5.4	6.4	7.1	4.9	7.9	8.9	18.2	22.3	28.8	2.7	7.8	13.1
Somalia	23.1		..	..	..	..	..	..	..	..	..	13.4	30.0	..
South Africa	..	0.1	0.2	0.2	0.2	0.3	0.3	0.3	0.3	0.3	0.4		0.1	0.3
Sudan	4.0	2.8	2.7	1.4	1.4	0.8	1.4	1.5	0.8	0.9	1.7	2.8	3.9	1.2
Swaziland	6.0	3.1	2.4	2.8	1.6	1.1	1.2	1.1	0.2	0.3	0.6	5.2	3.6	1.1
Tanzania	..	15.3	12.6	11.2	9.3	7.4	9.2	7.1	8.6	10.1	9.6	8.1	15.4	9.1
Togo	4.6	6.3	6.5	9.0	6.6	5.0	4.7	3.3	4.3	2.3	2.8	5.7	7.8	4.8
Uganda	3.4	10.8	8.6	7.4	6.1	7.0	5.9	6.0	9.8	6.8	8.0	1.7	5.3	7.1
Zambia	6.0	15.6	13.0	12.6	10.8	9.4	7.9	10.9	15.0	7.5	9.7	4.8	14.5	10.5
Zimbabwe	1.7	4.7	4.1	4.9	3.3	2.6	3.8	4.0	2.7	1.6	2.1	1.2	4.1	3.1
NORTH AFRICA	1.3	1.8	2.1	1.6	1.6	1.1	1.1	1.0	0.8	0.8	0.8	1.4	2.2	1.1
Algeria	0.3	0.3	0.6	0.7	0.6	0.4	0.3	0.2	0.1	0.0	0.2	0.4	0.3	0.3
Egypt, Arab Rep.	5.2	3.8	4.4	2.8	2.9	2.0	1.8	1.5	1.2	1.1	1.2	4.6	5.5	1.8
Libya	0.0	..	..	..	..	..	..	..	..	..	..	0.0	0.0	..
Morocco	1.0	1.6	1.0	1.1	1.1	0.6	0.7	0.9	0.9	1.0	0.6	1.4	1.9	0.9
Tunisia	1.8	0.9	0.5	0.3	0.2	0.4	0.5	0.5	0.8	0.9	0.7	2.5	1.6	0.5
ALL AFRICA	1.9	3.0	3.3	2.8	2.5	2.2	2.2	2.0	1.9	1.9	2.5	2.0	3.8	2.2

Note: Regional aggregates for aid include data for economies not specified elsewhere.

12-11. Net aid from multilateral donors as share of recipient GDP

	Percentage of GDP											Annual average		
	1980	1993	1994	1995	1996	1997	1998	1999	2000	2001	2002	75-84	85-94	95-MR
SUB-SAHARAN AFRICA	1.3	2.2	2.9	2.5	1.9	1.6	1.7	1.4	1.4	1.8	2.3	1.3	3.0	1.8
excluding South Africa	1.3	4.1	5.5	4.7	3.3	2.8	2.9	2.4	2.3	2.7	3.3	1.3	3.4	3.1
excl. S.Africa & Nigeria	2.1	4.6	6.5	5.6	4.0	3.3	3.4	2.9	2.9	3.4	4.1	2.0	4.0	3.7
Angola	..	2.6	5.6	3.5	2.4	1.7	1.9	2.2	1.3	1.2	1.2	..	1.6	1.9
Benin	3.8	6.6	7.4	4.8	5.3	3.4	2.7	3.9	2.2	5.4	2.9	3.3	5.8	3.8
Botswana	2.1	1.0	0.6	0.7	0.2	1.3	0.7	0.4	0.2	0.1	0.0	2.2	1.2	0.5
Burkina Faso	3.2	9.0	8.5	9.4	5.2	5.6	6.0	5.6	4.0	5.7	6.3	3.5	4.9	6.0
Burundi	5.9	10.0	22.3	18.2	4.9	1.9	2.7	3.1	7.6	12.0	12.2	5.2	11.1	7.8
Cameroon	1.1	0.1	4.2	1.2	1.5	1.9	2.3	2.0	1.9	1.6	2.1	1.0	1.0	1.8
Cape Verde	22.0	9.8	9.6	8.2	7.3	8.5	8.3	8.3	4.7	5.0	7.8	15.6	11.3	7.3
Central African Republic	4.2	4.1	8.4	3.8	4.2	3.0	6.1	5.6	2.4	1.9	1.9	4.4	6.2	3.6
Chad	1.5	5.2	9.2	7.6	10.7	8.4	5.1	7.6	5.5	6.8	8.2	3.6	7.1	7.5
Comoros	10.8	7.2	11.3	8.6	7.5	5.6	7.6	3.7	3.8	7.4	6.7	14.1	10.7	6.4
Congo, Dem. Rep. of	0.7	0.7	2.5	1.4	1.0	0.7	0.7	1.0	1.7	2.3	8.0	0.8	2.0	2.1
Congo, Rep. of	1.3	0.4	6.2	1.0	1.4	0.4	0.3	0.9	0.3	1.6	12.5	1.9	1.1	2.3
Côte d'Ivoire	0.6	0.5	9.3	4.4	4.2	1.8	3.7	0.6	1.0	0.1	2.0	0.5	1.8	2.2
Djibouti	..	6.2	4.7	4.5	4.3	3.7	3.3	3.5	3.6	..	..	..	4.9	3.8
Equatorial Guinea	..	16.5	10.6	7.3	2.9	1.3	0.8	0.6	0.2	0.0	0.3	0.7	14.9	1.7
Eritrea	..	3.8	9.3	8.4	4.1	3.7	5.1	6.8	8.6	17.9	15.1	..	6.6	8.7
Ethiopia	..	10.7	9.1	6.2	6.1	3.1	4.3	4.7	4.6	11.1	12.9	2.8	6.0	6.6
Gabon	0.2	0.1	0.5	0.2	0.3	0.2	0.2	0.3	0.5	0.4	0.4	0.2	0.2	0.3
Gambia, The	12.8	10.1	9.2	6.0	5.6	5.6	5.9	4.4	7.6	9.7	11.3	8.5	14.9	7.0
Ghana	1.3	5.2	4.0	4.6	4.4	2.7	4.3	3.2	4.5	4.8	3.9	1.4	5.0	4.1
Guinea	..	6.9	5.1	5.2	3.7	5.9	5.2	3.1	1.9	5.3	3.7	..	5.4	4.2
Guinea-Bissau	21.4	14.3	20.5	15.2	19.1	24.4	15.1	9.1	18.0	14.5	16.5	13.1	22.0	16.5
Kenya	1.6	9.8	3.9	3.0	2.7	1.4	1.2	0.5	2.1	1.7	0.8	1.2	3.9	1.7
Lesotho	7.1	8.3	8.4	5.6	5.4	3.9	3.4	0.7	1.9	3.6	6.7	8.7	9.6	3.9
Liberia	2.6	..	..	..	..	..	..	..	..	..	..	2.1	2.1	..
Madagascar	2.3	4.0	3.3	3.4	3.2	8.0	3.9	4.5	4.8	5.1	5.6	1.9	4.7	4.8
Malawi	5.5	16.2	18.2	14.8	9.4	6.7	13.3	11.8	10.0	11.7	7.5	4.8	13.8	10.7
Mali	5.8	5.5	11.8	10.9	7.7	7.2	4.5	4.6	2.5	5.0	5.2	5.6	7.5	6.0
Mauritania	5.1	14.3	14.6	11.3	16.6	14.1	10.8	13.0	13.8	18.6	21.4	7.6	9.7	14.9
Mauritius	0.7	0.0	0.2	0.4	0.5	0.7	0.5	0.9	0.2	0.1	0.4	1.2	0.3	0.5
Mozambique	1.0	18.3	21.3	15.7	11.7	9.6	8.5	5.4	6.9	6.1	11.0	1.3	11.5	9.4
Namibia	..	1.1	0.8	1.3	1.5	1.1	1.5	1.8	1.6	1.0	1.7	..	1.3	1.4
Niger	2.5	5.5	7.1	4.2	4.6	7.7	7.0	3.3	5.8	7.3	8.3	3.1	5.7	6.0
Nigeria	0.0	1.0	0.6	0.5	0.4	0.4	0.5	0.3	0.2	0.2	0.2	0.0	0.3	0.3
Rwanda	4.9	7.7	29.9	28.1	15.4	2.7	7.1	10.0	8.1	8.8	9.1	4.3	7.7	11.2
São Tomé and Principe	5.8	38.5	47.8	49.9	41.4	27.7	24.3	18.0	37.2	34.8	13.5	11.3	37.5	30.8
Senegal	2.6	2.2	4.5	5.7	3.8	2.8	4.5	2.4	3.2	4.1	3.9	3.2	3.9	3.8
Seychelles	2.3	2.6	1.2	0.5	1.6	1.1	1.0	1.0	1.4	0.8	0.6	1.3	2.0	1.0
Sierra Leone	2.7	13.3	22.3	15.7	12.0	9.0	7.5	2.0	10.5	23.5	16.0	2.1	7.3	12.0
Somalia	27.5	..	..	..	..	..	..	..	..	..	..	15.9	15.9	..
South Africa	..	0.1	0.1	0.0	0.0	0.1	0.1	0.1	0.1	0.1	0.3	..	0.1	0.1
Sudan	2.8	4.8	3.6	1.1	1.2	0.5	0.5	0.5	0.3	0.6	0.5	2.0	3.9	0.7
Swaziland	3.2	1.8	2.5	1.3	0.7	0.7	1.0	1.0	0.7	1.7	1.2	2.7	2.2	1.1
Tanzania	..	7.0	8.6	5.4	4.2	4.9	2.7	4.4	2.7	3.6	3.6	2.9	6.2	3.9
Togo	3.4	1.6	6.3	5.7	4.2	3.4	4.3	1.5	1.3	0.9	0.7	4.2	5.3	2.7
Uganda	5.6	8.1	9.9	7.0	4.9	5.9	4.0	3.9	4.0	7.2	2.9	2.4	7.1	5.0
Zambia	1.6	11.0	8.5	45.8	7.8	6.2	2.9	9.1	9.5	2.0	7.5	1.1	5.9	11.4
Zimbabwe	0.7	2.9	4.1	2.1	1.1	1.4	0.8	0.5	0.2	0.2	0.3	0.4	1.4	0.8
NORTH AFRICA	0.2	0.5	0.5	0.3	0.4	0.5	0.5	0.4	0.2	0.3	0.4	0.5	0.3	0.4
Algeria	0.0	0.2	0.1	0.1	0.1	0.1	0.5	0.0	0.1	0.2	0.2	0.1	0.1	0.2
Egypt, Arab Rep.	0.9	0.4	0.5	0.3	0.3	0.5	0.3	0.2	0.1	0.1	0.1	2.2	0.4	0.3
Libya	0.0	..	..	..	..	..	..	..	..	..	..	0.0	0.0	..
Morocco	0.4	1.0	0.9	0.4	0.6	0.6	0.7	0.9	0.4	0.4	0.8	0.3	0.4	0.6
Tunisia	0.3	0.7	0.3	0.2	0.6	0.8	0.4	0.8	0.4	1.0	1.3	0.4	0.6	0.7
ALL AFRICA	0.8	1.7	2.1	1.8	1.4	1.2	1.2	1.1	1.0	1.2	1.5	1.0	1.8	1.3

Note: Regional aggregates for aid include data for economies not specified elsewhere.

12-12. Net aid from all donors as share of recipient GDI

	Percentage of GDI											Annual average		
	1980	1993	1994	1995	1996	1997	1998	1999	2000	2001	2002	75-84	85-94	95-MR
SUB-SAHARAN AFRICA	20.9	35.1	37.7	32.2	26.9	24.6	23.8	22.3	23.4	24.1	31.8	22.2	50.7	26.1
excluding South Africa	20.9	60.0	68.7	59.5	44.9	40.5	35.8	33.2	34.8	33.4	42.4	22.2	56.3	40.6
excl. S.Africa & Nigeria	36.4	72.2	82.3	69.2	51.7	48.7	44.0	41.8	43.1	41.9	54.4	33.7	67.3	49.3
Angola	..	49.1	66.6	29.5	18.1	18.2	14.6	32.1	9.8	8.8	11.6	..	38.4	17.8
Benin	42.4	88.9	108.6	71.2	76.3	55.7	51.7	50.5	55.9	60.2	45.9	40.9	97.5	58.4
Botswana	25.0	10.8	7.5	7.7	6.2	8.3	6.4	4.4	3.0	2.6	2.9	29.6	20.9	5.2
Burkina Faso	72.9	110.2	113.6	87.3	61.8	56.5	52.7	59.6	57.0	73.7	82.8	64.1	75.8	66.4
Burundi	91.9	141.8	319.4	300.1	102.3	72.9	87.5	114.1	150.2	288.1	303.8	89.3	150.6	177.4
Cameroon	18.7	27.7	60.6	38.4	29.4	33.9	32.7	25.3	26.1	26.8	36.8	15.0	23.6	31.2
Cape Verde	116.9	81.4	68.3	56.3	96.4	99.9	121.7	112.1	89.9	73.8	68.5	95.0	114.8	89.8
Central African Republic	198.7	131.0	168.5	111.3	369.9	92.6	84.6	78.0	72.9	49.0	38.6	129.1	121.5	112.1
Chad	..	157.4	108.5	159.4	123.7	102.0	47.7	121.6	42.0	27.1	19.8	159.7	185.9	80.4
Comoros	105.7	96.1	101.1	92.6	88.1	81.1	90.7	64.4	70.2	95.1	101.9	114.1	117.3	85.5
Congo, Dem. Rep. of	29.8	94.6	53.5	37.0	10.3	102.8	112.2	91.0	123.5	99.5	199.5	23.1	63.1	97.0
Congo, Rep. of	15.1	21.8	65.5	16.2	62.7	52.0	12.6	21.7	4.9	10.2	59.7	19.5	28.9	30.0
Côte d'Ivoire	7.8	70.7	139.8	70.7	65.6	26.4	56.7	27.2	31.3	14.4	87.6	9.3	62.4	47.5
Djibouti	..	..	..	250.3	216.2	180.3	103.1	157.4	100.3	..	..	..	..	167.9
Equatorial Guinea	..	158.2	32.0	26.8	10.5	7.4	5.3	4.2	3.9	1.3	3.3	7.8	142.9	7.8
Eritrea	..	84.1	117.7	112.6	83.2	57.5	84.1	60.3	149.5	141.2	135.6	..	100.9	103.0
Ethiopia	..	122.6	127.6	93.0	80.6	53.3	59.1	58.4	67.0	96.3	105.2	37.2	94.1	76.6
Gabon	4.7	10.3	19.8	12.3	9.4	2.4	2.6	3.9	0.9	0.7	5.1	4.1	9.4	4.7
Gambia, The	84.7	110.5	106.0	60.5	44.1	55.1	50.4	43.6	68.6	77.5	79.0	100.5	177.0	59.9
Ghana	76.7	47.1	42.1	50.3	44.3	28.9	40.7	36.8	50.3	46.2	47.5	60.7	70.6	43.1
Guinea	..	69.8	67.9	68.2	33.4	42.7	47.7	31.1	22.4	41.9	46.4	..	69.0	41.7
Guinea-Bissau	190.7	129.2	340.7	209.2	290.0	212.4	409.5	139.1	233.3	150.5	198.7	158.2	169.6	230.3
Kenya	22.3	103.2	57.7	46.3	38.4	27.1	21.3	18.2	31.9	28.1	23.5	26.8	58.0	29.3
Lesotho	59.0	31.6	24.4	20.3	19.1	17.1	13.9	7.3	9.9	16.3	26.7	72.7	47.2	16.3
Liberia	32.1	..	..	..	..	..	..	..	..	..	..	44.5	94.0	..
Madagascar	38.1	94.0	89.1	87.1	76.7	183.5	87.1	64.7	55.2	43.7	59.4	47.1	108.1	82.2
Malawi	46.8	158.4	136.9	179.0	174.9	111.3	186.0	166.5	273.5	2,300.0	160.0	49.5	125.6	443.9
Mali	96.7	62.2	91.5	95.9	81.9	84.1	64.0	65.1	71.5	64.0	80.8	103.7	97.7	75.9
Mauritania	94.3	166.8	125.6	111.9	131.3	123.5	86.7	128.4	74.7	99.4	146.2	106.9	109.0	112.8
Mauritius	11.3	2.6	1.4	2.1	1.9	3.6	3.6	3.8	1.8	2.1	2.4	15.5	9.4	2.7
Mozambique	80.8	467.3	278.1	201.6	143.2	135.6	110.9	55.1	65.1	65.5	127.9	99.7	286.2	113.1
Namibia	..	32.9	19.8	25.2	23.3	22.6	20.7	22.7	22.9	14.7	19.3	0.0	17.4	21.4
Niger	24.1	334.4	232.2	199.4	132.7	166.1	124.7	90.7	108.8	114.9	107.7	84.2	183.9	130.6
Nigeria	0.3	5.8	4.1	4.6	3.8	3.2	2.6	1.9	2.5	2.2	3.1	0.6	4.0	3.0
Rwanda	82.8	107.8	952.2	404.8	234.9	89.8	118.8	112.2	101.4	95.2	109.2	85.9	172.5	158.3
São Tomé and Principe	49.8	277.4	242.9	271.9	188.3	154.7	192.1	150.4	173.0	272.8	194.7	115.6	313.1	199.7
Senegal	75.1	67.4	95.2	89.0	67.5	54.2	54.5	54.6	52.3	49.4	45.3	81.6	101.9	58.3
Seychelles	38.5	14.5	9.8	8.4	9.6	9.5	11.5	4.9	10.9	5.3	3.7	43.6	33.2	8.0
Sierra Leone	51.0	351.1	355.5	423.2	218.2	278.9	282.7	252.7	359.9	760.5	514.7	43.0	181.7	386.4
Somalia	169.3	..	..	..	..	..	..	..	..	..	..	156.0	196.4	..
South Africa	..	1.4	1.3	1.4	1.5	2.0	2.3	2.6	2.4	2.5	4.0	..	1.3	2.3
Sudan	96.5	38.5	28.0	15.9	11.1	9.0	7.3	10.9	11.3	8.2	13.3	61.4	76.5	10.9
Swaziland	24.6	22.3	23.5	21.3	7.8	9.6	11.4	11.2	5.1	13.4	11.6	25.1	28.5	11.4
Tanzania	..	88.8	86.8	84.4	81.2	82.5	86.2	73.8	63.9	80.0	78.7	..	102.1	78.8
Togo	28.1	105.0	84.8	91.1	57.1	51.3	43.7	26.6	27.3	16.8	17.0	39.6	81.8	41.4
Uganda	148.3	124.2	128.4	88.3	69.6	77.2	61.0	50.9	70.2	69.9	50.7	63.5	96.6	67.2
Zambia	35.2	177.0	260.3	367.3	145.1	107.0	65.7	113.4	131.5	47.9	99.4	34.1	159.4	134.7
Zimbabwe	14.5	33.3	34.3	35.2	23.4	22.0	26.6	27.6	19.6	23.2	29.2	9.3	28.4	25.8
NORTH AFRICA	7.2	11.1	11.7	8.5	9.5	7.3	6.4	5.4	4.4	4.6	5.3	9.4	11.2	6.4
Algeria	1.1	1.5	2.2	2.2	2.6	2.2	3.1	1.0	1.6	1.3	2.2	1.2	1.3	2.0
Egypt, Arab Rep.	22.0	31.2	31.2	19.5	19.6	12.1	9.2	7.0	5.6	5.7	6.2	33.9	29.7	10.6
Libya	0.2	..	..	..	..	..	..	..	..	..	..	0.2	..	..
Morocco	19.7	11.8	9.7	7.2	9.1	6.7	6.7	8.2	5.2	6.2	6.8	14.5	13.2	7.0
Tunisia	9.1	5.3	2.7	1.7	2.6	3.9	2.8	4.5	4.2	6.7	7.5	11.3	8.8	4.2
ALL AFRICA	13.4	25.2	27.5	23.2	20.5	17.8	16.1	14.5	14.6	14.9	19.3	14.4	28.8	17.6

Note: Regional aggregates for aid include data for economies not specified elsewhere.

12-13. Net aid from DAC donors as share of recipient GDI

	Percentage of GDI										Annual average		
	1980	1993	1994	1995	1996	1997	1998	1999	2000	2001	2002	75-84	85-94	95-MR
SUB-SAHARAN AFRICA	12.3	21.3	21.7	18.3	16.4	15.3	14.7	14.1	15.1	14.2	19.1	13.0	31.5	15.9
excluding South Africa	12.3	36.5	39.4	33.5	27.1	24.9	22.0	20.9	22.3	19.5	25.5	13.0	34.8	24.5
excl. S.Africa & Nigeria	21.6	44.4	47.5	39.2	31.4	30.1	27.3	26.5	27.6	24.5	32.6	19.7	41.6	29.9
Angola	..	25.4	33.1	17.1	11.3	11.6	9.4	20.9	6.0	5.5	7.9	..	21.8	11.2
Benin	16.8	45.6	60.2	45.0	43.6	37.3	36.3	28.5	44.6	31.7	29.1	21.0	53.9	37.0
Botswana	19.6	6.7	4.9	4.6	5.7	3.8	4.4	3.0	2.3	2.1	2.8	22.8	15.7	3.6
Burkina Faso	51.9	60.1	69.4	44.9	39.6	33.5	29.8	34.7	38.6	41.5	40.3	43.3	48.8	37.9
Burundi	46.8	82.1	111.0	113.1	62.5	49.5	57.7	79.9	66.3	114.7	149.4	48.1	70.0	86.6
Cameroon	12.1	26.9	33.0	29.9	20.0	22.4	19.9	14.8	14.7	18.2	25.4	10.1	17.4	20.7
Cape Verde	70.7	56.4	45.8	36.9	64.0	61.0	79.7	72.8	66.6	46.8	32.1	58.6	79.1	57.5
Central African Republic	134.5	88.4	94.4	80.8	262.7	62.4	39.9	39.1	51.3	35.3	25.5	84.4	68.1	74.6
Chad	..	102.0	52.7	85.7	50.9	43.2	21.2	41.8	17.1	10.6	5.7	86.5	104.9	34.5
Comoros	32.8	56.6	46.2	48.1	49.1	45.4	48.1	39.6	40.4	33.2	34.6	43.0	63.8	42.3
Congo, Dem. Rep. of	22.1	52.5	21.2	22.2	6.6	68.2	71.3	59.8	69.1	54.3	86.8	16.1	39.2	54.8
Congo, Rep. of	9.1	20.5	45.8	13.6	57.6	50.1	11.5	18.6	3.4	4.0	5.9	11.8	24.6	20.6
Côte d'Ivoire	5.6	65.5	71.9	42.3	30.6	13.8	28.7	22.2	22.3	13.5	68.1	7.3	43.3	30.2
Djibouti	..	..	..	189.5	157.9	131.2	79.4	116.1	59.2	..	..	..	..	122.2
Equatorial Guinea	..	83.0	17.7	17.3	7.9	5.5	4.4	3.1	3.3	1.3	2.2	..	88.0	5.6
Eritrea	..	60.5	71.6	71.5	66.7	37.7	49.1	32.6	95.1	76.1	71.0	..	66.1	62.5
Ethiopia	..	46.9	67.5	55.3	44.2	34.5	32.7	29.5	36.7	31.7	39.4	13.6	45.8	38.0
Gabon	4.2	9.9	17.6	11.6	8.5	1.9	2.2	2.8	0.9	0.6	3.5	3.4	8.6	4.0
Gambia, The	25.6	64.9	58.1	32.6	20.3	24.7	17.6	17.2	20.4	19.3	22.9	46.6	98.8	21.9
Ghana	42.8	23.6	25.5	27.7	23.8	17.1	21.7	21.5	31.5	28.0	29.6	32.8	32.4	25.1
Guinea	..	31.6	35.2	36.0	15.1	14.0	19.7	14.5	13.6	18.0	23.3	..	35.8	19.3
Guinea-Bissau	110.3	77.3	240.8	135.7	200.1	100.0	276.7	85.1	120.6	76.9	86.3	92.8	95.8	135.2
Kenya	15.6	48.4	34.1	28.9	22.3	18.2	14.2	14.9	18.2	16.4	17.2	20.7	36.3	18.8
Lesotho	39.9	16.2	9.5	11.0	9.0	8.3	7.4	6.0	5.9	8.6	10.4	43.4	26.8	8.3
Liberia	19.7	..	..	..	..	..	..	..	..	..	..	32.5	66.7	..
Madagascar	15.0	59.0	58.5	56.4	49.4	120.8	60.4	34.7	23.8	16.5	20.1	25.0	64.6	47.8
Malawi	24.7	50.5	73.0	90.9	93.9	56.4	87.1	84.9	165.0	1,114.7	95.4	26.2	55.2	223.5
Mali	47.5	37.8	50.4	50.5	49.6	50.3	43.5	43.5	59.6	37.8	44.0	55.7	60.1	47.3
Mauritania	28.7	100.6	60.1	61.2	47.6	50.1	33.4	52.0	29.1	30.2	60.3	25.5	58.3	45.5
Mauritius	8.6	2.7	0.7	1.0	0.1	0.2	1.7	0.5	1.1	0.8	0.4	10.3	7.9	0.7
Mozambique	54.8	322.1	169.9	132.3	89.0	88.9	76.0	40.6	46.3	50.6	103.3	74.1	205.2	78.4
Namibia	..	26.2	16.1	19.4	16.9	16.7	14.7	14.9	14.5	10.3	12.1	0.0	11.1	15.0
Niger	14.9	247.0	160.9	140.9	85.0	90.4	61.8	58.3	54.6	50.7	41.3	51.1	124.9	72.9
Nigeria	0.1	1.4	1.0	1.6	0.9	0.8	0.4	0.7	1.1	1.3	2.1	0.4	2.4	1.1
Rwanda	51.5	61.0	647.8	195.6	126.9	69.9	70.9	54.3	55.3	47.5	61.1	54.3	109.9	85.2
São Tomé and Principe	15.4	168.3	127.9	198.6	114.5	98.1	124.1	104.2	87.6	156.3	143.9	30.6	145.6	128.4
Senegal	51.9	49.0	70.7	53.4	45.6	37.4	31.4	42.4	35.6	26.8	24.5	50.5	67.3	37.1
Seychelles	32.4	5.1	5.5	7.1	4.0	3.5	8.2	1.8	1.9	3.2	1.7	38.5	24.0	3.9
Sierra Leone	31.8	178.5	69.4	122.2	79.4	97.4	141.4	205.6	228.1	367.8	328.1	24.2	90.7	196.3
Somalia	54.4	..	..	..	..	..	..	..	..	..	..	49.5	121.3	..
South Africa	..	0.9	0.9	1.2	1.2	1.7	1.9	1.9	1.8	1.8	2.3	..	0.9	1.7
Sudan	42.2	13.9	11.8	8.6	6.0	5.6	5.3	7.1	4.5	4.8	8.8	24.4	38.0	6.3
Swaziland	16.1	13.6	11.1	13.8	4.9	5.5	5.5	5.8	1.1	1.9	3.1	16.1	17.5	5.2
Tanzania	..	60.8	51.3	56.4	56.0	49.7	66.3	45.7	48.7	59.4	57.6	..	71.2	55.0
Togo	16.1	83.7	42.9	55.8	35.4	31.0	22.5	17.5	20.4	10.9	13.1	21.5	49.2	25.8
Uganda	55.2	70.8	58.8	44.8	38.1	41.7	36.2	30.8	49.6	34.0	37.1	25.5	39.3	39.0
Zambia	25.9	103.7	157.3	79.4	84.3	64.4	48.3	61.8	80.4	37.6	55.8	26.1	111.8	64.0
Zimbabwe	9.9	29.7	17.1	24.9	17.7	14.6	22.0	24.8	21.2	21.0	25.9	7.2	21.7	21.5
NORTH AFRICA	4.4	7.7	9.2	6.9	7.5	5.0	4.1	3.7	3.4	3.3	3.1	4.5	8.6	4.6
Algeria	0.7	1.0	1.9	2.1	2.3	1.7	1.1	0.6	0.5	0.2	0.7	0.9	1.0	1.2
Egypt, Arab Rep.	18.8	23.7	26.8	16.3	17.2	9.1	7.0	5.7	4.8	4.9	5.4	15.3	24.3	8.8
Libya	0.1	..	..	..	..	..	..	..	..	..	..	0.1	..	..
Morocco	4.1	7.0	4.9	5.1	5.5	3.1	3.2	4.0	3.6	4.1	2.3	5.5	8.3	3.9
Tunisia	6.1	2.9	1.9	1.3	0.9	1.4	1.9	1.8	2.8	3.3	2.3	8.0	6.1	2.0
ALL AFRICA	8.0	15.8	16.8	14.0	13.1	11.2	10.1	9.3	9.6	9.1	11.6	8.0	18.7	11.0

Note: Regional aggregates for aid include data for economies not specified elsewhere.

12-14. Net aid from multilateral donors as share of recipient GDI

	Percentage of GDI											Annual average		
	1980	1993	1994	1995	1996	1997	1998	1999	2000	2001	2002	75-84	85-94	95-MR
SUB-SAHARAN AFRICA	6.6	13.6	15.9	13.8	10.4	9.1	8.9	7.9	8.2	9.7	12.2	6.9	18.2	10.0
excluding South Africa	6.6	23.3	29.2	25.8	17.6	15.3	13.7	11.9	12.2	13.6	16.2	6.9	20.5	15.8
excl. S.Africa & Nigeria	11.4	27.7	34.7	29.9	20.1	18.1	16.5	14.9	15.0	17.0	20.9	10.5	24.5	19.0
Angola	..	23.1	33.5	12.4	6.8	6.5	5.3	11.2	3.6	3.4	3.8	..	16.5	6.6
Benin	24.8	43.2	46.8	24.5	31.1	18.4	15.8	22.3	11.5	28.1	16.2	19.5	42.7	21.0
Botswana	5.3	3.6	2.4	3.0	0.7	4.7	2.2	1.5	0.8	0.3	0.2	6.1	5.0	1.7
Burkina Faso	21.0	50.0	43.9	41.1	21.2	22.5	22.0	23.5	17.7	29.6	34.7	20.0	26.0	26.5
Burundi	42.2	61.2	211.4	189.9	41.0	23.8	30.6	34.1	83.8	173.3	154.3	39.0	79.3	91.3
Cameroon	5.0	0.8	27.7	8.4	9.6	11.6	13.0	10.7	11.6	8.8	11.4	4.3	6.2	10.6
Cape Verde	42.5	24.6	22.2	19.3	30.1	38.8	41.9	39.6	23.6	27.3	37.5	34.3	34.7	32.3
Central African Republic	60.5	40.7	72.1	28.2	96.7	30.2	44.7	39.0	21.7	13.7	13.0	42.9	51.6	35.9
Chad	..	53.4	55.3	73.4	71.5	56.6	25.1	75.4	24.6	16.5	13.9	69.7	80.5	44.6
Comoros	32.7	39.1	54.7	44.3	38.8	35.6	42.3	24.8	29.1	56.5	52.1	43.1	51.5	40.4
Congo, Dem. Rep. of	7.4	41.9	32.2	14.7	3.5	29.0	38.7	31.1	54.3	45.1	112.6	6.8	22.9	41.1
Congo, Rep. of	3.6	1.2	19.8	2.6	5.1	1.9	1.1	3.1	1.5	6.2	53.8	5.7	4.3	9.4
Côte d'Ivoire	2.2	5.1	67.8	28.3	35.0	12.6	28.0	4.9	9.0	0.9	19.4	2.0	19.1	17.3
Djibouti	..	..	..	53.1	47.3	39.4	21.5	39.3	27.7	..	..	..	..	38.0
Equatorial Guinea	..	75.2	14.3	9.5	2.6	2.0	0.9	1.2	0.6	0.1	1.1	5.3	53.0	2.2
Eritrea	..	22.5	36.9	37.1	15.0	12.0	19.1	20.1	46.6	63.8	57.0	..	29.7	33.8
Ethiopia	..	75.5	60.0	37.6	36.4	18.2	25.3	27.5	28.8	62.2	63.1	20.4	47.4	37.4
Gabon	0.6	0.4	2.1	0.8	1.1	0.7	0.5	1.1	1.8	1.3	1.6	0.5	0.7	1.1
Gambia, The	48.0	48.3	50.9	29.9	25.8	32.6	32.2	24.8	44.7	54.7	52.7	43.2	79.4	37.2
Ghana	23.7	23.3	16.9	23.1	20.6	11.1	18.8	15.1	18.6	18.0	17.6	24.9	38.1	17.8
Guinea	..	38.9	33.0	31.2	16.0	24.8	24.9	14.2	8.4	24.0	21.9	..	31.8	20.7
Guinea-Bissau	75.9	46.4	94.0	68.1	83.0	111.9	132.6	53.9	112.6	73.5	112.3	54.6	67.7	93.5
Kenya	6.7	55.2	23.8	17.0	15.9	8.8	7.1	3.1	13.3	11.4	5.7	5.7	21.4	10.3
Lesotho	19.1	14.8	14.7	9.3	9.4	7.4	6.8	1.6	4.3	8.1	16.7	28.8	20.1	8.0
Liberia	9.4	..	..	..	..	..	..	..	..	..	..	10.9	27.3	..
Madagascar	15.1	35.0	30.6	30.7	27.3	62.6	26.7	30.0	31.6	27.4	39.5	19.9	43.9	34.5
Malawi	22.1	107.0	62.7	87.0	81.1	55.3	98.5	79.9	104.7	1,125.2	60.4	23.3	69.3	211.5
Mali	37.4	25.0	43.3	47.8	33.6	34.9	21.5	21.6	12.2	23.9	27.6	38.7	34.7	27.9
Mauritania	19.3	69.1	70.2	58.4	89.1	80.1	56.9	73.3	45.6	69.8	86.6	30.4	44.6	70.0
Mauritius	2.7	0.1	0.7	1.3	2.1	2.5	2.0	3.4	0.6	0.6	2.0	4.7	1.3	1.8
Mozambique	16.3	143.7	107.6	68.9	53.8	46.9	35.1	14.6	18.8	14.6	24.5	22.5	79.8	34.7
Namibia	..	6.7	3.5	5.8	6.4	5.7	5.9	7.7	8.2	4.2	6.9	..	6.3	6.3
Niger	9.0	85.4	68.1	57.8	47.3	70.5	62.4	32.1	54.2	63.6	65.3	26.4	57.2	56.6
Nigeria	0.1	4.2	3.1	3.0	2.9	2.4	2.2	1.2	1.3	0.9	1.0	0.2	1.5	1.9
Rwanda	30.6	46.1	300.0	209.4	107.4	19.7	47.9	57.9	46.1	47.7	48.1	29.7	60.9	73.0
São Tomé and Principe	34.4	109.0	114.9	73.3	73.7	56.4	67.9	46.2	85.5	116.4	50.7	85.0	167.5	71.3
Senegal	22.6	16.5	24.3	33.9	20.6	15.6	22.9	11.7	17.3	22.7	19.7	25.0	30.5	20.6
Seychelles	6.1	9.0	4.4	1.6	4.1	3.4	2.9	2.3	5.0	2.0	2.0	4.4	8.4	2.9
Sierra Leone	16.7	172.3	285.9	299.7	133.7	179.1	134.3	45.9	131.8	388.0	182.8	16.3	87.5	186.9
Somalia	65.0	..	..	..	..	..	..	..	..	..	..	58.5	63.5	..
South Africa	..	0.5	0.4	0.2	0.2	0.3	0.4	0.7	0.7	0.7	1.7	..	0.4	0.6
Sudan	29.8	24.3	16.0	7.1	5.1	3.4	2.1	2.6	1.8	3.0	2.6	17.6	30.6	3.5
Swaziland	8.6	7.6	11.5	6.5	2.3	3.5	4.5	5.5	4.0	10.1	6.7	9.0	10.4	5.4
Tanzania	..	28.1	35.0	27.5	25.4	32.6	19.7	28.0	15.4	21.0	21.3	..	30.9	23.8
Togo	12.0	21.0	41.7	35.1	22.5	20.7	20.8	7.9	6.4	4.5	3.0	17.2	31.5	15.1
Uganda	91.3	53.1	67.3	42.3	30.6	35.3	24.8	20.0	20.2	35.7	13.3	34.7	54.2	27.8
Zambia	6.8	73.3	102.9	287.9	60.8	42.6	17.6	51.5	51.0	10.2	43.3	6.2	47.6	70.6
Zimbabwe	4.2	12.6	17.3	10.5	5.9	7.6	4.7	2.9	1.5	2.7	3.3	2.1	6.8	4.9
NORTH AFRICA	0.8	2.1	2.2	1.3	1.8	2.0	1.8	1.5	0.8	1.1	1.5	1.6	1.1	1.5
Algeria	0.1	0.6	0.3	0.3	0.3	0.4	1.9	0.2	0.5	0.7	0.6	0.1	0.2	0.6
Egypt, Arab Rep.	3.1	2.5	3.3	2.0	1.9	2.4	1.3	0.9	0.6	0.5	0.6	7.2	1.8	1.3
Libya	0.1	..	..	..	..	..	..	..	..	..	..	0.1	..	..
Morocco	1.4	4.5	4.4	1.9	3.2	3.1	3.1	3.8	1.6	1.7	3.0	1.3	1.9	2.7
Tunisia	1.0	2.6	1.3	0.9	2.5	2.9	1.5	2.9	1.3	3.4	4.6	1.4	2.1	2.5
ALL AFRICA	3.4	8.9	10.5	9.1	7.3	6.3	5.8	5.0	4.7	5.6	7.2	3.7	8.8	6.4

Note: Regional aggregates for aid include data for economies not specified elsewhere.

12-15. Net aid per capita from all donors

	U.S. dollars (current prices)											*Annual average*		
	1980	*1993*	*1994*	*1995*	*1996*	*1997*	*1998*	*1999*	*2000*	*2001*	*2002*	*75-84*	*85-94*	*95-MR*
SUB-SAHARAN AFRICA	22	32	34	32	28	24	23	21	20	21	28	18	33	25
excluding South Africa	22	34	36	34	29	25	24	21	21	22	29	18	33	26
excl. S.Africa & Nigeria	27	42	45	42	36	31	30	26	26	27	36	22	41	32
Angola	7	28	42	38	42	31	29	32	25	23	32	7	24	32
Benin	26	56	48	51	51	38	35	35	38	43	34	21	45	41
Botswana	117	92	59	60	48	77	66	37	18	17	22	91	102	43
Burkina Faso	30	49	44	49	41	35	37	36	30	34	40	24	38	38
Burundi	28	37	52	47	18	9	10	11	14	20	24	23	42	19
Cameroon	30	43	56	33	30	35	35	29	25	26	40	22	36	32
Cape Verde	223	323	326	307	298	277	316	323	216	173	201	144	298	264
Central African Republic	48	55	52	50	49	26	33	32	20	18	16	34	60	31
Chad	8	36	33	35	43	32	23	25	17	23	28	18	40	28
Comoros	129	105	81	85	78	53	66	39	34	48	55	119	115	57
Congo, Dem. Rep. of	15	4	6	4	4	3	3	3	4	5	16	11	13	5
Congo, Rep. of	51	45	127	43	142	86	20	42	10	21	115	46	58	60
Côte d'Ivoire	26	59	118	87	67	30	64	29	22	10	65	17	47	47
Djibouti	244	247	229	181	162	139	128	115	107	85	112	206	251	129
Equatorial Guinea	42	139	76	84	75	57	51	45	47	27	42	26	131	53
Eritrea	..	20	45	42	43	33	43	37	43	67	54	..	32	45
Ethiopia	6	20	20	16	14	10	11	10	11	17	19	5	18	13
Gabon	80	97	168	130	111	33	37	39	9	7	55	73	114	53
Gambia, The	85	81	65	42	32	33	32	26	37	40	44	58	101	36
Ghana	17	38	32	37	36	27	37	32	31	33	32	12	36	33
Guinea	20	65	56	63	44	55	51	33	21	37	32	15	52	42
Guinea-Bissau	75	84	151	100	148	99	74	39	59	42	41	63	105	75
Kenya	24	36	26	28	22	16	14	11	17	15	13	19	34	17
Lesotho	74	89	71	69	62	54	36	18	21	32	43	55	77	42
Liberia	52	47	24	45	62	26	24	31	22	12	16	40	40	30
Madagascar	26	29	22	23	26	59	33	24	21	23	23	16	29	29
Malawi	23	56	52	47	52	36	44	44	43	38	35	19	47	42
Mali	41	40	47	56	50	43	34	33	33	32	42	29	50	40
Mauritania	109	149	119	100	115	98	66	85	80	98	128	111	115	96
Mauritius	34	24	13	21	17	38	36	36	17	18	20	37	48	25
Mozambique	14	79	78	67	55	57	61	47	50	52	112	11	63	62
Namibia	..	98	86	117	111	96	102	98	81	57	68	0	58	91
Niger	30	41	43	30	27	34	29	18	20	23	26	30	47	26
Nigeria	1	3	2	2	2	2	2	1	1	1	2	1	2	2
Rwanda	30	47	136	123	82	32	48	50	42	38	44	26	49	57
São Tomé and Principe	44	373	388	638	352	240	198	190	236	254	169	72	317	285
Senegal	47	63	79	80	68	48	56	58	45	43	46	45	84	56
Seychelles	340	268	174	173	249	222	307	163	226	165	93	242	324	200
Sierra Leone	28	48	63	46	40	25	22	15	36	67	68	16	30	40
Somalia	67	115	70	26	12	10	10	14	12	17	21	46	72	15
South Africa	..	7	8	10	9	12	12	13	11	10	14	..	8	11
Sudan	32	17	15	9	8	5	7	8	7	6	11	28	32	7
Swaziland	89	65	66	65	36	29	35	28	13	27	23	60	58	32
Tanzania	37	34	34	30	29	30	31	30	30	37	35	28	37	32
Togo	36	26	33	50	40	31	30	16	15	9	11	32	51	25
Uganda	9	32	38	41	33	38	29	26	35	33	26	6	28	33
Zambia	55	103	83	229	67	66	37	64	80	35	63	35	77	80
Zimbabwe	23	45	50	43	32	28	21	20	14	13	15	15	38	23
NORTH AFRICA	31	30	30	23	26	22	23	20	16	17	20	31	35	21
Algeria	10	8	11	11	11	9	14	5	7	6	12	8	8	9
Egypt, Arab Rep.	34	43	47	35	37	33	32	25	21	19	19	44	52	28
Libya	5	1	1	1	2	1	1	1	3	2	2	3	2	2
Morocco	46	28	24	19	24	17	19	24	15	18	21	28	29	20
Tunisia	36	26	12	8	14	21	16	27	23	39	49	36	34	25
ALL AFRICA	24	31	34	31	27	24	23	20	20	20	27	20	33	24

Note: Regional aggregates for aid include data for economies not specified elsewhere.

12-16. Net aid per capita from DAC donors

	U.S. dollars (current prices)											Annual average		
	1980	1993	1994	1995	1996	1997	1998	1999	2000	2001	2002	75-84	85-94	95-MR
SUB-SAHARAN AFRICA	13	20	20	18	17	15	15	13	13	12	17	10	20	15
excluding South Africa	13	21	21	19	17	15	15	13	13	13	17	10	21	15
excl. S.Africa & Nigeria	16	26	26	24	22	19	19	17	17	16	22	13	26	19
Angola	5	15	21	22	26	20	18	21	15	14	22	4	14	20
Benin	10	29	27	32	29	26	24	20	31	23	21	11	25	26
Botswana	92	57	39	36	44	35	45	25	14	14	21	69	78	29
Burkina Faso	22	27	27	25	26	21	21	21	20	19	19	16	25	22
Burundi	14	21	18	18	11	6	7	8	6	8	12	12	20	9
Cameroon	20	42	30	26	20	23	21	17	14	18	28	15	27	21
Cape Verde	135	224	219	201	198	169	207	210	160	110	94	95	206	169
Central African Republic	32	37	29	36	35	17	16	16	14	13	10	22	33	20
Chad	5	23	16	19	18	13	10	8	7	9	8	10	23	12
Comoros	40	62	37	44	44	29	35	24	19	17	19	45	63	29
Congo, Dem. Rep. of	11	2	2	3	2	2	2	2	2	3	7	8	8	3
Congo, Rep. of	31	42	89	36	130	83	18	36	7	8	11	27	49	41
Côte d'Ivoire	19	54	61	52	31	16	32	24	16	10	50	13	33	29
Djibouti	107	173	167	137	118	101	98	85	63	41	53	122	164	87
Equatorial Guinea	5	73	42	54	56	42	42	33	40	28	28	14	76	40
Eritrea	..	14	27	26	35	21	25	20	27	36	28	..	21	27
Ethiopia	2	8	10	9	8	6	6	5	6	6	7	2	9	7
Gabon	71	93	150	122	99	26	31	28	9	6	38	61	104	45
Gambia, The	26	48	35	23	15	15	11	10	11	10	13	25	56	13
Ghana	10	19	20	20	19	16	20	18	19	20	20	7	17	19
Guinea	7	29	29	33	20	18	21	15	13	16	16	4	27	19
Guinea-Bissau	43	50	107	65	102	46	50	24	30	22	18	37	58	45
Kenya	17	17	15	17	13	11	10	9	10	9	9	15	22	11
Lesotho	50	45	28	37	29	26	19	15	12	17	17	34	43	22
Liberia	32	9	13	11	40	11	11	15	8	5	8	27	19	14
Madagascar	10	18	15	15	17	39	23	13	9	9	8	8	18	16
Malawi	12	18	28	24	28	18	21	23	26	19	21	10	20	22
Mali	20	24	26	30	30	25	23	22	28	19	23	16	30	25
Mauritania	33	90	57	55	42	40	25	35	31	30	53	28	61	39
Mauritius	26	24	7	10	1	2	17	4	10	7	3	24	40	7
Mozambique	9	54	48	44	34	37	42	34	35	40	90	8	45	45
Namibia	..	78	70	90	81	71	72	64	51	40	43	0	37	64
Niger	19	30	30	21	17	19	14	12	10	10	10	18	31	14
Nigeria	0	1	0	1	0	0	0	0	1	1	2	0	1	1
Rwanda	19	26	92	60	44	25	29	24	23	19	24	16	30	31
São Tomé and Principe	14	226	204	466	214	152	128	132	120	145	125	22	153	185
Senegal	33	46	58	48	46	33	32	45	31	23	25	28	56	35
Seychelles	286	93	98	146	103	82	218	60	40	100	44	212	235	99
Sierra Leone	18	25	12	13	14	9	11	12	23	33	43	8	15	20
Somalia	21	89	57	16	5	6	5	9	6	10	11	15	49	9
South Africa	..	5	6	8	8	10	10	9	8	7	8	..	5	9
Sudan	14	6	6	5	4	3	5	5	3	3	7	11	16	4
Swaziland	58	39	31	42	22	17	17	15	3	4	6	39	34	16
Tanzania	28	23	20	20	20	18	24	19	23	27	26	21	27	22
Togo	21	21	17	30	24	19	16	11	11	6	8	18	30	16
Uganda	3	18	17	21	18	21	17	16	25	16	19	2	11	19
Zambia	41	60	50	49	39	40	27	35	49	27	35	27	55	38
Zimbabwe	16	28	25	30	24	19	18	18	15	12	14	11	29	19
NORTH AFRICA	19	21	24	19	21	15	15	14	12	12	12	16	26	15
Algeria	6	5	9	10	9	7	5	3	2	1	4	6	6	5
Egypt, Arab Rep.	29	32	40	29	33	25	24	21	18	17	17	23	42	23
Libya	3	0	0	1	0	0	1	1	2	1	1	1	1	1
Morocco	10	17	12	13	15	8	9	12	10	12	7	10	19	11
Tunisia	25	14	8	6	5	8	11	11	16	19	15	25	23	11
ALL AFRICA	14	20	21	19	18	15	15	13	13	12	16	12	22	15

Note: Regional aggregates for aid include data for economies not specified elsewhere.

12-17. Net aid per capita from multilateral donors

	U.S. dollars (current prices)										Annual average		
	1980	*1993*	*1994*	*1995*	*1996*	*1997*	*1998*	*1999*	*2000*	*2001*	*2002*	*75-84*	*85-94*	*95-MR*
SUB-SAHARAN AFRICA	7	12	14	14	11	9	9	7	7	8	11	5	12	10
excluding South Africa	7	13	15	15	11	10	9	8	7	9	11	5	12	10
excl. S.Africa & Nigeria	9	16	19	18	14	12	11	9	9	11	14	7	15	12
Angola	2	13	21	16	16	11	10	11	9	9	10	3	10	12
Benin	15	27	21	18	21	13	11	15	8	20	12	10	20	15
Botswana	25	30	19	24	5	44	22	13	5	2	1	19	24	15
Burkina Faso	9	22	17	23	14	14	16	14	9	14	17	7	13	15
Burundi	13	16	34	30	7	3	4	3	8	12	12	10	22	10
Cameroon	8	1	26	7	10	12	14	12	11	9	12	6	8	11
Cape Verde	81	98	106	105	93	108	109	114	57	64	110	46	90	95
Central African Republic	15	17	22	13	13	8	18	16	6	5	5	12	26	10
Chad	3	12	17	16	25	18	12	15	10	14	20	7	17	16
Comoros	40	43	44	41	34	23	31	15	14	29	28	45	50	27
Congo, Dem. Rep. of	4	2	3	2	1	1	1	1	2	2	9	3	5	2
Congo, Rep. of	12	2	38	7	11	3	2	6	3	13	103	13	9	19
Côte d'Ivoire	7	4	57	35	36	14	32	5	6	1	14	4	15	18
Djibouti	29	54	41	38	35	30	27	29	30	44	56	30	46	36
Equatorial Guinea	37	66	34	30	18	15	8	12	7	1	14	17	53	13
Eritrea	..	5	14	14	8	7	10	12	13	30	23	..	10	15
Ethiopia	3	13	9	6	6	3	5	5	5	11	12	3	9	7
Gabon	10	3	18	8	13	10	7	11	19	13	17	8	8	12
Gambia, The	48	36	31	21	19	19	20	15	24	28	29	26	45	22
Ghana	5	19	13	17	17	10	17	13	11	13	12	5	19	14
Guinea	13	36	27	29	21	32	26	15	8	21	15	8	24	21
Guinea-Bissau	30	30	42	32	42	52	24	15	28	21	23	22	43	30
Kenya	7	19	11	10	9	5	5	2	7	6	3	4	12	6
Lesotho	24	42	43	31	31	24	18	4	9	16	27	21	34	20
Liberia	15	37	10	33	21	15	14	16	14	7	8	11	21	16
Madagascar	10	11	8	8	9	20	10	11	12	14	15	7	12	12
Malawi	11	38	24	23	24	18	23	21	17	19	13	8	26	20
Mali	16	16	22	28	20	18	11	11	6	12	14	11	18	15
Mauritania	22	62	67	52	78	64	43	49	49	69	76	30	46	60
Mauritius	8	1	7	12	20	26	20	31	6	5	16	12	7	17
Mozambique	3	24	30	23	21	20	19	12	14	12	21	3	18	18
Namibia	..	20	15	27	30	24	29	33	29	16	24	..	21	27
Niger	11	10	13	9	10	15	15	6	10	13	16	9	15	12
Nigeria	0	2	1	1	1	1	1	1	1	1	1	0	1	1
Rwanda	11	20	43	64	37	7	19	26	19	19	19	9	19	26
São Tomé and Principe	30	147	184	172	138	88	70	58	117	108	44	50	164	99
Senegal	14	15	20	30	21	14	24	13	15	20	20	14	26	19
Seychelles	54	166	78	33	107	79	77	77	104	64	50	25	83	74
Sierra Leone	9	24	50	32	24	16	10	3	13	34	24	7	14	20
Somalia	26	25	13	9	6	4	5	5	5	5	5	18	21	6
South Africa	..	2	2	2	1	2	2	4	3	3	6	..	2	3
Sudan	10	11	9	4	3	2	2	2	1	2	2	8	13	2
Swaziland	31	22	33	20	11	11	14	14	10	21	13	21	22	14
Tanzania	7	11	14	10	9	12	7	11	7	10	9	6	11	9
Togo	15	5	16	19	16	12	14	5	4	3	2	13	20	9
Uganda	5	14	20	20	14	17	12	10	10	17	7	4	16	13
Zambia	11	43	33	180	28	26	10	29	31	7	27	6	22	42
Zimbabwe	7	17	25	13	8	10	4	2	1	1	2	4	9	5
NORTH AFRICA	4	6	6	4	5	6	6	6	3	4	6	5	3	5
Algeria	1	3	2	1	1	2	9	1	2	3	3	1	1	3
Egypt, Arab Rep.	5	3	5	4	4	6	4	3	2	2	2	9	3	3
Libya	2	0	0	1	1	1	1	1	1	1	1	2	2	1
Morocco	3	11	11	5	9	8	9	11	5	5	10	2	4	8
Tunisia	4	13	6	5	13	16	8	17	8	20	29	4	8	14
ALL AFRICA	6	11	13	12	10	9	8	7	6	8	10	5	10	9

Note: Regional aggregates for aid include data for economies not specified elsewhere.

302

Figure 12-1. Total net ODA as a share of recipient GDP, 2002*

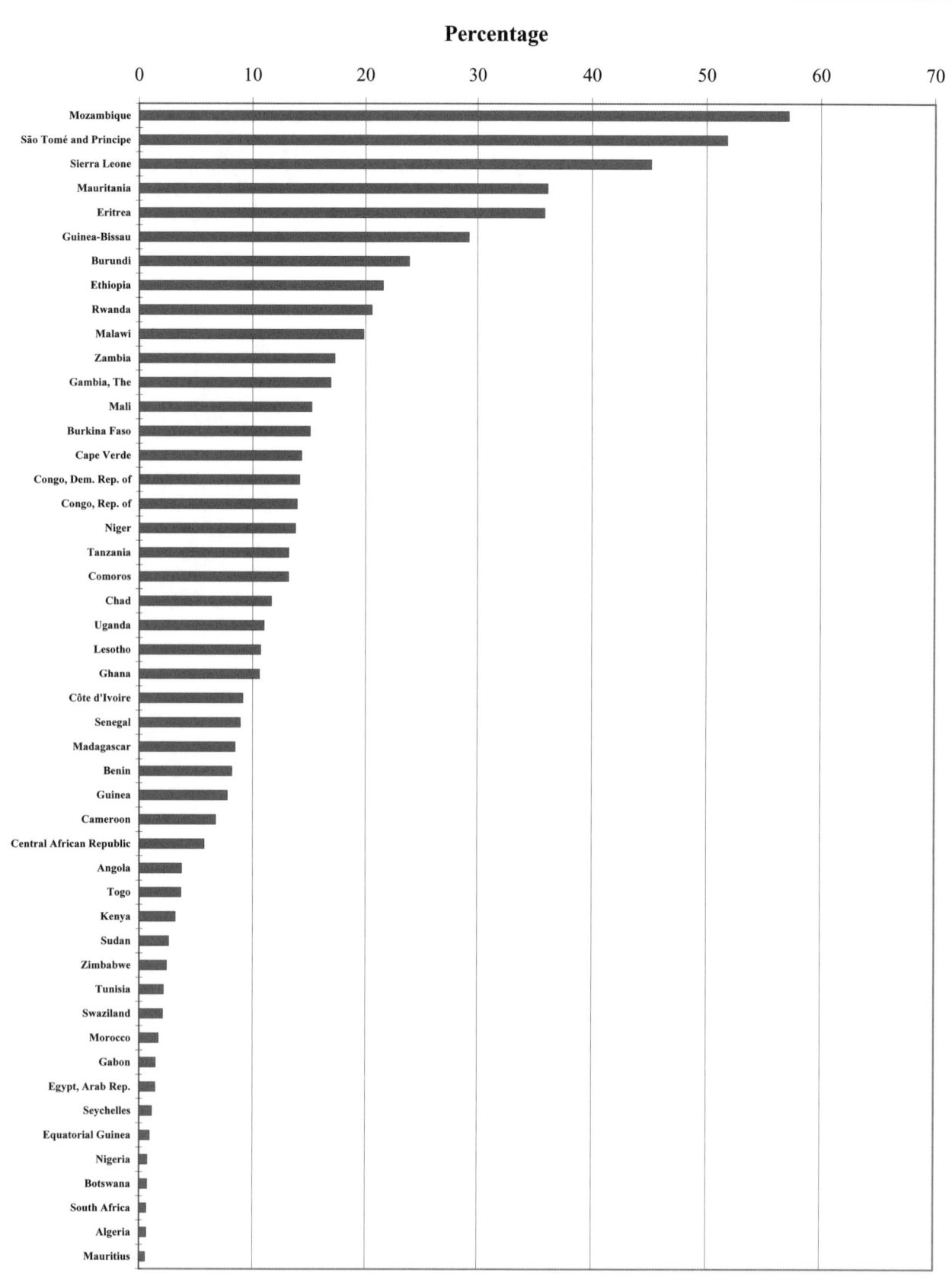

* Or most recent year available.

Figure 12-2. Total net aid per capita, 2002*

U.S. dollars

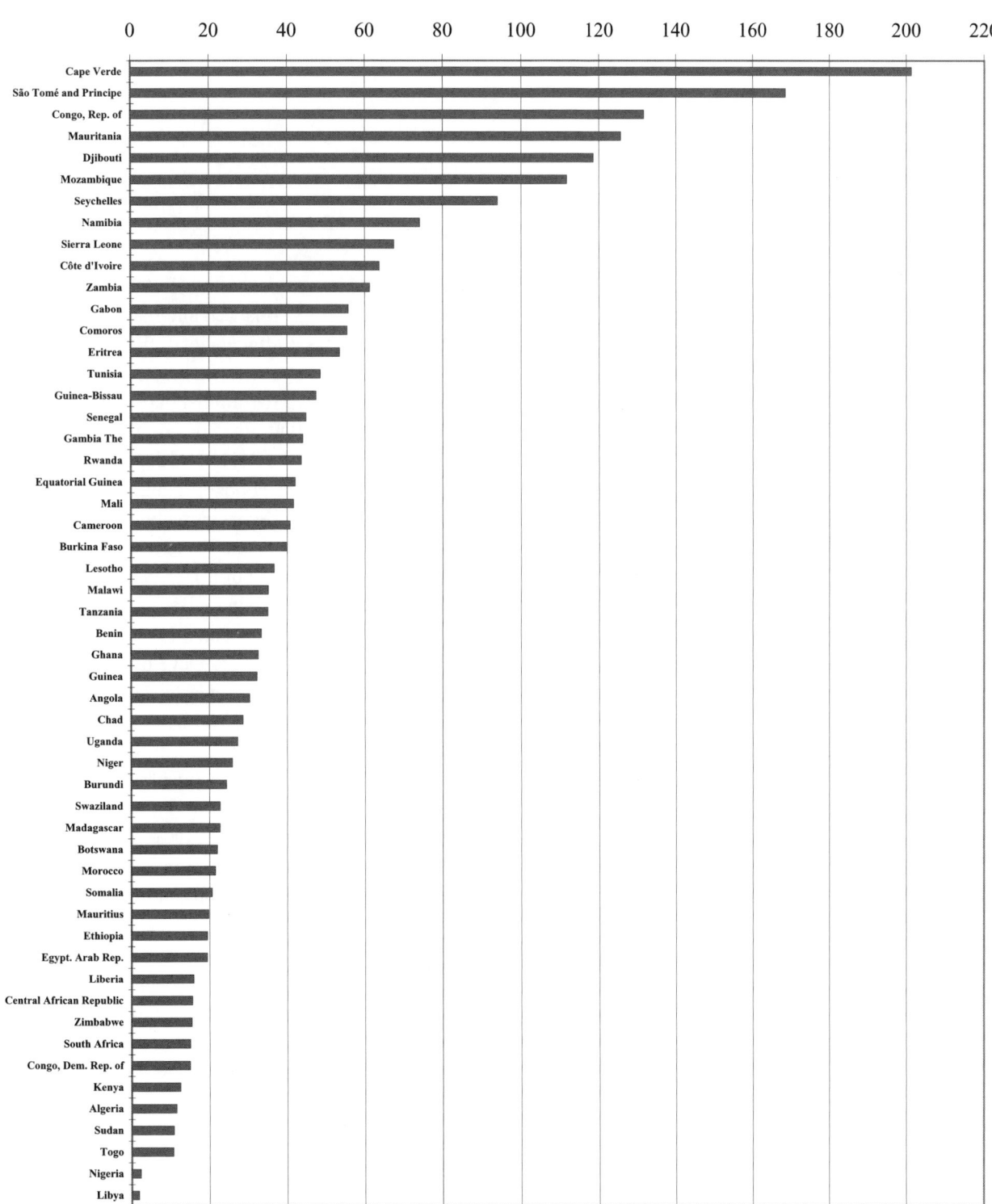

* Or most recent year available.

Technical notes

Tables

Table 12-1. Net aid from all donors, nominal. This table represents the total of Tables 12-2 through 12-4.

Table 12-2. Net aid from DAC donors, nominal. This table shows net aid from OECD's Development Assistance Committee (DAC) donors, which include Australia, Austria, Belgium, Canada, Denmark, Finland, France, the Federal Republic of Germany before reunification, Italy, Japan, the Netherlands, Norway, Sweden, Switzerland, the United Kingdom, and the United States (OECD data). (Ireland and New Zealand have been excluded in this compilation because their aid to Africa is negligible.)

Table 12-3. Net aid from non-DAC bilateral donors, nominal. This is net aid from Organization of Petroleum Exporting Countries (OPEC), the former Council for Mutual Economic Assistance (CMEA) countries, and China (OECD data). OPEC countries are Algeria, Iran, Iraq, Kuwait, Libya, Nigeria, Qatar, Saudi Arabia, the United Arab Emirates, and Venezuela. The former CMEA countries are Bulgaria, Czechoslovakia, the former German Democratic Republic, Hungary, Poland, Romania, and the former Soviet Union.

Table 12-4. Net aid from multilateral donors, nominal. This includes net aid, most notably from the African Development Fund, the European Development Fund for the Commission of the European Communities, the International Development Asso-

ciation (IDA), the International Fund for Agricultural Development, Arab/OPEC-financed multilateral agencies, and UN programs and agencies (OECD data). The UN programs and agencies include mainly the UN Technical Assistance Programme, the UN Development Programme (UNDP), the UN High Commissioner for Refugees, the UN Children's Fund (UNICEF), and the World Food Programme. Arab/OPEC-financed multilateral agencies include the Arab Bank for Economic Development in Africa, the Arab Fund for Economic and Social Development (AFESD), the Islamic Development Bank, the OPEC Fund for International Development, the Arab Authority for Agricultural Investment and Development, the Arab Fund for Technical Assistance to African and Arab Countries, and the Islamic Solidarity Fund. Aid flows from the IMF Trust Fund and Structural Adjustment Facility (SAF) are also included.

Tables 12-5, 12-6, 12-7, and 12-8. Net aid from all donors, from DAC donors, from non-DAC bilateral donors, and from multilateral donors (OECD data).

Tables 12-9, 12-10, and 12-11. Net aid from all donors, from DAC donors, and from multilateral donors as a share of recipient GDP. These tables show the relative importance of these aid flows to recipients' economies. They are obtained by dividing figures in Tables 12-1, 12-2, and 12-4 by GDP data from Table 2-5, which reflect current prices and exchange rates. For a given level of aid flows, devaluation of a recipient's currency may inflate the ratios shown in the table. Thus, trends for a given country and comparisons across countries that have implemented different exchange rate policies should be interpreted carefully.

Tables 12-12, 12-13, and 12-14. Net aid from all donors, from DAC donors, and from multilateral donors as a share of recipient GDI. These tables are obtained by dividing figures in Tables 12-1, 12-2, and 12-4 by GDI (World Bank country desks). These data highlight the relative importance of the indicated aid flows in maintaining and increasing investment in these economies. The same caveats mentioned above apply to their interpretation. Furthermore, aid flows do not exclusively finance investment (for example, food aid finances consumption), and the share of aid going to investment varies across countries.

Tables 12-15, 12-16, and 12-17. Net aid per capita from all donors, from DAC donors, and from multilateral donors. These data are calculated by dividing figures in Tables 12-1, 12-2, and 12-4 by midyear population (Table 1-2). These ratios offer some indication of the importance of aid flows in sustaining per capita income and consumption levels (shown in Tables 2-19 and 2-20, respectively), although bearing in mind that exchange rate fluctuations, the actual rise of aid flows, and other factors vary across countries and over time.

Figures

The following indicators have been used to derive the figures in this chapter.

Figure 12-1. Total net aid as a share of recipient GDP (Table 12-9).

Figure 12-2. Total net aid per capita (Table 12-15).

Methodology used for regional aggregations and period averages in Chapter 12

Table	Aggregations [a] (1)	(2)	Period averages [b] (1)	(2)
12-1	X		X	
12-2	X		X	
12-3	X		X	
12-4	X		X	
12-5	X			X
12-6	X			X
12-7	X			X
12-8	X			X
12-9		X	X	
12-10		X	X	
12-11		X	X	
12-12		X	X	
12-13		X	X	
12-14		X	X	
12-15		X	X	
12-16		X	X	
12-17		X	X	

Note: Regional aggregations are shown in the rows for Sub-Saharan Africa, North Africa, and All Africa. Period averages are shown in the last three columns. This table shows only the methodologies used in this chapter.

a. Regional aggregations: (1) simple total; (2) simple total of the first indicator divided by the simple total of the second indicator (same country coverage); (3) simple total of the gap-filled indicator; (4) simple total of the gap-filled main indicator divided by the simple total of the gap-filled secondary indicator; (5) simple total of the first gap-filled main indicator less the simple total of the second gap-filled main indicator, all divided by the simple total of the secondary indicator; (6) weighted total (by population); (7) median; (8) no aggregation; (9) simple arithmetic mean.

b. Period averages: (1) arithmetic mean (using the same series as shown in the table; i.e., ratio if the rest of the table is shown as ratio, level if the rest of the table is shown as level, growth rate if the rest is shown as growth rate); (2) least-squares growth rate (using main indicator); (3) least-squares growth rate (using main indicator in constant terms, with the rest of the table in current terms).

13

Social Indicators

This chapter provides indicators in the areas of demography, health, education, and gender issues in development. These indicators can be useful in evaluating and monitoring the social impact of development progress, aid flows, and structural adjustment policies.

The chapter presents such indicators as dependency ratio, urbanization, crude death rate, life expectancy at birth, infant mortality rate, child mortality rate, immunization rates for children, maternal death rate, and number of people per physician. These indicators are an indirect measure of the physical well-being of the population. In the same vein, such indicators as literacy rate among adults, school enrollment ratios by gender, and pupil-teacher ratio give some picture of the progress being made in education and training. Social indicators refer to phenomena that are inherently more qualitative than macroeconomic variables and thus need to be interpreted cautiously. Further caution is called for because of the particular limitations of the data. One of these limitations is the paucity—or even nonexistence—of data on certain indicators in many of the countries covered. This is especially true of indicators dealing with gender issues. Many countries have no data showing the gender breakdown of several social indicators.

Even when data are available, comparison among countries is limited because of varied practices in data gathering and reporting. Often the countries report survey data that cover different portions of the nation. Sometimes surveys are limited to only the urban areas—the largest cities—or the capital city alone. This is especially true of the health indicators. Such indicators as immunization rates for children under one year of age, percentage of births attended by health personnel, infant mortality rate, child mortality rate, and maternal death rate are often based on surveys of a handful of hospitals in the urban areas.

Another source of limitation is the definition of terms, which may differ from country to country. Some countries, for example, consider an institution as a "private school" only if it receives no form of financial support from the government, while others classify as "private" all schools not run by the government, whether or not they receive financial support from the government. In like manner, some countries include personnel other than doctors and trained nurses under "medical personnel."

Cultural norms may also affect the reported data. This is especially true for gender issues. In some countries, it is assumed that no woman can be the head of any household that also contains an adult male. In population censuses, therefore, enumerators and respondents simply take such assumptions for granted, reporting a male rather than a female as head of the household or family (see United Nations, *The World's Women: Trends and Statistics (1970–90)*. This distorts the true picture of the percentage of households headed by women.

The main source for this chapter is the *World Development Indicators* in the World Bank Statistical Information Management Analysis Database (SIMA), which contains electronic information as reported by a number of institutions and agencies in the socio-economic field, such as the United Nations, UNICEF, UNESCO, World Health Organization (WHO), the UNDP, the Joint United Nations Programme on HIV/AIDS (UNAIDS), and the Economic Commission for Africa (ECA). Other sources of data also include reports and publications on children, health, human development, education, and population from various agencies, including the World Bank.

In this chapter, columns headed by a period (for example, 1995–99) show data for the latest available year within the period.

13-1. Age and gender structure of the population

	Females as percentage of total population		Age groups as percentage of total population						Age dependency ratio	
			1980			2002				
	1980	2002	0-14	15-64	65+	0-14	15-64	65+	1980	2002
SUB-SAHARAN AFRICA	50.2	50.2	45.3	51.4	2.9	43.7	53.1	2.9	0.9	0.9
excluding South Africa	50.2	50.3	45.6	51.1	2.8	44.6	52.6	2.8	1.0	0.9
excl. S.Africa & Nigeria	50.3	50.3	45.7	50.9	2.8	44.8	52.4	2.9	1.0	0.9
Angola	50.8	50.5	44.7	52.5	2.9	50.0	52.7	3.1	0.9	1.0
Benin	50.7	50.7	45.1	50.8	4.1	45.7	52.2	2.7	1.0	0.9
Botswana	52.2	50.2	48.7	49.3	2.0	41.3	55.3	2.3	1.0	0.8
Burkina Faso	51.7	50.4	48.6	48.3	3.1	46.9	50.2	2.7	1.0	1.0
Burundi	51.9	51.0	44.7	51.8	3.5	45.6	51.7	2.6	0.9	0.9
Cameroon	50.6	50.0	44.1	52.0	3.6	40.8	54.3	3.6	0.9	0.8
Cape Verde	54.1	51.4	46.0	47.9	6.1	42.4	53.7	3.7	1.1	0.9
Central African Republic	51.9	51.2	41.7	54.4	4.0	42.2	54.7	3.5	0.8	0.8
Chad	50.9	50.5	44.3	52.2	3.4	47.6	47.1	2.8	0.8	1.1
Comoros	50.3	50.2	48.2	49.3	2.6	42.5	54.7	2.6	1.0	0.8
Congo, Dem. Rep. of	51.1	50.4	44.3	49.4	2.7	49.5	52.0	2.7	1.0	1.0
Congo, Rep. of	51.2	51.0	41.7	47.6	3.2	40.3	44.0	2.7	0.9	1.0
Côte d'Ivoire	48.5	49.2	45.8	51.8	2.4	42.2	56.1	2.6	1.0	0.8
Djibouti	53.3	52.6	41.9	56.2	1.9	40.7	50.9	2.9	0.9	0.9
Equatorial Guinea	51.0	50.6	40.7	54.3	4.1	43.4	52.6	3.7	0.8	0.9
Eritrea	50.4	50.4	44.2	53.1	2.6	45.0	52.4	2.6	..	0.9
Ethiopia	50.5	49.8	44.5	52.8	2.7	45.9	51.3	2.8	0.9	0.9
Gabon	50.8	50.4	34.1	59.1	6.3	39.4	52.8	5.5	0.7	0.9
Gambia, The	50.7	50.5	42.6	54.5	2.8	39.7	55.3	3.2	0.8	0.8
Ghana	50.4	50.2	44.6	50.0	2.7	41.6	52.1	4.4	0.9	0.9
Guinea	50.1	49.7	45.3	52.0	2.6	43.9	53.4	2.6	0.9	0.9
Guinea-Bissau	50.8	50.6	39.5	53.2	3.5	37.7	46.0	3.1	0.8	0.9
Kenya	50.3	49.8	50.1	47.0	2.9	42.4	54.5	2.7	1.1	0.8
Lesotho	51.3	50.3	44.2	58.5	3.9	46.2	65.7	5.0	0.9	0.8
Liberia	49.5	49.7	44.3	52.0	3.7	44.1	52.7	2.7	0.9	0.9
Madagascar	50.3	50.1	44.7	52.2	3.0	44.2	52.4	3.0	0.9	0.9
Malawi	51.6	50.8	47.5	50.2	2.3	44.6	51.8	3.5	1.0	0.9
Mali	51.2	50.9	46.8	50.7	2.6	46.7	49.8	2.9	1.0	1.0
Mauritania	50.7	50.4	42.1	51.3	2.9	44.0	53.5	3.2	0.9	0.9
Mauritius	50.7	50.5	35.6	60.8	3.6	25.2	68.4	6.3	0.6	0.5
Mozambique	50.8	51.4	44.1	52.7	3.2	42.4	53.6	3.6	0.9	0.9
Namibia	51.4	50.5	44.3	49.4	3.5	38.1	49.6	3.4	0.9	0.8
Niger	50.1	50.6	49.4	48.9	2.2	49.3	49.0	2.3	1.0	1.1
Nigeria	50.0	50.6	45.2	51.9	2.9	43.6	53.5	2.6	1.0	0.9
Rwanda	50.6	50.4	48.8	48.8	2.4	50.1	54.1	3.3	1.0	1.0
São Tomé and Principe	..	50.2	..	..	..	39.2	54.7	6.5	..	0.8
Senegal	50.0	50.2	45.3	51.8	2.8	44.6	54.0	2.7	0.9	0.9
Seychelles	..	49.4	..	..	..	27.8	64.2	7.1	..	0.5
Sierra Leone	51.0	50.9	43.0	53.9	3.1	44.0	53.2	2.6	0.9	0.9
Somalia	50.6	50.4	46.7	50.4	2.9	48.1	49.9	2.4	1.0	1.0
South Africa	50.3	51.7	41.8	55.1	3.1	30.7	60.4	4.3	0.7	0.6
Sudan	49.9	49.7	44.2	52.7	2.9	39.4	56.3	3.5	0.9	0.8
Swaziland	50.9	51.7	45.9	51.1	2.9	41.8	54.5	2.8	1.0	0.8
Tanzania	50.8	50.4	47.6	50.1	2.3	44.8	52.4	2.4	1.0	0.9
Togo	50.6	50.3	45.7	51.2	3.0	43.1	52.8	3.2	0.9	0.9
Uganda	50.3	50.0	47.9	49.6	2.5	46.6	46.7	1.8	1.0	1.0
Zambia	50.4	50.2	47.5	49.8	2.6	45.6	53.7	2.3	1.1	0.9
Zimbabwe	50.3	49.9	48.4	48.6	3.0	43.4	52.1	3.1	1.0	0.9
NORTH AFRICA	49.5	49.4	42.2	53.9	3.9	33.7	62.0	4.3	0.9	0.6
Algeria	50.4	49.4	46.5	49.6	3.9	34.7	61.5	4.0	1.0	0.6
Egypt, Arab Rep.	49.2	49.1	39.5	56.5	4.0	34.0	61.5	4.2	0.8	0.6
Libya	47.1	48.3	46.7	51.1	2.2	33.8	64.1	3.6	1.0	0.6
Morocco	49.9	50.0	43.2	52.7	4.1	33.5	62.2	4.3	0.9	0.6
Tunisia	49.3	49.5	41.6	54.6	3.8	28.2	65.9	6.0	0.8	0.5
ALL AFRICA	50.1	50.1	44.7	51.9	3.1	41.9	54.6	3.2	0.9	0.8

Note: Some age groups may not add up to 100% on account of rounding up error.

13-2. Poverty

	GDP per capita, based on PPP, 2002	Percentage of population living under US$ 1 a day, 1993-2000	National poverty headcount as % of population, 1984-2000	% of the population below 2/3 of national mean per capita income, 1991-1999		Gini coefficients, 1991-1997		Percentage of household income spent on food, 1991-1999
				Urban	Rural	Urban	Rural	
SUB-SAHARAN AFRICA	..	..	..	22	37	..	..	64
excluding South Africa	..	..	..	22	37	..	..	64
excl. S. Africa & Nigeria	..	..	..	22	37	..	..	64
Angola	2,053	..	..	..	..	..	..	..
Benin	1,032	..	33	..	..	..	..	..
Botswana	8,244	23	..	..	..	..	..	..
Burkina Faso	1,012	61	45	13	65	38	46	57
Burundi	613	58	36	..	..	..	..	..
Cameroon	1,712	33	40	..	..	..	..	55
Cape Verde	4,787	..	..	..	..	..	..	..
Central African Republic	1,198	67	..	33	77	51	63	60
Chad	1,008	..	64	..	..	..	..	..
Comoros	1,640	..	..	..	..	..	..	..
Congo, Dem. Rep. of	606	..	..	..	..	..	..	..
Congo, Rep. of	967	..	..	..	..	..	..	..
Côte d'Ivoire	1,500	12	37	29	51	39	33	48
Djibouti	2,028	..	45	38	84	38	39	43
Equatorial Guinea	..	..	..	..	..	..	..	..
Eritrea	958	69	53	..	..	..	..	..
Ethiopia	724	82	44	21	50	56	40	72
Gabon	6,349	..	..	..	..	..	..	..
Gambia, The	1,723	59	64	21	73	43	35	60
Ghana	2,050	45	31	22	37	34	36	39
Guinea	2,026	..	40	18	57	..	..	56
Guinea-Bissau	779	..	49	30	65	55	56	..
Kenya	992	23	42	14	53	51	52	71
Lesotho	2,272	43	49	..	..	..	..	..
Liberia	..	..	..	..	..	..	..	..
Madagascar	735	49	71	21	57	..	..	70
Malawi	586	42	65	..	..	..	57	..
Mali	878	73	64	8	64	53	55	75
Mauritania	1,511	29	46	18	56	34	33	70
Mauritius	10,530	..	11	..	..	..	..	..
Mozambique	..	38	69	..	..	..	..	..
Namibia	6,410	35	..	..	..	..	..	..
Niger	774	61	63	14	55	39	31	60
Nigeria	851	70	34	32	52	44	46	67
Rwanda	1,221	..	51	..	..	..	..	..
São Tomé and Principe	..	..	..	..	..	..	..	..
Senegal	1,535	26	33	14	66	..	..	61
Seychelles	..	..	..	..	..	..	..	..
Sierra Leone	509	..	68	..	..	..	50	..
Somalia	..	..	..	..	..	..	..	..
South Africa	10,132	7	..	40	86	..	..	56
Sudan	1,967	..	..	..	..	..	..	..
Swaziland	4,503	..	40	36	70	..	..	65
Tanzania	557	20	42	20	51	..	..	70
Togo	1,459	..	32	..	..	..	..	..
Uganda	1,354	82	55	16	46	35	44	63
Zambia	806	64	73	28	70	40	46	64
Zimbabwe	..	..	35	..	..	..	..	..
NORTH AFRICA	..	..	..	..	..	..	..	..
Algeria	5,536	2	23	..	..	..	..	..
Egypt, Arab Rep.	3,701	3	17	..	..	..	..	..
Libya	..	..	..	..	..	..	..	..
Morocco	3,767	2	19	..	..	..	..	..
Tunisia	6,579	2	8	..	..	..	..	..
ALL AFRICA	..	..	..	22	37	..	..	64

13-3. Income distribution

| | Share of income held by population groups | | | |
| | Richest 10% | Richest 20% | Poorest 10% | Poorest 20% |
	1989-00	1989-00	1989-00	1989-00
SUB-SAHARAN AFRICA	..	..	..	..
excluding South Africa	..	..	..	..
excl. S. Africa & Nigeria	..	..	..	..
Angola	..	..	..	..
Benin	..	..	..	..
Botswana	56.6	70.3	0.7	2.2
Burkina Faso	46.3	60.7	1.8	4.5
Burundi	32.8	48.0	1.7	5.1
Cameroon	36.5	53.0	1.8	4.6
Cape Verde	..	..	..	..
Central African Republic	47.7	65.0	0.7	2.0
Chad	..	..	..	..
Comoros	..	..	..	..
Congo, Dem. Rep. of	..	..	..	..
Congo, Rep. of	..	..	..	..
Côte d'Ivoire	28.8	44.3	3.1	7.1
Djibouti	29.9	45.4	2.3	6.3
Equatorial Guinea	..	..	..	..
Eritrea	..	..	..	..
Ethiopia	43.8	60.8	0.7	2.4
Gabon	..	..	..	..
Gambia, The	38.0	55.2	1.5	4.0
Ghana	30.0	46.6	2.1	5.6
Guinea	32.0	47.2	2.6	6.4
Guinea-Bissau	39.3	53.4	2.1	5.2
Kenya	36.1	51.2	2.3	5.6
Lesotho	53.6	70.7	0.5	1.4
Liberia	..	..	..	..
Madagascar	28.6	44.8	2.5	6.4
Malawi	42.2	56.1	1.9	4.9
Mali	40.4	56.2	1.8	4.6
Mauritania	28.4	44.1	2.5	6.4
Mauritius	..	..	..	..
Mozambique	31.7	46.5	2.5	6.5
Namibia	64.5	78.7	0.5	1.4
Niger	35.4	53.3	0.8	2.6
Nigeria	40.8	55.7	1.6	4.4
Rwanda	..	..	..	..
São Tomé and Principe	..	..	..	..
Senegal	33.5	48.2	2.6	6.4
Seychelles	..	..	..	..
Sierra Leone	43.6	63.4	0.5	1.1
Somalia	..	..	..	..
South Africa	46.9	66.5	0.7	2.0
Sudan	..	..	..	..
Swaziland	50.2	64.4	1.0	2.7
Tanzania	30.0	45.5	2.8	6.8
Togo	..	..	..	..
Uganda	29.8	44.9	3.0	7.1
Zambia	41.0	56.6	1.1	3.3
Zimbabwe	40.3	55.7	1.8	4.6
NORTH AFRICA	..	..	..	..
Algeria	26.8	42.6	2.8	7.0
Egypt, Arab Rep.	29.5	43.6	3.7	8.6
Libya	..	..	..	..
Morocco	30.9	46.6	2.6	6.5
Tunisia	31.8	47.9	2.3	5.7
ALL AFRICA	..	..	..	..

13-4. Urbanization

	Total population (millions)			Average annual percentage growth of total population			Urban population as percentage of total population			Average annual percentage growth of urban population		
	1980	1990	2002	1975-1979	1980-1990	1990-2002	1980	1990	2002	1975-1979	1980-1990	1990-2002
SUB-SAHARAN AFRICA	383.5	510.9	689.3	2.9	2.9	2.6	23.1	27.9	35.5	5.0	4.9	4.7
excluding South Africa	356.0	475.7	643.9	3.0	2.9	2.6	21.1	26.3	33.9	5.5	5.3	4.8
excl. S. Africa & Nigeria	284.8	379.5	511.1	3.0	2.9	2.5	19.7	24.1	30.8	5.4	5.1	4.7
Angola	7.0	9.3	13.1	2.5	3.0	2.8	20.9	27.6	35.5	5.9	6.1	5.3
Benin	3.5	4.7	6.6	2.5	3.1	2.8	27.3	34.5	43.7	7.3	5.6	5.0
Botswana	0.9	1.3	1.7	3.6	3.5	2.6	18.5	42.3	49.9	11.7	12.5	4.2
Burkina Faso	7.0	8.9	11.8	2.3	2.5	2.4	8.5	13.6	17.2	7.8	7.6	4.5
Burundi	4.1	5.5	7.1	2.1	2.8	2.2	4.3	6.3	9.6	8.4	6.8	5.9
Cameroon	8.8	11.7	15.8	3.0	2.9	2.6	31.4	40.3	50.4	6.6	5.5	4.4
Cape Verde	0.3	0.3	0.5	0.7	1.6	2.5	23.5	44.2	64.4	2.6	8.1	5.9
Central African Republic	2.3	2.9	3.8	2.3	2.5	2.3	35.1	37.5	42.2	3.3	3.2	3.3
Chad	4.5	5.8	8.3	2.0	2.7	3.1	18.8	21.0	24.5	6.2	3.8	4.3
Comoros	0.3	0.4	0.6	0.0	0.6	2.6	23.2	27.9	34.4	0.0	0.6	4.4
Congo, Dem. Rep. of	27.9	37.4	51.6	3.2	2.9	2.7	28.7	27.9	31.3	2.4	3.0	4.1
Congo, Rep. of	1.8	2.5	3.7	3.2	3.3	3.3	42.0	55.7	66.6	6.3	6.0	4.7
Côte d'Ivoire	8.2	11.8	16.5	4.0	3.7	2.9	34.7	39.8	44.5	5.9	5.2	4.0
Djibouti	0.3	0.5	0.7	7.9	4.5	3.2	74.2	81.0	84.4	9.6	5.1	3.2
Equatorial Guinea	0.2	0.4	0.5	-2.8	5.2	2.6	27.4	35.7	50.3	-2.5	8.0	5.7
Eritrea	2.4	3.1	4.3	2.7	2.8	2.7	13.8	15.8	19.5	4.3	4.2	4.5
Ethiopia	37.7	51.2	67.2	2.7	3.0	2.3	10.5	12.7	16.2	4.8	5.0	4.4
Gabon	0.7	1.0	1.3	3.3	3.2	2.8	49.6	68.1	82.9	7.9	6.5	4.5
Gambia, The	0.6	0.9	1.4	3.2	3.7	3.5	19.6	24.9	31.9	6.2	6.2	5.6
Ghana	11.0	15.3	20.3	2.1	3.4	2.5	31.2	33.5	36.7	2.5	4.2	3.2
Guinea	4.5	5.8	7.7	1.3	2.5	2.5	19.1	23.4	28.4	4.6	4.7	4.2
Guinea-Bissau	0.8	1.0	1.4	4.1	2.7	2.9	17.3	23.8	33.1	5.3	5.5	5.2
Kenya	16.6	23.4	31.3	3.8	3.5	2.5	16.1	24.0	35.2	8.4	7.8	5.9
Lesotho	1.3	1.6	1.8	2.3	2.2	1.0	13.4	20.1	29.5	6.7	6.4	5.3
Liberia	1.9	2.4	3.3	3.1	2.7	2.6	35.0	42.0	46.1	6.1	4.7	3.4
Madagascar	8.9	11.6	16.4	2.6	2.7	3.0	18.5	23.6	30.7	5.2	5.2	5.3
Malawi	6.2	8.5	10.7	3.3	3.3	2.0	9.1	11.6	15.5	7.1	5.8	4.5
Mali	6.6	8.5	11.4	2.2	2.5	2.5	18.5	23.8	31.5	4.8	5.1	4.9
Mauritania	1.6	2.0	2.8	2.5	2.4	2.7	27.7	44.0	60.3	9.3	7.5	5.8
Mauritius	1.0	1.1	1.2	1.6	0.9	1.1	42.4	40.5	41.9	1.3	0.5	1.4
Mozambique	12.1	14.2	18.4	2.8	1.7	2.2	13.1	21.1	34.3	11.6	6.8	6.6
Namibia	1.0	1.4	2.0	2.1	3.2	2.9	22.8	26.6	31.9	4.0	4.9	3.9
Niger	5.6	7.7	11.4	3.1	3.2	3.5	12.6	16.1	21.6	6.8	5.8	6.0
Nigeria	71.1	96.2	132.8	3.0	3.1	2.8	26.9	35.0	45.7	5.9	5.9	5.1
Rwanda	5.2	6.9	8.2	3.3	3.1	1.2	4.7	5.3	6.4	6.9	4.5	3.6
São Tomé and Principe	0.1	0.1	0.2	1.2	2.6	2.5	30.8	39.1	48.3	4.0	5.0	4.4
Senegal	5.5	7.3	9.8	2.9	2.9	2.5	35.7	40.0	48.8	3.7	4.0	4.4
Seychelles	0.1	0.1	0.1	1.9	0.8	1.5	40.8	53.5	65.3	6.0	3.7	3.3
Sierra Leone	3.2	4.0	5.2	2.0	2.1	2.3	24.1	30.0	38.0	4.7	4.4	4.4
Somalia	6.5	7.2	9.3	10.1	0.4	2.0	22.2	24.2	28.4	11.1	1.3	3.4
South Africa	27.6	35.2	45.3	2.2	2.5	2.2	48.1	48.8	58.4	2.2	2.6	3.4
Sudan	19.4	24.9	32.8	2.9	2.6	2.3	20.0	26.6	37.9	4.3	5.5	5.4
Swaziland	0.6	0.8	1.1	3.2	3.1	3.0	17.8	23.8	27.0	8.7	6.3	4.2
Tanzania	18.6	25.5	35.2	3.1	3.2	2.8	14.8	21.7	34.2	11.4	7.4	6.8
Togo	2.5	3.5	4.8	1.8	3.3	2.7	22.9	28.5	34.5	8.6	5.8	4.4
Uganda	12.8	17.4	24.6	2.7	3.0	2.9	8.8	11.2	14.9	3.8	4.8	5.6
Zambia	5.7	7.8	10.2	3.4	3.1	2.4	39.8	39.4	40.1	6.3	3.1	2.7
Zimbabwe	7.1	10.2	13.0	3.1	3.7	2.1	22.3	28.4	36.7	5.9	6.3	4.3
NORTH AFRICA	88.4	114.0	142.6	2.6	2.6	1.9	44.6	48.8	52.5	3.6	3.5	2.5
Algeria	18.7	25.0	31.3	3.1	3.0	1.9	43.5	51.4	58.3	4.5	4.8	3.0
Egypt, Arab Rep.	40.9	52.4	66.4	2.3	2.5	2.0	43.8	43.6	42.8	2.6	2.5	1.8
Libya	3.0	4.3	5.4	4.4	3.8	2.0	69.3	81.8	88.2	7.7	5.6	2.7
Morocco	19.4	24.0	29.6	2.3	2.2	1.8	41.3	48.4	56.7	4.1	3.8	3.2
Tunisia	6.4	8.2	9.8	2.5	2.5	1.6	51.5	57.9	66.8	3.4	3.7	2.8
ALL AFRICA	471.9	624.9	831.8	2.9	2.9	2.4	27.1	31.7	38.4	4.5	4.5	4.1

13-5. Components of population change

	Total fertility rate			Crude birth rate			Crude death rate		
	1985	1995	2002	1985	1995	2002	1985	1995	2002
SUB-SAHARAN AFRICA	6.4	5.6	5.0	45.6	41.7	38.6	16.1	15.4	17.6
excluding South Africa	6.7	5.8	5.2	46.5	42.7	39.5	16.6	15.8	17.5
excl. S. Africa & Nigeria	6.7	5.9	5.2	46.5	43.0	39.6	16.7	16.2	17.5
Angola	7.1	7.0	6.5	51.1	49.4	46.9	21.9	19.0	18.8
Benin	6.9	6.2	5.3	48.4	42.2	38.3	16.7	14.0	12.9
Botswana	5.6	4.6	3.8	41.8	35.1	29.7	8.4	12.4	22.8
Burkina Faso	7.3	6.8	6.3	47.3	45.8	43.2	19.1	18.8	19.3
Burundi	6.8	6.5	5.8	46.5	44.2	38.5	18.0	20.8	19.6
Cameroon	6.4	5.2	4.6	42.7	39.8	35.5	14.6	12.3	15.7
Cape Verde	6.0	4.1	3.5	37.6	35.6	30.8	10.5	6.9	5.4
Central African Republic	5.7	5.1	4.6	42.2	38.0	35.5	18.2	18.4	19.8
Chad	7.2	6.8	6.2	45.3	45.9	44.8	20.3	17.2	16.3
Comoros	6.9	4.8	4.1	45.3	35.7	32.0	16.1	9.5	7.8
Congo, Dem. Rep. of	6.7	6.5	5.9	48.1	47.0	45.1	15.0	14.9	17.7
Congo, Rep. of	6.3	6.3	5.8	44.1	44.5	41.2	15.2	14.8	14.2
Côte d'Ivoire	7.1	5.4	4.6	47.4	38.0	36.6	15.3	15.8	17.1
Djibouti	6.4	5.6	5.2	43.1	38.3	35.9	18.1	15.5	19.6
Equatorial Guinea	5.8	5.9	5.5	43.6	42.0	40.6	20.2	17.1	14.9
Eritrea	7.3	6.0	5.3	..	38.5	37.5	..	14.7	13.3
Ethiopia	7.1	6.2	5.5	50.9	47.1	42.4	20.1	20.1	20.1
Gabon	4.8	4.6	4.1	34.7	36.5	34.9	17.4	16.0	15.2
Gambia, The	6.3	5.5	4.8	47.2	43.2	36.8	21.7	15.7	13.8
Ghana	6.3	4.6	4.0	43.9	33.2	28.7	12.4	9.4	12.6
Guinea	6.2	5.6	5.0	47.8	42.5	37.7	22.4	18.0	16.7
Guinea-Bissau	6.0	6.0	5.6	45.2	44.9	39.3	23.7	20.9	19.8
Kenya	6.9	4.9	4.2	45.1	35.2	34.5	11.5	10.4	16.4
Lesotho	5.3	4.8	4.2	38.1	35.7	30.9	13.0	12.0	20.0
Liberia	6.8	6.5	5.8	46.8	46.7	43.1	16.2	20.4	19.6
Madagascar	6.6	5.9	5.2	46.3	43.6	38.6	15.1	12.4	11.9
Malawi	7.5	6.6	6.1	52.5	48.3	44.9	21.1	22.8	24.8
Mali	7.1	6.7	6.1	49.7	48.8	45.5	20.3	18.3	21.4
Mauritania	6.2	5.3	4.4	43.5	43.7	40.3	17.5	15.7	14.9
Mauritius	2.3	2.1	2.0	19.0	18.3	16.6	6.8	6.7	6.7
Mozambique	6.4	5.6	5.0	45.6	42.3	40.1	19.4	19.1	21.1
Namibia	5.7	5.3	4.8	39.5	36.9	35.4	12.6	11.9	20.5
Niger	8.0	7.5	7.1	56.1	53.6	49.4	23.8	21.2	19.7
Nigeria	6.5	5.7	5.1	46.6	41.6	39.1	16.0	14.5	17.4
Rwanda	7.7	6.5	5.7	47.2	43.5	43.5	17.4	23.5	21.6
São Tomé and Principe	..	4.8	4.3	37.4	36.7	30.7	9.7	9.3	9.0
Senegal	6.6	5.7	4.9	46.2	40.3	34.8	18.4	13.7	12.8
Seychelles	3.2	2.3	2.1	26.5	21.0	19.2	7.2	7.0	6.6
Sierra Leone	6.5	6.2	5.6	49.0	47.1	43.9	27.7	27.2	24.9
Somalia	7.3	7.3	6.9	51.7	52.2	49.9	21.0	21.1	16.8
South Africa	3.8	3.1	2.8	33.9	28.7	25.0	10.3	9.8	19.6
Sudan	5.8	5.1	4.4	39.9	36.8	33.0	15.1	12.7	10.3
Swaziland	5.8	4.9	4.2	42.6	38.5	34.8	13.0	10.5	18.3
Tanzania	6.5	5.8	5.0	45.7	41.8	38.2	14.2	14.8	18.2
Togo	6.9	5.4	4.9	44.6	41.2	33.9	15.3	15.6	14.5
Uganda	7.2	6.7	6.0	49.9	48.8	43.8	17.6	19.2	17.7
Zambia	6.7	5.9	5.1	48.0	43.2	38.5	14.4	17.4	23.1
Zimbabwe	5.8	4.1	3.7	41.4	33.0	28.8	11.2	11.8	21.3
NORTH AFRICA	4.9	3.5	2.9	36.4	26.6	22.7	10.4	7.0	5.7
Algeria	5.7	3.7	2.8	37.5	27.2	21.8	9.3	6.4	5.0
Egypt, Arab Rep.	4.6	3.6	3.1	36.7	27.2	24.2	11.6	7.6	6.1
Libya	6.3	3.9	3.3	37.4	27.4	26.8	7.5	4.7	4.4
Morocco	4.7	3.4	2.8	36.3	26.7	21.3	10.4	7.1	5.8
Tunisia	4.3	2.7	2.1	31.0	20.8	17.6	7.7	5.8	5.6
ALL AFRICA	6.1	5.2	4.6	43.9	39.0	35.8	15.1	13.9	15.6

13-6. Survival prospects

	Life expectancy at birth (years)		Infant mortality (per thousand)		Mortality of children under five years (per thousand)	Maternal mortality (per 100,000 live births)
	1990	*2002*	*1990*	*2001*	*2001*	*1999 or MR available*
SUB-SAHARAN AFRICA	50	46	110	103	169	1093
excluding South Africa	49	46	114	105	174	1155
excl. S. Africa & Nigeria	49	46	113	104	171	1170
Angola	45	47	166	154	260	1300
Benin	52	53	111	94	158	880
Botswana	57	38	45	80	110	480
Burkina Faso	45	43	118	104	197	1400
Burundi	44	42	114	114	190	1900
Cameroon	54	48	85	96	155	720
Cape Verde	65	69	45	29	38	190
Central African Republic	48	42	115	115	180	1200
Chad	46	48	118	117	200	1500
Comoros	56	61	88	59	79	570
Congo, Dem. Rep. of	52	45	128	129	205	940
Congo, Rep. of	51	52	83	81	108	1100
Côte d'Ivoire	50	48	100	102	175	1200
Djibouti	48	44	119	100	143	520
Equatorial Guinea	47	52	122	101	153	1400
Eritrea	49	51	92	67	111	1100
Ethiopia	45	42	128	97	166	871
Gabon	52	53	60	60	90	620
Gambia, The	49	53	103	91	126	1100
Ghana	57	55	74	57	100	590
Guinea	44	46	145	109	169	1200
Guinea-Bissau	42	45	153	130	211	910
Kenya	57	46	63	78	122	1300
Lesotho	58	43	102	91	132	530
Liberia	45	47	157	157	235	1000
Madagascar	53	55	103	84	136	580
Malawi	45	38	146	114	183	580
Mali	45	41	152	141	231	630
Mauritania	49	51	120	120	183	870
Mauritius	70	73	21	17	19	45
Mozambique	43	41	143	125	197	980
Namibia	58	42	65	55	67	370
Niger	45	46	191	156	265	920
Nigeria	49	45	114	110	183	1100
Rwanda	40	40	107	96	183	2300
São Tomé and Principe	62	66	69	57	74	..
Senegal	50	52	90	79	138	1200
Seychelles	70	73	17	13	17	..
Sierra Leone	35	37	185	182	316	2100
Somalia	42	47	133	133	225	1600
South Africa	62	46	45	56	71	340
Sudan	52	53	75	65	107	1500
Swaziland	57	44	77	106	149	370
Tanzania	50	43	102	104	165	1100
Togo	50	50	88	79	141	980
Uganda	47	43	100	79	124	1100
Zambia	49	37	108	112	202	870
Zimbabwe	56	39	53	76	123	610
NORTH AFRICA	65	70	62	35	42	205
Algeria	67	71	42	39	49	150
Egypt, Arab Rep.	63	69	76	35	41	170
Libya	68	72	34	16	19	120
Morocco	63	68	66	39	44	390
Tunisia	70	73	37	21	27	70
ALL AFRICA	53	50	104	96	155	924

13-7. HIV/AIDS estimates and data, end 2001

	Estimated number of people living with HIV/AIDS					AIDS Orphans	Estimated AIDS deaths
	Adults and children	Adults (15-49)	Adult rate (%)	Women (15-49)	Children (0-14)	Orphans (0-14), currently living	Adults and children
SUB-SAHARAN AFRICA	28,459,000	25,626,100	8.4	14,784,050	2,613,280	10,909,900	2,189,920
excluding South Africa	23,459,000	20,926,100	7.4	12,084,050	2,363,280	10,249,900	1,829,920
excl. S. Africa & Nigeria	19,959,000	17,726,100	7.7	10,384,050	2,093,280	9,249,900	1,659,920
Angola	350,000	320,000	5.5	190,000	37,000	100,000	24,000
Benin	120,000	110,000	3.6	67,000	12,000	34,000	8,100
Botswana	330,000	300,000	38.8	170,000	28,000	69,000	26,000
Burkina Faso	440,000	380,000	6.5	220,000	61,000	270,000	44,000
Burundi	390,000	330,000	8.3	190,000	55,000	240,000	40,000
Cameroon	920,000	860,000	11.8	500,000	69,000	210,000	53,000
Cape Verde	..	..	..			..	
Central African Republic	250,000	220,000	12.9	130,000	25,000	110,000	22,000
Chad	150,000	130,000	3.6	76,000	18,000	72,000	14,000
Comoros	..	..	..	..	..	..	..
Congo, Dem. Rep. of	1,300,000	1,100,000	4.9	670,000	170,000	930,000	120,000
Congo, Rep. of	110,000	99,000	7.2	59,000	15,000	78,000	11,000
Côte d'Ivoire	770,000	690,000	9.7	400,000	84,000	420,000	75,000
Djibouti	..	..	..	..	..	..	..
Equatorial Guinea	5,900	5,500	3.4	3,000	420	..	370
Eritrea	55,000	49,000	2.8	30,000	4,000	24,000	350
Ethiopia	2,100,000	1,900,000	6.4	1,100,000	230,000	990,000	160,000
Gabon	..	..	..			..	
Gambia, The	8,400	7,900	1.6	4,400	460	5,300	400
Ghana	360,000	330,000	3.0	170,000	34,000	200,000	28,000
Guinea	..	..	..	..	..	..	..
Guinea-Bissau	17,000	16,000	2.8	9,300	1,500	4,300	1,200
Kenya	2,500,000	2,300,000	15.0	1,400,000	220,000	890,000	190,000
Lesotho	360,000	330,000	31.0	180,000	27,000	73,000	25,000
Liberia	..	..	..	..	..	..	..
Madagascar	22,000	21,000	0.3	12,000	1,000	6,300	..
Malawi	850,000	780,000	15.0	440,000	65,000	470,000	80,000
Mali	110,000	100,000	1.7	54,000	13,000	70,000	11,000
Mauritania	..	..	..	..	..	..	..
Mauritius	700	700	0.1	350	..	..	..
Mozambique	1,100,000	1,000,000	13.0	630,000	80,000	420,000	60,000
Namibia	230,000	200,000	22.5	110,000	30,000	47,000	13,000
Niger	..	..	..	..	..	..	..
Nigeria	3,500,000	3,200,000	5.8	1,700,000	270,000	1,000,000	170,000
Rwanda	500,000	430,000	8.9	250,000	65,000	260,000	49,000
São Tomé and Principe	..	..	..	..	..	..	
Senegal	27,000	24,000	0.5	14,000	2,900	15,000	2,500
Seychelles	..	..	..	..	..	..	..
Sierra Leone	170,000	150,000	7.0	90,000	16,000	42,000	11,000
Somalia	43,000	43,000	1.0	..	..	..	..
South Africa	5,000,000	4,700,000	20.1	2,700,000	250,000	660,000	360,000
Sudan	450,000	410,000	2.6	230,000	30,000	62,000	23,000
Swaziland	170,000	150,000	33.4	89,000	14,000	35,000	12,000
Tanzania	1,500,000	1,300,000	7.8	750,000	170,000	810,000	140,000
Togo	150,000	130,000	6.0	76,000	15,000	63,000	12,000
Uganda	600,000	510,000	5.0	280,000	110,000	880,000	84,000
Zambia	1,200,000	1,000,000	21.5	590,000	150,000	570,000	120,000
Zimbabwe	2,300,000	2,000,000	33.7	1,200,000	240,000	780,000	200,000
NORTH AFRICA	..	41,000	0.05	..	..	..	..
Algeria	..	13,000	..	..	..	..	..
Egypt, Arab Rep.	8,000	8,000	<0.1	780	..	..	..
Libya	7,000	7,000	0.2	1,100	..	..	..
Morocco	13,000	13,000	0.1	2,000	..	..	..
Tunisia	..	..	..	..	..	..	..
ALL AFRICA	28,487,000	25,667,100	6.7	14,787,930	2,613,280	10,909,900	2,189,920

13-8. Immunization and ORT use

	Percentage of children (0-1 year) immunized against						ORT use among children under five (percentage)
	DPT			Measles			
	1991	*1996*	*2001**	*1991*	*1996*	*2001**	*1992-93*
SUB-SAHARAN AFRICA	50	52	49	54	54	54	..
excluding South Africa	48	50	47	52	53	53	50
excl. S. Africa & Nigeria	51	58	54	51	57	56	..
Angola	26	28	41	39	62	72	48
Benin	69	66	76	60	60	65	28
Botswana	88	83	87	88	89	83	64
Burkina Faso	53	37	41	69	40	46	15
Burundi	82	73	74	78	79	75	49
Cameroon	42	46	43	48	49	62	84
Cape Verde	..	..	78	76	66	72	5
Central African Republic	66	53	23	62	46	29	24
Chad	18	20	27	28	22	36	15
Comoros	..	..	70	40	43	70	70
Congo, Dem. Rep. of	..	..	40	17	21	46	46
Congo, Rep. of	74	37	31	64	42	35	67
Côte d'Ivoire	39	55	57	57	65	61	16
Djibouti	53	41	49	53	41	49	56
Equatorial Guinea	77	80	32	85	81	19	40
Eritrea	..	67	93	..	66	88	..
Ethiopia	21	55	56	17	54	52	68
Gabon	72	62	38	71	57	55	25
Gambia, The	..	..	96	87	94	90	51
Ghana	60	71	80	63	71	81	44
Guinea	36	48	43	42	61	52	82
Guinea-Bissau	63	53	47	52	49	48	26
Kenya	86	87	76	81	81	76	69
Lesotho	78	88	85	80	82	77	78
Liberia	..	..	62	..	..	78	15
Madagascar	53	49	55	54	46	55	26
Malawi	87	90	90	85	90	82	50
Mali	36	52	51	42	55	37	41
Mauritania	29	50	61	32	66	58	54
Mauritius	91	90	92	88	61	90	..
Mozambique	46	60	80	55	67	92	60
Namibia	69	70	63	76	61	58	75
Niger	19	23	31	28	38	51	17
Nigeria	39	26	26	57	38	40	80
Rwanda	91	89	86	89	76	78	36
São Tomé and Principe	..	..	82	77	57	69	50
Senegal	51	70	52	54	70	48	27
Seychelles	98	99	96	89	98	95	..
Sierra Leone	..	..	44	..	..	37	60
Somalia	20	21	33	30	33	38	78
South Africa	81	73	81	85	76	72	..
Sudan	63	56	46	57	59	67	47
Swaziland	79	82	77	80	82	72	85
Tanzania	..	..	85	79	78	83	83
Togo	73	50	64	69	48	58	33
Uganda	49	57	60	54	55	61	45
Zambia	79	87	78	80	86	85	90
Zimbabwe	87	90	75	87	88	68	..
NORTH AFRICA	80	88	89	87	92	95	24
Algeria	82	77	89	85	90	83	27
Egypt, Arab Rep.	76	90	99	89	92	97	34
Libya	..	..	94	87	93	93	80
Morocco	81	95	96	80	93	96	14
Tunisia	93	95	96	94	92	92	22
ALL AFRICA	55	57	54	59	59	59	48

Notes: ORT = Oral rehydration therapy; DPT = diphtheria, pertussis (whooping cough), and tetanus; * Or most recent available data.

13-9. Child malnutrition

	Percentage of children (1990-00)			Percentage of infants with low birth weight		Percentage of under-five (1990-00) suffering from moderate to severe		
	Exclusively breastfed, (0-3 months)	*Breastfed, plus other food, (6-9 months)*	*Still breastfeeding, (20-23 months)*	*1988*	*1993-00*	*Underweight*	*Wasting*	*Stunting*
SUB-SAHARAN AFRICA	29	63	47	..	..	..	..	..
excluding South Africa	29	63	47	..	..	..	..	..
excl. S. Africa & Nigeria	37	67	49	..	..	..	..	..
Angola	12	70	49	..	..	41	6	53
Benin	15	97	65	8	9	29	14	25
Botswana	39	82	23	8	..	13	11	29
Burkina Faso	12	44	81	..	..	34	13	29
Burundi	89	66	73	..	16	45	9	43
Cameroon	7	77	35	..	..	22	6	29
Cape Verde	18	..	..	..	..	14	6	16
Central African Republic	23	93	52	15	..	23	7	34
Chad	2	81	62	..	..	28	..	40
Comoros	5	87	45	..	..	25	8	34
Congo, Dem. Rep. of	32	40	64	..	20	34	10	45
Congo, Rep. of	43	95	27	..	..	..	..	..
Côte d'Ivoire	3	65	45	..	..	21	8	24
Djibouti	..	..	..	11	..	18	13	26
Equatorial Guinea	..	..	..	..	..	..	..	..
Eritrea	66	45	60	..	..	44	16	38
Ethiopia	63	77	75	..	9	47	10	51
Gabon	57	..	..	..	..	12	..	..
Gambia, The	..	8	58	..	..	17	6	14
Ghana	19	63	48	17	8	25	11	26
Guinea	52	..	15	25	13	33	12	29
Guinea-Bissau	..	..	..	..	..	25	5	..
Kenya	17	90	54	..	..	22	6	34
Lesotho	54	47	52	..	..	18	5	44
Liberia	15	17	25	..	..	..	..	..
Madagascar	61	93	49	10	15	40	7	48
Malawi	11	78	68	20	..	25	7	48
Mali	13	33	60	17	..	27	23	30
Mauritania	90	64	59	..	9	32	7	44
Mauritius	16	29	..	9	..	15	14	10
Mozambique	37	..	..	20	..	26	8	36
Namibia	22	65	23	..	..	26	9	29
Niger	1	67	52	..	..	40	21	41
Nigeria	2	52	43	20	..	31	9	43
Rwanda	90	68	85	..	..	24	4	42
São Tomé and Principe	..	..	..	..	..	..	..	26
Senegal	16	69	50	..	..	18	7	23
Seychelles	..	..	..	..	..	..	..	..
Sierra Leone	..	94	41	17	..	27	9	35
Somalia	..	..	..	..	16	26	..	30
South Africa	..	..	..	..	..	9	3	23
Sudan	14	45	44	15	15	35	17	36
Swaziland	37	51	20	..	..	10	..	..
Tanzania	41	93	53	13	..	29	7	43
Togo	15	25	99	20	..	25	..	34
Uganda	70	64	40	..	..	23	5	38
Zambia	27	88	43	..	10	24	4	42
Zimbabwe	16	93	26	..	11	13	6	21
NORTH AFRICA	45	34	..	..	..	14	..	..
Algeria	48	29	21	9	..	6	9	18
Egypt, Arab Rep.	53	37	..	..	..	4	5	30
Libya	..	..	..	..	..	5	3	15
Morocco	31	33	20	..	4	10	2	24
Tunisia	12	53	16	8	16	4	4	23
ALL AFRICA	32	59	45	..	..	..	..	..

13-10. Access to sanitation facilities

	Percentage of population with access to sanitation facilities					
	1990			2000		
	Total	Urban	Rural	Total	Urban	Rural
SUB-SAHARAN AFRICA	54	75	45	54	74	43
excluding South Africa	51	72	43	51	72	41
excl. S. Africa & Nigeria	50	73	43	50	74	40
Angola	..	..	..	44	70	30
Benin	20	46	6	23	46	6
Botswana	60	87	41	66	88	43
Burkina Faso	..	..	..	29	39	27
Burundi	87	65	89	88	68	90
Cameroon	77	97	64	79	92	66
Cape Verde	..	..	..	71	95	32
Central African Republic	24	38	16	25	38	16
Chad	18	70	4	29	81	13
Comoros	98	98	98	98	98	98
Congo, Dem. Rep. of	..	..	..	21	54	6
Congo, Rep. of	..	..	..	14	14	..
Côte d'Ivoire	46	70	29	52	71	35
Djibouti	..	..	..	91	99	50
Equatorial Guinea	..	..	..	53	60	46
Eritrea	..	..	..	13	66	1
Ethiopia	8	24	6	12	33	7
Gabon	..	..	..	53	55	43
Gambia, The	..	..	..	37	41	35
Ghana	61	56	64	72	74	70
Guinea	55	94	41	58	94	41
Guinea-Bissau	44	87	33	56	95	44
Kenya	80	91	77	87	96	82
Lesotho	..	..	..	49	72	40
Liberia	..	..	..	..	..	..
Madagascar	36	70	25	42	70	30
Malawi	73	96	70	76	96	70
Mali	70	95	62	69	93	58
Mauritania	30	44	19	33	44	19
Mauritius	100	100	100	99	100	99
Mozambique	..	..	..	43	68	26
Namibia	33	84	14	41	96	17
Niger	15	71	4	20	79	5
Nigeria	53	69	44	54	66	45
Rwanda	..	..	..	8	12	8
São Tomé and Principe	..	39	7	..	..	..
Senegal	57	86	38	70	94	48
Seychelles	..	..	..	..	..	..
Sierra Leone	..	..	..	66	88	53
Somalia	..	..	..	..	..	..
South Africa	86	93	80	87	93	80
Sudan	58	87	48	62	87	48
Swaziland	..	..	..	..	..	..
Tanzania	84	84	84	90	99	86
Togo	37	71	24	34	69	17
Uganda	84	96	82	79	93	77
Zambia	63	86	48	78	99	64
Zimbabwe	56	70	50	62	71	57
NORTH AFRICA	79	94	64	89	96	81
Algeria	..	..	..	92	99	81
Egypt, Arab Rep.	87	96	79	98	100	96
Libya	97	97	96	97	97	96
Morocco	58	88	31	68	86	44
Tunisia	76	96	48	84	96	62
ALL AFRICA	59	80	48	60	79	48

13-11. Access to safe water

	Percentage of population with access to safe water					
	1990			*2000**		
	Total	*Urban*	*Rural*	*Total*	*Urban*	*Rural*
SUB-SAHARAN AFRICA	53	86	40	58	83	45
excluding South Africa	50	84	38	56	81	44
excl. S. Africa & Nigeria	49	84	38	54	82	42
Angola	..	..	..	38	34	40
Benin	..	..	..	63	74	55
Botswana	93	100	88	95	100	90
Burkina Faso	53	74	50	42	66	37
Burundi	69	96	67	78	91	77
Cameroon	51	78	32	58	78	39
Cape Verde	..	..	..	74	64	89
Central African Republic	48	71	35	70	89	57
Chad	..	..	..	27	31	26
Comoros	88	97	84	96	98	95
Congo, Dem. Rep. of	..	..	..	45	89	26
Congo, Rep. of	..	..	..	51	71	17
Côte d'Ivoire	80	97	69	81	92	72
Djibouti	..	..	..	100	100	100
Equatorial Guinea	..	..	..	44	45	42
Eritrea	..	..	..	46	63	42
Ethiopia	25	80	17	24	81	12
Gabon	..	..	..	86	95	47
Gambia, The	..	..	..	62	80	53
Ghana	53	85	36	73	91	62
Guinea	45	72	36	48	72	36
Guinea-Bissau	..	..	..	56	79	49
Kenya	45	91	31	57	88	42
Lesotho	..	..	..	78	88	74
Liberia	..	..	..	..	..	..
Madagascar	44	85	31	47	85	31
Malawi	49	90	43	57	95	44
Mali	55	65	52	65	74	61
Mauritania	37	34	40	37	34	40
Mauritius	100	100	100	100	100	100
Mozambique	..	..	..	57	81	41
Namibia	72	98	63	77	100	67
Niger	53	65	51	59	70	56
Nigeria	53	83	37	62	78	49
Rwanda	..	..	..	41	60	40
São Tomé and Principe	..	100	61	..	..	..
Senegal	72	90	60	78	92	65
Seychelles	..	..	..	..	..	..
Sierra Leone	..	..	..	57	75	46
Somalia	..	..	..	..	..	..
South Africa	86	99	73	86	99	73
Sudan	67	86	60	70	86	69
Swaziland	..	..	..	..	..	..
Tanzania	38	76	28	68	90	57
Togo	51	82	38	54	85	38
Uganda	45	81	40	52	80	47
Zambia	52	88	28	64	88	48
Zimbabwe	78	99	69	83	100	73
NORTH AFRICA	86	93	80	90	95	83
Algeria	..	..	..	89	94	82
Egypt, Arab Rep.	94	97	92	97	99	96
Libya	71	72	68	72	72	68
Morocco	75	94	58	80	98	56
Tunisia	75	91	54	80	92	58
ALL AFRICA	59	88	46	64	86	50

* Or most recent year available.

13-12. Health expenditure

	Public expenditure as % of GDP, 1995-00	Private expenditure as % of GDP, 1995-00	Total expenditure		
			as % of GDP, 1995-00	per capita, US$, 1995-00	per capita PPP, international $, 1995-00
SUB-SAHARAN AFRICA	2.5	3.4	6.0	30	90
excluding South Africa	1.8	2.3	4.1	13	40
excl. S.Africa & Nigeria	2.1	2.5	4.6	15	46
Angola	2.0	1.6	3.6	24	..
Benin	1.6	1.6	3.2	11	29
Botswana	3.8	2.2	6.0	191	267
Burkina Faso	3.0	1.2	4.2	8	36
Burundi	1.6	1.5	3.1	3	21
Cameroon	1.1	3.2	4.3	24	77
Cape Verde	1.8	0.8	2.6	30	119
Central African Republic	1.4	1.5	2.9	8	33
Chad	2.5	0.6	3.1	6	25
Comoros	3.2	1.2	4.4	13	69
Congo, Dem. Rep. of	1.1	0.4	1.5	9	..
Congo, Rep. of	1.5	0.7	2.2	22	46
Côte d'Ivoire	1.0	1.7	2.7	16	62
Djibouti	4.2	2.8	7.0	56	..
Equatorial Guinea	2.3	1.1	3.4	54	163
Eritrea	2.8	1.5	4.3	9	..
Ethiopia	1.8	2.8	4.6	5	25
Gabon	2.1	0.9	3.0	120	198
Gambia, The	3.4	0.7	4.1	10	56
Ghana	2.2	2.0	4.2	11	85
Guinea	1.9	1.5	3.4	13	68
Guinea-Bissau	2.6	1.3	3.9	9	..
Kenya	1.8	6.5	8.3	28	79
Lesotho	5.2	1.1	6.3	28	..
Liberia	3.0	1.0	4.0	2	..
Madagascar	2.5	1.0	3.5	9	16
Malawi	3.6	4.0	7.6	11	36
Mali	2.2	2.7	4.9	10	30
Mauritania	3.4	0.9	4.3	14	74
Mauritius	1.9	1.5	3.4	134	302
Mozambique	2.7	1.6	4.3	9	28
Namibia	4.2	2.9	7.1	136	417
Niger	1.8	2.1	3.9	5	20
Nigeria	0.5	1.7	2.2	8	23
Rwanda	2.7	2.5	5.2	12	34
São Tomé and Principe	1.6	0.7	2.3	8	..
Senegal	2.6	2.0	4.6	22	61
Seychelles	4.1	2.1	6.2	440	..
Sierra Leone	2.6	1.7	4.3	6	27
Somalia	0.9	0.4	1.3	19	..
South Africa	3.7	5.1	8.8	255	623
Sudan	1.0	3.7	4.7	13	48
Swaziland	3.0	1.2	4.2	56	148
Tanzania	2.8	3.1	5.9	12	15
Togo	1.5	1.3	2.8	8	36
Uganda	1.5	2.4	3.9	10	65
Zambia	3.5	2.1	5.6	18	52
Zimbabwe	3.1	4.2	7.3	43	186
NORTH AFRICA	2.0	1.8	3.9	62	140
Algeria	3.0	0.6	3.6	64	216
Egypt, Arab Rep.	1.8	2.0	3.8	51	119
Libya	1.6	1.7	3.3	246	..
Morocco	1.3	3.2	4.5	50	134
Tunisia	2.9	2.6	5.5	110	287
ALL AFRICA	2.3	2.8	5.2	35	95

13-13. Health care

	Population per physician		Population per hospital bed		Percentage of births attended by trained health personnel	Percentage of population with access to health services
	1981	*1990-2000*	*1981*	*1990-2000*	*1990-2000*	*1990-2000*
SUB-SAHARAN AFRICA	..	..	..	1,304	..	..
excluding South Africa	..	..	..	1,304	..	..
excl. S.Africa & Nigeria	..	..	..	1,522	..	..
Angola	..	12,337	..	756	23	24
Benin	16,943	17,476	884	4,272	60	42
Botswana	7,452	4,274	..	635	99	..
Burkina Faso	55,742	26,317	..	706	31	..
Burundi	..	17,685	..	1,508	..	80
Cameroon	..	13,679	..	393	56	..
Cape Verde	..	5,851	..	635	89	..
Central African Republic	22,827	28,667	..	1,144	44	..
Chad	..	30,624	..	1,409	16	26
Comoros	..	13,632	..	362	62	..
Congo, Dem. Rep. of	..	14,631	..	708	70	59
Congo, Rep. of	..	4,496	..	334	50	..
Côte d'Ivoire	..	11,106	..	1,232	47	..
Djibouti	4,471	7,293	277	410	..	..
Equatorial Guinea	..	4,079	..	..	5	..
Eritrea	..	33,364	..	..	21	..
Ethiopia	88,118	35,096	..	4,141	10	51
Gabon	2,199	4,436	..	319	86	..
Gambia, The	..	28,286	..	1,637	44	..
Ghana	..	16,440	..	691	44	25
Guinea	45,460	7,691	..	1,816	35	45
Guinea-Bissau	..	6,694	527	727	25	..
Kenya	10,098	7,576	..	607	44	..
Lesotho	..	16,436	..	..	60	..
Liberia	9,454	43,667	..	..	..	..
Madagascar	10,061	9,345	..	1,068	46	..
Malawi	54,000	35,976	..	746	55	..
Mali	25,988	15,994	..	4,167	24	..
Mauritania	..	7,325	..	1,532	40	..
Mauritius	1,813	1,176	..	325	99	99
Mozambique	36,970	..	..	1,153	44	..
Namibia	..	3,562	..	..	76	..
Niger	..	30,350	..	8,506	16	30
Nigeria	..	5,208	..	599	42	67
Rwanda	32,315	25,192	676	604	31	..
São Tomé and Principe	2,395	2,143	..	210	..	..
Senegal	12,686	10,449	..	2,471	51	40
Seychelles	..	752	..	..	..	99
Sierra Leone	18,971	13,706	..	..	42	..
Somalia	24,382	24,918	..	1,327	34	..
South Africa	..	1,780	..	..	84	..
Sudan	9,944	11,167	1,152	923	86	70
Swaziland	..	6,636	..	..	56	55
Tanzania	..	24,400	..	1,123	36	93
Togo	20,587	13,027	..	662	51	..
Uganda	21,481	26,651	663	1,164	38	..
Zambia	7,913	14,323	287	..	47	..
Zimbabwe	7,222	7,194	..	1,959	73	..
NORTH AFRICA	5,936	1,120	570	620	..	88
Algeria	..	1,000	..	476	77	..
Egypt, Arab Rep.	733	625	483	476	61	99
Libya	612	779	207	232	94	100
Morocco	18,558	2,174	814	1,020	40	62
Tunisia	3,642	1,428	..	588	90	90
ALL AFRICA	..	..	..	1,133	..	..

13-14. Illiteracy rate

	Percentage of population 15 years of age and above that is illiterate								
	1990			*1997*			*2002*		
	Total	*Male*	*Female*	*Total*	*Male*	*Female*	*Total*	*Male*	*Female*
SUB-SAHARAN AFRICA	50	40	60	42	33	51	37	29	45
excluding South Africa	53	42	64	45	35	54	39	30	47
excl. S. Africa & Nigeria	54	42	64	46	36	55	40	31	49
Angola	..	..	..	..	..	..	..	..	..
Benin	74	62	85	66	52	79	60	45	74
Botswana	32	34	30	26	28	23	21	24	18
Burkina Faso	84	75	92	79	69	88	74	64	84
Burundi	63	52	73	55	46	64	50	42	56
Cameroon	42	31	52	33	24	41	26	19	33
Cape Verde	36	24	46	29	18	37	24	15	32
Central African Republic	67	53	79	57	44	70	50	38	62
Chad	72	63	81	62	53	71	54	45	62
Comoros	46	39	54	45	37	52	44	37	51
Congo, Dem. Rep. of	53	39	66	43	30	55	36	25	47
Congo, Rep. of	33	23	42	23	15	30	17	11	23
Côte d'Ivoire	61	49	74	54	43	66	49	39	60
Djibouti	47	33	60	39	27	50	33	23	43
Equatorial Guinea	27	14	39	20	9	30	15	7	23
Eritrea	54	42	65	47	35	58	42	31	53
Ethiopia	71	63	80	64	56	73	58	51	66
Gabon	..	..	..	..	..	..	..	..	..
Gambia, The	74	68	80	67	60	73	61	54	68
Ghana	42	30	53	32	23	42	26	18	34
Guinea	..	..	..	..	..	..	..	..	..
Guinea-Bissau	73	58	87	65	49	80	59	44	74
Kenya	29	19	39	21	13	28	16	10	21
Lesotho	22	35	11	18	29	7	16	26	6
Liberia	61	45	77	51	34	68	44	28	61
Madagascar	42	34	50	36	28	43	32	25	38
Malawi	48	31	64	42	27	57	38	24	51
Mali	81	72	90	77	67	86	73	62	83
Mauritania	65	54	76	61	51	72	59	49	69
Mauritius	20	15	25	17	13	20	15	12	18
Mozambique	67	51	82	59	43	75	54	38	69
Namibia	25	23	28	20	19	21	17	16	17
Niger	89	82	95	86	78	93	83	75	91
Nigeria	51	41	62	41	31	49	33	26	41
Rwanda	47	37	56	37	29	44	31	25	37
São Tomé and Principe	..	..	..	..	..	..	..	..	..
Senegal	72	62	81	65	55	75	61	51	70
Seychelles	..	..	..	..	..	..	..	..	..
Sierra Leone	..	..	..	..	..	..	..	..	..
Somalia	..	..	..	..	..	..	..	..	..
South Africa	19	18	20	16	15	17	14	13	15
Sudan	54	40	68	46	34	58	40	29	51
Swaziland	28	26	30	23	21	24	19	18	20
Tanzania	37	24	49	29	19	38	23	15	31
Togo	56	40	71	47	31	62	40	26	55
Uganda	44	31	57	36	25	47	31	21	41
Zambia	32	21	41	25	17	32	20	14	26
Zimbabwe	19	13	25	14	9	18	10	6	14
NORTH AFRICA	52	39	65	44	33	56	40	29	51
Algeria	47	36	59	37	27	47	31	22	40
Egypt, Arab Rep.	53	40	66	47	35	59	43	32	54
Libya	32	17	49	23	11	37	18	8	29
Morocco	61	47	75	54	41	67	49	37	62
Tunisia	41	28	53	33	22	44	27	17	37
ALL AFRICA	51	40	61	43	33	52	37	29	46

13-15. Primary school gross enrollment ratio

	Total			Males			Females		
	1985	*1995*	*1998-00*	*1985*	*1995*	*1998-00*	*1985*	*1995*	*1998-00*
SUB-SAHARAN AFRICA	76	76	87	86	83	94	67	69	81
excluding South Africa	76	71	72	86	79	79	67	64	65
excl. S. Africa & Nigeria	69	66	85	77	72	91	59	59	78
Angola	107	72	74	117	77	78	96	67	69
Benin	68	73	95	90	93	113	45	53	78
Botswana	105	108	108	100	107	108	111	109	108
Burkina Faso	27	40	44	34	48	52	20	31	37
Burundi	53	51	65	61	55	73	44	46	58
Cameroon	102	87	108	111	91	115	93	82	100
Cape Verde	116	140	139	119	140	140	112	140	137
Central African Republic	75	57	75	93	69	89	57	45	61
Chad	44	51	73	63	69	90	25	34	57
Comoros	82	75	86	93	81	92	70	68	80
Congo, Dem. Rep. of	87	67	47	105	78	49	68	56	44
Congo, Rep. of	147	114	97	154	120	101	141	109	93
Côte d'Ivoire	72	69	81	84	79	92	59	58	70
Djibouti	40	38	40	47	44	46	33	33	35
Equatorial Guinea	..	..	120	..	..	126	..	..	115
Eritrea	..	56	57	..	62	65	..	50	54
Ethiopia	38	37	64	45	48	76	30	27	52
Gabon	..	..	144	..	..	144	..	..	143
Gambia, The	68	77	82	84	87	86	52	67	78
Ghana	75	72	80	..	73	84	..	72	76
Guinea	34	48	67	47	62	78	22	33	56
Guinea-Bissau	64	66	83	85	83	99	43	48	66
Kenya	99	85	94	102	85	95	96	85	93
Lesotho	112	111	115	98	104	112	125	117	118
Liberia	..	25	118	..	30	140	..	20	96
Madagascar	..	92	103	..	92	105	..	91	101
Malawi	60	134	137	69	140	139	52	127	135
Mali	25	41	61	31	49	71	18	32	51
Mauritania	48	75	83	58	81	86	39	69	80
Mauritius	109	107	109	110	107	109	109	106	108
Mozambique	87	60	92	99	70	104	76	50	79
Namibia	..	133	112	..	132	112	..	134	113
Niger	26	29	35	33	36	42	18	22	29
Nigeria	104	93	..	115	103	..	92	83	..
Rwanda	63	94	119	65	95	119	61	93	118
São Tomé and Principe	..	..	..	..	..	..	..	..	..
Senegal	56	64	75	67	72	79	46	57	70
Seychelles	..	..	..	..	..	..	..	..	..
Sierra Leone	63	53	93	..	63	106	..	43	80
Somalia	14	10	..	18	13	..	9	7	..
South Africa	..	133	111	..	135	115	..	131	108
Sudan	52	50	55	61	54	59	42	46	51
Swaziland	102	121	125	104	124	128	100	118	121
Tanzania	75	67	77	76	68	78	74	66	76
Togo	93	119	124	115	140	138	71	97	110
Uganda	73	74	136	..	81	143	..	68	129
Zambia	105	89	78	111	91	80	98	86	76
Zimbabwe	136	114	95	141	116	96	131	113	93
NORTH AFRICA	88	100	103	99	107	107	77	93	99
Algeria	94	107	112	103	113	116	83	100	107
Egypt, Arab Rep.	85	100	100	94	106	103	76	93	96
Libya	109	118	116	113	118	115	104	118	117
Morocco	77	84	94	93	95	101	60	72	88
Tunisia	115	117	117	124	121	120	105	113	115
ALL AFRICA	79	80	91	89	87	97	69	73	85

13-16. Pupil progression

	Percentage of cohort reaching grade 5 (1998-99)			Progression to secondary school 1993		
	Total	Male	Female	Total	Male	Female
SUB-SAHARAN AFRICA	..	..	..	52	..	..
excluding South Africa	..	..	..	46	..	..
excl. S. Africa & Nigeria	..	..	..	..	..	..
Angola	4	3	4	..	..	..
Benin	84	89	78	..	..	..
Botswana	87	84	89	84	84	85
Burkina Faso	69	68	71	27	27	27
Burundi	58	59	58	11	12	11
Cameroon	81	72	93	..	..	..
Cape Verde	..	..	..	..	..	..
Central African Republic	..	..	..	..	..	..
Chad	54	58	48	47	..	..
Comoros	77	68	90	39	..	..
Congo, Dem. Rep. of	..	..	..	27	25	30
Congo, Rep. of	..	..	..	..	..	..
Côte d'Ivoire	91	91	90	33	..	..
Djibouti	77	71	85	38	..	..
Equatorial Guinea	16	14	19	..	..	..
Eritrea	..	..	..	80	85	74
Ethiopia	64	64	64	80	82	77
Gabon	..	..	..	..	..	..
Gambia, The	69	75	63	..	..	..
Ghana	66	67	65	..	..	..
Guinea	84	90	77	50	51	47
Guinea-Bissau	38	41	34	..	..	..
Kenya	71	70	73	41	..	..
Lesotho	75	68	80	71	..	..
Liberia	33	49	17	..	..	..
Madagascar	..	..	..	35	35	35
Malawi	49	55	43	15	..	..
Mali	95	100	86	63	64	60
Mauritania	61	68	55	32	34	28
Mauritius	..	..	..	51	49	54
Mozambique	..	..	..	39	39	39
Namibia	92	92	93	74	76	72
Niger	74	76	71	..	..	..
Nigeria	..	..	..	52	..	..
Rwanda	39	38	40	15	..	..
São Tomé and Principe	..	..	..	..	..	..
Senegal	72	75	69	..	..	..
Seychelles	..	..	..	100	..	..
Sierra Leone	..	..	..	..	..	..
Somalia	..	..	..	..	..	..
South Africa	65	66	63	90	87	91
Sudan	87	86	88	61	..	..
Swaziland	84	83	85	79	79	79
Tanzania	82	80	83	12	..	..
Togo	74	78	69	38	40	35
Uganda	..	44	46	32	..	..
Zambia	81	83	78	..	..	..
Zimbabwe	..	..	..	66	..	..
NORTH AFRICA	..	..	..	79	77	81
Algeria	97	97	98	80	77	82
Egypt, Arab Rep.	..	..	..	83	82	85
Libya	..	..	..	..	..	..
Morocco	80	79	81	81	79	84
Tunisia	93	92	94	62	62	63
ALL AFRICA	..	..	..	56	..	..

Notes: In the Seychelles a policy of automatic promotion is practiced at the primary level of education. Tanzanian figures refer to the mainland only.

13-17. Net primary enrollment ratio

	Total			Males			Females		
	1985	*1995*	*1999-00*	*1985*	*1995*	*1999-00*	*1985*	*1995*	*1999-00*
SUB-SAHARAN AFRICA	..	..	..	..	..	..	..	..	..
excluding South Africa	..	..	..	..	..	..	..	..	..
excl. S. Africa & Nigeria	..	..	68	..	..	71	..	..	66
Angola	..	..	37	..	..	39	..	..	35
Benin	53	60	70	71	75	83	36	44	57
Botswana	89	81	84	84	79	82	94	83	86
Burkina Faso	23	..	36	29	..	42	17	..	29
Burundi	41	..	54	47	..	59	36	..	49
Cameroon	..	..	..	..	..	..	..	..	..
Cape Verde	95	..	92	97	..	..	93	..	..
Central African Republic	61	..	55	75	..	64	47	..	45
Chad	..	40	58	..	..	70	..	..	47
Comoros	61	..	56	..	..	60	..	..	52
Congo, Dem. Rep. of	..	..	33	..	..	..	..	..	..
Congo, Rep. of	96	..	..	99	..	..	..	..	..
Côte d'Ivoire	..	53	64	..	61	73	..	45	55
Djibouti	31	32	33	37	37	37	26	28	28
Equatorial Guinea	..	..	72	..	..	76	..	..	68
Eritrea	..	31	38	..	32	44	..	29	38
Ethiopia	..	28	47	..	35	53	..	21	41
Gabon	..	..	88	..	..	89	..	..	87
Gambia, The	62	65	69	77	72	71	48	57	66
Ghana	..	..	58	..	..	60	..	..	57
Guinea	27	..	47	36	..	52	18	..	41
Guinea-Bissau	47	..	54	63	..	63	..	..	45
Kenya	91	..	69	92	..	68	..	..	69
Lesotho	72	71	78	62	65	75	82	76	82
Liberia	..	..	83	..	..	96	..	..	71
Madagascar	..	61	68	..	59	67	..	62	68
Malawi	43	..	101	46	..	97	41	..	104
Mali	20	31	..	..	38	..	..	25	..
Mauritania	..	57	64	..	61	66	..	53	62
Mauritius	100	96	95	100	96	95	101	96	95
Mozambique	51	40	54	56	45	59	47	34	50
Namibia	..	92	82	..	..	79	..	..	84
Niger	25	..	30	32	..	36	17	..	24
Nigeria	..	..	..	..	..	..	..	..	..
Rwanda	60	..	97	61	..	97	59	..	97
São Tomé and Principe	..	..	..	..	..	..	..	..	..
Senegal	48	54	63	57	60	66	39	48	60
Seychelles	..	..	..	..	..	..	..	..	..
Sierra Leone	..	..	65	..	..	68	..	..	63
Somalia	10	..	..	13	..	..	7	..	..
South Africa	..	..	89	..	..	90	..	..	88
Sudan	..	..	46	..	..	50	..	..	42
Swaziland	79	94	93	78	93	92	80	94	94
Tanzania	56	48	58	55	47	57	56	48	58
Togo	61	85	92	72	98	101	49	72	83
Uganda	..	..	84	..	..	85	..	..	84
Zambia	77	75	66	81	76	66	..	74	65
Zimbabwe	..	..	80	..	..	80	..	..	80
NORTH AFRICA	..	..	91	..	..	93	..	..	89
Algeria	86	95	98	94	99	100	78	91	97
Egypt, Arab Rep.	..	..	93	..	..	95	..	..	90
Libya	..	..	..	..	..	..	..	..	..
Morocco	61	72	78	73	81	82	48	63	74
Tunisia	93	98	99	99	100	100	87	95	99
ALL AFRICA	..	..	67	..	..	70	..	..	64

Note: Net enrollment ratios exceeding 100 percent indicate discrepancies between estimates of the school-age population and reported enrollment data.

13-18. Number of school teachers

	Primary						Secondary					
	Total teaching staff			Percentage females			Total teaching staff			Percentage females		
	1985	1995	2000	1985	1995	2000	1985	1995	2000	1985	1995	2000
SUB-SAHARAN AFRICA	..	..	..	34	42	39	..	..	..	..	..	..
excluding South Africa	..	..	..	34	39		..	..	..	..	..	..
excl. S. Africa & Nigeria	..	..	..	32	36	35	..	..	..	..	..	..
Angola	31,161	..	33,478	..	..	41	..	..	19,798	..	..	29
Benin	13,452	13,889	19,710	24	24	20	..	..	..	..	..	..
Botswana	6,980	12,306	12,135	78	78	81	1,675	6,670	9,407	40	43	46
Burkina Faso	6,091	14,037	19,007	25	24	23	..	..	6,432	..	..	20
Burundi	6,866	10,316	14,955	47	50	54	1,849	..	5,459	21	..	22
Cameroon	33,598	..	42,873	27	..	36	11,096	..	..	22	..	..
Cape Verde	1,493	..	3,193	..	..	63	..	..	..	..	..	..
Central African Republic	4,718	..	6,223	25	..	18	922	..	..	..	..	..
Chad	4,779	9,395	13,819	4	8	10	..	2,693	..	..	5	..
Comoros	1,901	1,508	2,723	21	..	17	..	..	..	..	..	..
Congo, Dem. Rep. of	..	..	..	..	..	..	..	..	..	..	..	..
Congo, Rep. of	7,745	7,060	9,880	30	36	41	6,322	7,173	7,668	..	16	9
Côte d'Ivoire	33,500	40,529	44,424	19	21	20	..	..	23,184	..	..	..
Djibouti	585	1,005	1,199	..	33	28	306	628	..	..	..	..
Equatorial Guinea	..	..	1,754	..	..	26	..	..	1,374	..	..	3
Eritrea	..	5,828	6,668	..	35	41	..	2,193	2,710	..	12	10
Ethiopia	50,922	89,189	121,077	26	28	30	15,861	25,984	..	..	10	..
Gabon	4,008	4,943	5,399	35	39	48	2,074	3,094	..	22	18	..
Gambia, The	2,979	4,118	4,186	36	29	29	695	1,547	2,207	..	17	17
Ghana	64,795	67,021	75,087	40	37	35	37,290	..	55,549	26	..	23
Guinea	7,605	11,875	19,244	19	25	25	4,642	..	..	7	..	..
Guinea-Bissau	..	..	..	..	..	..	..	..	..	..	..	..
Kenya	138,374	181,975	191,068	34	40	42	23,055	..	48,019	36	..	35
Lesotho	5,663	7,923	8,578	77	79	80	1,897	..	3,250	..	..	51
Liberia	..	..	..	..	..	..	..	..	..	..	..	..
Madagascar	..	44,145	46,482	..	51	54	..	..	..	..	..	..
Malawi	15,440	49,138	47,840	33	39	38	1,272	3,172	12,782	..	..	20
Mali	8,593	8,718	17,788	22	23	23	..	..	..	..	..	..
Mauritania	2,785	..	8,636	15	..	24	..	2,067	2,749	..	..	10
Mauritius	6,450	5,137	5,178	43	50	55	..	..	5,436	..	..	48
Mozambique	20,286	24,575	36,187	22	23	26	4,688	5,615	..	21	17	..
Namibia	..	..	12,327	..	..	67	..	..	5,164	..	..	46
Niger	7,383	11,285	15,668	33	33	33	..	3,548	4,127	..	21	18
Nigeria	308,072	423,059	..	41	47	..	105,003	..	..	28	..	..
Rwanda	14,896	..	28,698	44	..	51	3,120	..	..	9	..	..
São Tomé and Principe	..	..	649	..	..	62	..	..	..	..	..	..
Senegal	12,559	15,045	22,813	27	26	22	..	..	11,182	..	..	12
Seychelles	652	584	684	85	88	86	364	711	535	29	48	53
Sierra Leone	10,837	..	14,875	..	..	38	3,006	..	5,840	..	..	27
Somalia	10,338	..	..	45	..	..	2,786	..	..	11	..	..
South Africa	..	224,896	222,487	..	74	75	..	..	140,856	..	..	50
Sudan	50,089	95,184	..	44	60	..	23,035	..	..	33	..	..
Swaziland	4,107	5,917	6,544	80	76	75	..	..	..	..	..	..
Tanzania	92,586	105,280	107,111	..	43	45	5,267	12,198	..	..	25	..
Togo	10,049	16,217	27,523	20	14	12	4,351	5,389	9,339	13	..	10
Uganda	61,424	82,745	110,366	..	..	33	..	..	36,092	..	..	21
Zambia	27,302	38,528	35,348	43	43	50	..	..	..	..	..	..
Zimbabwe	56,067	63,475	66,440	43	44	48	..	27,458	34,162	..	36	48
NORTH AFRICA	..	..	..	43	47	76	..	..	..	33	39	43
Algeria	125,034	169,010	169,559	40	44	47	82,218	150,397	157,725	36	44	48
Egypt, Arab Rep.	194,929	302,916	352,911	48	53	109	187,580	369,107	490,648	35	40	40
Libya	63,122	..	..	56	..	..	10,765	..	..	19	..	..
Morocco	81,867	109,817	136,558	33	38	41	67,733	85,865	..	26	31	..
Tunisia	40,887	59,887	60,541	38	49	50	25,245	..	61,931	31	..	40
ALL AFRICA	..	..	..	36	43	48	..	..	..	..	..	..

Note: Figures include both part-time and full-time teachers.

13-19. Pupil/teacher ratio

	Number of pupils per teacher					
	Primary			Secondary		
	1985	1995	1999-00	1985	1995	1999-00
SUB-SAHARAN AFRICA	40	38	..	..	..	..
excluding South Africa	40	38	..	..	..	..
excl. S. Africa & Nigeria	39	39	45	..	..	..
Angola	31	..	35	..	..	20
Benin	33	52	54	..	..	23
Botswana	32	25	27	22	17	20
Burkina Faso	58	50	47	..	..	31
Burundi	56	50	50	14	..	21
Cameroon	51	..	63	31	..	..
Cape Verde	39	..	28	..	..	..
Central African Republic	66	..	74	64	..	..
Chad	71	63	71	..	35	32
Comoros	35	52	36	..	..	..
Congo, Dem. Rep. of	..	..	..	..	..	..
Congo, Rep. of	61	70	51	35	30	26
Côte d'Ivoire	36	41	48	..	..	29
Djibouti	43	36	36	23	19	21
Equatorial Guinea	..	..	42	..	..	25
Eritrea	..	41	45	..	37	52
Ethiopia	48	38	55	42	32	27
Gabon	46	51	49	21	26	..
Gambia, The	23	30	37	23	21	25
Ghana	23	33	33	20	..	19
Guinea	36	49	44	20	..	..
Guinea-Bissau	..	..	44	..	..	21
Kenya	34	32	33	20	..	17
Lesotho	55	48	48	20	..	23
Liberia	..	..	36	..	..	26
Madagascar	..	37	50	..	..	..
Malawi	61	59	56	30	45	38
Mali	34	78	63	..	..	..
Mauritania	51	..	42	..	25	28
Mauritius	22	24	26	..	..	19
Mozambique	62	58	64	32	33	33
Namibia	..	..	32	..	..	24
Niger	37	39	42	..	26	25
Nigeria	42	37	..	28	..	..
Rwanda	56	..	51	15	..	..
São Tomé and Principe	..	..	34	..	..	..
Senegal	46	58	51	..	..	23
Seychelles	22	17	15	11	13	14
Sierra Leone	39	..	44	32	..	27
Somalia	19	..	..	16	..	..
South Africa	..	36	33	..	..	29
Sudan	35	31	27	24	..	23
Swaziland	34	34	33	..	..	..
Tanzania	34	37	40	18	17	..
Togo	46	51	34	22	31	31
Uganda	34	35	59	..	..	17
Zambia	49	39	45	..	..	29
Zimbabwe	40	39	37	..	26	25
NORTH AFRICA	28	27	25	20	17	18
Algeria	28	27	28	22	17	19
Egypt, Arab Rep.	32	27	22	20	17	17
Libya	16	..	..	13	..	..
Morocco	28	28	28	18	16	17
Tunisia	32	25	23	18	..	18
ALL AFRICA	36	35	37	23	..	..

Note: Figures include both part-time and full-time teachers.

13-20. Secondary school gross enrollment ratio

	Total			Males			Females		
	1985	*1995*	*1999-00*	*1985*	*1995*	*1999-00*	*1985*	*1995*	*1999-00*
SUB-SAHARAN AFRICA	20	26	..	25	28	..	15	23	..
excluding South Africa	20	21	..	25	24	..	15	18	..
excl. S. Africa & Nigeria	16	18	..	21	21	23	12	15	19
Angola	14	12	15	..	15	18	..	10	13
Benin	18	16	22	26	22	30	10	9	14
Botswana	29	63	82	27	60	90	31	66	96
Burkina Faso	4	9	10	6	12	12	3	6	8
Burundi	4	7	..	5	8	12	2	5	9
Cameroon	23	26	..	28	30	..	18	21	..
Cape Verde	13	43	..	15	45	..	12	42	..
Central African Republic	16	10	..	24	14	..	8	6	..
Chad	6	9	11	10	15	18	2	4	5
Comoros	28	21	21	34	24	23	22	19	18
Congo, Dem. Rep. of	23	24	..	32	30	..	13	18	..
Congo, Rep. of	75	53	..	87	62	46	64	45	38
Côte d'Ivoire	20	23	..	28	31	30	12	15	17
Djibouti	12	13	15	14	15	13	9	11	17
Equatorial Guinea	..	..	31	..	..	43	..	..	19
Eritrea	..	19	28	..	22	34	..	16	23
Ethiopia	13	12	5	15	13	22	10	10	14
Gabon	..	..	..	..	..	61	..	..	58
Gambia, The	16	25	27	23	30	43	10	19	30
Ghana	40	34	..	49	39	40	30	28	32
Guinea	13	12	..	18	18	..	7	6	..
Guinea-Bissau	9	11	20	14	15	26	4	7	14
Kenya	21	24	..	26	26	32	16	22	29
Lesotho	23	31	28	19	25	30	28	37	36
Liberia	..	13	23	..	18	45	..	7	32
Madagascar	..	16	..	..	16	..	..	16	..
Malawi	6	17	..	8	21	40	4	12	31
Mali	6	11	..	9	14	..	4	7	..
Mauritania	15	16	18	22	21	22	8	11	20
Mauritius	49	62	107	51	60	79	46	64	75
Mozambique	7	7	14	10	9	14	5	5	9
Namibia	..	62	60	..	57	58	..	68	65
Niger	5	7	7	8	9	8	3	5	5
Nigeria	34	32	..	40	35	..	28	29	..
Rwanda	6	14	12	7	16	12	5	12	12
São Tomé and Principe	..	..	..	..	..	..	..	..	..
Senegal	14	16	..	18	20	21	9	12	14
Seychelles	..	..	..	..	..	..	..	..	..
Sierra Leone	18	17	24	24	21	29	12	12	24
Somalia	8	6	..	10	8	..	6	4	..
South Africa	..	95	90	..	88	83	..	103	91
Sudan	21	21	29	24	22	22	18	19	36
Swaziland	39	53	..	40	53	60	38	53	60
Tanzania	3	5	5	4	6	6	2	5	5
Togo	21	27	36	32	40	54	10	14	24
Uganda	10	12	..	13	15	21	7	9	16
Zambia	19	27	..	25	33	26	14	20	21
Zimbabwe	42	47	45	50	52	47	33	43	42
NORTH AFRICA	52	65	69	60	70	82	43	60	81
Algeria	51	62	67	59	66	68	44	59	73
Egypt, Arab Rep.	61	77	84	72	82	88	50	70	83
Libya	59	102	..	61	105	88	57	98	91
Morocco	35	39	39	42	44	44	28	33	35
Tunisia	39	60	75	46	62	76	32	58	80
ALL AFRICA	27	33	..	32	36	40	21	30	38

Note: *Secondary* refers to secondary general education.

13-21. Public expenditure on education

	As percentage of total public expenditure			As percentage of GDP		
	1980	1990	1998-00	1980	1990	1998-00
SUB-SAHARAN AFRICA	..	..	..	..	..	..
excluding South Africa	..	..	..	..	..	..
excl. S. Africa & Nigeria	..	..	..	..	..	..
Angola	..	..	..	..	3	2.7
Benin	..	..	..	..	..	3.2
Botswana	..	19	..	5.7	6	8.6
Burkina Faso	15.5	18	..	2.2	3	..
Burundi	..	..	..	..	3	3.4
Cameroon	..	..	..	3.2	3	3.2
Cape Verde	..	..	..	..	..	4.4
Central African Republic	..	..	..	..	2	1.9
Chad	..	..	..	..	..	2.0
Comoros	..	..	..	..	..	3.8
Congo, Dem. Rep. of	..	..	..	..	..	..
Congo, Rep. of	..	..	..	6.4	5	4.2
Côte d'Ivoire	..	30	..	6.9	..	4.6
Djibouti	..	..	..	..	4	3.5
Equatorial Guinea	..	..	..	..	..	0.6
Eritrea	..	..	..	..	..	7.4
Ethiopia	10.2	10	13.8	..	3	4.8
Gabon	..	..	..	2.5	..	3.9
Gambia, The	..	..	..	3.1	4	2.7
Ghana	..	..	..	3.1	3	4.1
Guinea	..	..	..	..	..	1.9
Guinea-Bissau	..	..	..	..	..	2.1
Kenya	22.9	23	..	6.5	7	6.4
Lesotho	..	17	..	7.5	6	10.1
Liberia	11.9	..	..	6.5	..	..
Madagascar	..	..	..	4.3	2	3.2
Malawi	..	..	..	3.1	3	4.1
Mali	..	..	..	3.4	..	2.8
Mauritania	..	..	..	..	..	3.0
Mauritius	..	..	..	5.5	4	3.5
Mozambique	..	..	..	2.5	3	2.4
Namibia	..	..	..	..	7	8.1
Niger	18.0	..	..	3.1	3	2.7
Nigeria	..	..	..	..	1	..
Rwanda	..	..	..	2.7	..	2.8
São Tomé and Principe	..	..	..	..	..	..
Senegal	..	..	..	..	4	3.2
Seychelles	..	..	..	5.6	8	7.6
Sierra Leone	..	..	..	3.7	..	1.0
Somalia	..	..	..	1.0	..	..
South Africa	..	..	..	..	6	5.5
Sudan	..	..	..	41.8	6	..
Swaziland	24.6	..	..	5.7	6	1.5
Tanzania	13.3	..	..	..	3	2.5
Togo	..	..	..	5.4	6	4.8
Uganda	..	..	27.0	1.2	1	4.0
Zambia	..	8	..	4.1	2	2.3
Zimbabwe	..	..	..	5.2	8	10.4
NORTH AFRICA	15.0	17	..	..	..	..
Algeria	..	..	..	7.6	5	..
Egypt, Arab Rep.	8.1	14	..	..	4	..
Libya	..	..	..	3.4	..	..
Morocco	17.3	18	..	5.9	5	5.5
Tunisia	17.0	17.0	..	5.2	6.0	6.8
ALL AFRICA	..	..	..	..	..	..

13-22. Economic opportunities of women

	Female / male ratio of participation in economic activity 1995	Female as percentage of male in occupational group, 1996*			
		Administrative and managerial	Professional and technical	Clerical and sales	Services
SUB-SAHARAN AFRICA	73	10	28	..	..
excluding South Africa	74	10	26	..	..
excl. S.Africa & Nigeria	78	..	..	..	..
Angola	87	..	..	..	..
Benin	93	..	..	..	..
Botswana	85	36	61	60	70
Burkina Faso	87	14	26	63	22
Burundi	97	13	30	..	..
Cameroon	60	10	24	37	31
Cape Verde	64	23	48	63	57
Central African Republic	88	9	19	59	12
Chad	80	..	..	..	..
Comoros	74	..	29	..	..
Congo, Dem. Rep. of	77	9	17	..	..
Congo, Rep. of	77	6	40	..	..
Côte d'Ivoire	49	29	..	..	..
Djibouti	..	2	20	..	..
Equatorial Guinea	55	2	27	..	..
Eritrea	90	17	30	48	43
Ethiopia	69	11	24	..	..
Gabon	80	..	..	..	..
Gambia, The	81	16	24	28	14
Ghana	103	9	36	59	68
Guinea	90	..	..	..	..
Guinea-Bissau	67	..	..	..	..
Kenya	85	..	..	..	..
Lesotho	58	33	57	144	209
Liberia	66	..	..	..	..
Madagascar	81	..	..	..	..
Malawi	96	5	35	33	28
Mali	87	20	19	57	41
Mauritania	77	8	21	25	45
Mauritius	46	23	38	49	28
Mozambique	94	11	20	..	..
Namibia	68	21	41	54	72
Niger	79	9	8	30	0
Nigeria	56	6	26	58	11
Rwanda	93	9	47	48	35
São Tomé and Principe	..	..	..	..	..
Senegal	74	..	..	..	..
Seychelles	..	29	58	59	59
Sierra Leone	57	8	32	66	15
Somalia	75	..	..	..	..
South Africa	60	17	47	..	196
Sudan	40	2	29	..	..
Swaziland	60	26	60	42	82
Tanzania	98	..	..	..	..
Togo	67	8	21	..	..
Uganda	91	..	..	..	..
Zambia	83	6	32	58	22
Zimbabwe	80	15	40	34	30
NORTH AFRICA	41	14	30	28	14
Algeria	32	6	28	11	19
Egypt, Arab Rep.	40	12	30	35	10
Libya	26	..	..	..	..
Morocco	53	26	31	28	17
Tunisia	44	13	36	33	17
ALL AFRICA	67	11	28	..	..

* Or most recent year available

13-23. Household and economic participation of women

	Percentage of households headed by women (latest available between 1991-99)	Percentage of women in occupational group 1991-99					
		Agriculture	Mining	Utilities & manufacturing	Construction, transport, storage & communications	Service industries	Community, social & personal services
SUB-SAHARAN AFRICA	..	..	..	..	..	..	..
excluding South Africa	..	..	..	..	..	..	..
excl. S.Africa & Nigeria	..	..	..	..	..	..	..
Angola	..	..	..	..	..	..	..
Benin	..	..	..	..	..	..	..
Botswana	..	2	1	12	9	35	41
Burkina Faso	6	..	..	..	..	..	..
Burundi	..	..	..	..	..	..	..
Cameroon	18	..	..	..	..	..	..
Cape Verde	..	..	..	..	..	..	..
Central African Republic	16	..	..	..	..	..	..
Chad	..	14	0	14	14	14	43
Comoros	..	..	..	..	..	..	..
Congo, Dem. Rep. of	..	..	..	..	..	..	..
Congo, Rep. of	..	..	..	..	..	..	..
Côte d'Ivoire	12	..	..	..	..	..	..
Djibouti	17	..	..	..	..	..	..
Equatorial Guinea	..	..	..	..	..	..	..
Eritrea	..	..	..	..	..	..	..
Ethiopia	18	10	0	24	6	10	50
Gabon	..	..	..	..	..	..	..
Gambia, The	1	..	..	..	..	..	..
Ghana	14	..	..	..	..	..	..
Guinea	8	..	..	..	..	..	..
Guinea-Bissau	10	..	..	..	..	..	..
Kenya	15	20	0	8	5	11	57
Lesotho	..	..	..	..	..	..	..
Liberia	..	..	..	..	..	..	..
Madagascar	18	..	..	..	..	..	..
Malawi	..	73	0	7	2	4	14
Mali	6	..	..	..	..	..	..
Mauritania	24	..	..	..	..	..	..
Mauritius	..	11	0	61	2	9	17
Mozambique	..	..	..	..	..	..	..
Namibia	..	..	..	..	..	..	..
Niger	6	5	5	20	25	25	25
Nigeria	13	..	..	..	..	..	..
Rwanda	..	..	..	..	..	..	..
São Tomé and Principe	..	..	..	..	..	..	..
Senegal	8	..	..	..	..	..	..
Seychelles	..	..	..	..	..	..	..
Sierra Leone	..	..	..	..	..	..	..
Somalia	..	..	..	..	..	..	..
South Africa	27	..	..	..	..	..	..
Sudan	..	..	..	..	..	..	..
Swaziland	26	23	1	16	4	20	36
Tanzania	11	..	..	..	..	..	..
Togo	..	..	..	..	..	..	..
Uganda	2	..	..	..	..	..	..
Zambia	19	..	..	..	..	..	..
Zimbabwe	..	38	1	7	4	9	..
NORTH AFRICA	..	36	0	21	2	8	32
Algeria	..	..	..	..	..	..	..
Egypt, Arab Rep.	..	47	0	7	2	8	36
Libya	..	..	..	..	..	..	..
Morocco	..	3	0	45	2	11	39
Tunisia	..	..	..	..	..	..	..
ALL AFRICA	..	..	..	..	..	..	..

Figure 13-1. Life expectancy, 2001

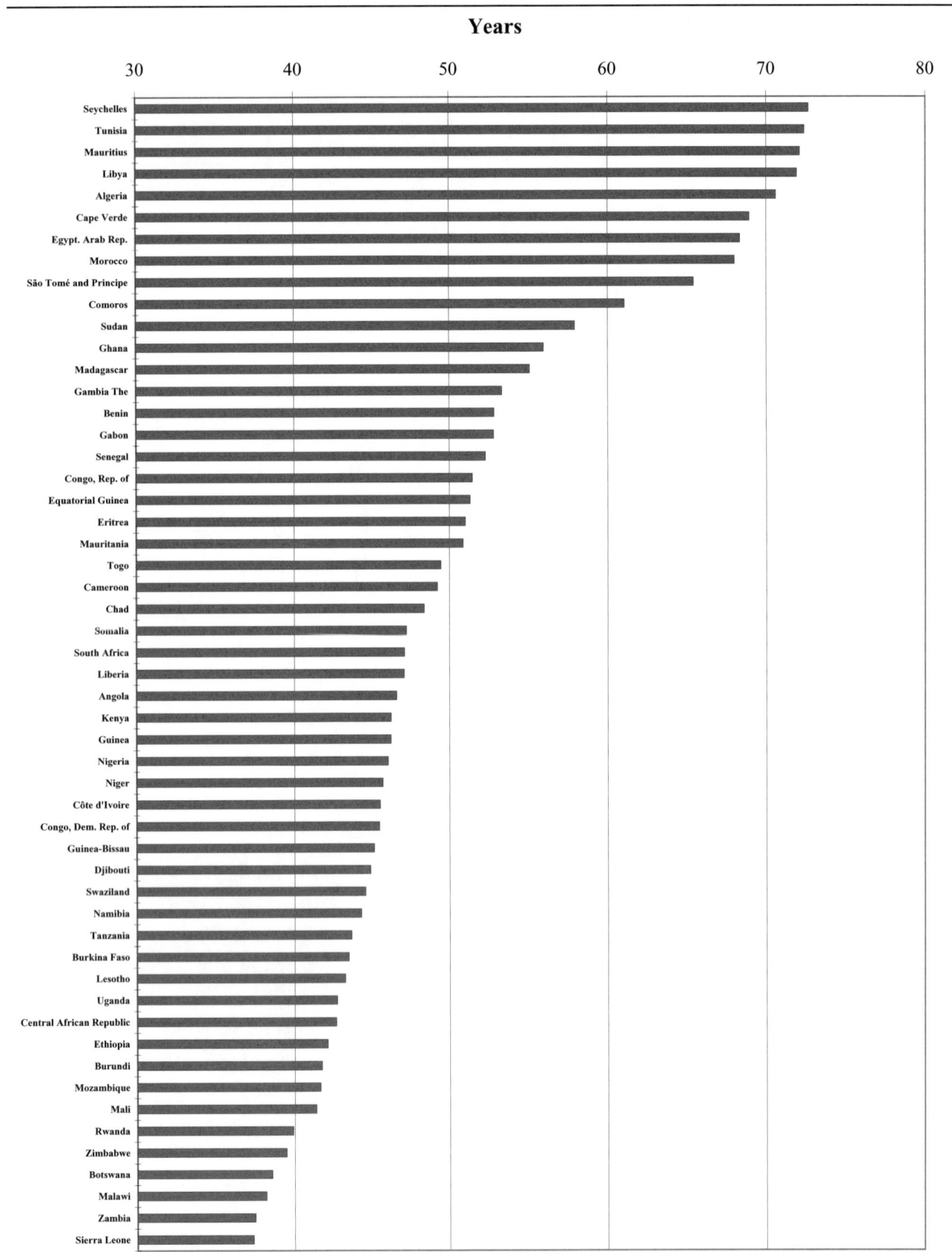

Figure 13-2. GDP per capita based on PPP, 2002

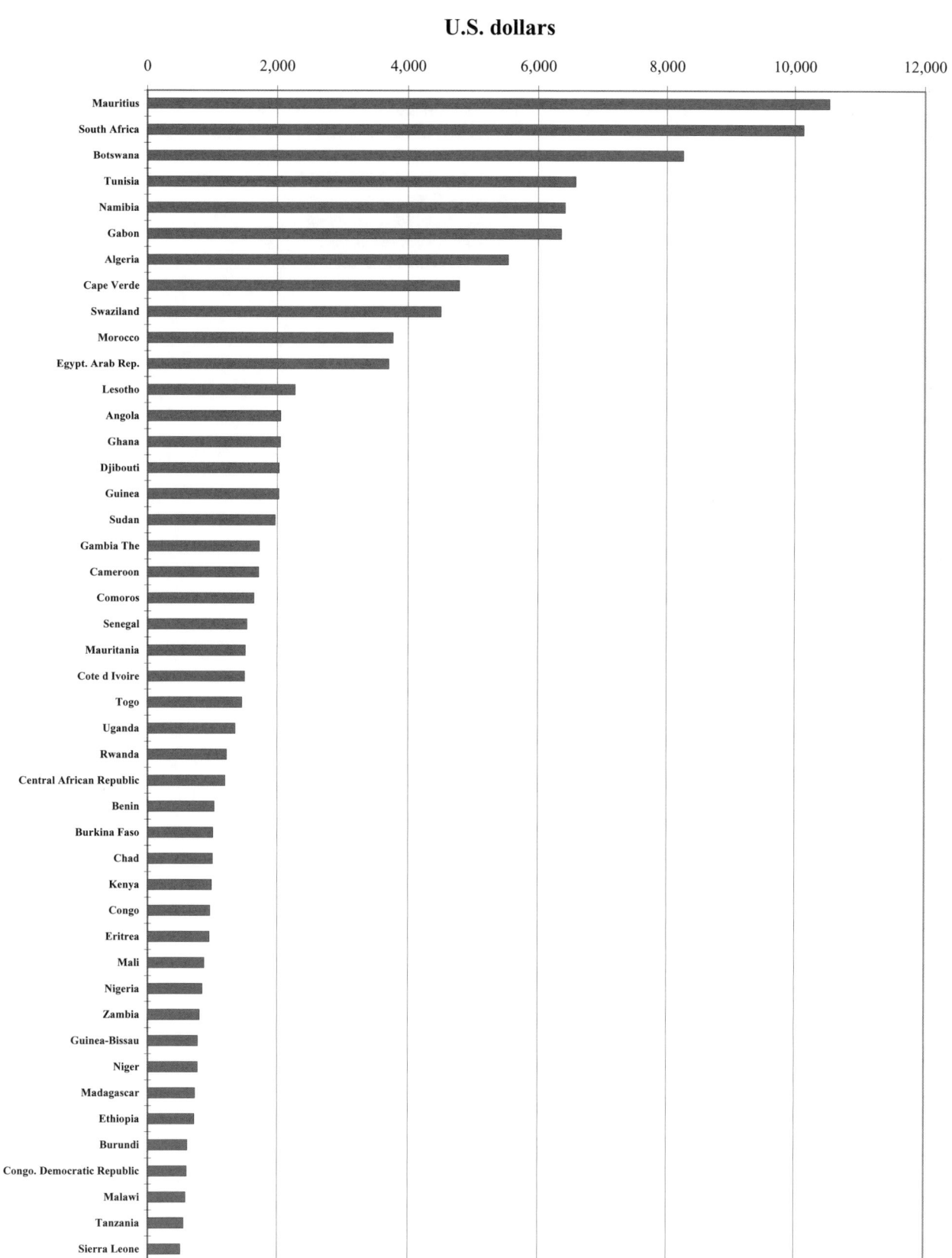

U.S. dollars

334

Figure 13-3. Urban population as a percentage of total population, 2002*

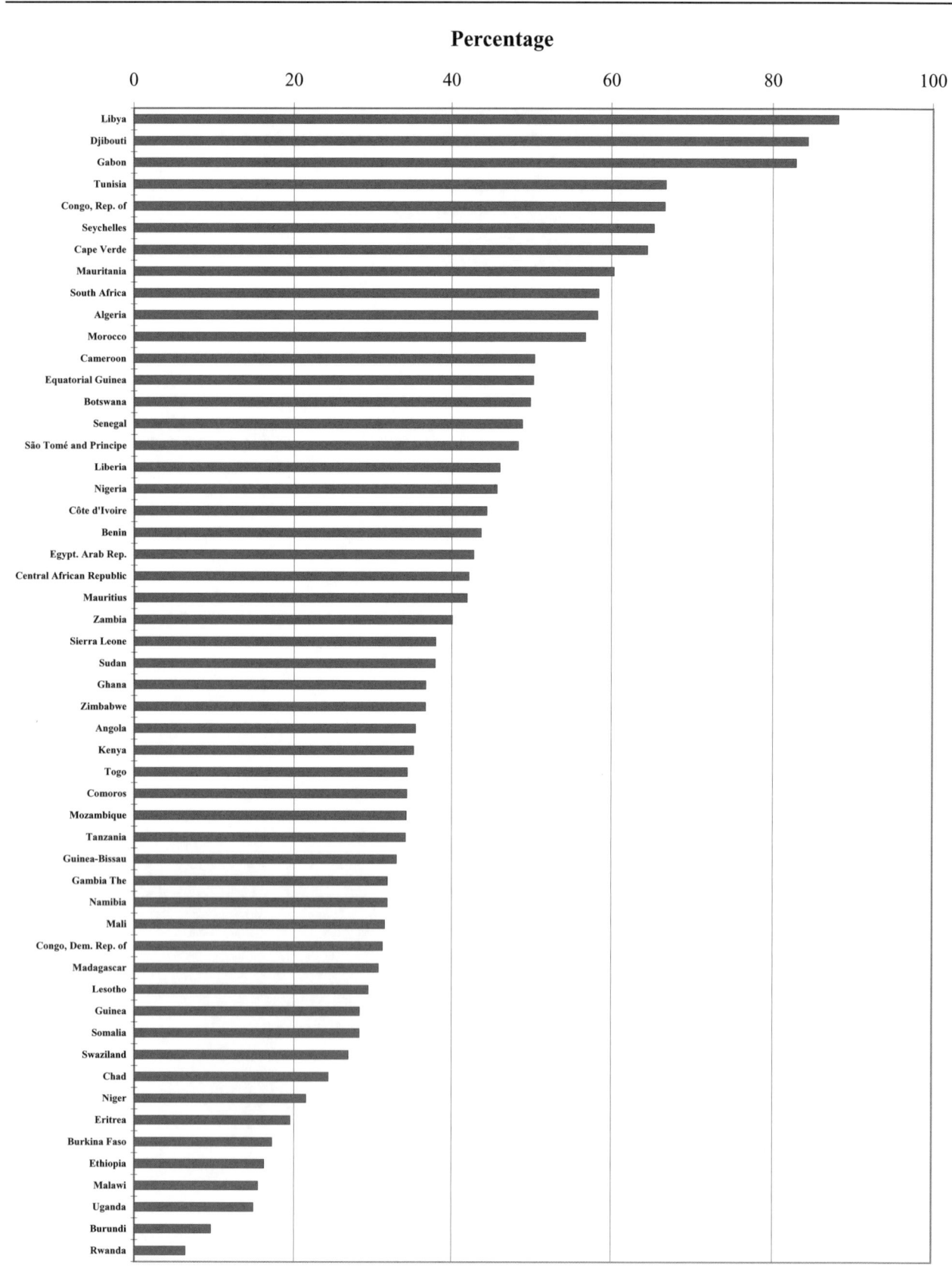

* Or most recent year available.

Figure 13-4. Primary school gross enrollement ratio, 2000*

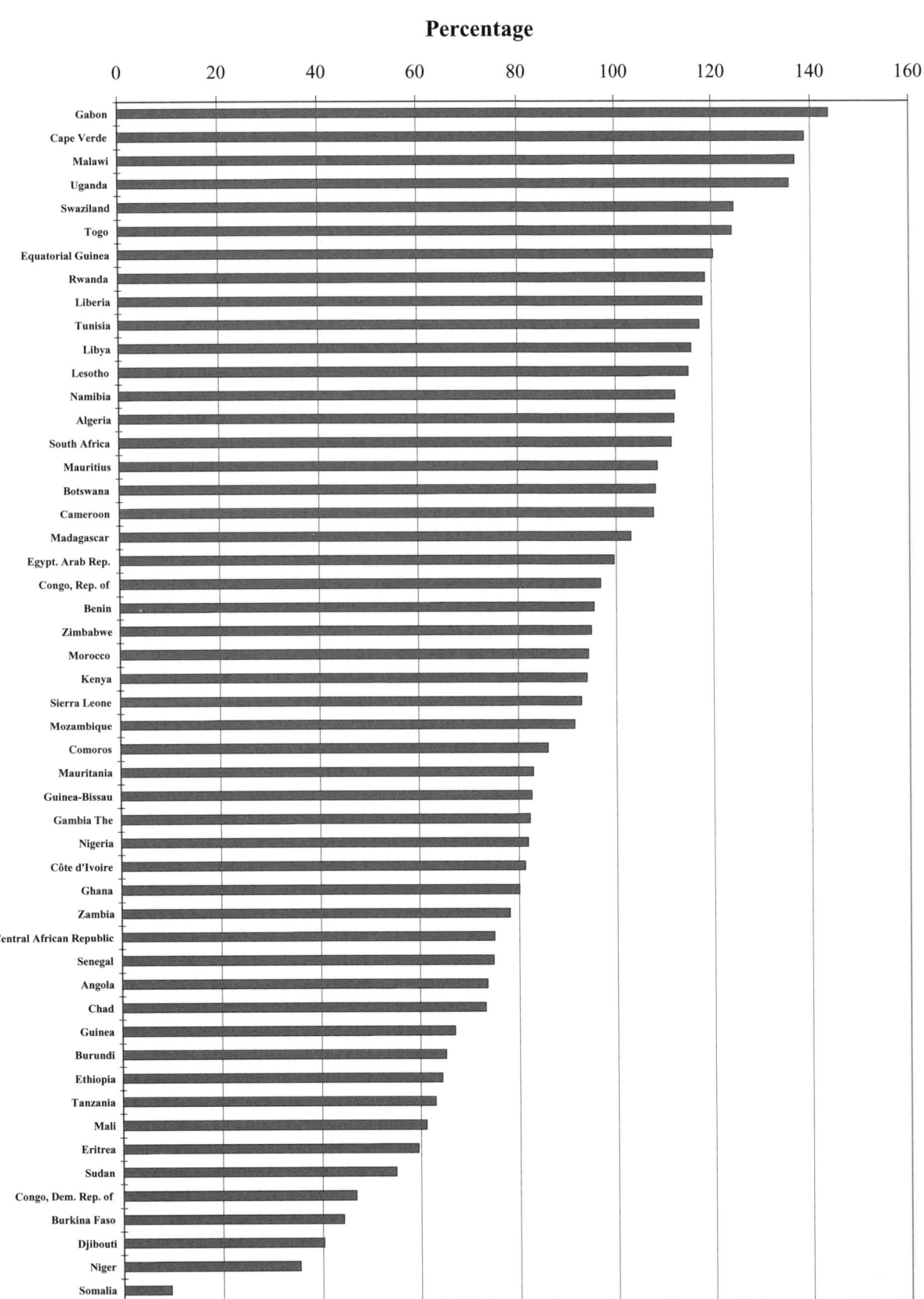

Percentage

* Or most recent year available.

Figure 13-5. Maternal mortality, 1999*

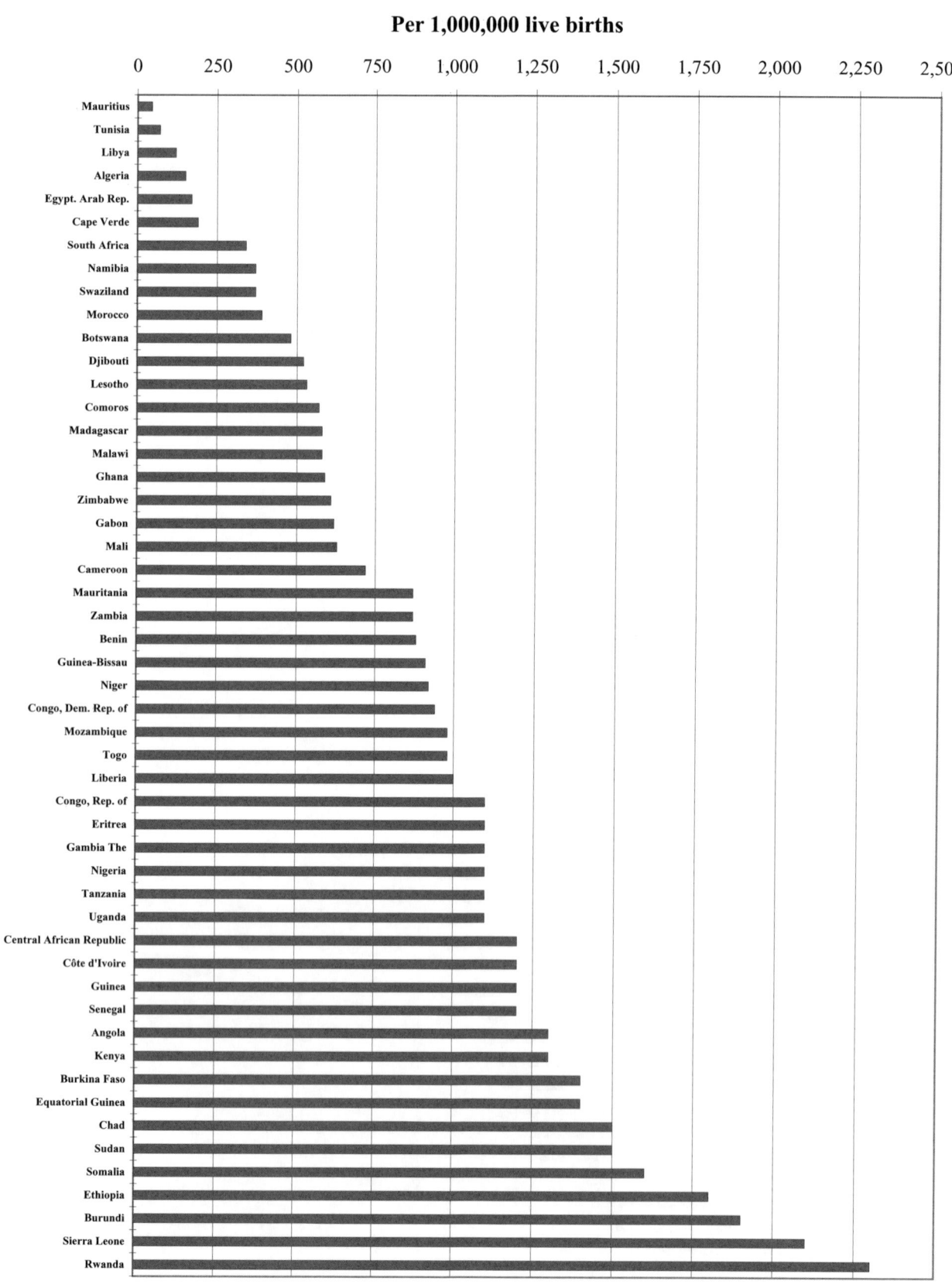

Per 1,000,000 live births

* Or most recent year available.

Technical notes

Tables

Table 13-1. Age and gender structure of the population. Age and gender structure of the population (UN and World Bank data) is the distribution of the total population according to age and gender. Only the female composition of the population is presented, as the male composition can easily be figured as the residual. Figures relate to midyear populations as estimated from the latest censuses. Age dependency ratio is calculated as the ratio of dependents—population under age 15 and above age 65—to the working age population—those aged 15 to 64.

Table 13-2. Poverty. This table presents selected indicators for comparing the incidence and extent of urban and rural poverty. The first indicator uses purchasing power parities rather than official exchange rates to calculate GDP per capita: a measure of the overall mean level of poverty at the national level. The next indicator is the national poverty head count, which shows the percentage of the population living below the poverty line deemed appropriate for the country by its authorities. The poverty line is defined as the level below which adequate standards of nutrition, shelter, and personal amenities cannot be assured. Since these levels are country specific, cross-country comparisons cannot be made. The next indicator, however, uses a relative concept of poverty, which does allow such comparisons. It shows the percentage of the urban and rural populations living on less than two-thirds of the mean national per capita income. Associated with these indicators are the urban and rural

Gini coefficients, which describe the level of inequality in urban and rural income distributions. The last indicator shows the percentage of household income spent on food (UNDP, World Bank, Penn World Tables, and National Household Surveys).

Table 13-3. Income distribution. These data present the share of income held by the richest and poorest population groups in a country (World Bank data and national household surveys).

Table 13-4. Urbanization. This table presents the number of persons living in urban areas as a percentage of the total population. Average annual percentage growth rates are shown separately for the urban population and the total population. The urban population percentages are based on the number of persons living in areas defined as "urban" according to national definitions of this concept. Since national definitions differ, cross-country comparisons should be made with caution (World Bank data).

Table 13-5. Components of population change. Three determinants of population change are presented here: total fertility rate, crude birth rate, and crude death rate. Crude birth rate is the number of births per 1,000 population in a given year. Crude death rate is the number of deaths per 1,000 population in a given year. Total fertility rate is the average number of children that would be born alive to a woman during her lifetime, if she were to bear children at each age in accordance with prevailing age-specific fertility rates (World Bank data).

Table 13-6. Survival prospects. This table shows four health-related indicators: life expectancy at birth, infant mortality rate, child mortality rate, and maternal mortality rate.

Life expectancy at birth is the number of years a newborn infant would live if prevailing patterns of mortality at the time of its birth were to stay the same throughout its life. Infant mortality rate is the number of deaths of infants under one year of age per 1,000 live births in a given year. Child mortality rate is the number of deaths of children under five years of age per 1,000 live births in a given year. Maternal mortality rate is the annual number of deaths of women from pregnancy-related causes per 100,000 live births.

Table 13-7. HIV/AIDS estimates and data, end 2001. Data reported on this table give the estimated number of people living with HIV/AIDS. The data are broken down into adults aged 15 and above, and children below the age of 15. Adult rate is the total number of adults (men and women) living with HIV/AIDS divided by the corresponding midyear population. Orphans are defined as children who lost their mother or both parents to AIDS when they were under the age of 15 (UNAIDS data).

Table 13-8. Immunization and ORT use. This is the percentage of children under one year of age immunized against tuberculosis, DPT, polio, and measles. It also gives the use rate of oral rehydration therapy (ORT) among children under five years of age. DPT refers to diphtheria, pertussis (whooping cough), and tetanus. ORT use is the percentage of all cases of diarrhea in children under five years of age treated with oral rehydration salts or an appropriate household solution (WHO data).

Table 13-9. Child malnutrition. Data reported in this table give the percentage of children and babies suffering from the nutrition-related problems of having low birthweight and being underweight, or suffering from wasting and stunting. Figures are also given on the extent of breastfeeding among nursing mothers.

Low birthweight refers to babies born weighing less than 2,500 grams. *Underweight* refers to children under the age of five weighing two standard deviations below the median weight for age of the reference population. *Wasting* refers to children of ages 12 through 23 months weighing two standard deviations below the median weight for height of the reference population. *Stunting* refers to children of ages 24 through 59 months standing two standard deviations below the median height-for-age of the reference population (UNDP various years, WHO and World Bank data).

Table 13-10. Access to sanitation facilities. Table 13-10 shows the percentage of the population with access to sanitation facilities (WHO data). Urban areas with access to sanitation facilities are defined as urban populations served by connections to public sewers or household systems, such as pit privies, pour-flush latrines, septic tanks, communal toilets, and other such facilities. Rural populations with access were defined as those with adequate disposal, such as pit privies and pour-flush latrines. Application of these definitions may vary, and comparisons can therefore be misleading.

Table 13-11. Access to safe water. This table refers to the percentage of the population with reasonable access to safe water supply, which includes treated surface waters or untreated but uncontaminated water, such as that from springs, sanitary wells, and protected boreholes. In an urban area, this may be a public fountain or standpost located not more than 200 meters away. In rural areas, it implies that members of the household do not have to spend a disproportionate part of the day fetching water. Data are presented separately for total, urban, and rural population (WHO data).

Table 13-12. Health expenditure. This table shows total health expenditure as percentage of GDP and on a per capita basis—both in U.S. dollars and PPP terms. The ratio to GDP is also shown for public and private expenditure. *Total expenditure* is the sum of public and private health expenditures. It covers the provision of health services (preventive and curative), family planning activities, nutrition activities, and emergency aid designated for health, but does not include provision of water and sanitation. *Public expenditure* consists of recurrent and capital spending from government (central and local) budgets, external borrowings and grants (including donations from international agencies and nongovernmental organizations, and social (or compulsory) health insurance funds. *Private expenditure* includes direct household (out-of-pocket) spending, private insurance, charitable donations, and direct service payments by private corporations (WHO, IMF, and World Bank data).

Table 13-13. Health care. Indicators presented here are population per physician, population per hospital bed, the percentage of births attended by trained health personnel, and access to health services. The figure for physicians includes, in addition to the total number of registered practitioners in the country, medical assistants whose medical training is less than that of qualified physicians, but who nevertheless dispense similar medical services, including simple surgical operations. The definition of recognized medical practitioners differs among countries. Hospital beds include inpatient beds available in public, private, general, and specialized hospitals and in rehabilitation centers. In most cases acute and chronic care are included. *Births attended* refers to births attended by physicians, nurses, midwives, trained primary healthcare workers, or trained traditional birth attendants. *Access to health services* refers to the percentage of the population that can reach appropriate local health services by the local transport in no more than one hour (WHO and World Bank data).

Table 13-14. Illiteracy rate. This table shows the share of illiterate adults in the total adult population aged 15 years and over. Literacy is defined as the ability to read and write. A person who can, with understanding, both read and write a short, simple statement about his everyday life is literate. Persons who can read, but cannot write, are included with illiterates. Figures are shown separately for males, females, and both genders combined (UNESCO data).

Tables 13-15. Primary school gross enrollment ratio. This is the total number of pupils enrolled at the primary level of education, regardless of age, ex-

pressed as a percentage of the population corresponding to the official school age of primary education in a given country. Data are given separately for males, females, and both genders combined. Figures shown may be more than 100 percent since total enrollment includes pupils above and pupils below the primary school age, as well as repeaters (UNESCO data).

Tables 13-16. Pupil progression. This table provides two education indicators. *Percentage of cohort reaching grade 5* shows the percentage of children starting primary school who eventually attain grade 4. The estimate is based on the Reconstructed Cohort Method, which uses data on enrollment and repeaters for two consecutive years. *Progression to secondary school* (general) is the number of new children in the first grade of secondary school (general) divided by the number of children enrolled in the final grade of primary school in the previous year (according to the country's duration of primary education (UNESCO and World Bank data).

Table 13-17. Net primary enrollment ratio. This is the ratio of the number of children of official school age enrolled in school to the number of children of official school age in the population (UNESCO data).

Table 13-18. Number of school teachers. Teachers in both public and private schools are covered in this table. Data refer to both full-time and part-time teachers, excluding other instructional personnel without teaching functions. Figures are shown here separately for primary and secondary schools. *Percentage females* means the number of female teachers expressed as a percentage of total teaching staff (UNESCO data).

Table 13-19. Pupil/teacher ratio. This ratio gives the average number of pupils per teacher. Figures are given separately for primary and secondary schools. As teaching staff includes both full-time and part-time teachers, comparability of this ratio between countries may be affected as the proportion of part-time teachers varies greatly from one country to another (UNESCO data).

Table 13-20. Secondary school gross enrollment ratio. This is the secondary school equivalent of the data presented in Table 13-15. It gives the total number of students enrolled at the secondary level of education, regardless of age, expressed as a percentage of the population corresponding to the official school age of secondary education. Data are presented separately for males, females, and both genders combined. *Secondary general education* refers to education in secondary schools that provides general or specialized instruction based upon at least four years of previous instruction at the first or primary level, but that does not specifically aim at preparing the pupils directly for a given trade or occupation. Such schools may be called high schools, middle schools, or lyceums and offer courses of study whose completion is a minimum condition for admission into universities. In some countries, some of these schools provide both academic and vocational training. These composite secondary schools are considered as equivalent to the academic type of secondary school and are thus classified as secondary *general* (UNESCO data).

Table 13-21. Public expenditure on education. This table presents public expenditure on education (UNESCO) first as a percentage of total public expenditure (IMF/*GFS*) and then as a percentage of current GDP (Table 2-5).

Table 13-22. Economic opportunities of women. This table shows two indicators. *Female/male ratio of participation in economic activity* shows the number of female workers in relation to the number of male workers. *Female/male ratio in occupational group* shows the breakdown of the first indicator for occupational categories (UNDP data).

Table 13-23. Household and economic participation of women. This table presents indicators on gender issues in development. *Households headed by women* (World Bank data) refers to families in which a woman is acknowledged as the head by the other members. The occupational statistics are based on the UN's, *Statistical Yearbook*.

Figures

The following indicators have been used to derive the figures in this chapter.

Figure 13-1. Life expectancy (Table 13-6).

Figure 13-2. GDP per capita, based on PPP, 2002 (Table 13-2).

Figure 13-3. Urban population as a percentage of total population (Table 13-4).

Figure 13-4. Primary school gross enrollment ratio (Table 13-15).

Figure 13-5. Maternal mortality (Table 13-6).

Methodology used for regional aggregations and period averages in Chapter 13

Table	Aggregations [a]					Period averages [b]	
	(1)	(2)	(6)	(7)	(8)	(1)	(2)
13-1							
Columns 1-8		x					
Columns 9-10			x				
13-2							
Columns 1, 3			x				
Columns 4, 5, 8				x			
Columns 2, 6-7					x		
13-3					x		
13-4							
Columns 1-3	x						
Columns 4-6							x
Columns 7-9			x				
Columns 10-12							x
13-5							
Columns 1-3			x				
Columns 4-6		x					
Columns 7-9		x					
13-6			x				
13-7	x						
13-8			x				
13-9			x				
13-10			x				
13-11			x				
13-12							
Columns 1-4			x				
Column 5					x		
13-13			x				
13-14			x				
13-15			x				
13-16			x				
13-17			x				
13-18							
Columns 1-3, 7-9					x		
Columns 4-6, 10-12			x				
13-19			x				
13-20			x				
13-21			x				
13-22			x				
13-23					x		

Note: Regional aggregations are shown in the rows for Sub-Saharan Africa, North Africa, and All Africa. Period averages are shown in the last three columns. This table shows only the methodologies used in this chapter.

  a. Regional aggregations: (1) simple total; (2) simple total of the first indicator divided by the simple total of the second indicator (same country coverage); (3) simple total of the gap-filled indicator; (4) simple total of the gap-filled main indicator divided by the simple total of the gap-filled secondary indicator; (5) simple total of the first gap-filled main indicator less the simple total of the second gap-filled main indicator, all divided by the simple total of the secondary indicator; (6) weighted total (by population); (7) median; (8) no aggregation; (9) simple arithmetic mean.

  b. Period averages: (1) arithmetic mean (using the same series as shown in the table; i.e., ratio if the rest of the table is shown as ratio, level if the rest of the table is shown as level, growth rate if the rest is shown as growth rate); (2) least-squares growth rate (using main indicator); (3) least-squares growth rate (using main indicator in constant terms, with the rest of the table in current terms).

14

Environmental Indicators

Data for this chapter were drawn entirely from the World Resources Institute and reflects tables published in their *World Resources 2002–2004: Decisions for Earth: Balance, Voice and Power*. It includes data on natural resources, their use by sector and the trends in their use, protected resources and those in danger of extinction, commercial energy production and its components, globally threatened species and protection, and management programs.

Until the early 1970s, environmental issues were mainly focused on problems of industrial countries and on such issues as water and air pollution, acid rain, and greenhouse gas emissions. Since the publication of the Club of Rome's *The Limit to Growth* in 1972, however, issues of natural resource depletion and degradation have received considerable attention in assessing environmental factors and their impacts on the development prospects of developing nations. At the national level, environmental concerns revolve around population expansion, desertification, deforestation, and the by-products of energy consumption.

Environmental destruction is not, however, confined by geographic borders. For instance, global warming, said to be caused by greenhouse gas emissions, has become a major global environmental concern. The issue of the greenhouse effect may be subject to controversy at the theoretical level and difficult to prove at the practical level. The fact that industrial wastes generated in one country cross frontiers and cause environmental damage to other nations is, however, widely acknowledged. Common interests, therefore, compel the international community to jointly work toward a common goal of preserving the environment.

Increasing emphasis on the links between the environment and development, both at the national and international levels, is reflected in the growing number of scientific and analytical studies. Challenging the hegemony of the SNA national income accounting convention, numerous scholarly endeavors are under way to integrate environmental consequences into national income calculations. The argument is made that the SNA methodology overstates national income levels for two reasons. First, it does not account for both the direct and indirect costs of drawing down natural resources. Second, it counts expenditure on resources for environmental protection activities as income. The changes both in methodology and emphasis have created an urgent demand for physical data. The information in this chapter aims to meet this growing demand, notwithstanding the limitations in data coverage and reliability.

The rate of deforestation is of particular concern because the cost of deforestation goes far beyond the losses of forest products, such as timber and fuelwood. There are equally significant indirect costs, including soil erosion; the substitution of animal and agricultural residues for cooking, which would otherwise be used for fertilizer; and climate changes. Deforestation is caused by many factors, including increased demand for settlement area, cultivation, fuelwood, or a combination thereof. The information in this chapter provides an empirical framework for assessing policy alternatives in reversing the continuing depletion of natural resources.

Data on roundwood production and consumption are important in monitoring the causes of deforestation. In addition, since roundwood is a primary source of energy in developing nations, data on roundwood consumption is essential in analyzing air pollution. For instance, for 1985–87, Africa used close to 88 percent of its roundwood production for fuel and charcoal production, while approximately 12 percent of the roundwood production went to industrial uses. To put these figures in perspective, the corresponding figures for Europe are 16 and 84 percent.

Information on freshwater resources available and on the extent and the methods of their uses can provide a partial basis for analyzing Africa's agricultural performance, its potential hydroelectric power, and its population's health conditions. Almost all Sub-Saharan African countries use a very small fraction of their internal renewable water resources. For example, Ethiopia, a nation that has suffered from repeated droughts, uses only 2 percent of its water resources. The major problem rests in the uneven geographic distribution of water resources with respect to population density and the state of freshwater drawing technology. The quality of water is as important as the quantity of water available. Water-related disease accounts for 80 percent of all sicknesses and for 90 percent of the 15 million deaths in developing countries each year.

Data on energy production are shown because of related environmental consequences. Biomass fuel, comprising wood fuel and animal and agricultural residues, accounts for 40 to 90 percent of total energy used in Sub-Saharan Africa.

Data on protected areas and endangered species indicate the intentions of countries to safeguard the environment and protect the use of natural resources for future generations.

14-1. Forest resources, 1990-2000

	Forest area								
	Total forest			Natural forest			Plantation		
	Extent (000 ha)		Annual % change	Extent (000 ha)		Annual % change	Extent (000 ha)		Annual % change
	1990	2000	1990-2000	1990	2000	1990-2000	1990	2000	1990-2000
SUB-SAHARAN AFRICA	..	..	..	..	..	..	..	..	..
excluding South Africa	..	..	..	..	..	..	..	..	..
excl. S. Africa & Nigeria	..	..	..	..	..	..	..	..	..
Angola	70,998	69,756	-0.2	70,858	69,615	-0.2	140	141	0.1
Benin	3,349	2,650	-2.3	3,248	2,538	-2.5	101	112	1.0
Botswana	13,611	12,427	-0.9	13,610	12,426	-0.9	1	1	4.1
Burkina Faso	7,241	7,089	-0.2	7,220	7,023	-0.3	22	67	11.3
Burundi	241	94	-9.0	189	21	-21.9	52	73	3.4
Cameroon	26,076	23,858	-0.9	25,998	23,778	-0.9	78	80	0.3
Cape Verde	35	85	9.3	0	0	..	35	85	8.9
Central African Republic	23,207	22,907	-0.1	..	22,903	..	..	..	..
Chad	13,509	12,692	-0.6	13,498	12,678	-0.6	11	14	2.5
Comoros	12	8	-4.3	11	7	-5.3	1	2	3.9
Congo, Dem. Rep. of	22,235	22,060	-0.4	140,435	135,110	-0.4	96	97	0.1
Congo, Rep. of	140,531	135,207	-0.1	22,209	21,977	-0.1	26	83	11.5
Côte d'Ivoire	9,766	7,117	-3.1	9,629	6,933	-3.3	137	184	2.9
Djibouti	6	6	0.0	..	..	..	..	..	..
Equatorial Guinea	1,858	1,752	-0.6	..	..	..	..	..	..
Eritrea	1,639	1,585	-0.3	1,639	1,563	-0.5	0	22	..
Ethiopia	4,996	4,593	-0.8	4,800	4,377	-0.9	196	216	1.0
Gabon	21,927	21,826	0.0	..	21,790	..	..	36	..
Gambia, The	436	481	1.0	..	479	..	..	..	..
Ghana	7,535	6,335	-1.7	7,476	6,259	-1.8	59	76	2.5
Guinea	7,276	6,929	-0.5	7,264	6,904	-0.5	12	25	7.4
Guinea-Bissau	2,403	2,187	-0.9	..	2,186	..	..	2	..
Kenya	18,027	17,096	-0.5	17,816	16,865	-0.5	212	232	0.9
Lesotho	14	14	0.0	14	0	..	0	14	..
Liberia	4,241	3,481	-2.0	4,124	3,363	-2.0	118	119	0.1
Madagascar	12,901	11,727	-0.9	12,608	11,378	-1.0	294	350	1.7
Malawi	3,269	2,562	-2.4	3,173	2,450	-2.6	96	112	1.5
Mali	14,179	13,186	-0.7	13,172	14,172	-0.7	8	15	6.6
Mauritania	415	317	-2.7	415	293	-3.5	0	25	..
Mauritius	17	16	-0.6	4	3	-3.4	13	13	0.2
Mozambique	31,238	30,601	-0.2	31,195	30,551	-0.2	43	50	1.5
Namibia	8,774	8,040	-0.9	..	8,040	..	..	0	..
Niger	1,945	1,328	-3.7	1,898	1,256	-4.1	48	73	4.2
Nigeria	17,501	13,517	-2.6	17,038	12,824	-2.8	463	693	4.0
Rwanda	457	307	-3.9	211	46	-15.2	246	261	0.6
São Tomé and Principe	27	27	0.0	..	..	..	..	..	..
Senegal	6,655	6,205	-0.7	6,501	5,942	-0.9	154	263	5.3
Seychelles	30	30	0.0	..	25	..	..	5	..
Sierra Leone	1,416	1,055	-2.9	..	1,049	..	..	6	..
Somalia	8,284	7,515	-1.0	..	7,512	..	..	3	..
South Africa	8,997	8,917	-0.1	7,563	7,363	-0.3	1,434	1,554	0.8
Sudan	71,216	61,627	-1.4	70,876	60,987	-1.5	341	641	..
Swaziland	464	522	1.2	..	362	..	..	161	..
Tanzania	39,724	38,811	-0.2	..	38,676	..	..	135	..
Togo	719	510	-3.4	687	472	-3.8	32	38	1.7
Uganda	5,103	4,190	-2.0	5,073	4,147	-2.0	30	43	3.6
Zambia	39,755	31,246	-2.4	39,699	31,171	-2.4	56	75	2.9
Zimbabwe	22,239	19,040	-1.5	22,120	18,899	-1.6	119	141	1.7
NORTH AFRICA	..	..	..	..	..	..	..	..	..
Algeria	1,879	2,145	1.3	1,456	1,427	-0.2	424	718	5.3
Egypt, Arab Rep.	52	72	3.3	0	0	0.0	52	72	3.3
Libya	311	358	1.4	190	190	0.0	..	..	..
Morocco	3,037	3,025	0.0	2,599	2,491	-0.4	438	534	2.0
Tunisia	499	510	0.2	436	308	-3.5	63	202	11.7
ALL AFRICA	702,272	649,641	-0.7	586,950	640,826	0.9	5,644	7,856	3.9

Sources: Food and Agriculture Organization of the United Nations and the United Nations Economic Commission for Europe.

Notes: 0 = zero or less than half the unit of measure; negative numbers indicate reduction in forest area;   .. = not available

14-2. Forest ecosystems, 1990-99

	Land area (000 ha) 1998	Original forest as a percentage of land area[a]	Closed forests — Forests as a precentage of original forest — Current forests[b] 1996	Closed forests — Frontier forests[c] 1996	Percentage frontier forests c/ threatened 1996	Forest ecosystems (1990-99) — Mangroves Area (000 ha)	Mangroves Percentage protected	Tropical forests Area (000 ha)	Tropical forests Percentage protected	Nontropical forests Area (000 ha)	Nontropical forests Percentage protected	Sparse trees and parkland Area (000 ha)	Sparse trees and parkland Percentage protected
SUB-SAHARAN AFRICA	..	..	..	..	..	..	..	..	..	..	..	..	..
excluding South Africa	..	..	..	..	..	..	..	..	..	..	..	..	..
excl. S. Africa & Nigeria	..	..	..	..	..	..	..	..	..	..	..	..	..
Angola	124,670	20	15	0	111	0	0	37,564	3	0	0	0	0
Benin	11,262	16	4	0	0	0	0	1,516	18	0	0	585	2
Botswana	58,173	2	100	0	0	0	0	12,123	2	0	0	0	0
Burkina Faso	27,400	0	0	0	0	0	0	0	0	0	0	5,667	16
Burundi	2,783	46	3	0	0	0	0	219	18	0	0	139	3
Cameroon	47,544	80	42	8	97	227	2	20,009	6	0	0	2,416	22
Cape Verde	403	..	..	..	..	..	..	..	..	..	..	1,451	..
Central African Republic	62,298	52	16	4	100	0	0	17,101	20	0	0	1,451	48
Chad	128,400	0	0	0	0	0	0	3,516	4	0	0	2,857	1
Comoros	223	50	0	0	0	..	..	..	..	..	..	..	..
Congo, Dem. Rep. of	234,486	83	60	16	70	22	0	135,071	7	0	0	172	40
Congo, Rep. of	34,200	100	68	29	65	19	76	24,321	4	0	0	0	0
Côte d'Ivoire	32,246	75	10	2	100	0	0	2,702	23	0	0	625	18
Djibouti	2,320	2	0	0	0	0	0	33	0	0	0	0	0
Equatorial Guinea	2,805	96	38	0	0	25	0	1,749	0	0	0	0	0
Eritrea	11,760	..	..	..	..	0	0	1	0	0	0	0	0
Ethiopia	110,430	25	17	0	0	0	0	11,937	19	0	0	4,804	21
Gabon	26,767	100	90	32	100	147	3	21,481	4	0	0	0	0
Gambia, The	1,130	39	62	0	0	51	5	188	5	0	0	244	2
Ghana	23,854	66	9	0	0	0	0	1,694	7	0	0	336	17
Guinea	24,586	76	5	0	0	316	0	3,073	1	0	0	2,723	1
Guinea-Bissau	3,612	100	34	0	0	317	0	1,141	0	0	0	550	0
Kenya	58,037	17	19	0	0	0	0	3,423	8	0	0	2,754	3
Lesotho	3,035	2	0	0	0	0	0	89	9	0	0	0	0
Liberia	11,137	100	44	0	0	0	0	3,149	3	0	0	1	0
Madagascar	58,704	93	13	0	0	310	0	6,940	6	0	0	0	0
Malawi	11,848	12	0	0	0	0	0	3,830	9	0	0	0	0
Mali	124,019	0	0	0	0	0	0	6,132	2	0	0	336	0
Mauritania	102,552	0	0	0	0	..	..	..	..	..	..	..	..
Mauritius	204	..	..	..	..	..	..	..	..	..	..	..	..
Mozambique	80,159	33	14	0	0	565	4	20,863	7	0	0	14,414	7
Namibia	82,429	0	95	0	0	0	0	3,436	11	0	0	0	0
Niger	126,700	0	0	0	0	0	0	27	16	0	0	0	0
Nigeria	92,377	45	11	1	100	1,145	0	11,634	7	0	0	10,588	4
Rwanda	2,634	36	16	0	0	0	0	291	77	0	0	162	2
São Tomé and Principe	96	33	71	0	0	0	0	30	0	0	0	0	0
Senegal	19,672	14	16	0	0	158	3	2,076	7	0	0	8,816	13
Seychelles	45	..	..	..	..	..	..	..	..	..	..	..	..
Sierra Leone	7,174	100	10	0	0	176	1	260	20	0	0	104	0
Somalia	63,766	4	0	0	0	0	0	11,800	1	0	0	1,530	1
South Africa	122,104	13	0	0	0	0	0	10,333	5	52	26	0	0
Sudan	250,581	1	0	0	0	0	0	12,288	12	0	0	5,870	9
Swaziland	1,736	22	0	0	0	0	0	286	3	0	0	0	0
Tanzania	94,509	22	9	0	0	323	0	14,356	16	0	0	583	3
Togo	5,679	33	7	0	0	0	0	224	3	0	0	91	9
Uganda	24,104	70	4	0	0	0	0	3,772	17	0	0	1,850	65
Zambia	75,261	7	70	0	0	0	0	21,989	32	0	0	39	14
Zimbabwe	39,076	7	67	0	0	0	0	15,397	12	0	0	0	0
NORTH AFRICA	..	..	..	..	..	..	..	..	..	..	..	..	..
Algeria	238,174	5	12	0	0	0	0	0	0	2,694	4	1	83
Egypt, Arab Rep.	100,145	1	0	0	0	0	0	134	0	4	0	0	0
Libya	175,954	1	0	0	0	0	0	0	0	53	0	0	0
Morocco	44,655	22	7	0	0	0	0	0	0	1,862	3	0	0
Tunisia	16,361	18	5	0	0	0	0	0	0	300	2	0	0
ALL AFRICA	3,004,279	23	34	8	77	3,801	1	448,197	9	8,249	2	69,710	11

Source: Food and Agriculture Organization of the United Nations.

Notes:
a. Original forest is that estimated to have covered the planet 8,000 years ago given current climate conditions.
b. Includes frontier and nonfrontier forests.
c. Frontier forests are large, relatively undisturbed forest ecosystems
0 = zero or less than half of the unit of measure; .. = not available

14-3. Wood production and trade, 1999-2001

| | Average annual roundwood production | | | | | | Average annual forest products production | | | | Trade in forest products | | |
| | Total roundwood | | Wood fuel | | Industrial roundwood | | Wood-based panels | | Paper and paperboard | | Import | Export | |
	Cubic meters (000) 1999-01	Percentage change since 1989-91	Cubic meters (000) 1999-01	Percentage change since 1989-91	Cubic meters (000) 1999-01	Percentage change since 1989-91	Cubic meters (000) 1999-01	Percentage change since 1989-91	Metric tons (000) 1999-01	Percentage change since 1989-91	Value (million US$) 1999-01	Value (million US$) 1989-91	Percentage of total exports [a] 2001
SUB-SAHARAN AFRICA	..	..	..	..	..	..	..	..	..	..	..	..	..
excluding South Africa	..	..	..	..	..	..	..	..	..	..	..	..	..
excl. S. Africa & Nigeria	..	..	..	..	..	..	..	..	..	..	..	..	..
Angola	4,274	34	3,158	30	1,116	28	16	0	0	..	0	3	0
Benin	6,246	7	5,914	6	332	18	..	..	..	..	0	12	6
Botswana	740	8	635	5	105	22	..	..	..	..	0	15	1
Burkina Faso	9,217	-4	8,624	-6	593	40	..	..	..	..	0	8	3
Burundi	6,539	11	6,208	6	331	189	..	..	..	..	0	2	5
Cameroon	10,954	3	9,109	18	1,845	-50	1,006	60	0	-100	0	21	1
Cape Verde	..	..	..	..	..	..	..	..	..	..	0	0	0
Central African Republic	2,977	-14	2,000	-42	977	..	113	82	..	..	0	0	0
Chad	6,635	28	5,874	24	761	29	..	..	..	..	0	2	1
Comoros	..	..	..	..	..	0	..	..	..	..	0	0	0
Congo, Dem. Rep. of	68,527	45	64,874	38	3,653	19	73	-52	3	200	0	4	0
Congo, Rep. of	2,405	0	1,154	17	1,251	-14	102	2	..	..	0	2	0
Côte d'Ivoire	11,912	11	8,550	11	3,362	8	975	3	..	..	6	57	2
Djibouti	..	..	..	0	..	0	..	..	..	..	0	0	..
Equatorial Guinea	811	31	447	0	364	74	19	-13	..	..	0	0	0
Eritrea	2,230	..	2,228	..	2	..	..	..	..	..	0	7	34
Ethiopia	89,817	23	87,360	20	2,457	35	86	150	11	39	3	0	0
Gabon	3,017	58	515	13	2,502	54	329	74	..	..	0	4	0
Gambia, The	686	32	573	..	113	..	..	..	..	..	0	2	1
Ghana	21,871	62	20,678	52	1,193	-4	789	48	..	..	0	20	1
Guinea	12,154	16	11,503	15	651	18	26	-63	..	..	0	5	1
Guinea-Bissau	592	4	422	0	170	15	..	..	..	..	0	0	0
Kenya	21,646	17	19,669	16	1,977	13	237	0	129	32	38	33	2
Lesotho	2,018	36	2,018	31	..	..	..	..	..	..	0	0	0
Liberia	4,954	12	4,617	30	337	-110	89	-17	..	..	0	0	..
Madagascar	9,738	23	9,638	30	100	-208	334	40	3	-45	2	9	1
Malawi	5,480	-1	4,960	-4	520	24	63	12	..	..	0	5	1
Mali	5,143	19	4,730	18	413	16	..	..	..	..	0	9	1
Mauritania	1,434	24	1,428	22	6	18	..	..	..	..	0	3	1
Mauritius	..	..	..	-14	..	-31	..	..	..	..	0	0	0
Mozambique	18,043	14	16,724	12	1,319	35	31	13	0	-100	5	5	1
Namibia	..	..	..	..	..	..	..	..	..	..	0	36	3
Niger	6,502	8	6,091	7	411	30	..	..	..	..	0	5	2
Nigeria	68,725	16	59,307	15	9,418	15	2,095	-28	19	-51	8	137	1
Rwanda	7,836	86	7,500	60	336	128	79	181	..	..	0	2	2
São Tomé and Principe	..	..	..	..	..	..	..	..	..	..	0	0	0
Senegal	5,908	11	5,114	9	794	22	..	..	..	..	0	44	4
Seychelles	..	..	..	..	..	..	..	..	..	..	0	0	0
Sierra Leone	5,436	13	5,312	13	124	-7	..	..	..	..	0	4	5
Somalia	9,318	46	9,208	38	110	11	14	0	..	..	0	1	..
South Africa	30,616	25	12,000	..	18,616	..	1,974	-11	2,116	11	590	439	1
Sudan	18,873	5	16,700	3	2,173	20	52	843	3	-47	6	18	1
Swaziland	..	..	..	0	..	-108	..	..	..	..	0	0	0
Tanzania	23,139	12	20,825	11	2,314	17	28	-84	25	-4	0	14	2
Togo	5,778	21	5,493	18	285	45	..	..	..	..	0	5	1
Uganda	37,318	20	34,143	15	3,175	60	269	717	3	13	0	18	4
Zambia	8,053	14	7,219	12	834	23	175	31	4	58	0	6	1
Zimbabwe	9,151	32	8,115	26	1,036	44	480	89	80	-6	69	33	2
NORTH AFRICA	..	..	..	..	..	..	..	..	..	..	..	..	..
Algeria	7,344	24	7,070	23	274	-3	62	0	36	-64	292	0	0
Egypt, Arab Rep.	16,447	17	16,179	15	268	87	135	114	414	92	765	13	0
Libya	652	2	536	..	116	..	..	..	6	0	31	0	..
Morocco	1,050	-86	479	-262	571	-36	118	-27	116	3	337	85	1
Tunisia	2,307	11	2,093	10	214	21	124	9	94	22	187	14	0
ALL AFRICA	..	..	..	..	..	..	..	..	..	..	..	..	..

Source: Food and Agriculture Organization of the United Nations.

Notes: a. Export values are from Table 5-1.

      0 = zero or less than half of the unit of measure;   .. = not available.

14-4. Freshwater resources and withdrawals, 1970-2002

	Annual internal renewable water resources		Annual river flows			Annual withdrawals			Sectoral withdrawals (percentage)		
	Total (cubic km)	Per capita 2002 (cubic meters)	From other countries (cubic km)	To other countries (cubic km)	Year of data	Total (cubic km)	Percentage of water resources	Per capita (cubic meters)	Domestic	Industrial	Agricultural
SUB-SAHARAN AFRICA	..	..	..	..	..	..	..	..	..	..	..
excluding South Africa	..	..	..	..	..	..	..	..	..	..	..
excl. S. Africa & Nigeria	..	..	..	..	..	..	..	..	..	..	..
Angola	184	13,203	..	..	1987	0.48	0.3	57	14	10	76
Benin	25	3,741	15.5	..	1994	0.15	1.4	28	23	10	67
Botswana	14	9,209	11.8	..	1992	0.11	3.8	81	32	20	48
Burkina Faso	13	1,024	..	..	1992	0.38	2.1	39	19	0	81
Burundi	4	538	..	..	1987	0.10	2.8	20	36	0	64
Cameroon	286	18,378	0.0	0.0	1987	0.40	0.1	38	46	19	35
Cape Verde	0	672	..	..	..	..	..	..	..	..	..
Central African Republic	..	..	..	..	1987	0.07	0.0	26	21	6	73
Chad	43	5,125	28.0	..	1990	0.19	1.3	33	16	2	82
Comoros	1	1,603	..	..	..	..	..	..	..	..	..
Congo, Dem. Rep. of	1,283	23,639	84.0	..	1994	0.36	0.0	8	61	16	23
Congo, Rep. of	832	259,547	610.0	..	1987	0.04	0.0	20	62	27	11
Côte d'Ivoire	81	4,853	1.0	..	1987	0.70	0.9	66	22	11	67
Djibouti	0	460	..	..	..	..	..	..	..	..	..
Equatorial Guinea	26	53,841	0.0	..	1987	0.01	0.0	30	81	13	6
Eritrea	6	1,578	6.0	..	..	..	..	..	..	..	..
Ethiopia	110	1,666	0.0	..	1987	2.20	2.0	50	11	3	86
Gabon	164	126,789	0.0	..	1987	0.06	0.0	70	72	22	6
Gambia, The	..	5,836	5.0	..	1990	0.03	1.0	33	7	2	91
Ghana	53	2,637	22.9	..	1970	0.30	1.0	35	35	13	52
Guinea	226	26,964	0.0	..	1987	0.74	0.3	141	10	3	87
Guinea-Bissau	31	24,670	11.0	..	1991	0.02	0.1	17	60	4	36
Kenya	30	947	10.0	..	1990	2.05	10.1	87	20	4	76
Lesotho	3	1,456	0.0	..	1987	0.05	1.0	31	22	22	56
Liberia	232	70,348	32.0	..	1987	0.13	0.1	54	27	13	60
Madagascar	337	19,925	0.0	..	1990	19.70	5.8	1694	1	0	99
Malawi	17	1,461	1.1	..	1994	0.94	5.4	98	10	3	86
Mali	100	8,320	40.0	..	1987	1.36	2.3	164	2	1	97
Mauritania	11	4,029	11.0	..	1990	16.30	4,075.0	8046	6	2	92
Mauritius	2	1,873	..	..	..	..	..	..	..	..	..
Mozambique	216	11,382	116.0	..	1992	0.61	0.6	40	9	2	89
Namibia	18	9,865	39.3	..	1990	0.25	4.0	185	29	3	68
Niger	34	2,891	29.0	..	1990	0.50	14.3	65	16	2	82
Nigeria	286	2,384	59.0	..	1990	4.00	1.8	46	31	15	54
Rwanda	5	638	..	..	1993	0.77	12.2	134	5	1	94
São Tomé and Principe	2	15,279	..	..	..	..	..	..	..	..	..
Senegal	39	3,977	13.0	..	1990	1.50	5.7	205	5	3	92
Seychelles	..	..	..	..	..	..	..	..	..	..	..
Sierra Leone	160	33,237	0.0	..	1987	0.37	0.2	98	7	4	89
Somalia	14	1,413	9.7	..	1987	0.81	13.5	115	3	0	97
South Africa	50	1,131	5.2	..	1990	13.30	29.7	391	17	11	72
Sudan	65	1,981	119.0	..	1995	17.80	50.9	669	5	1	94
Swaziland	3	2,785	..	..	..	..	..	..	..	..	..
Tanzania	91	2,472	9.0	..	1994	1.17	1.5	40	9	2	89
Togo	15	3,076	0.5	..	1987	0.09	0.8	28	62	13	25
Uganda	66	2,663	27.0	..	1970	0.20	0.5	20	32	8	60
Zambia	105	9,676	35.8	..	1994	1.71	2.1	214	16	7	77
Zimbabwe	20	1,530	5.9	..	1987	1.22	8.7	136	14	7	79
NORTH AFRICA											
Algeria	15	461	0.4	0.4	1990	4.50	32.4	180	25	15	60
Egypt, Arab Rep.	58	830	56.0	0.0	1993	55.10	2,395.7	920	6	8	86
Libya	1	109	0.0	0.0	1995	3.89	486.3	783	9	4	87
Morocco	29	936	0.0	0.2	1991	11.05	36.8	454	5	3	92
Tunisia	5	577	0.6	0.0	1996	2.83	80.4	312	13	2	86
ALL AFRICA											

Source: Food and Agriculture Organization of the United Nations.

Notes: 0 = zero or less than half of the unit of measure; .. = not available.

14-5. Marine and freshwater catches, aquaculture, balance of trade, and fish consumption

| | Average annual marine catch[a] | | Average annual freshwater catch[b] | | Average annual aquaculture production 1999-01 (metric tons) | | | | Average annual balance of trade[c] 1995-97 (million US$) | | | Per capita annual food supply from fish and seafood |
	(000 metric tons) 1998-00	% change since 1988-90	(000 metric tons) 1998-00	% change since 1988-90	Marine fish	Dia-dromous fish	Fresh-water fish	Mollusks & Crus-taceans	Fish	Mollusks and crustaceans	Fish meal	Total 2000 (kg)
SUB-SAHARAN AFRICA	..	..	..	..	..	..	..	..	..	..	..	..
excluding South Africa	..	..	..	..	..	..	..	..	..	..	..	..
excl. S. Africa & Nigeria	..	..	..	..	..	..	..	..	..	..	..	..
Angola	186	50	6	-25	..	..	..	..	-8	3	..	13
Benin	14	6	25	-6	..	..	..	..	-5	2	..	7
Botswana	..	..	0	-89	..	..	..	..	-5	0	0	6
Burkina Faso	..	..	8	7	..	..	12	..	-3	0	..	2
Burundi	..	..	11	-18	..	..	85	..	0	0	..	2
Cameroon	60	21	50	138	..	..	56	..	-22	2	0	12
Cape Verde	..	..	..	..	..	..	..	..	..	..	..	22
Central African Republic	..	..	15	14	..	..	..	..	..	..	..	4
Chad	..	..	84	31	..	..	..	..	..	0	..	7
Comoros	..	..	..	..	..	..	..	..	..	..	..	19
Congo, Dem. Rep. of	4	97	194	21	..	..	409	..	-27	7	..	6
Congo, Rep. of	21	-6	26	10	..	..	197	..	-50	..	..	20
Côte d'Ivoire	66	-2	12	-59	..	..	1,074	..	35	4	0	15
Djibouti	..	..	..	..	..	..	..	..	..	..	..	2
Equatorial Guinea	5	34	1	162	..	..	..	..	0	0	..	..
Eritrea	7	..	0	..	..	..	..	..	0	0	..	2
Ethiopia	..	..	15	365	..	..	..	..	0	..	..	0
Gabon	40	114	10	421	..	..	406	..	-9	7	..	50
Gambia, The	..	..	..	..	..	..	1	..	1	3	..	22
Ghana	385	24	78	24	..	..	4,633	..	64	2	..	31
Guinea	79	108	4	33	..	..	..	..	8	5	0	13
Guinea-Bissau	5	3	..	..	..	..	..	..	6	3	..	3
Kenya	6	-29	192	25	..	124	483	0	33	5	0	6
Lesotho	..	..	0	494	..	..	7	..	..	..	..	0
Liberia	9	3	4	-1	..	..	18	..	-2	0	..	7
Madagascar	99	47	30	-10	..	..	2,385	4,562	13	77	0	8
Malawi	..	..	44	-41	..	6	557	..	0	0	0	4
Mali	..	..	102	55	..	..	48	..	-1	..	..	8
Mauritania	33	-51	5	-17	..	..	..	..	22	105	..	9
Mauritius	..	..	..	..	1	..	39	33	..	..	..	24
Mozambique	26	-16	11	215	..	..	..	..	-5	74	..	3
Namibia	305	191	2	49	..	..	8	..	..	..	..	12
Niger	..	..	11	226	..	..	17	..	-1	0	..	1
Nigeria	316	66	137	46	..	..	23,951	..	-208	20	..	9
Rwanda	..	..	7	287	..	..	335	..	..	..	..	1
São Tomé and Principe	..	..	..	..	..	..	..	..	..	..	..	14
Senegal	379	42	27	47	..	..	104	50	206	73	3	28
Seychelles	..	..	..	..	..	..	..	311	..	..	..	58
Sierra Leone	50	32	16	0	..	..	30	..	13	10	..	12
Somalia	21	-2	0	-50	..	..	..	..	4	..	..	3
South Africa	596	-34	1	10	16	1,313	..	..	102	43	-37	6
Sudan	6	336	44	52	..	..	1,000	..	0	0	..	2
Swaziland	..	..	..	..	..	..	62	6	..	..	..	9
Tanzania	50	-4	280	-18	..	..	237	..	52	9	0	8
Togo	15	34	5	20	..	..	124	..	-23	5	..	12
Uganda	..	..	268	19	..	..	1,218	..	38	..	..	9
Zambia	..	..	68	6	..	..	4,207	..	0	0	0	7
Zimbabwe	..	..	14	-41	..	113	77	0	-15	-1	-1	2
NORTH AFRICA												
Algeria	98	-1	0	..	39	18	196	..	-7	2	..	4
Egypt, Arab Rep.	156	81	220	44	82,253	0	220,822	3	-108	0	..	13
Libya	33	45	0	..	..	..	..	..	21	0	..	6
Morocco	782	43	2	16	694	148	982	0	270	437	2	8
Tunisia	91	-4	1	291	900	16	536	0	8	77	0	10
ALL AFRICA												

Source: Food and Agriculture Organization of the United Nations.

Notes: a. Includes marine fish and diadromous fish caught in marine areas, as well as mollusks and crustacean

       b. Includes freshwater fish and diadromous fish caught in inland waters or low-salinity marine areas, as well as mollusks and crustacear

       c. Exports minus imports.

       0 = zero or less than half of the unit of measure; .. = not available.

14-6. Energy production by source

	From all sources			From non-renewable energy sources					Total electricity generated	
	(000 metric toe) [a]	*Percentage change since*	*Per capita (kg oil equivalent)*	*Solid fuels (000 metric toe)* [a]	*Liquid fuels (000 metric toe)* [a]	*Gaseous fuels (000 metric toe)* [a]	*Nuclear fuels (000 metric toe)* [a]	*Other sources (000 metric toe)* [a]	*(000 metric toe)* [a]	*% change since*
	1999	*1989*	*1999*	*1999*	*1999*	*1999*	*1999*	*1997*	*1997*	*1997*
SUB-SAHARAN AFRICA	..	..	..	..	..	..	..	..	..	..
excluding South Africa	..	..	..	..	..	..	..	..	..	..
excl. S. Africa & Nigeria	..	..	..	..	..	..	..	..	..	..
Angola	43,644	61	3,421	0	37,627	457	0	0	95	37
Benin	1,781	4	292	0	45	0	0	0	4	92
Botswana	..	..	..	..	..	..	..	..	..	..
Burkina Faso	..	..	..	..	..	..	..	..	..	..
Burundi	..	..	..	..	..	..	..	..	..	..
Cameroon	12,109	-4	832	0	6,945	0	0	0	269	25
Cape Verde	..	..	..	..	..	..	..	..	..	..
Central African Republic	..	..	..	..	..	..	..	..	..	..
Chad	..	..	..	..	..	..	..	..	..	..
Comoros	..	..	..	..	..	..	..	..	..	..
Congo, Dem. Rep. of	14,860	25	300	58	1,075	0	0	0	517	11
Congo, Rep. of	14,079	58	4,805	0	13,500	0	0	0	37	53
Côte d'Ivoire	6,023	82	384	0	493	1,267	0	0	276	55
Djibouti	..	..	..	..	..	..	..	..	..	..
Equatorial Guinea	..	..	..	..	..	..	..	..	..	..
Eritrea	467	..	132	0	0	0	0	..	..	..
Ethiopia	17,176	26	280	0	0	0	0	0	115	50
Gabon	17,842	60	14,881	0	16,813	68	0	0	87	13
Gambia, The	..	..	..	..	..	..	..	..	..	..
Ghana	5,640	32	299	0	0	0	0	0	529	26
Guinea	..	..	..	..	..	..	..	..	..	..
Guinea-Bissau	..	..	..	..	..	..	..	..	..	..
Kenya	12,051	19	401	0	0	0	0	0	364	60
Lesotho	..	..	..	..	..	..	..	..	..	..
Liberia	..	..	..	..	..	..	..	..	..	..
Madagascar	..	..	..	..	..	..	..	..	..	..
Malawi	..	..	..	..	..	..	..	..	..	..
Mali	..	..	..	..	..	..	..	..	..	..
Mauritania	..	..	..	..	..	..	..	..	..	..
Mauritius	..	..	..	..	..	..	..	..	..	..
Mozambique	7,067	2	394	11	0	0	0	0	86	199
Namibia	270	..	156	0	0	0	0		..	..
Niger	..	..	..	..	..	..	..	..	..	..
Nigeria	183,796	25	1,658	36	106,759	5,888	0	0	1,305	35
Rwanda	..	..	..	..	..	..	..	..	..	..
São Tomé and Principe	..	..	..	..	..	..	..	..	..	..
Senegal	1,684	27	183	0	1	5	0	0	108	52
Seychelles	..	..	..	..	..	..	..	..	..	..
Sierra Leone	..	..	..	..	..	..	..	..	..	..
Somalia	..	..	..	..	..	..	..	..	..	..
South Africa	143,993	26	3,368	126,253	348	1,518	3,345	0	17,866	38
Sudan	16,631	93	547	0	3,512	0	0	0	169	43
Swaziland	..	..	..	..	..	..	..	..	..	..
Tanzania	14,267	24	416	3	0	0	0	0	166	52
Togo	1,022	35	233	0	0	0	0	..	..	..
Uganda	..	..	..	..	..	..	..	..	..	..
Zambia	5,770	22	566	112	0	0	0	0	689	-8
Zimbabwe	8,723	11	703	2,983	0	0	0	0	628	15
NORTH AFRICA	..	..	..	..	..	..	..	..	..	..
Algeria	144,363	46	4,852	0	66,870	77,400	0	0	1,865	70
Egypt, Arab Rep	58,460	10	877	0	42,029	13,816	0	0	4,958	52
Libya	70,462	15	13,616	0	66,079	4,246	0	0	1,563	17
Morocco	615	-19	21	72	10	33	0	231	1,129	64
Tunisia	7,120	10	761	0	4,161	1,727	0	0	686	75
ALL AFRICA	..	..	..	..	..	..	..	..	..	..

Source: International Energy Agency (IEA)

Notes: a. Tons of oil equivalent. See technical notes for more information on toe

0 = zero or less than half of the unit of measure; .. = not available or indeterminate

14-7. Energy consumption by economic sector

	Energy consumption by economic sector (% of total consumption)															
	Industry				Transportation						Agriculture		Commercial and public services		Residential	
	All industries		Iron and steel		Total		Air		Road								
	1990	1999	1990	1999	1990	1999	1990	1999	1990	1999	1990	1999	1990	1999	1990	1999
SUB-SAHARAN AFRICA	..	..	..	..	..	..	..	..	..	..	..	..	..	..	..	..
excluding South Africa	..	..	..	..	..	..	..	..	..	..	..	..	..	..	..	..
excl. S. Africa & Nigeria																
Angola	41.2	11.9	0.0	0.0	41.2	12.0	20.6	5.3	20.6	6.8	0.5	0.0	7.4	4.9	7.2	70.5
Benin	16.0	3.4	0.0	0.0	66.7	19.0	15.9	2.1	50.8	16.6	0.0	0.0	0.4	8.4	17.3	62.8
Botswana	..	..	..	..	..	..	..	..	..	..	..	..	..	..	..	..
Burkina Faso	..	..	..	..	..	..	..	..	..	..	..	..	..	..	..	..
Burundi	..	..	..	..	..	..	..	..	..	..	..	..	..	..	..	..
Cameroon	14.5	17.0	0.0	0.0	54.5	11.0	4.5	1.1	50.0	9.5	0.0	0.0	2.0	0.5	22.3	70.8
Cape Verde	..	..	..	..	..	..	..	..	..	..	..	..	..	..	..	..
Central African Republic	..	..	..	..	..	..	..	..	..	..	..	..	..	..	..	..
Chad	..	..	..	..	..	..	..	..	..	..	..	..	..	..	..	..
Comoros	..	..	..	..	..	..	..	..	..	..	..	..	..	..	..	..
Congo, Dem. Rep. of	24.2	21.3	2.8	0.3	25.8	2.0	9.3	0.9	16.6	1.2	0.1	0.0	0.0	0.0	14.8	74.8
Congo, Rep. of	11.7	1.5	0.0	0.0	69.7	20.0	12.9	4.5	56.8	16.0	0.0	0.0	0.0	0.0	14.2	78.5
Côte d'Ivoire	21.4	8.0	0.0	0.0	49.4	15.0	9.2	2.4	35.1	11.2	5.7	2.0	9.4	12.8	7.6	63.0
Djibouti	..	..	..	..	..	..	..	..	..	..	..	..	..	..	..	..
Equatorial Guinea	..	..	..	..	..	..	..	..	..	..	..	..	..	..	..	..
Eritrea	..	3.6	..	0.0	..	14.0	..	1.6	..	12.6	..	0.1	..	11.8	..	69.3
Ethiopia	23.9	1.6	0.0	0.0	53.6	3.0	19.8	0.4	33.8	3.0	4.0	0.0	1.8	0.1	6.7	2.0
Gabon	22.3	22.4	0.0	0.0	50.8	18.0	17.8	6.2	28.8	10.3	0.0	0.0	3.5	0.9	16.4	54.2
Gambia, The	..	..	..	..	..	..	..	..	..	..	..	..	..	..	..	..
Ghana	15.7	11.9	0.0	0.0	13.3	13.0	1.3	1.1	11.5	10.9	0.8	0.7	0.3	0.2	67.9	66.5
Guinea	..	..	..	..	..	..	..	..	..	..	..	..	..	..	..	..
Guinea-Bissau	..	..	..	..	..	..	..	..	..	..	..	..	..	..	..	..
Kenya	25.8	11.4	0.0	0.0	53.2	12.0	13.1	4.6	38.5	6.8	2.7	6.7	1.0	0.7	11.7	68.6
Lesotho	..	..	..	..	..	..	..	..	..	..	..	..	..	..	..	..
Liberia	..	..	..	..	..	..	..	..	..	..	..	..	..	..	..	..
Madagascar	..	..	..	..	..	..	..	..	..	..	..	..	..	..	..	..
Malawi	..	..	..	..	..	..	..	..	..	..	..	..	..	..	..	..
Mali	..	..	..	..	..	..	..	..	..	..	..	..	..	..	..	..
Mauritania	..	..	..	..	..	..	..	..	..	..	..	..	..	..	..	..
Mauritius	..	..	..	..	..	..	..	..	..	..	..	..	..	..	..	..
Mozambique	12.7	23.4	0.0	0.0	27.5	4.0	10.8	0.4	16.7	3.6	8.9	0.1	34.5	0.4	11.5	71.6
Namibia	..	6.2	..	0.0	..	47.0	..	5.2	..	38.3	..	14.8	..	0.3	..	17.4
Niger	..	..	..	..	..	..	..	..	..	..	..	..	..	..	..	..
Nigeria	19.3	11.3	0.6	0.1	52.5	7.0	3.9	0.6	47.7	6.6	0.0	0.0	1.9	0.3	21.1	81.0
Rwanda	..	..	..	..	..	..	..	..	..	..	..	..	..	..	..	..
São Tomé and Principe	..	..	..	..	..	..	..	..	..	..	..	..	..	..	..	..
Senegal	17.6	17.5	0.0	0.0	61.2	24.0	23.8	8.0	34.1	14.1	8.7	2.8	1.3	0.6	9.1	54.7
Seychelles	..	..	..	..	..	..	..	..	..	..	..	..	..	..	..	..
Sierra Leone	..	..	..	..	..	..	..	..	..	..	..	..	..	..	..	..
Somalia	..	..	..	..	..	..	..	..	..	..	..	..	..	..	..	..
South Africa	50.7	46.2	16.0	10.3	21.0	24.0	1.5	2.8	18.8	20.5	2.5	3.1	4.7	3.7	20.4	20.9
Sudan	13.8	4.7	0.0	0.0	73.3	12.0	1.8	0.4	71.5	11.9	1.1	0.0	0.6	1.8	6.2	64.3
Swaziland	..	..	..	..	..	..	..	..	..	..	..	..	..	..	..	..
Tanzania	21.1	11.6	0.1	0.0	47.0	2.0	11.4	0.3	35.6	1.8	0.9	3.2	4.4	0.3	23.4	78.7
Togo	7.7	5.9	0.0	0.0	12.7	12.0	1.6	1.9	11.1	10.0	0.0	0.0	1.2	0.9	26.0	23.3
Uganda	..	..	..	..	..	..	..	..	..	..	..	..	..	..	..	..
Zambia	40.8	22.8	0.9	0.2	17.4	5.0	3.2	0.9	13.6	4.0	2.2	0.7	5.7	1.9	6.1	65.0
Zimbabwe	48.1	12.1	11.6	3.2	22.2	9.0	2.5	1.4	13.4	7.4	11.8	8.9	8.1	2.8	6.0	57.8
NORTH AFRICA	..	..	..	..	..	..	..	..	..	..	..	..	..	..	..	..
Algeria	25.2	24.6	3.5	3.0	38.3	21.0	2.8	2.2	32.9	13.9	0.0	0.0	0.0	0.0	24.6	31.6
Egypt, Arab Rep	47.6	44.3	1.7	2.0	21.2	22.0	2.4	1.7	18.8	20.2	0.5	0.7	0.0	2.8	23.5	24.1
Libya	36.6	33.6	0.0	0.0	32.4	39.0	3.1	3.5	29.3	35.8	0.0	0.0	0.0	0.0	8.5	10.0
Morocco	28.2	27.1	0.2	0.0	13.1	12.0	5.0	3.8	7.8	5.4	0.7	0.7	2.3	1.8	20.4	24.1
Tunisia	39.1	24.5	1.5	1.0	30.3	27.0	5.7	5.6	23.2	21.5	6.7	5.9	6.8	7.3	17.0	31.8
ALL AFRICA	..	..	..	..	..	..	..	..	..	..	..	..	..	..	..	..

Source: International Energy Agency (IEA)

Notes: 0 = zero or less than half of the unit of measure; .. = not available or indeterminate

14-8. CO₂ emissions from industrial processes, 1999

	CO₂ emissions (000 metric tons)							Per capita carbon emissions (kilograms) 1999
	Solid fuels 1999	Liquid fuels 1999	Gaseous fuels 1999	Gas flaring 1998	Cement manufacturing 1998	Total 1990	Total 1998	Total contribution since 1950 [a]	
SUB-SAHARAN AFRICA	..	..	..	..	..	..	..	..	..
excluding South Africa	..	..	..	..	..	..	..	..	..
excl. S. Africa & Nigeria	..	..	..	..	..	..	..	..	..
Angola	0	3,740	1,070	1,738	174	4,650	5,925	145,552	370
Benin	0	1,180	0	0	259	564	732	14,762	190
Botswana	..	..	..	9	0	2,415	3,778	51,505	..
Burkina Faso	..	..	..	0	20	1,008	1,009	14,682	..
Burundi	..	..	..	0	0	194	231	3,975	..
Cameroon	0	2,580	0	0	224	1,488	1,763	86,507	170
Cape Verde	..	..	..	0	0	0	84	121	..
Central African Republic	..	..	..	0	0	198	249	5,866	..
Chad	..	..	..	0	0	143	110	5,027	..
Comoros	..	..	..	0	0	66	70	..	..
Congo, Dem. Rep. of	880	1,570	0	0	60	4,096	2,434	142,475	40
Congo, Rep. of	0	370	0	167	0	2,037	1,820	40,161	120
Côte d'Ivoire	0	1,730	2,960	0	324	9,907	13,199	185,109	290
Djibouti	..	..	..	0	0	352	366	..	..
Equatorial Guinea	..	..	..	0	0	117	253	2,862	..
Eritrea	0	620	0	..	..	..	1,990	..	170
Ethiopia	0	2,930	0	0	411	2,964	2,820	66,509	40
Gabon	0	1,330	160	0	98	6,112	227	135,432	1,240
Gambia, The	..	..	..	0	0	191	4,357	4,481	..
Ghana	0	4,390	0	0	997	3,539	1,225	109,271	230
Guinea	..	..	..	0	130	1,011	231	32,445	..
Guinea-Bissau	..	..	..	0	0	209	9,131	4,477	..
Kenya	170	7,480	0	0	598	5,822	353	180,020	250
Lesotho	..	..	..	..	..	..	1,251	..	..
Liberia	..	..	..	0	5	465	747	33,189	..
Madagascar	..	..	..	0	60	945	485	37,860	..
Malawi	..	..	..	0	87	601	2,916	18,184	..
Mali	..	..	..	0	5	421	1,726	12,025	..
Mauritania	..	..	..	0	25	2,634	1,332	40,648	..
Mauritius	..	..	..	0	0	1,151	10	..	..
Mozambique	0	1,070	0	0	144	997	1,110	89,149	50
Namibia	10	2,200	0	0	10	..	78,455	..	1,280
Niger	..	..	..	0	18	1,048	2,231	20,863	..
Nigeria	140	25,950	12,300	40,203	1,345	88,665	511	1,944,327	340
Rwanda	..	..	..	2	7	528	7	9,167	..
São Tomé and Principe	..	..	..	0	0	66	77	..	..
Senegal	0	3,270	10	0	498	2,895	3,298	76,142	..
Seychelles	..	..	..	0	0	114	198	..	..
Sierra Leone	..	..	..	0	50	333	523	19,844	..
Somalia	..	..	..	0	0	18	0	13,747	..
South Africa	316,120	26,640	3,550	0	4,734	291,108	343,716	8,541,575	..
Sudan	0	5,390	0	0	150	3,459	3,597	137,001	..
Swaziland	..	..	..	0	0	425	399	..	..
Tanzania	8	0	7	0	150	2,272	2,227	61,694	..
Togo	0	880	0	0	281	689	882	17,023	..
Uganda	..	..	..	0	105	846	1,281	32,837	..
Zambia	400	1,490	0	0	199	2,444	1,559	111,151	..
Zimbabwe	9,520	4,130	0	0	548	16,646	14,072	369,232	..
NORTH AFRICA	..	..	..	..	..	..	..	..	..
Algeria	2,040	20,890	45,260	13,332	3,887	80,443	106,613	1,725,913	2,290
Egypt, Arab Rep	3,140	76,200	30,920	0	9,569	75,434	105,753	1,856,890	1,650
Libya	0	32,930	8,460	3,520	1,495	37,772	36,448	855,830	..
Morocco	8,590	19,350	80	0	3,588	23,486	32,035	558,859	950
Tunisia	360	10,210	6,150	259	2,287	13,260	22,364	318,035	..
ALL AFRICA	..	..	..	..	..	..	..	..	..

Sources: International Energy Agency (IEA), Carbon Dioxide Information Analysis Center (CDIAC)

Notes: Estimates are of the carbon dioxide emitted, 3.664 times the carbon it contains
a. Data are for 1998
0 = zero or less than half the unit of measure, .. = not available

14-9. Globally threatened species: mammals, birds, and higher plants, 1992-2002

	Mammals				Birds				Higher plants			
	Total number of known species			Number of species per 10,000 km²ᵃ	Total number of known species			Number of species per 10,000 km²ᵃ	Total number of known species			Number of species per 10,000 km²ᵃ
	All species	Endemic species	Threatened species		Breeding species	Endemic species	Threatened species		All species[b]	Endemic species	Threatened species	
SUB-SAHARAN AFRICA	..	..	..	..	..	..	..	..	..	..	..	..
excluding South Africa	..	..	..	..	..	..	..	..	..	..	..	..
excl. S. Africa & Nigeria	..	..	..	..	..	..	..	..	..	..	..	..
Angola	276	7	19	56	265	12	15	13	5,185	1,260	19	1,055
Benin	188	0	8	85	112	0	2	1	2,500	..	11	990
Botswana	164	0	6	43	184	1	7	7	2,151	17	..	563
Burkina Faso	147	0	7	49	138	0	2	1	1,100	..	2	369
Burundi	107	0	6	76	145	0	7	6	2,500	..	2	1,783
Cameroon	409	14	40	114	165	8	15	14	8,260	156	155	2,310
Cape Verde	5	..	3	7	42	4	2	3	774	86	2	..
Central African Republic	..	2	..	53	..	..	..	2	..	..	..	921
Chad	134	1	17	27	141	0	5	3	1,600	..	2	322
Comoros	12	..	2	20	43	14	9	6	721	136	5	..
Congo, Dem. Rep. of	450	28	40	74	345	24	28	26	11,007	1,100	55	1,818
Congo, Rep. of	200	2	15	62	130	0	3	3	6,000	1,200	33	1,870
Côte d'Ivoire	230	0	19	73	252	2	12	12	3,660	62	101	1,163
Djibouti	61	..	4	46	58	1	5	3	826	6	2	..
Equatorial Guinea	184	1	16	131	..	3	5	4	3,250	66	23	2,312
Eritrea	112	0	12	50	138	0	7	3	..	..	3	..
Ethiopia	277	31	35	54	262	..	16	20	6,603	..	22	1,398
Gabon	190	3	15	64	156	1	5	4	6,651	..	71	2,248
Gambia, The	117	0	..	112	..	..	..	1	..	..	..	935
Ghana	222	1	14	78	206	0	8	10	3,725	43	115	1,308
Guinea	190	1	12	66	109	0	10	12	3,000	88	21	1,043
Guinea-Bissau	108	0	3	71	235	0	..	1	1,000	12	4	655
Kenya	359	23	51	94	344	9	24	24	6,506	265	98	1,703
Lesotho	33	0	3	23	123	0	7	5	1,591	2	1	1,103
Liberia	193	0	17	87	146	1	11	13	2,200	103	46	993
Madagascar	141	93	50	37	172	105	27	28	9,505	6,500	162	2,479
Malawi	195	0	8	86	219	0	11	9	3,765	49	13	1,665
Mali	137	0	13	28	191	0	4	6	1,741	11	6	355
Mauritania	61	1	10	13	172	0	2	3	1,100	..	..	239
Mauritius	4	..	3	7	39	8	9	10	750	325	87	..
Mozambique	179	2	14	42	144	0	16	14	5,692	219	36	1,340
Namibia	250	3	15	58	201	3	11	8	3,174	687	5	942
Niger	131	0	11	27	125	0	3	2	1,460	..	2	238
Nigeria	274	4	27	62	286	2	9	9	4,715	205	119	1,059
Rwanda	151	0	9	110	200	0	9	6	2,288	26	3	1,664
São Tomé and Principe	8	..	3	17	50	25	9	9	895	134	27	..
Senegal	192	0	12	72	175	0	4	6	2,086	26	7	780
Seychelles	6	..	4	17	52	11	10	9	250	182	43	..
Sierra Leone	147	0	12	77	172	1	10	12	2,090	74	43	1,091
Somalia	171	12	19	43	179	11	10	8	3,028	500	17	768
South Africa	247	35	42	52	304	8	28	16	23,420	..	45	4,797
Sudan	267	11	23	43	280	1	6	9	3,137	50	17	507
Swaziland	47	..	4	39	378	0	5	6	2,715	4	3	..
Tanzania	316	15	42	70	229	24	33	30	10,008	1,122	235	2,231
Togo	196	0	9	110	117	0	..	1	3,085	..	9	1,739
Uganda	345	6	20	118	243	3	13	10	4,900	..	33	1,891
Zambia	233	3	11	56	252	2	11	10	4,747	211	8	1,141
Zimbabwe	270	0	11	81	229	0	10	9	4,440	95	14	1,325
NORTH AFRICA	..	..	..	..	..	..	..	..	..	..	..	..
Algeria	92	2	13	15	183	1	6	8	3,164	250	2	520
Egypt, Arab Rep	98	7	13	21	123	0	7	11	2,076	70	2	454
Libya	..	5	..	14	..	..	..	2	..	..	..	331
Morocco	105	4	16	30	..	0	9	11	3,675	625	2	1,049
Tunisia	78	1	11	31	165	0	5	6	2,196	..	..	873
ALL AFRICA	..	..	..	..	..	..	..	..	..	..	..	..

Source: United Nations Environment Programme-World Conservation Monitoring Centre (UNEP-WCMC), International Union for Conservation of Nature and Natural Resources (IUCN)

Notes: a. Values are standardized using a species-area curve.

       b. Flowering plants only.

       .. = not available

14-10. Globally threatened species: reptiles, amphibians, and fish, 1992-2003

	Reptiles				Amphibians				Freshwater fish	
	Total number of known species			No. of species per 10,000 km^{2a}	Total number of known species			No. of species per 10,000 km^{2a}	Total number of known species	
	All species	Endemic species	Threatened species		All species	Endemic species	Threatened species		All species	Threatened species^b
SUB-SAHARAN AFRICA	..	..	..	..	..	..	..	..	..	..
excluding South Africa	..	..	..	..	..	..	..	..	..	..
excl. S. Africa & Nigeria	..	..	..	..	..	..	..	..	..	..
Angola	227	19	4	..	78	22	..	..	108	..
Benin	97	1	1	..	2	0	..	..	84	..
Botswana	133	2	..	41	20	0	..	10	1	..
Burkina Faso	44	3	1	..	1	0	..	..	..	..
Burundi	79	0	..	..	18	2	..	..	5	..
Cameroon	210	21	1	51	171	66	1	53	138	27
Cape Verde	19	9	..	16	..	0	..	0	132	1
Central African Republic	..	..	..	33	..	..	..	12	..	..
Chad	52	1	1	1	3	0	..	..	1	..
Comoros	28	7	2	36	..	0	..	3	164	1
Congo, Dem. Rep. of	304	..	2	62	208	53	..	13	101	1
Congo, Rep. of	149	..	1	..	51	1	..	..	79	1
Côte d'Ivoire	125	3	2	..	38	3	1	..	111	..
Djibouti	85	0	..	27	6	0	..	2	166	1
Equatorial Guinea	91	4	2	..	29	2	1	..	83	..
Eritrea	87	1	6	38	5	2	..	8	102	..
Ethiopia	208	9	1	40	71	24	..	13	13	..
Gabon	130	3	1	..	35	4	..	..	104	1
Gambia, The	..	..	..	45	..	..	..	29	..	..
Ghana	131	1	2	..	33	4	..	..	90	..
Guinea	94	3	1	..	33	3	1	..	121	..
Guinea-Bissau	46	2	1	..	6	1	..	..	110	1
Kenya	261	18	5	50	63	10	..	23	314	18
Lesotho	41	2	..	..	6	0	..	..	2	1
Liberia	79	2	2	28	32	4	..	17	86	..
Madagascar	381	259	18	95	217	155	2	47	390	14
Malawi	108	7	..	55	46	3	..	31	163	..
Mali	106	4	1	3	30	1	..	..	2	1
Mauritania	72	1	2	..	3	0	..	..	117	..
Mauritius	35	11	4	19	2	0	..	0	430	1
Mozambique	195	5	5	39	52	1	..	15	524	4
Namibia	215	25	3	58	31	2	1	12	107	3
Niger	58	0	..	..	7	0	..	..	2	..
Nigeria	154	7	2	30	53	1	..	24	95	2
Rwanda	97	1	..	..	25	1	..	..	19	..
São Tomé and Principe	15	..	1	35	9	8	..	20	221	..
Senegal	91	1	6	37	22	1	..	1	150	1
Seychelles	38	14	4	103	12	11	4	33	480	..
Sierra Leone	67	1	3	..	35	2	..	..	99	..
Somalia	223	49	2	49	30	3	..	7	331	3
South Africa	364	97	19	65	117	49	9	22	629	29
Sudan	161	8	2	..	9	1	..	..	130	..
Swaziland	111	0	..	85	41	0	..	33	1	..
Tanzania	335	61	5	64	116	49	..	30	331	17
Togo	107	1	2	..	10	3	..	..	82	..
Uganda	165	2	..	52	43	1	..	17	49	27
Zambia	143	3	..	35	57	1	..	16	8	..
Zimbabwe	180	2	..	46	31	3	..	36	4	..
NORTH AFRICA	..	..	..	..	..	..	..	..	..	..
Algeria	97	4	2	13	11	0	..	2	100	1
Egypt, Arab Rep	108	0	6	18	11	0	..	1	284	..
Libya	..	..	..	10	..	..	..	1	..	..
Morocco	103	11	2	26	13	1	..	3	136	1
Tunisia	70	1	3	25	8	0	..	3	99	..
ALL AFRICA	..	..	..	..	..	..	..	..	..	..

Source: United Nations Environment Programme-World Conservation Monitoring Centre (UNEP-WCMC), International Union for Conservation of Nature and Natural Resources (IUCN)

Notes: a. Values are standardized using a species-area curve.
b. Threatened species include a few marine species
.. = not available

14-11. National protection of natural areas, 2003

	All protected areas (IUCN categories I-V)					Number of marine protected areas [a] (IUCN categories I-VI)		
			Percent	Number of areas at least:				
	Number	Area (000 ha)	of land area	100,000 ha in size	1 million ha in Size	Total	Littoral	Marine
SUB-SAHARAN AFRICA	..	..	..	..	..	..	..	..
excluding South Africa	..	..	..	..	..	..	..	..
excl. S. Africa & Nigeria	..	..	..	..	..	..	..	..
Angola	13	5,271	4.2	8	2	4	4	3
Benin	2	778	6.7	10	..	..	..	..
Botswana	12	10,499	18.1	31	3	..	..	..
Burkina Faso	12	3,135	11.5	8	1	..	..	..
Burundi	13	146	5.4	..	..	..	1	1
Cameroon	18	3,456	7	12	..	2	1	2
Cape Verde	..	0	0.0	..	..	3	2	..
Central African Republic	13	7,321	11.8	17	4	..	..	..
Chad	9	11,494	9.0	11	2	..	..	..
Comoros	..	40	24.3	..	..	..	..	..
Congo, Dem. Rep. of	15	..	..	23	7	1	1	0
Congo, Rep. of	9	4,860	14.1	8	2	..	1	1
Côte d'Ivoire	11	..	..	12	1	3	3	1
Djibouti	..	10	0.5	..	..	2	2	..
Equatorial Guinea	0	455	16.8	1	..	3	4	0
Eritrea	3	501	4	2	..	..	..	..
Ethiopia	21	5,518	4.9	28	3	..	..	..
Gabon	5	80	0.3	3	..	3	4	1
Gambia, The	6	..	..	..	..	..	5	3
Ghana	10	1,104	4.6	4	..	..	..	..
Guinea	3	164	1	1	..	1	0	1
Guinea-Bissau	0	0	0.0	..	..	2	2	1
Kenya	50	3,485	6.0	14	1	13	13	10
Lesotho	1	7	0.2	..	..	..	..	..
Liberia	1	129	1.3	5	..	1	..	..
Madagascar	40	1,404	2	3	..	7	3	1
Malawi	9	1,059	8.9	4	..	..	..	..
Mali	13	4,532	3.6	8	2	..	..	..
Mauritania	9	250	0.2	1	..	5	5	2
Mauritius	..	7	3.4	..	..	17	14	..
Mozambique	11	3,285	4	6	2	7	7	6
Namibia	20	3,214	3.9	5	1	4	4	0
Niger	6	9,694	8.2	4	2	..	..	..
Nigeria	27	3,254	3.6	19	..	..	..	..
Rwanda	6	194	7.7	..	..	..	..	..
São Tomé and Principe	..	..	..	..	..	..	..	..
Senegal	12	2,096	11	3	..	7	6	6
Seychelles	..	4	7.3	..	..	11	15	..
Sierra Leone	2	145	2.0	..	..	..	..	..
Somalia	2	180	0.3	1	..	2	2	2
South Africa	390	..	..	..	..	..	17	8
Sudan	11	8,616	3.5	13	4	2	0	2
Swaziland	..	35	2	..	..	..	..	..
Tanzania	39	13,787	14.6	69	6	26	8	8
Togo	9	429	7.5	2	..	1	0	1
Uganda	37	1,763	7.3	12	1	..	..	..
Zambia	35	6,366	8.4	58	4	..	..	..
Zimbabwe	48	3,103	7.9	14	1	..	..	..
NORTH AFRICA	..	..	..	..	..	..	..	..
Algeria	18	11,864	5.1	2	2	5	6	3
Egypt, Arab Rep.	16	4,536	4.6	9	1	25	16	6
Libya	8	..	..	..	..	..	2	3
Morocco	12	326	0.8	2	..	10	9	3
Tunisia	7	28	0.2	..	..	4	5	4
ALL AFRICA	..	..	..	..	..	..	..	..

Source: United Nations Environment Programme-World Conservation Monitoring Centre (UNEP-WCMC). International Union for Conservation of Nature and Natural Resources (IUCN)

Notes: a. Includes areas with substantial terrestrial components that reach the shore. An area can be both marine and littoral (see technical notes).

0 = zero or less than half the unit of measure.   .. = not available or indeterminate.

14-12. International protected areas, 2002

| | International protection systems | | | | | |
| | Biosphere reserves | | World Heritage sites | | Wetlands of international importance | |
	Number	Area (000 ha)	Number	Area (000 ha)	Number	Area (000 ha)
SUB-SAHARAN AFRICA	..	..	..	..	..	..
excluding South Africa	..	..	..	..	..	..
excl. S. Africa & Nigeria	..	..	..	..	..	..
Angola	..	..	0	0	..	..
Benin	1	623	0	0	2	139
Botswana	..	..	0	0	1	6,864
Burkina Faso	1	186	0	0	3	299
Burundi	..	..	0	0	1	1
Cameroon	3	876	1	526	..	..
Cape Verde	..	..	0	0	..	..
Central African Republic	2	1,640	..	..	..	..
Chad	..	..	0	0	2	1,843
Comoros	..	..	..	..	1	0
Congo, Dem. Rep. of	3	283	5	6,855	2	866
Congo, Rep. of	2	246	..	0	1	439
Côte d'Ivoire	2	1,770	3	1,504	1	19
Djibouti	..	..	..	..	..	..
Equatorial Guinea	..	..	..	..	..	..
Eritrea	..	..	..	..	..	..
Ethiopia	..	..	1	22	..	..
Gabon	1	15	0	0	3	1,080
Gambia, The	..	..	0	0	1	20
Ghana	1	8	0	0	6	178
Guinea	2	261	..	13	12	4,779
Guinea-Bissau	1	110	..	..	1	39
Kenya	5	1,335	2	300	4	91
Lesotho	..	..	..	..	..	..
Liberia	..	..	..	..	..	..
Madagascar	2	293	1	152	2	53
Malawi	1	45	1	9	1	225
Mali	1	2,500	1	400	3	162
Mauritania	..	..	1	1,200	2	1,231
Mauritius	1	4	0	0	1	0
Mozambique	..	..	0	0	..	..
Namibia	..	..	..	..	4	630
Niger	2	25,128	2	7,957	4	715
Nigeria	1	131	0	0	1	58
Rwanda	1	13	..	..	..	..
São Tomé and Principe	..	..	..	..	..	..
Senegal	3	1,094	2	929	4	100
Seychelles	..	..	2	35	..	..
Sierra Leone	..	..	..	..	1	295
Somalia	..	..	..	..	..	..
South Africa	..	3,371	..	..	..	..
Sudan	2	1,251	0	0	..	..
Swaziland	..	..	..	..	..	..
Tanzania	3	5,228	4	6,860	3	4,272
Togo	..	..	0	0	2	194
Uganda	1	247	2	132	1	15
Zambia	..	..	1	7	2	333
Zimbabwe	..	..	2	733	..	..
NORTH AFRICA	..	..	..	..	..	..
Algeria	3	7,312	1	8,000	13	1,866
Egypt, Arab Rep.	2	2,456	0	0	2	106
Libya	..	..	0	0	..	..
Morocco	2	9,754	0	0	4	14
Tunisia	4	74	1	13	1	13
ALL AFRICA						

Source: World Conservation Monitoring Centre (WCMC), United Nations Educational, Scientific, and Cultural Organization (UNESCO), and Ramsar Convention Bureau, Switzerland.

Notes: 0 = zero or less than half the unit of measure. .. = not available or indeterminate.

Technical notes

Tables

These notes are based on technical notes for each table as presented in *World Resources 2002–2004*. They have been edited and shortened for this volume. Readers are urged to consult the original source for details.

Table 14-1. Forest resources, 1990–2000. *Total forest* comprises all forest area for temperate countries and the sum of natural forest and plantation area categories.

FAO defines a *natural forest* as a forest composed primarily of indigenous (native) tree species. Natural forests include closed forest, where trees cover a high proportion of the ground and where grass does not form a continuous layer on the forest floor (e.g., broadleaved forests, coniferous forests, and bamboo forests), and open forest, which FAO defines as mixed forest/grasslands with at least 10 percent tree cover and a continuous grass layer on the forest floor. Natural forests encompass all stands except plantations and include stands that have been degraded to some degree by agriculture, fire, logging, and other factors.

Plantation refers to a forest stand established artificially by afforestation and reforestation for industrial and nonindustrial usage. Reforestation does not include regeneration of old tree crops (through either natural regeneration or forest management), although some countries may report regeneration as reforestation. Many trees are also planted for nonindustrial uses, such as village wood lots. Reforestation data often exclude this component. The data presented here reflect plantation survival rates as estimated by FAO.

Annual percentage change is shown as a percentage of the exponential growth rate. If negative, these figures reflect net deforestation, which is defined as the clearing of forest lands for all forms of agricultural uses (shifting cultivation, permanent agriculture, and ranching) and for other land uses such as settlements, other infrastructure, and mining. In tropical countries, this includes clearing that reduces tree crown cover to less than 10 percent. Deforestation, as defined here, does not reflect changes within the forest stand or site, such as selective logging (unless the forest cover is permanently reduced to less than 10 percent).

Table 14-2. Forest ecosystems, 1990–99. *Closed forests* exclude some woodlands and wooded savanna.

Original forest as a percentage of land area refers to the estimate of the percentage of land that would have been covered by closed forest about 8,000 years ago, assuming current climatic conditions, before large-scale disturbance by human society began.

Current forests refer to estimated closed forest cover within roughly the past 10 years (this varies by country). Only closed moist forests are given for Africa.

Frontier forests are large, relatively intact forest ecosystems. They represent undisturbed forest areas that are large enough to maintain all of their biodiversity, including viable populations of wide-ranging species associated with each forest type.

Percentage of frontier forests threatened refers to frontier forests where ongoing or planned human activities such as logging, mining, and other large-scale disturbances will eventually degrade the ecosystem through species decline or extinction, drastic changes in the forest's age structure, and so forth., and would result, if continued, in the violation of one of the above-mentioned criteria.

Tropical forests include all forests located between the Tropics of Cancer and Capricorn. All other forests are put into the *nontropical* category.

Percentage protected includes forest areas that fall within the protected areas in the world that are listed as the International Union for Conservation of Nature and Natural Resources' (IUCN's) management categories I-V.

Table 14-3. Wood production and trade, 1999–2001.

Total roundwood production refers to all wood in the rough, whether destined for industrial or fuelwood uses.

Industrial roundwood comprises all roundwood products other than fuelwood and charcoal.

Processed wood production includes sawn wood and panels.

Paper and paperboard includes newsprint, printing and writing paper, and other paper and paperboard.

Trade in forest products is the balance of imports minus exports.

Table 14-4. Freshwater resources and withdrawals, 1970–2002.

Annual internal renewable water resources refer to the average annual flow of rivers and groundwater generated from endogenous precipitation. Caution should be used when comparing different countries because these estimates are based on differing sources and dates. These annual averages also disguise large seasonal, inter-annual, and long-term variations. When data for annual river flows from and to other countries are not shown, the internal renewable water resources figure may include these flows. Per capita annual internal renewable water resource data were calculated using 2001 population estimates.

Annual withdrawals as a percentage of water resources refer to total water withdrawals, not counting evaporative losses from storage basins, as a percentage of internal renewable water resources and river flows from other countries. Water withdrawals also include water from desalination plants in countries where that source is a significant part of all water withdrawals.

Per capita annual withdrawals were calculated using national population data for the year of data shown for withdrawals.

Sectoral withdrawals are classified as domestic (drinking water, homes, commercial establishments, public services [for example, hospitals], and municipal use or provision); industry (including water withdrawn to cool thermoelectric plants); and agriculture (irrigation and livestock).

Table 14-5. Marine and freshwater catches, aquaculture, balance of trade, and fish consumption.

Marine and freshwater catches data refer to marine and freshwater fish, killed, caught, trapped, collected, bred, or cultivated for commercial, industrial, and subsistence use (catches from recreational activities are included where available). Crustaceans and mollusks are included. Statistics for mariculture, aquaculture, and other kinds of fish farming are included in the country totals. Figures are the national totals averaged over a three-year period; they include fish caught by a country's fleet anywhere in the world. Catches of freshwater species caught in low-salinity seas are included in the statistics of the appropriate marine area. Marine catch includes catches of diadromous (migratory between saltwater and freshwater) species.

Data are represented as nominal catches, which are the landings converted to a live-weight basis, that is, the weight when caught.

Landings for some countries are identical to catches.

Aquaculture is defined by FAO as "the farming of aquatic organisms, including fish, mollusks, crustaceans, and aquatic plants. Farming implies some form of intervention in the rearing process to enhance production, such as regular stocking, feeding, and protection from predators, etc. [It] also implies ownership of the stock being cultivated. . . ." Aquatic organisms that are exploitable by the public as a common property resource are included in the harvest of fisheries.

Marine fish include a variety of species groups such as mullets, sea basses, groupers, snappers, tunas, and mackerels. *Diadromous fish* include sturgeons, river eels, salmons, and trouts. *Freshwater fish* include carps, perches, catfish, and tilapias, among others. Mollusks include freshwater mollusks, oysters, mussels, scallops, clams, abalones, and cephalopods. *Crustaceans* include, among others, freshwater crustaceans, crabs, lobsters, shrimps, and prawns. Data on whales and other marine mammals are excluded from this table.

Balance of trade is defined as exports minus imports. Figures are the national totals averaged over a three-year period in millions of U.S. dollars. Imports are usually on a cost, insurance, and freight basis (c.i.f.) (i.e., insurance and freight costs added in). Exports are generally on a free-on-board basis (f.o.b.) —i.e., not including insurance or freight costs. A surplus of imports over exports is shown in parentheses. Trade in *fish* includes fish that is fresh, frozen, chilled, salted, or smoked, as well as fish products and preparations. Trade in *mollusks and crustaceans* includes mollusks and crustaceans that are fresh, chilled, smoked, or derived products. Trade in *fish meal* includes meals, solubles, and so on.

Per capita annual food supply from fish and seafood is the quantity of both freshwater and marine fish, seafood, and derived products available for human consumption. Data on aquatic plants and whale meat are excluded from the totals. The amount of fish and seafood actually consumed may be lower than the figures provided, depending on how much is lost during storage, preparation, and cooking, and on how much is discarded. Data are presented in kilograms per capita. Years shown are three-year averages.

Table 14-6. Energy production by source. All energy data are shown in a common unit of 1,000 metric tons of oil equivalent (toe) to facilitate comparisons of energy sourcing, consumption, substitution, and conservation. A toe is defined as 41.868 gigajoules.

Energy production from all sources is the amount of energy from all sources produced by each country in the year specified. In addition to solid, liquid, and gaseous fuels and nuclear electricity, the total also includes hydropower, geothermal, solar, wind, tidal, wave, combustible renewables and waste, and indigenous heat production from heat pumps. *Per capita* shows the amount produced per person for that country.

Energy production from *solid fuels* is the energy produced from all types of primary coal (i.e., hard coal or lignite). Peat is also included in the category.

Energy production from *liquid fuels* is energy produced from liquid fuels such as crude oil or natural gas liquids.

Energy production from *gaseous fuels* is the amount of energy produced from natural gas.

Energy production from *nuclear fuels* shows the primary heat equivalent of the electricity produced by nuclear power plants. Heat-to-electricity conversion efficiency is assumed to be 33 percent.

Total electricity generated is the toe equivalent of the electrical energy produced by thermal, nuclear, geothermal, hydropower (excluding pumped storage production), and other power plants. Electricity generated is not a primary energy source and should not be mistakenly added to the energy production from primary sources presented in this table. These data were converted from gigawatt-hours to toe using a conversion rate of 1Gwh = 86 toe.

Table 14-7. Energy consumption by economic sector. The *industry* sector includes energy consumption by the iron and steel industry, chemical industry, nonferrous metals basic industries, nonmetallic mineral products (glass, ceramic, cement, etc.), transport equipment, machinery, mining and quarrying, food and tobacco, paper, pulp and print, wood and wood products, construction, textile and leather, and any nonspecified industry.

Iron and steel consumption is the energy consumed by the iron and steel industry as a percentage of the total energy consumed by the country.

The *transportation* sector includes all fuel for air, road, and water transport except fuel used for international marine bunkers and for ocean, coastal, and inland fishing. *Air* transportation includes both international and domestic civil aviation. *Road* transportation includes all human and cargo transport along national road networks.

Agriculture refers to all agricultural and forestry activity, including ocean, coastal, and inland fishing.

Commercial and public services refer to service sectors such as stores, repair shops, and restaurants.

The *residential* sector includes household energy use.

The IEA reports that it can be difficult to distinguish accurately between the agriculture, commercial, and public services sectors and that a figure for "total energy use" is more accurate than totals for the individual sectors.

Table 14-8. CO$_2$ emissions from industrial processes, 1999. This table includes data on industrial additions to the carbon dioxide flux from solid fuels, liquid fuels, gas fuels, gas flaring, and cement manufacturing. The International Energy Agency (IEA) annually calculates emissions of carbon dioxide (CO$_2$) from the burning of fossil fuels for most of the countries of the world. The IEA presents data in four categories.

Total carbon dioxide emissions. Include emissions from combustion of all fossil fuels (whether solid, liquid, or gaseous) used by a country. Values are reported in thousand metric tons of CO$_2$.

Emissions from solid fuels. This shows the mass of CO$_2$ released in the combustion of all coal and coal-based products. Both primary (hard coal and lignite) and derived fuels (patent fuel, coke oven coke, gas coke, BKB, coke oven gas, gas works gas, and blast furnace gas) are included. Peat is also included in this category.

Liquid fuels. This represents emissions from combustion of crude oil, natural gas liquids, motor gasoline, gas/diesel oil, aviation gasoline, jet fuels, kerosene, refinery feedstocks, additives, refinery gas, ethane, LPG, heavy fuel oil, naphtha, white spirit, lubricants, bitumen, paraffin waxes, petroleum coke and other petroleum products.

Gaseous fuels. This shows emissions from combustion of natural gases (excluding natural gas liquids), occurring in underground deposits, consisting mainly of methane.

Per capita CO$_2$ emissions. These are the amount of CO$_2$ emitted, on average, from all sources for each person living in the specified country. These estimates do not include bunker fuels used for international transportation due to the difficulty of apportioning these fuels among the countries benefiting from that transport. Emissions are calculated by WRI using data from the IEA and population data from the Population Division of the Department of Economic and Social Affairs of the United Nations Secretariat.

Values for CO$_2$ emissions by source are calculated by the IEA using the methods and emission factors in the *Revised 1996 IPC Guidelines for National Greenhouse Gas Inventories* (available at http://www.ipc-nggip.iges.or.jp/public/gl/invs1.htm). The figures provided here are based on the reference approach, which calculates emissions from the carbon content of fuels supplied to a country's economy.

The reference approach captures refining, flaring, and other "fugitive emissions" that do not result directly from end-use fossil fuel combustion. Apparent consumption of fuel is calculated as production minus exports plus imports. Net stock changes are either added or subtracted. International marine and aviation bunkers (fuel used for international transport) are subtracted from national totals as well, as these figures are accounted for separately. The production of secondary fuels is not accounted for because the carbon contained in those fuels is already included in the primary fuel. However, imports and exports of secondary fuels are included in calculations. Stored carbon from fuels used for non-energy purposes is subtracted from the total carbon emissions. Emissions from biomass fuels are not included in these because the IPCC assumes that such emissions are equal sequestration during regrowth.

The Carbon Dioxide Information Analysis Center (CDIAC) calculates emissions of CO$_2$ from the burning of fossil fuels and the manufacture of cement in most of the countries of the world. During cement manufacture, cement in calcined to produce calcium oxide. In the process, 0.498 metric tons of CO$_2$ are released for each metric ton of cement produced.

Combustion of different fossil fuels releases CO$_2$ at different rates for the same levels of energy production. Burning oil released 1.5 times the amount of CO$_2$ released from burning natural gas; burning coal released about twice as much CO$_2$ as from burning natural gas.

Table 14-9. Globally threatened species: mammals, birds, and higher plants, 1992–2002. The total number of known species may include introductions in some instances. Data on mammals exclude cetaceans (whales and porpoises), except where otherwise indicated. Threatened bird species are listed for countries included within their breeding or wintering ranges. Higher plants refer to numbers of native vascular plant species, as totals are of full species only, rather than of species and subspecies. The number of endemic species refers to those species known to be found only within the countries listed. Figures are not necessarily comparable among countries because taxonomic concepts and the extent of knowledge vary (for the latter reason, country totals of species and endemics may be underestimates). In general, numbers of mammals and birds are fairly well known, while plants have not been as well inventoried.

The World Conservation Union classifies threatened and endangered species in six categories.

Endangered. "Taxa in danger of extinction and whose survival is unlikely if the causal factors continue operating."

Vulnerable. "Taxa believed likely to move into the endangered category in the near future if the causal factors continue operating."

Rare. "Taxa with world populations that are not at present endangered or vulnerable, but are at risk."

Indeterminate. "Taxa known to be endangered, vulnerable, or rare but where there is not enough information to say which of the three categories is appropriate."

Out of danger. "Taxa formerly included in one of the above categories, but which are now considered relatively secure because effective conservation measures have been taken or the previous threat to their survival has been removed."

Insufficiently known. "Taxa that are suspected but not definitely known to belong to any of the above categories."

The number of threatened species listed for all countries includes full species that are endangered, vulnerable, rare, indeterminate, and insufficiently known, but excludes introduced species or those known to be extinct.

Number of species per 10,000 square kilometers provides a relative estimate for comparing numbers of species among countries of differing size. Because the relationship between area and species number is nonlinear (that is, as the area sampled increases, the number of new species located decreases), a species-area curve has been used to standardize these species numbers.

Table 14-10. Globally threatened species: reptiles, amphibians, and fish, late 1990s. Threatened marine turtles and marine fish are excluded from country totals. Endangered fish species numbers do not include approximately 250 haplochromine and 2 tilapiine species of Lake Victoria cichlids, since the ranges of these species are undetermined.

The number of species per 10,000 square kilometers provides a relative estimate for comparing numbers of species among countries of differing size.

Table 14-11. National protection of natural areas, 2003. All protected areas combine natural areas in five World Conservation Union (formerly the International Union for Conservation of Nature and Natural Resources, [IUCN]), management categories (areas at least 1,000 hectares).

Totally protected areas are maintained in a natural state and are closed to extractive uses. They encompass the following three management categories: *category I*, scientific reserves and strict nature reserves; *category II*, national parks and provincial parks; and *category III*, natural monuments and natural landmarks.

Partially protected areas are areas that may be managed for specific uses, such as recreation or tourism, or areas that provide optimum conditions for certain species or communities of wildlife. Some extractive use within these areas is allowed. They encompass two management categories: *category IV*, managed nature reserves wildlife sanctuaries; and *category V*, protected landscapes and seascapes.

Protected areas between at least 100,000 hectares and 1 million hectares in size refer to all IUCN category I–V protected areas that fall within these two classifications.

IUCN has an additional management category, category VI, which includes areas "managed mainly for the sustainable use of natural ecosystems." These areas contain predominantly unmodified natural systems, managed to ensure long-term protection and maintenance of biological diversity, while also providing a sustainable flow of natural products and services to meet community needs.

Marine protected areas include protected areas in any of the IUCN categories (I–VI) that are marine or have a marine component. IUCN defines a "marine protected area" as "any area of intertidal or subtidal terrain, together with its overlying water and associated flora and fauna, historical and cultural features, which has been reserved by law or other effective means to protect part or all of the enclosed environment." Marine protected areas (MPAs) include areas that are fully marine as well as areas that have only a small area of intertidal land. Many of these MPAs have large terrestrial areas. The extent of the marine portion of most protected areas is rarely documented. The degree of protection varies from one country to another, and it may bear little relationship to the legal status of any site. The categories of *marine* and *littoral* are not exclusive. One protected area can be littoral and marine, therefore adding numbers under these two different categories may produce a higher number than the total for MPAs. Littoral is defined as any site that is known to incorporate at least some intertidal area. Such sites can also include marine and/or terrestrial elements. All sites with mangrove and saltmarsh communities are recorded as littoral. Marine is defined as any site that is known to incorporate at least some subtidal area permanently submerged under the ocean. Such sites can also include littoral and terrestrial elements. All sites with coral reefs and seagrasses are recorded as marine.

The values in this table do not include locally or provincially protected sites, or privately owned areas.

Table 14-12. International protected areas, 2002. Internationally protected areas usually include sites that are listed under national protection systems.

Biosphere reserves are representative of terrestrial and coastal environments that have been internationally recognized under the Man and the Biosphere Programme of UNESCO.

World heritage sites represent areas of "outstanding universal value" for their natural features, their cultural value, or for both natural and cultural values. The table includes only natural and mixed natural and cultural sites.

Any party to the Convention on Wetlands of International Importance, especially as it pertains to waterfowl habitat, agrees to respect the site's integrity and to establish wetland reserves can designate wetlands of international importance.

Marine and coastal protected areas refer to all protected areas greater than 1,000 hectares with littoral, coral, island, marine, or estuarine components. The area given is the whole protected area.

15

The Heavily Indebted Poor Countries (HIPC) Initiative

The Heavily Indebted Poor Countries (HIPC) debt initiative was proposed by the World Bank and IMF, and agreed to by governments around the world in the fall of 1996. It was the first comprehensive approach to reduce the external debt of the world's poorest, most heavily indebted countries, and represented an important step forward in placing debt relief within an overall framework of poverty reduction. While the initiative yielded significant early progress, multilateral organizations, bilateral creditors, HIPC governments, and civil society have been engaged in an intensive dialogue about the strengths and weaknesses of the program. A major review in 1999 has resulted in a significant enhancement of the original framework, and has produced a HIPC Initiative which is "deeper, broader, and faster."

Which countries qualify?
- The poorest countries, those that are only eligible for highly concessional assistance from the International Development Association (IDA)—the part of the World Bank that lends on highly concessional terms—and from the IMF's Poverty Reduction and Growth Facility (previously the Enhanced Structural Adjustment Facility).

- Those that also face an unsustainable debt situation even after the full application of traditional debt relief mechanisms (such as application of Naples terms under the Paris Club Agreement).

How the HIPC Initiative works
Under the enhanced framework, countries for which existing mechanisms would not achieve debt sustainability at the decision point will now receive assistance under the HIPC Initiative starting at the decision point.

In contrast to the original framework, where debt reduction was calculated on projections of debt stock at the completion point, relief under the new framework will be committed based on actual data at the decision point. This modification not only adds greater certainty to the calculations, but will in most cases increase the amount of relief actually provided, since most countries will reduce their net present value (NPV) debt-to-export and debt-to-revenue ratios between the decision and completion points.

In short, under the enhanced framework, the benefits of export and central government revenue will accrue fully to the country, allowing for greater investment in poverty reduction strategies.

362

Creditor participation

All creditors participate in providing exceptional assistance beyond current mechanisms as required to reach debt sustainability. Creditors share the costs of HIPC assistance based on broad and equitable burden sharing, and provide relief that is proportional to their share of the debt after the full application of traditional forms of debt relief; these forms include Naples terms from Paris Club creditors, which provide a 67 percent NPV reduction on eligible debt.

HIPC Eligible Countries (42 countries)

Africa (34 countries)
Angola
Benin
Burkina Faso
Burundi
Cameroon
Central African Republic
Chad
Comoros
Congo, Republic of
Congo, Democratic Republic
Côte d'Ivoire
Ethiopia
The Gambia
Ghana
Guinea
Guinea-Bissau
Kenya

Liberia
Madagascar
Malawi
Mali
Mauritania
Mozambique
Niger
Rwanda
São Tomé and Príncipe
Senegal
Sierra Leone
Somalia
Sudan
Tanzania
Togo
Uganda
Zambia

Latin America
Bolivia
Guyana
Honduras
Nicaragua

Asia (3 countries)
Lao, People's Dem. Rep.
Myanmar
Vietnam

Middle East
Yemen, Republic of

15-1. HIPC Initiative: flow chart

First Stage
Eligibility Requirements

- Paris Club provides flow rescheduling as per current Naples terms, i.e. rescheduling of debt service on eligible debt falling due during the three-year consolidation period (up to 67 percent reduction on eligible maturities on a net present value basis).

- Other bilateral and commercial creditors provide at least comparable treatment.

- Multilateral institutions continue to provide concessional financing in the framework of World Bank and IDMF-supported adjustment program.

- Country establishes three-year track record of good performance and develops together with civil society a Poverty Reduction Strategy Paper (PRSP); in early cases, an interim PRSP may be sufficient to reach the decision point.

Decision Point

EITHER EXIT   **OR**   **QUALIFICATION FOR ASSISTANCE**

Paris Club stock-of-debt operation under Naples terms (67% net present value reduction of eligible debt) and comparable treatment by other bilateral and commercial creditors
is adequate
for the country to reach sustainability by the decision point.

Sustainability targets: 150 percent of NPV of debt-to exports ratio; or 250 percent NPV of debt-to revenue ratio for country reaching qualifying threshold for the fiscal openness window (30 percent exports-to-GDP ratio and 15 percent revenue-to-GDP ratio).

====> Exit
(Country is not eligible for HIPC assistance.)

Hypothetical Paris Club stock-of-debt operation under Naples terms and comparable treatment by other bilateral and commercial creditors
is not sufficient
for the country to reach sustainability by the decision point. Countries request additional support under the HIPC Initiative. IMF and World Bank determine eligibility.

====> Decision Point

The International community commits sufficient assistance to reach sustainability targets. This relief can be delivered at the decision point and the remainder at the completion point when the country has implemented pre-agreed key structural and social reforms (triggers) provided the macroeconomic program remains on track.

Second Stage
The Interim Period

- Paris Club creditors provide interim relief (Cologne terms flows, i.e., 90% NPV of debt reduction on eligible debt) and other bilateral and commercial creditors provide at least comparable treatment.

- Some multilateral institutions, including World Bank and IMF, provide interim assistance (e.g., debt service reduction).

- Donors support interim assistance.

- Country establishes a second track record by implementing the Bank/IMF-supported programs, including the one-year implementation of a full PRSP (triggers). Length of this stage is determined by the speed by which country implements the triggers.

- Country also take steps to strengthen debt management.

"Floating" Completion Point

- Timing of completion point is tied to the implementation of policies determined at the decision point.

- All creditors provide the assistance determined at the decision point; interim debt relief provided between decision and completion points counts toward this assistance. Assistance is provided without further policy conditionality.

15-2. Grouping of African HIPC countries: status as of July 2003

African Heavily Indebted Poor Countries (32) [1]			
Benin	Congo, Rep. of *	Madagascar	Senegal
Burkina Faso	Côte d'Ivoire*	Malawi	Sierra Leone*
Burundi*	Ethiopia	Mali	Somalia*
Cameroon	The Gambia	Mauritania	Sudan*
Central African Republic*	Ghana	Mozambique	Tanzania
Chad	Guinea	Niger	Togo
Comoros*	Guinea-Bissau*	Rwanda*	Uganda
Congo, Dem. Rep. of*	Liberia*	Sao Tome and Principe	Zambia

COUNTRIES THAT HAVE REACHED COMPLETION POINT (7)	HIPC RELIEF APPROVED AT DECISION POINT (16)		COUNTRIES TO BE CONSIDERED (9)	
Benin	Cameroon	Madagascar	Burundi	Togo
Burkina Faso	Chad	Malawi	Central African Republic	
Mali	Congo, Dem. Rep. of	Niger	Comoros	
Mauritania	Ethiopia	Rwanda	Congo, Rep. of	
Mozambique	The Gambia	Sao Tome and Principe	Cote d'Ivoire	
Tanzania	Ghana	Senegal	Liberia	
Uganda	Guinea	Sierra Leone	Somalia	
	Guinea-Bissau	Zambia	Sudan	

Sources: HIPC documents; and IMF and World Bank staff estimates.

*Conflict-affected countries

1. Comoros has been added to the group as a preliminary assessment of its debt situation showed a potential need for HIPC debt.

15-3. External debt service for individual African HIPCs that reached decision points, by country, 1998-2005

	(In millions of U.S. dollars, unless otherwise indicated)							
	1998	*1999*	*2000*	*2001*	*2002*	*2003*	*2004*	*2005*
Benin								
Debt service paid	64	66	55	36				
Debt service due after enhanced HIPC Initiative relief [1]					32	30	30	34
Debt service/exports (in percent)	16	17	16	10	9	7	7	7
Debt service/government revenue (in percent)	17	17	15	9	7	6	6	6
Debt service/GDP (in percent)	3	3	2	2	1	1	1	1
Burkina Faso								
Debt service paid	57	61	48	33	42			
Debt service due after enhanced HIPC Initiative relief [1]						26	27	27
Debt service/exports (in percent)	18	24	23	15	18	9	8	8
Debt service/government revenue (in percent)	16	16	16	11	11	5	5	4
Debt service/GDP (in percent)	2	2	2	1	1	1	1	1
Cameroon [2,3]								
Debt service paid	401	401	437	261	233			
Debt service due after enhanced HIPC Initiative relief [1,5]						289	295	289
Debt service/exports (in percent)	18	15	16	10	9	10	10	10
Debt service/government revenue (in percent)	28	24	26	15	12	12	12	11
Debt service/GDP (in percent)	4	4	5	3	2	2	2	2
Chad [3]								
Debt service paid	26	30	32	18	29			
Debt service due after enhanced HIPC Initiative relief [1]						40	44	47
Debt service/exports (in percent)	8	12	14	8	13	10	3	2
Debt service/government revenue (in percent)	20	24	29	14	18	18	11	10
Debt service/GDP (in percent)	2	2	2	1	1	2	1	1
Congo, Dem. Rep. of [4]								
Debt service paid	1	3	-	-	34			
Debt service due after enhanced HIPC Initiative relief [1]						150	220	256
Debt service/exports (in percent)	0	0	-	-	3	16	23	22
Debt service/government revenue (in percent)	0	1	-	-	7	25	29	25
Debt service/GDP (in percent)	0	0	-	-	1	3	4	4
Ethiopia [3,5]								
Debt service paid	101	127	112	197	149			
Debt service due after enhanced HIPC Initiative relief [1]						88	89	88
Debt service/exports (in percent)	10	14	11	21	15	9	9	8
Debt service/government revenue (in percent)	9	11	10	16	12	6	6	5
Debt service/GDP (in percent)	2	2	2	3	2	1	1	1
Gambia, The [3]								
Debt service paid	26	20	13	16	16			
Debt service due after enhanced HIPC Initiative relief [1]						15	10	11
Debt service/exports (in percent)	12	15	12	14	12	11	7	8
Debt service/government revenue (in percent)	12	25	16	26	27	26	20	21
Debt service/GDP (in percent)	6	5	3	4	4	5	4	4
Ghana [3,6]								
Debt service paid	560	521	533	243	267			
Debt service due after enhanced HIPC Initiative relief [1]						163	104	112
Debt service/exports (in percent)	22	21	22	10	10	6	3	3
Debt service/government revenue (in percent)	41	53	78	26	39	17	10	8
Debt service/GDP (in percent)	7	7	11	5	4	2	1	1
Guinea [3]								
Debt service paid	128	132	144	75	85			
Debt service due after enhanced HIPC Initiative relief [1]						89	79	68
Debt service/exports (in percent)	15	18	20	9	11	10	9	7
Debt service/government revenue (in percent)	34	35	46	22	22	23	20	15
Debt service/GDP (in percent)	4	4	5	2	3	3	2	2
Guinea-Bissau [3]								
Debt service paid	7	6	13	0	5			
Debt service due after enhanced HIPC Initiative relief [1]						5	6	4
Debt service/exports (in percent)	23	11	19	1	8	8	8	4
Debt service/government revenue (in percent)	63	15	32	1	12	12	14	8
Debt service/GDP (in percent)	3	3	6	0	2	2	2	1
Madagascar [3,6]								
Debt service paid	166	106	65	45	50			
Debt service due after enhanced HIPC Initiative relief [1]						54	73	73
Debt service/exports (in percent)	21	12	5	3	7	5	6	6
Debt service/government revenue (in percent)	42	25	14	10	15	10	13	11
Debt service/GDP (in percent)	4	3	2	1	1	1	1	1
Malawi [3,7]								
Debt service paid	90	65	103	74	47			
Debt service due after enhanced HIPC Initiative relief [1]						67	39	51
Debt service/exports (in percent)	16	13	23	15	10	14	8	9
Debt service/government revenue (in percent)	22	21	35	24	14	19	10	12
Debt service/GDP (in percent)	5	4	6	4	2	4	2	2

Sources: HIPC country document; and World Bank and IMF staff estimates.

Note: The footnotes for this table are in the technical notes at the end of this chapter.

(Table continues on the following page.)

15-3. External debt service for individual African HIPCs that reached decision points, by country, 1998-2005 (continued)

	(In millions of U.S. dollars, unless otherwise indicated)							
	1998	*1999*	*2000*	*2001*	*2002*	*2003*	*2004*	*2005*
Mali								
Debt service paid	74	84	79	55	67			
Debt service due after enhanced HIPC Initiative relief [1]						59	63	66
Debt service/exports (in percent)	11	12	12	6	6	5	5	5
Debt service/government revenue (in percent)	17	20	21	13	12	8	8	8
Debt service/GDP (in percent)	3	3	3	2	2	2	2	1
Mauritania [7]								
Debt service paid	88	81	87	74	74			
Debt service due after enhanced HIPC Initiative relief [1]						54	60	61
Debt service/exports (in percent)	22	22	23	19	19	14	14	13
Debt service/government revenue (in percent)	35	30	36	37	20	17	18	17
Debt service/GDP (in percent)	10	8	9	8	7	5	5	5
Mozambique								
Debt service paid	104	60	18	27	42			
Debt service due after enhanced HIPC Initiative relief [1]						47	51	57
Debt service/exports (in percent)	41	9	2	3	4	4	3	3
Debt service/government revenue (in percent)	23	12	4	7	8	8	8	7
Debt service/GDP (in percent)	3	1	0	1	1	1	1	1
Niger [3]								
Debt service paid	17	19	22	34	53			
Debt service due after enhanced HIPC Initiative relief [1]						26	29	29
Debt service/exports (in percent)	5	6	8	12	17	7	8	8
Debt service/government revenue (in percent)	9	11	14	19	21	9	10	9
Debt service/GDP (in percent)	1	1	1	2	2	1	1	1
Rwanda [3, 5]								
Debt service paid	18	37	37	12	13			
Debt service due after enhanced HIPC Initiative relief [1]						13	16	15
Debt service/exports (in percent)	30	39	25	7	10	9	10	9
Debt service/government revenue (in percent)	16	23	23	6	6	6	6	6
Debt service/GDP (in percent)	2	2	2	1	1	1	1	1
São Tomé and Príncipe [3]								
Debt service paid	7	2	4	2	2			
Debt service due after enhanced HIPC Initiative relief [1]						3	2	1
Debt service/exports (in percent)	55	12	26	11	10	14	8	4
Debt service/government revenue (in percent)	84	21	42	18	16	23	11	5
Debt service/GDP (in percent)	16	4	8	4	4	5	3	1
Senegal								
Debt service paid	207	178	165	138	165			
Debt service due after enhanced HIPC Initiative relief [1]						146	141	139
Debt service/exports (in percent)	15	12	13	10	11	9	8	7
Debt service/government revenue (in percent)	26	22	21	17	16	13	12	11
Debt service/GDP (in percent)	4	4	4	3	3	2	2	2
Sierra Leone [3]								
Debt service paid	9	37	32	95	21			
Debt service due after enhanced HIPC Initiative relief [1]						16	29	24
Debt service/exports (in percent)	9	40	29	74	15	10	15	10
Debt service/government revenue (in percent)	18	77	44	89	18	13	28	14
Debt service/GDP (in percent)	1	5	5	12	3	3	4	2
Tanzania [5, 8]								
Debt service paid	224	193	154	92	109			
Debt service due after enhanced HIPC Initiative relief [1]						100	129	148
Debt service/exports (in percent)	21	16	12	6	7	6	7	7
Debt service/government revenue (in percent)	29	20	16	9	10	8	9	10
Debt service/GDP (in percent)	3	2	2	1	1	1	1	1
Uganda [5]								
Debt service paid	110	98	91	72	60			
Debt service due after enhanced HIPC Initiative relief [1]						100	129	148
Debt service/exports (in percent)	15	12	14	11	9	12	15	16
Debt service/government revenue (in percent)	16	13	14	12	8	13	16	17
Debt service/GDP (in percent)	2	2	2	1	1	2	2	2
Zambia [3, 9]								
Debt service paid	147	126	139	142	123			
Debt service due after enhanced HIPC Initiative relief [1]						187	223	210
Debt service/exports (in percent)	16	15	16	13	11	14	16	13
Debt service/government revenue (in percent)	24	23	30	22	20	27	31	28
Debt service/GDP (in percent)	5	4	4	4	3	5	5	5

Sources: HIPC country document; and World Bank and IMF staff estimates.

Note: The footnotes for this table are in the technical notes at the end of this chapter.

15-4. Committed debt relief and outlook for African HIPCs, status as of July 2003

(In millions of U.S. dollars) [1]

	Reduction in NPV terms			Nominal debt service relief			
	Original HIPC Initiative	Enhanced HIPC Initiative	Total	Original HIPC Initiative	Enhanced HIPC Initiative	Total	Date of approval
AFRICAN COUNTRIES THAT HAVE REACHED THEIR COMPLETION POINTS (7)							
TOTAL	**2,413**	**4,616**	**7,030**	**4,970**	**7,665**	**12,635**	
Benin	0	265	265	0	460	460	Mar-03
Burkina Faso [2]	229	324	553	400	530	930	Apr-02
Mali	121	417	539	220	675	895	Mar-03
Mauritania	0	622	622	0	1,100	1,100	Jun-02
Mozambique	1,716	306	2,022	3,700	600	4,300	Sep-01
Tanzania	0	2,026	2,026	0	3,000	3,000	Nov-01
Uganda	347	656	1,003	650	1,300	1,950	May-00
AFRICAN COUNTRIES THAT HAVE REACHED THEIR DECISION POINTS (16)							
TOTAL	**-**	**18,344**	**18,344**	**-**	**30,009**	**30,009**	
Cameroon	..	1,260	1,260	..	2,000	2,000	Oct-00
Chad	..	170	170	..	260	260	May-01
Congo, Dem. Rep. of	..	6,311	6,311	..	10,389	10,389	Jul-03
Ethiopia	..	1,275	1,275	..	1,930	1,930	Nov-01
Gambia, The	..	67	67	..	90	90	Dec-00
Ghana	0	2,186	2,186	0	3,700	3,700	Feb-02
Guinea	..	545	545	..	800	800	Dec-00
Guinea-Bissau	..	416	416	..	790	790	Dec-00
Madagascar	..	814	814	..	1,500	1,500	Dec-00
Malawi	..	643	643	..	1,000	1,000	Dec-00
Niger	..	521	521	..	900	900	Dec-00
Rwanda	..	452	452	..	800	800	Dec-00
São Tomé and Principe	..	97	97	..	200	200	Dec-00
Senegal	..	488	488	..	850	850	Jun-00
Sierra Leone	0	600	600	0	950	950	Mar-02
Zambia	..	2,499	2,499	..	3,850	3,850	Dec-00
AFRICAN COUNTRIES STILL TO BE CONSIDERED (9)							
Côte d'Ivoire [3]	345	..	345	800	..	800	
Burundi	..	..	..	..	..	..	
Central African Republic	..	..	..	..	..	..	
Comoros	..	..	..	..	..	..	
Congo, Rep. of	..	..	..	..	..	..	
Liberia	..	..	..	..	..	..	
Somalia	..	..	..	..	..	..	
Sudan	..	..	..	..	..	..	
Togo	..	..	..	..	..	..	
Memorandum item:							
Debt relief committed	**2,758**	**22,960**	**25,718**	**5,770**	**37,674**	**43,444**	

Sources: HIPC documents; and IMF and World Bank staff estimates.

1. Commited debt relief under the assumption of full participation of the creditors.

2. The assistance under the enhanced HIPC Initiative includes the topping up with the NPV calculated in the year of the completion point.

3. Preliminary document issued.

15-5. Poverty-reducing expenditure for African HIPCs that reached decision points[1]

(In millions of U.S. dollars)

	1999	2000	2001	2002	2003	2004	2005
		Actual		*Estimate*		*Projections*	
Benin							
Poverty-reducing expenditure	115	110	161	162	180	197	214
Poverty-reducing expenditure/government revenue (in percent)	30	29	42	35	34	34	34
Poverty-reducing expenditure/GDP (in percent)	5	5	7	6	6	6	6
Burkina Faso							
Poverty-reducing expenditure [2]	114	99	110	157	258	273	273
Poverty-reducing expenditure/government revenue (in percent)	30	32	36	42	53	49	43
Poverty-reducing expenditure/GDP (in percent)	4	4	4	5	7	6	6
Cameroon [3]							
Poverty-reducing expenditure	264	287	336	374	595	673	741
Poverty-reducing expenditure/government revenue (in percent)	16	17	19	19	25	27	29
Poverty-reducing expenditure/GDP (in percent)	3	3	4	4	5	5	5
Chad [3]							
Poverty-reducing expenditure [4]	190	149	192	236	320	367	404
Poverty-reducing expenditure/government revenue (in percent)	150	165	153	149	146	94	86
Poverty-reducing expenditure/GDP (in percent)	12	13	12	12	12	9	8
Congo, Dem. Rep. of [3]							
Poverty-reducing expenditure [5]	..	0	0	26	38	101	171
Poverty-reducing expenditure/government revenue (in percent)	..	0	0	6	6	13	16
Poverty-reducing expenditure/GDP (in percent)	..	0	0	0	1	2	3
Ethiopia [3]							
Poverty-reducing expenditure [6]	710	534	765	884	1,158	1,288	1,389
Poverty-reducing expenditure/government revenue (in percent)	61	44	64	73	82	87	84
Poverty-reducing expenditure/GDP (in percent)	11	8	12	15	18	18	18
Gambia, The [3]							
Poverty-reducing expenditure [7]	24	21	22	21	18	17	18
Poverty-reducing expenditure/government revenue (in percent)	30	27	36	35	32	34	34
Poverty-reducing expenditure/GDP (in percent)	5	5	6	6	6	6	6
Ghana [3]							
Poverty-reducing expenditure [8]	345	189	280	313	356	414	425
Poverty-reducing expenditure/government revenue (in percent)	35	52	30	30	25	24	25
Poverty-reducing expenditure/GDP (in percent)	4	7	5	5	5	5	5
Guinea [3]							
Poverty-reducing expenditure [9]	85	73	83	102	107	112	118
Poverty-reducing expenditure/government revenue (in percent)	23	22	24	26	28	28	26
Poverty-reducing expenditure/GDP (in percent)	2	2	3	3	3	3	3
Guinea-Bissau [3]							
Poverty-reducing expenditure [10]	..	..	..	6	9	8	10
Poverty-reducing expenditure/government revenue (in percent)	..	..	..	20	20	20	20
Poverty-reducing expenditure/GDP (in percent)	..	..	..	3	3	3	3
Madagascar [3]							
Poverty-reducing expenditure [11]	156	188	230	298	376	416	457
Poverty-reducing expenditure/government revenue (in percent)	37	41	50	91	73	72	70
Poverty-reducing expenditure/GDP (in percent)	4	5	5	7	8	8	8
Malawi [3]							
Poverty-reducing expenditure [12]	208	167	205	226	255	287	316
Poverty-reducing expenditure/government revenue (in percent)	66	56	66	68	72	71	73
Poverty-reducing expenditure/GDP (in percent)	12	10	12	12	14	15	15

(Table continues on the following page.)

Sources: HIPC country documents; and World Bank and IMF staff estimates.

Note: The footnotes for this table are in the technical notes at the end of this chapter.

15-5. Poverty-reducing expenditure for African HIPCs that reached decision points[1]

(In millions of U.S. dollars)

	1999	2000	2001	2002	2003	2004	2005
	Actual			*Estimate*	*Projections*		
Mali							
Poverty-reducing expenditure [13]	103	150	135	184	271	272	293
Poverty-reducing expenditure/government revenue (in percent)	24	39	31	33	38	35	34
Poverty-reducing expenditure/GDP (in percent)	4	6	5	6	7	7	7
Mauritania							
Poverty-reducing expenditure [14]	85	70	79	105	126	140	154
Poverty-reducing expenditure/government revenue (in percent)	35	29	39	28	39	41	43
Poverty-reducing expenditure/GDP (in percent)	9	7	8	11	11	12	12
Mozambique							
Poverty-Reducing Expenditure [15]	543	688	676	675	792	851	893
Poverty-Reducing Expenditure/Government Revenue (in percent)	53	157	167	133	135	126	117
Poverty-Reducing Expenditure/GDP (in percent)	6	19	20	19	19	17	16
Niger [3]							
Poverty-reducing expenditure [16]	104	84	95	119	180	197	211
Poverty-reducing expenditure/government revenue (in percent)	58	54	53	48	65	67	66
Poverty-reducing expenditure/GDP (in percent)	5	5	5	5	7	7	7
Rwanda [3]							
Poverty-reducing expenditure [17]	75	73	91	106	107	120	136
Poverty-reducing expenditure/government revenue (in percent)	40	46	48	54	48	49	52
Poverty-reducing expenditure/GDP (in percent)	4	4	5	6	6	7	7
São Tomé and Príncipe [3]							
Poverty-reducing expenditure	8	3	11	12	16	20	22
Poverty-reducing expenditure/government revenue (in percent)	88	37	100	96	116	104	94
Poverty-reducing expenditure/GDP (in percent)	17	7	22	22	27	29	28
Senegal							
Poverty-reducing expenditure	254	226	293	310	370	400	434
Poverty-reducing expenditure/government revenue (in percent)	31	28	36	31	34	33	33
Poverty-reducing expenditure/GDP (in percent)	5	5	6	6	6	6	6
Sierra Leone [3]							
Poverty-reducing expenditure [18]	..	23	37	57	65	..	..
Poverty-reducing expenditure/government revenue (in percent)	..	32	36	51	51	..	..
Poverty-reducing expenditure/GDP (in percent)	..	4	5	7	7	..	..
Tanzania							
Poverty-reducing expenditure [19]	412	525	581	805	971	1,250	1,314
Poverty-reducing expenditure/government revenue (in percent)	43	54	54	73	81	92	89
Poverty-reducing expenditure/GDP (in percent)	5	6	6	9	10	13	12
Uganda							
Poverty-reducing expenditure [20]	306	401	438	569	593	598	639
Poverty-reducing expenditure/government revenue (in percent)	40	60	71	80	79	76	75
Poverty-reducing expenditure/GDP (in percent)	5	7	8	10	10	10	10
Zambia [3]							
Poverty-reducing expenditure [21]	166	149	392	444	465	500	538
Poverty-reducing expenditure/government revenue (in percent)	30	32	60	72	67	70	70
Poverty-reducing expenditure/GDP (in percent)	5	5	11	12	12	12	12

Sources: HIPC country documents; and World Bank and IMF staff estimates.

Note: The footnotes for this table are in the technical notes at the end of this chapter.

Figure 15-1. Nominal Debt Service Relief for African Decision Point Countries*

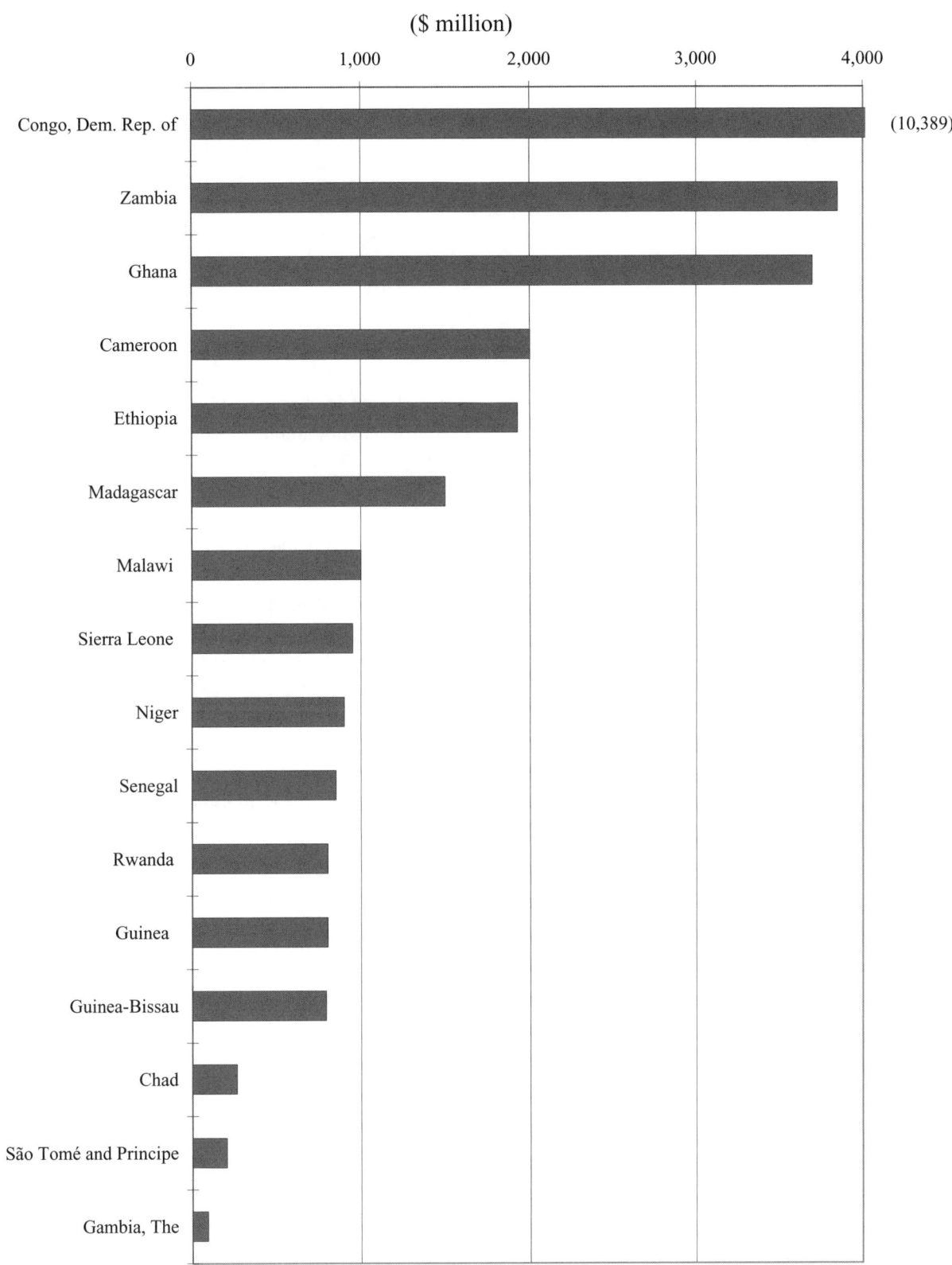

Source: HIPC decision point documents.

* Status as of July 2003.

Technical notes

Tables

Table 15.3 Debt service for individual African HIPCs that reached decision points, by country, 1998–2005

1. Debt service due after the full use of traditional debt relief mechanism and assistance under the enhanced HIPC Initiative. For Mozambique, these figures are also after additional bilateral assistance beyond HIPC.

2. On fiscal year basis (i.e., 2000 column shows FY 1999/2000).

3. The debt service figures for 2000 largely reflect pre-HIPC relief debt service because these countries did not reach their decision point until late in 2000 or later. Thus, the full impact of relief did not take effect until 2001 and thereafter.

4. Debt service is higher than anticipated at the decision point due to higher new borrowing than previously projected.

5. Debt service is lower than anticipated at the decision point due to lower financing needs than previously projected.

6. The relief for Madagascar is indicative and subject to change. The Madagasy authorities and Paris Club creditors would have to revisit the outstanding bilateral debt numbers. Also, minor adjustments must be incorporated in the case of three multilateral creditors. Consequently, the IMF Board approved US$790 million in HIPC relief with the understanding that Madagascar's exact level of HIPC assistance will be determined once such revisions are made.

7. Debt service figures differ from those in the decision point document because of exchange rate changes.

8. Debt service reflects some payments to commercial creditors and payments on moratorium interest not reflected in the completion point document.

Note: Debt service figures for 1998 and 1999 reflect debt relief already provided to Mozambique, and Uganda under the original framework.

The sources for this table are HIPC country documents and World Bank and IMF staff estimates.

Table 15.5 Poverty-reducing expenditure for African HIPCs that reached decision points

In 11 countries, poverty-reducing spending refers exclusively to public expenditure on health and education. In addition, poverty-reducing spending includes new programs to be financed partly with HIPC assistance in Benin, basic sanitary infrastructure in Bolivia, rural development and water supply in Burkina Faso, poverty-reducing affairs in Chad, poverty-related activities such as de-mining and rural development in Guinea-Bissau, funding for the Poverty-Reducing Impact Amelioration Program and Basic Needs Trust Fund in Guyana, Poverty-reducing safety net and rural development programs in Honduras, poverty reduction programs in Mauritania, other spending, including promotion of women in Senegal, water supply in both Tanzania and Uganda, and poverty-reducing safety nets, water and sanitation and disaster relief in Zambia.

1. The coverage of poverty-reducing expenditure varies across countries. If not indicated otherwise, poverty-reducing expenditure data refer to central government spending on health and education.

2. Data refer to central government spending on health care, primary education, promotion of women, "Solidarity" (employment program), social security, rural security, and other programs.

3. The figures for 2000 largely reflect social expenditure before HIPC relief, because these countries reached their decision points in late 2000 or in 2001. Thus, the full impact of HIPC relief for them will not be felt until 2001 and thereafter. Sierra Leone and the Democratic Republic of Congo reached their decision points in 2002 and 2003, respectively.

4. Data refer to domestically financed central government spending on health, education, rural development, infrastructure, and good governance.

5. Data refer to central government spending on health, education, and social protection.

6. Data refer to general government spending on education, health, and agriculture, and to poverty-related road spending.

7. Data refer to central government spending on education, health, and agriculture.

8. Data refer to central government expenditures on health and education. However, data may be incomplete because of missing data on donor support and internally generated funds.

9. Data refer to central government spending on justice, agriculture, fisheries and aquaculture, public works, urbanization, health and social affairs, primary education, and professional and technical education.

10. Previous estimates for Guinea-Bissau were based on budget data. Because of a very low execution rate those numbers tend to overstate the actual level of social spending and have been omitted here. The new estimate for 2002 is based on poverty-reducing expenditure outlays. These expenditures include outlays by the central government on education and health sectors.

11. Data refer to central government spending on health, education, and water.

12. Data refer to spending on education, health, social security and welfare services, and community and poverty-reducing development.

13. Data refer to central government spending on education and health, and funding for social safety nets.

14. Data refer to spending by central and local government on health, education, and poverty-reduction programs.

15. From 2000 onwards, data refer to general government spending on education, health, infrastructure, governance, agriculture, and macroeconomic management.

16. Data coverage has been revised to include only central government spending on health and education.

17. Data refer to recurrent priority expenditures by the central government, which include specified programs in the domains of internal affairs, agriculture, commerce, education, youth and sports, health, transport and communication, energy and water resources, gender, public service, lands and settlement, and support to local government.

18. From 2000 onwards, data refer to general government spending on health, education, social welfare, some economic services, and security-related spending.

19. Data refer to central government spending on education, health, water, agricultural research and extension, lands, roads, and judiciary.

20. Data refer to general government spending on education, health, Poverty Action Fund, and some donor-funded projects.

21. From 2001 onwards, the definition of poverty-reducing spending has been broadened to include housing, resettlement, and urban development; health; information services; employment and welfare; education and training; and general social expenditures.

Sources: HIPC country documents; and IMF staff estimates.

Note: The coverage of poverty-reducing expenditure varies across countries. All Poverty-Reducing data includes spending on health and education.

16

Household Welfare

While macroeconomic data about many African countries are published often, more disaggregated data are not frequently reported in statistical abstracts such as the *African Development Indicators*. This chapter addresses that issue by presenting statistics on poverty and some of its correlates at a sub-national level. These statistics are based upon household surveys rather than ministry-level data. The presentation of indicators is linked to the Millennium Development Goals to help in understanding the statistics. The tables that follow contain data for fourteen countries of Sub-Saharan Africa: Burundi, Burkina Faso, Côte d'Ivoire, Cameroon, Ethiopia, The Gambia, Ghana, Kenya, Madagascar, Mozambique, Malawi, São Tomé and Principe, Uganda, and Zambia.

This chapter is similar to one published in the 2000 *Africa Development Indicators*, but the underlying set of definitions and variables has changed. In addition, the presentation of this new set of indicators has been organized along the Millennium Development Goals. The definitions used in this presentation (see below) reflect the work of an ongoing project in the Africa Region's Operational Quality and Knowledge Services Unit: the Standardized Files and Standardized Indicators. The project, which builds upon earlier work, takes national statistical agencies' raw data files, as stored in the Africa Household Survey Databank, and performs consistency checks prior to

harmonizing the data, using a common dictionary. This process may include the computation of expenditure aggregates when they are not available to the unit. For more information on this project, please see the technical notes at the end of the chapter.

The definitions presented herein may diverge from those used in other publications, whether by the World Bank or a country's national statistical organization. This means that certain statistics may differ from those previously published. An example of this is enrollment rates; if the country bases them upon one definition of the age at which children should attend primary school while this report uses another, it is unlikely that the two statistics will be identical. Neither statistic is wrong; they are just different metrics and cannot be necessarily compared.

Selected definitions
National definitions of households are used, although most definitions do not differ markedly from those set forth by the United Nations. Additional information is available in the technical notes.

Expenditure quintiles are derived by ranking weighted sample individuals according to annual deflated per capita expenditure. When regional deflators are available, they are used, otherwise nominal expenditure is used. Individuals are used as the basis for estimating quintiles. Quintiles are constructed such that the first quintile represents the poorest 20 percent of the population, the second quintile the next poorest 20 percent (less poor), and so on; the fifth quintile represents the richest 20 percent of the population. The definition of expenditure varies from survey to survey. Please consult the technical notes for each survey for more details. The following surveys' data are presented with deflated expenditure quintiles: Côte d'Ivoire, Cameroon, Ghana, Kenya, Madagascar, Mozambique, and Malawi.

Demographic indicators

Number of households in each quintile varies because of differences in household size, although the total number of individuals in each quintile is the same.

Total population is a sampled population weighted by the cluster weights to give an estimate of the actual population size.

Education and literacy indicators (drawn from UNESCO definitions)

Net primary enrollment rate is the total number of children of primary school age enrolled in primary school as a proportion of the total number of children of primary school age. The age range varies by country. Please consult the technical notes for details.

Net secondary enrollment rate is the total number of children of secondary school age enrolled in secondary school as a proportion of the total number of children of secondary school age. The age range varies by country. Please consult the technical notes for details.

Literacy (adult) means the percentage of people aged 15 and above who can read and write a short, simple statement on their everyday life. The survey may have tested individuals to verify this, or may have used other methods. Please consult the technical notes for details.

Head of household indicators

Polygamous male-headed refers to male-headed household with more than one spouse. However, differences exist in the way in polygamous households are defined. Please consult the technical notes for details on each country's definition of a household.

De facto female-headed is defined as either (a) a household without a resident male head or where the husband is not present and the wife is the head by default and the main decision-maker in his absence; or (b) a household where the resident male head has lost most of his functions as the economic provider due to infirmity, inability to work, and so forth.

De jure female-headed refers to a single female-headed household where the household head has never been married, or is divorced or separated or widowed.

Household expenditure indicators

These indicators provide information on per capita expenditure in local currency (including the value of own-produced food consumed in the household and the imputed rent of homeowners when possible) and the share of food in household expenditures. These are computed as weighted averages of each household's per-capita expenditure, or as weighted ratios in the case of the shares.

Employment indicators

The *employment ratio* includes only persons who are employed and the unemployed aged 15–64 (inclusive), excluding the following categories: homemakers, retired, dependent, student, and other.

Formal employment is defined as wage employees in the government or formal private sector.

Informal employment is defined as those whose employment status is "informal" or "self-employed."

Anthropometric indicators

All three indicators are calculated for children who are less than 60 months old. Z-scores two standard deviations below the mean of reference population indicate that a child is *stunted* (height-for-age), *wasted* (weight-for-height), or *underweight* (weight-for-age). The reference is defined jointly by the National Center for Health Statistics and the Centers for Disease Control (both United States).

16-1. Burkina Faso

Expenditure Quintile

Indicators	Unit of measure	National total	Rural All	Q1	Q2	Q3	Q4	Q5	Urban All	Q1	Q2	Q3	Q4	Q5
Demographic Indicators														
Sample size (households)	Number	8,478	5,885	913	993	1,048	1,280	1,651	2,593	354	450	511	540	738
Total population	000s	10,597	8,830	1,766	1,765	1,767	1,766	1,766	1,767	353	354	353	353	354
Age dependency ratio	Number	1.0	1.1	1.2	1.2	1.1	1.1	0.9	0.7	1.0	0.8	0.7	0.6	0.5
Average household size	Number	7.6	8.2	10.3	10.1	9.1	7.6	5.7	5.6	8.0	6.5	5.7	5.4	4.0
Head of Household Characteristics														
Marital Status of head														
Monogamous male	Percent	53	51	44	44	50	55	57	60	53	59	62	66	57
Polygamous male	Percent	31	37	46	49	42	33	23	12	27	18	11	6	5
Single male	Percent	7	5	4	2	3	5	9	14	8	8	11	14	24
De facto female	Percent	2	2	1	1	1	2	3	3	3	3	3	3	4
De jure female	Percent	6	5	4	3	4	5	8	11	9	12	12	10	11
MDG1: Eradicate Extreme Poverty and Hunger														
Mean monthly expenditure	CFA francs	12,318	8,419	2,523	3,918	5,097	6,914	17,434	25,685	4,362	7,578	11,746	18,675	62,085
Mean monthly share on food	Percent	58	63	64	68	66	65	56	39	48	48	43	38	27
Mean monthly share on health	Percent	3	3	2	2	2	3	4	4	2	3	4	6	5
Mean monthly share on education	Percent	1	1	1	1	1	1	1	4	3	3	4	4	3
MDG2: Education and Literacy; MDG3: Promote Gender Equality														
Access to primary school (within 30 minutes)	Percent	59	52	47	48	50	49	59	84	75	84	85	84	89
Net primary enrollment rate														
Total	Percent	26	20	14	18	17	19	32	67	52	64	70	76	75
Male	Percent	30	23	18	24	20	22	37	69	53	70	70	77	81
Female	Percent	22	15	10	12	13	16	28	64	52	59	69	75	68
Net secondary enrollment rate														
Total	Percent	12	5	2	5	3	6	11	38	13	29	38	50	58
Male	Percent	13	7	4	5	4	7	15	41	13	33	39	58	68
Female	Percent	10	4	1	4	2	4	7	34	13	25	37	42	51
Tertiary enrollment rate	per 10,000	8	..	..	..	..	..	..	..	..	..	..	..	..
Adult literacy rate														
Total	Percent	18	10	5	8	9	10	18	51	23	34	48	62	78
Male	Percent	25	15	8	12	14	14	25	59	30	44	56	69	84
Female	Percent	13	6	3	5	5	6	12	42	15	25	40	54	71
Youth literacy rate														
Total	Percent	26	15	9	12	11	16	24	65	40	50	68	77	81
Male	Percent	32	20	13	17	15	21	32	72	49	62	76	81	89
Female	Percent	20	10	5	7	8	12	18	57	31	40	60	72	74
MDG4: Reduce Child Mortality; MDG5: Improve Maternal Health														
Proportion with time to market less than 5 km	Percent	78	72	73	72	71	69	75	97	93	97	97	98	99
Morbidity	Percent	7	6	4	5	6	7	10	11	7	9	11	12	15
Action taken when sick	Percent	41	39	29	29	34	37	51	49	35	45	45	52	57
Health provider ownership														
Public	Percent	83	85	84	85	85	82	86	79	75	87	81	78	75
Private - modern medicine	Percent	3	1	1	0	..	1	1	10	6	5	11	7	18
Private - traditional healers	Percent	11	12	12	10	14	16	10	4	16	3	4	4	2
Other	Percent	3	2	3	4	1	1	2	6	2	5	5	11	5
Child survival and malnutrition														
Birth assisted by trained staff	Percent	..	..	..	..	..	..	..	..	..	..	..	..	..
1-year-olds immunisation coverage	Percent	..	..	..	..	..	..	..	..	..	..	..	..	..
1-year-olds immunized against measles	Percent	..	..	..	..	..	..	..	..	..	..	..	..	..
Stunting (6-59 months)	Percent	43	46	46	44	46	50	43	28	32	37	27	22	17
Wasting (6-59 months)	Percent	24	24	24	22	25	24	25	23	19	15	21	35	26
Underweight (6-59 months)	Percent	50	52	53	49	54	56	50	34	38	37	30	38	26
MDG7: Ensure Environmental Sustainability														
Access to sanitation facilities	Percent	32	16	7	11	13	14	26	89	71	82	89	95	97
Proportion with time to Water Source less than 1 hour	Percent	78	73	67	72	74	72	77	96	88	94	97	98	99
Proportion with time to Market less than 1 hour	Percent	78	72	73	72	71	69	75	97	93	97	97	98	99
Access to improved water source														
Total	Percent	63	57	54	56	58	55	59	86	76	79	82	88	95
Pipe (own tap)	Percent	5	0	..	0	0	..	0	24	3	6	14	27	50
Pipe borne	Percent	16	5	4	3	4	4	8	53	56	61	58	56	41
Well (Protected)	Percent	42	52	50	53	55	52	51	9	17	12	11	5	4
Traditional Fuel Use														
Total	Percent	92	96	98	97	97	97	92	80	90	94	89	84	57
Firewood	Percent	87	91	95	94	93	92	85	74	88	92	87	78	46
Charcoal	Percent	5	5	3	4	4	4	7	6	1	2	3	7	11

Enquête Prioritaire Aupres des Menages II 1998.

16-2. Burundi

Expenditure Quintile

Indicators	Unit of measure	National total	Rural All	Q1	Q2	Q3	Q4	Q5	Urban All	Q1	Q2	Q3	Q4	Q5
Demographic Indicators														
Sample size (households)	Number	6,668	3,908	740	649	723	817	979	2,760	473	494	562	541	690
Total population	000s	6,026	5,717	1,143	1,153	1,135	1,143	1,144	309	62	62	62	62	62
Age dependency ratio	Number	1.1	1.1	1.4	1.2	1.2	1.0	0.9	0.7	1.1	0.9	0.7	0.6	0.4
Average household size	Number	4.9	4.9	5.5	5.5	5.1	4.7	4.0	4.8	6.4	6.1	5.0	4.7	3.3
Head of Household Characteristics														
Marital Status of head														
Monogamous male	Percent	68	68	57	67	71	71	74	66	62	72	68	68	61
Polygamous male	Percent	0	0	0	0	0	0	0	0	0	0	..	..	..
Single male	Percent	5	5	4	4	4	6	6	14	5	5	10	14	25
De facto female	Percent	3	3	2	1	5	3	4	3	4	3	4	4	3
De jure female	Percent	23	23	37	27	20	20	17	17	29	19	18	13	11
MDG1: Eradicate Extreme Poverty and Hunger														
Mean monthly expenditure	Burundi francs	6,574	5,438	1,438	2,925	4,221	5,910	10,765	27,314	4,454	9,137	15,444	26,007	58,137
Mean monthly share on food	Percent	74	75	69	77	77	77	75	48	59	58	52	44	37
Mean monthly share on health	Percent	2	2	3	2	2	2	2	3	3	3	3	2	2
Mean monthly share on education	Percent	1	1	2	1	1	1	1	3	4	4	3	4	2
MDG2: Education and Literacy; MDG3: Promote Gender Equality														
Access to primary school (within 30 minutes)	Percent	72	70	63	73	70	73	73	97	94	96	98	99	98
Net primary enrollment rate														
Total	Percent	56	55	40	50	59	63	66	83	67	84	90	93	94
Male	Percent	60	59	44	56	62	69	67	83	67	84	89	93	94
Female	Percent	51	50	36	44	55	57	65	83	66	83	91	93	94
Net secondary enrollment rate														
Total	Percent	9	7	2	4	7	13	11	48	14	34	56	74	74
Male	Percent	10	8	3	6	6	15	11	48	16	33	56	71	73
Female	Percent	9	7	1	3	8	12	11	48	13	35	56	76	74
Tertiary enrollment rate	per 10,000	11	..	..	..	..	..	..	..	..	..	..	..	..
Adult literacy rate														
Total	Percent	49	47	33	45	47	52	54	84	58	76	87	95	97
Male	Percent	58	56	43	55	55	61	62	90	70	85	90	97	98
Female	Percent	42	39	26	37	40	44	47	79	50	68	83	93	97
Youth literacy rate														
Total	Percent	71	70	55	71	66	77	77	90	72	88	91	98	99
Male	Percent	72	71	56	72	66	78	79	92	75	91	93	99	98
Female	Percent	71	70	55	70	66	77	76	89	69	86	90	97	100
MDG4: Reduce Child Mortality; MDG5: Improve Maternal Health														
Proportion with time to market less than 5 km	Percent	77	76	76	80	72	77	76	100	100	100	100	100	100
Morbidity	Percent	21	21	22	18	19	21	25	15	18	17	17	13	11
Action taken when sick	Percent	60	59	51	54	59	62	69	72	52	69	77	86	87
Health provider ownership														
Public	Percent	..	..	..	..	..	..	..	..	..	..	..	..	..
Private - modern medicine	Percent	..	..	..	..	..	..	..	..	..	..	..	..	..
Private - traditional healers	Percent	..	..	..	..	..	..	..	..	..	..	..	..	..
Other	Percent	..	..	..	..	..	..	..	..	..	..	..	..	..
Child survival and malnutrition														
Birth assisted by trained staff	Percent	..	..	..	..	..	..	..	..	..	..	..	..	..
1-year-olds immunisation coverage	Percent	..	..	..	..	..	..	..	..	..	..	..	..	..
1-year-olds immunized against measles	Percent	..	..	..	..	..	..	..	..	..	..	..	..	..
Stunting (6-59 months)	Percent	56	59	62	64	56	59	52	30	47	31	23	22	23
Wasting (6-59 months)	Percent	8	8	8	8	9	9	9	7	5	6	6	5	11
Underweight (6-59 months)	Percent	44	47	48	50	54	44	38	15	25	19	12	9	9
MDG7: Ensure Environmental Sustainability														
Access to sanitation facilities	Percent	..	..	..	..	..	..	..	..	..	..	..	..	..
Proportion with time to Water Source less than 1 hour	Percent	88	87	84	88	87	87	89	97	98	96	98	97	96
Proportion with time to Market less than 1 hour	Percent	77	76	76	80	72	77	76	100	100	100	100	100	100
Access to improved water source														
Total	Percent	85	84	80	83	85	84	87	98	94	96	98	99	100
Pipe (own tap)	Percent	4	1	1	1	0	1	2	57	11	28	50	76	88
Pipe borne	Percent	16	14	14	17	14	12	14	40	80	66	48	23	11
Well (Protected)	Percent	66	69	65	66	71	71	71	1	3	2	1	0	1
Traditional Fuel Use														
Total	Percent	99	99	100	100	98	100	98	97	99	100	99	98	93
Firewood	Percent	94	98	99	100	98	100	95	15	54	23	11	4	2
Charcoal	Percent	5	1	0	..	0	0	4	82	46	77	88	94	91

Étude Nationale sur les Conditions de Vie au Burundi, 1998.

Household Welfare

16-3. Cameroon

Indicators	Unit of measure	National total	Rural All	Rural Q1	Rural Q2	Rural Q3	Rural Q4	Rural Q5	Urban All	Urban Q1	Urban Q2	Urban Q3	Urban Q4	Urban Q5
Demographic Indicators														
Sample size (households)	Number	10,992	6,017	646	764	1,026	1,217	2,364	4,975	759	786	886	1,061	1,483
Total population	000s	15,473	10,089	2,019	2,016	2,019	2,018	2,018	5,383	1,077	1,076	1,076	1,076	1,078
Age dependency ratio	Number	0.9	1.0	1.4	1.3	1.1	0.9	0.6	0.7	1.0	0.8	0.7	0.5	0.4
Average household size	Number	5.0	5.0	7.2	6.8	5.5	5.0	3.0	4.9	7.3	6.3	5.7	4.5	3.1
Head of Household Characteristics														
Marital Status of head														
Monogamous male	Percent	44	46	50	50	50	48	40	40	47	49	46	38	32
Polygamous male	Percent	14	16	22	22	16	17	11	9	16	11	10	9	6
Single male	Percent	18	15	5	6	11	11	26	25	15	15	17	26	38
De facto female	Percent	4	4	5	5	5	4	3	4	5	4	5	4	4
De jure female	Percent	19	19	18	17	18	20	20	21	17	20	22	23	21
MDG1: Eradicate Extreme Poverty and Hunger														
Mean monthly expenditure	CFA francs	30,619	22,063	6,609	10,217	13,705	18,951	40,025	46,540	11,847	18,846	25,889	37,099	93,334
Mean monthly share on food	Percent	59	69	68	71	70	69	68	42	48	45	44	42	36
Mean monthly share on health	Percent	7	7	7	6	7	7	8	7	6	6	7	7	8
Mean monthly share on education	Percent	4	3	3	3	3	3	3	6	6	7	7	6	5
MDG2: Education and Literacy; MDG3: Promote Gender Equality														
Access to primary school (within 30 minutes)	Percent	85	79	75	77	79	77	83	96	96	96	96	95	96
Net primary enrollment rate														
Total	Percent	93	92	92	91	93	93	92	94	94	95	95	93	89
Male	Percent	93	93	93	92	94	93	90	94	94	95	95	94	91
Female	Percent	92	92	90	90	93	93	93	93	94	96	95	92	87
Net secondary enrollment rate														
Total	Percent	40	29	14	22	28	33	48	57	38	53	59	64	72
Male	Percent	39	29	15	22	28	33	49	55	35	49	59	64	73
Female	Percent	41	28	12	21	27	33	47	58	40	57	59	64	71
Tertiary enrollment rate	per 10,000	89	..	..	..	..	..	..	..	..	..	..	..	..
Adult literacy rate														
Total	Percent	68	56	50	50	55	58	62	88	76	85	89	92	94
Male	Percent	77	67	61	60	66	69	72	92	83	91	94	96	96
Female	Percent	60	47	42	42	46	49	51	83	70	80	84	88	92
Youth literacy rate														
Total	Percent	82	73	69	69	76	74	78	94	89	93	95	96	97
Male	Percent	88	82	76	78	85	84	85	96	90	95	97	97	98
Female	Percent	77	66	62	61	69	67	71	93	87	91	93	95	95
MDG4: Reduce Child Mortality; MDG5: Improve Maternal Health														
Proportion with time to market less than 5 km	Percent	90	85	82	85	84	86	88	99	99	99	99	100	99
Morbidity	Percent	31	31	28	29	31	33	35	31	30	31	31	30	33
Action taken when sick	Percent	..	..	..	..	..	..	..	..	..	..	..	..	..
Health provider ownership														
Public	Percent	53	55	53	53	53	59	58	48	44	49	51	49	48
Private - modern medicine	Percent	13	7	6	5	7	8	9	23	19	20	20	24	31
Private - traditional healers	Percent	15	18	18	21	21	15	14	11	18	12	9	7	6
Other	Percent	2	3	2	3	4	3	4	1	1	0	1	1	1
Child survival and malnutrition														
Birth assisted by trained staff	Percent	..	..	..	..	..	..	..	..	..	..	..	..	..
1-year-olds immunisation coverage	Percent	56	51	48	45	49	53	62	67	56	71	72	73	64
1-year-olds immunized against measles	Percent	62	57	55	54	55	56	67	73	59	74	78	82	73
Stunting (6-59 months)	Percent	53	59	69	56	61	53	50	39	48	42	40	29	29
Wasting (6-59 months)	Percent	8	8	7	12	9	7	5	8	9	10	7	9	5
Underweight (6-59 months)	Percent	25	30	32	30	30	30	26	13	17	18	9	12	8
MDG7: Ensure Environmental Sustainability														
Access to sanitation facilities	Percent	43	26	13	15	21	29	36	75	58	68	75	79	84
Proportion with time to Water Source less than 1 hour	Percent	68	75	71	80	73	74	76	56	56	59	61	57	50
Proportion with time to Market less than 1 hour	Percent	90	85	82	85	84	86	88	99	99	99	99	100	99
Access to improved water source														
Total	Percent	66	50	47	44	47	48	58	96	88	94	97	97	98
Pipe (own tap)	Percent	15	6	3	4	4	5	10	32	11	17	24	35	49
Pipe borne	Percent	27	14	12	11	11	13	17	52	58	62	59	51	41
Well (Protected)	Percent	24	31	32	30	32	30	31	12	19	15	14	10	8
Traditional Fuel Use														
Total	Percent	75	94	99	99	97	96	86	41	75	58	51	34	17
Firewood	Percent	75	93	99	99	96	96	85	40	75	58	49	33	16
Charcoal	Percent	0	0	..	..	0	0	0	1	0	1	2	1	1

Enquête Camerounaise Auprès des Ménages 2001.

16-4. Côte d'Ivoire

			Expenditure Quintile											
			Rural						Urban					
Indicators	Unit of measure	National total	All	Q1	Q2	Q3	Q4	Q5	All	Q1	Q2	Q3	Q4	Q5
Demographic Indicators														
Sample size (households)	Number	4,200	2,280	445	403	459	475	498	1,920	154	270	307	427	762
Total population	000s	16,816	9,225	2,724	2,173	1,880	1,470	978	7,590	578	1,143	1,471	1,889	2,509
Age dependency ratio	Number	0.8	1.0	1.2	1.2	0.9	0.8	0.7	0.7	1.0	1.0	0.8	0.6	0.5
Average household size	Number	5.7	5.9	8.3	6.9	6.1	5.0	3.6	5.6	8.5	7.7	6.7	5.7	3.9
Head of Household Characteristics														
Marital Status of head														
Monogamous male	Percent	58	58	49	63	62	57	59	58	51	52	65	66	55
Polygamous male	Percent	13	18	30	18	18	19	7	7	22	14	9	5	2
Single male	Percent	14	12	7	8	9	12	20	16	6	10	9	11	25
De facto female	Percent	3	2	1	2	3	3	2	5	7	5	5	4	4
De jure female	Percent	12	10	12	8	7	10	12	14	14	19	12	13	14
MDG1: Eradicate Extreme Poverty and Hunger														
Mean monthly expenditure	CFA francs	35,406	28,573	7,452	12,962	18,475	27,084	69,649	43,455	8,148	13,222	18,741	27,490	78,858
Mean monthly share on food	Percent	57	65	68	65	66	65	63	47	56	54	51	49	41
Mean monthly share on health	Percent	6	6	4	6	5	6	7	7	5	6	6	7	7
Mean monthly share on education	Percent	2	2	2	3	2	2	1	3	4	4	3	3	3
MDG2: Education and Literacy; MDG3: Promote Gender Equality														
Access to primary school (within 30 minutes)	Percent	..	..	..	..	..	..	..	..	..	..	..	..	..
Net primary enrollment rate														
Total	Percent	52	43	32	43	45	50	59	64	55	56	61	65	79
Male	Percent	55	47	37	45	51	52	65	67	58	59	66	68	84
Female	Percent	49	40	27	42	40	48	54	61	52	52	54	64	75
Net secondary enrollment rate														
Total	Percent	21	10	5	8	13	16	13	31	15	20	34	36	39
Male	Percent	26	14	7	10	18	21	20	40	20	23	45	48	51
Female	Percent	16	6	2	7	7	10	7	24	10	18	23	25	31
Tertiary enrollment rate	per 10,000	62	..	..	..	..	..	..	..	..	..	..	..	..
Adult literacy rate														
Total	Percent	48	33	24	31	34	38	43	64	44	56	61	64	76
Male	Percent	61	46	36	45	48	52	54	77	57	69	76	79	86
Female	Percent	35	21	14	18	21	24	31	51	32	44	45	52	65
Youth literacy rate														
Total	Percent	61	47	38	46	50	51	55	73	60	70	75	71	79
Male	Percent	72	59	48	59	61	64	65	86	71	79	88	89	91
Female	Percent	50	36	29	32	38	39	46	61	50	62	61	58	68
MDG4: Reduce Child Mortality; MDG5: Improve Maternal Health														
Proportion with time to market less than 5 km	Percent	..	..	..	..	..	..	..	..	..	..	..	..	..
Morbidity	Percent	15	14	11	11	14	17	17	16	13	14	14	17	20
Action taken when sick	Percent	54	48	35	51	48	51	58	60	43	55	58	65	65
Health provider ownership														
Public	Percent	..	..	..	..	..	..	..	..	..	..	..	..	..
Private - modern medicine	Percent	..	..	..	..	..	..	..	..	..	..	..	..	..
Private - traditional healers	Percent	..	..	..	..	..	..	..	..	..	..	..	..	..
Other	Percent	..	..	..	..	..	..	..	..	..	..	..	..	..
Child survival and malnutrition														
Birth assisted by trained staff	Percent	..	..	..	..	..	..	..	..	..	..	..	..	..
1-year-olds immunisation coverage	Percent	..	..	..	..	..	..	..	..	..	..	..	..	..
1-year-olds immunized against measles	Percent	..	..	..	..	..	..	..	..	..	..	..	..	..
Stunting (6-59 months)	Percent	..	..	..	..	..	..	..	..	..	..	..	..	..
Wasting (6-59 months)	Percent	..	..	..	..	..	..	..	..	..	..	..	..	..
Underweight (6-59 months)	Percent	..	..	..	..	..	..	..	..	..	..	..	..	..
MDG7: Ensure Environmental Sustainability														
Access to sanitation facilities	Percent	67	42	33	41	41	41	51	96	94	92	95	96	97
Proportion with time to Water Source less than 1 hour	Percent	..	..	..	..	..	..	..	..	..	..	..	..	..
Proportion with time to Market less than 1 hour	Percent	..	..	..	..	..	..	..	..	..	..	..	..	..
Access to improved water source														
Total	Percent	78	82	84	83	82	77	84	72	79	72	72	69	74
Pipe (own tap)	Percent	19	6	4	4	4	8	11	35	18	24	30	34	44
Pipe borne	Percent	7	2	1	2	3	2	3	13	3	11	9	14	16
Well (Protected)	Percent	51	73	79	77	76	68	69	25	58	37	33	22	14
Traditional Fuel Use														
Total	Percent	89	93	96	98	96	93	86	83	94	92	94	90	69
Firewood	Percent	64	90	96	97	95	88	79	32	75	57	44	29	13
Charcoal	Percent	25	3	0	1	2	4	7	51	19	35	50	60	56

Enquête Niveau de Vie des Ménages en Côte d'Ivoire 1998.

16-5. Ethiopia

| | | | Rural | | | | | | Urban | | | | | |
Indicators	Unit of measure	National total	All	Q1	Q2	Q3	Q4	Q5	All	Q1	Q2	Q3	Q4	Q5
Demographic Indicators														
Sample size (households)	Number	16,672	8,459	1,469	1,382	1,519	1,678	2,411	8,213	1,118	1,358	1,506	1,883	2,348
Total population	000s	54,756	47,531	9,502	9,513	9,504	9,507	9,505	7,225	1,446	1,443	1,446	1,445	1,445
Age dependency ratio	Number	1.0	1.1	1.3	1.2	1.1	1.0	0.8	0.7	1.0	0.9	0.8	0.6	0.5
Average household size	Number	4.9	4.9	5.9	5.4	5.2	4.8	3.8	4.5	5.6	5.1	4.7	4.3	3.5
Head of Household Characteristics														
Marital Status of head														
Monogamous male	Percent	68	71	75	72	74	74	64	48	53	50	50	49	41
Polygamous male	Percent	1	1	1	1	1	0	1	0	0	0	0	0	0
Single male	Percent	6	5	3	4	3	4	8	11	6	4	7	10	23
De facto female	Percent	1	1	1	1	1	0	1	3	2	4	4	3	2
De jure female	Percent	25	23	20	22	21	22	27	38	39	42	39	38	34
MDG1: Eradicate Extreme Poverty and Hunger														
Mean monthly expenditure	Ethiopian birr	103	93	42	60	75	95	161	162	49	76	103	147	346
Mean monthly share on food	Percent	66	68	72	71	69	68	62	55	66	62	59	53	43
Mean monthly share on health	Percent	1	1	1	1	1	1	1	1	1	1	1	1	1
Mean monthly share on education	Percent	1	0	0	0	0	0	0	2	2	1	2	2	2
MDG2: Education and Literacy; MDG3: Promote Gender Equality														
Access to primary school (within 30 minutes)	Percent	..	..	..	..	..	..	..	..	..	..	..	..	..
Net primary enrollment rate														
Total	Percent	30	25	19	23	29	25	32	75	66	70	76	84	85
Male	Percent	32	27	20	25	30	27	35	75	68	68	75	85	86
Female	Percent	29	22	18	20	28	21	29	75	64	71	77	82	84
Net secondary enrollment rate														
Total	Percent	9	3	2	3	3	3	5	40	30	36	41	50	47
Male	Percent	10	4	4	3	3	5	7	43	29	38	47	54	54
Female	Percent	8	2	1	2	2	2	3	38	30	35	36	46	42
Tertiary enrollment rate	per 10,000	10	..	..	..	..	..	..	..	..	..	..	..	..
Adult literacy rate														
Total	Percent	28	21	15	19	20	23	25	67	54	59	66	71	79
Male	Percent	41	34	26	32	33	39	39	81	70	75	80	86	91
Female	Percent	17	9	6	8	8	9	11	56	43	47	56	61	69
Youth literacy rate														
Total	Percent	39	29	24	32	29	30	31	84	80	81	86	87	86
Male	Percent	50	43	35	47	43	45	42	90	84	86	91	95	95
Female	Percent	28	17	12	17	16	16	20	80	76	78	82	81	81
MDG4: Reduce Child Mortality; MDG5: Improve Maternal Health														
Proportion with time to market less than 5 km	Percent	..	..	..	..	..	..	..	..	..	..	..	..	..
Morbidity	Percent	26	27	27	27	27	26	31	20	20	20	20	19	20
Action taken when sick	Percent	41	39	30	36	40	41	46	67	60	65	68	70	71
Health provider ownership														
Public	Percent	45	44	44	49	45	42	41	52	56	59	52	49	43
Private - modern medicine	Percent	45	45	46	40	46	46	48	42	36	36	41	43	51
Private - traditional healers	Percent	1	1	0	0	1	1	1	1	0	0	1	2	1
Other	Percent	6	7	6	7	5	9	7	4	4	3	4	3	4
Child survival and malnutrition														
Birth assisted by trained staff	Percent	..	..	..	..	..	..	..	..	..	..	..	..	..
1-year-olds immunisation coverage	Percent	45	41	35	48	42	38	45	85	81	81	84	96	88
1-year-olds immunized against measles	Percent	51	47	44	50	47	49	46	90	84	88	90	98	94
Stunting (6-59 months)	Percent	59	61	64	60	61	61	55	47	56	51	49	43	29
Wasting (6-59 months)	Percent	11	11	12	11	11	9	11	7	8	9	6	4	7
Underweight (6-59 months)	Percent	45	46	53	46	48	41	43	27	36	30	27	22	14
MDG7: Ensure Environmental Sustainability														
Access to sanitation facilities	Percent	18	9	8	8	8	10	11	73	49	64	74	80	87
Proportion with time to Water Source less than 1 hour	Percent	..	..	..	..	..	..	..	..	..	..	..	..	..
Proportion with time to Market less than 1 hour	Percent	..	..	..	..	..	..	..	..	..	..	..	..	..
Access to improved water source														
Total	Percent	29	19	15	18	18	19	21	92	83	91	93	92	96
Pipe (own tap)	Percent	0	0	0	0	0	0	0	1	1	1	1	2	2
Pipe borne	Percent	17	7	7	7	6	6	8	82	74	79	84	83	88
Well (Protected)	Percent	11	12	8	11	12	13	13	8	9	11	8	7	6
Traditional Fuel Use														
Total	Percent	77	78	82	78	77	78	77	66	80	74	70	65	51
Firewood	Percent	75	78	82	78	77	78	77	58	75	67	61	57	40
Charcoal	Percent	1	0	0	..	..	..	0	8	5	7	9	8	11

Welfare Monitoring Survey, 2000.

16-6. Gambia, The

Indicators	Unit of measure	National total	Rural All	Q1	Q2	Q3	Q4	Q5	Urban All	Q1	Q2	Q3	Q4	Q5
Demographic Indicators														
Sample size (households)	Number	1,958	933	138	158	166	191	280	1,025	119	148	177	230	351
Total population	000s	1,699	942	190	189	188	187	188	757	151	152	151	151	153
Age dependency ratio	Number	0.9	1.1	1.1	1.2	1.2	1.1	0.9	0.7	0.9	0.9	0.8	0.6	0.6
Average household size	Number	7.8	9.2	13.6	11.2	10.2	8.6	6.1	6.5	11.3	8.8	7.4	5.8	3.9
Head of Household Characteristics														
Marital Status of head														
Monogamous male	Percent	50	49	36	39	46	57	58	51	43	48	57	55	48
Polygamous male	Percent	27	38	55	48	42	31	28	17	38	27	17	14	8
Single male	Percent	7	4	4	4	2	2	6	10	6	3	6	8	18
De facto female	Percent	9	5	5	5	6	6	4	12	9	12	13	12	11
De jure female	Percent	7	3	1	3	4	4	4	10	4	9	7	10	14
MDG1: Eradicate Extreme Poverty and Hunger														
Mean monthly expenditure	Gambian dalasis	393	203	51	85	119	166	415	560	121	196	284	423	1,111
Mean monthly share on food	Percent	66	73	70	71	73	75	74	60	68	65	65	61	52
Mean monthly share on health	Percent	1	1	1	1	1	1	1	1	1	1	1	1	1
Mean monthly share on education	Percent	3	3	3	4	3	3	2	3	4	4	4	3	3
MDG2: Education and Literacy; MDG3: Promote Gender Equality														
Access to primary school (within 30 minutes)	Percent	..	..	..	..	..	..	..	..	..	..	..	..	..
Net primary enrollment rate														
Total	Percent	49	44	30	49	44	50	48	57	44	49	56	64	75
Male	Percent	51	47	37	50	45	50	53	59	46	58	57	62	75
Female	Percent	46	41	23	47	42	50	44	54	42	42	54	67	75
Net secondary enrollment rate														
Total	Percent	18	8	1	8	10	10	14	30	16	20	31	35	54
Male	Percent	22	11	1	11	15	12	18	36	21	28	34	40	57
Female	Percent	14	5	..	4	3	7	9	24	12	12	27	30	50
Tertiary enrollment rate	per 10,000	7	..	..	..	..	..	..	..	..	..	..	..	..
Adult literacy rate														
Total	Percent	..	..	..	..	..	..	..	..	..	..	..	..	..
Male	Percent	..	..	..	..	..	..	..	..	..	..	..	..	..
Female	Percent	..	..	..	..	..	..	..	..	..	..	..	..	..
Youth literacy rate														
Total	Percent	..	..	..	..	..	..	..	..	..	..	..	..	..
Male	Percent	..	..	..	..	..	..	..	..	..	..	..	..	..
Female	Percent	..	..	..	..	..	..	..	..	..	..	..	..	..
MDG4: Reduce Child Mortality; MDG5: Improve Maternal Health														
Proportion with time to market less than 5 km	Percent	..	..	..	..	..	..	..	..	..	..	..	..	..
Morbidity	Percent	7	8	8	7	8	9	9	6	4	5	6	7	5
Action taken when sick	Percent	75	72	72	69	79	75	65	81	78	85	86	81	78
Health provider ownership														
Public	Percent	82	82	84	80	82	80	87	82	77	88	90	78	75
Private - modern medicine	Percent	14	13	10	18	18	15	6	16	17	9	9	21	24
Private - traditional healers	Percent	3	4	6	2	1	6	7	2	6	3	1	1	1
Other	Percent	..	..	..	..	..	..	..	..	..	..	..	..	..
Child survival and malnutrition														
Birth assisted by trained staff	Percent	..	..	..	..	..	..	..	..	..	..	..	..	..
1-year-olds immunisation coverage	Percent	..	..	..	..	..	..	..	..	..	..	..	..	..
1-year-olds immunized against measles	Percent	..	..	..	..	..	..	..	..	..	..	..	..	..
Stunting (6-59 months)	Percent	24	28	34	21	27	29	31	17	27	21	15	10	12
Wasting (6-59 months)	Percent	7	8	8	6	9	7	8	7	3	7	5	10	13
Underweight (6-59 months)	Percent	21	26	33	22	23	26	27	13	14	14	17	11	9
MDG7: Ensure Environmental Sustainability														
Access to sanitation facilities	Percent	96	93	96	93	92	94	91	99	99	99	97	99	99
Proportion with time to Water Source less than 1 hour	Percent	..	..	..	..	..	..	..	..	..	..	..	..	..
Proportion with time to Market less than 1 hour	Percent	..	..	..	..	..	..	..	..	..	..	..	..	..
Access to improved water source														
Total	Percent	79	66	74	74	73	56	63	90	78	85	89	92	96
Pipe (own tap)	Percent	21	2	1	..	1	2	3	39	15	16	26	39	64
Pipe borne	Percent	38	25	19	23	32	24	25	50	60	65	63	52	31
Well (Protected)	Percent	20	40	54	51	40	31	34	2	4	4	1	1	1
Traditional Fuel Use														
Total	Percent	..	..	..	..	..	..	..	..	..	..	..	..	..
Firewood	Percent	..	..	..	..	..	..	..	..	..	..	..	..	..
Charcoal	Percent	..	..	..	..	..	..	..	..	..	..	..	..	..

Note: The column groups under "Expenditure Quintile" are Rural (All, Q1, Q2, Q3, Q4, Q5) and Urban (All, Q1, Q2, Q3, Q4, Q5).

The Gambia 1998 Household Poverty Survey.

16-7. Ghana

			Expenditure Quintile											
			Rural						Urban					
Indicators	Unit of measure	National total	All	Q1	Q2	Q3	Q4	Q5	All	Q1	Q2	Q3	Q4	Q5
Demographic Indicators														
Sample size (households)	Number	5,998	3,799	568	625	665	776	1,165	2,199	310	343	403	435	708
Total population	000s	18,239	11,493	2,295	2,191	2,267	2,241	2,500	6,746	1,150	1,265	1,331	1,440	1,559
Age dependency ratio	Number	0.9	1.0	1.2	1.2	1.1	1.0	0.7	0.8	1.1	0.9	0.8	0.7	0.5
Average household size	Number	4.4	4.7	6.3	5.7	5.3	4.7	3.1	4.0	5.7	5.2	4.5	4.3	2.6
Head of Household Characteristics														
Marital Status of head														
Monogamous male	Percent	53	56	63	57	63	57	48	48	49	54	54	57	37
Polygamous male	Percent	3	4	7	5	3	4	2	1	4	2	1	1	0
Single male	Percent	12	10	5	6	4	8	17	15	6	7	7	11	28
De facto female	Percent	12	10	8	10	13	9	10	14	20	12	15	14	12
De jure female	Percent	21	20	16	21	16	22	23	22	21	25	23	17	24
MDG1: Eradicate Extreme Poverty and Hunger														
Mean monthly expenditure	Ghanaian cedis	119,877	91,524	23,107	39,132	55,065	77,592	176,149	161,067	38,436	66,819	96,992	136,526	286,033
Mean monthly share on food	Percent	59	62	63	64	63	62	61	55	59	56	55	53	53
Mean monthly share on health	Percent	4	4	3	4	4	4	4	3	3	3	4	4	3
Mean monthly share on education	Percent	4	3	3	4	4	3	2	5	6	5	5	7	4
MDG2: Education and Literacy; MDG3: Promote Gender Equality														
Access to primary school (within 30 minutes)	Percent	..	..	..	..	..	..	..	..	..	..	..	..	..
Net primary enrollment rate														
Total	Percent	61	54	39	48	53	68	68	74	67	70	73	81	79
Male	Percent	61	53	38	50	50	70	64	77	68	76	73	87	79
Female	Percent	61	56	40	46	58	67	71	71	65	65	74	75	80
Net secondary enrollment rate														
Total	Percent	10	7	3	6	6	8	12	16	7	12	19	21	19
Male	Percent	11	8	3	6	10	10	12	16	5	10	22	21	23
Female	Percent	10	6	3	6	3	7	12	15	9	13	17	21	16
Tertiary enrollment rate	per 10,000	13	..	..	..	..	..	..	..	..	..	..	..	..
Adult literacy rate														
Total	Percent	53	43	24	35	44	50	55	67	45	59	64	75	82
Male	Percent	67	59	36	50	63	66	72	79	60	75	76	84	91
Female	Percent	40	29	13	23	28	36	39	57	34	47	54	67	73
Youth literacy rate														
Total	Percent	66	57	42	48	56	66	68	78	67	74	79	80	86
Male	Percent	73	65	47	56	69	77	77	85	74	80	86	87	91
Female	Percent	59	47	34	39	42	55	58	72	59	67	70	75	81
MDG4: Reduce Child Mortality; MDG5: Improve Maternal Health														
Proportion with time to market less than 5 km	Percent	100	100	100	100	100	100	100	100	100	100	100	100	100
Morbidity	Percent	26	28	24	26	27	28	34	23	23	22	21	22	27
Action taken when sick	Percent	44	40	33	37	39	39	47	53	42	49	53	56	62
Health provider ownership														
Public	Percent	47	47	47	39	59	47	45	46	50	49	38	52	45
Private - modern medicine	Percent	44	42	43	52	33	42	44	45	35	37	51	42	52
Private - traditional healers	Percent	5	6	8	6	4	7	5	5	9	6	7	3	2
Other	Percent	4	4	2	3	4	4	6	4	6	7	4	3	2
Child survival and malnutrition														
Birth assisted by trained staff	Percent	..	..	..	..	..	..	..	..	..	..	..	..	..
1-year-olds immunisation coverage	Percent	..	..	..	..	..	..	..	..	..	..	..	..	..
1-year-olds immunized against measles	Percent	..	..	..	..	..	..	..	..	..	..	..	..	..
Stunting (6-59 months)	Percent	..	..	..	..	..	..	..	..	..	..	..	..	..
Wasting (6-59 months)	Percent	..	..	..	..	..	..	..	..	..	..	..	..	..
Underweight (6-59 months)	Percent	..	..	..	..	..	..	..	..	..	..	..	..	..
MDG7: Ensure Environmental Sustainability														
Access to sanitation facilities	Percent	79	70	37	63	74	81	81	91	78	87	91	94	95
Proportion with time to Water Source less than 1 hour	Percent	..	..	..	..	..	..	..	..	..	..	..	..	..
Proportion with time to Market less than 1 hour	Percent	100	100	100	100	100	100	100	100	100	100	100	100	100
Access to improved water source														
Total	Percent	61	48	44	43	47	48	54	79	62	74	77	81	86
Pipe (own tap)	Percent	4	1	..	..	0	1	2	8	0	2	4	8	14
Pipe borne	Percent	40	19	7	15	15	19	29	70	60	70	71	72	72
Well (Protected)	Percent	17	28	38	28	32	29	22	1	2	3	2	2	1
Traditional Fuel Use														
Total	Percent	92	97	95	98	99	99	96	85	99	98	89	83	74
Firewood	Percent	57	81	93	91	89	83	65	23	64	37	24	17	6
Charcoal	Percent	35	16	2	7	10	16	31	62	35	61	65	66	68

Ghana Living Standards Survey 4 1998/1999.

16-8. Kenya

			Rural						Urban					
Indicators	Unit of	National total	All	Q1	Q2	Q3	Q4	Q5	All	Q1	Q2	Q3	Q4	Q5
Demographic Indicators														
Sample size (households)	Number	10,874	8,963	1,339	1,521	1,646	1,813	2,644	1,911	273	262	327	514	535
Total population	000s	25,468	21,490	4,298	4,299	4,293	4,303	4,298	3,978	797	793	798	795	795
Age dependency ratio	Number	0.9	1.0	1.3	1.1	1.0	0.9	0.7	0.6	1.0	0.8	0.5	0.4	0.3
Average household size	Number	4.6	4.9	6.4	5.8	5.4	4.8	3.3	3.5	5.3	4.3	3.8	2.9	2.5
Head of Household Characteristics														
Marital Status of head														
Monogamous male	Percent	58	56	57	55	57	59	53	66	76	63	58	64	68
Polygamous male	Percent	7	8	11	12	7	8	5	4	6	6	4	2	2
Single male	Percent	7	6	2	3	4	4	11	10	2	2	12	12	16
De facto female	Percent	12	14	16	14	14	15	11	4	6	3	5	4	2
De jure female	Percent	17	17	14	15	17	15	19	17	10	27	20	17	12
MDG1: Eradicate Extreme Poverty and Hunger														
Mean monthly expenditure	Kshs.	2,244	1,716	455	711	998	1,431	3,569	4,299	1,048	1,637	2,255	3,541	9,396
Mean monthly share on food	Percent	70	74	77	76	77	75	69	57	65	64	58	57	48
Mean monthly share on health	Percent	0	0	0	0	0	0	0	0	0	0	0	0	0
Mean monthly share on education	Percent	3	3	3	3	3	4	3	4	2	4	4	4	5
MDG2: Education and Literacy; MDG3: Promote Gender Equality														
Access to primary school (within 30 minutes)	Percent	69	63	57	63	62	64	66	91	88	89	93	90	95
Net primary enrollment rate														
Total	Percent	73	73	65	73	72	77	82	78	69	81	83	82	80
Male	Percent	72	71	64	71	69	77	82	77	66	87	81	78	74
Female	Percent	75	74	66	74	74	78	81	78	72	74	85	85	86
Net secondary enrollment rate														
Total	Percent	12	10	4	6	9	13	18	29	10	14	22	38	62
Male	Percent	12	9	3	5	8	13	19	36	18	13	34	42	73
Female	Percent	11	10	4	7	10	13	17	22	3	14	14	33	49
Tertiary enrollment rate	r 10,000	28	..	..	..	..	..	..	..	..	..	..	..	..
Adult literacy rate														
Total	Percent	78	75	67	72	74	78	79	92	87	91	94	93	95
Male	Percent	86	83	77	80	82	86	88	96	92	93	98	96	98
Female	Percent	71	67	59	64	67	71	71	89	83	89	89	90	91
Youth literacy rate														
Total	Percent	94	93	91	91	94	94	95	95	92	98	95	95	96
Male	Percent	95	94	92	93	96	95	96	98	95	99	99	98	98
Female	Percent	92	92	90	90	92	93	94	93	90	98	90	93	93
MDG4: Reduce Child Mortality; MDG5: Improve Maternal Health														
Proportion with time to market less than 5 km	Percent	82	78	77	79	78	77	79	99	99	98	99	99	100
Morbidity	Percent	16	15	12	15	14	17	18	17	14	13	22	17	21
Action taken when sick	Percent	90	90	86	89	87	93	92	92	88	93	96	96	88
Health provider ownership														
Public	Percent	32	31	34	30	38	28	27	36	54	35	31	39	28
Private - modern medicine	Percent	51	49	48	46	41	53	55	59	41	56	65	54	69
Private - traditional healers	Percent	3	3	3	4	4	3	1	2	3	1	2	2	0
Other	Percent	7	8	7	12	11	7	6	1	0	1	2	2	1
Child survival and malnutrition														
Birth assisted by trained staff	Percent	47	42	30	37	40	50	61	75	62	71	76	88	94
1-year-olds immunisation coverage	Percent	72	68	52	74	69	72	80	86	73	96	83	97	92
1-year-olds immunized against measles	Percent	83	80	69	80	83	83	91	92	87	96	91	100	92
Stunting (6-59 months)	Percent	38	40	50	40	34	35	35	32	44	31	26	28	21
Wasting (6-59 months)	Percent	6	6	7	5	8	6	6	5	5	7	8	2	2
Underweight (6-59 months)	Percent	22	24	32	26	21	19	19	13	20	12	14	7	8
MDG7: Ensure Environmental Sustainability														
Access to sanitation facilities	Percent	86	83	73	80	82	86	89	95	88	89	95	99	97
Proportion with time to Water Source less than 1 hour	Percent	68	62	53	59	61	61	68	92	89	96	90	92	94
Proportion with time to Market less than 1 hour	Percent	82	78	77	79	78	77	79	99	99	98	99	99	100
Access to improved water source														
Total	Percent	49	39	29	39	34	41	46	86	81	82	83	91	90
Pipe (own tap)	Percent	17	10	3	6	8	9	17	44	32	33	38	45	59
Pipe borne	Percent	19	14	10	15	10	14	17	40	42	46	44	45	30
Well (Protected)	Percent	13	16	16	18	17	18	12	2	6	3	1	1	1
Traditional Fuel Use														
Total	Percent	82	96	100	99	99	97	89	26	48	26	28	26	13
Firewood	Percent	73	91	99	97	97	93	78	5	16	5	2	4	2
Charcoal	Percent	8	5	1	2	2	4	11	21	32	21	26	22	12

Expenditure Quintile

Kenya Welfare Monitoring Survey III 1997.

16-9. Madagascar

Indicators	Unit of measure	National total	Rural All	Rural Q1	Rural Q2	Rural Q3	Rural Q4	Rural Q5	Urban All	Urban Q1	Urban Q2	Urban Q3	Urban Q4	Urban Q5
Demographic Indicators														
Sample size (households)	Number	5,120	2,880	452	495	554	622	757	2,240	298	367	415	487	673
Total population	000s	14,631	11,377	2,277	2,275	2,277	2,272	2,275	3,254	652	649	651	650	651
Age dependency ratio	Number	0.9	1.0	1.3	1.2	1.0	0.9	0.7	0.7	1.1	0.9	0.7	0.6	0.5
Average household size	Number	5.1	5.2	6.7	6.1	5.4	4.9	3.8	4.9	6.8	5.5	5.1	4.5	3.5
Head of Household Characteristics														
Marital Status of head														
Monogamous male	Percent	76	77	77	81	81	80	69	72	74	73	73	73	67
Polygamous male	Percent	..	..	..	..	..	..	..	..	..	..	..	..	..
Single male	Percent	7	7	5	4	4	6	12	6	3	5	3	7	12
De facto female	Percent	8	8	10	7	8	7	8	8	10	11	7	8	5
De jure female	Percent	10	9	8	8	7	8	11	14	13	11	17	12	16
MDG1: Eradicate Extreme Poverty and Hunger														
Mean monthly expenditure	Malagasy francs	67,747	54,210	15,780	26,142	36,507	51,866	108,173	112,001	26,008	47,759	72,121	107,535	226,090
Mean monthly share on food	Percent	72	75	75	77	76	77	73	63	68	65	63	62	60
Mean monthly share on health	Percent	3	3	3	3	3	3	3	4	4	4	4	4	4
Mean monthly share on education	Percent	2	2	2	2	2	1	1	3	3	4	4	3	2
MDG2: Education and Literacy; MDG3: Promote Gender Equality														
Access to primary school (within 30 minutes)	Percent	..	..	..	..	..	..	..	..	..	..	..	..	..
Net primary enrollment rate														
Total	Percent	67	64	52	66	64	64	77	82	67	78	84	94	97
Male	Percent	67	63	55	63	65	63	74	82	66	74	91	97	95
Female	Percent	68	64	50	68	64	65	81	82	68	81	79	92	98
Net secondary enrollment rate														
Total	Percent	10	6	2	4	4	6	16	24	6	18	24	34	46
Male	Percent	9	6	1	3	3	8	14	23	5	20	18	30	53
Female	Percent	11	6	2	4	5	4	19	25	8	16	28	37	40
Tertiary enrollment rate	per 10,000	8	..	..	..	..	..	..	..	..	..	..	..	..
Adult literacy rate														
Total	Percent	67	61	44	58	58	66	74	84	66	81	85	90	94
Male	Percent	71	66	49	64	62	71	77	87	68	86	87	93	95
Female	Percent	63	57	40	52	54	61	70	82	63	76	83	87	93
Youth literacy rate														
Total	Percent	70	64	47	60	63	72	78	87	69	89	91	91	95
Male	Percent	70	65	47	62	64	74	76	87	66	92	89	92	96
Female	Percent	70	64	48	58	63	71	79	88	72	86	93	91	94
MDG4: Reduce Child Mortality; MDG5: Improve Maternal Health														
Proportion with time to market less than 5 km	Percent	..	..	..	..	..	..	..	..	..	..	..	..	..
Morbidity	Percent	11	11	10	10	11	12	13	9	9	11	8	9	9
Action taken when sick	Percent	46	42	29	39	41	48	52	61	56	58	61	64	68
Health provider ownership														
Public	Percent	59	61	76	69	68	59	47	53	62	70	56	39	39
Private - modern medicine	Percent	32	30	20	22	23	32	42	36	23	21	36	48	53
Private - traditional healers	Percent	4	4	3	6	6	2	5	4	4	5	4	5	2
Other	Percent	2	3	1	2	2	3	4	1	1	2	1	1	1
Child survival and malnutrition														
Birth assisted by trained staff	Percent	..	..	..	..	..	..	..	..	..	..	..	..	..
1-year-olds immunisation coverage	Percent	61	57	45	57	51	63	76	76	70	78	63	84	91
1-year-olds immunized against measles	Percent	..	..	..	..	..	..	..	..	..	..	..	..	..
Stunting (6-59 months)	Percent	49	50	50	48	50	52	49	44	48	51	44	42	32
Wasting (6-59 months)	Percent	14	15	16	15	16	13	10	14	17	17	11	15	11
Underweight (6-59 months)	Percent	35	35	40	33	40	33	29	31	36	36	27	34	18
MDG7: Ensure Environmental Sustainability														
Access to sanitation facilities	Percent	52	43	32	36	39	46	54	80	60	70	81	84	93
Proportion with time to Water Source less than 1 hour	Percent	..	..	..	..	..	..	..	..	..	..	..	..	..
Proportion with time to Market less than 1 hour	Percent	..	..	..	..	..	..	..	..	..	..	..	..	..
Access to improved water source														
Total	Percent	24	10	3	6	6	10	19	70	43	57	71	76	85
Pipe (own tap)	Percent	4	1	..	..	..	1	2	15	1	3	7	16	32
Pipe borne	Percent	19	8	3	5	6	8	15	52	40	51	60	54	51
Well (Protected)	Percent	1	1	0	1	0	1	2	3	2	3	4	6	2
Traditional Fuel Use														
Total	Percent	98	99	99	99	99	98	98	95	98	98	97	96	89
Firewood	Percent	80	92	99	98	96	92	80	40	84	63	39	28	14
Charcoal	Percent	18	7	0	1	3	6	18	55	14	35	59	69	75

Enquête Prioritaire 1999.

16-10. Malawi

Expenditure Quintile

Indicators	Unit of measure	National total	Rural All	Q1	Q2	Q3	Q4	Q5	Urban All	Q1	Q2	Q3	Q4	Q5
Demographic Indicators														
Sample size (households)	Number	6,586	5,657	902	1,024	1,106	1,198	1,427	929	200	184	174	194	177
Total population	000s	9,795	8,795	1,760	1,759	1,758	1,759	1,759	1,000	200	200	200	200	200
Age dependency ratio	Number	0.9	0.9	1.2	1.0	0.9	0.8	0.7	0.6	0.9	0.7	0.6	0.5	0.4
Average household size	Number	4.4	4.4	5.3	4.8	4.5	4.2	3.6	4.1	5.4	4.5	4.2	3.5	3.6
Head of Household Characteristics														
Marital Status of head														
Monogamous male	Percent	68	68	65	68	71	70	66	70	78	80	75	65	56
Polygamous male	Percent	1	1	0	1	1	1	1	..	..	..	..	..	..
Single male	Percent	6	5	2	3	3	6	11	14	4	4	9	21	24
De facto female	Percent	7	8	10	8	8	6	7	3	5	3	2	2	4
De jure female	Percent	18	18	23	20	18	18	15	13	13	13	13	11	17
MDG1: Eradicate Extreme Poverty and Hunger														
Mean monthly expenditure	Malawi kwacha	431	308	91	155	218	310	637	1,456	298	510	759	1,212	3,820
Mean monthly share on food	Percent	71	74	78	77	77	75	67	42	56	52	46	40	26
Mean monthly share on health	Percent	1	1	1	1	1	1	1	2	1	2	1	2	2
Mean monthly share on education	Percent	0	0	0	0	0	0	1	2	0	1	1	1	4
MDG2: Education and Literacy; MDG3: Promote Gender Equality														
Access to primary school (within 30 minutes)	Percent	..	..	..	..	..	..	..	..	..	..	..	..	..
Net primary enrollment rate														
Total	Percent	62	61	60	58	59	61	68	70	70	63	76	75	68
Male	Percent	61	60	58	59	55	59	70	70	62	66	80	76	71
Female	Percent	63	62	63	57	62	63	66	70	80	60	72	73	65
Net secondary enrollment rate														
Total	Percent	5	3	1	3	2	3	6	20	11	13	21	20	34
Male	Percent	5	3	1	4	2	3	7	21	12	11	25	20	36
Female	Percent	5	3	..	3	2	3	5	19	9	15	16	19	33
Tertiary enrollment rate	per 10,000	4	..	..	..	..	..	..	..	..	..	..	..	..
Adult literacy rate														
Total	Percent	51	47	35	44	44	50	58	85	74	80	93	91	86
Male	Percent	62	58	47	55	55	61	68	89	83	88	96	90	86
Female	Percent	41	37	26	33	35	40	48	82	65	73	90	92	87
Youth literacy rate														
Total	Percent	63	59	50	57	57	63	66	88	79	84	96	94	87
Male	Percent	69	66	58	62	64	68	73	90	85	88	98	93	87
Female	Percent	58	54	42	53	51	58	61	87	75	81	95	95	87
MDG4: Reduce Child Mortality; MDG5: Improve Maternal Health														
Proportion with time to market less than 5 km	Percent	68	64	63	63	63	65	66	98	96	98	99	98	99
Morbidity	Percent	28	29	24	27	30	31	34	15	16	18	15	15	13
Action taken when sick	Percent	..	..	..	..	..	..	..	..	..	..	..	..	..
Health provider ownership														
Public	Percent	..	..	..	..	..	..	..	..	..	..	..	..	..
Private - modern medicine	Percent	..	..	..	..	..	..	..	..	..	..	..	..	..
Private - traditional healers	Percent	..	..	..	..	..	..	..	..	..	..	..	..	..
Other	Percent	..	..	..	..	..	..	..	..	..	..	..	..	..
Child survival and malnutrition														
Birth assisted by trained staff	Percent	..	..	..	..	..	..	..	..	..	..	..	..	..
1-year-olds immunisation coverage	Percent	87	86	89	85	83	90	84	97	91	100	100	100	100
1-year-olds immunized against measles	Percent	89	89	91	89	87	91	85	99	96	100	100	100	100
Stunting (6-59 months)	Percent	56	56	58	56	57	58	51	57	54	47	67	68	55
Wasting (6-59 months)	Percent	11	11	11	12	11	9	11	10	14	17	7	4	..
Underweight (6-59 months)	Percent	25	26	33	22	27	23	25	17	27	18	11	3	5
MDG7: Ensure Environmental Sustainability														
Access to sanitation facilities	Percent	..	..	..	..	..	..	..	..	..	..	..	..	..
Proportion with time to Water Source less than 1 hour	Percent	..	..	..	..	..	..	..	..	..	..	..	..	..
Proportion with time to Market less than 1 hour	Percent	68	64	63	63	63	65	66	98	96	98	99	98	99
Access to improved water source														
Total	Percent	50	45	47	46	43	43	46	89	79	83	92	96	93
Pipe (own tap)	Percent	6	1	0	0	1	1	3	43	13	22	44	49	72
Pipe borne	Percent	21	19	20	21	18	18	20	39	52	51	45	35	19
Well (Protected)	Percent	23	25	27	24	25	25	24	8	14	11	3	11	2
Traditional Fuel Use														
Total	Percent	94	98	99	99	97	97	96	67	94	88	78	59	29
Firewood	Percent	92	97	99	99	97	97	96	49	76	68	56	40	18
Charcoal	Percent	2	0	0	0	..	1	1	18	18	20	22	18	12

Malawi Integrated Household Survey 1997/1998.

Household Welfare

16-11. Mozambique

Indicators	Unit of measure	National total	Rural All	Rural Q1	Rural Q2	Rural Q3	Rural Q4	Rural Q5	Urban All	Urban Q1	Urban Q2	Urban Q3	Urban Q4	Urban Q5
Demographic Indicators														
Sample size (households)	Number	8,250	5,811	987	948	1,059	1,215	1,602	2,439	337	383	463	519	737
Total population	000s	15,867	12,634	2,527	2,518	2,536	2,527	2,527	3,233	646	647	647	647	646
Age dependency ratio	Number	0.9	0.9	1.2	1.1	1.0	0.9	0.6	0.9	1.3	1.1	0.9	0.8	0.6
Average household size	Number	4.8	4.7	6.6	5.8	5.1	4.3	3.2	5.5	6.2	6.1	5.7	5.2	4.5
Head of Household Characteristics														
Marital Status of head														
Monogamous male	Percent	65	65	66	68	67	66	60	66	63	71	67	65	65
Polygamous male	Percent	8	9	15	10	10	8	7	3	2	5	5	4	2
Single male	Percent	5	5	2	2	4	4	9	8	2	6	6	10	14
De facto female	Percent	6	6	5	9	6	6	7	5	7	4	5	5	6
De jure female	Percent	15	15	13	12	14	16	17	17	25	15	18	16	13
MDG1: Eradicate Extreme Poverty and Hunger														
Mean monthly expenditure	Mozambican meticais	192,481	182,572	53,118	86,604	119,027	164,442	350,674	237,861	52,180	93,179	132,226	203,191	592,973
Mean monthly share on food	Percent	68	70	68	71	72	71	69	59	63	65	61	60	51
Mean monthly share on health	Percent	0	0	0	0	0	0	0	1	1	1	0	0	0
Mean monthly share on education	Percent	0	0	1	1	0	0	0	1	2	1	1	1	1
MDG2: Education and Literacy; MDG3: Promote Gender Equality														
Access to primary school (within 30 minutes)	Percent	..	..	..	..	..	..	..	..	..	..	..	..	..
Net primary enrollment rate														
Total	Percent	36	32	25	30	33	36	39	54	34	48	60	68	71
Male	Percent	38	35	27	32	36	39	42	54	34	53	63	70	66
Female	Percent	33	29	22	27	31	33	35	53	34	43	57	67	76
Net secondary enrollment rate														
Total	Percent	10	5	3	3	6	7	7	26	11	15	23	34	44
Male	Percent	10	6	4	3	7	8	9	26	14	19	22	37	40
Female	Percent	9	4	2	3	4	5	5	25	8	11	24	31	47
Tertiary enrollment rate	per 10,000	7	..	..	..	..	..	..	..	..	..	..	..	..
Adult literacy rate														
Total	Percent	41	33	28	33	35	33	35	72	52	62	73	79	86
Male	Percent	58	51	44	51	53	52	53	84	70	80	84	88	94
Female	Percent	25	17	14	16	19	16	20	60	36	45	63	70	78
Youth literacy rate														
Total	Percent	51	42	35	42	47	39	45	82	71	75	83	86	90
Male	Percent	64	56	42	56	61	57	63	88	79	87	89	91	93
Female	Percent	40	29	28	28	34	25	32	76	61	65	78	82	88
MDG4: Reduce Child Mortality; MDG5: Improve Maternal Health														
Proportion with time to market less than 5 km	Percent	..	..	..	..	..	..	..	..	..	..	..	..	..
Morbidity	Percent	11	12	9	10	11	13	15	11	11	10	10	12	11
Action taken when sick	Percent	60	57	54	58	55	59	59	74	64	71	73	83	76
Health provider ownership														
Public	Percent	78	74	68	76	73	82	72	88	90	83	94	85	89
Private - modern medicine	Percent	6	5	3	6	6	4	6	9	10	13	4	13	7
Private - traditional healers	Percent	14	18	23	16	18	13	21	2	0	4	2	2	4
Other	Percent	2	2	6	2	2	1	1	0	..	0	0	0	0
Child survival and malnutrition														
Birth assisted by trained staff	Percent	..	..	..	..	..	..	..	..	..	..	..	..	..
1-year-olds immunisation coverage	Percent	43	35	30	32	36	38	41	76	82	53	86	85	80
1-year-olds immunized against measles	Percent	57	50	42	56	46	48	56	88	84	84	93	92	91
Stunting (6-59 months)	Percent	55	61	61	62	62	59	58	34	49	36	30	27	24
Wasting (6-59 months)	Percent	9	9	11	7	7	11	8	9	13	11	6	6	7
Underweight (6-59 months)	Percent	37	40	49	38	39	36	37	25	38	27	20	18	19
MDG7: Ensure Environmental Sustainability														
Access to sanitation facilities	Percent	35	29	26	29	28	29	29	67	44	55	70	76	81
Proportion with time to Water Source less than 1 hour	Percent	..	..	..	..	..	..	..	..	..	..	..	..	..
Proportion with time to Market less than 1 hour	Percent	..	..	..	..	..	..	..	..	..	..	..	..	..
Access to improved water source														
Total	Percent	18	11	9	8	10	10	14	51	42	40	48	53	65
Pipe (own tap)	Percent	2	0	0	0	0	0	1	9	0	2	5	9	25
Pipe borne	Percent	16	11	9	8	10	10	14	41	41	38	43	44	40
Well (Protected)	Percent	..	..	..	..	..	..	..	..	..	..	..	..	..
Traditional Fuel Use														
Total	Percent	97	99	99	99	99	98	99	87	97	96	94	86	70
Firewood	Percent	90	99	99	99	99	98	98	50	70	66	51	41	31
Charcoal	Percent	7	0	0	0	0	0	1	37	27	30	44	45	38

Inquérito Nacional aos Agregados Familiares Sobre as Condições de Vida 1996.

16-12. Sao Tome and Principe

			Expenditure Quintile											
			Rural						Urban					
Indicators	Unit of measure	National total	All	Q1	Q2	Q3	Q4	Q5	All	Q1	Q2	Q3	Q4	Q5
Demographic Indicators														
Sample size (households)	Number	2,416	1,173	179	197	215	244	338	1,243	187	202	242	264	348
Total population	000s	128	57	11	11	11	11	11	71	14	14	14	14	14
Age dependency ratio	Number	0.9	1.0	1.3	1.1	1.0	1.0	0.6	0.8	1.1	1.0	0.8	0.8	0.6
Average household size	Number	4.6	4.5	6.3	5.7	4.9	4.2	3.0	4.6	6.2	5.5	4.9	4.4	3.3
Head of Household Characteristics														
Marital Status of head														
Monogamous male	Percent	51	53	62	66	66	48	37	50	51	50	46	56	46
Polygamous male	Percent	..	..	..	..	..	..	..	..	..	..	..	..	..
Single male	Percent	16	18	9	5	10	16	36	15	4	9	12	14	26
De facto female	Percent	7	6	5	5	5	8	7	8	7	11	12	5	8
De jure female	Percent	25	23	25	24	19	27	20	27	37	29	30	25	20
MDG1: Eradicate Extreme Poverty and Hunger														
Mean monthly expenditure	Sao Tome and Principe	451,490	318,313	80,362	128,371	175,196	243,054	679,373	560,829	108,471	179,366	252,850	359,041	1,403,366
Mean monthly share on food	Percent	72	75	78	77	78	76	71	69	76	74	69	68	62
Mean monthly share on health	Percent	3	3	3	3	2	3	3	4	3	3	4	3	5
Mean monthly share on education	Percent	2	2	2	2	2	2	1	3	2	3	3	3	2
MDG2: Education and Literacy; MDG3: Promote Gender Equality														
Access to primary school (within 30 minutes)	Percent	34	33	46	44	37	35	16	35	51	39	35	38	23
Net primary enrollment rate														
Total	Percent	70	67	68	68	63	68	67	73	71	73	78	73	74
Male	Percent	71	70	67	75	62	71	70	73	72	71	75	80	66
Female	Percent	69	64	68	60	63	64	63	73	69	75	81	65	79
Net secondary enrollment rate														
Total	Percent	43	29	13	26	23	34	50	52	32	39	64	62	64
Male	Percent	43	29	15	24	24	42	47	52	30	41	65	66	66
Female	Percent	42	28	11	28	22	25	51	52	35	37	62	59	63
Tertiary enrollment rate	per 10,000	..	..	..	..	..	..	..	..	..	..	..	..	..
Adult literacy rate														
Total	Percent	83	80	76	82	79	77	85	86	78	83	85	89	91
Male	Percent	92	89	87	89	89	87	92	94	90	92	92	95	97
Female	Percent	76	72	67	76	70	69	77	79	68	75	80	84	84
Youth literacy rate														
Total	Percent	94	92	90	92	91	91	95	96	91	94	98	98	96
Male	Percent	95	93	95	91	90	94	96	96	94	96	97	98	98
Female	Percent	93	91	86	92	92	88	95	95	88	92	98	98	95
MDG4: Reduce Child Mortality; MDG5: Improve Maternal Health														
Proportion with time to market less than 5 km	Percent	87	81	74	73	80	86	86	92	90	88	91	93	94
Morbidity	Percent	18	15	12	14	14	17	20	19	12	19	19	22	24
Action taken when sick	Percent	48	45	41	45	40	50	47	50	38	44	50	56	57
Health provider ownership														
Public	Percent	70	81	94	88	78	83	68	64	80	78	68	62	53
Private - modern medicine	Percent	25	14	4	9	16	10	27	31	15	18	29	32	43
Private - traditional healers	Percent	3	2	..	3	..	3	4	4	5	1	3	6	2
Other	Percent	1	2	2	..	6	3	1	1	..	3	..	..	2
Child survival and malnutrition														
Birth assisted by trained staff	Percent	..	..	..	..	..	..	..	..	..	..	..	..	..
1-year-olds immunisation coverage	Percent	..	..	..	..	..	..	..	..	..	..	..	..	..
1-year-olds immunized against measles	Percent	..	..	..	..	..	..	..	..	..	..	..	..	..
Stunting (6-59 months)	Percent	..	..	..	..	..	..	..	..	..	..	..	..	..
Wasting (6-59 months)	Percent	..	..	..	..	..	..	..	..	..	..	..	..	..
Underweight (6-59 months)	Percent	..	..	..	..	..	..	..	..	..	..	..	..	..
MDG7: Ensure Environmental Sustainability														
Access to sanitation facilities	Percent	31	23	21	16	23	21	30	37	15	30	38	42	49
Proportion with time to Water Source less than 1 hour	Percent	88	93	93	94	93	95	92	84	82	80	87	86	85
Proportion with time to Market less than 1 hour	Percent	87	81	74	73	80	86	86	92	90	88	91	93	94
Access to improved water source														
Total	Percent	77	67	74	70	64	70	63	84	82	79	81	89	88
Pipe (own tap)	Percent	20	10	7	9	7	13	12	27	12	20	26	29	40
Pipe borne	Percent	8	13	19	15	15	11	10	4	4	3	5	5	4
Well (Protected)	Percent	49	44	48	46	42	46	41	53	65	56	49	56	43
Traditional Fuel Use														
Total	Percent	84	95	100	98	99	94	88	75	96	83	81	72	57
Firewood	Percent	73	91	98	96	97	90	82	59	88	74	63	50	36
Charcoal	Percent	11	4	1	2	2	4	6	16	8	9	18	22	20

Enquête Nationale sur les Conditions de Vie des Ménages, 2000.

Household Welfare

16-13. Uganda

			Rural						Urban					
Indicators	Unit of measure	National total	All	Q1	Q2	Q3	Q4	Q5	All	Q1	Q2	Q3	Q4	Q5
Demographic Indicators														
Sample size (households)	Number	10,696	8,344	1,233	1,456	1,621	1,833	2,201	2,352	562	470	444	498	378
Total population	000s	22,035	19,067	3,810	3,813	3,816	3,813	3,815	2,968	593	594	594	592	595
Age dependency ratio	Number	1.2	1.3	1.5	1.5	1.4	1.2	0.9	0.9	1.2	1.0	1.1	0.7	0.5
Average household size	Number	5.4	5.5	6.5	6.2	5.8	5.2	4.3	4.6	5.7	5.1	4.6	3.9	4.1
Head of Household Characteristics														
Marital Status of head														
Monogamous male	Percent	62	63	60	69	67	66	55	57	60	59	57	53	57
Polygamous male	Percent	2	3	3	3	3	2	2	0	1	0	1	..	0
Single male	Percent	9	8	3	4	4	7	18	11	4	10	11	16	14
De facto female	Percent	9	9	18	7	8	6	7	8	8	9	10	6	7
De jure female	Percent	18	17	17	17	17	18	18	23	27	22	21	25	22
MDG1: Eradicate Extreme Poverty and Hunger														
Mean monthly expenditure	Uganda shillings	28,291	21,491	6,692	11,069	15,155	20,997	43,759	64,718	15,999	28,028	40,751	62,152	153,618
Mean monthly share on food	Percent	57	59	63	61	60	60	55	43	52	48	45	41	32
Mean monthly share on health	Percent	4	4	3	4	4	4	5	3	3	3	3	3	3
Mean monthly share on education	Percent	3	3	2	2	3	3	4	6	4	6	6	6	6
MDG2: Education and Literacy; MDG3: Promote Gender Equality														
Access to primary school (within 30 minutes)	Percent	..	..	..	..	..	..	..	..	..	..	..	..	..
Net primary enrollment rate														
Total	Percent	63	61	50	61	62	67	70	74	64	73	77	79	80
Male	Percent	63	61	53	61	62	65	69	76	63	75	82	81	83
Female	Percent	62	61	46	61	63	69	71	72	65	71	72	77	77
Net secondary enrollment rate														
Total	Percent	13	10	3	6	8	11	23	29	17	20	30	40	36
Male	Percent	12	10	3	7	8	9	21	31	16	10	29	48	49
Female	Percent	14	11	3	5	8	13	24	28	18	29	30	34	29
Tertiary enrollment rate	per 10,000	17	..	..	..	..	..	..	..	..	..	..	..	..
Adult literacy rate														
Total	Percent	67	63	44	58	65	69	76	88	73	83	91	92	96
Male	Percent	79	76	63	74	79	79	83	93	84	88	96	94	99
Female	Percent	56	51	29	42	52	60	69	83	64	78	86	89	93
Youth literacy rate														
Total	Percent	79	76	56	72	79	82	87	92	86	85	93	96	95
Male	Percent	85	83	67	82	85	85	89	96	92	89	98	98	99
Female	Percent	74	70	44	60	73	78	86	89	83	82	89	93	93
MDG4: Reduce Child Mortality; MDG5: Improve Maternal Health														
Proportion with time to market less than 5 km	Percent	..	..	..	..	..	..	..	..	..	..	..	..	..
Morbidity	Percent	28	28	26	27	28	29	30	26	26	27	24	27	25
Action taken when sick	Percent	92	92	83	92	93	94	95	96	90	97	98	97	99
Health provider ownership														
Public	Percent	14	15	13	13	15	16	16	14	19	13	17	11	11
Private - modern medicine	Percent	17	17	14	17	17	16	20	16	17	10	17	27	10
Private - traditional healers	Percent	1	1	1	1	1	1	1	1	1	1	0	1	1
Other	Percent	68	67	71	69	67	68	63	69	63	76	66	62	79
Child survival and malnutrition														
Birth assisted by trained staff	Percent	..	..	..	..	..	..	..	..	..	..	..	..	..
1-year-olds immunisation coverage	Percent	..	..	..	..	..	..	..	..	..	..	..	..	..
1-year-olds immunized against measles	Percent	..	..	..	..	..	..	..	..	..	..	..	..	..
Stunting (6-59 months)	Percent	..	..	..	..	..	..	..	..	..	..	..	..	..
Wasting (6-59 months)	Percent	..	..	..	..	..	..	..	..	..	..	..	..	..
Underweight (6-59 months)	Percent	..	..	..	..	..	..	..	..	..	..	..	..	..
MDG7: Ensure Environmental Sustainability														
Access to sanitation facilities	Percent	86	84	58	82	88	91	93	99	94	99	100	100	100
Proportion with time to Water Source less than 1 hour	Percent	..	..	..	..	..	..	..	..	..	..	..	..	..
Proportion with time to Market less than 1 hour	Percent	..	..	..	..	..	..	..	..	..	..	..	..	..
Access to improved water source														
Total	Percent	58	52	49	51	50	53	55	93	84	90	94	97	98
Pipe (own tap)	Percent	2	1	0	0	1	1	1	7	2	2	3	6	19
Pipe borne	Percent	11	3	1	2	2	3	6	55	31	49	59	63	67
Well (Protected)	Percent	45	48	48	48	47	49	48	31	51	39	32	29	12
Traditional Fuel Use														
Total	Percent	98	99	100	99	99	99	98	90	96	96	94	88	78
Firewood	Percent	83	95	99	98	97	96	88	20	50	24	19	12	3
Charcoal	Percent	14	4	1	1	2	3	10	70	47	72	75	76	75

Uganda National Household Survey 1999/2000.

16-14. Zambia

Indicators	Unit of measure	National total	Rural All	Q1	Q2	Q3	Q4	Q5	Urban All	Q1	Q2	Q3	Q4	Q5
Demographic Indicators														
Sample size (households)	Number	16,422	8,317	1,414	1,461	1,561	1,655	2,226	8,105	1,298	1,384	1,518	1,752	2,153
Total population	000s	9,989	6,276	1,239	1,252	1,265	1,260	1,260	3,712	712	743	752	752	753
Age dependency ratio	Number	0.9	0.9	1.0	1.0	0.9	0.9	0.8	0.8	1.0	0.9	0.8	0.7	0.5
Average household size	Number	5.4	5.3	6.0	5.7	5.5	5.2	4.3	5.5	6.9	6.3	6.0	5.2	4.2
Head of Household Characteristics														
Marital Status of head														
Monogamous male	Percent	70	70	66	69	75	73	67	70	68	74	76	72	62
Polygamous male	Percent	..	..	..	..	..	..	..	..	..	..	..	..	..
Single male	Percent	7	6	3	5	4	7	11	10	6	6	7	9	17
De facto female	Percent	3	4	4	5	4	3	4	2	2	2	2	3	2
De jure female	Percent	19	19	26	21	17	17	18	18	23	18	16	16	19
MDG1: Eradicate Extreme Poverty and Hunger														
Mean monthly expenditure	Zambian kwacha	46,798	32,948	5,268	11,113	17,218	27,740	85,708	71,512	13,061	25,361	37,361	56,295	174,264
Mean monthly share on food	Percent	68	74	76	77	75	72	70	57	67	63	59	56	45
Mean monthly share on health	Percent	1	1	1	1	1	1	2	2	1	2	2	2	2
Mean monthly share on education	Percent	2	2	3	2	2	1	1	4	4	4	4	3	3
MDG2: Education and Literacy; MDG3: Promote Gender Equality														
Access to primary school (within 30 minutes)	Percent	..	..	..	..	..	..	..	..	..	..	..	..	..
Net primary enrollment rate														
Total	Percent	66	59	46	55	60	67	70	77	65	75	78	84	86
Male	Percent	65	59	49	56	59	66	70	77	64	77	77	82	87
Female	Percent	66	59	44	55	60	68	69	77	65	73	79	84	86
Net secondary enrollment rate														
Total	Percent	23	14	8	10	14	18	21	38	21	31	36	45	55
Male	Percent	25	16	10	11	16	20	24	40	21	33	38	52	58
Female	Percent	22	12	5	8	12	17	18	36	21	28	34	40	53
Tertiary enrollment rate	per 10,000	34	..	..	..	..	..	..	..	..	..	..	..	..
Adult literacy rate														
Total	Percent	..	..	..	..	..	..	..	..	..	..	..	..	..
Male	Percent	..	..	..	..	..	..	..	..	..	..	..	..	..
Female	Percent	..	..	..	..	..	..	..	..	..	..	..	..	..
Youth literacy rate														
Total	Percent	..	..	..	..	..	..	..	..	..	..	..	..	..
Male	Percent	..	..	..	..	..	..	..	..	..	..	..	..	..
Female	Percent	..	..	..	..	..	..	..	..	..	..	..	..	..
MDG4: Reduce Child Mortality; MDG5: Improve Maternal Health														
Proportion with time to market less than 5 km	Percent	..	..	..	..	..	..	..	..	..	..	..	..	..
Morbidity	Percent	11	12	9	12	12	14	15	10	10	9	8	10	11
Action taken when sick	Percent	37	33	30	31	31	34	38	46	38	43	43	45	56
Health provider ownership														
Public	Percent	..	..	..	..	..	..	..	..	..	..	..	..	..
Private - modern medicine	Percent	..	..	..	..	..	..	..	..	..	..	..	..	..
Private - traditional healers	Percent	..	..	..	..	..	..	..	..	..	..	..	..	..
Other	Percent	..	..	..	..	..	..	..	..	..	..	..	..	..
Child survival and malnutrition														
Birth assisted by trained staff	Percent	..	..	..	..	..	..	..	..	..	..	..	..	..
1-year-olds immunisation coverage	Percent	59	56	46	54	56	57	67	64	64	68	58	61	70
1-year-olds immunized against measles	Percent	89	87	79	88	88	90	92	94	95	92	93	92	95
Stunting (6-59 months)	Percent	62	66	70	65	65	62	65	57	64	64	55	54	45
Wasting (6-59 months)	Percent	6	6	8	5	6	5	5	5	6	5	5	5	5
Underweight (6-59 months)	Percent	27	30	37	30	32	26	24	23	31	27	20	20	14
MDG7: Ensure Environmental Sustainability														
Access to sanitation facilities	Percent	81	71	61	68	72	73	77	99	98	99	100	99	100
Proportion with time to Water Source less than 1 hour	Percent	..	..	..	..	..	..	..	..	..	..	..	..	..
Proportion with time to Market less than 1 hour	Percent	..	..	..	..	..	..	..	..	..	..	..	..	..
Access to improved water source														
Total	Percent	56	37	33	35	38	36	42	89	79	87	91	91	93
Pipe (own tap)	Percent	16	1	0	0	1	1	4	41	27	35	39	42	55
Pipe borne	Percent	17	4	3	3	3	4	5	40	41	42	43	43	32
Well (Protected)	Percent	23	32	29	31	34	31	33	8	11	9	8	7	6
Traditional Fuel Use														
Total	Percent	85	99	100	100	99	99	97	60	85	74	65	54	37
Firewood	Percent	62	90	95	93	91	89	84	12	29	11	9	6	8
Charcoal	Percent	23	9	5	7	9	9	13	48	57	63	56	47	29

Zambia Living Conditions Monitoring Survey II, 1998.

Technical notes

Burkina Faso

Data source. Burkina Faso's Institut National de la Statistique et de la Démographie carried out the "Enquête Prioritaire II sur les Conditions de Vie des Ménages au Burkina." Data were collected between May 1998 and August 1998. The project was funded by the Government of Burkina Faso, the World Bank, the African Development Bank (ADB), and the United Nations through the UNDP.

Household was defined as the basic socio-economic unit in which the different members—related or living in the same house or property—put together their resources and jointly meet their basic needs, including food, under the authority of one person who is recognized as the head.

Literacy. Household members aged five and up who could both read and write a simple sentence in any language were considered literate.

The survey had no information on the following topics: birth assistance and immunization.

Burundi

Data source. The Institut de Statistiques et d'Études économiques of Burundi, in conjunction with the UNDP, carried out the "Enquête Prioritaire—Étude nationale sur les conditions de vie des populations."

Household was defined as those people who habitually live and eat their meals in the same compound. One member is recognized as the head.

Literacy. Household members aged five and up who could both read and write were considered literate.

The survey had no information on the following topics: birth assistance, health provider ownership, and immunizations.

Cameroon

Data source. Cameroon's Bureau Central des Recensements et des Enquêtes of the Direction de la Statistique et de la Comptabilité carried out the "Enquête Camerounaise auprès des Ménages."

Household. Defined by the survey to be those people who live under the same roof, take their meals together or in little groups, put some or all of their incomes together for the group's spending purposes, at the head of household's discretion.

Literacy. Household members aged five and up who could both read and write were considered literate.

The survey had no information on the following topics: access to primary services.

Côte d'Ivoire

Data source. The Institut National de la Statistique carried out the "Enquête Niveau de Vie," a priority survey, in 1998.

Household. This was defined as a person or a group of people who live under the same roof, share the same meals, and recognize one person as the head.

Literacy. Household members aged five and up who could both read and write a simple sentence in any language were considered literate.

The survey had no information on the following topics: access to primary services, child survival and malnutrition, employment categories and job types, and health provider ownership.

Ethiopia

Data source. "The 1999/2000 Household Income, Consumption, and Expenditure Survey (HICES)" was carried out by the Central Statistical Office. The data collection process was carried out between June 1999 to February 2000.

Household. This was defined as a person or a group of people who live under the same roof, share the same meals, and recognize one person as the head.

Literacy. Persons were considered as literate if they could read and write a sentence in the national language.

The survey had no information on the following topics: access to primary school, and birth assisted by trained staff.

The Gambia

Data source. The Central Department of Statistics of the Ministry of Economic Planning and Industrial Development of Ghana carried out the "1998 National Household Poverty Survey," an integrated survey. Data was collected between April 1998 and May 1998.

Household. This was defined as the set of people who normally ate and lived together for six out of the twelve months prior to the survey.

Literacy. Such information is not reliably available for this survey; less than one in 1,100 who could have answered this question did so.

The survey had no information on the following topics: access to primary services, birth assisted by trained staff, cooking fuel, and immunization.

Ghana

Data source. The Ghana Statistical Service carried out the "Ghana Living Standards Survey IV," an integrated survey. Data collection was done between April 1988 and March 1989.

Household. In this survey, a household was defined as a group of people who have usually slept in the same dwelling and have taken their meals together for at least nine of the twelve months preceding the interview.

Literacy. Household members aged five and up who could both read and write a simple sentence in English or any local language were considered literate.

The survey had no information on the following topics: access to health center and primary school, and child survival and malnutrition.

Kenya

Data source. The Kenya Central Bureau of Statistics carried out data collection for the 1997 Welfare Monitoring Survey III, a priority survey, in March and April 1997.

Sample. Due to logistical and financial constraints, the survey did not adequately cover the North Eastern and parts of the Eastern provinces.

Household. This was defined as the set of people who normally ate and lived together for six out of the twelve months prior to the survey.

Literacy. Literacy was defined as the ability to read and write.

Madagascar

Data source. The Institut National de la Statistiques carried out the "Enquête Prioritaire auprès des ménages" in 1999. The project was funded by the government of Madagascar and the World Bank (IDA).

Household. This was defined as the set of people who have or do not have family links between them, who live and sleep in the same housing, and take their meals together regularly. The housing may be an individual house, an apartment, or one or more rooms in a larger building. The household is headed by one individual whose authority is recognized by all in the household.

Literacy. Household members aged five and up who had completed at least four years of primary school or could read and write were considered to be literate.

The survey had no information on the following topics: access to primary services, birth assisted by trained staff, immunization against measles, and owner occupancy rates.

Malawi

Data source. The Malawi National Statistics Office carried out the Integrated Household Survey from November 1997 to October 1998.

Household. This survey defined household as either a person living alone or a group of people, either related or unrelated, who lived together as a single unit in the sense that they have common housekeeping arrangements (that is, shared or were supported by a common budget). Someone who did not live with the household during the survey period was not counted as a current member of the household.

Literacy was defined as the ability to read and write a simple sentence for those who had not attended school in the past two months, and defined based upon educational attainment for those who had attended school in the past two months.

The survey had no information on the following topics: access to primary school, access to a water source, access to sanitation facilities, birth assisted by trained staff, and health provider ownership.

Mozambique

Data source. The Instituto Nacional de Estatistiqua carried out the Inquérito Nacional aos Agregados Familiares sobre as Condições de Vida, an integrated survey.

Household was defined as the set of people who partly or totally shared their expenditures, had not been absent for more than six months out of the previous year, and were not domestic help. In the case of polygamous households, each wife and her children were considered to be a separate household.

Literacy. Literacy was defined as their ability to read and write in Portuguese.

The survey had no information on the following topics: access to a health center, access to market, access to primary school, birth assisted by trained staff, immunization coverage, and expenditure on health or education.

São Tomé and Principe

Data source. The Instituto Nacional de Estatistica of the Ministério de Planomento, Finanças e Cooperaçao carried out the Enquête sur les Conditions de Vie des Ménages in 2000. The project was financed by the Government of São Tomé and Principe with assistance from the African Development Bank and the United Nations Development Program. Technical assistance was provided by the International Labor Organization.

Household. Defined by the survey as the set of people, related or not, who live together under the same roof, put their resources together, and address as a unit their primary needs, under the authority of one person whom they recognize as the head of the household.

Literacy. Defined as the ability to read and write a simple sentence.

The survey had no information on the following topics: child survival and malnutrition, and self-employment.

Uganda

Data source. The Uganda Bureau of Statistics carried out the National Household Survey. Data collection occurred between August 1999 and July 2000. The project was funded by the Government of Uganda and the World Bank. Statistics Denmark and the World Bank provided consultants for technical support.

Sample. The survey did not collect data in the Kitgum, Gulu, Kasese, and Bundibugio districts.

Household. Defined by the survey as those individuals who normally eat and live together.

Literacy. If individuals had answered questions about the ability to read and write, they were considered to be literate if they could do both. Otherwise, the level of education was used to make this determination.

The survey had no information on the following topics: access to primary school, access to a health center, access to market, and birth assisted by trained staff.

Zambia

Data source. The Zambian Central Statistical Office carried out the "Living Conditions Monitoring Survey II." Data collection was done between November 1998 and December 1998.

Household. A household was defined as a group of persons who normally cooked, ate, and lived together.

These people may or may not be related by blood, but make common provision for food or other essentials for living, and they have one person whom they all regarded as the head of the household.

Literacy. No information on literacy is available in the survey.

The survey had no information on the following topics: access to primary school, health provider ownership, and birth assisted by trained staff.

UNESCO class cohorts for the net enrollment statistics in Chapter 16

	Primary school		Secondary school	
Country	Entrance age	Duration	Entrance age	Duration
Burkina Faso	7	6	12	7
Burundi	7	6	13	7
Cameroon	6	6	12	7
Côte d'Ivoire	6	6	12	7
Ethiopia	7	4	11	8
Gambia, The	6	6	12	6
Ghana	6	6	12	6
Kenya	6	7	13	5
Madagascar	6	5	11	7
Malawi	6	4	10	8
Mozambique	6	5	11	7
São Tomé and Principe	7	6	13	6
Uganda	6	7	13	6
Zambia	7	7	14	5

Source: "Sub-Saharan Africa: Regional Report," UNESCO Institute for Statistics 2001.

Sample size and expenditure details for surveys covered in Chapter 16

		Number of Households			Expenditure Details		
Country	Survey Year	Rural	Urban	Items	Visits	Deflated	Aggregation**
Burkina Faso	1998	5,885	2,593	65	1	no	WB
Burundi	1998	3,908	2,760	41	1	no	NSO
Cameroon	2001	6,017	4,975	655	2	yes	NSO
Côte d'Ivoire	1998	2,280	1,920	73	1	yes	WB
Ethiopia	1999/2000	8,459	8,213	852	16	no	WB
Gambia, The	1998	933	1,025	165	2	no	NSO
Ghana	1998	3,799	2,199	127	6	yes	NSO
Kenya	1997	8,963	1,911	168	1	yes	WB
Madagascar	1999	2,880	2,240	111	1	yes	WB
Malawi	1997	5,657	929	131	1	yes	NSO
Mozambique	1996	5,811	2,439	125	2	yes	WB
São Tomé and Principe	2000	1,173	1,243	161	1	no	WB
Uganda	1999	8,344	2,352	131	1	no	WB
Zambia	1998	8,317	8,105	155	1	no	NSO

Notes:

(*) These are the sample sizes for the Standardized Files; the original sample size may be different.

(**) The abbreviation "WB" means that the data were aggregated at the World Bank; the abbreviation "NSO" means that the aggregation was done by the country's national statistical office. Rent was imputed for Kenya and São Tomé and Principe.

Bibliography

Association for the Development of African Education. 1995. *A Statistical Profile of Education in Sub-Saharan Africa, 1990–93*. Paris.

Candoy-Sekse, Rebecca. 1988. *Techniques of Privatization of State-Owned Enterprises. Volume III. Inventory of Country Experience and Reference Materials*. World Bank Technical Paper 90. Washington, D.C.

Central African Republic, Division of Statistics and Economic Studies. 1994. "Enquete prioritaire sur les conditions de vie des menages." Bangui.

Club of Rome. 1972. *The Limit to Growth*. Rome.

Côte d'Ivoire, Institut National de Statistique. 1994. "Enquete prioritaire." Abidjan.

Currency Data & Intelligence Inc. Monthly. *Global Currency Report*. New York.

Floyd, Robert, Clive Gray, and R. P. Short. 1984. *Public Enterprise in Mixed Economies: Some Macro-economic Aspects*. Washington, D.C.: International Monetary Fund.

Food and Agriculture Organization (FAO). 1987. *Agrostat Code Book*. Rome.

___. Various years. *Fertilizer Yearbook*. Rome.

___ Various years. *Food and Agriculture Organization Production Yearbook*. Rome.

___. Various years. *Food Aid in Figures*. Rome.

___. Various years. *Trade Yearbook*. Rome.

___. Various years. *Yearbook of Forest Products*. Rome.

Galal, Ahmed. 1990. "Public Enterprise Reform: A Challenge for the World Bank." PRE Working Paper 407. World Bank, Country Economics Department, Washington, D.C. Processed

___. 1991. *Public Enterprise Reform: Lessons from the Past and Issues for the Future*. World Bank Discussion Paper 119. Washington, D.C.

The Gambia, Ministry of Finance. 1993. "Report on the 1992 Priority Survey." Banjul.

Grootaert, Christian, and Timothy Marchant. 1991. *The Social Dimensions of Adjustment Priority Survey: An Instrument for the Rapid Identification and Monitoring of Policy Targeting Groups.* SDA Working Paper 12. Washington, D.C.: World Bank.

Guinea, Ministry of Planning and Finance. 1991. "Rapport Final: Enquete sur les informations prioritaire: Dimensions Sociales de l'Adjustment Structurel." Conakry.

Guinea-Bissau, National Institute of Statistics and Census. 1992. "Relatorio Final: Inquerito Ligeiro Junto as Familias." Bissau.

Hemming, Richard, and Ali M. Mansoor. 1988. *Privatization and Public Enterprises.* IMF Occasional Paper 56. Washington, D.C.

International Energy Agency (IEA). 1996. *Energy Statistics and Balances of Non-OECD Countries, 1993–94.* Paris.

International Labour Organization (ILO). annual. *Yearbook of Labor Statistics.* Geneva.

___. 1968. *International Standard Classification of Occupations.* Geneva.

___. 1987. *World Labor Report* 1. Oxford: Oxford University Press.

International Monetary Fund (IMF). 1986. *A Manual on Government Finance Statistics.* Washington, D.C.

___. 1993. *Balance of Payments Manual,* Fifth ed. Washington, D.C.

___. Various years. *Balance of Payments Yearbook.* Washington, D.C.

___. Various years. *Government Finance Statistics Yearbook.* Washington, D.C.

___. Monthly. *International Financial Statistics.* Washington, D.C.

___. Various issues. *Recent Economic Development.* Washington, D.C.

International Road Federation. 1995. *World Road Statistics, 1990–94.* Geneva.

International Telecommunication Union (ITU). *2003. World Telecommunication Development Report.* Geneva.

Jager, William, and Charles Humphreys. 1988. "The Effect of Policy Reforms on Africa." *American Journal of Agricultural Economics* 70 (50): 1036–43.

Kenya, Central Bureau of Statistics. 1993. "Welfare Monitoring Survey." Nairobi.

Metallgesellschaft AG. Various years. *Metallstatistik.* Frankfurt am Main.

Mukui, John Thinguri. 1994. "Kenya: Poverty Profiles, 1982–92." Prepared for the Office of the Vice-President and Ministry of Planning and National Development, Nairobi, Kenya.

Nair, Govindan, and Anastosios Filppides. 1988. "How Much Do State-Owned Enterprises Contribute to Public Sector Deficits in Developing Countries?" PPR Working Paper 45. World Bank, Development Economics Vice Presidency, Washington, D.C. Processed.

Organisation for Economic Co-operation and Development (OECD). Various issues. Geographical Distribution of Financial Flows to Developing Countries. Paris.

Republic of South Africa. 1990. *South Africa Statistics.* Pretoria: Government Printer.

Swanson, Daniel, and Teferra Wolde-Semait. 1989. *Africa's Public Enterprise Sector and Evidence of Reforms.* World Bank Technical Paper 95. Washington, D.C.

Uganda, Ministry of Finance and Economic Planning. 1993. "Report on the Uganda National Integrated Household Survey 1992–93." Entebbe.

United Nations. 1950. *Index Numbers of Industrial Production*. New York.

———. 1989. *Compendium of Statistics and Indicators on the Situation of Women*. New York.

———. 1992. *The World's Women, 1970–90*. New York.

———. Annual. *Population and Vital Statistics Report*. New York.

———. Various years. *International Trade Statistics Yearbook*. New York.

United Nations Children's Fund (UNICEF). annual. *The State of the World's Children*. New York.

United Nations Development Programme (UNDP). 1994. Human Development Report 1994. New York.

United Nations Development Programme and the World Bank. 1989. *African Economic and Financial Data*. Washington, D.C.

Joint United Nations Programme on HIV/AIDS (UNAIDS). June 2000. "Report on the Global HIV/AIDS Epidemic." Geneva.

United Nations Statistical Office (UNSO). 1975, 1986. "Standard International Trade Classification," revisions 2 and 3 (SITC, rev. 2 and 3). Statistical Papers, series M. no. 34, rev. 2 and 3. New York.

———. United Nations International Standard Classification of All Economic Activities, revision 2 (ISIC, rev. 2). New York.

———. Various years. *Energy Statistics Yearbook*. New York.

United Nations Educational, Scientific, and Cultural Organization (UNESCO). 1982. Conferences of Ministers of Education and Those Responsible for Economic Planning in African Member States. Paris.

———. 1986. *Regional Bulletin of Education Statistics BREDA – STAT*. Regional Office for Education in Africa. Paris.

———. 1989. *Trends and Projections of Enrollment by Level of Education and by Age, 1960–2025 (as assessed in 1989)*. Division of Statistics on Education. Paris.

———. 1990. *Basic Education and Literacy: World Statistical Indicators*. Paris.

———. Various years. *Statistical Yearbook*. Paris.

Wadda, Rohey, and Russel Craig. 1993. "Report on the 1992 Priority Survey." Central Statistics, Ministry of Finance and Economic Affairs, Banjul, The Gambia.

World Bank. 1988. *Education in Sub-Saharan Africa: Policies for Adjustment, Revitalization, and Expansion*. Washington, D.C.

———. 1992. *African Development Indicators*. Washington, D.C.

———. 1993a. "Africa Adjustment Study P.E. Sector Reform: Case Studies." Washington, D.C. Processed.

———. 1993b. "Public Enterprise Reform and Privatization in Africa." Washington, D.C. Processed.

———. 1994a. "Kenya Poverty Assessment." Eastern Africa Department, Africa Region. Washington, D.C.

———. 1994b. "A Statistical Profile of Education in Sub-Saharan Africa in the 1980s." Africa Technical Department. Washington, D.C. Processed.

___. 1994c. *World Population Projections, 1994–95.* Washington, D.C.

___. 1994d. "Zambia Poverty Assessment." Southern Africa Department. Washington D.C.

___. 1995. *Bureaucrats in Business.* New York: Oxford University Press.

___. Various years. *Commodity Trade and Price Trends.* Washington, D.C.

___. Various years. *Global Development Finance* (formerly *World Debt Tables* up to 1996).

___. Various years. *World Bank Atlas.* Washington, D.C.

___. Various years. World Debt Tables (until 1996; now Global Development Finance). Washington, D.C.

___. Various years. *World Development Indicators.* Washington, D.C.

___. Various years. *World Development Report.* New York: Oxford University Press.

World Resources Institute. 1996. *World Resources 1996–97.* Washington, D.C.

___. 1998. *World Resources, 1998–1999.* Washington, D.C.

___. 2000. *World Resources 2000–2001.* Washington, D.C.

___. 2002. *World Resources 2002–2004.* Washington, D.C.

World Bureau of Metal Statistics. monthly. *World Metal Statistics.* London.

World Health Organization (WHO). Various years. *World Health Statistics Annual.* Geneva.

___. Various issues. *World Health Statistics Quarterly.* Geneva.

Zambia, Central Statistical Office. 1993. "Social Dimensions of Adjustment: Priority Survey I, 1991." Lusaka.